Proceedings

The 19th IEEE Real-Time Systems Symposium

D1402442

Proceedings

The 19th IEEE Real-Time Systems Symposium

December 2 - 4, 1998
Madrid, Spain

Sponsored by
IEEE Computer Society Technical Committee on Real-Time Systems
The Technical University of Madrid

IEEE
COMPUTER
SOCIETY

Los Alamitos, California

Washington • Brussels • Tokyo

IEEE Computer Society Order Number PR09212
ISBN 0-8186-9212-X
ISBN 0-8186-9214-6 (microfiche)
ISSN 1052-8725
IEEE Order Plan Catalog Number 98CB36279

Additional copies may be ordered from:

IEEE Computer Society
Customer Service Center
10662 Los Vaqueros Circle
P.O. Box 3014
Los Alamitos, CA 90720-1314
Tel: + 1-714-821-8380
Fax: + 1-714-821-4641
E-mail: cs.books@computer.org

IEEE Service Center
445 Hoes Lane
P.O. Box 1331
Piscataway, NJ 08855-1331
Tel: + 1-732-981-1393
Fax: + 1-732-981-9667
mis.custserv@computer.org

IEEE Computer Society
Asia/Pacific Office
Watanabe Building,
1-4-2 Minami-Aoyama
Minato-ku, Tokyo 107-0062 JAPAN
Tel: + 81-3-3408-3118
Fax: + 81-3-3408-3553
tokyo.ofc@computer.org

Editorial production by Kristine Kelly

Cover art production by Joseph Daigle/Studio Productions

Printed in the United States of America by The Printing House

Table of Contents

Session 1: Keynote Talk

Session 2: Systems and Scheduling I

Session 3.A: Databases and Filesystems

Session 3.B: Systems Design and Development I

Foreword

Welcome to the 19th IEEE Real-Time Systems Symposium in Madrid!

The IEEE Real-Time Systems Symposium is the premier conference in the area of real-time systems. As in previous years, RTSS '98 includes papers on a variety of real-time issues, within a very broad spectrum of subjects: design methods, operating systems, scheduling, databases, communications, computer architecture, software engineering, fault tolerance, performance analysis, signal processing—and a lot more. As in previous years, this year's technical program is remarkably strong, featuring a healthy mixture of theoretical and applied results. Indeed, almost all RTSS proceedings include some of the best papers published in all of computer science and engineering. As you will see, 1998 will prove no exception to this fine tradition.

RTSS also provides a vibrant framework for researchers to exchange innovative ideas amongst old acquaintances, and to hear about new and challenging applications from invited speakers. One of the conference's unique qualities is the degree of interaction between people of different backgrounds. This has led to some fascinating developments, for example, verification theorists presenting general methods for schedulability analysis, and scheduling theorists contributing innovative techniques for systems design. Often an invited speaker will describe some problem in a highly complex application. Then a "pure" researcher will formalize the problem, solve it, and present the result at a future RTSS meeting. Likewise, we have seen many theoretical results from previous RTSS meetings getting used routinely in a wide variety of applications. Sometimes the case histories are presented at RTSS, thereby closing the loop. Last year's speech by Dave Wilner on the Pathfinder Project was just one example of this sort of feedback—albeit a very powerful example.

Recently there has been a rapid growth in the number of applications requiring real-time functionality, and interest in real-time systems has risen to a remarkable degree, spreading through academia and industry, and ultimately among the general public. Concepts published at previous RTSS meetings—once considered the arcane province of Ph.D. students—found their way into undergraduate textbooks, and then into books for non-specialists. RTSS has responded in kind, and gradually broadened its scope to accommodate new areas, and draw an increasingly diverse body of attendees.

In 1998, RTSS received a record number of submitted papers. There were 182 papers submitted in all, 80 more than in recent years and 50 more than any RTSS ever held. Of the 182 papers submitted, 45 top-quality papers were chosen to appear on the program. Many of these cover topics never presented at a previous RTSS, written by researchers attending the conference for the first time. We on the committee welcome you, and hope to see you back again next year.

Due to the extraordinary rise in paper submissions, the size of the program was also increased to include about 50% more papers than in recent years. This, in turn, led to our first parallel-session format. In planning the parallel sessions, we attempted to account for all the diverse interests represented in the real-time community, with the goal of offering "something for everyone" during each session. We hope we succeeded in achieving our goal.

There are many other new developments, a few of which deserve special mention. Firstly, we are very fortunate to have three excellent invited speakers at RTSS '98. The first day starts with a talk by David Martinez, who leads the Digital Radar Technology Group at MIT Lincoln Laboratory; David will discuss some of the challenging real-time issues involved in building high-performance radar processors. The second day's proceedings will be opened by Bran Selic, who is Vice for Advanced Technology at ObjecTime Ltd, and a co-founder of that company. Bran's talk will be on object-oriented design methods for real-time systems, and will include some first-hand insights into the evolution of the real-time features in the UML standard. The last day will be opened by an old friend of RTSS, Ted Baker, who is Professor and Chair of Computer Science at Florida State University. Ted will outline lessons learned from a decade of developing standardized runtimes and APIs for real-time systems, specifically in the context of Ada, POSIX and Java. We are delighted to have three keynote talks which complement each other so well, particularly since the speakers are leading experts in these areas.

Another development is the new face of the RTSS exhibition. Based on the success of last year's show, we included more demos in 1998, ranging across a wider variety of application areas. We have also set aside time in the main program for short presentations on these products and tools. Our hope is to foment more interactions between researchers and developers, and to help bring our technology to the attention of more real-time system engineers. Following the format from last year, we continue to have a work-in-progress track, to encourage dissemination of the most recent findings in experimental work.

Also, this year's PLRTIA '98 workshop should be very interesting. The workshop covers real-time programming languages in general, and is specifically targeting issues involved with real-time and embedded Java—a very timely topic. Moreover, since the most casual conversations on programming languages often lead to vigorous debates, the workshop should prove to be a lively affair indeed.

Many people worked hard to make this year's RTSS possible. First and foremost, we owe a large debt of gratitude to the Program Committee members. They signed on under an expectation of reviewing about 12-15 papers each—and ended up with a workload of 23 papers each. They took on this extra burden without complaint, and worked overtime to finish the job. Committee members carried out their work with a significant degree of care and thoroughness—and they finished on schedule. All papers were reviewed meticulously, and then were discussed at the meeting, in some cases three or four times apiece. We would also like to thank the outside reviewers for providing exceptional advice and assistance to the PC members; the workload couldn't have been handled without them.

This year we decided to use a 100% web-based submission and review process. The decision was highly fortuitous, given the record number of submissions and the number of reviews (838 processed, including revisions). In this regard, we would like to extend special thanks to Jeff Hollingsworth, whose prototype was the basis for the RTSS system, and whose consulting support was essential in building the full-scale submission/review toolset. As of this writing, 7 other conferences are using the system developed for RTSS.

We would also like to thank our colleagues on the conference committee for their help: Walt Heimerdinger for handling finances; Linda Buss for registration; Angel Alverez for Local Arrangements; Gerhard Fohler for organizing the exhibit; Steve Goddard for running the work-in-progress track; Juan de la Puente for doing the local finance work; Alejandro Alonso, Chao-Ju Jennifer Hou and Joseph Ng for their work as publicity chairs; and Alan Burns for helping put together the team in Europe.

Finally, we note that this is the second meeting within four years to be held in Europe. RTSS has always been IEEE's flagship *international* conference for real-time systems. Given the success of RTSS '98, we are happy and proud to report that we have truly earned that designation.

Welcome to Madrid, and we hope you enjoy RTSS '98!

General Chair
Kwei-Jay Lin
University of California, Irvine

Program Chair
Richard Gerber
University of Maryland

Conference Organization

General Chair
Kwei-Jay Lin, *University of California, Irvine*

Program Chair
Richard Gerber, *University of Maryland*

Finance Chair
Walt Heimerdinger, *Honeywell Technology Center*

Local Arrangements
Angel Alvarez, *Universidad Politécnica de Madrid*

Industrial Exhibit Chair
Gerhard Fohler, *Mälardalen University*

Work-In-Progresss Track Chair
Steve Goddard, *University of Nebraska*

Registration
Linda Buss

Local Treasurer
Juan A. de la Puente, *Universidad Politécnica de Madrid*

Publicity Co-Chairs
Alejandro Alonso, *Universidad Politécnica de Madrid*
Chao-Ju Jennifer Hou, *Ohio State University*
Joseph Ng, *Hong Kong Baptist University*

European Chair
Alan Burns, *University of York*

Ex-Officio
Doug Locke, *Lockheed Martin Corporation*

Program Committee

James Anderson, *University of North Carolina*

Azer Bestavros, *Boston University*

Sanjoy Baruah, *University of Vermont*

Giorgio Buttazzo, *Scuola Superiore Sant'Anna*

Gerhard Fohler, *Mälardalen University*

Michael Gonzalez Harbour, *Universidad Cantabria*

Jeffrey Hollingsworth, *University of Maryland*

Seongsoo Hong, *Seoul National University*

Farnam Jahanian, *University of Michigan*

Kevin Jeffay, *University of North Carolina*

Hermann Kopetz, *Vienna University of Technology*

Kim G. Larsen, *Aalborg University*

Insup Lee, *University of Pennsylvania*

Jane W.S. Liu, *University of Illinois*

Keith Marzullo, *University of California at San Diego*

Sang Lyul Min, *Seoul National University*

Al Mok, *University of Texas at Austin*

Ragunathan Rajkumar, *Carnegie Mellon University*

Jennifer Rexford, *AT&T Research*

Manas Saksena, *Concordia University*

Bran Selic, *ObjectTime, Ltd.*

Andy Wellings, *University of York*

David Wilner, *Wind River Systems*

Sergio Yovine, *CNRS/VERIMAG*

Hui Zhang, *Carnegie Mellon University*

Reviewers

Session 1: Keynote Talk

Future Challenges in the Development of Real-Time High Performance Embedded Systems

David Martinez, *MIT Lincoln Laboratory*

Abstract: The next advances in phased-array radars will be in the implementation of adaptive signal processing algorithms. As the need for battlefield superiority increases, many of the present military platforms will undergo major upgrades to commercial-off-the-shelf (COTS) computing technology. Supercomputers will play a very important role in these upgrades, due to the cost-to-performance ratio advantage provided by COTS parallel processors (relative to custom-built solutions), and also because they allow downloading different types of sensor array processing algorithms to the same platform. There will still be sections in the processing chain that cannot be economically solved with COTS processors. In these instances, we will employ COTS interfaces, but the processing will be performed using very large scale integration (VLSI) circuits, designed for application-specific functions.

Sensor array processing demands very high computation throughput in real-time. The typical computation throughput requirement ranges from 100 to 1000 billion operations per second (GOPS). These load demands arise from the need to process data through several compute-intensive operations, such as digital filtering, fast Fourier transforms, adaptive matrix inversion, and matrix multiplication over multiple sensor data channels. One can reach these levels of throughput by concatenating a large number of processors in a pipeline fashion. The problem, however, is that the demands are not just in computation throughput, but also in latency. Therefore, this application requires parallel processors that can meet both the computation and latency requirements.

Parallel computers, organized with a number of low-cost, off-the-shelf microprocessors, offer a very attractive solution. However, there are a number of challenges faced by parallel computers to reach the high computation rates demanded by the application. One important challenge is the ability to break up the application problem into enough degrees of parallelism (DOP) such that the processing tasks can be performed concurrently. The mapping of the algorithm and data onto the parallel processor is a very demanding and laborious task with today's processors. Another important challenge for these parallel computers is the ability to do a total exchange of the data within a minimum latency and a maximum bandwidth. This all-to-all communication is particularly important for sensor array processing, because the sequence of operations must be performed on multiple dimensions of the input sensor data. For example, digital data filtering is normally performed on a channel-by-channel independent basis. However, the matrix inversion is performed by combining multiple sensor channels. Therefore, a large bisection bandwidth, balanced with the total computational power of the machine, is needed to reach the requisite performance.

In this talk we describe the application of supercomputing systems to the very challenging problem of real-time sensor array processing. We discuss the computing technology areas that present the most challenge to today's high performance processors. We also share our experiences in prototyping a class of real-time embedded systems.

Profile: **DAVID MARTINEZ** received a B.S. degree in Electrical Engineering from New Mexico State University in 1976. He received the M.S. and E.E. degree in Electrical Engineering from MIT, jointly with the Woods Hole Oceanographic Institution in 1979. He completed an MBA degree from the Southern Methodist University in 1986. He worked at the Atlantic Richfield Co. in seismic signal processing from 1979 to 1988. During this time, he worked on algorithm development and technology field demonstrations. While at Atlantic Richfield Co., Mr. Martinez received the ARCO Special Achievement Award for the conception, management, and implementation of a multidisciplinary project. He holds three U.S. patents relating to seismic signal processing hardware. Mr. Martinez has worked at MIT Lincoln Laboratory since 1988. His areas of interest are in VLSI signal processing and high performance parallel processing systems. He has been responsible for managing the development of several complex real-time signal processor systems. In 1994-1995, he served as co-chairman on a national study to define the next generation real-time signal processor requirements for future surveillance enhancements to the Navy and Air Force airborne early warning systems. He was also the chairman for the second annual workshop on high performance embedded computing, held at MIT Lincoln Laboratory in September 1998. Mr. Martinez is the Group Leader of the Digital Radar Technology Group concentrating on signal processing and high performance embedded processor systems. He also served as an Associate Editor for *IEEE Signal Processing*

Session 2: Systems and Scheduling I

Integrating Multimedia Applications in Hard Real-Time Systems

Luca Abeni and Giorgio Buttazzo
Scuola Superiore S. Anna, Pisa
luca@hartik.sssup.it, giorgio@sssup.it

Abstract

This paper focuses on the problem of providing efficient run-time support to multimedia applications in a real-time system, where two types of tasks can coexist simultaneously: multimedia soft real-time tasks and hard real-time tasks. Hard tasks are guaranteed based on worst case execution times and minimum interarrival times, whereas multimedia and soft tasks are served based on mean parameters. The paper describes a server-based mechanism for scheduling soft and multimedia tasks without jeopardizing the a priori guarantee of hard real-time activities. The performance of the proposed method is compared with that of similar service mechanisms through extensive simulation experiments and several multimedia applications have been implemented on the HARTIK kernel.

1. Introduction

Continuous Media (CM) activities, such as audio and video streams, need real-time support because of their sensitivity to delay and jitter. On the other hand, however, the use of a hard real-time system for handling CM applications can be inappropriate for the following reasons:

- If a multimedia task manages compressed frames, the time for coding/decoding each frame can vary significantly, hence the worst case execution time (WCET) of the task can be much bigger than its mean execution time. Since hard real-time tasks are guaranteed based on their WCET (and not based on mean execution times), CM applications can cause a waste of the CPU resource.

- Providing a precise estimation of WCETs is very difficult even for those applications always running on the same hardware. This problem is even more critical for multimedia applications, which in general can run on a large number of different machines (think of a video conferencing system running on several different PC workstations).

- When data are received from an external device (for instance, a communication network) the interarrival time of the tasks that process such data may not be deterministic, so it may be impossible to determine a minimum interarrival time for such tasks. As a consequence, no a priori guarantee can be performed.

- Advanced multimedia systems tend to be more dynamic than classical real-time systems, so all the scheduling methodologies devised for static real-time systems are not suited for CM applications.

For the reasons mentioned above, a large part of the multimedia community continues to use classical operating systems, as Unix or Windows, to manage CM. Recently, some scheduling algorithms have been proposed [16, 6] to mix some form of real-time support with a notion of fairness, but they do not make use of conventional real-time theory. Since we are interested in systems based on a conventional RT scheduler (such as EDF or RM), we do not consider this kind of solutions.

In [8], Jeffay presents a hard real-time system based on EDF scheduling to be used as a test bed for video conference applications; the system can guarantee each task at its creation time based on its WCET and its minimum interarrival time. While a bound for the WCET can be found, the interarrival time may not have a lower bound, because of the unpredictability of the network (which may even reverse the order of messages at the reception site). For this reason, Jeffay in [7] introduces the Rate-Based Execution (RBE) task model, which is independent from the minimum interarrival time. Although this kind of task cannot be guaranteed to complete within a given deadline, it is possible to guarantee that it will not jeopardize the schedulability of other hard real-time tasks present in the system.

In [12], Mercer, Savage, and Tokuda propose a scheme based on CPU capacity reserves, where a fraction of the CPU bandwidth is reserved to each task. A reserve is a couple (C_i, T_i) indicating that a task τ_i can execute for at most C_i units of time in each period T_i. This approach removes the need of knowing the WCET of each task, because it fixes the maximum time that each task can execute in its period. Since the periodic scheduler is based on the Rate Monotonic algorithm, the classical schedulability analysis can be applied to guarantee hard tasks, if they are present. The only problem with this method is that overload situations on multimedia tasks are not handled efficiently. In fact, if a task instance executes for more than C_i units of time, the remaining portion of the instance is scheduled in background, prolonging its completion of an unpredictable time.

In [9], Kaneko et al. propose a scheme based on a periodic process (the multimedia server) dedicated to the service of all multimedia requests. This allows to nicely integrate multimedia tasks together with hard real-time tasks; however, being the server only one, it is not easy to control the QoS of each task.

In [3], Liu and Deng describe a scheduling hierarchy which allows hard real-time, soft real-time, and non real-time applications to coexist in the same system, and to be created dynamically. According to this approach, which uses the EDF scheduling algorithm as a low-level scheduler, each application is handled by a dedicated server, which can be a Constant Utilization Server [4] for tasks that do not use nonpreemptable sections or global resources, and a Total Bandwidth Server [13, 15] for the other tasks. This solution can be used to isolate the effects of overloads at the application level, rather than at the task level. Moreover, the method requires the knowledge of the WCET even for soft and non real-time tasks.

In this paper, we propose a scheduling methodology based on reserving a fraction of the processor bandwidth to each task (in a way similar to processor capacity reserves of Mercer et al.[12]). However, to efficiently handle the problem of task overloads, each task is scheduled by a dedicated server, which does not require the knowledge of the WCET and assigns a suitable deadline to the served task whenever the reserved time is consumed.

The rest of the paper is organized as follows: Section 2 specifies our notation, definitions and basic assumptions; Section 3 describes our scheduling scheme in detail and its formal properties; Section 4 compares the proposed algorithm with other server mechanisms, and presents some simulation results; Section 5 describes an implementation of the proposed algorithm on the HARTIK kernel and shows some experimental results; and, finally, Section 6 presents our conclusions and future work.

2. Terminology and assumptions

We consider a system consisting of three types of tasks: hard, soft, and non real-time tasks. Any task τ_i consists of a sequence of jobs $J_{i,j}$, where $r_{i,j}$ denotes the arrival time (or request time) of the jth job of task τ_i.

A hard real-time task is characterized by two additional parameters, (C_i, T_i), where C_i is the WCET of each job and T_i is the minimum interarrival time between successive jobs, so that $r_{i,j+1} \geq r_{i,j} + T_i$. The system must provide an a priori guarantee that all jobs of a hard task must complete before a given deadline $d_{i,j}$. In our model, the absolute deadline of each hard job $J_{i,j}$ is implicitly set at the value $d_{i,j} = r_{i,j} + T_i$.

A soft real-time task is also characterized by the parameters (C_i, T_i), however the timing constraints are more relaxed. In particular, for a soft task, C_i represents the *mean* execution time of each job, whereas T_i represents the *desired* activation period between successive jobs. For each soft job $J_{i,j}$, a soft deadline is set at time $d_{i,j} = r_{i,j} + T_i$. Since mean values are used for the computation time and minimum interarrival times are not known, soft tasks cannot be guaranteed a priori. In multimedia applications, soft deadline misses may decrease the QoS, but do not cause critical system faults.

The objective of the system is to minimize the mean tardiness of soft tasks, without jeopardizing the schedulability of the hard tasks. The tardiness $E_{i,j}$ of a job $J_{i,j}$ is defined as

$$E_{i,j} = max\{0, \; f_{i,j} - d_{i,j}\} \qquad (1)$$

where $f_{i,j}$ is the finishing time of job $J_{i,j}$.

Finally, a periodic task is a task (hard or soft) in which the interarrival time between successive jobs is exactly equal to T_i for all jobs ($r_{i,j+1} = r_{i,j} + T_i$). Periodic tasks do not have special treatment in this model.

Tasks that manage CM can be modeled as soft real-time tasks, because missing deadlines may decrease the QoS without causing catastrophic consequences. Moreover, CM activities are typically characterized by highly variable execution times, causing the WCET to be much greater than the mean execution time.

For the reasons mentioned above, treating CM tasks as hard real-time tasks is not appropriate, firstly because an underestimation of the WCET would compromise the guarantee done on the other tasks, and secondly because it would be very inefficient, since trying to guarantee a task with a WCET much greater than its mean execution time would cause a waste of the CPU resource.

This problem can be solved by a bandwidth reservation strategy, which assigns each soft task a maximum bandwidth, calculated using the mean execution time and the desired activation period, in order to increase CPU utilization. If a task needs more than its reserved bandwidth, it may slow down, but it will not jeopardize the schedulability of the hard real-time tasks. By isolating the effects of task overloads, hard tasks can be guaranteed using classical schedulability analysis [11].

To integrate hard and soft tasks in the same system, hard tasks are scheduled by the EDF algorithm based on their absolute deadlines, whereas each soft task is handled by a dedicated server, the *Constant Bandwidth Server* (CBS), whose behavior and properties are described in the next section.

3. The Constant Bandwidth Server

The service mechanisms that have inspired this work are the Dynamic Sporadic Server (DSS) [13, 5] and the Total Bandwidth Server (TBS) [13, 15]. As the DSS, the CBS guarantees that, if U_s is the fraction of processor time assigned to a server (i.e., its bandwidth), its contribution to the total utilization factor is no greater than U_s, even in the presence of overloads. Notice that this property is not valid for a TBS, nor for a Constant Utilization Server (CUS) [4], whose actual contributions are limited by U_s only under the assumption that all the served jobs execute no more than the declared WCET. With respect to the DSS, however, the CBS shows a much better performance, comparable with the one achievable by a TBS.

3.1. Definition of CBS

The CBS can be defined as follows:

- A CBS is characterized by a budget c_s and by a ordered pair (Q_s, T_s), where Q_s is the maximum budget and T_s is the period of the server. The ratio $U_s = Q_s/T_s$ is denoted as the server bandwidth. At each instant, a fixed deadline $d_{s,k}$ is associated with the server. At the beginning $d_{s,0} = 0$.

- Each served job $J_{i,j}$ is assigned a dynamic deadline $d_{i,j}$ equal to the current server deadline $d_{s,k}$.

- Whenever a served job executes, the budget c_s is decreased by the same amount.

- When $c_s = 0$, the server budget is recharged to the maximum value Q_s and a new server deadline is generated as $d_{s,k+1} = d_{s,k} + T_s$. Notice that there are no finite intervals of time in which the budget is equal to zero.

- A CBS is said to be active at time t if there are pending jobs (remember the budget c_s is always greater than 0); that is, if there exists a served job $J_{i,j}$ such that $r_{i,j} \leq t < f_{i,j}$. A CBS is said to be idle at time t if it is not active.

- When a job $J_{i,j}$ arrives and the server is active the request is enqueued in a queue of pending jobs according to a given (arbitrary) non-preemptive discipline (e.g., FIFO).

- When a job $J_{i,j}$ arrives and the server is idle, if $c_s \geq (d_{s,k} - r_{i,j})U_s$ the server generates a new deadline

$d_{s,k+1} = r_{i,j} + T_s$ and c_s is recharged to the maximum value Q_s, otherwise the job is served with the last server deadline $d_{s,k}$ using the current budget.

- When a job finishes, the next pending job, if any, is served using the current budget and deadline. If there are no pending jobs, the server becomes idle.

- At any instant, a job is assigned the last deadline generated by the server.

Figure 1 illustrates an example in which a hard periodic task, τ_1, is scheduled together with a soft task, τ_2, served by a CBS having a budget $Q_s = 2$ and a period $T_s = 7$. The first job of τ_2 arrives at time $r_1 = 2$, when the server is idle. Being $c_s \geq (d_{s,0} - r_1)U_s$, the job is assigned the deadline $d_{s,1} = r_1 + T_s = 9$ and c_s is recharged at $Q_s = 2$. At time $t_1 = 6$, the budget is exhausted, so a new deadline $d_{s,2} = d_{s,1} + T_s = 16$ is generated and c_s is replenished. At time r_2, the second job arrives when the server is active, so the request is enqueued. When the first job finishes, the second job is served with the actual server deadline ($d_{s,2} = 16$). At time $t_2 = 12$, the server budget is exhausted so a new server deadline $d_{s,3} = d_{s,2} + t_s = 23$ is generated and c_s is replenished to Q_s. The third job arrives at time $r_3 = 17$, when the server is idle and $c_s = 1 < (d_{s,3} - r_3)U_s = (23 - 17)\frac{2}{7} = 1.71$, so it is scheduled with the actual server deadline $d_{s,3}$ without changing the budget.

It is worth to notice that under a CBS a job J_j is assigned an absolute time-varying deadline d_j which can be postponed if the task requires more than the reserved bandwidth. Thus, each job J_j can be thought as consisting of a number of chunks $H_{j,k}$, each characterized by a release time $a_{j,k}$ and a fixed deadline $d_{j,k}$. An example of chunks produced by a CBS is shown in Figure 2. To simplify the notation, we will indicate all the chunks generated by a server with an increasing index k (in the example of Figure 2, $H_{1,1} = H_1$; $H_{1,2} = H_2$, $H_{2,1} = H_3$ and so on).

In order to provide a formal definition of the CBS, let a_k and d_k be the release time and the deadline of the kth chunk generated by the server, and let c and n be the actual server budget and the number of pending requests in the server queue (including the request currently being served). These variables are initialized as follows:

$$d_0 = 0 \quad c = 0 \quad n = 0 \quad k = 0$$

Using this notation, the server behavior can be described by the algorithm shown in Figure 3.

3.2. CBS properties

The proposed CBS service mechanism presents some interesting properties that make it suitable for supporting CM applications. The most important one, the *isolation property*, is formally expressed by the following theorem.

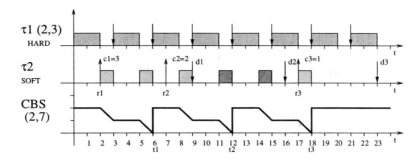

Figure 1. An example of CBS scheduling.

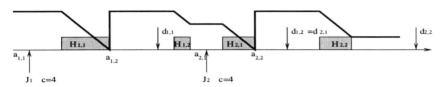

Figure 2. Example of jobs divided to chunks.

Theorem 1 *Given a set of n periodic hard tasks with processor utilization U_p and a CBS with processor utilization U_s, the whole set is schedulable by EDF if and only if*

$$U_p + U_s \leq 1.$$

Proof.
See [1]. □

The isolation property allows us to use a bandwidth reservation strategy to allocate a fraction of the CPU time to soft tasks whose computation time cannot be easily bounded. The most important consequence of this result is that such tasks can be scheduled together with hard tasks without affecting the a priori guarantee, even in the case in which soft requests exceed the expected load.

In addition to the isolation property, the CBS has the following characteristics.

- The CBS behaves as a plain EDF if the served task τ_i has parameters (C_i, T_i) such that $C_i \leq Q_s$ and $T_i = T_s$. This is formally stated by the following lemma.

    Lemma 1 *A hard task τ_i with parameters (C_i, T_i) is schedulable by a CBS with parameters $Q_s \geq C_i$ and $T_s = T_i$ if and only if τ_i is schedulable with EDF.*

Proof.
For any job of a hard task we have that $r_{i,j+1} - r_{i,j} = T_i$ and $c_{i,j} \leq Q_s$. Hence, by definition of the CBS, each hard job is assigned a deadline $d_{i,j} = r_{i,j} + T_i$

and it is scheduled with a budget $Q_s \geq C_i$. Moreover, since $c_{i,j} \leq Q_s$, each job finishes no later than the budget is exhausted, hence the deadline assigned to a job does not change and is exactly the same as the one used by EDF. □

- The CBS automatically reclaims any spare time caused by early completions. This is due to the fact that whenever the budget is exhausted, it is always immediately replenished at its full value and the server deadline is postponed. In this way, the server remains eligible and the budget can be exploited by the pending requests with the current deadline. *This is the main difference with respect to the processor capacity reserves* proposed by Mercer et al. [12].

- Knowing the statistical distribution of the computation time of a task served by a CBS, it is possible to perform a statistical guarantee, expressed in terms of probability for each served job to meet its deadline.

3.3. Statistical guarantee

To perform a statistical guarantee on soft tasks served by CBS, we can model a CBS as a queue, where each arriving job $J_{i,j}$ can be viewed as a request of $c_{i,j}$ time units. At any time, the request at the head of the queue is served using the current server deadline, so that it is guaranteed that Q_s units of time can be consumed within this deadline.

We analyze the following cases: a) variable computation time and constant inter-arrival time; and b) constant computation time and variable inter-arrival time.

```
When job J_j arrives at time r_j
    enqueue the request in the server queue;
    n = n + 1;
    if (n == 1) /* (the server is idle) */
        if (r_j + (c / Q_s) * T_s >= d_k)
            /*---------------Rule 1---------------*/
            k = k + 1;
            a_k = r_j;
            d_k = a_k + T_s;
            c = Q_s;
        else
            /*---------------Rule 2---------------*/
            k = k + 1;
            a_k = r_j;
            d_k = d_{k-1};
            /* c remains unchanged */
When job J_j terminates
    dequeue J_j from the server queue;
    n = n - 1;
    if (n != 0) serve the next job in the queue with deadline d_k;
When job J_j served by S_s executes for a time unit
    c = c - 1;
When (c == 0)
    /*---------------Rule 3---------------*/
    k = k + 1;
    a_k = actual_time();
    d_k = d_{k-1} + T_s;
    c = Q_s;
```

Figure 3. The CBS algorithm.

Case a.

If job interarrival times are constant and equal to T_s, and job execution times are randomly distributed with a given probability distribution function, the CBS can be modeled with a $D^G/D/1$ queue: every T_s units of time, a request of c_j units arrives and at most Q_s units can be served. We can define a random process v_j as follows:

$$\begin{cases} v_1 & = c_1 \\ v_j & = max\{0, v_{j-1} - Q_s\} + c_{i,j} \end{cases}$$

where v_j indicates the length of the queue (in time units) at time $(j-1)T_s$, that is the unit of times that are still to be served when job $J_{i,j}$ arrives. Hence, since Q_s units of time are served every period T_s, the job will finish no later than

$$d_{j_{max}} = r_{i,j} + \left\lceil \frac{v_j}{Q_s} \right\rceil T_s$$

which is also the latest deadline assigned by the server to job $J_{i,j}$.

If $\pi_k^{(j)} = P\{v_j = k\}$ is the state probability of process v_j and $C_h = P\{c_j = h\}$ is the probability that an arriving job requires h units of time (since c_j is time invariant, C_h does not depend on j), the value of $\pi_k^{(j)}$ can be calculated as follows:

$$\pi_k^{(j)} = P\{v_j = k\} = P\{max\{v_{j-1} - Q, 0\} + c_j = k\}$$

$$\pi_k^{(j)} = \sum_{h=-\infty}^{\infty} P\{max\{v_{j-1} - Q, 0\} + c_j = k \wedge v_{j-1} = h\}.$$

Being v_j greater than 0 by definition, the sum can be calculated for h going from 0 to infinity:

$$\pi_k^{(j)} = \sum_{h=0}^{\infty} P\{max\{h - Q, 0\} + c_j = k\} P\{v_{j-1} = h\}$$

$$= \sum_{h=0}^{Q} C_k \pi_h^{(j-1)} + \sum_{h=Q+1}^{\infty} P\{c_j = k - h + Q\} \pi_h^{(j-1)}$$

$$= \sum_{h=0}^{Q} C_k \pi_h^{(j-1)} + \sum_{h=Q+1}^{\infty} C_{k-h+Q} \pi_h^{(j-1)}.$$

Hence

$$\pi_k^{(j)} = \sum_{h=0}^{Q} C_k \pi_h^{(j-1)} + \sum_{h=Q+1}^{\infty} C_{k-h+Q} \pi_h^{(j-1)}. \quad (2)$$

Using a matrix notation, equation (2) can be written as

$$\Pi^{(j)} = M\Pi^{(j-1)} \quad (3)$$

where M and Π are described in Figure 4

8

$$M = \begin{pmatrix} \overbrace{\begin{matrix} C_0 & C_0 & . & . & . & C_0 \\ C_1 & C_1 & . & . & . & C_1 \\ C_2 & C_2 & . & . & . & C_2 \end{matrix}}^{Q+1} & \begin{matrix} 0 & 0 & . & . & . \\ C_0 & 0 & . & . & . \\ C_1 & C_0 & 0 & . & . \end{matrix} \\ . & . & . & . & . & . & . \end{pmatrix} \quad \text{and} \quad \Pi^{(j)} = \begin{pmatrix} \pi_0^{(j)} \\ \pi_1^{(j)} \\ \pi_2^{(j)} \\ . \end{pmatrix}$$

Figure 4. Matrix describing the Markov chain for case a)

Case b.

In the case in which jobs' execution times are constant and equal to Q_s ($\forall j, c_{i,j} = Q_s$) and jobs' interarrival times are distributed according to a given distribution function, each job is assigned a deadline $d_{i,j} = \max\{r_{i,j}, d_{i,j-1}\} + T_s$, identical to that assigned by a TBS. In this situation, the CBS can be modeled by a $G/D/1$ queue: jobs arrive in the queue with a randomly distributed arrival time and the server can process a request each T_s time units. If we define a random process w_j as $w_j = d_{i,j} - r_{i,j} - T_s$, the distribution of the relative deadlines $d_{i,j} - r_{i,j}$ of job $J_{i,j}$ can be computed from the distribution of w_j, because

$$d_{i,j} - r_{i,j} = w_{i,j} + T_s.$$

Since $d_{i,j} = max\{r_{i,j}, d_{i,j-1}\} + T_s$, we have

$$\begin{aligned} w_{j+1} &= d_{i,j+1} - T_s - r_{i,j+1} = \\ &= max\{r_{i,j+1}, d_{i,j}\} + T_s - T_s - r_{i,j+1} = \\ &= max\{0, d_{i,j} - r_{i,j+1}\} = \\ &= max\{0, r_{i,j} + w_j + T_s - r_{i,j+1}\} = \\ &= max\{0, w_j - a_{j+1} + T\} \end{aligned}$$

having defined $a_{j+1} = r_{i,j+1} - r_{i,j}$. Being a_j a stochastic stationary and time invariant process and w_j a Markov process, the matrix M describing the w_j Markov chain can be found. By defining $\pi_k^{(j)} = P\{w_j = k\}$ and $A_h = P\{a_j = h\}$, we have

$$\pi_k^{(j)} = P\{w_j = k\} =$$
$$= P\{\max\{0, w_{j-1} - a_j + T_s\} = k\}$$
$$= \sum_{h=-\infty}^{\infty} P\{\max\{0, w_{j-1} - a_j + T\} = k \wedge w_{j-1} = h\}$$
$$= \sum_{h=-\infty}^{\infty} P\{\max\{0, h - a_j + T\} = k\}P\{w_{j-1} = h\}$$

In order to simplify the calculus, we distinguish two cases: $k = 0$ and $k > 0$:

$$\pi_0^{(j)} = \sum_{h=-\infty}^{\infty} P\{h - a_j + T \leq 0\}P\{w_{j-1} = h\} =$$

$$= \sum_{h=-\infty}^{\infty} P\{a_j \geq h + T\}P\{w_{j-1} = h\} =$$
$$= \sum_{h=0}^{\infty} \sum_{r=h+T}^{\infty} P\{a_j = r\}\pi_h^{(j-1)} =$$
$$= \sum_{h=0}^{\infty} \sum_{r=h+T}^{\infty} A_r \pi_h^{(j-1)}$$

$\forall k > 0$,

$$\pi_k^{(j)} = \sum_{h=-\infty}^{\infty} P\{h - a_j + T = k\}P\{w_{j-1} = h\} =$$
$$= \sum_{h=-\infty}^{\infty} P\{a_j = h - k + T\}\pi_h^{(j-1)} =$$
$$= \sum_{h=0}^{\infty} A_{h-k+T}\pi_h^{(j-1)}$$

Thus, matrix M describing the Markov chain is shown in Figure 5. For a generic queue, it is known that the queue is stable (i.e., the number of elements in the queue do not diverge to infinity) if

$$\rho = \frac{mean\ interarrival\ rate}{mean\ service\ rate} < 1.$$

Hence, the stability can be achieved under the following conditions:

$$\begin{cases} \overline{c_{i,j}} & < \quad Q_s \quad \text{in case a)} \\ \overline{r_{i,j+1} - r_{i,j}} & > \quad T_s \quad \text{in case b)} \end{cases}$$

In general,

$$\frac{\overline{c_{i,j}}}{\overline{r_{i,j+1} - r_{i,j}}} < \frac{Q_s}{T_s}.$$

If this condition is not satisfied the difference between the deadline $d_{i,j}$ assigned by the server to a job $J_{i,j}$ and the job release time $r_{i,j}$ will increase indefinitely. This means that, for preserving the schedulability of the other tasks, τ_i will slow down in an unpredictable manner.

If a queue is stable, a stationary solution of the Markov chain describing the queue can be found; that is, there exists

9

$$M = \begin{pmatrix} \rho_0 & \rho_1 & \rho_2 & \cdot & & \cdot & \cdot & \cdot & \cdot & \cdot & \cdot & \cdot \\ A_{T+1} & A_T & A_{T-1} & \cdot & & \cdot & A_0 & 0 & 0 & \cdot & \cdot & \cdot \\ A_{T+2} & A_{T+1} & A_T & A_{T-1} & \cdot & A_1 & A_0 & 0 & 0 & \cdot & \cdot \\ A_{T+3} & A_{T+2} & A_{T+1} & A_T & \cdot & A_2 & C_1 & A_0 & 0 & 0 & \cdot \\ \cdot & \cdot & \cdot & \cdot & \cdot & \cdot & \cdot & \cdot & \cdot & \cdot & \cdot \end{pmatrix} \text{ with } \rho_i = \sum_{r=i+T}^{\infty} A_r.$$

Figure 5. Matrix describing the Markov chain for case b)

a solution Π such that $\Pi = \lim_{j\to\infty} \Pi^{(j)}$, and $\Pi = M\Pi$. This solution can be approximated by truncating matrix M (having infinite dimension) to an $N \times N$ matrix M' and solving the eigenvector problem $\Pi' = M'\Pi'$ with some numerical calculus technique.

The knowledge of the probability distribution function of the relative deadlines before which a multimedia task job is guaranteed to finish is useful for guaranteeing a QoS to each task and for choosing the right server parameters (Q_s, T_s) for each soft task.

4. Simulation results

In this section we compare the CBS with other similar service mechanisms, namely the Total Bandwidth Server (TBS) and the Dynamic Sporadic Server (DSS). The Constant Utilization Server (CUS) is not considered in the graphs because it is very similar to the TBS (indeed, slightly worse in performance).

The main difference between DSS and CBS is visible when the budget is exhausted. In fact, while the DSS becomes idle until the next replenishing time (that occurs at the server's deadline), the CBS remains eligible by increasing its deadline and replenishing the budget immediately. This difference in the replenishing time, causes a big difference in the performance offered by the two servers to soft real-time tasks. The TBS does not suffer from this problem, however *its correct behavior relies on the exact knowledge of job's WCETs, so it cannot be used for supporting CM applications*. Moreover, since the CBS automatically reclaims any available idle time coming from early completions, a reclaiming mechanism has also been added in the simulation of the TBS, as described in [14].

All the simulations presented in this section have been conducted on a hybrid task set consisting of 5 periodic hard tasks with fixed parameters and 5 soft tasks with variable execution times and interarrival times. The periods and the execution times of the periodic hard tasks are randomly generated in order to achieve a desired processor utilization factor U_{hard}, while their relative deadlines are equal to the periods. The execution and interarrival times of the soft tasks are uniformly distributed in order to obtain a mean soft load $\overline{U_{soft}} = \sum_i \frac{\overline{c_{i,j}}}{r_{i,j+1} - r_{i,j}}$ with $\overline{U_{soft}}$ going from 0

to $1 - U_{hard}$. All the soft tasks have the same relative deadline.

The metric used to measure the performance of the service algorithms is the mean tardiness $\overline{E_i}$ computed over all instances of each soft task. The reason for choosing such a metric is motivated by the fact that, as already mentioned above, in multimedia applications meeting all soft deadlines could be impossible or very inefficient. Thus, a more realistic objective is to guarantee all the hard tasks and minimize the mean time that soft tasks execute after their deadlines. Notice that, since all the soft tasks have the same relative deadline, the tardiness is not dependent on task's deadline.

In the first experiment, we compare the mean tardiness experienced by soft tasks when they are served by a CBS, a TBS and a DSS. In this test, the utilization factor of periodic hard tasks is $U_{hard} = 0.5$. The simulation results are illustrated in Figure 6, which shows that the performance of the DSS is dramatically worse than the one achieved by the CBS and TBS. This result was expected for the reasons explained above.

Figure 7 shows the same results, but without the DSS: the only difference is in the scale of the y-axis. In this figure, the TBS and CBS curves can be better distinguished, so we can see that the tardiness experienced by soft tasks under a CBS is slightly higher than that experienced using a TBS. However, the difference is so small that can be neglected for any practical purposes.

Figures 8 and 9 illustrate the results of similar experiments repeated with $U_{hard} = 0.7$ and $U_{hard} = 0.9$ respectively. As we can see, the major difference in the performance between CBS and TBS appears only for heavy hard loads. Fortunately, this situation is of little interest for most practical multimedia applications.

When $WCET_i >> \overline{c_{i,j}}$ the TBS can cause an underutilization of the processor. This fact can be observed in Figure 10, which shows the results of a fourth experiment, in which $U_{hard} = 0.6$, $\overline{U_{soft}} = 0.4$, the interarrival times are fixed, and the execution times of the soft tasks are uniformly distributed with an increasing variance.

As can be seen from the graph, CBS performs better than TBS when c_i varies a lot among the jobs.

10

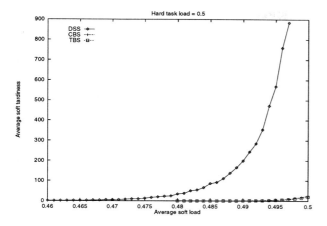

Figure 6. First experiment (TBS, CBS and DSS).

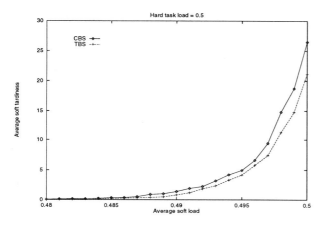

Figure 7. First experiment (TBS and CBS).

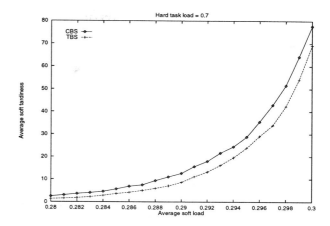

Figure 8. Second experiment.

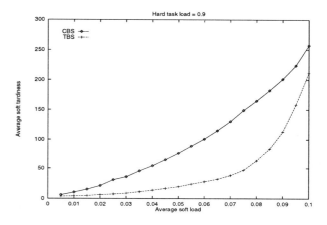

Figure 9. Third experiment.

5. Implementation and experimental results

The proposed CBS mechanism has been implemented on the HARTIK kernel [2, 10], to support some sample multimedia applications (see [1] for implementation details).

For example, an MPEG player has been executed using EDF, with and without CBS. The application consists of two periodic tasks: task τ_1 with a period $T_1 = 125ms$, corresponding to 8 frames per second (Fps), and task τ_2 with a period $T_2 = 30ms$ (33 Fps). Figure 11 reports the number of decoded frames as a function of time, when the two periodic tasks are scheduled by EDF, activating τ_2 at $t = 2000$. Since $C_1 = 49ms$, $C_2 = 53ms$ and $49/125 + 53/30 = 2.158 > 1$, when τ_2 is activated the system becomes overloaded. In fact, when τ_1 is the only task in the system, it runs at the required frame rate (8 Fps), but when at time $t = 2000$ τ_2 is activated, τ_1 slows down to $4.4Fps$, while τ_2 begins to execute at $17.96Fps$.

When τ_2 terminates, τ_1 increases its frame rate to its maximum value ($23, 8Fps$, that corresponds to a period of about $42ms$, which is the mean execution time for τ_1). After this transient interval, τ_1 returns to execute at $8Fps$.

Figure 12 shows the number of decoded frames as a function of time, when the same periodic tasks are scheduled by two CBSs with parameters $(Q_1, T_1) = (42, 125)$ and $(Q_2, T_2) = (19, 30)$. Being $42/125 + 19/30 = 0.969 < 1$, the two servers are schedulable, and being $Q_1 = 42 \simeq \overline{c_1}$, τ_1 will execute at a frame rate near to the required one.

From the figure we can see that the frame rate of τ_1 is about constant except for two little variations corresponding to the activation and the termination of τ_2 (remember that $Q = \overline{c}$ is a limit condition). This is obtained by slowing down the frame rate of τ_2 to 14.2 Fps: this task is clearly overloaded ($T_2 < \overline{c_2}$), so it is penalized by the CBS.

Notice that the proposed mechanism automatically arrange the task periods without using a-priori knowledge about the tasks' execution times. The only information used

11

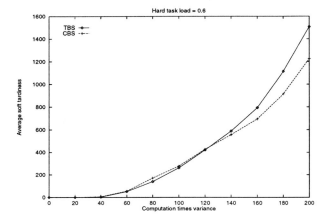

Figure 10. Fourth experiment.

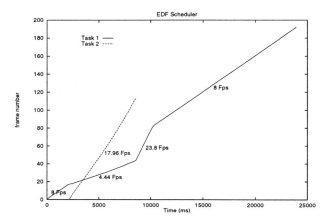

Figure 11. Two MPEG players scheduled by EDF.

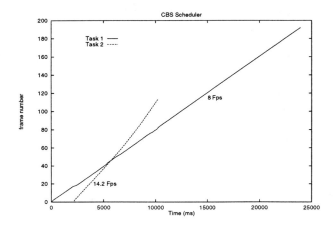

Figure 12. Two MPEG players scheduled by CBS.

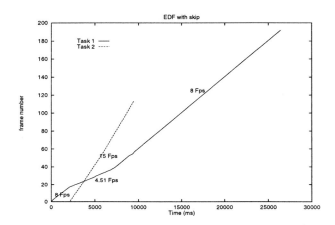

Figure 13. Two MPEG players scheduled by EDF with skip.

by the CBS is the couple (Q_i, T_i) and the estimation of task execution time given by the budget.

Figure 11 shows another undesirable effect: when τ_2 terminates, the frame rate of τ_1 increases to its maximum value (more than the required rate), in order to terminate in the same time instant in which it would terminate if τ_2 was not activated. This phenomenon causes an acceleration of the movie that appears unnatural and unpleasant. This problem can be solved using a skip strategy to serve soft tasks: when a job finishes after its absolute deadline, the next job is skipped.

As shown in Figure 13, a skip strategy eliminates accelerations in the movie, but it introduces another problem, which is presented in the next experiment, where the same movie is decoded by two identical tasks, with $\overline{U_{soft}} = 1$.

From Figure 14 it is easy to see that, although the two tasks have the same period, they proceed with different speed. This is due to the fact that the system is overloaded.

In fact, if

$$\overline{U_{soft}} = \frac{\overline{c_{1,j}}}{r_{1,j+1} - r_{1,j}} + \frac{\overline{c_{2,j}}}{r_{2,j+1} - r_{2,j}} = 1$$

then $U_{soft} = \frac{C_1}{T_1} + \frac{C_2}{T_2} > 1$.

Serving the two tasks by two identical CBSs with parameters $Q_s = \overline{c_{1,j}} = \overline{c_{2,j}}$ and $T_s = 2Q_s$, they proceed at the same rate (tasks' parameters are equal because the two tasks play the same video).

6. Conclusions

In this paper, we presented a novel service mechanism, the Constant Bandwidth Server, for integrating hard real-time and soft multimedia computing in a single system, under the EDF scheduling algorithm. The server has been

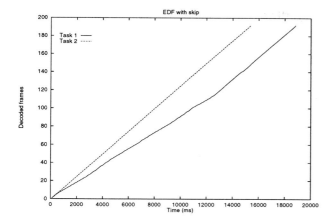

Figure 14. Two identical MPEG players scheduled by EDF with skip.

formally analyzed and compared with other known servers, obtaining very interesting results. The proposed model has also been implemented on the HARTIK kernel and used to support typical multimedia applications.

As a future work, in order to extend the proposed model to more general situations, the following issues need to be investigated. A concurrency control protocol needs to be integrated with the method to avoid priority inversion when accessing shared resources. The difference between the first and the current CBS deadline can be used as a kind of feedback for evaluating the request in excess and react accordingly adjusting the QoS in overload conditions. The CBS mechanism can be used to safely partition the CPU bandwidth among different applications that could coexist in the same system, as shown in [4]. A task can be used as a QoS manager to dynamically change the bandwidth reserved to each multimedia task. The strategies for changing the parameters of each CBS still have to be investigated.

References

[1] L. Abeni. Server mechanisms for multimedia applications. Technical Report RETIS TR98-01, Scuola Superiore S. Anna, 1998.

[2] G. C. Buttazzo. Hartik: A real-time kernel for robotics applications. In *IEEE Real-Time Systems Symposium*, December 1993.

[3] Z. Deng and J. W. S. Liu. Scheduling real-time applications in open envirovment. In *IEEE Real-Time Systems Symposium*, December 1997.

[4] Z. Deng, J. W. S. Liu, and J. Sun. A scheme for scheduling hard real-time applications in open system environment. In *Ninth Euromicro Workshop on Real-Time Systems*, 1997.

[5] T. M. Ghazalie and T. Baker. Aperiodic servers in a deadline scheduling environment. *Real-Time Systems*, 9, 1995.

[6] P. Goyal, X. Guo, and H. M. Vin. A hierarchical cpu scheduler for multimedia operating systems. In *2nd OSDI Symposium*, October 1996.

[7] K. Jeffay and D. Bennet. A rate-based execution abstraction for multimedia computing. In *Network and Operating System Support for Digital Audio and Video*, 1995.

[8] K. Jeffay, D. L. Stone, and F. D. Smith. Kernel support for live digital audio and video. *Computer Communications*, 15(6), 1992.

[9] H. Kaneko, J. A. Stankovic, S. Sen, and K. Ramamritham. Integrated scheduling of multimedia and hard real-time tasks. In *IEEE Real Time System Symposium*, December 1996.

[10] G. Lamastra, G. Lipari, G. Buttazzo, A. Casile, and F. Conticelli. Hartik 3.0: A portable system for developing real-time applications. In *Real-Time Computing Systems and Applications*, October 1997.

[11] C. L. Liu and J. Layland. Scheduling alghorithms for multiprogramming in a hard real-time environment. *Journal of the ACM*, 20(1), 1973.

[12] C. W. Mercer, S. Savage, and H. Tokuda. Processor capacity reserves for multimedia operating systems. Technical Report CMU-CS-93-157, Carnegie Mellon University, Pittsburg, May 1993.

[13] M. Spuri and G. Buttazzo. Scheduling aperiodic tasks in dynamic priority systems. *Real-Time Systems*, 10(2), 1996.

[14] M. Spuri, G. Buttazzo, and F. Sensini. Robust aperiodic scheduling under dynamic priority systems. In *IEEE Real-Time Systems Symposium*, December 1995.

[15] M. Spuri and G. C. Buttazzo. Efficient aperiodic service under the earliest deadline scheduling. In *IEEE Real-Time Systems Symposium*, December 1994.

[16] I. Stoica, H. Abdel-Wahab, K. Jeffay, S. K. Baruah, J. E. Gehrke, and C. G. Plaxton. A proportional share resource allocation algorithm for real-time, time-shared systems. In *IEEE Real Time System Symposium*, December 1996.

Isochronous Scheduling and its Application to Traffic Control

Masaaki Iwasaki, Tadashi Takeuchi, Masahiko Nakahara and Takahiro Nakano.

Systems Development Laboratory, Hitachi Ltd.

iwasaki@sdl.hitachi.co.jp

Abstract

Existing operating systems and communication protocols cannot achieve high quality video data transmission on an Ethernet, because they lack QoS assurance mechanisms for the shared medium. We have developed a kernel called Tactix to investigate new QoS assurance technologies that enable distributed continuous media applications.

In this paper, we focus on fixed bit rate video data transfer over an Ethernet, and we propose isochronous scheduling and its application to software traffic shaping. Furthermore, we present the results of measuring the service quality achieved by these technologies, which we obtained using ordinary personal computers and a shared mode 100-Mbps Ethernet. These indicate that the technologies enable multiple video streams (up to a total bandwidth of about 60 Mbps) and non-real-time background traffic to coexist on an Ethernet with a very low packet loss ratio and a transmission delay of less than a few milliseconds.

1. Introduction

The rapid progress of digital signal processing technologies is enabling the real-time transmission of video data over the Internet. Ethernet facilities widely available on LANs have a bandwidth of 10 or 100 Mbps today, so they are theoretically capable of transmitting video data compressed by MPEG or other methods. However, existing operating systems and communication protocols cannot achieve high quality video data transmission over an Ethernet, because they lack QoS assurance mechanisms for the shared medium. It is also believed that shared medium such as Ethernet is not adequate for real-time communication.

We have developed a kernel called Tactix from scratch to investigate new QoS assurance technologies that will enable real-time continuous media applications over networks including Ethernet. In this paper, we focus on fixed bit rate video data transfer over an Ethernet, and we propose isochronous scheduling and its application to software traffic shaping. Furthermore, we present the results of measuring the service quality achieved by these technologies. The results prove that these technologies enable high qual-

ity multiple video streams and non-real-time background traffic to coexist on an Ethernet.

In Section 2, we discuss Tactix kernel technologies including isochronous scheduling, fine-grain preemption and evaluation results for these technologies. In Section 3, we discuss Tactix communication technologies including Total Traffic Control Protocol and isochronous traffic shaping and their evaluation results.

2. Tactix Kernel Technologies

We designed Tactix as a real-time multi-threaded kernel suitable for continuous media processing[1,2,3]. Thus, it provides an asynchronous I/O function, a memory management function optimized for high throughput I/O, a low overhead synchronization function, and a real-time scheduling function. In this section, we focus on the real-time scheduling function of Tactix.

2.1. Limitations of Existing Technologies

Continuous media applications processing video data update the screen at constant intervals. Thus, the threads in those applications should be executed precisely and periodically. To achieve smooth video and audio playback on a computer system, an operating system must have accurate periodic scheduling of real-time threads (cyclic threads). Many scheduling algorithms have been proposed for this purpose; such as, rate monotonic scheduling [6], the earliest deadline first algorithm [7], the priority ceiling protocol [8], the deferrable server algorithm [10] or processor capacity reservation [9].

However, these scheduling mechanisms have the following drawbacks.

(a) Scheduling costs are increased in evaluating the priority of complicated constraints. For example, a scheduling queue should be scanned to search the thread with the least margin under its deadline conditions. In such a case, the scheduling costs are proportional to the number of ready state threads.

(b) When multiple cyclic threads coexist with multiple interrupt handlers driven by unpredictable sporadic events, it becomes difficult to satisfy their timing constraints simultaneously.

(c) If a thread exceeds the limit of its reserved CPU-time and continues execution, then successive deadline misses will occur because the activities of the other threads are affected by it.

Generally, it is difficult to keep the deadline miss ratio low in a multi-stream environment under heavy processor load caused by the frequent occurrence of external interrupts. For example, a video server is a system that faces this problem. Usually, a video server consists of multiple threads and each thread executes a dedicated task as shown in Fig. 1, and the server handles multiple streams simultaneously. Therefore, when many users are viewing and browsing the video contents, it is difficult to satisfy timing constraints required by both periodic activities and sporadic activities. If the periodic activities are executed with the highest priority, the scheduling delays of the sporadic activities result in response delay. This is a fatal problem for an interactive movie system. On the other hand, if the sporadic activities are executed with the highest priority, the periodic activities will experience frequent deadline misses and the playback quality will be degraded.

2.2. Isochronous Scheduling

In this section, we explain the design of an isochronous scheduling mechanism that solves the above problems. The maximum scheduling delay of this mechanism is less than few hundred microseconds even though multiple cyclic threads coexist with multiple interrupt handlers and normal threads.

In our design, we clearly separate the scheduling stage and the dispatching stage. We describe the scheduling stage in Section 2.2.1 and the dispatching stage in Section 2.2.2, and we discuss a mechanism that allows the coexistence of periodic activities and sporadic activities in Section 2.2.3.

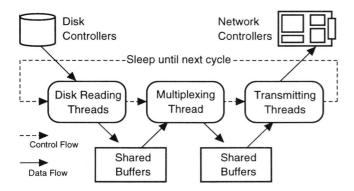

Fig. 1 Example of a video server application.

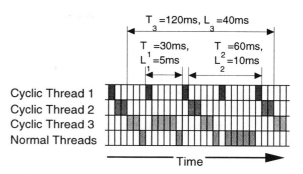

Fig. 2 Example of time-slot allocation.

2.2.1. Time-slot Reservation. We assume that a thread processing any continuous media can determine its execution period and the CPU-time in the period before it begins cyclic execution. Furthermore, though the CPU-time in a period may fluctuate to some extent, we assume that this has an upper limit.

We introduce an API named *start_cyclic_exec* so that each application can specify its timing constraints; that is, the execution period (T) and the CPU-time (L) in a period. In this API, the parameter *CPU-time in a period* means the upper bound of CPU-time reserved for the application's threads in a period.

The isochronous scheduler creates a time-slot table based on the time-constraint information specified by applications. The time-slot table is a reservation table for the CPU-time where the time sequence is divided into time-slots as shown in Fig. 2. Basically, each time-slot is assigned to a cyclic thread that can be executed in the interval.

The time-slot table is dynamically rebuilt when an application issues a *start_cyclic_exec* and a cyclic thread is added to the system, or when an application issues a *stop_cyclic_exec* and a cyclic thread is deleted from the system. When creating the time-slot table, the time-slots for a thread with a shorter period are allocated first. In the case of Fig. 2, allocation for thread1 is first, thread2 next, and thread3 last. If the required execution period is too long and it is not possible to allocate successive time-slots, discrete time-slots are allocated. Thread3 in Fig. 2 is an example of such a case. A CPU-time reservation request is rejected if the remaining processing capacity of the CPU is not sufficient when the request is issued.

Another important issue we have to consider is the granularity of a time-slot, because a shorter time-slot increases the timer interrupt overheads and a longer time-slot wastes the processor capacity. Therefore, we adjusted the length of a time-slot to about one tenth the timer interrupt interval. When we adjust the timer interrupt interval to 10 milliseconds, the length of a time-slot is set to 1 millisecond. An application can use the timer interrupt interval (10 milliseconds) as a unit of the period specification and the time-slot length (1 millisecond) as a unit of the CPU-time specification in a period. Kernel code checks the elapsed time of a current thread in an *enable_preempt* function (see Section 2.3.3) to detect the end of the reserved time-slots within a delay of about 100 microseconds.

The size of the time-slot table is proportional to the least common multiple of the periods specified by the applications. We have suppressed the increase in size of this table by restricting the available value for a period to be a power-of-two multiple of the timer interrupt interval.

2.2.2. Timer-driven Dispatch. As described in the previous section, the isochronous scheduler reserves the CPU-time for each cyclic thread by creating the time-slot table. The isochronous dispatcher, on the other hand, awakes the cyclic threads periodically with extremely small delay.

When the isochronous dispatcher is activated by any timer interrupt, it refers to the time-slot table to select and dispatch the cyclic thread that must be executed in the next time-slot with the highest priority. In each time-slot, there is only one cyclic thread that can be in a *raised state*. The other cyclic threads, except this raised-state thread, are kept in a *depressed state*. The raised-state thread is executed with the highest priority except the interrupt handlers, while the depressed-state threads are never executed until their allocated time-slot arrives.

If the reserved CPU-time is not exhausted in a period, the application can release the remaining CPU-time explicitly and the dispatcher will allocate it to any sporadic activities in a system. However, if there is not enough reserved CPU-time to complete the task in a period, a deadline-miss exception occurs. An exception handling thread is executed with normal priority so that it does not disturb the activities of the other cyclic threads, even though the exception is caused by a cyclic thread.

The isochronous dispatcher is activated by a hardware timer interrupt with an accurate constant interval, and each cyclic thread is awakened periodically according to the CPU-time reservation information kept in the time-slot table. The dispatcher itself does not need to evaluate the timing constraints of the activities in a system and it only looks up a time-slot table entry. This mechanism reduces the context switch costs and prevents a thread from consuming the CPU-time reserved for another cyclic thread.

2.2.3. Sporadic Event Handling. The next important issue we have to consider is the coexistence of the isochronous scheduling mechanism and a sporadic event handling mechanism such as an interrupt handler. In this section, we describe the Tactix kernel architecture related to this issue.

When the isochronous scheduler creates a time-slot table, some periods of the time-slots are intentionally reserved for sporadic activities to guarantee the minimum CPU-time required by them. Furthermore, when a cyclic thread has not exhausted the reserved CPU-time in a period, the isochronous dispatcher allocates the remaining CPU-time to the sporadic activities in a system as described in Section 2.2.2.

The upper bound of the response time for a sporadic event must be guaranteed, thus the interrupt handlers are divided into three layers; FLIH, SLIH and TLIH (first, second, and third level interrupt handlers, respectively).

FLIH and SLIH are given higher priority than the cyclic threads, and the priority of TLIH is lower than the priority of cyclic threads and higher than the priority of normal threads. Therefore, the execution overheads of FLIH and SLIH are minimized so that they do not waste the CPU-time reserved for cyclic threads, while the TLIH never disturbs the execution of a cyclic thread.

Each SLIH or TLIH is implemented as a thread, and they are resident in the kernel region that is shared by all address spaces. Therefore, all interrupt handlers are executable in a current address space without a process switch.

The FLIH does not share any kernel resources such as I/O buffers or queues with other threads. Thus, the FLIH is always executable immediately after the occurrence of external interrupts, even if the current thread is in a non-preemptable state. However, if the SLIH shares the kernel resources with other threads, then mutual exclusion for resource access is necessary. Therefore, we developed a fine-grain preemption mechanism which will be described in the next section to avoid the unpredictable delay caused by priority inversion.

2.3. Fine-grain Preemption

Generally, a multi-threaded kernel employs a mutual exclusion mechanism with a lock/unlock mechanism for shared resource access. However, if a context switch enforced by timer-driven dispatching occurs during execution of the critical section, it will cause priority inversion.

To avoid this problem, we developed a fine-grain preemption mechanism instead of a lock/unlock mechanism to achieve consistent access to the kernel resources. Thus, in principle, each thread executes the critical section in a non-preemptable state. If the current thread is in a non-preemptable state when a timer interrupt occurs, the dispatcher delays the context switch until the current thread reaches the next point of a state transition.

However, if preemption is disabled during the complete execution of a heavy system call such as process creation, the increase in the scheduling delay will disturb the periodic execution of cyclic threads. For example, if preemption is disabled during process creation, video playback will freeze during application launching.

To minimize this scheduling delay, we designed the structure of the Tactix kernel so that the maximum non-preemptable duration to execute a critical section would never exceed 100 microseconds. The following sections explain this fine-grain preemption approach.

2.3.1. Programming Constraint. First, we classified the system calls into two categories; the real-time class (RT class) and the non-real-time class (NRT class). The RT class includes light-weight system calls. Their costs are always predictable and rather small. The NRT class includes heavy system calls such as process creation, and their costs are usually unpredictable.

Next, we carefully designed the RT system calls so that their internal procedures would not need expensive resource allocation. Then, we have established a programming rule that any thread in a periodic execution mode could not issue NRT system calls. Thus, an application on Tactix must reserve the necessary resources using NRT system calls before its threads transit into the periodic execution mode. This programming constraint removes the unpredictable suspension of a cyclic thread caused by heavy resource allocation.

2.3.2. Serializer. The resource contention problems inside the NRT system calls are solved by a serializer. The serializer is the only thread that can access the significant shared resources in a Tactix kernel, and all requests using the NRT system calls from any user applications are accepted by the serializer through a FIFO queue. Therefore, the executions of the NRT system calls are serialized and no resource contentions occur.

Furthermore, the higher priority threads can preempt the execution of an NRT system call because the serializer itself has been designed to be preemptable with fine granularity as will be described in the next section.

2.3.3. Preemptable, Non-abortable State. We introduced a non-abortable state to make the execution of NRT system calls preemptable. A critical section that needs a lengthy duration to complete is executed in a *preemptable but non-abortable* state as shown in Fig. 3.

Each component of the Tactix kernel including the serializer is divided into non-preemptable code fragments. The execution of each code fragment is never preempted but the execution of the whole component may be preempted. However, the component may include shared resource accesses across the fragment boundary. If the execution of a thread is aborted at the fragment boundary, system consistency will be lost. Therefore, to prevent unexpected termination inside the preemptable critical section, each kernel thread issues a *disable_abort* at the beginning of the section, and it issues an *enable_abort* at the end of the section to restore its state. These primitives combined with the mechanism to be described in the next section are key parts

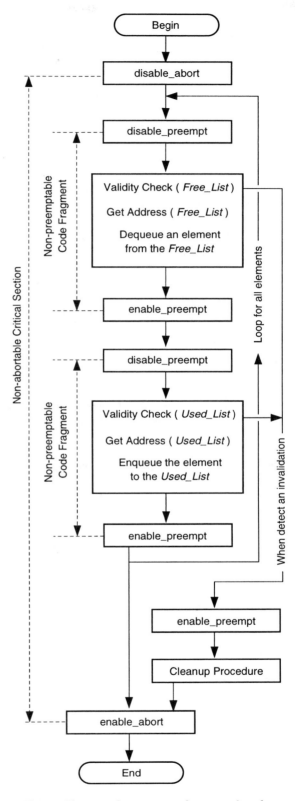

Fig. 3 Fine-grain preemption mechanism.

17

of fine-grain preemption.

2.3.4. Coherent Shared Resource Access. The mechanism described in the previous section is not complete when a shared resource is destroyed while a thread is accessing the resource across the fragment boundary.

When a user application causes an unrecoverable exception, all resources owned by this user process must be released. If a resource is shared among many processes, the deletion of the resource must be notified to all threads using it. In such a case, the usual kernel suspends the executions of all threads until these notifications have completed avoiding inconsistent access to the resource. Unfortunately, this operation causes undesirable suspension of the cyclic threads.

As shown in Fig. 3, we solved this problem by employing indirect resource access through using a unique resource identifier. *Free_List* and *Used_List* are shared resources in this example. The identifier must be converted to the resource address using the conversion function before the first resource access takes place in a non-preemptable code fragment. The obtained resource address is only available during temporal execution of the fragment.

The thread erasing the shared resource invalidates the corresponding entry for the identifier-to-address conversion. If the state of the shared resource is changed between the executions of two code fragments, the conversion fails and the thread trying to access the resource can detect that it is unavailable.

2.4. Evaluation of Scheduling Performance

In this section, we present the results of measuring the scheduling quality of the isochronous scheduler on Tactix.

2.4.1. Context Switch Cost. The isochronous scheduler separates the scheduling stage from the dispatching stage to reduce the cost of a context switch. Table 1 shows the measured context switch costs of the isochronous scheduler implemented on Tactix using a 133-MHz Pentium system. Each value includes kernel trapping, status saving for a current thread, looking up the time-slot table and selecting the next thread, changing priority for both the current thread and the next thread, and restoring the status and resuming execution for the next thread. The worst case values were measured by purging the TLB and cache intentionally just before the context switch.

These values prove that the increase in context switch cost to achieve isochronous dispatching is approximately 13 to 50 microseconds.

Table 2 Measured preemption granularities

System Call Function		microseconds
Process Manager	proc_create	46.8
	proc_delete	38.1
	proc_resume	22.1
	proc_suspend	23.5
	proc_get_info	4.2
	proc_set_info	3.1
	proc_get_my_pid	0
Thread Manager	thread_create	40.3
	thread_delete	48.5
	thread_resume	13.0
	thread_suspend	23.9
	thread_get_info	8.9
	thread_set_info	7.7
	thread_start_cyclic_exec	43.5
	thread_stop_cyclic_exec	35.0
	thread_raise_handoff	30.4
	thread_create_thread_group	27.5
	thread_delete_thread_group	20.9
	thread_get_my_tid	0
Virtual Memory Manager	vm_allocate_region	51.5
	vm_share_region	42.5
	vm_delete_region	49.6
	vm_get_region_info	11.8
	vm_set_region_info	48.1
Physical Memory Manager	pm_allocate_phys_page_set	55.9
	pm_share_phys_page_set	38.4
	pm_deallocate_phys_page_set	33.1
	pm_map_phys_page_set	50.6
	pm_unmap_phys_page_set	44.8
	pm_get_phys_page_set_info	12.7
	pm_set_phys_page_set_info	4.4
Event Box Manager	event_create_ebox	15.3
	event_delete_ebox	10.2
	event_init_and_ebox	45.2
	event_notify	46.2
	event_listen	33.2
	event_check_ebox	8.7

Table 1 Measured context switch costs

From	To	Best case	Worst case
Normal Thread	Normal Thread	23.5	42.0
Normal Thread	Cyclic Thread	50.5	74.3
Cyclic Thread	Normal Thread		
Cyclic Thread	Cyclic Thread	36.9	67.8

(microseconds)

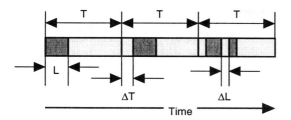

Fig. 4 Definition of scheduling jitter.

2.4.2. Preemption Granularity. Tactix employs a fine-grain preemption mechanism to avoid the priority inversion problem. Table 2 shows the maximum non-preemptable duration of each system call. These values were measured on a 133-MHz Pentium system, and cache and TLB were completely purged just before measurement. The units of all values are in microseconds. These results indicate that the maximum scheduling delay caused by the access conflicts of kernel resources is less than 60 microseconds.

2.4.3. Scheduling Jitter. The advantage of an isochronous scheduler will be obvious when a heavy I/O processing load is added to a processor while cyclic threads are being executed. In this experiment, the increase in scheduling jitter (ΔT in Fig. 4) and CPU-time (ΔL in Fig. 4) during a period is caused by the frequent occurrence of I/O interrupts for the communication processing. Figures 5 and 6 show the increases in ΔT and ΔL respectively. Executions of FLIH and SLIH increase ΔL though the ΔL is not counted as the part of the CPU-time executing a cyclic thread.

Four cyclic threads and a normal thread are executed concurrently in this case. Each cyclic thread requires an 8-millisecond reserved CPU-time during a 40-millisecond period and it executes an infinite memory copying loop that pollutes the processor cache. The normal thread receives packets at variable transfer rates, calculates their checksums, and sends them back at the same transfer rates without any packet loss. These threads are executed on a 200-MHz PentiumPro system, and the packets are transferred using a 100-Mbps Ethernet controller (DEC DC21141).

The horizontal axis of Fig. 5 represents the packet transfer rate in Mbps and the vertical axis represents the scheduling jitter (ΔT) in microseconds. Similarly, the vertical axis of Fig. 6 represents the increase in CPU-time (ΔL) during a period. The percentage values in both graphs indicate the probabilities that ΔT or ΔL in each cycle will not exceed the corresponding plotted value.

The results indicate that Tactix can schedule the cyclic threads precisely while executing communication processing that saturates a 100-Mbps Ethernet. The average scheduling jitters are less than 40 microseconds, and the maximum jitters will not exceed 150 microseconds with a probability of 99% under that condition.

Figures 7 and 8 shows the ΔT of RT-Mach using rate monotonic scheduling and earliest deadline first scheduling, respectively. The measurement conditions are identical to Fig. 5 including hardware constructions.

The ΔT of earliest deadline first scheduling is about 1/10 that of rate monotonic scheduling. However, it exceeds 1600 microseconds with the probability of 1% when the communication load is increased. The ΔT of isochronous scheduling shown in Fig. 5 is approximately 1/10 that of earliest deadline first scheduling shown in Fig. 8.

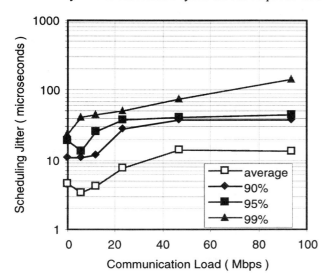

Fig. 5 Measured jitter of Tactix using isochronous scheduling.

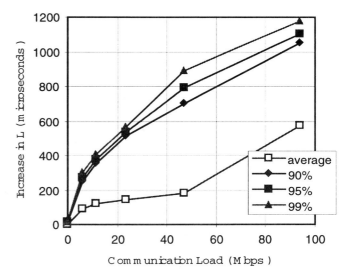

Fig. 6 Measured CPU-time increase in a period using isochronous scheduling.

19

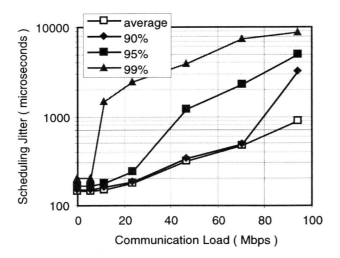

Fig. 7 Measured jitters of RT-Mach using rate-monotonic scheduling.

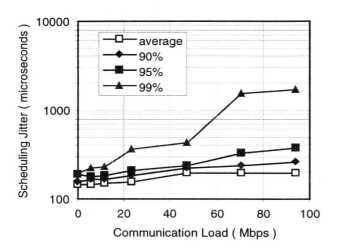

Fig. 8 Measured jitters of RT-Mach using earliest deadline first scheduling.

3. Tactix Communication Technology

As described in the previous sections, we developed an isochronous scheduling mechanism that enables the precise cyclic executions of multiple threads. In this section, we will progress to the application of this technology to real-time communication over the Ethernet [4,5]. The communication technologies proposed here enable the high quality transfer of multiple video data streams on an Ethernet segment without modifying the current hardware standards and the upper layer protocols.

In Section 3.1, we will, first, clarify the technical problems that must be solved to achieve real-time communication by examining the characteristics of the Ethernet. In

Section 3.2, we propose a software traffic shaping mechanism and a traffic control signaling protocol to solve these problems. Finally, in Section 3.3, we present the measurement results which confirm the effect of the proposed technologies.

3.1. Traffic Flow and QoS on an Ethernet

Ethernet hardware employs a collision detection and retransmission mechanism called CSMA/CD. Therefore, the concentration of traffic from many nodes in a short interval increases the probability of collisions, and it degrades the service quality of data transfer in an Ethernet segment.

In this section, we quantitatively analyze the relationship between traffic flow and service quality on an Ethernet. In the following discussion, we assume that many nodes share a single physical segment, or many nodes are connected by a shared hub (repeater hub) or hubs.

First of all, an appropriate traffic shaping mechanism is required to guarantee the service quality of data transfer on shared media such as the Ethernet. It is necessary to limit the total traffic flow in each short interval (T), and this interval T must be sufficiently small compared to the maximum allowable value of transfer delay (D). For example, when the value of D is 10 milliseconds and the value of T is 500 milliseconds, though the average traffic flow during the 500 milliseconds is low, a heavy traffic state may continue for more than 10 milliseconds and this will degrade the service quality. The total traffic flow in a physical segment is controlled by adjusting the amount of transmission data from each node in an interval T, and this value of T means the transmission triggering interval; the interval between the trigger of data transmission and the next trigger.

On the other hand, considering the occurrence of collisions during packet transmission, the transmission triggering interval T must be long enough so that the hardware retransmission mechanism can successfully transmit the

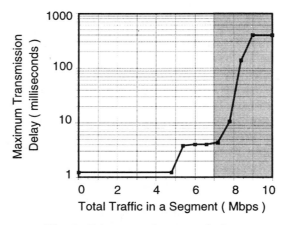

Fig. 9 Ethernet characteristics.

packet.

Taking the above constraints into consideration, we assumed 40 milliseconds to be the transmission triggering interval for a 10-Mbps Ethernet, and 5 or 10 milliseconds to be that for a 100-Mbps Ethernet in the following discussion.

Figure 9 shows the relationship between traffic and transfer delay on a 10-Mbps Ethernet calculated by computer simulation. The simulation condition reflects a situation where eight sender nodes transmit packets at the same specified rate on a single physical segment. We assumed that each node had a network interface device that was capable of successive transmissions of multiple packets by a single trigger from a device driver. The traffic flow was controlled by varying the number of transmitting packets during each transmission triggering interval. The horizontal axis of Fig. 9 represents the total amount of transmitted data from all nodes in 40 milliseconds, and the vertical axis represents the maximum transmission delay.

The simulation results indicated that if the total traffic was less than 50% of the physical bandwidth of the network, the occurrence of collisions would be very rare and the maximum delay negligibly small. Furthermore, the maximum delay is less than few milliseconds if the total traffic is less than 70% of the physical bandwidth.

However, if the total traffic exceeds 75% of the physical bandwidth, the increases in the maximum transfer delay become radical due to the frequent occurrence of transmission collisions. In such a situation, the hardware level retransmissions from each node increase the network busy ratio, and this results in the more frequent occurrence of collisions. Due to these positive feedback phenomena, the transfer delay exceeds a few hundred milliseconds. Furthermore, if the traffic increases further, the retransmission count exceeds 16 (the upper limit) and the packets are discarded. If the hardware retransmission fails and a software retransmission mechanism such as TCP is invoked, it becomes impossible to maintain the service quality required by interactive video applications.

3.2. TTCP and ITM

The above consideration indicates that Ethernet has the capability of high quality real-time data transmission, if the total traffic flow in a physical segment is suppressed so that it does not exceed a certain threshold. If the total traffic flow in a segment is less than 70% of its physical bandwidth, the hardware retransmission mechanism of the Ethernet guarantees the transmission of a packet within a few milliseconds.

In this section, we explain the design of the total traffic control protocol (TTCP) and the isochronous transmission mode (ITM). The basic idea of our design is to insert a soft-

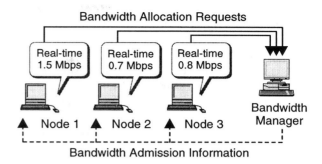

Fig. 10 Bandwidth reservation protocol.

ware filter between the network layer (IP layer) and the device driver layer so that the filter can suppress the excessive outgoing flow from a node. The TTCP is a signaling protocol that controls the filter to suppress the excess increases in total traffic flows for both real-time and non-real-time data transmissions in a segment. The ITM module is the filter itself, and it is a traffic shaping mechanism that avoids the concentrations in the traffic flows over a short interval (about 5-10 milliseconds). The TTCP and ITM can guarantee the QoS of real-time data transfer by reducing the probability of collisions in a segment.

3.2.1. Total Traffic Control. In this section, we explain a signaling protocol TTCP and the bandwidth allocation algorithm for the Total Traffic Control system.

We assume that there is a bandwidth manager (BM) on each physical segment as shown in Fig. 10. All nodes in the segment obtain the address of the BM at their boot time, and each node sends a bandwidth reservation request to the BM before it starts RT or NRT communication. The BM receives these requests and allocates the required bandwidth to each request.

The BM allocates a bandwidth to a logical port (socket) for RT communication, and it allocates a bandwidth to a node for NRT communication. Each node sends a reservation request with a specific value when it demands an RT

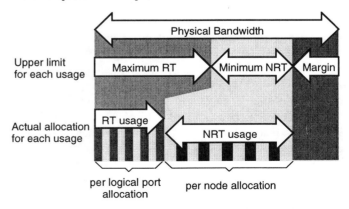

Fig. 11 Bandwidth limit and allocation.

bandwidth. On the other hand, each node sends a reservation request without a specific value when it demands an NRT bandwidth, then the BM determines an actual value for the NRT bandwidth.

As shown in Fig. 11, the BM allocates the bandwidth for RT communication prior to the bandwidth for NRT communication, if there is sufficient capacity remaining. The BM may refuse an RT bandwidth reservation request, if the required RT bandwidth exceeds the remaining capacity. After the whole RT bandwidth is allocated, the BM subtracts the total RT bandwidth and the bandwidth margin from the physical bandwidth to avoid jamming. Then, the BM divides the remaining bandwidth equally among the nodes demanding NRT bandwidth. In our experimental system using the 100-Mbps Ethernet, we set up a bandwidth margin of 20 Mbps, and an upper limit for total RT bandwidth of 50 Mbps, therefore, a 30-Mbps bandwidth at least was reserved for NRT communication.

The BM broadcasts the updated bandwidth admission information to all nodes in a segment after it has determined the new bandwidth allocation. If the BM has accepted a new reservation or release request from a node, it always broadcasts the updated admission information because this affects the NRT bandwidth of all nodes.

In the TTCP system, an RT bandwidth is not released until an application explicitly cancels the reservation. On the other hand, an NRT bandwidth is automatically released if no packets have transmitted from the node during a certain interval. Furthermore, if an application has terminated abnormally, all the RT bandwidth reserved by it is released.

Similarly, if a node is frozen by unexpected failure, all the bandwidth reserved for it is released. Each node periodically sends a message to the BM requiring continuation of the reservation in a specific interval (approximately 10 seconds), and the BM replies to this. If the BM does not receive this message from a node, it sends a message to it querying if the reservation is to continue. If the BM cannot get a reply to this message, it detects node failure and salvages the accidentally unreleased bandwidth.

3.2.2. Software Isochronous Transmission. The isochronous transmission mechanism built into each node provides outgoing flow control and traffic shaping facilities which obey the bandwidth admission information sent from the BM. As shown in Fig. 12, a small software module called ITM controls the amount of data injecting into a physical segment within a short interval (5-10 milliseconds for 100-Mbps Ehernet) so that the total traffic flow in the segment does not exceed a certain threshold.

The ITM module intercepts all transmission requests invoked by applications just before a device driver accepts them. The ITM module is implemented as a cyclic thread, and it is activated periodically with the transmission trig-

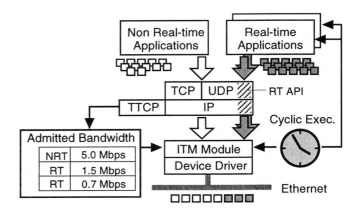

Fig. 12 Flow control by ITM module.

gering interval (After this, this interval is called the ITM period). In each ITM period, the ITM module only transmits packets corresponding to the admitted RT bandwidth for each logical port and the admitted NRT bandwidth for the node.

The start timing of the ITM period does not need to be synchronized for nodes in a segment, though the ITM period of all nodes should be identical. Therefore, transmission collision will occur during intervals shorter than the ITM period. However, each node can try several retransmissions during the interval, because the physical layer of the Ethernet has the retransmission mechanism. The probability of consecutive failure in these retransmissions is extremely low, because the average traffic flow in an ITM period is suppressed by the TTCP and ITM mechanism. Thus, each node can transmit all packets corresponding to the admitted bandwidth with a very high probability in each ITM period.

Furthermore, ITM improves the end-to-end reliability because the isochronous traffic shaping at the sender side reduces the receive buffer overflow at the receiver side.

3.3. Performance Evaluation of TTCP/ITM

In this section, we discuss the results of measuring real-time communication quality using the TTCP/ITM mechanism on Tactix. In Section 3.3.1, we investigate the transmission of 48-Mbps video data streams coexisting with burst NRT traffic on a 100-Mbps Ethernet. In Section 3.3.2, we investigate the relationship between the total traffic and the occurrence of collisions using eight active sender nodes.

3.3.1. Video data Transfer. The purpose of this real-time video data transfer experiment was to validate the effectiveness of TTCP/ITM. The NRT traffic flow is injected into the segment while the video server is transmitting the video data. Figure 13 is the configuration for the experimental system.

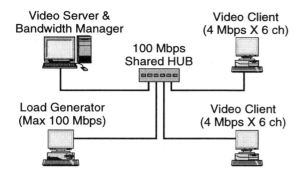

Fig. 13 Configuration of experimental VOD system.

All nodes are ordinary personal computers and they are connected by a 100Base-T half-duplex mode Ethernet through a shared hub. The bandwidth manager is configured as follows; the bandwidth margin is 10 Mbps, the minimum bandwidth for NRT communication is 10 Mbps, and the ITM period is 10 milliseconds.

In this experimental system, the video server transmits six video streams to each of the two video clients. Because the bit rate of each video stream is 4 Mbps, the total RT bandwidth occupied by the server is 48 Mbps. Each video client receives the six video streams and plays them back. Each client also monitors the successful packet arrival ratio. The traffic generator is capable of saturating the 100-Mbps Ethernet, and it injects the NRT traffic flow into the segment.

Figure 14 shows the outgoing traffic flow for the video server and that of the traffic generator without TTCP/ITM. Each vertical bar represents the flow during a 10 millisecond interval. When the elapsed time reaches the 100-millisecond point, the traffic generator starts NRT transmission and this interferes with video data transmission. In this situation, the successful packet arrival ratio falls to 50% - 80%, and frames are frequently lost.

Figure 15 shows the outgoing traffic flow for the video server and that of the traffic generator with TTCP/ITM. Identical to the above case, when the elapsed time reaches the 100-millisecond point, the traffic generator starts NRT transmission. However, here, the NRT traffic does not interfere with the video data transmission. In this situation, the successful packet arrival ratio stays at 100%, and the no frames are lost.

3.3.2. Collision Histogram. In the TTCP/ITM system, the important factor that determines the service quality of RT communication is not the number of nodes but the total traffic in a segment. This is because, if the number of active sender nodes is increased, the BM decreases the NRT bandwidth of each node to keep the total traffic in a segment constant.

The purpose of this measurement was to investigate the relationship between the service quality and the total traffic flow in a segment. The experimental system consisted of eight sender nodes as shown in Fig. 16, and all nodes were ordinary personal computers connected by a 100Base-T half-duplex mode Ethernet through a shared hub. In this measurement, all nodes reserved an identical bandwidth and started transmission simultaneously. We measured the frequency distribution of the occurrence count of consecutive collisions and the packet loss ratio while varying the traffic flow in a segment for 120 seconds.

The two patterns in Fig. 17 show the histogram of the occurrence count of consecutive collisions. The horizontal axis of Fig. 17 indicates the consecutive collisions count due to hardware level retransmission, and the vertical axis indicates the occurrence count. The front pattern corresponds to a situation where the total traffic flow is suppressed to 48

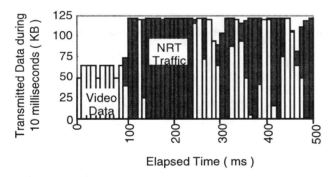

Fig. 14 Video-data transfer interfered by NRT traffic.

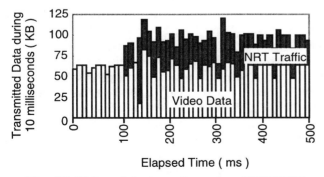

Fig. 15 Video-data transfer using TTCP/ITM.

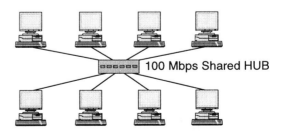

Fig. 16 Configuration of eight-sender system.

23

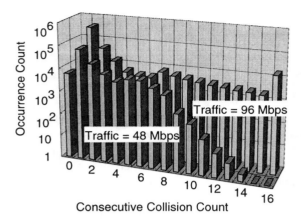

Fig. 17 Measured collision histogram.

Mbps, and the back one corresponds to a situation where the total traffic flow reaches 96 Mbps. These histogram patterns confirm that the hardware retransmission mechanism of the Ethernet is useful for real-time data transfer, if the total traffic flow is properly suppressed.

The solid line in Fig. 18 indicates the relationship between the transmission failure ratio and the total traffic flow in a segment. The transmission failure ratio means the probability that all sixteen time retransmissions have failed.

The dotted line in Fig. 18 indicates the increase in transmission failure ratio due to deadline miss. If the traffic in a segment increases too much, the Ethernet device cannot complete the transmissions of packets during an ITM period, and all packets for the next period are discarded.

Figure 18 indicates that the service quality of RT communication is adjustable depending on user requirements by varying the bandwidth margin. For example, the probability of deadline miss occurrence approaches zero if the total traffic flow is suppressed below 77 Mbps. Similarly, the packet loss ratio is kept below 0.01% if the total traffic

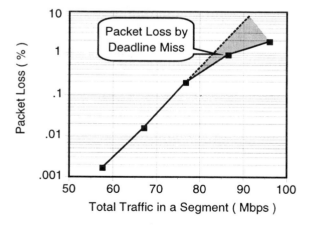

Fig. 18 Traffic vs. packet loss ratio.

flow is suppressed to 65 Mbps. Furthermore, this quality is sufficient for real-time transmission of digital video data such as MPEG1.

4. Related Work

4.1 Real-time Scheduling

Though the basic concept of isochronous scheduling is similar to processor capacity reservation [9], there is a significant difference between them. To satisfy the time constraints given by applications, processor capacity reservation uses a dynamic scheduling algorithm such as the earliest deadline first [7], which schedules and dispatches threads simultaneously. In contrast with this, our method clearly separates the scheduling stage and the dispatching stage to reduce the cost of a context switch.

The time-slot reservation at the scheduling stage resembles that of rate monotonic scheduling [6]. However, in our method, the execution delay caused by the frequent occurrence of sporadic events is never accumulated, because dispatching is tightly synchronized to timer interrupts.

Another important difference is the mutual exclusion mechanism for kernel resources. The priority ceiling protocol [8] or Rialto's real-time resource management [11] can reduce the execution delay caused by priority inversion to some extent, but this is very limited. Besides, they increase the scheduling costs dramatically. Fine-grain preemption guarantees an upper bound for execution delay caused by priority inversion (about 100 microseconds) with very low overheads.

4.2 Real-time Communication

Numerous research projects aimed at achieving the multimedia data communications have been planned and introduced over the last couple of years. For example, RTP [13] has been proposed as a transport layer protocol and RSVP [14] has been proposed as a resource reservation signaling protocol for multimedia communication, respectively.

RTP requires a lower layer protocol to guarantee reliability, correct ordering and the small jitter in the transmission of packets. Similarly, RSVP requires the lower layer to have appropriate flow control facilities. However, it is not very easy to satisfy these requirements.

There has been little research targeted to solve the problem for shared media such as the Ethernet. The approach of RETHER [12] is aimed at real-time communication on the Ethernet without modifying its hardware specifications. In contrast with TTCP/ITM, RETHER employs a token passing mechanism for bandwidth admission.

However, the nature of the token passing mechanism involves overall delays becoming sensitive to the processing capacity or load of each node. Moreover, if the token is lost due to node failure, it becomes difficult to maintain service quality. On the other hand, in TTCP/ITM, even if node failure occurs, the service qualities of communication among nodes are never degraded except for the failure node.

5. Conclusion

We have developed and demonstrated the performance of a kernel called Tactix which includes new QoS assurance technologies for high quality distributed continuous media applications. In this paper, we proposed isochronous scheduling and its application to software traffic control on the Ethernet. Furthermore, we were able to measure the service quality and the performance achieved by these technologies using ordinary personal computers, shared mode 100-Mbps Ethernet.

The results of evaluation prove the advantages of the proposed technologies. The isochronous scheduler can schedule the cyclic threads precisely while executing communication processing that saturates the 100-Mbps Ethernet. The average scheduling jitters are less than 40 microseconds, and the maximum jitters will not exceed 150 microseconds. TTCP/ITM enables the high quality transfer of multiple video data streams on an Ethernet segment without modifying the current hardware standards or the upper layer protocols. The packet loss ratio is kept below 0.01% if the total traffic flow is suppressed to 65 Mbps. This quality is sufficient for real-time transmission of digital video data such as MPEG1.

The bandwidth reservation by TTCP/ITM mechanism is valuable not only for real-time applications but also for non-real-time applications that need response time assurance. Furthermore, the combination of bandwidth reservation by TTCP/ITM and CPU-time reservation by isochronous scheduling will lead to high quality real-time routing.

References

[1] M. Iwasaki, T. Takeuchi, M. Nakahara, T. Nakano, S. Nakamura, S. Taguchi, and K. Serizawa, "Design and Evaluation of a Microkernel for Continuous Media Processing," IPSJ Computer System Symposium, Vol. 96, No. 7, pp. 99-104, Nov. 1996 (in Japanese).

[2] T. Takeuchi, M. Iwasaki, M. Nakahara, T. Nakano, and K. Serizawa, "A Design and Performance Evaluation of Isochronous Scheduler," IPSJ OS, Vol. 74, No. 26, pp. 147-152, Feb. 1997 (in Japanese).

[3] M. Iwasaki, T. Takeuchi, M. Nakahara, T. Nakano, S. Nakamura, S. Taguchi, and K. Serizawa, "A Micro-kernel for Isochronous Video data Transfer," Proc. of WWCA '97 Tsukuba, Lecture Notes in Computer Science, No. 1274, pp. 334-349, Springer, Mar. 1997.

[4] M. Iwasaki, T. Nakano, T. Takeuchi, and M. Nakahara, "QoS Assurance on an Ethernet using Isochronous Traffic Shaping," IPSJ DPS, Vol. 84, No. 3, pp. 13-18, Sep. 1997 (in Japanese).

[5] T. Nakano, M. Iwasaki, M. Nakahara, and T. Takeuchi, "Design and Implementation of a QoS Assurance Mechanism on an Ethernet," IPSJ Computer System Symposium, Vol. 97, No. 8, pp. 35-42, Nov. 1997 (in Japanese).

[6] C. L. Liu, and J. Layland, "Scheduling Algorithms for Multiprogramming in a Hard-real-time Environment," Journal of the ACM, Vol. 20, No. 1, Jan. 1973.

[7] M. Dertouzos, "Control Robotics: The Procedural Control of Physical Processes," Proc. IFIP Cong., 1974.

[8] L. Sha, R. Rajkumar, and J. P. Lehoczky, "Priority Inheritance Protocols: An Approach to Real-time Synchronization," IEEE Transactions on Computers, Vol. 39, No. 9, Sep. 1990.

[9] C. W. Mercer, S. Savage, and H. Tokuda, "Processor Capacity Reserves: Operating System Support for Multimedia Applications," Proc. Intl. Conf. on Multimedia Computing and Systems (ICMCS), pp. 90-99, 1994.

[10] J. K. Strosnider, J. P. Lehoczky, and L. Sha, "The Deferrable Server Algorithm for Enhanced Aperiodic Responsiveness in Hard Real-time Environments," IEEE Transactions on Computers, Vol. 44, No. 1, Sep. 1995.

[11] M.B. Jones, D. Rosu, and M. C. Rosu, "CPU Reservations and Time Constraints: Efficient, Predictable Scheduling of Independent Activities," ACM SOSP '97, Saint-Malo, France, Oct. 1997.

[12] C. Venkatramani, and T. Chiueh, "Design, Implementation, and Evaluation of a Software-based Real-time Ethernet Protocol," SIGCOMM '95 Cambridge, pp. 27-37, 1995.

[13] H. Schulzrinne, S. Casner, R. Frederick, and V. Jacobson, "RTP: A Transport Protocol for Real-time Applications," IETF RFC-1889, Jan. 1996.

[14] R. Braden, L. Zhang, S. Berson, S. Herzog, and S. Jamin, "Resource ReSerVation Protocol (RSVP) — Version 1 Functional Specification," IETF RFC-2205, Sep. 1997.

Schedulability Analysis for Tasks with Static and Dynamic Offsets

By: J.C. Palencia and M. González Harbour
Departamento de Electrónica y Computadores, Universidad de Cantabria, SPAIN

Abstract

In this paper we present an extension to current schedulability analysis techniques for periodic tasks with offsets, scheduled under a preemptive fixed priority scheduler. Previous techniques allowed only static offsets restricted to being smaller than the task periods. With the extension presented in this paper, we eliminate this restriction and we allow both static and dynamic offsets. The most significant application of this extension is in the analysis of multiprocessor and distributed systems. We show that we can achieve a significant increase of the maximum schedulable utilization by using the new technique, as opposed to using previously known worst-case analysis techniques for distributed systems.

1. Introduction

The collection of real-time analysis techniques for fixed-priority systems [1], historically known as rate monotonic analysis [3], represents a mature technology for obtaining guarantees about the timing requirements in hard real-time systems. Although it is possible to get higher utilization levels with dynamic priority scheduling algorithms, fixed priority systems are simpler to analyze and understand, and are supported in standard operating systems and compiler systems.

Rate monotonic analysis (RMA) allows an exact calculation of the worst-case response time of tasks in single-processor real time systems, including the effects of task synchronization [8], the presence of aperiodic tasks, the effects of deadlines before, at or after the periods of the tasks [2], precedence constraints and tasks with varying priorities [4], overhead analysis, etc. However, there are two related areas in which current RMA cannot provide exact

solutions to the response times: distributed hard real-time systems, and systems in which tasks suspend themselves. Current techniques for these systems are based on the assumption that all tasks are independent, and thus they lead to pessimistic results [10][6]. If an exact or a less pessimistic technique could be accomplished, this would enable more efficient use of the computing power available in these real-time systems.

Tindell developed in [11] a technique to calculate the worst-case response bound or an upper bound to it, for sets of tasks with static offsets. In his paper, the system is composed of periodic transactions, each containing several tasks. Each task is released after some time, called the offset, elapses since the arrival of the event that triggers the transaction. In [11], the task offsets are restricted to being smaller than the task's periods, and they are static. This is useful in those systems where task activations are timed precisely, at periodic intervals, to avoid the negative effects of jitter. However, a technique to calculate the worst-case response times of tasks sets with offsets could be very valuable to obtain a solution to the problems of task suspension and distributed systems if task offsets could be dynamic, i.e., if they could change from one activation to the next. For example, in distributed systems a task may be released when a previous task completes its execution and a message is received; this release time can vary from one period to the next. In addition, in distributed systems it is common that task deadlines are larger than the periods, and thus it is also very likely that task offsets might become larger than the task periods.

Consequently, in this paper we extend Tindell's analysis of tasks with static offsets in the following ways: we eliminate the restriction of task offsets being smaller than the period; we provide a formal basis that overcomes some defects in [11]; and most important, we extend the technique to cover the case in which task offsets may vary dynamically, and thus we make the technique directly applicable to the analysis of distributed systems and systems

This work has been supported in part by the *Comisión Interministerial de Ciencia y Tecnología* of the Spanish Government, under grant number TAP97-892

in which task suspend themselves. As we will show, in distributed systems the new technique allows a significant increase of the schedulable utilization of the CPU compared to the case when previous analysis techniques were used. This comes at no cost for the application, which will still be scheduled using fixed priorities.

The paper is organized as follows. In Section 2 we present the analysis for tasks with static offsets. We start with the computational model and discuss existing techniques for solving this problem. Then, we present our extension of Tindell's technique to allow task offsets to be larger than the periods. In Section 3 we extend this technique to the analysis of tasks with dynamic offsets. Then, in Section 4 we show how to apply this analysis to determine the schedulability of a distributed or multiprocessor real-time system. In Section 5 we compare the results obtained with our technique with the results obtained with previously known techniques; we will see that with the new technique the response times are significantly lower. Finally, in Section 6 we give our conclusions.

2. Analysis for Tasks with Static Offsets

2.1. Computational Model

The real-time system that we will consider for the analysis of tasks with static offsets is composed of a set of tasks executing in the same processor, which are grouped into entities that we will call *transactions* [11]. Each transaction Γ_i is activated by a periodic sequence of external events with period T_i, and contains a set of m_i tasks. The relative phasings between the different external events are arbitrary. Each task is activated (released) when a relative time —called the *offset*— elapses after the arrival of the external event. In this section of the paper we will assume that the offset is static, i.e., it does not change from one activation to the next. Each activation of a task releases the execution of one instance of that task, that we will call a *job*.

Figure 1 shows an example of such system: the horizontal axis represents time; down-pointing arrows represent the arrival of the external events associated to each transaction, while up-pointing arrows represent the activation times of each task; and shaded boxes represent task execution. We will assume that each task has its own unique priority, and that the task set is scheduled using a preemptive fixed priority scheduler. Notice that although offsets represent a kind of precedence constraints, in our analysis tasks are activated at a time equal to the arrival of the external event

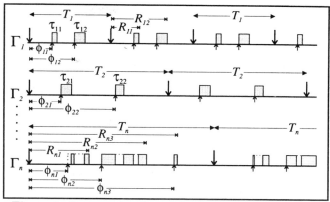

Figure 1. Computational model of a system composed of transactions with static offsets

plus the offset, and they execute at their assigned priority regardless of whether tasks of the same transaction and smaller offsets have finished or not.

Each task will be identified with two subscripts: the first one identifies the transaction to which it belongs, and the second one the position that the task occupies within the tasks of its transaction, when they are ordered by increasing offsets. In this way, τ_{ij} will be the j-th task of transaction Γ_i, with an offset of Φ_{ij} and a worst-case execution time of C_{ij}. In addition, we will allow each task to have jitter, that is to have its activation time delayed by an arbitrary amount of time between 0 and the maximum jitter for that task, which we will call J_{ij}. This means that the activation time of task τ_{ij} may occur at any time between $t_0+\Phi_{ij}$ and $t_0+\Phi_{ij}+J_{ij}$, where t_0 is the instant at which the external event arrived.

We will allow deadlines to be larger than the period, and thus at each time there may be several activations of the same task pending. We will also allow both the offset Φ_{ij} and the jitter J_{ij} to be larger than the period of its transaction, T_i. For each task τ_{ij} we define its response time as the difference between its completion time and the instant at which the associated external event arrived. The worst-case response time will be called R_{ij}. Each task may have an associated global deadline, D_{ij}, which is also relative to the arrival of the external event.

We will assume that if tasks synchronize for using shared resources in a mutually exclusive way they will be using a hard real-time synchronization protocol such as the priority ceiling protocol [8]. Under this assumption, the effects of lower priority tasks on a task under analysis τ_{ab} are bounded by an amount called the blocking term B_{ab}, calculated as the maximum of all the critical sections of lower priority tasks that have a priority ceiling higher than or equal to the priority of τ_{ab}. Analysis of systems with aperiodic tasks will be addressed in a future paper.

2.2. Current Response Time Analysis Techniques

The RMA analysis technique for tasks with jitter by Tindell and Clark [10], was extended by Tindell [11] to take into account the task offsets, and thus reduce the pessimism of the analysis. He obtained an exact schedulability analysis that was computationally intractable for large task sets, because of the high number of cases that had to be checked, which was exponentially dependent on the number of tasks. However, based upon this technique he developed an approximate upper bound for the worst-case response time, that could be obtained by analyzing a number of cases that was polynomially dependent on the number of tasks. Although the approximate upper bound is pessimistic, it is much closer to the exact solution than the original RMA technique.

However, Tindell's technique was restricted to task offsets being smaller than the associated task periods. In addition, although to our knowledge his results were correct, there were some defects in the development of his analysis; for example, Theorem 1 in [11] did not take into account jitter, and other results were based on this theorem. For these reasons, in this section of our paper we extend his technique to allow task offsets larger than the task periods, and we also formalize the technique via a complete set of proofs. Furthermore, we introduce a different kind of notation, which will help us in a future extension of our technique to further exploit precedence constraints among the tasks of a transaction.

Sun and Liu developed in [9] a technique similar to Tindell's analysis with offsets, and applied it to the analysis in multiprocessor systems, but their technique was restricted to offsets and deadlines smaller than the task periods, and it did not take into account the effects of jitter. Both [11] and this paper handle jitter for task activations, and deadlines larger than the task periods.

2.3. Exact Response-Time Analysis

In this subsection we will extend Tindell's technique for calculating an exact response time analysis of a set of tasks with static offsets [11], to allow offsets larger than the task periods, and we will formalize its development. Although the analysis will be intractable for large task sets because of the large number of cases that need to be considered, it will serve as the basis of the upper-bound approximation that

appears in Subsection 2.4.

For building the worst-case scenario for a task τ_{ab} under analysis, we must create a critical instant that leads to the worst-case busy period. A task τ_{ab} busy period is an interval of time during which the CPU is busy processing task τ_{ab} or higher priority tasks. For tasks with offsets, we must take into account that the critical instant may not include the simultaneous activation of all higher priority tasks, as it was the case when all tasks were independent. The existence of offsets makes it impossible for some sets of tasks to simultaneously become active.

When analyzing the response time of a particular task, the offset of a higher priority task may be changed by adding or subtracting whole periods of that latter task, without any effects on the response time of the lower priority tasks, since one instance of a task is indistinguishable from another instance. Therefore, in order to simplify the analysis, we will consider a reduced task offset, ϕ_{ij}, which is always within 0 and T_i:

$$\phi_{ij} = \Phi_{ij} \bmod T_i \qquad (1)$$

where function *mod* is the usual modulus operation, and where $\lfloor x \rfloor$ is the greatest integer number that is less than or equal to x. This result holds for all higher priority tasks, regardless of whether they belong to the same transaction as the task under analysis, or to different transactions. It also applies when calculating the interference of other jobs of the own task under analysis.

In order to derive the analysis technique, we will try to find out the contribution of each task to the worst-case response time, supposing that we know the time at which the critical instant occurs. Later, we will explore how to calculate the critical instant. Let us focus on the activation pattern of task τ_{ij}, and let us call its phase relation with the critical instant, ϕ, the time interval between the activation of transaction Γ_i that occurred immediately before or at the critical instant, and that critical instant. Notice that $0 \le \phi < T_i$.

In order to calculate the worst-case contribution of τ_{ij} to the response time of lower priority tasks we must categorize each instance of the task into one of the following sets:

- *Set 0*: Activations that occur before the critical instant and that cannot occur inside the busy period even with the maximum jitter delay.
- *Set 1*: Activations that occur before or at the critical instant and that can be delayed by an amount of jitter that causes them to coincide with the critical instant.
- *Set 2*: Activations that occur after the critical instant.

Figure 2 shows two possible scenarios for the alignment

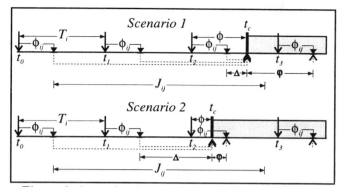

Figure 2. Scenarios for calculating the contribution of task τ_{ij} to the response time of lower priority tasks.

of the transaction T_i's arrival pattern and the critical instant. Scenario 1, in the upper part of the figure, corresponds to the case in which $\phi \geq \phi_{ij}$, and the lower part, Scenario 2, corresponds to $\phi < \phi_{ij}$. Dotted lines represent the actual jitter or delay in the activation time for each instance of the task. Time t_0 corresponds in both scenarios to the first event of Γ_i whose task τ_{ij} may be delayed by jitter until the critical instant, t_c (activations before t_0 would require a delay larger than the maximum jitter to occur at t_c). The event that occurs at t_1 may also be delayed by an amount that makes it coincide with the critical instant. The activation of τ_{ij} associated with the event that arrived at t_2, can be delayed until the critical instant in Scenario 1, but not in Scenario 2, because the offset ϕ_{ij} is larger than the relative phase ϕ between the event arrivals and the critical instant. For scenario 2, the job associated with the event arriving at t_2 must be included in Set 2.

Once the jobs of task τ_{ij} have been categorized into the three sets above, the calculation of the jitter terms that lead to the worst-case contribution of τ_{ij} to the response time of lower priority tasks is done according to the following theorem.

Theorem 1. Given a task τ_{ab} critical instant, t_c, and a phase relation ϕ between the arrival pattern of transaction Γ_i and the critical instant, the worst-case contribution of task τ_{ij} to the response time of τ_{ab} occurs when the activations in Set 1 have an amount of jitter such that they all occur at the critical instant, and when activations in Set 2 have an amount of jitter equal to zero.

Proof: By definition of the busy period, activations in Set 0 are not involved in it; otherwise, since they occur before the critical instant, the busy period would have started earlier.

For activations in Set 1, we must delay them with a jitter amount that causes them to occur inside the busy period.

But if this delay causes the activation to occur after the critical instant, it might fall outside the busy period. Thus, to ensure the maximum possible contribution to the busy period, the jitter amount must be such that the activation occurs at the critical instant.

For activations in Set 2, the larger the jitter delay they have, the more probability that the activation occurs outside the busy period. Thus, to ensure the worst possible contribution, the jitter amount for these activations must be zero.□

Under the conditions of Theorem 1, we will now calculate the number of activations of task τ_{ij} that belong to Set 1, and thus that may accumulate at the critical instant. We will call this number n_{ij} (in the example, the upper-part scenario had $n_{ij}=3$ and the lower-part scenario had $n_{ij}=2$). To calculate n_{ij}, we will define Δ as the difference in time between the time at which the last activation in Set 1 would have occurred if it had no jitter delay, and the critical instant. In the example of Figure 2, $\Delta = t_c - t_2 + \phi_{ij}$ for Scenario 1, and $\Delta = t_c - t_1 + \phi_{ij}$ for Scenario 2. It can be seen that:

$$\Delta = \begin{cases} \phi - \phi_{ij} & \text{if } \phi \geq \phi_{ij} \\ T_i + \phi - \phi_{ij} & \text{if } \phi < \phi_{ij} \end{cases} \quad (2)$$

or, equivalently:

$$\Delta = (\phi - \phi_{ij}) \bmod T_i \quad (3)$$

The first activation of τ_{ij} in Set 1 corresponds to the event arriving at t_0, which is the first one whose activation may occur at or after the critical instant. Therefore, this is the only activation that simultaneously verifies:

$$t_0 + \phi_{ij} + J_{ij} \geq t_c \quad (4)$$

and:

$$t_0 - T_i + \phi_{ij} + J_{ij} < t_c \quad (5)$$

By looking at Figure 2 we can see that:

$$t_c = t_0 + (n_{ij}-1)T_i + \phi_{ij} + \Delta \quad (6)$$

and replacing it in the two previous expressions we get:

$$\begin{aligned} t_0 + \phi_{ij} + J_{ij} &\geq t_0 + (n_{ij}-1)T_i + \phi_{ij} + \Delta \\ t_0 - T_i + \phi_{ij} + J_{ij} &< t_0 + (n_{ij}-1)T_i + \phi_{ij} + \Delta \end{aligned} \quad (7)$$

from which we get:

$$n_{ij}-1 \leq \frac{J_{ij}-\Delta}{T_i} \quad \text{and} \quad n_{ij}-1 > \frac{J_{ij}-\Delta}{T_i} - 1 \quad (8)$$

Given that n_{ij} is an integer number, the solution to the above two expressions is:

$$n_{ij} = \left\lfloor \frac{J_{ij}-\Delta}{T_i} \right\rfloor + 1 \quad (9)$$

In order to determine the effects of activations belonging

to Set 2, we need to know the time at which the first of them occurs; the others will occur at periodic intervals after the initial one. We will call φ the time difference between the critical instant and that first activation in Set 2. Given the definition of Δ we have:

$$\varphi = T_i - \Delta \tag{10}$$

We could have used φ in Equation (9) above to obtain:

$$n_{ij} = \left\lfloor \frac{J_{ij} + \varphi}{T_i} \right\rfloor \tag{11}$$

According to Theorem 1, the worst-case contribution of τ_{ij} to a busy period of a lower priority task is equivalent to n_{ij} activations at the critical instant, plus a sequence of periodic activations starting at φ time units after the critical instant. Without loss of generality, let's set the origin of time at the critical instant. Then, the worst-case contribution of task τ_{ij} to the response time of τ_{ab} at time t is determined by:

$$
\begin{aligned}
W(\tau_{ij}, \phi, t) &= n_{ij}(\phi) C_{ij} + \left\lceil \frac{t - \varphi(\phi)}{T_i} \right\rceil C_{ij} = \\
&= \left(\left\lfloor \frac{J_{ij} + \varphi(\phi)}{T_i} \right\rfloor + \left\lceil \frac{t - \varphi(\phi)}{T_i} \right\rceil \right) C_{ij}
\end{aligned}
\tag{12}
$$

with

$$\varphi(\phi) = T_i - (\phi - \phi_{ij}) \bmod T_i \tag{13}$$

The total interference of the tasks of transaction Γ_i on the execution of τ_{ab} is obtained by taking into account the contributions of all higher priority tasks:

$$W(\Gamma_i, \phi, t) = \sum_{\forall j \in hp_i(\tau_{ab})} W(\tau_{ij}, \phi, t) \tag{14}$$

where $hp_i(\tau_{ab})$ represents the set of tasks belonging to transaction Γ_i with priority greater than or equal to the priority of τ_{ab}.

Now, we must determine how to calculate ϕ, the phase between the arrival pattern of Γ_i and the critical instant. We will base this calculation on the following theorem:

Theorem 2. The worst-case contribution of transaction Γ_i to a task τ_{ab} critical instant is obtained when the first activation of some task τ_{ik} in $hp_i(\tau_{ab})$ that occurs within the busy period coincides with the critical instant, after having experienced the maximum possible delay, i.e., the maximum jitter, J_{ik}.

Proof. By definition of the busy period, right before the critical instant there are no pending tasks of priority higher than the priority of τ_{ab}. Now suppose that we choose a critical instant that does not coincide with the activation of some task in $hp_i(\tau_{ab})$. Let us focus on the first activation of

a task belonging to $hp_i(\tau_{ab})$ that occurs within the busy period, τ_{ik}. If we cause the arrival of the events of Γ_i to occur earlier while keeping the same activation patterns for all its tasks, until task τ_{ik} coincides with the critical instant, all the jobs of tasks belonging to $hp_i(\tau_{ab})$ that were in the busy period continue to be in that same busy period, but we have brought more jobs of those tasks, and perhaps other additional tasks, closer to the busy period, thus increasing the chance of additional interference on task τ_{ab}. Thus by making the first job of τ_{ik} coincide with the critical instant we can only make its contribution worse.

Now, we have to check that the worst-case contribution of transaction Γ_i is obtained when a job of a task τ_{ik} that initiates the critical instant has experienced the worst-case delay, equal to J_{ik}. Let us call I the set of jobs of tasks belonging to $hp_i(\tau_{ab})$ that initiate the busy period, and let us suppose that each of these jobs has a jitter value j_{il} less than the maximum for its associated task, J_{il}. Now let us move back (i.e., earlier in time) the event arrivals of transaction Γ_i, and simultaneously, increase the jitter delay of all the events in I by the same amount of time, so that all these jobs continue to be activated at the same time as before; jitter delays for all other jobs remain unchanged (and thus they are activated earlier). Under these conditions, we will move back the event arrivals until we reach the point when either: a) one of the jobs in I reaches its maximum jitter; or b) when a job in the busy period that did not belong to I gets aligned with the critical instant (because it is activated earlier). In case b), we insert the new job into set I, and we continue the process of moving back the event arrivals of Γ_i, in an iterative manner, until we reach condition a), under which one or more of the activations that start the busy period have experienced their maximum jitter. Notice that during this process, none of the activations that belonged to the busy period has been moved to a point before the critical instant, and thus all the jobs that belonged to the busy period remain in it. However, because the event arrivals of Γ_i now occur earlier, it is possible that jobs which previously occurred after the end of the busy period are now activated inside the busy period, thus making it longer and increasing the response times for the task under analysis, τ_{ab}. Therefore, the theorem follows.$\square$

By applying theorem 2, and supposing that we know that task τ_{ik} is one that originates the critical instant, we can determine the phase between the event arrivals and the critical instant:

$$\phi = (\phi_{ik} + J_{ik}) \bmod T_i \tag{15}$$

Substituting this expression in equation (13) we obtain

the phase φ_{ijk} between any task τ_{ij} and the critical instant created with τ_{ik}:

$$\varphi_{ijk} = \varphi(\phi) \Big|_{\phi = (\phi_a + J_a) \bmod T_i} = $$
$$= T_i - \left((\phi_{ik} + J_{ik}) \bmod T_i - \phi_{ij} \right) \bmod T_i \qquad (16)$$

and applying the properties of the modulus function,

$$\varphi_{ijk} = T_i - \left(\phi_{ik} + J_{ik} - \phi_{ij} \right) \bmod T_i \qquad (17)$$

Using this value, we can now obtain the expression of the worst-case contribution of transaction Γ_i when the critical instant is initiated with τ_{ik}. We will call this function $W_{ik}(t, \tau_{ab})$, and we obtain it by replacing (17) in equations (12), (13) and (14):

$$W_{ik}(\tau_{ab}, t) = W(\Gamma_i, \phi, t) \Big|_{\phi = (\phi_a + J_a) \bmod T_i} = $$
$$= \sum_{\forall j \in hp_i(\tau_{ab})} \left(\left\lfloor \frac{J_{ij} + \varphi_{ijk}}{T_i} \right\rfloor + \left\lceil \frac{t - \varphi_{ijk}}{T_i} \right\rceil \right) C_{ij} \qquad (18)$$

In order to obtain the worst-case response time of task τ_{ab} we need to apply the above function for all the transactions in the system. The main problem now is that for each transaction Γ_i we need to find the task τ_{ik} with which we create the critical instant. In order to perform an exact analysis, it is necessary to check all possible variations of one task out of every transaction, and choose the variation that leads to the worst response time for the task under analysis.

The number of variations, and thus of different critical instant possibilities that need to be checked, is determined by the number of tasks of priority higher than that of the task under analysis that exist in each transaction in the system. We also have to take into account that the task under analysis itself may originate the critical instant for its transaction. Thus, the total number of variations is:

$$N_v(\tau_{ab}) = \left(N_a(\tau_{ab}) + 1 \right) \cdot N_1(\tau_{ab}) \cdot N_2(\tau_{ab}) \ldots = $$
$$= \left(N_a(\tau_{ab}) + 1 \right) \cdot \prod_{\forall i \neq a} N_i(\tau_{ab}) \qquad (19)$$

where $N_i(\tau_{ab})$ is the number of tasks belonging to $hp_i(\tau_a)$. Each of the $N_v(\tau_{ab})$ variations is characterized by a tuple v of indexes, one for each transaction. Each index $v(i)$ identifies the task of transaction Γ_i that initiates the critical instant.

For convenience, we will number the jobs of the task under analysis using the letter p, with consecutive numbers ordered according to the activation time that they would have had if they had no jitter. In addition, we will assign the value $p=1$ to the activation of τ_{ab} that occurs in the interval $(0, T_a]$. This means that the activation that occurred in $(T_a, 2T_a]$ gets the value $p=2$, etc. Similarly, the activation that

would have occurred in the interval $(-T_a, 0]$ but that was delayed to the critical instant corresponds to $p=0$, the one in $(-2T_a, -T_a]$ to $p=-1$, etc. Notice that activations that occur after the critical instant are numbered with positive numbers, while previous activations have values of $p \leq 0$.

For each variation v we will obtain the completion time of each of the jobs of τ_{ab} in the busy period. This time, $w_{ab}^v(p)$ is obtained by considering the execution of τ_{ab} together with the interference from all the other tasks in the system:

$$w_{ab}^v(p) = B_{ab} + (p - p_{0,ab}^v + 1) C_{ab} + \sum_{\forall i} W_{iv(i)}\left(\tau_{ab}, w_{ab}^v(p) \right) \qquad (20)$$

where $p_{0,ab}^v$ corresponds to the lowest-numbered job, and is equal to:

$$p_{0,ab}^v = -\left\lfloor \frac{J_{ab} + \varphi_{abv(a)}}{T_a} \right\rfloor + 1 \qquad (21)$$

The solution to equation (20) is obtained as in the normal rate monotonic equation [10] by starting from a value of $w_{ab}^v(p) = 0$, and iterating until two consecutive iterations produce the same value. This analysis has to be repeated for all the jobs present in the busy period. The length of the busy period, which we will call L_{ab}^v, may be obtained with the following equation:

$$L_{ab}^v = B_{ab} + \left(\left\lceil \frac{L_{ab}^v - \varphi_{abv(a)}}{T_a} \right\rceil - p_{0,ab}^v + 1 \right) C_{ab} + \sum_{\forall i} W_{iv(i)}\left(\tau_{ab}, L_{ab}^v \right) (22)$$

which represents the first instant after the critical instant at which all jobs of τ_{ab} and of all higher priority tasks have been completed. With the length of the busy period, we can obtain the maximum value of p that we need to check:

$$p_{L,ab}^v = \left\lceil \frac{L_{ab}^v - \varphi_{abv(a)}}{T_a} \right\rceil \qquad (23)$$

The global response time is obtained by subtracting from the obtained completion time the instant at which the external event that activated the transaction arrived. According to our numbering scheme, the first activation of τ_{ab} after the critical instant corresponds to the value $p=1$ and, by definition, it corresponds to instant $\varphi_{abv(a)}$. Consequently the p-th activation occurs at $\varphi_{abv(a)} + (p-1)T_a$. Since the task is activated Φ_{ab} time units after the event arrival, the event arrival for each job p occurs at $\varphi_{abv(a)} + (p-1)T_a - \Phi_{ab}$. Therefore, the global worst-case response time for job p is:

$$R_{ab}^v(p) = w_{ab}^v(p) - \varphi_{abv(a)} - (p-1)T_a + \Phi_{ab} \qquad (24)$$

Notice that in the above equation we have to use the real

offset, Φ_{ab}, instead of the reduced offset ϕ_{ab}, which was used when calculating interference of higher-priority tasks on the task under analysis. To calculate the global worst-case response time for task τ_{ab} we must determine the maximum among all the potential critical instants examined:

$$R_{ab} = \max_{\forall v} \left[\max_{p=p_{0,ab}\cdots p_{L,ab}} \left(R_{ab}^v(p) \right) \right] \qquad (25)$$

By applying the described analysis to each task in the system we can obtain the global worst-case response times and, by comparing them with the deadlines, we can determine whether the system will meet or not its timing requirements. However, although the analysis technique is exact, it represents an NP-complete algorithm in which the number of cases to check grows exponentially with the number of tasks. This means that for most practical problems the algorithm is intractable and cannot be used. For this reason, in the following subsection we will use the upper-bound approximation that appears in [11], in which the number of cases to test is polynomially dependent on the number of tasks, at the price of providing pessimistic results. As it is shown in [11], these results will be much less pessimistic than the ones obtained with the current analysis techniques in [10].

2.4. Upper-Bound Approximation for Worst-Case Analysis

In [11], Tindell developed an approximate method that will enable us to obtain upper bounds for the global worst-case response times in a system composed of transactions with fixed offsets. Although the technique is not exact, the number of cases that need to be checked has a polynomial dependency on the number of tasks, which makes the method applicable even for relatively large systems. If the response times obtained with this method are smaller than the respective deadlines, the method gives guarantees that all timing requirements will be met.

The analysis is based on the exact technique developed in [11] and which we extended in the previous subsection. There, we obtained the equation that calculates the worst-case contribution of a transaction Γ_i on the response time of task τ_{ab} when the critical instant coincides with the activation of task τ_{ik}:

$$W_{ik}(\tau_{ab},t) = \sum_{\forall j \in hp_i(\tau_{ab})} \left(\left\lceil \frac{J_{ij}+\phi_{ijk}}{T_i} \right\rceil + \left\lceil \frac{t-\phi_{ijk}}{T_i} \right\rceil \right) C_{ij} \qquad (26)$$

The main problem with that analysis technique is that we

don't know which task τ_{ik} must be used to create the worst-case busy period. This caused us to have to check all possible variations. Tindell avoided it by obtaining an upper bound to the interference of the tasks of a transaction Γ_i in a busy period of duration w, as the maximum of all possible interferences that could be caused by considering each of the tasks of Γ_i as the one originating the busy period:

$$W_i^*(\tau_{ab},w) = \max_{\forall k \in hp_i(\tau_{ab})} W_{ik}(\tau_{ab},w) \qquad (27)$$

Therefore, using this function in the calculation of the response times, we can make sure that the time obtained is an upper bound for the contribution of the tasks of transaction Γ_i and thus it would not be necessary to calculate all the possible variations for k. By using one function like this for each transaction, we can calculate the global worst-case response time for a particular task by checking only a single case.

In order to introduce less pessimism, we will not use that function for the transaction to which the task under analysis belongs, but we will use the original transaction. Consequently, for the analysis we must consider all the possibilities of critical instants created with each of the tasks in the set $hp_a(\tau_{ab})$ plus τ_{ab}; the number of possibilities is small, equal to the number of tasks in $hp_a(\tau_{ab})$ plus one. For a critical instant created with τ_{ac}, the worst-case response time is determined by:

$$w_{abc}(p) = B_{ab}+(p-p_{0,abc}+1)C_{ab} + \\ + W_{ac}(\tau_{ab},w_{abc}(p)) + \sum_{\forall i \neq a} W_i^*(\tau_{ab},w_{abc}(p)) \qquad (28)$$

As it is shown in [11], this equation can be solved using the traditional RMA iterative method. Parameter $p_{0,abc}$ corresponds to the first activation that occurs at the critical instant:

$$p_{0,abc} = -\left\lfloor \frac{J_{ab}+\phi_{abc}}{T_a} \right\rfloor + 1 \qquad (29)$$

The length of the busy period is calculated as:

$$L_{abc} = B_{ab}+\left(\left\lceil \frac{L_{abc}-\phi_{abc}}{T_a} \right\rceil -p_{0,abc}+1 \right) C_{ab} + \\ + W_{ac}(\tau_{ab},L_{abc})+ \sum_{\forall i \neq a} W_i^*(\tau_{ab},L_{abc}) \qquad (30)$$

and from it:

$$p_{L,abc} = \left\lceil \frac{L_{abc}-\phi_{abc}}{T_a} \right\rceil \qquad (31)$$

The global worst-case response time is obtained by subtracting from the completion time the instant at which the associated event arrived:

$$R_{abc}(p) = w_{abc}(p) - \varphi_{abc} - (p-1)T_a + \Phi_{ab} \qquad (32)$$

And then we need to take the worst of all the response times obtained:

$$R_{ab} = \max_{\forall c \in hp_i(\tau_{ab}) \cup b} \left[\max_{p=p_{0,abc}..p_{L,abc}} \left(R_{abc}(p) \right) \right] \qquad (33)$$

Notice that this algorithm requires only inspecting a number of possible critical instants equal to the number of tasks in transaction Γ_i that have priorities larger than or equal to the priority of τ_{ab} (and including itself). It is usually a relatively small number, with which we obtain acceptable results, as it can be seen in [11].

3. Analysis for Tasks with Dynamic Offsets

In this section we will extend the analysis to include the case in which the system has tasks with dynamic offsets. As in the case with static offsets, the system is composed of a set of transactions that execute in the same processor. Each transaction Γ_i has a period of T_i and contains a set of m_i tasks with activation offset Φ_{ij}, execution time C_{ij}, and maximum jitter J_{ij}. However, in this case tasks offsets are allowed to vary dynamically, from one activation to the next, within a minimum and a maximum value: $\Phi_{ij} \in [\Phi_{ij.\,min}, \Phi_{ij.\,max}]$.

Dynamic offsets are useful in systems in which tasks suspend themselves or in distributed systems. For example, a task may execute for some time, and then suspend itself to read some data from a disk. Let us suppose that the suspension time is between S_{min} and S_{max}. We would then model this task as a transaction composed of two tasks: task τ_{i1} corresponding to the code before the suspension, and task τ_{i2} to the code after the suspension. The activation time of the second task depends on the completion time of the first task, plus the suspension time, and thus the offset for task τ_{i2} is variable in the interval $\Phi_{i2} \in [R_{i1}^b + S_{min}, R_{i1} + S_{max}]$, where R_{i1}^b and R_{i1} are, respectively, the best-case and worst-case response times of task τ_{i1}. The same kind of effect happens in distributed systems, when a task is activated upon the arrival of a message, which arrives at a variable time within a given time window. Distributed systems are considered in Section 4.

In the analysis for tasks with static offsets that was presented in Section 2, the activation phase represented the minimum interval of time that could exist between the arrival of the external event and the activation of the associated task. On the other hand, the jitter term represented the maximum delay that the task activation

could suffer, counted from the arrival of the external event plus the task's offset. Therefore, it is easy to notice that we can model the case in which the offsets may vary as a special case of a system with static offsets, by defining an equivalent static offset Φ'_{ij} and an associated equivalent jitter term J'_{ij}, for each task, in the following way:

$$\begin{aligned} \Phi'_{ij} &= \Phi_{ij.min} \\ J'_{ij} &= J_{ij} + \Phi_{ij.max} - \Phi_{ij.min} \end{aligned} \qquad (34)$$

Therefore, the analysis with static offsets can be applied to this equivalent transaction to obtain the worst-case response times. However, in most systems in which task offsets can vary dynamically, their minimum or maximum values, or both, are dependent on the response times of previous tasks in the transaction. For example, in a system with several suspending tasks like the one that was mentioned above, the minimum offset of the task after the suspension was a function of the best-case response time of a previous task in the same transaction, while the maximum offset was a function of the worst-case response of that same task:

$$\begin{aligned} \Phi'_{ij} &= \Phi_{ij.min} = R_{ij-1}^b + S_{min} \\ J'_{ij} &= J_{ij} + \Phi_{ij.max} - \Phi_{ij.min} = J_{ij} + R_{ij-1} - R_{ij-1}^b + S_{max} - S_{min} \end{aligned} \qquad (35)$$

The main problem is that the response times are dependent on the task offsets, and the task offsets depend on the response times. For R_{ij-1}^b, we can use any lower bound to the best-case response time. If task execution times can be arbitrarily small, this lower bound is zero. Otherwise, we can use the task's own best-case execution time. For a more detailed analysis of the best-case response time see [7].

So now our main problem is the calculation of the worst-case response times, which depend on the task offsets, which in turn depend on the worst-case response times. This is a problem similar to the calculation of response times in distributed systems, which depend on the task jitters, while the task jitters themselves depend on the response times. The solution to this problem appears in [10], and consists of starting from an initial value of response times of zero, and iterating over the analysis until a stable solution is achieved. The monotonic dependency of the response on the jitter terms determines the convergence of the method: the larger the jitter terms, the larger the response times, and viceversa.

In our case we will start with an initial value of the response time equal to zero, and thus an initial value for the jitter in the equivalent model of:

$$J'_{ij} = J_{ij} + S_{max} - S_{min} \qquad \forall i, \forall j \qquad (36)$$

Then, we apply the analysis using the technique for static

offsets with the equivalent offsets and jitter terms. In this way we obtain the response times of each task. Using these response times we re-calculate the equivalent jitter using (35), and with this new value we recalculate the response times. We continue this calculation in an iterative way until we obtain the same result in two successive iterations, that is:

$$R_{ij}^{(n+1)} = R_{ij}^{(n)} \qquad \forall i , \forall j \qquad (37)$$

We call this algorithm WCDO (worst-case analysis for dynamic offsets). It converges to a solution, if one exists, because of the monotonicity of the worst-case response times given in Eq. (25) with the jitter terms. This dependency is also in accordance with the results of Theorem 2.

4. Analysis of Multiprocessor and Distributed Systems

In multiprocessor and distributed systems it is usual that the system can be modeled with "transactions" composed of several tasks, like in the computational model described in Section 3. For example, in a system following the client-server architecture, a client task is activated by the arrival of an external event, and requests services from one or more servers, perhaps in different processors. This client task can be modeled as a transaction. Each piece of code between the service requests would be modeled as a task. Each portion of execution of a server in another processor is modeled as another task in the same transaction. Each task in the transaction, τ_{ij}, is activated by the completion of the previous task in its transaction τ_{ij-1}.

In a distributed system, the transmission times of the messages through the communications network must also be taken into the analysis. If we use a real-time network that is based on fixed priority messages like the CAN bus or point to point lines [5], we can model the network as if it was another processor, accounting the non-preemptability of the message packets as additional blocking time [6]. Thus, for simplicity, we will only talk about tasks and processors, although one or more of these processors may in fact be modeling a communications network. Other scheduling strategies for the messages in the network can also be adapted to our worst-case analysis.

Consequently, we will model the activities executing in a distributed system as transactions, each composed of a chain of tasks. Each task represents a task or a portion of a task executing in a processor, or a message transmitted through a communications network. The first task in the transaction is activated by the arrival of a periodic external event; let us suppose that this external event has no jitter. We will use a model similar to the one used for tasks that suspended themselves in Section 3, defining an equivalent offset and jitter term of zero for the task that initiates the transaction, and with the following values for each task that does not initiate the transaction:

$$\Phi'_{ij} = \Phi_{ij,min} = R_{ij-1}^{b}$$
$$J'_{ij} = J_{ij} + \Phi_{ij,max} - \Phi_{ij,min} = R_{ij-1} - R_{ij-1}^{b} \qquad (38)$$

where R_{ij-1}^{b} is a lower bound to the best-case response time of task, and R_{ij-1} is an upper bound for the worst-case response time.

Evidently, a task executing in a given processor cannot preempt tasks executing in other processors, and thus we must redefine the set $hp_i(\tau_{ab})$ of tasks that can preempt a given task τ_{ab} to contain only tasks that belong to the same processor as τ_{ab}:

$$hp_i(\tau_{ab}) = \{ j \in \Gamma_i \mid priority(\tau_{ij}) \geq priority(\tau_{ab})$$
$$\wedge processor(\tau_{ij}) = processor(\tau_{ab}) \} \qquad (39)$$

Using these equivalent offsets and jitter terms we can use the same iterative method that was presented in Section 3, algorithm WCDO, but using equation (38) to calculate the equivalent offsets and jitters, and starting with initial values of $J_{ij}=0$ and $\phi_{ij}=R_{ij-1}^{b}$ for each task. As before, convergence of the iterative algorithm is guaranteed by the monotonic dependency of the response times on the jitter terms.

In order to better understand the technique presented, we will illustrate it with a simple example. Consider the system that appears in Figure 3. Tasks 1, 3 and 5 are simple periodic tasks. Task 2 is a periodic task that suspends itself to request service from task 4. Right before the suspension, task 2 transmits a message, m_1, through the network, which is a serial line. Task 4 is activated at the arrival of this

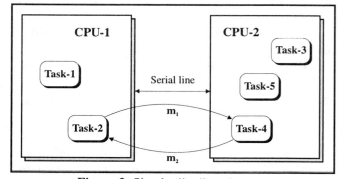

Figure 3. Simple distributed system

	Task	Original	C_i	T_i	D_i	Prio.
Γ_1	τ_{11}	task-1	4	20	20	High
Γ_2	τ_{21}	task-2_1	20			Low
	τ_{22}	m_1	25			-
	τ_{23}	task-4	15	150	150	Med
	τ_{24}	m_2	34			-
	τ_{25}	task-2_2	30			Low
Γ_3	τ_{31}	task-3	5	30	30	High
Γ_5	τ_{51}	task-5	100	200	200	Low

Table I. Timing parameters for the example

message at CPU-2; when it completes its execution it sends message m_2 back through the same serial line. Then, task 2 resumes its execution until completion. Task 2, task 4 and both messages can be modeled as a transaction with five tasks; the timing parameters of all the transactions and tasks are shown in Table I. The scheduling policy used in the network is FIFO; this can be easily modeled by assuming that, when analyzing each message, the other one has higher priority. We will assume that the execution times of each task, and the transmission times of each message are fixed, i.e., there is no difference between the best and the worst-case. This means that we can use the execution or transmission times as the local best-case response times for each associated task, and thus calculate the offset of each task as:

$$\Phi_{ij} = R^b_{ij} = \sum_{k=1..j-1} C_{ik} \qquad (40)$$

If we analyze the described system using the conventional analysis techniques in which we assume that each task is independent of the others, we get a response time for transaction Γ_2 of 266 time units, which is well past its end-to-end deadline of 150. However, if we apply the analysis technique described in this section, we obtain a worst-case response time for that same transaction of 145 time units, which makes the transaction schedulable (Table II shows the results of the analysis for the five tasks of transaction Γ_2). The reason for this difference is that in the original analysis the first portion of task 2 is preempted once by the second portion, and viceversa. The same happens for the messages in the network: each one preempts

task	Φ_{2j}	J_{2j}	R_{2j}
τ_{21}	0	0	28
τ_{22}	20	8	53
τ_{23}	45	8	73
τ_{24}	60	13	107
τ_{25}	94	13	145

Table II. Results for transaction Γ_2

the other one once. However, in practice, because of the task offsets, it is not possible that portion 2 of task 2 interferes with portion 1 or viceversa, nor it is possible that the messages interfere with each other. This is correctly taken into account by the analysis with dynamic offsets that we have developed in this paper.

5. Comparison with existing techniques

We have compared the results of the analysis for tasks with dynamic offsets with the results obtained using the current analysis technique for distributed systems, which assumes that each task is independent of the others [10]. For this purpose, we have conducted extensive simulations with different task sets whose execution times and periods were generated randomly. Priorities were assigned using the rate monotonic algorithm. The results of some of these simulations are shown in this section.

The first set of graphs (Figures 4 to 6) compares the response times obtained using Tindell and Clark's technique

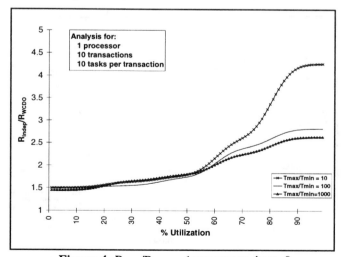

Figure 4. R_{indep}/R_{WCDO}, 1 processor, best=0

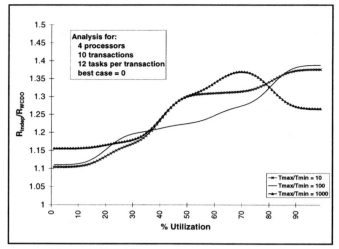

Figure 5. R_{indep}/R_{WCDO}, 4 processors, best=0

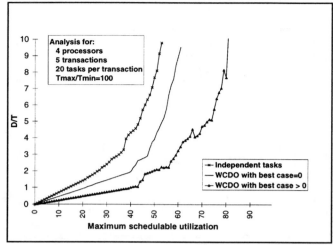

Figure 7. Max. Sched. Utilization, 100 tasks

for independent tasks, R_{indep}, with the response times obtained using algorithm WCDO, R_{WCDO}. In these figures, we show the average ratio R_{indep}/R_{WCDO} obtained for five simulated tasks sets for each point in the graph. The X axis represents processor utilization. Each figure presents the results for three different ratios of the maximum transaction period over the minimum transaction period, T_{max}/T_{min}. Figure 4 shows the results for a set of 10 transactions with 10 tasks per transaction, in one processor, for the case in which the best-case response times are considered negligible, and thus the task offsets are all zero. It can be seen that for normal utilization levels of around 70%, the response times with independent tasks are roughly between 2.2 and 2.6 times larger than in the analysis with dynamic offsets. The results with best case response times equal to the task execution times are the same for this case.

Figure 5 shows the results for a similar case, but running on four processors. We can see that as the number of tasks of the same transaction that are in the same processor diminishes, the benefits of the WCDO algorithm also diminish. However, these benefits are still significant, with response times between 1.27 and 1.37 times better for 70% utilization. Figure 6 shows the results for the same case as Figure 5, except that the best case response time of each task is considered equal to the sum of the execution times of itself and all its predecessor tasks in the same transaction. We can see that, in this case, the results are significantly better, with response times between 2 and 2.6 times better than in the analysis with independent tasks, for a utilization of 70%.

The second set of graphs (Figure 7 and Figure 8) compare the maximum schedulable utilization that can be

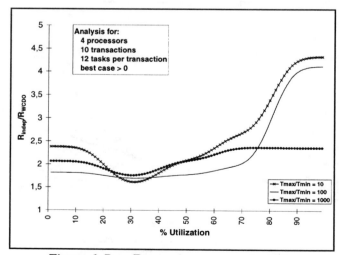

Figure 6. R_{indep}/R_{WCDO}, 4 processors, best>0

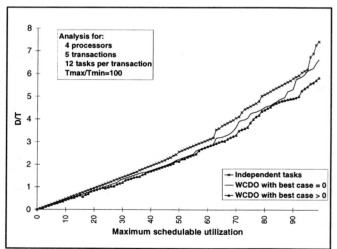

Figure 8. Max. Sched. Utilization, 60 tasks

obtained for a given task set using the analysis for independent tasks, algorithm WCDO with zero best case response times, and algorithm WCDO with best case response times equal to the task execution times. The maximum schedulable utilization is obtained by analyzing a system with low utilization and then increasing its utilization until the system no longer meets its deadlines. The maximum schedulable utilization is taken as the last of the task sets for which the deadlines were met. The simulations have been done for different ratios of deadlines over periods, D_i/T_i. Figure 7 shows the results for the simulation of a system with 4 processors, 5 transactions and 20 tasks per transaction, with $T_{max}/T_{min}=100$. Figure 8 shows the results for a similar task system, but with 12 tasks per transaction instead of 20. We can see that from values of $D_i/T_i=2$ and higher, we can get a increase of around 8% more schedulable utilization in the case of 12 tasks, and 25% more in the case of 20 tasks. We can see that, as the number of tasks of the same transaction that execute in the same processor increases, the benefits of the analysis with offsets also increase. It is also worth mentioning that for systems with several processors the results are better if we consider best-case response times larger than zero, although it is still possible to get benefits from our new analysis if we consider the best execution times equal to zero.

6. Conclusions

In this paper we have presented an extension to Tindell's technique for analyzing tasks with static offsets in the context of preemptive fixed-priority scheduling. Our extension consists of allowing the task offsets to be larger than the task periods, and formalizing the development of the technique. In addition, we have extended the technique to the case of dynamic offsets, which vary from one execution to the next. We have shown that the analysis for dynamic offsets is useful for analyzing systems with tasks that suspend themselves, as well as multiprocessor and distributed systems. In all these systems, tasks offsets are dependent on the response time of previous tasks in the same transaction. Through simulation results, we have shown that the benefits of the analysis for dynamic offsets over current analysis techniques for distributed systems are very high. The response times with the new technique are significantly lower. And the maximum schedulable utilization can be increased up to an additional 25% of schedulable utilization.

We are currently working on further extensions of the technique presented in this paper to include aperiodic tasks, as well as further exploiting the effects of the precedence constraints existing in distributed systems and other kinds of systems.

References

[1] M. Klein, T. Ralya, B. Pollak, R. Obenza, and M. González Harbour, "A Practitioner's Handbook for Real-Time Systems Analysis". Kluwer Academic Pub., 1993.

[2] J.P. Lehoczky, "Fixed Priority Scheduling of Periodic Task Sets with Arbitrary Deadlines". IEEE Real-Time Systems Symposium, 1990.

[3] C.L. Liu, and J.W. Layland, "Scheduling Algorithms for Multiprogramming in a Hard Real-Time Environment". Journal of the ACM, 20 (1), 1973, pp 46-61.

[4] M. González Harbour, M.H. Klein, and J.P. Lehoczky. "Fixed Priority Scheduling of Periodic Tasks with Varying Execution Priority". Proceedings of the IEEE Real-Time Systems Symposium, December 1991, pp. 116-128.

[5] J.J. Gutiérrez García, and M. González Harbour, "Increasing Schedulability in Distributed Hard Real-Time Systems". Proceedings of the 7th Euromicro Workshop on Real-Time Systems, Odense, Denmark, June 1995, pp. 99-106.

[6] J.C. Palencia Gutiérrez, J.J. Gutiérrez García, and M. González Harbour, "On the Schedulability Analysis for Distributed Hard Real-Time Systems". Proceedings of the 9th Euromicro Workshop on Real-Time Systems, Toledo, Spain, June 1997, pp. 136-143.

[7] J.C. Palencia Gutiérrez, J. J. Gutiérrez García, and M. González Harbour, "Best-Case Analysis for Improving the Worst-Case Schedulability Test for Distributed Hard Real-Time Systems". To appear in the proceedings of the 10th Euromicro Workshop on Real-Time Systems, Berlin, Germany, June 1998.

[8] L. Sha, R. Rajkumar, and J.P. Lehoczky. "Priority Inheritance Protocols: An approach to Real-Time Synchronization". IEEE Trans. on Computers, Sept. 1990.

[9] J. Sun and J. Liu, "Bounding the end-to-End Response Time in Multiprocessor Real-Time Systems", Proceedings of the Third Workshop on Parallel and Distributed Real-Time systems, Santa Barbara, CA, 1995.

[10] K. Tindell, and J. Clark, "Holistic Schedulability Analysis for Distributed Hard Real-Time Systems". Microprocessing & Microprogramming, Vol. 50, Nos.2-3, pp. 117-134, April 1994.

[11] K. Tindell, "Adding Time-Offsets to Schedulability Analysis", Technical Report YCS 221, Dept. of Computer Science, University of York, England, January 1994.

Session 3.A: Databases and Filesystems

Deadline-Modification-SCAN with Maximum-Scannable-Groups for Multimedia Real-Time Disk Scheduling

Ray-I Chang
Institute of Inform Science
Academia Sinica
Taipei, Taiwan, ROC
william@iis.sinica.edu.tw

Wei-Kuan Shih
Dept of Comp Science
National Tsing Hua Univ
HsinChu, Taiwan, ROC
wshih@cs.nthu.edu.tw

Ruei-Chuan Chang
Dept of Comp&Inform Science
National Chiao Tung Univ
HsinChu, Taiwan, ROC
rc@cc.nctu.edu.tw

Abstract

Real-time disk scheduling is important to multimedia systems support for digital audio and video. In these years, various approaches are presented to use the seek-optimizing scheme to improve the disk throughput of a real-time guaranteed schedule. However, as these conventional approaches apply SCAN only to the requests with the same deadline or within the same constant-sized group, their improvements are limited. In this paper, we introduce the DM-SCAN (deadline-modification-SCAN) algorithm with an idea of MSG (maximum-scannable-group). The proposed DM-SCAN method can apply SCAN to MSG iteratively by modifying request deadlines. We have implemented the DM-SCAN algorithm on UnixWare 2.01. Experiments show that DM-SCAN is significantly better than that of the best-known SCAN-EDF method in both the obtained disk throughput and the number of supported disk requests.

1. Introduction

Multimedia applications have become more and more popular [3-4]. In a multimedia system, large volume audio and video data require real-time services. Define the earliest time at which a request can be started as the *release time*. The latest time at which a request must be completed is the *deadline*. In a multimedia system, requests need to be served not only with high throughput to support lots of users but also with guaranteed real-time requirement [3] for continuous playback. To satisfy the real-time constraints, the request start-time should not be earlier than its release time and the request fulfill-time should not be later than its deadline. The design of a distributed multimedia system (see Fig. 1) focuses on the real-time network system and the real-time disk service system [1-2]. The problems of disk layout and real-time network transmission schedule were shown in [30] and [31]. Given the request media stream, we can decide the suitable disk layout and network transmission schedule to minimize allocated resources (buffer size, bandwidth, ..., etc.) with maximum resource utilization. In this paper, the real-time disk scheduling problem to balance the trade-off between satisfying real-time constraints and minimizing the disk service time is considered. It is an interesting and practical problem for real-time storage management.

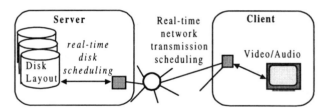

Fig. 1. The basic architecture of a distributed multimedia system. In this paper, we focus on the real-time disk scheduling problem.

The SCAN approach, which scans the disk surface to retrieve the request data block under disk head, has been proved to be an optimal disk scheduling algorithm [5-8]. However, since the additional real-time constraints are not considered, SCAN may not be suitable for real-time disk scheduling [9-15]. By modeling each real-time request as a task with a deadline, the EDF (earliest-deadline-first) method is optimal to schedule these tasks under the assumption of i.i.d. and exponential service times [16-19]. However, as the disk service time depends on the read/write head position as well as the scheduling result, the independent assumption no longer holds. The empoyment of EDF results in poor I/O throughput and requires an excessive seek time for real-time disk scheduling. In these years, different approaches are proposed to combine the seek-optimizing scheme and the real-time scheduling scheme to resolve the real-time disk scheduling problem [20-22, 32-36]. For example, in the best-known SCAN-EDF approach [20], they try to combine the SCAN scheme and the EDF schedule [23]. Given a real-time EDF schedule, SCAN-EDF reschedules the requests with the same deadlines by the seek-optimization SCAN scheme to reduce disk service time. Thus, the disk I/O throughput can be easily improved with guaranteed real-time requirements.

In this paper, a hard real-time disk-scheduling algorithm with dynamic request groups (called MSG, *maximum-scannable-group*) for rescheduling is proposed. Given an input schedule, we define MSG as *a set of consequent requests that can be successfully rescheduled by SCAN under guaranteed real-time requirements*. As MSG can identify the maximum request set for seek-optimizing, the obtained result would be better than that of the conventional approaches with constant-sized groups [24]. In this paper, we first give the definition of MSG. The theoretical proof of correctness is also presented. Then, we propose an O(n) algorithm to identify MSG (where n is the number of input requests). Requests in the same MSG can be easily rescheduled by SCAN to improve the I/O throughput with guaranteed real-time requirements. To apply the idea of MSG iteratively, a deadline-modification-SCAN (DM-SCAN) algorithm is proposed to modify request deadlines. By doing deadline-modification, we make sure that the rescheduled result can be applied for deciding MSG. This iterative DM-SCAN scheme is intuitively better than the best-known SCAN-EDF approach. Comparing to the obtained results, all simulations of DM-SCAN are convergent within n iterations to achieve over 14% improvements in I/O throughput. Besides, nearly 10% improvements can be obtained at the first iteration. The required time complexity O($n\log n$) is the same as SCAN-EDF (where n is the number of input requests).

The remainder of this paper is organized as follows. Section 2 introduces the real-time disk scheduling problem and reviews some conventional schemes. Section 3 gives the mathematical definition about MSG, and provides a formal illustration of the DM-SCAN algorithm. Then, some basic theoretical analyses are proposed to establish the properties of the proposed technique. Section 4 shows the experiment environments and obtained results. We have implemented the proposed algorithms on UnixWare 2.01 operating systems. The performance evaluation shows the effectiveness of the DM-SCAN scheme. Conclusion remark and future work are presented in Section 5.

2. Real-time disk scheduling

A real-time disk request T_i can be simply denoted as (r_i, d_i, a_i, b_i) where r_i is the release time, d_i is the deadline, a_i is the track location and b_i is the data capacity [25]. Define that $c_{j,i}$ is the execution time of request T_i when T_i is just served after request T_j. This serving sequence $T_j T_i$ is not pre-specified, but depends on the schedule result. The disk-head should seek from the track location a_j to track location a_i to retrieve the data block with size b_i. Given the disk layout [30] and the disk parameters [26-27], the start-time e_i and the fulfill-time f_i of request T_i can be computed as follows.

$$e_i = \max\{\, r_i, f_j \,\}$$
$$f_i = e_i + c_{j,i} \qquad (1)$$

A simple example to demonstrate the terminologies used and their relations is shown in Fig. 2. Notably, the start-time of a request should not be larger than its release time and its fulfill-time should not be later than its deadlines for real-time requirements.

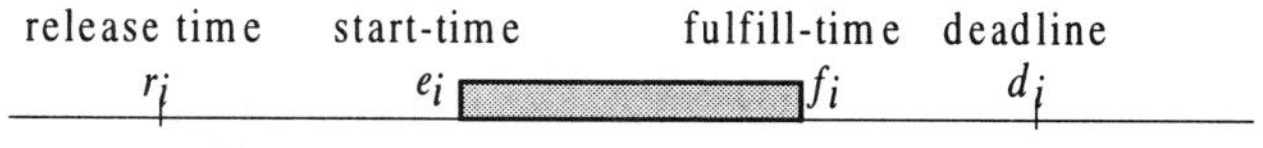

Fig. 2. A simple example to demonstrate the terminologies (release time, start-time, fulfill-time and deadline) used to represent a real-time task.

2.1. Problem definition

By considering a set of requests $T = \{T_0, T_1,..., T_n\}$ where n is the number of requests, the real-time disk scheduling problem can be defined as a process Z to find a feasible real-time schedule $T_{Z(0)}T_{Z(1)}...T_{Z(n)}$ with the maximum I/O throughput. In this paper, T_0 is a special request to represent the initial condition of disk arm. Without losing the generalization, we have $T_{Z(0)} = T_0 = (0, 0, 0, 0)$. Notably, in a multimedia system supported for digital audio and video [28-29], the scheduling result $T_Z = T_{Z(0)}T_{Z(1)}...T_{Z(n)}$ may be meaningless if the real-time requirements are not satisfied. It is a hard real-time problem. Assume that the request data size $b_i = b$ disk blocks (or b Mbits for a constant-data-length disk layout scheme [30]). The obtained I/O throughput for the applied algorithm Z can be measured by

$$(n * b / f_{Z(n)}) \qquad (2)$$

where $f_{Z(n)}$ is the schedule fulfill-time. To compare the performance with another algorithm X, the performance improvement of algorithm Z can be simply defined as

$$f_{Z/X} = (1 - f_{Z(n)}/f_{X(n)}) \times 100\% \qquad (3)$$

Notably, given a set of input requests, the obtained I/O throughput is just the inverse of schedule fulfill-time. By comparing Eq. (2) and (3), the problem objective for maximizing the I/O throughput of a feasible schedule can be simply defined as to minimize the schedule fulfill-time with guaranteed real-time requirements.

2.2. Conventional approaches

As the real-time disk scheduling problem was shown to be a NP-complete problem [38-40], various approaches have been proposed in these years to combine deadline information and disk service information in different ways. A comprehensive survey of the real-time disk scheduling problem in multimedia storage systems can be found in [35-36]. Considering the best-known SCAN-EDF schedule [20], requests are first sorted according to their deadlines and try to guarantee the correctness of real-time requirements. It is an EDF schedule with poor disk throughput. To improve the disk throughput, requests with the same deadlines are served with the SCAN order to reduce their disk-head seeking. SCAN-EDF can be easily implemented by modifying EDF slightly [20]. However, since the seek-optimizing scheme is applied only for requests with the same deadline, the obtained improvements are limited. Its efficiency depends upon how often the SCAN algorithm can be applied (i.e. how many requests have the same deadline). The simulation and implementation results can be found in [24]. To increase this probability, a sophisticated technique can be used to group requests that have the similar deadline together, and reschedule them according the SCAN order. However, it is hard to decide the best similarity measurement of deadlines. Besides, the real-time requirements may not be quaranteed after rescheduling.

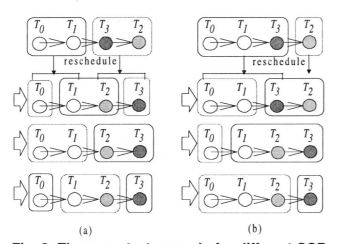

(a)   (b)

Fig. 3. The same test example for different SGR parameters: (a) group size 2, sliding size 1; (b) group size 3, sliding size 2.

In [41], we improve the SCAN-EDF approach by trying to reschedule the requests within the same constant-sized group by SCAN. It is called SGR(g, s) (*sliding-group-rescheduling*) where g is the group size (number of requests in a group) and $s \leq g$ is the sliding size. Assume that the initial real-time schedule is produced by EDF, and the applied groups are exclusive and consecutive to cover the whole schedule in each iteration. A simple example for SGR(2, 1) with group size 2 and sliding size 1 is shown in Fig. 3(a). In SGR, requests in each group are tried to reschedule by SCAN to reduce the schedule fulfill-time. As shown in group 2 of iteration one, T_3T_2 is rescheduled as T_2T_3. However, if the rescheduling result can not guarantee real-time requirements, the schedule would not be changed. We can repeatly improve the schedule result by the same procedure. In each iteration, groups will be slipped forward by s requests. An example for SGR(3, 2) with group size 3 and silding size 2 is shown in Fig. 3(b). The description of the SGR algorithm is shown in [24]. More detail discussions about the applied group size, sliding size and the number of iteration can be found in [41].

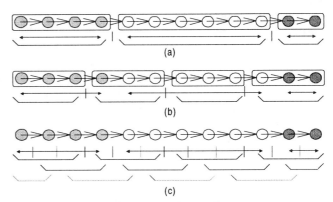

(a)

(b)

(c)

Fig. 4. (a) The ideal best request groups. (b) The constant-sized groups (group size = 3). (c) The sliding constant-sized groups (sliding size = 1).

Note that the group size used in a SGR schedule is a pre-specified constant. However, the best request groups for seek-optimizing (called *the best request groups*, for short) may be varying for different input schedules as shown in Fig. 4(a). Generally, doing seek-optimization on the maximum request groups would provide the largest benefit to disk throughput. If the group size is restricted to be a constant value, the best request groups may be partitioned into different request groups as shown in Fig. 4(b). The obtained performance improvements would be limited. Although the SGR algorithm has tried to improve the obtained results by sliding the request groups to cover the entire schedule (see Fig. 4(c)), the applied group size is still a pre-specified constant in each iteration. The obtained results would depend on the group size chosen for rescheduling. To analyze the effect of selected group size, we have tested the improvements of I/O throughput for different group sizes [24]. Our experiments show that the obtained results highly depend on the group size selected. Besides, the increasing of group size would not always lead to the increasing of performance improvement. It is hard to decide the best group size for these constant-group-sized approaches.

3. Deadline-modification SCAN

The difficulties in choosing a suitable group size for rescheduling motivate us to design an automatic group identification scheme. The proposed scheme should be able to compute the suitable request group for seek-optimizing with guaranteed real-time requirements. Define the *scannable-group* as a consequent request group that can be successfully scheduled by SCAN under the specified real-time constraints. In this paper, a linear-time algorithm is proposed to maximize the obtained scannable-group (called the *maximum-scannable-group, MSG*). Then, an iterative algorithm is introduced to identify and reschedule the maximum-scannable-group repeatedly. Before describing our proposed algorithms, notations used in this paper are summarized in Table 1.

Table 1. Some notations used in this paper.

T	a set of requests $T = \{T_0, T_1,..., T_n\}$
n	number of the input requests
T_i	a real-time disk request, $T_i = (r_i, d_i, a_i, b_i)$
r_i	release time of T_i
d_i	deadline of T_i
a_i	the track location of T_i
b_i	the data capacity of T_i
T_0	given as the initial condition of the disk arm
$c_{j,i}$	the service time of T_i when it's served after T_j
e_i	the start-time of T_i
f_i	the fulfill-time of T_i
T_Z	the schedule result of T by the algorithm Z, $T_Z = T_{Z(0)}T_{Z(1)}...T_{Z(n)}$
$f_{Z(n)}$	the schedule fulfill-time of T_Z
$f_{Z/X}$	improvement of T_Z when comparing with T_X, $f_{Z/X} = (1 - f_{Z(n)}/f_X(n)) \times 100\%$
G_i	the maximum-scannable-group started from T_i
S_G_i	the index of start request of G_i
E_G_i	the index of end request of G_i
$Z[i]$	the cumulated scan direction of G_i
S_i	the seek-optimized schedule result of G_i for T_i

3.1. Maximum-scannable-group

To avoid the incorrect partitioning of the best request groups, we should identify the rescheduling request groups as large as possible. In this paper, we first define the applied maximum-scannable-group (MSG) concept. Notably, in this paper, our definition of MSG are based

on an EDF input schedule. The applied MSG concept can be easily extended to redefine new MSG if the problem input is not an EDF schedule.

Definition: MSG
Given an EDF schedule $T_E = T_{E(0)}T_{E(1)}...T_{E(n)}$, the maximum-scannable-group G_i started from request T_i is defined as the maximum consequent request group $G_i = T_{E(i)}T_{E(i+1)}... T_{E(i+m)}$ which satisfies: $f_{E(k)} \le d_{E(i)}$ and $r_{E(k)} \le e_{E(i)}$ for $k = i$ to $i+m$. ❏

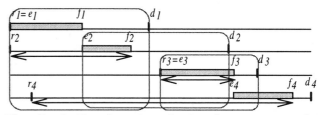

Fig. 5. A simple example to demonstrate the identification procedure of MSG.

Fig. 5 shows a simple example with the EDF schedule $T_0T_1T_2T_3T_4$. From the above definition for MSG, we have $G_0 = T_0$, $G_1 = T_1T_2$, $G_2 = T_2$, $G_3 = T_3$, and $G_4 = T_4$. Requests in MSG can be easily seek-optimized to improve the I/O throughput of the input schedule. In this paper, we didn't measure the likelihood of meeting deadlines, but just the time required to complete service for all of the requests.

Notably, in our proposed technique, the input schedule is not necessary to be feasible for guaranteed real-time requirements. We can produce a feasible schedule even when the input schedule isn't feasible. However, the reschedule results may be not feasible if the input schedule is not feasible. As the real-time requirements can be guaranteed only when the input schedule is feasible, the input schedule is assumed to be feasible in this paper. Given a feasible EDF schedule, we should prove that the seek-optimized reschedule result of MSG G_i can successfully improve the I/O throughput under guaranteed real-time requirements. The theoretical proof for our definition of MSG is given as follows.

Theorem: $T_E = T_{E(0)} T_{E(1)}...T_{E(n)}$ is a feasible EDF schedule with MSG $G_i = T_{E(i)}T_{E(i+1)}...T_{E(i+m)}$. Assume that $S_i = T_{S(i)}T_{S(i+1)}...T_{S(i+m)}$ is the seek-optimized reschedule result of G_i for $T_S = T_{E(0)}T_{E(1)}...T_{E(i-1)}T_{S(i)}$ $T_{S(i+1)}...T_{S(i+m)}T_{E(i+m+1)}...T_{E(n)}$. T_E can be rescheduled as T_S to improve the I/O throughput under guaranteed real-time requirements.

Proof:
(a) In the input schedule T_E, from the definition of the fulfill-time, we have

$f_{E(i+m)} = \max\{ \ldots \max\{e_{E(i)} + c_{E(i-1),E(i)}, r_{E(i+1)}\} \ldots\}$
$\qquad\qquad + c_{E(i+m-1),E(i+m)}.$

As G_i is an MSG, we have $r_{E(k)} \leq e_{E(i)}$ for $k = i$ to $i+m$. The above equation can be rewritten as

$$f_{E(i+m)} = e_{E(i)} + c_{E(i-1),E(i)} + c_{E(i),E(i+1)} + \ldots \qquad(4)$$
$$+ c_{E(i+m-1),E(i+m)}$$

In schedule T_S, the related fulfill-time of S_i is

$f_{S(i+m)} = \max\{ \ldots \max\{e_{S(i)} + c_{S(i-1),S(i)}, r_{S(i+1)}\} \ldots\}$
$\qquad\qquad + c_{S(i+m-1),S(i+m)}.$

Given $e_{E(i)} = r_{E(i)}$ or $f_{E(i-1)}$, we have $e_{S(i)} \leq e_{E(i)}$. Since S_i is a reschedule of G_i, we have $r_{S(x)} = r_{E(k)}$ for the given x and some a k in $[i, i+m]$. Thus, $r_{S(x)} \leq e_{E(i)}$ for $x = i$ to $i+m$. The above equation can be rewritten as

$$f_{S(i+m)} \leq e_{E(i)} + c_{S(i-1),S(i)} + c_{S(i),S(i+1)} + \ldots \qquad(5)$$
$$+ c_{S(i+m-1),S(i+m)}$$

Since S_i is a seek-optimized reschedule result of G_i for T_S, we have

$c_{S(i-1),S(i)} + c_{S(i),S(i+1)} + \ldots + c_{S(i+m-1),S(i+m)}$
$\leq c_{E(i-1),E(i)} + c_{E(i),E(i+1)} + \ldots + c_{E(i+m-1),E(i+m)} \qquad(6)$

$\Rightarrow$ From Eq. (5) and (6), we prove that the fulfill-time $f_{S(i+m)} \leq f_{E(i+m)}.$

(b) In schedule T_E, from the definition of MSG G_i, we have $f_{E(k)} \leq d_{E(i)}$ for all $k = i$ to $i+m$. As G_i is an EDF schedule, we also have $f_{E(k)} \leq f_{E(k+1)}$ and $d_{E(k)} \leq d_{E(k+1)}$ for all $k = i$ to $i+m-1$. These relations can be rewritten as

$$f_{E(i)} \leq f_{E(i+1)} \leq \ldots \leq f_{E(i+m)}$$
$$\leq d_{E(i)} \leq d_{E(i+1)} \leq \ldots \leq d_{E(i+m)} \qquad(7)$$

In schedule T_S, the fulfill-time $f_{S(k)} \leq f_{S(k+1)}$ for all $k = i$ to $i+m$. These relations can be written as

$$f_{S(i)} \leq f_{S(i+1)} \leq \ldots \leq f_{S(i+m)} \leq f_{E(i+m)} \qquad(8)$$

$\Rightarrow$ From Eq. (7) and (8), we can guarantee that the real-time constraints ($f_{S(k)} \leq d_{S(k)}$ for all k) are satisfied. As S_i is a seek-optimized reschedule result of G_i for T_S, the obtained I/O throughput of the rescheduled result T_S would not be smaller than that of the input schedule T_E. $\square$

The basic idea behinds the proposed algorithm is that the fulfill-time of the seek-optimized reschedule result would not be larger than that of the input schedule. Thus, we can focus only on the real-time constraints. In our definition, $f_{E(k)} \leq d_{E(i)}$ and $r_{E(k)} \leq e_{E(i)}$ for $k = i$ to $i+m$ are used to guarantee real-time requirements. In the next sub-section, we design an O(n) construction algorithms of MSG for rescheduling. Then, the deadline-modification-scan (DM-SCAN) algorithm is proposed to iteratively reschedule these MSG groups.

3.2. Identify MSG and MU_MSG in O(n)

Since G_i is defined as the MSG starting from $T_{E(i)}$, n

MSG groups are found in an input schedule with n requests. Before proposing our group identification algorithm, a basic property for the successive MSG groups is first introduced.

Property: Give a feasible EDF schedule $T_E = T_{E(0)}T_{E(1)} \ldots T_{E(n)}$. For each MSG $G_i = T_{E(i)}T_{E(i+1)} \ldots T_{E(i+m)}$, the sub-group $T_{E(x)}T_{E(x+1)} \ldots T_{E(i+m)}$ of G_i should be a part of G_x for $x = i+1$ to $i+m$.

Proof:
(a) Since $T_{E(0)}T_{E(1)} \ldots T_{E(n)}$ is a feasible EDF schedule, we have $d_{E(i)} \leq d_{E(i+1)}$ and $e_{E(i)} \leq e_{E(i+1)}$ for all i.
(b) As $G_i = T_{E(i)}T_{E(i+1)} \ldots T_{E(i+m)}$ is a MSG, we have $f_{E(k)} \leq d_{E(i)}$ and $r_{E(k)} \leq e_{E(i)}$ for $k = i$ to $i+m$.
$\Rightarrow$ From (a) and (b), it can be easily derived that $f_{E(k)} \leq d_{E(i)} \leq dd_{E(x)}$ and $r_{E(k)} \leq e_{E(i)} \leq e_{E(x)}$ for $x = i+1$ to $i+m$. Thus, the sub-group $T_{E(x)}T_{E(x+1)} \ldots T_{E(i+m)}$ of G_i should be a part of G_x. $\square$

From the above property, the n MSG groups can be easily identified by a one-pass O(n) algorithm. Define S_G_i and E_G_i as the start and the end request of G_i, the detail description about the group identification algorithm of MSG is shown as follows.

Algorithm: *MSG (maximum-scannable-group)*
/* INPUT: the EDF scheduling result $T_0 T_1 \ldots T_n$.
  OUTPUT: a set of MSG with S_G_i and E_G_i. */
$k := 1$;
for $i := 0$ **to** n **do begin**
  /* count the requests in the same MSG group */
  while (($r_k \leq e_i$) **and** ($f_k \leq d_i$) **and** ($k \leq n$)) **do** $k := k + 1$;
  /* G_i is defined as $T_i \ldots T_{k-1}$ */
  $S\_G_i := i$;
  $E\_G_i := k - 1$;
end /* next MSG group */

A MSG group is said to be a *scanned MSG (S_MSG)* if the requests in this group are seek-optimized. Otherwise, it is called an *un-scanned MSG (U_MSG)*. Notably, only U_MSG is necessary to be rescheduled by SCAN. In this paper, an O(n) algorithm is proposed to identify U_MSG for local seek-optimization. Note that these U_MSG groups are not mutually exclusive in nature. For example, we may have $G_i = T_i T_{i+1} \ldots T_j T_{j+1} \ldots T_{i+p}$ and $G_j = T_j T_{j+1} \ldots T_{i+p} \ldots T_{i+q}$. It is easy to show that these two MSG groups are not mutually exclusive ($G_i \cap G_j = \{T_j, T_{j+1}, \ldots, T_{i+p}\} \neq \varnothing$) and can not be rescheduled at the same time. In this paper, a procedure based on the first-come-first-serve (FCFS) policy is applied to select a set of *mutually-exclusive U_MSG (MU_MSG, for short) groups* for rescheduling. The detail description of this MU_MSG identification algorithm is shown as follows.

Algorithm: *MU_MSG*
/* INPUT: a set of MSG groups.
    OUTPUT: U_MSG, a subset of MSG. */
$Z[0] := 0$;
/* $Z[i]$ is the cumulated scan direction of G_i */
for $k := 1$ **to** n **do begin**
    if $(a_{k-1} \leq a_k)$ **then** *scan_direction* := 1;
                else *scan_direction* := -1;
    /* MSG is scanned iff the scan directions are
        +1,+1,...,+1 or -1,-1,...,-1 */
    $Z[k] := Z[k-1] +$ *scan_direction*;
end /* next request */
$i := 0$;
while $(i < n)$ **do begin**
    if $((|Z[E\_G_i] - Z[S\_G_i]| + 1) = size\ of\ G_i)$
    /* if G_i is seek-optimized */
        then $i := i + 1$; /* next group */
        else begin
            G_i is a MU_MSG
            /* can be rescheduled by SCAN; */
            $i := E\_G_i + 1$;
            /* next mutually exclusive group */
        end /* else */
end /* group */

In the previous sub-section, we have proved that real-time requirements of the disk I/O requests of the same MSG can be guaranteed after seek-optimizing. As described in the above algorithm, requests in MU_MSG can be directly seek-optimized by SCAN.

3.3. Deadline-modification-SCAN for MSG

Note that our algorithms are based on the assumptions that the input schedule is an EDF schedule. Algorithms described in this paper should be re-designed if the input schedule does not satisfy the EDF property. To iteratively improve the scheduling result by the same algorithm, the input schedule should be kept as an EDF schedule. To satisfy this requirement, we develop a deadline-modification-SCAN (DM-SCAN) algorithm to modify the deadlines of requests. After the deadlines are modified, we have a new EDF schedule. Therefore, we can iteratively reschedule the new MSG by the same approach to improve the I/O throughput. The original deadlines are restored after DM-SCAN. This entire algorithm can be described as follows.

Algorithm: *DM-SCAN*
/* INPUT: the scheduling result of EDF.
    OUTPUT: a real-time disk schedule. */
Store $d'_k := d_k$ for all requests T_k

/* d'_k backup real deadline d_k of T_k */
repeat
    Identify all the MSG groups from input schedule
    Identify all the MU_MSG groups from MSG groups
    /* local group seek-optimization */
    for $i := 1$ **to** n **do**
        if $(G_i$ is MU_MSG) **then** reschedule G_i by SCAN;
    /* deadline modification */
    for $k := n-1$ **down to** 1 **do**
        if $(d_k > d_{k+1})$ **then** $d_k := d_{k+1}$;
until (no deadline is modified); /* no more change */
Recover $d_k := d'_k$ for all requests T_k.
/* restore real deadlines */

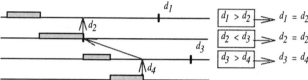

Fig. 6. A simple example to demonstrate the proposed deadline modification scheme.

A simple example to demonstrate the proposed deadline modification scheme is shown in Fig. 6. It is easy to show that these modified deadlines satisfy the EDF policy. Furthermore, as $f_i \leq f_{i+1}$ and $f_{i+1} \leq d_{i+1}$ for all the requests T_i, we can also show that $f_i \leq d_{i+1}$ and $f_i \leq d_i$. The obtained result is a feasible EDF schedule. Thus, the DM-SCAN algorithm is correct for iterative computing.

4. Experimental results

In this paper, the experimental results for DM-SCAN are presented to compare conventional approaches (they are implemented by us). Generally, the characteristic of the disk service time depends on the type of disk driver applied [1]. In this paper, a HP 97560 hard disk is applied for our performance evaluations. HP 97560 contains 1962 cylinders. It has 19 tracks-per-cylinder and 72 sectors-per-track with 512 bytes sector size. The rotation speed is 4002 RPM (rotations-per-minute). The detail disk model has been studied in [26-27]. In this paper, we apply this disk model to define the disk service time $c_{i,j}$ from request T_i to request T_j. Thus, given the seek distance $d_{i,j}$ as $|a_j - a_i|$. We have $c_{i,j} = 8 + 0.008d_{i,j}$ if $d_{i,j} > 383$. Otherwise, $c_{i,j} = 3.24 + 0.4(d_{i,j})^{1/2}$. In our experiments, the data access for each input request is assumed to be on one disk track (36 KB in HP 97560) without splitting across different cylinders. The detail descriptions about the disk layout scheme and the real-time network transmission scheme are shown in [24, 30-31]. We assume that the workloads of input requests are uniformly distributed on the disk surface. Requests' release times are randomly generated with proper deadlines assigned. Besides, only static request set (which presents all input requests before scheduling) is discussed. Solutions for the scheduling problems with dynamic-coming requests can be found in [24].

4.1. Number of iterations

In this paper, we first apply some test examples to evaluate the related performances for different reschedule iterations. For each approach, the same 100 test examples are presented. Each test example contains 10 randomly generated requests. The mean values for the obtained schedule fulfill-times are evaluated. Fig. 7 shows the obtained schedule fulfill-times for the iterative DM-SCAN and SGR approaches. They have the same time complexity. In SGR, the best group size (= 5) and the best sliding size (= 1) are assigned to achieve the best results. For the comparison purpose, the results for the non-iterative SCAN-EDF method are also presented.

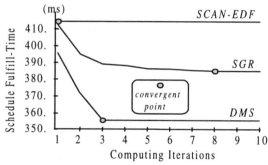

Fig. 7. The obtained schedule fulfill-time. Gray circle is the convergent time.

Not that, in an iterative algorithm such as DM-SCAN and SGR, the computing iterations required to convergence plays an important factor. As shown in Fig. 6, when we compare the convergence property of several different approaches, the proposed DM-SCAN method with dynamic MSG groups would be convergent after only 3 computing iterations. However, SGR with sliding constant-sized groups would require 8 computing iterations to enter the convergent state. DM-SCAN has better convergence property than SGR. It can achieve better results with less iteration times than the conventional approaches. Comparing the convergence results, the obtained schedule fulfill-times for the conventional SCAN-EDF and SGR approaches are 414.8 (ms) and 385.6 (ms), respectively. The proposed DM-SCAN method requires only 356.7 (ms) in the schedule fulfill-time. It can be found that, even at the first iteration (called *DM-SCAN-1*), the DM-SCAN method can obtain

better results than that of SGR or SCAN-EDF. Note that the time complexity of DM-SCAN-1 is O($n\log n$). It is the same as the time complexity of the well-known SCAN-EDF algorithm.

Table 2 shows the minimum, the maximum, and the average schedule fulfill-time obtained for different real-time disk scheduling approaches. In this table, we apply the same 100 test examples (each test example contains 10 randomly generated requests) to different solution approaches to keep the comparison as fair as possible. For each solution approach, the related improvements are also presented. In this paper, the measurement of I/O throughput improvement is compared to the obtained results of SCAN-EDF. The proposed DM-SCAN approach can achieve 14% improvements. Besides, 9% improvements are obtained at the first iteration (DM-SCAN-1). It is better than the SGR approach by applying n computing iterations (7% improvements).

Table 2. The minimum (min), maximum (max), and average (avg) schedule fulfill-time, and the improvement (imp) of the I/O throughput.

Algorithms	Schedule Fulfill-Time (msec)			
	min	max	avg	imp
DM-SCAN	289.27	402.36	356.74	14%
DM-SCAN-1	317.24	460.18	375.12	9%
SGR	291.37	462.70	385.63	7%
SCAN-EDF	377.06	462.70	414.84	=0%

* The applied group size of SGR is 5.
* The obtained improvement is related to EDF.

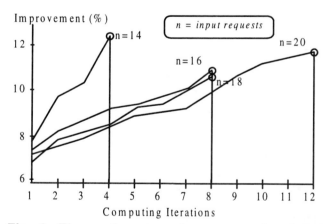

Fig. 8. The performance improvements of the DM-SCAN method with different problem sizes and different computing iterations.

4.2. Number of supported requests

To further demonstrate the capability of the proposed DM-SCAN method, we also apply DM-SCAN for different numbers of input requests. Three different test examples with 14, 16, 18, and 20 input requests are demonstrated with different computing iterations. The obtained performance improvements are shown in Fig. 8. In each point, the mean values of the I/O throughput improvements for 100 test examples (each test example contains 10 randomly generated requests) are applied. In the proposed DM-SCAN approach, all the test examples are found to be convergent before n computing iterations (n is the number of requests). We can simply set the maximum computing iterations of DM-SCAN to be the number of input requests.

More experiments about the DM-SCAN method with different numbers of input requests are shown in Fig. 9. The obtained results for SGR are presented for comparisons. Experiments show that the proposed DM-SCAN approach is better than SGR in almost all the test cases. Only when the applied problem size is relatively small (<< group size), SGR with a constant group size would be better than DM-SCAN. The possible reason for this irregular situation is that, in such small size problems, the sizes of the obtained MSG would be smaller than the pre-specified group size 5 of the SGR method. Thus, the SGR method would cover all the requests and have more chances to further improve the I/O throughput.

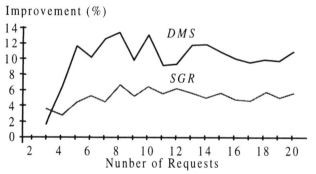

Fig. 9. Experiments for SGR and DM-SCAN with different numbers of input requests.

Notably, when the problem size is increased to 20 input requests, our experiments show that the proposed DM-SCAN method can achieve over 11% improvements for. However, the SGR method has only 6% improvements. Our experiment demonstrates that the proposed DM-SCAN approach is more suitable for handling large-sized problems than the conventional approaches. To further study the number of requests supported, Table 3 shows the minimum, the maximum and the average number of real-time requests that can be successfully scheduled by different approaches. To each test approach, the same 100 examples with a sequence of randomly-generated requests are applied. In each test

example, we try to increase the number of input requests to the test procedures until the related schedule result is not valid for real-time requirements. According to our experiment, the proposed DM-SCAN approach can support more requests than the conventional approaches. More descriptions about the SFTF algorithm and the FCFS method can be found in [24].

Table 3. The number of request supported for different scheduling policies.

Algorithms	Number of Supported Requests		
	min	max	avg
DM-SCAN	7	25	13.75
SCAN-EDF	4	24	10.21
EDF	3	24	9.87
SFTF	1	10	4.38
FCFS	1	10	4.11

* SFTF = shortest fulfill-time first.
* FCFS = first come first serve.

4.3. Implementation results

In this paper, we also implement the proposed DM-SCAN scheme on UnixWare 2.01 operating system to evaluate the performance of DM-SCAN on real world applications. Besides, we have also implemented the best-known SCAN-EDF scheme for comparisons. In the video server, there is one parent thread for dealing with the arrival multimedia services. After receiving a new service request, a new child thread is created by the parent thread. Then, the child thread starts sending the real-time disk requests periodically. The real-time disk scheduling algorithm is designed to handle these real-time disk requests. Then, a real-time network transmission scheme as shown in [31] can successfully send the retrieved data to the clients. Our implementation currently runs on a platform with Pentium-75 PC. The applied DASD device is a Seagate ST-31200N hard disk with an Adaptec SCSI-2742AT control card. Our programs are implemented on *portable device interface* (PDI) for the SCSI hard disk driver. Note that the PDI architecture can take the advantage to organize and standardize the processing flow of the device drivers. It has the same driver functionality to the same hard disk with different device interfaces (i.e. ESDI or SCSI). Besides, the driver functionality to the same SCSI controller would be also consistent although the hardware units are different. Based on this PDI architecture, our implementation can be easily ported to other UNIX-like systems. For supporting more video streams, we consider a software disk array system with 20 identical disk devices. For each hard disk, 20 KB/s bandwidth is required for serving one MPEG-I video stream.

We assume that the presented input requests are uniformly distributed over the disk with random arrivals and random deadlines. The same problem input is tested to different solution approaches for fair comparisons. Comparing to SCAN-EDF, Fig. 10 shows the obtained I/O throughput improvements of the proposed DM-SCAN approach. The obtained results for different request arrival rates (numbers of request) are shown. In each point, the mean value for 1000 test examples is presented. Our implementation results show than the proposed algorithms can obtain over 26% improvement in I/O throughput than that of the well-known SCAN-EDF approach. It is similar to our simulation results with over 23% improvement. The implementation results and the simulation results are match. More discussions about the detail system implementation and the evaluation for different system prototypes can be found in [24].

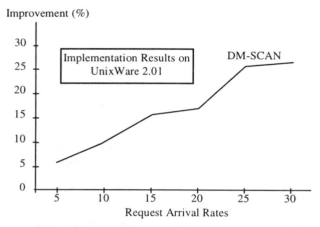

Improvement (%)

Request Arrival Rates

Fig. 10. The average improvement of DM-SCAN with different request arrival rates. (the obtained Implementation results on UnixWare 2.01)

5. Conclusion

In this paper, the DM-SCAN algorithm with a MSG concept is proposed to resolve the hard real-time disk scheduling problem. As conventional approaches only apply the seek-optimization procedure to the requests with the same deadline or within the same constant-sized group, the obtained improvements are limited. Our DM-SCAN algorithm can automatically and iteratively identify the suitable request group to minimize the schedule service times under some hard real-time requirements. The obtained simulation/implementation results are better than the conventional approaches.

Notably, although our problem input is defined as a feasible EDF schedule, DM-SCAN may produce a feasible schedule even when the input schedule isn't feasible. Th feasibility of problem input is used to guarantee the feasibility of output result. Considering a problem input that is not an EDF schedule, the applied DM-SCAN algorithm could be redefined by following the same MSG concept. It implies that, based on different problem input configurations, we can introduce a new MSG definition and a new DM-SCAN algorithm. How to further extend the concept of DM-SCAN and MSG is one of our future works. Besides, we can try to analyze the convergence property of the proposed algorithm theoretically. The considerations on the admission control scheme and the maximum number of requests supported can also be discussed.

Acknowledgements

The authors would like to thank the anonymous referees for their valuable suggestions about this paper.

References

[1] J.L. Peterson and A. Silberschatz, Operating System Concepts, 2nd Edition, Addison-Wesley, 1985.

[2] D.P. Anderson, Y. Osawa, and R. Govindan, "A file system for continuous media," *ACM Trans. Comp. Systems*, vol. 10, no. 4, pp.311-337, 1992.

[3] A. Dan, D. Sitaram and P. Shahabuddin, "Scheduling policies for an on-demand video server with batching," *Proc. ACM Multimedia Conf.*, pp. 15-22, 1994.

[4] D. B. Terry and D. C. Swinehart, "Managing stored voice in the etherphone system," *ACM Trans. Computer Systems*, vol. 6, no. 1, pp. 3-27, 1988.

[5] D.P. Anderson, Y. Osawa, and R. Govindan, "Real-time disk storage and retrieval of digital audio/video data," Tech. Report, Univ. of California, Berkeley, Dept. of Computer Science, 1991.

[6] D. P. Anderson, "Metascheduling for continuous media," *ACM Trans. Computer Systems*, vol. 11, no. 3, pp. 226-252, 1993.

[7] T. S. Chen, W. P. Yang, and R. C. T. Lee, "Amortized analysis of some disk scheduling algorithms: SSTF, SCAN, and *N*-StepSCAN," *BIT*, vol. 32 , pp.546-558, 1992.

[8] T. S. Chen and W. P. Yang, "Amortized analysis of disk scheduling algorithm V(R)*," *Journal of Inform. Science and Eng.*, vol. 8, pp.223-242, 1992.

[9] D.J. Gemmell, H.M. Vin, D.D. Kandlur, P.V. Rangan, L.A. Rowe, "Multimedia storage servers: a tutorial," *IEEE Computers*, pp. 40-49, 1995.

[10] P. V. Rangan and H. M. Vin, "Designing file systems for digital video and audio," *Proc. ACM Symp. Operating Systems*, pp. 81-94, 1991.

[11] D. J. Gemmell and S. Christodoulakis, "Principles

of delay sensitive multimedia data storage and retrieval," *ACM Trans. Information Systems*, vol. 10, no. 1, pp. 51-90, 1992.

[12] D. J. Gemmell and J. Han, "Multimedia network file servers: multichannel delay sensitive data retrieval," *Multimedia Systems*, vol. 1, no. 6, pp. 240-252, 1994.

[13] H.M. Vin and P.V. Rangan, "Designing file systems for digital video and audio," *Proc. ACM Symp. Operating System Principles*, pp. 81-94, 1991.

[14] P. Lougher and D. Shepherd, "The design of a storage server for continuous media," *The Computer Journal*, vol. 36, no. 1, pp. 32-42, 1993.

[15] P. V. Rangan and H. M. Vin, "Efficient storage techniques for digital continuous multimedia," *IEEE Trans. Knowledge and Data Engineering*, vol. 5, no. 4, pp. 564-573, 1993.

[16] T. H. Lin and W. Tarng, "Scheduling periodic and aperiodic tasks in hard real-time computing systems," *Proc. SIMMetrics Conf.*, pp. 31-38, 1991.

[17] M. Chen, D. D. Kandlur, and P. S. Yu, "Optimization of the grouped sliding scheduling (GSS) with heterogeneous multimedia streams," *Proc. ACM Multimedia Conf.*, pp. 235-242, 1993.

[18] J. P. Lehoczky, "Fixed priority scheduling of periodic task sets with arbitrary deadlines," *Proc. Real-Time Systems Symp.*, pp. 201-212, 1990.

[19] J. Yee and P. Varaiya, "Disk scheduling policies for real-time multimedia applications," Tech. Report, Univ. of California, Berkeley, Dept. of Computer Science, 1991.

[20] A. L. N. Reddy and J. Wyllie, "Disk scheduling in a multimedia I/O system," *Proc. ACM Multimedia Conf.*, pp. 225-233, 1993.

[21] A.L.N. Reddy and J. Wyllie, "I/O issues in a multimedia system," *IEEE Computers*, pp. 69-74, March 1994.

[22] K. Jeffay, D. F. Stanat, and C. U. Martel, "On nonpreemptive scheduling of periodic and sporadic tasks," *Proc. of Real-Time Systems Symp.*, pp. 129-139, 1991.

[23] C.L. Liu and J.W. Layland, "Scheduling algorithms for multiprogramming in a hard real-time environment," *Journal of ACM*, pp. 46-61, 1973.

[24] R. I. Chang, "Real-time disk scheduling in multimedia systems," Ph.D. Thesis, College of EE and CS, Dept. of CIS, NCTU, Taiwan, ROC.

[25] J. A. Stankovic and G. C. Buttazzo, "Implications of classical scheduling results for real-time systems," *IEEE Computer*, pp.16-25, June 1995.

[26] C. Ruemmler and J. Wilkes, "An introduction to disk drive modeling," *IEEE Computers*, pp. 16-28, March 1994.

[27] R. P. King, "Disk arm movement in anticipation of future requests," *ACM Trans. Computer Systems*, vol. 8, no. 3, pp. 214-229, 1990.

[28] A. Mok, "Fundamental design problems for the hard real-time environment," MIT Ph.D. Dissertation, Cambridge, MA, May 1983.

[29] W. K. Shih, J. W. S. Liu, and C. L. Liu, "Modified rate monotone algorithm for scheduling periodic jobs with deferred deadlines," Tech. Report, Univ. of Illinois, Urbana-Champaign, Dept. of Computer Science, Sept. 1992.

[30] Y. C. Wang, S. L. Tsao, R. I. Chang, M. C. Chen, J. M. Ho and M. T. Ko, "A fast data placement scheme for video server with zoned-disks," *Proc. SPIE Multimedia Storage and Archiving System*, pp. 92-102, 1997.

[31] R. I. Chang, M. C. Chen, J. M. Ho and M. T. Ko, "Optimizations of stored VBR video transmission on CBR channel," *Proc. SPIE Performance and Control of Network Systems*, pp. 382-392, 1997.

[32] S. Chen and M. Thapar, "I/O channel and real-time disk scheduling for video servers," *Proc. NOSSDAV*, pp. 113-122, 1996.

[33] R. I. Chang, W. K. Shih and R. C. Chang, "A new real-time disk scheduling algorithm and its application to multimedia systems," *Proc. 5th IEEE International Workshop on Interactive Distributed Multimedia Systems*, 1998.

[34] J. Yee and P. Varaiya, "Modeling and performance of real-time disk access policies", *Computer Communications*, vol. 18, no. 10, November 1995.

[35] S. J. Daigle and J. K. Srosnider, "Disk scheduling for continuous media data streams," *Proc. SPIE Conference on High-Speed Networking and Multimedia Computing*, 1996.

[36] R. Steinmetz, "Multimedia file systems survey: approaches for continuous media disk scheduling," Computer Communication, vol.18, no.3, pp.133-144, March 1995.

[37] K. Tindell and A. Burns, "Fixed priority scheduling of hard real-time multi-media disk traffic," *The Computer Journal*, vol. 37, no. 8, pp.691-697, 1994.

[38] H. M. Vin, A. Goyal and P. Goyal, "Algorithms for designing multimedia servers," Computer Comm., vol. 18, no. 3, pp. 192-203, March 1995.

[39] C.K. Wong, "Minimizing expected head movement in one dimension and two dimension mass storage system," Comput. Survery, vol. 12, no. 2, pp. 167-178, 1980.

[40] G. Neyer and P. Widmayer, "Singularities make spatial join scheduling hard," *Upper-Rhine-Region Algorithms Workshop*, 1997.

[41] R. I. Chang, W. K. Shih and R. C. Chang, "Real-time scheduling for continuous media retrieval with sliding-group-rescheduling," *submitted*, 1998.

Using Separate Algorithms to Process Read-Only Transactions in Real-Time Systems

Kwok-Wa Lam[1], Sang H. Son[2], Victor C. S. Lee[1] and Sheung-Lun Hung[1]

Department of Computer Science[1]
City University of Hong Kong,
83 Tat Chee Avenue, Kowloon,
Hong Kong.
kwlam@cs.cityu.edu.hk

Department of Computer Science[2]
University of Virginia,
Charlottesville, VA 22903,
U.S.A.
son@cs.virginia.edu

Abstract

In this paper, we investigate the approach of using separate algorithms to process read-only transactions in real-time systems. A read-only transaction (ROT) is a transaction that only reads, but does not update any data item. Since there is a significant proportion of ROTs in several real-time systems, it is important to investigate how to process ROTs effectively. Using an algorithm to process ROTs separately from update transactions may reduce the interference between ROTs and update transactions. This reduced interference alleviates the impact of concurrency control on real-time priority-driven scheduling and improves the timeliness of the system. Moreover, we explore the different consistency requirements of ROTs. Particularly, we define a weaker form of consistency, view consistency, which allows ROTs to perceive different serialization order of update transactions. While view consistency permits non-serializablility, ROTs are still ensured to see consistent data. We propose two robust algorithms for different consistency requirements of ROTs. The two algorithms are robust in the sense that they can be used in a compatible way so that a real-time system can provide different consistent data for different applications. The performance of two algorithms was examined through a series of simulation studies. The simulation results show that the two algorithms outperform the high-priority two-phase locking protocol.

Keywords: Concurrency control, transaction scheduling, real-time systems, database systems, serializability.

1. Introduction

A read-only transaction (ROT) is a transaction that only reads, but does not update any data items [2]. In real-time application domains, an ROT may be used to keep track of the movement of airplanes in a radar tracking system or to monitor the fluctuations of prices of stock shares in a stock trading system. ROTs can be processed with general concurrency control protocols that ensure serializability. Most previous studies on concurrency control protocols in real-time database systems (RTDBS) [5, 6, 9, 12] adopted this approach. That is, the concurrency control protocols do not differentiate ROTs from ordinary update transactions. In this approach, ROTs may be required to hold locks on large amount of data items for long periods of time, thus causing update transactions to suffer long delays. However, we believe that it is also possible to use separate algorithms to process ROTs effectively. In effect, a standard concurrency control protocol is used to process update transactions while a separate algorithm is used to process ROTs. With this approach, the separate algorithm can make use of the knowledge that ROTs will not update any data items.

Serializability is the standard notion of correctness in transaction processing [2]. Serializability preserves database consistency. That is, when transactions are processed in a serializable execution, then the database is guaranteed to remain in a consistent state. Serializability requires that concurrent transactions, including read-only ones, be scheduled in a serializable way. While this strictness of serializability is necessary for update transactions to maintain database consistency, it may place unnecessary restriction on processing ROTs. Consequently, this may have a negative impact on the system performance.

Serializability is often not necessary for some real-time systems which are, in most cases, deployed in mission-critical applications [1, 8, 14]. Using separate algorithms for ROTs can make use of the semantics of ROTs to provide a flexibility from the strictness of serializability in scheduling ROTs and to allow non-serializable executions of transactions. Furthermore, in some real-time applications, satisfying the timing constraints of transactions is the paramount objective. Some temporary and bounded inconsistencies may even be tolerated [1, 8, 13] so that a timely response to the environment can be provided. Thus, this unique characteristic of real-time applications make the approach of non-serializability a better candidate for transaction processing in RTDBS.

Therefore, to enhance the capability of the system of satisfying the timing constraints of real-time transactions, it may be desirable to relax the strictness of serializability to increase the amount of concurrency of processing transactions. Some research effort has been pursued in this direction and several protocols have been proposed to allow non-serializable execution of transactions to gain performance advantages [7, 8, 15, 16]. Their common objective is to reduce data contention thus allowing more execution schedules to speed up the processing of transactions. However, a common weakness of these protocols is that ROTs will read inconsistent data.

There is a significant proportion of ROTs in several real-time applications. For example, in stock trading systems, different ROTs are required to calculate a variety of technical indexes and summary data [11]. Thus, it is important to investigate how ROTs can be processed effectively. Using separate algorithms for ROTs could be a better approach to processing ROTs from update transactions. This approach reduces the interference between ROTs and update transactions so that the impact of blocking due to concurrency control on priority-driven scheduling in real-time systems can be decreased. This approach could also allow non-serializable executions of transactions. However, although non-serializability is allowed, ROTs should be guaranteed to read consistent data. It is essential that non-serializability must not compromise the consistency of ROTs because even bounded inconsistency may not be acceptable to some real-time applications.

In this paper, we investigate the approach of using separate algorithms for processing ROTs and non-serializable executions of transactions. The rest of the paper is organized as follows: Section 2 introduces some related work. In Section 3, we explore different consistency requirements of ROTs. Section 4 analyzes the criteria of different consistency requirements based on *read-from graph* analysis. In Section 5, we propose two algorithms for processing ROTs separately. We discuss the effectiveness of using separate algorithms and compare to standard concurrency control protocols in Section 6. We show the performance results of the two algorithms in Section 7 and conclude in Section 8.

2. Related Work

Epsilon-serializability [16] allows the uncommitted results of a transaction to be read by another transaction. Transactions are associated with limits of importing inconsistency and exporting inconsistency. A schedule is epsilon-serializable as long as there is no violation of importing and exporting inconsistency limits of any transaction and the schedule is serializable after removing queries. Son and Kouloumbis [15] adopted epsilon-serializability as the correctness criterion to provide higher degree of concurrency to real-time transactions in distributed replicated RTDBS. They proposed a new token-based replication control algorithm which integrates real-time scheduling with data replication control.

Kuo and Mok [7, 8] proposed a weaker correctness criterion, the notion of "similarity" for concurrency control for real-time transactions. In real-time database environment, the values of a data object represent different states of an entity in the real world. They observed that the values of a data object that are slightly different in age or in precision can be interchangeable as read data for transactions. They proposed a class of real-time concurrency control algorithms called SSP (Similarity Stack Protocol) based on the notion of similarity [8].

The rationale for this more liberal approach is that instances that are created at approximately the same time, are "similar" enough to be treated as the same instances.

The consistency model presented in [1, 13, 14] is an attempt to define another dimension of correctness criterion, the notion of external consistency. External consistency requires that the values of data objects which a transaction reads are accurate at some time within a bounded period of interval. The model is an extension of the imprecise computation model to real-time transaction model. They stressed that external consistency, i.e., a timely and externally consistent response, is more important than an out-of-date though internally consistent response. External consistency is achieved by sacrificing data consistency temporarily to some extent.

The objective of all these studies is to relax the strictness of serializability. With more knowledge of application characteristics available or when the timely response is the primary requirement, non-serializable execution of transactions becomes a better (or necessary) approach. However, the major weakness of these protocols is that (read-only) transactions must always tolerate bounded inconsistency of data, which may not be acceptable to some real-time applications. On the contrary, the protocols we propose in this paper ensure the consistency of data.

In fact, the semantics of ROTs has been exploited extensively to improve system efficiency in non-real-time database systems [3, 4]. For example, multiversion two-phase locking [3] is an extension of two-phase locking (2PL) with versioning to avoid the data contention problem of 2PL. In these studies, multiversions of data items in the databases are maintained to allow ROTs to run against past transaction consistent database states. The existence of multiversions of data items allows ROTs to serialize before all concurrent update transactions. The obvious advantage of this is that ROTs and update transactions do not conflict. The cost paid for it is the increased storage requirement and the overheads of retrieving old versions of data items in processing of ROTs.

3. Consistency Requirements of Read-Only Transactions

In this section, we investigate the consistency requirements of ROTs for different correctness criteria in RTDBS. A database is a set of data items which supports read and write operations. A transaction is a sequence of read and write operations. Each transaction must preserve consistency. A transaction, when run alone to completion without interference from other transactions, takes the database from one consistent state to another.

An ROT is a transaction that does not modify any data item. ROTs do not corrupt the eventual database state. However, if no control is imposed on the execution of ROTs together with update transactions, ROTs may read inconsistent data in their executions and produce incorrect results to users. We assume that it is possible *a priori* to distinguish ROTs from update transactions. Hence, transactions can be identified as read-only from their inception. Given this standard transaction model, we investigate two consistency requirements of ROTs.

We assume that the serializability of update transactions is maintained which can be guaranteed by standard concurrency control protocols.

3.1 Two Consistency Requirements

It is natural to conceive that the consistency requirement of ROTs comes from the requirement of serializability which is the standard correctness criterion of transaction processing. Under serializability, both update transactions and ROTs are indiscriminately considered as ordinary transactions and required to serialize with each other on the same serialization order of transactions. Serialization order is derived from topological sorting which determines a linear order consistent with the partial commitment order of transactions in the serialization graph. Moreover, serializability requires ROTs to serialize with each other. This serialization order of ROTs make ROTs read the database states which are produced by the same serialization order of update transactions. Otherwise, serializability will be violated. In other words, all ROTs perceive the same serialization order of update transactions. We call this requirement *strong consistency*.

Strong consistency could make it easy to understand the interactions among transactions. However, since ROTs do not modify any data item, it might be unnecessarily restrictive in processing ROTs. Obviously *strong consistency* can be guaranteed by standard concurrency control protocols which ensure serializability of transactions. Since most of them cannot produce all possible serializable executions of transactions, they are even more restrictive than *strong consistency* in processing ROTs. We will show later that it is more effective to use a separate algorithm to process ROTs from update transactions than to use standard concurrency control protocols for *strong consistency*.

As we mentioned earlier, serializability requires the set of committed update transactions to serialize on a serialization order. This set of the update transactions can be perceived by different ROTs in different perspectives. That means that the partial commitment order of the update transactions can be interpreted as a number of different serialization orders for different ROTs. These different serialization orders produce different consistent states because they represent different interpretations of serializable executions of update transactions.

We relax the requirement of *strong consistency* by allowing different ROTs to read different consistent states which are produced by different serialization orders of the same set of update transactions. Consequently, ROTs may not be required to serialize with one another. In other words, different ROTs may perceive different serialization order of update transactions. We call this requirement *view consistency*.

3.2 Strong Consistency vs View Consistency

To illustrate the difference between the requirements of *strong consistency* and *view consistency*, consider the following example:

Example 1: Suppose we have two ROTs, Q_1 and Q_2, and three update transactions U_3 and U_4 and U_5 as follows:

$Q_1 : r(x) r(y)$ $Q_2 : r(y) r(x)$

$U_3 : r(x) w(x)$ $U_4 : r(y) w(y)$ $U_5 : r(x) r(y) r(z) w(z)$

Consider the following schedule S1 and its serialization graph in Figure 1.

S1 : $r_1(x) r_2(y) r_3(x) w_3(x) c_3 r_4(y) w_4(y) c_4 r_5(x) r_5(y) r_5(z)$
$w_5(z) c_5 r_1(y) c_1 r_2(x) c_2$

where $r_i(x)$ and $w_i(x)$ denote transaction T_i reads and writes data item x respectively and c_i denotes the commitment of T_i.

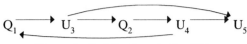

Figure 1 : Serialization graph of S1

In Figure 1, we can easily see that the execution of S1 does not satisfy the requirement of *strong consistency* because of the non-serializable execution of transactions which can be determined by having a cycle among ROTs and update transactions in the serialization graph. In particular, Q_1 and Q_2 read the database states which can not be produced by the same serialization order of update transactions. Thus, *strong consistency* does not allow processing Q_1 and Q_2 in this execution.

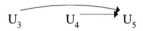

Figure 2 : Partial commitment order of U_3, U_4 and U_5

However, if we consider the partial commitment order of the update transactions only as shown in Figure 2, we can interpret different serialization orders of these update transactions. Two possible serialization orders are $\{U_3 \rightarrow U_4 \rightarrow U_5\}$ and $\{U_4 \rightarrow U_3 \rightarrow U_5\}$. If we consider Q_1 only together with the update transactions, we can observe that the values read by Q_1 are the result of complete execution of U_4 from its initiation. Q_1 reads consistent data because it is serialized with U_3, U_4 and U_5. The serialization order between them is $U_4 \rightarrow Q_1 \rightarrow U_3 \rightarrow U_5$ as shown in Figure 3a. Similarly, Q_2 reads the result of the complete execution of U_3 and is also serialized with the serialization order $U_3 \rightarrow Q_2 \rightarrow U_4 \rightarrow U_5$ as shown in Figure 3b. Clearly, Q_1 and Q_2 read different consistent states produced by different interpretations of serializable execution of U_3, U_4 and U_5. In other words, they perceive different serialization orders of U_3, U_4 and U_5. Thus, the execution of S1 satisfies the requirement of *view consistency*. Clearly, *view consistency* allows for non-serializable execution between ROTs and update transactions.

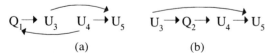

(a)   (b)

Figure 3 : Different interpretations of serialization order

Since serializability requires all transactions including ROTs to serialize on the same serialization order, ROTs are not allowed to be involved in a cycle in the serialization graph like the cycle $\{Q_1 \rightarrow U_3 \rightarrow Q_2 \rightarrow U_4 \rightarrow Q_1\}$ in S1. That is why *strong consistency* does not allow the different interpretations of serialization order of update transactions. Therefore, although two possible consistent states can be interpreted on the partial commitment order of S1, *strong consistency* only allows one of them to be visible to ROTs.

View consistency is a weaker requirement than *strong consistency* because ROTs are not required to perceive the same serialization order of update transactions. Therefore, the consistent states allowed by *strong consistency* are the subset of those allowed by *view consistency*. Although *view consistency* is a weaker requirement than *strong consistency*, it might be acceptable to some real-time applications.

4. Analysis of Consistency Requirement

In this section, we analyze the criteria of different consistency requirements. We assume that the uncommitted values of data items made by active transactions are not visible to other transactions. For the sake of exposition, we would like to analyze the *view consistency* requirement of ROTs first.

4.1 View Consistency Requirement

View consistency allows different ROTs to perceive different serialization orders of update transactions. It implies that ROTs do not need to serialize with each other. Hence, we can only investigate the interactions between an ROT and update transactions without taking other ROTs into consideration. In order to observe a consistent database state, an ROT must not see the partial effects of any update transaction. For each update transaction, the ROT must see all or none of its effects either directly or indirectly. In other words, if an ROT reads some data items written by an update transaction U, the ROT must either read all the data items from the update transaction or read none from it.

To help describe the analysis of an ROT reading partial-effects of an update transaction directly or indirectly, we define a *read-from (RF) graph* which is a directed graph and captures the relationships between an ROT and its associated update transactions. Each *RF-graph* is associated with an ROT. An *RF-graph* has a set of nodes $N = Q \cup U$, where Q denotes the ROT in question and U denotes the set of update transactions that may affect the database state read by the ROT. A directed edge is added ($U_j \rightarrow U_i$ or $U_j \rightarrow Q$) in an *RF-graph* of an ROT if an update transaction U_i or the ROT reads some data from another update transaction U_j. A directed edge will also be added ($Q \rightarrow U_i$) if the ROT has read a data item which is subsequently written by an update transaction U_i. We say that a transaction T_i reads from another transaction T_j if T_i reads a data item which is written by T_j. We call all the update transactions in an *RF-graph dependency transactions* of Q, denoted by $DT(Q)$. Hence, the directed edges capture the read-from relationships among transactions in an *RF-graph*. If there is a cycle in an *RF-graph*, we call it *RF-cycle*.

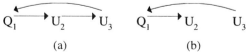

(a)   (b)

Figure 4 : RF-Graphs of Q_1 in S2 and S3

Consider the following schedule:

S2 : $r_1(x)$ $r_2(x)$ $w_2(x)$ c_2 $r_3(x)$ $r_3(y)$ $w_3(y)$ c_3 $r_1(y)$ c_1

In the schedule S2, Q_1 has read x before U_2 writes x. U_3 reads the new value of x written by U_2 to derive y which is, in turn, read by Q_1. It is easy to notice that S2 is a typical example of the inconsistent retrieval problem [2]. Q_1 has read an inconsistent data because Q_1 sees the partial effects of U_2 via U_3 indirectly. This situation is characterized by having an *RF-cycle* in the *RF-graph*. Figure 4a shows the *RF-cycle* for schedule S2.

Let's consider the following schedule S3:

S3 : $r_1(x)$ $r_2(y)$ $r_2(x)$ $w_2(x)$ c_2 $r_3(y)$ $w_3(y)$ c_3 $r_1(y)$ c_1

In the schedule S3, U_3 does not carry any partial effects of U_2 because they do not have read-from relationship. Figure 4b shows the *RF-graph* of S3 which contains no *RF-cycle*. In particular, the derivation of the new value of y does not have any dependency on U_2. Hence, Q_1 does not read any inconsistent data. However, U_2 and U_3 have read-write conflicts on y in S3. It is not difficult to see that the serialization graph of S3 is the same as that of S2. Figure 5 shows the serialization graph for S2 and S3. Clearly, the standard serialization graph is inadequate to characterize the inconsistent retrieval problem of an ROT. Thus, we need to modify it to characterize the correctness of *view consistency*. In [10], we have characterized the correctness criteria in terms of the extended serialization graph and proved the correctness of our protocols.

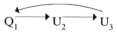

Figure 5 : Serialization Graph for S2 and S3

To analyze the synthesis of an *RF-cycle*, let's re-consider the schedule S2. U_2 initiates a "*partial-effect-chain*" when it commits before Q_1. U_3 which reads from U_2 carries the partial effects of U_2 to Q_1. An *RF-cycle* is therefore formed. It is important to notice that U_2 initiates a "*partial-effect-chain*". Without this initiation, an *RF-cycle* will never be formed. We call this *inconsistency threat instance* and the *dependency transaction* causing this instance *inconsistency threat (IT) transaction*. Hence, the passing of partial effects can only be made possible after this *inconsistency threat instance* occurs.

Based on the above analysis, an ROT will read inconsistent data if there exists an *RF-cycle* in the *RF-graph* of the ROT. For an ROT to read inconsistent data from the update transactions, we observe that the following two conditions must be true:

C1: An *inconsistency threat instance* occurs, i.e., the ROT has read some data items which are subsequently updated by an *IT transaction*.

C2: The ROT reads from a *dependency transaction* which has read from the *IT transaction* either directly or indirectly.

C1 stipulates the possible occurrence of the "partial-effect-chain" initiated by an *IT transaction*. C2 ensures that the passing of the partial-effects among *dependency transactions* must be in the order of directed edges in an *RF-cycle*. Otherwise, the partial-effects will never be carried to another *dependency transaction* from which the ROT will read. To avoid an ROT reading inconsistent data, it suffices to ensure that any one of the above two conditions is false. In other words, the objective of designing a new algorithm for *view consistency* is to prevent all these conditions from being true simultaneously.

4.2 Strong Consistency Requirement

We now turn our attention to the *strong consistency*. For the *strong consistency* requirement, all ROTs perceive the same serialization order of update transactions. Clearly, it is necessary to ensure that the two conditions in Section 4.1 cannot be true simultaneously for *strong consistency* requirement. However, it is not sufficient to satisfy the *strong consistency* requirement. To guarantee this, ROTs need to serialize with each other with respect to update transactions to prohibit non-serializable execution of transactions.

Consider Example 1 again. When Q_1 reads y from U_4, Q_1 is serialized after U_4. Since Q_2 has already read y before U_4 updates y, Q_2 is serialized before U_4. For the *strong consistency* requirement, Q_1 needs to be serialized after Q_2 at this point of execution. On the contrary, Q_2 needs to be serialized after Q_1 on reading x from U_3. A conflict arises between Q_1 and Q_2. Then, a conflict resolution protocol is needed to resolve the conflict, resulting in the abortion of one of either of Q_1 and Q_2. In effect, we need a way to impose a total ordering on the serialization order of ROTs. One simple technique suffices to achieve this. Each ROT is assigned a start-up timestamp when the ROT is initiated so that ROTs are serialized on this non-decreasing start-up timestamp. It means that old ROTs cannot read the data items from update transactions which have already read by younger ROTs. Obviously, this static determination of serialization order between ROTs at initiation places a restriction on conflict resolutions between ROTs, thus leading to some unnecessary aborts of ROTs. We will discuss a more flexible way to determine the total serialization order between ROTs dynamically. The objective of designing a new algorithm for *strong consistency* is to prevent the resulting serialization graph of the execution of transactions from having a cycle of all kinds, as required by serializability.

5. Algorithms for Read-Only Transactions

In this section, we present two algorithms which process ROTs separately from update transactions for *view consistency* and *strong consistency*. ROTs are guaranteed to read data for the two consistent requirements without interfering with update transactions. Recall that an underlying requirement of processing ROTs in the algorithms is that the execution of update transactions alone must be serializable, which is ensured by concurrency control protocols such as two-phase locking (2PL). Since these algorithms process ROTs separately from update transactions, they can be easily integrated with any concurrency control protocol. For simplicity, we assume that a transaction which writes a data item must have read the data item, i.e., the write set of a transaction is the subset of its read set.

With respect to an ROT, there are two sets of update transactions for the specified consistency requirement. The set of update transactions which should be placed before the ROT in the serialization order and the set of update transactions placed after the ROT. We call these two sets the *before set* and *after set* of the ROT respectively. Clearly, the ROT cannot read data items from an update transaction in its *after set*. Conversely, the ROT can only read data from its *before set*.

The basic mechanism of the two new algorithms is that for each ROT Q, we maintain a set of update transactions from which Q cannot read. That is, those update transactions need to be serialized after Q because of the consistency requirement. In other words, these update transactions would become the *after set* of Q on the serialization order. We denote this *after set* by AS(Q). We place an update transaction in this *after set* of an ROT only when the specified consistency requirement may be violated. Thus, ROTs always need to read the data items which are not written by the update transactions belonging to this *after set*. Otherwise, the ROT is aborted. Therefore, the difference between the new algorithms is the insertion rules for which update transactions need to be inserted into the *after set* of an ROT. There is a read rule for ROTs to read data items for both algorithms:

Read Rule : When an ROT wants to read a data item, the update transaction that has written the data item cannot be the *after set* of the ROT; otherwise the ROT is aborted.

5.1 View Consistency Algorithm

For the sake of exposition, we first describe our first algorithm which provides the *view consistency* requirement of ROTs. For *view consistency*, each ROT is allowed to define its own interpretation of the serialization order of update transactions. We will place an update transaction in the *after set* of an ROT only when the *view consistency* may be violated. An ROT always starts with an empty *after set*. Insertion of an update transaction into the *after set* of an ROT will only be carried out at the commit time of an update transaction.

As we discussed earlier, the objective of the new algorithm is to disallow the execution of update transactions to form an *RF-cycle*. Hence, it is necessary to keep track of these possible developments of *RF-cycles* for an ROT dynamically to determine whether a cycle will be formed. However, it is not necessary to do it explicitly. Recall that a cycle will be formed only if the two necessary conditions in Section 4.1 are all true at the same time. In particular, we should detect the *inconsistency threat instance*. In case of this occurrence, we should start to keep track of the passing of partial effects of the *IT transaction* among the *dependency transactions* to prevent an ROT reading from these *dependency transactions*.

The basic idea is that when an *inconsistency threat instance* occurs with respect to an ROT, the ROT cannot read from the *IT transaction* and all the *dependency transactions* which reads from the *IT transaction*. That is, all these transactions should be placed into the *after set* of the ROT. In this way, the *RF-cycle* with respect to an ROT will never be formed.

Let CRS(Q) be the set of data items that have been read by an ROT Q and $RS(T_i)$ and $WS(T_i)$ denote the read set and write set of transaction T_i respectively.

Algorithm 1 : When an update transaction U commits, it will be placed into the *after set* of an ROT, Q, under any of the following insertion rules:

R1 : Q has read the prior value of a data item that will be updated by U,

i.e., $WS(U) \cap CRS(Q) \neq \varnothing$

R2 : U reads a data item that has been written by another committed update transaction U' and U' is currently in the *after set* of Q,

i.e., $\exists_{U'} RS(U) \cap WS(U') \neq \varnothing$ and $U' \in AS(Q)$

In Algorithm 1, Rule R1 is to detect the *inconsistency thread instance*. Rule R2 is to keep track of the passing of the *partial-effects* of an *IT transaction* between the *dependency transactions* along the directed edges in *RF-cycles*. Recall that we do not assume the knowledge of data requirements of transactions. We cannot precisely recognize those *dependency transactions* which may really pose an inconsistency threat. Although some update transactions carry the partial effects, an ROT may not need to read from these update transactions. These update transactions will also be placed into the *after set* of an ROT in Algorithm 1. These additional insertions into the *after set* of an ROT are necessitated by the lack of complete knowledge of data requirements of the ROT. However, these insertions will not cause the unnecessary abort of an ROT. Since the ROT does not read from these update transactions, the abort of an ROT which is caused by the violation of the read rule, will never be caused by reading from these update transactions.

5.2 Strong Consistency Algorithm

In this section, we present another algorithm to process ROTs for *strong consistency* requirement. For *strong consistency*, ROTs perceive a single partial serialization order of update transactions. As we discussed earlier, we need to impose a total order on ROTs. In other words, ROTs need to be serialized with each other. Moreover, it is desirable that the serialization order between ROTs be determined dynamically instead of relying on the startup time. The problem is to find out when two ROTs needs to serialize with one another and how to serialize them.

It can be observed that even if two ROTs do not have same data items in their read sets, they may need to be serialized with each other. Figure 6 shows that although Q_1 and Q_2 do not read any same data item, they may constitute a cycle in the serialization graph. What we need is a way of breaking this cycle. The following technique suffices to solve this problem by adding a new insertion rule to Algorithm 1. Without loss of generalities, we assume that Q_1 starts to have read the prior value of some data item which U_3 updates. So, U_3 will be placed into the *after set* of Q_1. When U_4 commits, U_4 will also placed into the *after set* of Q_1 because of U_3. When Q_2 commits, the *after set* of Q_2 will contain U_5. We can easily see that Q_2 needs to serialized after Q_1 at this moment of execution because Q_2 has read from U_4 which have been in the

after set of Q_1. If Q_1 inherits the *after set* of Q_2, i.e. { U_5 }, when U_6 commits, U_6 will be placed into the *after set* of Q_1. Then Q_1 will not be allowed to read from U_6 later in its execution because U_6 is now in its *after set*. Hence, Q_1 needs to be aborted. This technique is better than the static determination of serialization order of ROTs based on start-up timestamp because the serialization order between ROTs is determined dynamically.

$$Q_1 \rightarrow U_3 \rightarrow U_4 \rightarrow Q_2 \rightarrow U_5 \rightarrow U_6$$

Figure 6 : A cycle involving two independent ROTs

Since the *after sets* of ROTs are inherited, the new algorithm consists of two parts of insertion rules. One part considers insertions of update transactions into the *after set* of an ROT and the other part is dealt with the inheritance of *after sets* of other ROTs by an ROT. In fact, the former part of the new algorithm includes the insertion rules of Algorithm 1 for *view consistency*.

Algorithm 2: There are two parts of insertion rules:

Part 1: When an update transaction U commits, the update transaction U is placed into the *after set* of an ROT, Q, if either R1 or R2 of Algorithms 1 or the following addition rule R3 is satisfied.

R3: U writes a data item that has been read by another committed update transaction U' and U' is currently in the *after set* of Q,

i.e., $\exists_{U'} WS(U) \cap RS(U') \neq \varnothing$ and $U' \in AS(Q)$

Part 2: When an ROT Q' commits, the *after set* of Q' is inherited by the ROT Q into its *after set*, if the following rule is satisfied:

R4: Q' has read from an update transaction U' which is currently in the *after set* of Q and Q has not read some data item from any update transactions in the *after set* of Q'. If Q has read from any update transactions in the *after set* of Q', Q is aborted.

i.e., $\exists_{U'} RS(Q') \cap WS(U') \neq \varnothing$ and $U' \in AS(Q)$ and $\forall_{U'' \in AS(Q')} CRS(Q) \cap WS(U'') = \varnothing$

The additional rule R3 considers the dependency edge due to read-write conflicts between update transactions. The additional rule R4 ensures that the cycle involving two ROTs will never occur because the *after set* of a committed ROT will always be included into the *after set* of all currently running ROTs if necessary. This eliminates an edge in the serialization graph from a currently running ROT to the committed ROT. The elimination of these cycles means that all ROTs will read database states which are produced by the same serialization order of update transactions. Algorithm 2 will place more additional update transactions into the *after set* of an ROT than Algorithm 1 because of the inheritance of the *after sets* of committed ROTs. Similar to Algorithm 1, these additional insertions will not cause the unnecessary abort of the ROT. It is because if these additional update transactions do not constitute a cycle involving the committed ROT, the running ROT will never read some data item written from the update transactions in the *after set* of the committed ROT.

6. Effectiveness of Using Algorithms for ROTs

Standard concurrency control protocols provide *strong consistency* of ROTs which comes from the requirement of serializability. Since most concurrency control protocols produce only a subset of serializable executions of transactions, they are even more restrictive in processing ROTs. As we claimed earlier, it is more effective to use separate algorithms to process ROTs than using standard concurrency control protocols. By effectiveness, we mean that using separate algorithm for ROTs allows higher degree of concurrency than standard concurrency control protocols. In other words, it allows some transaction schedules which cannot be produced by these protocols. We use Algorithm 2 for *strong consistency* to compare to two-phase locking (2PL) and optimistic concurrency control (OCC) protocols. To illustrate this, consider the following example:

Example 2: Suppose we have two ROTs, Q_1 and Q_2, and two update transactions U_3 and U_4 as follows:

$$Q_1 \; : \; r(x) \; r(y) \qquad Q_2 \; : \; r(y) \; r(x)$$
$$U_3 \; : \; r(x) \; w(x) \qquad U_4 \; : \; r(y) \; w(y)$$

Consider the following schedule S4 and its serialization graph in Figure 7.

$$S4 \; : \; r_1(x) \; r_2(y) \; r_2(x) \; r_3(x) \; w_3(x) \; c_3 \; r_4(y) \; w_4(y) \; c_4$$
$$r_1(y) \; c_1 \; c_2$$

In this example, S4 is a serializable schedule and can be allowed by Algorithm 2. Algorithm 2 allows ROTs and update transactions to execute without interference. This reduced interference between ROTs and update transactions alleviates the impact of concurrency control on the real-time priority-driven scheduling, thus providing more flexibility in scheduling transactions. If the same set of transactions are processed using standard 2PL, U_3 and U_4 will be blocked until Q_1 and Q_2 have finished. A priority inversion problem occurs if U_3 and U_4 have higher priorities than Q_1 and Q_2. On the other hand, if they are processed using optimistic concurrency control protocols with forward validation (OCC-FV) [2, 12], Q_1 and Q_2 will even be aborted. Hence, both 2PL and OCC-FV do not allow this schedule.

$$Q_1 \longrightarrow U_3 \longleftarrow Q_2 \longrightarrow U_4$$

Figure 7 : Serialization graph of S4

As reported in previous studies on real-time concurrency control, the optimistic approach is claimed to be more suitable for RTDBS than two-phase locking because of its nice properties of non-blocking and deferred conflict resolution. In [10], we illustrate that using a separate algorithm for ROTs together with OCC-FV is better than just using OCC-FV for all transactions. We use Algorithm 2 for comparison. We illustrate the superiority of Algorithm 2 over OCC-FV by proving that Algorithm 2 allows a superset of transaction schedules which can be allowed by OCC-FV.

7. Performance Evaluation

In this section, we present the performance results of the two algorithms compared to the standard two-phase locking with high-priority (2PL-HP) protocol from the simulation study.

7.1 Experimental Model

The simulation model consists of a firm real-time transaction generator, a ready queue, a block queue, a scheduler, a CPU and a disk resident database. The real-time transaction generator creates both read-only and update transactions following the Poisson distribution. Each transaction is modeled as a sequence of operations. The processing of an operation involves use of the CPU and access to data objects. The queuing discipline for CPU is earliest deadline first (EDF) while the queuing discipline for disk I/O is first come first served (FCFS). The scheduler assigns the CPU to the transaction at the head of the ready queue. Once a transaction misses its deadline, the transaction will be aborted.

7.1.1 Performance Measures

In RTDBS, the most important measure of performance is Miss Rate which indicates the probability of a transaction missing its deadline. Another useful measure is Restart Rate. It reflects the amount of resources spent on restarted transactions. Reducing Restart Rate not only saves resources, but also helps to soothe resource and data contention. In particular, it helps to analyze the usefulness of the algorithms because Restart Rate directly measures the amount of data conflicts between transactions. Response Time also enables us to understand the effectiveness of the algorithms. The meanings of Miss Rate and Restart Rate are defined as follows.

$$Miss\ Rate(MR) = \frac{N_{missed}}{N_{committed} + N_{missed}}$$

$$Re\ start\ Rate(RR) = \frac{N_{restarted}}{N_{committed} + N_{missed}}$$

where
N_{missed} = number of transactions missed their deadlines;
$N_{committed}$ = number of transactions committed;
$N_{restarted}$ = number of transactions being restarted.

7.1.2 Model Parameters

Table 1 summarizes the baseline settings of the model to be used in the simulation experiments. Long ROTs are used deliberately in order to intensify the data conflicts between the update transactions and ROTs. On the other hand, long update transactions are avoided because we would like to reduce the data conflicts among the update transactions. In addition, the same explanation is applied for the choice of the update transaction arrival rate. This baseline setting is intended to investigate the performance of the two algorithms in the environment where ROTs are dominant in the system. To assign a deadline to a transaction, the following worst execution time function is used.

$$Deadline = T_{gen} + (T_{cpu} + T_{disk}) * N_{oper} * (1 + SF)$$
where T_{gen} : current time of transaction generated.

Database size	200 data objects
Concurrency control	2PL with high priority, (2PL-HP)
Read only transaction size (N_{oper}) (number of operations)	15 – 20 (uniformly distributed)
Update transaction size	5 – 15 (uniformly distributed)
Update transaction arrival rate	1 transaction / second
Update transaction read probability	0.4
Slack factor (SF)	4 – 10
CPU time for each operation (T_{cpu})	10 msec
Disk I/O time (T_{disk})	20 msec

Table 1: The baseline setting

7.2 Performance results

Figure 8 gives the MRs of different algorithms as a function of ROT arrival rates. For each algorithm, the MRs of update transactions and ROTs are collected separately. It can be observed that the MRs increase as the ROT arrival rate increases. The MRs of both update transactions and ROTs are reduced significantly by using either Algorithm 1 or Algorithm 2. As to 2PL-HP protocol, both update transactions and ROTs would be restarted if they have data conflicts with high priority transactions. Therefore, using algorithms to process ROTs separately not only gives higher flexibility in processing ROTs by reducing data conflicts between update transactions and ROTs, but also helps update transactions to meet their deadlines because of reduced data conflicts. In general, the performance gain by ROTs is more significant than update transactions.

However, the performances of Algorithm 1 and Algorithm 2 are almost the same. In our investigation, we found that rule R1 is applied more frequently than rule R2 in using Algorithm 1. On the other hand, rules R3 and R4 are rarely applied in using Algorithm 2. This leads to the similar performance of both algorithms. Based on these findings, most cases of aborting an ROT are caused by the ROT reading inconsistent data directly from an update transaction which must be inserted by rule R1. The more update transactions are inserted by rule R1, the higher the probability of aborting the ROT because the Read rule is caused by these update transactions being in the *after set* of the ROT.

Figure 9 gives the RRs of the algorithms. It is noted that a restarted transaction can still meet its deadline if it has enough slack time. The RR can help to investigate the effectiveness of the algorithms. Since we use long ROTs in order to intensify the data conflicts between the update transactions and ROTs, the RR of the ROTs under 2PL-HP protocol is relatively higher than that of the update transactions even when the ROT arrival rate is low. The increase rate of the RR of ROTs is also higher. When either of the two algorithms is used, the RRs of ROTs drop to a low level. This can be explained by the reduced data conflicts. Since there is no data conflict among ROTs, the increase in the number of ROTs will not affect the RRs of ROTs under both separate algorithms. Moreover, using separate algorithms also helps to reduce the RRs of the update transactions by reducing the data conflicts between update transactions and ROTs.

Figure 10 gives the Response Time of the transactions. The major factors delaying a transaction execution are queuing time due to resource contention, blockings and transaction restarts due to data conflicts. Since there is no blocking for ROTs under both separate algorithms, the Response Time is reduced moderately. However, update transactions still suffer from blocking due to data conflicts among themselves. Hence, the amount of reduction in the Response Time of update transactions is marginal. The reduction in the RR also helps to reduce the Response Time of both update transactions and ROTs. Indirectly, resource contention is soothed because transaction restarts actually waste system resources. As a result, both separate algorithms help to reduce the Response Time of transactions, especially ROTs.

Figure 11 gives the MRs when the read ratio of the update transactions varies. The ROT arrival rate is fixed at 1.8 transactions per second to provide a relatively high workload environment. The read ratio of update transactions affects the amount of data conflicts in the system. When the read ratio is 1, update transactions become read-only ones and all transactions in the system become read-only transactions. In this case, both separate algorithms become useless since there is no data conflict between transactions. The MR is solely attributed to resource contention. As a result, the MRs of update transactions and ROTs are close to each other under 2PL-HP protocol and both separate algorithms.

As the read ratio of update transactions decreases, the amount of data conflicts is intensified leading to the increased MR. The effect of using separate algorithms becomes prominent. When the read ratio drops to zero, update transactions become write-only transactions where the performance improvement is the largest.

In the last experiment set, we fix the arrival rate of ROTs to investigate the performance of both algorithms in a situation dominated by update transactions by increasing the arrival rate of update transactions. In this experiment set, we fix the ROT arrival rate at 1 transaction per second. Figure 12 gives the MR in this environment. It can be noted that the amount of improvement in the MR of update transactions in using the two separate algorithms is reduced. In particular, when the arrival rate of the update transactions is high (2.4 transactions per second), the MR of update transactions is reduced from 41% to 37% only. The magnitude is comparatively smaller than that in Figure 8. On the other hand, the MR of ROTs is reduced from 51% to 18%.

In update transaction dominant situations, a large proportion of data conflicts is attributed to the data conflicts among update transactions which cannot be resolved by both separate algorithms. This is also illustrated in Figure 13 which shows the RR. Only a few percentage of reduction in the RR of update transactions can be observed whereas the RR of ROTs is reduced significantly.

8. Conclusions

An ROT is a transaction which does not update any data item. It may be more effective to process ROTs separately from other update transactions. We have defined different consistency requirements for ROTs : *strong consistency and view consistency*. *Strong consistency* restricts ROTs to perceive the same serialization order of update transactions, as required by serializability. *View consistency* allows ROTs to perceive different serialization orders of update transactions, thus permitting non-serializable execution of transactions. However, ROTs are still ensured to see consistent data, which is distinguished from other non-serializable algorithms that tolerate bounded inconsistency.

We have investigated the conditions under which an ROT may read inconsistent data based on the *RF-Graph* analysis for various consistency criteria. We have presented two algorithms to process ROTs separately for the *view consistency* and the *strong consistency* requirements. We argued for the case of using separate algorithms for ROTs, and even for *strong consistency* which can also be guaranteed by standard concurrency controls such as two-phase locking and optimistic concurrency control.

This paper showed that using algorithms to process ROTs separately is a viable approach to processing transactions in real-time systems. In our simulation studies, significant performance improvements of both separate algorithms in terms of various performance measures are shown compared to 2PL-HP protocol. It is especially true for ROTs although update transactions benefit from these algorithms as well. We found that most cases of ROTs reading inconsistent data are to read from an update transaction directly. Although both separate algorithms perform similarly, Algorithm 1 will be more useful in some environments, including distributed environments. When Algorithm 1 is used in distributed environments, it allows more locality of processing because an ROT does not need to serialize with other ROTs. However, Algorithm 2 lacks this property.

We are now developing another simulation model where both separate algorithms will be used in OCC protocols, particularly OCC-FV. It will be interesting to compare the impact of using separate algorithms on 2PL-HP protocol and OCC-FV. Also, we plan to extend our work to multiversion of data in RTDBS and investigate the temporal consistency of transactions. With multiversion data, *view consistency* provides a flexibility of choosing an appropriate version of data depending on temporal consistency requirement or logical consistency requirement.

References

[1] Audsley, N. C., A. Burns, M. F. Richardson, and A.J. Wellings, "Data Consistency in Hard Real-Time Systems", *Technical Report*, Department of Computer Science, University of York, 1993.

[2] Bernstein, P.A., V. Hadzilacos, and N. Goodman, "*Concurrency Control and Recovery in Database Systems*", Addison-Wesley, Reading, Mass, 1987.

[3] Chan, A., R. Gray, "Implementing Distributed Read-Only Transactions", *IEEE Transactions on Software Engineering*, 11(2), 1985.

[4] Garcia-Molina, H. and G. Wiederhold, "Read-Only Transactions in a Distributed Database", ACM Transactions on Database Systems, 7(2):209-234, 1982.

[5] Haritsa, J. R., M. J. Carey, and M. Livny, "Data Access Scheduling in Firm Real-time Database Systems," *Real-time Systems*, 4(3):203-242, 1992.

[6] Huang, J., J. A. Stankovic, K. Ramamritham, and D. Towley, "Experimental Evaluation of Real-Time Optimistic Concurrency Control Schemes," *Proc. of the 17th International Conference on Very Large Data Bases*, pp. 35-46, 1991.

[7] Kuo, T.W. and A.K. Mok, "Application Semantics and Concurrency Control of Real-Time Data Intensive Applications", *Proceedings of 13th IEEE Real-time Systems Symposium*, 1992.

[8] Kuo, T.W. and A.K. Mok, "SSP: A Semantics-based Protocol for Real-Time Data Access", *Proceedings of 14th IEEE Real-time Systems Symposium*, 1993.

[9] Lam, K.W., S.H. Son and S.L. Hung, "A Priority Ceiling Protocol with Dynamic Adjustment of Serialization Order", *Proceedings of the 13th International Conference on Data Engineering (ICDE'97)*, Birmingham, U.K., Apr 7-11, 1997.

[10] Lam, K.W., S.H. Son, Victor Lee and S.L. Hung, "Using Separate Algorithms to Process Read-Only Transactions in Real-Time Systems", Technical Report 98-10, Department of Computer Science, City University of Hong Kong, 1998.

[11] Lam, K.Y., T.W. Kuo and L. Shu, "On Using Similarity to Process Transactions in Stock Trading Systems", *Proceedings of the IEEE Workshop on Dependable and Real-Time E-Commerce Systems (DARE'98)*, Denver, U.S.A., 1998.

[12] Lee, J. and S.H. Son, "Using Dynamic Adjustment of Serialization Order for Real-time Database Systems," *Proceedings of 14th IEEE Real-time Systems Symposium*, 1993.

[13] Lin, K. J., S. Natarajan, and J. Liu, "Imprecise Results: Utilizing Partial Computations in Real-Time Systems", *Proceedings of the 8th IEEE Real-Time Systems Symposium*, 1987.

[14] Lin, K., "Consistency Issues in Real-Time Database Systems", *Proceedings of the 22nd Hawaii International Conference on Systems Science*, 1989.

[15] Son. S.H and S. Kouloumbis, "A Token-Based Synchronization Scheme for Distributed Real-Time Databases", *Information Systems*, Vol 18, No.6, 1993.

[16] Wu, K.L., P.S. Yu, and C. Pu, "Divergence Control for Epsilon Serializability", *Proceedings of the 8th International Conference on Data Engineering*, 1992.

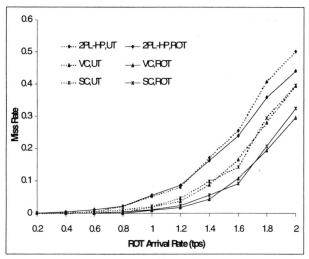

Figure 8: Miss Rate

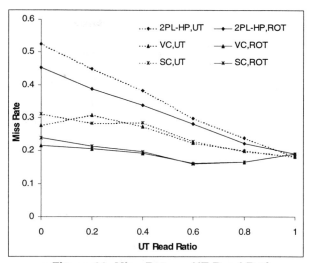

Figure 11: Miss Rate vs UT Read Ratio

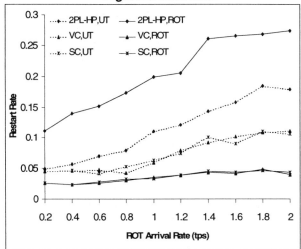

Figure 9: Restart Rate

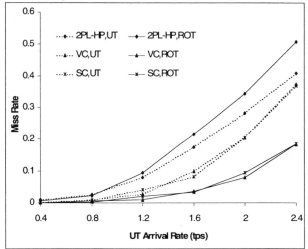

Figure 12: Miss Rate

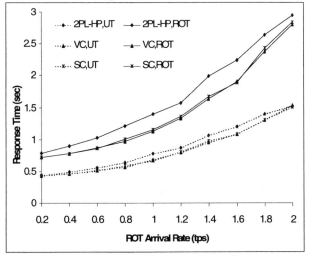

Figure 10: Response Time

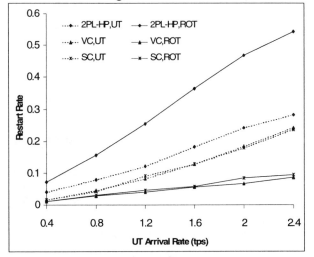

Figure 13: Restart Rate

Maintaining Temporal Coherency of Virtual Data Warehouses

Raghav Srinivasan   *Chao Liang*   *Krithi Ramamritham*

Dept of Computer Science, University of Massachusetts, Amherst, MA 01002

{raghav,cliang,krithi}@cs.umass.edu

Abstract

In Electronic Commerce applications such as stock trading, there is a need to consult sources available on the web for informed decision making. Because information such as stock prices keep changing, the web sources must be queried continually to maintain temporal coherency of the collected data, thereby avoiding decisions based on stale information. However, because network infrastructure has failed to keep pace with ever growing web traffic, the frequency of contacting web servers must be kept to a minimum. This paper presents adaptive approaches for the maintenance of temporal coherency of data gathered from web sources. Specifically, it introduces mechanisms to obtain timely updates from web sources, based on the dynamics of the data and the users' need for temporal accuracy, by judiciously combining push and pull technologies and by using virtual data warehouses to disseminate data within acceptable tolerance to clients. A virtual warehouse maintains temporal coherence, within the tolerance specified, by tracking the amount of change in the web sources, pulling the data from the sources at opportune times, and pushing them to the clients according to their temporal coherency requirements. The performance of these mechanisms is studied using real stock price traces. One of the attractive features of these mechanisms is that it does not require changes to either the web servers or to the HTTP protocol [1].

Keywords: Electronic Commerce, Temporal Correctness, Data warehouses, World Wide Web, Cache.

1. Introduction

Today many applications find it necessary to consult sources available on the web for informed decision making. Given the autonomy of many of these data sources, as well as the temporal nature of some of the data, it may not be possible to materialize the state of the world as represented in these data sources. Hence the data brought together from the various sources can at best be described as a *virtual warehouse (VW)*. The process of gathering data from distributed sources and maintaining their consistency has to be done efficiently and correctly. Applying workflow ideas, we have developed a system that gathers required information without a user explicitly asking for each and every piece of relevant information [KRGL97]. The collection and collation of relevant information is expressed via workflow specifications and the system automatically accesses the necessary sources. Knowing the format of an HTML page, this system has the capability to parse an HTTP reply and extract relevant information, such as stock prices, from the retrieved pages. It then integrates the necessary information using a CGI script and presents it to a user.

A challenging issue here is the maintenance of *temporal coherency*, that is, keeping the VW's deviation from the real world minimal in the temporal dimension. As an example, consider stock trading data. The need for a system that maintains temporal coherency of a VW containing information needed for intelligent decision making by stock investors is obvious. In practice, it is important to keep the data *only as up to date as is needed by the user* of a data item. For example, if a stock broker desires to sell stocks only when the price goes up by one dollar, smaller increases in the stock price will not be relevant, and hence, need not be communicated to him/her. Exploiting such requirements is one way to minimize network and system overheads incurred in the maintenance of temporal coherency. How this can be done is the subject of the paper.

We introduce mechanisms to obtain timely updates from web sources, based on the dynamics of the data and the users' need for temporal accuracy, by judiciously combining push and pull technologies and by using VWs to disseminate data within acceptable tolerance. Specifically, the virtual warehouses (maintained by client organizations) ensure the temporal coherence of data, within the tolerance specified, by tracking the amount of change in the web sources. Based on the changes observed and the tolerance specified by the different clients interested in the data, the VW determines the time for *pull*ing from the server next, and pushes newly acquired data to the clients according to their temporal coherency requirements.

[1] Supported by NSF grant IRI-9619588. Part of this work was done while the third author was at IIT, Mumbai, on leave from the Univ. of Mass. Amherst.

Of course, if the web sources themselves were aware of the clients' temporal coherency requirements and they were endowed with *push* capability, then we can avoid the need for mechanisms such as the ones proposed here. Unfortunately, this can lead to scalability problems and may also introduce the need to make changes to existing web servers (which do not have push capabilities) or to the HTTP protocol. Our mechanisms do not suffer from these disadvantages, making them especially attractive compared to other protocols that have been proposed for maintaining cache consistency in the Web context.

The rest of the paper is organized as follows - Section 2 explains the problem of maintaining temporal coherency, presents the issues involved in developing efficient solutions and discusses prior related work. Section 3 discusses different algorithms for determining *when* data sources must be contacted to obtain up-to-date data values so as to meet user-level temporal coherency requirements. Section 4 analyzes the performance of the algorithms using real-world stock market data streams. In Section 5, summarizing remarks and the directions for future work are presented.

2. Maintaining Temporal Coherency

In this Section, we discuss the problem of maintaining cache coherency and the issues involved in solving it. Finally, we discuss prior approaches to dealing with this problem.

2.1. The Problem

Consider a (stock trading) company that has many clients (i.e., stock brokers). Each broker focuses on one or more stocks and is interested in all the information needed to make decisions regarding those stocks, specifically, information about many different stocks, their competitors' stocks, company profiles, etc. So it is quite conceivable that information brought to serve the needs of one broker may be useful for another broker, especially if many of them are focusing on the same "hot stock" of the day. Also different brokers may have different temporal consistency requirements for the different stock prices that they are interested in. Under these circumstances, it makes practical sense to build a single VW for the whole company thereby serving the needs of the different clients from this single VW. Here, the state of the real-world objects is maintained in the web servers, and the images are maintained by the VW, and also in the users' (i.e., brokers') views. The VW acts as a *cache* containing the data from various web servers.

Temporal coherency is concerned with the relationship between an object in the real world and its image in a database [KRAM93, HZFJ98]. An interesting and challenging problem arises when we recognize that as time progresses, data in the warehouse gets more and more out of synch with the sources. That is, temporal coherency may be

lost as time progresses. This is especially true of the more dynamic (i.e., volatile) data such as stock prices.

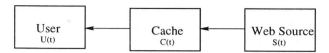

Figure 1. Real World Objects and their Images

Consider Figure 1. Here, $S(t)$ denotes the data source value, $C(t)$ and $U(t)$ denote the values at the cache and the user respectively – all at time t. In an application such as stock trading, users would rather remain oblivious to minor changes in stock prices. In terms of temporal coherency requirements, every user specifies a constraint, c, which means that changes of magnitude less than c in source data need not be informed to the user but the user should be aware of changes whose magnitude is greater than c. Thus, the system must guarantee

$$|U(t) - S(t)| < c$$

An example of a user constraint in the value domain is, *Update stock price of Company X whenever the stock price at the source changes by more than 50 cents*. An example of a user constraint in the time domain is, *Update the stock price relating to Company Y every 5 mins*. Either of these constraints can be easily satisfied if the server is aware of them. However, forcing the server to keep track of users' needs and to make it responsible for transmitting the changes to users leads to the scalability and fault-tolerance problems typically associated with stateful servers. Partly due to this, web sources are designed such that users will have to contact a server to obtain the latest state of the information maintained by the server. Thus, the problem of maintaining the user constraint translates to *how often* the source must be contacted. This is obviously straightforward when a user constraint is stated in the time domain. It is not, when constraints in the value domain must be translated into constraints with respect to the time domain, i.e., into requirements on *when* data at a client needs to be updated.

Thus, the issue is one of keeping the *deviation* of temporal coherency within user-specified bounds. We must employ efficient data refreshing schemes by which dynamic information such as stock prices can be provided to the brokers as prices change. This paper introduces mechanisms to achieve timely updates to the virtual warehouse, based on the dynamics of the data and the users' need for temporal accuracy, by judiciously combining push and pull technologies and by using *cache servers* to disseminate data within acceptable tolerance.

2.2. The Issues

As portrayed in Figure 1, to users, the cache server acts as a server while the web sources act as servers to the cache server. How to maintain consistency between the source, the cache and the user is the main issue addressed in this paper.

In a typical client-server environment, maintaining consistency of the client and the server can be achieved in one of two ways: 1) In the `Server Push` model, the source of the data, i.e., the server, *pushes* data to the client (whenever data changes at the source). In this model, the server can keep track of user requirements and push the data to a client at the appropriate time. Since the cache server maintains the cache and is the server for the clients we can use the server push mechanism to transmit data to the users. 2) In the `Client Pull` model, the client *pulls* data from the source (whenever it suspects that data might have changed at the source). So, consistency of the data at the client depends on how often the client polls the server. Too frequent polling may result in unnecessary overheads, and too infrequent polling might mean stale data.

This paper's contribution lies in the judicious combination of the two models. Today's web sources are "pull" based. Thus, we cannot use the server push technique to maintain consistency between the remote servers and our cache. Hence the cache must maintain its consistency by "pull"ing changes from the server. On the other hand, VW, i.e., the cache server, can be designed to pull data from the web servers and push them to the users.

Given this combination of `Client Pull` and `Server Push`, better performance can be obtained by updating a user's view only when the change is of interest to the user. That is, a user is allowed to specify consistency constraints, and we *push* new data to the user only when the change satisfies the constraints. For example, the user may specify that he is interested in a stock price change only when the price changes by at least a dollar. Note that even if the VW *pulls* data from remote servers when the change is less than a dollar, it *pushes* the changed data to the user only when the change exceeds a dollar. When the user is remote to the VW, this feature further reduces the incurred Internet traffic overhead.

To stay within the constraints imposed by today's web sources, we assume in the rest of the paper that these sources cannot be modified by us to "push" changes. Also, no change to the `http` *protocol must be required.* So, Let us look at the possible ways in which judicious "pull"ing can be accomplished with *current* web infrastructure.

The web infrastructure gives us two types of "hooks" that can be useful.

1. `Time-To-Live` (TTL) values, attached to cached objects (HTML pages). Upon its expiration, the source of the object can be contacted to update the page.

2. A source can be contacted with an `if-modified-since` (a header field in a `http`) request [BLET95]. This causes the server to respond to the request only if the requested object has been modified since the specified time. If it has not been modified, the client continues to use the cached object, else it caches the new object.

Given this, the crucial issue is the setting of the TTL values for each cached object.

For minimizing the incurred network overheads, the value of TTL must be high. But a low TTL value may compromise temporal consistency. Thus any TTL value must be judged depending on two factors - how well the cache consistency is maintained, and how often the remote servers are polled. Ideally, we must dynamically update this TTL value using an algorithm that decides the value depending on the present and past rates of source changes, with the goal of keeping remote requests to a minimum while maintaining the needed temporal accuracy of the data. An algorithm that achieves this is presented in Section 3 and evaluated in Section 4.

The next Section gives an overview of the related work to place the issues addressed in this paper in perspective.

2.3. Prior Work

[ABGM90] is one of the earliest papers relating to the topic of maintaining coherency between a data source and cached copies of the data. This paper discusses techniques whereby data sources can propagate, i.e, push, updates to clients based on their coherency requirements. This paper also discusses techniques whereby cached objects can be associated with expiration times so that clients themselves can invalidate their cached copies.

More recently, various coherency schemes have been proposed and investigated for caches on the World Wide Web where the sources are typically pull-based and stateless. Thus, the source is unaware of users' coherency requirements and users pull the required data from the sources.

A *Weak consistency* mechanism, *Client polling*, is discussed in [CATE92], where clients periodically poll the server to check if the cached objects have been modified. In the Alex protocol presented here, the client adopts an adaptive Time-To-Live(TTL) expiration time which is expressed as a percentage of the object's age. Simulation studies reported in [JGMS96] indicate that a weak-consistency approach like the Alex protocol ([CATE92]) would be the best for web caching. The main metric used here is network traffic. While the Alex protocol uses only the time for which the source data remained unchanged, given our desire to keep temporal consistency within specified limits, we need to also worry about the magnitude of the change.

A *strong consistency* mechanism, *Server invalidation*, is discussed in [CLPC97], where the server sends invalidation messages to all clients when an object is modified. This paper compares the performance of three cache consistency approaches, and concludes that the invalidation approach performs the best.

Whereas our goal is to develop a method that does not entail any server modifications or changes to the `http` protocol, invalidation based protocols as well as other proposed protocols (described next) for maintaining cache consistency either require changes to the web sources or to the `http` protocol.

A survey of various techniques used by web caches for maintaining coherence, including the popular "expiration mechanism", is found in [ADTP96]. It also discusses several extensions to this mechanism, but,as discussed in [RCKR98], these do not meet our needs. Another approach is for the cache server to piggyback a list of cached objects [BKCW97] whenever it communicates with a server. The list of objects piggybacked are those for which the expiration time is unknown or the heuristically-determined TTL has expired. The paper discusses two approaches to implement this mechanism within HTTP/1.1 (i.e., without any changes to the protocol), but the servers must be modified to implement this mechanism. [BKCW98] discusses a similar approach, where the servers partition the set of objects into *volumes*, and maintain version information for each volume. When responding to clients, the server piggybacks a list of volume objects modified since the client-supplied version. Again, implementation of this mechanism requires changes to existing web servers.

3. Choosing a good TTL

Note that different stocks fluctuate at different rates and that a particular stock may have different dynamic behaviors with the passage of time. The implication of this for us is that the tracking of different stocks will require one TTL per stock price data and that the TTL associated with a particular stock is likely to change with time. Also, given the nature of stock prices, the server has no way to know until when a particular stock price will prevail. So we assume that the server does not suggest an expiration time for the stock price. It is worth mentioning that even if it did, given that different users may have different temporal coherency requirements, the fact that the data will change at a certain time may be less interesting to a user than the magnitude of the change.

We first present several candidate approaches to select TTL values and finally present an adaptive approach that proves to be very effective.

3.1. Static TTL – based on a priori assumptions

One obvious approach is to choose a low value of TTL and use it throughout, thus ensuring that cache data seldom gets stale. But the drawback of this approach is that a low TTL implies contacting the web servers too often, thus increasing network overheads. On the other hand, a high TTL may compromise cache consistency, although it reduces the

network overhead. Thus a static TTL may not suffice. The only advantage of this approach is its simplicity, and this can be employed when source data changes are not rapid. However, for sources with time-varying data, a more dynamic TTL setting is necessary.

3.2. Semi-static TTL – based on observed maximum rate of change

One of the basic needs for maintaining temporal coherency is to be prepared to observe the quick changes that occur at the source. Suppose we do not know the rate at which changes occur at a source. A simple way to be prepared for quick changes is to adjust the TTL is to start with a large TTL and if the rate of change is more than can be observed by this TTL value, decrease the TTL value accordingly. This way, we can be prepared for the possibility of rapid changes at the sources.

Suppose $S(0)$, $S(1)$, ..., $S(l)$ denote the data values at the source at different points of time in chronological order. That is, $S(l)$ is the most recent value. Define,

$$change_i = |S(i) - S(i-1)|$$

Let $T_0, T_1, \ldots, T_l$ denote the TTL values that resulted in the respective W values.

Let the latest TTL value be T_l, and the latest data change, $change_l$. (Let the corresponding penultimate values be T_{l-1} and $change_{l-1}$).

Let

$$TTL_{est_l} = (T_l/change_l) \times c$$

That is, TTL_{est_l} is an estimate of the TTL value, based on the most recent observation, if we want to ensure that changes which are greater than or equal to c are not missed.

Let TTL_{mr} denote the most conservative TTL value used so far, i.e., the smallest TTL used so far. (This would have been set when the source changed rapidly.) This value is updated using

$$TTL_{mr} = Min(TTL_{mr}, TTL_{est_l})$$

This is the value of the new TTL. With this setting, the system is prepared even if the maximum rate of change observed so far recurs.

It is worth noting that the VW's computation of TTL_{mr}, based on the results of polling the source at specific points in time, is in fact an *estimate* of the maximum rate of change at the source. This is because, a stock price may change between two pollings at a rate higher than has been observed by the VW, but by the time the price is observed by the VW, the price comes down. This can happen if the TTL value is very large and hence the VW is unable to observe rapid changes in between two pollings. This suggests the need for setting TTL values which do not miss out on interesting changes and partly motivates the need to cap TTL values, as is done later. In general, a good understanding of the domain being observed, e.g., stock prices, will give indications about expected rate of change per unit time, given the constraints within which the domain operates. These can be used to set reasonable upper and lower bounds for TTL values.

Returning to the semi-static approach, it is pessimistic since it is based on the expected worst case rate of changes at the source. It will result in a large polling rate, especially if the worst-case does not occur often.

An alternative to the above semi-static approach is a dynamic approach wherein most recent changes, as opposed to the worst-case rate of change observed in the past, guide the selection of the TTL value.

3.3. Dynamic TTL_{dr} – based on the most recent source changes

An alternative to static or semi-static TTLs is to assume a low TTL initially, and adjust the value depending on recent observations of source data changes. That is, if the source data changes very often, use a low TTL, and if the source data changes slowly, use a high TTL. It assumes that recent changes are likely to be reflective of the changes in the near future.

As before, let TTL_{est_l} be a candidate for the next TTL value using only the most recent observations. Similarly, $TTL_{est_{l-1}}$ is a candidate for the next TTL value using only the penultimate observations[2]. TTL_{dr}, the new TTL value set by the *dynamic TTL* approach is given by

$$TTL_{dr} = (w \times TTL_{est_l}) + ((1 - w) \times TTL_{est_{l-1}})$$

where weight w ($0.5 \leq w < 1$, initially 0.5) is a measure of the relative change between the recent and the old changes, and is adjusted so that we have the *Recency* effect, i.e., more recent changes affect the new TTL more than the older changes [KLAH72]. w is computed as follows:

$$\delta = change_l / change_{l-1}$$

$$w = \begin{cases} \frac{\delta}{\delta+1} & \text{if } \delta > 1 \\ \frac{1}{\delta+1} & \text{otherwise} \end{cases}$$

Since $0.5 \leq w < 1$ (by definition), we always give at least half the weight to the estimate based on the most recent value. If the most recent change is much more (or much less) than the previous change, the weight w gets closer to 1, thus giving a larger weight to the recent value. In this way, TTL_{dr} is always in tune with the changes.

---

[2]It is important to note that although the method as shown here uses only two recent values of TTL, it can be easily extended to accommodate more values. Of course, this will mean that more history needs to be maintained by the VW.

3.4. Dynamic TTL_{ds} – based on keeping TTL within static bounds

While the above adjustment of TTLs to derive dynamic TTL values appears to be a good idea, there is a subtle need that this approach does not satisfy: When source remains unchanged for a long period, the above algorithm will result in very large TTL values. To rectify this problem, we can use a static *interval*, and allow the TTL to vary within the interval. When the source changes rapidly, TTL values tend to get closer to TTL_{min}, the low end of the interval. During quieter times, TTL tends to move towards TTL_{max}, the high end of the interval. TTL_{ds}, the new TTL set by this algorithm is

$$TTL_{ds} = Max(TTL_{min}, \ Min(TTL_{dr}, TTL_{max})).$$

The idea behind keeping the TTL value within a bounded interval is to allow the TTL to adapt to patterns of changes in source data but disallow it from assuming unreasonably low/high values.

3.5. An Adaptive approach

The adaptive algorithm uses the following factors to decide the new TTL.

1. Since we would like to keep TTL values bounded, TTL_{min} and TTL_{max} are used as static bounds.

2. Assuming that recent changes are likely to be reflective of the changes in the near future, TTL_{dr} is a candidate for the new TTL value.

3. The system must be in a position to handle the worst case rate of change that has been previously observed (that may be higher than has been witnessed in the recent past). So TTL_{mr} is also a candidate for the new TTL value.

With these in hand, the adaptive algorithm computes the new TTL to be,

$$TTL_{adaptive} = Max(TTL_{min}, \ Min(TTL_{max}, TTL_{dr}, TTL_{mr'}))$$

where, for reasons explained below, $TTL_{mr'}$, derived from TTL_{mr}, is used, instead of TTL_{mr} itself.

As was noted before, if the recent change tends to zero, TTL_{dr} will be very large, and before we contact the server next (when the large TTL expires), it is very likely that the source would have changed considerably. To avoid this, the estimated TTL is limited to be within TTL_{min} and TTL_{max}. However, since TTL_{max} is determined statically, it may not accurately reflect the current trend in source changes. This is the motivation behind $TTL_{mr'}$ defined as:

$$TTL_{mr'} = (f \times TTL_{mr}) + ((1 - f) \times TTL_{est_l})$$

where $0 \leq f \leq 1$ is the *fudge* factor. As defined earlier, TTL_{mr} corresponds to the fastest source change so far, and TTL_{est_l} corresponds to the recent change. Thus $TTL_{mr'}$ accommodates both of these, giving different weights to each of them depending on the f factor. If f is close to 0, we entirely rely on the recent trend; this will result in a loose upper bound if the recent source changes are slow. A high value of f is preferable, because this gives more weight to a conservative TTL (corresponding to a period when source changes were the fastest). That is, once the source has changed rapidly, we believe that the source has the *potential* for future rapid changes. Use of f allows us to control the pessimism that is unavoidable with the use of TTL_{mr}.

In summary, new TTL values are computed based on a combination of statically determined bounds, recent changes, and previously observed maximum rate of changes at the source.

Polling overhead incurred by the system, and the consistency guarantee provided critically depend on the *goodness* of the TTL values assigned to cached objects. Hence, an adaptive TTL (like ours) is expected to give considerable performance gains compared to the other candidate approaches. We next analyze the performance of the candidate algorithms and compare it with the performance of the adaptive algorithm.

4. Performance analysis

The algorithms introduced in the previous Section were evaluated using real world traces of stock prices to see how well they performed.

The presented results are based on stock price traces (i.e., history of stock prices) of a few companies obtained from `http://quote.yahoo.com`. We "cut out" the history for the time intervals listed in table 1 and experimented with the different mechanisms by determining the stock prices they would have observed had the source been live. This was done by noting the stock price in the trace at the time the "current" TTL expired. This is the price the source would have returned to the VW when contacted upon the expiry of the TTL, assuming that communication costs are negligible.

The graphs showing the performance metrics (defined in the next subsection) were obtained by averaging the results for these traces. We measured this average performance for different values of user constraint c, varying it from \$0.1 to \$0.7. The other graphs (TTL versus Time, and the graphs showing how the cache and the user display values follow the source) are based on the first trace from the list below. For these graphs, a value of \$0.6 was used as the user constraint.

Throughout this Section, the rate of change of the source is relative to the user constraint. For e.g., if the source

Table 1. Traces used for the Experiment

Company	Date	Time
IBM	May 7, 1998	10:00-13:00
IBM	Aug 6, 1998	10:00-13:00
IBM	Aug 6, 1998	13:00-16:00
Sun	Aug 6, 1998	10:00-13:00
HP	Aug 6, 1998	10:00-13:00
Sun	Aug 12, 1998	10:00-13:00
IBM	Aug 12, 1998	10:00-13:00
Microsoft	Aug 12, 1998	10:00-13:00

changes at 10 cents a minute, it is *slow* relative to $c = \$0.9$, but is *fast* relative to $c = \$0.05$.

We now describe the metrics used and then present and analyze the results.

4.1. Metrics used

Performance is judged by how well a temporal coherency mechanism minimizes two metrics -

- *#pollings*: the number of times the source is polled – this metric is an indication of the networking overhead incurred by the algorithm.

- *VProb*: probability that a user's temporal coherency requirement is violated. $VProb$ indicates the probability that the user will not be notified about changes that exceed c units (from what the user is currently aware of). It measures how well cache consistency is maintained relative to the requirement c.

While the first metric's semantics is clear, the second requires some explanation: In order to gauge how well cache consistency is maintained, we measure the duration for which the user is out of synch with the source data, when the price difference between source data and the value displayed to the user exceeds the user specified constraint. That is, $U(t)$ is different from $S(t)$, although $|U(t) - S(t)| \geq c$. Suppose this situation prevails continuously for a certain duration. Let $t_1, t_2, \ldots, t_n$ denote the durations when this happens. Let T denote the total time for which data was presented to a user. Then the consistency violation probability is computed as,

$$VProb = \sum_{i=1}^{n} t_i \bigg/ T$$

and is expressed as a percentage. This then indicates the percentage of time when a user's desire to be within c units of the source is not met.

The lower the $VProb$, the better the performance with respect to the cache consistency metric but higher the possible costs in terms of #pollings. There is clearly a tradeoff between the two metrics.

4.2. Performance comparison of the algorithms

Static TTL

One main attraction of a static TTL algorithm is its simplicity. If the rate at which the source changes is known, we can decide on a good TTL value, and use it throughout. But stock price variations are inherently unpredictable, and hence, choosing a good static TTL value is not trivial.

Figure 2 shows how the cache and the user displayed val-

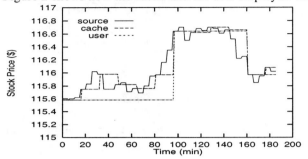

Figure 2. Changes with time – Static TTL = 16 min

ues change with time when a static TTL of 16 minutes is employed. This means that the cache is refreshed every 16 minutes at which point the cache value is compared with the user value. If the difference is more than c ($0.6 here), the user value is updated. If the source changes rapidly, this algorithm will not inform the user in time. This is what happens in the interval 75 to 95. Similarly, if the source changes very slowly, this algorithm will poll the source much more often than necessary.

In figure 2, the user requirement is violated around 90mins. But since the source is polled every 16mins, the violation is detected only at the next polling time which occurs at 96mins. A similar situation occurs between times 144 and 160.

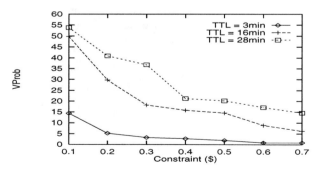

Figure 3. Violation probability, Static TTL

Figure 3 shows the performance of this algorithm for different values of static TTL. For low values (3 min), the curve for the probability of violation shows excellent performance, but the performance degrades with increasing

TTL values (28 min). We see that the number of times the source is polled is very large for low static TTL and gets better as we use higher values. This algorithm is ideal when the rate of change of source is well known. For e.g., if we know that the source changes rapidly, we can use a low static TTL value. If the source changes slowly, we employ high values. But when the rate at which the source changes is variable and unknown (the typical case for stock prices), this algorithm can perform poorly.

With respect to #pollings, a Static TTL of 3 mins results in a total of 60 pollings whereas 16 and 28 mins result in 10 and 6 respectively. Since we strive to achieve better temporal consistency by choosing low static TTL values, the number of pollings (and hence the networking overheads) increases a lot. As we can see here, if we use a low static value for a relatively quiet source, we end up incurring unnecessary overheads.

Semi-static TTL

We do not analyze the performance of the semi-static algorithm because in some ways it is similar to static TTL, except that the TTL values drop lower when the source changes faster than it did ever before. So, in this method, TTL values can only get lower with time. That is, if a source changes fast initially, and much slower later, this method will waste significant bandwidth.

In particular, for low values of c, even small changes at the source make the source appear *fast*, and this method assumes low TTL values. It then behaves as in the previous method (with a low static TTL value). So, this method is not really useful for low c values.

Dynamic TTL_{dr}, updates based on recent changes

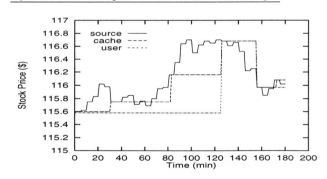

Figure 4. Changes with time, Dynamic TTL_{dr}

Figure 4 shows how the cache and the user displayed values change with time when this algorithm is used. The algorithm employs high TTL values when the source changes slowly. Because of the slow early changes, initial TTL values are high. (figure 7) . Because of this, the cache does not follow the source closely, and hence the probability of consistency violation is high (figure 5). Specifically, around

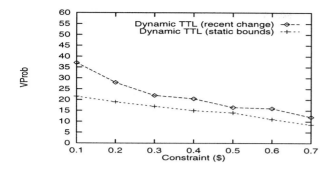

Figure 5. Violation probability, Dynamic TTL

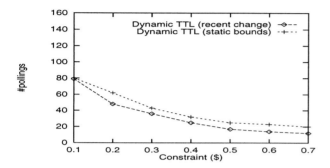

Figure 6. #Pollings, Dynamic TTL

80min, a TTL value of around 40mins is assumed (see figure 7). But in the next 40 mins, the source changes significantly, and the user is not informed even though the source has changed much more than $0.6 (see figure 4) compared to the user displayed values. We encounter this problem because the source didn't change much initially, and the algorithm assumed high TTL values. The next algorithm aims to address this problem.

Figure 6 shows #pollings for this algorithm. For low c values, most changes at the source appear fast. So, this method uses low TTL values, and hence, we have a greater number of pollings. For higher c values, the performance of this approach in terms of the number of pollings is much better.

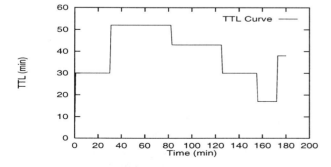

Figure 7. TTL adaptation, Dynamic TTL_{dr}

Dynamic TTL$_{ds}$, with static bounds ($TTL \in [1, 31]$)

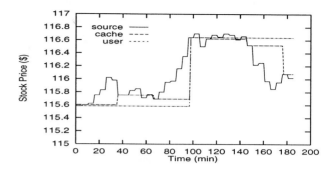

Figure 8. Changes with time, Dynamic TTL$_{ds}$

This is the same as the previous algorithm, except that we *statically* limit the TTL values. This is done to prevent the TTL values from assuming unreasonably high values. Depending on the rate of source changes, the TTL value will tend towards one end of the interval.

Figure 8 shows how the cache and the user displayed values change with time when this algorithm is used. When the system detects that the source changes rapidly, the cache is refreshed more often, and if the source is detected to change slowly, the cache is refreshed less frequently. As seen in figure 8, the user constraint is violated at around 90mins, and we detect this around 100mins. The upper bound on the TTL values helps us here; we would have assumed a higher TTL value around 50mins but for the upper bound (see figure 7). This helped us detect the violation earlier. Thus the upper bound solves, to some extent, the problem that surfaced in the previous algorithm. The next algorithm solves this problem to a greater degree.

Figures 5 and 6 show the performance of this algorithm. This algorithm performs worse than static TTL algorithm especially for higher 'c' values. This can be explained as follows. Initially, if the source changes slowly, the TTL value will assume the high end of the interval, and so the cache will not contact the source until this high value expires. If the high end of the interval was based on the slowest expected rate of change of the source, it is very likely that the source will change more rapidly when we assume a high TTL value. In such a case, the algorithm will fail to detect some changes. This explains the higher consistency violations recorded by this algorithm in figure 5. This observation is confirmed by the TTL adaptation curve shown in figure 9 where we see that the TTL value remains at the high end most of the time.

This algorithm is essentially the same as the previous method, except that we limit the TTL values. In the previous case, we found that the method assumed high TTL values and hence showed high probability of consistency violation. By using an upper bound, we have brought down the probability of consistency violation significantly (figure 5). The performance in terms of the number of pollings is not significantly more than the previous approach (figure 6).

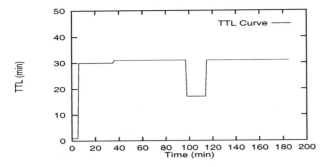

Figure 9. TTL adaptation, Dynamic TTL$_{ds}$

The algorithm's performance in terms of #pollings is comparable to the static TTL algorithm (with a static value of 16mins) for higher values of c, but the same cannot be said with respect to cache consistency maintenance.

Adaptive TTL

The problem with the previous algorithms was that we had to decide the TTL or the interval statically, depending on the expected patterns in source data changes. But typically, stock price changes are not predictable. In the adaptive algorithm, the key idea is to initially assume an arbitrary interval, and *update* not only the TTL value but also this interval depending on source data changes. (Presently, we alter the upper bound only.) We watch over the source and maintain the fastest rate of source change seen thus far. Using this, and the latest trend, we limit the upper bound. Since the latest trend could be in complete antithesis to rapid changes, it is better to give more weight to the bound based on the fastest rate. This can be achieved by using f values close to 1.

We added another embellishment to the adaptive algorithm - to limit the rate at which TTL can increase. But instead of using additive increase (used in TCP/IP), we allow multiplicative increase, but limit the factor of increase. Figure 10 shows the performance of the algorithm for different f values, when the new TTL is not allowed to be more than 2 times the previous estimate. The algorithm performs exceptionally well for higher values of f (0.9), producing very low values of $VProb$.

Figure 11 shows how the cache and the user displayed values change with time when the adaptive algorithm (using a f value of 0.9) is used. When the violation of the user constraint occurs around 90mins, this algorithm was working with a TTL value of only 9mins (see figure 12), and hence is able to detect this violation much earlier than the previous two algorithms. During the period from 100 to 140mins, the source changes very slowly, and the adaptive

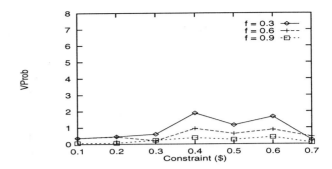

Figure 10. Violation probability, Adaptive TTL

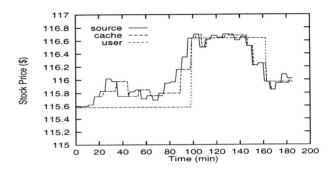

Figure 11. Changes with time, Adaptive TTL

algorithm assumes high TTL values (figure 12). But, the high TTL values are reached gradually in this period (instead of assuming high values suddenly), so as to not miss any potential change. (We limit the factor of increase to 2.) This way, the sudden decrease in the source value in the period from 140 to 160 mins is captured promptly by our algorithm. Note that in figure 12, there is a dip in this period. Thus the adaptive algorithm keeps a good watch on the source, without wasting too much bandwidth.

Figure 13 shows the #pollings of the adaptive algorithm for different f values. The #pollings for this algorithm for a f value of 0.3 is comparable to a static TTL of 3 min. But the consistency maintenance properties of this algorithm are much better than that of the static TTL (see figures 3 and 10). With higher f values, we employ increasingly pessimistic methods (Section 3.2), and hence the #pollings increases. But the performance in terms of the probability percentage improves with increasing f values (see figure 10). As we get more conservative, we use lower TTL values, and hence we get better consistency at the price of increased network overheads.

4.3. Summary of results

In Figures 14 and 15 we present an integrated view of the results presented so far. Not surprisingly, there is an almost inverse relationship between the number of pollings and the probability of violation.

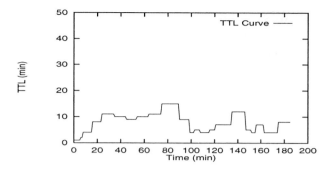

Figure 12. TTL adaptation, Adaptive TTL

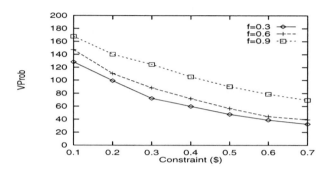

Figure 13. #Pollings, Adaptive TTL

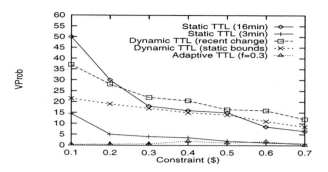

Figure 14. Violation probability

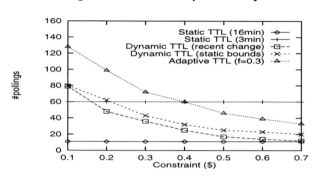

Figure 15. #Pollings

Adaptive TTL (with f=0.3, plotted in the graph, and for other f values as well) has the best $VProb$. In fact, even if we were to continuously poll a source, given the communication costs involved in practice, there is bound to be a certain amount of temporal violation in practice. Given this, we believe that the violation probability values (of 0–2%) resulting from the use of Adaptive TTL represent perhaps the best one can achieve.

Low Static TTL (say, 3 mins) has the next best $VProb$ values. But, notice that Adaptive TTL not only performs better across all c values tested, but it has a lower #pollings except for low c values (i.e., below 0.3). When Static TTL values are increased (to, say, 16 mins), their performance degrades further to an extent that at low values of c the Dynamic TTL algorithms are better.

Clearly, smaller static TTL values produce fewer temporal violations but result in a larger number of pollings for low to medium values of c. Even though Adaptive TTL also results in a large number of pollings, it produces a very low probability of violation.

In order to compare the relative cost of the superior performance of Adaptive TTL over Static TTL, we also computed the increase in cost (in terms of #pollings) per unit decrease in temporal violation (in terms of $VProb$). For example, at $c = 0.1$, $VProb$ for Adaptive TTL is close to 0 whereas for Static TTL of 16 mins it is close to 50. This performance is produced at the cost of 120 (i.e., 130 - 10)

additional pollings by Adaptive TTL. The cost per unit performance improvement is then 2.4 (i.e., 120/50). In fact, for different values of c this factor lies between 2 and 4 when Static TTL of 16 mins is compared to Adaptive TTL. This seems to be a reasonable price to pay for the increased cache consistency resulting from Adaptive TTL.

We conclude that for data such as stock prices, whose rate of change is unpredictable, it is best to use an adaptive algorithm. But rather than basing the TTL estimate solely on the most recent trend, the past trend must also be taken into account. To avoid using large TTL values, thus potentially missing sudden source changes, it is good to use an upper bound to limit the TTL estimates. But since a static upper bound may be problematic for stock prices, it is better to use an upper bound that gets tighter when the source changes faster than before. Also, even if the source changes are slow initially, assuming a high TTL value may result in poor performance. Hence the adaptive method is preferable. By limiting the rate at which TTL can increase, Adaptive TTL gets even better performance.

5. Conclusion and Future Work

We discussed the issues involved in maintaining temporal coherency of a virtual warehouse. A combination of Push (by the proxy server) and Pull (by the clients) maintain data consistency, both between the remote sources and the proxy server's cache, and between the cache and the results displayed at the clients' end. Clients are allowed to specify temporal constraints, so that the displayed results are updated only when the changes are of interest to the user.

We presented several approaches for setting TTL values and analyzed their performance. The adaptive algorithm's performance was shown to be much better than other algorithms that are less adaptive. We used two main factors in evaluating performance - how well cache consistency is guaranteed, and how many times the system contacts the data source.

There are several embellishments to the adaptive algorithm that we plan to explore. Presently, the adaptive algorithm keeps track of the TTL corresponding to the maximum rate of change at the source so far. This means that once the source changes rapidly, future TTL values will be quite conservative – and it gets tighter and tighter, when the source changes more rapidly than before. Suppose we believe that more recent trends are better indicators than trends indicated by *all* of history. Then the pessimism that is currently displayed by TTL_{mr} can be overcome by maintaining TTL_{mr} based on a fixed time into the past, instead of basing it on the entire past.

Also, currently, we update only the high end of the TTL interval. To obtain better performance in terms of the number of pollings, it is desirable to update the lower end of the interval as well (using the rate at which the source changes). We plan to explore these issues as part of our future work.

Finally, we are currently implementing a Virtual Warehouse architecture based on the ideas proposed so far. In it, data is brought from remote sources and maintained in the (cache of) the VW. Data from this cache is used to serve the needs of users who are connected to the VW via a network. The system consists of two main modules - the cache server, and the data manager. The cache server is responsible for getting data from the remote web sources, maintaining the cache, and informing the data manager when data in cache gets updated. The data manager is responsible for getting input from the user and updating the displayed results whenever user specified constraints have been satisfied. While there is one data manager per user, the cache server is common to all users. (Details of the implementation can be found in [RCKR98].)

With this implementation in hand, we plan to conduct experiments and make measurements of message overhead, processing overhead and actual performance of our mechanisms. We also plan to develop techniques to efficiently schedule the VW's requests that pull different pieces of information from web servers once the associated TTLs expire. This is especially of interest for those servers that are connected to the VW via a single link.

6. Acknowledgment

We thank Jennifer Rexford for her constructive comments on previous versions of the paper. We also thank the anonymous reviewers for their suggestions.

References

[ABGM90] R. Alonso, D. Barbara, and H. Garcia-Molina, Data Caching Issues in an Information Retrieval System, *ACM Trans. Database Systems,* September 1990.

[BLET95] T. Berners-Lee, Hypertext Transfer Protocol HTTP/1.0, *HTTP Working Group Internet Draft,* October 14, 1995.

[CATE92] A. Cate, Alex - A Global Filesystem, *Proceedings of the 1992 USENIX File System Workshop, Ann Arbor,MI,* May 1992.

[ADTP96] A. Dingle and T. Partl, Web Cache Coherence, *Proc Fifth Intnl WWW Conference,* May 1996.

[JGMS96] J. Gwertzman and M. Seltzer, World-wide Web cache consistency, *Proceedings of the 1996 USENIX Technical conference, San Diego, CA,* January 1996.

[KRGL97] M. Kamath, K. Ramamritham, N. Gehani, and D. Lieuwen, WorldFlow: A System for Building Global Transactional Workflows, *Proc. of 7th Intl. Workshop on High Performance Transaction Systems (HPTS),* 1997.

[KLAH72] A. Klopf, Brain Function and adaptive systems- a heterostatic theory,*Tech Report AFCRL-72-0164, Air Force Cambridge Research Laboratories, Bedford, MA,* 1972.

[BKCW97] B. Krishnamurthy and C. Wills, Study of Piggyback Cache Validation for Proxy Caches in the World Wide Web, *Proc. USENIX Symp. on Internet Technologies and Systems,* December 1997.

[BKCW98] B. Krishnamurthy and C. Wills, Piggyback Server Invalidation for Proxy Cache Coherency, *Proc. World Wide Web Conference,* April 1998.

[CLPC97] C. Liu and P. Cao, Maintaining Strong Cache Consistency in the World Wide Web, *Proceedings of ICDCS,* May 1997.

[KRAM93] K. Ramamritham, Real-Time Databases, *Journal of Distributed and Parallel Databases,* Volume 1, Number 2, pp.199- 226., 1993.

[RCKR98] R. Srinivasan, C. Liang, K. Ramamritham, *Maintaining Temporal Coherency in Virtual Warehouses,* University of Massachusetts, Amherst, Technical Report, September 1998.

[HZFJ98] H. Zou and F. Jahanian, Real-Time Primary-Backup (RTPB) Replication with Temporal Consistency Guarantees, *Proceedings of ICDCS,* May 1998.

Session 3.B: Systems Design and Development I

Specification and Modeling
of Dynamic, Distributed Real-time Systems

Lonnie R. Welch, Binoy Ravindran, Behrooz A. Shirazi and Carl Bruggeman
Computer Science and Engineering Dept.
The University of Texas at Arlington
Box 19015, Arlington, TX 76019-0015
{welch\binoy\shirazi\bruggema}@cse.uta.edu

Abstract

Time-constrained systems which operate in dynamic environments may have unknown worst-case scenarios, may have large variances in the sizes of the data and event sets that they process (and thus, have large variances in execution latencies and resource requirements), and may not be statically characterizable, even by time-invariant statistical distributions. This paper presents a specification language for describing environment-dependent features. Also presented is an abstract model that is constructed (statically) from the specifications, and is augmented (dynamically) with the state of environment-dependent features. The model is used to define techniques for QoS (quality-of-service) monitoring, QoS diagnosis, and resource allocation analysis. Experimental results show the effectiveness of the approach for specification of real-time QoS, detection and diagnosis of QoS failures, and restoration of acceptable QoS via reallocation of distributed computer and network resources.

1. Introduction

Many difficulties confront those who must engineer the emerging generation of real-time control systems. Such systems have rigorous Quality of Service (QoS) objectives. They must behave in a dependable manner, must respond to threats in a timely fashion and must provide continuous availability, even within hazardous and unknown environments. Furthermore, resources should be utilized in an efficient manner, and scalability must be provided to address the ever-increasing complexity of scenarios that confront such systems. The difficulties in engineering such systems arise from several phenomena, one of the most perplexing being the dynamic environments in which they must function. Systems which operate in dynamic environments may have unknown worst-case scenarios, may have large variances in the sizes of the data and event sets that they process (and thus, have large variances in execution latencies and resource requirements), and cannot be characterized (accurately) by constants, by intervals or even by time-invariant statistical distributions.

This paper presents techniques for specification and modeling of real-time Quality-of-Service for distributed systems that operate in dynamic environments. The techniques are based on a programming-language-independent meta-language for describing real-time QoS in terms of end-to-end paths through application programs. Constructs are provided for the specification and modeling of deterministic, stochastic, and dynamic characteristics of environment-dependent paths. The provision for description of periodic, transient and hybrid (transient-periodic) paths is also made. Another novel feature of the language is that it allows the description of multi-level timing constraints through (1) simple, cycle deadlines (which apply to a single cycle of a periodic, transient or transient-periodic path) and (2) super-period deadlines (which apply to multiple cycles of a transient-periodic path). The language and model also consider the scalability and fault tolerance features of the end-to-end paths and their application program constituents.

This is significantly different from other real-time application development languages and other real-time meta-languages. Real-time application development languages (e.g., Tomal [12], Pearl [17], Real-Time Euclid [13], RTC++ [9], Real-Time Concurrent C [7], Dicon [14], Chaos [3], Flex [16], TCEL [5], Ada95 [2], and MPL [19]) include a wide variety of features that allow assertion checking and code transformation to ensure adherence to timing constraints. Specification languages or "meta-languages" (such as ACSR [4], GCSR [1], [23], CaRT-Spec [27] and RTL [10]) formalize the expression of timing constraints and in some cases allow proofs of properties of programs based on these constraints. In [6], the features of [10] have been folded into an application development language. Our work is a specification meta-language that is application-language-independent. Rather than providing real-time support within a particular application language, it provides support for expressing timing constraints for *systems of application programs*, written in a melange of programming languages. Unlike previous work, in which timing constraints are associated at a relatively small granularity (e.g., task-level), our language allows timing constraints to be expressed the granularity of end-to-end *paths* which span many communicating programs.

Another way of categorizing real-time languages and models is in the way they permit characterization of a system's behavior when interacting with the physical environment. Prior work has typically assumed that the effects of the environment on the system can be modeled deterministically. Our work expands this to include systems that interact with environments that are either deterministic, stochastic, or dynamic. This is done by modeling interactions with the environment as data and event streams, that may have deterministic, stochastic or dynamic properties.

In order to handle dynamic environments, it is useful if the language includes features that can be related to dynamic mechanisms (such as those described in [20] [8] [21] [22] [24]) for monitoring, diagnosis and recovery. Language support for run-time monitoring of real-time programs has been addressed in [20], [6], [11], [13], and [2]. However, limited support was provided for diagnosis and recovery actions. Our work extends the language features pertaining to diagnosis of timing problems, and the migration or replication of software components to handle dynamic data stream or event stream loads (scalability). The specification language also provides support for fault-tolerance, an issue that has not been addressed in most real-time languages.

Previous real-time languages allow the description of behaviors that are purely periodic or aperiodic. Our work extends language support to describe hybrid behaviors such as the transient-periodic described in [26]. We also allow for multi-dimensional timing constraints, which, to our knowledge, cannot be described in any existing real-time language.

The remainder of the paper presents the specification language and shows how it is used for adaptive QoS management. Section 2 explains the software paradigm used in the specification language. In Section 3, we present the grammar of the specification language and illustrate its use with examples. Section 4 presents a static system model that is constructed from specifications. Section 5 defines a dynamic model, which is built at run-time by augmenting the static model with environment-dependent state. Use of the dynamic and static system models for adaptive resource and QoS management is illustrated in Section 6. Section 7 presents experimental results of applying the language, the models and the resource and QoS management techniques to a distributed real-time application.

2. The dynamic real-time path paradigm

This section presents the *dynamic real-time path paradigm.* A path-based real-time subsystem (see Figure 1) typically consists of a situation assessment path, an action initiation path and an action guidance path. The paths interact with the environment via evaluating streams of data from sensors, and by causing actuators to respond (in a timely manner) to events detected during evaluation of sensor data streams. The system operates in an environment that is either deterministic, stochastic or dynamic. A deterministic environment exhibits behavior that can be characterized by a constant value (see [19]). A stochastic environment behaves in a manner that can be characterized by a statistical distribution (see [15]). A dynamic environment (e.g., a war-fighting environment) depends on conditions which cannot be known in advance (see [22], [29]).

A (partial) air defense subsystem can be modeled using three dynamic paths: *threat detection, engagement,* and *missile guidance.* The *threat detection* path examines radar sensor data (radar tracks) and detects potential threats. The path consists of a radar sensor, a sensor data stream, a filtering program and an evaluation program. When a threat is detected and confirmed, the *engagement* path is activated, resulting in the firing of a missile to engage the threat. After a missile is in flight, the *missile guidance* path uses sensor data to track the threat, and issues guidance commands to the missile. The *missile guidance* path involves sensor hardware, software for filtering, software for evaluating & deciding, software for acting, and actuator hardware.

The remainder of this section describes the features of dynamic real-time *paths.* Recall that a path may be one of three types: situation assessment, action initiation, or ac-

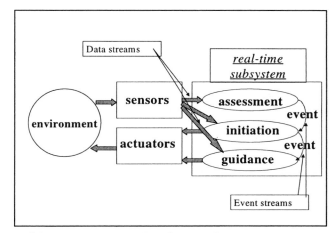

Figure 1. A real-time subsystem.

tion guidance. The first path type, situation assessment, *continuously* evaluates the elements of a sensor data stream to determine if environmental conditions are such that an action should be taken (if so, the action initiation path is notified). Thus, this type of path is called *continu-*

ous. Typically, there is a timeliness objective associated with completion of one review cycle of a continuous path, i.e., on the time to review all of the elements of one instance of a data stream. (Note: A data stream is produced by sampling the environment. One set of samples is called a data stream instance.)

The *threat detection* path of the air defense system is an example of a continuous path. It is a sensor-data-stream-driven path, with desired end-to-end cycle latencies for evaluation of radar track data. If it fails to meet the desired timeliness Quality of Service in a particular cycle, the path must continue to process track data, even though desired end-to-end latencies cannot be achieved. Peak loads cannot be known in advance for the *threat detection* path, since the maximum number of radar tracks can never be known. Furthermore, average loading of the path is a meaningless notion, since the variability in the sensor data stream size is very large (it may consist of zero tracks, or it may consist of thousands of tracks).

The second path type, action initiation, is driven by a stream of events sent by a continuous (situation assessment) path. It uses inputs from sensors to determine which actions should be taken and how the actions should be performed, notifies actuators to start performing the actions, and informs the action guidance path that an action has been initiated. We call this type of path *transient*, since it performs work in response to events. Typically, a timing objective is associated with the completion of the initiation sequence. The importance of the timing objective for a transient path is often very high, since performance of an action may be mission-critical or safety-critical.

For example, the *engagement* path of the air defense example is a transient path. It is activated by an event from the *threat detection* path, and has a QoS objective of end-to-end timeliness. The real-time QoS of this path has a higher priority than the real-time QoS of the continuous *threat detection* path.

The third path type, action guidance, is activated by an action initiation event, and is deactivated upon completion of the action. Action guidance repeatedly uses sensor inputs to monitor the progress of an actuator, to plan corrective actions needed to guide the actuator to its goal, and to issue commands to the actuator. This type of path is called *quasi-continuous,* since it behaves like a continuous path when it is active. A quasi-continuous path has *two timeliness objectives*: (1) cycle completion time: the duration of one iteration of the "monitor, plan, command" loop, and (2) action completion time (or deactivation time): the time by which the action must complete in order for success. Note that it is more critical to perform the required processing before the action completion deadline than it is to meet the completion time requirement for every cycle (although the two deadlines are certainly related). Thus, it is acceptable for the completion times of some cycles to violate the cycle deadline requirement, as long as the de-

sired actions are successfully completed by the deactivation deadline.

The *missile guidance* path of the air defense example is a quasi-continuous path. It is activated by the *missile launch* event. Once activated, the path continuously issues guidance commands to the missile until it detonates (the deactivation event). The required completion time for one iteration is dynamically determined, based on characteristics of the threat. If multiple threat engagements are active simultaneously, the threat engagement path is responsible for issuing guidance commands to all missiles that have been launched.

3. Grammar of the specification language

This section presents a specification language for describing the characteristics and requirements of dynamic, path-based real-time systems. The language provides abstractions to describe the properties of the software, such as hierarchical structure, inter-connectivity relationships, and run-time execution constraints. It also allows description of the physical structure or composition of the hardware such as LANs, hosts, interconnecting devices or ICs (such as bridges, hubs, and routers), and their statically known properties (e.g., peak capacities). Further, the Quality-of-Service requirements on various system components can be described. In this paper, we illustrate the concrete syntax to describe only the software and the Quality-of-Service objectives.

As shown in Figure 2, a subsystem is specified by describing its priority, sets of constituent applications and devices, a set of end-to-end real-time path definitions, and a graph representing the communication connectivity of the applications and devices. The non-terminals of the subsystem grammar are explained in a depth-first manner in the remainder of this section.

As seen in the grammar of Figure 2 and the example of Figure 3, the attributes of an application include boolean variables that indicate whether the application (1) can be replicated for survivability and (2) can support scalability via load sharing among replicas. Indications of whether an application combines its input stream (which may be received from different predecessor applications and/or devices), and splits its output stream (which may be distributed to different successor applications and/or devices) are also specified. Application attributes also include all information necessary to startup and shutdown applications (not elaborated in this paper). The connectivity of the subsystem describes the flow of data and events between the applications and devices of the subsystem, and is described as a sequence of ordered application and/or device pair names within parentheses. Alternately, one may use the square bracket set notation, which is a short hand to represent a complete graph.

The definition of a path (see Figure 4) includes a set of constituent applications, various attributes, QoS requirements and data/event stream definitions. The attributes of a path include priority, type, and importance. Path type, which defines the execution behavior of the path, is either continuous, transient, or quasi-continuous. The importance attribute (a string) is interpreted as the name of a dynamically linked library procedure that may be passed arguments such as priority and the current time, and returns an integer value that represents the importance of the path.

A real-time QoS specification includes timing con-

```
<sw-sub-system>::      Subsystem ID "{" Priority INT_LITERAL
                       ";" <appln-defn>+ <device-defn> { <path-
                       defn> }* <connectivity-descr> "}"
<appln-defn>::         Application ID "{" Scalable STRING ";"
                       Survivable STRING ";" Combining
                       STRING " ;"Splitting [NONE | EQUAL |
                       STRING]";" <startup-block>+ <shutdown-
                       block>+ "}"
<device-defn>          Device { ID "," }* ID ";" | λ
<connectivity-descr>:: Connectivity "{" <graph-defn>+ "}"
<graph-defn>::         <pair-wise-descr> | <complete-graph-descr>
                       | ID
<pair-wise-descr>::    "(" ID "," ID ")"
<complete-graph-descr>:: "[" { ID }+ "]"
```

Figure 2. Grammar for subsystems.

```
Application FilterManager { Scalable NO;  Survivable YES;  Combining NO;
                       Splitting  EQUAL; Startup{ ... }; Shutdown { ... } }
Device Sensor, Actuator;
Connectivity {  (Sensor, FilterManager) (FilterManager, Filter)
                (Filter, EvalDecideManager)
                (EvalDecideManager, EvalDecide) (EvalDecide, ActionManager)
                (EvalDecide,  MonitorGuideManager) (ActionManager, Action)
                (Action, Actuator) (MonitorGuideManager, MonitorGuide) }
```

Figure 3. Application, device and connectivity specifications.

straints such as simple deadlines, inter-processing times, throughputs, and super-period deadlines. A simple deadline is defined as the maximum end-to-end path latency during a cycle of a continuous or quasi-continuous path, or during an activation of a transient. Inter-processing time is defined as a maximum allowable time between processing of a particular element of a continuous or quasi-continuous path's data stream in successive cycles. The throughput requirement is defined as the minimum number of data items that the path must process during a unit period of time. A super-period deadline is defined as the maximum allowed latency for all cycles of a quasi-continuous path. A super-period deadline is specified as the name of a dynamically linked library procedure that is called dynamically to determine the estimated super-period deadline. Each timing constraint specification may also include items that relate to the dynamic monitoring of the constraint. These include minimum and maximum slack values (that must be maintained at run-time), the size of a moving window of measured samples that should be ob-

```
<path-defn>::      Path ID "{" <appn-set> <path-attribs>
                   <Real-TimeQoS><SurvivabilityQoS><stream-defns> "}"
<appn-set>::       Contains "{" { <app-name> ","}* <app-name> "}"
<app-name>::       ID
<path-attribs>::   Priority INT_LITERAL";" Type <path-type> ";"
                   Importance STRING";"
<path-type>::      Continuous | Transient | Quasi-Continuous
<Real-TimeQoS>::   Real-TimeQoS "{" <RTQoS-metric>+ "}"
<RTQoS-metric>::   SimpleDeadline FLOAT_LITERAL ";" <threshold>
                   | Inter-ProcessingTime FLOAT_LITERAL ";"
                       <threshold>
                   | Throughput INT_LITERAL ";"<threshold>
                   | Super-PeriodDeadline STRING ";" <threshold>
<threshold>::      MaxSlack INT_LITERAL";"
                   MinSlack INT_LITERAL ";"
                   MonitorWindowSize INT_LITERAL ";"
                   Violations INT_LITERAL ";" | λ
<SurvivabilityQoS>:: SurvivabilityQoS "{" Survivable STRING;
                   MinCopies INT_LITERAL "}"
<stream-defns>::   <DataStream-defn> | <EventStream-defn> |
                   <DataStream-defn> <EventStream-defn>
```

Figure 4. Grammar for paths.

```
Path Sensing {
    Contains {Sensor, FilterManager, Filter, EvalDecideManager, EvalDecide}
    Type Continuous;  Priority 2;  Importance "CalcImport";
    Real-TimeQoS {SimpleDeadline  4; //secs
                  MaxSlack 80; MinSlack 20; //PERCENT
                  MonitorWindowSize 20; Violations 15;
                  Inter-ProcessingTime 7; // secs
                  Throughput 200; // data elements per second }
    SurvivabilityQoS { Survivable YES; MinCopies 2; }
```

Figure 5. A path specification.

served, and the maximum tolerable number of violations (within the window).

Figure 4 also contains the grammar for describing survivability QoS. A survivability QoS specification includes a boolean variable that indicates (1) whether the path should be managed to ensure survivability and (2) the minimum required level of redundancy. Note that replicating a path entails replicating all of the applications that make up the path.

An example path specification is given in Figure 5. The "Sensing" path is continuous and has a priority of 2. It has a Simple Deadline of 4 seconds, which means that each review cycle must not have a latency that exceeds this amount. The MaxSlack and MinSlack definitions further constrain this requirement to the interval [0.8seconds, 3.2seconds]. If 15 out of the most recent 20 cycles violate this requirement, then corrective action by a resource manager is required. If the upper bound is exceeded, the corrective action would be to allocate more resources for the path. In the case where the lower bound is exceeded, the action would be to take away some of the resources of the path. The path inter-processing time is 7 seconds, meaning that no more than this amount of time should elapse between reviews of a particular data stream element in successive cycles. The path throughput must be at least 200 data stream elements per second. The path also requires

```
DataStream {                DataStream {
    Type Deterministic;         Type Stochastic;
    Size 40;}                   Size "/home/ uta/MGDataStream.data";}

EventStream {               EventStream {
    Type Dynamic; }             Type Stochastic;
                                Rate "Exponential 0.5" ; }
```

Figure 7. Specifications of streams.

```
<DataStream-defn>:: DataStream "{" Type [Deterministic | Stochastic | Dynamic ] ";"
                        Size <environ-descr> ";" "}"
<EventStream-defn>:: EventStream "{" Type [Deterministic | Stochastic | Dynamic ] ";"
                        Rate <environ-descr> ";" "}"
<environ-descr>:: INT_LITERAL
                    | "(" INT_LITERAL "," INT_LITERAL ")" | <pdf-descr> | λ
<pdf-descr>:: STRING | FILENAME
```

Figure 6. Grammar for streams.

the existence of at least 2 copies of each of its member applications at all times.

Figure 6 shows the grammar for describing stream properties. A corresponding specification is illustrated in Figure 7. The stream type can be deterministic, stochastic, or dynamic. The data stream size or event arrival rate of a deterministic stream is a constant (scalar or interval). A stochastic stream has a data stream size or an event arrival rate that is characterized by a probability distribution function. The distribution is described as a string containing the name of a distribution and its parameters, or is described as the name of a data file containing a data set that characterizes the stream's behavior. The data stream size or event arrival rate of a dynamic stream is not described in the specification, since it must be observed at run time.

4. Static system model

This section presents an overview of a static system model (which is constructed by a specification compiler) for a single subsystem.

A software subsystem, **SS,** consists of a set of applications **SS.A** = { $a_1, a_2,\ldots$ }, a set of devices (sensors and actuators) **SS.D** = { $d_1, d_2,\ldots$ }, a communication graph for applications and devices $\Gamma(SS) \in \Pi((SS.D \cup SS.A) \times (SS.D \cup SS.A))$, and a set of paths **SS.P** = { $P_1, P_2, P_3, \ldots$ }. (Note: Π denotes power set).

Each path P_i is represented as a type $\tau(P_i) \in$ {c, qc, t} (note that 'c', 'qc' and 't' denote 'continuous', 'quasi-continuous' and 'transient', respectively), a set of applications $P_i.A = \{a_{i,1}, a_{i,2},\ldots\}$ (where $P_i.A \subseteq SS(P_i).A$), a set of devices $P_i.D = \{d_{i,1}, d_{i,2},\ldots\}$ (where $P_i.D \subseteq SS(P_i).D$), a communication graph $\gamma(P_i) \in \Pi((P_i.D \cup P_i.A) \times (P_i.D \cup P_i.A))$ (note that $\gamma(P_i) \subseteq \Gamma(SS(P_i)))$, a data stream $P_i.DS$ (defined if $\tau(P_i) \in$ {c, qc}), and an event stream $P_i.ES$ (defined if $\tau(P_i) \in$ {t, qc}). $SS(P_i)$ denotes the subsystem in which path P_i is contained, $ROOT(G(P_i))$ is used to denote the root application node of $\gamma(P_i)$ (the node which

receives a data stream from a sensor or an event stream from an application) and $SINK(G(P_i))$ is used to represent the sink application of $\gamma(P_i)$ (the application which communicates with an actuator or sends an event to the root application of another path). The type of P_i's datastream is defined as $\tau(P_i.DS) \in$ {dynamic, stochastic, deterministic}. $\sigma(P_i.DS)$ denotes the size characteristics of P_i's data-stream.

The real-time QoS requirements of a path are: required latency of $\lambda_{REQ}(P_i)$ seconds, required throughput of $\theta_{REQ}(P_i)$ data stream elements/time, and required data inter-processing time of $\delta_{REQ}(P_i)$ (a maximum allowable time between processing of a particular element of $P_i.DS$ in successive cycles). To mask momentary QoS-spikes during QoS monitoring, a specification may define a sampling window and a maximum number of QoS violations to be tolerated within the window. $\omega(P_i)$ models the sampling window size and $\upsilon(P_i)$ represents the maximum allowable number of violations (within sampling window $\omega(P_i)$). $\psi(P_i) = [\psi_{min}(P_i), \psi_{max}(P_i)]$ is the required slack interval for each QoS requirement; i.e., it is required that the ratio (required QoS - actual QoS) : (required QoS) be no less than $\psi_{min}(P_i)$ and no greater than $\psi_{max}(P_i)$.

REPLICABLE($a_{i,j}$) --- has a true or false value to indicate if application $a_{i,j}$ can be replicated for the purpose of load sharing. **COMBINING($a_{i,j}$)** --- has the value of true or false, indicating if application $a_{i,j}$ combines the inputs from its predecessors before passing the values to successor(s). **SPLITTING($a_{i,j}$)** $\in$ (none, equal, non-equal) indicates whether an application splits it outputs among its successors, and if so, whether the outputs equally.

5. Dynamic system model

This section presents a model of such dynamic features as the current environment, its effect on QoS, a mapping of software to computation and communication hardware, and the number of replicas of each application.

The set of replicas of $a_{i,j}$ during cycle 'c' of P_i is defined as **REPLICAS** $(a_{i,j}, c) = \{a_{i,j,1}, a_{i,j,2}, \ldots\}$. The host to which $a_{i,j,k}$ is assigned during cycle 'c' of P_i is defined as **HOST** $(a_{i,j,k}, c, P_i)$, and the communication path (set of LANs and interconnection devices (ICs)) used during cycle 'c' of P_i for messages between applications $a_{i,j,x}$ and $a_{i,j,y}$ is represented as **COMMPATH** $(a_{i,j,x}, a_{i,j,y}, c, P_i)$.

The set of elements that constitutes a data stream can vary dynamically. $P_i.DS(c)=\{P_i.DS(c)_1, P_i.DS(c)_2,\ldots\}$ represents the set of elements in $P_i.DS$ during cycle 'c' of P_i. The **tactical load** (in number of data stream elements processed) of a (quasi)-continuous path P_i during it's c^{th} cycle is $|P_i.DS(c)|$. The processing of elements of a data stream may be divided among replicas of an application to exploit concurrency as a means of decreasing execution latency of a path. In successive stages of a path that has non-combining applications (applications which, after processing data received from a single predecessor, simply divide the data among their successors), data will arrive in batches to applications; hence, each application may process several batches of data during a single cycle. Thus, the model represents the batches of data processed by application/replica 'a' during cycle 'c'.as $P_i.DS(c, a)=\{P_i.DS(c, a)_1, P_i.DS(c, a)_2,...\}$ The cardinality $|P_i.DS(c).b(a)|$ is called the tactical load of 'a', and can be calculated by considering the REPLICAS, SPLITTING, and COMBINING attributes of the system model. The data stream elements contained in the jth batch of 'a' are denoted by $P_i.DS(c, a, j)=\{P_i.DS(c, a, j)_1, P_i.DS(c, a, j)_2,...\}$.

6. Dynamic QoS analysis techniques

This section illustrates the use of the dynamic and static system models for adaptive QoS management.

Monitoring of real-time QoS involves the collection of time stamped events sent from applications. The times when application/replica 'a' starts and ends processing batch 'j' of data during cycle 'c' of P_i are denoted by $s(P_i.DS(c, a, j))$ and $e(P_i.DS(c, a, j))$, respectively. The times when 'a' starts and ends processing of data stream element $P_i.DS(c, a)_k$ are represented as $s(P_i.DS(c, a)_k)$ and $e(P_i.DS(c, a)_k)$, respectively.

Observed real-time QoS metrics are defined in terms of these basic events as follows: (1) latency of path P_i during cycle 'c' = $\lambda_{OBS}(P_i, c)$ = {e($P_i.DS(c, a_{i,m,n}, j)$) – s($P_i.DS(c, a_{i,x,1}, 1)$) | $a_{i,m}$ = SINK($\gamma(P_i)$), $a_{i,x}$ = ROOT($\gamma(P_i)$)}; (2) throughput of P_i during cycle 'c' = $\theta_{OBS}(P_i, c)$ = $|P_i.DS(c)|$ / max($\lambda_{OBS}(P_i, c)$); (3) data-inter-processing time of application 'a' for datum $P_i.DS(c, a)_k$ during cycle 'c' = $\delta_{OBS}(P_i.DS(c, a)_k)$ = s($P_i.DS(c, a)_k$) - s($P_i.DS(c-1, a)_k$), for c > 1; (4) data-inter-processing time of application 'a' during cycle 'c' = $\delta_{OBS}(P_i.DS(c, a))$ = f($\delta_{OBS}(P_i.DS(c, a)_k)$), for all 'k' in the range [1, $|P_i.DS(c, a)|$]. (E.g., f can be defined as 'average' or as 'max'.); (5) data-inter-processing time of P_i during cycle 'c' = $\delta_{OBS}(P_i.DS(c))$ = f($\delta_{OBS}(P_i.DS(c, a))$), for all 'a' in $P_i.A$. (E.g., f can be defined as 'average' or as 'max'.)

Analysis of a time series of the real-time QoS metrics enables detection of QoS violations. An **overload** of a path occurs in any cycle 'c' wherein $\upsilon(P_i) \leq |\{d: c-d+1 < \omega(P_i) \wedge [\lambda_{REQ}(P_i) - max(\lambda_{OBS}(P_i,c))] / \lambda_{REQ}(P_i) < \psi_{min}(P_i)] \}|$. Similarly, an **underload** of a path occurs in any cycle 'c' wherein $\upsilon(P_i) \leq |\{d: c-d+1 < \omega(P_i) \wedge [\lambda_{REQ}(P_i) - max(\lambda_{OBS}(P_i,c))] / \lambda_{REQ}(P_i) > \psi_{max}(P_i)] \}|$.

When a path-level (end-to-end) real-time QoS violation occurs, diagnosis determine the cause(s) of the violation (i.e., identifies subpaths (application programs) that are experiencing significant slowdown). One diagnosis technique declares an application/replica 'a' to be unhealthy during cycle 'c' of path P_i if there exists another cycle 'd'

such that the following conditions hold. **Condition 1:** d < c. **Condition 2:** HOST (a, c, P_i) = HOST (a, d, P_i). **Condition 3:** $|P_i.DS(c, a)| = |P_i.DS(d, a)|$. **Condition 4:** $\forall f$: (f < c) $\wedge$ [HOST (a, c, P_i) = HOST (a, f, P_i) $\wedge$ [$|P_i.DS(c, a)| = |P_i.DS(f, a)|$] $\wedge$ max($\lambda_{OBS}(P_i, f)$) > max($\lambda_{OBS}(P_i, d)$). **Condition 5:** max($\lambda_{OBS}(P_i, d)$) < max($\lambda_{OBS}(P_i, c)$) - ϵ. Note: ϵ is the minimal difference between cycle latencies that is considered significant.

Following diagnosis, allocation analysis identifies and ranks recovery actions for the applications/replicas diagnosed as unhealthy. The first step of allocation analysis is to determine if the tactical load of an unhealthy application has significantly increased in the recent past. The tactical load of an application/replica 'a' has increased in the α cycles immediately prior to cycle 'c' by at least a significant amount 'Δ' when: $\exists d$: c>d $\wedge$ c-d<α+1 $\wedge$ ($|P_i.DS(c, a)|$ > $|P_i.DS(d, a)| + \Delta$). The tactical load change analysis is used to determine the appropriate allocation action for an unhealthy application as follows. **Replicate** an unhealthy application/replica 'a' when its tactical load has increased recently by a significant amount. We denote such an action as: act(a) = (a, replicate). **Move** an 'a' when its tactical has not increased recently by a significant amount. We denote such an action as: act(a) = (a, move). We define ACT={act_1, act_2,...} as the set of actions selected, where act_i is a pair (a,action) and denotes that 'action' is recommended for 'a'.

The second step of allocation analysis is to group actions which address the same cause of poor path QoS. All actions that move applications/replicas from a particular host are grouped, since any one of those actions will reduce the contention experienced by applications on the host. All actions that involve replication of a particular application 'a' are also grouped, since the addition of another replica of 'a' will cause a redistribution of load processed by the existing replicas of 'a'.

In addition to grouping related actions, the unhealthy applications are ranked in decreasing order by the degree of slowdown they are experiencing. The slowdown experienced by application 'a' during cycle 'c' of P_i is computed as $\xi(a, c, P_i)$ = max($\lambda_{OBS}(P_i, c)$) / max($\lambda_{OBS}(P_i, d)$), where 'd' is the cycle wherein 'a' exhibited its 'best' performance over all cycles wherein 'a' had the same tactical load as in cycle 'c'.

7. Experimental Results

This section presents two scenarios showing system behavior for the 'benchmark' situation assessment path (see Section 2, and also Figure 5) under different run-time scenarios. The path is hereafter referred to as the detect/sensing path. In the run-time scenarios, the adaptive resource management middleware monitors the real-time

QoS of the benchmark application, detects QoS violations, diagnoses cause(s) of poor QoS, and recovers accordingly.

Figure 8 depicts the overall architecture of the adaptive resource management system. In its current implementation, resource management is activated in 3 modes: during the initial system start-up process (to start application programs), when a path becomes unhealthy (i.e., a path latency exceeds the required deadline), and when an application program is terminated (due to hardware/software faults). A description of each of these resource management modes follows.

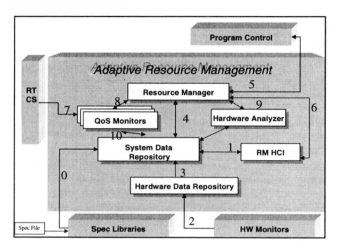

Figure 8. The resource management architecture.

The actions performed in *start-up mode* are as follows: (1) The System Data Repository (SDR) loads the user system specification file (via a compiler) into data structures (step 0 of Figure 8). (2) The SDR sends the compiled system description to the Resource Management (RM) HCI for display (step 1). (3) Hardware (HW) Monitors (which run on each host) periodically calculate load indices for hosts and LANS, and pass this information to the Hardware Data Repository (HDR) (step 2), which in turn passes such information to the SDR (step 3). (4) RM receives the system startup information from the SDR (step 4). (5) RM determines the initial hardware-to-software allocation and informs Program Control (PC) to start the Real-Time Control System (RTCS) application programs on specific hosts and LANs (step 5). (6) PC starts the programs (via daemons running on each host) and informs RM when finished (step 5). (7) RM sends startup information to the RM HCI for display (step 6). (8) RTCS application programs periodically send application profile information (time stamps and/or program/path latencies) to QoS Monitors (step 7). Global time is provided to the RTCS and to the QoS monitors via Network Time Protocol (NTP) [18].

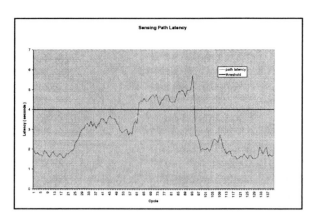

Figure 9. Sensing path latency (scenario I).

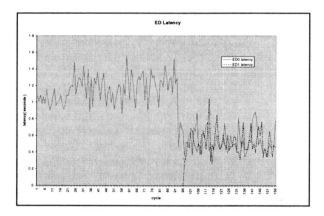

Figure 10. Latencies of the *filter* subpaths.

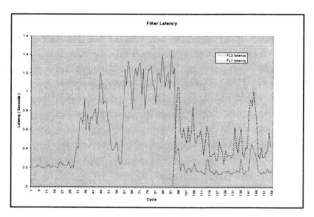

Figure 11. Latencies of *evaluate* subpaths.

The sequence performed during *QoS monitoring and enforcement mode* is: (1) If a path becomes unhealthy (misses its deadline), the QoS Monitors detect such a condition, diagnose the cause of poor health, and suggest actions (such as moving and/or replicating an application program(s)) to RM (step 8 of Figure 8). (2) RM selects the host onto which the unhealthy sub-path(s) needs to be replicated or moved, by choosing the host with the smallest load index. To enable this, the Hardware Analyzer (HA) ranks the hosts in ascending order by load index [25] and passes this information to the Resource Manager (step 9). (3) RM requests PC to enact the new allocation (step 5) and updates the RM HCI accordingly (step 6).

The actions taken in *program recovery mode* are: (1) If a sub-path (RTCS program) is terminated due to a hardware/software failure, PC detects this and informs RM (step 5 of Figure 8). (2) RM finds a healthy host with the smallest load index by querying HA (step 9). (3) RM restarts the terminated program on the healthy host by informing PC (step 5), and also notifies RM HCI to update the display (step 6 of Figure 8). To avoid thrashing via restarting a faulty piece of software ad infinitum, this step is only repeated a fixed number of times.

The remainder of this section describes two scenarios depicting the system behavior under different run-time conditions. The experiments were performed on a distributed network consisting of two Sun Sparc5 workstations (170MHZ processor, 32 MB RAM, 2GB disk, and Sun Solaris 2.5.1 configurations), named virginia and nujersy; and two Sun Ultra Sparc I workstations (167MHZ processor, 128MB RAM, 2GB disk, and Sun Solaris 2.5.1 configurations) named texas and desidrta. The hosts are connected via a 10/100MB per second ethernet network. The RTCS application consists of the Sensing path of the benchmark application with a simple deadline, λ_{REQ}(Sensing), of 4 seconds. The sensing path consists of a set of programs (called computation subpaths) that may be distributed, and which cooperate in pipeline fashion. The programs are: Sensor (a simulated radar), Filter Manager (FM), Evaluate and Decide Manger (EDM), Filter (FL), and Evaluate and Decide (ED).

The first experiment scenario is depicted in Figure 9, which shows a plot of the observed Sensing path latency (λ_{OBS}(Sensing, c)) and shows λ_{REQ}(Sensing) as a straight line. Initially, Sensor, FM, and EDM run on virginia, one copy of FL runs on texas, and one copy of ED runs on nujersy. RM and a QoS Monitor run on nujersy, SDR and PC run on texas, and HDR and HA run on desidrta.

As shown in Figure 9, the data stream size (i.e., the tactical load) of the sensing path during the initial execution cycles $c \in [1, 23)$ is 2000 elements; that is |Sensing.DS(c)| = 2000. The path latencies during this interval are below the required QoS threshold, i.e., λ_{OBS}(Sensing, c) < λ_{REQ}(Sensing), for $c \in [1, 23)$. At cycle c=23 the tactical load is incremented by 500, and the path latency increases.

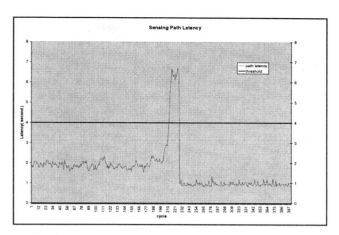

Figure 12. Sensing path latency (Scenario II).

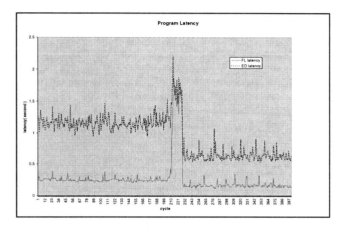

Figure 13. Latencies of FL and ED subpaths.

The tactical load is also incremented by 500 at cycle 55. From this cycle onward, the path latency gradually increases and finally exceeds the QoS threshold. Figures 10 and 11 show the corresponding latencies of the FL and ED subpaths, respectively. Increases in the latencies of these programs are seen to correspond with the increases in the tactical load of the path.

The QoS Monitor component of the adaptive resource management system detects the QoS violation during the [59, 79] cycle interval (shortly after the QoS violation as shown in Figure 9). In both of these experiments the sampling window size is 20 (ω(Sensing)=20), the number of acceptable violations per window is 15 (υ(Sensing)=15), and the minimum slack is 0% (ψ_{min}(Sensing)=0%). The QoS Monitor diagnoses the cause of poor health in cycle 79 and recommends replications of the FL and ED programs. The path monitor function has a latency of 1.135 μsec. and the path diagnosis function has a latency of 1.86 μsec. RM activates a copy of ED (ED1) on nujersy and a copy of FL (FL1) on texas at cycle 79. The latencies of

RM and PC are 211.2 and 1.84 μsec., respectively. Thus, all the resource re-allocation and enactment processes take place in one cycle of the sensing path. However, in the RTCS system, a newly activated application program takes several cycles to establish its communication sockets and thus the latency of the path does not immediately decrease. Figure 10 depicts how the latency of each copy of FL is reduced when a second copy of FL is initialized at cycle 92. Similarly, Figure 11 depicts how the latency of each copy of ED is reduced when a second copy of ED is initialized at cycle 95.

After the initialization of the replicas of the FL and ED programs, the path latency falls below the threshold around cycle 95 (Figure 9). Note that despite increasing the tactical load by a factor of 50%, the adaptive resource management system was able to adapt to this dynamic change and preserve the QoS requirement of the RTCS application.

Experiment scenario II begins with the sensing path complying with its QoS requirements. Instead of encountering a dynamic increase in tactical load, a dynamic system load increase is caused on one of the hosts, thereby increasing resource contention. The RTCS application programs are initially distributed as follows: Sensor and FL are assigned to virginia and FM, EDM, and ED are assigned to nujersy. Throughout this experiment, $|Sensing.DS(c)|=2000$, $\lambda_{REQ}(Sensing)=4$ sec., $\omega(Sensing)=20$, $\upsilon(Sensing)=15$, and $\psi_{min}(Sensing)=0\%$.

As shown in Figure 12, $\lambda_{OBS}(Sensing, c) < \lambda_{REQ}(Sensing)$, for $c \in [1, 208)$. At cycle 208, nujersy's load is increased by activating several computationally intensive applications. This causes $\lambda_{OBS}(Sensing, c)$ to increase and to eventually exceed the threshold of $\lambda_{REQ}(Sensing)$. Correspondingly, significant increases are observed in the latencies of the FL and ED subpaths (see Figure 13).

The QoS Monitor component of the adaptive resource management system detects the QoS violation during the [208, 228] cycle interval, diagnoses the cause of poor health (also during cycle 228) and recommends moving the FM, EDM, ED, and FL programs to another host. RM consults HA for host load indexes and decides to move the FM, EDM, ED, and FL programs to host texas. Figure 13 depicts how the latencies of the FL and ED programs are reduced after the move (cycle 228). Note that since no new application is activated in this scenario, the effect of resource re-allocation is almost immediate.

Finally, after some of the RTCS programs are moved to a host with a lower load, $\lambda_{OBS}(Sensing, c)$ falls below $\lambda_{REQ}(Sensing)$, for $c \geq 230$. Note that despite drastically increasing a host's load, the adaptive resource management system was able to adapt to this dynamic change and to preserve the QoS requirement of the RTCS application. It was also able to successfully diagnose causes of QoS violations.

Through the above two experiments the functionality of the resource management middleware has been validated, and its responsiveness to dynamic workload changes has been demonstrated. It should be noted that the observed variances in application latency may be improved further by the use of a real-time operating system. Additionally, it is planned to reduce the delayed effect of a reallocation action (replication) by redesigning the inter-process communication portion of the RTCS application. We have conducted several other experiments under other execution scenarios, such as simultaneous increases in tactical load and host loads, causing both moving and replicating of the programs. In every experiment, the middleware behaved as expected, successfully restoring the health of the RTCS applications (see [28] for more information).

8. Conclusions and future work

This paper has described the dynamic class of real-time systems, presented engineering techniques and tools appropriate for such systems, and demonstrated the utility of those tools for a dynamic real-time application. An important component of this paper is a specification language for real-time QoS. The language allows the description of environment-dependent application features, thereby facilitating the modeling and dynamic resource management of such systems. A model for static and dynamic aspects of such systems was presented, and dynamic QoS management techniques were defined in terms of the model. An example of the use of the specification language and the model for adaptive resource management of a dynamic real-time application was shown.

Ongoing work includes application of the tools and techniques to shipboard computing systems. Work is also being performed to develop and experimentally compare allocation algorithms and QoS forecasting algorithms.

9. Acknowledgements

This work was sponsored in part by DARPA/NCCOSC contract N66001-97-C-8250, and by NSWC/NCEE contracts NCEE/A303/41E-96 and NCEE/A303/50A-98.

The authors would like to thank scientists from NSWC for collaborative efforts which seeded the ideas presented in this paper. We are also indebted to the members of the Laboratory for Parallel and Distributed Real-time Systems at the University of Texas at Arlington.

10. References

[1] H. B-Abdallah, I. Lee and J-Y. Choi, A Graphical Language with Formal Semantics for the Specification and Analysis of Real-Time Systems, Proceedings of The IEEE Real-Time Systems Symposium, pages 276--286, December 1995.

[2] International Standard ANSI/ISO/IEC-8652:1995, Ada 95 Reference Manual, Intermetrics, Inc., January 1995.

[3] T. Bihari and P. Gopinath, Object-oriented real-time systems, IEEE Computer, 25(12):25--32, December 1992.

[4] J-Y. Choi, I. Lee, H-L. Xie, The Specification and Schedulability Analysis of Real-Time Systems using ACSR, Proceedings of The IEEE Real-Time Systems Symposium, pages 266--275, December 1995.

[5] R. Gerber and S. Hong, Semantics-based compiler transformations for enhanced schedulability, Proceedings of The IEEE Real-Time Systems Symposium, pages 232--242, December 1993.

[6] M. Gergeleit, J. Kaiser, and H. Streich, Checking timing constraints in distributed object-oriented programs, Proceedings of The Object-Oriented Real-Time Systems (OORTS) Workshop, October 1995.

[7] N. Gehani and K. Ramamritham, Real-Time Concurrent C: A language for programming dynamic real-time systems, Journal of Real-Time Systems, 3(4):377--405, December 1991.

[8] D. Hull, A. Shankar, K. Nahrstedt and J. W. S. Liu, An End-to-End QoS Model and Management Architecture, Proceedings of The IEEE Workshop on Middleware for Distributed Real-Time Systems and Services, pages 82-89, 1997. The 18th IEEE Real-Time Systems Symposium.

[9] Y. Ishikawa, H. Tokuda, and C. M. Mercer, An object-oriented real-time programming language, IEEE Computer, 25(10):66--73, October 1992.

[10] F. Jahanian and A. K.-L. Mok, Safety analysis of timing properties in real-time systems, IEEE Transactions on Software Engineering, 12(9):890--904, 1986.

[11] K. B. Kenny and K. J. Lin, Building flexible real-time systems using the Flex language, IEEE Computer, pages 70--78, May 1991.

[12] R. B. Kieburtz and J. L. Hennessy, Tomal - a high-level programming language for microprocessor process control applications, ACM SIGPLAN Notices, pages 127--134, April 1976.

[13] E. Kligerman and A. D. Stoyenko, Real-Time Euclid: A language for reliable real-time systems, IEEE Transactions on Software Engineering, 12(9):941--949, September 1986.

[14] I. Lee and V. Gehlot, Language constructs for distributed real-time systems, Proceedings of The IEEE Real-Time Systems Symposium, December 1985.

[15] J. P. Lehoczky, Real-Time Queueing Network Theory, Proceedings of The IEEE Real-Time Systems Symposium, pages 58--67, December 1997.

[16] K. J. Lin and S. Natarajan, Expressing and maintaining timing constraints in Flex, Proceedings of The 9th IEEE Real-Time Systems Symposium, pages 96--105, December 1988.

[17] T. Martin, Real-time programming language pearl - concept and characteristics, Proceedings of The IEEE Computer Society Second International Computer Software and Applications Conference (COMPSAC), pages 301--306, 1978.

[18] D. L. Mills, Improved Algorithms for Synchronizing Computer Network Clocks, IEEE/ACM Transactions on Networks, 3, June 1995.

[19] V. M. Nirkhe, S. K. Tripathi, A. K. Agrawala, Language Support for the Maruti Real-Time System, Proceedings of The 11th IEEE Real-Time Systems Symposium, pages 257--266, 1990.

[20] R. Rajkumar F. Jahanian and S. Raju, Run-time monitoring of timing constraints in distributed real-time systems, Journal of Real-Time Systems, 1994.

[21] R. Rajkumar, C. Lee, J. Lehoczky and D. Siewiorek, A Resource Allocation Model for QoS Management, Proceedings of The 18th IEEE Real-Time Systems Symposium, pages 298--307, 1997.

[22] D. Rosu, K. Schwan, S. Yalamanchili and R. Jha, On Adaptive Resource Allocation for Complex Real-Time Applications, Proceedings of The 18th IEEE Real-Time Systems Symposium, pages 320--329, December 1997.

[23] A. Shaw, Reasoning about time in higher-level language software, IEEE Transactions on Software Engineering, 15(7):875--889, July 1989.

[24] K. G. Shin and C.-J. Hou, Design and Evaluation of Effective Load Sharing in Distributed Real-Time Systems, IEEE Transactions on Parallel and Distributed Systems, 5(7), pages 704-719, July 1994.

[25] J. Song, Characterization of Load Indices for Unix Workstations, Master's Project, The University of Texas at Arlington, May 1998.

[26] S. Sommer and J. Potter, Operating system extensions for dynamic real-time applications, Proceedings of The IEEE Real-Time Systems Symposium, pages 45--50, December 1996.

[27] L. R. Welch, A. D. Stoyenko, and T. J. Marlowe, Response Time Prediction for Distributed Periodic Processes Specified in CaRT-Spec, Control Engineering Practice, 3(5), May 1995, pp. 651-664.

[28] L. R. Welch, P. Shirolkar, B. Shirazi, et al., Adaptive Resource Management For Scalable Dependable Real-Time Systems: Middleware Services and Applications to shipboard computing systems, Technical Report, TR-CSE-97-009, The University of Texas at Arlington, December 1997.

[29] L. R. Welch, B. A. Shirazi, B. Ravindran and C. Bruggeman, DeSiDeRaTa: QoS Management Technology for Dynamic, Scalable, Dependable, Real-Time Systems, Proceedings of The 15th IFAC Workshop on Distributed Computer Control Systems, September 1998.

Detailed Design of Avionics Control Software[*]

Ulf Nilsson, Siwert Streiffert, Anders Törne
Department of Computer and Information Science
Linköping University, S-581 83 Linköping, SWEDEN
{ulfni, siwst, andto}@ida.liu.se

Abstract

Avionics control systems are typical real-time systems – automatic control algorithms are realized as periodic computations where strict requirements on the timing can be derived by a control analysis. The requirements are effectively end-to-end timing requirements on the computation – from sensory input to actuator output – and have to be transformed into a detailed control software design. This analysis, together with a resource and performance analysis, is required early in the development process – neither hardware nor prototypes of the software can be assumed to exist – in order to estimate the cost of development and the cost of hardware to meet customer requirements. The paper investigates the applicability of a method (the period calibration method) to transform the end-to-end requirements of an avionics control software, into a design consisting of a set of periodic tasks with buffered data flows. The experience is discussed and shortcomings of the method are analysed.

1. Introduction

An *avionics control system* is a typical real-time system involving many difficult decisions regarding the balance between performance, flexibility, production costs, maintenance costs, engineering effort, and total system functionality. Several of these decisions are made very early in the design process or have to be approximated during a quotation process. Typical decisions are the control laws, the partitioning of software and hardware functionality, the selection of basic hardware components and the architectural decisions regarding the software organization.

During *control design* the operational requirements on the total system are transformed into a set of derived functional (e.g. control laws) and non-functional (e.g. end-to-end timing) requirements. During *preliminary software design* a functional software design is made and a hardware platform is selected. Then the functional design and the timing requirements are mapped to the computational resources and the communication mechanisms are decided. During the *detailed software design* the functionality (possibly refined) for each computational resource is transformed into a set of periodic tasks, with timing attributes determined from the timing requirements. Finally an implementation specification for the software can be generated (*software module design*). The software/hardware functional partitioning problem is not considered in this work – all control functionality is assumed to be implemented in software.

The goal of each design phase is to find a feasible[1] design while optimizing with respect to *non-strict* requirements, like minimizing life cycle costs (for obvious reasons), minimizing the constraints on later design phases (to make it easier to find a design), and minimizing the resource requirements (to simplify future extensions).

The design problem can be decomposed into:
- generating an "optimal" proposal for a feasible design – the synthesis problem. If the proposal satisfies the strict requirements by construction, then no analysis is needed.
- analyzing if the proposed design is feasible, i.e., if it satisfies the strict requirements – the analysis problem. Industrially the synthesis and analysis are done iteratively until a satisfactory design is found. The design often has to be approximated during a quotation process. Neither hardware nor prototypes of the software can therefore be assumed to exist. This means, for example, that required attributes, like the *WCET*s, for a correct analysis of timing requirements have to be estimated.

If a design is found infeasible or problematic during control, preliminary or detailed design, the problem will be reiterated in a preceding phase, and a change of requirements will be made. Early design errors which

---

[*] This work was done on commission from Saab Dynamics AB.

1. A feasible design is one that satisfies the strict requirements – i.e., requirements that are either satisfied or not.

cause problems in later phases will therefore be costly when the complexity of the design increases. To increase the quality of early designs it is therefore crucial to develop tools and methods to support the generation of the design and the verification of the requirements.

Design methods for real-time software normally only provide a notation for the model of the design, a description of inputs/outputs for each phase in the development process, and general descriptions of how to perform the phases. The tools do often lack support for functional and/or timing verification (analysis). Even more rare is support for generating the designs (synthesis) given input requirements.

Typical design methods are HRT-HOOD (cf. [5, 6]) and the MARS method (cf. [11, 14]). HRT-HOOD requires a method to estimate (or determine) *WCET*s and a decision on scheduling strategy. HRT-HOOD is more general than MARS, since MARS has the hardware architecture and programming environment defined together with the method. On the other hand it is easier to incorporate synthesis and analysis tools (like a WCET-analyzer) with MARS.

The long term intention of our research is to investigate, evaluate and improve industrially usable computerized support for real-time system design, that complements the used design method. This paper describes a feasibility study of a method (the period calibration method [8]) and tool to support synthesis during the detailed design phase. The objectives (related to the presentation in this paper) were:

- to evaluate the selected method.
- to investigate tool support for the method.
- analyze the benefits and drawbacks.

We also assume that the control analysis has resulted in functional and timing requirements (strict requirements) on the software/hardware realization and that the preliminary design has been made. It is furthermore assumed that the algorithmic realization of the control laws is straightforward during modular design and therefore does not strongly interfere with the earlier phases.

The work presented here was made in cooperation with Swedish aerospace industry, as a continuation on an earlier project which investigated early estimation of worst case execution times, methods to develop control software, and ways to do schedulability analysis (cf. [4]).

This feasibility study first briefly presents the period calibration method. In Section 3 the actual case is presented. The tool used in the case study and the resulting implementation are presented in Sections 4 and 5. Finally we analyze benefits and drawbacks of the method.

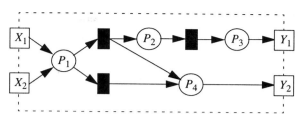

Figure 1: An asynchronous task graph showing the subtasks and the communication buffers (in black).

2. The Synthesis Method

In this section we give a brief account of the synthesis method used – for a detailed account see Gerber, Hong and Saksena [8]. In this paper we refer to the method as the *GHS-method* after the authors of the main report, since the feasibility study investigated the method presented there and not later extensions or modifications. Later work of the authors refer to the general method as the *period calibration method*.

The synthesis method results in a detailed design (an Asynchronous Task Graph, ATG) composed of a number of interacting and communicating *tasks*, ultimately receiving data from external inputs and delivering data to external outputs, as illustrated in Figure 1.

The GHS-method assumes that end-to-end and internal timing requirements can be quantitatively described by means of algebraic equations and inequalities relating unknown variables. The unknown variables correspond to attributes of internal computations while the end-to-end requirements and worst case execution times are assumed to be known.

2.1. The Input of the Method

The method requires the following as input:
- A task graph describing the dataflow dependencies between the external inputs and outputs, and all intermediate tasks, similar to Figure 1.
- The *WCET* (denoted e_i) of each task.
- A set of end-to-end timing requirements on the system.

The end-to-end requirements
The end-to-end requirements are assumed to belong to one of the following three categories (see [8] for details):
- *Freshness requirements* (or *propagation delays*), $F(Y \mid X)$, bound the time for data to flow through the system from input X to output Y.
- *Correlation requirements*, $C(Y \mid X_1, X_2)$, limit the difference in sampling time between several inputs used to produce the same output.

- *Separation requirements* give the *lower, l(Y)*, and *upper, u(Y)*, time bound between consecutive values output on *Y*.

2.2. The Output of the Method

The method gives the following as output:

- A set of tasks with *offsets (O_i), deadlines (D_i)* and *periods (T_i)*. The tasks include those given as input, plus possibly some new or transformed tasks;
- A set of data buffers with determined parameters for communication between tasks;
- An Asynchronous Task Graph (ATG) connecting tasks and buffers, as illustrated in Figure 1;
- A partial order of *priorities* to guarantee precedence constraints for internal tasks.

The method may also fail in producing these outputs.

If all tasks can be scheduled according to their attributes, then all of the end-to-end requirements will be met. Furthermore, the processor utilization is guaranteed to be below a maximum value (as discussed in the next section).

2.3. The Transformation

The transformation of the GHS-method from input to output deals with two main issues: creation of the ATG and derivation of task attributes. The structure of the ATG produced by the GHS-method is generally the same as the task graph provided as input, but extended by additional sampling tasks. If the attainable utilization proves to be too high, further restructuring of the graph may be necessary. A method named *task replication* that duplicates critical paths of the graph is described in [8]. This may relax the constraints on the solution and may facilitate finding a solution. Task replication was not examined in this case study, since the overall level of utilization was not a subject of concern.

In order to satisfy the *correlation* requirements one or more *sampling tasks* are added to the graph. The freshness constraints for inputs used to compute the same output, cannot differ more than the correlation for the same inputs. Thus the freshness constraints are trimmed to prevent this. The approach in the GHS-method is to actually make all such correlated freshness constraints equal.

The technique for dealing with freshness and separation requirements is to derive – from the given end-to-end requirements and the structure of the ATG – a set of constraints (algebraic equations with inequalities) on periods, deadlines, and offsets of each task. A constraint solver is then used to obtain explicit solutions to the constraints. The details may be found in [8], and are summarized below.

The solution to the algebraic inequalities is further constrained by the following constraints:

- harmonicity – the period of each task should be a multiple of the period of all preceding tasks in the graph;
- utilization – namely $U \le U_{max}$.

The first requirement makes it possible to design the communication between consecutive tasks so that the tasks execute independently (but in sequence) using asynchronous data buffers. The second requirement is natural in avionics control systems. Both requirements impose non-linear constraints in periods – harmonization expressed as $T_i \cdot N = T_j$ ($N = 1, 2, \ldots$) and utilization U expressed as:

$$U = \sum \frac{e_i}{T_i}$$

By elimination of offset and deadline variables (using Fourier-Motzkin elimination [7, 8]), a (still non-linear) set of inequalities only in periods is obtained which extends the solution space. A period solution to the original set is also a solution to the eliminated set, but not the opposite. By use of various heuristics the solution space for the periods can be restricted. To select one of the remaining solutions the selection criterion may for example be to choose the solution to the reduced problem that minimizes the utilization.

The offsets and deadlines are then reintroduced and instantiated through a set of optimization criteria aiming to maximize the probability of schedulability.

3. The Case Study

A full account of the intermediary results achieved during the application of the method cannot be given here due to space restrictions.

The example was provided by Swedish aerospace industry as a typical example of an avionics control system. The example was specified in a form adapted to the application of the GHS method – a computation graph, specification of in- and out-signals, maximal computational delays, correlations between insignals, and output separation requirements, and worst case execution times.

Some information was not available for confidentiality reasons, and was therefore invented (by industry) with the restriction that data *could* correspond to an actual design case. This issue will be further discussed later.

The computation graph is given in Figure 4, together with the end-to-end timing requirements. The computation graph differs from the graph used in the GHS-method in that it contains cyclic dependencies. For a direct application of the GHS-method these must be eliminated. No specific information was used to do this, but the choice was arbitrary. This issue will be further discussed below.

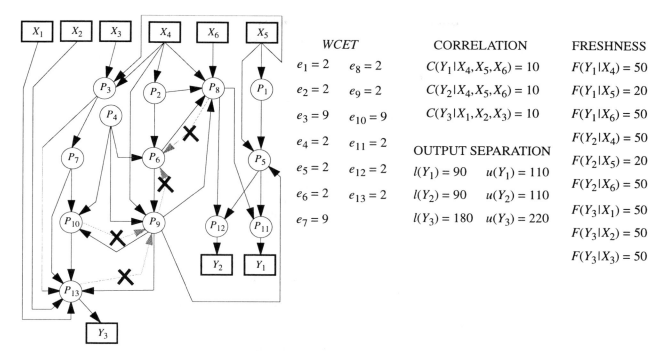

The following data accompany the figure:

WCET		CORRELATION	FRESHNESS
$e_1 = 2$	$e_8 = 2$	$C(Y_1|X_4,X_5,X_6) = 10$	$F(Y_1|X_4) = 50$
$e_2 = 2$	$e_9 = 2$	$C(Y_2|X_4,X_5,X_6) = 10$	$F(Y_1|X_5) = 20$
$e_3 = 9$	$e_{10} = 9$	$C(Y_3|X_1,X_2,X_3) = 10$	$F(Y_1|X_6) = 50$
$e_4 = 2$	$e_{11} = 2$		$F(Y_2|X_4) = 50$
$e_5 = 2$	$e_{12} = 2$	OUTPUT SEPARATION	$F(Y_2|X_5) = 20$
$e_6 = 2$	$e_{13} = 2$	$l(Y_1) = 90 \quad u(Y_1) = 110$	$F(Y_2|X_6) = 50$
$e_7 = 9$		$l(Y_2) = 90 \quad u(Y_2) = 110$	$F(Y_3|X_1) = 50$
		$l(Y_3) = 180 \quad u(Y_3) = 220$	$F(Y_3|X_2) = 50$
			$F(Y_3|X_3) = 50$

Figure 2: Computation graph for an avionics control system and related end-to-end timing requirements. Deleted dependencies are crossed out. (All timings are in milli-seconds.)

Another minor difference is the existence of a computation that lacks insignal (P_4). The reason for this is that this computation depends only on the global clock. The GHS-method can handle this by the constraints on period via harmonicity and utilization constraints.

All in- and out-signals were continuous.

3.1. Application of the Method

Gerber et al [8] propose a series of actions to perform the actual transformation from end-to-end constraints (input) to task-specific parameters (output). These actions where executed for the case study and are described below:

- First two sampling-tasks P_{s1} and P_{s2} are introduced that sample from inputs $\{X_1, X_2, X_3\}$ and $\{X_4, X_5, X_6\}$ respectively, and secondly, the freshness constraints $F(Y_1|X_i)$ and $F(Y_2|X_i)$ are trimmed (from 50 ms to 20 ms) as described in Section 2.3.

- Then the task graph is used to set up a number of constraints involving the *period* (T_i), *offset* (O_i) and *deadline* (D_i) of each task P_i. Each chain imposes *harmonicity constraints, e.g.,* $T_3 = N \cdot T_{s1}$, on the periods. The *correlation constraints* relate offsets and deadlines of the sampling tasks, e.g., $D_{s1} - O_{s1} \le 10$. The *freshness constraints* restrict the earliest sampling to the latest output time, e.g., $D_{13} - O_{s1} \le 50$. Note that not all computation chains had a defined freshness

constraint – X_4 to Y_3 and X_5 to Y_3 were not specified. The precedence requirements are realized by *precedence constraints* only for input and output tasks ($D_{s1} \le D_3 - e_3$, $D_3 \le O_{13}$). Intermediary tasks all have $O_i = 0$ and are given a *priority ordering* so that the precedence requirements are satisfied. The output *separation constraints* have to consider that output can occur at any time between offset and deadline for an output task, e.g., $(T_{13} + D_{13}) - O_{13} \le 220$ and $(T_{13} - D_{13}) + O_{13} \ge 180$. The *execution time constraints* guarantee that each task gets a large enough window of execution, e.g., for input/output tasks

$$O_{s1} + e_{s1} \le D_{s1} \quad O_{s1} \ge 0 \quad D_{s1} \le T_{s1}$$
$$O_{13} + e_{13} \le D_{13} \quad O_{13} \ge 0 \quad D_{13} \le T_{13}$$

and for intermediary tasks

$$O_{s1} + e_{s1} + e_3 \le D_3 \quad D_3 \le T_3$$

The resulting number of equations and inequalities was approximately 100.

- Next the constraints are transformed by Fourier-Motzkin elimination of offsets and deadlines, resulting in equations in periods and harmonicity variables only. The harmonicity constraints and the utilization constraint are added to the constraint set (Figure 3).

- Then the T:s are resolved so that they satisfy the resulting system of inequalities. In [8] this task is supported in part by a set of heuristics. If the designer chooses, say, a maximum allowable utilization of 0.7, the heuristics will delete *some* points in *T*-space that violate this assumption, but not necessarily (and not likely) *all* such points. Likewise the heuristics will remove *some* solutions that violate the harmonic constraints.

Applying the heuristics does not necessarily result in a unique value for each T_i, but rather a reduced solution space. It is up to the designer to select among these. The selected point in *T*-space should be checked to satisfy the original set of constraints, the harmonicity constraints and to imply a low enough utilization. In the current study we applied the heuristics manually. When the tool, described in Chapter 4, was applied, a depth first search strategy was used, without applying the solution space reduction heuristics. The same periods were achieved.

- Next the *O*:s and *D*:s and their corresponding constraints are reintroduced and an effort is made to maximize schedulability. This is done by a greedy heuristic that tries to maximize the execution window of every task by minimizing *O*:s and maximizing *D*:s as they are reintroduced in a certain order:

First, the execution window (*D–O*) of all input tasks are maximized.

Next, the execution window of all output tasks are maximized.

Then the offset of all input tasks are minimized.

Next the deadline of all output tasks are maximized.

Finally, the deadlines of the intermediate tasks, sorted in topological order, are maximized.

$$T_{s1} \geq 1 \quad T_{s2} \geq 1 \quad T_1 \geq 3 \quad T_2 \geq 3 \quad T_3 \geq 10 \quad T_4 \geq 0$$
$$T_5 \geq 9 \quad T_6 \geq 0 \quad T_7 \geq 19 \quad T_8 \geq 9 \quad T_9 \geq 7 \quad T_{10} \geq 28$$
$$92 \leq T_{11} \leq 108 \quad 92 \leq T_{12} \leq 108 \quad 182 \leq T_{13} \leq 218$$

$$\frac{e_{s1}}{T_{s1}} + \frac{e_{s2}}{T_{s2}} + \frac{e_1}{T_1} + \frac{e_2}{T_2} + \frac{e_3}{T_3} + \dots + \frac{e_{13}}{T_{13}} \leq U_{max}$$

$$T_3 = n_1 T_{s1} \quad T_{13} = n_2 T_{s1} \quad T_1 = n_3 T_{s2} \quad T_2 = n_4 T_{s2}$$
$$T_3 = n_5 T_{s2} \quad T_5 = n_6 T_{s2} \quad T_8 = n_7 T_{s2} \quad T_9 = n_8 T_{s2}$$
$$T_5 = n_9 T_1 \quad T_6 = n_{10} T_2 \quad T_8 = n_{11} T_2 \quad T_7 = n_{12} T_3$$
$$T_{13} = n_{13} T_3 \quad T_{11} = n_{14} T_5 \quad T_{12} = n_{15} T_5 \quad T_8 = n_{16} T_6$$
$$T_9 = n_{17} T_6 \quad T_{10} = n_{18} T_7 \quad T_{13} = n_{19} T_7 \quad T_{11} = n_{20} T_8$$
$$T_{12} = n_{21} T_8 \quad T_5 = n_{22} T_9 \quad T_8 = n_{23} T_9 \quad T_{10} = n_{24} T_9$$
$$T_{13} = n_{25} T_9 \quad T_{13} = n_{26} T_{10} \quad n_i \in \{1, 2, 3, \dots\}$$

Figure 3: The complete set of constraints after Fourier-Motzkin elimination

There is no guarantee that the solution actually maximizes schedulability.

The constraints were set up and solved by means of a CLP-tool (see Chapter 4.). The initial (non-schedulable) solution together with a final solution are presented in Table 1.

- The design can now be analyzed w.r.t. schedulability. Note that utilization based schedulability analysis cannot be used since synchronization between tasks makes them dependent. Some problems were experienced at this stage so that the original problem had to be reformulated, see next section. The final solution using fixed priority scheduling is shown in Figure 4.

- If the derived set of parameters results in a schedulable set of tasks, asynchronous buffers can be allocated.

Table 1 : The solution using the GHS-method. Values in parentheses are derived using additional constraints resulting in a schedulable solution (with priorities).

P_i	e_i	T_i	O_i	D_i	Pri_i
$s1$	1	216	0	10	2
$s2$	1	108	0	10	1
1	2	108	0	108	4
2	2	108	0	108	3
3	9	216	0	46 (48)	12
4	2	108	0	108	5
5	2	108	0	18 (16)	9
6	2	108	0	108	6
7	9	216	0	46 (48)	13
8	2	108	0	18 (16)	8
9	2	108	0	46 (48)	7
10	9	216	0	46 (48)	14
11	2	108	18 (16)	20 (18)	10
12	2	108	18	20	11
13	2	216	46 (48)	50	15

3.2. Schedulability

Even if the average utilization was low (0.315), it is obvious from Table 1 that task 11 and 12 compete for the same window of execution in the initial solution. The utilization is at least 200 per cent in that window. The recommended approach given by the GHS-method in this situation is to transform the task graph, as described in Section 2.3. However, it is not obvious how this would solve the problem in our case. Instead a new inequality is added that guarantees that P_{11} executes before P_{12}, e.g., $D_{11} \leq O_{12}$. Furthermore, the sum of the *WCET*s of task 10 and its predecessors is greater (47 ms) than the deadline of task 10 (46 ms). Two additional constraints were there-

86

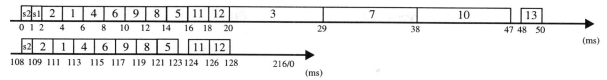

Figure 4: Timing diagram for the scheduled tasks according to the solution of the example.

fore added to set the offset and deadline of task 13; $O_{13} = 48$ and $D_{13} = 50$. It can be shown that the solution to the more constrained problem (derived using the same method as originally) is schedulable, given a certain order of priorities. (See Figure 4 and Table 1.)

3.3. Asynchronous Buffer Design

The buffers decouple the tasks and guarantee that producers and consumers of data never access the same location at the same time. As a result, locking is not required and tasks are never blocked by lower priority tasks. The design of the buffers presented no problem, and was straightforward using the GHS-method.

4. The Tool

The synthesis of *offsets*, *deadlines* and *periods* was supported by a small *constraint logic program* (see e.g. Marriott and Stuckey [13] or Jaffar and Maher [9]) implemented in SICStus Prolog [20]. Constraint logic programming (CLP) is a family of programming languages that combine logic programming with special-purpose algorithms for solving equations and inequations over various algebraic domains. In this particular project we used CLP(Q) – logic programming with linear constraints over the *rational* numbers. The combination of a general purpose programming language (with built-in search) and constraint solving provides a flexible and powerful tool for solving this type of problems – the prototype implementation consisted of less than 300 lines of code and was written in less than a day. Running the program on the example task graph (plus the sampling tasks that were added manually) took approximately 2.5 seconds on a 200MHz Pentium Pro running Linux.

The input to the program – the asynchronous task graph and the end-to-end requirements – was specified by means of a logic program; input tasks, output tasks and the execution time of all tasks were specified as follows:

task(s1, 1).   *input(s1).*   *output(p11).*
task(s2, 1).   *input(s2).*   *output(p12).*
task(p1, 2).   *input(p4).*   *output(p13).*
   ...
task(p13, 2).

The internal structure of the ATG was specified by relating the tasks to the list all of the immediate predecessors in the graph.

pred(p1, [s2]).
pred(p2, [s2]).
pred(p3, [s1, s2]).
   ...
pred(p12, [p5, p8]).
pred(p13, [s1, p3, p7, p9, p10]).

Finally the external requirements were specified:

freshness(p13, s1, 50).   *separation(p11, 90, 110).*
freshness(p12, s2, 20).   *separation(p12, 90, 110).*
freshness(p11, s2, 20).   *separation(p13, 180, 220).*

correlation(s1, 10).
correlation(s2, 10).

The main procedure of the program was responsible for *setting up* the constraints, and then *solving* them in accordance with the GHS-method:

$$\textit{main(Tasks, Utilization) :-} \qquad (1)$$
$$\textit{create\_variables(Tasks)}, \qquad (2)$$
$$\textit{setup\_correlation(Tasks)}, \qquad (3)$$
$$\textit{setup\_freshness(Tasks)}, \qquad (4)$$
$$\textit{setup\_separation(Tasks)}, \qquad (5)$$
$$\textit{setup\_execution(Tasks)}, \qquad (6)$$
$$\textit{setup\_harmonicity(Tasks, Harm)}, \qquad (7)$$
$$\textit{solve\_constraints(Tasks, Harm, Utilization)}. \qquad (8)$$

The predicate *create_variables(Tasks)* in line 1 was responsible for creating and initializing the unknowns (*offset*, *deadline* and *period*) for each task in the task graph. The variables were kept in *Tasks* (as an association list).

In lines 2–7 the different types of constraints (correlation, freshness etc.) were set up. For instance, the code for setting up the correlation constraints looked as follows:

setup_correlation(Tasks) :-
    collect_correlation(List),
    setup_corr_loop(List, Tasks).

First we collect the list of all tasks that need to be correlated and the corresponding correlation value. Then we traverse this list and set up the correlation constraint that restricts the window of execution of tasks that sample several inputs:

setup_corr_loop([ ], *Tasks*).
setup_corr_loop([*c(Task, Corr)* | *Rest*], *Tasks*) :-
    get_task(Task, Tasks, [Offset,Deadline,Period]),
    { *Deadline – Offset =< Corr* },
    setup_corr_loop(Rest, Tasks).

For each pair of task-correlation in the list we retrieve the associated offset and deadline (using *get_task*/3) and set up the constraint *Deadline – Offset =< Corr*.

The last step – before solving the constraints – was to generate and set up the constraints containing the integer-valued variables that govern the harmonicity of the system (line 7). The process of setting up the constraints was completely deterministic and driven by the structure of the ATG. Only the last step – actually finding a solution to the constraints (line 8) – is non-deterministic. This is also the most difficult part of the process computationally; it involved solving several non-linear constraints. Although CLP(Q) accepts non-linear constraints there is no support for solving or even checking the satisfiability of non-linear constraints. However, by exploiting the non-determinism of logic programming it was possible to reduce the problem to a linear one by systematically labeling the harmonicity variables using a depth first search. Solving the constraints was then easy.

5. The Implementation

An investigation of how to implement the detailed design in Ada 95 was made. Ada 95 [1] supports monotone time with a resolution of 1 ms and monotonicity of 50 years to safely implement cyclic tasks and offsets. It also supports static priorities and pre-emptive scheduling. The implementation framework contains three packages – one for the generic task scheduling administration, one for the application code and one for initialization. Exception handlers can be associated with missed deadlines

6. Discussion

In this section we present conclusions from the project and discuss ideas for extensions. Finally we present some related work.

6.1. Evaluation of the Method

Problem Specification

The example problem was specified by industry in a form prepared with the GHS-method in mind. The information was partly available, but sometimes in alternative forms. Some of the input data was therefore estimated, like *WCET* for the different tasks. The initial task graph contained several feedbacks which had to be eliminated. For confidentiality reasons, the original specification is not available to the authors, and no statement can presently be made about how well the method *really* fits industrial practice. However, the problem formulation, the problems encountered during the application of the method and the solution itself has parallels in industrial experience.

The Method

The GHS-method generates periods, deadlines and offsets, such that *if the solution is schedulable*, the implementation is guaranteed to satisfy the end-to-end timing requirements. However, the method may generate a solution which is not schedulable or it may fail to generate a solution at all – even when there is a schedulable solution. The problem then has to be transformed and the method must be applied to the transformed problem.

The method fails if:
- the constraint-set is unsatisfiable because of too tight external requirements or too high *WCET*s;
- the heuristics fail to produce a set of periods as the solution to the reduced problem, for example due to a too low maximal utilization requirement.
- all possible sets of period solutions to the reduced problem fail to result in a solution to offsets and deadlines.
- all solutions from the method to the complete problem given as periods, offset and deadlines cannot be scheduled.

None of the failures are critical or unexpected. There are two possible approaches to handle a failure:
- to change the end-to-end requirements by reapplying the preliminary design (or negotiating the control requirements) and applying the method for detailed design synthesis again *or*
- to make a transformation of the ATG [8] that conserves the satisfiability of the functional requirements and apply the method again.

In our case we had to tighten the initial (estimated) *WCET*s in order to avoid the first type of failure.

The most difficult type of failure is the last – *the method does not guarantee schedulability*. As demonstrated by this case, several additional constraints had to be added to make the solution schedulable. These constraints cannot easily be derived; but having a flexible tool to experiment with helped considerably.

Task Communication

Because of the asynchronous buffers the GHS-method imposes no locking between tasks accessing the same buffer. This is a major advantage of the method. If the correlation constraints are non-critical the buffers can even be reduced to a single slot as discussed in [12].

Priority Assignment and Schedulability

The GHS-method [8], assumes priority based scheduling, since the precedence constraints for intermediate tasks are guaranteed by the priority on the intermediate tasks. However, precedence can be realized in other ways and the method does not inherently assume the use of a specific method for scheduling.

An analysis for schedulability using priority based scheduling must instantiate priorities for all tasks. As the schedulability must be guaranteed for the solution to the end-to-end requirements, a method must be given to assign priorities, for example optimal priority assignment.

It can be anticipated that the schedulability analysis requires significant effort (given a task set characterized by periods, WCETs, deadlines and offsets) and is it not clear how to integrate the synthesis method with the analysis, except that a straightforward iterative method can be used. The problem of estimating schedulability during synthesis is not easy, to say the least. In [17] a gain factor for the response time is maximized when allocating time budgets to single tasks in a distributed real-time system, while satisfying schedulability and the end-to-end timing requirements. The gain factor is used as an estimate of individual task schedulability.

Generally it can be said that schedulability analysis for task sets containing precedence constraints and offsets is hard to do for the general case. Different exact and approximate (but conservative) methods are proposed that make different assumptions about the task set (cf. [3, 10, 21]). A systematic method to select method for schedulability analysis given a task set with certain characteristics and a scheduling method calls for further research.

The simplest method is to assume that the tasks are independent. The worst scheduling case then corresponds to simultaneous release of all tasks with higher (or equal) priority to the one for which the response time is analysed. This would, however, be too pessimistic for the general control example where the chains of computations can be long.

The Space of Solutions

Even if the method significantly reduces the space of solutions, the example can still be solved using 10^7 combinations of periods. The solution for offsets and deadlines in the example was relatively easy to find, but the worst case scenario will not be easily solved – in particular if the schedulability analysis is resource demanding. More analysis of the complexity and perhaps other heuristics should be investigated further. An alternative heuristics for the period assignment sub-problem is described in [16].

Constraint Logic Programming

To support the method we implemented the main ideas in SICStus Prolog with constraints over the rationals. The experience was encouraging – CLP offers great flexibility and the time spent on developing a working prototype was short (less than a day). Although SICStus Prolog implements constraint handling only by means of Prolog libraries the time to compute a solution was short – only 2.5 seconds on a 200MHz Pentium Pro for our example. A dedicated constraint system like CHIP (e.g. [2]) is likely to improve on this.

A problem that still lacks a satisfactory solution, however, is what *heuristics* to use when solving non-linear constraints. In our case the reduced non-linear sub-problem for the periods was reasonably small and with some user intervention (setting an upper bound on the harmonicity variables) it was possible to come up with a reasonable solution using bounded, exhaustive depth-first search. However, for larger problems it is necessary to employ more intelligent search strategies (e.g. branch-and-bound) or non-exhaustive search.

6.2. Extensions

Feedback

The original computation graph contained cycles. The cycles are typical for control systems, since state information from one cycle must be transferred to the next cycle. In the current work this was handled in an ad hoc way, by excluding some of the dependencies from the graph.

A more satisfactory approach would be to consider state as input/output data. The end-to-end timing requirements then become functions of period (instead of constant), as output from one cycle must finish before the value is used as input to a computation in the next calculation. This means that the cyclic, directed graph is transformed into an acyclic directed graph, where the output buffer of the state calculating task becomes both the input and output buffer of a computational chain – one for each use of the state variable.

Consider two tasks – τ_i with period T_i, that produces state data and τ_j with period T_j, that consumes data in the next "cycle". Since the feedback results in a cyclic graph, τ_i also consumes data produced by τ_j (perhaps after some intermediary calculations) in the same cycle. Let τ_i^0 be an instance of τ_i that consumes data produced by the instance τ_j^0. τ_i^0 then produces state data used in a later instance of τ_j. The constraint becomes a constraint on the deadline of τ_i^0, as the calculated state value must be available before it is used. The deadline constraint will correspond to the worst case for all τ_j that consumes state data produced by τ_i:

$$\forall j \{ D_i \leq \min(k_j T_j + \phi_j + \Phi_{ij}) \}$$
$$\text{where} \quad k_j > (O_i + e_i - \phi_j - \Phi_{ij})/T_j$$

Here Φ_{ij} is the phase shift between the start of period for τ_j^0 and start of period for τ_i^0. k_j enumerates the instances of τ_j and may be treated as integer variables, but this increases the non-linearity in the equations. For $k_j = 0$ it can be assumed that the corresponding period instance for τ_j is the first instance starting after the beginnning of the period instance for τ_i^0, i.e., Φ_{ij} are all positive. To minimize, all Φ_{ij} can be assumed to be zero, as this corresponds to the worst case.

ϕ_j is the minimum delay time in a period before τ_j may start (minimum in-period phase shift). The in-period phase shift is due to the delay of τ_j caused by predecessor tasks. O_i is the offset of τ_i. Observe that it is now an output task.

In the current project there was no time to investigate this approach further since is changes the end-to-end constraints significantly so the GHS-method would not be directly applicable.

Constraint Logic Programming

The flexibility of constraint logic programming opens up new possibilities. The GHS-method strictly requires that end-to-end requirements and *WCET*s for the tasks are known – only task periods, deadlines, and offsets are allowed to be unknown. This is not always the case in an industrial setting – in the early design phases it is just as adequate to ask – "What is the maximum possible *WCET* for a certain computation?" or "What is the minimum computational delay from A to B?". For this purpose, CLP makes less assumptions about what is input and what is output to the problem. The problem formulation would be basically the same no matter what the unknowns are. However the heuristics may, of course, vary from case to case.

The GHS-method assumes a specific form for the final solution (harmonicity, no feedback), and makes no assumptions about other parameters, like the choice of

scheduling method. To find the "best" design, experimentation by relaxing or varying assumptions is needed. CLP has the flexibility to support such experiments. It could, for example, be interesting to:

- investigate how feedback influences the choice of heuristics.
- investigate other heuristics for choice of "best" solution or how to handle non-linear equations, where some manual manipulation was required.
- experiment with other constraint domains and a dedicated CLP-system like CHIP. One domain that seems particularly interesting is *finite domains*; CLP(fd) contains efficient constraint solvers over finite intervals of integers and has been successfully applied to e.g. scheduling and resource allocation problems.

6.3. Related Work

The method used in this work (the period calibration method [8]) has been further extended by the original authors. In [18] the method is applied to a *distributed system*. In this work the period assignment uses fixed task allocation and similar utilization bounds as in the single processor case, but for each processor. The end-to-end deadlines then have to be allocated to each task. This is done by calculating the response times for each task and asserting the allocated deadlines to be a maximal constant factor times the response time, while the constraints on the end-to-end deadline are satisfied. Fixed priority scheduling is used to calculate the response times and the priorities are varied until a satisfactory solution is found. When the deadlines have been asserted the offsets for the tasks are calculated. The method is approximate and heuristically based.

A case study is conducted in [12], which investigates the applicability of the method and the effect of latency, periods and output jitter on the quality of the system control. A similar study of the effects of latency and sampling frequencies was made in [15]. In [19] an effort is made to optimize the quality of control by using optimal control theory and increase the processor utilization.

Our case study does not investigate the control quality, but focus the applicability of the method in existing industrial design environments. Industrial practice is that the bounds given by control design on output separation, correlation and freshness are upper bounds. Normally 2-4 samples per rise time (first and second order linear systems), i.e., $2 < T_r/h < 4$, where T_r is the rise time and h is the sampling period, is satisfactory. The analysis of the effect of end-to-end requirements on control quality and stability can be integrated into the control design [22] and reliable (but negotiable) bounds can be achieved. In this work it is assumed that the timing requirements developed during control design are strict and that the utilization is minimized to simplify future system extensions and changes.

7. Conclusions

We have applied a method (the period calibration method [8]) for the detailed design of a task set which satisfies a set of end-to-end constraints to a typical example of avionics control software. The general conclusion is that the method does provide a feasible way to do this. The asynchronous communication is particularly appreciated.

The general approach to restrict the design architecture, for example by assuming that periods are multiples of a basic period – as opposed to assuming general periods (read: related like the primes) – to obtain a problem that is easier to solve is attractive, particularly for industrial use.

Some discrepancies where noticed in the way the problem was formulated. In particular it was noticed that the utilization is unsatisfactory as an inverse estimate of schedulability, since the method generated a solution which was easily seen to be unschedulable.

Also, the strict view on what is input and what is output of the GHS-method must be relaxed.

The project gave a positive response on the use of methods such as this for automatizing detailed design of control software, but also generated several issues that have to be investigated before actually recommending industrial production use.

Acknowledgments

We would like to thank Saab Dynamics AB for providing support and Lars-Åke Classon in particular for discussions and for supplying the specification for the case study. Thanks are also due to the anonymous reviewers and Manas Saksena for valuable comments on the paper.

References

[1] Ada 95 Reference Manual, ISO/IEC 8652:1995(E)

[2] Aggoun, A. and Beldiceanu, N. Overview of the CHIP Compiler System. In Benhamou and Colmerauer (ed), *Constraint Logic Programming: Selected Research*, 421–435, The MIT Press, 1993.

[3] Bate I., Burns A., Schedulability Analysis of Fixed priority Real-Time Systems with Offsets, in *Proc. of 9th Euromicro Workshop on Real-Time Systems*, Toledo, June 1997, IEEE Computer Society.

[4] Bonnier, S., Kalmelid, S. and Törne, A., Control System Design – An Overview of Timing Analysis Methods and Tools, restricted availability, contact the authors of the current report for authorization procedure.

[5] Burns, A., and Wellings, A. *HRT-HOOD^{TM}: A Structured Design Method for Hard Real-Time Ada Systems.* Elsevier, 1995.

[6] Burns, A., and Wellings, A. HRT-HOOD: A Structured Design Method for Hard Real-Time Systems. *Real-Time Systems*, 6:73-114, 1994.

[7] Dantzig, G., Eaves, B. Fourier-Motzkin Elimination and its Dual. *Journal of Combinatorial Theory (A)*, 14:288-297, 1973

[8] Gerber, R., Hong, S., and Saksena, M., Guaranteeing Real-Time Requirements With Resource-Based Calibration of Periodic Processes. *IEEE Transactions on Software Engineering*, 21(7):579 - 592, July 1995.

[9] Jaffar, J. and Maher, M. Constraint Logic Programming: A Survey. *J. Logic Programming*, 19/20:503–582, 1993.

[10] Klein, M.H., Ralya, T., Pollak, B., Obenza., R., Gonzalez Harbour, M., *A Practitioner's Handbook for Real-Time Analysis*, Kluwer Acad Publ, 1993.

[11] Kopetz, H., Zainlinger, R., Fohler, G., Kantz, H., Puschner, P., and Schutz, W. The Design of Real-Time Systems: From Specification to Implementation and Verification. *Software Engineering Journal*, 6(3): 72-82, May 1991.

[12] Kim, N., Ryu, M., Hong, S., Saksena, M., Choi, C-H. and Shin, H., Visual Assessment of a Real-Time System Design: A Case Study on a CNC-controller, In *Proc IEEE Real-Time Systems Symposium*, Dec 1996.

[13] Marriott, K. and Stuckey, P. *Programming with Constraints: An Introduction*. The MIT Press, 1998.

[14] Pospischil, G., Puschner, P., Vrchoticky, A., and Zainlinger, R. Developing Real-Time Tasks with Predictable Timing. *IEEE Software*, 35–44, September 1992.

[15] Ryu, M., Hong, S. and Saksena, M., Streamlining Real-Time Controller Design: From Performance Specifications to End-to-End Timing Constraints, In *Proc, IEEE Real-Time Technology and Applications Symposium*, Montreal, June 1997.

[16] Ryu, M. and Hong, S., A Period Calibration Algorithm for Embedded Digital Controllers. Seoul National University, SNU-EE-TR-96-1, October 1996.

[17] Saksena, M. and Hong, S., An Engineering Approach to Decomposing End-to-End Delays on a Distributed Real-Time System, In *Proc, IEEE Workshop on Parallel and Distributed Real-Time Systems*, April 1996.

[18] Saksena, M. and Hong, S., Resource Conscious design of Distributed Real-Time Systems – An End-to-End Approach, In *Proc. IEEE Int'l Conf on Engineering of Complex Computer Systems*, Oct 1996.

[19] Seto, D., Lehoczky, J., Sha, L.and Shin, K., On Task Schedulability in Real-Time Control Systems, In *Proc IEEE Real-Time Systems Symposium*, Dec 1996.

[20] Swedish Institute of Computer Science. *SICStus Prolog User's Manual*. Release 3#6. 1995.

[21] Tindell K., Adding Time-Offsets to Schedulability Analysis, Internal report, University of York, Computer Science Dept, YCS-94-221.

[22] Åström, K.J. and Wittenmark, B., *Computer Controlled Systems – Theory and Design*, Prentice Hall 1984.

Schedulability Analysis for Automated Implementations of Real-Time Object-Oriented Models

M. Saksena[*]   A. Ptak[†]   P. Freedman[‡]   P. Rodziewicz[§]

Abstract

The increasing complexity of real-time software has led to a recent trend in the use of high-level modeling languages for development of real-time software. One representative example is the modeling language ROOM (real-time object-oriented modeling), which provides features such as object-orientation, state machine description of behaviors, formal semantics for executability of models, and possibility of automated code generation. However, these modeling languages largely ignore the timeliness aspect of real-time systems, and fail to provide any guidance for a designer to a priori predict and analyze temporal behavior.

In this paper we consider schedulability analysis for automated implementations of ROOM models, based on the ObjecTime toolset. This work builds on results presented in [8], where we developed some guidelines for the design and implementation of real-time object-oriented models. Using the guidelines, we have modified the run-time system library provided by the ObjecTime toolset to make it amenable to schedulability analysis. Based on the modified toolset, we show how a ROOM model can be analyzed for schedulability, taking into account the implementation overheads and structure. The analysis is validated experimentally, first using simple periodic models, and then using a large case study of a train tilting system.

1 Introduction

In a recent article entitled "The Challenges of Real-Time Software Design" [11], Selic and Ward use the words *event-driven* and *time-driven* to describe two basic 'styles' of real-time software. The time-driven style corresponds to using cyclic activities triggered by time. This software style is naturally suited for the implementation of periodic activities, such as software implementation of control-loop behavior in embedded control systems. In contrast, software written in event-driven style typically waits for an event to arrive, reacts to it by performing an appropriate computation, and then enters a dormant state waiting for the next event. The event-driven style naturally suits implementation of reactive behavior, associated with (often unpredictable) discrete events in the external system.

The time-driven style has evolved to develop methods that can predict *timeliness* aspects of a system, and is particularly suitable for systems whose performance critically depends on meeting deadlines. The predictability of event-arrivals makes it easier to do such analysis. The maturity of real-time scheduling theory [5] has led to a range of techniques, mostly based on fixed priority scheduling theory, that a designer/developer can use to perform timing and schedulability analysis of a time-driven real-time system. In contrast to time-driven software style, the event-driven software style has evolved largely to deal with the complexity arising from asynchrony, concurrency, and the inherent non-determinism due to the two. In order to deal with this complexity, various modeling languages have evolved using modeling features such as (1) object-orientation, with finite state machines to model object behavior, (2) visual modeling, with formal semantics (enabling executability of models), (3) use-cases or scenarios to model system behavior, and (4) associated CASE tools to facilitate model development, provide executability of models, as well as partially or completely automate code generation.

In reality most systems contain both time-driven and event-driven components. For example, consider computerized control systems. The control loops and other data flow paths are typical of the time-driven parts of such systems. On the other hand, such a system must also react to discrete external events such as operator commands, changes in the operating conditions, and various types of exceptions and equipment failures. In fact, most of the complexity of such a system is in this reactive component of a system. Moreover, there are timing constraints to be respected for the reactive component as well. Therefore, as systems be-

---

[*]Department of Computer Science, Concordia University, Montreal, Canada. Email: manas@cs.concordia.ca.

[†]Centre de recherche informatique de Montreal (CRIM), and Canadian Space Agency, Montreal, Canada. Email: aptak@crim.ca.

[‡]Centre de recherche informatique de Montreal (CRIM), Email: freedman@crim.ca.

[§]Centre de recherche informatique de Montreal (CRIM) and Concordia University, Email: rodziew@cs.concordia.ca

come increasingly complex, it is our view that one must be able to use high level modeling languages to deal with the complexity of software, and still be able to subject critical components of the system to timing and schedulability analysis.

Unfortunately, little attention has been paid to the integration of schedulability analysis into the analysis and development tools for real-time modeling languages. This is, in part, due to the very nature of event-driven software – that is the asynchrony and non-determinism. In the absence of deterministic arrival of events, it is hard to determine response times, and thus hard to analyze a system for real-time performance. On the other hand, in a recent paper [8], we showed that it is possible to perform such analysis. The key is to realize that even though a given system may be processing many events in a state-dependent manner, only a relatively small number of event-sequences are time-critical and need to be analyzed for timeliness. Thus, if we can (1) prioritize events to reflect their time-criticality, and (2) implement a system that bounds priority inversions for event-processing, then it becomes simpler to analyze the time behavior of the time-critical event-sequences. The key aspects of our guidelines presented in [8] were the need for (1) preemptability of event processing, which requires multiple threads of control performing event-processing, and (2) managing thread priorities dynamically to minimize and bound priority inversions for event-processing. In other words, threads of control and thread priorities must be viewed as artifacts of implementation for preemptability, and events and event-priorities must be viewed as design elements.

In this paper, we present our experience with the application of the guidelines presented in [8] for implementation of real-time object-oriented models. As in [8], our work uses the ROOM modeling language [9] and the ObjecTime Developer Toolset from ObjecTime Inc. The ROOM modeling language and the ObjecTime Developer Toolset are representative of the new generation of modeling and development tools for event-driven real-time software. Rhapsody from i-Logix (http://www.ilogix.com), and ObjectGeode from Verilog (http://www.verilogusa.com/og/og.htm) are other similar tools, and by and large the results presented here are equally applicable for systems developed using those tools. Also, the modeling concepts of ROOM are compatible with the Unified Modeling Language (UML) developed by a consortium of companies, including Rational, i-Logix and ObjecTime, and recently standardized by Object Management Group (OMG). Indeed, a recent joint press release from ObjecTime and Rational states that "Rational and ObjecTime are defining a comprehensive approach for the application of UML to the development of complex real-time systems." A recent white paper [10] also describes how the ROOM modeling concepts may be derived from the general UML modeling concepts, and suggests a domain specific specialization of UML for real-time based on ROOM modeling language.

The main contribution of this paper is in presenting experimental evidence of the soundness of the ideas presented in [8] showing that it is possible to perform a priori schedulability analysis of automated implementations of real-time object-oriented software models. We have modified ObjecTime's run-time system in accordance with the guidelines presented in [8], and then used the implementation to develop a schedulability analysis model taking into account the implementation aspects and the overheads. This model is then used to illustrate how schedulability analysis can be performed for a simple set of periodic tasks; we also validate the model through measurements. To illustrate the generality of the approach, we also present a case study of a train tilting system to illustrate to what extent the approach scales to complex ROOM models. The train tilting system modeled here represents a realistic and representative (future generation) computerized control system. Previous work on the application of ROOM/ObjecTime for the development of the train tilting system [2] had revealed serious timing problems due to the use of static thread priorities.

2 Overview of ROOM Concepts

Modeling of systems with ROOM is performed by designing *actors*, which are encapsulated, concurrent objects, communicating via point-to-point links. Inter-actor communication is performed exclusively by sending and receiving *messages* via interface objects called *ports*. A message is a tuple consisting of a signal name, a message body (i.e., data associated with the message), and an associated message priority.

The behavior of an actor is represented by an extended state machine called a *ROOMchart*, based on the statechart formalism [3]. Each actor remains dormant until an *event* occurs, i.e., when a *message* is received by an actor. Incoming messages trigger transitions associated with the actor's finite state machine. Actions may be associated with transitions, as well as entry and exit points of a state. The sending of messages to other actors is initiated by an action. The finite state machine behavior model imposes that only one transition at a time can be executed by each actor. As a consequence, a *run-to-completion* paradigm applies to state transitions. This implies that the processing of a message cannot be preempted by the arrival of a new (higher priority) message for the same actor. However, as explained later, in a multi-threaded implementation, the processing may be preempted by other higher priority threads.

ROOM supports the notion of a *composite* state, which can be decomposed into substates. Decomposition of a state into substates can be taken upto an arbitrary level in a recursive manner. The current state of such a system is defined by a nested chain of states called a *state context*. The behavior is said to be simultaneously "in" all of these states.

Transitions on the innermost current state take precedence over equivalent transitions in higher scopes. An event for which no transition is triggered at all levels of the state hierarchy is discarded, unless it is explicitly deferred.

ROOM also provides the concept of a layered architecture. A layer provides a set of services to the entities in the layer above. The linkage between layers is done at discrete contact points called *service access points* (SAPs) in the upper layer which uses the services, and *service provisioning points* (SPPs) at the layer providing the services. Each service access point is connected to a service provision point in the layer below (there can be a many to one mapping), and the end points of each such connection must have matching service points.

The bottom layer in ROOM models is provided by the ROOM virtual machine, which provides, among other things, a *communications service* and a *timing service*. The communications service provides the services to establish and manage connections between ROOM actors. The timing service may be used to set and cancel timers, both one-shot and periodic. The ROOM virtual machine is also responsible for interfacing to other external (non-ROOM) environments such as specialized hardware or other software components and systems.

3 Implementation of ROOM Models

ROOM run-time systems provide an implementation of the ROOM virtual machine, and are responsible for providing the mechanisms that support the ROOM paradigm as well as the services needed by ROOM models. The ObjecTime Developer Toolset is a CASE tool that provides a fully integrated development environment to support the ROOM methodology, with features such as graphical and textual editing for actor construction, and C++ code generation from the model [9]. The ObjecTime toolset includes a target run-time system (TargetRTS) [7], which is linked with the application code to provide a stand-alone executable that may be run on either a workstation (emulation) environment, or on a target environment with an underlying real-time operating system such as VxWorks, QNX, pSOS, and VRTX.

3.1 Single vs Multi-Threaded Implementation

The simplest approach to implement a real-time system designed in ROOM is to cast all actors into a single thread. Thus, processing takes place in event priority order, and the only source of priority inversion is due to the *run-to-completion* semantics of the concurrency model. Therefore, the maximum blocking time by lower priority tasks is limited by the most "time-consuming" transition in the entire system. In many systems, this is perfectly tolerable, and

leads to a simple, low overhead approach to implementation. This would be true, for example, in systems which are primarily reactive, and where the processing requirements are largely related to state changes.

This simple approach, however, ceases to be effective when the *time-driven* functionality is incorporated into a system designed in ROOM. In such systems, it is not surprising to find compute-intensive functions (e.g., signal processing functions), and the need for preemption becomes imperative to avoid significant priority inversions for higher priority event processing. A multiple thread configuration may then be used to manage preemption. In a multi-threaded configuration, each actor is mapped to one of the application defined threads. Each thread runs as a message handler for the actors that it controls. A thread may then be preempted by another thread depending on thread priorities and the scheduling of threads by the underlying operating system. Threads are also useful if a segment of code makes a blocking call to external functions. Note however, that a multi-threaded configuration comes with its own costs. In particular, inter-thread message passing is an order of magnitude more expensive than intra-thread message passing. Also, one must take into account the cost of preemption and synchronization when considering performance.

3.2 Multi-Threaded Implementation and Thread Priorities

In a multi-threaded implementation, there are two levels of priority scheduling. Within the context of a single thread, the processing of events takes place in message/event priority order. This ordering is enforced by the message handling loop provided by the run-time system. Across the whole system, the operating system schedules the threads in thread priority order. We assume that the underlying operating system supports preemptive priority scheduling, and the thread priorities are under application control.

This two-level scheduling can result in priority inversions if thread priorities are not appropriately controlled. As noted earlier, *the processing associated with messages represents the "tasks" in the system, and accordingly, message priorities are the "real" application priorities*. Threads and thread priorities, on the other hand, are artifacts of an implementation. Ideally, processing across the whole system should be driven by the message priorities, and there is a priority inversion whenever a higher priority message processing is blocked by lower priority message processing (whether in the same thread or another thread). The TargetRTS supplied by ObjecTime allows an application designer to choose thread priorities, but these priorities are static. This can lead to priority inversions since (in general) each actor, and hence each thread, will be processing messages of different priorities.

Still, many systems may be designed successfully, and

indeed are, with this capability. One way to use it effectively would be to design a system such that the functionality of the system is partitioned into "control" actors (where most event processing is non compute-intensive), and "data-processing" actors (i.e., where processing may be compute-intensive, but state machines are simple, and the actor does not receive many different types of messages) parts. All "control" actors can then be mapped to a single "control" thread, while, other data-processing actors may be mapped to separate thread to manage preemption. A data processing actor can then be assigned a priority depending on the time criticality of the function it implements. The control thread can be assigned the highest priority (presumably, it will be handling all kinds of emergency messages, which require the tightest response times). While, there is some priority inversion, it may be acceptable if the aggregate low-priority workload on the control thread is not sufficient to cause missed deadlines in the data processing actors.

Dynamic Thread Priorities. It is not hard to imagine systems where a static thread priority approach would fail to work. The train tilting system presented in Section 5 is one such example. It may not be possible to nicely separate the control and data-processing functionalities into separate actors. Even when this is possible, there may be sufficient low priority workload in the control thread that can lead to missed deadlines for other data processing activities. This may happen, for example, because of various kinds of system monitoring and other background functions, which must be done in the control actors. Note that, while each of these system monitoring activities may be relatively small, the aggregate of all such activities (over a time interval of interest) may be large, and can cause significant priority inversion.

This problem was identified in [8], and it was suggested that the run-time system should automatically manage thread priorities to reflect the priority of pending messages for the thread. Thus, each thread can have a dynamic priority, which is increased whenever a higher priority message arrives for one of the actors managed by the thread. Likewise, the priority of a thread can be automatically adjusted to that of the highest priority queued message when the thread finished processing a message. With sufficient thread priorities, this simple scheme gives the advantage of preemptability offered by multiple threads, without the problems of priority inversions as described above. Of course, one must also take into account the costs of changing thread priorities.

3.3 Implementation of Dynamic Priority Threads in TargetRTS

We have made changes to the TargetRTS provided with the ObjecTime Developer Toolset to dynamically adjust thread priorities as described above. These modifications

were made in consultation with the developers at ObjecTime. Here, we only briefly discuss the implementation aspects. Our implementation was carried out on Solaris operating system, using real-time priorities[1]. In Solaris, real-time priorities are fixed priorities (i.e., not changed by the kernel) and are higher than other thread/process priorities. These priorities can be changed from the application (with super-user privileges) using the priocntl() system call.

A thread[2] running with a real-time priority cannot be preempted by other threads running in the *time-sharing* or *system* class. Most user processes/threads run in the time-sharing class, while kernel threads run in the system class. Thus, a real-time thread in Solaris can only be preempted by other (higher-priority) real-time threads and interrupts.

The TargetRTS from ObjecTime uses a *controller* object to control a thread's execution. That is, each application thread has a controller object, and uses an underlying operating system thread to execute. The controller object is responsible for managing the message queues and implementing the message handling loop. In each iteration of the loop, it processes the current highest priority waiting message by invoking the behavior (Finite State Machine code) of the destination actor. The very nature of the message handling code ensures the run-to-completion semantics.

Our changes to the run-time system primarily consisted of (1) changing the threads implementation so that the threads are run in the real-time class with real-time priorities, and (2) changing the controller object implementation to dynamically adjust the priority of the underlying thread. There were a number of other minor changes made as well, such as increasing the number of priority levels, as well as instrumentation of the run-time system for timing purposes. We made minimal changes to the structure of the system such that ROOM models built with the ObjecTime toolset could be compiled with the modified run-time system.

4 Schedulability Analysis of ROOM Models

In this section we analyze ROOM model implementations and show how they may be subjected to schedulability analysis based on real-time scheduling theory [1, 5, 12]. Rather than develop a comprehensive schedulability analysis model, we just show how simple periodic tasks can be implemented and analyzed. The generalizations to the simple periodic task model take the same approach as has been done in the real-time scheduling literature.

---

[1] The TargetRTS provided by ObjecTime for Solaris does not use the real-time priorities.

[2] Threads in in ObjecTime are bound (to kernel threads) user-level threads. Such threads are termed light-weight processes in Solaris.

4.1 Implementing Periodic Activities

A ROOM model implemented using the ObjecTime toolset and using the `TargetRTS` consists of a single *TimerThread*, and one or more application threads (by default, there is a single MainThread which controls all actors). The TimerThread controls a *timer actor*, which implements the timing services provided by the ROOM virtual machine. The timer actor receives requests for timing services sent through timing SAPs, and manages the timers set up by actors. The TimerThread blocks for the length of the shortest timeout or until a new request is received. Upon return, it checks for expired timeouts, if any, and sends timeout messages (at the priority specified when the timer was set) to the appropriate destination actor.

Periodic activities can be implemented within any actor by setting a periodic timer through the timing service. The system then delivers a *timeout* message to the actor once every specified time period. Figure 1 shows the message flow for periodic timers. The figure on the left shows the normal message passing for periodic timers. For each periodic timeout, there are two messages: a *timeout* message sent from the timer actor, and an *informAt* message sent to the timer actor. Each *informAt* message contains the next timer expiry time, which is calculated based on the previous expiry time and the period of the timer. Before re-arming, a check is made for missed-timeouts (i.e., those timeouts whose expiry time has passed), and no messages are sent for the missed timeout intervals. A count of these missed timeouts can be requested by the application. The figure on the right shows the effect of a missed timeout.

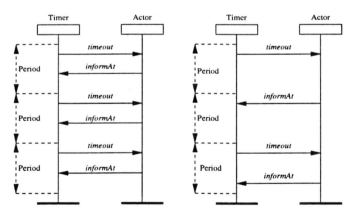

Figure 1. Message Sequence Chart(s) for Periodic Timers. The figure on left shows the normal behavior. The figure on right shows the effect of a delayed re-arming, which results in missed timeout messages.

4.2 Schedulability Analysis

In this section, we consider the timing and schedulability analysis for a set of periodic activities. We will assume that each periodic activity is implemented using a periodic timer on a separate actor. The state machine of such a periodic actor is trivial; it simply responds to the timeout messages. When the timeout message is delivered, the computation associated with the periodic activity is performed on a transition. We will further assume that the computation neither blocks nor sends a message to another actor. The basic model can easily be extended for more complex systems, as has been done in real-time scheduling theory literature [12, 5].

Let $\tau_1, \tau, \ldots, \tau_n$ be a set of periodic tasks as described above. Each task τ_i is characterized by its period T_i, and its computation time C_i. Further, let the priorities of the tasks be such that task τ_i has a higher priority than task τ_j, whenever $i < j$. Also, let Γ_i denote the thread to which a task τ_i is allocated. Then, if R_i denotes the worst-case response time for task τ_i, it can be calculated (ignoring all overheads, and assuming $R_i < T_i$) using the following equation [12].

$$R_i = \sum_{j<i} I^j(R_i) + C_i + B_i$$

where $I^j(R_i)$ represents the interference from higher priority task τ_j, and B_i represents the blocking time from lower priority tasks. Typically, through the use of priority inheritance protocols, the blocking time can be bounded. The interference from a higher priority task over a time window of W can be bounded by:

$$I^j(W) = \lceil \frac{W}{T_j} \rceil * C_j$$

Here, the first term represents the maximum number of instances of task τ_j that can arrive during an interval of length W.

The basic equations have to be modified to take into account (a) the overheads due to context switching, (b) the overheads of timeout processing, and (c) release jitter. Here we develop a simple extension of the model to take into account these factors. This model will then be used to predict response times. Figure 1 is useful to understand the additional overheads due to higher priority tasks. Recall that in our implementation, the timer actor runs in a separate TimerThread. Therefore, the message passing associated with timeouts involves inter-thread message sends, and context switches. Also, to minimize release jitter, we run the TimerThread at the highest priority, and all *informAt* messages are sent at the highest priority as well. The *timeout* messages, on the other hand, are sent at the priority requested by the application. Thus, in a simple periodic task model, each periodic actor can set up a timer with a priority equal to the task priority.

We define the following parameters to account for the implementation artifacts and overheads into our response time analysis. This is a relatively simple approximation to the overheads, but we have found that it works reasonably well in predicting response times.

- **Timeout Processing** ($C_{timeout}$): In this parameter, we lump in all the overhead associated with the processing of a timer expiry in the TimerThread. Most of this overhead is in the sending of the *timeout* message to the receiving thread, which involves accessing its message queues, as well as changing the thread's priority, if needed.

- **Re-arming Timer** (C_{rearm}): This is an even more coarse-grained parameter, and here we lump in the entire overhead of re-arming a timer. This overhead includes (a) the overhead of sending *informAt* message to the TimerThread, (b) a context switch overhead to the TimerThread, (c) the processing associated with the *informAt* message in the TimerThread, and finally (d) a context switch back to the task.

- **Context-Switch Time** (C_{cs}): This parameter is used to account for the context switch overheads.

- **Inter-Thread Message Send Time** (C_{send}): This parameter models the overheads associated with sending a message to another thread.

Interference from Higher Priority Tasks. For each higher priority task, there is an additional overhead of $C_{timeout} + C_{rearm}$, every time the timer expires for a higher priority task. In addition, we should also charge three additional context switches, one to the TimerThread, one from the TimerThread to the task, and finally another one when processing of the higher priority task is completed. Thus, the interference from higher priority tasks can be calculated as:

$$I^j(W) = \lceil \frac{W}{T_j} \rceil * (C_j + C_{timeout} + C_{rearm} + 3C_{cs})$$

Blocking Time from Lower Priority Tasks. There are several sources of blocking in this model. The first source of blocking comes from the run-to-completion semantics, which we will refer to as B_i^{RTC}, and which is given by the following equation.

$$B_i^{RTC} = \max C_j :: \Gamma_i = \Gamma_j$$

The next source of blocking comes from the processing of timer expiry for timers set for lower priority tasks. This is because, the timer expiry activates the Timer Thread, which

runs at the highest priority in the system. Thus, for each lower priority task, a blocking time of $C_{timeout} + 2C_{cs}$ must be added for each instance of the task that arrives within the response time interval. We do not need to take the re-arming of the timer into account, since the control must switch to the lower priority task for that to begin. We refer to this blocking as B_i^{TIMER}, and it is given by:

$$B_i^{TIMER}(W) = \sum_{j>i} \lceil \frac{W}{T_j} \rceil * C_{timeout} + 2C_{cs})$$

It is also possible that when the higher priority task is released, some low priority task is in the process of re-arming its expired timer. If the Timer thread is running, then this will delay the release of the task. We will refer to this as B_i^{REARM}, and this is bounded by the processing time associated with an *informAt* message.

Finally, there is also blocking possible due to access to shared message queues. The message queues of an actor (actually a controller) are accessed by other threads during an inter-thread send operation. Thus, a blocking is incurred if a task is activated when a lower priority task is sending a message to this thread. Using Immediate Priority Ceiling Inheritance Protocol [1], this blocking time can be bounded to the cost of one inter-thread send operation. We refer to this blocking time as: B_i^{MQ}.

In our implementation, we access shared message queues at the highest priority. This ensures that a higher priority task can be blocked by either the Timer re-arming or message queue access, but not both. Thus, the total blocking time experienced by a task is given by:

$$B_i(R_i) = B_i^{TIMER}(R_i) + B_i^{RTC} + \max(B_i^{MQ}, B_i^{REARM})$$

Response Time Calculation. Given the interference from higher priority tasks, and the blocking from lower priority tasks, it is simple to calculate the response time of a task. The computation time of a task must now include the additional overheads, and is given by:

$$C_i' = C_i + 3C_{cs} + C_{timeout} + C_{rearm}$$

Also, we must include the effect of clock release jitter (J_i), since the task's release may be delayed by the operating system due to the granularity of its system clock.

Then, the worst case response time of a task is given by the following equation (assuming $R_i < T_i$):

$$R_i(W) = \sum_{j<i} I^j(R_i) + C_i' + B_i(R_i) + J_i$$

4.3 Experimental Results

In order to validate the model, we implemented periodic models with N periodic tasks. Each periodic task was implemented as described above. We first estimated the parameters $C_{timeout}$, and C_{rearm}, and then used the estimated parameters to predict response times for tasks in a periodic task set. The predicted response times were then compared with the measured response times. Each periodic task executed a spinloop, as given below, with loopCount decided based on its desired execution time [4].

```
while (i < loopCount) { j = &i; i++; }
```

All our experiments were done on a Sun UltraSPARC-I, with a 167MHz clock, 128MB main memory, and running Solaris 2.5. Using measurements, it was estimated that 10.3 loops were required for each microsecond of execution time. For tasks of 10ms or higher execution time, this resulted in less than 1% difference in the actual measured times. All our timing was done using the `clock_gettime` call provided in Solaris (the same call is used in the `TargetRTS` for the timing services). The overhead for the `clock_gettime` call was measured to be between 652 and 759 nanoseconds. The clock's resolution (as provided by the `clock_getres` call) was 1 microsecond. Over a range of experiments, we found that the clock release jitter could be as high as 10 milliseconds. The values of the parameters were estimated as follows (all values are rounded up and expressed in microseconds).

$$C_{timeout} = 140, \quad C_{rearm} = 405, \quad C_{cs} = 135, \quad C_{send} = 110$$

Here, we present the results of only one of the periodic task sets for illustration purposes. This task set consisted of 5 tasks, with periods and execution times listed in Table 1. The table also shows the predicted and the measured worst case response times. A release time jitter of 10ms was used in the calculation of predicted response time, although in this particular run, the jitter was approximately 5.5 ms.

Task	C_i	T_i	$R_i(predicted)$	$R_i(measured)$
τ_1	5	50	17.455	11.727
τ_2	12	50	29.995	23.858
τ_3	15	100	45.535	39.277
τ_4	20	100	84.975	75.431
τ_5	35	200	195.215	181.516

Table 1. Predicted and Measured Response Times for a Set of Periodic Tasks

The table shows that the measured worst-case response times fall below the predicted response times, as desired. The numbers also reveal the conservative nature of the analysis, and the overestimation was found to be largely due to (a) overestimation of the clock release jitter, and (b) some of the overheads are overestimated, since when two tasks are to be released at roughly the same time, the full overheads of timeout processing are not applicable. This is because the TimerThread processes all expired timeouts when it wakes up. In any case, the timing results reveal that in this simple case of periodic activities, the implementation of the model is quite predictable. The case study in the next section shows that this temporal determinism is preserved even in large complex systems with many actors, complex state machines, and large number of events and state dependent event processing.

5 Train Tilting System: A Case Study

In this section, we show how the analysis technique developed above can be applied to a real-life system using the example of a train tilting system. The train tilting control system is typical of computerized control systems, and includes both *time-driven* and *event-driven* behavior. Much of the software complexity of the system is in the *reactive* aspects of the system, and includes behavior related to handling operator inputs, error and limit checking, detecting alarms and failures, and failure recovery procedures. The use of ROOM modeling language, along with the visual development environment of ObjecTime Developer toolset greatly helped in the development effort. On the other hand, the system has strict timing requirements as well, both for the nominal control loop behavior as well as for reacting to external events (especially those related to failure).

Our insight into train tilting systems has evolved through our work in software development automation for embedded control systems. A preliminary ROOM model was developed at CRIM as part of a project involving the evaluation of ROOM and ObjecTime for the software development of new generation embedded control systems, in collaboration with Bombardier's Transportation Equipment Group, North America's leading mass transit company. The train tilting system described here extends that preliminary model based on our vision of how such tilting technology is evolving, with an emphasis on additional functionality. As a result, this new model does not necessarily reflect Bombardier's current or planned technologies.

5.1 Train Tilting Systems

New-generation train tilting technology allows passenger trains to travel faster on conventional (non-banked) tracks, making medium-speed train service more competitive with airlines for passenger travel [6]. By physically tilting the body of the passenger cars during the curves, the permissible train speed in the curves may be increased without exceeding the maximum allowable transient and steady state lateral acceleration experienced by the passengers. Advanced tilting systems permit train speeds in excess of 240 km/h, a significant improvement over the conventional train speed limit of 160 km/h.

Such a medium-speed train typically consists of a non-tilting locomotive pulling from two to four tilting passenger cars. Each tilting car is mounted on two trucks, with each truck composed of two axles and four wheels with a primary and secondary suspension system. Local tilting control for each car is provided by a feedback control system using servo-valves and displacement transducers on the electro-hydraulic actuators. The master tilt controller, situated in the locomotive and connected to the closed-loop tilting controllers and monitoring equipment in each car, controls the operation of all the car tilting controllers. Inertial-based instruments, situated between the primary and secondary suspension systems on the lead truck of the locomotive, provide curve-sensing data at periodic intervals. The master tilt controller calculates the tilt angles for each of the cars in the train. By placing the curve sensing subsystem on the lead truck of the locomotive, the master tilting controller has 300 milliseconds lead-time to process sensor data and calculate the tilt setpoint for the first passenger car (based on the typical locomotive length of 20 m and a train speed of 240 km/h). Each following passenger car will tilt 375 milliseconds later than the preceding one (based on the typical car length of 25 m).

The train operating environment is particularly harsh due to vibration, extreme operating temperature ranges, contamination from dirt, snow and ice, and infrequent maintenance intervals. Inertial-based sensor data is accurate but noisy. Curve data is over-sampled to allow for data filtering and rejection of erroneous measurements. Sensor, actuator and communications failures are possible; Fault-tolerance is achieved by replication of critical components and self-diagnosis at the locomotive, car and train level. On actuator failure in any car, tilting is automatically deactivated and all cars are returned to the upright position and mechanically locked in place. Robustness is achieved by self-calibration of sensors and self-test routines. The tilting master controller continually receives equipment status information via the onboard network. The train speed must be immediately reduced to the slower non-tilting speed limit in the event of a failure in any part of the tilting system.

5.2 Tilting System ROOM Model

Figure 2 shows the top-level structural view of our ROOM model of the train tilting system. The model includes actors for various sensors: one for the inertial sensor (TiltingMasterSensor) and one for speed (TrainSpeedSensor). The TiltingMasterSensor includes a CurveDataProcessor actor (not shown in the figure) for statistical filtering of the sensor data. There are actors representing the 3 passenger cars (TiltingCarControllers). The TiltingLocoConsole actor is used for operator console and display functions. It

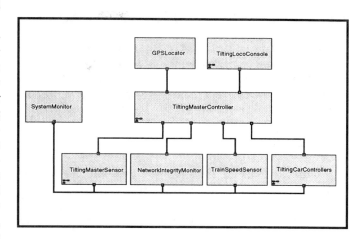

Figure 2. Top Level Structural View of the Train Tilting System

includes a DisplayProcessor actor (not shown in the figure) for processing and rendering graphical data on the console. Also, a communications network monitor (NetworkIntegrityMonitor) is used for monitoring the integrity of the network. A position reference system (GPSLocator) incorporating a Global Positioning System (GPS) receiver provides a secondary means of curve detection and allows predictive control, independent of the inertial sensing system, by locating the train's actual position on a predefined map of the train route. A train-wide system monitor (SystemMonitor) collects event logs and status information for all system components, which is used for predictive maintenance purposes. The TiltingMasterController (TMC) is the master tilting controller with interfaces to all other components. It is a hierarchical actor, and consists of two component actors, a TiltingDataProcessor (TDP) and a ModelBasedController (MBC) actor. The TiltingDataProcessor computes tilt commands based on the current speed, the inertial curve data, and the predictive curve data from the GPS system. The ModelBasedController actor takes these tilt commands and modulates them based on a model of the actuation system (feed-forward control).

The TMC behaviour is principally reactive, and consists of four principal modes of operation: Stop, Startup, Run and Fault. The controller enters the Stop state upon initialization, and it will remain in the Stop position until a START command is issued from the operator console (the TiltingLocoConsole). A START command will cause a transition to the Start-up mode, following which transitions will occur to either the Run or Fault state according to events originating in the external environment. At any time, a STOP command from the operator console will cause the TMC to return to the Stop state. A STOP command is required to recover from the Fault state.

Due to space constraints, it is impossible to give complete details of the system behavior. Instead, we focus on the behavior of the system in the nominal (RUN) state, focusing on the time-critical event sequences. These are described in the next section.

5.3 Event sequences

In the RUN mode, there are several event sequences of interest. We classify the time-critical event-sequences into two categories: (1) those that are responsible for monitoring correct operation of the system, and (2) those that constitute the main "data processing" part of the system.

5.3.1 Monitoring Event Sequences

The monitoring event sequences monitor the state of the devices and operator input. In case of failure, and/or operator command to stop the system, a quick response is needed for these event sequences to shut down the system. In the current model, we have three such monitoring event-sequences.

Onboard Network Integrity Monitoring: The onboard communications network integrity is monitored at 50 millisecond intervals by requesting a reply from the network interfaces on each passenger car. If no reply is received on any one of the interfaces, a message is sent to the Tilting-MasterController. The TMC transitions to the Fault mode, disabling the tilting system, and sends a message to the OperatorDisplay in the TiltingLocoConsole.

Car Tilting Control System Status Monitoring: The car tilting control system status (including hydraulic system temperature, level and pressure and actuator displacement, and preventative maintenance information) is sent at 100 millisecond intervals to the TiltingMasterController. In the event of a fault or critical failure, the TMC transitions to the Fault mode, disabling the tilting system, and sends a message to the OperatorDisplay in the TiltingLocoConsole.

Operator Input Monitoring: The Operator input is polled once every 100 milliseconds, and any operator command is dispatched to the TiltingMasterController.

5.3.2 Data Processing Event Sequences.

The data processing event sequences constitute the main control loop functions. The control loop behavior results in sending tilt commands to the TiltingCarControllers. The tilt commands are computed based on the curve sensor values, the current speed of the train, and the predicted track curvature using the GPS position reference system. The main control loop is driven by the sampling of the curve sensor values, while the GPS and speed update are carried out asynchronously.

Curve Sensor Update: The curve sensor update event sequence constitutes the primary control loop function in the system. The event sequence is triggered by the sampling of the curve sensor values in the TiltingMasterSensor (TMS) every 50ms. The sampled values are sent to the CurveDataProcessor (CDP), grouped in a sensor data frame, which uses statistical averaging over a 5-second sliding window. We refer to this part of the event sequence as the *Curve Data Filtering* event sequence. A message sequence chart depicting the message flow for this event sequence is given in Figure 3.

The sensor is twice over-sampled to allow for rejection of one incomplete or out-of-range sensor data frame. Thus, every second filtered sensor frame (i.e., once every 100ms) is sent to the TiltingDataProcessor (TDP), which combines the TMS sensor data with the GPS location information (which is updated once per second) and the train speed (updated at 100 millisecond intervals) to calculate the new tilting setpoints for each of the passenger cars. The new tilt setpoints are then modulated by the ModelBasedController (MBC) and sent to the TiltingMasterController (TMC). The TMC formats the control value from the MBC with other control information and sends it to the individual TiltingCarControllers over the onboard network. The TCC's update their local closed-loop control setpoint based on the value received. We refer to this part of the event sequence as the *Update Tilt Angles* event-sequence.

Finally, the event sequence also includes an update of the tilt commands being sent to the TiltingLocoConsole for operator display, where a display processor actor is responsible for graphical rendering of the data on the operator's console. This part of the event sequence is referred to as the *Display Update* event-sequence.

Train Speed Sensor Update: The train speed is sampled at 100 millisecond intervals and is sent to the master tilting controller to determine the desired tilting angle and the time delay between tilting commands for each of the passenger cars. The TrainSpeedSensor samples the speed on expiry of a timer and a message containing the speed value with warning and error flags is sent to the TiltingDataProcessor. The speed sensor sets the warning flag on intermittent errors and the previous reading is resent. The speed sensor sets the error flag on repeated errors and will cause the tilting controller to disable the tilting system. In the model, the train speed is read from a data file and the timing service provides the timer expiry event.

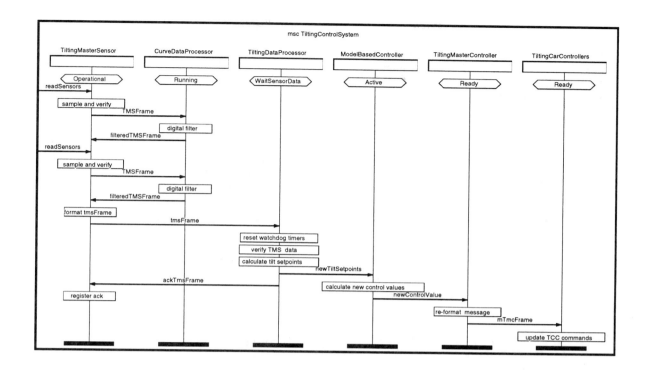

Figure 3. Message Sequence Chart for the Curve Sensor Update Event Sequence

GPS Position Reference Update: The GPS position reference system provides a secondary curve input to the tilting system, independent of the noise-prone inertial sensor, which is used to predict the required tilting angle based on a predefined database of the train route). The GPSLocator receives a position reference update at 1 second intervals from a stand-alone GPS receiver. A message containing the train position and predicted track curvature (determined from a predefined database of the train route) is sent to the TiltingMasterController. The tiltingMasterController forwards the message to the TiltingDataProcessor (where it is used to determine the tilting angle) and to the TiltingLocoConsole which forwards it to the OperatorDisplay. In the model, the behaviour is triggered by a timeout from the timing service.

5.4 Experimental Results

We conducted our experimental results with this model using curve sensor data recorded over an actual section of track between Montreal and Kingston to drive the model. This resulted in a run of approximately 100 seconds. Many of the new functionalities in the model (e.g., the GPS system, the Model Based Controller, and the Curve Data Processor) and some of the old functionality in the model had dummy code, using spin loops as used in Section 4.

Table 2 shows the assignment of priorities to the event sequences. All the monitoring event sequences were given a high priority (2) since any of them may result in stopping

the control loop behavior by moving the system from RUN mode to STOP or FAULT mode. A tight response time is required in such cases. The other priorities are assigned according to the time period of the event sequence. The Display Update portion of the Curve Sensor Update event sequence is given a lower priority since this is a soft real-time task. All other events in the system were given lower priorities. Priority 1 was used for the TimerThread; this ensured that it ran whenever it was made ready.

For threads assignment, the CurveDataProcessor, GPSLocator, DisplayProcessor, and the ModelBasedController actors were each placed in separate threads, since they contained code segments with large execution times (15 ms or more). All other actors were put in one thread.

Table 2 presents the minimum, maximum, and average of the measured response times. Due to the difficulty of measuring exact execution times, we have not calculated the predicted response times. Instead, we show the approximate execution times associated with the event-sequences to give the reader an idea of expected response times. We find that, by and large, the response times are quite predictable, and as one would expect. There are a few anomalous cases, where the maximum response time for some of the high priority event sequences is significantly more than the average. A detailed examination of the timing trace revealed that this was a combination of (a) clock jitter, and (b) run-to-completion blocking due to the background system mon-

Event Sequence	Priority	T	C	R^{min}	R^{max}	$R^{average}$
Onboard Network Integrity Monitoring	2	50	1	2.723	18.837	3.938
Car Tilting Control System Status Monitoring	2	500	1	1.844	2.440	3.047
Operator Input Monitoring	2	100	1	2.267	5.463	2.984
Curve Sensor Update						
Curve Data Filtering	3	50	16	18.413	34.537	19.664
Update Tilt Angles	4	100	22	40.166	73.990	42.177
Display Update	7	100	25	83.295	246.207	114.265
Train Speed Sensor Update	5	100	1	19.791	24.510	20.528
GPS Position Reference Update	6	1000	51	126.506	131.541	127.257

Table 2. Event Sequences for the Train Tilting System

itoring tasks. This resulted in a net additional delay of about 15 ms, and happened only occasionally. Overall we find that the execution of the model was quite predictable, and this was revealed by hand-inspection of the detailed timing traces.

We also tested the case when the system is moved to a FAULT state due to faults in the network (detected by NetworkIntegrityMonitor) and the cars (detected by Tilting-CarController), and found that due to the high priority of the events they were processed promptly and the shutdown message was received by the Tilting Car Controllers within 5-10 ms.

6 Concluding Remarks

We have presented our experience with the application of schedulability analysis to automated implementation of ROOM models. The work builds on our previous paper [8] which presented some guidelines on how priority inversions can be avoided to make schedulability analysis feasible. In this paper, we presented experimental evidence that it is indeed possible to make the temporal behavior of automated implementations of ROOM models sufficiently predictable so that a priori timing and schedulability analysis can be performed.

While our work was done in the context of a specific modeling language (ROOM) and its commercial toolset (Objec-Time Developer), the results are widely applicable. This is partly because of the standardization of the Unified Modeling Language (UML), and the fact that ROOM concepts are compatible with Real-Time UML. Moreover, other industry leaders in such tools (e.g., iLogix and Verlog) have products featuring similar modeling capabilities and code generation facilities.

We hope that the results of this work will lead to an integration of the divergent styles of real-time software development, such that in the future real-time software development can benefit from the strengths of both the event-driven and the time-driven styles through integrated toolsets which pro-

vide rich modeling capabilities on one hand, and timing and schedulability analysis tools on the other. In the future, we also hope to release the train tilting system model as a benchmark for other researchers.

References

[1] A. Burns and A. Wellings. *Real-time Systems: Specification, Verification and Analysis*, chapter Advanced Fixed Priority Scheduling, pages 32–65. Prentice Hall, 1996.

[2] P. Freedman. Investigating the suitability of objectime for the software development of embedded control systems. In *Proceedings, ObjecTime Worksop on Research in Real-Time Object-Oriented Modeling*, January 1998.

[3] D. Harel. Statecharts: A visual approach to complex systems. *Science of Computer Programming*, 1987.

[4] D. Katcher, H. Arakawa, and J. Strosnider. Engineering and Analysis of Fixed Priority Schedulers. *IEEE Transactions on Software Engineering*, 19(9), September 1993.

[5] M. H. Klein, T. Ralya, B. Pollak, R. Obenza, and M. G. Harbour. *A Practitioner's Handbook for Real-Time Analysis*. Kluwer Academic Publishers, 1993.

[6] D. Lanoix. Bombardier's New Generation Tilting System. *IEEE Canadian Review*, Spring/Summer 1995.

[7] ObjecTime Limited. ObjecTime TargetRTS Guide. ObjecTime Limited, Kanata, Canada.

[8] M. Saksena, P. Freedman, and P. Rodziewicz. Guidelines for Automated Implementation of Executable Object Oriented Models for Real-Time Embedded Contol Systems. In *Proceedings, IEEE Real-Time Systems Symposium*, 1997.

[9] B. Selic, G. Gullekson, and P. T. Ward. *Real-Time Object-Oriented Modeling*. John Wiley and Sons, 1994.

[10] B. Selic and J. Rumbaugh. Using UML for Modeling Complex Real-Time Systems. White Paper, Published by Objec-Time, and available from www.objectime.com, March 1998.

[11] B. Selic and P. Ward. The challenges of real-time software design. *Embedded Systems Programming*, pages 66–82, October 1996.

[12] K. Tindell, A. Burns, and A. Wellings. An extendible approach for analysing fixed priority hard real-time tasks. *The Journal of Real-Time Systems*, 6(2):133–152, Mar. 1994.

Session 4.A: Scheduling and Analysis I

A Better Polynomial-Time Schedulability Test for Real-Time Multiframe Tasks

Ching-Chih Jason Han
BroadVision, Inc.
585 Broadway
Redwood City, CA 94063
cchan@broadvision.com

Abstract

The well-known real-time periodic task model first studied by Liu and Layland [11] assumes that each task τ has a worst-case computation time C and each execution (instance) of the task takes no more than C time units. Based on the worst-case computation time assumption, Liu and Layland derived a utilization bound under which all task sets are schedulable by the fixed-priority scheduling scheme. The assumption and the derived utilization bound are, however, too pessimistic when the average computation times of the tasks are smaller than their worst-case computation times. To improve the schedulability test for such kind of task sets, Mok and Chen proposed a multiframe task model [12, 13] for characterizing real-time tasks whose computation times vary instance by instance. They also derived an improved utilization bound for multiframe task sets.

Although Mok and Chen's utilization bound is better than Liu and Layland's bound, it is still too pessimistic in the sense that a lot of feasible task sets may not be found schedulable using their utilization bound.

In [4], we proposed a new, better polynomial-time schedulability test for periodic task model. We found that similar technique can be applied to multiframe task model. In this paper, we discuss how the previously-proposed schedulability test can be modified for multiframe task model. We also show that our schedulability test is much better than using Mok and Chen's utilization bound by giving theoretical reasoning and presenting thorough performance evaluation results.

1. Introduction

In the well-known real-time periodic task model [1, 6, 8–11], each task τ is characterized by three parameters (C, T, ϕ), where C is the worst-case computation time, T the period, and ϕ the *release time* (the phasing relative to time 0) of task τ. Although this model is reasonable for tasks whose actual computation times do not change significantly instance by instance, it is too pessimistic for applications in which tasks' average computation times are smaller than their worst-case computation times. One of such kind of applications is the transmission of MPEG-coded video frames. In MPEG coding standard, there are three kinds of video frames: I-frame, P-frame, and B-frame. The maximum size of I-frames is usually much larger than those of P- and B-frames, and all the frames follow a fixed pattern, such as "IBBPBBPBBIBBP···". For this kind of applications, it will be too conservative if we use the maximum size of all the frames to compute the worst-case transmission time for all frames.

To further illustrate this point, consider a real-time task set $\mathcal{T} = \{\tau_1, \tau_2\}$. Suppose τ_1 has a release time 0 and a period 3 time units, and takes time no more than 2 time units for the first, third, fifth, ... executions and no more than 1 time unit for all the other executions. Also, suppose τ_2 has a release time 0 and a period 5 time units, and takes time no more than 2 time units for all the executions. Using Liu and Layland's periodic task model, we have $\mathcal{T} = \{\tau_i = (C_i, T_i, \phi_i) \mid i = 1, 2\} = \{(2,3,0), (2,5,0)\}$ since τ_1's worst-case computation time is 2. It it easy to see that $\mathcal{T}$ will not be found schedulable using periodic task model (note that $2/3 + 2/5 > 1$) even though it is indeed schedulable. However, if we take into account the fact that τ_1's worst-case computation time varies from one instance to another we may be able to use some other better schedulability tests to find out the feasibility of $\mathcal{T}$.

To remedy this drawback of periodic task model, Mok and Chen proposed the following *multiframe* task model in [12, 13].

Definition 1 A real-time multiframe task τ is a 3-tuple (Γ, T, ϕ), where Γ is a vector of N computation times $(C^0, C^1, \ldots, C^{N-1})$ for some $N \geq 1$, T is the period, and ϕ is the release time of task τ. The j-th execution/instance of task τ takes time no more than $C^{((j-1) \bmod N)}$ time units. □

Using Mok and Chen's multiframe task model, the aforementioned example is denoted as $\mathcal{T} = \{\tau_i = (\Gamma_i, T_i, \phi_i) \mid i = 1, 2\} = \{((2, 1), 3, 0), ((2), 5, 0)\}$.

Mok and Chen also derived a utilization bound for multiframe task sets. However, their bound is still too pessimistic. For example, their utilization bound is never larger than 1, but under multiframe task model a lot of task sets with *peak utilization* (to be formally defined later) larger than 1 are still schedulable. (Note that the aforementioned example has a peak utilization $2/3 + 2/5 > 1$ and is schedulable, but will not be found feasible using Mok and Chen's utilization bound.) This implies that Mok and Chen's utilization bound, although is an improvement over the well-known utilization bound derived for the periodic task model, in most cases, will not help us to find out the schedulability of a feasible task set.

In this paper, we study the schedulability analysis for multiframe task model under *fixed-priority* scheduling scheme[1] and propose a better schedulability test that can be done in polynomial time for a set of multiframe tasks. We show that a lot of feasible multiframe task sets, especially those with peak utilization larger than 1, cannot be found feasible by using Mok and Chen's utilization bound but can be found feasible using our schedulability test. Extensive performance evaluation has also been conducted and the results are presented in this paper.

The remainder of the paper is organized as follows. In Section 2, we briefly summarize the previously-known results for periodic and multiframe tasks. In Section 3, we prove our main result that given a multiframe task set $\mathcal{T}$ if there exists another task set $\mathcal{T}'$ which satisfies a certain condition and is schedulable, then the original task set $\mathcal{T}$ is also schedulable. In Section 4, we present two polynomial-time algorithms for finding such a task set $\mathcal{T}'$. In Section 5, we present our performance evaluation results, which show that a lot of task sets that are schedulable but do not pass the schedulability test using Mok and Chen's utilization bound can pass our schedulability test. The paper concludes with Section 6.

2. Background

We consider a set of n real-time multiframe tasks $\mathcal{T} = \{\tau_1, \tau_2, \ldots, \tau_n\}$. Each instance/execution of a multiframe task is called a *job*. The j-th job τ_{ij} of the i-th task τ_i has a worst-case computation time $C_i^{((j-1) \bmod N_i)}$. τ_{ij} is ready for execution at its *ready (request)* time $r_{ij} = \phi_i + (j - 1) \cdot T_i$ and must be completed before its deadline $d_{ij} = \phi_i + j \cdot T_i$, where $\phi_i, 0 \leq \phi_i < T_i$, is the *release time* (phasing relative to 0) of τ_i. Moreover, we assume that tasks (jobs) are *preemptable*, i.e., the execution of a job can be

preempted by any job of higher priority. However, tasks (jobs) do not suspend themselves before their completion. It is easy to see that the traditional periodic task model is a special case of the multiframe task model with $N_i = 1$ for all i. Therefore, any results derived for multiframe task model in this paper as well as in [12, 13] can also be applied to periodic task model.

For ease of discussion, Mok and Chen first defined a special case of multiframe task sets [12], called *accumulatively monotonic (AM)*, and concentrated on the schedulability analysis of AM task sets.

Definition 2 A vector of computation times $\Gamma_i = (C_i^0, C_i^1, \ldots, C_i^{N_i-1})$ is said to be *accumulatively monotonic (AM)* if there exists an $m_i \in \{0, 1, \ldots, N_i - 1\}$ such that for all $k, l \in \{0, 1, \ldots, N_i-1\}$, $\sum_{j=m_i}^{m_i+k} C_i^{(j \bmod N_i)} \geq \sum_{j=l}^{l+k} C_i^{(j \bmod N_i)}$. A multiframe task τ_i is said to be AM if its vector of computation times is AM. The frame that has the largest worst-case computation time $C_i^{m_i}$ is called the *peak frame* of τ_i. Also, a task set is said to be AM if all of its tasks are AM. $\square$

In the following discussion, unless otherwise specified, we assume that all multiframe tasks are AM. Note that the MPEG video frame transmission application mentioned in Section 1 is a good example of AM multiframe task sets.

Mok and Chen later generalized their results for a more general case [13] of multiframe task sets by presenting a technique for transforming a more general multiframe task set into an AM task set [13]. Their transformation is also valid in the context of this paper. However, due to the space limitation, the validity of their transformation for our results will be omitted from this paper and will be reported in a full paper.

Given a set of (periodic/multiframe) tasks and a scheduling algorithm, the *response time* of a job of a certain task is defined to be the time span between the request time and the completion time of the job. Liu and Layland [11] defined a *critical instant* of a task to be a time instant at which a job for that task will have the largest response time. We will also call a job of a certain task requested at a critical instant of the task a *critical instance* of the task. From the definition of critical instance, it is easy to see that if a critical instance of a task meets its deadline, then all jobs (instances) of the task will meet their corresponding deadlines.

Liu and Layland proved a theorem (Theorem 1 in [11]) that given a set of periodic tasks and a fixed-priority scheduling algorithm, a critical instant of any task occurs whenever the task is requested simultaneously with the requests of all higher priority tasks. Mok and Chen generalized this theorem and showed that given a set of (AM) multiframe tasks and a fixed-priority scheduling algorithm, a critical instant of any task occurs whenever the task's peak frame is requested simultaneously with the requests

---

[1] A fixed-priority scheduling scheme assigns a fixed priority to each task before run-time. During run-time the task with the highest priority among all ready tasks will execute at any time.

of the peak frames of all higher priority tasks. A corollary of the theorem is that a worst-case phasing occurs when $\phi_1 + m_1 \cdot T_1 = \phi_2 + m_2 \cdot T_2 = \cdots = \phi_n + m_n \cdot T_n$. Therefore, without loss of generality, in the following discussion we assume that $m_i = 0$ (i.e., the first frame of each task is a peak frame for that task) and $\phi_i = 0$ for all i. We will then drop ϕ_i from the parameter list of task τ_i.

Liu and Layland [11] and Mok and Chen [12, 13] showed that the *rate-monotonic* (RM) algorithm is optimal for fixed-priority scheduling scheme for periodic and multiframe tasks, respectively. The RM algorithm assigns priorities to tasks according to their periods. Tasks with shorter periods get higher priorities. Since the periods of tasks are fixed, their priorities are also fixed.

For periodic task sets, Liu and Layland further defined C_i/T_i to be the *utilization (factor)* of task τ_i and $U(\mathcal{T}) = \sum_{i=1}^{n} C_i/T_i$ the *total utilization* of task set $\mathcal{T}$, and showed that the least upper bound for a task set to be feasibly scheduled by the RM algorithm is $L(n) = n(2^{1/n} - 1)$, i.e., if $U(\mathcal{T}) \leq L(n)$ then the task set is guaranteed to be schedulable by the RM algorithm.

Mok and Chen defined the following notation

$$\gamma_i = \begin{cases} C_i^0/C_i^1 & \text{if } N_i > 1 \\ 1 & \text{otherwise} \end{cases} \tag{1}$$

for all i and $\gamma = \min_{i=1}^{n} \gamma_i$, and generalized Liu and Layland's result to multiframe task set that if $U^m(\mathcal{T}) = \sum_{i=1}^{n} C_i^0/T_i \leq M(n,\gamma) = \gamma \cdot n((\frac{\gamma+1}{\gamma})^{1/n} - 1)$ then the multiframe task set $\mathcal{T}$ is guaranteed to be schedulable by RM, where $U^m(\mathcal{T})$ is called the *peak utilization* of task set $\mathcal{T}$.

It is easy to see that Mok and Chen's bound $M(n,\gamma)$ subsumes Liu and Layland's bound $L(n)$ (when $\gamma = 1$ the two bounds are the same). Note, however, that if the peak utilization $U^m(\mathcal{T})$ of $\mathcal{T}$ is larger than $M(n,\gamma)$, it is still not known whether or not the task set $\mathcal{T}$ can be feasibly scheduled by RM. In fact, a lot of task sets with peak (total) utilizations larger than $M(n,\gamma)$ ($L(n)$) are schedulable by RM. In other words, this bound $M(n,\gamma)$ as well as Liu and Layland's bound $L(n)$ is too pessimistic since it only characterizes the worst-case situation. This situation is more significant in multiframe task model than in periodic task model since a lot of multiframe task sets with peak utilizations larger than 1 are still schedulable by RM but $M(n,\gamma)$ is never larger than 1 ($M(n,\gamma) \to 1$ when $n \to \infty$ and $\gamma \to \infty$). As a result, Mok and Chen's utilization bound $M(n,\gamma)$ is only of theoretical interest but does not give us much help in most cases.

Joseph and Pandya [5] and Lehoczky *et al.* [6] studied the exact characteristics of fixed-priority scheduling scheme and derived a necessary and sufficient condition for a set of periodic tasks to be schedulable by a fixed-priority scheduling algorithm. Their results are briefly summarized in the following.

Let $\mathcal{T} = \{\tau_i = (C_i, T_i) \mid 1 \leq i \leq n\}$ be a set of periodic tasks to be scheduled by a fixed-priority scheduling algorithm. Assume that the tasks are indexed in such a way that τ_i has a higher priority than τ_j if $i < j$. Consider a task $\tau_k, 1 \leq k \leq n$. The cumulative processing demand by task $\tau_i, 1 \leq i \leq k$, during the time interval $[0, t]$ is

$$W_k(t) = \sum_{i=1}^{k} C_i \lceil \frac{t}{T_i} \rceil.$$

According to Liu and Layland's result, if the first job (critical instance) of task τ_k meets its deadline, then all of the jobs of τ_k will meet their corresponding deadlines. The first job of τ_k will meet its deadline if and only if there exists a time instant t such that $0 \leq t \leq T_k$ and $W_k(t) \leq t$, i.e.,

$$\min_{0 \leq t \leq T_k} \sum_{i=1}^{k} C_i \lceil \frac{t}{T_i} \rceil \leq t. \tag{2}$$

To test the above inequality for each k, $1 \leq k \leq n$, only a finite number of time instants need to be checked. Lehoczky *et al.* [6] showed that only the time instants in the set $\{j \cdot T_i \mid i = 1, 2, \ldots, k; j = 1, 2, \ldots, \lfloor \frac{T_k}{T_i} \rfloor\}$ need to be checked. Joseph and Pandya [5] showed that only the sequence of time instants, $t_0, t_1, \ldots$, where $t_0 = \sum_{i=1}^{k} C_i$, and $t_j = W_k(t_{j-1})$, for all $j \geq 1$ need to be checked until either $t_\ell = t_{\ell+1} \leq T_i$ or $t_\ell \geq T_i$, for some ℓ. The former case means that t_ℓ is the completion time of the first job of τ_k, and the latter case means that the first job of τ_k cannot meet its deadline.

Although the above schedulability condition is a necessary and sufficient condition for testing the schedulability of a periodic task set under any fixed-priority scheduling algorithm and can be easily generalized for testing multiframe task sets, its pseudo-polynomial time[2] complexity [14, 15] restricts its practical use.

In [4], we proposed a new schedulability test for periodic task sets which is proven to be better than Liu and Layland's utilization bound $L(n)$ and can be done in polynomial time. Specifically, we first proved that given a periodic task set $\mathcal{T} = \{(C_i, T_i) \mid 1 \leq i \leq n\}$, if there exists another task set $\mathcal{T}' = \{(C_i' = C_i, T_i') \mid 1 \leq i \leq n\}$ with a total utilization $U(\mathcal{T}') \leq 1$ which also satisfies the following condition:

Condition A $T_i' \leq T_i$ for all $i = 1, 2, \ldots, n$, and T_i' evenly divides T_{i+1}', denoted as $T_i' \mid T_j'$, (thus, $T_i' \leq T_{i+1}'$) for all $i = 1, 2, \ldots, n-1$,   □

then the task set $\mathcal{T}$ is schedulable by RM. We then presented two polynomial-time algorithms that, given a task set $\mathcal{T}$, find another task set $\mathcal{T}'$ satisfying Condition A.

---

[2]For the definition of pseudo-polynomial time, please refer to [2].

We found that similar technique can be applied to multiframe tasks as well. In what follows we discuss how to modify our polynomial-time schedulability test originally proposed for periodic tasks to multiframe tasks and discuss its performance by giving thorough simulation results. Note that the modification is nontrivial, especially for the period transformation algorithms and the proofs of the validity of the schedulability test.

3. Main result

Since we consider only fixed-priority scheduling algorithms in this paper, in the following discussion, unless otherwise specified we assume that the tasks in a task set $\mathcal{T} = \{\tau_i = (\Gamma_i, T_i) \mid 1 \leq i \leq n\}$ are indexed in such a way that if $i < j$ than τ_i has a higher priority than τ_j. Therefore, if we say that a task set $\mathcal{T} = \{\tau_i = (\Gamma_i, T_i) \mid 1 \leq i \leq n\}$ is to be scheduled by the RM algorithm, it implies that $T_1 \leq T_2 \leq \cdots \leq T_n$. In other words, $\mathcal{T}$ specifies not only the task set itself but also the fixed-priority scheduling algorithm to be used to schedule the task set.

As mentioned earlier, it has been proven in [13] that if a multiframe task set can be feasibly scheduled by any fixed-priority scheduling algorithm it can also be feasibly scheduled by the RM algorithm, i.e., RM is optimal for scheduling multiframe task sets. Therefore, in the following discussion, we consider only the RM algorithm (and hence, $T_1 \leq T_2 \leq \cdots \leq T_n$).

Let $\mathcal{T} = \{\tau_i = (\Gamma_i, T_i) \mid 1 \leq i \leq n\}$ be an AM task set and $\mathcal{T}' = \{\tau_i' = (\Gamma_i', T_i') \mid 1 \leq i \leq n\}$ be another task set such that $\Gamma_i' = \Gamma_i$ for all i and Condition A (see Section 2) holds. Since $T_i' \mid T_j'$ for all $i < j$, $\mathcal{T}'$ is a *harmonic* task set. (Note that since $\Gamma_i' = \Gamma_i$ for all i, $\mathcal{T}'$ also satisfies the AM property.) It is well-known that a harmonic periodic task set with total utilization less than or equal to one can be feasibly scheduled by the RM algorithm [7]. A similar result can also be derived for harmonic multiframe task set (which satisfies the AM property). Theorem 1 states this generalization.

Before proving the correctness of Theorem 1, we first give the following lemma, which is an easy generalization of the necessary and sufficient schedulability condition summarized in Section 2 (see Eq. (2)).

Lemma 1 Given a multiframe task set, $\mathcal{T} = \{\tau_i = (\Gamma_i, T_i) \mid 1 \leq i \leq n\}$, which satisfies the AM property, if there exists a time instant t_k such that $0 \leq t_k \leq T_k$ and

$$W_k(t_k) = \sum_{i=1}^{k} \sum_{j=1}^{\lceil \frac{t_k}{T_i} \rceil} C_i^{((j-1) \bmod N_i)} \leq t_k,$$

for all $1 \leq k \leq n$, then $\mathcal{T}$ is schedulable by RM.

Proof: Note that the cumulative processing demand by task τ_i, $1 \leq i \leq k$, during the time interval $[0, t_k]$ is $W_k(t_k)$. According to Mok and Chen's result, if the peak frame (i.e., the first job) of task τ_k meets its deadline, then all of the jobs of τ_k will meet their corresponding deadlines. The first job of τ_k will meet its deadline if and only if there exists a time instant t_k such that $0 \leq t_k \leq T_k$ and $W_k(t_k) \leq t_k$. The lemma thus follows directly from Mok and Chen's result. $\square$

Theorem 1 Given a harmonic multiframe task set, $\mathcal{T} = \{\tau_i = (\Gamma_i, T_i) \mid 1 \leq i \leq n\}$, which satisfies the AM property, if for all $1 \leq k \leq n$

$$W_k(T_k) = \sum_{i=1}^{k} \sum_{j=1}^{\frac{T_k}{T_i}} C_i^{((j-1) \bmod N_i)} \leq T_k, \qquad (3)$$

then $\mathcal{T}$ is schedulable by RM.

Proof: Since $T_i \mid T_j$ for all $i \leq j$, the first job of τ_k will meet its deadline if and only if $W_k(T_k) \leq T_k$. The theorem thus follows from Lemma 1. $\square$

Using the above theorem we can test whether or not a harmonic AM task set is schedulable by RM in polynomial time. Specifically, we have the following theorem.

Theorem 2 Using Theorem 1, the schedulability of a harmonic AM task set can be checked in $O(n(n+\max_{i=1}^n N_i))$ time.

Proof: In Eq. (3), if we let $\frac{T_k}{T_i} = q \cdot N_i + r$, for some integers q and r, $0 \leq r < N_i$, we have $\sum_{j=1}^{\frac{T_k}{T_i}} C_i^{((j-1) \bmod N_i)} = q \cdot \sum_{j=0}^{N_i-1} C_i^j + \sum_{j=0}^{r-1} C_i^j$. It takes $O(N_i)$ time to compute all the prefix sums, $\sum_{x=0}^{y} C_i^x$, $0 \leq y \leq N_i - 1$, of vector Γ_i. After all the prefix sums of Γ_l, $1 \leq l \leq n$, have been computed, it takes $O(k)$ time to check whether or not τ_k can meet its deadline. Therefore, to check if the task set is schedulable takes time $O(n^2 + \sum_{i=1}^{n} N_i) \leq O(n(n + \max_{i=1}^n N_i))$. $\square$

Note that with carefully designed data structures and algorithms, the above time complexity can be further reduced. However, the reduction of the time complexity is beyond the scope of this paper since our major intent in this paper is to show that the proposed schedulability test can be done in polynomial time.[3]

With the above two theorems, we can now present our main theorem:

Theorem 3 Given an AM task set $\mathcal{T} = \{(\Gamma_i, T_i) \mid 1 \leq i \leq n\}$, if there exists another task set $\mathcal{T}' = \{(\Gamma_i' = \Gamma_i, T_i') \mid 1 \leq i \leq n\}$ which satisfies Condition A and $\mathcal{T}'$ is schedulable by RM, then so is $\mathcal{T}$. $\square$

Note, however, that the converse may not be true, i.e., the feasibility of $\mathcal{T}$ under RM does not imply that there

---

[3] The same claim also applies to Theorems 5 and 7.

exists a task set $\mathcal{T}'$ which satisfies Condition A and $\mathcal{T}'$ is schedulable by RM. For example, the task set $\{((1,1,1,0.5),2),((1,1,0.5),3),((1,0.5),6)\}$ is schedulable by RM, but no task set satisfying Condition A is schedulable by RM.

To prove the above theorem, we actually establish a more general theorem (Theorem 4). First, we need the following lemma.

Lemma 2 Given two multiframe task sets $\mathcal{T}$ and $\mathcal{T}'$ with $T_i' \leq T_i$ and $\Gamma_i' = \Gamma_i$ for $1 \leq i \leq n$ and an integer k, $1 \leq k \leq n$, if there exists a time instant t', $0 \leq t' \leq T_k'$, such that $W_k'(t') = \sum_{i=1}^{k}\sum_{j=1}^{\lceil \frac{t'}{T_i'} \rceil} C_i^{((j-1) \bmod N_i)} \leq t'$, then there also exists a time instant t, $0 \leq t \leq T_k$, such that $W_k(t) = \sum_{i=1}^{k}\sum_{j=1}^{\lceil \frac{t}{T_i} \rceil} C_i^{((j-1) \bmod N_i)} \leq t$.

Proof: Intuitively, since $\mathcal{T}'$ has more stringent deadline constraints (i.e., smaller periods) than $\mathcal{T}$, it is expected that $\mathcal{T}'$ is harder to schedule than $\mathcal{T}$.

Since $T_i' \leq T_i$ and $\Gamma_i' = \Gamma_i$ for $1 \leq i \leq n$, we have

$$\sum_{i=1}^{k}\sum_{j=1}^{\lceil \frac{t'}{T_i} \rceil} C_i^{((j-1) \bmod N_i)} \leq \sum_{i=1}^{k}\sum_{j=1}^{\lceil \frac{t'}{T_i'} \rceil} C_i^{((j-1) \bmod N_i)}$$
$$\leq t' \leq T_k' \leq T_k.$$

Therefore, t' is such a time instant. $\square$

We can now prove our general theorem.

Theorem 4 Given an AM task set $\mathcal{T}$, if there exists another (AM) task set $\mathcal{T}'$ such that $T_i' \leq T_i$ and $\Gamma_i' = \Gamma_i$, for $1 \leq i \leq n$, and $\mathcal{T}'$ is schedulable by RM, then $\mathcal{T}$ is also schedulable by RM.

Proof: According to Lemma 1, given a task set $\mathcal{T} = \{\tau_1, \tau_2, \ldots, \tau_n\}$ with $T_i \leq T_{i+1}$ for $1 \leq i \leq n-1$, $\mathcal{T}$ is schedulable by RM if and only if $C_1^0 \leq T_1$ and there exists a time instant t_k, $0 \leq t_k \leq T_k$, such that $W_k(t_k) = \sum_{i=1}^{k}\sum_{j=1}^{\lceil \frac{t_k}{T_i} \rceil} C_i^{((j-1) \bmod N_i)} \leq t_k$ for all $k = 2, 3, \ldots, n$.

We prove the theorem by showing that (1) $C_1^0 \leq T_1$, and (2) there exists a time instant t_k, $0 \leq t_k \leq T_k$, such that $W_k(t_k) \leq t_k$, for $k = 2, 3, \ldots, n$.
(1) Since $\mathcal{T}'$ is schedulable by RM, $C_1^0 \leq T_1'$, and hence $C_1^0 \leq T_1' \leq T_1$.
(2) Since $\mathcal{T}'$ is schedulable by RM, we know that there exists a time instant t_k', $0 \leq t_k' \leq T_k'$, such that $W_k'(t_k') = \sum_{i=1}^{k}\sum_{j=1}^{\lceil \frac{t_k'}{T_i'} \rceil} C_i^{((j-1) \bmod N_i)} \leq t_k'$, for $k = 2, 3, \ldots, n$. By Lemma 2, we have that there exists a time instant t_k, $0 \leq t_k \leq T_k$, such that $W_k(t_k) \leq t_k$, for $k = 2, 3, \ldots, n$.

From (1) and (2), we conclude that $\mathcal{T}$ is schedulable by RM. $\square$

It is easy to see that Theorem 3 is just a special case of

Theorem 4, and hence, the correctness of Theorem 3 follows directly from Theorem 4.

According to Theorem 3, given an AM task set $\mathcal{T} = \{\tau_i = (\Gamma_i, T_i) \mid 1 \leq i \leq n\}$, if we can find another multiframe task set $\mathcal{T}' = \{\tau_i' = (\Gamma_i, T_i') \mid 1 \leq i \leq n\}$ such that $T_i' \leq T_i$ for all $i = 1, 2, \ldots, n$, $T_i' \mid T_{i+1}'$ (thus, $T_i' \leq T_{i+1}'$) for all $i = 1, 2, \ldots, n-1$, <u>and</u> $\mathcal{T}'$ is schedulable by RM then we know that $\mathcal{T}$ is also schedulable by RM. To check whether or not $\mathcal{T}'$ is schedulable by RM, we can use Theorem 1, which can be done in polynomial time (Theorem 2).

Now, the problem is, given a task set $\mathcal{T}$, how to find (in polynomial time) another task set $\mathcal{T}'$ which satisfies Condition A and is easy to schedule. For periodic task sets, we have designed two algorithms **Sr** [3] and DCT [4], for finding such a task set $\mathcal{T}'$. Similar technique can be applied to handle multiframe task sets. In the next section, we show how to modify **Sr** and DCT and use them together with Theorem 3 to check the schedulability of a multiframe task set scheduled by the RM algorithm.

4. Finding a task set $\mathcal{T}'$ satisfying Condition A

4.1. Specialization operation Sr

The first algorithm we proposed to find a task set $\mathcal{T}'$ that satisfies Condition A is called *specialization operation* **Sr**. Given a multiframe task set $\mathcal{T} = \{\tau_i = (\Gamma_i, T_i) \mid 1 \leq i \leq n\}$, **Sr** derives for each period T_i another period T_i' according to the following formula.

$$T_i' = r \cdot 2^{j_i} \leq T_i < r \cdot 2^{j_i+1} = 2 \cdot T_i',$$

where r is a real number chosen from the range $(T_1/2, T_1]$, and j_i is an integer. We say that the specialization operation is done with respect to r. Note that after r is fixed, j_i for $1 \leq i \leq n$ are all fixed. That is, $j_i = \lfloor \log(T_i/r) \rfloor$ and

$$T_i' = r \cdot 2^{\lfloor \log(T_i/r) \rfloor}. \tag{4}$$

Also note that there is no need to choose an r for $r \leq T_1/2$ since in such a case, the result of the operation with respect to r is the same as that with respect to $2r$.

Fig. 1 illustrates the specialization operation **Sr**. It is easy to see that $T_i' \leq T_i$ for all i and $T_i' \mid T_j'$ for all $i < j$. Since $T_i' \leq T_i$ for all i, $\mathcal{T}'$ is more difficult to schedule than $\mathcal{T}$. The problem is how we can find an r such that $\mathcal{T}'$ will be the easiest one to schedule among all possible transformed task sets.

Let r^* be a real number chosen from the range $(T_1/2, T_1]$ such that the task set $\mathcal{T}'$ derived by specializing $\mathcal{T}$ with respect to r^* is schedulable by RM. If no such number exists, then r^* is undefined.

Sr uses the following algorithm to find an r^* and then derive the new periods T_i', for all i, using r^*. Define

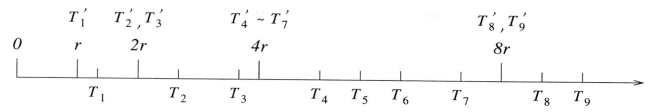

Figure 1. Illustration of the specialization operation Sr.

$l_i = T_i/2^{\lceil \log(T_i/T_1) \rceil}$ (note that $T_1/2 < l_i \leq T_1$), for $1 \leq i \leq n$. Let $k_1 < k_2 < \cdots < k_u$, $u \leq n$, be the sorted sequence of l_i's with duplicates removed. Since $l_1 = T_1$, we know that $k_u = T_1$. We call $\{k_1, k_2, \ldots, k_u\}$ the *special base* of $\mathcal{T}$. For convenience of discussion, we define $k_0 = T_1/2$. We will prove that an r^* can always be found in the special base, i.e., there exists an $r^* = k_v$, for some $v \in \{1, 2, \ldots, u\}$. Let $\mathcal{T}(r)$ denote the task set after $\mathcal{T}$ is specialized with respect to r. We can check the schedulability of the task sets $\mathcal{T}(r)$ for $r = k_v$, $1 \leq v \leq u$ (see Theorem 2), select an r value, if exists, such that $\mathcal{T}(r)$ is schedulable by RM, and use that r value to transform the periods of task set $\mathcal{T}$. With this algorithm, **Sr** can be done in time $O(n^2(n + \max N_i))$ (Theorem 5).

The rationale behind the claim that only the numbers in the special base of $\mathcal{T}$ need to be considered in finding r^* is as follows. Given an r, $T_1/2 < r \leq T_1$, we define the *r-based subset*, π_r, of $\mathcal{T}$ as follows.

$$\pi_r = \{\tau_i \in \mathcal{T} \mid T_i = r \cdot 2^j, \text{ for some integer } j \geq 0\}. \quad (5)$$

It is easy to see that $\pi_r \neq \emptyset$ if and only if $r = k_v$, for $1 \leq v \leq u$. Recall that when $\{T_1, T_2, \ldots, T_n\}$ is specialized with respect to r, every T_i is specialized to a number $T_i' = r \cdot 2^{\lfloor \log(T_i/r) \rfloor}$ (Eq. (4)). The reason we define the r-based subsets of $\mathcal{T}$ as in Eq. (5) is that for every task $T_i \in \pi_{k_v}$, $T_i = l_i \cdot 2^{\lceil \log(T_i/T_1) \rceil} = k_v \cdot 2^{\lfloor \log(T_i/k_v) \rfloor}$ (because $l_i = k_v$ and $\log(T_i/k_v) = \lfloor \log(T_i/k_v) \rfloor = \lceil \log(T_i/T_1) \rceil$ is an integer); as a result, if $r = k_v$, T_i will be specialized to itself (i.e., $T_i' = T_i$). This also gives the intuition why we only need to choose r^* from the special base $\{k_1, k_2, \ldots, k_u\}$ of $\mathcal{T}$. More formally, we prove the following lemma.

Lemma 3 If $k_{v-1} < r < k_v$, for some v, $1 \leq v \leq u$, and $r \neq k_0$, then $\mathcal{T}(r)$ is schedulable by RM implies that $\mathcal{T}(k_v)$ is also schedulable by RM.

Proof: Let $T_i(r)$ denote the period of τ_i after the task set is specialized with respect to r. It is easy to see that, for $k_{v-1} < r < k_v$, $T_i(r) < T_i(k_v)$ for all i. According to Theorem 4, if $\mathcal{T}(r)$ is schedulable by RM, so is $\mathcal{T}(k_v)$. $\quad\square$

Corollary 1 If r^* exists, then there is one which falls in the special base of $\mathcal{T}$.

Proof: The corollary follows directly from Lemma 3. $\quad\square$

/* Input: $\mathcal{T} = \{\tau_i = (\Gamma_i, T_i) \mid 1 \leq i \leq n\}$, where $\mathcal{T}$ is an AM task set and $T_i \leq T_j, \forall i < j$. */
/* Output: r^* and $\mathcal{T}' = \mathcal{T}(r^*)$. */
1. **for** $i := 1$ **to** n **do** $l_i = T_i/2^{\lceil \log(T_i/T_1) \rceil}$;
2. sort $(l_1, l_2, \ldots, l_n)$ into nondecreasing order and remove duplicates; let $(k_1, k_2, \ldots, k_u)$ be the resulting sequence;
3. **for** $v := 1$ **to** u **do**
4.   derive $\mathcal{T}(k_v)$;
5.   use Theorem 1 to check the feasibility of $\mathcal{T}(k_v)$;
6.   if $\mathcal{T}(k_v)$ is feasible, output $r^* = k_v$ and $\mathcal{T}(k_v)$ and stop;
7. **end**
8. output "unable to find a feasible harmonic set for $\mathcal{T}$".

Figure 2. The specialization operation Sr.

Thus, to find an r^*, if exists, so that $\mathcal{T}(r^*)$ is schedulable by RM, we only need to compute $\mathcal{T}(k_v)$, for all k_v in the special base of $\mathcal{T}$.

To summarize the above results, we list the pseudo-code of **Sr** in Fig. 2, and prove its time complexity in Theorem 5.

Theorem 5 The time complexity of the specialization operation **Sr** is $O(n^2(n + \max N_i))$.

Proof: Note that the time complexity of the algorithm is dominated by the for-loop, which, in turn, is dominated by Step 5. From Theorem 2, we know that Step 5 can be done in time $O(n(n + \max N_i))$. Therefore the whole algorithm can be done in time $O(un(n + \max N_i)) \leq O(n^2(n + \max N_i))$. $\quad\square$

4.2. Algorithm DCT

As mentioned in the previous section, in the specialization operation **Sr**, an r^*, if exists, always falls in the special base $\{k_1, k_2, \ldots, k_u\}$, i.e., $r^* = k_\ell$ for some $1 \leq \ell \leq u$. Moreover, the periods of all the tasks in $\pi_{r^*} = \pi_{k_\ell}$ do not change after the specialization operation, i.e., $T_i' = T_i$ for all $\tau_i \in \pi_{k_\ell}$. In fact, we proved the following theorem in [4].

/* Input: $\mathcal{T} = \{\tau_i = (\Gamma_i, T_i) \mid 1 \leq i \leq n\}$, where $\mathcal{T}$ is a multiframe task set and $T_i \leq T_j, \forall i < j$. */
/* Output: $\mathcal{T}' = \{\tau_i' = (\Gamma_i, T_i') \mid 1 \leq i \leq n\}$, where $T_i' \leq T_i, \forall i$ and $T_i' \mid T_j', \forall i < j$ */
1. **for** $f := 1$ **to** n **do** {
2. $Z_f := T_f$;
3.   **for** $i := f + 1$ **to** n **do**
4. $Z_i := Z_{i-1} \cdot \lfloor T_i / Z_{i-1} \rfloor$;
5.   **for** $i := f - 1$ **downto** 1 **do**
6. $Z_i := \frac{Z_{i+1}}{\lceil Z_{i+1}/T_i \rceil}$;
7.   **if** $\{(\Gamma_i, Z_i) \mid 1 \leq i \leq n\}$ is feasible **then**
8.   **for** $i := 1$ **to** n **do** $T_i' := Z_i$;
9.   output $\{(\Gamma_i, T_i') \mid 1 \leq i \leq n\}$ and stop;
10.   **endif**
11. }
12. output "unable to find a feasible harmonic set for $\mathcal{T}$".

Figure 3. Algorithm DCT.

Theorem 6 Let $\{T_1^*, T_2^*, \ldots, T_n^*\}$ be a set of periods satisfying Condition A and

$$\sum_{i=1}^{n} \frac{C_i}{T_i^*} \leq \sum_{i=1}^{n} \frac{C_i}{T_i'}$$

for any other set of periods $\{T_1', T_2', \ldots, T_n'\}$ satisfying Condition A. Then, there must exist an index ℓ such that $T_\ell^* = T_\ell$. $\square$

Motivated by the above theorem we can modify the algorithm DCT proposed in [4] to find a $\mathcal{T}'$ for multiframe task set $\mathcal{T}$. The DCT algorithm is shown in Fig. 3. The DCT algorithm is quite simple. For each f, $1 \leq f \leq n$, we first fix T_f' at T_f and then recursively transform T_i, for each $i > f$, to the largest integral multiple of T_{i-1}' that is less than or equal to T_i, i.e.,

$$T_i' = T_{i-1}' \cdot \lfloor T_i / T_{i-1}' \rfloor, \text{for } i = f+1, f+2, \ldots, n. \quad (6)$$

Similarly, we recursively transform T_i, for each $i < f$, to the largest divisor of T_{i+1}' that is less than or equal to T_i, i.e.,

$$T_i' = \frac{T_{i+1}'}{\lceil T_{i+1}'/T_i \rceil}, \text{for } i = f-1, f-2, \ldots, 1. \quad (7)$$

The f that results in a feasible transformed task set will be the final index of T_i whose transformed value T_i' is fixed at T_i.

The time complexity of Algorithm DCT is given in the following theorem.

Theorem 7 The time complexity of Algorithm DCT is $O(n^2(n + \max N_i))$.

Proof: The time complexity of the outer for-loop is dominated by Step 7. By Theorem 2, we know that checking the schedulability of a harmonic task set can be done in time $O(n(n + \max N_i))$. Since the index of the outer for-loop goes from 1 to n, the whole algorithm can be done in time $O(n^2(n + \max N_i))$. $\square$

4.3. The proposed schedulability test

Given a multiframe task set $\mathcal{T}$, if its peak utilization $U^m(\mathcal{T}) \leq M(n, \gamma)$, then according to Mok and Chen's result, we know that it is schedulable by RM. However, as mentioned earlier, $U^m(\mathcal{T}) > M(n, \gamma)$ does not necessarily mean that the task set $\mathcal{T}$ is not schedulable by RM. According to Theorem 3, as long as we can find a transformed task set $\mathcal{T}'$ which is schedulable by RM, we know that $\mathcal{T}$ is also schedulable by RM. To check if there exists a feasible transformed task set $\mathcal{T}'$, we can apply **Sr** and/or DCT to $\mathcal{T}$, both of which can be done in $O(n^2(n + \max N_i))$ time (Theorems 5 and 7). If either or both of them can find a feasible transformed task set, then by Theorem 3 the original task set $\mathcal{T}$ is also schedulable by RM.

The reason that Mok and Chen's utilization bound $M(n, \gamma)$ is too conservative is twofold. First, according to the definition of γ_i (Eq. (1)), only the first two frames of each task are considered in deriving $M(n, \gamma)$, and the fact that the subsequent frames may have even smaller worst-case computation times is not taken into account. Secondly, according to the definition of γ ($\gamma = \min \gamma_i$), it is too conservative to take only the minimum of γ_i, for $1 \leq i \leq n$, since the smallest γ_i can lower the value of $M(n, \gamma)$ even if all the other γ_i's are very large. The above two factors reduce the advantages of using the multiframe task model since only the "worst" pair of (C_i^0, C_i^1) is considered in deriving the utilization bound.

We think that the drawback of Mok and Chen's schedulability test is due to the "closed-form" utilization bound. Our schedulability test does not rely on a closed-form utilization bound and can also be done in polynomial time. Therefore, in conclusion, our schedulability test which use Theorem 3 and **Sr** and/or DCT to check if a multiframe task set is schedulable by RM is better than using the pessimistic closed-form utilization bound $M(n, \gamma)$ (which was proved by performance evaluation whose results are presented in Section 5), and is faster than the pseudo-polynomial time necessary and sufficient condition discussed in Section 2 and Lemma 1.

5. Performance evaluation

We conducted extensive simulation to evaluate the improvement of our schedulability tests over Mok and Chen's utilization bound. Our performance evaluation is conducted as follows. We first randomly generate a number of (AM) multiframe task sets and use the necessary and sufficient condition proposed by Lehoczky *et al.* and generalized in Lemma 1 to find out those task sets that are schedulable by RM[4] but have peak utilizations larger than Mok and Chen's utilization bound $M(n, \gamma)$. We then apply our schedulability tests (**Sr** and DCT) to these feasible task sets and calculate the percentage of the task sets that are reported as schedulable by our schedulability tests.

The difficulty of our performance evaluation lies in the random generation of feasible AM multiframe task sets. Each AM task set, $\mathcal{T} = \{\tau_i = (\Gamma_i, T_i) \mid 1 \leq i \leq n\}$, has several parameters — the number of tasks, n, in the task set $\mathcal{T}$, the period, T_i, of each task τ_i, the number of computation times, N_i, in the computation time vector Γ_i, and the computation times, C_i^j, $0 \leq j \leq N_i - 1$, of each vector Γ_i, $1 \leq i \leq n$. These parameters are highly correlated. In order to generate feasible task sets we cannot just generate these parameters arbitrarily. For example, if the average peak frame utilization of the tasks in $\mathcal{T}$ is C/T then the peak utilization of $\mathcal{T}$ is nC/T. In order to generate a feasible task set $\mathcal{T}$, the total (not peak) utilization of $\mathcal{T}$ should take a reasonable value. Therefore, each task's frame utilizations should be generated according to the number of tasks n in $\mathcal{T}$ (and, to be more precisely, its γ_i value as well). Also, in Mok and Chen's utilization bound $M(n, \gamma)$, γ is defined as $\gamma = \min_i \gamma_i$, where $\gamma_i = C_i^0/C_i^1$ if $N_i > 1$ and $\gamma_i = 1$ otherwise. Since we are studying multiframe tasks we consider only the case that $N_i > 1$. Moreover, for simplicity, we assume $N_i = 2$ for all $1 \leq i \leq n$. As discussed in Section 4.3, this assumption ignores the fact that subsequent computation times, C_i^j, $j > 1$, in an AM task is usually smaller than C_i^0 and C_i^1, and hence, the net effect of the assumption is underestimating the performance of our schedulability tests. However, the simulation results showed that even with this assumption our schedulability tests are still much better than Mok and Chen's utilization bound $M(n, \gamma)$.

In summary, the task sets in our simulation are generated as follows. Given the number of tasks, n, in the task set $\mathcal{T}$, we first randomly generate for each task τ_i, $1 \leq i \leq n$, its period T_i from the range $[T\_low, T\_high]$, its peak frame computation time C_i^0 from the range $[U\_low \cdot T_i/n, U\_high \cdot T_i/n]$, and its γ_i value from the range $[\gamma\_low, \gamma\_high]$. We then calculate the second frame computation time $C_i^1 = C_i^0/\gamma_i$ for each task τ_i. As a result, the inputs to our simulation program are a set of pre-selected values for n, and the range pairs: (T_low, T_high), (U_low, U_high), and $(\gamma\_low, \gamma\_high)$, where $[U\_low, U\_high]$ is our "target" range for

the peak utilization of each generated task set $\mathcal{T}$.

5.1. Simulation results

In each run of the simulation, we first select a number of values for n and fix the values of (T_low, T_high), (U_low, U_high), and $(\gamma\_low, \gamma\_high)$. We then use the methods described above to randomly generate 1,000 task sets for each selected value of n, find out those task sets which are feasible but have peak utilizations larger than $M(n, \gamma)$, apply our schedulability tests to these task sets, and calculate the percentages of the task sets that are found feasible by our schedulability tests (**Sr** and DCT). The simulation is repeated for different inputs and the results are depicted in Figs. 4–6. In each figure, the x-axis is the number of tasks n and the y-axis is the percentage of the task sets that pass our schedulability tests among the feasible task sets that do not pass the test using Mok and Chen's utilization bound $M(n, \gamma)$.

Fig. 4 shows the results for $[T\_low, T\_high] = [10, 1000]$, $[U\_low, U\_high] = [0.75, 1.5]$, and $[\gamma\_low, \gamma\_high] = [5, 10]$, $[5, 50]$ and $[50, 100]$ for (a), (b), and (c), respectively. Fig. 5 shows the results for $[\gamma\_low, \gamma\_high] = [10, 50]$, $[U\_low, U\_high] = [0.75, 1.5]$, and $[T\_low, T\_high] = [10, 100]$, $[10, 1000]$ and $[10, 10000]$ for (a), (b), and (c), respectively. Fig. 6 shows the results for $[T\_low, T\_high] = [10, 1000]$, $[\gamma\_low, \gamma\_high] = [20, 100]$, and $[U\_low, U\_high] = [0.75, 1.5]$, $[0.85, 1.5]$ and $[0.9, 1.5]$ for (a), (b), and (c), respectively.

We can see from these figures that in general when n increases the performance of our schedulability tests decreases. However, there is still a high probability (in most cases, 40%–90%) that our tests will be able to find out the feasible task sets (which can not be found out by using Mok and Chen's utilization bound). Another general observation is that **Sr** usually performs better than DCT, except when n is small (e.g., $n = 2$).

From Fig. 4, we can see that if the γ value increases, the performance of our schedulability tests also increases. With a large value of γ, about 75%–90% of the feasible task sets with peak utilizations larger than $M(n, \gamma)$ can still be found schedulable using **Sr**. However, the performance increase of DCT is not so significant as **Sr**. From Fig. 5, we can see that if the variance of the periods in a task set increases, the performance of DCT decreases. However, the performance of **Sr** does not change much. From Fig. 6, we can see that if the peak utilizations of the task sets increase, the performance of both **Sr** and DCT decreases and the difference between the two tests becomes smaller.

As the original idea of proposing the multiframe task model is to explore the possibility of taking into account the cases when tasks' average computation times are much smaller than their worst-case computation times, it is rea-

---

[4]Note that since the schedulability test using the necessary and sufficient condition takes pseudo-polynomial time, it is impossible for us to test the feasibility of a task set with a very large number of tasks. Therefore, in our simulation the number of tasks, n, ranges from 2 to 100 only.

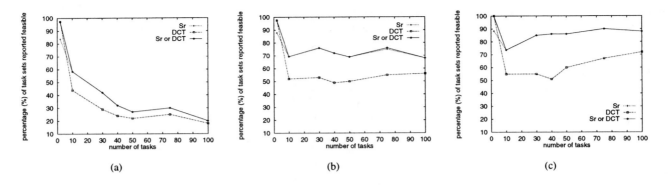

Figure 4. Performance evaluation results (with increasing γ value).

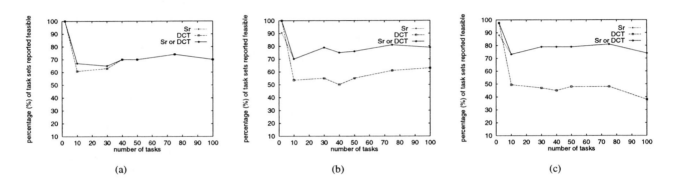

Figure 5. Performance evaluation results (with increasing period variance).

sonable to assume that in such kind of real-time task sets the γ value is usually very large. In such cases, our schedulability tests perform much better than the tests using a closed-form utilization bound like $M(n, \gamma)$.

6. Conclusion

Mok and Chen proposed the multiframe task model to remedy a drawback of the traditional periodic task model in characterizing task sets whose average computation times are smaller than the worst-case computation times. They also derived a utilization bound for multiframe task sets which is an improvement over the well-known Liu and Layland's utilization bound. However, the schedulability test based on Mok and Chen's new utilization bound is still too pessimistic. A theoretical reasoning (Section 4.3) and experimental evidences (Section 5) for the drawback of the schedulability test using Mok and Chen's utilization bound are discussed/presented in this paper.

In this paper, we also proposed a better polynomial-time schedulability test for multiframe task sets scheduled by fixed-priority scheduling algorithms. We showed that our schedulability test is much better than using Mok and

Chen's utilization bound in the sense that if a feasible task set has a peak utilization larger than their bound, our schedulability test will still answer positively with a very high probability.

The proposed schedulability test does not rely on closed-form utilization bounds, and hence, does not have the restrictions imposed on schedulability tests based on certain utilization bounds. We have demonstrated that this kind of non-closed-form schedulability tests are very powerful and efficient in analyzing the schedulabilities of periodic and multiframe real-time tasks, and we believe that similar technique can be applied to other types of real-time tasks and hence it is a new direction for real-time schedulability analysis worthy of further investigation.

References

[1] S.-C. Cheng, J. A. Stankovic, and K. Ramamritham. Scheduling algorithms for hard real-time systems — a brief survey. In *Tutorial Hard Real-Time systems*, pages 150–173. IEEE, 1988.

[2] M. Garey and D. Johnson. *Computer and Intractability: A Guide to the Theory of NP-Completeness*. Freeman, San Francisco, CA, 1979.

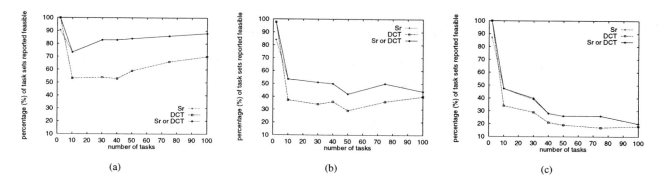

Figure 6. Performance evaluation results (with increasing peak utilization value).

[3] C.-C. Han, K.-J. Lin, and C.-J. Hou. Distance-constrained scheduling and its applications to real-time systems. *IEEE Trans. on Computers*, 45(7):814–826, July 1996.

[4] C.-C. Han and H. ying Tyan. A better polynomial-time schedulability test for real-time fixed-priority scheduling algorithms. In *IEEE Real-Time Systems Symposium*, San Fransco, December 1997.

[5] M. Joseph and P. Pandya. Finding response times in a real-time system. *The Computer Journal, British Computer Society*, 29(5):390–395, October 1986.

[6] J. Lehoczky, L. Sha, and Y. Ding. The rate monotonic scheduling algorithm: Exact characterization and average case behavior. In *Proc. of the Real-Time Systems Symposium*, pages 166–171, Santa Monica, CA, December 1989.

[7] J. P. Lehoczky, L. Sha, J. K. Strosnider, and H. Tokuda. Fixed priority scheduling theory for hard real-time systems. In A. M. van Tilborg and G. M. Koob, editors, *Foundations of Real-Time Computing: Scheduling and Resource Management*, chapter 1, pages 1–30. Kluwer Academic Publishers, Boston, 1991.

[8] D. W. Leinbaugh. Guaranteed response time in a hard real-time environment. *IEEE Transactions on Software Engineering*, January 1980.

[9] J. Y.-T. Leung and M. L. Merrill. A note on preemptive scheduling of periodic, real-time tasks. *Information Processing Letters*, 11(3):115–118, November 1980.

[10] J. Y.-T. Leung and J. Whitehead. On the complexity of fixed-priority scheduling of periodic, real-time tasks. *Performance Evaluation*, 2:237–250, 1982.

[11] C. L. Liu and J. W. Layland. Scheduling algorithms for multiprogramming in a hard real-time environment. *Journal of ACM*, 20(1):46–61, January 1973.

[12] A. K. Mok and D. Chen. A multiframe model for real-time tasks. In *IEEE Real-Time Systems Symposium*, pages 22–29, Dec. 1996.

[13] A. K. Mok and D. Chen. A multiframe model for real-time tasks. *IEEE Trans. on Software Engineering*, to appear.

[14] K. W. Tindell. Using offset information to analyze static priority pre-emptively scheduled task sets. Technical Report YCS 182, Department of Computer Science, University of York, 1992.

[15] K. W. Tindell, A. Burns, and A. J. Wellings. An extendible approach for analyzing fixed priority hard real-time tasks. *Real-Time Systems Journal*, 6:133–151, 1994.

A general model for recurring real-time tasks[*]

Sanjoy K. Baruah
The University of Vermont

Abstract

A new model for hard-real-time tasks — the **recurring real-time task** model — is introduced. This model generalizes earlier models such as the sporadic task model and the generalized multiframe task model. An algorithm is presented for feasibility-analysis of a system of independent recurring real-time tasks in a preemptive uniprocessor environment.

Keywords: Hard-real-time scheduling; conditional code; feasibility analysis; processor demand criteria.

1 Introduction

Real-time computer systems may be defined as those where the correctness of a computation depends upon both the result of the computation, and the time at which this result is obtained. A *uniprocessor* hard-real-time system consists of a number of *hard-real-time tasks* that share a single processor. Each hard-real-time task generates a sequence of *jobs*; each job is characterized by three attributes — a *ready time*, a (worst case) *execution requirement*, and a *deadline*, with the interpretation that the job must be executed on the shared processor for an amount of time equal to its execution requirement between its ready time and its deadline. (For ease of exposition, we restrict our attention in this paper to systems where these attributes are always integer-valued; however, all our results extend in a direct manner to systems where the attribute values are arbitrary real numbers.) Different models for hard-real-time tasks place different constraints upon the permissible values for these job attributes; for example, the *sporadic task model* [1] mandates that the

ready times of successive jobs of a task be at least a specified time-interval apart, and that all jobs have the same execution-requirement, and a deadline that is the same amount of time after the ready-time.

Feasibility-analysis in hard-real-time scheduling is concerned with the following problem: given the specifications for a system of hard-real-time tasks, how do we determine whether the tasks can be scheduled in such a manner that all the jobs complete by their deadlines?

§ 1. Demand Bound Function. In recent years, considerable effort has been devoted to the study of systems of *independent tasks* (i.e., the attributes of the jobs being generated by a particular task are completely independent of the jobs being generated by other tasks in the system) in *preemptive* (i.e., a job executing on the processor can be interrupted at any instant in time, and it's execution resumed later with no cost or penalty) *uniprocessor* environments. A standard methodology for doing feasibility-analysis in such systems has emerged, centered around the idea of *processor demand criteria* [2, page 102]. We provide a brief introduction to this methodology below; for further details, consult [2].

For our purposes, processor demand criteria can be formalized into the notion of a demand bound function:

Definition 1 (Demand Bound Function) *Let T be a task, and t a non-negative integer. The* demand bound function $\mathrm{dbf}(T, t)$ *denotes the maximum cumulative execution requirement by jobs of T that have both ready times and deadlines within any time interval of duration t.*

The demand bound function quantifies the maximum amount of processor time that can be requested by jobs of a task in any interval of a given size. In task systems

[*]This research has been supported in part by the National Science Foundation (Grant Nos. CCR-9704206 and CDA-9720676).

comprised of *independent* real-time tasks (i.e., task systems in which the attributes of the jobs generated each task are completely independent of the jobs generated by the other tasks), a necessary and sufficient conditions for a system of real-time tasks Γ to be feasible is that

$$\left(\sum_{T \in \Gamma} \mathsf{dbf}(T, t) \ \leq \ t \right) \tag{1}$$

for all $t \geq 0$.

Thus using the processor demand criteria methodology, feasibility-analysis for systems of independent real-time tasks reduces to the following two questions:

Q1: How do we efficiently compute the demand bound function dbf?

Q2: Since it is clearly impractical to explicitly verify (1) for <u>all</u> $t \geq 0$, how do we choose a small *testing set* for t — a set of values of t such that verifying (1) for each t in the testing set is sufficient to establish that (1) holds for all $t \geq 0$?

§ 2. Conditional real-time code.

Embedded real-time processes are typically implemented as some event-driven code embedded within an infinite loop. The first step in the feasibility-analysis of such real-time code involves obtaining an equivalent task model for the code. Processes which are implemented as straight-line code (i.e., code with no conditional branches) within the infinite loop can often be transformed to sporadic tasks [1, 3, 4] or generalized multi-frame tasks [5]. In many event-driven real-time application systems, however, the timing requirements are not representable as straight-line code; instead, the action to be taken upon the occurrence of an external event depends upon other factors (such as the current state of the system, the values of certain external variables, etc), which can only be determined at run-time:

```
for (;;){
when (external event):
    perform e_o units of work over the next d_o time units;
    if (C)       /* Condition C depends upon the state of the
                    system, and of the environment, at the time
                    the external event occurs, and cannot hence
                    be evaluated at compile-time. */
        perform e_1 units of work over the next d_1 time units;
    else
        perform e_2 units of work over the next d_2 time units;
}
```

Traditionally, feasibility analysis for such conditional code is done by assuming the worst-case behavior — i.e., by analyzing the system when the code takes the branch that makes the most rigorous demands upon the system resources. Unfortunately, it is not always clear which branch corresponds to the worst-case behavior, and indeed the "worst" behavior often depends upon circumstances external to the task. Consider the above example with $e_o = 0$, $e_1 = 2$, $d_1 = 2$, $e_2 = 4$, and $d_2 = 5$. If there were to be another job with $(e = 1, d = 1)$ executing simultaneously with this branching job, then the (e_1, d_1) branch represents the worse behavior; if, instead, the other job had requirements $(e = 2, d = 5)$, then the (e_2, d_2) branch is the worse one. Thus the worst-case behavior such of a task cannot be identified in isolation, without taking into account the behaviors of all other tasks in the system. A direct approach of considering all combinations of possible behaviors for all the tasks in a system would quickly result in combinatorial explosion and rapidly prove computationally intractable — this problem is enormously further aggravated when the tasks are permitted to *recur* periodically. This research is directed at devising efficient feasibility tests for systems of tasks each of which may be comprised of such conditional code.

§ 3. System Model.

A recurring real-time task T is represented by a *task graph* $G(T)$ and a *period* $P(T)$. The task graph $G(T)$ is a directed acyclic graph (DAG) with a unique source vertex – a vertex with no incoming edges, and a unique sink vertex – a vertex with no outgoing edges. Each vertex in this DAG represents a subtask, and each edge represents a possible flow of control. Each vertex u is labelled by two integer parameters $e(u)$ and $d(u)$ with the following interpretation: every time subtask u is <u>triggered</u>, a job is generated with ready-time equal to the triggering-time of the subtask, an execution requirement of $e(u)$ time units and a deadline $d(u)$ time-units after the triggering-time. Each edge (u, v) is labelled by an integer parameter $p(u, v)$ denoting the minimum amount of time that must elapse after vertex u is triggered, before vertex v can be triggered.

In informal language, the semantics of execution of a recurring real-time task may be described as follows: When a subtask u is triggered it generates a job which needs to be executed on the shared processor for $e(u)$

units of the next $d(u)$ units of time. Initially the source vertex of the DAG may be triggered at any time. Suppose that vertex u is triggered at time t

- if u is <u>not</u> the sink vertex of $G(T)$, then the next vertex of $G(T)$ to be triggered is some vertex v such that (u, v) is an edge in $G(T)$; vertex v is triggered at or after time $t + p(u, v)$.

- if u is the sink vertex of $G(T)$, then the next vertex of $G(T)$ to be triggered is the source vertex; it can be triggered at any time after t subject to the constraint that at least $P(T)$ time units should have elapsed since its last triggering.

More formally, let us use a 3-tuple (T, t, u) to denote the fact that subtask (or vertex) u of recurring real-time task T is triggered at time-instant t; such a 3-tuple will be called an <u>event</u>.

Let $$\sigma(T)$$
denote a (possibly infinite) sequence of events of task T; i.e., $\sigma(T)$ is a sequence of 3-tuples. Event sequence $\sigma(T) = [(T, t_1, u_1), (T, t_2, u_2), (T, t_3, u_3), \ldots,]$ is said to be a <u>legal</u> event sequence if and only if the following conditions are satisfied:

- If u_i is not the sink vertex of $G(T)$, then

    1. (u_i, u_{i+1}) is an edge in the DAG $G(T)$, and
    2. $t_{i+1} - t_i$ is at least as large as $p(u_i, u_{i+1})$.

- If u_i is the sink vertex of $G(T)$, then

    1. u_{i+1} is the source node in $G(T)$, and
    2. if there is an event (T, t_j, u_j), $j < i$, in the event-sequence such that $u_j = u_{i+1}$ (i.e., the source node has occurred previously in the event sequence) then $t_{i+1} - t_j \geq P(T)$.

In this paper, we will further restrict legal event sequences to satisfy the constraint that $t_i + d(u_i) \leq t_{i+1}$ for all $i \geq 1$; i.e., we will assume that all legal event sequences satisfy what is sometimes referred to as the *Frame Separation property* [6]. However, we note that this is <u>not</u> a necessary restriction on our model, in that our results continue to hold in its absence (although some of the complexity bounds will change). For vertices u other than the sink vertex, the frame separation property is equivalent to having $p(u, v) \geq d(u)$ for all v such that (u, v) is an edge; with respect to the sink vertex t, it is necessary (but not sufficient) that a time

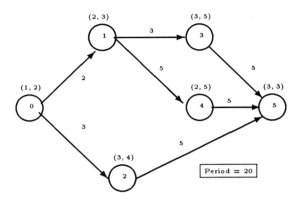

Figure 1. An example recurring real-time task

interval of length $d(t)$ elapse after t is triggered prior to the subsequent triggering of the source node.

A *system of recurring real-time tasks* consists of several independent recurring real-time tasks, which are to be preemptively scheduled on a single processor.

An example recurring real-time task is depicted graphically in Figure 1. Each vertex is labelled with the name of the subtask – vertex 0 is the source vertex, and vertex 5 the sink vertex. The ordered pair above each vertex u represents the vertex's execution requirement and the relative deadline – $(e(u), d(u))$. The single integer on each edge (u, v) represents the associated inter-triggering separation $p(u, v)$. The period of the task — the minimum time that must elapse between successive triggerings of the source node — is 20.

§ 4. Significance of this research. The recurring real-time task model is, in our opinion, the logical culmination to the succession of models that have been developed to represent recurring tasks with minimum separation constraints. As was pointed out by Mok & Chen [7], the simplest model — each task characterized by an execution requirement e and a minimum separation p (deadlines are "implicit," i.e., they are assumed to occur p units after the frame's arrival) — is an extension of the periodic task model of Liu & Layland [8]. Mok's generalization [1] explicitly added the deadline d, with the interpretation that the deadline of a frame occurs d time units after its arrival; in the notation of this paper, tasks in these two elementary models have task graphs consisting of a single vertex. The multi-

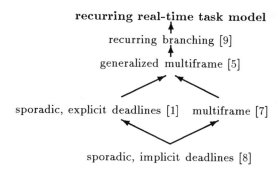

recurring real-time task model

recurring branching [9]

generalized multiframe [5]

sporadic, explicit deadlines [1]   multiframe [7]

sporadic, implicit deadlines [8]

Figure 2. Relationship between the various sporadic task models

frame model of Mok & Chen [7] permitted each task to cycle through a given finite sequence of frame execution times, but did away with the explicit deadline(s). The gmf-task model [5] adds explicit deadlines to the multiframe model, and, for good measure, permits the minimum separations, too, to cycle through a given finite sequence of values — the equivalent task-graph is restricted to being a chain of vertices. The recurring branching task model, introduced in [9], is a further generalization in that it permits the modelling of certain restricted forms of conditional ("if-then-else" and "case") real-time code which can be represented by task-graphs that are directed trees. The relationship between the various models for sporadic tasks is graphically shown in Figure 2, where "A → B" denotes that the model B is a generalization of model A (the "→" relation is, of course, transitive).

§ 5. Organization of this paper. As stated in § 1 above, the feasibility question for systems of independent tasks to be preemptively scheduled on a uniprocessor reduces to the following two questions: (i) How do we efficiently compute the demand bound function dbf for individual tasks?, and (ii) How do we efficiently go about verifying whether Inequality (1) holds for all $t \geq 0$?

In the remainder of this paper, we answer these questions for systems of recurring real-time tasks. In Section 2, we will describe an algorithm for preprocessing a task T to generate certain data-structures, such that $\mathsf{dbf}(T, t)$ can be efficiently computed – in constant time – from these data-structures for any value of t. In Section 3, we will prove that Inequality (1) holds for re-

curring real-time task system Γ for all $t \geq 0$ if and only if it holds for all t in the range $[0, 1, \ldots, \mathsf{lmt}]$, where lmt is a constant whose value depends upon the exact characteristics of the tasks in Γ. Further, we will see in Section 3 that for most systems of recurring real-time tasks, lmt turns out to be reasonably small, and will derive an exact formula for computing it. Hence once we have the data-structures for efficiently computing $\mathsf{dbf}(T, t)$ in place for each T in Γ, a feasibility test for Γ is easily implemented:

for $\hat{t} = 1, 2, 3, \ldots, \mathsf{lmt}$
    if $(\sum_{T \in \Gamma} \mathsf{dbf}(T, \hat{t})) > \hat{t}$ return "infeasible"
return "feasible"

2 Determining the demand bound function

Let $[t_s, t_f)$ be an interval of duration $\hat{t}$ (i.e, $t_f - t_s = \hat{t}$) such that the total cumulative execution requirement by jobs of T over $[t_s, t_f)$ is the maximum possible for any legal event sequence. Consider some such legal event sequence, and let $\sigma_o(T)$ denote those events in this event sequence such that each event (T, t, u) in $\sigma_o(T)$ has $t \geq t_s$ and $(t + d(u)) \leq t_f$. Then by definition of the demand bound function,

$$\mathsf{dbf}(T, \hat{t}) = \sum_{(T, t, u) \in \sigma_o(T)} e(u) .$$

Let $\sigma_1(T)$ be obtained from $\sigma_o(T)$ as follows. Suppose that $\sigma_o = [(T, t_1, u_1), (T, t_2, u_2), (T, t_3, u_3), \ldots, (T, t_n, u_n)]$. Then $\sigma_1 = [(T, t'_1, u_1), (T, t'_2, u_2), (T, t'_3, u_3), \ldots, (T, t'_n, u_n)]$, where $t'_1 = 0$, and the value of t'_{i+1} is determined in the following manner:

- If u_i is not the sink vertex, then $t'_{i+1} = t'_i + p(u_i, u_{i+1})$

- Else, u_i is the sink vertex

  - if there is no integer $j < i$ such that u_j is the source vertex in $\sigma_o(T)$, then $t'_{i+1} = t'_i + d(u_i)$,

  - else, let j denote the largest integer smaller than i such that u_j is the sink vertex in $\sigma_o(T)$; $t'_{i+1} = t'_j + P(T)$.

That is, $\sigma_1(T)$ is obtained from $\sigma_o(T)$ by triggering the first event at time 0 and subsequent events as early

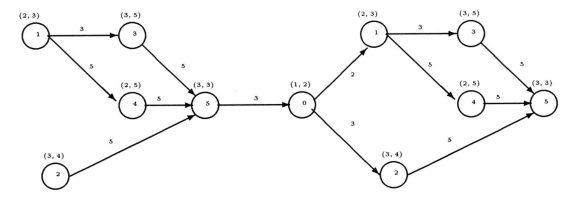

Figure 3. Determining "short" critical event sequences for the example task of Figure 1.

as is legal. Since the events that are triggered in $\sigma_o(T)$ and $\sigma_1(T)$ are exactly the same, we have

$$\mathsf{dbf}(T, \hat{t}) = \sum_{(T,t,u) \in \sigma_o(T)} e(u) = \sum_{(T,t,u) \in \sigma_1(T)} e(u) \ . \quad (2)$$

We will refer to an event sequence such as $\sigma_1(T)$ as a **critical event sequence** for interval-length $\hat{t}$. That is, $\sigma(T) = [(T, t_1, u_1), (T, t_2, u_2), (T, t_3, u_3), \ldots, (T, t_n, u_n)]$ is a *critical event sequence for interval-length* $\hat{t}$ if and only if

1. The first event in $\sigma(T)$ is triggered at time 0; i.e., $t_1 = 0$,

2. Each subsequent event is triggered as soon as is legal,

3. All events in $\sigma(T)$ have deadlines at or before time $\hat{t}$, and

4. $\mathsf{dbf}(T, \hat{t}) = \displaystyle\sum_{(T,t,u) \in \sigma(T)} e(u)$.

We are now ready to describe our method for computing $\mathsf{dbf}(T, t)$. For small values of t, we will build (Section 2.1) lookup tables from which $\mathsf{dbf}(T, t)$ can be directly obtained. For larger t, we will show (Section 2.2) that the critical event-sequence exhibits a regular "repeating" pattern — a consequence of the recurring nature of the task. We will take advantage of this fact to reduce the problem of computing $\mathsf{dbf}(T, t)$ for large t to the problem of computing $\mathsf{dbf}(T, t)$ for small t; this can once again be done, as in Section 2.1, by table-lookup using the data structures that have already been built.

2.1 Computing $\mathsf{dbf}(T, t)$ for small values of t

Let us first attempt to compute $\mathsf{dbf}(T, \hat{t})$ for small values of $\hat{t}$. In particular, we will consider values of $\hat{t}$ such that, in the critical event-sequence for interval-length $\hat{t}$, *the source vertex is either not triggered at all, or is triggered exactly once*. To obtain all such event sequences, consider the graph obtained by taking two copies of the DAG, adding an edge from the sink vertex of one copy to the source vertex of the other copy and labelling this edge with the deadline of the sink vertex, and then deleting the source vertex of the first copy (see Figure 3 for this process applied to the example task of Figure 1). Now every path in this new graph corresponds to one of our event sequences (with certain event-sequences —those in which the source vertex is not triggered at all— repeated twice: once from each copy of the original DAG). Hence enumerating all event sequences reduces to enumerating all paths of a DAG. This is a problem that has been extensively studied by graph theorists (see, e.g., [10, Chapter 3], for a survey), and simple recursive algorithms are known for enumerating all paths in time that is linear in the total length (in terms of the number of vertices) of all the paths.

We use this recursive algorithm as the basis of a procedure that examines all such event sequences. Let $(u_1, u_2, \ldots, u_\ell)$ be a path in this enhanced graph — observe that the source vertex appears at most once in this path. The corresponding critical event sequence is

$$\sigma(T) = [(T, t_1, u_1), (T, t_2, u_2), (T, t_3, u_3), \ldots, (T, t_\ell, u_\ell)],$$

where $t_1 = 0$ and $t_{i+1} = t_i + p(u_i, u_{i+1})$. For each such sequence $\sigma(T) = [(T, t_1, u_1), (T, t_2, u_2), (T, t_3, u_3), \ldots, (T, t_\ell, u_\ell)]$, we compute an ordered pair (e, d) such that

$e = \displaystyle\sum_{(T,t,u) \in \sigma(T)} e(u)$, and $d = t_\ell + d(u_\ell)$. Intuitively, the ordered pair (e, d) indicates that e is a lower bound on $\mathsf{dbf}(T, d)$ — the event sequence from which this ordered pair was computed is witness to this fact. These ordered pairs are directed into two separate lists — List0(T), consisting of ordered pairs corresponding to event sequences that do *not* contain the source vertex, and List1(T), consisting of ordered pairs corresponding to event sequences that contain the source vertex exactly once.

Having generated List0(T) and List1(T), the next steps are to

1. Sort the lists in non-decreasing order, according to the following rule: (e_1, d_1) is "less than" (e_2, d_2) if $(d_1 < d_2)$ or $((d_1 = d_2) \wedge (e_1 > e_2))$.

2. Compress the sorted lists according to the following rule: ordered pair (e_i, d_i) is deleted from a list if there exists an ordered pair (e_j, d_j) in the list, $j < i$, for which $e_j \geq e_i$.

It is straightforward to show that the ordered pairs remaining in List0(T) and List1(T) after these (sorting and deleting) steps are exactly the ordered pairs (e, d) such that $\mathsf{dbf}(T, d) = e$. Hence, for any $\hat{t}$ such that the critical event sequence for interval-length $\hat{t}$ contains the source vertex at most once, $\mathsf{dbf}(T, \hat{t})$ can now be determined from these two lists as follows:

$$\mathsf{dbf}(T, \hat{t}) = \max\{e_i \mid (e_i, d_i) \text{ is an ordered pair} \\ \text{in List0(T) or List1(T), and } d_i \leq \hat{t}\}$$

2.2 Computing $\mathsf{dbf}(T, t)$ for any t

Next, let us consider values of $\hat{t}$ such that the critical-sequence $\sigma(T)$ for interval-length $\hat{t}$ contains the source vertex two or more times. Let t'_s and t'_f denote the earliest and latest time-instants respectively in $[0, \hat{t})$ when the source vertex s of T is triggered in $\sigma(T)$. That is, t'_s is the minimum t such that (T, t, s) is in $\sigma(T)$, and t'_f is the maximum t such that (T, t, s) is in $\sigma(T)$ (Figure 4).

$\mathsf{dbf}(T, \hat{t})$ can be represented as the sum of three terms, with the processor demands over intervals $[0, t'_s)$, $[t'_s, t'_f)$, and $[t'_f, t)$ being represented by the first, sec-

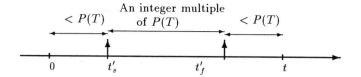

Figure 4. Instants t'_s and t'_f are the first and last ready-times of the root-node in the critical event sequence for interval-length t.

ond, and third terms respectively:

$$\left(\sum_{(T,t,R) \in \sigma(T) \,\wedge\, t < t'_s} e(R) \right) \quad (3)$$

$$+ \left(\sum_{(T,t,R) \in \sigma(T) \,\wedge\, t'_s \leq t < t'_f} e(R) \right)$$

$$+ \left(\sum_{(T,t,R) \in \sigma(T) \,\wedge\, t'_f \leq t} e(R) \right) .$$

The middle term of this expression covers an interval that may be arbitrarily large, but is guaranteed to be of duration a multiple of $P(T)$; i.e., $t'_f - t'_s$ is an integer multiple of $P(T)$. The processor demand over this interval is easily computed:

$$\left(\sum_{(T,t,u) \in \sigma(T) \,\wedge\, t'_s \leq t < t'_f} e(u) \right) = \frac{t'_f - t'_s}{P(T)} \cdot E(T) , \quad (4)$$

where $E(T)$ denotes the maximum cumulative execution requirement on a path from the source vertex to the sink vertex (both inclusive), and is thus equal to the largest execution requirement for T between successive triggerings of the source vertex. (For the example task T in Figure 1, $E(T)$ is 9.)

Consider the event sequence obtained by "removing" the time-interval $[t'_s, t'_f)$ from $\sigma(T)$. That is, consider the new event sequence obtained from $\sigma(T)$ by the following rules:

- include all events $(T, t, u) \in \sigma(T)$, for which $t < t'_s$.

- exclude all events $(T, t, u) \in \sigma(T)$, for which $t'_s \leq t < t'_f$.

- for each event $(T, t, u) \in \sigma(T)$ with $t \geq t'_f$, include the event $(T, t - (t'_f - t'_s), u)$.

Observe that this new event-sequence

1. contains exactly the subtasks contributing to the first and third terms in Expression 3;

2. has <u>one</u> triggering of the root subtask, corresponding to the triggering of the root subtask at time t'_f in $\sigma(T)$, and

3. is exactly the critical event sequence for interval-length $\hat{t} - (t'_f - t'_s)$.

Based upon this observation and Equation 3 above, we conclude that

$$\mathsf{dbf}(T, \hat{t}) = \frac{t'_f - t'_s}{P(T)} \cdot E(T) + \mathsf{dbf}(T, \hat{t} - (t'_f - t'_s)) \; ; \; (5)$$

furthermore, $\mathsf{dbf}(T, \hat{t} - (t'_f - t'_s))$ can be determined from $\mathsf{List1}(T)$ using the method described in Section 2.1 above. Thus the problem of determining $\mathsf{dbf}(T, \hat{t})$ reduces to the problem of determining $\mathsf{dbf}(T, \hat{t} - (t'_f - t'_s))$, *provided we know what the value of $\hat{t} - (t'_f - t'_s)$ is.* We do know that this interval of length $\hat{t} - (t'_f - t'_s)$ contains exactly one triggering of the root subtask; hence, $\hat{t} - (t'_f - t'_s)$ must be strictly less than $2P(T)$; we also know that $(t'_f - t'_s)$ is a multiple of $P(T)$. These two facts together imply that $\hat{t} - (t'_f - t'_s)$ is either $\hat{t} \bmod P(T)$, or $P(T) + \hat{t} \bmod P(T)$; we consider both possibilities, and choose the one that yields the largest value for $\mathsf{dbf}(T, \hat{t})$ in Equation 5. That is,

$$\mathsf{dbf}(T, \hat{t}) = \max \{$$
$$\quad (\hat{t} \text{ div } P(T)) \cdot E(T) + \mathsf{dbf}(\hat{t} \bmod P(T))$$
$$\quad (\hat{t} \text{ div } P(T) - 1) \cdot E(T) + \mathsf{dbf}(P(T) + \hat{t} \bmod P(T))$$
$$\}$$

where div is the integer divide function, and the dbf computations on the right hand side are done by looking up table $\mathsf{List1}(T)$ only.

3   Determining lmt

Recall that we'd discussed in the Introduction how one can easily design a feasibility test for a recurring real-time task system based upon the processor demand criteria methodology, provided $\mathsf{dbf}(T, t)$ can be efficiently computed:

for $\hat{t} = 1, 2, 3, \ldots, \mathsf{lmt}$
    (where lmt is a constant whose value depends upon the exact characteristics of the tasks in the system)
    if ($\sum_{\text{all tasks } T} \mathsf{dbf}(T, \hat{t})) > \hat{t}$ return "infeasible"
return "feasible"

We now address the issue of determining lmt. For recurring real-time task T and positive integer t, let $\rho_{\mathrm{ave}}(T)$ and $\mathsf{Dbf}(T, t)$ be defined as follows:

$$\rho_{\mathrm{ave}}(T) \stackrel{\text{def}}{=} E(T)/P(T)$$
$$\mathsf{Dbf}(T, t) \stackrel{\text{def}}{=} t \cdot \rho_{\mathrm{ave}}(T) + 2E(T)$$

It is not difficult to see that $\mathsf{Dbf}(T, t)$ is an upper bound on $\mathsf{dbf}(T, t)$ — this follows from Equation 3, and the observation that the second term in the summation is no larger than $t \cdot \rho_{\mathrm{ave}}(T)$ while the first and third terms are each no larger than $E(T)$.

If system Γ of recurring real-time tasks is infeasible, then there must exist a $\hat{t}$ such that

$$\sum_{T \in \Gamma} \mathsf{dbf}(T, \hat{t}) > \hat{t}$$
$$\Rightarrow \sum_{T \in \Gamma} \mathsf{Dbf}(T, \hat{t}) > \hat{t} \; (\text{Since } \mathsf{Dbf}(T, t) \geq \mathsf{dbf}(T, t))$$
$$\Rightarrow \hat{t} \sum_{T \in \Gamma} \rho_{\mathrm{ave}}(T) + 2 \sum_{T \in \Gamma} E(T) > \hat{t}$$
$$\Rightarrow \hat{t} < \frac{2 \sum_{T \in \Gamma} E(T)}{1 - \sum_{T \in \Gamma} \rho_{\mathrm{ave}}(T)} \qquad (6)$$

Hence if Γ is infeasible, a $\hat{t}$ satisfying Inequality 6 will be discovered during the feasibility test above. Equivalently, if the feasibility test has not returned "infeasible" for all values of $\hat{t}$ satisfying Inequality 6, we can conclude that Γ is feasible. Thus, lmt is set equal to

$$\frac{2 \sum_{T \in \Gamma} E(T)}{1 - \sum_{T \in \Gamma} \rho_{\mathrm{ave}}(T)}$$

Any system with $\sum_{T \in \Gamma} \rho_{\mathrm{ave}}(T) > 1$ is infeasible. If $\sum_{T \in \Gamma} \rho_{\mathrm{ave}}(T)$ is bounded by a constant strictly less than one, then this bound is pseudopolynomial in the representation of the input problem instance.

A note on complexity

As we'd pointed out in the introduction, the processor demand criteria methodology reduces feasibility-analysis to the following two questions:

Q1: How do we efficiently compute the demand bound function dbf? and

Q2: How do we choose a small *testing set* for t — a set of values of t such that verifying (1) for each t in the testing set is sufficient to establish that (1) holds for all $t \geq 0$?

Q2 was answered in Section 3, using techniques essentially identical to the ones used previously in [3, 4, 5, 9]. As in [3, 4, 5, 9], this step takes time pseudopolynomial in the representation of the input problem instance.

In answering Q1, we had to enumerate all paths in a DAG (Section 2.1). This takes time linear in the total length of all paths in the enhanced DAG (which is obtained by taking two copies of the DAG and adding an edge from the sink of one copy to the source of the other copy). Unfortunately, there may in general be an exponential number of such paths (as many as $\mathcal{O}(\sqrt{k}^{\sqrt{k}})$, for a DAG with k vertices); consequently, this procedure could end up taking time exponential in the size of the task representation. The recurring real-time task model therefore deviates from the trend established in earlier work with respect to the sporadic, multiframe, and branching models, in that feasibility-analysis need no longer be a pseudo-polynomial time operation.

In defense of this model, however, we point out the following:

- In many large application systems, each individual task is not too large — this is a consequence of the general object-oriented or "modular" approach to system design, in which systems are implemented as a large number of interacting objects. Since the complexity is exponential only in the size of *individual* tasks rather than the size of the entire system of tasks, feasibility analysis of such systems remains tractable.

- Furthermore, efficient polynomial-time algorithms are known (see, e.g, [10]) for determining how many paths there are in a DAG. Hence with respect to a particular task, one can pre-compute how many critical event sequences are going to have to be analyzed *prior* to actually enumerating them —- if this number is unacceptably high, the task can be redesigned (e.g, broken up into smaller tasks) by the applications system designer prior to feasibility analysis.

- It should also be noted that the recurring real-time task model is a *generalization* of previous models; as such, this methodology can be used to model and analyze sporadic, multiframe, and branching tasks as well (in which case the DAGs are a single node, a chain, or a tree respectively). For such tasks, the number of critical event sequences that need to be examined is polynomial in the size of the input – a consequence of the fact that chains and trees have a polynomial number of paths. Thus, our method of analysis is no more expensive than previous methods for systems that could be modelled using these previous models. This fact renders our model particularly useful in application systems where most of the tasks can be modelled as chains or trees, but a few tasks need the full expressive power of DAGs. Previous modelling techniques would fail to model such a system; using our model, however, we can construct a model for the system, while paying the exponential runtime cost for just a few — hopefully, not-too-large — tasks.

- In any case, the current trend towards the widespread and inexpensive availability of powerful computing resources makes possible the use of algorithmic techniques that were previously considered computationally intractable. This research fits in with the recent general approach of using extensive computer simulation for feasibility determination, and to design, implement, and test feasibility-analysis algorithms and heuristics that would have been considered impractical a few years ago, but now deserve consideration for inclusion in the toolbox of real-time application system developers.

4 Conclusions

As real-time safety-critical application software requirements have become increasingly more complex, there is an increasing need for formal models of real-time processes that satisfy the contradictory properties of (i) being powerful enough to model these complex requirements, and (ii) being efficiently analyzable to ensure that the application systems being designed satisfy basic safety properties. With these twin goals in mind, there has been considerable work done in designing new and powerful models of real-time tasks for which feasibility-analysis remains efficiently do-able. This includes the sporadic tasks model, the multiframe tasks model, and the branching tasks model — this list is by no means exhaustive.

In all of these models, "tractable" has been assumed to mean in polynomial or at worst pseudo-polynomial time. The current explosion in computing capacity – today's desktop personal computers are computationally more powerful than the mainframes of a few years ago – has however forced a re-evaluation of this interpretation of tractability. With this in mind, there has recently been a willingness to explore the use of exponential-time algorithms, particularly on problems that are usually *small*, which must be solved *off-line* rather than at run-time, and for which some estimate of the total run-time can be efficiently determined a priori.

The task model introduced in this paper — the **recurring real-time task model** — is an instance of this approach. By permitting exponential-time off-line analysis on individual (hopefully, rather small) tasks, we have designed a task model that is significantly more general and more powerful than earlier models, and have devised a feasibility-test for a system of such tasks. We have implemented and tested our feasibility-test — the algorithms are simple and easy to code, and the run-time behavior is very satisfactory.

Acknowledgements

The presentation of this research was substantially improved with the help of the comments provided by the anonymous reviewers.

This research builds upon previous work done jointly with Rod Howell, Al Mok, Lou Rosier, Deji Chen, and Sergey Gorinsky.

References

[1] A. K. Mok. *Fundamental Design Problems of Distributed Systems for The Hard-Real-Time Environment.* PhD thesis, Laboratory for Computer Science, Massachusetts Institute of Technology, 1983. Available as Technical Report No. MIT/LCS/TR-297.

[2] Giorgio C. Buttazzo. *Hard Real-Time Computing Systems: Predictable Scheduling Algorithms and Applications.* Kluwer Academic Publishers, 101 Philip Drive, Assinippi Park Norwell, MA 02061, USA, 1997.

[3] S. Baruah, A. Mok, and L. Rosier. The preemptive scheduling of sporadic, real-time tasks on one processor. In *Proceedings of the 11th Real-Time Systems Symposium*, pages 182–190, Orlando, Florida, 1990. IEEE Computer Society Press.

[4] Sanjoy Baruah. *The Uniprocessor Scheduling of Sporadic Real-Time Tasks.* PhD thesis, Department of Computer Science, The University of Texas at Austin, 1993.

[5] Sanjoy Baruah, Deji Chen, Sergey Gorinsky, and Aloysius Mok. Generalized multiframe tasks. *Real-Time Systems: The International Journal of Time-Critical Computing.* To appear.

[6] Hiroaki Takada and Ken Sakamura. Schedulability of generalized multiframe task sets under static priority assignment. In *Proceedings of the Fourth International Workshop on Real-Time Computing Systems and Applications*, pages 80–86, Taipei, Taiwan, October 1997.

[7] Aloysius K. Mok and Deji Chen. A multiframe model for real-time tasks. In *Proceedings of the 17th Real-Time Systems Symposium*, Washington, DC, 1996. IEEE Computer Society Press.

[8] C. Liu and J. Layland. Scheduling algorithms for multiprogramming in a hard real-time environment. *Journal of the ACM*, 20(1):46–61, 1973.

[9] Sanjoy Baruah. Feasibility analysis of recurring branching tasks. In *Proceedings of the Tenth Euromicro Workshop on Real-time Systems*, pages 138–145, Berlin, Germany, June 1998.

[10] Bernard Carre. *Graphs and Networks.* Oxford Applied Mathematics and Computing Science Series. Oxford University Press, 1979.

Statistical Rate Monotonic Scheduling*

Alia Atlas[†]
Dept of Internetwork Research
BBN Technologies
Cambridge, MA 02138

Azer Bestavros
Computer Science Department
Boston University
Boston, MA 02215

{akatlas, best}@cs.bu.edu

Abstract

Statistical Rate Monotonic Scheduling (SRMS) is a generalization of the classical RMS results of Liu and Layland [10] for periodic tasks with highly variable execution times and statistical QoS requirements. The main tenet of SRMS is that the variability in task resource requirements could be smoothed through aggregation to yield guaranteed QoS. This aggregation is done over time for a given task and across multiple tasks for a given period of time. Similar to RMS, SRMS has two components: a feasibility test and a scheduling algorithm. SRMS feasibility test ensures that it is possible for a given periodic task set to share a given resource without violating any of the statistical QoS constraints imposed on each task in the set. The SRMS scheduling algorithm consists of two parts: a job admission controller and a scheduler. The SRMS scheduler is a simple, preemptive, fixed-priority scheduler. The SRMS job admission controller manages the QoS delivered to the various tasks through admit/reject and priority assignment decisions. In particular, it ensures the important property of task isolation, whereby tasks do not infringe on each other.

1. Introduction

Traditional scheduling and resource management algorithms devised for periodic real-time task systems have focused on strict "hard" deadline semantics, whereby a set of periodic tasks is deemed *schedulable* if every instance of every task in the set is guaranteed to meet its deadline. An optimal fixed-priority algorithm is the classical Rate Monotonic Scheduling (RMS) algorithm of Liu and Layland[10]. To ensure the satisfaction of the hard deadlines imposed on periodic tasks, RMS requires that either the periodic resource requirement of each task be constant, or the periodic worst-case resource requirement of each task be known *a priori*. Given such knowledge, RMS guarantees the satisfaction of all deadlines, provided that a simple schedulability condition is satisfied. Using RMS on an unschedulable task system will improve

utilization, but will not provide clear predictability of which tasks will miss their deadlines. Indeed, because RMS couples period and priority, tasks with longer periods will miss deadlines more frequently than tasks with shorter periods—the criticality of the tasks is ignored.

There are many real-time, periodic applications in which (1) tasks have highly variable utilization requirements, and (2) deadlines are firm. For such applications, RMS is too restrictive in assuming a constant resource requirement, and it provides a more stringent guarantee on deadlines than is necessary. In particular, for such applications missing a deadline may be acceptable, as long as (say) a specified percentage of the deadlines are met. This flexibility—coupled with the variability in resource utilization—suggests that the worst-case resource requirement need not be planned for. An important class of such applications is the multiplexing of real-time multimedia streams on a shared fixed-bandwidth channel. For such an application, it is obvious that (1) the individual streams may have highly variable bandwidth requirements, and (2) missing deadlines, while not desirable, is not fatal. Using RMS for arbitrating a shared communication channel amongst the various streams is impractical, as it would result in very poor utilization.

This paper presents Statistical Rate Monotonic Scheduling (SRMS), a generalization of RMS that allows the scheduling of periodic tasks with highly variable execution times and statistical QoS requirements. SRMS maximizes the utilization of the resources being managed. In particular, it wastes no resource bandwidth on jobs that will miss their deadlines, due to overload conditions, resulting from excessive variability in execution times. SRMS is cognizant of the value of the various tasks in the system. Thus, it ensures that under overload conditions, the deterioration in QoS suffered by the various tasks is inversely proportional to their value.

2. Related Work

SRMS uses a schedulability analysis similar to that of RMS. This makes many of the schedulability results obtained for RMS applicable to SRMS as well. Examples of such results include the less restrictive, though more complex, ex-

*This work was partially supported by NSF grant CCR-9706685.
[†]Research completed while co-author was at Boston University.

act schedulability test by Lehoczky, Sha and Ding [9] and the less accurate but faster polynomial-time schedulability test by Han and Tyan [7].

SRMS relaxes the pivotal assumption of RMS—namely that the resource requirement of a periodic task is fixed. Several other relaxations of this assumption have been explored in the literature. The execution time of real-time tasks has been examined and modeled [21, 5]. In [6], Chung, Liu and Lin defined incremental tasks, where the value to the system increases with the amount of time given to the task, until the deadline occurs. In [12], Mok and Chen presented the multiframe model, where each task has a sequence of resource requirements which it iterates through. In [18], Tan and Hsu used feedback to control the resource requirements of tasks and admission control to prevent overload.

When a system has variable resource requirements, overload is expected to occur. When a system is in overload, the goal of the scheduling algorithm must be revisited since meeting *all* deadlines becomes impossible. Possible system goals include maximizing the number of deadlines met [3], maximizing the effective processor utilization [3], and completing all critical work [18, 8]. In [11], Marucheck and Strosnider provided a taxonomy of scheduling algorithms with varying levels of overload and criticality cognizance. To deal with overload, Koren and Shasha introduced the skip factor in [8], where occasionally a job can be skipped. This was expanded to (n m)-hard deadlines by Bernat and Burns in [4], where the relaxed deadline requirement allowed increased responsiveness for aperiodic tasks.[1]

Dealing with variable execution requirements introduces an unpredictability akin to that introduced when aperiodic tasks are to be executed along with RMS-scheduled periodic tasks. This latter problem has been examined in a number of studies. Proposed solutions include the polling server [14], the deferrable server [17], the sporadic server [15], the extended priority exchange algorithm [16], and slack stealing [13]. The latter keeps exact track of the slack available in the system at every priority and reclaims unused execution time.

The work of Tia *et al.* [20] is most closely related to SRMS in that it considered the problem of scheduling periodic tasks with variable resource requirements and soft deadlines. In their study, Tia *et al.* presented the transform-task method, which uses a threshold value to separate jobs guaranteed under the RMS schedulability condition from those which would require additional work. Jobs that fall under the threshold are guaranteed to meet their deadlines by RMS. The other jobs are split into two parts. The first part is considered as a periodic job with a resource requirement equal to the threshold; the second part is considered to be a sporadic job and is scheduled via the sporadic server when the periodic part has completed. In [20], an analysis was given for the probability that the sporadic job would meet its deadline. However, the sporadic jobs are served in FIFO order,

disregarding any sort of intertask fairness. Finally, no jobs are ever rejected, because the deadlines are soft and all work must be completed.

Motivated by the work in [20], we considered a similar approach, Slack Stealing Job Admission Control (SSJAC) [2], where tasks have firm deadlines and slack stealing was used to admit or reject jobs. Associated with each task is a threshold. Jobs with resource requirements below the threshold were automatically admitted. Jobs with resource requirements above that threshold were considered for admittance based upon the slack in the system at their priority level. SSJAC is discussed in more detail in section 5.2 as we pit it against SRMS for performance comparison purposes.

3. Statistical Rate Monotonic Scheduling

3.1. SRMS Task Model

The SRMS task model we use in this paper extends the RMS's task model and the semiperiodic task model given by Tia *et al.* [20]. We start with the following basic definitions.

Definition 1 *A periodic task, τ_i, is a three-tuple, $(P_i, f_i(x), Q_i)$, where P_i is the task's period, $f_i(x)$ is the probability density function (PDF) for the task's periodic resource utilization requirement, and Q_i is the task's requested Quality of Service (QoS).*

Without loss of generality, we assume that tasks are ordered rate monotonically. Task 1, τ_1, is the task with the shortest period, P_1. The task with the longest period is τ_n, where n is the total number of tasks in the system. The shorter the period, the higher the task's priority.[2] At the start of every P_i units of time, a new instance of task τ_i (a *job* of task τ_i) is available and has a firm deadline at the end of that period. Thus, the jth job of task i—denoted by $\tau_{i,j}$—is released and ready at time $(j-1) * P_i$ and its firm deadline is at time $j * P_i$. Its ready time is denoted by $r_{i,j}$ and its deadline is denoted by $d_{i,j}$.[3]

Definition 2 *The superperiod of τ_i is P_{i+1}, the period of the next lower priority task, τ_{i+1}.*

We assume that the resource requirements for all jobs of a given task are independent and identically distributed (iid) random variables. The distribution is characterized using the probability density function (PDF), $f(x)$. Obviously, it is impossible for a job to require more than 100% of the resource. Thus, $x > P \leadsto f(x) = 0$. We assume that the resource requirement for a job is known when the job is released and that such a requirement is accurate.[4] The resource requirement for the jth job of the ith task is denoted by $e_{i,j}$.

---

[1] Out of any consecutive m jobs, at least n must meet their deadlines.

[2] It is important to note that the "priority" of a task is not (and should not) be mistaken for the "value" (or importance) of a task. In particular, the manner in which a resource is allotted to various tasks depends on both task priority and value.

[3] While this model does not include non-zero task phases, the small modification necessary to support them is described in subsection 3.3.

[4] If this assumption cannot be ensured, then a policing mechanism could be employed, whereby when a task is given the resource, an interrupt is set so that the task is interrupted at the end of its "requested" time to ensure that it does not use more than what it had requested upon its release.

The third element of a task specification under the SRMS paradigm is its requested Quality of Service (QoS). For the purpose of this paper, we restrict QoS to the following definition.[5]

Definition 3 *The quality of service $QoS(\tau_i)$ for a task τ_i is defined as the probability that in an arbitrarily long execution history, a randomly selected job of τ_i will meet its deadline.*

To enable tasks to meet their requested QoS, SRMS assigns to each task τ_i an allowance, which is replenished periodically (every superperiod) to a preset value a_i. Task allowances are set through the QoS negotiation process (*i.e.* SRMS schedulability analysis). In particular, as we will show later in this section, there is a one-to-one correspondence between the allowance extended to a task and the QoS it achieves. A task set is schedulable under SRMS if the QoS of every task in the task set is satisfied through a feasible assignment of allowances.

Definition 4 *A set of tasks $\tau_1, \tau_2, ..., \tau_n$ is said to be schedulable under SRMS, if every task τ_i is guaranteed to receive its allowance a_i at the beginning of every one of its superperiods. Thus, a schedulable task set is one in which every task achieves its specified/negotiated QoS.*

3.2. Overview of SRMS Scheduling Algorithm

The SRMS algorithm consists of two parts: a job admission controller and a scheduler. Like RMS, the SRMS scheduler is a simple, preemptive, fixed-priority scheduler, which assigns the resource to the job with the highest priority that is in need of the resource. The SRMS job admission controller is responsible for maintaining the QoS requirements of the various tasks through admit/reject and priority assignment decisions. In particular, it ensures the important property of *task isolation*, whereby tasks do not infringe upon each other's guaranteed allowances. Job admission control occurs at a job's release time. All admitted jobs are guaranteed to meet their deadlines through a priority assignment that is rate monotonic (similar to RMS). Jobs that are not admitted may be either discarded, or allowed to execute at a priority lower than that of all admitted jobs.[6]

SRMS consists of an analyzable core and several extensions to optimize performance. In the remainder of this section we consider each of these components, starting with SRMS core, which we henceforth term *Basic SRMS*.

3.3. Basic SRMS with Harmonic Task Sets

One of the main tenets of SRMS is that *the variability in task resource requirements could be smoothed through aggregation*. To simplify the analysis of the gains possible through such aggregation, we start with an examination of Basic SRMS for harmonic task sets. We consider non-harmonic task sets later in subsection 3.4.

---

[5]Other definitions which allow for closed-form schedulability analysis include (for example) restricting the execution history to a finite window.

[6]This is discussed in more details in section 4.

Definition 5 *A task set is harmonic if, for any two tasks τ_i and τ_j, $P_i < P_j \Rightarrow P_i | P_j$.*

Basic SRMS is based upon the following task transformation. A task, τ_i, with period, P_i, is transformed into a task with a longer period, P_{i+1}. If the original task was assumed to have a fixed resource requirement, t_i, then the new resource requirement is $t_i * \frac{P_{i+1}}{P_i} = a_i$.

Lemma 1 *If a task system, $((P_1, t_1), ..., (P_i, t_i), (P_{i+1}, t_{i+1}), ...(P_n, t_n))$, is schedulable according to RMS, then the transformed task system $((P_1, t_1), ..., (P_{i+1}, t_i * \frac{P_{i+1}}{P_i}), (P_{i+1}, t_{i+1}), ...(P_n, t_n))$ is also schedulable.*

This task transformation depends upon the ability to arbitrarily break ties between two tasks with the same period, so that either can be given the higher priority. Therefore, it is possible to transform task τ_i to have the same period as task τ_{i+1} and still maintain a higher priority. If task τ_i were transformed to have a period longer than P_{i+1}, then either it would have a lower priority than τ_{i+1} and miss deadlines, or it would have a higher priority and could cause τ_{i+1} to miss deadlines. Therefore, the maximum interval over which jobs can be aggregated is the period of the next lowest priority task.

In the SRMS model presented, task phases are not considered, but little modification is necessary to support them. The task transformation is valid with non-zero task phases. The sole difference is that with phases, the start of a task's superperiod does not align with the release of a job of the next lower priority task. That is the start of the first superperiod for task τ_i occurs at $r_{i,1}$, not at $r_{i+1,1}$.

The task transformation above is meaningless for the last task in the system, τ_n. The goal of the task transformation is to aggregate as many jobs as possible without causing lower priority jobs to miss their deadlines. Task τ_n has no lower priority jobs to be concerned over and can therefore have an arbitrarily large superperiod. To visualize this, imagine that there is a task τ_{n+1} with no resource requirement and an arbitrarily large period.

In SRMS job admission control is used to ensure that: (1) no task is using more of the resource than it has been guaranteed, and (2) no task is admitted if it cannot be guaranteed to meet its deadline. The first of the above two goals prevents higher priority tasks from infringing on the QoS promised to lower priority ones. The second goal maximizes the useful utilization of the resource by disallowing the use of the resource by any job that cannot be guaranteed to finish by its firm deadline.

SRMS job admission control works as follows. At the beginning of each superperiod, a task τ_i has its budget b_i replenished up to its allowance a_i. When a job $\tau_{i,j}$ is admitted to the system, its resource requirement $e_{i,j}$ is debited from the task's current budget. A job $\tau_{i,j}$ released at time $r_{i,j}$ and requesting $e_{i,j}$ units of resource time is admitted if the following two conditions (corresponding respectively to the two goals explained above) hold: (1) $e_{i,j}$ is less than b_i, and (2) $e_{i,j}$ is less than the time remaining in the period after all higher priority tasks have claimed their allowances. This leads to the following admissibility condition for a job $\tau_{i,j}$:

$$(e_{i,j} \leq b_i) \quad \wedge \quad (e_{i,j} \leq P_i - \sum_{j=1}^{i-1} \frac{a_j * P_i}{P_{j+1}})$$

Schedulability Analysis: In SRMS, each task is assigned an allowance, a_i, which is the amount of time the resource is assigned to that task during its superperiod.[7] For schedulability analysis purposes, the allowance takes the place of the constant resource requirement in RMS. Thus, under SRMS, a necessary and sufficient condition for a *harmonic* task set to be schedulable is that:

$$\sum_{i=1}^{n} \frac{a_i}{P_{i+1}} \leq 1$$

Moreover, according to RMS and Lemma 1, a transformed task is guaranteed to receive at least its allowance every superperiod. To be able to relate the QoS achieved by a given allowance, it is necessary to determine how many jobs available during a superperiod can be completed, given that allowance. Recall, that under Basic SRMS, periods are harmonic and thus no *overlap* jobs exist. For our calculations, we will assume that the probability distribution function is truncated, so that no impossible jobs are submitted to the system.[8]

As illustrated in figure 1, a job $\tau_{i,j}$ can fall into $\frac{P_{i+1}}{P_i}$ different *phases* within the superperiod P_{i+1}. The probability that $\tau_{i,j}$ will be admitted is dependent on the phase in which it falls. To explain this, it suffices to observe that the first job in the superperiod has a replenished budget and has the best chance of making its deadline, while the last job in the superperiod has a smaller chance, because the budget is likely to have been depleted.

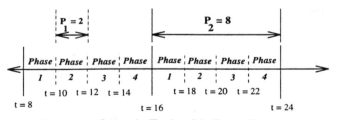

Figure 1. Sample Task with Four Phases

An arbitrary job $\tau_{i,j}$ has an equal probability of being in any given phase out of the possible $\frac{P_{i+1}}{P_i}$ phases within the superperiod P_{i+1}. To explain this, it suffices to note that in an infinite execution of task τ_i, there will be an equal number

of jobs in each phase, and thus a uniform distribution for the phase of a randomly selected job is reasonable.

Let $S_{i,k} = 1$ ($S_{i,k} = 0$) denote the event that a job $\tau_{i,j}$ released at the beginning of phase k of a superperiod of task τ_i is admitted (not admitted) to the system. Now, we proceed to compute $P(S_{i,k} = 1)$—the probability of admitting a job in the kth phase of a superperiod of task τ_i (i.e. the probability of success).

Recall that a_i is the allowance made available to task τ_i at the start of its superperiod P_{i+1}, which is the start of the first phase. Obviously, a job $\tau_{i,j}$ released in this first phase (i.e. $k = 1$) will be admitted only if its requested utilization is less than or equal to a_i. This leads to the following relationship.

$$P(S_{i,1} = 1) \quad = \quad P(e_{i,j} \leq a_i)$$

For a job $\tau_{i,j}$ released in the second phase (i.e. $k = 2$), two possibilities exist, depending on whether the job released in the first phase was admitted or not admitted. This leads to the following relationship.

$$\begin{aligned} P(S_{i,2} = 1) \quad &= \quad P(e_{i,j-1} \leq a_i) * P(e_{i,j-1} + e_{i,j} \leq a_i) \\ &+ P(e_{i,j-1} > a_i) * P(e_{i,j} \leq a_i) \\ \cdots \quad &= \quad \cdots \end{aligned}$$

Obviously, each $P(S_{i,k} = 1)$ can be calculated as the sum of 2^{k-1} different terms, where each term expresses a particular history of previous jobs being admitted and/or rejected (i.e. deadlines met and/or missed). Thus, to calculate $P(S_{i,3} = 1)$, the sum of the probabilities of all possible histories, where the job in the third phase meets its deadline, must be calculated. The set of possible histories are $((1,1,1), (1,0,1), (0,1,1), (0,0,1))$, where 1 represents a met deadline and 0 represents a missed deadline.

We are now ready to define the QoS guarantee that SRMS is able to extend to an arbitrary set of tasks with harmonic periods.

Theorem 1 *Given a task set with harmonic periods, the probability that an arbitrary job $\tau_{i,j}$ of task τ_i will be admitted is the QoS function of τ_i.*

$$QoS(\tau_i) = \frac{P_i}{P_{i+1}} * \sum_{k=1}^{\frac{P_{i+1}}{P_i}} P(S_{i,k} = 1)$$

Theorem 1 follows from the assumption that an arbitrary job has an equal probability of being in any given phase. The value thus calculated, $QoS(\tau_i)$, is the statistical guarantee which harmonic RMS provides on the probability that an arbitrary job will not miss its deadline.

3.4. Basic SRMS with Arbitrary Periods

Previously, we assumed that the task set is harmonic. When task periods are harmonic, it is impossible for the release time and deadline of a job to be in different superperiods. When task periods are not harmonic, this situation is possible—a

---

[7]The superperiod of the last task, which would be P_{n+1}, is not defined. It can be specified by the user. In practice, we have used $5 * P_n$ successfully. If all tasks in the system are expected to be in overload, then the superperiod of the last task should be shorter.

[8]In practice, if a job with an infeasible resource requirement is submitted, it must automatically be rejected.

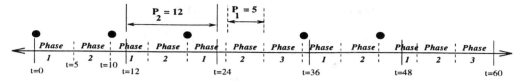

Figure 2. Phases for Task with Overlap Jobs

job could overlap two superperiods.[9] To generalize Basic SRMS to schedule task systems with arbitrary periods, we must determine how *overlap jobs* should be treated.

Definition 6 *A job $\tau_{i,j}$ whose release time is in one superperiod and whose deadline is in the next superperiod is called an* overlap *job.*

First, we explain the subtlety involved in dealing with overlap jobs. The primary purpose of job admission control in Basic SRMS is to prevent the variability in resource utilization by a high priority task from disturbing other lower priority tasks. This is done by ensuring that the high priority task does not consume more than its allocated budget within each of its superperiod. Now consider the advent of an overlap job. By definition, an overlap job is one that is released in one superperiod (the release superperiod) and whose deadline is in the next (the deadline superperiod). Figure 2 shows a task which has overlap jobs. The difficulty in making admission decisions for overlap jobs is due to the simple fact that any resource use charged to a given budget *must* be completed within the superperiod of that budget. The fact that overlap jobs span two superperiods complicates that process. There are three possibilities for admitting an overlap job, which we consider below.

If the overlap job is to be admitted based on the available budget in the release superperiod, then (in order not to disturb lower priority tasks) the overlap job must complete its execution before the end of the release superperiod. This may or may not be possible. If possible, the overlap job is admitted and the budget of the release superperiod is debited.

If the overlap job is to be admitted based on the available budget in the deadline superperiod, then (in order not to disturb lower priority tasks) the execution of the overlap job must be delayed until the beginning of the deadline superperiod, or at least until the job of the next lower priority task has finished its execution and thus is not subject to being infringed upon by the overlap job. Again, this may or may not be possible. If possible, the overlap job is admitted, but not permitted to run until after some delay, and the budget of the deadline superperiod is debited.

Finally, for the purpose of admission control and debiting the appropriate budgets, it would be possible to combine the above two possibilities by splitting the overlap job into two components. The first would be admitted at release time and allowed to execute against the budget available in the release superperiod. The second would be delayed until the

beginning of the deadline superperiod and allowed to execute against the budget available in that deadline superperiod. Again, this may or may not be possible. If possible, the overlap job would be admitted, otherwise it would be rejected. We did not implement this in SRMS due to the additional complexity required in the scheduler.

Schedulability Analysis: The evaluation of the feasibility of achieving the requested QoS for a SRMS task system with arbitrary periods is an elaboration of the schedulability analysis for a harmonic task system presented in subsection 3.3. The additional complexity is caused by an analysis of the behavior for overlap jobs. Due to space limitations, we do not include this analysis here. Interested readers are referred to the derivations and formulae in [1].

4. Extensions to Basic SRMS

In this section we examine a number of extensions that optimize the performance of the Basic SRMS algorithms presented in the previous section. For the remainder of this paper, we use SRMS to refer to the Basic SRMS algorithm (whether or not the task set is harmonic) when augmented with all of the extensions presented in this section.

Time Inheritance: At the start of each superperiod, a task's budget is replenished. However, that task (say τ_i) may have time leftover in the budget of its previous superperiod. In Basic SRMS, this unused budget is simply discarded. But, does it have to be? To answer this question, we first note that such leftover time can only be spent by a task with priority lower than that of τ_i. Task τ_i can't use the leftover allowance because such use may adversely affect τ_{i+1}. In particular, using this leftover time by τ_i may result in tasks of priority i and higher getting more than their fair share (i.e. reserved percentage) of the resource during the superperiod P_{i+1}. However, if τ_{i+1} is not also ending a superperiod, then τ_{i+1} *can* spend this leftover time. Such use won't affect τ_{i+2} because it will not result in exceeding the percentage of the resource reserved for tasks with priority higher than that of τ_{i+2}.[10]

Time inheritance is another instance of the SRMS concept of "smoothing the variability in resource usage through aggregation". In Basic SRMS, this aggregation was done over time for a single task (see Lemma 1). Using the time inheritance extension of SRMS, this aggregation is done across tasks. Figure 3 shows an example where time inheritance occurs twice.

---

[9]Again, if task τ_i has a non-zero phase, the start of the first superperiod is aligned with the release time of the first job $\tau_{i,1}$, not with the release of job $\tau_{i+1,1}$.

[10]Clearly, the last task in the system merely discards any unused allowance when it replenishes its budget.

127

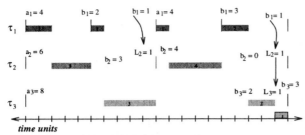

time units

Figure 3. Illustration of Time Inheritance

Second Chance Priorities: In Basic SRMS, it is possible to reject a job (1) because its budget is depleted, or (2) because the admission controller cannot guarantee that such job (if scheduled) will have enough time (leftover from higher priority tasks) to meet its deadline. The above two conditions—while sufficient to satisfy the task isolation and efficient resource utilization properties of SRMS—may be unnecessarily stringent. Namely, it is possible that a job may be rejected and still be allowed to use the resource *without* jeopardizing the task isolation and efficient resource utilization properties of SRMS. The admission controller pessimistically assumes that other tasks in the system will use their maximum allowances. If the other tasks do not, then "idle times" may be available to complete the job *despite* the job's failure to satisfy one (or even both) of the above conditions. Thus, rather than simply discarding rejected jobs, it would may be advantageous to give those jobs a *second chance*. This is the motivation for the following extension.

Each task has two possible priorities, either HIGH (and admitted) or LOW (and rejected). If a job is admitted, then the priority is set to HIGH and the allowance is debited. Otherwise, the priority is set to LOW and the allowance is unchanged. This splits the tasks into two RM-ordered priority bands. First, the HIGH priority tasks are scheduled; then, if there is time, the LOW priority tasks are scheduled. This gives guaranteed jobs highest priority, and still permits a best-effort attempt on the rejected jobs. For example, given two tasks with periods of 5 and 8 respectively, a HIGH priority job with period 8 is scheduled after a HIGH priority job with period 5 and before a LOW priority job with period 5.

5. Performance Evaluation of SRMS

To evaluate the performance of SRMS, we developed a simulator to run a periodic task system subject to the model and assumptions discussed in section 3.1.

5.1. Simulation Model and Performance Metrics

In our experiments, we made a number of simplifying assumptions. These assumptions were necessary to allow for a more straightforward interpretation of the simulation results, by eliminating conditions or factors that are not of paramount interest to the subject matter of this paper (e.g. effects of task criticality). First, we assumed that all tasks demand the same average percentage utilization of the resource be-

ing managed. In other words, the ratio $\frac{E(e_{i,k})}{P_i}$ for all tasks is constant. Second, the probability distributions used to generate the resource requirements were of the same type[11] (but with different parameters) for each task in the system. Also, these distributions were truncated so that no infeasible jobs were submitted to the system. Third, we assumed that all tasks were of equal criticality/importance, which implies that the assignment of allowances $(a_1, a_2, \ldots)$ to the tasks in the system should not reflect any preferability due to the task's "value" to the system.

To compare algorithms and discuss their characteristics, we define a few performance measures. In the following definitions, the number of tasks in the system is n.

Definition 7 *The job failure rate (JFR) is the average percentage of missed deadlines.*[12]

$$JFR = \frac{1}{n} * \sum_{i=1}^{n} \frac{\tau_i \ missed \ jobs}{\tau_i \ jobs}$$

We chose to use the job failure rate because it gives all tasks equal priority. Using a completion count gives unfair importance to tasks with shorter periods, because in any time interval, those tasks will release more jobs than tasks with longer periods. Naturally, this job failure rate assumes that all tasks are of equal criticality and require the same QoS.

With the assumption that all tasks require the same performance, there is a need to describe how fair the system is. For example, in RMS it is quite possible that the highest priority task meets all its deadlines and the lowest priority task meets none. Intertask unfairness describes how unfair the scheduling algorithm is.

Definition 8 *The intertask unfairness is a measure of how unfair the scheduling algorithm is to the different tasks. It is the standard deviation of the percent of missed jobs.*

$$Intertask \ Unfairness = \sqrt{\frac{\sum_{i=1}^{n} (\frac{\tau_i \ missed \ jobs}{\tau_i \ jobs} - JFR)^2}{n}}$$

Finally, we consider the average utilization requested of the system and the average useful utilization achievable by a scheduling algorithm. Note that the achievable utilization is an average, and some overloaded intervals may occur even when the requested utilization is within the schedulability requirement of RMS.

Definition 9 *The requested utilization is the sum of all jobs' resource requirements divided by the time interval during which scheduling occurs.*

Definition 10 *The achievable utilization is the sum of all successful jobs' resource requirements divided by the time interval during which scheduling occurs.*

---

[11] We considered a variety of such distributions as will be evident later in this section.

[12] This is the opposite of the **job completion rate** used in [11], which is the average percentage of met deadlines.

5.2. Algorithms Considered for Comparison

To evaluate the performance of SRMS, it was necessary to identify algorithms against which SRMS should be compared. This was challenging, as there are no algorithms in the literature addressing the problem of scheduling periodic tasks with highly-variable resource requirements under firm-deadline semantics, subject to minimal QoS requirements. We decided to use three algorithms: RMS, SSJAC, and an Oracle. We justify these choices below.

Rate Monotonic Scheduling: SRMS and RMS are alike in many aspects. Both employ a fixed priority preemptive scheduler, with priorities being assigned in a rate monotonic fashion. Despite the fact that RMS was designed for hard deadlines (as opposed to firm) and constant (as opposed to highly variable) resource requirements, we decided to use it to provide a baseline (a performance lower bound) of what is readily achievable using RMS.

Slack Stealing Job Admission Control: As described in section 2, SSJAC [2] uses slack-stealing to determine whether to admit jobs with resource requirements above a set threshold. Like SRMS, when a job is released, it must undergo admission control. If the job's resource requirement is below the threshold, then it is automatically admitted. Otherwise, it is conceptually "split" into two parts. The first has a resource requirement equal to the allowance and the second part has a resource requirement equal to difference between the originally requested resource requirement and the threshold. The second part is treated as a sporadic task with the same priority, release time, and deadline; it is considered for admittance using the slack in the system. If there is adequate slack to admit such a sporadic task, then the job (with both of its parts) is admitted to the system. Otherwise, the job is rejected. For SSJAC, we chose to calculate the available slack myopically so that no aperiodic servers are necessary. Once a job is admitted to the system, it runs completely at its original priority. To reclaim unspent resource time, we used Thuel's slack reclaimer [19].

SSJAC could be considered as an evolution of the *transform-task* method introduced by Tia *et al.* in [20]. For this problem, the performance of SSJAC subsumes that of the transform-task method. In SSJAC, any job which is not guaranteed to meet its deadline is discarded. This is the correct approach when dealing with firm deadlines—in contrast to the transform-task method's approach of completing all jobs, even if the deadline is missed, which is useful for soft (but not firm) deadlines. Second, rather than using the sporadic server, which has no guarantees, SSJAC uses slack stealing enabling the use of accurate job admission control with immediate results at a job's release time. The main drawback of SSJAC (when compared to the transform-task method) is the high overhead of slack stealing. However, in our experiments, we completely neglected overhead, thus giving SSJAC (as a representative of competing algorithms) a tremendous advantage over SRMS which has a constant overhead.

Oracles for Establishing Performance Upper Bounds: We found it interesting to consider, not merely how SRMS performed against RMS and SSJAC, but also how close is SRMS' performance to the "best possible" performance. To this end, we developed an omniscient oracle for systems with harmonic periods. The oracle accepts different value functions for each job, and will optimize the schedule accordingly. Three value functions are particularly useful. First, the optimal completion count is determined by assigning an equal value to each job of each task. We denote by OPT-J the oracle under this "all-jobs-are-equal" value function. Second, the optimal JFR is determined by using a function that values tasks equally by assigning to each job a value equal to its period. Thus, in any interval of time, each task has the same total value assigned to its jobs. We denote by OPT-T the oracle under this "all-tasks-are-equal" value function. Finally, the optimal effective processor utilization is determined by setting a job's value equal to its resource requirement. We denote by OPT-U the oracle under this "all-resource-cycles-are-equal" value function.

5.3. Simulation Experiments:

We will discuss two of the sets of simulation experiments that we conducted. The first set, *harmonic 5-Tasks*, contained five periodic tasks with harmonic periods.[13] The first period was fixed, and the remaining periods were chosen randomly, so that the ratio between adjacent periods was an *integer* uniformly distributed between two and four. The second set, *arbitrary 5-Tasks*, contained five periodic tasks with arbitrary (i.e. non-harmonic) periods. The first period was fixed, and the remaining periods were randomly chosen, with the ratio between adjacent periods being a *real number* uniformly distributed between two and six.

For our experiments, we pre-determined the resource requirement of each job, so that all algorithms were run on the identical scheduling problem. While we ran sets of different random systems, the results presented below show one run of a given set of randomly generated systems and are representative. We have also run experiments for significantly longer and shorter simulation periods, with comparable results.

Our experiments were run with different probability distributions used to generate the variable resource requests. We considered exponential, gamma, poisson, normal, uniform, and pareto distributions, as well as constant resource requirements, to determine if the gross behavior of the algorithms changed. We found that it did not. In this paper we restrict our presentation to the results we obtained for the poisson distribution. The poisson distribution was chosen because it is frequently used to model data arrivals. In real-time systems, a periodic task may well be responsible for processing all events that arrive within a period of time (hence the variability in execution requirements).

---

[13] The small size of our task sets was chosen to permit comparison against the *optimal oracles* discussed earlier.

Experiments with Harmonic Task Sets: First, we compare the performance of the various algorithms to those of the oracles we developed for harmonic task sets. Figure 4 shows that OPT-J forms a clear performance upper bound for RMS. This is expected since OPT-J maximizes the completion count. RMS attempts to maximize the completion count by giving preference to tasks with shorter periods (i.e. those likely to contribute "more" to the completion count due to their frequent jobs).

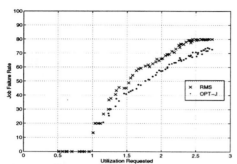

Figure 4. JFR of RMS vs OPT-J for *harmonic 5-Tasks* **with poisson PDFs.**

While RMS attempts to optimize the completion count, both SRMS and SSJAC do not. With all tasks given the same percentage utilization (and requesting the same percentage utilization), both SRMS and SSJAC attempt to fairly distribute the resource among all tasks. This is similar to the function maximized by OPT-T, which gives each task equal value. Figure 5 shows that OPT-T forms a clear performance upper bound for both SRMS and SSJAC.

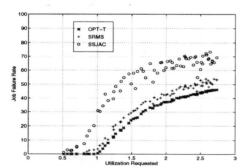

Figure 5. JFR of SRMS/SSJAC vs OPT-T for *harmonic 5-Tasks* **with poisson PDFs.**

We also compared the performance of SRMS, RMS and SSJAC, as shown in Figures 4 and 5. As expected, SRMS outperformed both RMS and SSJAC by a wide margin. Two factors contribute to SRMS superiority. First, SRMS attempts to assign the resource fairly to all tasks. Thus, no outlier tasks significantly reduce the job failure rate, and deadlines are missed fairly by the different tasks. Second, the ratio between adjacent periods is guaranteed to be at least two. This permits aggregation of at least two jobs, which increases the smoothing gained (we will discuss the significance of the ratio between adjacent periods at the end of this section).

As mentioned previously, RMS attempts to maximize the completion count which does not result in the maximization of the job failure rate. However, when the system is not in overload RMS may have performance superior to SRMS. This is because SRMS is pessimistic and more reactive to potential overload than RMS; SRMS may reject a job that could actually make its deadline without damaging effects if it were scheduled at an accepted priority. This can occur if one task in the system is in overload, but the others are not, and the overall system is not in overload.

SSJAC gains most of its advantage by scheduling the extra one third of the utilization which SRMS and RMS cannot guarantee. However, with harmonic periods, full utilization can be auctioned by both RMS and SRMS. Therefore, SSJAC edge is not likely to be evident when the task set is harmonic. Additionally, SSJAC can only acquire extra slack from the past. It cannot schedule an extra long job with the assumption that it can steal that time from the future, as SRMS does. Nonetheless, it does succeed in preventing one task from harming a guaranteed job of another task. In serious overload, SSJAC does perform better than RMS.

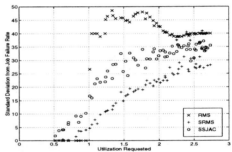

Figure 6. Intertask Unfairness for *harmonic 5-Tasks* **with poisson PDFs.**

Looking at the intertask unfairness shown in Figure 6, similar patterns apply. RMS is completely fair until it becomes overloaded. This is the case because no jobs miss their deadlines! However, as soon as deadlines are missed, the intertask unfairness for RMS rises rapidly, because RMS is extremely unfair in penalizing lower priority tasks. As the system becomes more overloaded, SRMS' intertask unfairness increases, but still manages to be the least of all three algorithms. SRMS' unfairness increases because of time inheritance; tasks with shorter periods will have jobs rejected. The unspent budgets of those tasks are added to the budgets of lower-priority (longer-period) tasks, thus improving the outlook for those tasks, and hence increasing SRMS' intertask unfairness. SSJAC exhibits an intertask unfairness between RMS and SRMS. SSJAC is better than RMS, because a set percentage of jobs for every task are admitted, since their requirements are below the threshold. However, SSJAC performs worse than SRMS because it distributes its slack on a FCFS basis.

Experiments with Arbitrary (non-harmonic) Task Sets: The results for task sets with arbitrary (non-harmonic) periods were similar to those obtained for harmonic task sets. As evident in Figure 7, RMS performs best before overload. As soon as overload occurs, SRMS has the best job failure rate throughout most of the overloaded area. However, when the overload becomes severe, SSJAC occasionally does better than SRMS. We believe that this is due to two factors. First, SSJAC usually has significant slack to distribute, which is the unguaranteed time, nearly a third of the resource. Second, in overload, SSJAC will reclaim even more time to redistribute, because more jobs will be rejected and not take any of their guaranteed allowances.

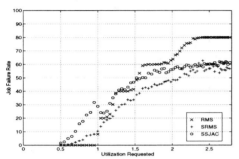

Figure 7. JFR for *arbitrary 5-Tasks* **with poisson PDFs.**

Figure 8 shows that the intertask unfairness observed for task sets with arbitrary periods is also similar to that observed for harmonic task sets. The main difference is that SSJAC may have better performance than SRMS under serious overload. For a few experiments, even RMS achieved lower unfairness.

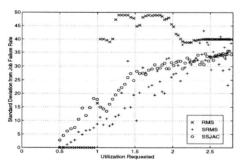

Figure 8. Intertask Unfairness for *arbitrary 5-Tasks* **with poisson PDFs.**

Figure 9 shows the achievable utilization for arbitrary task sets. Until overload is reached, RMS (again) delivers the best utilization with SRMS a close second. In overload, SRMS is a clear winner. This result is somewhat surprising. Although SSJAC can distribute nearly an extra one third of the utilization, it does not do better than SRMS.

5.4. Effect of Aggregation

As we iterated several times in this paper, one of the main tenets of SRMS is that the variability in periodic resource utilization for a given task can be smoothed through aggre-

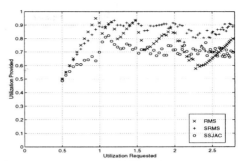

Figure 9. Resource Utilization for *arbitrary 5-Tasks* **with poisson PDFs.**

gation over time (see Lemma 1) and across tasks (see the extensions in section 4). Such an aggregation is most (least) effective when the ratio of adjacent periods (i.e. P_{i+1}/P_i) is large (small).

Although we could not include them in this paper (for space limitations), we have conducted extensive experiments to study the sensitivity of SRMS to the ratio of adjacent periods. We found that SSJAC does slightly better than SRMS in overload as long as the ratio of adjacent periods is less than two. The regions and shape of the intersection varies depending upon the probability distribution examined. While this is interesting for characterizing the algorithms, the overhead needed for SSJAC is *significantly* higher than that of SRMS, making SRMS much more attractive even when the ratio of adjacent periods is less than two.

6. The SRMS Workbench

For demonstration purposes, we have packaged: (1) the SRMS schedulability analyzer (QoS negotiator), and (2) our SRMS simulator (Basic SRMS + all extensions) into a Java Applet that can be executed remotely on any Java-capable Internet browser. For comparison, a RMS simulator and a SSJAC simulator are included.

Through a simple GUI, the *SRMS Workbench* allows users to specify a set of periodic tasks, each with (a) its own period, (b) the distributional characteristics of its periodic resource requirements (e.g. Poisson, Pareto, Normal, Exponential, Gamma, etc.), (c) its desired QoS as a lower bound on the percentage of deadlines to be met, and (d) a criticality/importance index indicating the value of the task (relative to other tasks in the task set). Once the task set is specified, the SRMS Workbench allows the user to check for schedulability under SRMS. If the task set is schedulable, the SRMS Workbench generates the appropriate allowance for each task and allows the user to create an animated simulation of the task system, which can be executed and profiled. If the task set is not schedulable, the SRMS Workbench informs the user of that fact and suggest (as part of the QoS negotiation) an alternative set of *feasible* QoS requirements that reflects the specified criticality/importance index of the tasks in the task set.

The SRMS Workbench is available at: `http://www.cs.bu.edu/groups/realtime/SRMSworkbench`

7. Conclusion and Future Work

In this paper, we have introduced Statistical Rate Monotonic Scheduling (SRMS)—an algorithm that schedules firm-deadline periodic tasks with variable resource requirements. In addition to providing a predictable scheduling algorithm for this type of periodic task, SRMS is value-cognizant, overload-cognizant, predictable, configurable and enforces task isolation. The job admission control used in SRMS introduces a low overhead of constant complexity. SRMS maximizes useful system utilization by not wasting resources on jobs which will fail. The SRMS enforces task isolation, so that no task can adversely affect another task. This permits SRMS to be overload-cognizant on an individual task basis; the responses caused by the overload only affect the misbehaving task. Additionally, quality of service (QoS) guarantees can be specified for each task[1]. SRMS also permits intratask fairness; a job with a large resource requirement can still be admitted, and a job with a small resource requirement can be rejected.

Our current work focuses on deploying SRMS in working real-time environments. In particular, we are examing a framework where the task set is allowed to change dynamically (i.e. new periodic tasks can enter the system and old ones can leave). To that end, we are designing an API suitable for SRMS, which would allow for QoS specification, negotiation, and for on-line task admission control, including notification of job admission or rejection decisions.

We plan to analyze the case of tasks where the deadlines are either shorter or longer than their periods. The former case for hard deadlines has been solved using deadline monotonic scheduling. We believe that a similar approach will work for SRMS; the key detail is defining the correct task transformation. The case of deadlines longer than their deadlines is more easily solved; the solution for RMS involves different priority bands of rate-monotonically ordered tasks. SRMS already has such bands for accepted and rejected jobs. To transform SRMS to have more bands would not be difficult. The complexity will come from determining when and which budgets should be debited to support a given job.

References

[1] A. K. Atlas and A. Bestavros. Multiplexing vbr traffic flows with guaranteed application-level qos using statistical rate monotonic scheduling. Technical Report BUCS-TR-98-011, Boston University, Computer Science Department, 1998.

[2] A. K. Atlas and A. Bestavros. Slack stealing job admission control. Technical Report BUCS-TR-98-009, Boston University, Computer Science Department, 1998.

[3] S. Baruah, J. Haritsa, and N. Sharma. On line scheduling to maximize task completions. In *Real-Time Systems Symposium*, pages 228–237, Dec. 1994. URL is http://www.emba.uvm.edu/ sanjoy/Papers/cc-jnl.ps.

[4] G. Bernat and A. Burns. Combining (n m)-hard deadlines and dual priority scheduling. In *Real-Time Systems Symposium*, pages 46–57, 1997.

[5] K. Bradley and J. K. Strosnider. An application of complex task modeling. In *Real-Time Technology and Applications Symposium*, pages 85–90, June 1998.

[6] J.-Y. Chung, J. W. S. Liu, and K.-J. Lin. Scheduling periodic jobs that allow imprecise results. *IEEE Transactions on Computers*, 39(9):1156–1174, Sept. 1990.

[7] C.-C. Han and H. ying Tyan. A better polynomial-time schedulability test for real-time fixed-priority scheduling algorithms. In *Real-Time Systems Symposium*, pages 36–45, 1997.

[8] G. Koren and D. Shasha. Skip-over: Algorithms and complexity for overloaded systems that allow skips. In *Real-Time Systems Symposium*, 1995.

[9] J. Lehoczky, L. Sha, and Y. Ding. The rate monotonic scheduling algorithm: Exact characterization and average case behavior. In *Real-Time Systems Symposium*, pages 166–171, 1989.

[10] C. Liu and J. Layland. Scheduling algorithms for multiprogramming in a hard-real-time environment. *Journal of the ACM*, 20(1), 1973.

[11] M. Marucheck and J. Strosnider. An evaluation of the graceful degradation properties of real-time schedulers. In *The Twenty Fifth Annual International Symposium on Fault-Tolerant Computing*, June 1995.

[12] A. K. Mok and D. Chen. A multiframe model for real-time tasks. In *Real-Time Systems Symposium*. IEEE Computer Society Press, Dec. 1996.

[13] S. Ramos-Thuel and J. P. Lehoczky. Algorithms for scheduling hard aperiodic tasks in fixed-priority systems using slack stealing. In *Real-Time Systems Symposium*. IEEE Computer Society Press, Dec. 1994.

[14] K. G. Shin and Y.-C. Chang. A reservation-based algorithm for scheduling both periodic and aperiodic real-time tasks. *IEEE Transactions on Computers*, 44:1405–1419, Dec. 1995.

[15] B. Sprunt. *Aperiodic task scheduling for real-time systems*. PhD thesis, Department of Electrical and Computer Engineering, Carnegie Mellon University, Pittsburgh, PA, Aug. 1990.

[16] B. Sprunt, J. Lehoczky, and L. Sha. Exploiting unused periodic time for aperiodic service using the extended priority exchange algorithm. In *Real-Time Systems Symposium*, 1988.

[17] J. K. Strosnider. *Highly responsive real-time token rings*. PhD thesis, Department of Electrical and Computer Engineering, Carnegie Mellon University, Pittsburgh, PA, Aug. 1988.

[18] T. G. Tan and W. Hsu. Scheduling multimedia applications under overload and non-deterministic conditions. In *Real-Time Technology and Applications Symposium*, June 1997.

[19] S. R. Thuel. *Enhancing Fault Tolerance of Real-Time Systems through Time Redundancy*. PhD thesis, Carnegie Mellon University, May 1993.

[20] T. Tia, Z. Deng, M. Shankar, M. Storch, J. Sun, L.-C. Wu, and J. W.-S. Liu. Probabilistic performance guarantees for real-time tasks with varying computation times. In *Real-Time Technology and Applications Symposium*, pages 164–173, May 1995.

[21] M. Woodbury. Analysis of the execution time of real-time tasks. In *Real-Time Systems Symposium*, pages 89–96, 1986.

Session 4.B: Timing Analysis and Compiler Techniques

Testing the Results of Static Worst-Case Execution-Time Analysis [*]

P. Puschner and R. Nossal[†]

Technische Universität Wien, A-1040 Wien, Austria

peter@vmars.tuwien.ac.at

Abstract

Analytically derived worst-case execution time (WCET) bounds are prone to errors, because they often rely on information provided by the user. This paper presents a method for testing the results of static WCET analysis. The proposed test method is a black-box test method that uses a genetic algorithm (GA) for test-case generation. Important properties of the method are (a) that it requires minimal information about possible input data from the user and (b) that the GA guides data generation into directions that have a good chance to yield the real WCET of the program under test. Experimental results show that GA-based testing produces results of high quality.

1 Introduction

The knowledge of task execution times is crucial for the development and verification of dependable real-time systems. This information must be available to allocate resources, to guide scheduling decisions, and to demonstrate the temporal correctness of real-time application programs.

In recent years researchers developed concepts and tools for computing worst-case execution time (WCET) information for real-time tasks by static analysis [11, 21, 12, 15]. These tools derive WCET bounds for tasks as follows: they analyze the code of the tasks for possible execution paths and then model the timing of the code on the target hardware. While the latter step of the analysis can be fully automated, the first step usually has to be supported by the programmer — the programmer annotates the task code with information about the possible execution paths. Due to this need for human interaction, WCET analysis is prone to er-

rors. The correctness of the results of static WCET analysis must therefore be tested.

We developed a task-test method that increases the confidence on the results of static WCET analysis. This method executes the task under test, compares the execution times of the test runs to the computed WCET bound, and reports a timing error if a measured time exceeds the computed bound. The data generator for the tests is based on a genetic algorithm (GA). It generates test data that promise to yield long execution times based on feedback about the execution times of the task in the preceding test runs.

The proposed test method uses a test data generation paradigm known as *dynamic test data generation* [17]. Dynamic test data generation treats parts of a program under test as functions. These functions are evaluated by executing the tested program. The returned function values indicate the quality of test data with respect to a given criterion. Test data generation tries to find inputs that maximize (or minimize) the function values to fulfill this criterion. Dynamic test data generation thus maps the problem of generating test data onto the well-known problem of function maximization. For WCET testing the function to be maximized is the function that yields the execution time of the task for given input data. We realize this function by measuring the execution time of the task.

Note that our test method, like any dynamic test generation method, has its limits. Most tasks will have a vast input space, of which only a small number of inputs are tested within the available test time. Given such a limited set of input samples, no search strategy can guarantee that the tests hit the WCET or even yield tight estimates. Therefore, if WCET tests for a task do not invalidate the result of static WCET analysis, then this may increase the *confidence* in the correctness of the computed WCET bound. Such a result, however, *never guarantees* the absence of a failure.

Dynamic test data generation was introduced in [17]. An extension of this idea can be found in [14]. The first approaches to dynamic test data generation used

---

[*]This work has been supported by the Austrian Science Fund (Fonds zur Förderung der wissenschaftlichen Forschung) under contract P12476-INF".

[†]R. Nossal is now with Siemens AG, Regensburg, Germany.

simple, local search strategies that got easily stuck in local maxima or minima. To avoid this problem, more sophisticated global search techniques were introduced. Jones et al. [9] and McGraw et al. [16] use Genetic Algorithms (GA) for dynamic test case generation, and in [25] WCET testing is presented as an example for GA-based testing.

The problem of real-time systems testing was covered in various publications [7, 2, 5, 23]. None of them, however, addressed the issue of testing the timing of single tasks. Only recently, researchers started to work on methods for testing execution-time bounds. Work, very similar to ours, gives a detailed description of GA-based WCET testing [27, 26] and compares evolutionary testing to static WCET analysis [18]. The here-presented work describes a novel test environment for dynamic WCET tests. The paper focuses on GA-based testing and compares its results to those of random testing, best-effort testing, and static analysis. Also, it demonstrates shortcomings of GA-based test data generation by means of a set of test programs we designed.

Section 2 describes our test environment and the proposed test approach. Section 3 focuses on the use of GAs for WCET testing. It gives a short introduction to GAs and shows how we apply them for controlling the tests and generating test data. Section 4 describes our experiments which compared GA-based testing to other test methods. It presents the lessons we learned from these experiments. Section 5 summarizes and concludes the paper.

2 Test Environment

The test environment consists of the target computer system, the host computer system, and a high-resolution timer/counter.[1] The target computer system has the same hardware timing characteristics (CPU clock rate, memory access times, etc.) as the computer on which the software under test will be executed in the real application. During the tests the task under evaluation executes on this system and the properties of interest—the start and the stop events of tasks generated at the beginning and the end of the tasks—are observed. The host computer system is a PC that accommodates the software development tools, the user interface of the test environment, and the test control software. The timer counts the number of CPU clock ticks between the start and stop events generated for the task under investigation. The durations measured by the timer are corrected on the host

---
[1]We use an external counter since not all target boards have timers that provide the clock resolution we are interested in.

system to account for the constant overhead of the instructions that trigger the timer and start the task.

Note, that the environment is conceived for embedded target systems with scarce CPU and memory resources. We execute a small software system on the target and use the host for the resource-intensive operations. For targets with sufficient resources the host is not needed; the entire software can run on the target.

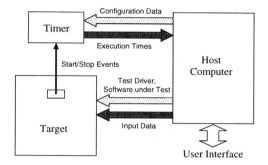

Figure 1. The test environment

Figure 1 shows the setup of the test environment as well as its data paths. Dotted arrows mark the data paths for initializations, gray arrows show the data flow during the operation of the test system.

2.1 Software Components

The most important software components of the test environment are, on the one hand, the *task* under investigation and a simple *test driver* that reside on the target system and, on the other hand, the *user interface* and the *test control software* on the host system.

The test environment assumes that the *tested task* is a so-called *simple task* [13]. A simple task communicates with other tasks and the environment solely by the exchange of messages. The operating system assures that all input messages of the task are available at the point in time the task starts. Outputs are written to the output message buffers of the task. The output message buffers are emptied by the operating system after the completion of the task. Thus all tasks execute completely without blocking I/O, synchronization, and communication.

The simple task model precludes that one task blocks another active task. It allows us to test the timing of single tasks in separation. As in the real application, the test environment provides the inputs to the tested task before the task starts. For repetitive tasks with a state, the task execution times may depend on the values of the state variables at task activation time. To handle state dependencies, the test environment also sets the state variables of the tasks before execution. Thus, for the test environment the interface of a task comprises not only the inputs and outputs of the task, but also includes the task state.

The *test driver* receives the test data for the task from the host. For each set of input data it copies the data to the input buffers of the task and executes the task. To support the timing measurements the test driver generates trigger signals for the timer. It writes to an output port, immediately before the task starts and after the task has terminated. Further, the test driver watches the proper termination of the task. It sets a local timeout to some value greater than the WCET (e.g., 2*WCET) before it generates the task-start signal and starts the task. The purpose of this timeout is to avoid that the tests get stuck in an endless loop of a faulty task being tested.

Via the *user interface* the programmer selects the task to be tested together with the description of the task interface and the computed WCET bound. Further he/she defines the test termination criteria, starts, and controls the tests by means of this interface.

The *test control software* implements the main control function for the tests. It obtains the measured task execution times from the timer and evaluates them against the WCET. It repeatedly issues calls to the *test data generator* to produce new test data and it sends these test data to the target. Finally, the test control software evaluates the termination criteria and decides about the termination of the tests. In the approach described in this paper a GA realizes the main functions of the test control software (see Section 3).

2.2 Testing Steps

The following information is needed to start a WCET-test suite for a task:

- A specification of the interface of the task. This description comprises all input, output, and state data items together with their types, ranges, and the specified relations between the different data values.

- The code of the task to be tested.

- The WCET bound of the task computed by static WCET analysis.

The tests consist of two phases. In the *initialization phase* the programmer selects the task to be tested. The user interface of the test environment displays the task interface and the WCET bound and allows the programmer to refine the interface description. Further

the programmer defines the stopping criteria for the tests (see Section 3.3.3).

After the task selection, the programming environment generates task-specific versions of the test control software and the test driver. To this end, it reads the input-data description of the task and instantiates the available templates for the test control software and the test driver accordingly.

Finally, the test driver and the task are linked and loaded onto the target. The timer is initialized. After completion of these steps the test driver is ready to receive input data sets and to start test execution.

In the *test phase* the timer measures the durations between start and stop events and transmits the results to the host. The test control software, executing on the host, reads the measured execution times, evaluates the stopping criteria for the tests, calls the test data generator, and sends the new test data to the test driver on the target. The test driver, in turn, executes the tested task with the data received from the host.

3 Test Control and Data Generation

This section deals with the issue of generating test data. After an introduction, it describes Genetic Algorithms in general before it takes a closer look at their adaptation for use in a WCET test environment. Finally, the characteristics of the test setup are discussed.

3.1 Heuristic Generation of Test Data

It is obvious that, due to the large number of input data sets, an exhaustive application of all data sets is impossible. Thus, a method must be used to heuristically derive test data sets that lead to a long or even better the worst-case execution time of the task under test. Stochastic optimization methods like Genetic Algorithms (GA) [8], Simulated Annealing [10], or Tabu Search [3] are perfectly suited for this purpose. They facilitate a goal-oriented optimization without the danger of being stuck in local optima like traditional hill climbing. The major advantage of GAs over the other two methods is that it exploits different parts of the search space at the same time, a feature that is referred to as the *inherent parallelism* of GAs. Because of this characteristic, GAs allow to quickly narrow down the search space to promising regions. Neighborhood search methods like Simulated Annealing and Tabu Search, on the other hand, are superior for systematic evaluation of the search space.

For the first implementation we selected GAs as test data generator. Alternatively, we consider to enhance the test data generator with a neighborhood search for future implementations. In this case the GA identifies the regions of long execution times, which are then exploited by the neighborhood search.

3.2 Introduction to Genetic Algorithms

Genetic Algorithms (GA) [8] are a stochastic method used to solve NP-hard optimization problems in many fields. GAs constitute a so-called "uninformed" search strategy. This term refers to the fact that the algorithm itself does not have any knowledge on the problem it solves. The problem specific knowledge is entirely incorporated into the *fitness function*, which calculates a basic *fitness value* of a candidate solution produced by the GA; additional constraints can be incorporated into the function by so-called *penalty terms*. A penalty term reduces the fitness of a solution provided that it violates a constraint. The resulting, overall fitness value is used as a feedback to the algorithm.

A problem to be solved by a GA has to be *encoded* into bit strings. Each bit string, called a *gene* encodes one part of the information on the problem solution. Genes are grouped to *chromosomes*; one or more chromosomes form an *individual*. Each individual encodes a complete solution to the given problem. The quality of this solution, i.e., the fitness of the individual is assessed by the fitness function. A certain number of individuals form a *population*.

The GA imitates the process of evolution of nature by taking one population as parent generation and creating an offspring generation. The algorithm selects the best, i.e., fittest, individuals of the parent population. Here the fitness of an individual comes into play. The better the fitness value of an individual, the greater is the probability that it is selected for reproduction. After the selection the GA *mutates* some of the genes of the selected individuals by flipping bits according to a given mutation rate and performs *cross-over* between the individuals by swapping parts of chromosomes. As a result of this process a new population, a child generation, is created, which is then evaluated. The whole process iterates until a solution of sufficient quality is found.

While the GA is capable of generating new solutions to a problem that has been properly encoded, the derivation of an encoding scheme and the selection of a fitness function are up to the user. The major difference between conventional optimization techniques like the various branch-and-bound approaches and GAs is the way a solution is generated. Whereas with conventional methods the user must provide the knowledge on how to construct a solution, it is sufficient to know

how to assess a given solution with GAs. The "construction" of new solutions is autonomously done by the GA.

For a comprehensive description of GAs and their function the reader is referred to [24, 4]. The GA-library that forms the basis of the GA used in the test environment is presented in [19].

3.3 GA-Adaptation for WCET Testing

In the following we will concentrate on the "intelligence" of the GA, i.e., the problem encoding and the fitness function, which have to be defined by the user. Both have to be adapted such that the GA can operate as an input data generator for the actual test driver.

3.3.1 Problem Encoding

The GA is dedicated to produce sets of test data, which are handed to the task under test. Hence the individuals must represent the input data space of the tested task.

One gene is used for each input data item of the task. The value range of the gene must reflect the value range of the input data. However, regardless of the actual data type of an input data item, the GA is only capable of handling integer values. If the input data item has a different type an appropriate mapping must be applied. The following table lists possible input data types and their encoding as integer genes.

Table 1. Encoding of various data types

Data Type	Encoding
Integer	1 gene
Char	1 gene with value range 0 to 255
String(n)	n character genes
Fixed point number	2 genes, 1 representing integer part, 1 representing fractional part
Floating point number	3 genes, 1 representing integer part of mantissa, 1 fractional part of mantissa, 1 representing exponent

Complex data types like arrays or structures are encoded as sets of the above basic types.

The next step in the encoding hierarchy are chromosomes. There is no general rule how to arrange the input data to form chromosomes. The simplest way is to devise one chromosome, which comprises all input data items. Depending on the shape of the particular input space more sophisticated encoding schemes can be applied. In the matrix multiplication example, which will be presented in Section 4, the input space is made up of two equally sized matrices. In this case we constructed a GA that uses two chromosomes, one for each matrix.

The set of all chromosomes forms one individual. Each individual thus represents one complete set of input data for the task to be tested.

3.3.2 Fitness Function

The evolutionary process inherent to GAs creates new individuals in each generation. Each of these individuals is handed to the fitness function, which conducts the assessment of its quality. The fitness value of an individual is fed back to the GA to guide the further evolution.

For the purpose of deriving execution time bounds, the fitness of an individual (i.e., of a set of input data) is given by the *execution time* that the task under test needs to process the input data. The larger the execution time for a set of input data, the better is the fitness value of this data set. Hence the fitness of a set of input data is determined by executing the task under test with the given input data and measuring its execution time. The GA tries to maximize the fitness value, thus eventually arriving at the WCET or at an execution time close to the WCET.

Note that there is a fundamental difference between conventional applications of GAs for optimization and the test strategy presented in this paper. When normally applying a GA, the primary interest is in the individual that yielded the optimal performance. This individual represents the optimal solution to the given problem. The actual performance of the solution is only of secondary importance. In the GA-application shown in this paper, however, the significance of the individual and its performance is reversed. As the whole test setup is dedicated to assessing the correctness of WCET bounds, the main concern here is the performance of an individual, since it stands for the execution time of the tested task with the given input data. The set of input data items that yield this execution time, i.e., the individual itself, is only of importance if we are interested in more details of the scenario that caused the worst case. Such detailed information is, for example, helpful if we have to investigate why the results of static WCET analysis did not hold against the measured times.

3.3.3 Stopping Criterion

Two types of stopping criteria are common for GAs, (1) a certain fitness threshold is reached, or (2) a max-

imum number of generations, that has been specified by the user, has been reached. For our purpose we have replaced the second criterion by stopping after a maximum number of individuals, because this can be easier related to the size of the input space.

At first glance criterion 1 seems well suited for our purpose. Since the setup aims at assessing the analytically derived WCET-bounds, stopping the test when the bound is reached appears to be a reasonable stopping criterion. If, however, the analytically derived WCET bound is smaller than the actual WCET of the task, the test would never discover this failure.

To levy this difficulty we suggest a stopping criterion that is made up of the two basic criteria. First, we apply the maximum number of individuals criterion. We choose the number of individuals in relation to the size of the input space, i.e., the larger the input space the greater the maximum number of individuals. Second, the fitness threshold is set to a value slightly beyond the analytically derived WCET bound, i.e., $threshold = WCET_{analytic} + \epsilon$, where ϵ is a small positive number. Using a fitness threshold that is greater than the WCET bound derived from static analysis causes the GA to stop if the analytically-derived WCET bound is exceeded, i.e., the GA discovered a failure.

3.4 Properties of the Test Setup

Goal-Directed Test Data Generation. Compared to random testing the GA-based strategy operates in a goal-directed manner. While in the beginning it tests a variety of different input patterns, the evolutionary process directs the testing into promising directions that are likely to produce longer execution times. This guidance is inherent to the GA, which tries to maximize the fitness of individuals.

Code Inspection Not Required. The inherent guidance, which has just been mentioned, also relieves the user from evaluating the task under test in order to exploit input data yielding longer execution time. While other methods of test data generation force the user to carefully inspect the task to find such data sets, the GA-based approach does not require any code review. Promising sets of input data are discovered by "chance" and are automatically explored further.

Portability. While static WCET analysis needs a special compiler and exact knowledge about the timing characteristics of the target hardware (instruction timing, memory access times, etc.), the GA test strategy, like the other dynamic test-generation methods, is independent from the used programming language and compiler. To adapt it to a specific target hardware, a relatively small number of changes is needed. The test driver has to be ported to the new target and the table of the GA that describes the basic data types has to be adapted for the new target environment. The rest of the software remains unchanged.

4 Experiments

We carried out extensive simulations to demonstrate that the GA-based test approach is well-suited for testing WCET bounds. The simulations replaced the target machine part of the original MC68000 test setup, i.e., the tasks were executed in a simulation environment on a workstation.

By using a simulation environment we could focus our observations on that part of the task execution times that are not constant for every execution (e.g., for the matrix multiplication task, see below, we concentrated on the execution time differences caused by the variable number of steps of multiply instructions). Thus, we did not have to carry the constant parts of the task execution time through our evaluations, which simplified the evaluations. Only for the program with the most complex structure (Heapsort) we measured the execution times in CPU clock cycles.

4.1 Test Techniques

We evaluated the results of the GA-based test method against the results of three other methods for the assessment of execution times.

Random Testing. The GA for test data generation is replaced by a random data generator. Like GA-based testing, random testing is a black box test method. Random testing starts with the same knowledge about the program under test as GA-controlled testing, i.e., it needs the same information from the user (task interface description and termination criterion). It therefore serves as a kind of benchmark for the GA-based test strategy.

Best Effort Data Generation. This step, which was conducted before we started the GA-based tests, aimed at finding the real worst-case execution time for every program configuration under test. Best effort data generation is not a test generation strategy, but comprises the sum of our efforts to generate worst-case input data. Depending on the complexity of the task under test we used different methods, like complete or partial

systematic test data generation, data generation based on code inspection, and trial and error for execution time assessment. Yet, we could not be sure that the results of the best effort analysis really yielded the WCET of the tasks (see below).

Static WCET Analysis. The GA-based test method has been devised to test the results of static WCET analysis. Therefore we had, of course, to perform static WCET analysis for each task [22, 20]. The results of static WCET analysis serve as further reference values for judging the quality of the GA-based test method.

Since both GA-based Testing and Random Testing use stochastic methods for data generation, the results of single tests with these test approaches are of limited value. To reduce this stochastic uncertainty, we evaluated each test configuration ten times for the GA-based and the random test.

4.2 Algorithms

We used seven programs with diverse execution-time characteristics for our evaluations. To get a broad range of different problem complexities for the GA, we tested the programs with various input spaces. The programs were executed in a number of configurations with diverse numbers of input elements and with different value ranges for the individual input elements.

Heapsort. This test program implements the Heapsort algorithm. The input to the program consists of n integers that have to be sorted by the algorithm. We tested Heapsort for three different array sizes, with n being 10, 25, and 50, respectively. For all configurations the input data items were in the range $[0..5n)$.

Matmul. Matmul[2] multiplies two matrices. Its input data space consists of two n by n integer matrices, i.e., $2 * n^2$ data elements. Matmul was tested with the following array sizes and value ranges for the array elements:

	array size	value range
1	5×5	0..255
2	5×5	0..65535
3	10×10	0..255

---

[2]The use of Matmul and Matcnt was inspired by the use of equally-named programs in [6]. The programs used in our work have a similar functionality as the programs in [6]. They are, however, not identical with the programs documented there.

Matcnt. `Matcnt` counts the number of elements of a matrix that have values in the upper half of the given value range. `Matcnt` assumes one n by n matrix as input. The configurations tested for `Matcnt` were the same as for `Matmul`.

DES. DES (data encryption standard) is an implementation of the algorithm that UNIX systems use for password encoding [1]. DES has two input parameters, an eight-character password and a two-character "salt"-string.

SimXT1, SimXT2, SimXT3. The three *SimXT* programs were implemented to test how the GA behaves for programs with "malignant" execution-time characteristics. The three algorithms have similar execution patterns. Their execution times depend on two input parameters, x and y, as follows: $exec\_time = C1 * ones(x) + C2 * x + C3 * ones(y) + C4 * y$, where the function *ones* counts the number of ones in the binary representation of its argument and $C1$ to $C4$ are constants that differ between *SimXT*-versions. The constants $C1$ to $C4$ and the ranges for the input data were chosen such that the configurations yielded problems of diverse difficulty for the test-generation GA.

	$C1$	$C2$	$C3$	$C4$
SimXT1	15	2	10	1
SimXT2	3	5	4	1
SimXT3	1	2	1	4

For each of the three simulation programs the input value ranges were [0..99] in configuration 1 and [0..129] in configuration 2.

As discussed in Section 3 the maximum number of individuals has to be defined for each test run. This termination criterion heavily influences the duration of the test and the probability that a faulty WCET bound can be discovered. Table 2 lists the number of individuals used as stopping criterion in the experiments.

Table 2. Maximum number of individuals applied as stopping criterion

Program	No. of Individuals
Heapsort	20000000
Matmul, Matcnt	4000000
DES	100000
SimXT1, SimXT2, SimXT3	10000

4.3 Results

Table 3 lists the results of our experiments. Columns 1 and 2 display the names of the tested programs and the configuration numbers. Columns 3 to 5 show the results of the GA-based tests. *Max.* is the global maximum of the execution times measured in all tests, *Avg.* is the average of the maxima measured in the ten test series, and *StdDev.* is the standard deviation of these maxima. Columns 6 and 7 display the results of the random tests. The meanings of *Max.* and *Avg.* are the same as for the GA-based tests. Columns 8 and 9 present the results from the best-effort data generation and from static WCET analysis.

4.3.1 Discussion of Results

Size of the Input Space: The GA-based method yields good WCET-estimates even for input-data spaces that are large compared to the number of tested individuals. This is best illustrated by the results of `Matcnt` and `Heapsort`. For `Matcnt` the GA returned the real WCET in all configurations, and even for `Heapsort` with 50 elements the average of the maxima derived by the GA-method underestimates the WCET bound from static analysis only by approximately 5%. Of further interest are the results of `Matmul`. The results suggest that the size of the input space of configuration 1 is at the limit of the GA's capabilities for obtaining the WCET. While the maximum and average result of configuration 1 are within 0.1% of the real WCET, the other configurations are much farther away from the optimum. Better results could be obtained only by drastically increasing the number of tested individuals.

GA-based Testing vs. Random Testing: For all programs except for *SimXT3*, GA-based testing performed equal or better than random testing (the results of the *SimXT* programs will be discussed in detail in a dedicated section below). The difference of the results of GA-based testing and random testing strongly depends on the relation of the size of the input space to the number of test-data sets generated in each test. If the number of test-data sets is large relative to the size of the input space, random testing yields similar results as GA-based testing (see configuration 1 of `Heapsort` and `Matcnt`, configurations 1 and 2). For large input-data spaces the goal-directed, GA-based approach clearly outperforms the random method (see `Heapsort`, configurations 2 and 3, and `Matmul`).

GA-based Testing and Static Analysis: The GA-based tests did not invalidate any of the WCET bounds from static analysis. Nevertheless, the fact that the results of the GA-based tests come very close to, or in many test cases hit the actual WCETs lets us assume

Table 3. Results of the execution-time tests. Except for `Heapsort` all numbers are given in abstract time units. For `Heapsort` the execution time is measured in CPU cycles.

Program	Conf.	Results of GA Tests			Random		Best Eff.	WCET
		Max.	Avg.	StdDev.	Max.	Avg.	Max.	Bound
Heapsort	1	10906	10906	0	10906	10906	10906	11610
Heapsort	2	41798	41554	282.5	37214	36554	41796	43320
Heapsort	3	106294	104307	2960.7	84396	83411	106963	109818
Matmul	1	1000	999	3.2	770	753	1000	1000
Matmul	2	1865	1853	13.4	1285	1259	2000	2000
Matmul	3	7880	7756	74.1	5340	5266	8000	8000
Matcnt	1	25	25	0	25	24	25	25
Matcnt	2	25	25	0	25	24	25	25
Matcnt	3	100	100	0	76	74	100	100
DES		62	60	1.7	59	56	62	63
SimXT1	1	438	438	0	438	433	438	438
SimXT1	2	559	559	0	559	553	559	559
SimXT2	1	632	631.6	1.26	632	630	632	632
SimXT2	2	817	816.2	2.53	817	813	817	817
SimXT3	1	608	601	1.89	608	606	608	608
SimXT3	2	785	782	1.41	785	783	785	785

that the GA-based method would detect an erroneous under-estimation of the WCET with high probability.

GA-based Testing vs. Best Effort Data Generation: As mentioned, the purpose of best-effort data generation was to complement static analysis and to approximate the real WCET of programs as good as possible. For all programs but `Heapsort` this method yielded the WCET and confirmed the result of static analysis. Comparing the best-effort and the GA-based method, the most impressive observation for us is definitely the result of `Heapsort`, configuration 2: The execution-time maximum measured in the GA-based tests was two CPU cycles greater than the execution time of the best-effort solution, i.e., the GA identified a better approximation to the real WCET than we had found in the extensive best-effort assessment.

Influence of Input Data on the GA Behavior

The quality of the test result of the GA-based approach largely depends on how the tested program uses its input data items. In order to understand this influence one has to know an important property of GAs. GAs allow a fast convergence towards optimal values—in this case large execution times—if different individuals yield different fitness values. If, on the other hand, a large number of individuals have the same fitness, the algorithm "tumbles" around, creating new individuals without increasing or even decreasing the fitness.

Of particular interest for the convergence is on the one hand the size of the input data space, while on the other hand one has to distinguish between programs that operate on the actual value of an input data item and programs that take into account the distribution of values. Programs with small input spaces that depend on the actual value of an input data item in general exhibit a fast convergence. For this type of program each set of input data out of a small range results in different fitness values. Hence the GA can quickly arrive at a high quality execution time bound. An example for a program of this category is `SimXT1`.

The opposite end of the range is marked by programs that have large input spaces and take into account mainly the input value distribution. In these cases many sets of input data out of a large space are alike and have the same or similar execution times. The GA is not guided into promising directions and takes a long time to explore the input space. An example for the latter category is `Heapsort`. If `Heapsort` sorts 10 numbers between 0 and 50 each, there are numerous test cases that yield approximately equal results. Consider, the case where the first nine number are 0, 1, 2, 3, 4, 5, 6, 7, and 8. In principle all test cases with the tenth input parameter in the range [9..50] are the same, yet they increase the input space.

4.3.2 Discussion of Malignant Test Scenarios

This section gives a closer look at the results for the *SimXT* programs. Although the principal structure of these programs is the same, the quality of the results derived by the GA differs: While the GA found the optimal solution in all tests for *SimXT1*, it failed to find the WCETs for a number of executions of *SimXT2* and *SimXT3* (see Table 3).

To get more details about the behavior of the GA for the three programs, we ran a further series of tests. This time we did not limit the maximum number of individuals tested, since we wanted to find out how many individuals were needed to obtain the WCET for each of the programs and configurations. Table 4 displays the results of the 10 tests for each configuration. The figures show the number of individuals the GA had to generate, on the average, until it found a solution (`Avg`) and the standard deviation of these numbers (`StdDev`).

Table 4. Number of individuals required for deriving the execution time bound

Program	Conf.	No. of Evaluations Avg	StdDev
SimXT1	1	3050	2404.6
SimXT1	2	3411	2197.4
SimXT2	1	13638	22279.1
SimXT2	2	4104	3755.6
SimXT3	1	61306	64953.0
SimXT3	2	522910	530038.5

For `SimXT1` and the second version of `SimXT2` the GA needs a small number of evaluations to find the WCET. The first configuration of `SimXT2` as well as both configurations of `SimXT3`, however, require a large number of evaluations to arrive at the WCET. These numbers are even greater than the actual size of the input data space, which indicates that the GA has problems with these scenarios.

Table 5 shows the input data that yield the WCET for all configurations of the *SimXT* programs. First, note that for the configurations requiring a large number of evaluations the input values producing the WCET are at the upper bounds of the respective input spaces. Second, note that the worst-case input values are always slightly greater than a "big" power of 2 (129 = *128 + 1*) or greater than a sum of "big" powers of 2 (99 = *64 + 32 + 3*). A "big" power of 2 means that within the allowed input space this number is represented by one of the most significant bits.

Table 5. Input values that lead to the WCET

Program	Conf.	Parameter Values x	y
SimXT1	1	95	95
SimXT1	2	127	127
SimXT2	1	*99*	95
SimXT2	2	127	127
SimXT3	1	*99*	*99*
SimXT3	2	127	*129*

The first observation implies that the GA cannot approach the solutions (99 and 129, respectively) from greater values, as greater values are outside the input space. The second observation indicates that a large number of bits has to be flipped in order to move from input values that are only little smaller than the worst-case inputs to the worst-case input values themselves. For example, seven bits have to be flipped to change the inputs from 127 to 129. Changes that affect a large number of bits at the same time are, however, very unlikely. Furthermore, the input values that have similar bit patterns as the worst-case input values yield significantly smaller execution times than the worst-case inputs. The input values that are composed of big powers of 2 form local maxima for the search of the GA that attract the GA and reduce the survival probability of input values with bit patterns similar to the worst-case patterns. Thus the GA gets stuck and takes long time to construct the worst-case inputs.

5 Summary and Conclusion

In this paper we introduced a black-box test strategy for testing the WCET bounds computed from static WCET analysis. This test strategy relies on a Genetic Algorithm (GA) for the goal-oriented generation of test cases: By means of its feedback mechanism the GA effectively guides test-data generation into directions that have a high chance to yield the real WCET of the program under test.

The experiments carried out to evaluate the proposed test method have shown that test data generation based on GAs is well suited for WCET tests. The results achieved by the GA-based approach compare favorably to execution time bounds derived from static WCET analysis and similar techniques and outperform random testing by far. In particular for programs with large input spaces the GA-based method creates test cases of significantly better quality than random testing, i.e., the execution times of the GA-generated test data are significantly closer to the WCET than the execution time of the random test data.

In the future we will further investigate into problems of GA-based testing that we identified in our experiments. We will focus on problems that the GA has with certain execution-time distributions of the input-data space and with the bit-coding of input data. A special "adaptive" mutation rate will be applied to overcome the problems of the GA with large plateaus of equal fitness function values. Since the tested task represents the fitness function and its execution time the fitness value, strict monotony of the function cannot be assumed. Furthermore, we plan to develop mechanisms that detect anomalies in the behavior of the GA and identify special problem cases.

Acknowledgements

We would like to thank Christian Ebner, Richard Gerber, our shepherd Michael Gonzalez Harbour, and the anonymous reviewers for their valuable comments on earlier versions of the paper.

References

[1] S. Garfinkel and G. Spafford. *Practical UNIX Security*. O'Reilly and Associates Inc., Sebastopol, CA, 1991.

[2] R. L. Glass. Real-time: The "lost world" of software debugging and testing. *Comm. of the ACM*, 23(5):264–271, May 1980.

[3] F. Glover, E. Taillard, and D. de Werra. User's guide to tabu search. *Annals of Operations Research*, 41, 1993.

[4] D. Goldberg. *Genetic Algorithms in Search, Optimization and Machine Learning*. Addison-Wesley, 1989.

[5] H. Gomaa. Software development of real-time systems. *Communications of the ACM*, 29(7):657–668, July 1986.

[6] C. A. Healy, D. B. Whalley, and M. G. Harmon. Integrating the timing analysis of pipelining and instruction caching. In *Proc. 16th Real-Time Systems Symposium*, pages 288–297, Dec. 1995.

[7] C. R. Hill. A real-time microprocessor debugging technique. *ACM SIGSOFT Software Engineering Notes*, 8(4):145–148, Aug. 1983. Proc. ACM SIGSOFT/SIGPLAN Software Engineering Symp. on High-Level Debugging.

[8] J. Holland. *Adaptation in Natural and Artificial Systems*. The Univ. of Michigan Press, Ann Arbor, 1975.

[9] B. Jones, H. Sthamer, and D. Eyres. Automatic structural testing using genetic algorithms. *Software Engineering Journal*, 11(5):299–306, 1996.

[10] S. Kirkpatrick, C. Gelatt, and M. Veechi. Optimization by simulated annealing. *Science*, 220:671–680, May 1983.

[11] E. Kligerman and A. Stoyenko. Real-time euclid: A language for reliable real-time systems. *IEEE Transactions on Software Eng.*, SE-12(9):941–949, Sep. 1986.

[12] L. Ko, C. Healy, E. Ratliff, and M. Harmon. Supporting the specification and analysis of timing constraints. In *Proceedings of the IEEE Real-Time Technology and Applications Symposium*, pages 170–178, June 1996.

[13] H. Kopetz. *Real-Time Systems*. Kluwer, 1997.

[14] B. Korel. Automated software test data generation. *IEEE Transactions on Software Engineering*, 16(8):870–879, Aug. 1990.

[15] Y. S. Li, S. Malik, and A. Wolfe. Cache modeling for real-time software: Beyond direct mapped instruction caches. In *Proc. 17th Real-Time Systems Symposium*, Dec. 1996.

[16] G. McGraw, C. Michael, and M. Schatz. Generating software test data by evolution. Technical Report RSTR-018-97-01, Reliable Software Technologies Corporation, 21515 Ridgetop Circle, Suite 250, Sterling, VA 20166, Feb. 1998.

[17] W. Miller and D. Spooner. Automatic generation of floating point test data. *IEEE Transactions on Software Engineering*, SE-2(3):223–226, Mar. 1976.

[18] F. Müller and J. Wegener. A comparison of static analysis and evolutionary testing for the verification of timing constraints. In *Proc. of the 4th Real-Time Technology and Applications Symposium*, pages 144–154, Denver, CO, USA, June 1998.

[19] R. Nossal and T. Galla. Solving NP-Complete Problems in Real-Time System Design by Multichromosome Genetic Algorithms. In *Proceedings of the SIGPLAN 1997 Workshop on Languages, Compilers, and Tools for Real-Time Systems*, pages 68–76. ACM SIGPLAN, June 1997.

[20] P. Puschner. Worst-Case Execution Time Analysis at Low Cost. *Control Engineering Practice*, 6(1):129–135, Jan. 1998.

[21] P. Puschner and C. Koza. Calculating the Maximum Execution Time of Real-Time Programs. *Real-Time Systems*, 1(2):159–176, Sep. 1989.

[22] P. Puschner and A. Schedl. Computing Maximum Task Execution Times — A Graph-Based Approach. *Real-Time Systems*, 13(1):67–91, July 1997.

[23] W. Schütz. *The Testability of Distributed Real-Time Systems*. Kluwer, Boston, MA, USA, 1993.

[24] M. Srinivas and L. Patnaik. Genetic Algorithms: A Survey. *IEEE Computer*, pages 17–26, June 1994.

[25] N. Tracey, J. Clark, and K. Mander. The way forward for unifying dynamic test case generation: The optimization-based approach. In *Proc. of the 1998 IFIP International Workshop on Dependable Computing and Its Applications*, pages 169–180, Johannesburg, South Africa, 1998.

[26] J. Wegener and M. Grochtmann. Verifying timing constraints of real-time systems by means of evolutionary testing. *Real-Time Systems*, to appear.

[27] J. Wegener, H. Sthamer, B. Jones, and D. Eyres. Testing real-time systems using genetic algorithms. *Software Quality Journal*, 6(2):127–135, June 1997.

Combining Abstract Interpretation and ILP for Microarchitecture Modelling and Program Path Analysis

Henrik Theiling and Christian Ferdinand
Universität des Saarlandes / Fachbereich Informatik
Postfach 15 11 50 / D-66041 Saarbrücken / Germany
{theiling,ferdi}@cs.uni-sb.de

Abstract

Abstract interpretation (AI) and integer linear programming (ILP) are two techniques which were used independently from each other for worst case execution time (WCET) approximation.

With AI one can compute interesting properties of programs. It can be implemented efficiently and yields provably correct results. Previous work has shown that it is suitable for cache behaviour prediction of memory references of a program.

By using ILP the structure of a program and the program path can be described easily and in a very natural way. A set of constraints describes the overall structure of the program and solving the constraints yields very precise results. However, when modelling microarchitectural components like caches or pipelines the complexity of the solving process can increase dramatically.

Our approach uses AI to model the microarchitecture's behaviour and ILP for finding worst case program paths using the results of the AI. This combines the advantages of both approaches.

1. Introduction

Caches are used to improve the access times of fast microprocessors to relatively slow main memories. By providing faster access to recently referenced regions of memory, they can reduce the number of cycles a processor is waiting for data. Caching is used for more or less all general purpose processors and, with increasing application sizes, it becomes increasingly relevant and used for high performance microcontrollers and DSPs.

Programs with hard real-time constraints have to be subjected to a schedulability analysis. It has to be determined whether all timing constraints can be satisfied. The degree of success for such a timing validation [13] depends on tight WCET estimations. For example, for hardware with caches, the typical worst case assumption is that all accesses miss the cache. This is an overly pessimistic assumption which leads to a waste of hardware resources.

For this reason the cache behaviour must be taken into account when finding the WCET. Earlier work [1, 6, 4, 5] describes how a cache analysis can efficiently be implemented using AI.

The results of the cache analysis must be combined with the results of a worst case program path analysis. In our approach we use the fine grained results of the cache analysis by AI for the generation of integer constraints to find the worst case program path. In this way, each technique is used to solve the problem it can handle best.

For the practical experiments, we used executables produced by a standard optimising compiler in order to provide WCET bounds for executables that meet the goal of exploiting system resources best.

2. Program analysis by AI

Program analysis is a widely used technique to determine runtime properties of a given program without actually executing it. Such information is used for example in optimising compilers [14] to enable code improving transformations.

A program analyser takes a program as input and computes some interesting properties. Most of these properties are undecidable. Hence, both correctness and completeness of the computed information are not achievable together. Program analysis makes no compromise on the correctness side; optimising transformations rely on the computed information. It cannot thus guarantee completeness. The quality of the computed information, usually called its *precision*, should be as good as possible.

There is a well developed theory of static program analysis called *abstract interpretation* [3]. With this theory, correctness of a program analysis can easily be derived. According to this theory a program analysis is determined by an *abstract semantics*.

Usually the meaning of a language is given as functions for the statements of the language computing over a concrete domain. A domain is a complete partially ordered set of values. For such a semantics, an abstract version consists of a new simpler abstract domain and simpler abstract functions which define the abstract meaning for every program statement.

The program analyser generator PAG [2] offers the possibility of generating a program analyser from a description of the abstract domain and of the abstract semantic functions in two high level languages, one for the domains and the other for the semantic functions. Domains can be constructed inductively starting from simple domains using operators like constructing power sets and function domains. The semantic functions are described in a functional language which combines high expressiveness with efficient implementation. Additionally the user has to supply a join function combining two domain values into one. This function is applied whenever a point in the program has two (or more) possible execution predecessors.

3. Cache memories

A cache can be characterised by three major parameters:

- *capacity* is the number of bytes it may contain.

- *line size* (also called block size) is the number of contiguous bytes that are transferred from memory on a cache miss. The cache can hold at most $n = capacity/line\ size$ blocks.

- *associativity* is the number of cache locations where a particular block may reside.
  $n/associativity$ is the number of *sets* of a cache.

If a block can reside in any cache location, then the cache is called *fully associative*. If a block can reside in exactly one location, then it is called *direct mapped*. If a block can reside in exactly A locations, then the cache is called A-*way set associative*.

The fully associative and the direct mapped caches are special cases of the A-way set associative cache where $A = n$ and $A = 1$ resp.

In the case of an associative cache, a cache line has to be selected for replacement when the cache is full and the processor requests further data. This is done according to a replacement strategy. Common strategies are *LRU* (Least Recently Used), *FIFO* (First In First Out), and *random*.

The set where a memory block may reside in the cache is uniquely determined by the address of the memory block, i. e., the behaviour of the sets is independent of each other. The behaviour of an A-way set associative cache is completely described by the behaviour of its n/A fully associative sets[1].

For the sake of space, we restrict our description to the semantics of fully associative caches with LRU replacement strategy. More complete descriptions that explicitly describe direct mapped and A-way set associative caches can be found in [1] and [4].

---

[1]This holds also for direct mapped caches where $A = 1$.

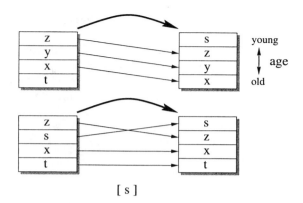

[s]

Figure 1. Update of a concrete fully associative (sub-) cache.

4. Cache semantics

In the following, we consider a (fully associative) cache as a set of cache lines $L = \{l_1, \ldots, l_n\}$, and the store as a set of memory blocks $S = \{s_1, \ldots, s_m\}$.

To indicate the absence of any memory block in a cache line, we introduce a new element I; $S' = S \cup \{I\}$.

Definition 1 (concrete cache state)
A *(concrete) cache state* is a function $c : L \to S'$.
C_c denotes the set of all concrete cache states.

If $c(l_x) = s_y$ for a concrete cache state c, then x describes the relative age of the memory block according to the LRU replacement strategy and not the physical position in the cache hardware (see Figure 1).

The *update* function describes the side effect on the cache of referencing the memory. The LRU replacement strategy is modelled by putting the most recently referenced memory block in the first position l_1. If the referenced memory block s_x is in the cache already, then all memory blocks in the cache that have been more recently used than s_x increase their relative age by one, i. e., they are shifted by one position to the next cache line. If the memory block s_x is not in the cache already, then all memory blocks in the cache are shifted and the oldest, i. e., least recently used memory block is removed from the cache.

Definition 2 (cache update) A cache update function $\mathcal{U} : C_c \times S \to C_c$ describes the new cache state for a given cache state and a referenced memory block.

Updates of fully associative caches with LRU replacement strategy are modelled as in Figure 1.

Control flow representation

We represent programs by control flow graphs consisting of nodes and typed edges. The nodes represent *basic blocks*[2]. For each basic block, the sequence of references to memory is known[3], i.e., there exists a mapping from control flow nodes to sequences of memory blocks: $L : V \to S^*$.

We can describe the working of a cache with the help of the update function $\mathcal{U}$. Therefore, we extend $\mathcal{U}$ to sequences of memory references: $\mathcal{U}(c, \langle s_{x_1}, \ldots, s_{x_y} \rangle) = \mathcal{U}(\ldots(\mathcal{U}(c, s_{x_1}))\ldots, s_{x_y})$.

The cache state for a path $(k_1, \ldots, k_p)$ in the control flow graph is given by applying $\mathcal{U}$ to the initial cache state c_I that maps all cache lines to I and the concatenation of all sequences of memory references along the path: $\mathcal{U}(c_I, L(k_1) \circ \ldots \circ L(k_p))$.

Abstract semantics

The domain for our AI consists of *abstract cache states*:

Definition 3 (abstract cache state) An *abstract cache state* $\hat{c} : L \to 2^S$ maps cache lines to sets of the memory blocks. $\hat{C}$ denotes the set of all abstract cache states.

We will present three analyses. The **must analysis** determines a set of memory blocks that are in the cache at a given program point under all circumstances. The **may analysis** determines all memory blocks that may be in the cache at a given program point. The latter analysis is used to guarantee the absence of a memory block in the cache. The **persistence analysis** determines memory blocks that will never be removed from the cache after having been loaded into it.

The analyses are used to compute a categorisation for each memory reference that describes its cache behaviour. The categories are described in Table 1.

The abstract semantic functions describe the effects of a control flow node on an element of the abstract domain. The **abstract cache update** function $\hat{\mathcal{U}}$ for abstract cache states is an extension of the cache update function $\mathcal{U}$ to abstract cache states.

On control flow nodes with at least two[4] predecessors, *join*-functions are used to combine the abstract cache states.

Definition 4 (join function) A *join function* $\hat{\jmath} : \hat{C} \times \hat{C} \mapsto \hat{C}$ combines two abstract cache states.

---

[2]A basic block is a sequence (of fragments) of instructions in which control flow enters at the beginning and leaves at the end without halt or possibility of branching except at the end. For our cache analysis, it is most convenient to have one memory reference per control flow node. Therefore, our nodes may represent the different fragments of machine instructions that access memory. For non-precisely determined addresses of data references, one can use a set of possibly referenced memory blocks.

[3]This is appropriate for instruction caches and can be too restricted for data caches and combined caches. See [1, 4] for weaker restrictions.

[4]Our join functions are associative. On nodes with more than two predecessors, the join function is used iteratively.

Category	Abb.	Meaning
always hit	ah	The memory reference will always result in a cache hit.
always miss	am	The memory reference will always result in a cache miss.
persistent	pers	The memory reference could neither be classified as ah nor am. But the second and all further executions of the memory reference will always result in a cache hit.
not classified	nc	The memory reference could neither be classified as ah, am nor pers.

Table 1. Categorisations of memory references.

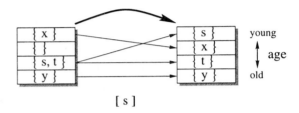

[s]

Figure 2. Update of an abstract fully associative (sub-) cache.

4.1. Must analysis

To determine whether a memory block is definitely in the cache we use abstract cache states where the positions of the memory blocks in the abstract cache state are upper bounds of the *ages* of the memory blocks. $\hat{c}(l_x) = \{s_y, \ldots, s_z\}$ means the memory blocks $s_y, \ldots, s_z$ are in the cache. $s_y, \ldots, s_z$ will stay in the cache at least for the next $n - x$ references to memory blocks that are not in the cache or are *older* than $s_y, \ldots, s_z$, whereby s_a is older than s_b means: $\exists l_x, l_y : s_a \in \hat{c}(l_x), s_b \in \hat{c}(l_y), x > y$.

We use the abstract cache update function depicted in Figure 2.

The join function is similar to set intersection. A memory block only stays in the abstract cache if it is in both operand abstract caches states. It gets the oldest age if it has two different ages (see Figure 3).

The solution of the must analysis computed by the PAG generated analysers by fixpoint iteration is interpreted as follows: Let $\hat{c}$ be an abstract cache state at a control flow node k that references a memory block s_x. If $s_x \in \hat{c}(l_y)$ for a cache line l_y then s_x is definitely in the cache. A reference to s_x is categorised as *always hit* (ah).

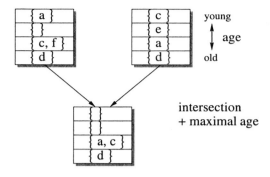

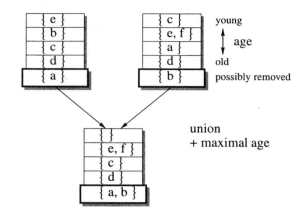

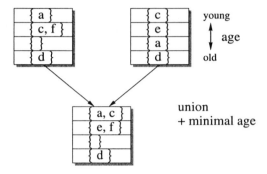

Figure 3. Join for the must analysis.

Figure 4. Join for the may analysis.

Figure 5. Join for the persistence analysis.

4.2. May analysis

To determine whether a memory block s_x is never in the cache we compute the set of all memory blocks that *may* be in the cache. We use abstract cache states where the positions of the memory blocks in the abstract cache state are lower bounds of the *ages* of the memory blocks. $\hat{c}(l_x) = \{s_y, \ldots, s_z\}$ means the memory blocks $s_y, \ldots, s_z$ may be in the cache. A memory block $s_w \in \{s_y, \ldots, s_z\}$ will be removed from the cache after at most $n - x + 1$ references to memory blocks that are not in the cache or are *older or the same age* than s_w, if there are no memory references to s_w. s_a is older or same age than s_b means: $\exists l_x, l_y : s_a \in \hat{c}(l_x), s_b \in \hat{c}(l_y), x \geqq y$.

We use the following join function: The join function is similar to set union. If a memory block s has two different ages in the two abstract cache states then the join function takes the youngest age (see Figure 4).

The solution of the may analysis computed by the PAG generated analysers is interpreted as follows: Let $\hat{c}$ be an abstract cache state at a control flow node k that references a memory block s_x. If s_x is not in $\hat{c}(l_y)$ for an arbitrary l_y then it is definitely not in the cache. A reference to s_x is categorised as *always miss* (am).

4.3. Persistence analysis

To improve the prediction we use the classification pers (*persistent*)[5], which means that a first execution of a memory reference may result in either a hit or a miss, but all non-first executions will result in hits[6]. An abstract cache state $\hat{c}$ at a control flow node k that references a memory block s_x is interpreted in the following way: If $s_x \in \hat{c}(l_y)$ for $y \in \{1, \ldots, n\}$ then s_x would not have been replaced if it had been in the cache. If a reference to s_x cannot be categorised as ah, then it is categorised as pers. When a memory block gets too old, it is moved into an additional virtual cache line $l_\top$ which holds those cache lines that could once have been removed from the cache.

The join function is similar to set union. If a memory block s has two different ages in the two abstract cache states then the join function takes the youngest age (see Figure 5).

The solution of the persistence analysis is interpreted as follows: Let $\hat{c}$ be an abstract cache state at a control flow node k that references a memory block s_x. If s_x is not in $\hat{c}(l_\top)$, it can definitely not be removed from the cache. A reference to s_x is categorised as pers.

4.4. Termination of the analysis

There are only a finite number of cache lines and for each program a finite number of memory blocks. This means the domain of abstract cache states $\hat{c} : L \to 2^S$ is finite. Hence, every ascending chain is finite. Additionally, the abstract cache update functions $\hat{\mathcal{U}}$ and the join functions $\hat{\mathcal{J}}$ are monotonic. This guarantees that our analysis will terminate.

---

[5]This improvement is described in [4]
[6]This is similar to the 'first miss' classification as found in [11].

147

5. Analysis of loops and recursive procedures

Loops and recursive procedures are of special interest, since programs spend most of their runtime there.

A loop often iterates more than once. Since the execution of the loop body usually changes the cache contents, it is useful to distinguish the first iteration from others.

For our analysis of cache behaviour we treat loops as procedures to be able to use existing methods for the interprocedural analysis (see Figure 6).

$$
\begin{array}{lll}
& \texttt{proc loop}_L\texttt{();} & \\
\vdots & \texttt{if } P \texttt{ then} & \\
\texttt{while } P \texttt{ do} & \quad BODY & \\
\quad BODY \implies & \quad \texttt{loop}_L\texttt{();} & (2) \\
\texttt{end;} & \texttt{end} & \\
& \vdots & \\
& \texttt{loop}_L\texttt{();} & (1) \\
& \vdots &
\end{array}
$$

Figure 6. Loop transformation.

In the presence of (recursive) procedures, a memory reference can be executed in different execution contexts. An execution context corresponds to a path in the call graph of a program.

The interprocedural analysis methods differ in which execution contexts are distinguished for a memory reference within a procedure. Widely used is the *callstring approach* whose applicability to cache behaviour prediction is limited [4].

To get more precise results for the cache behaviour prediction, we have developed the **VIVU approach** which has been implemented with the mapping mechanism of PAG as described in [2]. Paths through the call graph that only differ in the number of repeated passes through a cycle are not distinguished. It can be compared with a combination of *virtual inlining* of all non-recursive procedures and *virtual unrolling* of the first iterations of all recursive procedures including loops. The results of the VIVU approach can naturally be combined with the results of a path analysis to predict the WCET of a program.

6. Program path analysis

A problem formulated in ILP consists of two parts: the cost function, and constraints on the variables used in the cost function. Our cost function represents the number of CPU cycles in the worst case. Correspondingly, it will be maximised. Each variable in the cost function will represent the execution count of one basic block of the program and will be weighted by the execution time of that basic

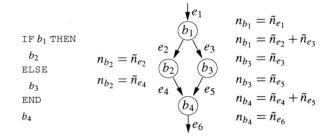

Figure 7. Constraints that can automatically be generated from the control flow graph. $b_1 \ldots b_4$ are the basic blocks whose execution counts are $n_{b_1} \ldots n_{b_4}$. The basic principle is that the execution count of a basic block equals the sum of the traversal counts of its incoming edges and also of its outgoing edges.

block. Additionally, we will use variables corresponding to the traversal counts of the edges in the control flow graph.

Looking at the control flow graph of the program under examination, integer constraints describing how often basic blocks are executed relative to each other can automatically be generated. Figure 7 shows how constraints can be generated for a simple `if`-statement.

However, additional information about the program provided by the user is usually needed, as the problem of finding the worst case program path is unsolvable in the general case. Loop and recursion bounds cannot always be inferred automatically and must therefore be provided by the user.

The ILP approach for program path analysis has the advantage that users are able to describe in precise terms virtually anything they know about the program. In our system arbitrary integer constraints can be added by the user to improve the analysis.

In our program path analysis we use the VIVU approach described in [4, 5, 6] to distinguish first iterations of loops (or calls to functions) and all other iterations (or recursive calls).

The system first generates the obvious constraints automatically and then adds user supplied constraints to tighten the WCET bounds.

6.1. Generating constraints

A description of how to generate constraints for program path analysis is given in [8]. In the following we will show how to use this together with the VIVU analysis to distinguish execution contexts, so how the cost function can be generated, how to generate the constraints that describe the relation between basic blocks and thereby bounding the cost function, and how to incorporate the cache analysis by AI.

In our approach a basic block is considered in different contexts for which separate constraints are generated. A context is determined by the execution stack, i. e., the function calls and loops along the corresponding path in the control flow graph to the instruction. It is represented as a sequence of first and recursive function calls ($C[c]$ and $R[c]$) and first and other executions of loops ($F[\ell]$ and $O[\ell]$) for each basic block c calling a function and each (virtually) transformed loop ℓ of a program.

Definition 5 (Context) Let $calls(\mathcal{P})$ be the set of basic blocks of program $\mathcal{P}$ that contain a call to a function of $\mathcal{P}$. Let $loops(\mathcal{P})$ be the set of loops of $\mathcal{P}$. The set $\mathcal{T}$ of all contexts is defined as follows:

$$\mathcal{T} = \{C[c], R[c], F[\ell], O[\ell] \mid$$
$$c \in calls\ (\mathcal{P}), \ell \in loops\ (\mathcal{P})\}^*$$

In Figure 8 a simple loop is shown that will be used to demonstrate the generation of constraints.

Definition 6 Let n_b be the execution count of basic block b and let $\tau(b) \subseteq \mathcal{T}$ be the set of distinguished execution contexts of b. Let n_b^ϑ be the execution counts for each context $\vartheta \in \tau(b)$ and let $\tilde{n}_e^\vartheta$ be the traversal count for an edge e in a context ϑ.

Generally, each simple constraint for n_b, like those in Figure 7, will be generated for each n_b^ϑ. Following this general rule, we obtain the following simple constraints for basic block b_H in Figure 8:

$$n_{b_H}^{F[\ell]} = \tilde{n}_{h_1}^{F[\ell]} + \tilde{n}_{g_1}^{F[\ell]}$$
$$n_{b_H}^{O[\ell]} = \tilde{n}_{h_1}^{O[\ell]} + \tilde{n}_{g_1}^{O[\ell]}$$

At basic block s we generate the following constraint for its incoming edge:

$$n_{b_S}^\varepsilon = \tilde{n}_{g_1}^\varepsilon$$

An edge has the same contexts as the corresponding basic block. Therefore, g_1 is considered in two different sets of contexts depending on the basic block it belongs to when the constraint is generated.

6.2. Cost function

The cost function computes how many CPU cycles the program will take to execute in the worst case. A basic block can take different times to execute for each of its contexts so we define the cost function as follows.

The cache analysis presented earlier in this paper calculated a categorisation (ah, am, nc or pers) for each basic block in each VIVU context. This categorisation defines a worst case execution time for each basic block in all of its contexts. These execution times are the basis for the cost

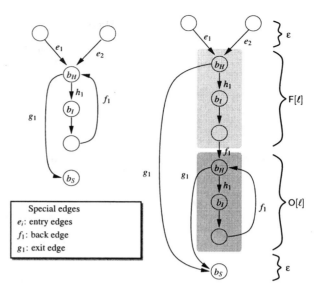

Figure 8. A simple loop (left). Virtually unrolled once on the right.

function of the generated ILP to weigh the basic blocks on the paths in the program.

Let t_b^ϑ be the execution time of basic block b in any of its contexts $\vartheta \in \tau(b)$.

Then the cost function is

$$fmax = \sum_b \sum_{\vartheta \in \tau(b)} t_b^\vartheta \cdot n_b^\vartheta. \quad (1)$$

The next two sections deal with constraints to describe the control flow between blocks with different contexts.

6.2.1. Loops

For loops, special constraints are generated. Let b_H be the first basic block executed in a loop ℓ, called the *head* of the loop.

Let e_i be the edges that enter the loop ℓ. For each context ϑ of an arbitrary e_i there must be two contexts of b_H which have the same prefix but either $F[\ell]$ or $O[\ell]$ appended:

$$\vartheta \circ F[\ell] \quad (2)$$
$$\vartheta \circ O[\ell]$$

The constraints generated for control flow entering ℓ are distinguished by the first and all other iterations. The first iteration of ℓ is naturally entered from outside ℓ. So the constraint for each ϑ looks like this:

$$n_{b_H}^{\vartheta \circ F[\ell]} = \sum_{e_i} \tilde{n}_{e_i}^\vartheta \quad (3)$$

In our example we obtain:

$$n_{b_H}^{F[\ell]} = \tilde{n}_{e_1}^\varepsilon + \tilde{n}_{e_2}^\varepsilon$$

Let f_i be the back edges of ℓ, i.e., those edges that jump back to the beginning of the loop from inside the loop. All non-first iterations of loop ℓ are entered from inside the loop via these back edges either from the first or from other iterations. This is described by the following constraint:

$$n_{b_H}^{\vartheta \circ O[\ell]} = \sum_{f_i} \left(\tilde{n}_{f_i}^{\vartheta \circ F[\ell]} + \tilde{n}_{f_i}^{\vartheta \circ O[\ell]} \right) \quad (4)$$

In the example in Figure 8 there is only one back edge, correspondingly, we generate the following constraint:

$$n_{b_H}^{O[\ell]} = \tilde{n}_{f_1}^{F[\ell]} + \tilde{n}_{f_1}^{O[\ell]}$$

We also need special constraints for exiting a loop, so we introduce a constraint for each exit edge g_i of loop ℓ and for each context ϑ:

$$\tilde{n}_{g_i}^{\vartheta} = \tilde{n}_{g_i}^{\vartheta \circ F[\ell]} + \tilde{n}_{g_i}^{\vartheta \circ O[\ell]} \quad (5)$$

The context ϑ outside our example loop is the empty context, so we obtain:

$$\tilde{n}_{g_1}^{\varepsilon} = \tilde{n}_{g_1}^{F[\ell]} + \tilde{n}_{g_1}^{O[\ell]}$$

This constraint links together the two views on the exit edges from inside and outside the loop ℓ.

6.2.2. Loop bounds

First we have to define what it means when a loop is executed k times. We used an executable produced by an optimising standard compiler as input for our analysis so this issue is not as easy as it may appear at first sight. In fact we have to identify some *inner* basic block, i.e., one that does not belong to the loop's exit condition check which is usually executed once more than the whole loop. There are various types of loops, those that test the condition at the beginning, e.g. while() {...} in the C programming language, those that test the condition at the end of the loop, e.g. do {...} while() loops in C, or even in the middle of the loop, e.g. if (...) break;.

There are two factors that complicate the analysis. Firstly, C programmers usually like to use break and return inside loops and, secondly, the compiler sometimes optimises quite fancily. The first problem can be solved by user provided additional constraints.

There are still some open problems with optimising compilers, as can be seen from the experimental results. The compiler optimisation problem could perhaps be solved by the help of the compiler itself. In our case the compiler very often inferred that the first iteration is always executed and, therefore, either unrolled it once or moved the condition test from the beginning to the end of the loop.

Because the problem of finding an inner basic block of a loop couldn't be solved in all the cases, and because we

have to guarantee that the analysis doesn't calculate time bounds that are below the WCET, we had to leave the problem of defining which basic block is an inner basic block of the loop with the user. We will therefore assume that b_I is the first basic block of the body of the loop. Then b_I is executed as many times as the loop is iterated.

Let e_i be the entry edges to ℓ. Let k be the maximal number of iterations of ℓ. Then we use the following constraint for each context ϑ of e_i to bound the number of iterations of ℓ:

$$n_{b_I}^{\vartheta \circ F[\ell]} + n_{b_I}^{\vartheta \circ O[\ell]} \leq k \cdot \sum_{e_i} \tilde{n}_{e_i}^{\vartheta} \quad (6)$$

Assuming our example loop will be executed 10 times at the most, we generate the following constraint:

$$n_{b_I}^{F[\ell]} + n_{b_I}^{O[\ell]} \leq 10 \cdot \left(\tilde{n}_{e_1}^{\varepsilon} + \tilde{n}_{e_2}^{\varepsilon} \right)$$

6.2.3. Functions

We now describe the generation of the constraints necessary to link together functions.

Without loss of generality we assume that the first basic block of a function is executed as many times as the function is called. This is not the case if the first basic block of the function is also the first basic block of a loop in that function. But in that case we can simply introduce an empty basic block not belonging to the loop at the beginning of such a function.

We now generate the constraints for the fact that each function's first basic block is executed as many times as the function is called. We distinguish each context according to the VIVU analysis.

Let b_C be an arbitrary basic block from which the first basic block b_φ of a function φ is called. For each context $\vartheta \in \tau(b_C)$ there is at least one context $\vartheta \circ C[b_C]$ of b_φ. If φ is called recursively, there is also a context $\vartheta \circ R[b_C]$. For each context ϑ of b_C we generate one constraint:

$$n_{b_C}^{\vartheta} = n_{b_\varphi}^{\vartheta \circ C[b_C]} \quad (7)$$

For recursive calls we need a recursion bound b which must be supplied by the user. In many cases, b could be found by a data flow analysis. If the compiler optimises by inlining functions we meet similar problems as for loop unrolling. In order to overcome these problems, we had to switch off function inlining.

For each $\vartheta \in \tau(b_C)$ we generate the following constraint which bounds the number of calls to φ:

$$n_{b_\varphi}^{\vartheta \circ C[b_C]} + n_{b_\varphi}^{\vartheta \circ R[b_C]} \leq b \cdot n_{b_C}^{\vartheta} \quad (8)$$

6.2.4. Handling the categorisation pers

To handle pers correctly we have to change the cost function and add additional constraints, because a basic block in a context ϑ has two different execution times, one for the first execution that might be a miss, and one for all other references which will be hits.

We define $\hat{n}_b^\vartheta$ to count all but the first execution of b in context ϑ. The relation between n_b^ϑ and $\hat{n}_b^\vartheta$ is:

$$n_b^\vartheta = \hat{n}_b^\vartheta = 0 \quad \vee \quad \left(n_b^\vartheta > 0 \quad \wedge \quad \hat{n}_b^\vartheta = n_b^\vartheta - 1\right). \quad (9)$$

Since this relation contains an $\vee$ operator, the formulation in ILP is not straightforward. However, $\hat{n}_b^\vartheta$ will have a negative coefficient in the cost function and the above constraints will be the only ones for $\hat{n}_b^\vartheta$. Therefore, we can formulate (9) as follows:

$$\hat{n}_b^\vartheta \geq n_b^\vartheta - 1 \quad (10)$$

Next we introduce $\hat{t}_b^\vartheta$ to be the time that b executes faster in all non-first executions compared to the first execution in context ϑ.

The new times must be incorporated into the cost function. Its definition changes as follows.

Let k_i be the number of distinguished contexts for basic block i and m the number of basic blocks in the program. Then the cost function is

$$fmax = \sum_b \sum_{\vartheta \in \tau(b)} \left(t_b^\vartheta \cdot n_b^\vartheta - \hat{t}_b^\vartheta \cdot n_b^\vartheta\right). \quad (11)$$

7. Implementation

The cache analysis techniques are implemented with the help of the program analyser generator PAG. The cache analyser gets the executable and a specification of the instruction cache as input and produces a categorisation of the instruction/context pairs in the input program.

The program path analysis consists of about 9 500 lines of C++ code. It includes a C++ parser to read the user annotations and an interpreter for a Lisp-like language that provides an easy way of specifying loop and recursion bounds as well as additional constraints.

The frontend of our analyser reads a Sun SPARC executable in a.out format. The Sun SPARC is a RISC architecture with a uniform instruction size of four bytes. Our implementation is based on the Executable Editing Library (EEL) of the Wisconsin Architectural Research Tool Set (WARTS)[7].

The profiles used for comparison with our program path analysis were produced with the help of qpt2 (Quick program Profiler and Tracer) that is part of the WARTS distribution.

To solve the integer constraints generated by the program path analyser we used lp_solve[8].

---

[7] The WARTS home page containing EEL and qpt2 is reachable via http://www.cs.wisc.edu/~larus/warts.html

[8] lp_solve was written by Michel Berkelaar and is freely available at ftp://ftp.es.ele.tue.nl/pub/lp_solve

Name	Description	#lines	#bytes
fac	recursive calculation of factorials	16	96
prime	test of several numbers to be prime*	34	228
sort	Bubble sort implementation*	123	236
matmul	5 × 5 matrix multiplication	46	240
circle	circle drawing routine	200	1240
jfdctint	JPEG forward discrete cos transform	392	1476
stats	two array sums, mean, variance, standard derivation, and linear correlation	186	1512
ndes	data encryption*	287	1944

* with worst case input

Table 2. List of the test programs we used. The number of lines of the source code and the number of bytes of the compiled code when compiling with -O2 are given.

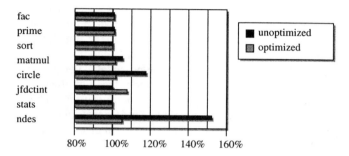

Figure 9. Prediction accuracy of the WCET of several test programs. The WCET is normalised to 100%. The programs were tested with gcc using both no optimisation and -O2.

For our experiments we used parts of the program suites of Frank Müller, some of the programs of Yau-Tsun Steven Li, and some additional programs (see Table 2). The programs were compiled using the GNU C compiler version 2.7.2 under SunOS 4.1.4 with either -O0 or -O2.

8. Experimental results

To test the accuracy of our system we first predicted the hits and misses for each instruction in the test programs. We assumed an instruction cache with a size of 1k byte, a level of associativity of 4, and a line size of 16 bytes.

For each instruction in each context the cache analyser predicted whether the instruction was always going to be in the cache (ah), or never be in the cache (am), whether it will be persistent (pers) or not classified (nc). To make this information usable for the program path analysis we assume an idealised virtual hardware that executes all instructions that result in an instruction cache hit in one cycle and all instructions that result in an instruction cache miss in 10 cycles. Accordingly, for instructions classified as pers the first execution was assumed to take 10 cycles, all further ones only one.

For each basic block b in each context $\vartheta \in \tau(b)$ we defined t_b^ϑ to be the sum of the instruction execution times of the idealised hardware and $\hat{t}_b^\vartheta$ the sum of the speed-up in all non-first executions. With this information the program was then first traced with worst case input (as far as applicable) and then analysed by generating the set of constraints and the cost function described in section 6. The resulting set of constraints was then solved using the ILP solver.

The results of the cost function which represents the worst case execution time are compared to the measured cache behaviour (the number of hits and misses) obtained by simulation. Figure 9 presents the overestimation of the analysis. The overestimation is caused by unknown cache behaviour (classifications nc and pers) on the one hand and by misprediction of worst case paths in if-statements and loops (mainly for the loop condition checks) on the other hand. For technical reasons, calls to library functions are not taken into account by the simulation and therefore also ignored by the cost function in the practical experiments.

Figure 9 shows that the prediction does not always become worse when using compiler optimisation. This is quite surprising as the generated set of constraints is definitely more pessimistic when the compiler optimises the code due to unrolled loops and the like which the analyser is not aware of. However, it seems that because the code shrinks with optimisation, the cache analysis becomes better, so that the more pessimistic set of constraints does not lead to worse analyses. Comparing the execution counts of the trace with our prediction, without taking into account the cache behaviour, our prediction is slightly worse. For ndes, the cache prediction yielded many nc classifications due to the bigger executable at compiler optimisation level -OO. This is the reason for the overestimation. For other test programs, like jfdctint, the more pessimistic program path analysis lead to an overestimation for executables compiled with optimisation. An interface to the compiler that provides information about the compiler optimisations would help to eliminate this overestimation.

For programs without conditionally executed code apart from the loops like matmul, stats etc.the overestimation of our analysis is small. Except for loop bounds, no additional user constraints were necessary. For sort and ndes we had to add additional constraints to reach good results. E. g. the triangular loop structure in sort looked like this:

```
a
FOR i:= 1 TO N-1 DO
    FOR j:= N DOWN TO i+1 DO
        b
```

This can be described by the following constraint:

$$n_b = \frac{(N-1) \cdot N}{2} n_a \qquad (12)$$

The analysis of any of the test programs takes only a few seconds on a SUN UltraSPARC with 168 MHz, although

| Name | problem size | | CPU cycles | | accuracy |
	variables	constraints	predicted	traced	[%]
fac	61	53	25756	25600	100.61
prime	274	238	62507	61940	100.92
sort	110	104	2503726	2503646	100.00
matmul	123	103	1908	1879	101.54
circle	53	49	1945	1912	101.73
jfdctint	49	46	4587	4259	107.70
stats	148	135	150592	150578	100.01
ndes	625	540	54148	51478	105.19

Table 3. Results of the program path analysis with optimisation level -O2.

ndes compiled without optimisation takes around 80s to be solved (with 705 constraints). Table 3 shows an overview of the test results with a compiler optimisation level of -O2.

9. Related work

The work of Arnold, Müller, Whalley, and Harmon has been one of the starting points of our work. [11] describes a data flow analysis for the prediction of instruction cache behaviour of programs for direct mapped caches.

In [7, 8, 9] Yau-Tsun Steven Li, Sharad Malik, and Andrew Wolfe describe how integer linear programming can be used to solve the problem of finding worst case program paths and how this can be extended to cache memories and pipelines[9]. Their work inspired us to use integer constraints for finding worst case program paths because of the users being able to formulate nearly everything they know about the program. In our approach we can additionally take advantage of the VIVU analysis. This enables the user to provide constraints separately for different contexts. In the approach of Li, Malik and Wolfe, the cache behaviour prediction with integer constraints leads to quite large sets of constraints when the level of associativity is increased, and leads to prohibitively high analysis times. This was the reason for us to use abstract interpretation for this kind of problem which was shown (in [4]) to compute the results quickly for any level of associativity. The sets of constraints are smaller than those reported in [9] and the estimated WCETs are equally tight. The threat of user provided constraints that destroy the structure of the ILP leading to very high solving times still remains although it did not occur with our test programmes.

Widely based on [9], Greger Ottoson and Mikael Sjödin [12] have tried to develop a framework to estimate WCETs for architectures with pipelines, instruction and data caches. Unlike the approach of Li, Malik, and Wolfe, they are not restricted to linear constraints but use logical constraints (formulas) to model microarchitectural properties. Nevertheless, they experience the same problems. In an experi-

---

[9]See http://www.ee.princeton.edu/~yauli/cinderella-3.0/

152

ment to predict the cache behaviour of a very small program they report analysis times of several hours.

In [10], Lim et al. describe a general framework for the computation of WCETs of programs in the presence of pipelines and cache memories. Two kinds of pipeline and cache state information are associated with every program construct for which timing equations can be formulated. One describes the pipeline and cache state when the program construct is finished. The other can be combined with the state information from the previous construct to refine the WCET computation for that program construct. Unlike our method that is based on well explored theories and tools for AI, the set of timing equations must be explicitly solved. An approximation to the solution for the set of timing equations has been proposed. The usage of an input and output state provides a way for a modularisation for the timing analysis.

10. Conclusion and future work

We have shown how it is possible to use the results from a cache analysis by AI (presented in [1, 4, 5, 6]) for the calculation of worst case program paths using integer linear programming. Our implementation can be used even for optimising compilers and uses the VIVU analysis to distinguish different execution contexts. By using WCETs for basic blocks as input it is not limited to cache analyses but can use results from any microarchitecture simulation.

There is still room for further research. We are currently developing a pipeline analysis that will be integrated into the existing analysers.

Another area of research is the development of an appropriate interface to the compiler. The compiler should produce a description of the applied optimisations, which can be used in our analyser.

Furthermore, we are developing a data flow analysis to be able to predict bounds for simple loops and recursions. In our experiments many loops had a fixed start and end value for the iteration counter. Again an interface to the compiler would help, since it must obviously use such information when rearranging the code.

11. Acknowledgements

We would like to thank Mark D. Hill, James R. Larus, Alvin R. Lebeck, Madhusudhan Talluri, and David A. Wood for making available the Wisconsin architectural research tool set (WARTS), Thomas Ramrath for the implementation of the PAG frontend for SPARC executables, Yau-Tsun Steven Li and Frank Müller for providing their benchmark programs, Martin Alt for an early implementation of the cache analysis, and Joanne Capstick for her proof-reading.

References

[1] M. Alt, C. Ferdinand, F. Martin, and R. Wilhelm. Cache Behavior Prediction by Abstract Interpretation. In *Proceedings of SAS'96, Static Analysis Symposium*, LNCS 1145, pages 52–66. Springer, Sept. 1996.

[2] M. Alt and F. Martin. Generation of Efficient Interprocedural Analyzers with PAG. In *Proceedings of SAS'95, Static Analysis Symposium*, LNCS 983, pages 33–50. Springer, Sept. 1995.

[3] P. Cousot and R. Cousot. Abstract Interpretation: A Unified Lattice Model for Static Analysis of Programs by Construction or Approximation of Fixpoints. In *Proceedings of the 4th ACM Symposium on Principles of Programming Languages*, pages 238–252, Jan. 1977.

[4] C. Ferdinand. Cache Behavior Prediction for Real-Time Systems. Dissertation, Universität des Saarlandes, Sept. 1997.

[5] C. Ferdinand, F. Martin, and R. Wilhelm. Applying Compiler Techniques to Cache Behavior Prediction. In *Proceedings of the ACM SIGPLAN Workshop on Language, Compiler and Tool Support for Real-Time Systems*, pages 37–46, June 1997.

[6] C. Ferdinand, F. Martin, and R. Wilhelm. Cache Behavior Prediction by Abstract Interpretation. *Science of Computer Programming*, 1998. Selected for SAS'96 special issue.

[7] Y.-T. S. Li and S. Malik. Performance Analysis of Embedded Software Using Implicit Path Enumeration. In *Proceedings of the 32nd ACM/IEEE Design Automation Conference*, pages 456–461, June 1995.

[8] Y.-T. S. Li, S. Malik, and A. Wolfe. Efficient Microarchitecture Modeling and Path Analysis for Real-Time Software. In *Proceedings of the IEEE Real-Time Systems Symposium*, pages 298–307, Dec. 1995.

[9] Y.-T. S. Li, S. Malik, and A. Wolfe. Cache Modeling for Real-Time Software: Beyond Direct Mapped Instruction Caches. In *Proceedings of the IEEE Real-Time Systems Symposium*, Dec. 1996.

[10] S.-S. Lim, Y. H. Bae, G. T. Jang, B.-D. Rhee, S. L. Min, C. Y. Park, H. Shin, K. Park, S.-M. Moon, and C. S. Kim. An Accurate Worst Case Timing Analysis for RISC Processors. *IEEE Transactions on Software Engineering*, 21(7):593–604, July 1995.

[11] F. Mueller, D. B. Whalley, and M. Harmon. Predicting Instruction Cache Behavior. In *Proceedings of the ACM SIGPLAN Workshop on Language, Compiler and Tool Support for Real-Time Systems*, 1994.

[12] G. Ottoson and M. Sjödin. Worst-Case Execution Time Analysis for Modern Hardware Architectures. In *Proceedings of the ACM SIGPLAN Workshop on Language, Compiler and Tool Support for Real-Time Systems*, pages 47–55, June 1997.

[13] J. A. Stankovic. *Real-Time and Embedded Systems*. ACM 50th Anniversary Report on Real-Time Computing Research, 1996. http://www-ccs.cs.umass.edu/sdcr/rt.ps.

[14] R. Wilhelm and D. Maurer. *Compiler Design*. International Computer Science Series. Addison–Wesley, 1995. Second Printing.

Compiler Optimizations for Real Time Execution of Loops on Limited Memory Embedded Systems *

Sundaram Anantharaman[†] and Santosh Pande
PO Box 210030, Department of ECECS, University of Cincinnati
Cincinnati, OH 45221–0030 E-mail: {asundara,santosh}@ececs.uc.edu

Abstract

We propose a framework to carry out an efficient data partitioning for global arrays on limited on-chip memory embedded systems. The key problem addressed in this work is how to perform a good partitioning of data references encountered in loops between on-chip and off-chip memory to meet the demands of real time response by keeping run time overheads of remote access to a minimum. We introduce a concept of footprint to precisely calculate the memory demands of references at compile time and compute a profit value of a reference using its access frequency and reuse factor. We then develop a methodology based on 0/1 knapsack algorithm to partition the references in the local/remote memory. We show the performance improvements due to our approach and compare the results.

1 Introduction

Embedded systems are often characterized by limited resources like memory, computing power and band-width of communication. Memory on embedded systems is especially limited due to its high power consumption. Typically on-chip memory available on embedded Digital Signal Processing (DSP) processors such as TMS320C2x series is quite small (of the order of 1 or 2 KB) [10]. Also a part of the local memory of the embedded device is used up by the code generated for an application and this makes lesser memory available for the data segment of the application (for example, in TMS320C2x, 288 words are reserved for data memory and the remaining 256 words can be configured as either program or data memory). On the other hand, most of the applications (such as image processing codes, data compression/uncompression codes etc.) that execute on these systems are memory–intensive. In such cases, the data segment of such applications is split across the on-chip and off-chip memory. This re-

sults in remote (off-chip) memory references which are expensive and can lead to significant degradation in real time response for these devices. This necessitates an efficient data partitioning compilation method. The issue of data segment partitioning on embedded systems must be addressed in conjunction with the need for low run time overheads for fast real time response and also small code size. This is the focus of our work.

The next section discussion the related work in the area of data partitioning and locality, while the section 3 discusses the outline of our approach. Section 4 defines terms and definitions. In section 5 we discuss our methodology and algorithms to solve the problem. Finally section 6 discusses results and conclusions.

2 Related work

Most compiler optimizations have focussed on decreasing the code size or have focussed on techniques to fit the code in the available memory on an embedded device through different techniques. Bowman et al [3] have attempted code mapping problem by overlapping program portions. Devadas et al [6] have attempted code size optimization by addressing the problem of instruction selection in code generation. Recently, Kolson, Nicolau, Dutt and Kennedy have developed an optimal register allocation algorithm through loop unrolling [5]. However, these approaches focus on code size or register allocation issues and not on data segment partitioning.

Data partitioning has been extensively examined in parallel computing especially in the field of data parallel programs. The issues examined in these partitioning are how to efficiently distribute and align data across processors so as to achieve a workload balance and reduce interprocessor communication. Some of the other typical uses of data partitioning are to enhance cache performance [7]. Wolf and Lam [11] have focussed on data locality of a loop nest in parallel programs, by transforming the code via interchange, reversal, skewing and tiling to minimize memory latency.

Data partitioning on memory scarce embedded de-

---

*This was partially supported by NSF grant number CCR 9696129

[†]Currently with Microsoft Inc., 1, Microsoft Way, WA98052

vices is a challenging problem mainly due to a very limited amount of memory available on the device and also due to tight requirements on real time response and code size. Thus, a new approach needs to be designed so that an efficient code could be generated obeying all these constraints. In this paper, we develop a new scheme for data partitioning based on a concept of compile time definable data partitions (called footprint) that do not need run time address resolution.

3   An Outline of Approach

Following is the outline of our approach:
- We first identify the footprint to be associated with each array reference within loop nest. We use Fourier Motzkin method to compute footprints in the presence of compile time unknown loop bounds. In order to compute the footprint for multiple references of an array that could occur within a loop nest, we first classify the references, determine their overlaps, and then compute the footprint associated with them. A footprint associated with a group of references represents the tightest polytope that surrounds lattice elements accessed by those references. We then precisely compute the size of footprint in terms of the number of lattice points enclosed.
- After identifying the footprints, we associate a profit value that reflects the access frequency of lattice points, enclosed in the footprint corresponding to the underlying references.
- Using the size of footprint, profit-value and memory available on the embedded device as input parameters to a variation of 0/1 Knapsack algorithm we determine the set of footprints that can be fitted locally.
- We then relax the problem for simpler address calculation. We calculate a simple bounding box enclosing each footprint which would help simplifying address calculation. The following is the motivation behind this relaxation. All data accesses of a array reference can be served by the footprint of the reference. Consequently fitting just the footprint on the local machine can suffice the needs of a array reference. However the address calculation within the footprint will be very complex due to the the shape of the footprint. We overcome this by using a bounding box which is rectangular in shape with each side aligned parallel to the respective axis of the index variable. This allows the traditional base+offset calculation to be applied, resulting in several opportunities for common sub-expression elimination etc., to make address calculation very efficient. This efficient address calculation is very essential for real time response of the generated code.
- Using the above set of footprints, we enumerate the set of corresponding bounding boxes that can be fit-

ted on the local machine. An exhaustive version of 0/1 knapsack is used in this case to find the optimal solution viz. the set of bounding boxes that could be locally fitted. Exhaustive solution is justified since the size of input that we are dealing with is small in this case due to elimination done using footprints in the previous step.

The following discussion explains the motivation behind our approach that computes precise footprint values instead of using simple bounding boxes.

A simpler and straightforward approach could be to identify the bounding boxes associated with each reference and use them directly to compute 0/1 solution. We claim that our approach of identifying the set of bounding boxes from the set of footprints is more beneficial than using just the bounding boxes in the 0/1 Knapsack algorithm. This is due to the fact that the knapsack is more closely packed by using object with small granularity in a 0.5-bounded solution (one may note that 0/1 knapsack problem is NP-hard and we have to resort to such a bounded solution to make this analysis tractable). This was concluded by a study by Sarkar et al [9]. This allows *generation* of a better solution using a bounded version of the algorithm; this solution can then be relaxed to the corresponding bounding boxes. The following example clearly demonstrates the superiority of solution found using our approach as against using the simpler approach of directly using the bounding boxes.

```
for j = 1 to 10
    for i = 1 to 6
        A[ i/3, i] = i ;
    endfor
    for i = 1 to 8
        B[1,j] = B[2, i+1] + 2*i;
    endfor
    for i = 1 to 4
        C[1,i] = C[2, i+1] + A[i/2, i]
                + B[1, i] + B[2, i+1];
    endfor
    C[1,j/4] = j;
endfor
```

Table 1 lists the profits, footprint sizes and the bounding box sizes associated with the references in the above piece of code. Let us assume this code is to be executed in an device with a memory capacity of 30. If we decide to perform the selection by using just the bounding boxes, the 0.5-bounded knapsack algorithm will select references B and C. Thus the profit achieved is 230. Using footprint sizes as a criteria results in the selection of references A, B, and C. Relaxing this to fit the corresponding bounding boxes will let us fit the bounding boxes of reference A and B on the device. The profit

155

	Ref A	Ref B	Ref C
Profit	100	240	90
Footprint size	6	16	8
Bounding Box size	12	18	10

Table 1. Table of References

achieved by this method is 240 as against 230 obtained by using bounding boxes. Thus, for a heuristic-based solution approach it is important to aim first at a solution using precise footprint values and then relaxing the solution to bounding boxes. The major contribution of our work is thus, the identification of the footprint of each reference, devising a framework for its 0/1 solution, and then relaxing it to enclosing bounded boxes for simplifying address calculation.

4 Terms and Definitions

We now define some terms that are used in developing our framework.

Definition of G matrix The statement in the loop body can have array references of the form A[g(i_1, i_2, i_3)] where the index function is g $: Z^l \longrightarrow Z^d$, l is the loop nesting with indices i_1, i_2 and i_3 and d is the dimension of the array A. We also assume that the array index expressions are affine function of loop indices. In other words, the index function can be expressed as
$g(\vec{i}) = \vec{i}G + a$
where **G** is a l x d matrix with integer entries and a is an integer constant vector of length d, termed offset vector.

Definition of L matrix
An l dimensional square integer matrix **L** defines the l dimensional iteration space.

Null space of a matrix
Null space of a matrix $\mathbf{A}^{n \times m}$ is the set $\{x^m | Ax = 0\}$.

Data footprint of a reference
Data footprint of a reference within a loop defines the region which includes all the array elements accessed by the reference during the loop execution. A formal definition of Data footprint of a reference g(i) is the polytope P in real space obtained by substituting the bounds of the loop index vector $\vec{i}$. Thus polytope P can be defined by a set of hyper-planes $\{A\vec{x} \geq \vec{k} | \vec{x}, \vec{k} \in IR^d\}$, where, $\vec{k} = g(\vec{I})$ where $\vec{I}$ is the extreme value of $\vec{i}$.

As seen above, the footprint of a reference is calculated by using the index vector of a reference to transform the iteration space spanned by the loop. The iteration space spanned by a loop can be calculated by using the loop bounds given by extreme value of $\vec{i}$. However, in many cases the loop bounds are compile time unknowns that could prohibit precise calculation of $\vec{i}$ and thus the footprints. We could use Fourier-

Motzkin projection of the index vectors of array references and array bounds to determine legal loop bounds and the footprints based on them. Consider the following example.

```
int A[1..100, 1..100]
int B[1..10, 1..10]
for i = c1 to c2
    for j = c3 to c4
        A[i+j,j-4] = B[i,j];
    endfor
endfor
```

Using the Fourier Motzkin method and array bounds, we can attempt to determine legal limits on c1, c2, c3 and c4 which are compile time unknown.

The values of i and j can range from 1 to 10 within the loop since the legal array bounds for B are 1 (lower) and 10 (upper) in both dimensions. Adding the constraints due to A can further tighten the legal loop bounds. The loop index variable j must be lower bounded by 5 since it would lead to an illegal reference in A[i+j,j-4] otherwise. Thus, index variable i goes from 1 to 10 and j can go from 5 to 10 using the above constraints. This allows in turn to precisely compute the footprints for A and B. This gives the lower and upper bounds for (i+j) to be 6 and 20; similarly, the lower and upper bounds for j-4 are 1 and 6. Thus, the footprint for A has a size of 15 x 6 which can be found by using the above bounds for (i+j) and (j-4). Footprint of B can be similarly found. It can be seen that the actual footprint of A for the given loop is much smaller than the actual declaration and can lead to a better utilization of memory when used in data partitioning.

The next step is to determine a cumulative footprint of multiple references of the same variable referenced multiple times within a loop. We introduce the following definitions that assist us in computing the cumulative footprint. The framework which uses these definitions is developed in the next section.

Intersecting references
Two references A[$g_1(\vec{i})$] and A[$g_2(\vec{i})$] are said to be intersecting if there are two integer vectors $(\vec{i_1})$, $(\vec{i_2})$ such that $g_1(\vec{i_1}) = g_2(\vec{i_2})$.

Uniformly generated references
Two references A[g_1] and A[g_2] are said to be uniformly generated if $g_1(\vec{i}) = (\vec{i})\mathbf{G} + a_1$ and $g_2(\vec{i}) = (\vec{i})\mathbf{G} + a_2$ where **G** is a linear transformation and a_1 and a_2 are integer constants.

Uniformly intersecting references
Two array references are uniformly intersecting if they are both intersecting and uniformly generated.

Spread of a set of vectors
Given a set of d-dimensional offset vectors $a_r 1 \leq r \leq R$, $spread(a_1, \ldots \ldots a_R)$ is a vector of the same di-

mension as the offset vectors, whose k-th component is given by $max_r(a_{r,k}) - min_r(a_{r,k}), \forall k \in 1, \ldots \ldots d$.

5 Theoretical framework of our approach

We first discuss our approach to compute the loop bounds that are unknown at compile time. We then develop the criteria for classification of references. After classification we develop a methodology to calculate the footprint of each reference. We then discuss how to compute profit-values that can be associated with a footprint and methods to calculate them. Finally we present a partitioning algorithm based on 0/1 knapsack problem.

5.1 Computing loop bounds

Loop bounds define the iteration space and the trip count of a loop. In order to calculate the footprint of a reference and the profit value which is based on the trip count, we need to compute the legal limits on the loop bounds as illustrated in the above example. We use the following approach to compute the limits on loop bounds of a loop-nest that are unknown at compile time:

- We first enlist all the array references that are within the given loop-nest.
- We determine the upper and the lower bound of each array, that is in the above list. This can be obtained from the declaration of the array.
- Using the index vector of array references and the array bounds from the declaration of the array, we construct a matrix.
- This matrix is used by the Fourier-Motzkin algorithm to determine the legal range of the index variables using elimination. These index variables reflect the limits on loop bounds of the loop-nest which can then be used for footprint computation.

5.2 Classification of references

After determining loop bound limits, we classify references according to Figure 1. This classification of references is done so as to identify references that can be combined depending upon the category they fall. References are combined if there is a significant overlap in their footprints.

After representing each reference in matrix format resulting in the **G** and offset matrices, we classify each reference as either Uniformly generated or Non-uniformly generated. This can be established after examining the **G** matrix of each reference. Uniformly generated references can be further classified as intersecting or non-intersecting by examining the **G** matrix. We use Omega Test [8] based on Fourier-Motzkin projections to determine whether there exists a non-empty integer solution. If a non empty integer solution exists the references are intersecting.

Uniformly generated intersecting references with offset differences : References which are uniformly generated and are intersecting have offset differences. These references are combined together and the cumulative footprint is determined. Such references are treated together and the size of the cumulative footprint is determined to be used by the knapsack algorithm.

Uniformly generated but non-intersecting references : References uniformly generated but which are non-intersecting are considered as separate references. This leads to evaluating the size of footprint, profit-value for each reference separately. The enclosing bounding box and their size is determined for each reference.

Non-uniformly generated but fully overlapping references : Two references are fully overlapping references, if the footprint of one of the references completely encloses the footprint of the other reference. This can be easily determined by checking the corresponding polytope first in real spaces and then (if needed) in integer spaces. We use Fourier-Motzkin projections to determine whether references are overlapping. References that overlap are combined.

5.3 Bounding Box

Every footprint associated with a reference is a polytope, whose sides/edges need not be parallel to the coordinate axes. Fitting such an footprint on the embedded device, will demand a complex address translation mechanism. This is due to the fact that array elements within an array are accessed linearly from the base of the array. We overcome this issue by considering a bounding box that will enclose the footprint. This bounding box has all its sides/edges parallel to the coordinate axes. Data elements within this bounding box can be accessed linearly from the base of this bounding box. Array references that were combined after classification are treated together, thus a combined bounding box is calculated for these set of references.

5.3.1 Building bounding box

Array-slice of each reference is found by calculating the vertices of the polytope. These vertices can be determined by substituting the lower and upper bounds of the loop on to the index expression. Bounding box that encloses this polytope is established by considering the extreme vertices on each coordinate axes.

5.3.2 Size of Bounding box

Once the extreme vertices of the bounding box is obtained the number of lattice points in the bounding box can be determined by primitive techniques. This will be used by the data partitioning algorithm to determine the actual amount of memory needed to fit the

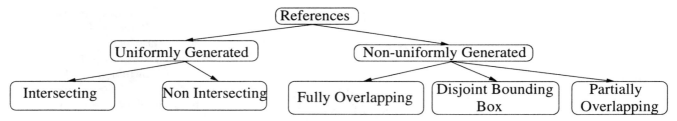

Figure 1. Classification of references

array locally on embedded device. After determining the bounding boxes of each reference or each set of reference the Non-uniformly generated references can be further classified depending upon their bounding boxes.

5.3.3 Non-uniformly generated references with disjoint bounding box

References that are non-uniformly generated and with disjoint bounding box are considered separately for evaluating the size of the footprint profit-value, and size of bounding box.

5.3.4 Non-uniformly generated references with partial overlapping

References which are non-uniformly generated, but have their footprints overlapping partially fall in this category. Partial overlapping can also happen due to the overlapping of the bounding boxes, but not the footprints. We will consider each reference in this category as a separate reference thus calculating the size of footprint, profit-value and the bounding box for each reference.

Figure 2 illustrates the different overlapping cases discussed above.

5.4 Calculating the size of an footprint of a reference

After the above classification, each reference or set of references that are combined will be associated with a footprint. The next step is to calculate the size of the footprint. To calculate the size of the footprint we need to determine the number of lattice points in the corresponding polytope. In order to determining the number of lattice points, we classify references according to their **G** matrices.

- **G** matrix that is Unimodular and Invertible.
- **G** matrix that is Non-unimodular and Invertible.
- **G** matrix that is Non-unimodular and Non-invertible.

5.4.1 G matrix that is Unimodular and Invertible

We will consider two cases :
- **Single reference**

The number of lattice points in the footprint of this reference is given by $|\det(\mathbf{D})|$, where $\mathbf{D} = \mathbf{LG}$.

- **Cumulative number of lattice points in the footprint of a set of uniformly intersecting references**

Consider the case of two references, in which one of the offset vectors is (0,0). The cumulative number of lattice points in the footprint of these two uniformly intersecting references can be found by

$$|\det\mathbf{D}| + \sum_{k=1}^{d} |\det\mathbf{D}_{\mathbf{k}\longrightarrow\mathbf{a}}|$$

where **D** is the matrix obtained by the product of **L** and **G** and $D_{k\longrightarrow a}$ is the matrix obtained by replacing the k th row of **D** by 'a'.

Consider the case of multiple references. The basic approach for estimating the cumulative footprint size involves deriving an effective offset vector 'a' that captures the combined effects of multiple offset vectors when there are several overlapping footprints resulting from a set of uniformly intersecting references. According to a theorem stated by Agarwal et. al. [1, 2] we have the following:

Given a matrix **L** representing the loop bounds and a unimodular reference matrix **G**, the size of the cumulative footprint with respect to a set of uniformly intersecting references specified by the reference matrix **G** and a set of offset vectors $a_1, \dots a_r$ is approximately

$$|\det D| + \sum_{k=1}^{d} |\det\mathbf{D}_{\mathbf{k}\longrightarrow\hat{\mathbf{a}}}|$$

where $\hat{a} = spread_D(a_1, a_2 \dots, a_r)$ and $\mathbf{D}_{\mathbf{k}\longrightarrow\hat{\mathbf{a}}}$ is the matrix obtained by replacing the k th row of **D** by $\hat{a}$.

5.4.2 G matrix that is Non-unimodular and Invertible

A **G** matrix that is non-unimodular and invertible implies that not every integer point in the hyper-parallelepiped **D** is an image of an iteration point in **L**. We are however interested in the total number of points enclosed by polytope, which also includes the points that are not referenced, but are within the polytope. The number of lattice points can be calculated by the same methodology used to calculate the number of lattice points when the **G** matrix is unimodular and invertible.

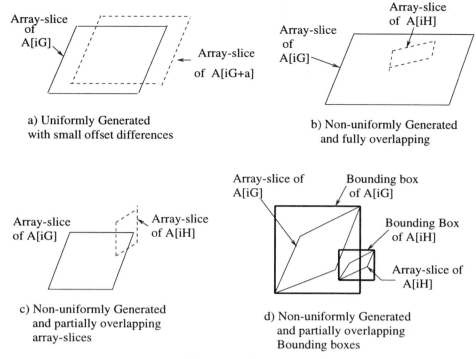

a) Uniformly Generated
with small offset differences

b) Non-uniformly Generated
and fully overlapping

c) Non-uniformly Generated
and partially overlapping
array-slices

d) Non-uniformly Generated
and partially overlapping
Bounding boxes

Figure 2. Overlapping and intersecting footprints

5.4.3 G matrix that is Non-unimodular and Non-invertible

In this subsection we calculate the number of lattice points when **G** matrix is non-unimodular and non-invertible. We restrict this case only to two dimensional references since the calculation in higher dimensions is highly combinatorial. In order to determine the number of lattice points enclosed by the corresponding polygon, we use Pick's theorem [4].

Pick's Theorem: The area of any simple polygon **P** in $I\!R^2$ (not necessarily convex) whose vertices are lattice points is

$$Area = l_1 + \frac{l_0}{2} - 1$$

where

l_1 : Number of lattice points in the interior of the polygon

l_0 : Number of lattice points on the boundary of the polygon

Given the vertices of a line, n_0-number of points on this line can be calculated by using the formula

$$n_0 = 1 + gcd((x_2 - x_1)(y_2 - y_1))$$

where (x_1, y_1) and (x_2, y_2) are the end points of a line. The number of lattice points on the boundary of the polygon can be determined by the above formula and the vertices of the polygon. The area of any polygon can be determined using primitive techniques of geometry. Once the number of lattice points on the boundary and the area of the polygon is found, Pick's theorem is used to calculate the total number of lattice points. Pick's theorem does not hold in a space of more than two dimensions. The situation becomes very complicated and involves many intractable problems.

5.5 Profit-value of a reference

Each array reference is associated with a profit-value to reflect the benefit of fitting the footprint associated with this reference on the embedded device. In other words the profit-value of a reference will exhibit the reuse of a footprint. To calculate the profit-value we use the following two approaches.

5.5.1 Profit-value using the loop size

Every reference within a loop has a footprint associated with it. Therefore during each iteration of the loop, a reference will access one data element from the footprint. Thus the trip-count of the enclosing loop is the count of the number of times the footprint is referenced. This gives a measure of the profit-value. The following is an example to calculate the profit-value using trip-count.

```
for i = 0 to 10
    A[2i] = .....;
end for
```

Trip-count of the loop = 10

Size of the footprint = 20 (as the reference spans from 0 to 20).

Profit-value = trip-count = 10(as only 10 data elements in the array slice are referenced).

However, the profit value computed in this manner is not a precise measure of the remote references saved. A more precise measure is obtained by estimating the exact number of distinct references within the footprint of a array reference. [1]

5.5.2 Profit-value using the number of distinct references

In this approach to calculate the profit-value, we find the number of distinct references within an footprint. Not every data element in an footprint is accessed during the execution of the loop.

```
for i = 1 to 10
    for j = 1 to 10
        A[2i, 2i] = .... ;
    end for
end for
```

Trip-count of the loop = 10 * 10 = 100.
Size of the footprint = 20 * 20 = 400.
Number of distinct references = 10 (Only alternative diagonal elements of the footprint).
Profit-value = Number of distinct references = 10.
We determine the profit-value of a reference by computing the number of distinct accesses made by the reference. We have devised an empirical algorithm to compute the number of distinct data elements accessed in an footprint. This empirical algorithm finds the number of distinct elements accessed by array references that are 2-dimensional. The motivation behind the following algorithm is that the distinct references are a reflection of temporal reuse which depends upon the null vector of the reference matrix $\mathbf{G}$.

Algorithm for computing the number of distinct references

• Compute the determinant of the reference matrix-$\mathbf{G}$.
• If determinant is not 0, then there does not exists a Null vector for this reference. This means there is no temporal reuse and the number of data elements accessed is equal to the total trip count of the enclosing loops.
• Determine the reference matrix-$\mathbf{G}$ matrix, Null Vector for this reference-$\mathbf{N}$ matrix, and the loop size matrix-$\mathbf{B}$ matrix.
• Initialize the DistRef (DistRef is a counter for distinct references) to 0.
• Initialize rn to 1, where rn is the row number.
• Multiply the rn^{th} row of the $\mathbf{N}$ matrix with all rows of $\mathbf{B}$ matrix excepting the rn^{th} row.

---

[1]The justification of using the distinct references is that remote references could always be cached on the local memory the first time they are used; thus, *actual* number of remote accesses is given by the number of distinct references

• Add the value obtained from step 4 to DistRef.
• Subtract the rn^{th} row of the $\mathbf{B}$ matrix by the rn^{th} row of the $\mathbf{N}$ matrix
• Increment rn and repeat steps 4,5,6 as long as rn is lesser or equal to the number of rows in $\mathbf{N}$ matrix. This algorithm can be illustrated by an example.

```
for i= 1 to k1
    for j = 1 to k2
        a[ai+bj, di+ej];
    }
}
```

$$\mathbf{G} = \begin{pmatrix} a & b \\ d & e \end{pmatrix} \quad \mathbf{N} = \begin{pmatrix} n_1 \\ n_2 \end{pmatrix} \quad \mathbf{B} = \begin{pmatrix} k1 \\ k2 \end{pmatrix}$$

DistRef = 0 and rn = 1
First iteration through step 4
$n1 \times k2$
First iteration through step 5
DistRef = DistRef + $n1 \times k2$
First iteration through step 6
$$\mathbf{B} = \begin{pmatrix} k1 - n1 \\ k2 \end{pmatrix}$$
Second iteration will result in
DistRef = DistRef + $n2 \times (k1 - n1)$
$$\mathbf{B} = \begin{pmatrix} k1 - n1 \\ k2 - n2 \end{pmatrix}$$

5.6 0/1 Knapsack Algorithm

Finally we use the above information about footprint sizes and profit values to decide 0/1 partitioning which is a 0/1 knapsack problem. In the 0/1 knapsack problem we are given n objects and a knapsack of finite capacity $\mathbf{M}$. Object i, $(1 \leq i \leq n)$, has a weight $\mathbf{W}[i]$ and a profit $\mathbf{P}[i]$. The problem is to maximize the total profit of the subset of the objects which can be packed into the knapsack without exceeding its capacity $\mathbf{M}$. Stated more formally, the problem is to maximize $\sum_{i=1}^{n} \mathbf{P}[i]\mathbf{X}[i]$ subject to $\sum_{i=1}^{n} \mathbf{W}[i]\mathbf{X}[i] \leq \mathbf{M}$, and $\mathbf{X}[i] \in \{0, 1\}$, $1 \leq i \leq n$. The knapsack problem is similar to our problem of selecting the footprints that can be fitted in the local embedded device. The objects in the knapsack problem can be mapped to footprints in ours, the weight to the size of array slices, the profit to profit-value of a reference, and the capacity to the memory available on the embedded device.

The 0/1 knapsack problem is known to be NP-hard and hence any algorithm which guarantees to provide optimal solution is believed to be computationally no less than semi-exhaustive in nature. We use the algorithm proposed by U.K. Sarkar et al [9](please refer to this paper for a detailed discussion about the algorithm), which is a greedy procedure whose solution is guaranteed to be 0.5-bounded.

5.7 Data partitioning

We now describe the data partitioning algorithm:

- For each footprint evaluate the ratio $\frac{Profit-value}{Footprintsize}$
- The sorted ratios above and the size of the memory are given as input to the 0/1 knapsack algorithm proposed by Sarkar et al [9]. This knapsack algorithm should output the set of footprints that can be accommodated on the local machine.
- For the set of footprints selected we then relax the condition by computing their bounding boxes to simplify address calculation. If all the corresponding bounding boxes can be fitted in the memory the solution is found; else, we select the optimal subset of bounding boxes by exhaustively enumerating solutions (since this is done only for the footprints selected in the previous step, the algorithm is quite fast).
- Compute the resulting profit by adding up the corresponding profit of each bounding box chosen by the algorithm.

5.7.1 Extended case for Non-uniformly generated references with partial overlapping

After the data partitioning algorithm has computed the solution, it is possible that there is some memory not occupied in the embedded device. This may happen because the amount of memory remaining is not sufficient to accommodate any remaining footprint (bounding box). Under this scenario, we determine whether any of the remaining references that are not accommodated have a partial overlapping with any reference that has been accommodated. When a non-accommodated reference has a partial overlapping with a accommodated reference, then we determine a bounding box that can accommodate both these references and attempt to fit this resulting bounding box on the embedded device. However if this resulting bounding box cannot be fitted on the embedded device, then we proceed with the original data partitioning.

6 Results

6.1 Performance Evaluation

We evaluated our methodology by simulating an embedded system framework discussed above using the Tiny Loop Restructuring Research Tool. We tested our implementation using the sample test routine below.

```
function foo(){
1   short a(1:100, 1:100), b(1:100, 1:100)
2   short e(1:100, 1:100), f(1:100, 1:100)
3   short c(1:20, 1:20),d(1:20, 1:20)
4   integer n, n1, n2, n3, n4
5   for i=1,n do
6     for j = 1, n1 do
7       a(2*i+j,j+5) = c(i,j);
8     endfor
```

```
9   endfor
10  for i=1,n2 do
11    for j = 1, n3 do
12      b(4*i+j, 2*j) = d(2*i,2*j);
13    endfor
14  endfor
15  for i=1,50 do
16    for j = 1, 50 do
17      f(i+j, j) = f(i+j+1,j+2);
18    endfor
19  endfor
20  for i=1,10 do
21    for j = 1, 10 do
22      e(i+j, i+j) = a(i+4,j+5) + f(i+2,j)
                      +b(4*i+j,2*j)+c(i,j)
                      +d(2*i,2*j) ;
23    endfor
24  endfor
}
```

In the above code fragment, there are four loop nests, of which there are two with compile-time unknown loop bounds. We first compute the unknown loop bounds using Fourier-Motzkin projections. The loop bounds for the first loop nest ranges with i from 1 to 20 and j from 1 to 20 while the loop bounds of the second loop nest ranges with i from 1 to 10 and j from 1 to 10. Array references f(i+j, j) and f(i+j+1,j+2) are classified as uniformly intersecting, while other references are classified as non-uniformly generated. The uniformly intersecting references are combined and treated as a single reference. The cumulative footprint and the cumulative bounding box is determined for these references. Other references are treated separately. References to a, f, b, c, d in line 25 is overlapped by references to the corresponding arrays in the previous lines. After classifying the references, we compute the precise footprint of the references. Table 2 gives the final list of references with the corresponding number of lattice points in the footprints(Actual Pts), and the cumulative number of points(Cumm. pts) in cases where the footprints are combined. References 'f' being uniformly intersecting are combined. Therefore only the 'f' row has a cumulative number of points. These precise footprints are given as input to the 0/1 knapsack algorithm to determine the set of footprints that can be fitted locally, thus minimizing the remote references. We further select references from this set whose bounding box can be accommodated in the local memory of embedded processor. We compare our method against each of the following allocation strategies.

- **Conventional allocation without optimization**

In a conventional allocation array definitions are first

Loop-nest	Ref	Actual pts	Cumm. pts
1	a	780	NA
	c	400	NA
2	b	694	NA
	d	361	NA
3	f	2500	2650
4	e	19	NA

Table 2. Table of References

examined to determine the arrays that can be fitted locally on the embedded device. These arrays are examined in the sequence of their definitions. There are no analyses performed on the access pattern to find the footprint or bounding box. Therefore the entire array is considered for each definition. Arrays are fitted on the local device according to the available memory.

- **Conventional allocation with 0/1 knapsack**

This strategy is similar to the above method except that it analyzes all the definitions using 0/1 knapsack. With each definition we associate a profit that is the sum of the trip-count of the loops in which this array variable is referenced. Using the entire array's size and profit value we use a variation of 0/1 knapsack algorithm to determine the arrays that can be fitted locally.

- **Trip Count**

In this approach we apply our methodology to perform optimization. We first use Fourier-Motzkin to compute the limits on unknown loop bound (without which we will be forced to consider the entire array size for references within a loop-nest with unknown loop bounds). Using the computed limits on loop bounds, we associate with each reference a profit value which is the trip count of the loop-nest. The 0/1 knapsack uses the precise footprint to compute a solution and then uses that to relax to the corresponding bounding box using exhaustive version of 0/1 knapsack as explained earlier.

- **Distinct points**

This approach is same as above except that the profit value associated with a reference is not the trip count but the number of distinct points accessed by each reference. Thus, the profit associated with references in this case are more precise taking into consideration data re-use and thus attempting to maximize locality. This is our improved allocation algorithm.

- **Bounding box**

This approach is the same as one based on trip count (explained above) except that it directly uses bounding boxes as input to the knapsack algorithm to compute the final 0/1 solution and does not use footprints or distinct reference computations.

We evaluate our methodology by comparing the results obtained by using the precise footprint that uses profit based on trip counts and based on distinct references against the conventional methods (with and without 0/1 optimization). We also compare the results obtained by directly using the bounding box as against the approach which first computes a solution using precise footprint and then relaxes it to corresponding bounding boxes. To evaluate our methodology we have varied the memory from 400 bytes to 2000 bytes. This is typically the amount of memory available on embedded processors. TMS320C2x, a popular DSP chip from Texax Instruments, provides a total of 544 16-bit words of on-chip data RAM [10] . We assume that the 'short' data type occupies one byte on the target embedded processor. We also assumed the memory latency to be 150 nanosecs for local access and 150 millisecs for remote access.

In graph(a) we observe that our methods (based on distinct references and trip counts) lead to lesser loop completion time than any other approaches. The loop completion time is least when the distinct references are used instead of trip-count of the loop. This is due to the fact that distinct references reflect data-reuse. Therefore the number of data elements is less than the trip-count. This allows us to pack more references locally. Graph(b) which shows percentage of remote accesses which are also least for our methods. Thus, our analysis leads to better loop completion time and lesser remote references than conventional methods which do not perform this analysis.

In graph(c) and graph(d), we compare two approaches as follows. The first approach is based on computing the local/remote partition using precise footprint sizes first and then relaxing the problem for choosing an appropriate subset of corresponding bounding boxes; whereas the second one is based on directly choosing a set of bounding boxes that could fit locally. We observe that when the memory available is low, using the precise footprint and then relaxing it to the corresponding bounding box results in better performance. This is due to the fact that at low memory availability the footprints are more fine grain and lead to a better usage of the local memory. The exhaustive enumeration which relaxes the solution to the corresponding bounding boxes maintains the quality of the solution. This also shows that although it is much simpler to compute and use bounding boxes, it is worthwhile undertaking computation of footprints since generated solutions using polynomial bounded versions of knapsack are quite sensitive to distribution of inputs; the more fine grained they are is the better.

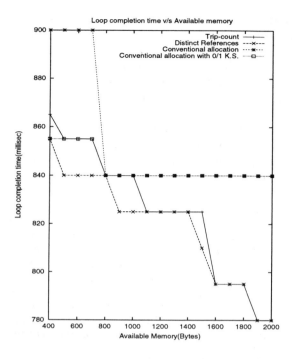

Figure 3. Graph (a)

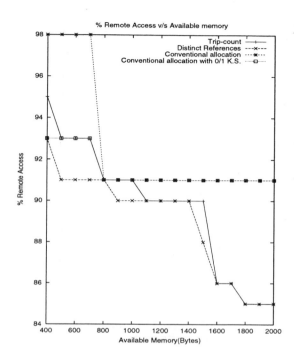

Figure 4. Graph (b)

Finally the percentage of remnant space in the memory (knapsack) is a measure of quality of solution. Please refer to graph (e) for a comparison of memory utilization for different methods. As can be seen, the memory utilization for our footprint based approaches which use trip count and distinct references are better than the one which use bounding box as well as the one based on conventional allocation strategy discussed earlier. The memory utilization for approaches which use trip count, distinct reference and bounding boxes vary between to 60 % to 100 % whereas for the conventional approach it deteriorates with increasing available memory size. As the size of available memory increases, approaches which use trip count, distinct references and bounding boxes show a consistent memory utilization between 90 to 100 %. In general, the footprint based approach which uses distinct references gives the best memory utilization followed by the one which uses trip counts followed the one which uses bounding boxes followed by the conventional one.

7 Conclusion

In this work, we have developed a framework for performing compile time analysis to determine efficient data partitioning of array references in loops on limited memory embedded systems. Through experimental evaluation, we have shown that our methodology performs about 10 to 15 % better than the conventional allocation strategies that do not perform detailed

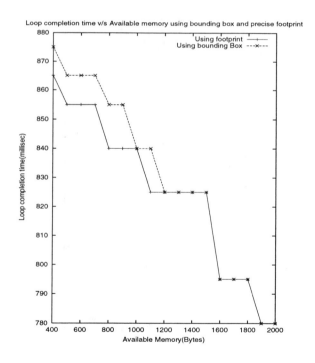

Figure 5. Graph (c)

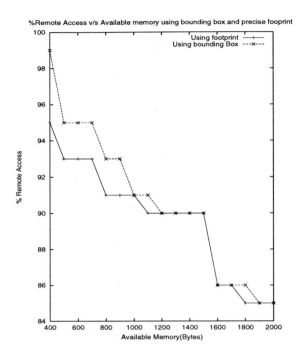

Figure 6. Graph (d)

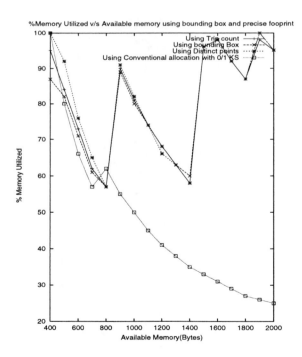

Figure 7. Graph (e)

analysis proposed here. We also show that at low memory capacities (which is typically the case in embedded processors), the allocation strategy based on precise footprints and distinct references performs the best by saving a significant number of remote references improving the loop completion time by a large degree.

8 Acknowledgments

We would like to sincerely thank Prof. George Purdy for pointing us to Pick's theorem and for his help in our understanding of it.

References

[1] A. Agarwal, D. Kranz, and V. Natarajan. Automatic partitioning of parallel loops and data arrays for distributed shared memory multiprocessors. In *International Conferrence on Parallel Processing*, 1993.

[2] R. Barua, D. Kranz, and A. Agarwal. Communication-minimal partitioning of parallel loops and data arrays for cache-coherent distributed-memory multiprocessors. In *Languages and Compilers for Parallel Computing*, August 1996.

[3] R. L. Bowman, E. J. Ratliff, and D. B. Whalley. Decreasing process memory requirements by overlapping program portions. In *Proceedings of the Hawaii International Conference on System Sciences*, pages 115–124, January 1998.

[4] R. Graham, M. Grotschel, and L.Lovasz. Handbook of combinatorics-volume 1, The MIT Press. page 947.

[5] D. J. Kolson, A. Nicolau, N. Dutt, and K. Kennedy. Optimal register assignment to loops for embedded code generation. In *ACM Transaction on Design Automation of Electronic Systems*, pages 251–279, April 1996.

[6] S. Liao, S. Devadas, K. Keutzer, and S. Tjiang. Instruction selection using binate covering for code size optim ization. In *International Conference on Computer-Aided Design*, 1995.

[7] F. Mueller. Compiler support for software-based cache partitioning. In *Workshop on Languages, Compilers and Tools for Real-time Systems*, June 1995.

[8] W. Pugh. The Omega Test: A fast and practical integer programming algorithm for dependence analysis. In *Supercomputing '91*, 1991.

[9] U. K. Sarkar, P. P. Chakrabarti, S. Ghose, and S. C. DeSarkar. A simple 0.5-bounded greedy algorithm for the 0/1 knapsack problem. In *Information Processing Letters*, pages 173–177, May 1992.

[10] Texas Instruments. *TMS320C2x User's Guide*, 1993.

[11] M. E. Wolf and M. S. Lam. A data locality optimizing algorithm. In *Programming Language Design and Implementation*, June 1991.

Session 5: Keynote Talk

Animated Structures: Real-Time, Objects, and the UML
Bran Selic, *ObjecTime, Ltd.*

Abstract: A real-time system is one that continuously responds to events originating in the physical world. This persistent quality implies that the structural aspects of real-time systems are, at the very least, as important as their dynamic characteristics. This is the primary reason why the object paradigm, with its emphasis on creating structures of collaborating parts, is particularly suitable for real-time applications. Despite this obvious affinity, the object paradigm is penetrating into the real-time domain more slowly than in other disciplines. This can be traced to the fact that early object-oriented programming languages mostly neglected issues that are crucial to execution. real-time developers, such as concurrency modeling and efficient

However, the new generation of object technologies is actively addressing such issues. We review the state of the art of these technologies - most notably the emerging Unified Modeling Language (UML) standard - and show how they are evolving to meet the needs of real-time developers. In fact, they present an outstanding opportunity to embark on a program that will consolidate the current body of real-time techniques into a common framework and that will provide a platform for the yet more complex real-time systems of the future.

Profile: **BRAN SELIC** is the Vice President of Advanced Technology at ObjecTime Limited. He has over 25 years of experience in constructing large-scale real-time systems in a number of different disciplines including telecommunications, aerospace, and robotics. He is the principal author of the popular book, "Real-Time Object-Oriented Modeling" that describes how the object paradigm can be used effectively in real-time applications. Most recently, he has been active in the specification of the Unified Modeling Language (UML) standard for object-oriented analysis and design.

Session 6: Systems and Scheduling II

The Time-Triggered Model of Computation

H. Kopetz
Technische Universität Wien, Austria
hk@vmars.tuwien.ac.at

Abstract

The Time-Triggered (TT) model of computation is a model for the representation and analysis of the design of large hard real-time systems. Central to this model is the concept of temporal accuracy of real-time information. The TT-model consists of four building blocks, interfaces that contain temporally accurate data, a communication subsystem that connects interfaces, a host computer that reads input data from interfaces and writes output data to interfaces, and a transducer that transforms the information representation in the environment into the digital form of the interface and vice versa. These four building blocks can be used recursively to describe arbitrary large hard real-time systems. The TT-model separates cleanly the design of the interaction pattern among components from the design of the components themselves. It thus supports a compositional design. In the final section the TT-model is compared to the client-server model.

Keywords: Real-time system, design representation, time-triggered, client-server model, temporal accuracy of data.

1. Introduction

With the advent of cost-effective microcomputers on a single silicon die, distributed architectures are becoming the norm in real-time applications. The integration of a sensor, transducer and signal-processing within a single unit has led to the concept of a smart sensor that acts as a node in a real-time network. Many such intelligent sensor, actuator, and computational nodes are interconnected to form a cluster that provides the services of the real-time computer system. Such a distributed real-time computer system must produce the intended results within a specified window of real-time. In this paper we focus on real-time systems where a single failure to produce results on time constitutes a system failure, i.e., on *hard real-time systems*. Hard real-time systems are fundamentally different from soft real-time systems, where the occasional violation of a deadline is tolerated. Hard real-time systems are more difficult to understand and to design than soft real-time systems because the designer must consider two dimensions of the design problem simultaneously: the value dimension and the time dimension of each result. One will only succeed in designing large hard real-time systems systematically if there is a reduced representation, a system model, of such a large system that captures the essential properties of the design problem while abstracting from irrelevant detail.

A distributed computer system consists of nodes interconnected by a communication systems. The prevalent computational model for the description of distributed applications is the client-server model. In the client-server model, one node, acting as a client node, requests a service from another remote node, acting as a service node, using the services of the interconnection network. The client-server model has evolved over many years from the field of non-time critical distributed applications. The Open System Foundation (OSF 1992) and the CORBA (OMG 1993) initiative try to standardize client-server interfaces to achieve application interoperability in all types of networks. Recently, an initiative has been started to extend the client-server model to the domain of real-time systems(OMG 1998). Extending the client-server model to cater for real-time applications is difficult, because the fundamental notions of time and timeliness are missing from the original client-server model. It has yet to be demonstrated whether these fundamental notions can be integrated into the client-server model as an addendum. It is our belief that a computational model of a distributed real-time computer system must be based around the notion of time as a first order concept. The TT-model discussed in this paper is such a computational model in that it is based on time and timeliness of real-time information. The objective of the TT-Model is to provide the means for the high-level description of large real-time systems. The model focuses on the temporal accuracy of the data elements in the interfaces between the subsystems.

It is the objective of this paper to present a time-triggered (TT) model for the representation of large

168

distributed real-time systems. The rest of this paper is organized as follows. In the next section we introduce the concepts of real-time (RT) entities and real-time (RT) images and define the temporal accuracy relationship between an RT entity and the corresponding RT image. After a short discussion about layering versus partitioning, the building blocks and the structure of the TT-model are introduced in the core Section 4. The relation between the TT-model of computation and the time-triggered architecture as an implementation architecture is discussed in Section 5. Section 6 gives an example of a TT system model. Section 7 compares the TT-model with the client server model of a distributed computation. Finally, Section 8 concludes the paper.

2. Temporal Accuracy of Information

At the core of the TT-model is the notion of the temporal accuracy of real-time data. Real-time data loses its validity as time progresses. In order to refine this notion, the concepts of a real-time (RT) entity and of a real-time (RT) image as a picture of a RT entity are introduced (Kopetz 1997).

Real-time Entity: A controlled object, e.g., a car or an industrial plant, changes its state as a function of time. If we freeze time, we can describe the current state of the controlled object by recording the values of its state variables at that moment. We are normally not interested in *all* state variables, but only in the *subset* of state variables that is *significant* for our purpose. A significant state variable is called a *real-time (RT) entity*. Every RT entity is in the *sphere of control (SOC)* of a subsystem, i.e., it belongs to a subsystem that has the authority to change the value of this RT entity. Outside its sphere of control, the value of an RT entity can be observed, but cannot be modified.

A *real-time (RT) entity* is thus a state variable of relevance for the given purpose, and is located either in the SOC within the environment or in the SOC within the computer system. Examples of RT entities are the flow of a liquid in a pipe (in the SOC of the controlled object), the setpoint of a control loop (in the SOC of the operator), and the intended position of a control valve (in the SOC of the real-time computer). An RT entity has static attributes that do not change during the lifetime of the RT entity, and has dynamic attributes that change with time. Examples of static attributes are the name, the type, the value domain, and the maximum rate of change. The value set at a particular point in time is the most important dynamic attribute. Another example of a dynamic attribute is the rate of change at a chosen point in time.

Observation: The information about the state of an RT entity at a particular point in time is captured by the notion of an *observation*. An observation is an *atomic data structure*

$$Observation = <Name, t_{obs}, Value>$$

consisting of the name of the RT entity, the point in real time when the observation was made (t_{obs}), and the observed value of the RT entity. A continuous RT entity can be observed at any point in time while a discrete RT entity can only be observed when the state of this RT is not changing.

Real-time Image: A *real-time (RT) image* is a *current* picture of an RT entity. An RT image is valid at a given point in time if it is an accurate representation of the corresponding RT entity, both in the value and the time domains. While an observation records a fact that remains valid forever (a statement about an RT entity that has been observed at a particular point in time), the validity of an RT image is *time-dependent* and thus likely to be invalidated by the progression of real-time.

Temporal Accuracy: *Temporal accuracy* is the relationship between an RT entity and its associated RT image (Kopetz and Kim 1990). The temporal accuracy of an RT image is defined by referring to the *recent history* of observations of the related RT entity. A recent history RH_i at time t_i is an ordered set of time points $\{t_i, t_{i-1}, t_{i-2}, \ldots t_{i-k}\}$, where the length of the recent history, $d_{acc} = z(t_i) - z(t_{i-k})$, is called the *temporal accuracy interval* or the *temporal accuracy*. ($z(e)$ is the timestamp of event e generated by a reference clock z). Assume that the RT entity has been observed at every time point of the recent history. An RT image is temporally accurate at the present time t_i if

$$\exists\, t_j \in RH_i: Value\,(RT\,image\,at\,t_i) = Value\,(RT\,entity\,at\,t_j)$$

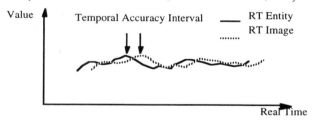

Figure 1: Time lag between RTentity and RTimage.

The present value of a temporally accurate RT image is a member of the set of values that the RT entity had in its recent history. Because the transmission of an observation message from the observing node to the receiving node takes some amount of time, the RT image lags behind the RT entity (See Figure 1).

The size of the admissible temporal accuracy interval is determined by the dynamics of the RT entity in the controlled object. The delay between the observation of the RT entity and the use of the RT image causes an error, *error(t)* of the RT image that can be approximated by the product of the gradient of the value *v* of the RT entity multiplied by the length of the interval between the observation and its use:

$$error(t) = \frac{dv(t)}{dt}(z(t_{use}) - z(t_{obs}))$$

If a temporally valid RT image is used, the worst-case error,

$$error = \left(\max_{\forall t} \frac{dv(t)}{dt} d_{acc}\right),$$

is given by the product of the maximum gradient and the temporal accuracy d_{acc}. In a balanced design, this worst-case error caused by the temporal delay is in the same order of magnitude as the worst-case measurement error in the value domain, and is typically a fraction of a percentage point of the full range of the measured variable.

State Estimation: The most important future point in time where the RT image must be in close agreement with the corresponding RT entity is t_{use}, the point in time where the value of the RT image is used to cause an action in the environment. If the time it takes to transport an observation from a node that observes a RT entity to another node that performs a computation and the output to the environment is longer than the temporal accuracy interval d_{acc}, then the state of the RT image at the time of use t_{use} must be estimated by a process called state estimation. State estimation involves the building of a model of an RT entity inside a computer to compute the probable state of an RT image at a selected future point in time. State estimation is a powerful technique to extend the temporal accuracy interval of an RT image, i.e., to bring the RT image into better agreement with the RT entity.

If the behavior of an RT entity can be described by a continuous and differentiable function $v(t)$, the first derivative dv/dt is sometimes sufficient in order to obtain a reasonable estimate of the state of the RT entity at the point t_{use} in the neighborhood of the point of observation:

$$v(t_{use}) \approx v(t_{obs}) + (t_{use} - t_{obs})dv/dt$$

If the precision of such a simple approximation is not adequate, a more elaborate series expansion around t_{obs} can be carried out. In other cases a more detailed mathematical model of the process in the controlled object may be required. The execution of such a mathematical model can demand considerable processing resources.

The most important dynamic input to the state estimation model is the precise length of the time interval $[t_{obs}, t_{use}]$. Because t_{obs} and t_{use} are normally recorded at different nodes of a distributed system, a communication protocol with small jitter (the jitter of a communication protocol is the difference between the maximum and the minimum protocol execution time) or a global time-base with a good precision is a prerequisite for state estimation. This prerequisite is an important requirement for the design of a field bus.

3. Layering versus Partitioning

Model building implies the design of a framework that can be used to describe the reality at an abstract, i.e. less detailed, level. Two kinds of structuring of a computer system can be distinguished to reduce the system complexity: *horizontal* versus *vertical* structuring.

(i) Horizontal structuring (or *layering*) is related to the process of stepwise abstraction, of defining successive hierarchically-ordered new layers that are reduced representations of the system. Many software-engineering techniques (e.g., structured programming, virtual machines) propose one or another form of horizontal structuring.

(ii) Vertical structuring is related to the process of *partitioning* a large system into a number of *nearly* independent subsystems with their own resources (CPUs, memory, software) and with *well-specified interfaces* (in the temporal and value domain) among these subsystems so that these subsystems can be validated in isolation of each other. In distributed real-time systems *clusters* and *nodes* are the tangible units of partitioning.

While in a central computer system, layering is the common technique to combat complexity, the designer of a distributed computer system can take advantage of both techniques. In the following section we focus on system partitioning.

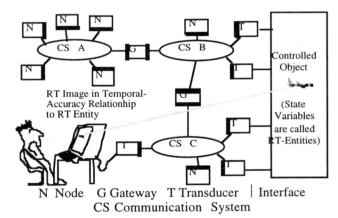

N Node   G Gateway   T Transducer | Interface
CS Communication System

Figure 2: A distributed computer system consisting of three computational and two environment clusters.

A large distributed computer application is normally partitioned into clusters. Some clusters are in the environment, e.g., the process that is to be controlled, and some clusters form the controlling computer system, the computational clusters (Figure 2). Each computational cluster consists of a set of nodes N that are interconnected by a communication system. A node that is a member of two clusters--we call such a node a gateway node G-- provides the interconnection between these two clusters. A node that transduces information from/to an environmental cluster is called a *transducer* T. Figure 2 shows a system consisting of three computational and two environment clusters.

From the point of view of design, a real-time system is first partitioned into nearly decomposable subsystems of high inner connectivity and low external connectivity. Some of these subsystems are then mapped into clusters and nodes of the distributed computer system. In a second step, each node can be structured internally according to the layering technique.

In many embedded applications this partitioning of a distributed computer system into nodes and clusters is dictated by the structure and the constraints of the controlled object. For example, in a distributed vehicle system it is expedient to assign a distinct node--or even a complete cluster--to the control of the engine, to the control of the brakes and to the control of the body electronics. Such a functional partitioning of the hardware can lead to a number of advantages concerning composability, error containment, and reusability:

(i)   In a partitioned system, where few computational tasks share a processor, there is a reduced need for resource multiplexing. Resource multiplexing introduces complexity and temporal unpredictability into the system behavior. It is thus easier to arrive at tight execution time bounds of computations if there is only limited resource sharing among the tasks of a node.

(ii) The abstractions of partitioned systems also hold in case of failures. While in a layered system, it is difficult to define clean error-containment regions for the case of a fault in a shared resource (e.g., the CPU), the partitions (nodes and clusters) of a distributed system coincide with the units of failures where small and observable interfaces (the message interfaces) around these error-containment regions facilitate the error detection and error containment.

(iii) The complexity of an implementation of a partition can be hidden behind the precise specification of the communication network interface between the partition and the rest of the world. The attributes of data objects (value and temporal) that are contained in this interface can form the core of such a precise interface specification.

(iv) The future availability of highly integrated system chips makes partitioning and clustering economically and conceptually attractive. The economic attractiveness is a consequence of the immense economies of scale of the semiconductor industry. The conceptual attractiveness results from reusing the same design pattern over and over again.

4. The TT Model of Computation

The Time–Triggered (TT) model of computation is based on partitioning a large distributed computer system into nearly autonomous subsystems with small and stable interfaces between these subsystems. It describes a large real-time system by the repetitive use of the following four basic building blocks:

(i)   An *interface*, i.e., a boundary between two subsystems,

(ii) A *communication system* that connects interfaces,

(iii) A *host computer* that reads data from one or more interfaces, processes the data and writes data into one or more interfaces, and

(iv) A *transducer* that connects an RT entity in the environment to an interface or vice versa.

It is assumed that each one of these building blocks has access to a globally synchronized time base of sufficient precision. In the following sections we describe these building blocks in more detail. Section 5 relates these basic building blocks to the physical units, i.e., the nodes and the clusters of a distributed computer system.

4.1   Interface

The most important concept of the TT-model is the interface. An interface consists of a memory element that is shared between two interfacing subsystems and that contains valid RT images of the relevant RT entities. An interface can be viewed as a dual-ported memory, where the information-producing subsystem updates the RT image periodically in order to ensure that the RT image in the interface is valid. The information-consuming subsystem reads this temporally accurate information whenever needed.

Temporal Firewall: The concept of a *temporal firewall* (Kopetz and Nossal 1997) has been developed to describe the properties of interfaces in the TT-model. We distinguish between two types of temporal firewalls, *phase-insensitive (PI)* and *phase-sensitive (PS)* temporal firewall.

*A **PI temporal firewall** is a unidirectional **data-sharing interface** with **state-data semantics** where **at least one** of the interfacing subsystems accesses the temporal firewall according to an **a priori known time-triggered schedule** and where at all points in time the information contained in the temporal firewall can be assumed to be **temporally accurate** for at least d_{acc} time units into the future.*

There are no control signals crossing a temporal firewall. The information provider has to update the RT image in the temporal firewall according to the dynamics of the corresponding RT entity. If the information-

171

providing subsystem ceases to operate, the information in the temporal firewall is likely to become invalidated by the passage of time.

If a user (e.g., a process in a host computer) uses a data-element of a PI temporal firewall within d_{acc} interval time units after reading then the result will be temporally valid at the time of use. Such users can access the data items of the temporal firewall at arbitrary instants without running the risk that the RT image will become invalid before it is used.

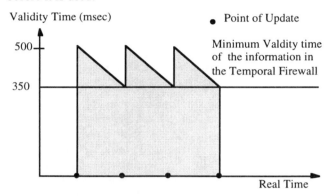

Figure 3: Information validity in the PI firewall of the previous example.

Example: Consider an RT-entity that denotes the temperature of the oil in an engine. The temperature changes at most 1 % of the range per second. An accuracy in the value domain of .5 % is required. Assuming that the measurement is precise at the point of observation, d_{acc} is 500 msec at the instant of observation. If it takes 50 msec to transport the RT image to the temporal firewall of the receiver and the update period is 100 msec, then the remaining d_{acc} in a PI temporal firewall is 350 msec. If the update period is 50 msec, then d_{acc} is 400 msec.

If a system designer intends to make full use of the temporal validity of the firewall information at the point of update, the user tasks must be synchronized with the update points.

*A **PS temporal firewall** is a unidirectional **data-sharing interface** with **state-data semantics** where the **information producer** accesses the temporal firewall according to an **a priori known time-triggered schedule** and where the information contained in the temporal firewall is **temporally accurate** for at least d_{acc} time units into the future at the instant when the information producer delivers the information to the temporal firewall.*

When a user reads information from a PS temporal firewall it must ensure that the time interval between its use of the information and the point in time of information delivery by the producer is less than d_{acc}

time unit or it must perform state estimation. The name "phase-sensitive" temporal firewall expresses the need for a user task to synchronize its start of execution with the *a priori* known instant of information delivery.

Example: Consider an RT-entity that denotes the position of a crankshaft of an engine. The maximum speed of the engine is 6000 revolutions per minute, i.e., one revolution per 10 msec. The required accuracy of the position measurement for fuel injection is about .1 degree, corresponding in the time domain to a temporal accuracy of about 3 μsec. With these parameters it is not feasible to built an PI firewall, since it is impossible to use the RT-image within 3 μsec after it has been observed. In this application a PS firewall with state estimation is required. Since an engine operation is regular, it is possible to estimate the future state of the position of the crankshaft provided the position, the speed, and the acceleration of the crankshaft is known at the point of observation. The producer of this information knows *a priori* when precisely the information will be delivered at the consumer's firewall. It can perform the state estimation of the position, the speed, and the acceleration for the instant when the RT image is made available to the consumer's firewall. The consumer can then perform a second state estimation to estimate the position of the crankshaft at the time of use t_{use} when the output signal to open the valve is relayed to the I/O circuitry.

Task scheduling is simpler if the temporal firewall is phase insensitive than if it is phase sensitive. It depends on the temporal properties of the application and the available communication resources whether the simpler PI temporal firewall can be designed.

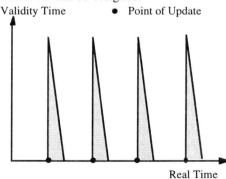

Figure 4: Information validity in the PS firewall of the previous example.

Stable Properties: The following stable properties characterize a temporal firewall. In the TT-model it is assumed that knowledge about these properties is available *a priori* to all interfacing subsystems:

(i)   The addresses (names) and the syntactic structure of the data items in the temporal firewall. The meaning of the data items is associated with these names.

(ii) The points on the global time base when the data items in the temporal firewall are accessed by the TT subsystem. This information enables the avoidance of race conditions between the producer and the consumer. A race condition could lead to a loss of replica determinism in replicated temporal firewalls.

(iii) The temporal accuracy d_{acc} of the data items in the temporal firewall. This knowledge is important to guide the information consumer about the minimum rate of sampling the temporal firewall. The absolute time-points when the TT subsystem accesses the temporal firewall are reference points for the temporal accuracy of the information in the PS temporal firewall and can be used as the basis for state estimation.

Producer Obligation: The producer of the RT-images stored in the temporal firewall is responsible that the *a priori* guaranteed temporal accuracy of the RT-images is *always* given. It must update the state information with such a frequency that the guaranteed temporal accuracy is maintained, in the case of a PI firewall even immediately before the point of update. In case the producer of the information is the TT subsystem, the producer is allowed to access the temporal firewall only at the *a priori* established time points t to avoid race conditions for access to the temporal firewall. In case the producer of the information is not the TT subsystem, the producer is allowed to access the temporal firewall at any point in time outside a *critical interval* around t.. The duration of this critical interval is *[t-2g, t+d_{acd}+2g]*, where t is the *a priori* known access instant of the consumer, d_{acd} is the access duration of the consumer, and g is the granularity of the global time [Kopetz 1997, p.55].

Consumer Obligation: Based on the *a priori* knowledge about the temporal accuracy of the RT images in the temporal firewall, the consumer must sample the information in the temporal firewall with a sampling rate that ensures that the accessed information is temporally accurate at its *time of use* of this information. The consumer is only allowed to access the information in the temporal firewall when it knows (based on the *a priori* knowledge) that the producer is not accessing it. If the consumer violates these access constraints, replica determinism may be lost, or, in the worst case, the consumed information may be corrupted.

The implementation of protected-shared objects (PSO) can avoid information corruption, but cannot guarantee replica determinism for the following reason: If two replicas perform an exclusive operation on a PSO at about the same time, it cannot be guaranteed that the temporal order of access to the PSO is the same in both replicas. In

case it is different, a loss of replica determinism between these two replicas may occur.

4.2 Communication System

The time-triggered communication system connects interfaces and transports data elements from one interface to one or more other interfaces within *a priori* known deterministic time bounds. The semantics of the transported data is state-message semantics, i.e., a new version of a message replaces the current version in the receiving interfaces. State messages are not consumed on reading. There is thus no queuing of messages in the interfaces. The points in time when a message is taken from the sending interface and is delivered to the receiving interfaces are stored in dispatching tables. The contents of these dispatching tables are designed before run time and are *common knowledge* to all communicating partners. The temporal properties of the interfaces are thus precisely specified and do not change during the operation of the communication system.

The computational interaction pattern between the nodes of a cluster is reduced to the deterministic interaction between interfaces, established by the time-triggered communication system. The precise specification of the temporal and value properties of the interfaces can be developed without any knowledge about the (local) host implementation. The TT-model thus supports composability and host heterogeneity.

The operation of the time-triggered communication system between interfaces can be compared to the operation of a train system between stations. There is an *a priori* known time table that informs the clients about when a train is expected to arrive at a station and when a train will leave a station. The train system operates deterministically and independently from the activity at the stations and is synchronized with a known time standard. The client has to adapt to the time schedule of the train system.

4.3 Host Computer

A host computer is an encapsulated computational machine including one or more processing units, a memory, system software and application software. The host computer reads the input data from one or more interfaces and writes the output data into one or more interfaces. The instants when input data to the host computer are delivered at the interfaces and when output data from the host computer are fetched from the interfaces are known *a priori*. If a host computer has to react to a specific state change (event) it has to periodically sample the respective interface data items and trigger some action if the anticipated state change has been observed. The sphere of temporal control is thus always within the host computer and not delegated to the outside of the host computer.

The notion of an interrupt, i.e., an external event that interrupts a computation in a host computer, is foreign to the TT-model. The processing of such an external interrupt would consume an unpredictable amount of computational resources of the host computer and would thus conflict with the predictability requirement.

4.4 Transducer

A transducer translates the environment's representation of an RT entity to the digital format of the corresponding RT image that is stored in the associated interface and vice versa. The time delay between sampling the RT entity in the environment and writing the RT image into the interface is constant and known *a priori*. Transducers are introduced to model the input/output system of a real-time system. From the modeling point of view it does not matter whether the I/O device is an analog sensor or a human operator behind a terminal. What is relevant is (i) that the I/O data is available in the corresponding interface within a known time-interval after it has been created and (ii) how long this RT image is temporally valid. The same reasoning, but in the opposite direction, applies to the output data generated by the computer system.

5. Implementation Issues

The TT-model described in this paper is a conceptual model for the design representation and the analysis of large real-time systems. Such a design representation of a system can only be implemented effectively if the semantic gap between this design representation and an object architecture can be bridged without intricated transformations that destroy the understandable structure of the design representation. The Time-Triggered Architecture (TTA) (Kopetz 1998) is an exemplary architecture for the implementation of the TT-model.

Node

Figure 5 depicts the structure of a standard TTA node. A standard node consists of two subsystems, a host computer and a time-triggered communication protocol (TTP) controller with a controller internal data structure (the message descriptor list MEDL) that determines when a message must be sent or received.

The host computer of the node corresponds with the host computer in the TT model. It is a self-contained computer with its own operating system and the application software. It interfaces to the communication controller via the communication network interface CNI. The CNI is the concrete implementation of the interface building block of the TT model.

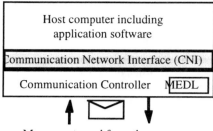

Messages to and from the
real-time communication system

Figure 5: Structure of a standard TTA node.

The set of communication controllers of all nodes within a cluster, including the physical media, forms the communication system of the cluster. Every node contains a part of the communication system. If a node is a gateway node (see Figure 2) it contains two communication controllers and thus is a member of two clusters. A transducer node can be considered as a special gateway node that contains an I/O interface to an environment cluster.

Services of the Communication System

The time triggered communication protocol TTP provides the clock synchronization service that is needed for the implementation of the TT-model. The TTP communication controller contains its own data structure, the message descriptor list MEDL, that specifies the global interaction pattern among the nodes of a cluster and the temporal and value parameters of the communication network interface (CNI). There are a number of mechanisms in the TTP controller to increase the dependability. To avoid that a malicious host can interfere with the global communication system, the MEDL is not made accessible from the host computer. The TTP controller contains two independent physical channels such that the loss or disturbance of one channel can be tolerated. A special device in the TTP controller, the bus guardian, ensures that the controller will not access the bus outside its planned time slot, even if the controller itself becomes faulty(Temple 1998).

6. Example

Consider the example of an air traffic control system consisting of three computational and two environment clusters as shown in Figure 2. Cluster B and Cluster C interface to complex radar equipment that monitors the airspace. Cluster A, a computation cluster, dynamically computes some safety parameters, e.g., the expected future distance of the observed planes in order to avoid mid-air collisions. Cluster C interfaces to the operator.

The main interest of the operator at its interface is the temporally accurate display of the RT images of the RT entities that are in the monitored airspace. Figure 6 tries to capture this abstraction. Similarly, the computational cluster A needs the up-to-date attributes of the RT images to perform the collision avoidance calculations.

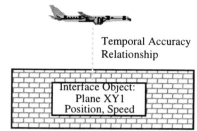

Temporal Accuracy
Relationship

Interface Object:
Plane XY1
Position, Speed

Figure 6: Temporal firewall data at operator interface.

A high-level requirements analysis of such a system must first try to capture all relevant RT entities. It then proceeds by identifying the temporal firewalls and the RT images that must be contained in each of these firewalls. In the next step the required temporal validity of the RT images in the temporal firewalls must be established. The points in time when the interface objects are accessed (read or write) by the TT communication system will be determined by the schedule of the time-triggered communication system that transports the RT images between the interfaces.

At this point the architecture design phase is completed. The global interaction patterns among all subsystems have been established. The temporal and value attributes of all interfaces are precisely specified despite the fact that no knowledge about the hardware architecture, the operating system and the application software structure of the hosts is yet available (nor needed). The precise interface specification is sufficient to specify, implement and validate the interaction patterns among the components. The TT-model thus supports a compositional design.

In the next phase, the component design phase, the given interface specifications are taken as constraints for the development of the host and the transducer subsystems. The development of these subsystems can proceed in parallel, because the interactions among the subsystems are known and fully specified in the temporal domain and in the value domain at this phase of the design.

The host systems interfacing to the temporal firewalls can be heterogeneous computer systems or even legacy systems, provided they meet the temporal firewall specifications. Each subsystem can be based on a different hardware architecture and can use a different real-time operating system. As long as the value and temporal attributes of the interface objects in the temporal firewalls are satisfied, the interoperability of the subsystems is guaranteed. Each subsystem can be tested in isolation with respect to the interface specification.

During system integration the subsystems are integrated with the communication system to perform the system function. The interface properties are not modified by this integration. System integration is therefore a straightforward process, as has been demonstrated in an industrial application (Hedenetz and Belschner 1998).

7. The Client-Server Model versus the TT Model

In this section the TT-model is compared to the most widely used model for the description of distributed real-time systems, the client-server model. The client-server model assumes that one application, the *client*, requests the services from another application, the *server*, that can be at a different node of the distributed system. The client-server model provides a process-based horizontal service interface to the client at the API (application program interface) within the client node (Figure 7). Its focus is on the request-response transactions between a client process and a server process, possibly using the services of some intermediate brokers.

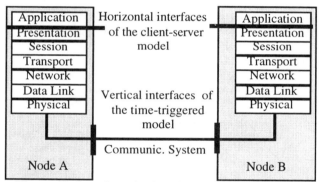

Figure 7: Interfaces in the client-server and the TT model.

In contrast, the TT model provides a state based vertical interface (Figure 7) at the boundary of a host, describing the temporal and value properties of the data exchanged between the interfacing partners. The internal structure of the interfacing subsystems is of subordinate concern to the TT model. Table 1 compares the characteristics of the two models.

The key problem in the application of the client-server model to distributed hard real-time systems is the missing phase control among the initiations of the remote client-server requests. Since the start-of-transaction commands are not globally coordinated there is always the possibility of a *critical instant* (Liu and Layland 1973) when all clients request services from the global communication system and the servers at the same point in time. No matter what scheduling strategy is employed, some transactions will have to wait for resources until other transactions have completed. This unpredictable jitter caused by these global interactions destroys the temporal composability.

Characteristic	Client-Server	TT-Model
Focus	Process based	State based
Structuring	horizontal-layer	vertical-partition
Driven by	Event messages	Sampling of states
Locus of Control	Global system wide events	Local within subsystem
Temporal concern	Timely request response transactions	Temporal accuracy of interface data
Temporal composability	Not supported	Supported

Table 1: Comparison of Client-Server model and TT-model.

One solution that has been proposed to solve this problem is the provision of as many resources as are required at the critical instant. This is a considerably more expensive solution than the *a priori* coordination of the interactions as performed in the TTA. Furthermore, it does not lead to composable design. From the economic viewpoint it is important to make the right choice about the implementation architecture (Table 2) for a soft and hard real-time application.

Architecture	Hard real-time application	Soft real-time application
Time-Triggered Architecture	adequate	Too expensive, because there is no need to provide all the resources required to handle all specified load and fault scenarios.
Client-Server Architecture	Too expensive, because the fear that the computer system might miss its deadline at the critical instant leads to the installation of hardware overcapacity with a low resource utilization.	adequate

Table 2: Choice of implementation architecture for hard and soft real-time systems.

Since many applications contain soft real-time functions and hard real-time functions in parallel, it can be economical to partition the system into a hard real-time partition and a soft real-time partition with a gateway between these partitions. The hard real-time parts of the system can be designed according to the TT paradigm and the soft real-time parts according to the client-server paradigm.

8. Conclusion

At the core of the TT-model are precisely specified interfaces and a predictable time-triggered communication system that decouples the interactions among the subsystems of a large distributed hard real-time system from the data processing functions at the nodes. The communication system defines the precise interaction patterns among these subsystems in the temporal domain and in the value domain. It transports RT images from one interface to another interface and does not have any knowledge about the hardware environment, the software environment, or the application task structure in the subsystems behind the interfaces.

The TT-model supports a two-phase design methodology, an architecture design phase and a component design phase. The interaction patterns among the subsystems and the precise temporal and value attributes of the interface objects are defined during an architecture design phase. For the ensuing component design phase, these interface specifications are considered to be implementation constraints. Since the temporal properties of the interface specifications do not change during system integration, the TT-model is composable and supports the constructive implementation of large real-time systems.

In the final section, the TT model has been compared with the client server. It is proposed to partition large real-time systems that contain soft and hard real-time functions into a hard real-time partition and a soft real-time partition.

A prerequisite for the implementation of the TT-model is the availability of an implementation of the time-triggered communication system model. Such a time-triggered communication system based on the TTP protocol has been developed and implemented at the Technische Universität Wien during the last ten years. The future availability of VLSI controllers for TTP will open many new opportunities for the constructive design of large real-time systems.

Acknowledgments

Constructive comments on an earlier version of this paper by Brian Randell and Peter Puschner are warmly acknowledged. This paper has been supported by the ESPRIT LTR project DEVA, by the ESPRIT OMI project TTA, by the Brite Euram project X-by-Wire.

References

Hedenetz, B. and R. Belschner (1998). "Brake by Wire" without Mechanical Backup by Using a TTP Communication Network. *SAE World Congress*, Detroit Michigan. SAE Press, Warrendale, PA, USA.

Kopetz, H. and K. Kim (1990). Temporal Uncertainties in Interactions among Real-Time Objects. *Proc. 9th Symposium on Reliable Distributed Systems*, Huntsville, AL, USA. IEEE Computer Society Press. pp. 165-174.

Kopetz, H. (1997). *Real-Time Systems, Design Principles for Distributed Embedded Applications; ISBN: 0-7923-9894-7*. Boston. Kluwer Academic Publishers.

Kopetz, H. (1998). A Comparison of CAN and TTP. Technische Universität Wien, Institut für Technische Informatik.

Kopetz, H. (1998). The Time-Triggered Architecture. *ISORC 1998*, Kyoto, Japan. IEEE Press.

Kopetz, H. and R. Nosssal (1997). Temporal Firewalls in Large Distributed Real-Time Systems. *Proceedings of IEEE Workshop on Future Trends in Distributed Computing*, Tunis, Tunesia. IEEE Press.

Liu, C. L. and J. W. Layland (1973). Scheduling Algorithms for Multiprogramming in a Hard-Real-Time Environment. *J. of the ACM*. Vol. **20**. pp. 46-61.

OMG (1993). Object Managment Group: The common object request broker, architecture and specification (CORBA). Object Management Group, Framingham, Mass.

OMG(1998). Real-Time CORBA, Request for Proposals. Object Management Group, Framingham, Mass.

OSF, 9. (1992). *Introduction to OSF DCE, Open System Fondation*. Englewood Cliffs, N.J. Prentice Hall.

Temple, C. (1998). Avoiding the Babbling Idiot Failure in a Time-Triggered Communication System. *Fault Tolerant Comp. Symp. 28*, Munich, Germany. IEEE Press.

Synthesis Techniques for Low-Power Hard Real-Time Systems on Variable Voltage Processors

Inki Hong†, Gang Qu†, Miodrag Potkonjak†, and Mani B. Srivastava‡
†Computer Science Department, University of California, Los Angeles, CA 90095-1596 USA
‡Electrical Engineering Department, University of California, Los Angeles, CA 90095-1596 USA

Abstract

The energy efficiency of systems-on-a-chip can be much improved if one were to vary the supply voltage dynamically at run time. In this paper we describe the synthesis of systems-on-a-chip based on core processors, while treating voltage (and correspondingly, the clock frequency) as a variable to be scheduled along with the computation tasks during the static scheduling step. In addition to describing the complete synthesis design flow for these variable voltage systems, we focus on the problem of doing the voltage scheduling while taking into account the inherent limitation on the rates at which the voltage and clock frequency can be changed by the power supply controllers and clock generators. Taking these limits on rate of change into account is crucial since changing the voltage by even a volt may take time equivalent to 100s to 10,000s of instructions on modern processors. We present both an exact but impractical formulation of this scheduling problem as a set of non-linear equations, as well as a heuristic approach based on reduction to an optimally solvable restricted ordered scheduling problem. Using various task mixes drawn from a set of nine real-life applications, our results show that we are able to reduce power consumption to within 7% of the lower bound obtained by imposing no limit at the rate of change of voltage and clock frequencies.

1 Introduction

In recent years the demand for portable battery-operated computing and communication devices has made low power consumption an essential design attribute. The power reduction approaches that have emerged so far include reduction of switched capacitance, activity based system shutdown, and aggressive supply voltage reduction via exploitation of quadratic dependence of power on voltage together with parallelism and pipelining to recoup lost throughput. However, aggressive supply voltage reduction [1],the most powerful of these techniques, is usable only if throughput (data sample rate) is the sole metric of speed. A single tight latency constraint, as is often present in embedded systems, renders the technique ineffective.

The problem outlined above really arises because conventional systems are designed with a fixed supply voltage. However, there is no fundamental reason that the supply voltage has to be fixed. Instead, it can in principle be varied dynamically at run time. Indeed, advances in power supply technology makes it possible to vary the generated supply voltage dynamically under external control. While many CMOS circuits have always been capable of operating over a range of supply voltages, it is the recent progress in power supply circuits [21, 9] that has made feasible systems with dynamically variable supply voltages. Since both the power consumed and the speed (maximal clock frequency) are a function of the supply voltage, such *variable voltage* systems can be made to operate at different points along their power *vs.* speed curves in a controlled fashion.

In particular a static or dynamic scheduler, in addition to its conventional task of scheduling the computation operations on hardware resources, may also schedule changes in voltage as a function of timing constraints and changing system state. Such voltage scheduling would allow for much higher energy efficiency (lower power) for a wider class of applications than is possible by operating the system at one or two fixed points on the power-speed curve, as is done by conventional approaches of supply voltage reduction to a fixed value [1] and system shutdown [25]. The benefits of quadratic dependence of power on voltage thus become available even in event driven systems as well as in the presence of joint latency and throughput constraints

In this paper, we develop the first approach for power minimization of scheduling, instruction and data cache size determination, and processor core selection. We establish the theoretical framework for designing variable voltage systems by treating voltage as an optimization degree of freedom for the applications with real-time constraints and providing the optimal variable voltage scheduling algorithm for some special cases, where the speed overhead for changing voltages is explicitly accounted for. We develop an effective scheduling heuristic for a general case based on the optimal algorithm for the restricted problem. By selecting the most efficient voltage profile in the presence of multiple timing constraints under the realistic variable voltage hardware model, our algorithms result in significant savings in energy.

The rest of the paper is organized in the following way. Section 2 presents the related work. Section 3 explains the necessary background. Section 4 discusses the variable voltage scheduling problem and provides an optimal solution to some special cases. The global design flow of the novel synthesis approach is presented in Section 5. In Section 6 we establish the computational complexities of the variable voltage scheduling problem and propose an effective heuristic based on the optimal algorithm for some special cases. Section 7 presents experimental data. Section 8 concludes.

2 Related work

Low power system synthesis has emerged as an important area of research in last 5 years. Several good reviews on power estimation and minimization techniques exist [20, 23]. We review the research results relevant to low power systems based on dynamically variable voltage hardware.

2.1 Variable voltage system and design issues

Of direct relevance to our research is the prior research activity on technology, circuits, and techniques for variable voltage systems. At the technology level, efficient DC-DC converters that allow the output voltage to be rapidly changed under external control have recently been developed [21, 26].

At the hardware design level, research work has been performed on chips with dynamically variable supply voltage that can be adjusted based on (i) process and temperature variations, and (ii) processing load as measured by the number of data samples queued in the input (or output) buffer. Dynamically adapting voltage (and the clock frequency), to operate at the point of lowest power consumption for given temperature and process parameters was first suggested by Macken et. al. [19]. Nielsen et al. [22] extended the dynamic voltage adaptation idea to take into account data dependent computation times in self-timed circuits. Recently, researchers at MIT [9] have extended the idea of voltage adaptation based on data dependent computation time from [22] to synchronously clocked circuits. Because these approaches rely on run-time reactive approaches to dynamic voltage adaptation, they work fine only where *average throughput*. is the metric of performance. Therefore, these approaches are inapplicable to hard real time systems such as embedded control applications with strict timing requirements.

There has been research on scheduling strategies for adjusting CPU speed so as to reduce power consumption. Most existing work is in the context of non-real-time workstation-like environment. Weiser et al. [29] proposed an approach where time is divided into 10-50 msec intervals, and the CPU clock speed (and voltage) is adjusted by the task-level scheduler based on the processor utilization over the preceding interval. Govil et al. [8] enhanced [29] by proposing and comparing several predictive and non-predictive approaches for voltage changes, and concluded that smoothing helps more than prediction. Finally, Yao et al. [31] described an off-line minimum energy scheduling algorithm and an on-line average rate heuristic for job scheduling with preemption for independent processes with deadlines under the assumption that the supply voltage can be changed arbitrarily without any timing and power overhead.

Hong et al. [10] proposed an approach for the low power core-based real-time system-on-chip based on dynamically variable voltage hardware. While they developed the *non-preemptive* variable voltage scheduling heuristic with the assumption of zero delay in changing voltage levels, in this paper we focus on the *preemptive* variable voltage scheduling while taking into account the inherent limitation on the rates at which voltage and clock frequency can be changed by the power supply controllers and clock generators.

2.2 System level and behavioral level power estimation

Landman and Rabaey have performed the work on the macro and micro level power estimation [16]. The work at Princeton and Fujitsu on the estimation of power consumption for programmable processors [28] is of particular relevance. Evans and Franzon [5] and Su and Despain [27] have proposed power estimation model for cache, specifically for SRAM.

2.3 System level and behavioral level power optimization

One well known technique that results in substantial power reduction is reducing the voltage to reduce the switching power, which is the dominant source of power dissipation in CMOS circuit and is proportional to V_{dd}^2 where V_{dd} is the supply voltage [1]. However, this reduction came with a speed penalty due to increased gate delays. The gate delay is proportional to $\frac{V_{dd}}{(V_{dd}-V_T)^2}$, where V_T is the threshold voltage [1]. Chandrakasan et al. [1] have shown that the strategy of operating at a fixed reduced voltage can be coupled with architectural level parallelism and pipelining to compensate for lower clock rate due to voltage reduction so that the overall throughput remains the same but the overall power is still lowered, although at the cost of increased latency.

Microprocessor core	Clock (MHz)	MIPS	Technology (μm)	Area (mm^2)	Power diss. (mW) (Volt.)
StrongARM	233	266	0.35	4.3	300 (1.65)
ARM, 7	40	36	0.6	5.9	200 (5)
ARM, 7 Low-Power	27	24	0.6	3.8	45 (3.3)
LSI Logic, TR4101	81	30	0.35	2	81 (3.3)
LSI Logic, CW4001	60	53	0.5	3.5	120 (3.3)
LSI Logic, CW4011	80	120	0.5	7	280 (3.3)
DSP Group, Oak	80	80	0.6	8.4	190 (5)
NEC, R4100	40	40	0.35	5.4	120 (3.3)
Toshiba, R3900	50	50	0.6	15	400 (3.3)
Motorola, 68000	33	16	0.5	4.4	35 (3.3)
PowerPC, 403	33	41	0.5	7.5	40 (3.3)
ARM 710 (ARM7 / 8KB)	40	72	0.6	34	424 (5)
SA-110 (StrongARM / 32KB)	200	230	0.35	50	900 (1.65)

Table 1. The performance, area, and power data for a subset of processor cores.

Several researchers have addressed the issue of power in event-driven systems, and proposed various techniques for shutting down the system or parts of the system [25, 12, 4]. Compilation techniques for low power software have emerged for both general-purpose computation [28] and DSP computations [11]. Numerous behavioral synthesis research efforts have also addressed power minimization [23].

Four research groups have addressed the use of multiple (in their software implementation restricted to two or three) different voltages [2, 13, 18, 24]. They used the term "variable voltage" for a fixed number of simultaneously available voltages.

3 Preliminaries

3.1 Task model

A set $\mathcal{T}$ of independent tasks is to be executed on a system-on-chip. Each task $T_i \in \mathcal{T}$ is associated with the following parameters:

- a_i its arrival time
- d_i its deadline
- p_i its period
- W_i its required number of CPU cycles

We assume, without loss of generality, that all tasks have identical periods. When this is not the case, a simple preprocessing step and application of the least common multiple (LCM) theorem [17] transforms an arbitrary set of periods to this design scenario in polynomial time. As the consequence, when the LCM theorem is applied, there may be a need to run several iterations of a given task within this overall period.

3.2 Variable voltage hardware model

The variable voltage generated by the DC-DC switching regulators in the power supply cannot instantaneously make a transition from one voltage to another. For example, [21] reported transition times of 6 msec/volt for a DC-DC switching converter. In personal communications with

the authors, researchers at MIT and Berkeley have reported transitions times of 10 to 100 microsec/volt.

Dual to the supply voltage variation is the accompanying variation of the clock frequency. The time overhead associated with voltage switching is significant in the order of 100s to 10000s of instructions in modern microprocessor. Fortunately, the computation itself can continue during the voltage and frequency change period. However, the speed overhead during the transition period must be explicitly accounted for.

As suggested in [21], we employ a linear model to describe the speed overhead. The maximum rate of voltage change is specified for the power supply regulator, and we can make a transition from a voltage to any other voltages within the maximum rate.

3.3 Power model

It is well known that there are three principal components of power consumption in CMOS integrated circuits: switching power, short-circuit power, and leakage power. The switching power, which dominates power consumption, is given by $P = \alpha C_L V_{dd}^2 f_{clock}$, as indicated earlier. αC_L is defined to be effective switched capacitance. It is also known that reduced voltage operation comes at the cost of reduced throughput [1]. The gate delay T follows the following formula: $T = k \frac{V_{dd}}{(V_{dd} - V_T)^2}$ where k is a constant [1] and V_T is the threshold voltage. From these equations together with the observation that the speed is proportional to f and inversely proportional to the gate delay, the power vs. speed curve can be derived. In particular, the normalized power P_n (= 1 at $V_{dd} = V_{ref}$) as a function of the normalized speed S_n (= 1 at $V_{dd} = V_{ref}$). For example, assuming $V_{ref} = 3.3$ volts and $V_T = 0.8$ volts, the power vs. speed curve follows the following equation:

$$P_n = 0.164 \cdot S_n^3 + \sqrt{0.893 \cdot S_n^2 + 1.512 \cdot S_n} \cdot (0.173 \cdot S_n^2 + 0.147 \cdot S_n) + 0.277 \cdot S_n^2 + 0.059 \cdot S_n$$

By varying V_{dd}, the system can be made to operate at different points along this curve. From the equation, it is easy to see that the power is a convex function of speed.

3.4 Target architecture

Several factors combine to influence system performance: instruction and data cache miss rates and penalty, processor performance, and system clock speed. Power dissipation of the system is estimated using processor power dissipation per instruction and the number of executed instructions per task, supply voltage, energy required for cache read, write, and off-chip data access as well as the profiling information about the number of cache and off-chip accesses.

Data on microprocessor cores have been extracted from manufacturer's datasheets as well as from the CPU Center Info web site [3]. A sample of the collected data is presented in Table 1, The last two rows of the table show two integrated microprocessor products with on-chip caches and their system performance data. We assume that the processor cores follow the power model described in the preceding subsection.

Cache size	Line size						
	8B	16B	32B	64B	128B	256B	512B
512B	6.07	5.99	6.02	-	-	-	-
1KB	6.44	6.13	6.07	6.23	-	-	-
2KB	6.88	6.52	6.36	6.34	6.51	-	-
4KB	7.67	7.02	6.66	6.49	6.56	7.35	-
8KB	8.34	7.81	7.21	6.99	6.91	7.65	9.40
16KB	9.30	8.58	8.00	7.62	7.54	8.14	9.80
32KB	1.04e-08	9.45	8.91	8.59	8.69	9.30	10.04

Table 2. A subset of the cache latency model: minimal cycle time (ns) for various direct-mapped caches with variable line sizes.

We use CACTI [30] as a cache delay estimation tool with respect to the main cache design choices: size, associativity, and line size. The energy model has been adopted from [5] and [27]. The overall cache model has been scaled with respect to actual industrial implementations. Caches typically found in current embedded systems range from 128B to 32KB. Although larger caches correspond to higher hit rates, their power consumption is proportionally higher, resulting in an interesting design trade-off. Higher cache associativity results in significantly higher access time. We use a recently developed compiler strategy which efficiently minimizes the number of cache conflicts that considers direct-mapped caches [14]. We have experimented with 2-way set associative caches which did not dominate comparable direct-mapped caches in a single case. Cache line size was also variable in our experimentations. Its variations corresponded to the following trade-off: larger line size results in higher cache miss penalty delay and higher power consumption by the sense amplifiers and column decoders, while smaller line size results in large cache decoder power consumption. Extreme values result in significantly increased access time. We estimated the cache miss penalty based on the operating frequency of the system and external bus width and clock for each system investigated. This penalty ranged between 4 and 20 system clock cycles. Write-back was adopted in opposed to write-through, since it is proven

	No optimizations			Block buffering, sub-banking and Gray code addressing [27]		
Cache size	8B	16B	32B	8B	16B	32B
512B	0.330	0.378	0.468	0.291	0.322	0.401
1KB	0.356	0.394	0.463	0.295	0.299	0.345
2KB	0.422	0.444	0.489	0.317	0.271	0.271
4KB	0.651	0.666	0.694	0.456	0.334	0.273
8KB	1.146	1.156	1.175	0.769	0.504	0.347
16KB	2.158	2.164	2.174	1.412	0.869	0.530
32KB	4.198	4.202	4.209	2.702	1.608	0.922

Table 3. A subset of the cache power consumption model: power consumption (nJ) estimation for various direct-mapped caches with variable line sizes.

to provide superior performance and especially power savings in uniprocessor systems at increased hardware cost [15]. Each of the processors considered is able to issue at most a single instruction per clock period. Thus, caches were designed to have a single access port. A subset of the cache model data is given in Tables 2 and 3. Cache access delay and power consumption model were computed for a number of organizations and sizes, assuming the feature size of 0.5 μm and typical six transistors per CMOS SRAM cell implementation. The nominal energy consumption per single off-chip memory access, $98nJ$, is adopted from [6].

4 Theory of variable voltage scheduling: special solvable cases

Yao, Demers and Shenker [31] have provided the optimal preemptive static scheduling algorithm for a set of independent tasks with arbitrary arrival times and deadlines. The algorithm is based on the concept of critical regions and the tasks in critical regions are scheduled by the earliest deadline first (EDF) algorithm. The running time of the algorithm is $O(nlog^2n)$ for n tasks. When there is a limit on the maximum voltage change rates, then the problem becomes NP-complete, which is shown by the reduction from the SEQUENCING WITH DEADLINES AND SETUP TIMES problem in page 238 of [7]. In this Section, we discuss some special cases which can be solved optimally.

We find the speed function $S(t)$ of the processor to minimize the energy consumption during the time period $[t_1, t_2]$. The voltage function $V(t)$ can be easily obtained from $S(t)$ [1]. We assume that the speed of the processor can be changed between S_{min} and S_{max} with a maximum change rate K, i.e., at any time t, the speed $S(t)$ satisfies:

$$S_{min} \leq S(t) \leq S_{max} \qquad (1)$$
$$|S'(t)| \leq K \qquad (2)$$

The *amount of work* that the processor completes during time interval $[t_1, t_2]$ is given by:

$$W = \int_{t_1}^{t_2} S(t)\, dt \qquad (3)$$

The *power*, or energy consumed per unit time, is a convex function $P(S)$ of the processor's speed. The function

P(S) depends on the technology considered. The total energy consumed during the time interval $[t_1, t_2]$ is:

$$E = \int_{t_1}^{t_2} P(S(t)) \, dt \qquad (4)$$

Lemma 1. Starting with speed S_0, the work W that the processor can complete, in the time interval $[t_1, t_2]$, falls into the range $[W_{min}, W_{max}]$, with

$$W_{min} = S_c(t_2 - t_1) + \frac{(S_0 - S_c)^2}{2K}$$
$$W_{max} = S_d(t_2 - t_1) - \frac{(S_0 - S_d)^2}{2K}$$

where $S_c = max(S_{min}, S_0 - K(t_2 - t_1))$ and $S_d = min(S_{max}, S_0 + K(t_2 - t_1))$.

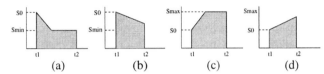

Figure 1. Illustrated W_{min}, W_{max} for Lemma 1.
(a) W_{min} if $S_0 - K(t_2 - t_1) < S_{min}$
(b) W_{min} if $S_0 - K(t_2 - t_1) \geq S_{min}$
(c) W_{max} if $S_0 + K(t_2 - t_1) \geq S_{max}$
(d) W_{max} if $S_0 + K(t_2 - t_1) < S_{max}$

Since power is a convex function of the processor's speed, it is obvious that if we can start from any speed, to complete a given workload W in any time interval of fixed length Δt, we should run our processor at the constant speed $\frac{W}{\Delta t}$. When we do not have the freedom to choose the starting speed, the following theorem shows that the best we can do is to change the speed as fast and early as possible until we reach a critical point, then keep the constant speed.

Theorem 1. With the same constraints as in Lemma 1, for any workload $W \in [W_{min}, W_{max}]$, there is a unique speed function $S : [t_1, t_2] \to [S_{min}, S_{max}]$ such that (1), (2), and (3) are all satisfied and the energy (4) is minimized. Moreover, $S(t)$ is defined as:
if $W_{min} \leq W \leq S_0(t_2 - t_1)$,
$$S(t) = \begin{cases} S_0 - K(t - t_1), & \text{if } t_1 \leq t \leq t_c; \\ S_0 - K(t_c - t_1), & \text{if } t_c < t \leq t_2. \end{cases}$$
where $t_c = t_2 - \sqrt{(t_2 - t_1)^2 + \frac{2}{K}[W - S_0(t_2 - t_1)]}$.
and if $S_0(t_2 - t_1) \leq W \leq W_{max}$,
$$S(t) = \begin{cases} S_0 + K(t - t_1), & \text{if } t_1 \leq t \leq t_c; \\ S_0 + K(t_c - t_1), & \text{if } t_c < t \leq t_2. \end{cases}$$
where $t_c = t_2 - \sqrt{(t_2 - t_1)^2 - \frac{2}{K}[W - S_0(t_2 - t_1)]}$.

Next we consider the case when there is a finishing speed constraint. Similarly, we have the following results:

Lemma 2. Starting with speed S_0, to reach the finishing speed S_1 at the end of the time interval $[t_1, t_2]$, the work W that the processor has to complete falls into the range $[W_{min}, W_{max}]$, with

$$W_{min} = S_c(t_2 - t_1) + \frac{(S_0 - S_c)^2}{2K} + \frac{(S_1 - S_c)^2}{2K}$$

$$W_{max} = S_d(t_2 - t_1) - \frac{(S_0 - S_d)^2}{2K} - \frac{(S_1 - S_d)^2}{2K}$$

where $S_c = max(S_{min}, \frac{(S_0 + S_1)}{2} - K\frac{(t_2 - t_1)}{2})$ and $S_d = min(S_{max}, \frac{(S_0 + S_1)}{2} + K\frac{(t_2 - t_1)}{2})$.

Theorem 2. With the same constraints as in Lemma 2, for any workload $W \in [W_{min}, W_{max}]$, there is a unique speed function $S : [t_1, t_2] \to [S_{min}, S_{max}]$ such that (1), (2), and (3) are satisfied and the energy (4) is minimized. The speed function will be a step function that satisfies the following:
if $W_{min} \leq W \leq W_1$,
$$S(t) = \begin{cases} S_0 - K(t - t_1), & \text{if } t_1 \leq t \leq x_1; \\ S_0 - K(x_1 - t_1), & \text{if } x_1 < t \leq x_2; \\ S_1 - K(t_2 - t), & \text{if } x_2 < t \leq t_2. \end{cases}$$
if $W_1 \leq W \leq W_2$,
$$S(t) = \begin{cases} S_0 + K(t - t_1), & \text{if } t_1 \leq t \leq x_1; \\ S_0 + K(x_1 - t_1), & \text{if } x_1 < t \leq x_2; \\ S_1 - K(t_2 - t), & \text{if } x_2 < t \leq t_2. \end{cases}$$
and if $W_2 \leq W \leq W_{max}$,
$$S(t) = \begin{cases} S_0 + K(t - t_1), & \text{if } t_1 \leq t \leq x_1; \\ S_0 + K(x_1 - t_1), & \text{if } x_1 < t \leq x_2; \\ S_1 + K(t_2 - t), & \text{if } x_2 < t \leq t_2. \end{cases}$$
where W_1, W_2, x_1, x_2 are constants.

From Theorem 2, it is simple to see that the speed functions which minimize energy are of some restricted shapes. For example, if $S_1 > S_0$, then $S(t)$ has to be one of the following seven shapes in Figure 2.

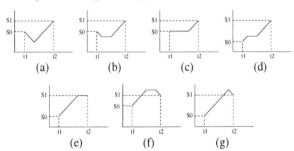

Figure 2. All possible shapes of an optimal speed function when $S_1 > S_0$.

We consider the following scheduling problem:
Ordered Scheduling Problem (OSP): Given a partition $0 = t_0 < t_1 < t_2 < \ldots < t_{n-1} < t_n = t$ of the time interval $[0, t]$, there is a workload W_i to be completed during the interval $[t_{i-1}, t_i]$, we want to find the speed function $S : [0, t] \to [S_{min}, S_{max}]$, such that:
(i) $S(0) = S_0$,
(ii) $S_{min} \leq S(t) \leq S_{max}$,
(ii) $|S'(t)| \leq K$,
(iv) $W_i = \int_{t_{i-1}}^{t_i} S(t) \, dt$, and
(v) $E = \int_0^t P(S(t)) \, dt$ is minimized.
For this problem, we can use the following approach. Let $S(t)$ be a speed function that we are looking for and $x_i = S(t_i)$ for $i = 1, 2, \cdots, n$. Using the Theorem 2,

we can express $S(t)$ as a function of unknown variables $x_1, x_2, \cdots, x_n$. Now we can plug this expression into (v), get a system of (non-linear) equations involving x_i's from the first order condition to minimize the energy function (v). The system of (non-linear) equations is solved by using some numerical method, if the closed form solution can not be found. The speed function $S(t)$ is determined by the formulae in Theorem 2 and the solution(s) of the system of (non-linear) equations.

There are a few comments to be made about this approach. First, this approach is impractical since the (non-linear) system of equations is very difficult to be solved in many cases. Secondly, when applying Theorem 2 in this approach, we have to check another condition: $W_{min}(x_{i-1}, x_i) \leq W_i \leq W_{max}(x_{i-1}, x_i)$, which will make the problem even more difficult. Thirdly, since the solution(s) to the (non-linear) system of equations is the potential candidate for our minimization problem, we have to apply (at least) the second order condition to check it. Finally, there are still some more mathematical details that we have to take into consideration, e.g., the continuity and differentiability of the power function. Therefore, some good heuristics will be more useful in real life.

We note that the following special case of the OSP problem can be solved optimally.

Restricted Ordered Scheduling Problem (ROSP): With the same constraints as in the OSP problem, $S(t_i)$ for $i = 1, 2, \cdots, n$ are additionally given.

It is trivial to see that the Theorem 2 provides an optimal speed function for the ROSP problem.

5 Global design flow

In this Section we describe the global flow of the proposed synthesis system and explain the function of each subtask and how these subtasks are combined into a synthesis system.

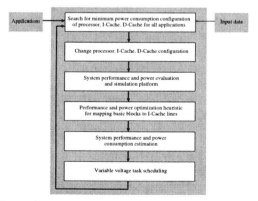

Figure 3. The global flow of the synthesis approach.

Figure 3 illustrates the synthesis system. The goal is to choose the configuration of processor, I-cache, and D-cache

and the variable voltage task schedule with minimum power consumption which satisfy the timing requirements of multiple preemptive tasks. To accurately predict the system performance and power consumption for target applications, we employ the approach which integrates the optimization, simulation, modeling, and profiling tools, as shown in Figure 5. The synthesis technique considers each non-dominated microprocessor core and competitive cache configuration, and selects the hardware setup which requires minimal power consumption and satisfies the individual performance requirements of all target applications. The application-driven search for a low-power core and cache system requires usage of trace-driven cache simulation for each promising point considered in the design space. We attack this problem by carefully scanning the design space using search algorithms with sharp bounds and by providing powerful algorithmic performance and power estimation techniques. The search algorithm to find an energy-efficient system configuration is described using the pseudo-code shown in Figure 4.

Sort processor cores in a list L in an increasing order of $\frac{EnergyPerInstruction}{SystemClockFrequency}$ at the nominal voltage 5V
Delete the dominated processor cores from L
For each processor core in L in the order of appearance
  For I-cache = 512B..32KB and CacheLineSize = 8B..512B
    For D-cache = 512B..32KB and CacheLineSize = 8B..512B
      Check bounds; if exceeded **break**;
      If (current I- and D-cache configuration has never been evaluated)
        Evaluate performance and power consumption
      Using the cache system analysis, evaluate the power consumption of the entire system using variable voltage task scheduling
      Memorize Configuration C if power consumption is minimal

---

Figure 4. Pseudo code for the search of power efficient system configuration.

Since performance and power evaluation of a single processor, I- and D-cache configuration requires a time-consuming trace-driven simulation, the goal of our search technique is to reduce the number of evaluated cache systems using sharp bounds for cache system performance and power estimations. However, a particular cache system is evaluated using trace-driven simulation only once since the data retrieved from such simulation can be used for overall system power consumption estimation for different embedded processor cores with minor additional computational expenses.

The algorithm excludes from further consideration processor cores dominated by other processor cores. One processor type dominates another if it consumes less power at higher frequency and results in higher MIPS performance at the same nominal power supply. The competitive processors are then sorted in ascending order with respect to their power consumption per instruction and frequency ratio. Microprocessors which seem to be more power-efficient are, therefore, given priority in the search process. This step provides later on sharper bounds for search termination. The search for the most efficient cache configuration is bounded with sharp bounds. A bound is determined by measuring the number of conflict misses and comparing the energy required to fetch the data from off-chip memory due to measured conflict misses and the power that would have been consumed by twice larger cache for the same number of cache accesses assuming zero cache conflicts. We terminate further increase of the cache structure when the power consumption due to larger cache would be larger than the energy consumed by the current best solution. Similarly, another bound is defined at the point when the energy required to fetch the data from off-chip memory due to conflict cache misses for twice smaller cache with the assumption of zero-energy consumption per cache access, is larger than the energy required for both fetching data from cache and off-chip memory in the case of the current cache structure. We abort further decrease of the cache structure if the amount of energy required to bring the data due to additional cache misses from off-chip memory is larger than the energy consumed by the current best solution.

When evaluating competitive hardware configurations, the target applications are scheduled with the variable voltage task scheduler using the predicted system performance and power on the configuration considered.

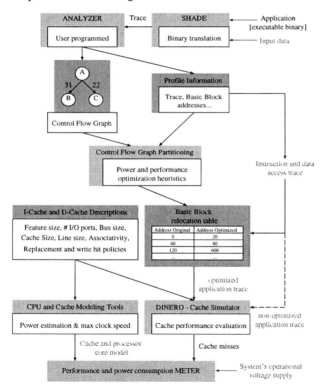

Figure 5. The system performance and power evaluation and simulation platform.

To estimate the system performance and power on the configuration under consideration, we use the system performance and power evaluation and simulation platform based on SHADE and DINEROIII [14, 15]. SHADE is a tracing tool which allows users to define custom trace analyzers and thus collect rich information on runtime events. SHADE currently profiles only SPARC binaries. The executable binary program is dynamically translated into host machine code. The tool also provides a stream of data to the translated code which is directly executed to simulate and trace the original application code. A custom analyzer composed of approximately 2,500 lines of C code, is linked to SHADE to control and analyze the generated trace information. The analyzer sources relevant trace information from SHADE and builds a control flow graph (CFG) corresponding to the dynamically executed code. The analysis consists of two passes. The first pass determines the boundaries of basic blocks, while the second pass constructs a CFG by adding control flow information between basic blocks. We also collect the frequencies of control transfers through each basic block, and branch temporal correlation. Once the CFG is obtained, an algorithm is employed to reposition application basic blocks in such a way that instruction cache misses and cache decoder switching activity are minimized. Our experimentation uses a basic block relocation look up table to simulate the relocation of basic blocks in main memory. An entry in the basic block relocation table consists of two elements: the original and optimized starting address of the basic block. To simulate cache performance of a given application and data stream, we use a trace-driven cache simulator DINEROIII. Cache is described using a number of qualitative and quantitative parameters such as instruction and data cache size, replacement policy, associativity, etc.

The system optimization process is composed of a sequence of activations of these tools. The SHADE analyzer traces program and data memory references as well as the CFG. The CFG is used to drive the code reposition module which produces a new application mapping table. Stream of references are sent to a program that uses the basic block relocation look-up table to map from the original address space into the optimized address space. The re-mapped trace of addresses, along with all unmodified data memory references, is sent to DINEROIII for cache simulation.

6 Variable voltage scheduling

In this Section, we first formulate the *variable voltage scheduling* problem to minimize power consumption and propose an efficient and effective heuristic for the problem.

6.1 Problem formulation

Let $\mathcal{T}$ be a set of tasks and, associated with each task $T_i \in \mathcal{T}$ are a_i its arrival time, d_i its deadline and, W_i its workload, e.g., CPU cycles required. We are using a single variable voltage (variable speed) processor as described in Section 4 to execute the set $\mathcal{T}$. Let $t_0 = min\{a_i : T_i \in \mathcal{T}\}$

and $t_1 = max\{d_i : T_i \in \mathcal{T}\}$. A *scheduler* of $\mathcal{T}$ is a pair of functions defined on $[t_0, t_1]$, such that for any $t \in [t_0, t_1]$, $S(t)$ is the speed of the processor and $T(t)$ is the task being processed at time t. A scheduler is *feasible* if

- $\int_{a_i}^{d_i} S(t)\delta(T(t), T_i)\, dt \geq W_i$,
  where $\delta(x, y)$ is 1 if $x = y$ and 0 otherwise.
- $S(t) \in [S_{min}, S_{max}]$
- $|S'(t)| \leq K$

The *scheduling problem* is to determine, for any given set of tasks, whether there is a feasible scheduler. The *power minimization problem* is to find a feasible scheduler such that the total energy consumed E is minimized, where $E = \int_{t_0}^{t_1} P(S(t))\, dt$.

6.2 Heuristic scheduler for a single preemptive variable voltage processor

As described in Section 4, the preemptive scheduling of a set of independent tasks with arbitrary arrival times and deadlines on a *variable voltage* processor with a limit on the maximum voltage change rates is an NP-complete task. We have developed an efficient and effective heuristic for the general variable voltage task scheduling problem, which leverages on the least-constraining most-constrained heuristic paradigm as well as the optimal algorithm for the ROSP problem in Section 4 in order to obtain competitive solutions. The algorithm is described using the pseudo-code shown in Figure 6.

Input: a set of m tasks $\mathcal{T} = \{(a_i, d_i, W_i)\}$, the processor's speed range $[S_{min}, S_{max}]$ and the maximal speed change rate K.

Output: a feasible scheduler which minimizes the power consumption to complete $\mathcal{T}$.

1. Use the critical regions [31] to find a partition $0 = t_0 < t_1 < \cdots < t_{n-1} < t_n = t$ of the time interval $[0, t]$
2. Assign the workload W_i for the task T_i in the interval $[t_{j-1}, t_j]$ if T_i appears exactly once in the partition.
3. **REPEAT** {
4.   Determine the priority of the remaining tasks.
5.   Assign the workload to all time intervals of the task T_i with the highest priority in a least constraining way.
6. } **UNTIL** (All tasks are assigned its workload)
7. Find an optimal solution to the corresponding ROSP problem.
8. Relax constraints on $S(t_i)$'s and improve the solution.

Figure 6. Pseudo code for the variable voltage task scheduling algorithm.

The global flow of the heuristic consists of the following three phases. The heuristic first reduces the problem to the ROSP problem by carefully scheduling the tasks and assigning the workload using the most constrained least constraining heuristic paradigm. Next, the reduced problem is solved optimally. Finally, the solution is further improved by relaxing the starting and finishing speed constraints from the ROSP problem.

Step 1 can be performed in polynomial time using the algorithm given in [31]. In step 2, we first assign the full workload for the tasks with only one time interval. In step 4, the constrainedness of a task T_i is determined by the $COST$ function:

$$COST(T_i) = \sum_{j=1}^{p} ((S_{L(i_j)} - S_{i_j})^2 + (S_{R(i_j)} - S_{i_j})^2).$$

i_j is the jth time interval for the task T_i with p time intervals. $L(i_j)(R(i_j))$ is the left(right) neighboring time interval to the time interval i_j. $S_{i_j} = \frac{WORK_{i_j}}{length\ of\ time\ interval\ i_j}$, where $WORK_{i_j} = W_i \times \frac{length\ of\ time\ interval\ i_j}{length\ of\ all\ time\ intervals\ of\ T_i}$, if i_j is not already assigned workload and $WORK_{i_j}$ is as assigned otherwise. In step 5, we assign the workload to all time intervals of the task T_i with the highest priority in such a way that it minimizes the $COST(T_i)$.

In step 7, we can get a scheduler which is feasible as well as optimal subject to the condition that *at time t_i, we have to operate the processor at speed $S(t_i)$*. Note that this condition is not necessary for the original problem. Then we may apply the approach described in Section 4 to the OSP problem and find the optimized values for each $S(t_i)$. As discussed in Section 4, however, this approach may not be practical. Thus, in step 8, we relax constraints on $S(t_i)$'s from step 7 and improve the solution. The optimal scheduler for the ROSP problem provides the local optimal speed functions in each interval $[t_{i-1}, t_i]$ which are given by Theorem 2. Recall the shapes of the speed functions given in Theorem 2. For example, if we have a speed function consisting of a shape (a) followed by a shape (b), then it will create a "pike" at the joint point. In this case, if we use a slower speed at the joint point, the speed function can be smoothed. Further calculation shows that this "pike" can be completely eliminated with a slower speed. Based on this observation, in step 8, the local optimal solution obtained from step 7 approaches the global optimal by eliminating all the "pikes".

7 Experimental results

7.1 Design descriptions

We used nine applications to demonstrate the effectiveness of the approach. All nine applications are in public domain and can be obtained via the Internet.

JPEG encoder/decoder from the Independent JPEG Group implements JPEG baseline, extended-sequential, and progressive compression processes. We used integer DCT for decoding a JPEG file to a PPM file. Integer DCT and progressive compression process options were used for compression.

GSM encoder/decoder (Technische Universität, Berlin) is an implementation of the European GSM 06.10 provisional standard for full-rate speech transcoding, prI-ETS 300 036, which uses RPE/LTP (residual pulse excitation/long

Task Set	Processor Core	I-cache		D-cache		Energy Consumption (J)		
		Cache Size	Block Size	Cache Size	Block Size	Lower Bound	New Approach	[31]+ROSP
10 tasks	LSI CW4001	512B	64B	1KB	128B	**2.39**	**2.48**	**3.05**
	LSI CW4001	512B	64B	1KB	128B	**2.39**	**2.48**	**3.05**
20 tasks	LSI TR4101	512B	64B	4KB	32B	**10.6**	**11.8**	**13.9**
	Motorola 68000	1KB	128B	2KB	64B	10.9	11.5	14.1
30 tasks	PowerPC403	1KB	32B	2KB	64B	**45.3**	**49.0**	**61.2**
	LSI CW4011	1KB	64B	2KB	64B	46.5	**48.1**	63.9
40 tasks	PowerPC403	1KB	32B	2KB	32B	**72.6**	**78.2**	**87.5**
	PowerPC403	1KB	32B	2KB	32B	**72.6**	**78.2**	**87.5**
50 tasks	LSI CW4011	1KB	64B	2KB	64B	**100.2**	**108.6**	**128.6**
	LSI CW4011	1KB	64B	2KB	64B	**100.2**	**108.6**	**128.6**

Table 4. The most power-efficient configurations obtained by the proposed approach.

term prediction) coding at 13 kbit/sec. A 16 bit linear PCM data file is used to measure execution parameters of the GSM encoder. The measurement of the GSM decoder execution characteristics was done using the output of the GSM encoder.

EPIC (Efficient Pyramid Image Coder), from University of Pennsylvanian, implements lossy image compression and decompression utilities.

Mipmap, Osdemo, and Texgen from University of Wisconsin use a 3-D graphic library called Mesa. Osdemo is a demo program that draws a set of simple polygons using the Mesa 3-D rendering pipe. Finally, Texgen renders a texture mapped version of the Utah teapot.

7.2 Experimental data

The processor cores described in Table 1 are used with the assumption that they can be operated at the dynamically variable [0.8, 5.0] V supply voltage. Performance and power consumption data have been scaled according to the performance *vs.* voltage and power *vs.* voltage relationships, respectively. The limit on the voltage change rate is assumed to be 10000 instructions/volt for all processor cores. We consider several different mixes of the above nine applications. The details of the application mixes and deadlines are provided in the technical report version of this paper.

The most power-efficient processor, I-cache and D-cache configurations for the target scenarios by the proposed allocation heuristic using Yao's optimal preemptive scheduling algorithm with no limit on voltage change rates, Yao's optimal preemptive scheduling algorithm with the ROSP solution taking into account the rate change limits, and our scheduling heuristic with limit on voltage change rates, respectively, are described in Table 4. For each task set, the first row represents the best configuration for the proposed allocation heuristic using Yao's optimal preemptive scheduling algorithm with no limit on voltage change rates, while the second row provides the best configuration for the proposed allocation heuristic using our scheduling heuristic. Columns 7, 8, and 9 provide the energy consumption of the

target scenarios by Yao's optimal scheduling algorithm under ideal condition, our scheduling heuristic, and Yao's optimal scheduling algorithm with the ROSP solution under rate change limits, respectively, where the numbers in bold represent the best energy consumption achieved for each algorithm.

Our approach resulted in only **6.8** % more energy consumption over the power consumption lower bound which was obtained by using Yao's optimal preemptive scheduling algorithm with no limit on voltage change rates, which always results in a solution better than or equal to the optimal preemptive solution with any limit on voltage change rates. Our approach also resulted in **20.2** % reduction in energy consumption from Yao's optimal preemptive scheduling algorithm with the ROSP solution under the rate change limits. Among the five application mixes, three cases resulted in the same configurations for both scheduling algorithms, while their actual task schedules were different.

8 Conclusion

Voltage is an important dimension that, with appropriate CAD tools and schedulers, can be actively manipulated at run time instead of just the static optimization of a fixed voltage as is currently done. However, for this to happen, the CAD tools must incorporate an understanding of the limitations inherent to variable voltage hardware. In this paper we have accomplished this by describing, in the context of a core-processor based system-on-a-chip synthesis design flow, a scheduler that not only schedules a set of computation tasks on hardware resources but also schedules changes in voltage (and correspondingly the clock frequency) while meeting constraints on the rate of voltage change imposed by the voltage regulator. Our results show that the proposed heuristic algorithm is extremely effective and is within 7% of the best possible variable voltage hardware system. Moreover, our research for the first time formalizes how synthesis tools might leverage run-time controlled variation of supply voltage while taking into account inherent limitations of the physical voltage and clock regulation circuits.

References

[1] A. P. Chandrakasan, S. Sheng, and R.W. Broderson. Low-power CMOS digital design. *IEEE Journal of Solid-State Circuits*, 27(4):473–484, 1992.

[2] J.-M. Chang and M. Pedram. Energy minimization using multiple supply voltages. In *International Symposium on Low Power Electronics and Design*, pages 157–162, 1996.

[3] http://infopad.eecs.berkeley.edu/CIC/.

[4] F. Douglis, P. Krishnan, and B. Bershad. Adaptive disk spin-down policies for mobile computers. In *USENIX Symposium on Mobile and Location-Independent Computing*, pages 121–137, 1995.

[5] R.J. Evans and P.D. Franzon. Energy consumption modeling and optimization for SRAM's. *IEEE Journal of Solid-State Circuits*, 30(5):571–579, 1995.

[6] R. Fromm, S. Perissakis, N. Cardwell, C. Kozyrakis, B. McGaughy, D. Patterson, T. Anderson, and K. Yelick. The energy efficiency of IRAM architectures. In *International Symposium on Computer Architecture*, pages 327–337, 1997.

[7] M.R. Garey and D.S. Johnson. *Computer and Intractability: A Guide to the theory of NP-Completeness*. W. H. Freeman & Co., New York, NY, 1979.

[8] K. Govil, E. Chan, and H. Wasserman. Comparing algorithms for dynamic speed-setting of a low-power CPU. In *ACM International Conference on Mobile Computing and Networking*, pages 13–25, 1995.

[9] V. Gutnik and A. Chandrakasan. An efficient controller for variable supply-voltage low power processing. In *Symposium on VLSI Circuits*, pages 158–159, 1996.

[10] I. Hong, D. Kirovski, G. Qu, M. Potkonjak, and M. Srivastava. Power optimization of variable voltage core-based systems. In *Design Automation Conference*, pages 176–181, 1998.

[11] I. Hong, M. Potonjak, and R. Karri. Power optimization using divide-and-conquer techniques for minimization of the number of operations. In *IEEE/ACM International Conference on Computer-Aided Design*, pages 108–113, 1997.

[12] C. Hwang and A.C.-H. Wu. A predictive system shutdown method for energy saving of event-driven computation. In *IEEE/ACM International Conference on Computer-Aided Design*, pages 28–32, 1997.

[13] M. C. Johnson and K. Roy. Datapath scheduling with multiple supply voltages and level converters. *ACM Transactions on Design Automation of Electronic Systems*, 2(3), 1997.

[14] D. Kirovski, C. Lee, W. Mangione-Smith, and M. Potkonjak. Application-driven synthesis of core-based systems. In *IEEE/ACM International Conference on Computer-Aided Design*, pages 104–107, 1997.

[15] D. Kirovski, C. Lee, W. Mangione-Smith, and M. Potkonjak. Synthesis of power efficient systems-on-silicon. In *Asia and South Pacific Design Automation Conference*, 1998.

[16] P. E. Landman and J. M. Rabaey. Activity-sensitive architectural power analysis. *IEEE Transactions on Computer-Aided Design of Integrated Circuits and Systems*, 15(6):571–587, 1996.

[17] E. L. Lawler and C. U. Martel. Scheduling periodically occuring tasks on multiple processors. *Information Processing Letters*, 12(1):9–12, 1981.

[18] Y.-R. Lin, C.-T. Hwang, and A.C.-H Wu. Scheduling techniques for variable voltage low power designs. *ACM Transactions on design Automation of Electronic Systems*, 2(2):81–97, 1997.

[19] P. Macken, M. Degrauwe, M. Van Paemel, and H. Oguey. A voltage reduction technique for digital systems. In *IEEE International Solid-State Circuits Conference*, pages 238–239, 1990.

[20] F. N. Najm. A survey of power estimation techniques in VLSI circuits. *IEEE Transactions on VLSI Systems*, 2(4):446–455, 1994.

[21] W. Namgoong, M. Yu, and T. Meng. A high-efficiency variable-voltage CMOS dynamic DC-DC switching regulator. In *IEEE International Solid-State Circuits Conference*, pages 380–381, 1997.

[22] L. S. Nielsen, C. Niessen, J. Sparso, and K. van Berkel. Low-power operation using self-timed circuits and adaptive scaling of the supply voltage. *IEEE Transactions on Very Large Scale Integration (VLSI) Systems*, 2(4):391–397, 1994.

[23] M. Pedram. Power minimization in IC design: principles and applications. *ACM Transactions on Design Automation of Electronic Systems*, 1(1):3–56, 1996.

[24] S. Raje and M. Sarrafzadeh. Variable voltage scheduling. In *International Symposium on Low Power Design*, pages 9–14, 1995.

[25] M. Srivastava, A. P. Chandrakasan, and R. W. Brodersen. Predictive system shutdown and other architectural techniques for energy efficient programmable computation. *IEEE Transactions on VLSI Systems*, 4(1):42–55, 1996.

[26] A. J. Stratakos, S. R. Sanders, and R. W. Brodersen. A low-voltage CMOS DC-DC converter for a portable battery-operated system. In *Power Electronics Specialist Conference*, volume 1, pages 619–626, 1994.

[27] C.-L. Su and A.M. Despain. Cache design trade-offs for power and performance optimization: a case study. In *International Symposium on Low Power Design*, pages 63–68, 1995.

[28] V. Tiwari, S. Malik, and A. Wolfe. Power analysis of embedded software: a first step towards software power minimization. *IEEE Transactions on VLSI Systems*, 2(4):437–445, 1994.

[29] M. Weiser, B. Welch, A. Demers, and S. Shenker. Scheduling for reduced CPU energy. In *USENIX Symposium on Operating Systems Design and Implementation*, pages 13–23, 1994.

[30] S.J.E. Wilton and N.P. Jouppi. CACTI: an enhanced cache access and cycle time model. *IEEE Journal of Solid-State Circuits*, 31(5):677–688, 1996.

[31] F. Yao, A. Demers, and S. Shenker. A scheduling model for reduced CPU energy. In *IEEE Annual Foundations of Computer Science*, pages 374–382, 1995.

Task Period Selection and Schedulability in Real-Time Systems *

Danbing Seto[1], John P. Lehoczky[2], and Lui Sha[1]
[1] Software Engineering Institute, [2] Department of Statistics
Carnegie Mellon University
Pittsburgh, PA 15213

Abstract

In many real-time applications, especially those involving computer-controlled systems, the application tasks often have a maximal acceptable latency, and small latency is preferred to large. The interaction between choosing task periods to meet the individual latency requirements and scheduling the resulting task set was investigated in [4] using dynamic priority scheduling methods. In this paper, we present algorithms based on static priority scheduling methods to determine optimal periods for each task in the task set. The solution to the period selection problem optimizes a system-wide performance measure subject to meeting the maximal acceptable latency requirements of each task. This paper also contributes to a new aspect of rate monotonic scheduling, the optimal design of task periods in connection with application related timing specifications and task set schedulability.

1   Introduction

Many real-time computer-controlled applications are developed in two isolated steps: (1) the design of application specific computation modules and (2) the implementation of these modules. In the design stage, the computation modules are designed to fulfill the control objectives of the application, and each module is assigned a period which will guarantee that a certain performance level will be achieved. In the implementation stage, the computation modules are treated as real-time periodic tasks and scheduled using the periods that were determined in the design stage. Task set schedulability is completely determined by the given periods, task execution times, and the scheduling algorithm. These two stages are isolated in the sense that the choice of task period in the design stage is made with no concern for task schedulability requirements in the implementation stage. It is possible that the resulting set of computation modules may not be schedulable. Even they are schedulable, the performance of the overall system may not be optimal in terms of making full use of the underline computing resource.

A better overall system design can be achieved by taking into account the task schedulability at design time. In many real-time applications, there often exists an acceptable range of periods for each computing task, with the largest period still meeting the latency requirements of the task. For example, a real-time control system may have multiple control processes whose sampling frequencies can be chosen from a range of frequencies such that the control objective of each control process is accomplished. Moreover, different choices of frequency will generally result in different task performances as the task executes. By *performance*, we mean a measure of how well a task achieves its objective, or an aggregate measure of how well the overall system meets its overall objective. In practice, the period for each computing task is usually chosen to satisfy certain performance requirements. In choosing the periods, two principles will generally apply: (1) the period of each task will be bounded above by some value corresponding to the maximal permissible latency requirement associated with the task, and (2) the performance of a task is often inversely related to the task's period, i.e., the shorter the period, the better the performance. For the class of tasks for which (1) and (2) apply, it is obvious that task periods should be chosen to be as small as possible, to satisfy the upper bound conditions and to satisfy schedulability conditions. This leads to an optimization problem: for a set of real-time periodic tasks to determine periods for those tasks which will maximize an overall system performance measure subject to satisfying the maximal task periods and task set schedulability requirements. The periods which optimize the performance are called *optimal periods*.

The integration of task schedulability and system performance has been investigated by Locke [2] using best-effort scheduling methods, and by Gerber, Hong and Saksena [1] who focused on distributed systems. An optimal solution to the problem of allocating and scheduling communicating periodic tasks in distributed real-time systems was developed by Peng, Shin and Abdelzaher [3], where the max-

---

*This research was supported in part by the Office of Naval Research under contracts N00014-92-J-1524 and F19628-95-C-0003, and by the Software Engineering Institute of Carnegie Mellon University.

imum normalized task response time, i.e., the system hazard, is minimized subject to the intercommunication constraints among the tasks to be allocated and scheduled. The present paper is an extension of the paper by Seto, Lehoczky, Sha and Shin [4] who developed an algorithm to determine optimal task periods assuming tasks were scheduled by the earliest deadline first (edf) algorithm. The use of the edf algorithm to schedule periodic tasks with deadlines equal to task periods ensures that 100% schedulable processor utilization can be achieved. Unfortunately, many real-time computer operating systems only support static priority scheduling. Consequently, it is important to obtain a solution to this task period design problem for the optimal static scheduling algorithm, the rate monotonic algorithm (RMA). When RMA is used, task set feasibility becomes an issue because the RMA algorithm only supports full schedulability when the task periods are harmonic. Furthermore, task periods that result in high schedulable utilization may not necessarily also maximize the system performance index. While the optimal RMA periods can be found by inspection in very simple cases, a general algorithm is needed to address this problem.

In this paper, we present a search algorithm for the optimal periods when the tasks are scheduled with RMA. In particular, we first develop an algorithm to search all the possible periods for which the set of tasks are schedulable with RMA. We will show that these periods, although there are infinite many of them, can be specified by a finite set of period ranges. Then, from these period ranges, we identify the set of optimal periods. It is important to note that finding the set of all possible periods for which a task set is RMA schedulable is of independent interest even without any consideration of selecting the optimal periods from that set. Indeed, it could be a necessary step in the development of an integrated design when the system performance characteristics are not known. In addition, it provides the design engineer with the feasible periods that can be used for a variety of purposes, for example, performance trade-off, multiple rate selection, etc. The algorithm for searching the ranges of possible periods for RMA schedulability is developed by formulating the RMA schedulability testing algorithm reported in [5] as an integer programming problem, from which a finite collection of sets of integers can be obtained. These integers represent the number of times each task executes before the task with the lowest priority completes. Based on these sets of integers, the ranges of possible periods can be derived using a *branch and bound* approach . For ease of exposition, we define the following concepts and notation. For a set of tasks $\{\tau_1, .., \tau_p\}$ having upper bounds on their periods given by $[T_{m1}, .., T_{mp}]$, *a set of feasible periods* refers to an array of periods $[T_1, .., T_p]$ which satisfies the condition $T_1 \leq T_{m1}, .., T_p \leq T_{mp}$ and results in all tasks being schedulable using RMA. *A set of ranges of feasible periods* S_p is a set of arrays $[T_1, .., T_p]$ such that all the tasks can

be scheduled by RMA with periods chosen from S_p, and it can be expressed as:

$$S_p = \{[T_1, .., T_p] : L_j \leq T_j \leq U_j, \ j = 1, .., p\}$$

with L_j and $U_j \leq T_{mj}$ the lower and the upper limits of the period ranges. In the rest of the paper, all aspects of schedulability are with respect to RMA scheduling.

The paper is organized as follows. In section 2, we present an algorithm to determine the sets of ranges of feasible periods for a given set of tasks. In particular, we consider two cases: the task set is specified with a required priority order, and the task set is specified without any specific required priority order. In section 3, we choose the optimal periods from the sets of ranges of feasible periods such that a performance measure is optimized. Conclusions are given in section 4.

2 Task Periods for RMA Schedulability

In this section, we study the problem of finding all the periods $[T_1, .., T_p]$ for a set of tasks $\{\tau_1, .., \tau_p\}$ with upper bounds on their periods $[T_{m1}, .., T_{mp}]$ such that they can be scheduled with RMA. To achieve this, we need to first determine the priority order for these tasks. According to RMA, a task with a relatively short period should be assigned a relatively high priority. Since the task periods are not given, in principle, all $p!$ permutations of the priority orders should be considered. In the algorithm proposed next, we use a branch and bound approach to search the feasible periods for the given task set tasks. As a result, the number of the possible permutations can be significantly less than $p!$. We first describe an algorithm to determine the periods for a given priority order, and then investigate the periods for all possible priority orders.

2.1 Task Periods for RMA Schedulability with A Priority Order

Problem Statement: Given a set of periodic tasks $\{\tau_1, .., \tau_p\}$ with execution times $C_1, .., C_p$ and period upper bounds $T_{m1}, .., T_{mp}$, suppose the set of tasks is schedulable with the maximum periods $T_{m1}, .., T_{mp}$. Find all the possible periods $T_1, .., T_p$, satisfying $T_1 \leq \cdots \leq T_p$, and $T_1 \leq T_{m1}, .., T_p \leq T_{mp}$, such that all the tasks are schedulable.

We start with the schedulability conditions for a set of tasks with fixed periods $T_1 \leq \cdots \leq T_p$, and use a schedulability testing algorithm reported in [5]. According to RMA, for any task τ_k, $1 \leq k \leq p$, the tasks $\tau_1, .., \tau_{k-1}$ have higher priorities than τ_k, and at time t, the total cumulative demand on CPU time by these k tasks is given by

$$w_k(t) = \sum_{j=1}^{k} C_j \left\lceil \frac{t}{T_j} \right\rceil$$

The conditions for a set of tasks to be schedulable are summarized in the following lemma.

Lemma 2.1 A set of tasks $\{\tau_1, .., \tau_p\}$ with execution times $C_1, .., C_p$ and periods $T_1 \leq \cdot\cdot \leq T_p$ is schedulable if and only if for each task k, $k = 1, .., p$, the iterative sequence

$$t_0^k = \sum_{j=1}^{k} C_j, \quad t_1^k = w_k(t_0^k), \quad t_2^k = w_k(t_1^k), \cdot\cdot$$

converges to a t_c^k, i.e., $t_c^k = w_k(t_c^k)$ and $t_c^k \leq T_k$.

Note that for each i, $t_i^k = \sum_{j=1}^{k} n_j C_j$ where $n_1, .., n_k$ are integers. Thus the schedulability conditions can be reformulated as follows.

Proposition 2.1 A set of tasks $\{\tau_1, .., \tau_p\}$ with execution times $C_1, .., C_p$ and periods $T_1 \leq \cdot \leq T_p$ is schedulable if and only if for each task k, $k = 1, .., p$, there exists a set of integers $[n_1, .., n_k]$ with $n_k = 1$ such that

$$\sum_{j=1}^{k} n_j C_j \leq n_i T_i, \quad i = 1, .., k \quad (1)$$

Proof: For sufficiency, we show that the set of tasks is schedulable if conditions in (1) are satisfied. For each task τ_k, it is clear that the integer n_j, $j = 1, .., k-1$, in (1) is the number of times that task τ_k is preempted by task τ_j. Then conditions in (1) imply that task τ_k will complete at time $t_c^k = \sum_{j=1}^{k} n_j C_j$ with n_j preemptions by tasks τ_j, $j = 1, .., k-1$, and $t_c^k \leq T_k$. Therefore, task τ_k is schedulable. As this holds for all $k = 1, .., p$, the task set is schedulable.

For necessity, we prove that the schedulability of the task set implies condition (1). For each task τ_k in the task set, the schedulability of τ_k indicates that the completion time of τ_k is given by $t_c^k = \sum_{j=1}^{k} n_j C_j$ with $n_k = 1$, and $t_c^k \leq T_k$. Thus, before its completion, task τ_k will be preempted n_j times by the higher priority tasks τ_j, $j = 1, .., k-1$. Since each task τ_i, $i = 1, .., k$, will execute n_i times before τ_k completes, we conclude that $t_c^k \leq n_i T_i$, $i = 1, .., k$, which are exactly the equations given in (1).

Remark 2.1 Proposition 2.1 is equivalent to Lemma 2.1 in terms of task schedulability. It represents the schedulability conditions in terms of the existence of a set of integers. This formulation provides the basis for an integer programming algorithm for searching possible periods which guarantee task schedulability.

Remark 2.2 The set of integers which satisfies the conditions in (1) for one task **may** not be unique, i.e., for a given set of periods $[T_1, .., T_k]$ with $T_1 \leq \cdot\cdot \leq T_k$, there could be multiple sets of integers satisfying the conditions in (1). Among those sets of integers, only the one which gives the smallest completion time for task k, i.e., $t_c^k = \sum_{j=1}^{k} n_j C_j$, has a real meaning in terms of task execution. As we described in the proof of Proposition 2.1, the integers in that set indicate how many times tasks $\tau_1, .., \tau_k$ will execute before task τ_k completes.

Example 2.1 To illustrate Proposition 2.1, we determine the schedulability of a set of tasks $\{\tau_1, \tau_2, \tau_3\}$ with the following two cases

C_i	1	5	7
T_i	4	10	29

and

C_i	1	5	7
T_i	4	12	29

where C_i, T_i, $i = 1, 2, 3$, are the tasks' execution times and periods, respectively. For τ_3 to be schedulable, we check the existence of a set of integers $[n_1, n_2, 1]$ such that conditions in (1) are satisfied. Let $t_c = n_1 C_1 + n_2 C_2 + C_3$ and $B = \min\{n_1 T_1, n_2 T_2, T_3\}$. Then the conditions in (1) can be written as $t_c \leq B$. In the first case, we obtain the following results:

n_1	n_2	t_c	B
≥ 1	1	≥ 13	≤ 10
2,3	2	19, 20	8, 12
≥ 4	2	≥ 21	≤ 20
3,4,5,6,7	3	25, 26, 27, 28, 29	12, 16, 20, 24, 28
≥ 8	3	≥ 30	29
≥ 4	≥ 4	29	≤ 28

Apparently, none of the sets of integers will satisfy the condition $t_c \leq B$, and hence, the task set with the given execution times and periods is not schedulable. For the second case, we obtain:

n_1	n_2	t_c	B
≥ 1	1	≥ 13	≤ 12
2, 3, 4, 5	2	19, 20, 21, 22	8, 12, 16, 20
6	2	23	24
7	2	24	24
≥ 8	2	≥ 25	24
3, 4, 5, 6, 7	3	25, 26, 27, 28, 29	12, 16, 20, 24, 28
≥ 8	3	≥ 30	29
≥ 4	≥ 4	≥ 31	29

In this case, the sets of integers $[6, 2, 1]$ and $[7, 2, 1]$ satisfy the condition $t_c \leq B$, which indicates that task τ_3 is schedulable. Similarly, for τ_2 schedulability, we obtain

$$n_1 = 2, 3, 4, 5, 6, \text{ or } 7, \text{ and } n_2 = 1.$$

Since the schedulability of τ_1 is guaranteed by $C_1 < T_1$, we conclude that all the tasks are schedulable. According to Remark 2.2, only the sets of integers $[6, 2, 1]$ and $[7, 2, 1]$ have real meaning in terms of task execution.

We now consider the schedulability problem with changeable periods by investigating the relation between the sets of integers and the ranges of feasible periods. Suppose a set of tasks is given as described in the Problem Statement. It is easy to see that the sets of integers in (1) will be infinite if the periods can be freely chosen, which implies that the algorithms for searching the sets of feasible periods may not terminate. However, when the periods are constrained to lie below their upper bounds, then the number of possible sets of integers becomes finite, and this makes possible an integer programming approach. In fact, the sets of eligible integers for τ_k to be schedulable must satisfy the following conditions:

$$n_k \equiv 1, \quad \sum_{j=1}^{k} n_j C_j \leq n_i T_{mi}, \quad i = 1, .., k. \quad (2)$$

and they are possibly not unique. It is worth emphasizing that the multiplicity of the set of integers described here is different from the case discussed in Remark 2.2 where a set of periods is fixed and given. Here different sets of integers may result in different sets of ranges of periods as described in below. Our objective is to identify all the possible ranges of periods for the tasks to be schedulable. Since the task set is assumed to be schedulable with the maximum periods, conditions in (2) for $k = 1$ are always satisfied. Suppose there exist R_k sets of integers satisfying (2) for task τ_k, and let N_k^r be the rth set among them. Then we write $N_k^r = [n_1^{kr}, ..., n_k^{kr}]$, $r = 1, .., R_k$, and rewrite (2) in an equivalent form:

$$n_k^{kr} \equiv 1, \quad D_k^r \leq \min\{n_i^{kr} T_{mi}, \ i = 1, .., k\} \quad (3)$$

where $D_k^r = \sum_{j=1}^{k} n_j^{kr} C_j$ is the total demand for CPU time for task τ_k to complete, with the number of preemptions n_j^{kr}, caused by τ_j, $j = 1, .., k$. According to the relations in (1), the set of ranges of periods corresponding to the set of integers N_k^r is given by:

$$S_k^r = \{[T_1, .., T_k] : \frac{D_k^r}{n_i^{kr}} \leq T_i \leq T_{mi}, \ i = 1, .., k\} \quad (4)$$

Apparently, when R_k has the trivial value zero, neither the task τ_k nor the task set is schedulable.

The above analysis provides the basis for developing an integer programming algorithm to search for all the sets of feasible periods. In fact, for each task τ_k, $k = 2, .., p$, sets of integers N_k^r, $r = 1, .., R_k$, can be found from (3). Corresponding to each N_k^r, a set of ranges of periods S_k^r can be derived as in (4), which contains all the possible periods with which task τ_k is guaranteed to complete before its deadline, and it will be preempted n_j^{kr} times by task τ_j, $j = 1, .., k - 1$, during its execution. To make the whole task set schedulable, the intersections of the sets of ranges of periods derived for different tasks needs to be considered. Specifically, with R_k sets of ranges of periods

for each task τ_k, $k \geq 2$, there would be a total of $\prod_{k=2}^{p} R_k$ different intersections, which can be written as

$$I_{j_2 \cdots j_p} = \bigcap_{k=2}^{p} S_k^{j_k}, \quad j_i = 1, .., R_i, \ i = 2, .., p \quad (5)$$

Since the period ranges given in (4) only affect the periods of the tasks involved, the intersection of $S_{k_1}^{r_{k_1}}$ with $S_{k_2}^{r_{k_2}}$, $k_1 < k_2$, only intersects the first k_1 ranges between these two sets and leaves the remaining $k_2 - k_1$ ranges from $S_k^{r_{k_2}}$ unchanged. Eq. (5) gives the complete sets of ranges of feasible periods.

Example 2.2 To demonstrate the procedure to obtain the set of ranges of feasible periods, we consider the second case of Example 2.1, and we use the given set of periods as the upper bounds of the periods, i.e., $[T_{m1}, T_{m2}, T_{m3}] = [4, 12, 29]$. As calculated earlier, we found that task τ_3 and τ_2 are schedulable with the upper bounds of periods and obtained the sets of integers:

$$N_3^1 = [6, 2, 1], \quad N_3^2 = [7, 2, 1],$$
$$N_2^r = [r + 1, 1], \quad r = 1, .., 6$$

These integers correspond to the ranges of periods for τ_3 to be schedulable:

With N_3^1 :

3.83	$\leq$	T_1	$\leq$ 4
11.5	$\leq$	T_2	$\leq$ 12
23	$\leq$	T_3	$\leq$ 29

With N_3^2 :

3.43	$\leq$	T_1	$\leq$ 4
		T_2	$=$ 12
24	$\leq$	T_3	$\leq$ 29

and for τ_2 to be schedulable:

With N_2^1 :

3.5	$\leq$	T_1	$\leq$ 4
7	$\leq$	T_2	$\leq$ 12

With N_2^2 :

2.67	$\leq$	T_1	$\leq$ 4
8	$\leq$	T_2	$\leq$ 12

With N_2^3 :

2.25	$\leq$	T_1	$\leq$ 4
9	$\leq$	T_2	$\leq$ 12

With N_2^4 :

2.0	$\leq$	T_1	$\leq$ 4
10	$\leq$	T_2	$\leq$ 12

With N_2^5 :

1.83	$\leq$	T_1	$\leq$ 4
11	$\leq$	T_2	$\leq$ 12

With N_2^6 :

1.71	$\leq$	T_1	$\leq$ 4
12	$\leq$	T_2	$\leq$ 12

Intersecting each of the sets of ranges of periods for τ_3 with the sets for τ_2, we obtain the final sets of ranges of feasible periods:

3.83	$\leq$	T_1	$\leq$ 4
11.5	$\leq$	T_2	$\leq$ 12
23	$\leq$	T_3	$\leq$ 29

3.43	$\leq$	T_1	$\leq$ 4
		T_2	$=$ 12
24	$\leq$	T_3	$\leq$ 29

In deriving these final sets, we have excluded any set that can be contained in these two sets. This will be elaborated on later.

We now develop an integer programming algorithm for finding all the feasible periods for a given set of tasks with a fixed priority order. As shown earlier, deriving the sets of integers from (3) and the corresponding ranges of periods from (4) for each task's schedulability is fairly straight-forward, but constructing the intersections as in (5) could be computationally intensive. To reduce the computation, we apply the branch and bound approach in the construction. Specifically, starting from task p, we consider all the intersections of $S_p^{j_p}$ with $S_{p-1}^{j_{p-1}}$ for all $j_p = 1, .., R_p$, $j_{p-1} = 1, .., R_{p-1}$. Among the resulting sets of ranges of periods, some of them may be contained by the others. Suppose A and B are two sets from these intersections, and $A \subset B$. As further intersections are taken, for instance, $A \cap S_{p-2}^{j_{p-2}}$ and $B \cap S_{p-2}^{j_{p-2}}$, it is clear that $(A \cap S_{p-2}^{j_{p-2}}) \subset (B \cap S_{p-2}^{j_{p-2}})$. Namely, any further intersection starting from A will be contained in the same intersection starting with B. Therefore, all further intersections starting from A can be ignored once A is discovered to be contained in another set. This may reduce computation significantly. A complete algorithm is described in below.

Algorithm 2.1 Searching for All Feasible Periods with A Fixed Priority Order $T_1 \leq \cdots \leq T_p$

Step 1: Determine the sets of integers. For each task k, $k = 2, .., p$, we search for the sets of integers $N_k^r = [n_1^{kr}, .., n_{k-1}^{kr}, 1]$, $r = 1, .., R_k$, such that (3) is satisfied. Since $T_1 \leq \cdots \leq T_p$, only $n_1^{kr} \geq \cdots n_{k-1}^{kr} \geq 1$ needs to be considered.

Step 2: Derive the ranges of periods. For each N_k^r obtained from Step 1, we compute the set of ranges of periods S_k^r from (4). In addition, we define $k \times 2$ matrices B_k^r, $r = 1, .., k$, to represent the lower limits of the ranges of periods in S_k^r, $L_j^{kr} = D_k^r / n_j^{kr}$, $j = 1, .., R_k$, and the upper limits $T_{m1}, .., T_{mk}$. Namely,

$$B_k^r = \begin{bmatrix} L_1^{kr}, ..., L_k^{kr} \\ T_{m1}, ..., T_{mk} \end{bmatrix}^T$$

Therefore, each set of the ranges of periods, S_k^j, can be specified by the corresponding matrix B_k^r.

Step 3: Intersect the sets of ranges of periods. In this step, we construct a sequence of intersections from $S_p^{j_p}$ to $S_2^{j_2}$, i.e.,

$$(\cdots((S_p^{j_p} \cap S_{p-1}^{j_{p-1}}) \cap S_{p-2}^{j_{p-2}}) \cap \cdots \cap S_2^{j_2}).$$

Let $\mathcal{I}$ be a set of $p \times 2$ matrices that contain the limits of the resulting intersections, i.e.,

$$\mathcal{I} = \{\{I_{\alpha\beta}^r\}, r = 1, .., N\}$$

where $\alpha = 1, .., p$, $\beta = 1, 2$, $I_{\alpha 1}^r$ and $I_{\alpha 2}^r$ are the lower and upper limits of the range of period T_α in the kth intersection, respectively, and N is the number of intersections

specified in $\mathcal{I}$. Starting with $S_p^{j_p}$, we initialize $\mathcal{I}$ to contain all $B_p^{j_p}$, $j_p = 1, .., R_p$. Then we intersect each of the intersections specified by the corresponding element in $\mathcal{I}$ with each set of ranges of periods for task τ_k, specified by the corresponding matrix $B_k^{j_k}$, $k = p - 1, .., 2$. In particular, the intersection of the set specified by $\{I_{\alpha\beta}^r\}$ with $S_k^{j_k}$ can be specified by a $p \times 2$ matrix given by

$$\begin{bmatrix} \max\{I_{11}^r, L_1^{kj_k}\} & T_{m1} \\ \vdots & \vdots \\ \max\{I_{k1}^r, L_k^{kj_k}\} & T_{mk} \\ I_{(k+1)1}^r & T_{m(k+1)} \\ \vdots & \vdots \\ I_{p1}^r & T_{mp} \end{bmatrix}$$

For ease of exposition, we will refer the above matrix manipulation as $\mathcal{I} \cap B_k^{j_k}$. After all the intersections of $\mathcal{I}$ with $B_k^{j_k}$, $j_k = 1, .., R_k$, have been taken, we obtain a new set $\mathcal{I}$ with $N \times R_k$ intersections. Among these intersections, we delete those that can be contained by the others. For example, if $\{I_{\alpha\beta}^{r_1}\}$ and $\{I_{\alpha\beta}^{r_2}\}$ are two elements in the newly derived $\mathcal{I}$, we say $\{I_{\alpha\beta}^{r_1}\}$ is contained in $\{I_{\alpha\beta}^{r_2}\}$ if for all $\alpha = 1, .., p$, $\{I_{\alpha 1}^{r_1}\} \geq \{I_{\alpha 1}^{r_2}\}$, and $\{I_{\alpha\beta}^{r_1}\}$ will be eliminated from the set $\mathcal{I}$. Then the resulting $\mathcal{I}$ will have a reduced number of elements and this set will be used to intersect further with $B_{k-1}^{j_{k-1}}$. Repeat this step until all $S_2^{j_2}$, $j_2 = 1, .., R_2$, have been intersected with $\mathcal{I}$. Then the final set $\mathcal{I}$ specifies all the sets of ranges of feasible periods for the order of $T_1 \leq \cdots \leq T_p$.

Remark 2.3 While the sets of feasible periods obtained from Algorithm 2.1 contains all the periods for which the set of tasks is schedulable, the sets of ranges of feasible periods specified in the final set $\mathcal{I}$ may overlap. This implies that there exists some set of periods which can be simultaneously obtained from different sets of integers. In other words, there will be multiple sets of integers satisfying (3) with the same set of periods as discussed in Remark 2.2. For example, consider a set of tasks $\{\tau_1, \tau_2\}$ with execution times $C = [10, 20]$. From (4), we obtain the ranges of periods summarized in the following table, for $n_1 = 1, 2, 3$.

$n_1 = 1$	$n_1 = 2$	$n_1 = 3$
$T_1 \geq 30$	$20 \leq T_1$	$16.66 \leq T_1$
$T_2 \geq 30$	$T_2 \geq 40$	$T_3 \geq 50$

Apparently, the sets of ranges of periods obtained from the sets of integers $[1, 1]$ and $[2, 1]$ overlap in the ranges $30 \leq T_1$ and $T_2 \geq 40$. Therefore, any periods chosen from these overlapped ranges will have two sets of integers which both satisfy the conditions in (1). Although it would be nice to have exclusive sets of ranges of feasible periods, it is not necessary as far as task schedulability is concerned. As discussed in Remark 2.2, once the set of periods is determined, the set of integers, i.e., the actual

47.00	50.00	47.50	50.00	47.00	50.00	50.00	50.00
80.00	80.00	78.33	80.00	78.33	80.00	62.50	80.00
80.00	100.00	95.00	100.00	78.33	100.00	83.33	100.00
117.50	166.67	117.50	166.67	125.00	166.67	125.00	166.67
235.00	250.00	235.00	250.00	235.00	250.00	250.00	250.00

Figure 1: Elements of set $\mathcal{I}$ for Example 2.3. Each block is a matrix in $\mathcal{I}$.

number of execution of each task, is fixed with the one yielding the smallest completion time of the task with the longest period.

Example 2.3 Consider a set of tasks $\{\tau_1, .., \tau_5\}$ with computation time $C_1, .., C_5$ and the upper bounds of period $T_{m1}, .., T_{m5}$ given in the following table. Find all the feasible periods with the priority order $T_1 \leq \cdots \leq T_5$.

	τ_1	τ_2	τ_3	τ_4	τ_5
C_i (ms)	10	15	20	25	30
T_{mi} (ms)	50	80	100	166.67	250

Following Algorithm 2.1, we find that the number of sets of integers for each task to be schedulable are $R_5 = 2$, $R_4 = 10$, $R_3 = 9$, $R_2 = 6$, and these sets of integers would result in $6 \cdot 9 \cdot 10 \cdot 2 = 1080$ possible sets of ranges of feasible periods. By using the branch and bound approach, most of the intermediate ranges will be eliminated at an earlier stage and the final number of sets of ranges of feasible periods will be reduced to 4. The final ranges of feasible periods specified in $\mathcal{I}$ are given in Fig. 1.

Example 2.4 Consider a set of tasks $\{\tau_1, .., \tau_5\}$ with real-time data given in the following table. The period of task τ_5 is required to be fixed as given. Find all the feasible periods $[T_1, .., T_4]$ with the priority order $T_1 \leq \cdots \leq T_5$.

	τ_1	τ_2	τ_3	τ_4	τ_5
C_i (ms)	10	10	10	10	5
T_{mi} (ms)	50	55.56	66.67	100	100

Again, the number of sets of integers for each task to be schedulable is obtained from Algorithm 2.1 as $R_5 = 9$, $R_4 = 10$, $R_3 = 5$, $R_2 = 4$, and there are totally 12 sets of ranges of feasible periods specified in set $\mathcal{I}$, and they are listed in Fig. 2.

While both examples are scheduled with the fixed priority order the same as the order of the maximum periods, the numbers of final sets of ranges of feasible periods are different significantly. Such differences are a consequence of the utilization levels that each set of tasks can have. For the first example, the allowable utilization is constrained in

27.50	50.00	32.50	50.00	37.50	50.00	28.33	50.00
55.00	55.56	32.50	55.56	37.50	55.56	42.50	55.56
55.00	66.67	65.00	66.67	37.50	66.67	42.50	66.67
55.00	100.00	65.00	100.00	75.00	100.00	85.00	100.00
100.00	100.00	100.00	100.00	100.00	100.00	100.00	100.00

23.75	50.00	31.67	50.00	42.50	50.00	40.00	50.00
47.50	55.56	31.67	55.56	42.50	55.56	47.50	55.56
47.50	66.67	47.50	66.67	42.50	66.67	47.50	66.67
95.00	100.00	95.00	100.00	42.50	100.00	47.50	100.00
100.00	100.00	100.00	100.00	100.00	100.00	100.00	100.00

31.67	50.00	31.67	50.00	35.00	50.00	31.67	50.00
50.00	55.56	47.50	55.56	47.50	55.56	47.50	55.56
50.00	66.67	60.00	66.67	47.50	66.67	47.50	66.67
50.00	100.00	60.00	100.00	70.00	100.00	80.00	100.00
100.00	100.00	100.00	100.00	100.00	100.00	100.00	100.00

Figure 2: Elements of set $\mathcal{I}$ for Example 2.4. Each block is a matrix in $\mathcal{I}$.

the range [0.8575, 1], while the second example has a larger range [0.63, 1]. Therefore, there is a wider choice of periods in the second example than the first one. The difference on the allowable utilization will have a large impact when the tasks are scheduled without any prescribed priority order, as will be addressed in the subsequent section.

2.2 Task Periods for RMA Schedulability with No Prescribed Priority Order

We now move on to investigate the schedulability of a given set of tasks without a prescribed priority order of task execution. Again, we are searching for the possible periods for all the tasks to be schedulable.

Problem Statement: Given a set of periodic tasks $\{\tau_1, .., \tau_p\}$ with execution time $C_1, .., C_p$ and upper bounds of periods $T_{m1}, .., T_{mp}$. Suppose the set of tasks is schedulable with the maximum periods $T_{m1}, .., T_{mp}$. Find all the possible periods $T_1, .., T_p$ satisfying the condition $T_1 \leq T_{m1}, .., T_p \leq T_{mp}$ so that all the tasks are schedulable. Without loss of generality, we assume $T_{m1} \leq \cdots \leq T_{mp}$.

As a direct use of Algorithm 2.1, one could arrange the periods in $p!$ different priority orders, and run through the algorithm for each one of them to find out the ranges of periods. The resulting period ranges will cover all the periods, arranged in all orders, such that the set of tasks is schedulable. Undoubtedly, this will involve a huge amount of computation, and it is not always necessary. In most cases, a large number of the permutations of the priority order may result in the ranges of feasible periods which can be contained by the ones obtained from other permutations. Therefore, one can use the branch and bound approach to eliminate some of the permutations in the search. A *branch* for the current problem is defined as a particular order of task priority, represented by the order of the periods as $T_{i_1} \leq \cdots \leq T_{i_p}$, where $1 \leq i_j \leq p$, $\forall j = 1, .., p$, and $i_1, .., i_p$ are distinguished. By a *priority level*, we mean that a task at this level will have the ith highest priority among all the tasks. To apply the branch and bound approach, we make the following observations.

1. Suppose $r < p$ tasks are chosen to run last with a fixed priority order $T_{i_{p-r+1}} \leq \cdots \leq T_{i_p}$, and the remaining tasks have an unrestricted priority order. Then the condition in (3) can be modified to generate all the sets of integers with all possible priority orders of the $p - r$ tasks such that the ranges of periods derived from the integers to provide all the possible periods for those r task to be schedulable. Specifically, for task τ_{i_k} to be schedulable, $i_k \in \{i_{p-r+1}, .., i_p\}$, the set of integers $n_{i_1}, .., n_{i_k}$ must satisfy the following condition:

$$\begin{cases} \sum_{j=1}^{k} n_{i_j} C_{i_j} \leq \min\{n_i T_{mi}, \forall i \in \{i_1, .. i_k\}\} \\ n_{i_{p-r+1}} \leq \cdots \leq n_{i_k} \equiv 1 \end{cases}$$
(6)

From these sets of integers, we obtain all the possible ranges of periods for tasks $\tau_{i_1}, .., \tau_{i_k}$ as in (4) such that τ_{i_k} is schedulable given its priority in the fixed priority order. Furthermore, by running through this procedure for all $i_k \in \{i_{p-r+1}, .., i_p\}$, and taking intersections of the resulting sets of ranges of periods from task to task as described in Algorithm 2.1, we obtain all the possible sets of ranges of periods for all tasks that guarantee the schedulability of those r tasks as the last to run with the fixed priority order. We will call the problem of finding all the possible ranges of periods for this set of tasks the *partially-fixed-order problem*. The case of only one tasks being chosen as the last to run is also a partially-fixed-order problem since the order of that task is fixed.

2. Again, assume the same as in the first observation. Let $\sigma = < j_{p-r+1}, .., j_p >$ represent a permutation of the fixed priority order $T_{p-r+1} \leq \cdots \leq T_p$, and $\mathcal{I}_\sigma$ be the set of $p \times 2$ matrices that contains the limits of all the possible ranges of periods obtained from solving the partially-fixed-order problem with the fixed priority specified by σ. Then $\mathcal{I}_\sigma$ specifies a set of ranges of periods that contain all the sets of ranges of feasible periods obtained from all the possible priority orders with last r tasks fixed as given.

To summarize, we conclude that, if the set of ranges of periods specified by $\mathcal{I}_\sigma$ turns out to be contained in some set of ranges of feasible periods that have been considered, then no more permutation of $< *, .., *, \sigma >$ needs to be investigated, where $< *, .., * >$ represents all permutations of period for tasks $\tau_{i_1}, .., \tau_{i_{p-r}}$ and $< *, .., *, \sigma > = < *, .., *, j_{p-r+1}, .., j_p >$ if $\sigma = < j_{p-r+1}, .., j_p >$. In this case, all the permutations $< *, .., *, \sigma >$ are considered to be checked in the sense of generating feasible periods.

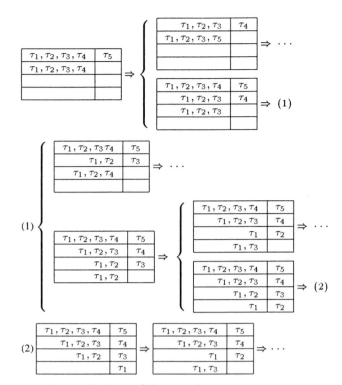

Figure 3: Some of the steps from the algorithm

We now develop an integer programming algorithm with the branch and bound approach utilizing the properties described above. Let $\mathcal{I}$ be the set of $p \times 2$ matrices that contains the limits of ranges of feasible periods. Starting with a fixed order of period, say the order same as the maximum periods, i.e., $\sigma = < 2, .., p >$, we derive a set of ranges of feasible periods specified by $\mathcal{I}_\sigma$ and initialize $\mathcal{I} = \mathcal{I}_\sigma$. For each priority level, we associate with it a list of candidate tasks to be scheduled with this priority. Starting from $\sigma = < 2, .., p >$, we go through a sequence of permutations of priority and for each permutation, we derive the set $\mathcal{I}_\sigma$. If some elements in $\mathcal{I}_\sigma$ can not be contained by any element in $\mathcal{I}$, we add them in $\mathcal{I}_\sigma$ to $\mathcal{I}$ if σ is a permutation of $p - 1$ tasks; otherwise, we proceed with a new permutation $< \gamma, \sigma >$, where γ is the index of a candidate task that can run just before the tasks ordered by σ. τ_γ will be withdrawn from the list of candidates. A new element in $\mathcal{I}_\sigma$ is the one that can not be contained by any element in $\mathcal{I}$. If $\mathcal{I}_\sigma$ does not contain any new elements, i.e., all the elements in $\mathcal{I}_\sigma$ can be contained by some elements in $\mathcal{I}$, there is no need to pursue any further check with permutations $< *, .., *, \sigma >$, and we change the permutation $\sigma = < j_{p-r+1}, .., j_p >$ by replacing j_{p-r+1} with the index of a task from the list of candidates. Such a task will be removed from the list of candidates once it is placed in the fixed order. If no more candidate task are in the list, we replace j_{p-r+2} with a new one and proceed with $\sigma = < j_{p-r+2}, .., j_p >$. This procedure is repeated until all the permutation are considered to be checked in the sense of generating feasible periods.

To illustrate some of the steps in this algorithm, we consider a task set with five tasks. Construct a block with two columns: the left column lists the candidate tasks at each of the priority levels 2,..,5, and the right column gives the permutations of priority to be checked, i.e., σ. The lower the task is in the block, the higher is its priority. When the algorithm proceeds, the content in the block changes as shown in Fig. 3. To start, we pick τ_5 as the last to run and set $\sigma = <5>$. Then tasks $\tau_1, .., \tau_4$ will be the candidates at the priority levels 4 and 5. Derive $\mathcal{I}_\sigma$ and compare it with set $\mathcal{I}$ which is initialized as $\mathcal{I}_{<2,..,5>}$. If $\mathcal{I}_\sigma$ has no new element, a new task is chosen from the list of candidate tasks at priority level 5, say τ_4, and removed from the list. The list of candidate tasks at priority level 4 is then modified by taking out τ_4 and adding τ_5. The algorithm continues with $\mathcal{I}_{<4>}$. If $\mathcal{I}_\sigma$ contains some new elements, a task with higher priority is picked from the list of candidate tasks at priority level 4, say τ_4, and removed from the list. A new list of candidate tasks at priority level 3 is established by using the list at the priority level 4, and we move on with $\sigma = <4,5>$. Suppose both $\mathcal{I}_{<4,5>}$ and $\mathcal{I}_{<3,4,5>}$ will have some new elements. Then $\mathcal{I}_{<2,3,4,5>}$ will be derived and all its elements will be contained by some elements in $\mathcal{I}$. This is the path indicated by $\cdots \Rightarrow (1) \Rightarrow (2) \Rightarrow \cdots$. To proceed after $\sigma = <2,3,4,5>$, we replace τ_2 by τ_1 as the second task to run, and derive $\mathcal{I}_{<1,3,4,5>}$. If $\mathcal{I}_{<1,3,4,5>}$ contains some new elements, add them to $\mathcal{I}$. Since there is no more candidate at priority level 2, we pick a new task, say τ_3, as the 3rd task to run, and proceed in the similar manner as earlier. A formal description of the algorithm is given as below.

Algorithm 2.2 Searching for All Feasible Periods with All the Possible Priority Orders:

Variables

$To\_Be\_Checked$: a p element array, and each element $To\_Be\_Checked[i]$, $i = 2, .., p$, contains a list of the candidate tasks at priority level i.

γ_i : the highest index of the task among the tasks contained in $To\_Be\_Checked[i]$.

r : the number of tasks involved in σ.

Init:

- Derive $\mathcal{I}_{<2,..,p>}$ and initialize $\mathcal{I} = \mathcal{I}_{<2,..,p>}$;
- $To\_Be\_Checked[i] = \{\tau_k, k = 1, .., p - 1\}$, $i = p, p - 1$;
- $\sigma = <p>$ and $r = 1$.

# of Orders Checked	σ	# of New Matrices in I_σ	# of Matrices obtained in I
1	<5>	1	4
2	<4,5>	0	4
3	<3,5>	0	4
4	<2,5>	0	4
5	<15>	0	4
6	<4>	0	4
7	<3>	0	4
8	<2>	0	4
9	<1>	0	4

Figure 4: The ranges of feasible periods for the set of tasks in Example 2.3 with all possible priority orders.

Step 1:

- Solve the partially-fixed-order problem for $\mathcal{I}_\sigma$.
- If $\mathcal{I}_\sigma$ has no new element, go to Step 2;
- Otherwise
  If $r = p - 1$, add the new elements to $\mathcal{I}$;
  If $r < p - 1$, $r = r + 1$;
  go to Step 2.

Step 2:

- $v = p - r + 1$;
- If $To\_Be\_Checked[v]$ is empty and $r = 1$
  the search is over. $\mathcal{I}$ specifies all the ranges of feasible periods with all the priority orders;
- If $To\_Be\_Checked[v]$ is empty and $r > 1$
  $r = r - 1$ and empty $To\_Be\_Checked[v - 1]$;
  go back to Step 2;
- If $To\_Be\_Checked[v]$ is not empty
  If $r < p - 1$
  $To\_Be\_Checked[v - 1]$
  $= \{To\_Be\_Checked[v] - \{\tau_{\gamma_v}\}, \tau_{j_v}\}$;
  $\sigma = <\gamma_v, j_{v+1}, .., j_p>$;
  eliminate γ_v from $To\_Be\_Checked[v]$;
  go to Step 1.

We now apply Algorithm 2.2 in Examples 2.3 and 2.4 to find all the sets of ranges of feasible periods with all the possible orders of priority. Results are shown in Fig. 5. Due to the limitation of space, we only present the number of sets of ranges of periods at various steps as the algorithm proceeds without showing the actual ranges. In the first example, we initialize $\mathcal{I} = \mathcal{I}_{<2,..,5>}$. Starting with $\sigma = <5>$ and $r = 1$, we see that $\mathcal{I}_\sigma$ has one new element and that leads to the check of the new permutation $\sigma = <4,5>$. Since $\mathcal{I}_{<4,5>}$ does not give any new element, $\sigma = <3,5>$ is considered afterwards. As none of $\sigma = <3,5>, <2,5>$ and $<1,5>$ generate any new element in $\mathcal{I}_\sigma$, all the branches $<*,..,*,5>$ are checked, and the task at priority level 5 is replaced. Further calculation shows that none of $\mathcal{I}_\sigma$, $\sigma = <4>, .., <1>$, have any new element, and therefore, the algorithm terminates. To conclude, we see that there are four sets of ranges of feasible periods, all of them obtained from $\mathcal{I}_{<2,..,5>}$, and only 9 out of 120 (5!) permutations are checked.

# of Orders Checked	σ	# of New Matrices in I_σ	# of Matrices obtained in I
1	<5>	10	13
2	<4,5>	15	13
3	<3,4,5>	7	13
4	<2,3,4,5>	0	13
5	<1,3,4,5>	7	20
6	<2,4,5>	7	20
7	<3,2,4,5>	1	21
8	<1,2,4,5>	6	27
9	<1,4,5>	1	27
10	<3,1,4,5>	1	28
11	<2,1,4,5>	0	28
12	<3,5>	2	28
13	<4,3,5>	0	28
14	<2,3,5>	2	28
15	<4,2,3,5>	0	28
16	<1,2,3,5>	2	30
17	<1,3,5>	0	30
18	<2,5>	0	30
19	<1,5>	0	30
20	<4>	21	30
21	<5,4>	15	30
22	<3,5,4>	8	30
23	<2,3,5,4>	6	36
24	<1,3,5,4>	2	38
25	<2,5,4>	5	38
26	<3,2,5,4>	3	41
27	<1,2,5,4>	2	43
28	<1,5,4>	2	43
29	<3,1,5,4>	2	45
30	<2,1,5,4>	0	45
31	<3,4>	16	45
32	<5,3,4>	1	45
33	<2,5,3,4>	1	46
34	<1,5,3,4>	0	46
35	<2,3,4>	10	46
36	<5,2,3,4>	3	49
37	<1,2,3,4>	7	56
38	<1,3,4>	5	56
39	<5,1,3,4>	3	59
40	<2,1,3,4>	2	61
41	<2,4,>	4	61
42	<5,2,4>	0	61
43	<3,2,4>	0	61
44	<1,2,4>	4	61
45	<5,1,2,4>	2	63
46	<3,1,2,4>	2	65
47	<1,4>	0	65
48	<3>	0	65
49	<2>	0	65
50	<1>	0	65

Figure 5: The ranges of feasible periods for the set of tasks in Example 2.4 with all possible priority orders.

For the second example, we assume that the period of task τ_5 can be changed as well. Again, we initialize $I = I_{<2,..,5>}$ with 13 sets of ranges of feasible periods. Following the steps of the algorithm, we find that all of I_σ, $\sigma = <5>$, $<4,5>$ and $<3,4,5>$, contain some new elements, and that leads to the check of $I_{<2,3,4,5>}$, which, of course, will not have any new element. Replacing τ_2 by τ_1, the candidate at priority level 2, we derive $I_{<1,3,4,5>}$ and get 7 new elements. These new elements are then added to I. It is worth emphasizing that the new elements from I_σ are added to I only when σ is a permutation of $p - 1$ tasks, which implies that all the tasks are schedulable with the priority order specified by σ. As σ involves less than $p - 1$ tasks, only those tasks being specified have guaranteed schedulability, and as a result, the ranges of periods specified in I_σ may not all be feasible. To conclude the example, we notice that the permutations $\sigma = <*,..*,5>$ and $\sigma = <*,..,*,4>$ both generate many new elements, while $\sigma = <*,..*,3>$, $<*,..,*,2>$ and $<*,..,*,1>$ give none. This can be explained intuitively by taking a look at the period bounds. In fact, the upper bounds of T_1, T_2 and T_3 are almost one half of the bounds for T_4 and T_5, and therefore, using one of T_1, T_2 or T_3 as the lower priority task would constrain the ranges of feasible periods much more than making T_4 or T_5 as the lower priority tasks. In the end, there are 65

sets of ranges of feasible periods derived, and 50 permutations have been checked, which is 42% of 5!. Comparing to the result from Example 2.3, where the number of permutations checked is only 7.5% of 5!, we conclude that the more the utilization is constrained, the more effective is the proposed algorithm.

3 The Optimal Periods for RMA Schedulability

In this section, we address the issue of finding the periods for a set of tasks such that the given performance measure of the overall system is optimized and the task set is schedulable using RMA. In particular, we will focus on the class of systems in which the performance index for each task can be described by a monotonically increasing function of task period, which we will call a cost function. It is desirable to have a lower cost for each task. Such classes of systems have been discussed in [4] where the tasks are control law computations and the cost functions are defined as the difference on a performance index evaluated using continuous and digitized control laws. A precise description of the problem is given by the following:

Problem Statement: Given a set of periodic tasks $\tau_1, .., \tau_p$ with execution times $C_1, .., C_p$, upper bounds of periods $T_{m1}, .., T_{mp}$, and a cost function for the overall system, $J(T_1, .., T_p)$, with $\partial J / \partial T_i \geq 0$, $\forall 0 < T_i \leq T_{mi}$. Suppose the set of tasks is schedulable with the maximum periods. Let $T = [T_1, .., T_p]$. Find the set of optimal periods T^* such that $J(T)$ is minimized and all the tasks are schedulable.

The optimization problem can be solved after all the feasible periods have been found using the search algorithm proposed in the last section. Since all the sets of ranges of feasible periods are specified by matrices in I, all the feasible periods are given by

$$I_{j1}^i \leq T_j \leq T_{mj}, \quad j = 1, .., p, \qquad (7)$$

where $i = 1, .., N$ and N is the total number of matrices in I. Then the optimal solution to the periods is obtained as:

$$T^* = \min_{T \in \{L_i, \ i=1,..,M\}} \{J(T)\}, \quad L_i = [I_{11}^i, .., I_{p1}^i].$$

While the optimal solution can be obtained by checking all the possible periods which guarantee RMA schedulability, it is not necessary to do so if finding the optimal periods is the sole objective. In fact, the search algorithm presented in last section can be easily modified to provide the set of optimal periods. Suppose a set of tasks is given without any prescribed priority order. In last section, we have discovered that for any permutation of priority σ, the sets of ranges of periods specified by $\mathcal{I}_\sigma$ will contain all the sets of ranges of periods corresponding to permutations $<*,..,*,\sigma>$. Since only the lower limits of the periods in each set are of interest as far as minimizing $J(T)$ is concerned, none of the sets of ranges of periods would possibly result in an optimal solution if the ones specified by $\mathcal{I}_\sigma$ do not. Therefore, if none of the $J(T)$ evaluated with the sets of the lower limits of periods specified by $\mathcal{I}_\sigma$ has a smaller value than some $J(T)$ already obtained, the whole branch specified by permutations $<*,..,*,\sigma>$ can be eliminated from further consideration. Let L_σ^{min} be the set of lower limits of periods specified by $\mathcal{I}_\sigma$ which gives the smallest value of $J(T)$ among all the sets of periods specified in $\mathcal{I}_\sigma$. By taking into account the evaluation of $J(T)$, we modify the algorithm given in last section as follows:

Algorithm 3.1 Searching for the Optimal Feasible Periods:

Init:

- Derive $\mathcal{I}_{<2,..,p>}$ and evaluate $J(T)$ to obtain $L_{<2,..,p>}^{min}$;
- Initialize $T^* = L_{<2,..,p>}^{min}$;
- $To\_Be\_Checked[i] = \{\tau_k, \ k = 1,..,i-1\}$, $\forall i = p, p-1$.
- $\sigma = <p>$ and $r = 1$.

Step 1:

- Solve the partially-fixed-order problem for $\mathcal{I}_\sigma$.
- Evaluate $J(T)$ to find L_σ^{min};
- If $L_\sigma^{min} \geq T^*$, got to Step 2;
- Otherwise
  If $r = p-1$, $T^* = L_\sigma^{min}$ and go to Step 2;
  If $r < p-1$, $r = r+1$ and go to Step 2.

Step 2:

- $v = p - r + 1$;
- If $To\_Be\_Checked[v]$ is empty and $r = 1$
  the search is over and
  T^* contains the set of optimal periods;
- If $To\_Be\_Checked[v]$ is empty and $r > 1$
  $r = r - 1$ and empty $To\_Be\_Checked[v-1]$;
  go back to Step 2;
- If $To\_Be\_Checked[v]$ is not empty
  If $r < p-1$
  $To\_Be\_Checked[v-1]$
  $= \{To\_Be\_Checked[v] - \{\tau_{\gamma_v}\}, \tau_{j_v}\}$;
  $\sigma = <\gamma_v, j_{v+1}, .., j_p>$;
  eliminate γ_v from $To\_Be\_Checked[v]$;
  go to Step 1.

Again, Algorithm 3.1 is illustrated by the examples presented earlier. As before, we reassign the tasks' indices

Results of Example 2.3

# of Orders Checked	σ	# of Matrices obtained in $\mathcal{I}_\sigma$	Optimal Cost
1	<5>	2	0.19965
2	<4,5>	4	0.19965
3	<3,5>	1	0.19965
4	<2,5>	1	0.19965
5	<1,5>	1	0.19965
6	<4>	1	0.19965
7	<3>	1	0.19965
8	<2>	1	0.19965
9	<1>	1	0.19965

Final Result:
    Optimal cost: 0.19965
    Optimal Periods: [47, 80, 80, 117.5, 235]

Results of Example 2.4

# of Orders Checked	σ	# of Matrices obtained in $\mathcal{I}_\sigma$	Optimal Cost
1	<5>	18	0.02048
2	<4>	34	0.02048
3	<3>	4	0.02048
4	<2>	3	0.02048
5	<1>	2	0.02048

Final Result:
    Optimal cost: 0.02048
    Optimal Periods: [23.75, 47.5, 47.5, 95, 100]

Figure 6: Illustration of finding the optimal feasible periods for a set of task with no particular priority order.

such that $T_{m1} \leq \cdots \leq T_{mp}$. We assume both examples have a cost function given by $J(T) = \sum_{i=1}^5 \alpha_i e^{-\beta_i/T_i}$ with parameters for Example 2.3

α_i	0.67	1.33	2.0	2.67	3.33
β_i	0.3	0.4	0.5	0.6	0.7

for Example 2.4

α_i	1	2	5	3	0
β_i	0.1	0.3	0.5	0.7	0

As can be seen in Fig. 6, where the results are shown, the search terminated much faster than the search for feasible periods, when the check of minimum value of $J(T)$, evaluated with each set of ranges of periods, is used for branching. This will be the case only when the true optimal value of $J(T)$ is found, but not confirmed, at an earlier stage. In both examples, the minimum value of $J(T)$ was obtained from the range of feasible periods specified by $\mathcal{I}_{1..5}$, the set derived first.

4 Conclusion

In this paper, we studied the issue of choosing the periods for a given set of real-time periodic tasks such that the performance of the system is optimized in the sense that a given cost function is minimized, and all the tasks are schedulable with RMA. The problem is solved by finding all the sets of periods with which the set of tasks is schedulable with RMA, and then identifying the set of periods, among all the possible sets, that minimizes the cost function. To find the possible periods that render the RMA schedulability for the task set, the testing algorithm reported in [5] is formulated as an integer programming problem. By solving this integer programming problem with the branch and bound approach, all the possible periods for RMA schedulability are obtained, described by a finite number of sets of ranges of feasible periods. An algorithm to find all the feasible periods with a given order of priority is developed first, and based on that, an algorithm for searching for all the feasible periods with all the possible priority orders is presented. The results obtained from the latter algorithm cover all the sets of periods that make the task set schedulable with RMA. From the derived sets of ranges of feasible periods, the optimal periods are determined by evaluating the cost function with all the lower limits of these ranges. Moreover, by incorporating the evaluation of the cost function in the search algorithm, the optimal periods can be obtained without actually deriving all the possible ranges of periods.

The contributions of the paper are three-fold. First, it addresses the issue of RMA schedulability from an alternative perspective, namely, reformulating the schedulability conditions as the existence of a set of integers. Such a formulation transforms task schedulability into an integer programming problem, which enables the use of a class of branch and bound search algorithms.

Second, finding all the feasible periods and making them available in the design stage of an application would reduce the gap between design and implementation. By presenting the computing resource constraint as a range of feasible periods for the tasks in the task set, the designer could carry out the task design in a systematic manner, and the resulting task set will be guaranteed to be schedulable. For example, in a control application, the control algorithm can be designed subject to the constraint on sampling frequency, given as the ranges of feasible frequencies.

Third, using the optimal periods for the tasks would make a better use of the limited resource with respect to some given performance measure. Raising the efficiency of resource usage is an important issue in practice. In some applications, the number of computing devices is limited due to certain space, weight and power constraints, and therefore, adding more facilities may not be a solution to accommodate the increase of tasks' frequencies as required for performance improvement. In other cases, if the computing device is one element of a mass produced system (for example computer controllers in automobiles), then the cost of the computing device may be a major concern.

In such applications, using a high speed computing device to allow for high task sampling frequencies and ease of schedulability may not be an acceptable solution because of its cost impact on the final product. In both situations, it would be desirable to determine the best performance that the system can achieve with the given available computing resource, and how to make the system improve its performance by achieving a higher level utilization of the available resource. The approaches presented in this paper provide a solution to these concerns when RMA is used for scheduling.

The efficiency of the search algorithm proposed in this paper depends on applications, as can be seen from the examples. They are efficient when the utilization is constrained. The number of the task, on the other hand, does not play a significant role here, opposed to what one would expect. In the case of a more restrictive utilization being given, the algorithms will rapidly finish their search no matter how many tasks are involved. On the other hand, when the system contains a large number of tasks and they have a low level utilization of the computing resource, it would take a long time for the algorithm to complete the search, and the result obtained, for instance the sets of ranges of feasible periods, could be a large set of different possibilities. Therefore, we conclude that the algorithms developed in this paper are efficient for reasonably structured engineering applications.

References

[1] Gerber, R., Hong, S. and Saksena, M., "Guaranteeing end-to-end timing constraints by calibrating Intermediate Processes," *Proceedings of the IEEE Real-Time Systems Symposium*, December, 1994.

[2] Locke, C. D., "Best-effort decision making for real-time scheduling." Ph.D. Dissertation, Computer Science Department, Carnegie Mellon University, 1986.

[3] D.-T. Peng, K. G. Shin, and T. K. Abdelzaher, "Assignment and Scheduling Communicating Periodic Tasks in Distributed Real-Time Systems," *IEEE Transactions on Software Engineering*, Vol. 23, No. 12, December, 1997.

[4] Seto, D., J. P. Lehoczky, L. Sha, and K. G. Shin, "On Task Schedulability in Real-Time Control System," in the *Proceedings of 17th Real-Time Systems Symposium*, pp. 13-21, December, 1996.

[5] Sha, L., Rajkumar, R. and Sathaye, S. S., "Generalized rate-monotonic scheduling theory: A framework for developing real-time systems," *Proceedings of the IEEE*, Vol. 82, No. 1, January, 1994.

Session 7.A: Testing, Verification and Analysis I

Automatic Testing of Reactive Systems *

Pascal Raymond, Xavier Nicollin, Nicolas Halbwachs
Vérimag,† Grenoble - France
{*raymond,nicollin,halbwachs*} *@imag.fr*

Daniel Weber
Schneider Electric, Grenoble - France
daniel_weber@mail.schneider.fr

Abstract

This paper addresses the problem of automatizing the production of test sequences for reactive systems. We particularly focus on two points: (1) generating relevant inputs, with respect to some knowledge about the environment in which the system is intended to run; (2) checking the correctness of the test results, according to the expected behavior of the system. We propose to use synchronous observers to express both the relevance and the correctness of the test sequences. In particular, the relevance observer is used to randomly choose inputs satisfying temporal assumptions about the environment. These assumptions may involve both Boolean and linear numerical constraints. A prototype tool, called LURETTE, *has been developed and experimented, which works on observers written in the* LUSTRE *programming language.*

1   Introduction

The term *reactive system* was introduced by David Harel and Amir Pnueli [13], and is now commonly accepted to designate systems that permanently interact with their environment, and to distinguish them from *transformational systems* (e.g., compilers).

In this paper, we understand this term in a more restrictive way, distinguishing between "*interactive*" and "*reactive*" systems: *interactive systems* permanently communicate with their environment, but at their own speed (e.g., operating systems, data base interface, web server), while *reactive systems* have to react to an environment which cannot wait. Typical examples appear when the environment is a physical process (e.g., process control in industry, power plants; embedded systems in trains, aircrafts...). In contrast with most interactive systems, reactive systems are generally *deterministic*: from an abstract point of view, the ex-

ecution of a reactive system can be viewed as an infinite sequence of input/output vectors, where, at each step, the output values are completely determined by the past and present inputs. This is the point of view of synchronous programming languages [5, 2, 15], and we will adopt it throughout the paper. Notice that, with this point of view, the "real-time" constraints on the system generally reduce to a maximal reaction time; they are clearly separated from its functional requirements.

Because of their application domain, reactive systems are intrinsically critical. They need to be strongly validated before being run in their actual environment. All the techniques and tools that can increase confidence in the design of reactive systems are of high interest: high level, special purpose, languages for their specification and design, compilers for automatic coding, validation techniques, both for the code and the specification.

The most appealing validation approach is formal verification, which intends to prove that the system satisfies some given properties. This approach is intrinsically limited by theoretical problems of decidability (in particular, because of numerical aspects of the system), and technical problems of cost (time and space necessary for the proof). There are, roughly speaking, two approaches to formal verification. Techniques based on general *theorem proving* make use of inference systems with deductive rules. Such techniques generally involve a great amount of user interaction. The second approach is based on *model checking*. The proof is made by an exhaustive exploration of a finite abstraction of the system. The proof is partial, but conservative, in the sense that if the model meets the properties, then so does the real system, otherwise the result is unconclusive. These techniques are (mostly) automatic, but they are dramatically limited by the "size explosion" of the models.

Program testing is a more popular validation technique, which is complementary to formal verification. Their goals are rather different, since testing aims at finding bugs, but cannot generally provide any absolute, positive result. The classical approaches to testing focus on the following aspects:

- *Glass-box vs Black-box:* Some techniques assume a

---

*This work has been partially supported by the ESPRIT-LTR project "SYRF".

† Verimag is a joint laboratory of Université Joseph Fourier (Grenoble I), CNRS and INPG (*www-verimag.imag.fr*).

full knowledge of the program under test (Glass-box, or structural testing), while others suppose that (almost) nothing is known about it (Black-box, or functional testing).

- *Unit - Integration - System:* The test process is generally hierarchical. First, the functionality of small components is widely tested (unit testing); then the interaction between those components is tested (integration testing); and finally, the whole system is tested "in place" (this last step is in general unfeasible for embedded systems, so the test is performed in a simulated environment).

Our approach does not really fall into this classification. Our main goal is to concentrate on the complementarity of the verification and test methods. Program testing is the only way of increasing the confidence about systems that are outside the scope of formal verification. So, in our opinion, a tool devoted to program testing should concentrate on cases where formal verification fails:

- programs with significant numerical aspects, which cannot be abstracted away;
- programs the source code of which is not necessarily available — e.g., because it is partly written in languages that are not supported by verification tools;
- programs which are used as specifications, and are implemented by hand (e.g., distributed implementations from centralized programs).

Amazingly, testing of reactive programs has not been widely studied. In particular, little attention seems to have been paid to the fact that such a system is embedded into a specific environment, with which it forms a *closed loop*: at a given instant, constraints on the current inputs may depend on the exact past behavior of the system. This distinguishes our approach from those based on temporal logic specifications (e.g., [17, 14]). The most advanced works on the subject [24, 19, 20, 9, 18] either assume a full knowledge of the program under test, or do not deal with numerical programs. Notice also that we are only interested in testing the functional behavior of the system. As mentionned before, the real-time aspects are a clearly separated concern (maximum reaction time) which is not considered here (see, e.g., [7, 23] for references on testing real-time constraints).

In this paper, we follow a *black-box* approach, since the program is not supposed to be fully known. Moreover, we will focus on the problem of automatic generation and analysis of test sequences, without distinguishing between unit, integration and system testing. The problems we are trying to solve are:

- Producing *realistic* inputs, with respect to the environment in which the system will be embedded.
- Moreover those sequences must be *interesting* for the user, who generally has some goal in mind.

- Analyzing outputs, to check whether the test has passed successfully.

To solve these problems, we will make use of some results coming from the field of formal verification. In particular, we propose that both the relevance of inputs and the success of testing be described by means of *synchronous observers*. Synchronous observers are programs implementing acceptors of sequences. They are used in synchronous program verification to specify program properties and assumption about the environment.

A *test sequence generator* (in short, a *tester*) is built from these observers and the interface of the program under test. A run of the tester generates one input test sequence together with the corresponding outputs and the flag indicating if the test has passed.

The paper is organized as follows. Section 2 focuses on the problem of producing relevant input sequences. The solution we propose yields an algorithm which is the core of a tester. We introduce in section 3 the specification of oracles defining the expected behavior of the system. They may be used to check whether a test succeeds or fails. We present in section 4 a tool called Lurette, developed at Verimag following these principles. Finally, section 5 provides some ideas for future work.

Throughout the paper, we will use a simple example to illustrate our approach. Let us consider a program which is intended to regulate a physical value (for instance a temperature). It takes as input the numerical variable u (to be regulated), and has two Boolean outputs p(lus) and m(inus), which control the physical process (for instance a heater) producing u (see Fig. 1).

The regulator is intended to maintain u inside a given interval (e.g., $[10, 25]$). Clearly, the program alone cannot satisfy this property, which requires a cooperation between the program and its environment. In order to generate realistic test sequences, we have to know assumptions about the behavior of the heater. The most obvious is that the heater obeys the program: if the program sends the p (resp. m) command, the temperature is intended to increase (resp. decrease). Moreover, we can have information on the way the temperature may vary (e.g., bounds on its derivative).

2 Modeling the environment

2.1 General framework

A reactive program is intended to run in a given environment, the properties of which are partially known and should obviously be taken into account during the testing process: test cases submitted to the program must satisfy the known properties of the actual environment. This is what we call the *realism* constraint. Moreover, even if a test

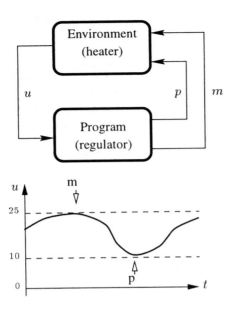

Figure 1: A regulator and its environment

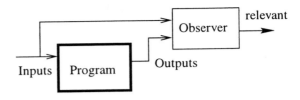

Figure 2: An observer of the relevance

case is realistic according to a given environment, it may be not *interesting*: the user usually has in mind a more or less precise goal. Distinguishing between *realism* and *interest* of test cases is surely relevant, from a methodologic point of view; however, technically speaking, there is no real difference: the test cases must satisfy constraints. In the following, we use the word *relevance* to talk about both *realism* and/or *interest*.

Examples of relevance constraints may be: "*two Boolean inputs are exclusive*", or "*a numerical input is always between 0 and 100*". More complex constraints deal with the temporal behavior of the variables: e.g., "*a Boolean input cannot be true at two consecutive instants*". Finally, the constraints on the environment may depend on the outputs of the considered program. As said before, in the heater example, the variation of the temperature (i.e., the environment) depends on the commands sent by the regulator program. Thus, from a general point of view, relevance constraints are any temporal properties involving the inputs/outputs of the considered reactive program.

2.1.1 Synchronous observers

The first problem addressed in this section is "how can the user describe such constraints?"

Our approach consists in using *synchronous observers*: observers have been proposed to describe properties in the framework of formal verification [22, 12]. A synchronous observer is a reactive program, taking as inputs the inputs/outputs of the program it observes, and computing a single Boolean output (Fig. 2) telling if the considered prop-

erty is satisfied. The property is considered to be violated as soon as the observer answers "false". In terms of temporal logic, the class of properties that can be expressed by such observers are the *safety properties*.

In our opinion, this description approach has several advantages:

- There is no need to learn a new and complex formalism (such as temporal logics): in some sense, if you can program you can express properties.

- Modeling the environment is sometimes as difficult as designing the program itself. Since the model is a program, it can be analyzed and tested in order to increase the confidence in its adequacy.

As for any deterministic reactive program, the abstract behaviors of both the observer and the program can be described in terms of state/transition systems. A state S of a reactive program is a valuation of all its internal variables. A fundamental feature of a deterministic program is that, at each instant t, its state S_t is completely determined by the sequence of inputs received before t. Moreover, both the current output o_t and the next state S_{t+1} are completely determined by the current input i_t and the current state S_t[1].

In the case of the synchronous composition of a program and its observer, a global state of the system is a pair $\langle S_P, S_\Omega \rangle$ consisting of a state of the program P under test, and a state of the observer Ω.

The structure of S_P is unknown, since P is considered as a black box. We just suppose that we are able to *initialize* the program, and to *execute* it step by step, by calling its transition procedure. Given a current value for the input, such a procedure computes the corresponding output and modifies the internal state of the program. In fact, we will often suppose that we have two distinct procedures, one for computing the output, and one for modifying the state. This assumption is a basic feature in the considered scope (i.e., for programs obtained by compiling synchronous languages such as Lustre 4.1). It can always be satisfyed, either by storing the state as a memory dump, or by retrieving the state by running again the program on the same input sequence. Moreover, this assumption is not crucial: it just

---

[1]i_t (resp. o_t) is actually the vector of input (resp., output) values of the program. In the following, we write "the input" and "the output" for "the vector of inputs" and "the output".

allows us to define more efficient algorithms that can "test" several inputs without changing the state of the program. The three primitives are:

- An *initialization procedure*, init$_P$, putting P in its initial state;

- An *output function* o = out$_P(i)$ providing the output o computed by the program in its current state for a given input i; we suppose that the program may compute its outputs without changing its state.

- A *next-state procedure*, next$_P(i)$, making P change to its next state according to a given input i.

On the contrary, we have a complete knowledge of the observer Ω. Its initial state is noted S_Ω^0, and its behavior is given by the two functions $\rho = \Omega_O(i, o, S_\Omega)$ computing its output (the value of the Boolean "relevant") and $S_\Omega' = \Omega_N(i, o, S_\Omega)$ computing its next state.

A *relevant test sequence* is a sequence of inputs $(i_1, i_2, \ldots, i_n)$ which results in a sequence of outputs $(\langle o_1, \rho_1 \rangle, \langle o_2, \rho_2 \rangle, \ldots, \langle o_n, \rho_n \rangle)$ of the pair $\langle P, \Omega \rangle$ such that: $\forall i,\ \rho_i = true$.

Intuitively, the observer behaves as a "language acceptor": the relevant sequences (i.e., the accepted language) are those for which the output of the observer is always *true*. Note that, in this way, we can only express *safety properties*.

Observers may be written in any formal language equivalent to the state/transition model. In our tool, we use the language Lustre. Before presenting a concrete example, we recall the useful aspects of this language.

2.1.2 Overview of the language Lustre

Lustre [10, 11] is a synchronous data-flow language. Each expression or variable denotes a *flow*, i.e., a function of discrete time (the positive natural numbers). The Lustre equation x = 2*y + z means: "*at each instant t, $x_t = 2 \times y_t + z_t$*". Lustre expressions are built from variables, constants (interpreted as constant flows), usual arithmetic and logical operators (considered as applying pointwise to flows), and two specific operators: the *previous* operator introduces a unit delay, and the *followed-by* operator is used to initialize flows. Let E and F be two Lustre expressions, then pre E and E -> F are Lustre expressions and we have at any instant $t > 1$:

- $(\text{pre E})_t = E_{t-1}$, while $(\text{pre E})_1$ is undefined.

- $(E \to F)_t = F_t$, while $(E \to F)_1 = E_1$.

For instance, the recursive Lustre equation "n = 0 -> pre n + 1" defines n as the flow of naturals "*0, 1, 2 ...*", and the equation "k = true -> not pre k" describes the oscillating Boolean flow "*true, false, true, false ...*".

A Lustre program is structured into *nodes*. A node defines its output parameters as functions of its input parameters. This definition is given by an unordered set of equations, possibly involving local variables. Once declared, a node may be instanciated in an expression, just like any predefined operator. For instance, the following node will be used to check whether a variable X belongs to an interval [LB, HB]:

```
node in_interval(X, LB, HB : real)
returns(S : bool);
let
    S = (X >= LB) and (X <= HB);
tel
```

2.1.3 Example: writing an observer in Lustre

Let us now consider more precisely the example of the heater. The inputs of our observer are the temperature u (the input of the program under test) and the commands plus and minus emitted by the program. The local variable heat_on defines at each instant the state of the heater, while the local variable dudt holds the slope of the temperature. We suppose that, in a realistic environment, the slope of the temperature may vary between 0 and 2 if the heater is on, and between -5 and 0 otherwise. Moreover, we wish to concentrate on "interesting" environments, where, e.g., the temperature is initially between 15 and 20, and where the heater is initially running. The Lustre code of such an observer may be:

```
node obs(u : real; plus, minus : bool)
returns (relevant : bool);
var heat_on : bool; dudt : real;
let
    heat_on = true -> if plus then true
                      else if minus then false
                      else pre heat_on;
    dudt = u - pre u;
    relevant = in_interval(u, 15, 20) ->
                if heat_on then
                    in_interval(dudt, 0, 2)
                else in_interval(dudt, -5, 0);
tel
```

For instance, the equation of heat_on states that it is initially true, and then it is set to true whenever plus is true, otherwise it is set to false whenever minus is true, otherwise it keeps its previous value. The slope dudt is defined to be always the difference between the current value and the previous value of u.

Note that such a Lustre program fits the state/transition model. Intuitively, the state variables of the program are the pre expressions; there is also an implicit state variable in the -> operator: E -> F can be interpreted as if init then E else F, where init$_1$ = *true*, and init$_t$ =

false $\forall t > 1$. All other variables (including the output) are then defined as pointwise functions of inputs and state variables.

2.2 Exploiting the observer

The problem addressed in this section is "how to exploit the observer in order to generate relevant test sequences?" The simplest solution consists in randomly generating input values and using the observer to reject those which are not relevant, as done by the following algorithm:

```
σ := ε; S_Ω := S_Ω^0; init_P;   initializations
repeat
  repeat
    i := Random;              select randomly an input value
    o := out_P(i);           get the output of the program
    ρ := Ω_O(i, o, S_Ω);     compute relevance
  until ρ = true;            stop when relevant
  σ := σ · i;                extend the sequence
  next_P(i);                 make the program progress
  S_Ω := Ω_N(i, o, S_Ω);     compute next state of the observer
until Length(σ) = MaxLength ;
```

MaxLength is a parameter of the algorithm allowing the length of the sequence to be limited.

This algorithm is quite ineffective (and rather stupid). For instance, if the observer has to check the equality of two real input values, the probability of randomly satisfying the constraint is null.

This is why we propose, rather, to transform the observer (which is an acceptor) into a *generator* of relevant input sequences. Intuitively, this consists in finding a solution of the equation $\Omega_O(i, \text{out}_P(i), S_\Omega) = true$. In order to solve this equation, we have to introduce some restrictions:

- Since the program is considered as a black box, the function out_P is unknown. So we cannot solve an equation involving this function. The first restriction is that the value of ρ at instant t may not depend on that of $o = \text{out}_P(i)$ at instant t. That is, the output function of the observer should be $\rho = \Omega_O(i, S_\Omega)$. However, the next state S'_Ω may still depend instantaneously on o: the transition function remains $S'_\Omega = \Omega_N(i, o, S_\Omega)$.

- With this first restriction, the problem is reduced to solving the equation: given a state S_Ω, find some i such that $\Omega_O(i, S_\Omega) = true$. Such a problem is in general undecidable (in particular because of numerical constraints). We restrict ourselves to a decidable subproblem: we will only consider equations involving logical operators and *linear constraints*.

In the sequel, we will note $i = \text{Choose}(\Omega, S_\Omega)$ a function which selects a solution of the equation for a given observer Ω and a given state S_Ω.

The general algorithm for test sequence generation is the following; it is parameterized by the **Choose** function (more precisely studied in §2.4) and by the constant **MaxLength**.

```
σ := ε; S_Ω := S_Ω^0; init_P;   initializations
repeat
  i := Choose (Ω, S_Ω);      select an input value
  o := out_P(i);             get the output of the program
  σ := σ · i;                extend the sequence
  next_P(i);                 make the program progress
  S_Ω := Ω_N(i, o, S_Ω);     compute next state of the observer
until Length(σ) = MaxLength ;
```

2.3 Example: generating a test sequence for the heater

Let us come back to the example of the heater. As it is written, the observer node (see §2.1.3) does not satisfy the first constraint: the value of `relevant` instantaneously depends on the program outputs `plus` and `minus` (via the local variable `heat_on`). We must slightly modify the observer by introducing delay operators in the definition of `heat_on`:

```
heat_on = true ->
          if (pre plus) then true
          else if (pre minus) then false
          else (pre heat_on);
```

The new observer is *not equivalent to the previous one*: the `heat_on` variable still represents the state of the heater, but with a delay. In practice, this restriction is not very important.

Here are some steps of a test sequence generation:

1st step. We start with the initial state of the observer where the implicit state variable `init` is true (i.e., we consider the left-hand argument of arrow operators). We have:
```
heat_on = true,
relevant = in_interval(u, 15, 20).
```
According to the definition of the node `in_interval`, `relevant` is then equivalent to the following constraint: $(u \geq 15) \wedge (u \leq 20)$. This constraint is linear and can be solved. More precisely, the **Choose** function builds an internal representation of the whole set of numerical solutions (in fact, a *polyhedron*) and randomly chooses a value in this set, for instance 18.2. Then, a step of the program is executed with this value; let us suppose it returns:
```
plus = minus = false.
```

2nd step. The internal state is now given by:
- `init` = `false` from now on,
- `pre u` = `18.2` is the value chosen at the previous step,

- `pre plus = pre minus = false` are the values returned by the program at the previous step,
- `pre heat_on = true` is the value computed at the previous step.

In this state (i.e., with these "pre" values) we have:
`heat_on = pre heat_on = true`, and
`relevant = in_interval(dudt, 0, 2)`
with `dudt = u - 18.2`. The numerical constraints are:
$(u - 18.2 \geq 0) \wedge (u - 18.2 \leq 2)$, i.e.
$(u \geq 18.2) \wedge (u \leq 20.2)$.
Suppose that the algorithm selects $u = 19.9$. Then, we run a step of the program and we obtain (for instance):
`plus = minus = false`.

3rd step. Now the state of the observer is given by:
- `pre u = 19.9`
- `pre plus = pre minus = false`
- `pre heat_on = true`

So we have:
`heat_on = true`, and
`relevant = in_interval(dudt, 0, 2)`.
The constraints are then: $(u \geq 19.9) \wedge (u \leq 21.9)$. Assume that $u = 21.5$ is randomly chosen, and that the program returns:
`plus = false, minus = true`.

4th step. The state is now given by: `pre u = 21.5, pre plus = false, pre minus = true, pre heat_on = true`.
So we have: `heat_on = false`, and `relevant = in_interval(dudt, -5, 0)`, which implies: $(u \geq 16.5) \wedge (u \leq 21.5)$; so we can choose $u = 17.4$, and so on ...

2.4 The Choose function

This technical section presents our realization of the Choose function more precisely.

For a given state S_t, the value of the observer's output ρ is given by a Boolean function ρ_t depending only on the current input values: $\rho_t(i) = \Omega_O(i, S_t)$. The input variables are either Boolean or numerical. Let I_B be the set of Boolean inputs, and I_N the set of numerical inputs.

The first step consists in clearly separating the Boolean and numerical parts of the function. We express the output as a purely Boolean function of I_B augmented by a (minimal) set C of auxiliary Boolean variables, each of which representing a linear constraint: $\rho_t : I_B \times C \to \mathbb{B}$. Each constraint variable c is defined as a function $c : I_N \to \mathbb{B}$ of the form:

$$\sum_{x \in I_N} \alpha_x x + \beta \bowtie 0$$

where $\bowtie$ is $>$ or $\geq$.

> **Example:** Let us consider the following Lustre definition:
>
> ```
> relevant = (X = 0) ->
>            if A then (B or (X > Y))
>            else (X + Y <= 10) and
>                 (X * pre Y < 12);
> ```
>
> where A and B are Boolean inputs and X and Y are numerical input. We suppose that we are in a non-initial state, where the value of `pre Y` is 3. The Choose function identifies 3 linear constraints:
>
> $$C_1 = (X > Y) \quad C_2 = (X + Y <= 10) \quad C_3 = (X < 4)$$
>
> The observer's output in the current state is interpreted as a Boolean function over A, B, C_1, C_2 and C_3:
>
> $$\rho_t = A \wedge (B \vee C_1) \vee \neg A \wedge C_2 \wedge C_3$$

The search for an input value such that ρ_t is true is performed in two steps: we concentrate first on the Boolean part, and then on the numerical constraints.

The Boolean choice is made as in [19]: we randomly choose a value for the variables $\langle I_B, C \rangle$ such that $\rho_t = true$. This choice is made using the Binary Decision Diagram (or bdd [1, 3]) of ρ_t. A bdd is a concise representation of the Shannon decomposition of a Boolean function.

> **Example:** The bdd of our example is shown below (more precisely, we have represented the Shannon tree of the function; in a bdd common sub-graphs are shared).
>
>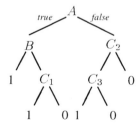
>
> Each node is labeled with a variable, its left-hand subtree corresponds to the "true" value of the variable, while the right-hand subtree corresponds to the false value. Leaves are either 1 (i.e., the always true function) or 0 (the always false function).
>
> Each path in the bdd leading to the 1 leaf gives a monomial satisfying the formula. Here, there are 3 such paths:
>
> $$A \wedge B \quad A \wedge \neg B \wedge C_1 \quad \neg A \wedge C_2 \wedge C_3$$

Finding a value for $\langle I_B, C \rangle$ is made by randomly choosing a path in the bdd leading to the leaf "1". This search is quite simple, but raises a problem of fairness: if the choice is made with a $1/2$ probability on each node of the bdd, the probability for each path to be chosen is of the form $1/2^n$. Those kinds of probabilities are intrinsically unfair: it may happen that the same path be chosen "half of the time" or, on the contrary, that a path be (almost) "never" chosen. In order to avoid this problem, we use classical techniques of weighted graphs.

The numerical choice. Once a Boolean monomial, satisfying the formula, has been selected, it directly provides the value of all Boolean inputs (if some variables do not appear in the corresponding monomial, their values are chosen randomly). Let us now focus on the numerical part: the selected monomial, reduced to the variables in C, involves a conjunction of linear constraints. The set of points (i.e., values of numerical inputs) satisfying such a linear system is a convex polyhedron, that can be efficiently represented and manipulated in terms of its frame (vertices and extremal rays [6, 16]).

If the polyhedron is empty, this means that the whole Boolean monomial was a bad choice (numerical unfeasibility): the corresponding leaf in the bdd is set to "0", and another monomial is randomly chosen. Otherwise, the polyhedron representation allows us to select a point using several heuristics: limit values (vertices or edges), or random selection inside the polyhedron.

Example: Suppose that the selected monomial is $\neg A \land C_2 \land C_3$. The value of A is imposed by this choice: $A = false$. The value of B is randomly selected, for instance $B = true$. Then, the induced linear constraint is: $(X + Y <= 10) \land (X < 4)$. The corresponding polyhedron is shown below. The polyhedron is in gray; the corresponding frame consists of one vertex $(4, 6)$ and two rays, represented as vectors with white arrows.

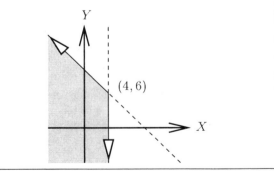

---

3 Analyzing outputs

The second important part of the testing process consists in using the test sequences to validate the program or to detect its faults. This involves running the program with each input sequence and analyzing the corresponding output sequence it produces. The later part requires the presence of an *oracle* which compares the outputs with the expected ones. This comparison may be more complex than a simple point-to-point equality. For instance, one may expect that, for a given input sequence, the value of some numerical output at some instant be in some interval, or that some Boolean output become true after some condition and within a given delay.

The oracle is often a human being, but, in many cases, it may be automatized by a program, which may be as "simple" as consulting association tables between inputs and outputs, or more complicated, involving temporal properties on the input/output sequence. We propose to describe the oracle using the synchronous observer technique.

3.1 The oracle as a synchronous observer

An oracle may always be viewed as a synchronous observer in the sense of section 2.1.1. Indeed, we can consider that it observes the input and output sequences and produces at each instant a Boolean answer `correct` stating that the two sequences satisfy the properties up to the current instant (Fig. 3).

Example: A typical property that can checked on the heater, is that the observed temperature u always remains between two given constants (for instance 10 and 25). The Lustre code of such an observer may be:

```
node oracle(u:   real; plus, minus:   bool)
returns (ok :   bool);
let
  ok = in_interval(u, 10, 25);
tel
```

This framework is very similar to that of the environment's observer, that will thereafter be called the *assertion*, in order to avoid confusion. In both cases, the observers express properties of "good" interactions between the program and its environment: the assertion (resp., the oracle) expresses what is under the responsibility of the environment (resp., of the program) in a satisfactory interaction.

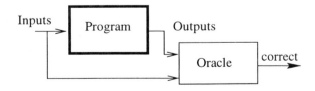

Figure 3: An oracle as a synchronous observer

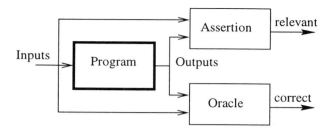

Figure 4: The complete framework of test generation

Another important remark is that there is no need to wait until the end of the test generation to start analyzing the correctness of the result: the assertion and the oracle may be put together in a unified framework (Fig. 4).

3.2 Using the oracle

The oracle and the assertion are very similar, but they are used quite differently in the testing process. We only need to execute the oracle, so there is no restriction on the way it is written. In particular, the `correct` output may depend instantaneously on both inputs and outputs of the program, and the function defining `correct` may be arbitrarily complicated.

In fact, the oracle is used in a way similar to that of the program under test: this observer can be viewed as a "black-box", and we only have access to it via primitives similar to those of the program interface:

- The procedure init_Γ puts the oracle in its initial state;
- The function $\text{out}_\Gamma(i, o)$ provides the `correct` output of the oracle in its current state for the values (i, o) of the program's inputs/outputs;
- The procedure $\text{next}_\Gamma(i, o)$ makes the oracle advance to its next state, according to the values of (i, o).

The use of the oracle is integrated in the generation algorithm; thus the correctness of the test can be checked during the test generation. The $out_\Gamma(i, o)$ function is computed at each step to check whether the current values meet the property; if they do not, the generation is stopped, and the current sequence is returned as a counter-example.

A more clever use the oracle observer is to try several input values at each step, exploiting the fact that both the program and the oracle may be called for their outputs, without modifying their internal states. In the following algorithm, we use a function $\text{SelectPoints}(\Omega, S_\Omega)$, returning a finite set of "notable" points in the underlying polyhedron (e.g., the vertices). All these points are "tested" and, if no counter-example is found, a random point is chosen to complete the sequence.

We obtain the following algorithm:

$$\begin{aligned}
&\sigma := \varepsilon;\ S_\Omega := S_\Omega^0;\ \text{init}_P;\ \text{init}_\Gamma; && \textit{Initializations} \\
&\text{repeat} \\
&\quad \text{for each } i && \textit{Test several} \\
&\quad \text{in SelectPoints}\ (\Omega, S_\Omega)\ \text{do} && \textit{... interesting points} \\
&\qquad o := \text{out}_P(i); \\
&\qquad \text{if } \neg\ \text{out}_\Gamma(i, o) && \textit{Stop with a} \\
&\qquad \text{then Stop}(\sigma \cdot i); && \textit{... counter-example} \\
&\quad \text{end}; \\
&\quad i := \text{Choose}\ (\Omega, S_\Omega); && \textit{Select an input to} \\
&&& \textit{... complete the sequence} \\
&\quad o := \text{out}_P(i); && \textit{Get the output} \\
&&& \textit{... of the program} \\
&\quad \text{if } \neg\ \text{out}_\Gamma(i, o) && \textit{Stop with a} \\
&\quad \text{then Stop}(\sigma \cdot i); && \textit{... counter-example} \\
&\quad \sigma := \sigma \cdot i; && \textit{Extend the sequence} \\
&\quad \text{next}_P(i); && \textit{Make the program progress} \\
&\quad \text{next}_\Gamma(i, o); && \textit{Make the oracle progress} \\
&\quad S_\Omega := \Omega_N(i, o, S_\Omega); && \textit{Compute next state} \\
&&& \textit{... of the observer} \\
&\text{until Length}(\sigma) = \text{MaxLength}\ ;
\end{aligned}$$

4 Putting it all together: the Lurette tool

A prototype tool, called Lurette, has been developed, following the ideas presented in this paper. The concrete realization of such a tool raises some technical problems which are sketched in this section.

4.1 Building a test generator

The program under test is a "C" file, supposed to implement a reactive program. In general, such programs are the "object code" obtained by the compilation of higher level languages such as Lustre. In order to use such a file, the Lurette tool must be able to extract a minimal set of informations:

- The names and types of its inputs/outputs, in order to "connect" them to the observers;
- The way of calling (or simulating the calls of) the procedures init_P, $\text{out}_P(i)$ and $\text{next}_P(i)$.

For the time being, Lurette is able to extract these informations from the C code generated by two different compilers:

- The academic *Lustre Compiler*, which is a free tool developed at Verimag;
- The *SCADE Code Generator*, which is an industrial tool distributed by the Verilog company. The SCADE environment is based on a graphical implementation of the Lustre language.

Note that this (small) list could be extended to any other language dedicated to reactive programs, given the convention used by its compilers. For instance, accepting code coming from other synchronous programming languages (like Esterel [2] or Signal [15]) would be easy since the academic compilers of those languages use (almost) common objet codes [21, 4].

Once the needed informations are extracted, the C program is compiled and linked with the *Lurette library*, which includes the Choose function, and bdd and polyhedron packages. The result is an executable *test generator* (or "tester"), dedicated to the given reactive program.

4.2   Calling a test generator

The tester implements the algorithm presented in section 3.2. It takes as input the description of the two observers (assertion and oracle), and the parameter giving the maximum length of the test sequence.

The assertion observer must be fully analyzed by the tester, so it must be written in a high level language with a well-defined semantics. The tester first makes some static analysis on this observer; in particular, it checks that its output does not depend instantaneously on the outputs of the tested program, and that all the involved numerical constraints are linear.

The oracle observer is dynamically loaded, instead of being linked with the tester. This way, the user can manage the test production by means of pairs assertion/oracle. The drawback of this choice is that the oracle must be interpreted instead of being compiled. So, even if not necessary in principle, this observer must be given (just like the assertion) in a high level language. However, the restrictions on the oracle are weaker: the output may instantaneously depend on both inputs and outputs of the program, and the code may be as complicated as needed. For the time being, both observers must be written either in Lustre or in SCADE.

5   Conclusion: experiment and future work

We have proposed a method to automatically generate and analyze test sequences for reactive deterministic systems. It is based on the use of synchronous observers to describe both the constraints on the environment (assertion) and the expected properties of the program under test (oracle). The main problem is to randomly generate inputs satisfying the assertion, which can be a complex temporal property, involving both Boolean and numerical constraints. This problem is solved by restricting ourselves to linear constraints, and by using bdds- and polyhedra-based techniques, which make the generation particularly efficient. At this time, we have got an experimental workbench (the

Lurette prototype) connected to both an academic language (Lustre) and an industrial design tool (SCADE).

An experiment has been made on a case study provided by the Schneider Electric company. The program, written using the SCADE environment (very close to Lustre) is interesting for several reasons:

- The scope of this application is very critical (control/command in a nuclear power plant).
- Its size is significant: it has 29 inputs, 50 outputs, and corresponds to a data-flow network of 1000 operators. Once compiled, it results in a C program of 2600 lines.

- Numerical aspects are important in the program. Moreover some numerical procedures are directly written in C, therefore it is (almost) impossible to perform formal verification.

We wrote three assertion observers in Lustre, according to the knowledge of the Schneider Electric engineers. Each observer is a data-flow network with about 130 operators and leads to an internal model of 40 Boolean constraints (i.e. bdds) on 40 Boolean variables, and 15 linear constraints on 9 numerical variables. We have observed that the test generator runs very fast: sequences of hundreds inputs were generated in a few seconds.

An oracle was written in Lustre: it observes about 20 safety properties, extracted from the software requirement specifications. Those properties were not violated by the generated test. Note that we did not expect to find bugs in this software, that is actually running in a nuclear power plant.

A lot of work remains to be done. The most urgent is to evaluate and increase the quality of test selection (function Choose). There are several, commonly accepted, criteria for evaluating the quality of a set of test sequences:

- The *test coverage* is a measure of the part of the code that is actually executed by the test sequences. Several kinds of measures can be used, generally based on the control structure of the code (exercised statements, condition–to–condition paths, etc..).
- The *mutation analysis* [8] consists in introducing slight changes in a program, and in measuring the ratio of such changes that are detected by a given set of test cases.

Another important goal is to take *test objectives* into account during the generation of the test. For the moment, we only deal with *invariant* constraints (i.e., safety properties): the input sequence is build step-by-step in such a way that the assertion remains true. An additional, much more difficult, criterion would be to drive the generation in such a way that a property eventually becomes true (liveness property). Such a goal-directed generation requires some knowledge about the program under test. We can at least exploit the test objective to avoid generating sequences that have no chance to reach the goal, whatever the behavior of the program. Another approach is to use the oracle as an approximation of the program.

References

[1] S. B. Akers. Binary decision diagrams. *IEEE Transactions on Computers*, C-27(6), 1978.

[2] G. Berry and G. Gonthier. The Esterel synchronous programming language: Design, semantics, implementation. *Science of Computer Programming*, 19(2):87–152, 1992.

[3] R. E. Bryant. Graph-based algorithms for boolean function manipulation. *IEEE Transactions on Computers*, C-35(8):677–692, 1986.

[4] C2A-SYNCHRON. The common format of synchronous languages – The declarative code DC. Technical report, Eureka-SYNCHRON Project, October 1995.

[5] P. Caspi, D. Pilaud, N. Halbwachs, and J. Plaice. LUSTRE: a declarative language for programming synchronous systems. In *14th ACM Symposium on Principles of Programming Languages, POPL'87*, München, January 1987.

[6] N. V. Chernikova. Algorithm for discovering the set of all solutions of a linear programming problem. *U.S.S.R. Computational Mathematics and Mathematical Physics*, 8(6):282–293, 1968.

[7] D. Clarke and I. Lee. Testing real-time constraints in a process algebraic setting. In *Proceedings of the 17th International Conference on Software Engineering*, 1995.

[8] R. A. DeMillo. Mutation analysis as a tool for software quality assurance. In *COMPSAC'80*, Chicago, October 1980.

[9] J.-C. Fernandez, C. Jard, T. Jéron, and C. Viho. Using on-the-fly verification techniques for the generation of test suites. In R. Alur and T. Henzinger, editors, *8th International Conference on Computer Aided Verification, CAV'96*, Rutgers (N.J.), 1996.

[10] N. Halbwachs, P. Caspi, P. Raymond, and D. Pilaud. The synchronous dataflow programming language LUSTRE. *Proceedings of the IEEE*, 79(9):1305–1320, September 1991.

[11] N. Halbwachs, F. Lagnier, and C. Ratel. Programming and verifying real-time systems by means of the synchronous data-flow programming language LUSTRE. *IEEE Transactions on Software Engineering, Special Issue on the Specification and Analysis of Real-Time Systems*, September 1992.

[12] N. Halbwachs, F. Lagnier, and P. Raymond. Synchronous observers and the verification of reactive systems. In M. Nivat, C. Rattray, T. Rus, and G. Scollo, editors, *Third Int. Conf. on Algebraic Methodology and Software Technology, AMAST'93*, Twente, June 1993. Workshops in Computing, Springer Verlag.

[13] D. Harel and A. Pnueli. On the development of reactive systems. In *Logic and Models of Concurrent Systems*, NATO Advanced Study Institute on Logics and Models for Verification and Specification of Concurrent Systems. Springer Verlag, 1985.

[14] L. J. Jagadeesan, A. Porter, C. Puchol, J. C. Ramming, and L. G. Votta. Specification-based testing of reactive software: Tools and experiments. In *Proceedings of the 19th International Conference on Software Engineering (ICSE '97)*, pages 525–537, Berlin - Heidelberg - New York, May 1997. Springer.

[15] P. LeGuernic, A. Benveniste, P. Bournai, and T. Gautier. SIGNAL, a data flow oriented language for signal processing. *IEEE-ASSP*, 34(2):362–374, 1986.

[16] H. LeVerge. A note on Chernikova's algorithm. Research Report 635, IRISA, February 1992.

[17] S. Morasca, A. Morzenti, and P. S. Pietro. Generating functional test cases in-the-large for time-critical systems from logic-based specifications. In *ISSTA 1996, ACM-SIGSOFT International Symposium on Software Testing and Analysis*, San Diego, CA, January 1996.

[18] M. Müllerburg, L. Holenderski, and O. Maffeis. Systematic testing and formal verification to validate reactive programs. *Software Quality Journal*, 4(4), 1995.

[19] F. Ouabdesselam and I. Parissis. Testing synchronous critical software. In *5th International Symposium on Software Reliability Engineering (ISSRE'94)*, Monterey, USA, November 1994.

[20] F. Ouabdesselam and P. Parissis. Testing safety properties of synchronous reactive software. In *7th International Software Quality Week*, San Francisco, May 1994.

[21] J. A. Plaice and J.-B. Saint. The LUSTRE-ESTEREL portable format. Unpublished report, INRIA, Sophia Antipolis, 1987.

[22] C. Ratel, N. Halbwachs, and P. Raymond. Programming and verifying critical systems by means of the synchronous data-flow programming language LUSTRE. In *ACM-SIGSOFT'91 Conference on Software for Critical Systems*, New Orleans, December 1991.

[23] J. Springintveld, F. Vaandrager, and P. D'Argenio. Testing timed automata. Technical Report CTIT 97-17, University of Twente, 1997. Also as CSI Report R9712, University of Nijmegen.

[24] P. Thevenod-Fosse, C. Mazuet, and Y. Crouzet. On statistical testing of synchronous data flow programs. In *1st European Dependable Computing Conference (EDCC-1)*, pages 250–67, Berlin, Germany, 1994.

Analyzing Non-deterministic Real-Time Systems with (max,+) Algebra [*]

Guillaume P. Brat
The University of Texas at Austin
Dept. of Electrical and Computer Engineering
Austin, Texas 78712, USA
gbrat@pine.ece.utexas.edu

Vijay K. Garg
The University of Texas at Austin
Dept. of Electrical and Computer Engineering
Austin, Texas 78712, USA
garg@ece.utexas.edu

Abstract

We describe a hierarchical technique that allows a class of non-deterministic timed Petri nets to be analyzed using the (max,+) algebra of periodic signals. We show that the timing and controllability analysis of such systems is possible via the use of (sup- and) inf-convolution operations within the (max,+) framework. We apply this technique to the verification of timing constraints in an intelligent structural control system and compare our technique to other modeling tools for real-time systems.

1. Introduction

There is a growing body of work showing the usefulness of the (max,+) algebra [1, 3, 4, 13, 7]) to analyze timed event graph models and deterministic real-time systems. The strongest criticism about these approaches is their failure to cope with non-deterministic systems. This work extends the (max,+) algebra of periodic signals [4] to the analysis of non-deterministic real-time systems.

We are aware of only one work that has applied the (max,+) algebra to non-deterministic, timed Petri nets [6]. In that work, the (max,+) algebra is applied to variable routing event graphs in which places are allowed to have many successors under the following restrictions. First, the function allocating tokens to the successors of a given place has to be deterministic. Second, places with multiple successors are not allowed within cycles. Our work aims at lifting those two restrictions, thus facilitating the analysis of non-deterministic systems.

We propose a hierarchical technique that replaces subnets with non-deterministic features by single places with delays that capture the non-deterministic behavior. The result of this reduction is a deterministic Petri net that is ana-

lyzable using the (max,+) algebra of signals. This technique applies to a class of real-time systems that are also analyzable by well-known modeling tools such as Modechart [18], HyTech [17], timed automata [16], Uppaal [19], KRONOS [10], SCR [15], CSR [14], PARAGON [2] and other techniques based on temporal logics. Due to length limitations, we limit our comparison to Modechart which is well known and has been compared to the other above-mentioned techniques.

There are two main advantages to the (max,+) algebra of signals over these existing techniques. First, unlike existing techniques, our algebra does not require the construction of large state spaces to prove timing properties. For example in Modechart, a state consists of a combination of the active modes at a given time and the values of the global variables at that time. This potentially leads to large graphs with sizes that are usually reduced by pruning based on the timing constraints in the modeled system. In the (max,+) algebra, the behavioral information of a system is captured by $N \times N$ closure matrices where N is the number of events in the modeled system. These matrices, which are built using an $O(N^3)$ algorithm, contain the necessary information to compute all time occurrences of all the events in the system. Moreover, this technique tolerates system decomposition which can further reduce the cost of the analysis [5]. These features make the (max,+) algebra of signals less prone to state explosion than other traditional techniques. Second, the analysis techniques available in the (max,+) algebra of signals include algorithms to compute optimal controllers for real-time discrete event systems (DES). Similar work can be done using symbolic methods within the framework of timed automata [11]. However, we are not aware of any efficient implementation of that work yet. Control synthesis is not demonstrated in this paper, but examples are given in [3, 5, 7, 8].

Unfortunately, there are some drawbacks to our technique. The (max,+) algebra of signals applies only to these systems in which events are eventually periodic. Therefore, our technique handles sporadic events in a manner similar

---

[*]supported in part by the NSF Grants ECS-9414780, CCR-9520540, TRW faculty assistantship award, a General Motors Fellowship, and an IBM grant

to the way sporadic tasks are handled in scheduling algorithms for periodic tasks; the timing behavior of a sporadic event has to be bound by periodic signals. Note also that HYTECH, SCR, and timed automata have been applied to the verification of hybrid systems, which is not possible at this time with our technique.

The organization of this paper is as follows. Section 2 explains our motivation for extending the current model. Section 3 provides background information on the (max,+) algebra and timed event graphs. Then, Section 4 describes our analysis technique, the role of convolution in capturing non-determinism and our reduction technique. Section 5 explains how to perform controllability analysis of non-deterministic systems. Section 6 describes our implementation. Section 7 details the analysis of an intelligent structural control system originally described in [12]. Finally, Section 8 presents our conclusions and future work.

2. Motivation

As a motivating example, we apply our analysis technique to an intelligent structural control system initially defined in [12] using Modechart for specification and Temporal CCS for verification. The goal of this system is to counteract the effects of earthquakes on buildings. It computes forces that need to be applied to a structure to counter its external excitations.

The system consists of three interacting components. A sensor monitors the state of the system (e.g., accelerations and displacement); a controller computes the appropriate forces needed to counter external excitations of the structure, and an actuator applies these forces to the structure. The algorithm described in [12] is a pulse control algorithm. Pulses are sent to the structure (via the actuator) to control the structure's excitation. The magnitude of each pulse is computed based on the state variables of the system. The pulse control algorithm provides satisfactory performance if the time between pulses is bounded by $T_0/8$ and $T_0/2$ where T_0 is the natural period of the structure (in this case, $T_0 = 290$ time units (t.u.)). Moreover, it is required in [12] that 135 t.u. elapse between two consecutive pulse calculations. The goal of the analysis is to ensure that both conditions are met.

Figure 1 illustrates the timed Petri net (PN) for the whole system. Time is associated with places, i.e, a token cannot participate in the enabling of the downstream transitions of a place until it has spent a minimum amount of time in that place. For readability, zero delays are omitted in Figure 1. Observe that the subnet for the controller (area delimited by dotted lines) includes some non-deterministic choices (transitions t_5 and t_{11} have the same upstream place). It also synchronizes with two deterministic subnets representing the sensor (area with evenly dashed lines) and the actuator

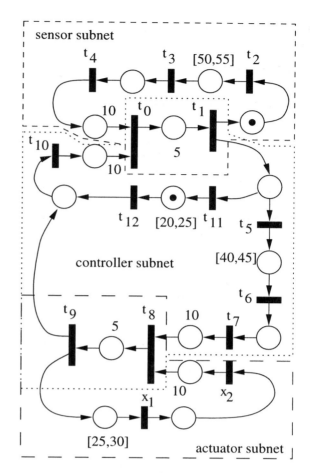

Figure 1. Timed Petri net for an intelligent structural control system

(area with extended dashed lines). The subnet between transitions t_5 and t_9 describes the control actions taken upon getting values from the sensors. The pulse control algorithm computes control values that are then transmitted to the actuator via a synchronization on transition t_8. If the minimum separation time (135 t.u.) constraint on successive calculations of control values is not satisfied, the values acquired by the controller are discarded and the controller goes through an internal updating phase; this is represented by the subnet between transitions t_{11} and t_{12}.

The (max,+) algebra of signals provides an interesting analysis framework to analyze the timing behavior of real-time DES that can be modeled by timed event graphs (TEG) [4, 5]. Unfortunately, TEG belong to a class of deterministic timed PN in which places have exactly one upstream transition and one downstream transition. This is not the case in our example and many other practical real-time systems. Therefore, in this work, we extend the (max,+) algebra of signals so that it applies to non-deterministic timed Petri nets (which we call non-deterministic timed event graphs).

3. Background

3.1 Introduction to (max,+) algebra

This section is a short introduction to the (max,+) algebra for DES. Further details can be found in [1, 7, 13].

Let $\varepsilon = -\infty$, $e = 0$, and Z be the union of the set of integers and $\{\varepsilon\}$. Let $+$ be the conventional addition on Z given that, for all $a \in Z$, $a + \varepsilon = \varepsilon + a = \varepsilon$. Define two binary operations in Z, $\oplus$ and $\otimes$, such that, for all $a, b \in Z$, $a \oplus b = \max(a, b)$ and $a \otimes b = a + b$. The $\oplus$ operator is commutative, associative, idempotent, and ε is its identity element. The $\otimes$ operator is associative, distributive over $\oplus$, e is its identity element, and ε is absorbing with respect to $\otimes$. $(Z, \oplus, \otimes)$ forms a dioid called the (max,+) algebra.

In [1, 7, 13], the (max,+) algebra has been applied to the modeling of DES. Systems are described by matrices (called delay matrices) that defines delays between events. Therefore, indices in delay matrices correspond to events in DES. Let x be the vector representing the time sequences corresponding to all (say N) events in a DES. Let v be a vector defining the earliest times at which the events can occur. Let A be the delay matrix. Then, x is a solution to the following set of equations:

$$x_i = \bigoplus_{1 \leq j \leq N} A_{ij} x_j \oplus v_i, \text{ where } 1 \leq i \leq N.$$

According to [9], this system of equations can be written as

$$x = Ax \oplus v,$$

the least solution of which is $A^* v$ where $A^* = \bigoplus_{k \geq 0} A^k$. The closure matrix, A^*, gives the maximum delay between transitions along infinite paths. The solution $x = A^* v$ gives the earliest times at which the transitions may fire.

We illustrate these concepts with a manufacturing process example (see Figure 2). Upon arrival ($x_1(k)$ is the time of the kth arrival), parts are first set-up in a machine queue, and then worked in order of arrival. Let $x_2(k)$ represent the departure of the kth part from the queue, and $x_3(k)$ its completion time. Each action (i.e, setting the part (s), working it (w), and resetting the machine (r)) takes a certain amount of time. Moreover, the part interarrival time is represented by a. Then, assuming that $r(0) = \varepsilon$, the system is described by the following equations.

$$
\begin{aligned}
x_1(k) &= x_1(k-1) + a(k-1) + v_1 \\
x_2(k) &= \max\{x_1(k) + s, x_3(k-1) + r(k-1)\} + v_2 \\
x_3(k) &= x_2(k) + w + v_3
\end{aligned}
$$

which translates into the following matrix form:

$$
\begin{pmatrix} x_1 \\ x_2 \\ x_3 \end{pmatrix} = \begin{pmatrix} a\gamma & \varepsilon & \varepsilon \\ s & \varepsilon & r\gamma \\ \varepsilon & w & \varepsilon \end{pmatrix} \begin{pmatrix} x_1 \\ x_2 \\ x_3 \end{pmatrix} \oplus \begin{pmatrix} v_1 \\ v_2 \\ v_3 \end{pmatrix}.
$$

The backshift operator, denoted by γ, is used when the value of a state variable at index k depends on the value of a state variable at index $k - 1$ (as in the expression for x_1 and x_2).

In [4, 5], we define a (max,+) algebra over the set $\mathcal{Z}$ of periodic signals. Signals are finite representations of ultimately periodic, infinite sequences. A signal is defined by two lists of integers capturing the transitory part (or aperiodic finite subsequence) and the period of a periodic sequence. Each element of these lists represents a time difference between two consecutive values of the sequence. For alternative finite representations of infinite sequences see [13]. For example, the sequence

$$X = \{1, 3, 6, 9, 12, \ldots\}$$

is represented by the signal

$$x = ((1, 2); (3)).$$

Note that symbols for signals are in lower case and that the corresponding sequences are the same symbols in upper case.

In [4, 5], delays can vary in a periodic manner over time. Therefore, they are also described by periodic signals (called delay signals). Delay signals are subject to the following restrictions: the sum of their periodic steps is equal to 0 and the values in their underlying sequences cannot be negative. The delay function associated with a given delay, say d, is written as δ_d. Delays in the manufacturing process example are not always constant. For example, on one hand, the interarrival time a varies over time. It alternates between five and seven. Therefore, the associated delay function is δ_a where $a = ((7); (-2, 2))$, which corresponds to the delay sequence $A = \{7, 5, 7, 5, \ldots\}$. On the other hand, The setting time s is constant and equal to one. Therefore, the corresponding delay function is δ_s where $s = ((1); (0))$, which corresponds to $S = \{1, 1, 1, 1, \ldots\}$. The other delays are characterized by $w = ((4); (0))$ and $r = ((); (4, -3, 0, 0, 0))$. The effect of γ on a signal is to increment all indices by one, e.g., $\gamma[((1, 2); (3))] = ((\varepsilon, 1, 2); (3))$. In the manufacturing process example, the equations yield the sequence

$$X_3 = \{5, 10, 17, 22, 29, 37, 42, 47, 53, 58, 66, 71, 77, \ldots\}$$

which represents the times of occurrence for the event x_3. The corresponding signal is

$$x_3 = ((5, 5, 7); (5, 7, 8, 5, 5, 6, 5, 8, 5, 6)).$$

3.2 Timed event graphs

This section gives a brief description of timed event graphs; further details can be found in [1, 20] among others.

An event graph is a Petri net in which places have only one upstream transition and one downstream transition. A timed event graph (TEG) is an event graph in which enabling delays are associated with places. An enabling delay, or simply a delay, is the minimum amount of time (possibly zero) a token has to spend in a place before it can participate in the enabling of the downstream transition of the place. TEGs can be used to describe the temporal behavior of DES. Transitions model events. The temporal behavior is captured by a delay matrix. The entries of these matrices are the delays specified in the places. Therefore, the delay matrix of the manufacturing process example corresponds to the TEG in Figure 2. In our terminology, a place with-

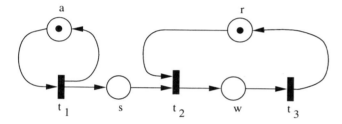

Figure 2. Manufacturing process example.

out incoming (outgoing) arcs is a source (sink respectively) place. Similarly, a transition without incoming (outgoing) arcs is a source (sink respectively) transition.

4. Non-deterministic Timed Event Graphs

This section describes how (max,+) algebra analysis techniques can be extended to a class of timed PNs with non-deterministic constructs.

Our strategy is quite simple. We identify the smallest subnet encompassing the scope of some non-deterministic constructs and replace it by a single place. The delay of this place reflects the possibility of selecting any alternative paths in the replaced non-deterministic subnet. This is done in two steps. First, reduce each alternative path to a single place (Section 4.2). Second, combine all these "alternative" places into a single place using some convolution on their delays (Section 4.3). First, we define what class of Petri nets can be analyzed with our technique.

4.1. Model definition

We now define our non-deterministic extension to TEGs. Figure 3 representing the intelligent structural control system without the actuator illustrates our definitions.

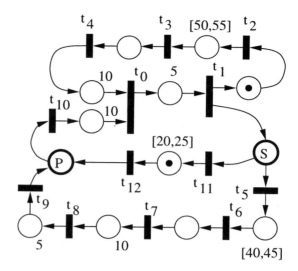

Figure 3. Non-deterministic TEG for the intelligent control system

Definition 1 (Balanced Acyclic TEG)
A balanced, acyclic TEG, say B, is a TEG without any directed cycles such that

- *B has one source transition (called $sourcetr(B)$) and one sink transition (called $sinktr(B)$), and*

- *any two paths between any two transitions have the same number of tokens.*

In Figure 3, there are two balanced, acyclic TEGs. The first one is the path between transitions t_{11} and t_{12}. The second one is defined by the path from transition t_5 to transition t_9.

Definition 2 (Alternative TEG)
An alternative TEG consists of

- *a source place and a sink place with no initial tokens,*

- *a finite set $\mathcal{B}$ of balanced acyclic TEGs ($\mathcal{B} = \{B_1, B_2, \ldots, B_n\}$), and*

- *for all $B_i \in \mathcal{B}$, there are arcs from the source place to $sourcetr(B_i)$ and from $sinktr(B_i)$ to the sink place.*

In Figure 3, there is one alternative TEG (corresponding to most of the controller) whose sink and source places (shown in bold) are named P and S.

Definition 3 (Non-Deterministic TEG)
A non-deterministic TEG is a PN that can be derived from a TEG by finite applications of the following rules:

- *pick a place, and*

- *replace it by an alternative TEG.*

The Petri net described in Figure 3 is a non-deterministic TEG.

Observe that the non-deterministic behavior started in the source place of an alternative TEG ends at its sink place. The absence of connectivity between balanced, acyclic TEGs of a same alternative TEG is motivated by the desire to avoid deadlocks. If a deadlock occurs within an alternative TEG, it results from a deadlock within one of its balanced, acyclic TEGs, and not from interactions between the balanced, acyclic TEGs.

4.2. Reduction of balanced acyclic TEGs

This subsection studies the reduction of TEGs to nets with a single source (sink) transition and a single place with a, possibly, non-zero delay. As described in [4], star-delay operations have to be used to analyze cycles in TEGs. Since the computation of a star-delay operation depends on its input signal, subnets with cycles are not reducible, hence they are excluded from the definition of acyclic TEGs.

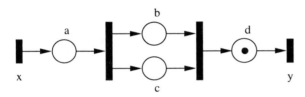

Figure 4. Example of an acyclic TEG

Consider an acyclic TEG with a single source transition and a single sink transition. The structure of this TEG consists of the places, and transitions composing the graph as well as the initial tokens present in places. Such a net can be completely described by a (max,+) expression consisting of max, delay and backshift operations. For example, the net displayed in Figure 4 can be described by the following (max,+) expression where x and y are the input and output signals respectively and a, b, c, and d are delay signals:

$$y = \delta_d \gamma (\delta_b \oplus \delta_c) \delta_a [x]$$

Definition 4 (Reducibility)
An acyclic TEG with a single source transition x and a single sink transition y is reducible if its (max,+) expression can be written

$$y = \delta_a \gamma^i [x] \qquad (1)$$

where a is a delay and i is a positive integer.

The interpretation of $y = \delta_a \gamma^i [x]$ is that of a net with a single source transition x, a single sink transition y, and a single place with delay signal a and i initial tokens. Any expression of this form is called a primitive form.

Theorem 1 *Any balanced acyclic TEG is reducible.*

Proof:
First, observe that the composition of two delay operations can be reduced to a single delay operation, i.e., let d and d' be two delay signals and x be an input signal,

$$\delta_d(\delta_{d'}[x]) = \delta_{d \odot d'}[x]$$

where $d \odot d' = \delta_d[d']$.

As shown in [5], for any delay signal d and any input signal x,

$$\gamma \delta_d[x] = \delta_{(\gamma d)}[\gamma(x)].$$

Therefore, the composition of delays and backshift can be reduced to a primitive form. Also,

$$\forall x, y \in \mathcal{Z}, x \oplus y \in \mathcal{Z}, \text{ and}$$

$$\forall x, y \in \mathcal{Z}, \gamma(x \oplus y) = \gamma(x) \oplus \gamma(y).$$

Therefore, the composition of delays and backshift as operands of a maximization can be reduced to a primitive form as long as the numbers of backshifts in the operands match.

∎

Note that if the numbers of backshifts are different in operands of a maximization, then the expression cannot be reduced to a primitive form. Consider the expression

$$y = (\delta_a \gamma \oplus \delta_b)[x]$$

where a and b are two delay signals and x is an input signal. Let A, B, and X be the underlying sequences of a, b, and x respectively. For $k \geq 2$,

$$
\begin{aligned}
Y[k] &= (A[k] + X[k-1]) \oplus (B[k] + X[k]) \\
&= (A[k] + X[k-1] - X[k] + X[k]) \oplus \\
&\qquad (B[k] + X[k]) \\
&= ((A[k] + X[k-1] - X[k]) \oplus B[k]) + X[k]
\end{aligned}
$$

This shows that $Y[k]$ can not be obtained by adding a delay, independent of X, to $X[k]$. Therefore, this expression is not reducible. For example, if there is an initial token in place b, but not in place c, in the acyclic net in Figure 4, then the net is not reducible.

4.3. Convolution of primitive forms

In this section, we assume that balanced, acyclic TEGs are reduced to single places each characterized by a delay as shown in the previous section.

We now define the cumulative delay $C(d, i)$ at index i of a delay d (with underlying sequence D) as

$$C(d, i) = \sum_{j=1}^{i} D[j].$$

$C(d, i)$ is the cumulative sum of all the delays incurred after i tokens have passed through the place of delay d. We call cumulative delay sequence $C(d)$ the sequence $\{C(d, 1), C(d, 2), \ldots\}$. It is equivalent to the sequence obtained by applying a delay sequence to a zero input signal. For example, consider the delay signal

$$a = ((7); (-2, 2))$$

in the manufacturing example. Its underlying delay sequence is

$$A = \{7, 5, 7, 5, 7, 5, \ldots\}.$$

The associated cumulative sequence is given by

$$C(a) = \{7, 12, 19, 24, 31, 36, \ldots\}.$$

Our goal is to eventually replace every alternative TEG by a single place. To characterize the delay of such a place, we examine the cumulative delay sequence within an alternative TEG. Let d be the delay signal associated with an alternative TEG (consisting of two balanced, acyclic TEGs in their primitive forms consisting of delay signals d_1 and d_2) once it has been reduced to a single place. The convolutive sum $C(d, i, j)$, where

$$C(d, i, j) = C(d_1, j) + C(d_2, i - j),$$

is the cumulative delay at index i when the alternative delay d_1 has been selected j times while the first i tokens passed through the alternative TEG. $C(d, i, j)$ is the result of applying one of all the possible decision strategies in the place creating the non-determinism. Obviously, $C(d, i)$ is a function of the $C(d, i, j)$. Since $C(d, i, j)$ is under a convolutive form, we view $C(d, i)$ as the result of applying some type of convolution on the cumulative sums of the delays of the balanced, acyclic TEGs of the alternative TEG. In fact, Section 5 shows that the inf-convolution and the sup-convolution (obtained by taking the inf, and sup respectively, of the $C(d, i, j)$ at each index i) are two convolutions that play a critical role in computing the controllability of lower and upper bound specifications.

Let $\oslash$ be a commutative, associative operator on integers such that the traditional arithmetic addition distributes over $\oslash$, e.g., min or max. The operator $\oslash$ defines a decision function that determines a path (hence, a delay signal d) in the alternative TEG. The cumulative delay sequence $C(d)$ in the alternative TEG once it is reduced to the delay d from the alternative delays is defined as follows. For any $i \geq 1$,

$$C(d, i) = \oslash_{j=1}^{i} C(d, i, j).$$

The elements D, for $i \geq 1$, of the delay sequence D are given by the following equations:

$$D[1] = C(d, 1)$$
$$D[i] = C(d, i) - C(d, i - 1), \text{ for } i > 1$$

The signal d is easily derived from the sequence D as described in [5].

For example, the delay signal $d_1 = ((4); (2, -2))$ has for delay sequence $D_1 = \{4, 6, 4, 6, 4, 6, \ldots\}$ which yields the cumulative sequence

$$C(d_1) = \{4, 10, 14, 20, 24, 30, \ldots\}.$$

Similarly, the delay signal $d_2 = ((5); (1, -1))$ has for delay sequence $D_2 = \{5, 6, 5, 6, 5, 6, \ldots\}$ which yields the cumulative sequence

$$C(d_2) = \{5, 11, 16, 22, 27, 33, \ldots\}.$$

The cumulative delay sequence of the signal d corresponding to the inf-convolution of d_1 and d_2 is computed by taking the inf-convolution of $C(d_1)$ and $C(d_2)$. Thus, $C(d, 1) = \min\{4, 5\}$, $C(d, 2) = \min\{10, 4 + 5, 11\}$, $C(d, 3) = \min\{14, 10 + 5, 4 + 11, 16\}$, and so on. Therefore, it yields

$$C(d) = \{4, 9, 14, 19, 24, 29, \ldots\}$$

which corresponds to the delay sequence $D = \{4, 5, 5, \ldots\}$ and the delay signal $d = ((4, 1); (0))$.

We now establish the fact that the convolution of periodic signals results in a periodic signal. First, define a pure periodic delay signal as a signal whose underlying sequence has no transitory subsequence (hence, in the signal form, the list for the transitory sequence contains only one step).

Lemma 1 *The convolution of two pure periodic delay signals results in a periodic delay signal.*

Proof: Let $\oslash$ be a commutative and associative operator such that the traditional arithmetic addition distributes over $\oslash$. Without loss of generality, consider two periodic signals x and y the periods of which are of the same length m. Recall that the sum of the periodic steps of a periodic delay signal is zero. Since x and y are pure periodic signals, they are fully characterized by the first m elements of their underlying sequence. Let $P_x = \sum_{i=1}^{m} X[i]$ and $P_y = \sum_{i=1}^{m} Y[i]$.

As shown above,

$$C(d, k) = \oslash_{j=1}^{k} C(d, k, j).$$

It can be shown that, for any $j, k \geq 1$,

$$\text{either,} \quad C(d, k + m, j) = C(d, k, j) + P_x$$
$$\text{or,} \quad C(d, k + m, j) = C(d, k, j) + P_y.$$

Therefore,

$$C(d, k + m) = C(d, k) + P_x \oslash P_y. \qquad (2)$$

Since $P_x \oslash P_y$ is constant, the cumulative delay sequence $C(d)$ is periodic, and so are the delay sequence D and the signal d.

■

Theorem 2 *The convolution of two periodic delay signals results in a periodic delay signal.*

Proof: The proof is similar to the proof of Lemma 1. Let $\oslash$ be a commutative and associative operator such that the traditional arithmetic addition distributes over $\oslash$. Assume, without loss of generality, that the signals, say x and y, are homogeneous, i.e., the lengths of their transitory sequence are equal (to n) and the lengths of their period are also equal (to m). An algorithm to homogenize signals is given in [5].

It can be shown that, for any index $k > 2n + m$, the equality (2), in the proof of Theorem 2, holds again. Therefore, the value of the $\oslash$-convolution of x and y at index k is periodic for any $k > 2n + m$.

■

5. Controllability Analysis

Using the (max,+) algebra framework, the controllability of a system can be analyzed. A controllable event is defined to be an event whose occurrences can be delayed (but not hastened). An uncontrollable event is an event that cannot be hastened nor directly delayed. The only means of delaying an uncontrollable event is to delay a controllable event that causes the delay of the uncontrollable event. Controllable events can be specified using a diagonal matrix I_c (of equal size to the transition matrix) in which diagonal elements are either ε when the event is uncontrollable or e when the event is controllable. The remaining elements of I_c are equal to ε.

If y is a vector of signals defining the control signals for all events in a system, $I_c y$ defines the valid control signals (a control signal is valid if it applies to a controllable event). Moreover, if A is the transition matrix of the system and v the initial firing times for every transition, then $A^*(I_c y \oplus v)$ represents the earliest occurrence times of the events when the system is under the control law defined by I_c and y. Thus, if y is a vector of signals specifying the desired timing behavior of the events in the system, one can compute the controllability of y with respect to the system defined by the matrices A and I_c and the initial vector v by comparing the value of $A^*(I_c y \oplus v)$ to y.

5.1. Lower and upper bound specifications

Assume that y is a vector defining a lower bound specification, i.e., the occurrence times of the events in the system are greater or equal to y. Then,

$$A^*(I_c y \oplus v) \geq y$$

is a controllability test for the lower bound specification y.

Denote the inf-convolution operator by $\sqcap$. Since $\sqcap$ provides the smallest value of all the possible convolutions, it is trivial to show that, for any convolution operator $\oslash$,

$$A_\oslash^*(I_c y \oplus v) \geq A_\sqcap^*(I_c y \oplus v)$$

where $A_\oslash$ is the transition matrix resulting from applying $\oslash$ to the delays of the non-deterministic subnet. Therefore, a lower bound specification y is controllable, if

$$A_\sqcap^*(I_c y \oplus v) \geq y.$$

The convolution $\sqcup$ defined by the sup operator can also be used to compute the controllability of an upper bound specification. Given an upper bound specification y,

$$A_\sqcup^*(I_c y \oplus v) \leq y.$$

6. Implementation

Our goal is to automate all phases of the analysis process. We are therefore extending our tool (maxplus), which implements the (max,+) algebra of periodic signals with algorithms to compute convolution operations on delay signals, an algorithm to reduce a single input-single output, acyclic TEG to a single delay, and an algorithm to check the reducibility of a subnet

6.1. Convolution operations

It is easy to derive from the proof of Lemma 1 that the length of the period of the signal resulting from the convolution of two pure periodic signals is the lowest common multiple of the lengths of their period. Moreover, the length of the transitory sequence is bounded by the size of the period. Therefore, we can derive the algorithm in Figure 5 where m is the common length of the periods of the two input signals, and *trans* and *prev* are integer arrays of size m. The function *convolutivesum* takes for inputs two periodic signals and an index. It computes the convolutive sums of the signals at the specified index. The complexity of *convolutivesum* is $O(k)$ where k is a given index. Therefore, the complexity of *convolution* is $O(m^2)$.

Using results from the proof of Theorem 2, the *convolution* algorithm can be modified to handle any periodic delay

```
convolution(signal x,y): signal z
{   1. previous := 0; cumul := 0;
    2. for i from 1 to 2m do
        current := convolutivesum(x,y,i) - previous;
        if (i ≤ m)
            trans[i] := current - cumul;
            cumul += trans[i];
        if (i > m)
            per[i] := current - cumul;
            cumul += per[i];
        previous += current;
    3. z := (trans;per); }
```

Figure 5. Algorithm for the convolution of periodic signals

signal without changing its overall complexity: make *trans* an integer array of size $2n$, *per* an integer array of size m, and change the tests of both *if* statements to reflect those new bounds. Still, the modified algorithm does not handle the presence of initial tokens in balanced, acyclic TEGs.

Assume that there are two balanced, acyclic TEGs corresponding to two signals x and y of underlying sequences X and Y respectively that contain n_x and n_y initial tokens respectively. It is obvious that the first $n_x + n_y$ steps of the signal z corresponding to the convolution of x and y have to result from the convolution of the first n_x steps of x and the first n_y steps of y. The remaining steps can be computed by replacing the first n_x steps of x by their sum and respectively the first n_y steps of y by their sum, and by computing the convolution of the modified signals.

6.2. Reducibility of balanced, acyclic TEGs

There are two important steps in the reduction of balanced, acyclic TEGs to single places. First, one needs to check if the subnets are reducible (i.e., no loops and a balanced number of tokens in concurrent paths). Second, the reduction itself has to take place. This can be performed by using the algebraic simplification rules discussed in Section 4.2. We now describe an algorithm to check the reducibility of a balanced, acyclic TEG.

Detecting the presence of a cycle within a subnet is an easy operation that can be performed in $O(|V| + |E|)$ operations using a depth-first search algorithm. E is the set of edges in the subnet, and V is the set of vertices. Detecting an unbalanced number of tokens in concurrent activities can also be performed using a depth-first search algorithm (with $O(|V| + |E|)$) complexity) given in Figure 6. The idea is as follows. Consider the weighted, directed graph where

- the vertices are the transitions of the acyclic TEG,

- there is an arc from a vertex to another if there is a place connecting the corresponding transitions in the TEG, and

- the weight $w(a)$ of that arc a is the number of tokens initially present in that place.

Assume that *Cnt* is an array of integers, whose elements are initialized to -1, indexed by the vertices of the graph. Define the function $w : V \times V \to N$ (where N is the set of natural number) that associates its weight to an arc. Algorithm 6

```
reducible(vertex u, int tokens): boolean
{
    1. if (Cnt[u] = -1)
        then Cnt[u] := tokens;
            for each vertex v successor of u do
                if not reducible(v, Cnt[u]+w(u,v));
                then return FALSE;
    2. if (Cnt[u] ≠ tokens)
        then return FALSE;
    3. return TRUE;
}
```

Figure 6. Algorithm for checking reducibility

starts with the source transition and 0 as arguments.

7. Example

In this section, we apply our analysis technique to the intelligent structural control system example defined in [12]. Our goal is to verify that the time between control pulses is bounded by $T_0/8$ and $T_0/2$ where T_0 is 290 t.u. and that consecutive calculations of the actuator values are separated by at least 135 t.u.

Figure 3 illustrates the non-deterministic TEG for the sensor and the controller. The actuator needs to synchronize with the controller. However, the timing constraints in the actuator net are such that it cannot affect the behavior of the controller. Therefore, we need not model the actuator when analyzing the timing of the sensor and the controller. This makes all the balanced, acyclic TEGs reducible. Note that all timing values are integer constants that correspond to constant signals. The constant c corresponds to the signal $((c); (0))$. Intervals represent ranges of possible delays.

The balanced, acyclic TEG for the calculation of the pulse can be reduced to a single place with a cumulative delay ranging from 55 to 60 t.u. However, the resulting PN is still not analyzable. The alternative TEG must be replaced by a single place whose delay d is the result of some convolution operation on the delays in the balanced, acyclic TEGs. Once this is done, we obtain the reduced TEG in Figure 7.

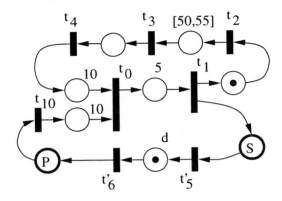

Figure 7. Reduced TEG for the intelligent structural control system

Using the inf- and sup-convolutions to compute lower and upper bounds on the timing behavior in the alternative TEG, we find that

$$((20); (0)) \leq d \leq ((25, 35); (0))$$

which yields

$$((0, 85); (65)) \leq t_6' \leq ((0, 130); (75)).$$

The lower bound $(((0, 85); (65)))$ corresponds to a decision function in place S that always selects t_{11} as its downstream transition. Since the goal is to generate pulses, t_5 should be selected at some point in time. Therefore, inf-convolution is not a desirable decision function in S. Moreover, the upper bound $(((0, 130); (75)))$ shows that the constant selection of t_5 as the output of S results in a separation time between calculations as low as 75, which violates our requirements. Clearly, deciding the output of S requires some control.

Computing a decision function for S cannot be done automatically in this case. However, we can observe that the sum of the minimum cycling time in the updating cycle (65) and the minimum cycling time in the pulse calculation cycle (70) is 135. Therefore, a decision function alternating between the updating cycle (65 to 70 t.u. because of the synchronization with the sensor cycle) and the calculation cycle (70 to 75 t.u.) of the controller should result in a separation time of at least 135 t.u. between successive pulse calculations. Let u and c be the delay signals (and U and C their underlying sequences) in the updating cycle and the calculation cycle respectively of the controller. Define delay d such that its underlying sequence D is as follows:

$$\forall i > 0 : D[i] = \begin{cases} U[(i + 1)/2] & \text{if } i \text{ is odd} \\ C[i/2] & \text{otherwise} \end{cases}$$

Then,

$$d \in [((20); (35, -35)), ((25); (35, -35))]$$

which yields the following bounds on D:

$$\{20, 55, 20, 55, \ldots\} \leq D \leq \{25, 60, 25, 60, \ldots\}.$$

Using the new definition of delay d, we obtain

$$((0, 120); (35, 100)) \leq t_6' \leq ((0, 130); (40, 105))$$

Passes through the calculation loop correspond to the even-indexed events. Therefore, the separation time between two calculations is always greater than or equal to 135.

We now show how to compute the timing occurrences of events in the actuator. Figure 8 illustrates the TEG for the actuator. The synchronization between the controller and the actuator is handled as follows: the actuator is modeled as a stand-alone TEG and its synchronization with the controller via a non-zero initial value for transition x_3. In gen-

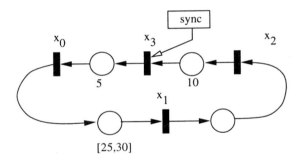

Figure 8. Event graph for the actuator of the intelligent structural control system

eral, initial values are constant, and therefore, they impact only the first values of the event signals. However, as shown in [4] and Section 5, non-constant initial values serve as synchronization points at all indices in the event signals. An initial value v for an event signal x guarantees that $x \geq v$. Therefore, making the signal corresponding to transition t_8 the initial value for transition x_3 actually enforces the synchronization between the controller and the actuator. Let A be the transition matrix of the actuator subnet. Let the initial vector v be such that $v[0] = v[1] = v[2] = e$ and $v[3] = t_8$. Then, the event signals for x_i ($i = 0, \ldots 3$) are given by A^*v.

The value of transition t_8 can be computed from the value of transition t_6'. Let T_8 be the underlying sequence corresponding to transition t_8. Then,

$$\forall i > 0 : T_8[i] = T_6'[2i] - 5.$$

Using this result, we find that

$$x_1 = [((75); (135)), ((80); (145))]$$

We can now check the correctness of the system. Given that X_1 is the underlying sequence of signal x_1, the system is correct if the following inequation is verified:

$$\forall i > 0 : T_0/8 \leq X_1[i+1] - X_1[i] \leq T_0/2.$$

Since $T_0 = 290$, the inequation becomes

$$\forall i > 0 : 37 \leq X_1[i+1] - X_1[i] \leq 145.$$

Observe that the value $X_1[i+1] - X_1[i]$ is the value of the elements (or steps) in the period and transitory sequence of signal x_1. Therefore, the proof of correctness is reduced to verifying that the value of any step in signal x_1 is between 37 and 145, which is the case.

8. Conclusions

In this work, we have illustrated how the (max,+) algebra of signals can be used to verify the timing correctness of real-time discrete event systems. In doing so, we introduced a hierarchical analysis technique that allows the use of the (max,+) algebra on non-deterministic Petri nets. This allowed us to model and verify the correctness of an intelligent structural control system [12]. Future work will focus on extending the analysis capabilities for non-deterministic systems and on defining composition techniques to further reduce the cost of analysis.

References

[1] F. Baccelli, G. Cohen, G. Olsder, and J.-P. Quadrat. *Synchronization and Linearity: an Algebra for Discrete Event Systems*. John Wiley and Sons, 1992.

[2] H. Ben-Abdallah, I. Lee, and J.-Y. Choi. A graphical language with formal semantics for the specifications and analysis of real-time systems. In *Proceedings of the 16th IEEE Real-Time Systems Symposium*, pages 276–286, Raleigh Durham, North Carolina, December 1995.

[3] G. P. Brat and V. K. Garg. A (max,+) algebra for non-stationary periodic timed discrete event systems. In *Proceedings of the International Workshop on Discrete Event Systems*, pages 237–242, Cagliari, Italy, August 1998.

[4] G. P. Brat and V. K. Garg. A max-plus algebra of signals for the supervisory control of real-time discrete event systems. In *Proceedings of the 9th Symposium of the International Federation of Automatic Control on Information Control in Manufacturing*, Nancy-Metz, France, June 1998.

[5] G. P. Brat and V. K. Garg. A max-plus algebra of signals for the supervisory control of real-time discrete event systems. Technical Report TR-PDS-1998-001, Department of Electrical and Computer Engineering, University of Texas at Austin, USA, January 1998.

[6] D. D. Cofer and V. K. Garg. A timed model for the control of discrete event systems involving decisions in the max-plus algebra. In *Proceedings of the 31st IEEE Conference on Decision and Control*, pages 3363–3368, Tuczon, Arizona, 1992.

[7] D. D. Cofer and V. K. Garg. A max-algebra solution to the supervisory control problem for real-time discrete event systems. In *Lecture Notes in Control and Information Sciences 199: 11th International Conference on Analysis and Optimization of Systems*, pages 283–289, 1994.

[8] D. D. Cofer and V. K. Garg. Supervisory control of real-time discrete event systems using lattice theory. In *Proceedings of the 33rd IEEE Conference on Decision and Control*, pages 978–983, December 1994.

[9] G. Cohen, P. Moller, J.-P. Quadrat, and M. Viot. Dating and counting events in discrete event systems. In *Proceedings of the 25th IEEE Conference on Decision and Control*, pages 988–993, 1986.

[10] C. Daws and S. Yovine. Two examples of verification of multirate timed automata with KRONOS. In *Proceedings of the 16th IEEE Real-Time Systems Symposium*, pages 66–75, Pisa, Italy, Dec. 1995.

[11] E. Asarin, O. Maler, and A. Pnueli. Symbolic controller synthesis for discrete and timed systems. In A. N. P. Antsaklis, W. Kohn and S. Sastry, editors, *Hybrid Systems II*, pages 1–20. LNCS 999, Springer-Verlag, 1995.

[12] W. M. Elseaidy, R. Cleaveland, and J. W. B. Junior. Verifying an intelligent structural control system: A case study. In *Proceedings of the 15th IEEE Real-Time Systems Symposium*, pages 271–275, San Juan, Puerto Rico, December 1994.

[13] S. Gaubert. *Théorie Linéaire des Systèmes dans les Dioïdes*. PhD thesis, Ecole des Mines de Paris, Paris, 1992.

[14] R. Gerber, I. Lee, and A. Zwarico. Communicating Shared Resources: A model for distributed real-time systems. In *Proceedings of the 12th IEEE Real-Time Systems Symposium*, pages 68–78, Santa Monica, California, December 1989.

[15] C. Heitmeier, A. Bull, C. Gasarch, and B. Labaw. SCR: A toolset for specifying and analyzing requirements. In *Proceedings of the Tenth Annual Conference on Computer Assurance (COMPASS '95)*, pages 109–122, Gaithersburg, Maryland, June 1995.

[16] C. Heitmeier and N. Lynch. The generalized railroad crossing: A case study in formal verification of real-time systems. In *Proceedings of the 15th IEEE Real-Time Systems Symposium*, pages 120–131, San Juan, Puerto Rico, December 1994.

[17] T. A. Henzinger, P.-H. Ho, and H. Wong-Toi. HYTECH: The next generation. In *Proceedings of the 16th IEEE Real-Time Systems Symposium*, pages 56–65, Raleigh Durham, North Carolina, December 1995.

[18] F. Jahanian and D. Stuart. A method for verifying properties of Modechart specifications. In *Proceedings of the 9th IEEE Real-Time Systems Symposium*, pages 12–21, Los Alamitos, CA, July 1988.

[19] K. G. Larsen, P. Petterson, and Wang Yi. Compositional and symbolic model-checking of real-time systems. In *Proceedings of the 16th IEEE Real-Time Systems Symposium*, pages 76–87, Pisa, Italy, Dec. 1995.

[20] T. Murata. Petri nets: Properties, analysis, and applications. *Proceedings of the IEEE*, 77(1):541–580, 1989.

Timed Test Cases Generation Based on State Characterization Technique[1]

Abdeslam En-Nouaary, Rachida Dssouli
Départ. d'IRO, Université de Montréal,
C.P. 6128, succ. Centre-ville,
Montréal, P.Q., H3C 3J7, Canada
{ennouaar, dssouli}@iro.umontreal.ca

Ferhat Khendek
Electrical and Computer Engineering,
Concordia University, 1455 Maisonneuve Blvd. W.,
Montreal, Quebec H3G 1M8,
khendek@ece.concordia.ca

Abdelkader Elqortobi
Départ. d'IRO, Université de Montréal,
C.P. 6128, succ. Centre-ville,
Montréal, P.Q., H3C 3J7, Canada
elqortob@iro.umontreal.ca

Abstract

Real-time reactive systems interact with their environment, using inputs and outputs, within specified time constraints. For such systems, a functional misbehavior or a deviation from the specified time constraints may have catastrophic consequences. Therefore, ensuring the correctness of real-time systems becomes very important. In this paper, we introduce the potential faults which can be encountered in a timed system implementation. We adapt an existing test cases generation technique, based on state characterization set, to generate timed test cases from a timed system specification. We model a timed system with a Timed Input Output Automaton (TIOA), *which is a variant of Alur and Dill model. In order to generate the timed test suite, the TIOA is first transformed into a* Nondeterministic Timed Finite State Machine (NTFSM) *with a given granularity. We illustrate our method with an example.*

Key-words : *Testing, Specification, Implementation, Timed Automata, Real-Time Systems.*

1. Introduction

Nowadays, important safety-critical and real-time systems, such as patient monitoring systems, plant control systems, air traffic control systems, are controlled by software systems. We also witness the rapid development and deployment of new time dependent applications such as multimedia communications. The functions of such systems are time constrained. Ensuring their correctness, i.e. function correctly within specified time intervals, is a difficult and complex task.

Formal methods are often used to cope with complexity. Many formal models have been proposed for timed systems [1, 16]. They are mainly real-time enrichments of well known models, such as Finite State Machines, Petri Net, etc. The misbehaviors of time dependent systems are often due to the non respect of timing constraints. Different verification techniques have been proposed in the literature (see [1] for instance). The verification techniques deal with the specification of the system under consideration and they aim to ensure that the designed specification satisfies predefined functional and timing requirements. The correctness of the system specification does not guarantee the correctness of its implementation. Testing is an important activity which aims to ensure the quality of the implementation. Testing procedure consists of generating test suites and applying them to the implementation which is referred to as an *Implementation Under Test (IUT)*. In this paper, we focus on functional testing that considers the IUT as a *black box*.

Contrary to the (untimed) finite state models, test cases generation and testing of timed systems is still a new research area which is being investigated by different teams with different backgrounds [15, 12, 6, 18, 9].

In [15], the authors propose a tool for the generation of test cases from specifications given as temporal logic formulas extended with time measures. However, the generated test cases cover only integer values.

Liu proposes a testing methodology which takes into account timers and counters [12]. This approach does not deal with the timed specifications in general.

[1]This work is partially supported by NSERC Grants #OG20629188 for Dssouli and #OGP0194234 for Khendek.

220

In [6], the authors introduce a framework for the testing of the constraints in timed systems. They derive test cases from a specification described in the form of a constraint graph (CG). These test cases satisfy some test criteria for real-time systems. However, the constraint graph is restricted to the description of a minimum and a maximum allowable delays between input/output events in the execution of a system, following Taylor's and Dasarathy's classification of timing requirements [20, 7].

In [18], the authors present a theoretical framework for testing timed automata. This is the first real approach for the generation of test cases from timed finite state models using methods developed for untimed models. In fact, the W-method [5] is used for the generation of test cases. The approach proposed in [18] is based on previous work by Čerāns [4] for the reduction of the test of a region automata into the test of a subautomata, referred to as *Grid Automata*. The model used as basis for test cases generation assumes that outputs can occur only on integer values of clocks. The number of test cases generated using this method can be very large.

In [9], we present a simple method for timed test sequence generation which is based on the transition tour of the entire region graph of the control part. We identify a state only by one empirical value for each clock and we show how to execute the obtained timed test cases.

In this paper, we first present the fault model for timed systems. Then, we present the algorithm for test cases generation. The model we use to specify timed systems is the *Timed Input Output Automaton (TIOA)*, a variant of [1, 17, 14], in which clocks are real-valued variables, increase synchronously at the same speed and measure the amount of time elapsed since last initialization or reset. In addition, this model consists of all clocks having bounded domains [19] to indicate that clock values are relevant only under a certain integer constant. In order to generate timed test suites, we proceed as follows: First, as in [1] we use the region graph as a semantic of the TIOA to explicit the elapsing of time and the relationship between clocks. Secondly, we sample the region graph for a defined granularity in a way that each state has an outgoing transition labeled with the same delay (i.e. the granularity of sampling). This leads to a reduction of the region graph into a *Grid Automata*, which is then transformed into a *Nondeterministic Timed Finite State Machine (NTFSM)*. Finally, we adapt well known methods [10, 13] for the generation of test cases. As a result of these transformations, our test algorithm has a good fault coverage and a certainly practical value.

The remainder of this paper is structured as follows. Section 2 is devoted to the notations and definitions we use in addition to the syntax and the semantics of TIOA. Section 3 presents our fault model for timed systems. Section 4 describes our algorithm for sampling the region automata.

Section 5 presents the timed test cases generation method illustrated with an example. In Section 6, we conclude.

2. Definitions and Notations

In the subsequent sections of the paper, $\mathbf{R}$ denotes the set of reals, $\mathbf{R}^{\geq 0}$ the set of nonnegative reals, $\mathbf{R}^{+\infty} = \mathbf{R}^{\geq 0} \cup \{+\infty\}$, $\mathbf{N}$ the set of nonnegative integers and $\mathbf{N}^{+\infty} = \mathbf{N} \cup \{+\infty\}$. For $t \in \mathbf{R}^{\geq 0}$, $\lfloor t \rfloor$ denotes the largest number in $\mathbf{N}$ that is not greater than t, and $\lceil t \rceil$ denotes the smallest number in $\mathbf{N}$ that is not smaller than t. With $\{t\}$ we denote the fractional part of t. An interval I is a convex subset of $\mathbf{R}^{+\infty}$. An integer interval is an interval I with its both bounds ($Inf(I)$ and $Sup(I)$) are in $\mathbf{N}^{+\infty}$. An integer interval I is said to be left (respectively right) open if $Inf(I) \notin I$ and $Sup(I) \in I$ (respectively $Inf(I) \in I$ and $Sup(I) \notin I$). An integer interval is said to be open if it is simultaneously left and right open. We use $+\infty$ with ∞ as synonyms.

The concatenation of two finite sets V_1 and V_2 is denoted by "." and defined as follows:$V_1.V_2 = \{v_1.v_2 \mid v_1 \in V_1 \wedge v_2 \in V_2\}$, where $v_1.v_2$ stands also for the concatenation of the sequences v_1 and v_2. Let V^n denotes n-times concatenation of V ($V^n = V.V^{n-1}$). The notation $X[k]$ is used to define the set $\{\varepsilon\} \cup X \cup X^2 \cup ... \cup X^k$, where k is a nonnegative integer and ϵ is the empty sequence.

Definition 2.1 Timed Input Output Automaton

A Timed Input Output Automaton (TIOA) A is a tuple $(\Sigma_A, L_A, l_A^0, C_A, T_A)$, where :

- Σ_A is a finite alphabet composed of input actions begining with "?" and denoted by I_A, and output actions begining with "!" and denoted by O_A,
- L_A is a finite set of locations,
- $l_A^0 \in L_A$ is the initial location,
- C_A is a finite set of clocks all initialized to zero in l_A^0,
- $T_A \subseteq L_A \times L_A \times \Sigma_A \times 2^{C_A} \times \Phi(C_A)$ is the set of transitions.

A tuple $(l, l', \{?, !\}a, \lambda, G) \in T_A$, denoted in the rest of the paper with $l \xrightarrow{\{?,!\}a, \lambda, G}_A l'$, represents a transition from location l to location l' on action $\{?, !\}a$. The subset $\lambda \subseteq C_A$ specifies the clocks to be reset with this transition, and $G \in \Phi(C_A)$ is a clock guard (time constraint) for the execution of the transition. The term $\Phi(C_A)$ denotes the set of all guards over C_A, built using boolean conjunction over atomic formulas of the form $x < m$, $x > m$, $x = m$, and $x \leq m$, where $x \in C_A$ and $m \in \mathbf{N}$. The operator $\leq$ is particularly used in output action constraints. The choice of naturals as bounds in constraints will help us, later, in the discretization of the set of reals into integer intervals, reducing thereby the state space of timed systems. In this definition, we assume that each clock $x \in C_A$ has a domain $[0, C_x] \cup \{\infty\}$, where C_x is the largest integer constraint appearing in a constraint over x in the automaton, i.e $C_x = max\{c \mid ((x \leq c) \vee (x \geq c))$ *is a constraint over* $x\}$. This means that each clock x is relevant only under the integer constant C_x. We will represent each clock value greater than this constant by ∞, and we write : $\forall \varepsilon > 0, \forall x \in C_A, C_x + \varepsilon = \infty$.

In the following sections, we will omit the subscripts of the elements of A when these are implicit from the context.

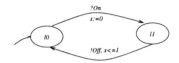

Figure 1. A TIOA Example.

For illustration purposes, we consider the 1-clock TIOA given in Figure 1. The automaton has two locations named l_0 and l_1, one clock, x and two transitions. The transition from l_1 to l_0 has Off as output action, and a guard condition $x \leq 1$ while the transition from l_0 to l_1 can execute on input On at any time and resets clock x to zero.

In order to present the semantic model of the TIOA, we need to define the notions of clock valuation and state of a TIOA.

Definition 2.2 Clock valuation
A clock valuation over a set of clocks C is a map v that assigns to each clock $x \in C$ a value in $\mathbf{R}^{+\infty}$. We denote the set of clock valuation by $V(C)$.

Definition 2.3 Satisfaction of a clock guard
A clock valuation v satisfies a clock guard G, denoted $v \models G$, if and only if G holds under v.

For $d \in \mathbf{R}^{\geq 0}$, $v + d$ denotes the clock valuation which assigns a value $v(x) + d$ to each clock x. For $X \subseteq C$, $[X \mapsto d]v$ denotes the clock valuation for C which assigns the value d to each $x \in X$, and agrees with v over the rest of the clocks.

A state of an TIOA A is a pair (l, v) consisting of a location $l \in L_A$ and a clock valuation $v \in V(C_A)$. The pair (l_A^0, v_0), where $v_0(x) = 0$ for each clock $x \in C_A$, represents the initial state of A.

The semantic model of a TIOA A is given by a timed labeled transition system $S_t(A)$ that consists of the state set S_A, the label set $\mathbf{R}^{\geq 0} \cup \Sigma_A$, both input/output actions and time increments, and the transition relation $\xrightarrow{a}$, for $a \in \mathbf{R}^{\geq 0} \cup \Sigma_A$.

Since the timed labeled transition system $S_t(A)$ is infinite, because of the infinity delay transitions, it cannot be used for test generation. The solution is therefore the reduction of the number of states in the system. For that, we use

an equivalence relation [1] on the set of clock valuations $V(C_A)$ in order to cluster equivalent states of $S_t(A)$ into equivalent classes.

Definition 2.4 Clock region
Let $A = (\Sigma_A, L_A, l_A^0, C_A, T_A)$ be a timed input output automaton, v and $v' \in V(C_A)$; we say $v \sim v'$ iff :

1) $\forall x_i \in C_A, \lfloor v(x_i) \rfloor = \lfloor v'(x_i) \rfloor$
2) $\forall x_i, x_j \in C_A \mid ((v(x_i) \neq \infty) \wedge (v(x_j) \neq \infty)),$
$(\{v(x_i)\} \leq \{v(x_j)\} \Leftrightarrow \{v'(x_i)\} \leq \{v'(x_j)\})$
3) $\forall x_i \in C_A \mid v(x_i) \neq \infty, (\{v(x_i)\} = 0 \Leftrightarrow \{v'(x_i)\} = 0)$

A clock region for A is an equivalence class of clock valuations induced by $\sim$. Let $[v]$ denotes the clock region to which v belongs.

The set of regions for a TIOA with two clocks, x and y where $D_x = [0, 1] \cup \{\infty\}$ and $D_y = [0, 1] \cup \{\infty\}$, is given in Figure 2. For instance, the clock valuations $v_1 = (x = 1/2, y = 1/4)$ and $v_2 = (x = 1/10, y = 1/12)$ have the same behaviors when time progresses. For this specific example given in Figure 2, we distinguish between three kinds of clock regions: the corner points ($\{1, 2, 3, 4\}$), the open line segments ($\{5, 6, 7, 8, 9, 10, 11, 12, 13\}$), and the open regions ($\{14, 15, 16, 17, 18\}$).

An upper bound for the number of clock regions has been given in [1]. This number can be largely optimized to the exact number [8].

Definition 2.5 Region Automaton
Let $A = (\Sigma_A, L_A, l_A^0, C_A, T_A)$ be a timed input output automaton. A region automaton of A is an automaton $RA = (\Sigma_{RA}, S_{RA}, s_{RA}^0, T_{RA})$ where:

- $\Sigma_{RA} = \Sigma_A \cup \mathbf{R}^{>0}$,
- $S_{RA} = \{\langle l, [v] \rangle \mid l \in L_A \wedge v \in V(C_A)\}$,
- $s_{RA}^0 = \langle l_A^0, [v_0] \rangle$, *where* $v_0(x) = 0$ *for all* $x \in C_A$,
- R_A *has a transition* $s \xrightarrow{\{?,!\}a} s'$, *from* $s = \langle l, [v] \rangle$ *to* $s' = \langle l', [v'] \rangle$ *on action* $\{?,!\}a \in \Sigma_A$ *iff there is a transition* $l \xrightarrow{\{?,!\}a, \lambda, G}_A l'$ *such that* $v \models G$ *and* $v' = [\lambda \mapsto 0]v$.
- R_A *has a delay transition* $s \xrightarrow{d} s'$, *from* $s = \langle l, [v] \rangle$ *to* $s' = \langle l, [v'] \rangle$ *on time increment* $d > 0$, *iff* $[v'] = [v + d]$.

The region automaton is a partition of the uncountable state space of the timed automaton into a finite number of clock regions, a set of equivalent states in other words. The region automaton is at the heart of any verification or testing technique for timed systems (see for example [1, 17, 18, 9]). This automaton corresponds in a certain manner to the reachability analysis graph of the timed system. Our definition of region automaton is slightly different from the definition in [1]. We take into account the delay transitions.

The corresponding region automaton for the TIOA given in Figure 1 is shown in Figure 3.

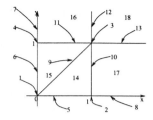

Figure 2. Clock regions.

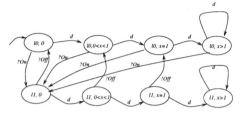

Figure 3. Region Automaton of the TIOA given in Figure 1.

No	Spec.	Impl. Faults
1	$\langle l, t \rangle \xrightarrow{\{?,!\}a}$	$\langle l, t - \varepsilon \rangle \xrightarrow{\{?,!\}a}$, $\langle l, t + \varepsilon \rangle \xrightarrow{\{?,!\}a}$
2	$\langle l,]t, t'[\rangle \xrightarrow{\{?,!\}a}$	$\langle l, [t, t'[\rangle \xrightarrow{\{?,!\}a}$, $\langle l,]t, t'] \rangle \xrightarrow{\{?,!\}a}$, $\langle l,]t - \varepsilon, t'[\rangle \xrightarrow{\{?,!\}a}$, $\langle l,]t, t' + \varepsilon[\rangle \xrightarrow{\{?,!\}a}$
3	$\langle l,]t, t'[\rangle \xrightarrow{?a}$	$\langle l,]t + \varepsilon, t'[\rangle \xrightarrow{?a}$, $\langle l,]t, t' - \varepsilon[\rangle \xrightarrow{?a}$
4	$\langle l, x < y \rangle \xrightarrow{\{?,!\}a}$	$\langle l, x = y \rangle \xrightarrow{\{?,!\}a}$, $\langle l, x > y \rangle \xrightarrow{\{?,!\}a}$
5	$\langle l, x = y \rangle \xrightarrow{\{?,!\}a}$	$\langle l, x < y \rangle \xrightarrow{\{?,!\}a}$, $\langle l, x > y \rangle \xrightarrow{\{?,!\}a}$

Figure 4. Possible Timing Faults.

3. The Fault Model For Timed Systems

The fault model is an important aspect for a testing activity, especially for the evaluation of the fault coverage of a given testing approach [2]. Different faults may be encountered in the implementation of a timed system. We distinguish between simple and multiple faults. In this section, We will list, discuss and classify the simple faults within the semantic framework of the region automata. The potential simple faults in an implementation can be classified into two categories:

- Timing faults: due to the non respect of the time constraints under which the timed system should make its transitions. In this category, we find the restriction and the enlargement of time constraints as kinds of faults.

- Transfer/Output faults: This category concerns the faults related to both input and output actions and is similar to the well known fault model for FSMs[2].

3.1. Timing faults

The timing faults are the most important faults since they are the most frequent and the most difficult ones to detect. They include "1-Clock timing faults" and "Multi-Clocks timing faults".

3.1.1 1-Clock timing fault

. This kind of timing faults concerns only one clock at a time. We will study it in relation to the clock regions.

- "Corner point fault": It is related to the corner points that are represented in the graph of clock region by points with integer coordinates. The possible faults of a clock in this case are represented in Figure 4(row 1). These faults occur when we have in the specification of the timed system an input action (respectively an output action) that can occur exactly at integer time t while the implementation of the system does not accept the input action (respectively does not respond with the output action) at time t. For example, the implementation of the specification given in Figure 3 may not accept the input action $?On$ exactly at one unit of time since it was in its initial state, but it can do it ε-time units before or after, for some $\varepsilon > 0$.

- "Interval fault": It is related to the other clock region types where at least one clock takes values in an open integer interval I. In this case, the possible faults of such clocks are given in Figure 4(rows 2 and 3). These faults occur when at least one interval bound is modified in the implementation of a timed constraint for an action. The enlargement of the allowable time interval is considered a fault for both input and output actions. However, its restriction is viewed as a fault for input actions only, since the implementation of a transition $\langle l,]t, t'[\rangle \xrightarrow{!a}$ in a way that the system responds always before $t' - \varepsilon$ or after $t + \varepsilon$ (i.e. as $\langle l,]t + \varepsilon, t'[\rangle \xrightarrow{!a}, \langle l,]t, t' - \varepsilon[\rangle \xrightarrow{!a}$), for $\varepsilon > 0$, is considered as a valid reduction and is not seen as a fault. As an example of the enlargement of the allowable time interval, an implementation of the specification given in Figure 3 can perform the output action

$!Off$ when the clock x value is greater than 1.

3.1.2 Multi-Clocks timing faults

In the previous subsection, we focussed only on simple timing faults that concern only one clock regardless of the other clocks. In order to be complete, another type of timing faults may occur when the relation between clocks in a clock region does not hold. For illustration, let us consider again the example in Figure 4(rows 4 and 5). The specification indicates that clock x is less than (respectively equal to) clock y, while the implementation changes this ordering to $x > y$ or $x = y$ (respectively to $x > y$ or $x < y$).

Notice that since TIOA is more general than CG, our fault model for timed constraints includes the one presented in [6].

3.2. Transfer/Output action faults

Similarly to the untimed systems [2], some transfer/output action faults may occur in an implementation of a timed specification.

3.2.1 Transfer faults

They are related to the input actions. An implementation is said to have a transfer fault if from a state s and on an input action $?a$, the implementation enters a state s'' while it is expected to reach a state s' ($s' \neq s''$).

3.2.2 Output faults

This kind of faults concerns the output actions. An implementation is said to have an output fault if in a state s, the implementation responds by a sequence of output actions different from the expected one.

3.3. Multiple Faults

We define a multiple fault as a combination of timing faults and/or transfer/output action faults. Notice that we can neither estimate nor enumerate the potential multiple faults. However, for practical purposes, an upper bound should be assumed in order to avoid the consideration of infinite set of faulty implementations.

4. Sampling Region Automaton

Sampling has been introduced in [11] for the verification of real-time systems while the concept of *Grid Automata* has been proposed in [18]. A *Grid Automata* is defined as

a subautomaton of the region automata. In order to generate test cases, the *Grid Automata* is derived from the region automata. Since the region automaton is formed with locations of TIOA and clock regions, a set of clock valuations having the same behavior, inferred with respect to the equivalence relation $\sim$ defined previously (see definition 2.4), the idea behind the construction of the grid automaton is to represent each clock region with a finite set of clock valuations, referred to as the *representatives* of the clock region. For this reason, we define the grid points with granularity $1/k$ [11].

Definition 4.1 Set of Grids
Let $k \in N$, we define the set of grids with granularity $1/k$ to be the set $N_k = \{m/k | m \in N\}$. We extend this notion in the usual way to any vector of elements to define the grid points with granularity $1/k$ as the set $N_k^n = \{\bar{r} | 1 \leq i \leq n, r_i \in N_k\}$.

The set of representatives of each clock region is determined from the set of grid points. The properties of sampling are studied in [11]. In particular, it is proven that for each clock region of a n-clock TIOA, there exists a set of its representatives in the grid points with granularity at most $1/(n+1)$. But, in order to reach all clock regions in the region automaton from the clock region of its initial state for $(n \geq 2)$, we have to use grid points with granularity at most $1/(n+2)$. In fact, the granularity of grid points constitutes the steps by which the clocks are authorized to pass from one clock region to another one, allowing thereby the automaton to make transitions from one location to another. The construction of the grid automata leads to the explicit extension of the alphabet of the automaton with delay actions of value $1/(n+2)$ (or $1/(n+1)$ if $n = 1$).

For illustration, consider again the TIOA A of Figure 1. The automaton has one clock, x. Therefore, the grid points we calculate are of granularity $1/2$. For our example, the set of representatives is $\{(0), (1/2), (1), (\infty)\}$. To

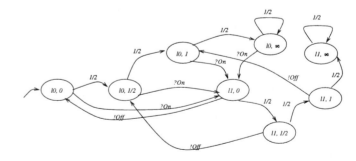

Figure 5. The grid automaton of the TIOA given in Figure 1.

derive the grid automata of Figure 5, we proceed in many

steps. Given an n-clock TIOA, we first derive the maximal granularity we can use (if $n = 1$ then the granularity is $1/2$ else the granularity is $1/(n + 2)$). In a second step, we create the initial state formed with the initial location of the TIOA and a valuation that sets all clocks to zero. In a third step, we create all states reachable from the initial state with repetitive $1/(n + 2)$ (or $1/(n + 1)$ if $n = 1$) delay transitions. Then, for each state (l, v), create a transition $((l, v), \{!, ?\}a, (l', [\lambda \mapsto 0]v))$ for each transition $(l, l', \{!, ?\}a, \lambda, G)$ in the TIOA such that v satisfies G. Afterwards, we repeat the same process starting with state $(l', [\lambda \mapsto 0]v)$.

The Sampling Algorithm:
INPUT : - A k-clock TIOA $A = (\Sigma, L, l^0, C, T)$.
OUTPUT: - A grid automaton.
STEP0: Compute the granularity to use:
    $granul \leftarrow$ if $k = 1$ then $1/2$ else $1/(k + 2)$.
STEP1: Initialize the sets to use:
    $R_S \leftarrow (l_0, v_0(x) = 0) \forall x \in C$ (Reachable States)
    $H_S \leftarrow \emptyset$ (Handled States)
STEP2: Construct the grid automata:
    While $R_S \backslash H_S \neq \emptyset$ do
      Get a state $s = (l, v)$ from $R_S \backslash H_S$
      $H_S \leftarrow H_S \cup \{s\}$
      For each $t = (l, l', \{!, ?\}a, \lambda, G) \in T$ do
        If $v \models G$ then Add $((l, v), \{!, ?\}a, (l', [\lambda \mapsto 0]v))$
          if it does not exist
          $R_S \leftarrow R_S \cup \{(l', [\lambda \mapsto 0]v)\}$ if it does not exist
        EndIf
      EndFor
      If $((v(x) + granul) \leq \infty \forall x \in C)$ then
      Add $((l, v), granul, (l', (v + granul)))$
        if it does not exist
        $R_S \leftarrow R_S \cup \{(l, (v + granul))\}$ if does not exist
      EndIf
    EndWhile

Except for the granularity, our algorithm constructs a grid automata similar to the one obtained in [18] by the definition of the grid automata for a given TIOA. The complexity of our algorithm is exponential in terms of the number of clocks and the integer constants used in the TIOA. This is inherent for any verification or testing method based on the region automata.

5. Timed Test Generation

Prior to the introduction of the test cases generation method, we will first introduce our testing hypothesis, our test model and the conformance relation which is relating the implementation to the specification in the case of successful testing.

5.1. Testing hypothesis

As in [5, 10, 18, 13], we make few assumptions about the specification (a TIOA A) and the implementation under test. Some of these assumptions are necessary for the existence of the characterization set for the generation of test cases. Other assumptions are necessary for the testing of the implementation.

- It is deterministic on the set of alphabet, i.e., from any location we cannot have two transitions labeled by the same action and whose time constraints can be satisfied simultaneously.

- from each location, we cannot have more than one outgoing transition labeled by an output action and whose time constraints can be satisfied simultaneously, or an outgoing transition labeled by output action and another one labeled by an input action and their time constraints can be satisfied simultaneously.

- For testing the implementation, we have to bring it back to its initial state after each single test case in order to apply the next test case. Therefore, we assume the existence of the reset action which always brings the implementation to its initial state. We also assume there is no outgoing transition from the initial location labeled with an output action only.

- It is completely specified over the set of inputs I, otherwise we complete it by adding a self-loop transition for each non-specified input. Notice that with this completion, we assume that the implementation does never refuse inputs.

- complete-testing assumption: It is possible, by applying a given input sequence to a given implementation a finite number of time, to cover all execution paths that can traversed by this sequence.

5.2. Timed Test Model

The region graph defines in a certain manner the semantics of the TIOA model. However, it is very difficult to test since it does not explicit how to handle the clock variables. For this reason, we propose a testable model which consists, as in hardware, of two parts (see Figure 6): the *control part* and the *clock part*.

The control part represents the communication of the timed system with its environment by receiving the inputs and responding with outputs. The clock part handles the clock variables used in the specification of the timed system. Each clock variable gives rise to a process to perform the operations on the variable. The communication between the two parts is achieved with the exchange of the

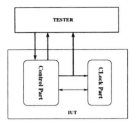

Figure 6. Timed Test Model.

predefined internal signals *PleaseValue*, *GetValue* and *ResetClock*. When the control part receives an input from the environment, it checks whether or not the input constraint is satisfied. It sends the *PleaseValue* signal to the involved clock processes asking for the clock values. After the reception of this signal, each process computes the current value of its clock and passes it to the control part using the signal *GetValue*. To reset a clock to zero, the control part sends the signal *ResetClock* to the corresponding clock process. In this model, we explicitly distinguish the *ResetClock* channel from the other signals channel because *ResetClock* is the only internal signal we want to observe. We are assuming a synchronous communication.

This test model seems to be general. It represents an efficient and a simple manner to implement real-time systems. It is also a suitable model for testing a real-time system. In fact, it makes explicit the reset to zero of clocks with the execution of transitions.

5.3. Conformance Relation

The starting point for conformance testing is the definition of the conformance relation between an IUT and the specification. Many conformance relations have been introduced and used to generate test cases from FSM and LTS models [10, 13, 3]. Conformance relations assume that the environment behaves accordingly to the reference specification and the verdict for whether or not the IUT conforms to the specification is given by observing the implementation reactions (i.e. outputs) to the applied inputs. To test an implementation of a real-time system, we have to check whether or not the IUT when stimulated with inputs responds with expected outputs within the allowable time intervals. Contrary to the untimed case, the controllability of the time at which an output is produced is difficult or impossible without time stamp instrumentation. To avoid this problem, we will not focus on which exact time an output is produced but we ensure if or not it occurs in the allowable time interval. This is guaranteed by the use of $\leq$ in output constraints and the transformation of the grid automata into an equivalent *nondeterministic timed FSM*

(NTFSM). In this transformation, the action corresponding to the elapsing of time is interpreted as an input action. Following this interpretation, during testing, the testers (Upper and Lower Testers) will check regularly the implementation output queue looking for an output. The transformation of the grid automata into an NTFSM is based on the two schemes shown in Figure 7. Notice that this transformation preserves the expressed behavior and one can easily prove the equivalence between the grid automata and the NTFSM. As an example, the NTFSM corresponding to the

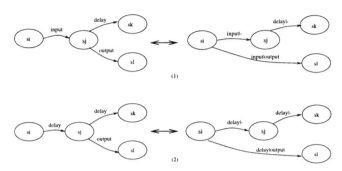

Figure 7. The Basic Transformation Schemes

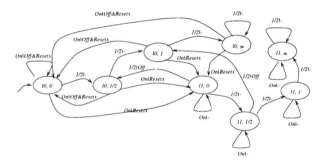

Figure 8. The NTFSM Corresponding to the Grid Automata of Figure 5.

grid automata of Figure 5 is shown in Figure 8. Note that the obtained NTFSM is nondeterministic. In this NTFSM model we distinguish between two categories of states:

- States that are connected only by delay transitions: these states have the same first component and an incoming $1/(n + 2)$-delay transition. They cannot be distinguished by any input sequence because they are sub-states of the same super-state. However, the semantic of time distinguishes these states if no clock has been reset to zero during the last $1/(n + 2)$-unit of time. The semantics of time guarantees that by letting the time elapse with $1/(n + 2)$-unit, we change the state of the system. Furthermore, the model we use ensures whether or not a clock has been reset to zero.

- States that are identified by other input transitions as in the FSM model.

The set of time connected states and the set of input identified states are denoted by S_T and S_I respectively. As an example, the states $\{(l_0, 0), (l_1, 0)\}$ in the Figure 8 are *input identified* while the states $\{\{(l_0, 0), (l_0, 1/2), (l_0, 1), (l_0, \infty)\}, \{(l_1, 0), (l_1, 1/2), (l_1, 1), (l_1, \infty)\}\}$ are *time connected*.

Based on the previous distinction between states, we define the conformance relation between an IUT and its specification as a trace-equivalence for nondeterministic FSM[13]. Notice that we are dealing automatically with an *observable nondeterminism*. The trace-equivalence relation is based on the notion of traces of a state. By definition, a sequence of input/output actions σ is a trace of a state s if the automaton can evolve from s to another state s' on σ. We denote the set of traces of a state s by $traces(s)$ and we say that two states s and s' are trace-equivalence, notation $s =_{trace} s'$, if and only if $traces(s) = traces(s')$. Furthermore, two NTFSM's S and I with their respective initial states s_0 and i_0, are trace-equivalence, notation $S =_{trace} I$, if and only if $s_0 =_{trace} i_0$. The trace-equivalence is an equivalence relation. Moreover, we believe that the trace-equivalence relation is sufficient to cover all the faults discussed in section 3. The formal study of the fault coverage of our method is left for future investigations.

5.4. Test Algorithm

As mentioned previously, by constructing the grid automata we explicitly extend the alphabet of the TIOA with the delay action $1/(n + 2)$ in a way that each state has a transition labeled with this action and can be completely specified for the other input actions. Furthermore, we use our test model to make explicit the reset to zero operation on clocks. Therefore, we can apply the state characterization technique to generate timed test suites for the control part of our test model. The state characterization methods generate test cases that are conceptually applied in two phases. The first phase checks if all the states defined in the specification are identifiable in the implementation. The second phase checks if all transitions defined in the specification are implemented correctly. In general, the second phase does not check for the transitions which are already covered by test cases in the first phase.

For the generation of timed test cases, we have adapted the generalized W_p method [13]. This algorithm uses many sets which are simple to determine and their definitions are as follows:

Definition 5.1 State Cover
A set $Q \subseteq I^*$ is a state cover of an NTFSM A if, for every state S_i, Q contains an input sequence that brings the machine A from the initial state S_0 to S_i.

Definition 5.2 Transition Cover
A set $P \subseteq I^*$ is a transition cover of an NTFSM A if, for every transition $S_i \xrightarrow{a|b}_A S_j$, P contains an input sequence x and $x.a$ that bring the machine A from the initial state S_0 to S_i and S_j, respectively. We note that $Q \subseteq P$.

Definition 5.3 Delay Sequence Set
A set $D \subseteq (\{1/(n + 2)\} \cup I)^*$ is a delay sequence set of an NTFSM A if, for every transition $S_i \xrightarrow{1/(n+2)|b}_A S_j$, D contains an input sequence x and $x.1/(n + 2)$ that bring the machine A from the initial state S_0 to S_i and S_j, respectively. We note that $D \subseteq P$.

Definition 5.4 Characterization Set
A set $W \subseteq I^*$ is a characterization set for an NTFSM iff $\forall S_i, S_j \in S_I, i \neq j \Rightarrow \exists x$ such that: $x \in Tr(S_i)$ xor $x \in Tr(S_j)$, and $x{\restriction}I^* \in W$, where $x{\restriction}I^*$ denotes the projection of x on I^* obtained by removing the output actions from x. With the completeness assumption, this means $(x{\restriction}I^*)$ applied to S_i and S_j will yield different output traces.

Definition 5.5 Prefix Set
Let V be a set of input sequences. We define the prefix set of V as follows: $Pref(V) = \{t_1 \mid t_1 \neq \varepsilon \& t_2 \in I^* \& t_1.t_2 \in V\}$.

Definition 5.6 State Identification Set
Given an NTFSM and a characterization set W, $\{W_0, W_1, ..., W_{n-1}\}$ is said to be a set of identification sets if, for $i = 0, 1, ..., n-1$, W_i is a preferably minimal set such that: $W_i \subseteq Pref(W)$ and for $j = 0, 1, ..., n-1$, $(j \neq i \Rightarrow \exists x \in Tr(S_i)$ xor $Tr(S_j)$ and $x{\restriction}I^* \in W_i)$.

The generalized Wp adapted algorithm:
INPUTs:
- A k-clock TIOA A with an alphabet $\Sigma = I \cup O$,
- A number of states, m, in the IUT M ($m \geq n$),
OUTPUTs:
- A test suite for the IUT M.
STEP0: Construct a grid automata from the TIOA with an alphabet $\Sigma \cup \{1/(k + 2)\}$ and n states, using the algorithm given in section 4,
STEP1: Transform the resulting grid automata into an NTFSM as shown in section 5.3,
STEP2: Determine the sets of timed connected and input identified states S_T and S_I respectively.
STEP3: Construct the set cover Q that includes the set of delay sequences D for S_T,
STEP4: Construct a characterization set W and the set of state identification set $\{W_0, W_1, ..., W_{n-1}\}$ of S.
STEP5: Construct two sets P and R such that: $P = Q.I[1]$ and $R = P \backslash Q$.
STEP6: Construct the timed test suite $\prod$ as follows: $\prod = \prod 1 \cup \prod 2$, where

$\prod 1 = Q.I[m - n].W,$
$\prod 2 = R.I^{m-n} \oplus \{W_0, W_1, ..., W_{n-1}\}$, where
$R.I^{m-n} \oplus \{W_0, W_1, ..., W_{n-1}\} =$
$\qquad \bigcup \{x \mid I\}.W_i.$
$S_0 \xrightarrow{x} S_i \& x \mid I \in R.I^{m-n}$
STEP7: Return $\prod$.

The algorithm generates test cases to check the conformance of an implementation to the specification given as TIOA. Since the grid automata is a subautomaton of the region automata, the generated test cases ensures the correct behavior of the grid automata in the implementation but do not cover the entire region automata. Therefore, the *uniformity* assumption is needed in order to claim the conformance (trace-equivalence) of IUT to its specification. The uniformity assumption means that if the implementation behaves correctly on some points in a clock region it does the same in the remaining points of the clock region. Under this assumption, an implementation that passes successfully the test cases generated by the algorithm is claimed to be conform to the region automata. However, the absence of the uniformity reduces the quality of testing in the sense that the implementation passing successfully the test is only trace-equivalent to the grid automata (or its equivalent NTFSM) which is contained in the region automata. As a consequence, a subset of the faults introduced in section 3 may not be detected. In order to cover all these faults we have to use a very small granularity in the construction of the grid automata. However, the use of a small granularity leads to a very large number of test cases and renders the method impracticable. For this reason, we aimed, since the beginning of our work, to use an appropriate granularity and come out with a practical timed test cases generation method.

The timed test cases generated by the algorithm for the *TIOA* in Figure 1 are given in Figure 9. For the sake of simplicity, we assume that the number of states in the IUT is equal to the number of states in the reference specification. Notice that, in general, the number of states in the IUT can be larger than the number of states in the specification. In this case, we can fix a reasonable upper bound for this number and the method will generate longer test cases.

A faulty implementation

In order to illustrate how the generated timed test cases will detect faults in an faulty implementation, let us consider the implementation given in Figure 10.
This implementation contains two faults. The first one is the violation of time constraint on input On in state $(l_0, 0 < x < 1)$, i.e. the IUT does not accept input On in location l_0 when the value of clock x is between 0 and 1. The second fault is a transfer fault. After responding with output Off in state $(l_1, x = 1)$, the IUT remains in its current state instead of entering the state $(l_0, x = 1)$. Both faults are drawn in Bold. When we apply the timed test sequences $1/2.On$ and $1/2.On.1/2.1/2.On$ to this faulty implementation, we observe respectively the output sequences $\varepsilon. \varepsilon$ and $\varepsilon.\varepsilon.\varepsilon.Off. \varepsilon$ which are different from the expected ones: $\varepsilon.Off.Resetx$ and $\varepsilon.\varepsilon.\varepsilon.Off.Off$ respectively. Here, the unexpected outputs are written in bold. For each test case, the comparison of the actual output sequence with the expected one yields to the detection of the fault.

6. Conclusions and future work

We introduced a method for the derivation of test cases for real-time systems described by a TIOA, a variant of the Alur and Dill model. In order to generate the test cases, we first discussed the model at the syntactic and semantic levels. Then, we studied the fault model for real-time systems and described a timed test model. For the generation of the test cases, we made explicit the elapsing of time by sampling the region graph with a known granularity and obtained a reduction called the grid automata. Furthermore, to ensure a good coverage of the potential faults for a timed system, we transformed the grid automata into an observable nondeterministic finite state machine and we generated test cases from the resulting automata using a generation technique based on the state characterization sets. The non-determinism in the resulting automata is completely due to the non-controlability of outputs. The exact time at which the IUT responds with outputs remains unknown, only the respect or the violation of the time constraints is important.

Our approach has been implemented. We are currently working on the generalization of our approach to nondeterministic TIOA, communicating TIOAs and TIOA extended with variables.

References

[1] R. Alur and D. Dill. A theory of timed automata. *Theoretical Comput. Sci.*, 126:183–235, 1994.

[2] G. V. Bochmann, A. Das, R. Dssouli, M. Dubuc, A. Ghedamsi, and G. Luo. Fault model in testing. In *Proceedings of the 4th IFIP TC6 International Workshop Protocol Test System*, 1992.

[3] E. Brinksma, G. Scollo, and C. Steenbergen. LOTOS Specification, Their Implementations and Their Tests. In B. Sarikaya and G. Bochmann, editors, *Protocol Specification, Testing, and Verification, VI*, Montreal, Québec, Canada, June 10-13, 1986, pages 349–360. North-Holland, 1986.

[4] K. Čerāns. Decidability of bisimulation equivalences for parallel timer processes. In G. v. Bochmann and D. Probst, editors, *Proceedings of the 4th International Workshop on Computer Aided Verification*, Montreal, Canada, volume 663 of *Lecture Notes in Computer Science*, pages 302–315. Springer-Verlag, 1992.

[5] T. Chow. Testing software design modeled by finite-state machines. *IEEE Trans. Softw. Eng.*, SE-4(3):178–187, 1978.

[6] D. Clarke and I. Lee. Automatic generation of tests for timing constraints from requirements. In *Proceedings of the Third International Workshop on Object-Oriented Real-Time Dependable Systems,* Newport Beach, California, Feb. 1997.

[7] B. Dasarathy. Timing constraints of real-time systems: Constructs for expressing them, methods of validating them. *IEEE transactions on Software Engineering*, 11(1):80–86, January 1985.

[8] A. Elqortobi, A. En-Nouaary, and G. V. Bochmann. Dénombrement du nombre des régions dans un automate temporisé. Technical Report TR-1116, Département IRO, Université de Montréal, Montréal, Canada, Jan. 1998.

[9] A. En-Nouaary, R. Dssouli, and A. Elqortobi. Génération de Tests Temporisés. In *Proceedings of the 6th Colloque Francophone de l'ingénierie des Protocoles, HERMES, ISBN 2-86601-639-4, 1997.*

[10] S. Fujiwara, G. Bochmann, F. Khendek, M. Amalou, and A. Ghedamsi. Test selection based on finite-state models. *IEEE Transactions Software Engineering*, SE-17, NO. 6:591–603, 1991.

[11] K. Larsen and W. Yi. Time abstracted bisimulation: Implicit specifications and decidability. In *Proceedings Mathematical Foundations of Programming Semantics (MFPS 9),* volume 802 of *Lecture Notes in Computer Science*, New Orleans, USA, Apr. 1993. Springer-Verlag.

[12] F. Liu. Test generation based on an fsm model with timers and counters. Master thesis, Département d'Informatique et de Recherche Opérationnelle, Université de Montréal, 1993.

[13] G. Luo, G. V. Bochmann, and A. Petrenko. Test selection based on communicating nondeterministic finite-state machines using a generalized wp-method. *IEEE Transactions Software Engineering*, SE-20, NO. 2:149–162, 1994.

[14] N. Lynch and H. Attiya. Using mappings to prove timing properties. *Distributed Computing*, 6(2):121–139, 1992.

[15] D. Mandrioli, S. Morasca, and A. Morzenti. Generating test cases for real-time systems from logic specifications. *ACM Trans. Comput. Syst.*, 13(4):365–398, Nov. 1995.

[16] P. Merlin and D. Farber. Recoverability of communication protocols. *IEEE transactions on Communication Protocols*, 24(9), 1976.

[17] X. Nicollin, J. Sifakis, and S. Yovine. Compiling real-time specifications into extended automata. *IEEE transactions on Software Engineering*, 18(9):794–804, September 1992.

[18] J. Springintveld, F. Vaadranger, and P. Dargenio. Testing timed automata. Technical Report CTIT97-17, University of Twente, Amesterdam, 1997.

[19] J. Springintveld and F. Vaandrager. Minimizable timed automata. In B. Jonsson and J. Parrow, editors, *Proceedings of the 4th International School and Symposium on Formal Techniques in Real Time and Fault Tolerant Systems,* Uppsala, Sweden, volume 1135 of *Lecture Notes in Computer Science*. Springer-Verlag, 1996.

[20] B. Taylor. Introducing Real-time Constraints into Requirements and High Level Design of Operating Systems. In *In Proceedings 1980 Nat. Telecommunications Conference,Houston, TX, volume 1*, pages 18.5.1–18.5.5, 1980.

The Timed Connected States
$\{\{(l_0,0),(l_0,1/2),(l_0,1),(l_0,\infty)\},$ $\{(l_1,0),(l_1,1/2),(l_1,1),(l_1,\infty)\}\}$
The Input Identified States
$\{(l_0,0),(l_1,0)\}$
The Transition Cover P
$\{\varepsilon,1/2,1/2.1/2,1/2.1/2.1/2,1/2.On,1/2.On.1/2,$ $1/2.On.1/2.1/2,On,1/2.1/2.On,1/2.1/2.1/2.On,$ $1/2.On.On,1/2.1/2.1/2.1/2,1/2.On.1/2.On,1/2.$ $On.1/2.1/2.On,1/2.On.1/2.1/2.1/2,1/2.On.1/2.$ $1/2.1/2.On,1/2.On.1/2.1/2.1/2.1/2\}$
The State Cover Q
$\{\varepsilon,1/2,1/2.1/2,1/2.1/2.1/2,1/2.On,1/2.On.1/2,$ $1/2.On.1/2.1/2,1/2.On.1/2.1/2.1/2\}$
The Delay Sequence Set D
$\{1/2,1/2.1/2,1/2.1/2.1/2,1/2.On.1/2,1/2.On.1/2.$ $1/2,1/2.On.1/2.1/2.1/2\}$
The R Set
$\{On,1/2.1/2.On,1/2.1/2.1/2.On,1/2.On.On,1/2.$ $On.1/2.On,1/2.1/2.1/2.1/2,1/2.On.1/2.On,$ $1/2.On.1/2.1/2.On,1/2.On.1/2.1/2.1/2.1/2\}$
The Set Characterization W
$\{1/2,On\}$
The State Identification Sets W_i
$W_0=W_1=W_2=W_3=W_6=W_7=\{On\}and$ $W_4=W_5=\{1/2\}$
Test Cases $\prod 1$:
$\{1/2,On,1/2.1/2.1/2,1/2.1/2.1/2.1/2,1/2.On.1/2,$ $1/2.On.1/2.1/2,1/2.1/2.On,1/2.1/2.1/2.On,1/2.On.$ $On,1/2.On.1/2.On,1/2.On,1/2.1/2,1/2.On.1/2.1/2.$ $1/2,1/2.On.1/2.On,1/2.On.1/2.1/2.On.1/2,$ $1/2.On.1/2.1/2.On.On,1/2.On.1/2.1/2.1/2.$ $1/2,1/2.On.1/2.1/2.1/2.On\}$
Test Cases $\prod 2$:
$\{On.On,On.1/2,1/2.1/2.On.On,1/2.1/2.On.1/2,1/2.$ $1/2.1/2.On.On,1/2.1/2.1/2.On.1/2,1/2.On.On.On,$ $1/2.On.On.1/2,1/2.On.1/2.On.On,1/2.On.1/2.On.$ $1/2,1/2.1/2.1/2.1/2.On,1/2.On.1/2.1/2.On.On,1/2.$ $On.1/2.1/2.On.On,1/2.On.1/2.On.1/2.On,1/2.$ $On.1/2.1/2.On.1/2,1/2.On.1/2.1/2.1/2.On\}$

Figure 9. Timed Test Cases for the NTFSM of Figure 8

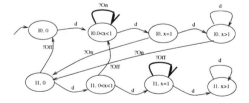

Figure 10. A Faulty Implementation for the Specification Given in Figure 3

Session 7.B: Operating Systems and Services

General Data Streaming *

Frank W. Miller
Pete Keleher
Dept. of Computer Science
Univ. of Maryland, College Park
{fwmiller,keleher}@cs.umd.edu

Satish K. Tripathi
College of Engineering
Univ. of California, Riverside
tripathi@engr.ucr.edu

Abstract

This work presents a new I/O system design and implementation targeted at applications that perform data streaming. The approach yields true zero-copy transfers between I/O devices in many instances. We give a general characterization of I/O elements and provide a framework that allows analysis of the potential for zero-copy transfers. Finally, we describe the design, implementation, and performance of a prototype I/O system in a real-time, embeddable, 32-bit operating system whose design is based on the presented analysis to minimize data copying.

1 Introduction

A variety of computer applications display a behavior termed *data streaming* where data is repetitively moved from one input/output (I/O) device to another. This work increases performance using mechanisms that couple I/O devices together tightly devices within the operating system kernel. In current systems, data copies decouple the transfer characteristics of I/O devices. However, data copies have a detrimental effect on performance. The design and implementation of streaming presented here eliminates data copies by passing data between I/O devices by reference.

The proposed design is quite general, applying to I/O systems for a wide range of operating system types, from embedded systems to personal (PC) class and workstation class computers. The initial implementation has been performed in an embeddable, 32-bit, real-time operating system. While predictability is the primary goal for the design of embedded, real-time operating systems, such systems are also generally resource constrained. The elimination of data copies frees both CPU and memory resources that can be used for other

purposes. As such, the performance gains achieved using the techniques presented here should be of great value to real-time operating system designers.

This work makes several contributions. 1) A small set of general parameters that may be used to characterize *any* I/O channels to be used as stream endpoints is given. 2) A general analysis of data streaming based on an orthogonal matching of these parameters is provided. 3) A set of algorithms designed to minimize data copies for each of the analytical cases is presented. 4) A large set of performance results taken from the prototype operating system that enumerate a representative set of I/O channel pairings and uniformly show throughput improvements are presented.

The rest of the paper is organized as follows. Section 2 provides motivation and context in related work. Section 3 presents a set of parameters for characterizing I/O channels and a general analysis of data streaming. Section 4 presents a set of algorithms which provide optimized streaming based on the analysis in Section 3. Section 5 provides a performance evaluation of a representative sample of an orthogonal matching of I/O channels. Finally, Section 6 discusses some observations and current work.

2 Related Work

The major motivation for the design and implementation presented here is an explosion in the number of different types of peripheral I/O devices that can be attached to modern day computer systems and the desire to support their data transfers as efficiently as possible. In embedded real-time systems, there is an almost infinite array of I/O devices in use as sensor/effector equipment. With respect to PCs and workstations, it was not so long ago that such a system consisted of a CPU, memory, disk, keyboard, display, and perhaps an Ethernet adapter. More recently, cameras, scanners, CD-ROMs and DVDs, microphones, sound

---

*Partial funding provided by NSF Grant CCR 9318933, IBM, and ASSERT grant from DOD.

cards with their associated amplifiers and/or speakers, all types of pointing devices, joysticks, projectors, modems, ISDN, all types of network adapters ({regular, fast, really fast} Ethernet, FDDI, ATM, Frame Relay, cable modems, etc.), and more are available and in widespread use.

Data streaming can occur at a variety of levels. Architectures such as I_2O [8] allow for *peer-to-peer streaming* across a backplane bus. The major advantage is performance but it comes at a price. System complexity and cost are significantly higher since code to manage the organization of data being moved across the backplane must be pushed into the devices and coordinated with the main system. For this reason, much of the work in data streaming has focused on *main memory streaming* where data passes through main memory on its way between peripheral devices.

In main memory streaming, the goal is to copy the data while it is in memory as few times as possible, with zero copy the ultimate goal. Much of the recent work in streaming has focused on the problem of *cross address space* copies. Brustolini and Steenkiste's *Genie* and Pai's work with *IO-lite* [14] which is based on Druschel's `fbufs` [4] are recent examples of the use of page remapping to move data residing in main memory across protection boundaries while avoiding data copies in streaming applications.

Reducing cross address space copies is important, however, in embedded systems, a significant number of applications do not make use of virtual memory addressing. Further, the cross address space works do not address the resulting situation where data transfers between I/O devices are now tightly coupled. The analysis and mechanism presented in this work complements the solutions proposed to address the cross address space problem, i.e. it simply assumes that data is brought into memory from one device and sent out another. It works regardless of how many times the data is moved across address space boundaries.

The primary influence on the I/O system design has been the streaming work performed at UCSD [5, 6]. Fall's proof-of-concept when coupling I/O from similar channels together within a BSD-variant operating system kernel provided performance improvements that are echoed here. However, his approach has been expanded in this work to encompass orthogonal pairing between any I/O elements in the system. The central issue arising from this extension is the need to deal with the dislike characteristics of tightly coupled I/O channels.

case	
case 1	T^{in} = fix $\wedge T^{out}$ = fix $\wedge B^{in}$ = B^{out}
	T^{in} = fix $\wedge T^{out}$ = var $\wedge B^{in}$ = B^{out}
	T^{in} = fix $\wedge T^{out}$ = var $\wedge B^{in}$ < B^{out}
	T^{in} = var $\wedge T^{out}$ = var $\wedge B^{in}$ = B^{out}
	T^{in} = var $\wedge T^{out}$ = var $\wedge B^{in}$ < B^{out}
case 2	T^{in} = fix $\wedge T^{out}$ = var $\wedge B^{in}$ > B^{out}
	T^{in} = var $\wedge T^{out}$ = var $\wedge B^{in}$ > B^{out}
case 3	T^{in} = fix $\wedge T^{out}$ = fix $\wedge B^{in}$ > B^{out}
case 4	T^{in} = fix $\wedge T^{out}$ = fix $\wedge B^{in}$ < B^{out}
	T^{in} = var $\wedge T^{out}$ = fix $\wedge B^{in}$ = B^{out}
	T^{in} = var $\wedge T^{out}$ = fix $\wedge B^{in}$ < B^{out}
	T^{in} = var $\wedge T^{out}$ = fix $\wedge B^{in}$ > B^{out}

Table 1. Static Parameter Combinations

3 Streaming Analysis

Define a device as any hardware that performs data movement, typically, between a peripheral and main memory. A device driver is defined as the lowest level software that controls a device. A device and either and *input channel* or an *output channel* specify a stream endpoint, either a *source* or a *sink*.

Each device has a value, B, associated with it that corresponds to the *maximum* contiguous block of memory required for a data transfer. Define b to be the amount of data moved during some transfer. If the transfer size associated with a device must be constant and equal to its block size, i.e. $b = B$ for all transfers, the device is said to require *fixed block transfers*. Hard disks and CD-ROM drives are examples of fixed block devices. If the block size can vary up to the maximum, i.e. $b \leq B$, the device is said to allow *variable block transfers*. Network adapters and video cards are examples of variable block devices.

We characterize each I/O channel with two paramters, the *block type*, T, which can take on the values `fix` (fixed) or `var` (variable) and the *maximum block size*, B. Both parameters are static, i.e. they do not vary from transfer to transfer.

Figure 1 is a list of all possible combinations that result when the parameters for source and sink channels are coupled. These twelve cases reduce to four that provide algorithmic oppurtunities to optimize throughput for streaming.

We define a *stream* as a half-duplex channel between a source and sink. The source provides a sequence of M transfers where each transfer has a size b^{in}. The stream delivers to the sink a sequence of N transfers each with size b^{out}. Consider the following analysis of generalized streaming using the two static parameters to maximize throughput.

Case 1 $(T^{in} = \texttt{fix} \wedge T^{out} = \texttt{fix} \wedge B^{in} = B^{out}) \vee (T^{out} = \texttt{var} \wedge B^{in} \leq B^{out})$

In this first case, either both the source and sink have the same fixed block type or the output block type is variable and the input block size is smaller than the output block size. Input blocks can be output directly. We have $N = M$ and no data copies are required since the input buffer can always be output directly. An illustration of this streaming case is given in case 1 of Figure 1.

Case 2 $T^{out} = \mathtt{var} \wedge B^{in} > B^{out}$

In this case, the output block type is variable and the input block size is larger than the output block size. The stream divides the input block into $\lfloor \frac{B^{in}}{B^{out}} \rfloor$ output blocks of size B^{out} and a single output block holding the remainder, $b^{out} = B^{in} - \lfloor \frac{B^{in}}{B^{out}} \rfloor B^{out}$. Note that the solid lines indicate that *reference buffers* are used to generate multiple output blocks for each input block. An illustration of this streaming case is given in case 2 of Figure 1.

Case 3 $T^{in} = \mathtt{fix} \wedge T^{out} = \mathtt{fix} \wedge B^{in} > B^{out}$

In this case, both the input and output block types are fixed and the input block size is greater than the output block size. The stream divides input blocks into smaller blocks for output. The number of output blocks required to empty an input block is $\frac{B^{in}}{B^{out}}$ which may be non-integral. Since output blocks must be filled, they may contain fractions of input blocks. For every $\frac{L}{B^{out}}$ output blocks, $\frac{L}{B^{in}} - 1$ copies of input data to an output block must be performed. The segments of data framed by dashed lines must be copied from an input buffer to an output buffer. An illustration of this streaming case is given in case 3 of Figure 1.

Case 4 $(T^{in} = \mathtt{fix} \wedge T^{out} = \mathtt{fix} \wedge B^{in} < B^{out}) \vee (T^{in} = \mathtt{var} \wedge T^{out} = \mathtt{fix})$

In the final case, either both the input and output block types are fixed and the input block size is smaller than the output block type or the input block type is variable and the output block type is fixed. In both situations, blocks must be aggregated to fill the larger output blocks. The number of input blocks that fill an output block is given by $\frac{B^{out}}{B^{in}}$. If this result is non-integral, input blocks must be split.

Define $L = lcm(B^{in}, B^{out})$ to the least common multiple of B^{in} and B^{out}. Observe that for every $\frac{L}{B^{in}}$ input blocks, $\frac{L}{B^{out}}$ blocks will be output. Furthermore, for every $\frac{L}{B^{out}}$ output blocks,

one copy of data from an input block to an output block can be avoided. An illustration of this streaming case is given in case 4 of Figure 1.

4 Streaming Algorithms

A set of algorithms whose goal is to provide the efficient streaming presented in the previous section is now given. These algorithms make assumptions about the design of the I/O system. First, access to all I/O elements is performed through a common applications programming interface (API). Second, a common buffer representation is used by all system I/O elements.

The *Roadrunner* I/O architecture utilizes a common interface to all I/O elements. This is accomplished using a global file system (or $\mathtt{fs}$) layer which is supported by specific file system implementations. This architecture is based on work from several sources. The use of the file system name space to address various elements of the system is reminiscent of Plan 9/Inferno [15]. The internal implementation is based primarily on the $\mathtt{vnodes}$ [10, 16, 17] architecture present in 4.4BSD [11] (among others) and the stackable architectures proposed by Heidemann and Popek [7].

The most significant design element is the use of a common buffer representation by all I/O elements. Figure 2 illustrates the design of the common buffer representation and Table ?? lists the routines used by the kernel to manage them. Buffers have two parts, a descriptor and an optional data block. The fields of the descriptor are partitioned into those used for referencing data in a data block and those used for caching. The $\mathtt{data}$ field points at the beginning of an allocated data block. The $\mathtt{size}$ field contains the length of the allocated block. The $\mathtt{start}$ and $\mathtt{len}$ fields mark where useful data is contained in the allocated block. The $\mathtt{pos}$ field is used to provide an offset into the start of the useful data. The $\mathtt{devno}$ (or device number), and $\mathtt{blkno}$ (or block number), fields are used for caching. These two fields are combined in a hash function that allows quick insertion and retrieval of buffers into and out of hash table managed buffer pools. I/O elements use *move semantics* when managing buffers, i.e. a buffer only resides in the global cache when it is *not* owned by some file descriptor.

The algorithm presented here conceptually "overlays" a stream of input buffers onto a stream of output buffers. The overall structure of this algorithm is given in Figure 3.

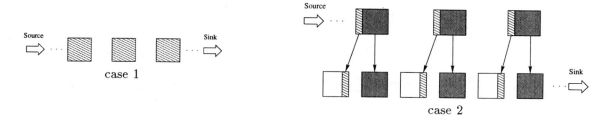

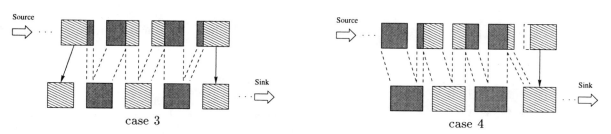

Figure 1. The set of streaming cases derived from the static parameter combinations.

```
int stream(int in, int out)
{
    int infilesize;
    int inblktype, outblktype;
    int inbufsize, outbufsize;
                        Get channel paramters

    if ((inblktype == FIX && outblktype == FIX && inbufsize == outbufsize) ||
        (outblktype == VAR && inbufsize <= outbufsize)) {
                          Case 1 stream

    } else if (outblktype == VAR && inbufsize > outbufsize) {
                          Case 2 stream

    } else if (inblktype == FIX && outblktype == FIX && inbufsize > outbufsize) {
                          Case 3 stream

    } else if ((inblktype == FIX && outblktype == FIX && inbufsize < outbufsize) ||
        (inblktype == VAR && outblktype == FIX)) {
                          Case 4 stream

    }
}
```

Figure 3. The overall structure of the overlay algorithm

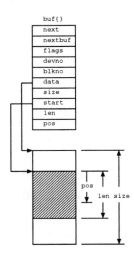

Figure 2. Common buffer representation.

Routine	Description
bread()	Retrieve cached buffer
bput()	Enter buffer in cache
balloc()	Blocking get buffer descriptor *only*
_balloc()	Non-blocking get buffer descriptor *only*
bget()	Blocking get buffer with data block
_bget()	Non-blocking get buffer with data block
bfree()	Release buffer to the free list
brel()	Enter buffer in cache or release to free list

Table 2. Common Buffer Management Routines

4.1   Case 1

This simplest cases occur when either the input and output block types are fixed and the input and output buffer sizes are equal or the output block type is variable, and the input buffer size is less or equal to the output buffer size. In these instances, input buffers can be output directly using the simple algorithm in Figure 4. This algorithm implements exactly the behavior specified in case 1 of Figure 1. The system call, **read(in, b)**, reads data from the input channel, **in**, into the buffer, **b**. The system call, **write(out, b)**, writes data to the output channel, **out**, using the buffer, **b**. [1] Since input buffers are output directly, no data copies are required.

4.2   Case 2

This case occurs when the output block type is variable and the input block size is greater than the output block size. In these instances, the algorithm given in Figure 5 can be executed. It's operation matches exactly the analysis given in case 2 of Figure 1.

The algorithm repetitively fetches a buffer, **bin**, from the input channel and progresses through its data sending it to the output channel. The buffer, **bout** is a *reference buffer*, i.e. its descriptor is used to progress through areas of data in **bin**. The maximum block size for **bout** is used until the end of the data has been reached in **bin**. In this last output transfer, the amount of data sent will be **inbufsize** *mod* **outbufsize**. Since all output buffers are passed by reference, no data copies are required.

4.3   Case 3

This case occurs when the input and output block types are both fixed and the input buffer size is greater than the output buffer size. The algorithm given in Figure 6 is based on the analysis in case 3 of Figure 1 but does not match its operation exactly.

The key observation made when developing this algorithm is that it is very likely that the input buffer size is a multiple of the output buffer size. If this is so, it is desirable to have the algorithm behave similarly to case 2, i.e. passing partitions of the input blocks by reference. Only when the input block size is not a multiple of the output block size should copying be performed. Fortunately, the case where a multiple is present is common. An example is when a file is copied

---

[1]The specifications for **read()** and **write()** have been condensed for clarity in this presentation.

```
int n;
for (n = 0; n < infilesize;) {
    b = bget(inbufsize);
    read(in, b);
    write(out, b);
    n += inbufsize;
}
```

Figure 4. The case 1 stream algorithm

```
int n;
for (n = 0; n < infilesize;) {
    if (bin == NULL) {
        bin = bget(inbufsize);
        read(in, bin);
    }
    bout = balloc();
    bout->start = bin->start + bin->pos;
    if (bin->len - bin->pos >= outbufsize) {
        bout->len = outbufsize;
        n += outbufsize;
        bin->pos += outbufsize;
    } else {
        bout->len = bin->len - bin->pos;
        n += bin->len - bin->pos;
        brel(bin);
        bin = NULL;
    }
    write(out, bout);
}
```

Figure 5. The case 2 stream algorithm

between disk file systems that utilize a different block size.

The algorithm again repetitively reads blocks from input channel. In this algorithm case, however, a separate inner **for** loop is used to progress through the data in each input block. There are four cases that occur as it progresses through data in each input block. They are defined by the guards on the inner and outer **if** statements.

The first two cases occur when no output block is currently being filled. In the first case, the amount of data in the input block is greater than or equal to the size of an output block. A reference buffer is defined and sent out the output channel. The second case occurs when the amount of data left in the input block is less than the size of an output buffer. The remainder of the input block is copied into a new output buffer and the algorithm proceeds to the next input block.

The second two cases occur when there is an as yet unfilled output block that was carried over. This can happen as a result of the second or fourth cases. In the third case, there is enough data in the input block to fill the remainder of the output block. The data is copied and the filled output block is sent to the output channel. The fourth case occurs when the data remaining in the input block will not fill the carried over output buffer. This action taken is similar to case 2.

If the input buffer size is a multiple of the output buffer size, the first case is the only one that is ever executed and no data copies are required. If however, the input buffer size is not a multiple of the output buffer size, the situation in case 2 of Figure 1 occurs, i.e. a copy is avoided only when the least common multiple of the two buffer sizes occurs.

4.4 Case 4

This case occurs when the input and output block types are both fixed and the input buffer size is less than the output buffer size or the input block type is variable and the output block type is fixed. The algorithm given in Figure 7 is based on the analysis in case 4 of Figure 1 but does not match its operation exactly.

In this case, one copy must always be performed. For the first part of this case, it is necessary to aggregate smaller input blocks into larger output blocks. In the second part, since it is impractical to expect that the the data in variable input blocks will have repetitive sizes, all the variable input data must be aggregated into the fixed output buffers.

This case also proceeds by looping over input buffers. During each iteration, however, it is possible that an input or output buffer may have been carried

```
int n;
for (n = 0; n < infilesize;) {
    bin = bget(inbufsize);
    read(in, bin);
    while (bin->pos < bin->len)
        if (bout == NULL) {
            if (bin->len - bin->pos >= outbufsize) {
                bout = balloc();
                bout->start = bin->start + bin->pos;
                bout->len = outbufsize;
                write(out, bout);
                n += outbufsize;
                bin->pos += outbufsize;
            } else {
                bout = bget(outbufsize);
                bcopy(bout->start,
                        bin->start + bin->pos,
                        bin->len - bin->pos);
                bout->len = outbufsize;
                bout->pos = bin->len - bin->pos;
                n += bin->len - bin->pos;
                break;
            }
        } else {
            if (bin->len - bin->pos >= bout->len - bout->pos) {
                bcopy(bout->start + bout->pos,
                        bin->start + bin->pos,
                        bout->len - bout->pos);
                n += bout->len - bout->pos;
                bin->pos += bout->len - bout->pos;
                write(out, bout);
            } else {
                bcopy(bout->start + bout->pos,
                        bin->start + bin->pos,
                        bin->len - bin->pos);
                bout->pos += bin->len - bin->pos;
                n += bin->len - bin->pos;
                break;
            }
        }
    brel(bin);
}
```

Figure 6. The case 3 stream algorithm

over. If not, the required buffer is allocated. If there is enough input data to fill the output buffer, the data is copied and the buffer is sent to the output channel. The input buffer carries over. Otherwise, the output data is copied and the output buffer is carried over.

5 Performance

Performance measurements, especially apples to apples comparisons are difficult in this work for a number of reasons. Probably most important is that we are not aware of any other systems with an I/O subsystem designed to do generalized coupling of I/O elements within the kernel in the manner being described here. The approach that has been taken is to provide two sets of measurements for a subset of an orthogonal coupling of a representative set of I/O endpoints. The first set *simulates* the environment found in most current systems, i.e. it uses read()/write() system calls to perform streaming transfers. The second set uses the appropriate streaming algorithm.

All of the performance measurements presented were made on the same machine, an IBM PC/350, that includes a 75 MHz Pentium with 256 Kbyte second level cache, 16 Mbytes of memory, an 800 Mbyte EIDE hard disk, and an SMC EtherPower 10BaseT PCI Ethernet adapter. While this machine is dated compared to those currently available, it is important to note that the absolute figures in these measurements are not as important as the *relative* results, those using the streaming interface versus those using the traditional read()/write() interface.

A list of the file systems and devices used as stream endpoints is given in Figure 3. The /dev/null device is accessed through the devfs file system. It provides a variable block type with a maximum block size of 4096 bytes. The UDP and TCP file systems provides endpoints utilizing the DEC tulip based PCI Ethernet adapter. The UDP endpoint uses a variable block type with a maximum of 1446 bytes The TCP endpoint uses a variable block type with a maximum of 4096 bytes. Two DOS compatible file systems are used that reside on the same hard disk in different partitions. Both have a fixed block type with one having a block size of 2048 bytes and the other a block size of 4096 bytes.

Table 4 shows how these endpoints can be combined for streaming. There are two types of cells in this matrix. Those cells that contain only a single number give the streaming case exercised when the corresponding endpoints are combined. For example, when the

```
int n;
for (n = 0; n < infilesize;) {
    if (bin == NULL) {
        bin = bget(inbufsize);
        read(in, bin);
    }
    if (bout == NULL) {
        bout = bget(outbufsize);
        bout->len = outbufsize;
    }
    if (bin->len - bin->pos >= bout->len - bout->pos) {
        bcopy(bout->start + bout->pos,
            bin->start + bin->pos,
            bout->len - bout->pos);
        n += bout->len - bout->pos;
        bin->pos += bout->len - bout->pos;
        write(out, bout);
    } else {
        bcopy(bout->start + bout->pos,
            bin->start + bin->pos,
            bin->len - bin->pos);
        n += bin->len - bin->pos;
        bout->pos += bin->len - bin->pos;
        brel(bin);
        bin = NULL;
    }
}
```

Figure 7. The case 4 stream algorithm

Endpoint	File System/Device	Blk Type	Max. Size
1	devfs/null	var	4096
2	udpfs/tulip	var	1446
3	tcpfs/tulip	var	4096
4	dosfs/wd disk	fix	2048
5	dosfs/wd disk	fix	4096

Table 3. Stream endpoints used in measurements

		Destination				
		1	2	3	4	5
Source	1	1	2	1	4/9	4
	2	1	4	1	4	4
	3	1	4	4	4	4
	4	1/8	2	1/13	1/10	4/12
	5	1	2	1	3/11	1

Table 4. Endpoint combinations for measurements. Cells containing a single number give the streaming case used for the endpoint combination. Cells containing two numbers separated by a slash give the streaming case and the figure number for measurements taken for the endpoint combination.

DOS file system with block size 2048 bytes is used a source and the UDP endpoint is used a sink, the case 2 streaming algorithm applies. Those cells that contain two numbers separated by a slash give the streaming case and the figure number of measurements presented for that endpoint combination. For example, when the DOS file system with block size 2048 bytes is used as a source and the TCP endpoint is used as a sink, the case 1 streaming algorithm applies and measurements taken for this case are presented in Figure 13.

Figure 8 shows the baseline performance of the IDE disk in the test machine. Because disk I/O transfers take so long compared to memory movements, speedups are heavily dependent on the use of caching. The improvements are good when the cache is in play, i.e. the file, or portions of it, reside in the cache. The improvements are modest when disk I/O dominates the transfers. Consider the points for a 1 MB cache when a 512 KB file is read. The streaming transfers are accomplished at a rate of 30.5 Mbps while the read()/write() transfers yield a throughput of 22.6 Mbps. Streaming yields a 35% improvement in this case. However, if the same cache size is used

to transfer a 1 MB file, the best throughput for a streaming transfer is 1.9 Mbps versus 1.7 Mbps for the read()/write() transfers. Streaming yields only a 6% improvement here.

Figure 9 illustrates the effect of the overall cache size for a given data block size during file writes. Since delayed writes are occurring, disk operations do not come into play until the file size exceeds the cache size. When the file fits into the cache, speedups are in the neighborhood of 79%. When the file size exceeds the cache size, bget() calls must flush buffers, i.e. write the dirty contents to disk, before filling them with new data. This results in the significantly reduced speedup of approximately 5%.

The remaining sets of measurements provide results for applications that make use of the streaming algorithms. Figures 10, 11, and 12 give speedups for execution of the file copy program, cp, and Figure 13

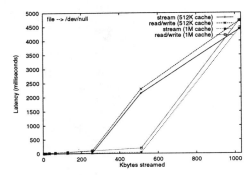

Figure 8. File read stream

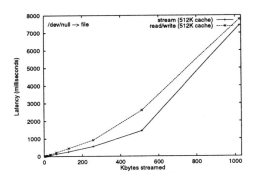

Figure 9. File write stream

gives the speedups associated with the *Roadrunner* web server, `httpd`.

In Figure 10, a copy from one place to another on the same file system is presented. Improvements here range from 33% for the case of a 1 MB file and 512 KB cache to 75% for a 512 KB file and 1 MB cache to 77% for a 1 MB file and 1 MB cache. In Figure 11, a file is copied from a file system with a buffer size of 4096 bytes to a file system with a buffer size of 2048 bytes. The performance improvements for the input buffer greater than the output buffer are the best of any of the algorithm cases. Consider the data points for the 256 KB cache size. The `read()/write()` performance is 1.25 Mbps for a 256 KB file, 608 Kbps for a 512 KB file, and 535 Kbps for a 1 MB file. The stream performance is 1.4 Mbps for a 256 KB file, 1.29 Mbps for a 512 KB file, and 1.2 Mbps for a 1 MB file. These throughputs yield 12.5%, 87%, and 124% speedups, respectively. In Figure 12, a file is copied from a file system with a buffer size of 2048 bytes to a file system with a buffer size of 4096 bytes. The speedups here, while uniform, are modest. This is to be expected since this stream uses case 4, where copies are always required.

There is an interesting dynamic here with the cached blocks in Figures 10 and 11. When `read()/write()` is used, a block is brought into the cache for the input channel and another block is entered in the cache for the output channel. When streaming is used, a single block is entered in the cache. The block is originally brought in for the input channel but is then passed by reference to the output channel. When this happens, the input channel reference goes away. This halves the cache utilization for the stream and explains why the performance of the 1 MB file and 1 MB cache hasn't yet dropped off as in the case of the 1 MB file and 512 KB cache. The tradeoff is that future references to the same input block will require another disk reference.

The speedups in Figure 13 vary depending on the retrieved file size. A best case speedup of 505% has been observed when a file that is less than or equal to the TCP send buffer size resides in the global cache. More modest improvements of 26% are observed for large files. It should be noted that these results are particularly impressive given that in the web server, a modifed XINU [2] implementation is being used. This implementation contains few of the optimizations present in BSD derived stacks, such as no-copy send and receive buffers, optimized checksums and header prediction.

6 Conclusion

We have presented a general framework that characterizes the need for copying in systems that perform data streaming. We have demonstrated analytically that true zero-copy data transfers can be used in many instances and described the performance of a prototype implementation in a real-time, embeddable, 32-bit operating system. We have shown that zero-copy transfers uniformly improve performance in our environment. It is important to note that these improvements are hardware independent. The I/O system design and streaming algorithms are characteristics of our operating system architecture and should provide speedups on any hardware platform on which they are used.

Our approach does have potential drawbacks. First, the exclusive use of *move* semantics eliminates the possibility of concurrent access to a single buffer, which reduces the number of expensive I/O operations performed. Work is currently under way to extend the common buffer design to allow concurrent access to data blocks. Second, performance improvements are greater when I/O transfer times are close to data copy times, and this is not generally the case for disk I/O.

Finally, we have implemented an entirely new I/O system from scratch in order to prototype this design approach. The I/O system was made small, fast, and inherently extensible by using a stackable `vnode`-based

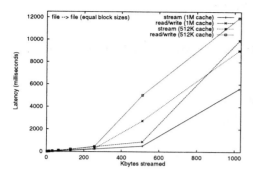

Figure 10. File copy stream, $B^{in} = B^{out}$

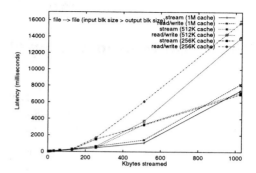

Figure 11. File copy stream, $B^{in} > B^{out}$

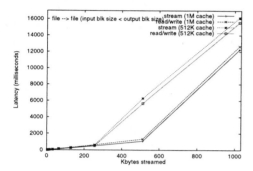

Figure 12. File copy stream, $B^{in} < B^{out}$

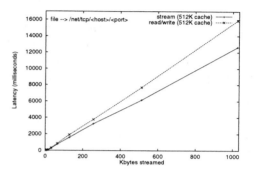

Figure 13. Web server stream

design. While the *Roadrunner* system is targeted at embedded system development, we do have a set of tools that allow self-hosted development. The authors are prepared to make the complete sources for the *Roadrunner* system available for further research.

References

[1] Brustolini, J. and Steenkiste, P., "Effects of Buffering Semantics on I/O Performance", *Proc. of 2nd Symposium on Operating System Design and Implementation (OSDI)*, 1996.

[2] Comer, D., *Internetworking with TCP/IP: Volume II*, Prentice-Hall, 1995.

[3] Cornfed Systems, Inc., Roadrunner *Operating System Reference*, 1998.

[4] Druschel, P., "Operating System Support for High-Speed Communication", *CACM*, *39*, 9, 1996.

[5] Fall, K. and Pasquale, J., "Improving Continuous-Media Playback Performance with In-Kernel Data Paths", *Proc. of the Intl. Conference on Multimedia Computing and Systems (ICMCS)*, 1994.

[6] Fall, K., *A Peer-to-Peer I/O System in Support of I/O Intensive Workloads*, Ph.D. Dissertation, University of California, San Diego, 1994.

[7] Heidemann, J. and Popek, G, "File-System Development with Stackable Layers", *ACM Transactions on Computer Systems*, *12*, 1, 1994.

[8] I$_2$O Special Interest Group, *Intelligent I/O for Enterprise Computing*, Presentation by I$_2$O SIG Member Representatives at Fall '97 COMDEX, 1997.

[9] Intel Corp., *80386 Programmer's Guide*, 1994.

[10] Kleinman, S., "Vnodes: An Architecture for Multiple File System Types in Sun UNIX", *Proc. of the Summer 1986 Conference*, USENIX, 1986.

[11] McKusick, M., Bostic, K., Karels, M., and Quarterman, J., *The Design and Implementation of the 4.4BSD Operating System*, Addison-Wesley, 1996.

[12] Miller, F. W. and Tripathi, S. K., "An Integrated Input/Output System for Kernel Data Streaming", *Proc. of the SPIE/ACM Multimedia Computing and Networking (MMCN)*, 1998.

[13] Miller, F. W., *Input/Output System Design for Streaming*, Ph.D. Dissertation, University of Maryland, College Park, 1998.

[14] Pai V., Druschel P., and Zwaenopoel, W., IO-lite: *A Unified I/O Buffering and Caching System*, TR97-294, Rice University, 1997.

[15] Pike, R., Presotto, D., Thompson, K., and Trickey H., "Plan 9 from Bell Labs", *Plan 9: The Documents - Volume 2*, AT&T Bell Laboratories, 1995.

[16] Rosenthal, D., "Evolving the Vnode Interface", *Proc. of the Summer 1990 Conference*, USENIX, 1990.

[17] Skinner, G. and Wong, T., "Stacking Vnodes: A Progress Report", *Proc. of the Summer 1993 Conference*, USENIX, 1993.

Design and Implementation of a Real-Time ATM-Based Protocol Server

Martin Borriss   Hermann Härtig
Dresden University of Technology
Operating Systems Group
{borriss,haertig}@os.inf.tu-dresden.de

Abstract

This paper describes design and implementation of L^4ATM, an ATM (Asynchronous Transfer Mode) based networking server. While ATM emphasizes deterministic high-speed communication, applications can not yet fully utilize its potential. We demonstrate an architecture—and a corresponding implementation—to resolve this dilemma by developing implementable resource quantification techniques and QoS (Quality Of Service) management algorithms for host resources.

L^4ATM has been built in the context of DROPS (Dresden Real-Time OPerating System). DROPS supports coexisting real-time and time-sharing applications in a μkernel environment.

Evaluating L^4ATM's implementation in a real-world environment, we show that (i) performance guarantees are maintained under heavy time-sharing load, and (ii) the implementation outperforms a standard OS significantly.

1. Introduction

This section introduces the DROPS architecture [12] and states design criteria applying to all sub-projects within the DROPS context.

1.1. Motivation

Applications with real-time requirements, such as multimedia applications, can be supported by end systems in two contradictory ways: (1) Use standard (e.g., non-real-time capable) operating systems software on hosts equipped with vast amounts of resources to account for the worst case; (2) Alternatively, use real-time-aware operating system software, thus providing performance guarantees to real-time applications while using less powerful hardware compared to the first approach.

This research was supported in part by the Deutsche Forschungsgemeinschaft (DFG) through the Sonderforschungsbereich 358.

Firstly, we believe that the second alternative is technologically more desirable. Secondly, we feel that—although complex—building such a system is attainable and practical. This observation has guided the design of DROPS. The remainder of Section 1 reviews DROPS' essentials.

1.2. DROPS architecture

Based on the L4 μkernel [17], DROPS incorporates multiple OS personalities: Standard time-sharing tasks use the L^4Linux server [13], a port of the monolithic Linux kernel to the L4 μkernel. In contrast, real-time applications are free to use dedicated real-time servers for predictable performance. Drivers run in user space. Resource manager components are responsible for enforcing and monitoring host resource reservation, such as buffer space, processing times, cache utilization and I/O-bandwidth. Figure 1 shows the system architecture.

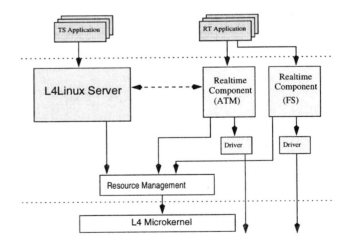

Figure 1. Simplified DROPS architecture.

The L^4Linux server provides the environment for standard time-sharing applications and buys us (1) support for a broad range of hardware devices, and (2) binary compatibility to Linux. With the exception of the Linux scheduler, only architecture-dependent parts needed to be modified to adapt Linux to the L4-μkernel. System call traps are redirected via the L4 μkernel (*trampoline mechanism*). Hardware interrupts are translated into IPC messages to dedicated threads. To control interrupt latency, protection of critical regions within the L^{4}Linux server is done by using explicit synchronization instead of blocking interrupts. Host memory is divided at boot time between the L^{4}Linux server and real-time components, taking cache access characteristics into account [10].

1.3. Real-time model

Similar to the *path abstraction* in the experimental Scout [21] system and to the concept of *compound sessions* by Anderson's LBAP model [4], real-time components can be lined up in chains. The DROPS model is based on jitter constrained streams [9], an abstraction on numerous parameter sets (such as the QoS parameters defined for ATM networks [23]). The model develops quantitative techniques for resource management, for example, computation of required buffer space to compensate for jitter (Section 2.3).

The data model builds on L4' virtual memory management concept of *flexpage* mapping operations [11], resembling *fbufs* [7], but extending it with the capability of precisely timed revoke operations of page mappings.

Each real time component must provide the uniform DROPS interface, but is free to offer additional interfaces.

Scheduling in the L4 μkernel uses static priorities. On top of that, the model provides a flexible periodic scheduling framework. Applications may reserve a certain priority level within a given interval for a number of cycles. For the reserved cycles, priority of the application will be temporarily raised. Time-sharing processes (that is, low-priority processes) are granted unused or remaining cycles. A call-back mechanism provides feedback to applications, allowing them to scale their requirements as appropriate.

The remainder of this paper discusses design, implementation and performance of one such real-time component, the L^{4}ATM protocol server.

2. L^{4}ATM design

While network hardware support is necessary to offer QoS guarantees to applications, it is not sufficient. To guarantee tight bounds on throughput, delay and jitter, operating system support is mandatory. Operating system and host protocol implementations must provide mechanisms for the management of local resources necessary to pass performance guarantees on to application level. We identified relevant host resources for protocol processing, in particular: CPU time, host buffer space, network bandwidth, cache [18], I/O-bandwidth and memory bandwidth. The machine-global resource manager enforces reservation. Additionally, time-sharing applications are conceptually integrated into the resource management design to allow strict separation from guaranteed services.

Requirements. Applications using L^{4}ATM require: (1) Guaranteed throughput; (2) Bounded latency; and (3) Bounded jitter. These requirements are expressed in terms of a traffic specification and mapped to actual resource reservation by the host (within L^{4}ATM and driver) and by the network (within ATM switches).

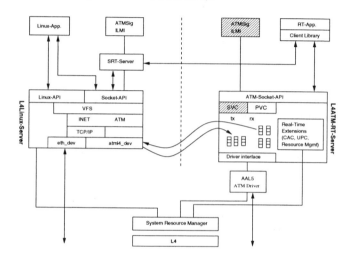

Figure 2. Integration of the L^{4}ATM protocol server into the DROPS framework.

For practical reasons we rejected the full implementation of heavy-weight transport protocols in favor of a native ATM protocol stack. Figure 2 shows the overall design and its integration into the DROPS framework. Note that API calls unsupported by real-time servers are transparently redirected to L^{4}Linux by the client library and a "SRT server" task. ATM signalling is performed by a Linux daemon, which is part of the Linux-ATM distribution [3].

2.1. Process structure

For L^{4}ATM, we chose a multi-threaded design. ATM connections are associated with dedicated *worker threads*. Using BSD-socket terminology, worker threads handle `read()` and `write()` calls. Additionally, traffic management algorithms (with the exception of admission control) run in worker thread context.

A *service thread* handles non-time-critical requests, such as connection establishment, admission control, and connection tear-down.

Finally, a *pseudo interrupt thread* takes incoming protocol data units from the hardware driver, buffers messages if necessary and triggers activation of a worker thread blocking on this connection.

The resulting concurrent server is scalable and fits well to L4's synchronous IPC. Most importantly, however, an efficient implementation of real-time policies is possible (i.e., per-connection priorities and L^4ATM's *thread suspension* technique used for enforcing resource reservation). Thread support—conforming to POSIX threads—for L^4ATM is contained in the platform dependent layer, providing an 1:1 mapping of pthreads to L4's kernel threads. Synchronization primitives (mutexes) support priority inheritance to avoid priority inversion.

2.2. Data transfer

To achieve low communication latencies and preserve the high bandwidth offered by network hardware, our design reduces data copying costs as much as possible without compromising protocol functionality and system integrity.

Transmit data path. Traditionally, the data path looks as follows: Application data is copied into protocol memory. Protocol buffers are then copied by the network interface card into the internal send FIFO and are transmitted. No CPU involvement is necessary for the last data copy (DMA). Thus, write() calls are possible with a single CPU-initiated copy. Additionally, L^4ATM offers another, zero-copy, interface. Using the page re-mapping scheme, the copy operation between application and L^4ATM is avoided and replaced by a temporary or permanent mapping operation (Figure 3).

Figure 3. Data path for write().

Receive data path. L^4ATM employs both a two-copy architecture (for the standard read()-interface) and a single-copy architecture (for the real-time interface). As can be seen from Figure 4, read() calls require an extra data copy. Typically, a receive interrupt activity has to identify the higher-level protocol of a PDU, allocate buffer memory, copy the PDU into the protocol buffer and return the old buffer to the ATM device driver. In addition, receive control flow is divided into the pseudo interrupt activity and the read() activity initiated by the receiving application, which blocks until data arrives. It is feasible to get rid of

this last CPU-initiated data copy, even without special support by the ATM board. However, explicit synchronization and feedback are necessary to signal possible buffer re-use to the hardware driver, requiring knowledge and cooperation by the application.

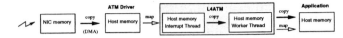

Figure 4. Data path for read().

L^4ATM uses linear buffers, similar to Linux' sk_buffs. For the single-copy and zero-copy variants, protocol buffers carry only a reference to the actual user buffer.

2.3. Real-time extensions

Real-time behavior is implemented by inserting a set of traffic management algorithms into L^4ATM, which implement functionality to enforce meeting of QoS objectives of connections compliant to their traffic specification.

Based on resource requirements computed from the specified traffic parameters, *Connection Admission Control* decides on feasibility of new guaranteed connections, maintains resource utilization statistics and triggers actual resource reservation. *Usage Parameter Control (UPC)* detects non-conforming connections and triggers the local policing function. Note that UPC applies to both real-time and non-real time traffic. Non-conforming connections (i.e., connections exceeding their reserved bandwidth) are subject to policing. The *policing function* provides flow control by restricting the data rate.

Traffic parameters. To express bandwidth and jitter requirements, applications submit a parameter set to the protocol, using the setsockopt() call. The parameter set contains: (1) A qualitative description of the requested service, expressed in terms of ATM traffic classes. ATM potentially supports Constant Bit Rate (CBR) service, real-time Variable Bit Rate (rt-VBR) service and a number of non-real-time service classes. (2) Maximum data rate. (3) Sustainable data rate. This is intended for support of staggering streams and maps to the rt-VBR traffic class. For streams with constant data rate, both rates are equal. (4) Maximum service data unit length. (5) Delay variation tolerance (DTV). Applications announce their sensibility regarding jitter.

The purpose of this parameter set is twofold: Firstly, L^4ATM performs local admission control, triggers resource reservation and initializes local management information used for the UPC algorithm. Secondly, the same parameter set is signalled to the network to be used for ATM-level admission control and resource allocation.

Integration of time-sharing applications. Applications without guaranteed performance potentially suffer from two handicaps. First, real-time connections use higher priorities than all non-real-time connections, controlling latency. Note that, due to the use of the priority inheritance protocol for mutexes, waiting time at critical sections for high-priority worker threads is bounded. Second, non-real-time connections share the remaining unreserved bandwidth, which is dynamically adapted on start and termination of guaranteed connections. For non-real-time traffic a minimum amount of host resources must be available to allow at least discarding data.

Design of traffic management algorithms is discussed next, implementation issues are described in Section 3.

2.4. Admission control

Admission control for the protocol is designed to manage the resources CPU, buffer space and network bandwidth. From application-supplied parameters and parameters configured statically (such as maximum available network bandwidth) and dynamically (such as CPU speed) required CPU time and parameters for UPC are determined. In case a new connection cannot be accommodated, admission control recommends a modified traffic parameter set to the client, in order to ease re-negotiation.

Buffer space. Buffer space needed for a connection is computed from the following traffic parameters: For transmitting real-time connections, transmit buffers are sized according to the maximum service data unit. For real-time receiving, receive buffers sizes are determined from both bandwidth parameters and the jitter tolerance specified by the client, as can be seen from the following example.

Using the generalized framework developed in [9]: Let $\mathcal{D}$ be the minimum inter-arrival time of two conforming packets, defined by the reciprocal of the maximum data rate: $D = \frac{1}{R_{max}}$. Let $\mathcal{T}$ be the average inter-arrival time of two conforming packets, defined by the reciprocal of the sustainable data rate: $T = \frac{1}{R_{avg}}$. Further, let τ be the maximum acceptable delay variation, $\mathcal{L}$ be the maximum burst length and $\mathcal{P}$ be the buffer size. Then, the following holds[1]:

$$\mathcal{L} = 1 + \left\lfloor \frac{\tau}{\mathcal{T} - \mathcal{D}} \right\rfloor \tag{1}$$

$$\mathcal{P} = \left\lceil \frac{\tau}{\mathcal{T}} \right\rceil \tag{2}$$

As an example, consider a request which adheres to the following traffic parameters: $R_{max} = 125Mbps$, $R_{avg} = 93.75Mbps$, a data size of $max\_sdu = 8192$ bytes and

---

[1]We have to refer to [9] for a complete treatment.

a delay variation tolerance of $\tau = 2ms$. Plugging in the numbers, Equations 1 and 2 yield a maximum burst size of $\mathcal{L} = 13$ packets and a required buffer size $\mathcal{P} = 24$ KB.

L^4ATM also maintains network bandwidth utilization. Contrary to network devices, L^4ATM has knowledge of the locally achievable throughput. Otherwise, considering a fast network interface, networking hardware may accept bandwidth reservations which cannot be preserved by host systems. Furthermore, this concept allows bandwidth management in environments not supporting network level bandwidth negotiation, for instance due to limited support in network interface cards or in a statically configured ATM environment (using Permanent Virtual Circuits (PVCs) where no dynamic QoS negotiation takes place).

2.5. Usage parameter control and policing

Both algorithms are closely related and are in practice often implemented together. While admission control ensures that enough resources are available for this connection, UPC is responsible for detection of non-conforming connections, that is, connections exceeding their requested bandwidth. After detection of non-conforming traffic policing takes over and guarantees isolation of non-conforming traffic. UPC and policing are always performed in worker thread context.

Packet-based UPC requires a granularity which we find too fine to be implemented in practice.[2] Therefore, L^4ATM adopts a mechanism comparable to a token bucket scheme. Each real-time connection has a control interval associated with it. At the beginning of each interval, the connection receives new credit[3]. When transferring data, connections are conforming to their traffic specification as long as enough credits for the current PDU are left. If not, the policing function, which is described below, takes over. Note that this credit-based scheme behaves oblivious. That is, connections do not receive additional credit for using less than its reserved share in earlier intervals.

Worker threads exceeding their announced peak rate are suspended until the start of the next interval (at that point the connection receives new credits). In combination with a synchronous API, this design enforces flow control.

Finding the optimum interval length involves a tradeoff between accuracy of rate control and burst size ("clumping" of packets). Long intervals yield more exact rate control for bursty streams and induce less overhead for the UPC algorithm itself. On the contrary, short intervals bound the maximum burst size and have a smoothing effect on the data

---

[2]For example, when requesting an 80 Mbps stream consisting of 8 KB-sized packets, average inter-arrival time for a single packet is 0.78 ms.

[3]Credits and intervals are direction-specific, that is, connections may maintain separate credits and intervals for both directions, provided that real-time service has been requested for both directions.

stream. Figure 5 illustrates this for a connection which has 50% reserved bandwidth.

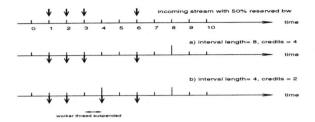

Figure 5. Influence of interval length.

It can be seen that for an asynchronous interface (e.g., the DROPS stream model and the receive direction from the network) short intervals potentially lead to dismission of packets considered conforming when using longer intervals[4]. In practice, very short intervals additionally suffer from rounding errors.

2.6. Driver interaction

This section closes by describing protocol interaction with the driver. The hardware driver provides two IPC interfaces, a send interface and a receive interface. Current design and implementation uses a synchronous send interface, which eases transmit buffer management due to its implicit feedback. That is, using page re-mapping techniques, the application's buffer (or any other producer's buffer) is transmitted to the driver interface, where the ATM board performs AAL processing (e.g., segmentation and checksumming) and transfers the data via DMA into its transmit FIFO queue. On return from this operation, the application's buffer can be recycled safely.

On data receive, the ATM board reassembles the PDU and copies it (via DMA) into host-resident buffers. These buffers are handed to the driver by the protocol on startup. The board triggers an interrupt, causing the ATM driver's receive thread to transmit a reference to this buffer. The pseudo-interrupt thread within the protocol classifies the PDU, physically copies the buffer into a connection-specific buffer and calls wake_up() on this connection.

Driver real-time support. To allow for separation of real-time from best-effort traffic, the driver uses two receive buffer pools. The protocol conveys knowledge about the nature (guaranteed or best effort) of a new connection to the driver when opening a connection. This allows for early discard of non-guaranteed traffic on system overload induced

---

[4]In the example, assume the packet at time 6 arrives early at time 4. Depending on available buffer space, this packet could be dismissed in scenario b), but not in scenario a).

by arriving ATM traffic. While the protocol has more information available for making competent QoS decisions, consistent real-time support on all system level maps well into a general DROPS paradigm. Particularly, on hosts with fast networking hardware attached, real-time support already at the driver level is imperative.

While the above scheme is not yet implemented in the driver, the Linux version of the PCA-200E driver already supports the simple cell rate control mechanism offered by the hardware.

2.7. Application interfaces

The interface provided by L[4]ATM is based on L4's synchronous IPC. Two principal application interfaces are included, which are encapsulated by a library.

Socket Interface. To ease usage of L[4]ATM and—because the synchronous nature of most socket-level calls maps well to L4's IPC—a BSD-socket compatible interface is provided. Initial test applications and applications ported to native L4 are expected to primarily use this interface. The interface handles both real-time and time-sharing services. Users convey traffic parameters via the setsockopt() call, similar to the design of Linux' ATM API [2]. It is important to note that no QoS-related knowledge (except the traffic spec) is needed by applications. The API is extended by calls where user↔L[4]ATM data transfer is performed via map operations. All measurements in Section 4 have been performed using this interface.

DROPS Stream Interface. To allow interoperability with other DROPS components, the design contains an asynchronous interface based on timed page mapping and page unmapping operations. No explicit flow control is provided here, applications are expected to be able to reserve their resources and conform to their traffic specification. Implementation of this interface is yet incomplete.

L[4]Linux Interface. As seen by L[4]Linux server, L[4]ATM behaves like a device driver. Data is transmitted via a worker thread. For receive, no buffering of Linux traffic is performed in L[4]ATM, since L[4]Linux handles buffering itself.

3. Implementation

Implementation of L[4]ATM's design is fairly complete. This section reviews selected aspects and mentions remaining discrepancies compared to the design.

Traffic management algorithms work well and exact (see Section 4). Static ATM connections (PVCs) are fully functional. Transparent usage by the L[4]Linux server (including SVCs, IP encapsulation) is stable. Support for DROPS-type chains is yet untested. Driver real-time mechanisms are implemented at the moment.

Hardware. Development platform for the DROPS project are Intel PCs. Testing and measurements (Section 4) were performed on off-the-shelf Pentium-90 machines[5] and Pentium Pro-200 machines[6]. All machines included FORE PCA-200E PCI network interface adapters. The boards support a line rate of 155.52 Mbps and are capable of AAL5 processing in hardware and bus-master DMA transfer. The machines are physically connected to a FORE ASX-200WG ATM switch using OC-3 optical fiber.

Software. The ATM device driver for Linux has been developed in our group and is freely available [5]. The L[4]ATM version is a port of the Linux driver [6].

Protocol implementation is based on the ATM suite for Linux [3]. As a first step, the Linux implementation has been moved to user level [24]. The L4-specific platform-dependent layer of L[4]ATM is built using an early version of the OSKit distribution of the University of Utah [8], a port of the Linux Pthread implementation and a library rebuilding some of typical Linux' kernel functionality (e.g., sleep_on() and wake_up()) with L4 primitives.

3.1. Resource management

Until we attain more detailed experience using the real-time components a few simplifying assumptions are used in the implementation. Resource amounts are assumed to be linear[7]. In particular, this applies to network bandwidth, buffer space and processor as resources.

Due to requirements for DMA-able buffers (i.e., contiguous physical memory) cache-partitioning schemes are not applied yet.

For simplicity, admission control manages utilization of resources independently. We use known dependency relations of resources. For instance, PCI bus and memory bus usage is strongly correlated with CPU usage. Therefore—lacking better techniques—strong dependencies among resources allow a reasonable approximation in practice.

The assumptions made reduce the number of resources considered in the implementation to CPU time, network bandwidth and buffer space.

CPU time. Machine speed is measured at protocol initialization time. Average cycles needed for protocol and driver processing have been measured. The implementation bases admission control on linear CPU utilization. Measured values for maximum achievable transmit and receive bandwidth are the basis for CPU resource management. For example, a slow P-90 machine has peak transmit rates of

about 133 Mbps and peak receive rates of about 90 Mbps in the current non-optimized implementation. Increase in processing time for small packets is compensated for by introduction of a scaling factor λ. Equation 3 is used on the P90 (σ denotes packet size):

$$\lambda \approx \begin{cases} 1 & \text{if } \sigma \geq 4096 \\ -\frac{1}{1878}\sigma + 3.238 & 1024 \leq \sigma < 4096 \\ \frac{2201}{\sigma} & 0 < \sigma < 1024 \\ 0 & \text{otherwise} \end{cases} \quad (3)$$

Total CPU time $\mathcal{U}$ needed for L[4]ATM and ATM driver processing of n transmit flows and m receive flows is thus computed as follows:

$$\mathcal{U} = \frac{\sum_{i=1}^{n} t_i \lambda_i}{t_{max}} + \frac{\sum_{j=1}^{m} r_j \lambda_j}{r_{max}} \quad (4)$$

In Equation 4, t_i indicates a guaranteed transmit flow, r_i a guaranteed receive flow, t_{max} maximum achievable transmit bandwidth and r_{max} maximum achievable receive bandwidth. $\mathcal{U} = 1$ indicates full CPU utilization.

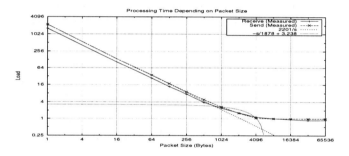

Figure 6. CPU load for a 40 Mbps transmit connection (P90).

Enforcement of CPU reservation is not yet integrated in the current prototype, but implementation of DROPS' scheduling framework and system-global CPU resource management is underway. CPU time reservation is emulated using priority hierarchies in conjunction with the policing function.

A temporary solution is used for the problem of incoming traffic overloading the receiving machine. A high-priority driver will consume all available CPU time, transmit incoming data to the protocol's *pseudo interrupt thread* which will buffer the data for readers. However, readers will get preempted almost instantly by the driver, leading to excessive data loss due to overflowing buffers in the protocol. A workaround, using a low priority for the device driver, has proved satisfactory in the implementation. Obviously, the problem will be permanently solved by integrated scheduling support, driver real-time support and appropriate configuration of the network.

---

[5] 256 KB Cache, 64 MByte RAM, Intel Neptune-based boards

[6] 256 KB Cache, 64 MByte RAM, ASUS main boards P/I-XP6NP5

[7] That is, CPU time required for a 80 Mbps flow is assumed to be twice as high as for a 40 Mbps connection.

Management of network bandwidth and core buffers are handled straightforward. L^{4}ATM is configured with the maximum achievable network bandwidth and mainly keeps track of the bandwidth used. Actual reservation is handled by the network either statically or dynamically. Buffer space is computed based on application-provided traffic parameters. Allocation and deallocation of buffer space is performed by the system's resource manager.

3.2. Implementation of UPC and policing

For Usage Parameter Control, values for interval length and credits are chosen based on the delay variation tolerance requested by the client (see Section 2.5). For jitter sensitive applications, small intervals (equaling 2 PDUs) are chosen, for the default case the algorithm tries to fit the equivalent of 10 PDUs into an interval, while jitter insensitive applications use larger intervals (equaling 50 PDUs).

When performing UPC, the current interval is determined by reading the L4 kernel's real-time clock. Thread suspension is implemented using L4 IPC, specifying a relative timeout. Thus, the suspended thread is woken up by the L4 kernel at the beginning of the next interval, when it resumes execution. Using the L4 real-time clock implies a maximum resolution of 2 ms on our test hardware.

3.3. Building the data path

When setting up connection parameters via the `setsockopt()` interface, L^{4}ATM establishes distinct permanently mapped memory segments for the transmit and receive direction. This has the advantage of speed and faster IPC compared to temporary mappings. Furthermore, it does not suffer from alignment restrictions. The driver interface is copy-free for the transmit direction (see Section 2.2). For the receive path, the current implementation still features one extra copy compared to the design presented.

Transmit and receive buffers are implemented as ring lists, where only current index position and data size are exchanged between L^{4}ATM and client library.

4. Evaluation

L^{4}ATM has matured during numerous stress tests performed in the last few months. While a multi-threaded design is traditionally prone to sporadic synchronization errors (implementing synchronization primitives used up a significant share of total programming time), L^{4}ATM routinely handles a number of concurrent `read()` and `write()` connections under competing load when running overnight.

Real-time overhead. At run time, additional cost is introduced by the call to the UPC function for each packet. The overhead associated with this function has been measured: It takes slightly more than 300 CPU cycles to call the UPC function, read the μkernel's real-time clock, check the conformity of the current packet, adjust connection credits and return to the caller. Cycles required on the P90 for the *complete* send path are in the range of 11577 . . . 351060, depending on packet size. No visible run time overhead is expected by the real time extensions. This has been verified experimentally.

Throughput. Using 8 KB sized packets, Table 1 compares throughput for L^{4}ATM against native ATM performance under Linux on the same hardware (P90).

		Avg	Max	Min
L^{4}ATM	RX	79.8	84.2	74.2
	TX	130.6	130.6	130.6
Linux	RX	58.3	62.8	52.4
	TX	129.5	130.6	126.4

Table 1. Throughput for 8 KB packets for Linux and L^{4}ATM.

Performance of L^{4}ATM was very satisfactory. Send performance is close to the maximum AAL5 rate. Average receive performance of L^{4}ATM was found to be 36.8 % higher compared with Linux. L^{4}ATM's gain is due to the smarter (e.g., more efficient) distribution of processing time: In Linux, data is enqueued in socket specific buffers by an interrupt service routine. A problem occurs when incoming ATM load is high. For the remaining path within the Linux kernel and within the application available processing time is not sufficient. Thus, a number of packets is dropped by Linux' interrupt thread due to the unavailability of buffer space at the socket queue. In contrast, L^{4}ATM makes sure that enough processing time is available for the *worker thread*. (Applications get guaranteed processing time by means of either DROPS' scheduling framework or static priorities.) This advantage outweighs the additional IPC operations required compared to Linux' in-kernel driver.

4.1. Predictability

Regarding deterministic behavior, Table 2 presents the requested sustainable data rate versus perceived data rates for two concurrent writer applications. After requesting a rate, both applications sent with full speed (In all scenarios in this section, applications are "dumb"—sending data in tight loops without QoS awareness.). L^{4}ATM transparently performs adaptation to the requested rate. The first two columns show the rate as requested by the application;

the third column the maximum data unit size specified by the application; the forth and fifth column displays interval length and credits chosen for UPC; the sixth column shows the data rate as measured by the writing application and the last column shows the received data rate on the peer machine.

Requested rate (Bytes)	Requested rate (Mbps)	Data size (Bytes)	Interval length (ms)	Credits (Bytes)	Rate sent	Peer rate
$8 * 10^6$	61.03	8192	10	79990	60.98	60.89
$3 * 10^6$	22.89	4096	13	39000	22.91	22.90

Table 2. Precision of UPC and policing algorithm for concurrent real-time `write()`.

Pre-scheduled writers. The previous measurement has sparked interest in the following question: How does L^4ATM's predictability depend on number and aggregated load imposed by several competing clients? To answer this question, a schedule has been pre-configured which tries to maximize the number of different combinations of concurrently running clients. During the total duration of about 4 hours, competing connections are periodically set up and terminated. Figure 7 shows the schedule used and gives information on the individual connections.

Figure 7. Concurrent writer schedule.

Results are given in Figure 8. Dots denote the received data rate as measured on the peer machine.

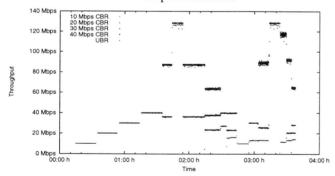

Figure 8. Five pre-scheduled concurrent writers.

During the first 80 minutes, the real-time connections ran separately. As expected from previous measurements,

L^4ATM enforces the requested bandwidth perfectly. At the later stages of the measurement, competition between the connections exists.

The upper part of the plot displays the remaining bandwidth used by the UBR connection. On start and termination of real-time connections, L^4ATM's admission control decreases or increases the rate available for all best effort connections.

4.2. Separation—AIM

The commercial AIM multiuser benchmark suite VII [1] simulates typical multi-user application load. Using a set of subtests, relevant components of an operating system are stressed. The load mix used by AIM is designed to resemble typical system load. While increasing system load until response time becomes unacceptable (*cross-over*), the number of jobs handled by the system is measured[8].

A P90 machine ran both the time-sharing L^4Linux server and the L^4ATM server concurrently on top of the L4 μkernel. A fast peer machine (Pentium Pro 200 machine running Linux) was connected via a standard OC-3 multimode fiber and a FORE ASX-200WG ATM switch.

The test duration for the complete AIM measurement (until occurrence of cross-over) is about 10 hours. A L4 real-time application requested a guaranteed ATM connection with a constant bandwidth of 40 Mbps with 8 KB sized datagrams. Within a total time frame of 22 hours, about 5000 spot checks on received throughput on the peer machine—each consisting of 10000 datagrams or 80 MB data—were made.

Performance degradation of time-sharing component. Figure 9 compares the performance of L^4Linux in terms of jobs processed per minute.

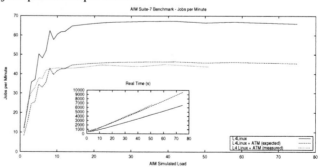

Figure 9. Achieved performance of the concurrently running time-sharing OS server.

In the top-most curve no real-time jobs exist—L^4Linux uses all hardware resources fully. Cross-over occurs at a

---

[8]The measurements are not certified by AIM Technology.

load index of 75. Under concurrent real-time ATM load (see lower curve), system performance was expected to suffer by about 31.2 %[9]. Both estimated and measured performance are given. As can be seen from the graph, time-sharing system performance measured closely fits the estimate.

ATM performance under heavy local load. The second question of interest concerns L^4ATM's ability to preserve guarantees under heavy time-sharing competition. Figure 10 shows the bandwidth received on a peer machine. During measurement of samples 1...2398 AIM load increased until crossover occurred. At sample 2399, the AIM benchmark was completed. Except for periodic maintenance services in L^4Linux, only protocol processing was running on the test machine at this stage.

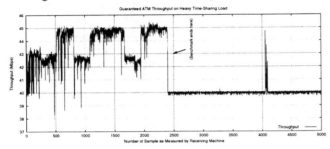

Figure 10. Measured throughput for guaranteed ATM connection under heavy concurrent load.

As can be seen from the results, L^4ATM always meets or exceeds the reserved rate, even under high load. However, the measurement also reveals an anomaly: While L^4ATM exactly meets the reserved bandwidth when using the machine exclusively, it exceeds the reserved bandwidth under extreme load conditions. This unexpected behavior is caused by the L4 μkernel, which wakes up suspended threads under this circumstances prematurely.

5. Related work

Similar to DROPS, Rialto [14] envisions coexisting real-time applications and time-sharing applications. Both pragmatic and practical assumptions have been made to aid actual implementation.

A theoretical model for QoS management has been proposed by [22] which intends to improve resource utilization for a single resource for perceived quality by the user. DROPS focuses on determining resource requirements, enforcing reservations and protection against time-sharing tasks. We do not explicitly optimize resource utilization,

rather we provide techniques for integration of component-specific parameters sets into a generalized model.

Issues in designing zero-copy user-level protocols are subject of, for example, the U-NET project [25]. An experimental setup for a zero-copy architecture using ATM hardware is described in [15].

In the context of Real-Time Mach [16] many related aspects were subject to research. Predictable protocol processing has been attempted by separating protocol code from the Mach UNIX server [20] and linking it to applications (instead of a dedicated task protecting protocol code). Contrary to L^4ATM, resource reservation issues exclusively apply to processor time. The problem of priority inversion is addressed by dynamic adaptation of thread priority (instead of per-connection threads). Resource requirements are estimated by monitoring (instead of measuring). Applications are expected to scale (instead of L^4ATM's assumption on "dumb" applications).

A related approach with very similar goals on designing end system's communication subsystem is proposed in [19], based on the x-kernel. A thread-per-connection model is favored there, too. L^4ATM improves on this approach in several ways: (1) Multitasking in L^4ATM is fully preemptive, and not cooperative. (2) Suspending threads in the L^4ATM implementation is work-preserving (e.g., no busy waiting is involved). (3) Guarantees in L^4ATM hold under existence of exclusively misbehaving time-sharing or real-time applications. (4) L^4ATM uses an off-the-shelf network adapter (as opposed to a software null device).

6. Conclusion and future work

The DROPS architecture, simultaneously supporting real-time and time-sharing applications, has been introduced. DROPS integrates multiple personalities, one such component—an ATM-based protocol server targeting deterministic network communication support—is the centerpiece of the work presented.

Design and implementation of L^4ATM has been discussed and selected aspects of the implementation on top of the L4 μkernel have been described.

Experiences with L^4ATM give us reason to be optimistic. Using highly implementable, efficient L4-based techniques for host resource management, UPC and policing, a running system has matured. Applications are provided with a standard interface, and do not need particular QoS awareness.

L^4ATM outperforms classic monolithic kernels in terms of throughput. Traffic management algorithms have been shown to work in real-world scenarios, enforcing precise control over requested rates.

Separation from time-sharing traffic has been demonstrated by running a benchmark on the time-sharing L^4Linux server. Overhead caused by implementation of

---

[9]Based on L^4ATM's resource requirements estimate.

real-time support is well below 1 %, except for very small packet sizes.

The mechanisms designed and implemented have been integrated into a prototype "DROPS chain" (a media server formed by a real-time file system and L⁴ATM) and have passed initial tests. We expect to learn more from refining this scenario.

The main future task involves integration of DROPS' scheduling mechanisms. Experiments with staggering streams will lead to refinement of interval length determination. Porting Linux' ATM signalling support to native L4—to allow for generic propagation of traffic parameters to the network—is a useful implementation step.

7. Acknowledgements

We are indebted to the members of the DROPS group at TU Dresden for supporting design, implementation, evaluation, integration and presentation of L⁴ATM. Among them, Michael Hohmuth, Jean Wolter, Sven Rudolph and Uwe Dannowski deserve special mention.

We also thank the anonymous reviewers for their comments, in particular for their helpful critical remarks.

Finally, the Linux-ATM effort by Werner Almesberger served as code base for the protocol.

References

[1] AIM Technology. *AIM Multiuser Benchmark Suite VII.*

[2] W. Almesberger. Linux ATM API (Version 0.4). Technical report, LRC Lausanne, 1996.

[3] W. Almesberger. ATM on Linux. http://lrcwww.epfl.ch/linux-atm/, 1997.

[4] D. P. Anderson. Metascheduling for Continuous Media. *ACM Transactions on Computer Systems*, 11(3):226–252, August 1993.

[5] M. Borriss and U. Dannowski. Linux Support for FORE Systems PCA-200E NIC. http://os.inf.tu-dresden.de/project/atm/, 1997.

[6] U. Dannowski. An ATM Driver for DROPS. Term paper (Großer Beleg)—Dresden University of Technology., 1998.

[7] P. Druschel and L. L. Peterson. Fbufs: A High Bandwidth Cross-Domain Transfer Facility. In *ACM Symposium On Operating System Principles (SOSP)*, 1993.

[8] B. Ford, G. Back, G. Benson, J. Lepreau, A. Lin, and O. Shivers. The Flux OSKit: A Substrate for Kernel and Language Research. In *ACM Symposium On Operating System Principles (SOSP)*, Saint Malo, France, December 1997.

[9] C.-J. Hamann. On the Quantitative Specification of Jitter Constrained Periodic Streams. In *MASCOTS*, Haifa, Israel, January 1997.

[10] H. Härtig, M. Hohmuth, and J. Wolter. Taming Linux. In *Proceedings of the 5th Annual Australasian Conference on Parallel And Real-Time Systems (PART '98)*, Adelaide, Australia, September 1998.

[11] H. Härtig, J. Wolter, and J. Liedtke. Flexible-Sized Page Objects. In *5th International Workshop on Object Orientation in Operating Systems (IWOOOS)*, pages 102–106, Seattle, WA, Oct. 1996.

[12] H. Härtig, R. Baumgartl, M.Borriss, C.-J. Hamann, M. Hohmuth, F. Mehnert, L. Reuther, S. Schönberg, and J. Wolter. DROPS - OS Support for Distributed Multimedia Applications. In *Eighth ACM SIGOPS European Workshop*, Sintra, Portugal, September 1998.

[13] H. Härtig, M. Hohmuth, J. Liedtke, S. Schönberg, and J. Wolter. The Performance of μ-Kernel Based Systems. In *ACM Symposium On Operating System Principles (SOSP)*, Saint Malo, France, December 1997.

[14] M. B. Jones, P. J. Leach, R. P. Draves, and J. S. B. III. Support for User-Centric Modular Real-Time Resource Management in the Rialto Operating System. In *Network And Operating System Support for Audio and Video (NOSSDAV)*, 1995.

[15] H. Kitamura, K. Taniguchi, H. Sakamoto, and T. Nishida. A New OS Architecture for High Performance Communication over ATM networks. In *Network And Operating System Support for Audio and Video (NOSSDAV)*, 1995.

[16] T. Kitayama, T. Nakajima, and H. Tokuda. RT-IPC: An IPC extension for Real-Time Mach. In *Proceedings of the Winter 1992 USENIX Conference*, pages 91–104, Sept. 1993.

[17] J. Liedtke. On μ-Kernel Construction. In *ACM Symposium On Operating System Principles (SOSP)*, Copper Mountains, CO, December 1995.

[18] J. Liedtke, H. Härtig, and M. Hohmuth. OS Controlled Cache Predictability for Real-Time Systems. In *Third IEEE Real-time Technology and Applications Symposium (RTAS'97)*, Montreal, Canada, June 1997.

[19] A. Mehra, A. Indiresan, and K. G. Shin. Structuring Communication Software for Quality of Service Guarantees. In *17th IEEE Real-Time Systems Symposium (RTSS)*, December 1996.

[20] C. W. Mercer, J. Zelenka, and R. Rajkumar. On Predictable Operating System Protocol Processing. Technical Report CMU-CS-94-165, School of Computer Science, Carnegie Mellon University, May 1994.

[21] D. Mosberger and L. L. Peterson. Making Paths Explicit in the Scout Operating System. In *Operating System Design and Implementation*, 1997.

[22] R. Rajkumar, C. Lee, J. Lehoczky, and D. Siewiorek. A Resource Allocation Model for QoS Management. In *IEEE Real-Time Systems Symposium*, December 1997.

[23] S. Sathaye, editor. *Traffic Management Specification Version 4.0*. ATM Forum Technical Committee, Traffic Management Working Group, 1996.

[24] G. Vattrodt. Entwicklung einer ATM-basierten Echtzeitkomponente auf dem Mikrokern L4 (in German). Master's thesis, Dresden University of Technology, 1997.

[25] T. von Eicken, A. Basu, V. Buch, and W. Vogels. U-Net: A User-Level Network Interface for Parallel and Distributed Computing. In *ACM Symposium On Operating System Principles (SOSP)*, Copper Mountains, CO, December 1995.

Session 8.A: Testing, Verification and Analysis II

Membership Questions for Timed and Hybrid Automata

R. Alur *
University of Pennsylvania & Bell Labs
alur@cis.upenn.edu

R.P. Kurshan
Bell Labs
k@research.bell-labs.com

M. Viswanathan †
University of Pennsylvania
maheshv@cis.upenn.edu

Abstract

Timed and hybrid automata are extensions of finite-state machines for formal modeling of embedded systems with both discrete and continuous components. Reachability problems for these automata are well studied and have been implemented in verification tools. In this paper, for the purpose of effective error reporting and testing, we consider the membership problems for such automata. We consider different types of membership problems depending on whether the path (i.e. edge-sequence), or the trace (i.e. event-sequence), or the timed trace (i.e. timestamped event-sequence), is specified. We give comprehensive results regarding the complexity of these membership questions for different types of automata, such as timed automata and linear hybrid automata, with and without ϵ-transitions.

In particular, we give an efficient $O(n \cdot m^2)$ algorithm for generating timestamps corresponding a path of length n in a timed automaton with m clocks. This algorithm is implemented in the verifier COSPAN to improve its diagnostic feedback during timing verification. Second, we show that for automata without ϵ-transitions, the membership question is NP-complete for different types of automata whether or not the timestamps are specified along with the trace. Third, we show that for automata with ϵ-transitions, the membership question is as hard as the reachability question even for timed traces: it is PSPACE-complete for timed automata, and undecidable for slight generalizations.

1. Introduction

Finite state machines are widely used in the modeling of systems for analysis of performance and reliability. Descriptions using FSMs are useful to represent the flow of control (as opposed to data manipulation) and are amenable to formal analyses such as testing and model checking. Traditional definitions of FSMs do not admit an explicit modeling of time, and are thus, unsuitable for describing real-time systems whose correctness depends on relative magnitudes of different delays. Consequently, timed automata [3] were introduced as a formal notation to model the behavior of real-time systems. Its definition provides a natural way to annotate FSMs with timing constraints using finitely many real-valued *clock variables*. For describing *hybrid systems*, dynamical systems whose behavior exhibits both discrete and continuous change, we need to model evolution of continuous variables such as temperature and pressure. A *hybrid automaton* [2] is a mathematical model for hybrid systems, which combines, in a single formalism, automaton transitions for capturing discrete change with differential equations for capturing continuous change.

In recent years, there has been extensive research on timed and hybrid automata (see [8, 1] for surveys). The focus of this research has been on their application to modeling and verification of real-time and hybrid systems. The best studied problem is the *reachability* question: given an automaton A and a set T of target states, is there an execution of the automaton starting in an initial state and ending in a target set? It turns out that, for timed automata, the reachability problem is decidable (in PSPACE), and the solution relies on the construction of a finite quotient of the infinite space of clock valuations. Most generalizations of timed automata have undecidable reachability problem. However, for a subclass of hybrid automata called *linear hybrid automata*, we can obtain a semi-decision procedure using a symbolic fix-point computation procedure that ma-

---

*Supported in part by NSF CAREER award CCR97-34115, and DARPA/NASA grant NAG2-1214

†Supported by grants ARO DAAG55-98-1-0393, ONR N00014-97-1-0505 (MURI), and NSF CCR-9619910

		Timed Traces	Untimed Traces	Timestamps
Timed Automata	w/o ϵ-transitions	NP-complete	NP-complete	$O(n \cdot m^2)$
	with ϵ-transitions	PSPACE-complete	PSPACE-complete	
Timed Automata with linear constraints	w/o ϵ-transitions	NP-complete	NP-complete	P
	with ϵ-transitions	undecidable	undecidable	
Linear Hybrid Automata	w/o ϵ-transitions	NP-complete	NP-complete	P
	with ϵ-transitions	undecidable	undecidable	

Figure 1. Summary of results

nipulates state-sets represented by linear constraints. For both timed and hybrid automata, a variety of of optimizations of the basic procedure have been investigated, and have been implemented in tools such as COSPAN [5], KRONOS [6], UPPAAL [11], and HYTECH [9]. These tools have been demonstrated to be useful for modeling and analysis in case-studies involving asynchronous circuits, distributed protocols, and real-time scheduling.

In this paper, we consider *membership* questions for timed and hybrid automata. In the membership question, we are given an automaton A and some partial information about a possible execution of the automaton A, and we are required to determine if there is an execution consistent with the given partial information. In particular, we consider the following three problems for various classes of hybrid automata:

1. *Timestamp generation:* Given a *path*, i.e. a sequence of edges, of the automaton, we wish to check if there is a corresponding execution, and if so, generate a possible sequence of time values at which the individual edges are traversed.

2. *Timed traces:* Given a *timed trace*, i.e. a sequence of events together with the corresponding timestamps, we wish to check if there is a corresponding execution.

3. *Untimed traces:* Given a *trace*, i.e. a sequence of events, we wish to check if there is a corresponding execution.

Our motivation for studying the first problem is reporting of counterexamples during timing verification: once the verification tool determines the sequence of transitions that leads to a violation of the safety property, the timestamp generation algorithm can be used to augment it with timestamps, thereby providing greater diagnostic feedback. The motivation for studying the last two problems is testing: a trace or a timed trace can be used as a test to check consistency of the model. This paper studies these three problems for timed automata, timed automata with linear constraints, and linear hybrid automata. For the last two problems, the complexity depends on whether or not the automaton has "hidden" ϵ-transitions. The results are summarized in Figure 1.

The timestamp generation problem for linear hybrid automata reduces to finding a solution to a set of linear inequalities. For a timed automaton, the inequalities are of a special form, and consequently, the problem reduces to computing shortest paths in a weighted digraph (with possibly negative cost cycles). Instead of using standard algorithms for this problem, we present a more efficient solution that exploits the structure of our problem better. The running time of our algorithm is $O(n \cdot m^2)$, where n is the length of the path and m is the number of clocks in the timed automaton. Note that an $O(n \cdot m^2)$ algorithm for checking whether there is an execution corresponding a given sequence of edges was already known (see, for instance, [4]), however, generating timestamps in $O(n \cdot m^2)$ requires a nontrivial modification. The timestamp generation algorithm for timed automata has been implemented in the tool COSPAN to improve its error-reporting capability.

The second set of results concerns automata in which all the edges are labeled with observable events (no ϵ-transitions). We show that for timed automata as well as linear hybrid automata, checking consistency of timed as well as untimed traces is NP-complete. The fact that all these problems are in the same class is noteworthy: specifying timestamps together with the trace does not help, and the problem is NP-hard even for timed automata.

Finally, we present results concerning automata with ϵ-transitions. Here again our results indicate that specifying timestamps together with the trace has no influence on the complexity of the membership problem. We show that the membership problem for timed automata is no easier than the reachability problem, and is PSPACE-complete. Surprisingly, the membership problem for linear hybrid automata is undecidable just like its reachability problem. This result is proved by establishing a stronger result: for timed automata with linear constraints—a restricted class of linear hybrid automata, the *bounded reachability* problem, namely, given an automaton A, a location u_f, and a deadline d, is there an execution from an initial state of A that leads to location u_f before time d, is undecidable.

2. Timed and Hybrid Automata

A hybrid automaton [2] is a formal model to describe reactive systems with discrete and continuous components. It consists of a graph wherein the system evolves continuously while at a vertex, and experiences discrete changes in the edges.

Definition 1 A hybrid automaton H consists of the following seven components.

- A finite set of real valued variables X. The cardinality of X is called the *dimension* of H. We denote by $\dot{X}$, and X', the set of variables representing the first derivatives with time and the set of variables representing the values after a discrete change, respectively, of the variables in X. A *valuation* ν is a function that assigns a real value $\nu(x)$ to each variable $x \in X$.

- A finite directed multi-graph (V, E). The vertices are called the *control modes* while the edges are called the *control switches*.

- A function *init*, that assigns to each vertex $v \in V$, a predicate $init_v$, whose free variables are from X. This describes the set of valid initial values for the variables.

- A function *inv*, that assigns to each vertex v, a predicate inv_v whose free variables are from X. This predicate describes the invariant condition for each control mode.

- A function *flow*, that assigns to each vertex v, a predicate $flow_v$ whose free variables are $X \cup \dot{X}$. This describes the way variables change in each state.

- A function *jump*, that maps a predicate $jump_e$ to each control switch $e \in E$, whose free variables are from $X \cup X'$.

- A finite set Σ (not containing ϵ) of events and an edge labeling function *event* that assigns to each control switch an event from $\Sigma \cup \{\epsilon\}$. Here ϵ denotes an unobservable transition. □

During an execution of a hybrid automaton, its state, which is given by the control mode and the value of its variables, can change in one of two ways. A *discrete* change causes the automaton to change both its control mode and the values of its variables according to the *jump* function. Otherwise, a *time delay*, causes only the value of variables to change according to the flow predicate. The execution behavior is defined more formally below.

Definition 2 For states $q_1 = (v_1, \nu_1)$ and $q_2 = (v_2, \nu_2)$ of the automaton A, an edge $e = (v_1, v_2)$, and real number t, we say $q_1 \to_t^e q_2$, if there is a function $\nu : [0, t] \to V$, where V is the set of valuations, having the following properties:

- $\nu(0) = \nu_1$.

- For all $0 \leq t' \leq t$, $inv_{v_1}(\nu(t'))$, and $flow_{v_1}(\dot{\nu}(t'))$, i.e., while the automaton is in control mode v_1 it satisfies the invariance and flow conditions.

- The edge e can be taken at time t to go to state q_2: $jump_e(\nu(t), \nu_2)$ holds.

For states $q_1 = (v_1, \nu_1)$ and $q_2 = (v_2, \nu_2)$ of the automaton A, an event a from $\Sigma \cup \{\epsilon\}$, and real number t, we say $q_1 \to_t^a q_2$ if there is an edge e such that $q_1 \to_t^e q_2$ and $event(e) = a$. □

We will denote the ith member of a sequence σ by σ_i.

Definition 3 For a sequence π of edges, a run of a hybrid automaton A from a state q, is a pair (ρ, τ), where ρ is a sequence of states, and τ is a sequence on real numbers, such that

- The sequences π, ρ, and τ are of same length,

- $\rho_0 = q$, and

- For every i, $\rho_i \to_{\tau_i}^{\pi_i} \rho_{i+1}$.

The total time of the run is $\sum_i \tau_i$. □

To define runs of an automaton on a sequence of events, we must account for the possibility of taking a sequence of ϵ-labeled edges between successive events.

Definition 4 For states q_1, q_2 of the automaton A, an event $a \in \Sigma$, and a real number t, we say $q_1 \Rightarrow_t^a q_2$, if there exists a run starting from q_1 and ending at q_2, for the sequence $\epsilon^n a \epsilon^m$, for some n, m, where the total time of the run is t. In other words, there is a run that takes an arbitrary (finite) number of unobservable transitions before and after taking a control switch labeled a, to reach q_2 after t units of time.

For a sequence σ of events, a run of a hybrid automaton A from a state q over σ, is a pair (ρ, τ), where ρ is a sequence of states, and τ is a sequence of real numbers, such that

- $\rho_0 = q$, and

- For every i, $\rho_i \Rightarrow_{\tau_i}^{\sigma_i} \rho_{i+1}$. □

Example 1 Consider the hybrid automaton described in Figure 2. It models a system that controls the percentage of oxygen and carbon-dioxide in the room. The variables o and c represent the volume of oxygen and carbon-dioxide. When the system is in the control mode "Off", oxygen is consumed to produce carbon-dioxide and other gases (which have not been modeled). This is reflected by

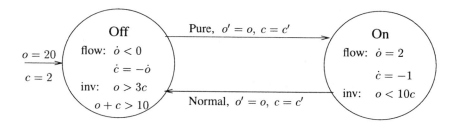

Figure 2. Example of a Hybrid automaton

the fact that the rate at which carbon-dioxide increases is related to the rate at which oxygen is consumed. The system can remain in this control mode as long as there is enough oxygen compared to the carbon-dioxide ($o > 3c$), and the total volume of the other gases in the room is not too much (i.e. $o+c > 10$). In the control mode "On", the system turns on the purifier which pumps in oxygen and takes out the carbon-dioxide. The two control switches "Pure" and "Normal" can be taken at any time and these leave the volumes of the gases unchanged. Initially the system is assumed to be in "Off" mode, with the value $o = 20$ and $c = 2$ for the variables. □

We will now define some special classes of hybrid automata. Recall, that a *linear inequality* over a set of variables X is an inequality involving linear terms of the variables in X.

Definition 5 A linear hybrid automaton is a hybrid automaton, where, for any control mode v and switch e,

- The predicates $init_v$, inv_v, and $jump_e$ are conjunctions of linear inequalities [1] over X, and

- The predicate $flow_v$ is a conjunction of linear inequalities over $\dot{X}$. □

The automaton in Example 1 is an example of an linear hybrid automaton.

Definition 6 A variable $x \in X$ is a clock if for every control mode v, $flow_v : \dot{x} = 1$ (in other words, value of x increases uniformly with time), and if every discrete change either resets x to 0 or leaves it unchanged.

A timed automaton with linear constraints is a linear hybrid automaton all of whose variables are clocks.

A timed automaton is a linear hybrid automaton all of whose variables are clocks and whose linear expressions

are boolean combinations of inequalities of the form $x \, \theta \, k$, where θ is a comparison operator and k is an integer constant. □

For a class $\mathcal{H}$ of hybrid automata we define different membership problems depending on whether we are given a sequence of edges or a sequence of events or a sequence of events together with corresponding timestamps.

Timestamp Generation	Given an automaton $A \in \mathcal{H}$ and a sequence π of edges, check if there is a run (ρ, τ) of A on π starting from some initial state, and if so, output the time sequence τ.
Timed Traces	Given an automaton $A \in \mathcal{H}$, a sequence of events σ and a sequence of real numbers τ, check if there is a run (ρ, τ) of A on σ starting from some initial state.
Untimed Traces	Given an automaton $A \in \mathcal{H}$ and a sequence of events σ, check if there is a run (ρ, τ) of A on σ starting from some initial state.

3. Generating Timestamps

In this section, we consider the problem of checking whether a sequence of edges can be taken, and if so, generating a corresponding consistent sequence of timestamps.

3.1. Timed Automata

We are given a timed automaton A and a sequence π of edges of A, and we wish to determine if A has a run over π, and if so, determine a possible sequence τ of timestamps at which the edges in π can be taken.

3.1.1 Graph-theoretic formulation

The problem timestamp generation for timed automata can be reformulated as a graph theoretic problem. We will first

---

[1] In literature, most papers consider $init_v$, inv_v, $flow_v$, and $jump_e$ to be any boolean combination of linear inequalities. Though in this paper we consider these predicates to be only conjunctions, our algorithms and proofs can be easily modified to handle to more general case. See footnote in proof of Proposition 5.

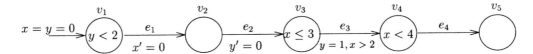

Figure 3. A sample path in a timed automaton

illustrate this through an example, before giving the formal translation of this problem into a graph theoretic one.

Example 2 Consider the sample path shown in Figure 3. If we denote the initial time by t_0, and the time at which edge e_i is traversed by t_i, then the path is traversable iff the following set of constraints has a solution:

$$t_0 \leq t_1 \leq t_2 \leq t_3 \leq t_4, \ t_1 - t_0 < 2,$$

$$t_3 - t_1 \leq 3, \ t_4 - t_1 < 4, \ t_3 - t_2 = 1, \ t_3 - t_1 > 2.$$

Furthermore, a solution to the above set can be used to construct the desired timestamps. To solve this problem, we can consider the weighted graph shown in Figure 4. Note that for an upper bound constraint such as $t_3 - t_1 \leq 3$, we put an edge from node 3 to 1 with cost 3, and for a lower bound constraint such as $t_3 - t_1 > 2$, we put an edge from 1 to 3 with cost -2^-. The superscript "-" indicates that the corresponding constraint is strict. The set of constraints is not consistent if there is a cycle with total cost 0^- or less. If there is no negative cost cycle, then let $d(0, i)$ denote the cost of the shortest path from 0 to node i. Setting $t_i = -d(0, i)$ gives a feasible solution to the set of constraints. □

Now we formalize the graph theoretic formulation of the problem. Assume that the sequence π contains n edges $e_1, \ldots e_n$, where the edge $e_i = (v_i, v_{i+1})$. Recall that a timed automaton uses constraints of the form $x\theta k$ for a clock x and a comparison operator θ. A lower bound on x is a constraint of the form $x > k$ or $x \geq k$, while an upper bound on x is a constraint of the form $x < k$ or $x \leq k$ (a constraint $x = k$ is modeled as the conjunction $x \leq k \wedge x \geq k$). For vertex v_i, the invariant $inv(v_i)$ is a conjunction of lower and upper bound constraints. For edge e_i, the jump predicate $jump(e_i)$ contains lower and upper bound constraints on some of the clocks (unprimed values), and resets some of the clocks. Let λ_i denote the set of clocks reset on edge e_i, and let λ_0 contain all the clocks. For a clock x and index i, let $last_i^x$ denote the position where the clock x has been reset most recently before i. That is, $last_i^x = j$ if $j < i$ and $x \in \lambda_j$ and $x \notin \lambda_k$ for $j < k < i$.

The lower and upper bound constraints can be strict or non-strict. In order to deal with different types of bounds

uniformly, we define the domain of bounds, similar to [7], to be the set

$$\mathcal{B} = \{\ldots - 2, -1, 0, 1, 2, \ldots\} \cup$$
$$\{\ldots - 2^-, -1^-, 0^-, 1^-, 2^-, \ldots\} \cup$$
$$\{-\infty, \infty\}.$$

For a constraint of the form $x \leq k$, upper bound on x is k, while for a constraint of the form $x < k$, upper bound on x is k^-. Similarly, for a constraint of the form $x \geq k$, lower bound on x is k, while for a constraint of the form $x > k$, lower bound on x is k^-. To compute shortest paths, we need to add bounds and compare bounds. The ordering $<$ over the integers is extended to $\mathcal{B}$ by the following law: for any integer a, $-\infty < a^- < a < (a + 1)^- < \infty$. The addition operation $+$ over integers is extended to $\mathcal{B}$ by: (i) for all $b \in \mathcal{B}$, $b + \infty = \infty$, (ii) for all $b \in \mathcal{B}$ with $b \neq \infty$, $b + (-\infty) = -\infty$, and (iii) for integers a and b, $a + b^- = a^- + b = a^- + b^- = (a + b)^-$.

Generating timestamps corresponding to the path π reduces to computing shortest paths in the graph G defined below. The graph has $n + 1$ nodes numbered 0 through n. The edges are defined by the following rules

1. Monotonicity: for each node $0 \leq i < n$, there is an edge from node i to node $i + 1$ with cost 0.

2. Upper bounds: for each clock x and position $1 \leq i \leq n$, if k is the upper bound on x in $jump(e_i)$ or in $inv(v_i)$, then there is an edge from node i to node $last_i^x$ with cost k.

3. Lower bounds: for each clock x and position $1 \leq i \leq n$, if k is the lower bound on x in $jump(e_i)$ or in $inv(v_{i+1})$ then there is an edge from node $last_i^x$ to i with cost $-k$.

Proposition 1 *The timed automaton A has a run over the path π of edges iff the graph G defined above has no negative cost cycle. Furthermore, if G has no negative cost cycle, then for $1 \leq i \leq n$, let d_i denote the shortest path from node 0 to node i. Then, the sequence $-d_1, d_1 - d_2, d_2 - d_3, \ldots d_{n-1} - d_n$ is a feasible time sequence corresponding to π.* □

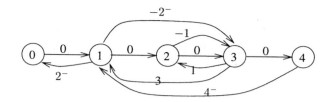

Figure 4. The weighted graph for the path of Figure 2

3.1.2 An efficient algorithm for timestamp generation

We have shown that generating timestamps reduces to finding negative-cost cycles and shortest paths in graph G. Let n be the length of the given sequence of edges and m be the number of clocks in A. In our applications, m usually denotes the number of processes, and is quite small, while n can be quite large. Consequently, instead of using standard algorithms for computing shortest distances in a weighted graph, we present an algorithm that exploits the structure of our problem in a better way.

For two nodes i and j in graph G, let $cost(i, j)$ denote the weight of the edge from node i to node j (if there are multiple edges between a pair of nodes, we need to consider only the one with minimum cost). For $1 \leq i \leq n$, define the subgraph G_i to consist of nodes numbered 0 through i. Let $d_i(j, l)$, for $0 \leq j, l \leq i$ denote the cost of the shortest path from j to l in the graph G_i. In particular, $d_i(0, i)$ is the cost of the shortest path from 0 to i without visiting a vertex numbered higher than i.

Let $V_i \subseteq \{0, \ldots i\}$ contain the node 0, the node i, and any other node of G_i that has an edge to some node outside G_i. Note that for a node $0 < j < i$ to be in V_i, there must be some position $l > i$ and a clock x with $last_l^x = j$. Consequently, besides 0 and i, V_i can contain at most one node per clock, and has at most $m + 2$ nodes. The nodes not in V_i are "internal" to the subgraph G_i. From the graph G_i let us define another weighted graph H_i, called the *reduced graph* of G_i, as follows: the set of nodes is V_i, and for every pair of nodes j and l in V_i there is an edge from j to l with cost equal to the cost $d_i(j, l)$ of the shortest path from j to l in the graph G_i (note that this cost can be ∞ if there is no path from j to l, and can be $-\infty$ if there is no "shortest" path because of a negative cost cycle).

The algorithm for generating timestamps is outlined in Figure 5. In the first phase, the algorithm successively computes the reduced graphs H_1, H_2, and so on. While implementing the algorithm, each such graph is represented by the matrix M that gives, for every pair of nodes, the cost of the edge connecting them (the entries in the matrix are from the domain $\mathcal{B}$). Since the number of vertices in a reduced graph is bounded by $m + 2$, the size of the matrix M is $(m + 2) \times (m + 2)$. Consider the matrix M representing the reduced graph H_{i-1}. Step 1 corresponds to adding an extra row and column to M. At step 2, we need to check if the updated matrix has a negative cost cycle, and if not, compute the new shortest distances. Observe that, for any pair of vertices j and l, the new shortest distance between j and l is different from the old one, only if the new shortest path visits the new vertex i. This fact can be used to compute the new shortest distances efficiently in time $O(m^2)$. Step 3 ensures that the updated matrix M stores only the nodes that are external to H_i. In particular, if a clock x gets reset on edge e_i, then the node $last_i^x$ can become internal, and get deleted.

The shortest distances computed during the first phase are stored in the array C and the matrix D: at the end of the first phase, for each node i, $C[i]$ equals $d_i(0, i)$, and for each clock x, $D[i][x]$ equals $d_i(last_i^x, i)$. The distance $C[i]$ computed at the end of the first phase does not consider paths to node i that visit vertices numbered higher than i. Such paths are accounted for in the second phase. First note that the distance $d(0, n)$ equals $d_n(0, n)$, and thus, the entry $C[n]$ contains the optimal shortest path to the last node n. Observe that the shortest path from 0 to a node i is either contained in G_i (and hence equals $d_i(0, i)$), or consists of a shortest path from 0 to a node $j > i$, an edge from j to some vertex l in V_i, and shortest path from l to i in G_i: $d(0, i)$ equals

$$min\{d_i(0, i), min_{j>i,l \in V_i}\{d(0, j) + d_i(l, i) + cost(j, l)\}\}$$

The second phase consists of a loop that processes nodes in decreasing order starting from n. Just before processing node i, we know that the entries $C[j]$ for nodes j numbered higher than i, denote the true costs $d(0, j)$. Furthermore, the entries $C[l]$ for nodes $l \in V_i$ have been updated to reflect edges from nodes numbered higher than i: for each $l \in V_i$ and $j > i$, $C[l]$ is at most the sum of $C[j]$ and the cost of the edge from j to l. Consequently, the correct value of $d(0, i)$ can be computed as shown in the algorithm.

Proposition 2 *At the end of the execution of the algorithm of Figure 5, for each i, the value $C[i]$ equals the cost $d(0, i)$ of the shortest path from 0 to i in the graph G.* □

The running time of the first phase is $O(n \cdot m^2)$, while of the second phase is $O(n \cdot m)$.

Input: A timed automaton A and a sequence π of edges.

Output: Decides if A has a run over π, and if so, outputs a sequence τ of timestamps.

Data structures: M: $(m+2) \times (m+2)$ matrix; C: array of length n; D: $n \times m$ matrix

Algorithm:

Phase One:

    Initialize M to denote the graph with a single node 0.

    For $i := 1$ **to** n **do**

        { **Comment**: M denotes the graph H_{i-1} }

        1. To M, add the node i and all edges of H_i involving node i.

        2. Compute new shortest distances within M.

            If a negative cost cycle is detected, stop (there is no run over π).

        3. Remove all the nodes not in V_i.

        4. Set $C[i]$ to shortest distance from 0 to i in M.

        5. For each clock x, set $D[i][x]$ to shortest distance from $last_i^x$ to i in M.

Phase Two:

    For $i := n$ **downto** 1 **do**

        { **Comment**: $C[j]$ for $j > i$ denotes the shortest distance $d(0, j)$ }

        { **Comment**: for $l \in V_i$ and $j > i$, $C[l] \leq C[j] + cost(j, l)$}

        For each clock x **do**

            $C[i] = min(C[i], C[last_i^x] + D[i][x])$;

        For each clock x **do**

            $C[last_i^x] = min(C[last_i^x], C[i] + cost(i, last_i^x))$;

Figure 5. Algorithm for generating timestamps in timed automata

Theorem 3 *Given a timed automaton A with m clocks, and a sequence of π of n edges, the timestamp generation problem can be solved in time $O(n \cdot m^2)$ time.* $\square$

3.1.3 Implementation in COSPAN

The timestamp generation algorithm is implemented in the tool COSPAN. We begin with an overview of COSPAN, a model checker based on the theory of ω-automata developed at Bell Labs. The system to be verified is modeled as a collection of coordinating processes described in the language S/R [10]. The semantics of such a model M is the ω-language $L(M)$ corresponding to the infinite executions of the model. The property to be checked is described as another process T, and the model M satisfies the property T if the language of the product of M and T is empty. The language-emptiness test can be performed via a variety of highly optimized algorithms such as on-the-fly enumerative search and symbolic search using binary decision diagrams. In the real-time extension of COSPAN[5], real-time constraints are expressed by associating lower and upper bounds on the time spent by a process in a local state. An execution is timing-consistent if its steps can be assigned real-valued timestamps that satisfy all the specified bounds. The semantics of a timed S/R model M with a table B of bounds is, then, the set $L(M, B)$ of executions of M that are timing-consistent with the bounds-table B. The timing verification problem corresponds to checking emptiness of the language $L(M \otimes T, B)$ for a suitably chosen process T. A variety of correctness requirements such as invariants, absence of deadlocks, liveness, and bounded response, can be modeled in S/R. The expressiveness of timed S/R is the same as that of timed automata [3]. For checking emptiness of the language $L(M, B)$, the verifier automatically constructs another automaton A_B, also as a S/R process, which when composed with the original model, rules out executions that do not satisfy the timing constraints: $L(M \otimes A_B)$ equals $L(M, B)$. The existence of such a finite-state constraining automaton A_B follows from the so-called region construction for timed automata [3].

As explained above, the timing verification problem reduces to language emptiness problem, which in turn is a reachability problem. If the model does not satisfy the property the tool reports a *counterexample* that consists of a path consisting of states and events. The counterexample provides debugging information that is helpful is isolating the problem, and is of crucial importance in practice. The input to the timestamp generation algorithm is the counterexample reported by COSPAN. The timestamp generation algorithm computes the sequence of time values corresponding to the path, and outputs the counterexample together with timestamps. Thus, it enhances the error reporting capabilities of COSPAN. In practice, the running time of the timestamp generation algorithm is much smaller than the model checking algorithm that generates the path corresponding to the counterexample.

3.2. Linear Hybrid Automata

Theorem 4 *The timestamp generation problem, for the class of linear hybrid automata, can be solved in polynomial time.*

Proof: Given a sequence π of edges and a linear hybrid automaton A, the problem of timestamp generation can be reduced to that of solving a linear programming problem. If λ is the sequence of control modes of A that are visited when traversing the sequence of edges π, then the linear program is defined as follows.

For each variable $x \in X$ and control mode λ_i in the sequence λ, we will introduce variables x_{λ_i}, x'_{λ_i}, and τ_{λ_i} in the linear programming formulation. Intuitively, the variables x'_{λ_i} and x_{λ_i} denote the value of the variable x of the automaton, at the time of entering and leaving the control mode λ_i, respectively. The variable τ_{λ_i} denotes the total time spent in control mode λ_i during the run. Let ν_i and ν'_i denote the vector of variables x_{λ_i} and x'_{λ_i}, respectively, for $x \in X$. We will now introduce constraints corresponding to the predicates associated with the control modes and switches of A. Since (λ_0, ν_0) is the initial state of this run, we will have constraints $init_{\lambda_0}(\nu_0)$ which will ensure that the valuation ν_0 is a valid initial valuation. For the invariance predicate inv_{λ_i}, we will introduce linear constraints $inv_{\lambda_i}(\nu'_i)$ and $inv_{\lambda_i}(\nu_i)$. For a flow condition of the form $\sum_j a_j \cdot \dot{x}_j \leq k$, we add constraints $\sum_j a_j(\frac{x_{j\lambda_i} - x'_{j\lambda_i}}{\tau_{\lambda_i}}) \leq k$ and for each predicate $jump_{e_i}$, where $e_i = (\lambda_i, \lambda_{i+1})$ and $label(e_i) = \sigma_i$, we have constraints $jump_{e_i}(\nu_i, \nu'_{i+1})$. These constraints essentially check that if we assume that in each control mode λ_i of the run, the variables evolve along the straight line joining ν'_i and ν_i then that will correspond to a correct execution of the automaton A.

So clearly if the above linear programming problem has a solution then (ρ, τ), where τ is the sequence $\tau_{\lambda_1}, \tau_{\lambda_2}, \ldots$, and ρ is the sequence $(\lambda_1, \nu_1), (\lambda_2, \nu_2), \ldots$, is a run of A on σ. Furthermore, if there is an execution in which, in each control mode, the variables evolve so that the invariance and flow conditions are not violated, then the straight line evolution from ν'_i to ν_i would also conform to the invariance and flow conditions. This follows from the central limit theorem in calculus and the fact that the predicate inv_{ρ_i} defines a convex region. Since the solution of a linear program can be found in polynomial time [12], the the timestamp generation problem in in P. $\qquad \square$

Remark: The timestamp generation problem for timed automata with linear constraints also can be solved by reducing it to solving a similar linear programming problem. We cannot do much better than this because the linear programming formulation for timestamp generation, in the cases of linear hybrid automata and timed automata with linear constraints, does not have a special form like in the case of timed automata. $\qquad \square$

Example 3 Consider the hybrid automaton given in Example 1, and suppose we want to see if there is valid run of the automaton on the sequence of edges "Pure, Normal". The sequence of control modes is then Off, On, Off. The existence of a run can be reduced to the feasibility of the following linear program.

$$o'_{\text{Off}_1} = 20 \quad c'_{\text{Off}_1} = 2 \ \} \ \text{initial condition}$$

$$\left.\begin{array}{ll} o'_{\text{Off}_1} = 20 & c'_{\text{Off}_1} = 2 \\ o'_{\text{Off}_1} > 3 \cdot c'_{\text{Off}_1} & o'_{\text{Off}_1} + c'_{\text{Off}_1} > 10 \\ o_{\text{Off}_1} > 3 \cdot c_{\text{Off}_1} & o_{\text{Off}_1} + c_{\text{Off}_1} > 10 \\ \frac{o_{\text{Off}_1} - o'_{\text{Off}_1}}{\tau_{\text{Off}_1}} < 0 & \frac{c_{\text{Off}_1} - c'_{\text{Off}_1}}{\tau_{\text{Off}_1}} = -\left[\frac{o_{\text{Off}_1} - o'_{\text{Off}_1}}{\tau_{\text{Off}_1}}\right] \end{array}\right\} \text{Mode Off}$$

$$\left.\begin{array}{ll} o'_{\text{On}} = o_{\text{Off}_1} & c'_{\text{On}} = c_{\text{Off}_1} \\ o_{\text{On}} < 10 \cdot c'_{\text{On}} & o_{\text{On}} < 10 \cdot c_{\text{On}} \\ \frac{o_{\text{On}} - o'_{\text{On}}}{\tau_{\text{On}}} = 2 & \frac{c_{\text{On}} - c'_{\text{On}}}{\tau_{\text{On}}} = -1 \end{array}\right\} \text{Mode On}$$

$$\left.\begin{array}{ll} o'_{\text{Off}_2} = o_{\text{On}} & c'_{\text{Off}_2} = c_{\text{On}} \\ o_{\text{Off}_2} > 3 \cdot c'_{\text{Off}_2} & o'_{\text{Off}_2} + c'_{\text{Off}_2} > 10 \\ o_{\text{Off}_2} > 3 \cdot c_{\text{Off}_2} & o_{\text{Off}_2} + c_{\text{Off}_2} > 10 \\ \frac{o_{\text{Off}_2} - o'_{\text{Off}_2}}{\tau_{\text{Off}_2}} < 0 & \frac{c_{\text{Off}_2} - c'_{\text{Off}_2}}{\tau_{\text{Off}_2}} = -\left[\frac{o_{\text{Off}_2} - o'_{\text{Off}_2}}{\tau_{\text{Off}_2}}\right] \end{array}\right\} \text{Mode Off}$$

4. Automata without unobservable transitions

In this section we will investigate the complexity of membership questions for automata that do not have ϵ-transitions.

Proposition 5 *The problem of membership of untimed traces for linear hybrid automata is in NP.*

Proof: In order to check if a sequence of events σ is an untimed trace of a linear hybrid automaton A, our algorithm will first guess a sequence λ of control modes that the automaton A visits in a run on σ. Once we have guessed a sequence of control modes, the problem of checking if there is a sequence of real numbers τ, and a sequence of valuations ν such that (ρ, τ) (where $\rho_i = (\lambda_i, \nu_i)$) is a run on σ is then reduced to checking the feasibility of a linear programming problem, defined in a manner similar to that in the proof of Theorem 4.[2] $\qquad \square$

---

[2]In the more general case, when the invariant predicate is a boolean combination of linear inequalities, the predicate defines a union of convex regions. The algorithm then will guess not only the sequence of control modes λ that are visited, but will also guess the sequence of convex regions visited, for each control mode. The linear program will then have additional variables, for each control mode, that will correspond to the values of the clock and the variables of the automaton, at the time of entering and leaving each convex region.

Proposition 6 *The problem of membership of timed traces for timed automata is NP-hard.*

Proof: We will reduce the *directed hamiltonian path* problem to the problem of membership of timed traces. In the directed hamiltonian path problem, we are given a graph G and we want to know if there is a directed path in G that visits each vertex exactly once.

Now the control graph of the timed automaton A that we will construct will be exactly the same as the graph G that is input to the directed hamiltonian path problem. The idea will be to ensure that transitions of the timed automaton are taken after every time unit and that when we visit a vertex v of the graph G, we "mark" the vertex. The way we will "mark" the vertex is by resetting a clock x_v corresponding to the vertex v.

More formally, the automaton A will have clocks y and z, and clocks x_v corresponding to each vertex v of G. Clock y will be used mark out 1 unit of time since the last transition, while z will be used to store the total time elapsed since the start of execution. The clocks x_v will be used to mark the vertices visited. All the edges in the control graph will be labeled a. A transition from u to v will check if $(y = 1)$ i.e., 1 unit of time has passed, and if $(x_v = z)$ i.e., the vertex v has not been visited. Taking the transition from u to v will have the effect of resetting the clocks y and x_u. It can be easily seen that the string $a.a.\ldots.a$ with timing sequence $1, 1, \ldots, 1$ is a valid timed trace of A if and only if G has a directed hamiltonian path. $\square$

The following theorem then can be seen as an immediate corollary of propositions 5 and 6.

Theorem 7 *The problems of membership of timed traces and untimed traces for linear hybrid automata, timed automata with linear constraints, and timed automata are NP-complete.* $\square$

5. Automata with unobservable transitions

We will now examine the question of membership of traces with ϵ-transitions for various classes of hybrid automata. This problem is closely related to the well-studied problem of control mode reachability.

Definition 7 The reachability problem for a class $\mathcal{H}$ of hybrid automata asks, given an automaton A from class $\mathcal{H}$ and a control mode v of the automaton, if there exists a run (ρ, τ) for some trace σ such that $(v, \nu) = \rho_i$ for some i and valuation ν. $\square$

The problem of membership of untimed traces with ϵ-transitions is, in some sense, "equivalent" to the reachability problem. Clearly, the reachability problem can be reduced to a problem of membership of untimed traces with

ϵ-transitions. Now, if we have a membership problem, then we simply guess a sequence of states ρ and then check if ρ_{i+1} is reachable from ρ'_i, where ρ'_i is the state such that $\rho_i \rightarrow^{\sigma_i} \rho'_i$. Since we know that the reachability problem is PSPACE-complete for timed automata [3], and is undecidable for timed automata with linear constraints [3] and linear hybrid automata [2], we get the following theorem as a corollary of the above observation.

Theorem 8 *The problem of membership of untimed traces with ϵ-transitions is PSPACE-complete for timed automata and is undecidable for timed automata with linear constraints and linear hybrid automata.* $\square$

Similarly, the problem of membership of timed traces with ϵ-transitions is "equivalent" to the bounded reachability problem. In the bounded reachability problem, we are given an automaton A, a control mode v and time t, and we want to know if we can reach the control mode v at time t.

Proposition 9 *The bounded reachability problem for timed automata is PSPACE-complete.*

Proof: This result essentially follows from Savitch's theorem and from the PSPACE-completeness proof of reachability for timed automata [3]. In [3], they reduce the question of deciding whether a given linear bounded automaton M accepts a given input string to the reachability problem for timed automata.

In the construction, a computation of M is encoded by a word

$$\sigma_1^1 a_0 \ldots \sigma_n^1 a_0 \sigma_1^2 a_0 \ldots \sigma_n^2 a_0 \ldots \sigma_1^j a_0 \ldots \sigma_n^j a_0 \ldots$$

where $\sigma_1^j \sigma_2^j \ldots \sigma_n^j$ encodes the jth configuration of the machine M. One tries to ensure that the time difference between successive a_0's is some constant $k + 1$ (depending on the tape alphabet of M), while the time difference between σ_i^j and the preceding a_0 encodes the symbol σ_i^j. The timed automaton then reaches a special control mode q_f precisely when the word encodes an accepting computation of M.

Observe that in the above construction, the timed automaton processes each configuration of the machine M in a fixed time of $n \cdot (k + 1)$. Now from Savitch's theorem, we know that a linear bounded automaton has at most 2^{cn} configurations, where c is a constant. Therefore, we know that the timed automaton reaches the control mode q_f at time $n \cdot (k + 1) \cdot 2^{cn}$ if and only if the linear bounded automaton accepts the input string. (If the computation of M has less than 2^{cn} configurations then in the timed automaton we will simply idle in some control state q_i until the time is $n \cdot (k + 1) \cdot 2^{cn}$.) Since $n \cdot (k + 1) \cdot 2^{cn}$ can be written using polynomially many bits, this is a polynomial time reduction. Hence, the bounded reachability problem for timed automata is PSPACE-complete. $\square$

The bounded reachability problem, which shall now investigate, turns out to be undecidable for even the class of timed automata with linear constraints. The proof shall use the fact that the halting problem for two-counter machines is undecidable.

A two-counter machine has a finite sequence of instructions and two unbounded counters. Each instruction can be one of three kinds; branching conditionally based upon the value of a certain counter being 0, or incrementing a counter, or decrementing a counter. Initially the counters are assumed to be 0. Now, it is known that the halting problem for two-counter machines is undecidable. We shall use this fact in our proofs.

Proposition 10 *The bounded reachability problem for timed automata with linear constraints is undecidable.*

Proof: The proof is very similar to the undecidability proof of the reachability problem for 2-rate timed systems in [2]. We shall encode the computation of a two-counter machine M by a timed automaton with linear constraints, A. The control mode of A encodes the program counter of M, while the value of the counters is encoded by two clocks x_1 and x_2. Every step of the two-counter machine is simulated in $k < 1$ time units, where k is a constant that is nondeterministically chosen by the automaton in the first step; hence in one time unit the automaton simulates approximately $\frac{1}{k}$ steps of the two-counter machine. The way we measure out k units of time is by using two clocks — y_o and y_e. The absolute value of the difference between these two clocks will always be k; at the start of each odd step we will reset the clock y_o when $y_o = 2 \cdot y_e$, and at the start of each even step, we will reset the clock y_e when $y_e = 2 \cdot y_o$. A counter value of n at the ith step in the computation of machine M is encoded by the clock x_1 (or x_2) having the value $\frac{k}{2^n}$ at time $i \cdot k$.

Testing for the counter being zero essentially is checking to see if $x_1 = k$ (or $x_2 = k$); this can be done by comparing x_1 (or x_2) to $y_e - y_o$, if it is the odd step, and to $y_o - y_e$ if it is an even step. Now suppose the value of the clock x_1 is $\frac{k}{2^n}$ at time $i \cdot k$. If the value of the counter remains unchanged in the next step of computation, then simply reset the clock x_1 when its value becomes k (i.e. at time $(i+1) \cdot k - \frac{k}{2^n}$), and that way its value at time $(i+1) \cdot k$ will be $\frac{k}{2^n}$. If the value of the counter is to be incremented, then we reset a clock z at the time when $x_1 = k$, and reset x_1 at some time after $(i+1) \cdot k - \frac{k}{2^n}$ but before $(i+1) \cdot k$. At time $(i+1) \cdot k$, we test if $z = 2 \cdot x_1$, and this will ensure that the value of x_1 is $\frac{1}{2} \cdot \frac{k}{2^n} = \frac{k}{2^{n+1}}$. In order to decrement the counter in the ith step, we first nondeterministically reset a clock z in the interval $((i-1) \cdot k, i \cdot k - \frac{k}{2^n})$ and check if at time $k \cdot i$, $z = 2 \cdot x_1$. This will ensure that the value of z at time $k \cdot i$ represents the counter value $i - 1$. We will then reset x_1

when $z = k$, and so at time $(i+1) \cdot k$, the value of x_1 is $\frac{k}{2^{n-1}}$.

Now, it can be seen that at time 1 the automaton A will reach a particular control mode q_f if and only if the two-counter machine M halts. Hence, the bounded reachability problem for timed automata with linear constraints is undecidable. ☐

The propositions 9 and 10 imply the following theorem.

Theorem 11 *The problem of membership of timed traces with ϵ-transitions is PSPACE-complete for timed automata, and is undecidable for timed automata with linear constraints and linear hybrid automata.* ☐

Acknowledgements.

We thank Sampath Kannan, Insup Lee, and Mihalis Yannakakis for fruitful discussions.

References

[1] R. Alur. Timed automata. In *NATO ASI Summer School on Verification of Digital and Hybrid Systems*. 1998. To appear. Available at www.cis.upenn.edu/ alur/Nato97.ps.gz.

[2] R. Alur, C. Courcoubetis, N. Halbwachs, T. Henzinger, P. Ho, X. Nicollin, A. Olivero, J. Sifakis, and S. Yovine. The algorithmic analysis of hybrid systems. *Theoretical Computer Science*, 138:3–34, 1995.

[3] R. Alur and D. Dill. A theory of timed automata. *Theoretical Computer Science*, 126:183–235, 1994.

[4] R. Alur, A. Itai, R. Kurshan, and M. Yannakakis. Timing verification by successive approximation. *Information and Computation*, 118(1):142–157, 1995.

[5] R. Alur and R. Kurshan. Timing analysis in COSPAN. In *Hybrid Systems III: Control and Verification*, LNCS 1066, pages 220–231. Springer-Verlag, 1996.

[6] C. Daws, A. Olivero, S. Tripakis, and S. Yovine. The tool KRONOS. In *Hybrid Systems III: Verification and Control*, LNCS 1066, pages 208–219. Springer-Verlag, 1996.

[7] D. Dill. Timing assumptions and verification of finite-state concurrent systems. In J. Sifakis, editor, *Automatic Verification Methods for Finite State Systems*, LNCS 407, pages 197–212. Springer–Verlag, 1989.

[8] T. Henzinger. The theory of hybrid automata. In *Proceedings of the 11th IEEE Symposium on Logic in Computer Science*, pages 278–293, 1996.

[9] T. Henzinger, P. Ho, and H. Wong-Toi. HYTECH: a model checker for hybrid systems. *Software Tools for Technology Transfer*, 1, 1997.

[10] R. Kurshan. *Computer-aided Verification of Coordinating Processes: the automata-theoretic approach*. Princeton University Press, 1994.

[11] K. Larsen, P. Pettersson, and W. Yi. UPPAAL in a nutshell. *Springer International Journal of Software Tools for Technology Transfer*, 1, 1997.

[12] C. Papadimitriou and K. Steiglitz. *Combinatorial optimization: Algorithms and complexity*. Prentice-Hall, 1982.

On Checking Timed Automata for Linear Duration Invariants[*]

Victor Adrian Braberman
FCEyN-UBA, Argentina
vbraber@dc.uba.ar

Dang Van Hung
The United Nations University
UNU/IIST, P.O.Box 3058 Macau
dvh@iist.unu.edu

Abstract

In this work, we address the problem of verifying a Timed Automaton for a real-time property written in Duration Calculus in the form of Linear Duration Invariants. We present a conservative method for solving the problem using the linear programming techniques. First, we provide a procedure to translate Timed Automata into a sort of regular expressions for timed languages. Then, we extend the linear programming-based approaches in [10] to this algebraic notation for the timed automata. Our results in this paper are more general than the ones presented in [10]. Namely, Timed Automata are our starting point, and we can provide an accurate answer to the problem for a larger class of them.

1. Introduction

Timed Automata [2] (TA) are one of the most widely used formalisms to model real-time systems. Linear Duration Invariants (LDI) are a fragment of Duration Calculus (DC) [7] used to express linear constraints on the accumulated time for the presence of system states. They are first presented in [17] where it is shown that the reachability problem of the Integration Graphs, a class of Hybrid Automata, can be reduced to the verification of TA for LDI.

Our goal is to develop a technique to verify algorithmically real-time systems modeled as TA for this kind of real-time properties. To our knowledge, the existing theoretical methods which work for the whole class of TA seem to be useless even for a small example because of their high complexity.

In [17], the authors present an algorithm for solving the problem, based on two techniques: digitization and mixed

linear integer programming. Digitization is a way to obtain a discrete time automaton which generates the integer runs of the original dense time version. Naive digitization is based on the region graph construction which produces huge graphs depending on the size of the constants involved in comparisons [2]. Besides, mixed linear integer programming techniques possess high complexity. A realated problem is treated in [1], the computation of accumulated delays. It does not cover the case of negative coefficients for durations and it is even more complex than the one presented in [17] for checking the "possitive" LDI. In [11] a general approach for model checking discrete Duration Calculus is presented. This approach is based on the inclusion of regular languages. Obtaining regular languages through digitization of TA as well as transforming DC formula into finite state automata are the main sources of its high complexity.

In order to obtain more practical algorithms, several proposals based on linear programming techniques were presented [8, 10, 14]. The common idea is to represent real-time systems by means of some sort of timed regular expression. These works are based on the fact that if the expression to verify is finite, i.e. there is no repetition in the expression, the verification can done by using a linear programming procedure (i.e., maximizing the body of the LDI subject to the timing constraints in the form of linear inequalities on variables which stand for the duration of each location visit). Therefore, most of the research effort is devoted to reduce the infinite case to the finite one, i.e. to eliminate repetition. The strength of these techniques is the reuse of well studied and efficient set of linear programming tools avoiding digitization. Their weakness lies on the fact that the starting points are those regular expressions which can only represent a small class of TA.

In this paper, we achieve our goal by generalizing the ideas of these methods for TA. In order to cope with them, we present an algebraic formalism for expressing the behaviour of the whole class of TA along with a translation procedure. Based on the translation results, we provide conservative analysis ("yes" , "no", "don't know" answers) to the problems using linear programming techniques and

---
[*]The paper was written during the fellowship of the first author with The United Nations University, International Institute for Software Technology from September 1997 to March 1998. He is partially supported by KIT125 and ARTE,PIC 11-00000-01856, ANPCyT. The second author is on leave from Institute of Information Technology, Hanoi, Vietnam

avoiding digitization. Compared to the methods in [8, 10], our method can work directly on the whole class of TA and give the accurate answer to the problem for a subclass larger than any previously defined in these approaches. The paper is organized as follows. In the next section, we recall some basic notions of TA and LDI. A new algebraic formalism, Time Constrained Regular Expressions (TC-RE), for expressing the behaviour of TA is given in Section 3. Our model-checking procedure is presented in Section 4. Conclusions are summarized in the last section of the paper.

2. Basic notations

First, we introduce some basic notations for sequences that will be used in the sequel.

Let s be a sequence. Then, $|s|$ will denote the length (i.e. number of elements) and s_i ($0 \leq i \leq |s| - 1$) will denote the ith element of the sequence s. For $0 \leq i \leq j \leq |s| - 1$, let $s_{i]}$ denote the prefix of s that ends with the ith element, $s_{[i}$ the suffix of s that starts from the ith element and $s_{[i,j]}$ the subsequence that starts from the ith element and ends with the jth element inclusively. If the sequence s is not empty, its last element (i.e. $s_{|s|-1}$) will be denoted by $last(s)$. The concatenation of two sequences s and s' will be denoted by ss', and a sequence with a single element will be identified with its element. Given a set E, a subset T of E and a sequence s over E, $T \cap s$ will denote the intersection between T and the underlying set of s. $last\_T\_in\_s$ will denote the natural number k such that $s_k \in T$ and $\forall l, k < l < |s|$ it holds that $s_l \notin T$.

In this paper, by "time sequence" we mean a nondecreasing sequence of non negative reals. For our convenience, we define the operation $\lhd$ between time sequences as follows. For time sequences τ' and τ, $\tau' \lhd \tau \overset{def}{=} \tau' \tau''$, where $\tau'' \overset{def}{=} (\tau_0 + \tau'_{|\tau'|-1})(\tau_1 + \tau'_{|\tau'|-1}) \ldots (\eta_{|\tau|-1} + \tau'_{|\tau'|-1})$. Intuitively, the sequence τ is translated by the last element of τ' and is then concatenated to the sequence τ' to give the result of this operation. For example, $(0\ 2\ 3\ 5.5) \lhd (1\ 5.3) = (0\ 2\ 3\ 5.5\ 6.5\ 11.8)$

2.1. Timed automata

Definition 1 (Timed Automata) *A timed automaton is a tuple $A = (Q, C, L, \Omega, S, Inv)$ where Q is a finite set of locations, C is a finite set of clock variables, L is a finite set of labels, Ω is a set of edges (see bellow), $S \subseteq Q$ is a set of initial locations, and Inv is a function from the set of locations to conjunctions of tests of the form $x \leq c$ (the invariant of a location), where $c \in N$ and x is a clock variable. An edge is a tuple (q, ϕ, ρ, l, q') where $q, q' \in Q$, $\rho \subseteq C$ (clocks reset), l is a label, and ϕ (guard) is a conjunction of tests of the form $x \sim c$, where x is a clock variable, $\sim \in \{\leq, \geq\}$*

($\leq$ for deadline and $\geq$ for delay test) and $c \in N$. (In order to simplify the presentation, we assume there is at most one edge for each pair of locations.)

Usually, systems are specified as nets of time automata running in parallel, which are synchronized at the transitions that have the same label. The location set of the parallel composition is the cartesian product of the sets of locations of both automata. The invariant of a location is the conjunction of the invariants of the components. The condition of synchronized transitions is the conjunction of the local conditions, while the clock reset is the union of the local clock resets.

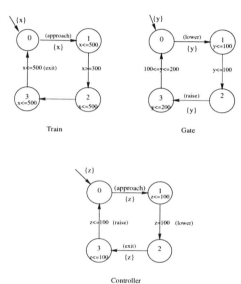

Figure 1. The Railroad Crossing System

Example 1 *Figure 1 shows the three components of the Railroad Crossing System as presented in [16]. They are synchronized at the labels **approach, exit, lower, down**. When a train approaches the crossing, it sends a signal **approach** to the Controller and enters the crossing at least 300 time units later. When leaving the crossing, it sends a signal **exit** to the Controller within 500 time units after the signal **approach** has been sent. The Controller sends a signal **lower** to the gate exactly 100 time units after it has received the signal **approach**, and sends a signal **raise** within 100 time units after it has received the signal **exit**. The gate responds to the signal **lower** by moving down within 100 time units, and responds to the signal **raise** by moving up between 100 and 200 time units.*

Now, we define the finite timed language to express the behaviour of TA.

Definition 2 *A Timed word over an alphabet E is a pair (σ, τ), where σ is a finite sequence of elements of E, τ is a* finite time sequence both having the same length. A set of timed words over E is called a timed language over E.

The set of *transitions* over an alphabet Q, denoted by T_Q, is defined as the set $(Q \cup \{\bot\}) \times Q$. The symbol $\bot$ will serve to denote starting transitions of automata. Let π_1, π_2 denote the projections of the first and the second component of a transition respectively.

Let A be a timed automaton as in Definition 1. A *clock valuation* is a function $v : C \to \Re_{\geq 0}$. In this paper, we also consider clock valuations as clock-indexed vectors. For a clock valuation v and a set $\rho \subseteq C$ let $Reset_\rho(v)$ denote the valuation defined by

$$Reset_\rho(v)(c) = \begin{cases} 0 & \text{if } c \in \rho, \\ v(c) & \text{otherwise.} \end{cases}$$

We use $\mathbf{1}$ to denote the unit vector $(1, \ldots, 1)$, and $\mathbf{0}$ to denote the 0-vector $(0, \ldots, 0)$ of dimension $|C|$.

A *state* of the timed automaton A is a pair $(q, v) \in Q \times (C \to \Re_{\geq 0})$ for which $Inv(q)$ holds on v.

A *run* of the automaton A is a sequence

$$r = (q_0, v_0) \overset{\omega_1, \tau_1}{\leadsto} (q_1, v_1) \overset{\omega_2, \tau_2}{\leadsto} \ldots \overset{\omega_n, \tau_n}{\leadsto} (q_n, v_n),$$

where (q_i, v_i) are states of A, $\omega_i \in \Omega$, $\tau_i \in \Re_{\geq 0}$ satisfying

Initialization: $q_0 \in S$; $v_0 = \mathbf{0}$; $\tau_0 = 0$

Monotonicity: $0 \leq \tau_i \leq \tau_{i+1}$ for all natural numbers $i < n$

Succession: $1 \leq i \leq n$; $\omega_i = (q_{i-1}, \phi_i, \rho_i, l_i, q_i)$, where the condition $\phi_i(v_{i-1} + (\tau_i - \tau_{i-1})\mathbf{1})$ holds, $v_i = Reset_\rho(v_{i-1} + (\tau_i - \tau_{i-1})\mathbf{1})$, and $Inv(q_{i-1}(v_{i-1} + t\mathbf{1})$ holds for all $0 \leq t \leq \tau_i - \tau_{i-1}$

The timed word over the alphabet T_Q accepted by the run r above is defined as

$$((\bot, q_0), (q_0, q_1), \ldots, (q_{n-1}, q_n), \tau_0 \tau_1 \ldots \tau_n).$$

The timed language $L(A)$ of the timed automaton A is the set of finite timed words over T_Q which have an accepting run. We will only consider in this paper *Non-zeno* Automata (see. [12]), i.e. those automata for which, given any real number t, any finite run can be extended to a run with the time $\tau_n > t$ (time can progress).

2.2. Linear duration invariants

In order to model a real-time system, the automaton A is usually associated with a mapping $\lambda : Q \to 2^P$ which assigns a set of propositional letters to each location which should be interpreted as *true* when the automaton stays at the location.

Example 2 *For the composition automaton of the previous example (whose locations are triples indicating local locations of its three components), let $P = \{Up, Down, MovingUp, MovingDown\}$ and λ be*

$$\lambda((q_1, q_2, q_3)) = \begin{cases} \{Up\} & \textit{if } q_2 = 0 \\ \{MovingDown\} & \textit{if } q_2 = 1 \\ \{Down\} & \textit{if } q_2 = 2 \\ \{MovingUp\} & \textit{if } q_2 = 3 \end{cases}$$

Linear Duration Invariants (LDI) are a family of real-time properties that predicate over the runs of timed automata. LDI are DC formulas of the form

$$\Pi \overset{\text{def}}{=} l \leq \int 1 \leq u \Rightarrow \sum_{b \in B} c_b \int b \leq M,$$

where B is a finite set of boolean expressions over P, l, c_b and M are reals, and u is either real or ∞. Given a run of the automaton A, the expression $\int b$ stands for the accumulated time in the run where the expression b evaluates to *true*, i.e. the time that the automaton stays in a location s for which $\lambda(s) \Rightarrow b$. The LDI Π is satisfied by the automaton A when $\sum_{b \in B} c_b \int b$, the duration expression, is less than or equal to M for those runs of A whose 'time length' (τ_n) lies between l and u. Formally,

$$A \models_\lambda \Pi \overset{\text{def}}{=} \forall (\sigma, \tau) \in L(A) : \\ l \leq last(\tau) \leq u \Rightarrow f_{\Pi, \lambda}^\sigma(\tau) \leq M,$$

where

$$f_{\Pi, \lambda}^\sigma(\tau) \overset{\text{def}}{=} \alpha(\pi_1(\sigma_0))\tau_0 + \\ \sum_{1 \leq i < |\sigma|} \alpha(\pi_1(\sigma_i))(\tau_i - \tau_{i-1})$$

$$\alpha(q) \overset{\text{def}}{=} \sum_{\{b \in B \mid \lambda(q) \Rightarrow b\}} c_b$$

(α assigns to each location the contribution it makes to the linear duration expression.)

Example 3 *Let*

$$\Pi \overset{\text{def}}{=} 0 \leq \int 1 < \infty \Rightarrow \\ -3 \int (Down \vee Up) + 2 \\ \int (MovingDown \vee MovingUp) \leq 1000.$$

For the composition automaton of Example 1 the mapping α associated to the mapping λ is

$$\alpha((q_1, q_2, q_3)) = \begin{cases} -3 & \textit{if } q_2 = 0 \\ 2 & \textit{if } q_2 = 1 \\ -3 & \textit{if } q_2 = 2 \\ 2 & \textit{if } q_2 = 3 \end{cases}.$$

Let $\sigma = (\bot, 000) (000, 101) (101, 112) (112, 122)$; $\tau = 0\,600\,700\,850)$. Then $f_{\Pi, \lambda}^\sigma(\tau) = -3 \times 600 + -3 \times 100 + 2 \times 150$.

Since LDIs are universal properties, it is obvious that for any automata A and A' $L(A) \subseteq L(A') \Rightarrow A' \models_\lambda \Pi \Rightarrow A \models_\lambda \Pi$.

2.3. Simplification of the problem

We apply a simple conversion to the problem in order to get rid of time bounds in the LDI property. Suppose we want to verify a LDI for all those runs A of "time length" between l and u. We define a new automaton A' from A by making the following changes to A:

- Add a new clock, z,

- Add to all invariants the condition $z \leq u$,

- Add a new "trap" location, *final*. Associate the invariant *True* to this location and add to it a self loop with the *true* condition and the empty set of reset clock variables (stuttering step).

- Add edges from all original locations to the trap location with the condition $l \leq z \leq u$ and the empty set of reset clock variables.

- Extend λ by assigning any value to *final* (lets call this extension λ').

It is easy to see that the obtained automaton A' has the property that its runs ended in the trap location *final* are exactly the same runs which are relevant to the LDI satisfaction. That is,

$$A \models_\lambda \Pi \iff \begin{aligned} &\forall (\sigma, \tau) \in L(A'): \\ &((\pi_1(last(\sigma)) \neq ``final" \land \\ &\pi_2(last(\sigma)) = ``final") \\ &\Rightarrow f_{\Pi,\lambda'}(\sigma, \tau) \leq M). \end{aligned}$$

It is obvious that if the original automaton A is non-zeno then so is the automaton A'. Moreover, every run of the automaton A' is a prefix of a run leading to the trap location.

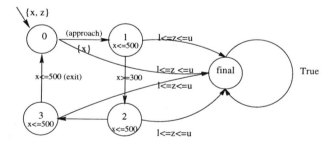

Figure 2. Adding a Trap Location

3 Time constrained regular expressions

In this section, we give a descriptive and algebraic representation of the behaviour of TA which will be called Timed Constrained Regular Expressions (TC-RE). TC-RE

provides us the necessary insight to formulate the principles of our model checking algorithm proposed later in this paper.

Definition 3 *A TC-RE over an alphabet Q is a tuple $M = (R, \Delta)$ where R is a regular expression over the alphabet T_Q and Δ is a finite set of triples of the form $(T, t, \sim c)$, where $T \subseteq T_Q$ (i.e. is a finite set of transitions over Q), $t \in T_Q$, $\sim \in \{\leq, \geq\}$ and $c \in Q$.*

The intuition behind this definition is that the regular expression (see [13]) R gives the potential untimed sequences of transitions, while Δ establishes a set of constraints on the distance between transition occurrences. A tuple $(T, t, \sim c)$ in Δ is the analogous of a clock test associated to the transition t (which appears as the second component of the tuple). Then, the first component, T (hereafter called a clock), is the set of transitions which reset that clock. Roughly speaking, $\sim c$ is a time constraint on the distance between t and the closest previous T-transition.

Definition 4 *Given a TC-RE (R, Δ) over Q. The language $L(R, \Delta)$ represented by (R, Δ) is the set of timed words (σ, τ) over T_Q that satisfy:*

- *$\sigma \in R$ (σ is a transition sequence described by the regular expression),*

- *$\tau_0 = 0$ (initialization),*

- *$\forall 0 \leq i < |\sigma|:$ $((T, \sigma_i, \sim c) \in \Delta \land (T \cap \sigma_{i-1]} \neq \emptyset$ $\Rightarrow \tau_i - \tau_{last\_T\_in\_\sigma_{i-1]}} \sim c))$ (i.e. τ satisfies the time constraints on the distance between event instances).*

Hereafter, we write $\tau \in Sol(\sigma, \Delta)$ to express that (σ, τ) is a timed word satisfying the conditions of the last two items of Definition 4.

Example 4 *Let $R = (\perp, 0)\,((0,1)(1,2)(2,3)(3,0))^*$,*

$$\Delta = \left\{ \begin{array}{l} (\{(\perp, 0), (0, 1)\}, (1, 2), \geq 300), \\ (\{(\perp, 0), (0, 1)\}, (1, 2), \leq 500), \\ (\{(\perp, 0), (0, 1)\}, (2, 3), \leq 500), \\ (\{(\perp, 0), (0, 1)\}, (3, 0), \geq 300) \end{array} \right\}.$$

Then, (R, Δ) is a TC-RE that represents all the timed words leading to the location 0 of the automaton "Train" in Fig. 1

The notion of TC-RE leads to a clear separation between the untimed structure and the timing constraints. The structured nature of traditional Regular Expressions (RE) is extremely helpful for developing the principles of our algorithm (see [3] for another approach that adds an intersection operator to define timed RE). The following facts are obvious from the above definition.

Fact 1 *Let R and R' be equivalent REs (i.e. they recognize the same language), and let Δ be a set of constraints. Then $L(R, \Delta) = L(R', \Delta)$.*

Fact 2 $L(R, \Delta \cup \{(T, t, \sim c)\}) \subseteq L(R, \Delta)$.

3.1. Verifying finite TC-RE for LDI

In this section, we want to illustrate the formerly introduced concept by showing how to solve the model checking problem for finite TC-REs. That is, we deal with the case of TC-REs where first component is a RE with no occurrence of the star (Kleene closure). Finiteness implies that the RE can be rewritten as a finite union of words. The LDI must be satisfied for all the words in which the RE can be decomposed into. Given a word σ and a set of time constraints Δ, we can associate to it a set of variables and a set of linear constraints $C(\sigma, \Delta)$ such that its solutions is precisely the set $Sol(\sigma, \Delta)$. Formally, the set $C(\sigma, \Delta)$ of inequalities on the variable set $(x_i)_{i < |\sigma|}$ is defined by

$$
\left\{ x_i - x_{last\ T\ in\ \sigma_{i-1]}} \sim c \left| \begin{array}{l} i < |\sigma| \wedge \\ (T, \sigma_i, \sim c) \in \Delta \wedge \\ T \cap \sigma_{i-1]} \neq \emptyset \end{array} \right. \right\}
$$
$$
\cup \ \{x_{i+1} - x_i \geq 0 \mid i + 1 < |\sigma|\}
$$
$$
\cup \ \{x_0 = 0\}.
$$

Thus, checking the LDI Π under mapping λ over (σ, Δ) is exactly the same as checking whether the maximum of the function $f^{\sigma}_{\Pi, \lambda}(x)$ subject to $C(\sigma, \Delta)$ is less than or equal to M which can be solved by linear programming techniques. Note that all words of a finite RE can be checked in parallel.

Example 5 *Let σ be $(\perp, 1)(1, 2)(2, 3)(3, 4)(4, 11)$, and let Δ be as in the previous example. Then $C(\sigma, \Delta)$ is the set of the following inequalities:*

$$
0 = x_0, x_1 - x_0 \geq 0, x_2 - x_1 \geq 0,
$$
$$
x_3 - x_2 \geq 0, x_4 - x_3 \geq 0, x_2 - x_1 = 100,
$$
$$
x_3 - x_2 \leq 300, x_4 - x_0 \geq 0.
$$

Let Π be as in Example 3. It is easy to see that the maximum of the linear duration expression is 0, and that it is reached at $(x_0 = 0,\ x_1 = 0,\ x_2 = 100,\ x_3 = 400,\ x_4 = 400)$.

4. Principles for our model checking algorithm

In this section, we show that it is straightforward to derive from the timed automaton A' a TC-RE that defines the set of timed words of A' which lead to the final trap location. However, we want a TC-RE with a 'good' properties which allow a simple treatment of Kleene closured subexpressions in our verification procedure. Such a TC-RE is said to be

'well-behaved and operational' TC-RE. The first step of our model checking procedure is to obtain a 'well-behaved and operational' TC-RE from the input timed automaton. Then, if it is finite we can apply linear programming techniques to solve the model checking problem as shown before. For the infinite case, we present, in next sections, some techniques for either infering that the LDI is violated or reducing the original expression to a finite TC-RE which is equivalent to the original one for the LDI (in the sense that $(R, \Delta) \models_\lambda \Pi$ iff $(R', \Delta') \models_\lambda \Pi$). In the following sections, we give more details of our idea.

4.1. Well-behaved and operational TC-RE

Definition 5 *A TC-RE (R, Δ) is a Well-Behaved TC-RE (WB-TC-RE) if it satisfies the following properties:*

Fusion Closure *For any transitions t, t' such that $\pi_2(t) = \pi_2(t')$, and for any sequences of transitions σ, σ', θ and θ' it holds that $(\sigma t \theta \in R \wedge \sigma' t' \theta' \in R) \Rightarrow (\sigma t \theta' \in R \wedge \sigma' t' \theta \in R)$.*

Feasibility *$\forall \sigma \in R : Sol(\sigma, \Delta) \neq \emptyset$.*

Reachability Equivalence *Let $\sigma \in R$, $i < k < |\sigma|$, $(T, \sigma_k, \sim c) \in \Delta$ such that $last\_T\_in\_\sigma_{k-1]} \leq i$. Let MC be the maximum of the constants appearing in a time constraint in Δ. There exist for the location $l = \pi_2(\sigma_i)$ and the set T two constants MAX^l_T and MIN^l_T in $[0, MC] \cup \{\infty\}$ such that for all $\theta \in Prefix(R)$ satisfying $\pi_2(last(\theta)) = l$ it holds that*

- *$(Max\{last(\tau) - \tau_{last\_T\_in\_\theta} \mid \tau \in Sol(\theta, \Delta)\} \geq MC \wedge MAX^l_T = \infty) \vee (Max\{last(\tau) - \tau_{lastTin\theta} \mid \tau \in Sol(\theta, \Delta)\} = MAX^l_T)$, and*

- *$(Min\{last(\tau) - \tau_{last\_T\_in\_\theta} \mid \tau \in Sol(\theta, \Delta)\} > MC \wedge MIN^l_T = \infty) \vee (Min\{last(\tau) - \tau_{lastTin\theta} \mid \tau \in Sol(\theta, \Delta)\} = MIN^l_T)$.*

The first property is natural since symbols are pairs of locations. The second property avoids the case in which words described by the RE have no associated solution for the timing constraints imposed by Δ. The last property means that the maximum (resp. minimum) value for a clock T that might be tested in the future is the same for all paths leading to l. This maximum (resp. minimum) is denoted MAX^l_T (resp. MIN^l_T)[1]. Note that all values greater than MC are equated to ∞. The last property has many interesting technical corollaries and greatly simplifies the way we treat cycles (Kleene closured subexpressions). Roughly speaking, these properties imply that the number of iterations does not affect, and is not affected by timing constraints (see [6]).

---

[1] Actually, this is a simplified version of the Reachability Equivalence property. In [6] we also require the same property for the difference of each pair of clocks which might be tested in the future.

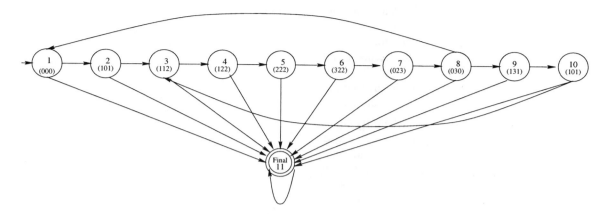

Figure 3. The Reachability Graph

Thus, our algorithm can, in some extent, analyse Kleene closured subexpressions locally. These properties can be achieved for a timed automaton using techniques explained in the next section.

Example 6 *Let*

$$R = (\bot,0)(0,1)(1,2)((2,3)(3,2))^*(2,4)$$

$$\Delta = \left\{ \begin{array}{c} (\{(\bot,0)\},(0,1),\geq 100), \\ (\{(0,1)\},(1,2),\geq 3), \\ (\{(1,2),(3,2)\},(2,3),\geq 50), \\ (\{(\bot,0)\},(2,4),\geq 100) \end{array} \right\}.$$

Then, (R,Δ) *is a WB-TC-RE. Furthermore,* $MAX^2_{\{(\bot,0)\}} = MIN^2_{\{(\bot,0)\}} = \infty.$

Definition 6 *A TC-RC (R,Δ) is operational iff it satisfies the following condition: for all $\sigma \in R$, $0 \leq i < |\sigma|$, $\tau \in Sol(\sigma_{i]},\Delta)$ there exists a sequence of transitions θ such that $(\sigma_{i]}\theta,\tau') \in L(R,\Delta)$ and $\tau = \tau'_{i]}$*

Operationality means that partial solutions are part of total solutions. It is intimately connected to non-zenoness. Note that the TC-RE in the previous example is also operational since for any compatible time assignment for some prefix of R there is always a way to extend it so that it reaches location 4. In the next section, we show how to obtain a well-behaved and operational TC-RE from a timed automaton that satisfies Non-zenoness. This TC-RE will recognize the relevant language of timed words leading to final locations.

4.2. Problem transformation in terms of well behaved and operational TC-RE

Given a timed automaton B and a set of final locations, we could apply a simple procedure derived from the proof of Kleene theorem [13, 3] to B to obtain a regular expression that recognizes all the untimed words of transitions which lead to the final locations (without using the stuttering step at final locations).

Then, Δ is obtained in a simple way as follows.
For each edge, (q,ϕ,ρ,l,q'), follow this procedure:

- For each test $x \sim c \in \rho$ add the tuple $(T,(q,q'),\sim c)$ to Δ, where T is the set of transitions that reset the clock x (remember that this set includes also initial ones, i.e. $(\bot,s) \in T$ for all $s \in S$).

- For each test $x \leq c \in Inv(q)$ add the tuple $(T,(q,q'),\leq c)$ to Δ, where T is the set of transitions that reset the clock x including the the initial ones as above.

We call the TC-RE constructed from B in this way $\Delta Kleene(B)$. Then we have the following observation

Fact 3 $A \models_\lambda \Pi$ *iff* $(\forall(\sigma,\tau) \in L(\Delta Kleene(A'))$: $f^{\sigma'}_{\Pi,\lambda}(\tau) \leq M)$, *where A', λ are the automaton and the mapping obtained by following the procedure of section 2.3 and the set of final locations is $\{final\}$.*

Therefore, in order to verify for the LDI (described earlier) of the timed automaton A, all we have to do is check whether $f^\sigma_{\Pi,\lambda}(\tau) \leq M$ is satisfied by all the timed words described by the obtained TC-RE. But, is the obtained TC-RE well behaved and operational?.

Since symbols are pairs of locations, the resulting language has the **Fusion Closure** property.

And also, since every run of A' is a prefix of a run leading to the trap state (this property comes from the fact that A is non-zeno), it is easy to see that the obtained TC-RE is **operational**.

The last two properties of well-behavedness are not guaranteed if we apply the Kleene procedure to an arbitrary timed automaton. Fortunately, most of the symbolic state space representations (e.g. [21, 16, 20]) produce automata where all paths are feasible and, moreover, for which reachability equivalence holds. Given a timed automaton, these techniques produce an automaton which represents all the reachable timed states of the original one. Generally, the resulting automaton is much smaller than the Region Graph. The Reachability Graph is among such kind of automata.

Let us illustrate the idea of using the Reachability Graph [16] technique. The Reachability Graph is a well known concept in many timed formalisms [15, 5]. In particular, given a timed automaton A, the Reachability Graph $RG(A)$ of A can be seen as an automaton that accepts (up to renaming, let us call it β) the same language as A. It is built by unfolding symbolically the original graph in such a way that the language accepted by the underlying graph is feasible. This implies immediately the **feasibility** of its associated TC-RE. Moreover, the procedure equates paths when they satisfy the **reachability equivalence** property [16]. The $\Delta Kleene(RG(A'))$ is built taking those locations l of $RG(A')$ such that $\beta(l) = final$ as the set of final locations. It is not difficult to see that $\Delta Kleene(RG(A'))$ is **operational** as well. This is derived from the fact that runs of $RG(A')$ are, up to renaming, the runs of A'. Therefore, every run of $RG(A')$ is the prefix of a run leading to a trap location.

So, from the automaton $RG(A')$, we obtain a well-behaved and operational TC-RE (R, Δ), where R is a regular expression on the set of transitions T_Q over the set of locations of the graph, $Q = \{q_1, q_2, \ldots, q_n\}$. As it was mentioned earlier, R is obtained following the procedure of the Kleene theorem proof [13]. Namely, R can be obtained as the union of the RE R_{ij}^n, where q_i is an initial location and q_j is a final one, and R_{ij}^n is the set of words that lead the automaton $RG(A')$ from location q_i to location q_j. For any $k, j, i \leq n$ R_{ij}^k is the set of words that lead the automaton $RG(A')$ from location q_i to location q_j without passing at locations in $\{q_{k+1} \ldots q_n\}$, and it is defined inductively as: $R_{ij}^k \overset{\text{def}}{=} R_{ik}^{k-1}(R_{kk}^{k-1})^* R_{kj}^{k-1} \oplus R_{ik}^{k-1} R_{kj}^{k-1}$; R_{ij}^0 is $\{(q_i, q_j)\}$ if such transition exists, it is $\{\epsilon\}$ if $i = j$ and it is the empty set otherwise.

Example 7 *The reachability graph for the timed automaton* $(train\|gate\|controller)'$ *is shown in Figure 3, where a final location and an extra clock for the observation interval* $[0, \infty)$ *were added. A TC-RE that accepts all the time words of the RG in Figure 3, which lead to the location 11 (final) is the following:*

$$
\begin{aligned}
R \;=\; & R_{1,11}^7 \oplus R_{1,8}^7 (R_{8,8}^7)^* R_{8,11}^7 \oplus \\
& R_{1,8}^7 (R_{8,8}^7)^* (8,9)(9,11) \oplus \\
& R_{1,8}^7 (R_{8,8}^7)^* (8,9)(9,10)(R_{10,10}^9)^* R_{10,11}^9,
\end{aligned}
$$

where

$$
R_{1,11}^7 = \begin{pmatrix} (1,11)\oplus \\ \ldots \oplus \\ (1,2)(2,3)\ldots(7,11) \end{pmatrix}
$$

$$
\begin{aligned}
R_{1,8}^7 &= (1,2)(2,3)\ldots(7,8) \\
R_{8,8}^7 &= (8,1)(1,2)(2,3)\ldots(7,8)
\end{aligned}
$$

$$
R_{8,11}^7 = \begin{pmatrix} (8,11)\oplus \\ \ldots \oplus \\ (8,1)(1,2)\ldots(7,11) \end{pmatrix}
$$

$$
R_{10,10}^9 = (10,1)R_{1,8}^7(R_{8,8}^7)^*(8,9)(9,10)
$$

$$
R_{10,11}^9 = \begin{pmatrix} (10,11)\oplus \\ \ldots \oplus \\ (10,3)(3,4)\ldots(R_{8,8}^7)^*(8,11)\oplus \\ (10,3)(3,4)\ldots(R_{8,8}^7)^*(8,9)(9,11) \end{pmatrix}
$$

and

$$
\Delta \overset{\text{def}}{=} \left\{ \begin{array}{c}
(\{(\bot,1),(1,2)\},(2,3),\geq 100), \\
(\{(\bot,1)\},(1,11),\geq 0), \\
(\{(\bot,1),(1,2)\},(2,3),\leq 100), \\
(\{(\bot,1)\},(2,11),\geq 0), \\
(\{(\bot,1),(2,3),(10,3)\},(3,4),\leq 300), \\
(\{(\bot,1)\},(3,11),\geq 0), \\
(\{(\bot,1),(1,2),(8,9)\},(4,5),\leq 500), \\
(\{(\bot,1)\},(4,11),\geq 0), \\
(\{(\bot,1),(1,2),(8,9)\},(4,5),\geq 300), \\
(\{(\bot,1)\},(5,11),\geq 0), \\
(\{(\bot,1),(1,2),(8,9)\},(5,6),\leq 500), \\
(\{(\bot,1)\},(3,11),\geq 0), \\
(\{(\bot,1),(1,2),(8,9)\},(6,7),\leq 300), \\
(\{(\bot,1)\},(6,11),\geq 0), \\
(\{(\bot,1),(6,7)\},(7,8),\leq 100), \\
(\{(\bot,1)\},(7,11),\geq 0), \\
(\{(\bot,1),(7,8)\},(8,9),\leq 200), \\
(\{(\bot,1)\},(8,11),\geq 0), \\
(\{(\bot,1),(7,8)\},(9,10),\geq 100), \\
(\{(\bot,1)\},(11,11),\geq 0), \\
(\{(\bot,1),(7,8)\},(9,10),\leq 100), \\
(\{(\bot,1),(8,9)\},(10,3),\geq 100), \\
(\{(\bot,1),(8,9)\},(10,3),\leq 100), \\
(\{(\bot,1),(7,8)\},(8,1),\geq 100), \\
(\{(\bot,1),(7,8)\},(8,1),\leq 200)
\end{array} \right\}
$$

Now we formulate the main result of this section.

Lemma 1 $\Delta Kleene(RG(A'))$ *is a well-behaved and operational TC-RE for which*

$$
A \models_\lambda \Pi \quad iff \quad (\forall(\sigma,\tau) \in L(\Delta Kleene(RG(A')))) : \\
f_{\Pi,\lambda'\beta}^\sigma(\tau) \leq M)
$$

270

4.3. Past-independence

In this section, we present some necessary concepts to explain our checking algorithm. As it will be shown later in this paper, our algorithm processes, in a bottom up fashion, the Kleene closured subexpressions trying to reduce them into a finite subexpression or to find a counterexample, i.e. a violation of the LDI. Due to the global nature of timing constraints, it is hard to analyse compositionally the TC-RE. Valid time assignments for a word having a past context may depend on the values of clocks which are tested with no previous reset in the word. These clocks are called "Free Clocks".

Definition 7 (Free Clocks) $FreeClocks(\sigma, \Delta) \stackrel{\text{def}}{=} \{T \mid 0 \le i < |\sigma| \wedge (T, \sigma_i, \sim c) \in \Delta \wedge T \cap \sigma_{i-1]} = \emptyset\}$.

However, there are some cases where we can analyse locally a word and then draw some valid conclusions.

Definition 8 (Past-Independence) Let (R, Δ) be a TC-RE. Let $\theta\sigma \in Prefix(R)$. We say that σ is past-independent iff for all time sequences τ it holds that $\exists \tau' \in Sol(\theta, \Delta) : \tau' \lhd \tau \in Sol(\theta\sigma, \Delta)$ implies that $\forall \gamma\sigma \in Prefix(R) : \forall \tau'' \in Sol(\gamma, \Delta) : \tau'' \lhd \tau \in Sol(\gamma\sigma, \Delta)$.

The past-independency means that a solution (τ) for a valid past context (θ, τ') for a word (σ) is a solution for any valid past context (γ, τ'') for the word (σ).

If the maximum and minimum values for the free clocks of σ coincide (i.e. $MAX_T^l = MAX_T^l$ for all $T \in FreeClocks(\sigma, \Delta)$) then σ is past-independent since the values are known constants when entering the first location of the word (i.e. the free clocks have fixed values). If the word σ satisfies this sufficient condition then the following inequality system $\hat{C}(\sigma, \Delta)$ on the variable set $(\tau_i)_{i<|\sigma|}$ provides all the valid time assignments τ for σ as subword of a word in R

$$\left\{ \tau_i - \tau_{last\ T\ in\ \sigma_{i-1]}} \sim c \left| \begin{array}{l} i < |\sigma| \wedge \\ (T, \sigma_i, \sim c) \in \Delta \wedge \\ T \cap \sigma_{i-1]} \neq \emptyset \end{array} \right. \right\}$$
$$\cup$$
$$\{\tau_{i+1} - \tau_i \geq 0 \mid i+1 < |\sigma|\}$$
$$\cup$$
$$\left\{ \tau_i + MAX_T^{\pi_1(\sigma_0)} \sim c \left| \begin{array}{l} i < |\sigma| \wedge \\ (T, \sigma_i, \sim c) \in \Delta \wedge \\ T \cap \sigma_{i-1]} = \emptyset \end{array} \right. \right\}$$

We have the following results.

Theorem 1 Let (R, Δ) be an operational WB-TC-RE, let A^* be a subexpression of R where $\theta \in A$ is a non-transient (i.e time always elapses from the start transition to the last

one [2]) and past-independent word such that the maximum value for the $f_{\Pi,\lambda}^\theta$ subject to $\hat{C}(\theta, \Delta)$ is greater than 0 then $(R, \Delta) \not\models_\lambda \Pi$.

That is, if we detect a word θ of a Kleene closured subexpression such that the maximum value for the duration expression is greater than zero and the word is past-independent, we can conclude that the LDI is violated by the whole expression. In fact, the duration expression will not be bounded (because we can repeat that timed word as many times as we want).

Theorem 2 Let (R, Δ) be a WB-TC-RE, let A^* be a subexpression of R such that all $\theta \in A$ are non-transient and past-independent words satisfying that the maximum value for the duration expression $f_{\Pi,\lambda}^\theta$ subject to $\hat{C}(\theta, \Delta)$ is less than or equal to zero. Then, by replacing A^* in R with $\epsilon \oplus A \oplus AA$, we get a regular expression R' for which $(R, \Delta) \models_\lambda \Pi$ iff $(R', \Delta) \models_\lambda \Pi$.

This complementary result states that the Kleene closured subexpression can be replaced by some unfolds of the subexpression in order to obtain an equivalent expression w.r.t. the LDI (the repetitions do not contribute to the duration expression).

4.4. The basic algorithm

We have shown in previous sections how the original problem can be transformed into the verification of an operational WB-TC-RE for a LDI. Given the TC-RE (well-behaved and operational), a theoretical algorithm would process, in a bottom up fashion, the Kleene closured subexpressions. Under the hypothesis of Theorems 1 and 2 it is possible to either reduce the TC-RE into a finite expression or find a violation of the LDI. A scheme for our whole method is shown in Figure 4.

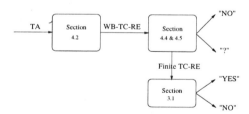

Figure 4. The whole picture

In this section, we present a sketch of an on-the-fly algorithm that shows that it is not necessary to translate the whole automaton $RC(A')$ to the TC-RE at the beginning. We use an n^3-matrix to store $R_{i,j}^k$:

---

[2] A word σ is non transient for Δ iff $\exists i < |\sigma| : \exists (T, \sigma_i, \geq c) \in \Delta : c > 0 \wedge T \cap \sigma_{i-1]} \neq \emptyset$

for $i, j \leq n$ **do**
$\quad R_{ij}^0 :=$ **if** (q_i, q_j) is a transition **then** $\{(i, j)\}$ **else** $\emptyset$
od.
for $k = 1 \, to \, n$ **do**
$\quad$ **if** $R_{kk}^{k-1} \neq \emptyset$ **then**
$\quad\quad$ **if** $\exists \theta \in R_{kk}^{k-1}$ that satisfy the conditions of
$\quad\quad$ Theorem 1
$\quad\quad$ **then** EXIT with RESULT False
$\quad\quad$ **else** $Cycle_k := (\epsilon \oplus R_{kk}^{k-1} \oplus R_{kk}^{k-1} R_{kk}^{k-1})$
$\quad\quad$ **fi**
$\quad$ **else**
$\quad\quad$ $Cicle_k := \epsilon$
$\quad$ **fi**
$\quad$ **for** $i, j \leq n$ **do**
$\quad\quad$ $R_{ij}^k := R_{ik}^{k-1} Cicle_k R_{kj}^{k-1} \cup R_{ij}^{k-1}.$
$\quad$ **od**
od
Hence, from Theorems 1 and 2, with this procedure

- We either obtain a Finite TC-RE (no occurrence of Kleene closure) that is equivalent up to the LDI to the original one, (See its treatment in section 3.1),

- or we discover a violation for the LDI (counter example).

Therefore, the algorithm works for a class of automata where all cycles are non-transient and past-independent. We believe that the first hypothesis is not very restrictive in practice. The latter requires, for example, that 'freeclocks' of the body of a cycle have fixed values independently of the path leading to the cycle. In the next section, we present some techniques to convert non independent iterations into independent ones.

Note that the calculus of each $R_{i,j}^k$ for a fixed k can be done in parallel. It is also possible to chose among several strategies of calculus reuse for the sets $R_{i,j}^k$ (e.g. either the sets of words can be stored explicitly in the matrix in order to avoid recalculation or they can be stored symbolically and calculated by demand).

Example 8 *Consider the automaton in Fig 3. Observe that first the algorithm analyses* $R_{8\,8}^7 = (8, 1)(1, 2) \ldots (1, 8)$ *(the less complex Kleene closured subexpression). It is past-independent since its only 'freeclock'* $T = \{(\perp, 1), (7, 8)\}$ *has fixed* $MAX_T^8 = MIN_T^8 = 0$ *when entering the location 8. It is easy to see that the maximum of the duration expression is greater than 0. In fact, the automaton can remain at the locations* 1, 4, 5, 6 *and* 7 *for* 0 *time units whereas it can remain* 100 *time units in location* 2, 300 *time units in location* 3 *and* 200 *time units in location* 8. *The value of the objective function of the LDI (in Example 3) is* 700 *in this case. The algorithm concludes that the invariant is not satisfied.*

4.5. Obtaining past-independent iterations

This section proposes some manipulations that can be used to obtain past-independent iterations from dependent ones:

- By applying the rewritting rule $(PB)^* \equiv P(BP)^* B \oplus \epsilon$, in many cases we obtain past-independent subwords BP.

- Conservative treatment. The basic idea is to eliminate non fixed 'freeclocks' from the iterations to make them past independent. Let σ_i be a transition such that there is a $(T, \sigma_i, \sim c) \in \Delta$ for which $T \cap \sigma_{i-1]} = \emptyset$ and $MAX_T^{\pi_1(\sigma_0)} \neq MIN_T^{\pi_1(\sigma_0)}$. Then we can simply eliminate these kind of tuples from Δ to achieve the past independency [3]. These manipulations produce a TC-RE whose language is a superset of the original one (see Fact 2). Therefore this step is conservative and any counterexample found using an altered subexpression must be checked for inclusion into the original language. Thus, there are cases where the procedure is not able to produce a yes/no response ("don't know").

5 Conclusions and discussions

We have presented a procedure for verifying LDI of a timed automaton A with non-transient cycles. Our achievements can be summarized as follows.

- From the procedure, it is not difficult to see that when the upper bound of the premise in the LDI is finite (i.e $u < \infty$) the translation procedure $(\Delta Kleene(RG(A')))$ leads to finite TC-REs thus enabling an accurate verification.

- We can also verify the cases $u = \infty$, without digitization, when cycles in the automaton can be rewritten in terms of past-independent iterations. Some identified classes such as the Alternating RQ automata fulfill the condition of independent iterations [18]. In general, this condition is also satisfied when the tests in a cycle are always preceded by a reset in the cycle. There are some results to treat special cases which do not require past-independence to detect the violation of the invariant (e.g. the duration expression is greater than zero for any time assignment of an iteration). Some of them are shown in [6] but are not covered in this article because of the lack of space.

---

[3] Actually, the procedure first renames the transition σ_i producing a new (R', Δ') and a new mapping λ' such that: $(R', \Delta') \models_{\lambda'} \Pi$ iff $(R, \Delta) \models_\lambda \Pi$ (see [6]). This renaming is done to achieve a local elimination. Otherwise, tests which are not troublesome for past-independence would be eliminated.

- For $u = \infty$ we can verify conservatively the whole class of TA with non transient cycles avoiding digitization (This is the first proposal that avoids digitization to verify LDI and that copes with TA as model of real-time systems).

- We strongly believe that in the near future we will be able to verify accurately the whole class of TA with non-transient cycles adding a local digitization technique to convert non past-independent iterations into independent ones (using the possible integer values of free clocks).

The use of the algorithm is still an empirical exercise. Although the estimated worst case complexity is not better than the procedure shown in [17] there are some encouraging observations. First of all, techniques of [21, 16, 20] produce graphs which are, generally, much smaller than the Region Graph. The complexity of our RE conversion procedure seems to depend on the number of transitions and it is not necessarily exponential on the number of nodes. Also, the algorithm works on the fly and many steps can be done in parallel. Note also that, since the work is based on the reachability graph construction, it could be easily migrated to other formalisms like real-time versions of Petri Nets [5] and ModeCharts [15]. As future work, we would like to adapt some recently presented optimization techniques to our framework (e.g. [9, 19, 4]). In particular, we believe that partial order techniques (see. [4]) can be adapted to check LDI which deppend on the locations of just one automaton of a parallel composition.

Acknowledgements: We thank Pablo Giambiagi, Gerardo Schneider, Miguel Felder and Helena Cavanagh for their useful comments.

References

[1] R. Alur, C. Courcoubetis, and T. Henzinger. Computing accumulated delays in real-time systems. In *Proceedings of 5th International Conference on Computer Aided Verification, CAV'93*, number 697 in Lecture Notes in Computer Science, pages 181–193. Springer-Verlag, 1993.

[2] R. Alur and D. Dill. A theory of timed automata. *Theoretical Comput. Sci.*, (126):183–235, 1994.

[3] E. Asarin, O. Maler, and P. Caspi. A kleene theorem for timed automata. In *Proceedings of Logics In Computer Science*, 1997.

[4] J. Bengtsson, B. Jonsson, J. Lilius, and W. Yi. Partial order reductions for timed systems. In *Proceedings of CONCUR'98*, September 1998.

[5] B. Berthomieu and M. Diaz. Modeling and verification of time dependent systems using time petri nets. *IEEE Trans. Softw. Eng.*, 17(3), March 1991.

[6] V. A. Braberman and D. V. Hung. On checking timed automata for linear duration invariants. TR 135, UNU-IIST, February 1998.

[7] Z. Chaochen, C. Hoare, and A. Ravn. A calculus of durations. *Information Processing Letters*, 5(40), 1991.

[8] Z. Chaochen, Z. Jingzhong, Y. Lu, and L. Xiaoshan. Linear duration invariants. In *Formal Techniques in Real-Time and Fault-Tolerant systems*, volume 863 of *Lecture Notes in Computer Science*, 1994.

[9] C. Daws and S. Yovine. Reducing the number of clock variables of timed automata. In *Proceedings of the 17th inter. IEEE Real-Time Systems Symposium*, December 1996.

[10] L. X. Dong and D. V. Hung. Checking linear duration invariants by linear programming. In *Concurrency and Paralellism, Programming, Networking, and Securiry*, volume 1179 of *Lecture Notes in Computer Science*, pages 321–332, December 1996.

[11] M. Hansen. Model-checking discrete duration calculus. *Formal Aspects of Computing*, 6(A):826–846, Nov-Dec 1994.

[12] T. Henzinger, X. Nicollin, J. Sifakis, and S. Yovine. Symbolic model checking for real-time systems. *Information and Computation*, 2(111):193–244, 1994.

[13] J. Hopcroft and J. Ulman. *Introduction to Automata Theory, Languages and Computation*. Adison-Wesley, 1979.

[14] D. V. Hung and P. H. Thai. On checking parallel real-time systems for linear duration invariants. In I. C. S. Press, editor, *Proceedings of the Inter. Symposium on Software Engineering for Parallel and Distributed Systems*, pages 61–71, 1998.

[15] F. Jahanian and D. Stuart. A method for verifying properties of modechart specifications. In *Proceedings of the 9th Inter. IEEE Real-Time Systems Symposium*, 1988.

[16] I. Kang, I. Lee, , and Y. Kim. An efficient space generation for the analysis of real-time systems. In *Proceedings of the Inter. Symposium on Software Testing and Analisys*, 1996.

[17] Y. Kesten, A. Pnueli, J. Sifakis, and S. Yovine. Integration graphs: a class of decidable hybrid systems. In *Proceedings of Workshop on Theory of Hybrid Systems*, volume 736 of *Lecture Notes in Computer Science*, pages 179–208. Springer-Verlag, June 1992.

[18] W. Lam and R. Brayton. Alternating rq timed automata. In *Proceedings of the 5th Inter. Conference on Computer Aided Verification*, volume 697 of *Lecture Notes in Computer Science*, pages 236–252. Springer-Verlag, June/July 1993.

[19] K. Larsen, F.Larsson, P. Pettersson, and W. Yi. Efficient verification of real-time systems: Compact data structure and state-space reduction. In *Proceedings of the 18th Inter. IEEE Real-Time Systems Symposium*, December 1997.

[20] S. Tripakis and S. Yovine. Analysis of timed systems based on time-abstracting bisimulations. In *Proceedings of the 8th Inter. Conference On Computer Aided verification, CAV'96*, volume 1102 of *Lecture Notes in Computer Science*. Springer-Verlag, July 1996.

[21] M. Yannakakis and D. Lee. An eficient alghorithm for minimizing real-time transition systems. In *Proceedings of the 5th Inter. Conference On Computer Aided verification, CAV'93*, volume 697 of *Lecture Notes in Computer Science*, pages 220–224. Springer-Verlag, June/July 1993.

Schedulability Analysis of Acyclic Processes

Michael J. Meyer and Howard Wong-Toi*

Abstract

This paper describes the analysis of worst-case execution times for a class of acyclic processes that can express precedence constraints and internal computational delays. The motivation for our work comes from hardware designs where a scheduler allocates exclusive access to a memory bus. Blocks that execute concurrently generate read and write requests. The timing of these requests may depend on factors such as bus contention, internal buffering, internal timing delays, and pipelining. Adaptations of our proposed method have enabled the verification of the timing performance of all subprocesses of an industrial MPEG-2 audio/video decoder chip. The method is accurate enough to produce guaranteed deadlines that are within 1% of those obtained through performance simulation.

1 Introduction

We study real-time systems consisting of several processes that require shared use of a common resource. A scheduler is used to assign mutually exclusive access to the resource among those processes contending for it. It should ensure that each process meets its hard real-time constraints. Validating the correctness of such systems may be critical for safety reasons (e.g., in transportation controllers), or for guaranteed performance (e.g., in multimedia applications). There is a vast body of literature studying the design and correctness of scheduling algorithms for real-time systems, e.g., [LL73, LW82, XP90, ABD+95, Ram96]. The system is commonly decomposed into a fixed number of tasks. The tasks are usually generated according to some simple scheme. For example, tasks may have fixed execution times, and they may be periodic (they are generated every Δ time units), or sporadic (they are generated with a separation of at least Δ).

We consider here fixed-priority dynamic scheduling. See [ABD+95] for an excellent survey. There exist feasibility tests that determine whether sets of tasks are schedulable under various scheduling strate-

gies [Ser72, LL73, SLR86]. We use instead a very successful alternative methodology that computes the worst-case execution time (WCET) of each task and compares it to its deadline.

In this paper, we extend WCET analysis methods to processes where tasks have conjunctive precedence constraints (a task may not be executed until *all* its predecessor tasks have executed), release times are not periodic (but may depend on the completion times of other tasks), and tasks within the same process can preempt one another. In addition, once a task has been requested on the shared resource, computation can commence without having to wait for the task to be completed, i.e., the shared resource is not the only means of performing computation in our model.

Our motivation stems from the performance analysis of an MPEG-2 decoder chip. MPEG-2 is an international standard for the digital compression of streams of video and audio signals [HPN97]. It enables broadcast-quality transmission of video, as well as enhanced multimedia applications on PCs. In previous work, a performance simulation of the decoder chip indicated that its behavior was likely to meet its specification. Here, we are interested in obtaining hard guarantees of performance.

The shared resource in our system is the memory bus. Computation is performed using custom hardware. The chip has blocks to decode and present audio and video data. These blocks must read and write the data to external memory via a shared bus. Each block represents a process that can execute several tasks in parallel. Within blocks, there are precedence constraints between reading memory, writing memory, and computation for decoding data. The hardware implementation is pipelined, with requests for the bus occurring at times dictated by the status of the data-processing pipeline.

We propose a simple class of acyclic processes that is sufficiently expressive for modeling the decoder chip, yet still admits an efficient and accurate algorithm for bounding worst-case execution times. The key idea behind the analysis is to account for task preemptions along *paths* of actions. For accuracy, it is important that our analysis consider the effect of preemption on sequences of actions rather than on individual actions

---

* Cadence Berkeley Labs, 2001 Addison Street, Third Floor, Berkeley, CA 94704, USA. {mjm,howard}@cadence.com.

only—otherwise delay due to a preempting task may be counted multiple times in a single execution.

The methodology has been used to verify that all processes in the MPEG-2 chip do indeed meet their performance deadlines. Furthermore, the method is accurate enough to produce guaranteed deadlines that are within 1% of those obtained through performance simulation.

Related work

Our system could be specified using existing models in the literature. For example, schedulability analysis is possible using process algebras such as ACSR [CLX95] or a multiple-agent version of RTSL [FC93]. Process algebra specifications are converted to their underlying state graphs, and then analyzed using state-space exploration, which is subject to computational complexity. Our WCET analysis avoids this complexity.

In the past, the basic WCET analysis framework has been extended in various ways, although not to a process model capable of specifying our hardware blocks. For example, Sun and Liu consider arbitrary release times and variable execution times [SL96]. Audsley et al. discuss distributed task precedence but with tasks arriving at the same time [ABR+93]. They also offer suggestions to avoid analyzing cases where tasks interfere with one another on the same processor. Balarin and Sangiovanni-Vincentelli consider embedded reactive systems with disjunctive precedence constraints (a task can execute whenever one of its predecessors completes) and no internal computational delays [BSV97]. Leinbaugh and Yamini consider an expressive class of distributed real-time systems with computation and communication delays [LY86]. However, their model disallows processes that wait for acknowledgement of their own service requests.

2 Process model

2.1 Syntax

We provide a simple language for specifying processes which share a single common resource. A process is essentially a directed acyclic graph (DAG) with its nodes labeled with actions. Actions can represent time-consuming computations, instantaneous requests for service on the shared resource, or waiting for service completion of a request. Actions cannot be executed until all "preceding" actions have completed. Before giving formal definitions, we provide an example of a process.

Example 2.1 Figure 1 depicts a process in which the first action is to compute for 3 time units. The process then branches into two parallel threads. The

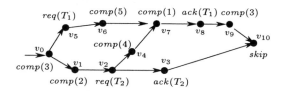

Figure 1: Example process $\mathcal{P}_0$

upper one instantly requests service, then computes for 5 time units. If the $comp(4)$ action has not yet completed, it then waits before proceeding. Otherwise, the action $comp(1)$ starts. The lower branch out of node v_0 computes for 2 time units, and then requests service via the $req(T_2)$ action. It then splits into two threads. One computes for 4 time units. It must complete before the $comp(1)$ action can be enabled. The other thread waits for acknowledgement that the service requested by the $req(T_2)$ action has been completed. After the completion of the $comp(1)$ action, the thread waits for completion of service of the $req(T_1)$ action, denoted by the $ack(T_1)$ action, and then performs some additional computation. After this computation, and the acknowledgement of the $req(T_2)$ service completion, the process ends. ∎

A *process* $\mathcal{P}$ consists of a task set $\mathcal{T}_\mathcal{P}$ and a labeled DAG $G_\mathcal{P}$. The task set consists of a finite set $\{T_1, \ldots, T_n\}$ of tasks. Each task T_i, identified by its index i, has a nonnegative integer priority π_i (the highest priority is 0), and a positive integer service time c_i. The set of action labels $Act(\mathcal{P})$ for the process $\mathcal{P}$ is $\{skip, comp\} \cup \bigcup_{i=1..n}\{req(T_i), ack(T_i)\}$. The DAG $G_\mathcal{P} = (V, E)$ has a finite set V of vertices (nodes), and a set $E \subseteq V \times V$ of edges. We write $s \to t$ to denote that $(s, t) \in E$, and call s a *predecessor* of t, and t a *successor* of s. If there exists a sequence $s_1, s_2, \ldots, s_m$ of $m > 1$ nodes such that (a) $s = s_1$, (b) $s_i \to s_{i+1}$ for $i \in 1..m-1$, and (c) $t = s_m$, then t is a *descendant* of s and s is an *ancestor* of t, denoted $s \twoheadrightarrow t$. The sequence is referred to as a *path* from s to t. The graph $G_\mathcal{P}$ has no cycles, i.e., there does not exist a node s such that $s \twoheadrightarrow s$. Let $succ(s)$ denote the set of successors of node s, and by overloading notation we denote the successors of a set A of nodes by $succ(A)$. A node is a *source* node of the DAG G if it has no predecessors, and a *sink* node if it has no successors. Each node is labeled with an action in $Act(\mathcal{P})$.

For simplicity, we require that for each $i \in 1..n$ there is exactly one node, r_i say, labeled $req(T_i)$. In other words, we disallow repeated requests of the same task. We can model repeated tasks: each task instance must be assigned a different task identifier.

Without loss of generality, we make the following requirements on every process.

1. There is a unique *source* node, which is denoted $source(\mathcal{P})$, and a unique *sink* node, which is denoted $sink(\mathcal{P})$.

2. The sink node is labeled with the *skip* action.

3. There is exactly one node, a_i say, labeled $ack(T_i)$. Furthermore $r_i \twoheadrightarrow a_i$.

For syntactic convenience, we pictorially represent a sequence of n nodes labeled *comp* with a single node labeled $comp(n)$.

The restriction to acyclic graphs means that a process cannot explicitly model iteration. This shortcoming in modeling is not an obstacle to analysis: it can be handled in two ways. First, an iterating process can be unwrapped an arbitrary number of times into a long acyclic process. The number of unwrappings can be bounded by the period of time we are considering. Second, our analysis method allows for explicit handling of processes that restart upon termination.

2.2 Semantics

Each process executes repeatedly. Processes are sporadic, in that once a process completes execution (i.e., it reaches its sink node), it waits a nondeterministic time before restarting (i.e., it resumes at its source node at some unknown future time).

Intuitively, the semantics of the internal behavior of a process are straightforward. The *comp* action causes execution of the current thread to idle for one time unit. The request action $req(T_i)$ takes no time to execute. If this is not a realistic assumption, a fixed computation time for the request can be added before the request. The $req(T_i)$ action involves sending a request for c_i time units of service on the common resource at the integer priority π_i. The $ack(T_i)$ action represents waiting (possibly no time) until the task T_i has had c_i units of time allocated to it on the shared resource. Parallel threads of a process are assumed to execute concurrently. Thus if two threads are at the start of different $comp(1)$ actions, they will *both* complete their actions after one time unit has passed. The *comp* actions do not require access to the shared resource. An action at a node cannot take place until the actions at all predecessor nodes have completed.

Scheduler

The semantics of the system depends on the scheduling policy chosen. We provide semantics for a preemptive fixed-priority scheduler in which priorities are positive integer values, with priority π_1 being higher than π_2 if $\pi_1 < \pi_2$. Thus the prior-

ity 0 represents the highest priority. Given a collection $\{\mathcal{P}_1, \ldots, \mathcal{P}_m\}$ of m processes with the set $\mathcal{T} = \{T_1, \ldots, T_n\}$ of tasks, the state of the scheduler is a pair $\langle sched, queue \rangle$ where $sched$ is a map from $\bigcup_{j=1..n} \mathcal{T}_j$ to $\{-1, 0, 1, \ldots\}$, and $queue$ is a map taking each priority π to a queue $queue(\pi)$. The map $sched$ encodes the amount of processing time already allocated to each task. The map $queue$ encodes a service ordering among tasks with the same priority. Consider a task T. If $sched(T) = -1$, then the task has not yet been requested in this invocation of the process it belongs to. Otherwise, the task has been requested and $sched(T)$ denotes the amount of processing time that has currently been assigned to T.

The state of the scheduler changes as follows. When the action $req(T_i)$ is executed, the state of the scheduler remains unchanged except that $sched(T_i)$ is changed from -1 to 0, and T_i is placed at the end of the queue for tasks of priority π_i.

Whenever one time unit passes, the scheduler picks among all tasks T_i for which $0 \leq sched(T_i) \leq c_i - 1$, if any, that task T_j with the highest priority and first in its priority queue, and increments $sched(T_j)$ by 1. If $sched(T_j)$ reaches the service time c_j, then T_j is removed from the queue for priority π_j. The initial state of the scheduler assigns the value -1 to all tasks. The action $ack(T)$ may be executed whenever $sched(T) = c_T$. The scheduler state remains unchanged.

Process and system states

A *state* of a process $\mathcal{P}_j$ is a subset of its nodes. The nodes in the state represent the currently active "threads". The *initial* state is the singleton containing the source node. Not all states are reachable; nor do all states even have a reasonable interpretation.

A *state* of the system — consisting of the parallel composition of the set $\{\mathcal{P}_1, \ldots, \mathcal{P}_m\}$ of processes together with the scheduler — is a tuple $\langle S, sched, queue \rangle$, where S is a union of states for each $\mathcal{P}_j$, and $\langle sched, queue \rangle$ is a state of the scheduler. The initial state consists of the initial state of each process and of the scheduler.

A node v is *instantaneous* in state $\langle S, sched, queue \rangle$ if $v \in S$ and either (a) it is labeled with either *skip* or $req(T_i)$ for some i, or (b) it is labeled with $ack(T_i)$ and $sched(T_i) = c_i$. The action at an instantaneous node can be executed immediately without further passage of time.

Executions

We are now ready to define the executions of the closed system consisting of the scheduler and the processes. A state $\langle S', sched', queue' \rangle$ is a *successor* of the state $\langle S, sched, queue \rangle$ if either of the two following conditions hold:

1. [Instantaneous step] There exists an instantaneous node $v \in S$ and either of the following two conditions hold:

   (a) [Process restart] The node v is $sink(\mathcal{P})$ for some process $\mathcal{P}$ and the following three conditions hold:

      i. $S' = S \cup source(P) - \{v\}$.
      ii. For all tasks $T \in \mathcal{T}_P$, $sched'(T) = -1$, and for all tasks $T \notin \mathcal{T}_P$, $sched'(T) = sched(T)$.
      iii. $queue' = queue$.

   (b) [Internal process step] The node v is not a sink and the following three conditions hold:

      i. $S' = S \cup succ(v) - \{v\}$.
      ii. If v is labeled $req(T)$, then $sched'(T) = 0$ and for all tasks $\hat{T} \neq T$, $sched'(\hat{T}) = sched(\hat{T})$, else for all tasks $\hat{T}$, $sched'(\hat{T}) = sched(\hat{T})$.
      iii. $queue' = queue$ unless v is labeled with $req(T)$ in which case $queue'$ differs from $queue$ only in that T is inserted at the tail of the queue for its priority.

2. [Unit time step] The only instantaneous nodes in S are sink nodes and the following two conditions hold:

   (a) The set $S' = S \cup succ(CompNodes(S)) - CompNodes(S)$, where $CompNodes(S)$ is the set of nodes in S whose labels are $comp$.

   (b) Let $\tilde{\mathcal{T}}$ be the set of tasks T for which $0 \leq sched(T) < c_T$. Let T be the task that has highest priority among the tasks in $\hat{\mathcal{T}}$ and is at the head of its queue. Then $sched'(T) = sched(T) + 1$ and for all tasks $\hat{T} \neq T$, $sched'(\hat{T}) = sched(\hat{T})$. We say that T is being serviced during this time step. We have $queue'$ the same as $queue$ unless $sched'(T) = c_T$, in which case it differs only in that T is deleted from its queue.

An *execution* of the system is a finite sequence $q_1, q_2, \ldots, q_r$ of states such that q_1 is the initial state and for $j \in 1..r-1$, we have q_{j+1} is a successor of q_j. For an execution η, the *duration* or *execution time* $time(\eta)$ of η is the number of states q_j among the $q_1..q_{r-1}$ such that q_{j+1} is a unit time step successor of the state q_j.

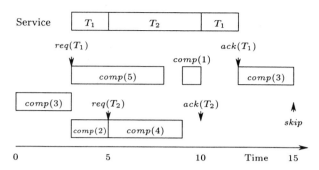

Figure 2: Execution for process $\mathcal{P}_0$ of Figure 1

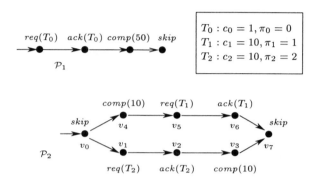

Figure 3: Example system

Example 2.2 Figure 2 depicts the execution of process $\mathcal{P}_0$ of Figure 1 under the assumption that this process is the sole process in the system. The task T_1 has service time 4 and priority 1 and the task T_2 has service time 5 and priority 0. At time 5, the request for T_2 at node v_2 preempts T_1, and then the computation at v_4 for 4 time units begins. Meanwhile, the computation of length 5 time units of the upper thread continues. At time 9, both delays at the predecessor nodes for node v_7 have completed, and the 1 time unit computation at this node can proceed. The computation taking 3 time units does not begin until time 12 when T_1's service is complete. Finally, the process completes at time 15. ∎

3 Schedule validation

We use worst-case analysis of execution times to provide a conservative (but not necessarily tight) upper bound on the execution time of a process. We assume that our system requirements place a deadline on the completion of every process. When examining a particular process, we must consider not only the effect of higher priority tasks from other processes, but also the effect of tasks within the process itself. The following example motivates our discussion.

277

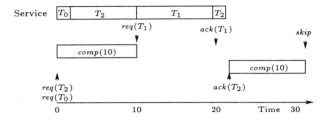

Figure 4: Execution of system consisting of $\mathcal{P}_1$ and $\mathcal{P}_2$

Example 3.1 Consider the system consisting of the processes $\mathcal{P}_1$ and $\mathcal{P}_2$ in Figure 3. Our goal is to verify that $\mathcal{P}_2$ completes within 35 time units of when it starts. We separate service time due to other processes (here $\mathcal{P}_1$) and service time due to the process itself (here $\mathcal{P}_2$). Over a 35 time unit period, there can be at most one servicing of $\mathcal{P}_1$'s request. Hence, during an execution of $\mathcal{P}_2$, there is at most 1 time unit spent servicing tasks from $\mathcal{P}_1$. It is not sound to calculate the execution time of process $\mathcal{P}_2$ independently, and then add the service time from $\mathcal{P}_1$. Such an analysis would give a cost of $20 + 1 = 21$ time units. The problem is that the timing of the service of T_0 in $\mathcal{P}_1$ can cause a long delay in $\mathcal{P}_2$. See Figure 4. The T_0 request occurs at time 0, and ends at time 1. Then the request $req(T_2)$ starts being served. At time 10, the process $\mathcal{P}_2$ submits the request $req(T_1)$ which preempts the service of task T_2 one time unit before its completion. Then the task T_1 completes at time 20, followed by the task T_2 at time 21. The computational delay of 10 time units after the $ack(T_2)$ event causes the process $\mathcal{P}_2$ to complete at time 31. A conservative, but very loose, bound can be obtained by removing all parallelism from the process, and determining the time bound for all requests and all computational delays. This results in a upper bound of 40 time units from $\mathcal{P}_2$ plus an additional 2 for $\mathcal{P}_1$. ∎

Our method provides conservative bounds on process execution times at the same time as taking into account parallelism. An *execution of a process* $\mathcal{P}$ in a system of processes is a sequential fragment of an execution of the system such that (1) at the beginning of the fragment the process $\mathcal{P}$ is at its source node, (2) at the end it is at its sink node, and (3) it never returns to the source node after leaving it.

We define the worst-case execution time of a process $\mathcal{P}$, denoted $\text{WCET}(\mathcal{P})$, to be the maximum execution time $time(\eta)$ over all executions η of $\mathcal{P}$.

We separate the time of an execution of a process into two parts. A task is *external* to a process if it does not lie in that process's task set. Since the process is running concurrently with other processes, a typical execution of $\mathcal{P}$ will include some times during which external tasks are being serviced by the shared resource. Let the lowest priority task of $\mathcal{P}$ have priority π_{min}. For a given execution η of $\mathcal{P}$, let the *external execution time* $ext\_time(\eta)$ denote the total amount of time during which external tasks of priority higher than π_{min} are being serviced while tasks in $\mathcal{P}$ are waiting for service. Define the *internal execution time* of an execution η, denoted $int\_time(\eta)$, to be $time(\eta) - ext\_time(\eta)$. For example, the execution depicted in Figure 4 of process $\mathcal{P}_2$ has an internal execution time of 30, and an external execution time of 1 due to process $\mathcal{P}_1$.

We define the *worst-case internal execution time* $\text{WCIET}(\mathcal{P})$ of a process $\mathcal{P}$ as the maximal internal execution time $int\_time(\eta)$ over all executions η of $\mathcal{P}$.

Given a finite set $\{\mathcal{P}_1, \ldots, \mathcal{P}_m\}$ of sporadic processes, the system requirement is that each instance of $\mathcal{P}_j$ complete within deadline D_j time units, i.e., that the time for every execution of the process $\mathcal{P}_j$ is no more than D_j. Our methodology performs the following steps for each process $\mathcal{P}$.

Step 1. We determine an upper bound on $\text{WCIET}(\mathcal{P})$. This step is independent of the other processes.

Step 2. We determine an upper bound on $\text{WCET}(\mathcal{P})$. We use the bound on $\text{WCIET}(\mathcal{P})$ and add the service time for all potential preempting tasks from other processes. This second step is essentially the usual WCET analysis, except that we must first determine a lower bound on the execution time for each process in order to bound the number of occurrences of each process over a given time interval.

These two steps are now explained in more detail in the next two sections.

4   Bounding internal execution time

We show how to bound the internal execution times under a preemptive scheduling policy with fixed priorities. Nonpreemptive scheduling policies can be handled with minor extensions to the framework.

A task in $\mathcal{P}$ with a low priority may be affected by a higher priority request, $req(T)$ say, within $\mathcal{P}$. Recall Example 3.1. Thus for each task T in $\mathcal{P}$, we consider its effect on other tasks within $\mathcal{P}$. We first determine an overapproximation of the set of tasks that may be affected by the servicing of T. To do so, we assume a worst-case scenario, based on the structure only of the DAG of the process. Specifically, the servicing of T cannot preempt any task that is known to be serviced before $req(T)$ or after $ack(T)$. This motivates the following definition. The *parallel scope* $Par(T)$ of a task T is the set of nodes $V - descendants(a) - ancestors(r)$, where the node $a \in V$ is labeled with $ack(T)$, the node r is labeled with $req(T)$, the set $descendants(v) \subseteq V$ is the set of descendant nodes of v, and the set $ancestors(v) \subseteq V$ is the set of ancestor nodes of v.

For example, in $\mathcal{P}_0$ of Figure 1, we have $Par(T_1) = \{v_1..v_8\}$ and $Par(T_2) = \{v_2..v_9\}$. For process $\mathcal{P}_2$ in Figure 3, we have $Par(T_1) = \{v_1, v_2, v_3, v_5, v_6\}$ and $Par(T_2) = \{v_1, v_2, v_4, v_5, v_6\}$.

The following proposition states that the set $Par(T)$ of a task is conservative.

Proposition 4.1 *For all executions η of $\mathcal{P}$, for all states $s = \langle S, sched, queue \rangle$ along η, and for all tasks T_i of $\mathcal{P}$, if $sched(T_i) \in \{0, \ldots, c_i - 1\}$, then every node v of $\mathcal{P}$ that lies in S is in $Par(T_i)$.* ∎

4.1 A characterization of WCIETs

Bounds on the internal execution time of an execution can be obtained by considering the paths in the DAG of the process. A *complete path* of the process $\mathcal{P}$ is a path from the source to the sink in the DAG $G_{\mathcal{P}}$. Given an execution η of $\mathcal{P}$, the *dwelling time* $dwell(\eta, v)$ of η at node v is the number of consecutive pairs of states (q, q') in η such that there is a time step between q and q' and v occurs in both q and q'.

Lemma 4.2 *Let η be an execution of $\mathcal{P}$. Then $time(\eta)$ is the maximum over all complete paths p of $\mathcal{P}$ of the sum of the dwelling times $dwell(\eta, v)$ for each node in p.*

Proof sketch. The "start" time at each node is the maximum of the "completion" times of each of its predecessors. Since $\mathcal{P}$ has an underlying DAG, the completion time at the sink can be obtained (and bounded) by summing the times spent at each node along a critical path constructed backwards from sink to source. ∎

The basic cost $cost(v)$ of a node v is 0 if it is labeled with a *req* or *skip*, is 1 if it is labeled with *comp*, and is c_i if it is labeled with $ack(T_i)$. Let p be a complete path of $\mathcal{P}$. The *basic cost* $cost(p)$ of the path p is the sum of the costs $cost(v)$ of all nodes v along p. Let $\hat{\mathcal{T}}(p)$ be the subset of tasks T_i in $\mathcal{P}$ such that the node labeled with $ack(T_i)$ does not appear on p, and there exists some node v along p labeled with some $ack(T_j)$ such that $v \in Par(T_i)$ and T_i is of higher priority than T_j. Let $added(p)$ be the sum of the service times of the tasks in $\hat{\mathcal{T}}(p)$. Define $max\_path\_cost(\mathcal{P})$ to be the maximum of $cost(p) + added(p)$ over all complete paths p of $\mathcal{P}$.

Proposition 4.3 *The $WCIET(\mathcal{P})$ is bounded above by $max\_path\_cost(\mathcal{P})$.*

Proof. Let η be an execution of $\mathcal{P}$. By definition, $int\_time(\eta) = time(\eta) - ext\_time(\eta)$. By Lemma 4.2, it follows that $int\_time(\eta)$ is bounded above by the maximum over all complete paths p of the sum of the times spent at each node in p minus $ext\_time(\eta)$. For each complete path p, this sum is bounded above by $cost(p) + added(p) + ext\_time(\eta)$, since the time spent at each node v is no more than the time due to computational delay, added delay due to internal task preemption, and preemption by higher priority tasks from other processes. The result follows. ∎

This proposition immediately implies an algorithm for finding upper bounds for WCIETs. One enumerates all paths p to bound the value of $cost(p) + added(p)$. However, the number of paths in a process may be exponential in the number of nodes. While it not known whether computing this particular bound is NP-complete, mild generalizations of the problem are NP-hard.

4.2 An edge-based algorithm

We present an algorithm that is computationally efficient, but may in practice be less accurate than the path-based algorithm suggested above. Our proposed solution to the complexity problem is to account for the effects of preemption not along paths, but along edges, since this can be done locally. Let the subset $E' \subseteq E$ of edges in the DAG $G = (V, E)$ of $\mathcal{P}$ be a *preemption cut-set* for task T iff every complete path in G includes at least one edge in E' if it passes through a node with label $ack(T')$ for some T' with lower priority than T. For example, if T_2 has higher priority than T_1 in $\mathcal{P}_0$ of Figure 1, then $\{(v_4, v_7), (v_6, v_7)\}$ and $\{(v_7, v_8)\}$ are both preemption cut-sets for T_2.

We can bound $added(p)$ over a complete path p by summing across all its edges e, adding in the service time for task T whenever e lies in the preemption cut-set of T. Let $\mathcal{E} = \{E_1 \ldots E_n\}$ be such that each E_i is a preemption cut-set for task T_i. Define $added_{\mathcal{E}}(v, v')$ to be $\sum_{i=1..n} added_{E_i}(v, v')$ where $added_{E_i}(v, v') = c_i$ if $(v, v') \in E_i$ and 0 otherwise. For all complete paths p, the sum of the $added_{\mathcal{E}}(e)$ over the edges e in p is an upper bound on $added(p)$. Our conservative algorithm appears in Figure 5. It takes a process $\mathcal{P}$ as input, and outputs an upper bound on $WCIET(\mathcal{P})$. It sweeps forward, assigning the time $wciet(v)$ to each node v once all its predecessor nodes have been assigned times.

Theorem 4.4 *The WCIET Algorithm is correct, i.e., given a process $\mathcal{P}$ as input, it outputs an upper bound on $WCIET(\mathcal{P})$.* ∎

```
WCIET Algorithm
Choose set ℰ of preemption cut-sets for process 𝒫
wciet(source(𝒫)) := 0
marked := {source(𝒫)}
new := {source(𝒫)}
repeat
  last := new
  new := {}
  for each v ∈ last
    for each v' in succ(v)
      if pred(v') ⊆ marked then
        wciet(v') := cost(v') +
              max_{v̂∈pred(v')}{wciet(v̂) + added_ℰ(v̂, v')}
        new := new ∪ {v'}
        marked := marked ∪ {v'}
      endif
    endfor
  endfor
until marked = V
output wciet(sink(𝒫))
```

Figure 5: Algorithm to bound WCIET($\mathcal{P}$)

Using $\{(v_1, v_2)\}$ as the preemption cut-set for T_1, the WCIET Algorithm outputs 30, obtained by assigning 0 to v_0 and v_1, 20 to v_2, and 30 to v_3 and the sink v_7.

Finding a set of edges that satisfies the preemption cut-set definition is easy. One can always take the set of edges that are going out from the parallel scope. Thus the algorithm can be performed in polynomial time. This choice of preemption cut-set has the advantage that every traversing path encounters only one edge in the set. In general though, there may not be preemption cut-sets such that the WCIET Algorithm gives tight bounds on $max\_path\_cost(\mathcal{P})$. Finding good cut-sets may be difficult.

An alternative approach to reducing complexity associates added costs to a subset of nodes, rather than to a subset of edges. Choosing edges, however, provides greater flexibility. In any case, the important point is to have preemption by a specific task accounted for at most once along any given path, if possible. Naively assigning added costs to every node that lies within the parallel scope of higher priority tasks is unnecessarily conservative.

5 Bounding total execution time

Bounding the total execution time of a process is done using mild modification to traditional WCET analysis [ABD+95]: thus we state the method without elaboration. The primary differences are that

(1) the bound on the WCIET of a process is taken in place of a prespecified execution time, (2) lower time bounds for the execution of other processes must be computed since processes are not given with specific minimal separation times, and (3) due to unpredictable release times, one additional instance of each task is accounted for. Let the WCIET of process $\mathcal{P}$ be bounded above by K. We need to compute the maximal amount of time that higher priority external tasks could be receiving service while $\mathcal{P}$ is undergoing an execution. Let $\{T_1, \ldots, T_d\}$ be the external tasks with higher priority than the lowest priority task in $\mathcal{P}$. Let P_i be a lower bound on the execution time of the process containing task T_i, for each $i = 1..d$. Then an upper bound on the WCET of a process is obtained by finding solutions to the formula

$$W = K + \sum_{i=1..d} (\lceil W/P_i \rceil + 1) \cdot c_i. \qquad (1)$$

The minimal solution for this equation can be found by treating it as an assignment and iterating from an initial value of K for the W on the righthand side. The process $\mathcal{P}$ completes before its deadline D if $W \leq D$.

Theorem 5.1 *Given a process $\mathcal{P}$, the WCET($\mathcal{P}$) is bounded above by any W satisfying Equation 1.*

Proof. There can be at most $(\lceil W/P_i \rceil + 1)$ instances of task T_i being serviced in any interval of duration W. For all executions η, K bounds $int\_time(\eta)$ and the summation term bounds $ext\_time(\eta)$. ∎

The expression $(\lceil W/P_i \rceil + 1) \cdot c_i$ in Equation 1 can be tightened in various ways. For example, if the task T_i is known to complete before some deadline, then it might be possible to bound the number of instances of servicing of the task T_i to fewer than $\lceil W/P_i \rceil + 1$.

The above methodology can be adapted for non-preemptive scheduling policies. One then considers the effect of a task on all tasks with acknowledgements in its parallel scope, regardless of priority.

6 Pipelined processes

Typical dataflow-like processes rely on pipelining for efficiency. A process may receive streams of items of data and be required to perform a series of computational steps on each item. We briefly discuss the modeling and analysis of pipelined processes.

Example 6.1 Consider the schematic in Figure 6. The processing unit sends a read request, which requires 5 time units of service, and starts computing for 8 time units. After receiving acknowledgement of the read, it computes for 5 time units before making a request to write data for 5 time units, and then

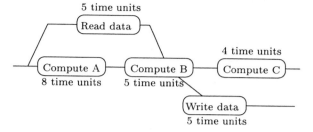

Figure 6: Schematic of pipelined process

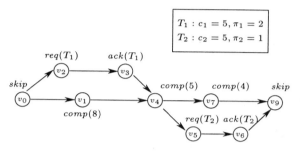

Figure 7: Process $\mathcal{P}_{basic}$

computes for a further 4 time units. The basic process can be modeled as shown in Figure 7. Execution of this process takes at least 18 time units, as can be seen from the sum of the costs along the path $v_0 \rightarrow v_1 \rightarrow v_4 \rightarrow v_5 \rightarrow v_6 \rightarrow v_9$.

Now suppose the process operates in a pipelined fashion, with a buffer between the "Compute A" and "Compute B" stages, between the "Read" and the "Compute B" stage, between the "Compute B" and "Compute C" stages, and between the "Compute B" and the "Write" stage. The interpretation is that once the "Compute A" unit completes, the data it has processed resides in the buffer between "Compute A" and "Compute B". When "Compute B" completes, it removes data from the buffer in front of it and places revised data in the buffers ahead of it, i.e., before the "Compute C" and "Write" stages. The "Compute A" stage can commence its execution on the next item of data as soon as two things occur: it must complete its execution on the current data item and the "Compute B" stage must also have completed and therefore have no further use of the data in the buffer.

The pipelined process is modeled by unwrapping the pipe to replicate the stages, giving rise to one instance of the basic process per data item being processed. An unwrapping of three replications of the basic process is shown in Figure 8. The node (task) of the ith replication of the basic process that corresponds to the node v (task T) in the basic process will be denoted (v, i) $((T, i))$, for $i \geq 0$. For space

reasons, the task (T, i) is denoted T^i in the figure. The dotted edges denote precedence edges modeling the operation of the pipeline. For instance, the dotted edge from (v_1, i) to $(v_1, i + 1)$ denotes the fact that the "Compute A" stage cannot commence processing the next $(i + 1)$th data item until it has finished processing the ith data item. The dotted edge from (v_4, i) to $(v_1, i + 1)$ indicates that the buffer containing the ith data item must be freed by completion of the "Compute B" stage before "Compute A" starts processing the $(i + 1)$th item. The pipelined process is now analyzed using the WCIET Algorithm. The parallel scope of (T_2, i) is $\{(v_5, i), (v_6, i), (v_7, i), (v_1, i + 1), (v_2, i + 1), (v_3, i + 1)\} \cup \{(v_0, j) \mid j > i\}$. We use $\{((v_2, i + 1), (v_3, i + 1))\}$ as the preemption cut-set for (T_2, i). The $wciet$ assignments are indicated in boldface in the figure. ∎

In our example, we considered only single buffering between pipeline stages. Larger buffers can easily be handled. In this case, there would be edges modeling precedence that spanned to more than just the adjacent replication.

Given a basic process $\mathcal{P}$, a process $\mathcal{P}'$ is a k-unwrapping of $\mathcal{P}$ if the following five conditions hold:

1. Its set of nodes is $V_{\mathcal{P}} \times \{0..k-1\} \cup \{v_{source}, v_{sink}\}$, where the additional nodes v_{source} and v_{sink} are the new source node and sink node, connected to the basic source and sink nodes in the expected way. Nodes of the form (v, r) are said to belong to the rth replication of $\mathcal{P}$.

2. Its task set is $\mathcal{T}_{\mathcal{P}} \times \{0..k-1\}$, i.e., the task set is replicated k times. The task (T, k') has the same priority and service time as T.

3. The labels on nodes match. Whenever node v in $\mathcal{P}$ is labeled with $req(T)$, then each (v, k') is labeled with $req(T, k')$, etc.

4. The edges within every replication match those of the basic process, i.e., for all $0 \leq \hat{k} < k$, the pair $((v, \hat{k}), (v', \hat{k}))$ is an edge in $\mathcal{P}$ iff (v, v') is an edge in $\mathcal{P}'$.

5. The added precedence relations are consistent across all replications, i.e., for all $b \geq 1$, for all $\hat{k} < k - b$, $((v, \hat{k}), (v', \hat{k} + b))$ is an edge of $\mathcal{P}'$ iff $((v, \tilde{k}), (v', \tilde{k} + b))$ is an edge of $\mathcal{P}'$ for all $0 \leq \tilde{k} < k - b$.

Given an unwrapping of a pipelined process, one may now perform WCET analysis as shown in the previous section. The analysis however may be inefficient, since the basic process may have been replicated a large number of times, as would be the case when

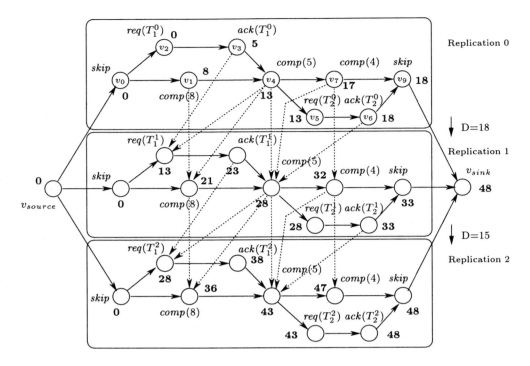

Figure 8: Unwrapped pipelined process with *wciets* of nodes in boldface

examining the average rate of throughput of a pipeline in the presence of other tasks with very large periods. This is because we need to consider large numbers of replications in order to minimize the average effect of widely-spaced preemptions of external tasks.

We give a stopping condition that prevents computation of *wciets* across unnecessarily many replications. The following theorem states that under certain conditions if the *wciets* of all nodes in a replication are bounded by some time D within the *wciets* of the matching nodes in the previous replication, then all successive replications have *wciets* separated at most by the appropriate multiple of D. The following definition is used to ensure that all possible task preemptions among the various replications are considered. A k-unwrapping $\mathcal{P}'$ of $\mathcal{P}$ is *d-bounded* if for all nodes (v_1, k_1) and (v_2, k_2), if (v_2, k_2) is in the parallel scope of (v_1, k_1) or $(v_1, k_1) \rightarrow (v_2, k_2)$, then $k_2 \leq k_1 + d$. When computing *wciets* for nodes in the k_2th replication of a basic process $\mathcal{P}$ with a d-bounded unwrapping, it suffices to consider the effect of tasks in replications $k_2 - d$ or higher.

A set of preemption cut-sets is *consistent* across replications in a k-unwrapping if for all $k_1, k_2, k_3 < k - 1$, the edge $((v_1, k_1), (v_2, k_2))$ is in the preemption cut-set for (T, k_3) iff the edge $((v_1, k_1 + 1), (v_2, k_2 + 1))$ is in the preemption cut-set for $(T, k_3 + 1)$.

Theorem 6.1 *Let $\mathcal{P}'$ be a d-bounded k-unwrapping of the basic process $\mathcal{P}$. Suppose there exists an integer k' such that $d \leq k' < k$, an integer $D \geq 0$, and a set $\mathcal{E}$ of consistent preemption cut-sets for which the WCIET Algorithm assigns wciets to nodes in $\mathcal{P}'$ such that for all $b \in 1..d$, for all nodes v of the basic process $\mathcal{P}$, $wciet(v, k' - b + 1) \leq wciet(v, k' - b) + D$. Then there exists a choice $\mathcal{E}'$ of preemption cut-sets such that for all k'' such that $k' \leq k'' < k$, for all nodes v in $\mathcal{P}$, $wciet(v, k'') \leq wciet(v, k') + (k'' - k')D$.*

Proof. Consider the value that the WCIET Algorithm assigns to the node $(v, k' + 1)$. Since $k' \geq d$ and $\mathcal{P}'$ is d-bounded, for every predecessor node $(\hat{v}, \hat{k}+1)$ of $(v, k' + 1)$, there is a predecessor node $(\hat{v}, \hat{k})$ of (v, k'). By hypothesis, $wciet(\hat{v}, \hat{k} + 1) \leq wciet(\hat{v}, \hat{k}) + D$.

Since $\mathcal{P}'$ is d-bounded and $\mathcal{E}$ is consistent, whenever $(\hat{v}, \hat{k} + 1), (v, k' + 1)$ is in the preemption cut-set of a task $(\tilde{T}, \tilde{k}+1)$, then $((\hat{v}, \hat{k}), (v, k'))$ is in the preemption cut-set for $(\tilde{T}, \tilde{k})$. Thus $added_{\mathcal{E}}((\hat{v}, \hat{k}+1), (v, k'+1)) \leq added_{\mathcal{E}}((\hat{v}, \hat{k}), (v, k'))$.

Putting it all together, we see that the computation of $wciet(v, k' + 1) \leq wciet(v, k') + D$, since, compared to the k'th replication, the matching predecessor nodes for $(v, k' + 1)$ have *wciets* within D of those for the predecessors of (v, k'), and the corresponding $added_{\mathcal{E}}$ values are no greater than for the previ-

282

ous replication. An inductive argument concludes the proof. ∎

Thus one may run the WCIET Algorithm and terminate as soon as at least $d + 1$ replications in a d-bounded unwrapping have been processed. In our example, we have $d = 1$ and $k' = 1$, and the D value obtained between replications 1 and 2 is 15. Since the preemption cut-set at one replication belongs to a task from the prior replication, any k-unwrapping will have the same *wciet*s assigned to the first few replications as those shown in Figure 8. We therefore conclude that a k-unwrapping of $\mathcal{P}_{basic}$ would have WCIET no more than $15k + 18$. Although not true for this example, it is possible that iterating for more replications than for $k' = d$ may give better results.

7   Discussion

Adaptations of the method described here have enabled the verification of the timing performance of all subprocesses of an industrial MPEG-2 video decoder chip. This chip has nine processes running concurrently. The maximum number of nodes in a process is in the order of thousands, and the number of nodes in the basic unpipelined video process is in the order of hundreds. The primary effort was in the modeling phase. Particularly helpful would have been tool support to generate a system of our acyclic processes from the simulation models built for performance analysis. Instead, this work was done by hand.

The WCIET analysis was also carried out manually. While implementing the algorithm would have been straightforward, we relied instead on the structure of the processes to simplify summation of the costs over the worst-case paths.

Further work includes the development of algorithms for better bounds on the parallel scope of tasks. These could exploit information about time delays or the completion times of individual tasks within a process. It would be useful to design practical heuristics for choosing good preemption cut-sets. Currently, the choice is purely manual and ad hoc. We are also investigating generalizations of the class of processes that can be modeled and analyzed. For instance, we expect our method to extend to multiple shared resources with little additional cost in computational complexity.

References

[ABD+95] N. C. Audsley, A. Burns, R. I. Davis, K. W. Tindell, and A. J. Wellings. Fixed priority preemptive scheduling: An historical perspective. *Real-Time Systems*, 8:173–198, 1995.

[ABR+93] N. Audsley, A. Burns, M. Richardson, K. Tindell, and A. J. Wellings. Applying new scheduling theory to static priority pre-emptive scheduling. *Software Engineering Journal*, pages 284–292, September 1993.

[BSV97] F. Balarin and A. Sangiovanni-Vincentelli. Schedule validation for embedded reactive real-time systems. In *DAC 97: 34th Design Automation Conference*, pages 52–7. ACM, Inc., 1997.

[CLX95] J.-Y. Choi, I. Lee, and H.-L. Xie. The specification and schedulability analysis of real-time systems using ACSR. In *RTSS 95: Proceedings of the 16th Real-Time Systems Symposium*, pages 266–275. IEEE Computer Society Press, 1995.

[FC93] A. N. Fredette and R. Cleaveland. RTSL: A language for real-time schedulability analysis. In *RTSS 93: Proceedings of 14th Real-time Systems Symposium*, pages 274–283. IEEE Computer Society Press, 1993.

[HPN97] B. Haskell, A. Puri, and A. Netravali. *Digital Video: An Introduction to MPEG-2*. Chapman and Hall, 1997.

[LL73] C. Liu and J. Layland. Scheduling algorithms for multiprogramming in a hard real-time environment. *Journal of the Association of Computing Machinery*, 20:46–61, 1973.

[LW82] J. Y.-T. Leung and J. Whitehead. On the complexity of fixed-priority scheduling of periodic, real-time tasks. *Performance Evaluation*, 2(4):237–250, 1982.

[LY86] D. W. Leinbaugh and M.-R. Yamini. Guaranteed response times in a distributed hard-real-time environment. *IEEE Transactions on Software Engineering*, SE-12(12):1139–1144, 1986.

[Ram96] K. Ramamritham. Dynamic priority scheduling. In M. Joseph, editor, *Real-Time Systems*, pages 66–96. Prentice Hall, London, 1996.

[Ser72] O. Serlin. Scheduling of time critical processes. In *Proceedings of AFIPS Spring Computing Conference*, pages 925–932, 1972.

[SL96] J. Sun and J. W. S. Liu. Bounding completion times of jobs with arbitrary release times and variable execution times. In *RTSS 96: Proceedings of 17th Real-time Systems Symposium*, pages 2–12. IEEE Computer Society, 1996.

[SLR86] L. Sha, J. P. Lehoczky, and R. Rajkumar. Solutions for some practical problems in prioritized preemptive scheduling. In *RTSS 86: Proceedings of 7th Real-time Systems Symposium*, pages 181–191. IEEE Computer Society, 1986.

[XP90] J. Xu and D. Parnas. Scheduling processors with release times, deadline, precedence, and exclusion relations. *IEEE Transactions on Software Engineering*, 16(3):360–9, 1990.

Session 8.B: Quality of Service Issues

Elastic Task Model For Adaptive Rate Control

Giorgio C. Buttazzo, Giuseppe Lipari, and Luca Abeni
Scuola Superiore S. Anna, Pisa, Italy
{giorgio,lipari}@sssup.it, luca@hartik.sssup.it

Abstract

An increasing number of real-time applications, related to multimedia and adaptive control systems, require greater flexibility than classical real-time theory usually permits. In this paper we present a novel periodic task model, in which tasks' periods are treated as springs, with given elastic coefficients. Under this framework, periodic tasks can intentionally change their execution rate to provide different quality of service, and the other tasks can automatically adapt their periods to keep the system underloaded. The proposed model can also be used to handle overload conditions in a more flexible way, and provide a simple and efficient mechanism for controlling the quality of service of the system as a function of the current load.

1. Introduction

Periodic activities represent the major computational demand in many real-time applications, since they provide a simple way to enforce timing constraints through rate control. For instance, in digital control systems, periodic tasks are associated with sensory data acquisition, low-level servoing, control loops, action planning, and system monitoring. In such applications, a necessary condition for guaranteeing the stability of the controlled system is that each periodic task is executed at a constant rate, whose value is computed at the design stage based on the characteristics of the environment and on the required performance. For critical control applications (i.e., those whose failure may cause catastrophic consequences), the feasibility of the schedule has to be guaranteed a priori and no task can change its period while the system is running.

Such a rigid framework in which periodic tasks operate is also determined by the schedulability analysis that must be performed on the task set to guarantee its feasibility under the imposed constraints. To simplify the analysis, in fact, some feasibility tests for periodic tasks are based on quite rigid assumptions. For example, in the original Liu and Layland's paper [7] on the Rate Monotonic (RM) and the

Earliest Deadline First (EDF) algorithms, a periodic task τ_i is modeled as a cyclical processor activity characterized by two parameters, the computation time C_i and the period T_i, which are considered to be constant for all task instances. This is a reasonable assumption for most real-time control systems, but it can be too restrictive for other applications.

For example, in multimedia systems timing constraints can be more flexible and dynamic than control theory usually permits. Activities such as voice sampling, image acquisition, sound generation, data compression, and video playing, are performed periodically, but their execution rates are not as rigid as in control applications. Missing a deadline while displaying an MPEG video may decrease the quality of service (QoS), but does not cause critical system faults. Depending on the requested QoS, tasks may increase or decrease their execution rate to accommodate the requirements of other concurrent activities.

If a multimedia task manages compressed frames, the time for coding/decoding each frame can vary significantly, hence the worst-case execution time (WCET) of the task can be much bigger than its mean execution time. Since hard real-time tasks are guaranteed based on their WCET (and not based on mean execution times), multimedia activities can cause a waste of the CPU resource, if treated as "rigid" hard real-time tasks.

In order to provide theoretical support for such applications, some work has been done to deal with tasks with variable computation times. In [18] a probabilistic guarantee is performed on tasks whose execution times have known distribution. In [17], the authors provide an upper bound of completion times of jobs chains with variable execution times and arbitrary release times. In [9], a guarantee is computed for tasks whose jobs are characterized by variable computation times and interarrival times, occurring with a cyclical pattern. In [8], a capacity reservation technique is used to handle tasks with variable computation time and bound their computational demand.

Even in some control application, there are situations in which periodic tasks could be executed at different rates in different operating conditions. For example, in a flight control system, the sampling rate of the altimeters is a function of the current altitude of the aircraft: the lower the altitude, the higher the sampling frequency. A similar need arises in robotic applications in which robots have to work in unknown environments where trajectories are planned based on the current sensory information. If a robot is equipped with proximity sensors, in order to maintain a desired performance, the acquisition rate of the sensors must increase whenever the robot is approaching an obstacle.

In other situations, the possibility of varying tasks' rates increases the flexibility of the system in handling overload conditions, providing a more general admission control mechanism. For example, whenever a new task cannot be guaranteed by the system, instead of rejecting the task, the system can try to reduce the utilizations of the other tasks (by increasing their periods in a controlled fashion) to decrease the total load and accommodate the new request. Unfortunately, there is no uniform approach for dealing with these situations. For example, Kuo and Mok [4] propose a load scaling technique to gracefully degrade the workload of a system by adjusting the periods of processes. In this work, tasks are assumed to be equally important and the objective is to minimize the number of fundamental frequencies to improve schedulability under static priority assignments. In [12], Nakajima and Tezuka show how a real-time system can be used to support an adaptive application: whenever a deadline miss is detected, the period of the failed task is increased. In [13], Seto et al. change tasks' periods within a specified range to minimize a performance index defined over the task set. This approach is effective at a design stage to optimize the performance of a discrete control system, but cannot be used for on-line load adjustment. In [6], Lee, Rajkumar and Mercer propose a number of policies to dynamically adjust the tasks' rates in overload conditions. In [1], Abdelzaher, Atkins, and Shin present a model for QoS negotiation to meet both predictability and graceful degradation requirements in cases of overload. In this model, the QoS is specified as a set of negotiation options, in terms of rewards and rejection penalties. In [10, 11], Nakajima shows how a multimedia activity can adapt its requirements during transient overloads by scaling down its rate or its computational demand. However, it is not clear how the the QoS can be increased when the system is underloaded.

Although these approaches may lead to interesting results in specific applications, we believe that a more general framework can be used to avoid a proliferation of policies and treat different applications in a uniform fashion.

In this paper we present a novel framework, the elastic model, which has the following advantages:

- it allows tasks to intentionally change their execution rate to provide different quality of service;

- it can handle overload situations in a more flexible way;

- it provides a simple and efficient method for controlling the quality of service of the system as a function of the current load.

The rest of the paper is organized as follows. Section 2 presents the elastic task model. Section 3 illustrates the equivalence of the model with a mechanical system of linear springs. Section 4 describes the guarantee algorithm for a set of elastic tasks. Section 5 presents some theoretical results which validate the proposed model. Section 6 illustrates some experimental results achieved on the HARTIK kernel. Finally, Section 7 contains our conclusions and future work.

2. The elastic model

The basic idea behind the elastic model proposed in this paper is to consider each task as flexible as a spring with a given rigidity coefficient and length constraints. In particular, the utilization of a task is treated as an elastic parameter, whose value can be modified by changing the period or the computation time. To simplify the presentation of the model, in this paper we assume that the computation is fixed, while the period can be varied within a specified range.

Each task is characterized by five parameters: a computation time C_i, a nominal period T_{i_0}, a minimum period $T_{i_{min}}$, a maximum period $T_{i_{max}}$, and an elastic coefficient $e_i \geq 0$, which specifies the flexibility of the task to vary its utilization for adapting the system to a new feasible rate configuration. The greater e_i, the more elastic the task. Thus, an elastic task is denoted as:

$$\tau_i(C_i, T_{i_0}, T_{i_{min}}, T_{i_{max}}, e_i).$$

In the following, T_i will denote the actual period of task τ_i, which is constrained to be in the range $[T_{i_{min}}, T_{i_{max}}]$. Any task can vary its period according to its needs within the specified range. Any variation, however, is subject to an *elastic* guarantee and is accepted only if there exists a feasible schedule in which all the other periods are within their range. Consider, for example, a set of three tasks, whose parameters are shown in Table 1. With the nominal periods, the task set is schedulable by EDF since

$$U_p = \frac{10}{20} + \frac{10}{40} + \frac{15}{70} = 0.964 < 1.$$

If task τ_3 reduces its period to 50, no feasible schedule exists, since the utilization would be greater than 1:

$$U_p = \frac{10}{20} + \frac{10}{40} + \frac{15}{50} = 1.05 > 1.$$

However, notice that a feasible schedule exists ($U_p = 0.977$) for $T_1 = 22$, $T_2 = 45$, and $T_3 = 50$, hence the system can accept the higher request rate of τ_3 by slightly decreasing

Task	C_i	T_{i_0}	$T_{i_{min}}$	$T_{i_{max}}$	e_i
τ_1	10	20	20	25	1
τ_2	10	40	40	50	1
τ_3	15	70	35	80	1

Table 1. Task set parameters used for the example.

the rates of τ_1 and τ_2. Task τ_3 can even run with a period $T_3 = 40$, since a feasible schedule exists with periods T_1 and T_2 within their range. In fact, when $T_1 = 24$, $T_2 = 50$, and $T_3 = 40$, $U_p = 0.992$. Finally, notice that if τ_3 requires to run with a period $T_3 = 35$, there is no feasible schedule with periods T_1 and T_2 within their range, hence the request of τ_3 to execute with a period $T_3 = 35$ must be rejected.

Clearly, for a given value of T_3, there can be many different period configurations which lead to a feasible schedule, hence one of the possible feasible configurations must be selected. The great advantage of using an elastic model is that the policy for selecting a solution is implicitly encoded in the elastic coefficients provided by the user. Thus, each task is varied based on its current elastic status and a feasible configuration is found, if there exists one.

As another example, consider the same set of three tasks with their nominal periods, but suppose that a new periodic task $\tau_4(5, 30, 30, 30, 0)$ enters the system at time t. In a rigid scheduling framework, τ_4 (or some other task selected by a more sophisticated rejection policy) must be rejected, because the new task set is not schedulable, being

$$U_p = \sum_{i=1}^{4} \frac{C_i}{T_{i_0}} = 1.131 > 1.$$

Using an elastic model, however, τ_4 can be accepted if the periods of the other tasks can be increased in such a way that the total utilization is less than one and all the periods are within their range. In our specific example, the period configuration given by $T_1 = 23$, $T_2 = 50$, $T_3 = 80$, $T_4 = 30$, creates a total utilization $U_p = 0.989$, hence τ_4 can be accepted.

The elastic model also works in the other direction. Whenever a periodic task terminates or decreases its rate, all the tasks that have been previously "compressed" can increase their utilization or even return to their nominal periods, depending on the amount of released bandwidth.

It is worth to observe that the elastic model is more general than the classic Liu and Layland's task model, so it does not prevent a user from defining hard real-time tasks. In fact, a task having $T_{i_{min}} = T_{i_{max}} = T_{i_0}$ is equivalent to a hard real-time task with fixed period, independently of its

elastic coefficient. A task with $e_i = 0$ can arbitrarily vary its period within its specified range, but it cannot be varied by the system during load reconfiguration.

3. Equivalence with a spring system

To understand how an elastic guarantee is performed in this model, it is convenient to compare an elastic task τ_i with a linear spring S_i characterized by a rigidity coefficient k_i, a nominal length x_{i_0}, a minimum length $x_{i_{min}}$ and a maximum length $x_{i_{max}}$. In the following, x_i will denote the actual length of spring S_i, which is constrained to be in the range $[x_{i_{min}}, x_{i_{max}}]$.

In this comparison, the length x_i of the spring is equivalent to the task's utilization factor $U_i = C_i/T_i$, and the rigidity coefficient k_i is equivalent to the inverse of task's elasticity ($k_i = 1/e_i$). Hence, a set of n tasks with total utilization factor $U_p = \sum_{i=1}^{n} U_i$ can be viewed as a sequence of n springs with total length $L = \sum_{i=1}^{n} x_i$.

Using the same notation introduced by Liu and Layland [7], let U_{lub}^A be the *least upper bound* of the total utilization factor for a given scheduling algorithm A (we recall that for n tasks $U_{lub}^{RM} = n(2^{1/n} - 1)$ and $U_{lub}^{EDF} = 1$). Hence, a task set can be schedulable by A if $U_p \leq U_{lub}^A$. Under EDF, such a schedulability condition becomes necessary and sufficient.

Under the elastic model, given a scheduling algorithm A and a set of n tasks with $U_p > U_{lub}^A$, the objective of the guarantee is to compress tasks' utilization factors in order to achieve a new utilization $U_p' \leq U_{lub}^A$ such that all the periods are within their ranges. In the linear spring system, this is equivalent of compressing the springs so that the new total length L' is less than or equal to a given maximum length L_{max}. More formally, in the spring system the problem can be stated as follows.

> Given a set of n springs with known rigidity and length constraints, if $L > L_{max}$, find a set of new lengths x_i' such that $x_i' \in [x_{i_{min}}, x_{i_{max}}]$ and $L' = L_d$, where L_d is any arbitrary desired length such that $L_d < L_{max}$.

For the sake of clarity, we first solve the problem for a spring system without length constraints, then we show how the solution can be modified by introducing length constraints, and finally we show how the solution can be adapted to the case of a task set.

3.1 Springs with no length constraints

Consider a set Γ of n springs with nominal length x_{i_0} and rigidity coefficient k_i positioned one after the other, as depicted in Figure 1. Let L_0 be the total length of the array, that is the sum of the nominal lengths: $L_0 = \sum_{i=1}^{n} x_{i_0}$. If

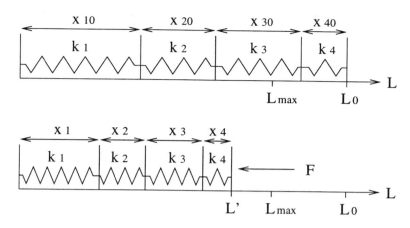

Figure 1. A linear spring system: the total length is L_0 when springs are uncompressed (a); and $L < L_0$ when springs are compressed (b).

the array is compressed so that its total length is equal to a desired length L_d ($0 < L_d < L_0$), the first problem we want to solve is to find the new length x_i of each spring, assuming that for all i, $0 < x_i < x_{i_0}$. Being L_d the total length of the compressed array of springs, we have:

$$L_d = \sum_{i=1}^{n} x_i. \qquad (1)$$

If F is the force that keeps a spring in its compressed state, then, for the equilibrium of the system, it must be:

$$\forall i \quad F = k_i(x_{i_0} - x_i). \qquad (2)$$

Solving the equations (1) and (2) for the unknown x_1, x_2, ..., x_n, we have:

$$\forall i \quad x_i = x_{i_0} - (L_0 - L_d)\frac{K_{//}}{k_i} \qquad (3)$$

where

$$K_{//} = \frac{1}{\sum_{i=1}^{n} \frac{1}{k_i}}. \qquad (4)$$

3.2 Introducing length constraints

If each spring has a length constraint, in the sense that its length cannot be less than a minimum value $x_{i_{min}}$, then the problem of finding the values x_i requires an iterative solution. In fact, if during compression one or more springs reach their minimum length, the additional compression force will only deform the remaining springs. Thus, at each instant, the set Γ can be divided into two subsets: a set Γ_f of fixed springs having minimum length, and a set Γ_v of variable springs that can still be compressed. Applying

equations (3) and (4) to the set Γ_v of variable springs, we have

$$\forall S_i \in \Gamma_v \quad x_i = x_{i_0} - (L_0 - L_d + L_f)\frac{K_v}{k_i} \qquad (5)$$

where

$$L_f = \sum_{S_i \in \Gamma_f} x_{i_{min}} \qquad (6)$$

$$K_v = \frac{1}{\sum_{S_i \in \Gamma_v} \frac{1}{k_i}}. \qquad (7)$$

Whenever there exists some spring for which equation (5) gives $x_i < x_{i_{min}}$, the length of that spring has to be fixed at its minimum value, sets Γ_f and Γ_v must be updated, and equations (5), (6) and (7) recomputed for the new set Γ_v. If there exists a feasible solution, that is, if the desired final length L_d is greater than or equal to the minimum possible length of the array $L_{min} = \sum_{i=1}^{n} x_{i_{min}}$, the iterative process ends when each value computed by equations (5) is greater than or equal to its corresponding minimum $x_{i_{min}}$. The complete algorithm for compressing a set Γ of n springs with length constraints up to a desired length L_d is shown in Figure 2.

4. Compressing tasks' utilizations

When dealing with a set of elastic tasks, equations (5), (6) and (7) can be rewritten by substituting all length parameters with the corresponding utilization factors, and the rigidity coefficients k_i and K_v with the corresponding elastic coefficients e_i and E_v. Similarly, at each instant, the set Γ of periodic tasks can be divided into two subsets: a set Γ_f of fixed tasks having minimum utilization, and a set Γ_v of variable tasks that can still be compressed. If $U_{i_0} = C_i/T_{i_0}$

```
Algorithm Spring_compress(Γ, L_d) {

    L_0 = Σ_{i=1}^n x_{i_0};
    L_min = Σ_{i=1}^n x_{i_min};
    if (L_d < L_min) return INFEASIBLE;

    do {

        Γ_f = {S_i | x_i = x_{i_min}};
        Γ_v = Γ - Γ_f;

        L_f = Σ_{S_i ∈ Γ_f} x_{i_min};
        K_v = 1 / Σ_{S_i ∈ Γ_v} 1/k_i;

        ok = 1;
        for (each S_i ∈ Γ_v) {
            x_i = x_{i_0} - (L_0 - L_d + L_f)K_v/k_i;
            if (x_i < x_{i_min}) {
                x_i = x_{i_min};
                ok = 0;
            }
        }

    } while (ok == 0);
    return FEASIBLE;
}
```

Figure 2. Algorithm for compressing a set of springs with length constraints.

```
Algorithm Task_compress(Γ, U_d) {

    U_0 = Σ_{i=1}^n C_i/T_{i_0};
    U_min = Σ_{i=1}^n C_i/T_{i_max};
    if (U_d < U_min) return INFEASIBLE;

    do {

        U_f = E_v = 0;
        for (each τ_i) {
            if ((e_i == 0) or (T_i == T_{i_max}))
                U_f = U_f + U_i;
            else E_v = E_v + e_i;
        }

        ok = 1;
        for (each τ_i ∈ Γ_v) {
            if ((e_i > 0) and (T_i < T_{i_max})) {
                U_i = U_{i_0} - (U_0 - U_d + U_f)e_i/E_v;
                T_i = C_i/U_i;
                if (T_i > T_{i_max}) {
                    T_i = T_{i_max};
                    ok = 0;
                }
            }
        }

    } while (ok == 0);
    return FEASIBLE;
}
```

Figure 3. Algorithm for compressing a set of elastic tasks.

is the nominal utilization of task τ_i, U_0 is the sum of all the nominal utilizations, and U_f is the total utilization factor of tasks in Γ_f, then to achieve a desired utilization $U_d < U_0$ each task has to be compressed up to the following utilization:

$$\forall \tau_i \in \Gamma_v \quad U_i = U_{i_0} - (U_0 - U_d + U_f)\frac{e_i}{E_v} \qquad (8)$$

where

$$U_f = \sum_{\tau_i \in \Gamma_f} U_{i_min} \qquad (9)$$

$$E_v = \sum_{\tau_i \in \Gamma_v} e_i. \qquad (10)$$

If there exist tasks for which $U_i < U_{i_min}$, then the period of those tasks has to be fixed at its maximum value T_{i_max} (so that $U_i = U_{i_min}$), sets Γ_f and Γ_v must be updated (hence, U_f and E_v recomputed), and equation (8) applied

again to the tasks in Γ_v. If there exists a feasible solution, that is, if the desired utilization U_d is greater than or equal to the minimum possible utilization $U_{min} = \sum_{i=1}^n \frac{C_i}{T_{i_max}}$, the iterative process ends when each value computed by equation (8) is greater than or equal to its corresponding minimum U_{i_min}. The algorithm[1] for compressing a set Γ of n elastic tasks up to a desired utilization U_d is shown in Figure 3.

4.1 Decompression

All tasks' utilizations that have been compressed to cope with an overload situation can return toward their nominal

---

[1]The actual implementation of the algorithm contains more checks on tasks' variables, which are not shown here to simplify its description.

values when the overload is over. Let Γ_c be the subset of compressed tasks (that is, the set of tasks with $T_i > T_{i_0}$), let Γ_a be the set of remaining tasks in Γ (that is, the set of tasks with $T_i \leq T_{i_0}$), and let U_d be the current processor utilization of Γ. Whenever a task in Γ_a decreases its rate or returns to its nominal period, all tasks in Γ_c can expand their utilizations according to their elastic coefficients, so that the processor utilization is kept at the value of U_d.

Now, let U_c be the total utilization of Γ_c, let U_a be the total utilization of Γ_a, and let U_{c_0} be the total utilization of tasks in Γ_c at their nominal periods. It can easily be seen that if $U_{c_0} + U_a \leq U_{lub}$ all tasks in Γ_c can return to their nominal periods. On the other hand, if $U_{c_0} + U_a > U_{lub}$, then the release operation of the tasks in Γ_c can be viewed as a compression, where $\Gamma_f = \Gamma_a$ and $\Gamma_v = \Gamma_c$. Hence, it can still be performed by using equations (8), (9) and (10) and the algorithm presented in Figure 3.

5. Theoretical validation of the model

In this section we derive some theoretical results which validate the elastic guarantee algorithm that can be performed with this method. In particular, we show that if tasks' periods are changed at opportune instants the task set remains schedulable and no deadline is missed. The following lemmas state two properties of the EDF algorithm that are useful for proving the main theorem.

Lemma 1 *In any feasible EDF schedule σ, the following condition holds:*

$$\forall t > 0 \quad \sum_{i=1}^{n} \frac{\gamma_i(t)}{t} \geq U_p$$

where $U_p = \sum_{i=1}^{n} C_i/T_i$ and $\gamma_i(t)$ is the cumulative time executed by all the instances of task τ_i up to t.

Proof.
If $\sigma(t) = IDLE$, we have that

$$f(t) = \frac{\sum_{i=1}^{n} \gamma_i(t)}{t} = \frac{\sum_{i=1}^{n} \left\lceil \frac{t}{T_i} \right\rceil C_i}{t} \geq \frac{t \sum_{i=1}^{n} \frac{C_i}{T_i}}{t} = U_p.$$

If $\sigma(t) \neq IDLE$:

$$\begin{aligned}
f(t+1) &= \frac{\sum_{i=1}^{n} \gamma_i(t+1)}{t+1} = \frac{\sum_{i=1}^{n} \gamma_i(t) + 1}{t+1} = \\
&= \frac{f(t)t+1}{t+1} = f(t) + \frac{1-f(t)}{t+1} \geq f(t).
\end{aligned}$$

Moreover, being $\sigma(0) \neq IDLE$ and $f(1) = 1 \geq U_p$ (because the system is feasible), we have that, for all $t > 0$, $f(t) \geq U_p$. $\square$

Lemma 2 *In any feasible EDF schedule σ, the following condition holds:*

$$\forall t > 0 \quad \sum_{i=1}^{n} c_i(t) \leq \sum_{i=1}^{n} [\nu_i(t) - t] U_i.$$

where $U_i = C_i/T_i$, $c_i(t)$ is the remaining execution time of the current instance of task τ_i at time t, and $\nu_i(t)$ is the next release time of τ_i greater than or equal to t.

Proof.
By definition of $c_i(t)$, we have

$$\begin{aligned}
c_i(t) &= \left\lceil \frac{t}{T_i} \right\rceil C_i - \gamma_i(t) \\
\nu_i(t) &= \left\lceil \frac{t}{T_i} \right\rceil T_i
\end{aligned}$$

and, by Lemma 1,

$$\begin{aligned}
\sum_{i=1}^{n} c_i(t) &= \sum_{i=1}^{n} \left(\left\lceil \frac{t}{T_i} \right\rceil C_i - \gamma_i(t) \right) \leq \\
&\leq \sum_{i=1}^{n} \left(\left\lceil \frac{t}{T_i} \right\rceil C_i - t U_i \right) = \\
&= \sum_{i=1}^{n} \left(T_i \left\lceil \frac{t}{T_i} \right\rceil - t \right) U_i = \\
&= \sum_{i=1}^{n} (\nu_i(t) - t) U_i.
\end{aligned}$$

$\square$

The following theorem states a property of decompression: if at time t all the periods are increased from T_i to T_i', then the total utilization factor is decreased from U_p to $U_p' = \sum_{i=1}^{n} \frac{C_i}{T_i'}$.

Theorem 1 *Given a feasible task set Γ, with total utilization factor $U_p = \sum_{i=1}^{n} \frac{C_i}{T_i} \leq 1$, if at time t all the periods are increased from T_i to $T_i' \geq T_i$, then for all $L > 0$,*

$$D(t, t+L) \leq L U_p'$$

where $D(t_1, t_2)$ is the total processor demand of Γ in $[t_1, t_2]$, and $U_p' = \sum_{i=1}^{n} \frac{C_i}{T_i'}$.

Proof.
As task periods are increased at time t, the new release time of task τ_i is:

$$\nu_i'(t) = \nu_i(t) - T_i + T_i'.$$

291

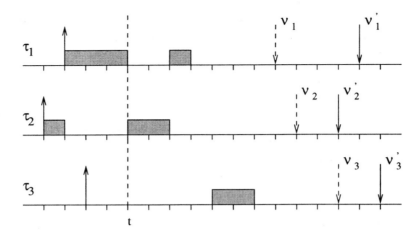

Figure 4. Example of n tasks that simultaneously increase their periods at time t.

The total demand in $[t, t+L]$ is given by the total execution time of the instances released after or at t with deadlines less than or equal to $t + L$, plus the remaining execution times of the current active instances. The situation considered in the proof is illustrated in Figure 4.

Using the result of Lemma 2 we can write:

$$
\begin{aligned}
D(t, t+L) &= \sum_{i=1}^{n} \left\lfloor \frac{t + L - \nu_i'(t)}{T_i'} \right\rfloor C_i + \sum_{i=1}^{n} c_i(t) \leq \\
&\leq \sum_{i=1}^{n} \left\lfloor \frac{t + L - \nu_i'(t)}{T_i'} \right\rfloor C_i + \sum_{i=1}^{n} [\nu_i(t) - t] U_i \leq \\
&\leq \sum_{i=1}^{n} [t + L - \nu_i'(t)] U_i' + \sum_{i=1}^{n} [\nu_i(t) - t] U_i = \\
&= \sum LU_i' + \sum_{i=1}^{n} [\nu_i(t) U_i - \nu_i'(t) U_i' - t U_i + t U_i'] = \\
&= LU_p' + A.
\end{aligned}
$$

Now, we show that $A \leq 0$.

$$
\begin{aligned}
A &= \sum_{i=1}^{n} \left[\nu_i(t) U_i - \nu_i'(t) \frac{T_i}{T_i'} U_i - t U_i + t U_i \frac{T_i}{T_i'} \right] = \\
&= \sum_{i=1}^{n} U_i \left[\nu_i'(t) - T_i' + T_i - \nu_i'(t) \frac{T_i}{T_i'} - t \left(1 - \frac{T_i}{T_i'} \right) \right] \\
&= \sum_{i=1}^{n} U_i [\nu_i'(t) - t - T_i''] \left(1 - \frac{T_i}{T_i'} \right) \leq 0.
\end{aligned}
$$

Hence,

$$
D(t, t+L) \leq LU_p'.
$$

□

Notice that the property stated by Theorem 1 does not hold in case of compression. This can be seen in the example illustrated in Figure 5, where two tasks, τ_1 and τ_2, with computation times 3 and 2, and periods 10 and 3, start at time 0. The processor utilization is $U_p = \frac{29}{30}$, thus the task set is schedulable by EDF. At time $t = 14$, τ_1 changes its period from $T_1 = 10$ to $T_1' = 5$. As a consequence, to keep the system schedulable, the period of τ_2 is increased from $T_2 = 3$ to $T_2' = 6$. The new processor utilization is $U_p' = \frac{28}{30}$, so the task set is still feasible; but, if we change the periods immediately, task τ_1 misses its deadline at time $t = 15$.

In other words, the period of a compressed task can be decreased only at its next release time. Thus, when the QoS manager receives a request of period variation, it calculates the new periods according to the elastic model: if the new configuration is found to be feasible (i.e., $U_p' < 1$), then it increases the periods of the decompressed tasks immediately, but decreases the periods of the compressed tasks only at their next release time. Theorem 1 ensures that the total processor demand in any interval $[t, t+L]$ will never exceed LU_p and no deadline will be missed.

6. Experimental results

The elastic task model has been implemented on top of the HARTIK kernel [2, 5], to perform some experiments on multimedia applications and verify the results predicted by the theory. In particular, the elastic guarantee mechanism has been implemented as a high priority task, the QoS manager, activated by the other tasks when they are created or when they want to change their period. Whenever activated, the QoS manager calculates the new periods and changes them atomically. According to the result of Theorem 1, periods are changed at the next release time of the task whose period is decreased. If more tasks ask to decrease their period, the QoS manager will change them, if possible, at their next release time.

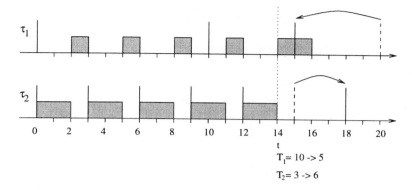

T₁= 10 -> 5

T₂= 3 -> 6

Figure 5. A task can miss its deadline if a period is decreased at arbitrary time.

Task	C_i	T_{i_0}	$T_{i_{min}}$	$T_{i_{max}}$	e_i
τ_1	24	100	30	500	1
τ_2	24	100	30	500	1
τ_3	24	100	30	500	1.5
τ_4	24	100	30	500	2

Table 2. Task set parameters used for the first experiment. Periods and computation times are expressed in milliseconds.

Task	C_i	T_{i_0}	$T_{i_{min}}$	$T_{i_{max}}$	e_i
τ_1	30	100	30	500	1
τ_2	60	200	30	500	1
τ_3	90	300	30	500	1
τ_4	24	50	30	500	1

Table 3. Task set parameters used for the second experiment. Periods and computation times are expressed in milliseconds.

In the first experiment, four periodic tasks are created at time $t = 0$. Tasks' parameters are shown in Table 2, while the actual number of instances executed by each task as a function of time is shown in Figure 6. All the tasks start executing at their nominal period and, at time $t_1 = 10sec$, τ_1 decreases its period to $T'_1 = 33msec$. We recall that a task cannot decrease its period by itself, but must perform a request to the QoS manager, that checks the feasibility of the request and calculates the new periods for all the tasks in the system. So, at time t_1, since the schedule is found to be feasible, the period of τ_1 is decreased and the periods of τ_2, τ_3 and τ_4 are increased according to their elastic coefficients. The values of all the periods are indicated in the graph.

At time $t_2 = 20sec$, τ_1 returns to its nominal period, so the QoS manager can change the periods of the other tasks to their initial values, as shown in the graph. In this manner, the QoS manager ensures that when a task requires to change its period, the task set remains schedulable and the variation of each task period can be controlled by the elastic factor.

In the second experiment, we tested the elastic model as an admission control policy. Three tasks start executing at time $t = 0$ at their nominal period, while a fourth task starts at time $t_1 = 10sec$. Tasks' parameters are shown in Table 3. When τ_4 is started, the task set is not schedulable

with the current periods, thus the QoS manager, in order to accommodate the request of τ_4, increases the periods of the other tasks according to the elastic model. The actual execution rates of the tasks are shown in Figure 7. Notice that, although the first three tasks have the same elastic coefficients, their periods are changed by a different amount, because tasks have different utilization factors.

7. Conclusions

In this paper we presented a flexible scheduling theory, in which periodic tasks are treated as springs, with given elastic coefficients. Under this framework, periodic tasks can intentionally change their execution rate to provide different quality of service, and the other tasks can automatically adapt their periods to keep the system underloaded. The proposed model can also be used to handle overload situations in a more flexible way. In fact, whenever a new task cannot be guaranteed by the system, instead of rejecting the task, the system can try to reduce the utilizations of the other tasks (by increasing their periods in a controlled fashion) to decrease the total load and accommodate the new request. As soon as a transient overload condition is over (because

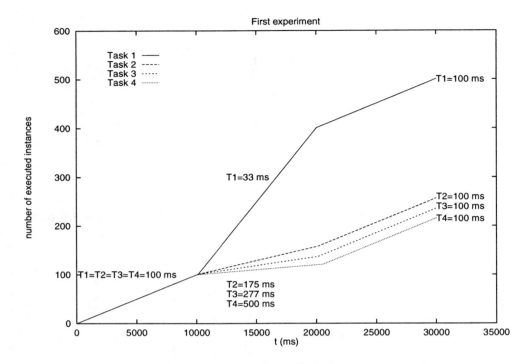

Figure 6. Dynamic period change.

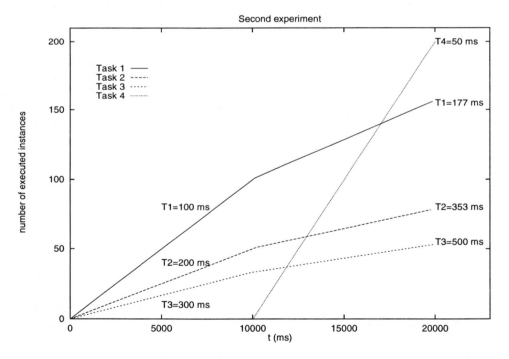

Figure 7. Dynamic task activation.

a task terminates or voluntarily increases its period) all the compressed tasks may expand up to their original utilization, eventually recovering their nominal periods.

The major advantage of the proposed method is that the policy for selecting a solution is implicitly encoded in the elastic coefficients provided by the user. Each task is varied based on its current elastic status and a feasible configuration is found, if there exists one.

The elastic model is extremely useful for supporting both multimedia systems and control applications, in which the execution rates of some computational activities have to be dynamically tuned as a function of the current system state. Furthermore, the elastic mechanism can easily be implemented on top of classical real-time kernels, and can be used under fixed or dynamic priority scheduling algorithms. The experimental results shown in this paper have been conducted by implementing the elastic mechanism on the HARTIK kernel [2, 5].

As a future work, we are investigating the possibility of extending this method for dealing with tasks having deadlines less than periods, variable execution time, and subject to resource constraints.

References

[1] T.F. Abdelzaher, E.M. Atkins, and K.G. Shin, "QoS Negotiation in Real-Time Systems and Its Applications to Automated Flight Control," *Proceedings of the IEEE Real-Time Technology and Applications Symposium*, Montreal, Canada, June 1997.

[2] G. Buttazzo, "HARTIK: A Real-Time Kernel for Robotics Applications", *Proceedings of the 14th IEEE Real-Time Systems Symposium*, Raleigh-Durham, pp. 201–205, December 1993.

[3] M.L. Dertouzos, "Control Robotics: the Procedural Control of Physical Processes," *Information Processing*, 74, North-Holland, Publishing Company, 1974.

[4] T.-W. Kuo and A. K, Mok, "Load Adjustment in Adaptive Real-Time Systems," *Proceedings of the 12th IEEE Real-Time Systems Symposium*, December 1991.

[5] G. Lamastra, G. Lipari, G. Buttazzo, A. Casile, and F. Conticelli, "HARTIK 3.0: A Portable System for Developing Real-Time Applications," *Proceedings of the IEEE Real-Time Computing Systems and Applications*, Taipei, Taiwan, October 1997.

[6] C. Lee, R. Rajkumar, and C. Mercer, "Experiences with Processor Reservation and Dynamic QOS in Real-Time Mach," *Proceedings of Multimedia Japan 96*, April 1996.

[7] C.L. Liu and J.W. Layland, "Scheduling Algorithms for Multiprogramming in a Hard real-Time Environment," *Journal of the ACM* 20(1), 1973, pp. 40–61.

[8] C. W. Mercer, S. Savage, and H. Tokuda, "Processor Capacity Reserves for Multimedia Operating Systems" *Proceedings of the IEEE International Conference on Multimedia Computing and Systems*, May 1994.

[9] A. K. Mok and D. Chen, "A multiframe model for real-time tasks," *Proceedings of IEEE Real-Time System Symposium*, Washington, December 1996.

[10] T. Nakajima, "Dynamic QOS Control and Resource Reservation," *IEICE, RTP'98*, 1998.

[11] T. Nakajima, "Resource Reservation for Adaptive QOS Mapping in Real-Time Mach," *Sixth International Workshop on Parallel and Distributed Real-Time Systems*, April 1998.

[12] T. Nakajima and H. Tezuka, "A Continuous Media Application supporting Dynamic QOS Control on Real-Time Mach," *Proceedings of the ACM Multimedia '94*, 1994.

[13] D. Seto, J.P. Lehoczky, L. Sha, and K.G. Shin, "On Task Schedulability in Real-Time Control Systems," *Proceedings of the IEEE Real-Time Systems Symposium*, December 1997.

[14] M. Spuri, and G.C. Buttazzo, "Efficient Aperiodic Service under Earliest Deadline Scheduling", *Proceedings of IEEE Real-Time System Symposium*, San Juan, Portorico, December 1994.

[15] M. Spuri, G.C. Buttazzo, and F. Sensini, "Robust Aperiodic Scheduling under Dynamic Priority Systems", *Proceedings of the IEEE Real-Time Systems Symposium*, Pisa, Italy, December 1995.

[16] M. Spuri and G.C. Buttazzo, "Scheduling Aperiodic Tasks in Dynamic Priority Systems," *Real-Time Systems*, 10(2), 1996.

[17] J. Sun and J.W.S. Liu, "Bounding Completion Times of Jobs with Arbitrary Release Times and Variable Execution Times", *Proceedings of IEEE Real-Time System Symposium*, December 1996.

[18] T.-S. Tia, Z. Deng, M. Shankar, M. Storch, J. Sun, L.-C. Wu, and J.W.-S. Liu, "Probabilistic Performance Guarantee for Real-Time Tasks with Varying Computation Times," *Proceedings of IEEE Real-Time Technology and Applications Symposium*, Chicago, Illinois, January 1995.

Practical Solutions for QoS-based Resource Allocation Problems*

Ragunathan (Raj) Rajkumar, Chen Lee, John P. Lehoczky[†], Daniel P. Siewiorek
Department of Computer Science
[†]Department of Statistics
Carnegie Mellon University
Pittsburgh, PA 15213
{raj+, clee, dps}@cs.cmu.edu, [†]jpl@stat.cmu.edu

Abstract: The QoS-based Resource Allocation Model (Q-RAM) proposed in [20] presented an analytical approach for satisfying multiple quality-of-service dimensions in a resource-constrained environment. Using this model, available system resources can be apportioned across multiple applications such that the net utility that accrues to the end-users of those applications is maximized. In this paper, we present several practical solutions to allocation problems that were beyond the limited scope of [20]. First, we show that the Q-RAM problem of finding the optimal resource allocation to satisfy multiple QoS dimensions (at least one of which is dependent on another) is NP-hard. We then present a polynomial solution for this resource allocation problem which yields a solution within a provably fixed and short distance from the optimal allocation. Secondly, [20] dealt mainly with the problem of apportioning a single resource to satisfy multiple QoS dimensions. In this paper, we study the converse problem of apportioning multiple resources to satisfy a single QoS dimension. In practice, this problem becomes complicated, since a single QoS dimension perceived by the user can be satisfied using different combinations of available resources. We show that this problem can be formulated as a mixed integer programming problem that can be solved efficiently to yield an optimal resource allocation. Finally, we also present the run-times of these optimizations to illustrate how these solutions can be applied in practice. We expect that a good understanding of these solutions will yield insights into the general problem of apportioning multiple resources to satisfy simultaneously multiple QoS dimensions of multiple concurrent applications.

1. Introduction

Several applications have the ability to provide better performance and quality of service if a larger share of system resources is made available to them. Such examples abound in many domains. Feedback control systems can provide bet-

ter control at higher rates of sampling and control actuation. Multimedia systems using audio and video streams can provide better audio/video quality at higher resolution and/or very low end-to-end delays. Tracking applications can track objects at higher precision and accuracy if radar tracks are generated and processed at higher frequencies. In many cases, computationally intensive algorithms can provide better results than their less-demanding counterparts. Even interactive systems can provide excellent response times to users if more processing and I/O resources are made available. Conversely, many applications can still prove to be useful and acceptable in practive even though the resources needed for their maximal performance are *not* available. For instance, a 30 frames/second video rate would be ideal for human viewing, but a smooth 12 fps video rate suffices under many conditions.

The QoS-based Resource Allocation Model (Q-RAM) proposed in [20] addressed the following question: "How does one allocate available resources to multiple concurrent applications?". This question was posed in the context where applications can operate at high levels of quality or acceptably lower levels of quality based on the resources allocated to them. The novelty of Q-RAM is that it allows multiple Quality of Service requirements such as timeliness, cryptography and reliable data delivery to be addressed and traded off against each other.

In this paper, we address some significant and open problems posed by Q-RAM. For example, much of the QoS work focuses on allocating a single time-shared resource such as network bandwidth. In real-time and multimedia systems, applications may need to have simultaneous access to multiple resources such as processing cycles, memory, network bandwidth and disk bandwidth, in order to satisfy their needs. The solutions that we provide turn out to be very efficent to be used in practice.

1.1. Q-RAM: The QoS-based Resource Allocation Model

We now provide a brief overview of Q-RAM referring the reader to [20] for more details. The goal of Q-RAM is to ad-

This work was supported in part by the Defense Advanced Research Projects Agency under agreements E30602-97-2-0287 and N66001-97-C-8527, and in part by the Office of Naval Research under agreement N00014-92-J-1524.

dress two problems:

- Satisfy the simultaneous requirements of multiple applications along multiple QoS dimensions such as timeliness, cryptography, data quality and reliable packet delivery, and

- Allow applications access to multiple resources such as CPU, disk bandwidth, network bandwidth, memory, etc. simultaneously.

Q-RAM uses a dynamic and adaptive application framework where each application requires a certain minimum resource allocation to perform acceptably. An application may also improve its performance with larger resource allocations. This improvement in performance is measured by a *utility function*.

Q-RAM considers a system in which multiple applications, each with its own set of requirements along multiple QoS dimensions, are contending for resources.

- Each application may have a minimum and/or a maximum need along each QoS dimension such as timeliness, security, data quality and dependability.

- An application may require access to multiple resource types such as CPU, disk bandwidth, network bandwidth and memory.

- Each resource allocation adds some utility to the application and the system, with utility monotonically increasing with resource allocation.

- System resources are limited so that the maximal demands of all applications often cannot be satisfied simultaneously.

With the Q-RAM specifications, a resource allocation decision will be made for each application such that an overall system-level objective (called *utility*) is maximized.

The system consists of n applications $\{\tau_1, \tau_2, \cdots, \tau_n\}$, $n \geq 1$, and m resources $\{\mathbf{R}_1, \mathbf{R}_2, \cdots, \mathbf{R}_m\}$, $m \geq 1$. Each resource $\mathbf{R}_j$ has a finite capacity and can be shared, either temporally or spatially. CPU and network bandwidth, for example, would be time-shared resources, while memory would be a spatially shared resource.

Let the portion of resource $\mathbf{R}_j$ allocated to application τ_i be denoted by $R_{i,j}$. We enforce $\sum_{i=1}^{n} R_{i,j} \leq \mathbf{R}_j$. The following definitions are used:

- The *application utility*, U_i, of an application τ_i is defined to be the value that is accrued by the system when τ_i is allocated $\mathbf{R}^i = (R_{i,1}, R_{i,j}, \cdots, R_{i,m})$. In other words, $U_i = U_i(\mathbf{R}^i)$. U_i is referred to as the *utility function* of τ_i. This utility function defines a surface along which the application can operate based on the resources allocated to it.

- Each application τ_i has a relative importance specified by a weight w_i, $1 \leq i \leq n$.

- The *total system utility* $\mathbf{U}(\mathbf{R}^1, \cdots, \mathbf{R}^n)$ is defined to be the sum of the weighted application utilities, i.e. $\mathbf{U}(\mathbf{R}^1, \cdots, \mathbf{R}^n) = \sum_{i=1}^{n} w_i U_i(\mathbf{R}^i)$.

- Each application τ_i needs to satisfy requirements along d QoS dimensions $\{Q_1, Q_2, \cdots, Q_d\}$, $d \geq 1$.

- The *dimensional resource utility* $U_{i,k} = U_{i,k}(\mathbf{R}^i)$ of an application τ_i is defined to be the value that is accrued by the system when τ_i is allocated $\mathbf{R}^i$ for use on QoS dimension Q_k, $1 \leq k \leq d$.

- [1]An application, τ_i, has *minimal resource requirements on QoS dimension* Q_k. These minimal requirements are denoted by $R_i^{min_k} = \{R_{i,1}^{min_k}, R_{i,2}^{min_k}, \cdots, R_{i,m}^{min_k}\}$ where $R_{i,j}^{min_k} \geq 0, 0 \leq j \leq m$.

- An application, τ_i, is said to be *feasible* if it is allocated a minimum set of resources for every QoS dimension. We denote the total minimum requirements by $\mathbf{R}_i^{min} = \{R_{i,1}^{min}, R_{i,2}^{min}, \cdots, R_{i,m}^{min}\}$ where $R_{i,j}^{min} = \sum_{k=1}^{d} R_{i,j}^{min_k}$, $1 \leq j \leq m$.

The assumptions of Q-RAM that are used in this paper are:

- The applications are independent of one another.

- The available system resources are sufficient to meet the minimal resource requirements of each application on *all* QoS dimensions.

- The utility functions U_i and $U_{i,k}$ are nondecreasing in each of their arguments. In some cases, we will assume that these functions are concave and have two continuous derivatives.

Resource allocation schemes presented in [20] assumed a single resource and thereby solved only the simpler problem dealing with multiple QoS dimensions. Resource allocation schemes in the presence of multiple resources were beyond its scope but are the subject of Section 3 in this paper.

1.2. The Objective

The objective of Q-RAM is to make resource allocations to each application such that the total system utility is maximized under the constraint that *every* application is feasible with respect to each QoS dimension. Stated formally, it determines $\{R_{i,j}, 1 \leq i \leq n, 1 \leq j \leq m\}$ such that $R_{i,j} \geq \sum_{k=1}^{d} R_{i,j}^{min_k}$ and $\mathbf{U}$ is maximal among all such possible allocations.

Each application has a relative weight w_i, but this can be ignored in the optimization step without loss of generality (by scaling an application's utility values by the same weight).

---

[1]This aspect is stated as a simplification; by choosing different implementation schemes, the minimum requirement on a resource may change. Please see Section 3.

1.3. Related Work

Significant research has been carried out for making resource allocations to satisfy specific application-level requirements. The domain of operations research in particular has spawned over several decades multiple resource allocation problems. For example, [8] characterizes several problems and formally summarizes known solutions to these problems. Other work can be classified into various categories. The problem of allocating appropriate resource capacity to achieve a specific level of QoS for an application has been studied in various contexts. For example, [6] studies the problem of how to allocate network packet processing capacity assuming bursty traffic and finite buffers. In [10], the problem of the establishment of real-time communication channels is studied as an admission control problem. The Spring Kernel [24] uses on-line admission control to guarantee essential tasks upon arrival.

With the advent of asynchronous transfer mode networks and their deployment by telephone companies, Quality of Service in terms of bandwidth and timeliness guarantees has been studied in depth (e.g. see [2, 3]). Like most research on real-time scheduling theory [16, 11], QoS research in networks focus on a single QoS dimension (like timeliness or bandwidth guarantees). In addition, network and real-time scheduling research have typically focused on a *single* resource type like network bandwidth and CPU cycles respectively. In contrast, we focus on multiple QoS dimensions spanning timeliness, cryptography, and application quality requirements. We also focus on making resource allocation decisions across multiple resource *types* including processor compute cycles, network bandwidth, and disk bandwidth.

Various system-wide schemes have been studied to arbitrate resource allocation among contending applications. In [1], a distributed pool of processors is used to guarantee timeliness for real-time applications using admission control and load-sharing techniques. The Rialto operating system [9] presents a modular OS approach, the goal of which is to maximize the user's perceived utility of the system, instead of maximizing the performance of any particular application. No theoretical basis is provided to maximize system utility. A QoS manager is used in the RT-Mach operating system to allocate resources to application, each of which can operate at any resource allocation point within minimum and maximum thresholds [15]. Applications are ranked according to their semantic importance, and different adjustment policies are used to obtain or negotiate a particular resource allocation. Q-RAM can also be considered to be a broad generalization of [17] and [23]. A multi-dimensional QoS problem from a tracking perspective is summarized in [12].

1.4. Organization of the Paper

The rest of this paper is organized as follows. In Section 2, we show that the Q-RAM problem of finding the optimal resource allocation to satisfy multiple QoS dimensions (at least one of which is dependent on another) is NP-hard. We then present a polynomial solution for this resource allocation problem which yields a solution within a provably fixed and short distance from the optimal allocation. In Section 3, we study the problem of apportioning multiple resources to satisfy a single QoS dimension. This problem becomes complicated, since resources can be traded off against each other and still yield the same utility. We formulate this problem as a mixed integer programming problem that can be solved efficiently to yield an optimal resource allocation. In Section 4, we present our concluding remarks and discuss problems that remain unsolved.

2. Multiple QoS Dimensions and A Single Resource

The work reported in [20] provided optimal and near-optimal resource allocation schemes for applications which need a single resource, but need to satisfy one or more QoS dimensions. Specifically, optimal resource allocation schemes were provided for the two cases of

1. a single resource and a single QoS dimension, and

2. a single resource and multiple independent QoS dimensions.

Finally, a greedy and sub-optimal algorithm was proposed for the case of a single resource and two or more QoS dimensions, where one QoS dimension is discrete and dependent on another.[2]

In this section, we further study this latter problem of a single resource and a dependent and discrete QoS dimension. We refer to this problem as DDQSRP (Dependent Discrete Dimension and Single Resource Problem). For the sake of simplicity and practicality, we assume that the utility curve is linear from R_i^{min} to a maximum resource requirement R_i^{max} beyond which it becomes flat. An example of the individual dimensional utility functions for two QoS dimensions, one independent and another dependent, and their aggregated application utility function are illustrated in Figure 1. The first or lowermost curve represents the utility curve for the application when a base scheme (such as no encryption) is used. The second curve represents the utility curve when (say) encryption using 40 bits is used. Additional utility is accrued by the use of encryption, which results in a positive vertical offset at the beginning of the curve. At the same time, additional compute cycles are expended to perform encryption resulting in the lateral shift of the curve to the right. In addition, as data volume increases with improved QoS on the base dimension, the encryption cost increases correspondingly. This results in a "flattening" with respect to the curve of the base scheme. This flattening effect is even more pronounced for the third curve, corresponding to (say) encryption using 128 bits.

---

[2]A QoS dimension, Q_a, is said to be dependent on another dimension, Q_b, if a change along the dimension Q_b will increase the resource demands to achieve the quality level previously achieved along Q_a.

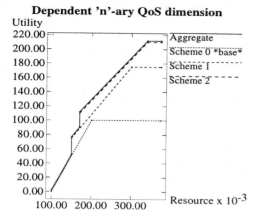

Figure 1. One 3-ary QoS dimension w/ min-linear-max.

We now show that the general problem of finding an optimal resource allocation for applications with these non-concave piecewise linear utility functions is NP-hard.

Theorem 1 *Finding the optimal resource allocation with dependent and discrete QoS dimensions is NP-Hard.*

Proof: We prove this by showing that the inexact 0-1 knapsack problem which is known to be NP-hard (see for example [18]) maps directly to a special case of our QoS problem. The inexact 0-1 knapsack problem is as follows:

Maximize $\sum_{i=1}^{n} v_i$
Subject to:

$$\sum_{i=1}^{n} R_i \leq \mathbf{R}$$

where there are n objects each with size R_i and value v_i, and $\mathbf{R}$ is the size of the knapsack.

The above problem is identical to the following special case of our problem. Suppose each of the users in our QoS allocation has a utility function which is a step function with a single discontinuity, that is

$$U_i(r) = \begin{cases} 0 & \text{if } r < R_i \\ v_i & \text{if } r \geq R_i. \end{cases}$$

Thus user i receives a utility value of v_i if and only if R_i units of additional resource are allocated. A total of $\mathbf{R}$ additional units of resource are available for allocation.

An identity transformation makes the inexact 0-1 knapsack problem a special case of our QoS problem. $\square$

We now provide a polynomial algorithm which yields a solution for this resource allocation problem within a provably fixed and short distance from the optimal allocation. This algorithm uses the "natural" boundary of the set of discontinuities in these utility functions. This boundary is the smallest

concave function lying on or above the aggregate utility function. We shall refer to this boundary as the "concave majorant".

2.1. Convex Hulls, Majorants and the Q-RAM Utility Function

The *convex hull* of a set of points in the plane is the smallest convex polygon containing all the points (for example, see [22]). Several algorithms, such as the Graham's Scan [22], Jarvis' March [7], etc., determine the convex hull of a set of points. In our case, the concave majorant is a subset of the path on the convex hull of the points on the aggregate utility curve starting from the minimum resource allocation point to a point with the highest achieved value of utility. Some examples of these concave majorants are presented in Figure 2. Minor variations of the convex hull algorithms can be used to determine the needed concave majorants as follows:

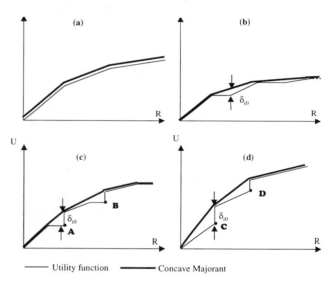

Figure 2. Examples of Concave Majorants for Q-RAM Utility Curves. δ_{i0} **represents the maximum vertical separation of the convex majorant from application** τ_i**'s aggregate utility curve.**

Consider the discontinuity points *A, B, C, D, E, F, G, H* and *I* corresponding to a utility function similar to the one in Figure 2-(c) plotted separately in Figure 3-(a) and 3-(b).

Jarvis' March. Figure 3-(c) illustrates how the variant of the Jarvis' March works. Start from the minimum resource allocation point (A) which is known to be in our path. From there, travel to the point with the weakest right turn (highest slope) drawing line segment 1 shown in 3-(c). Repeat until we run out of points, drawing line segments

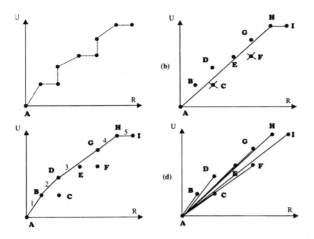

Figure 3. Using Jarvis' March (c) and Graham's Scan (d) for Determining Concave Majorants.

2, 3 4 and 5. This algorithm is conceptually simple but is of complexity $O(n^2)$.

Graham's Scan. Figure 3-(d) illustrates how Graham's Scan works. Again, start from the minimum resource allocation point A which is known to be in our path. Draw lines from this point to all other points and sort them according to their slopes. Travel to B, the point along the highest slope. From there, travel to D, the point with the next highest slope. If ABD is not concave, backtrack to the previous point where concavity is still true and draw a line from there to D; else, continue. Travel to the next unvisited point with the highest slope. Backtracking when necessary, repeat until either no points remain or a maximal point is reached. This algorithm is of complexity $O(n \log n)$ in general and $O(n)$ with pre-sorted points.

Both Jarvis' March and the Graham's Scan algorithms described above can be optimized further under Q-RAM as shown in Figure 3-(b). Draw a line from the starting point (A) to one of the maximal points (H is preferable but I is acceptable as well). Any points that lie below this line can be ignored by both of the above schemes.

2.2. Polynomial Concave Majorant Optimization Algorithm for DDQSRP

1. For each application, determine the convex hull of the points on its utility function.

2. Pick the subset of the path on the convex hull starting from the minimum resource allocation point to the maximal resource allocation point. That is, obtain the concave majorant of the aggregate utility function.

3. Run the algorithm as described in [20] using the Kuhn-Tucker conditions (see [19], chapter 5): Allocate the available resource to each application in decreasing order of the slope of the concave majorant until the resource runs out or all applications obtain their maximum useful resource allocation. This yields an optimal resource allocation based on the concave majorants.

The determination of the concave majorant has a computational complexity of $O(n)$ (or $O(n \log n)$ if the discontinuity points are not pre-sorted). The resource allocation algorithm has a computational complexity of $O(k \log k)$ where $k = nm$ where n is the number of applications and m is the number of discontinuities in each concave majorant.

We now prove that the above algorithm yields a resource allocation that is within a short distance of the optimal resource allocation.

Remark: The Q-RAM utility model assumes that the utility gains due to the introduction of an n-ary and dependent QoS dimension are also themselves non-decreasing and concave.

Notation: Let the maximum vertical separation of the convex majorant from application τ_i's aggregate utility curve be δ_i.

Notation: Let $\delta_0 = max_{1 \leq i \leq n} \delta_i$.

Theorem 2 *The maximum deviation from the optimal resource allocation for DDQSRP using the polynomial concave majorant algorithm is δ_0.*

Proof:
The proof is based on the properties of the concave majorant. First, the vertex points on a concave majorant are points from the original point set. Therefore, in our case, each of the discontinuity points on the concave majorant also corresponds to a discrete point on the aggregate utility function.

Second, by definition, the concave majorant is piece-wise concave. The Kuhn-Tucker conditions are used to allocate the available resource first to the application with the maximum slope at its allocation point. When this is carried out on piece-wise concave functions, all but *at most one* of the applications will be at one of the discontinuity points [20].

Finally, the application of the Kuhn-Tucker conditions leads to an optimal resource allocation if the concave majorants are treated as the actual utility curves. Let the total utility obtained on the concave majorants be $U_{majorant}$. Let the actual total utility obtained by the applications be U_{actual}. Let the total utility obtained by an optimal allocation on the actual utility curves be $U_{optimal}$. Since at most one resource allocation point may lie above an actual utility curve, and the concave majorants lie at or above the actual utility curves, we have,

$$U_{majorant} \geq U_{actual}$$

Since the concave majorants lie at or above the actual utility curves, and $U_{majorant}$ is optimal for the concave majorants, we must have

$$U_{majorant} \geq U_{optimal}$$

We therefore have,

$$U_{majorant} \geq U_{optimal} \geq U_{actual}$$

The largest difference between the utility obtained on the concave majorants and the actual utility occurs when U_{actual} is separated from $U_{optimal}$ by the maximal vertical distance between the concave majorant and an actual utility curve. The maximal separation between an aggregate utility function and its concave majorant cannot be larger than δ_0. The theorem follows. $\square$.

It is possible that δ_0 can be large in some systems, since the inclusion of a scheme (such as cryptography to encrypt sensitive data) may yield significant utility for an application. In such cases, it may seem acceptable to treat the inclusion of the scheme as the minimum requirement for the application. Correspondingly, δ_0 can be reduced. Even if this were not possible, it is encouraging to note that a simple polynomial algorithm yields a resource allocation that is close to the optimal resource allocation, which would take an exponential amount of time to find.

A brute-force exponential algorithm to find the exact optimal resource allocation for DDQSRP is outlined in [21].

3. Single QoS Dimension and Multiple Resources

In this section, we will study the problem of apportioning shares of multiple resources to multiple concurrent applications each of which has to satisfy only a single QoS dimension. We will first motivate the problem and define the solution space available to a resource allocation scheme which is meant to solve this problem.

3.1. The Multiple Resource Problem

Consider an audio-conferencing application where an audio stream is being transmitted from a source to a destination. The stream must be processed at the source processor, transmitted across the network (across one or more hops) and must then be processed again by the destination for playback on a speaker. For the audio stream to be processed on time, all elements on its path would require adequate resources. The sampling rate of the audio stream is a QoS dimension of interest in this context. If sufficient resources are available on the end-processors and the intermediate network elements, a higher audio sampling rate is desirable. However, beyond a CD-Quality sampling rate, any increased utility to the users is very marginal. In other words, this QoS dimension fits the requirements of Q-RAM.

Consider multiple such streams in the system (such as an IP telephony service provider). The goal of Q-RAM is to allocate available resources to each of these streams such that the overall accrued utility is maximized. This problem may seem straightforward and a direct converse of the multiple QoS dimension/single resource problem solved earlier in Section 2.

However, one key aspect of this problem tends to be complicated and is discussed next.

3.2. Resource Trade-Offs

Tradeoffs across resources are possible. If processing resources are (relatively) scarce, and network bandwidth is plentiful, the source node may transmit the data in raw form consuming less processor cycles and more network bandwidth. Conversely, if processing resources are relatively plentiful and network bandwidth meager, available processor cycles can be used to compress the data and thereby consume less of the network bandwidth. Different compression schemes also make different tradeoffs with more compression time spent leading to higher compression ratios.

Consider the application utility function defined in Figure 4-(a). As the sampling rate increases, utility improves but beyond a point, it saturates and flattens. For the sake of illustration, consider only two resources (CPU cycles and network bandwidth) and two schemes (with and without compression). In addition, assume that the compression is lossless such that there is no perceived QoS difference to the user whether compression is used or not. The resource consumption functions for this data stream on the CPU and network bandwidth resources are plotted in Figure 4-(b). If no compression is used, demand on the CPU is less and demand on the network bandwidth is higher. The converse is true if compression is used. In either case, the demands on the two resources increase as the sampling rate is increased.

We assume in the rest of this section that the resource consumption functions are linear. As a result, the resource utility functions which combine the application utility function and the resource consumption functions are as plotted in Figure 4-(c). It is informative to note that points marked (1) on the resource utility functions are chosen in tandem; that is, if point (1) is chosen on the CPU utility function, point (1) *must* be chosen on the network bandwidth utility function. The same holds true for points (2), (3) and (4) respectively (and all other pairs of points inbetween).

In general, a total of M schemes is assumed to be available, with $M = 2$ in the example of Figure 4.

3.3. Notation

We shall use the following notation in this section.

Notation: $\mathbf{R}_j$ is the amount available on resource j.

Notation: a_{ik}^j represents the minimum resource demand for application τ_i on resource j when scheme k is used to satisfy the application requirements.

Notation: b_{ik}^j represents the additional resource demand (beyond the minimum requirement of a_{ik}^j) that application τ_i can fruitfully use on resource j when scheme k is in use. In other words, if application τ_i were allocated more than $a_{ik}^j + b_{ik}^j$ amount of resource j, no additional increase in utility will accrue.

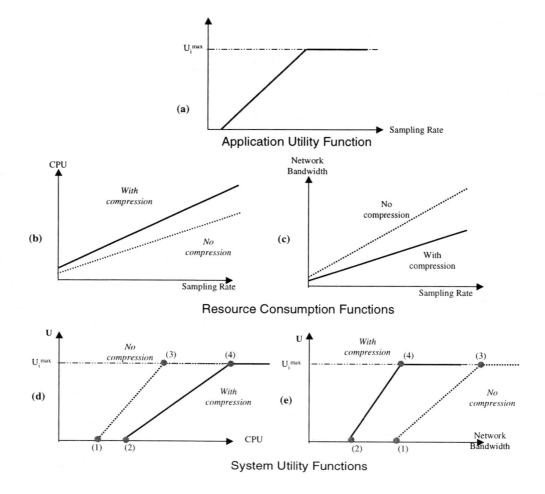

Figure 4. Resource Tradeoffs and Its Impact on Utility Functions.

Notation: u_{ik} is the maximum utility accrued by application τ_i when scheme k is used.

3.4. The Case of $M = 4$

Let (X_i, Y_i) represent $M = 4$ possible schemes for achieving a given quality of service. For example, consider the following. Data is transmitted as is (no compression) and 3 possible compression schemes using different amounts of resources and thereby generating different amounts of data.

Each application τ_i, $1 \leq i \leq n$, has an associated maximal value u_{ik}, $1 \leq k \leq 4$, when scheme k is chosen. Let F_i be the fraction of τ_i's useful range of resource allocation (above its minimal allocation), with $0 \leq F_i \leq 1$.[3]

---

[3] That is, if τ_i is allocated a total r_i^j of resource $\mathbf{R}_j$ under scheme k, for any k, $F_i = (r_i^j - a_{ik}^j) \div b_{ik}^j$. Q-RAM assumes that $r_i^j \geq a_{ik}^j$ for some value of k.

Objective: maximize

$$\sum_{i=1}^{n} (u_{i1} F_i X_i Y_i + u_{i2} F_i (1 - X_i) Y_i + u_{i3} F_i X_i (1 - Y_i) + u_{i4} F_i (1 - X_i)(1 - Y_i))$$

subject to:

$$0 \leq F_i \leq 1 \text{ and resource constraints.}$$

Let $1 \leq j \leq m$ index resources, and X_i, $Y_i = 0$ or 1. Since $\mathbf{R}_j$ is the amount available on resource j, the resource constraints can be stated as follows.

Resource Constraints:

$\forall j, 1 \leq j \leq m,$

$$\sum_{i=1}^{n}(a_{i1}^j + b_{i1}^j F_i)X_i Y_i + \sum_{i=1}^{n}(a_{i2}^j + b_{i2}^j F_i)(1 - X_i)Y_i$$

$$+ \sum_{i=1}^{n}(a_{i3}^j + b_{i3}^j F_i)X_i(1 - Y_i)$$

$$+ \sum_{i=1}^{n}(a_{i4}^j + b_{i4}^j F_i)(1 - X_i)(1 - Y_i) \leq \mathbf{R}_j$$

Expanding, the jth resource constraint becomes

$$\sum_{i=1}^{n} a_{i4}^j + \sum_{i=1}^{n} b_{i4}^j F_i$$

$$+ \sum_{i=1}^{n}(a_{i1}^j - a_{i2}^j - a_{i3}^j + a_{i4}^j)X_i Y_i$$

$$+ \sum_{i=1}^{n}(b_{i1}^j - b_{i2}^j - b_{i3}^j + b_{i4}^j)X_i Y_i F_i$$

$$+ \sum_{i=1}^{n}(a_{i3}^j - a_{i4}^j)X_i + \sum_{i=1}^{n}(a_{i2}^j - a_{i4}^j)Y_i$$

$$+ \sum_{i=1}^{n}(b_{i3}^j - b_{i4}^j)X_i F_i + \sum_{i=1}^{n}(b_{i2}^j - b_{i4}^j)Y_i F_i \leq \mathbf{R}_j$$

The objective function and these resource constraints are non-linear in $\{F_i\}$, $\{X_i\}$ and $\{Y_i\}$ containing terms of the form $X_i F_i$, $Y_i F_i$, $X_i Y_i F_i$ and $X_i Y_i$. These constraints can be linearized by introducing substitutions and adding extra (linear) constraints to the problem[4].

We use the following substitutions:

$$X_i Y_i = Z_i$$

$$X_i F_i = f_i$$

$$Y_i F_i = g_i$$

$$Z_i F_i = h_i$$

Note that $X_i Y_i F_i = Z_i F_i = h_i$.
The objective function now becomes

$$\sum_{i=1}^{n}(u_{i4}F_i + (u_{i1} - u_{i2})Z_i + (u_{i2} - u_{i4})f_i$$

$$+ (u_{i3} - u_{i4})g_i + (u_{i4} - u_{i3})h_i)$$

which is linear in the new variables, and we insert the following additional constraints:

[4]We would like to thank Professor Egan Balas of the Graduate School of Industrial Administration at Carnegie Mellon University for suggesting the linearization technique for the case of $M = 2$ upon which this is based.

$f_i \geq 0$
$g_i \geq 0$
$h_i \geq 0$
$f_i - F_i \leq 0$
$g_i - F_i \leq 0$
$h_i - Z_i \leq 0$
$-f_i + F_i + X_i \leq 1$
$-g_i + F_i + Y_i \leq 1$
$-h_i + F_i + Z_i \leq 1.$

We also need to enforce

$$X_i Y_i = Z_i$$

where X_i, Y_i, Z_i are *binary* 0-1 variables. This can be done by adding the constraints

$Z_i - X_i \leq 0$
$Z_i - Y_i \leq 0$
$X_i + Y_i - Z_i \leq 1$

The optimal resource allocation problem we call the Multi-Resource Single QoS dimension Problem (MRSQP) thus reduces to the following.

Multi-Resource Single QoS Dimension Problem (MRSQP):

Objective: maximize

$$\sum_{i=1}^{n}(u_{i4}F_i + (u_{i1} - u_{i2})Z_i + (u_{i2} - u_{i4})f_i$$

$$+ (u_{i3} - u_{i4})g_i + (u_{i4} - u_{i3})h_i)$$

subject to:
$\forall j, 1 \leq j \leq m,$

$$\sum_{i=1}^{n} a_{i4}^j + \sum_{i=1}^{n} b_{i4}^j F_i + \sum_{i=1}^{n}(a_{i1}^j - a_{i2}^j - a_{i3}^j + a_{i4}^j)Z_i$$

$$+ \sum_{i=1}^{n}(b_{i1}^j - b_{i2}^j - b_{i3}^j + b_{i4}^j)h_i$$

$$+ \sum_{i=1}^{n}(a_{i3}^j - a_{i4}^j)X_i + \sum_{i=1}^{n}(a_{i2}^j - a_{i4}^j)Y_i$$

$$+ \sum_{i=1}^{n}(b_{i3}^j - b_{i4}^j)f_i + \sum_{i=1}^{n}(b_{i2}^j - b_{i4}^j)g_i \leq \mathbf{R}_j$$

where $X_i, Y_i, Z_i (1 \leq i \leq n)$ are binary 0-1 variables, and for $1 \leq i \leq n,$

$$f_i \geq 0$$
$$f_i - Fi \leq 0$$
$$f_i - X_i \leq 0$$
$$-f_i + F_i + X_i \leq 1$$

$$g_i \geq 0$$
$$g_i - Fi \leq 0$$
$$g_i - Y_i \leq 0$$
$$-g_i + F_i + Y_i \leq 1$$

$$h_i \geq 0$$
$$h_i - Fi \leq 0$$
$$h_i - Z_i \leq 0$$
$$-h_i + F_i + Z_i \leq 1$$

$$Z_i - X_i \leq 0$$
$$Z_i - Y_i \leq 0$$
$$X_i + Y_i - Z_i \leq 1$$

MRSQP can be efficiently solved using standard optimization techniques for mixed integer programming. This is particularly so for problems where the number of applications is relatively small (a few tens at most). Commercial software packages that are available for these purposes include *lindo* [14], *gino* [13], *C-Whiz* [5] and *CPlex* [4]. We provide a brief evaluation of how efficiently this linear mixed integer programming problem can be solved in Section 3.7.

3.5. Dealing with $M \neq 4$

The definition of MRSQP in Section 3.4 assumed that $M = 4$ schemes were available to support and implement a particular QoS dimension. The problem scales readily if $M = 2^p$, where p is a positive integer. The binary variables X_i and Y_i are then replaced by the binary variables $X_{il}, 1 \leq i \leq n$ and $1 \leq l \leq p$ and the linearization process is repeated after the objective function is expanded accordingly.

If M is *not* a power of 2, pick the smallest integer p such that $2^p > M$ and define the objective function and constraints assuming that 2^p schemes are available (as described above). Then, set $u_{ik} = -1$ and $a_{ik}^j = 0, (M + 1) \leq k \leq 2^p, 1 \leq j \leq m$. The optimization will be forced away from choosing the non-existent schemes.[5]

3.6. Dealing with The Same Utilities for All M Schemes

Suppose that all alternative schemes available for implementing the QoS dimension provide the same maximal utility to each application. For example, consider a bulky real-time data stream being transmitted and the end-to-end delay of the data stream is the QoS dimension under consideration. In addition, the data must be received at its destination without any loss. There can be several options available. The data can be

---

[5]Alternatively, one can also assign $\forall i, 1 \leq i \leq n, b_{ik}^j = \infty, (M + 1) \leq k \leq 2^p$.

transmitted as is, or it can be compressed using any one of several available lossless compression schemes (such as "zip" with different compression factors). Any scheme chosen impacts the demand on processing and network resources differently. However, since there is no data loss in the compression, at the receiver site, the utility derived from each scheme is the same (for a given end-to-end delay).

Under such conditions, where $u_{i1} = u_{i2} = u_{i3} = u_{i4} = u_i$, the objective function of MRSQP can be simplified as follows:

Objective:

$$\text{maximize} \sum_{i=1}^{n} u_i F_i$$

subject to $0 \leq F_i \leq 1$ and the exact same constraints as MRSQP.

The outlines of a heuristic that is expected to give practically very acceptable but suboptimal results at much higher speeds than the mixed integer programming solution defined above is presented in [21]. As a result, it may be used even within a non-preemptive kernel, for example.

3.7. Solving MRSQP in Practice

As shown in Section 3.4, MRSQP is expressed as a linearized mixed integer programming problem. However, it must be noted that integer programming problems can still potentially have long execution times. In order to obtain some insights into its run-time efficiency, we solved these problems in a commercially available optimization package called CPLEX [4] for some sample situations. We used a 266MHz Pentium with 64MB of memory for performing the optimization.

In MRSQP, the number of constraints in the problem is 62 when 10 applications are considered, and 122 when 20 applications are considered simultaneously. The results are summarized in Table 1.

The first two columns of Table 1 represent inputs to MRSQP, defining the objective function, the resource constraints and the number of schemes (M) available to support the specified QoS. The number of iterations exercised by the optimizer, the time spent in pre-solving the problem (where redundant constraints are eliminated and pseudo-cost variables are selected) and the time to solve the problem are listed in the last three columns respectively.

We drew some of the following conclusions based on our observations:

- The solution times of about 20 *ms* is a strong indicator that this mixed integer programming problem can be solved in real-time for online decision making of resource allocation. We found that in most cases, the solution is found in about 0.02 seconds, but we suspect that the running time is often much less since the resolution of the clock itself is 0.01 seconds.

- The solution time in the small 10s of milliseconds also indicates that such a decision should *not* be computed as a

# of Applications	M	# of Iterations	Pre-solve Time (s)	Solution Time (s)
10	2	41	0.00	0.01
10	2	43	0.01	0.02
10	2	29	0.01	0.03
10	2	30	0.00	0.01
10	2	42	0.00	0.01
20	2	63	0.01	0.03
20	2	68	0.01	0.01
20	2	53	0.01	0.02
20	2	61	0.01	0.02

Table 1. The Run-Time Efficiency of Solving MRSQP.

long critical section in a non-preemptive kernel. Instead, this decision should be made by a resource manager running preemptively in user space. This is the architecture of the QoS manager used in RT-Mach [15].

- Another interesting observation from these and many other similar experiments was that all applications except for one application have their $F_i = 0$ or 1. Under relatively rare conditions, two applications have their $F_i \neq 0$ or 1. We have yet to see a case where three applications have their $F_i \neq 0$ or 1. We expect that this observation can form the basis of an efficient heuristic that can be used to solve substantially larger problems in real-time.

4. Concluding Remarks

In this paper, we have presented practical solutions to some important problems that were not addressed by the QoS-based Resource Allocation Model of [20]. For example, this prior work presented only a greedy algorithm to apportion an available resource across multiple applications to satisfy multiple QoS dimensions (at least one of which is dependent on another). We have shown in this paper that the problem of finding the optimal resource allocation is NP-hard and present a brute-force scheme to find this allocation. However, a simple polynomial algorithm based on computational geometry allowed us to find a solution within a provably fixed and very short distance from the optimal allocation. We have also studied the problem of apportioning multiple resources to satisfy a single QoS dimension, the converse of a problem solved in [20]. This problem is rather interesting because resources can be traded against each other while satisfying the same QoS requirement. We solve this problem as a linear mixed integer programming problem that is solvable efficiently using commercially available software packages and libraries to obtain an optimal resource allocation.

We expect that a deep understanding of these and related solutions will yield insights into the general problem of apportioning multiple resources to satisfy simultaneously multiple QoS dimensions of multiple concurrent applications. In addition, extending some of these solutions to higher dimensions remains to be carried out. We are also exploring heuristics that can be used to solve MRSQP at even higher efficiencies (for use inside a real-time kernel for example). Finally, a significant amount of empirical work must be done to determine resource consumption functions.

Acknowledgments

The authors would like to thank the other members of the Amaranth project at Carnegie Mellon University.

References

[1] E. M. Atkins T. F. Abdelzaher and Kang Shin. Qos negotiation in real-time systems and its application to automated flight control. In *The Proceedings of the IEEE Real-time Technology and Applications Symposium*, June 1997.

[2] J. C. R. Bennett, D. C. Stephens and H. Zhang. *High Speed, Scalable, and Accurate Implementation of Fair Queueing Algorithms in ATM Networks.* ICNP '97.

[3] J. C. R. Bennett and H. Zhang. Hierarchical Packet Fair Queueing Algorithms. *IEEE/ACM Transactions on Networking*, 5(5):675-689, Oct 1997. Also in Proceedings of SIGCOMM'96, Aug, 1997.

[4] Using the CPLEX Callable Library. Using the CPLEX Base System with CPLEX Barrier and Mixed Integer Solver Options. CPLEX Division, ILOG Inc., 1997.

[5] C-Whiz Manual. *C-Whiz Linear Programming Optimizer*. Ketron Management Science, July 1994.

[6] R. Guérin, H. Ahmadi, and M. Naghshineh. Equivalent capacity and its application to bandwidth allocation in high-speed networks. *IEEE Journal on Selected Areas in Communications*, September 1991.

[7] T. Cormen, C. Leiserson, R. Rivest *Introduction to Algorithms*. The MIT Press, 1990. ISBN 0-262-03141-8 (MIT Press), ISBN 0-07-013143-0 (McGraw-Hill)

[8] T. Ibaraki and N. Katoh. *Resource Allocation Problems: Algorithmic Approaches*. MIT Press, 1988. ISBN 0-262-09027-9.

[9] M. B. Jones and P. J. Leach. Modular real-time resource management in the rialto operating system. Technical Report MSR-TR-95-16, Microsoft Research, Advanced Technology Division, May 1995.

[10] K. G. Shin D. D. Kandlur and D. Ferrari. Real-time communication in multi-hop networks. *IEEE Transactions on Parallel and Distributed Systems*, pages 1044–1056, Oct 1994.

[11] M. H. Klein, T. Ralya, B. Pollak, R. Obenza, and M. G. Harbour. *A Practitioner's Handbook for Real-Time Analysis: Guide to Rate-Monotonic Analysis for Real-Time Systems*. Kluwer Academic Publishers, 1993. ISBN 0-7923-9361-9.

[12] T. F. Lawrence. The Quality of Service Model and High Assurance. *Workshop on High Assurance Systems*, July 1997.

[13] J. Liebman, L. Lasdon, L. Schrage and A. Waren. *Modeling and Optimization with GINO*. The Scientific Press, 1988.

[14] Lindo Manual. *Optimization Modeling with LINDO*. 5th Edition. Duxbury Press, 1997.

[15] C. Lee, R. Rajkumar, and C. Mercer. Experiences with processor reservation and dynamic qos in real-time mach. *In the proceedings of Multimedia Japan 96*, April 1996.

[16] C. L. Liu and Layland J. W. Scheduling algorithms for multiprogramming in a hard real time environment. *JACM*, 20 (1):46 – 61, 1973.

[17] J. W. S. Liu, K-J Lin, R. Bettati, D. Hull, and A. Yu. *Use of Imprecise Computation to Enhance Dependability of Real-Time Systems*. Kluwer Academic Publishers, 1994.

[18] R. Neopolitan, and K. Naimipour. *Foundations of Algorithms*. 2nd Edition, Jones and Bartlett, 1998. ISBN 0-7637-0620-5.

[19] A. L. Peressini, R. E. Sullivan, and Jr. J. J. Uhl. *Convex Programming and the Karish-Kuhn-Tucker conditions*, chapter 5. Springer-Verlag, 1980.

[20] R. Rajkumar, C. Lee, J. P. Lehoczky, and D. P. Siewiorek. A QoS-based Resource Allocation Model In *Proceedings of the IEEE Real-Time Systems Symposium*. December, 1998.

[21] R. Rajkumar, C. Lee, J. P. Lehoczky, and D. P. Siewiorek. Some Solutions for QoS-based Resource Allocation In *Technical Report, Department of Computer Science, Carnegie Mellon University*. June, 1998.

[22] R. Sedgewick. *Algorithms in C*. Addison Wesley, 1990. ISBN 0-201-51425-7.

[23] D. Seto, J. P. Lehoczky, L. Sha, and K.G. Shin. On task schedulability in real-time control systems. *IEEE Real-Time System Symposium*, December 1996.

[24] J. A. Stankovic and K. Ramamritham. The design of the spring kernel. In *Proceedings of the Real-Time Systems Symposium*, Dec 1987.

A Dynamic Quality of Service Middleware Agent for Mediating Application Resource Usage

Scott Brandt, Gary Nutt
University of Colorado at Boulder
{sbrandt,nutt}@cs.colorado.edu

Toby Berk
Florida International University
berkt@cs.fiu.edu

James Mankovich
Hewlett Packard
jman@cs.colorado.edu

Abstract

High-bandwidth applications with time-dependent resource requirements demand certain resource level assurances in order to operate correctly. Quality of Service resource management techniques are being successfully developed that allow network systems to provide such assurances. These solutions generally assume that the operating system at either end of the network is capable of handling the throughput requirements of the applications. However, real operating systems have to manage many concurrent applications with varying resource requirements. Without specialized support, the operating system cannot guarantee the resources needed for any particular application. In support of these kinds of applications we have developed a middleware agent called a dynamic QoS manager (DQM) that mediates application resource usage so as to ensure that applications get the resources they need in order to provide adequate performance. The DQM employs a variety of algorithms to determine application resource allocations. Using application QoS levels, it provides for resource availability based algorithmic variation within applications and varying application periods. It also allows for inaccurate application resource usage estimates through a technique we have developed called dynamic estimate refinement. This paper discusses new developments in the design of the DQM and presents results showing DQM performance with both real and synthetic applications.

1 Introduction

High-bandwidth applications with time-dependent resource requirements such as continuous media demand certain resource level assurances in order to operate correctly. Quality of Service (QoS) resource management techniques are being successfully developed that allow network systems to provide such assurances. These solutions generally assume that the operating system at either end of the network is capable of handling the throughput requirements of the applications. However, real operating systems have to manage many concurrent applications with varying resource requirements. Without specialized support, the operating system cannot guarantee the resources needed for any particular application.

Applications with such time-dependent resource requirements are often referred to as *soft real-time*. QoS techniques, originally developed in the context of network bandwidth utilization and packet loss management, have been successfully applied to the domain of soft real-time processing. A QoS system provides a *guarantee* that a certain amount (or quality) of resources will be available when they are needed. In the strictest sense these guarantees are hard; an application is guaranteed to get all of the resources it has requested, assuming the request is satisfiable with the currently available (i.e. uncommitted) resources. Because an application must reserve the resources it needs at the time that it enters the system, the hard nature of the guarantees requires that the application make a worst-case estimate of its resource needs. However, many such applications can and often do run perfectly well with significantly less resources.

The nature of soft real-time processing is such that the processes do not need such a strict guarantee, only a reasonable assurance that their resource needs will be largely met by the operating system. Operating system researchers have been developing techniques for softening the strict guarantees of such systems so as to allow more applications to run simultaneously, with the expectation that their average case performance will be acceptable and the understanding that worst-case behavior may result in some missed deadlines, loss of data, or other similar consequences. Since these are operating system mechanisms, and since they are based on worst-case estimates, an application is generally required to operate within its worst case estimate (i.e. if the operating system is to make assurances about the use of its resources, it must generally enforce the resource management policy that it adopts).

Operating systems designers have been creating mechanisms to support QoS-based soft real-time application execution. These mechanisms provide a variety of interfaces for determining the amount of resources that will be allocated to an application, allowing a process to a) *negotiate* with the operating system for a specific amount of resources as in RT Mach [19] and Rialto [13][14]; b) specify a *range* of resource allocations as in MMOSS [7]; or c) specify a measure of application *importance* that can be used to compute a fair resource allocation as in SMART [21][22]. These systems all provide a mechanism that can be used to dynamically reduce the resource allotment granted to the running applications. In creating these resource management mechanisms, operating systems developers have assumed that it is possible for applications to adjust their behavior according to the availability of resources, but without providing a general model of application development for such an environment. In the extreme, the applications may be forced to dynamically adapt to a strategy in which the resource allocation is less than that required for average-case execution.

We are exploring a middleware solution which takes an approach in which applications cooperate with the operating system in their use of system resources. This approach is in contrast with the operating system approach in which utilization outside the worst case requires enforcement (as opposed to cooperation). This distinction, cooperation versus enforcement, is a philosophical difference in our approach when compared to existing operating system approaches to achieving soft real-time. The assumption of cooperation should be completely adequate for those circumstances in which all processes in the system are owned by a single user or manager (as in a multimedia server or proxy). In a more general system, some

level of enforcement will likely prove to be required. One goal of this work is to determine the minimum set of real-time system services required to support soft real-time application execution. In pushing our cooperative approach we have already found that relatively few real-time services are really required.

In previous papers [3][11][24][25] we introduced our notion of QoS levels (called *execution levels*), a method for managing soft real-time application execution in an environments with varying QoS allocations. With execution levels, each application is constructed using a set of strategies for achieving its goals, ordered by their relative resource usage and the relative quality of their output. We also demonstrated the feasibility of cooperative middleware based QoS management and discussed our prototype middleware execution level based QoS resource manager called the *Dynamic QoS Resource Manager* (DQM) and examined a set of representative QoS allocation algorithms within this context. In so doing, we have demonstrated that a real-time scheduler such as the one provided by RT Mach is not required to support soft real-time execution of QoS level-based applications.

In continuing our research in this area, we have extended the DQM in several ways that bring it significantly closer to our goal of a viable middleware QoS resource management agent. In our earlier work we used synthetic programs to experiment with the DQM, though now our tests are driven using working applications (two mpeg players). We have also enhanced the DQM: we added dynamic application period management capabilities and we have fully generalized the level management by adding level-raising capabilities. Once these capabilities were added, we discovered that middleware QoS management requires accurate application resource usage estimates. To deal with this problem we have developed a technique called *dynamic estimate refinement*. We ran into a number of other issues related to the placement of the DQM as a middleware application, including its lack of fine-grained application resource usage information and its lack of a QoS allocation enforcement mechanism. Taken together, these omissions result in significant differences in the way the DQM must function and in the resulting execution of the applications themselves, as compared with OS based QoS solutions.

This paper presents the results of our continued DQM development. We briefly review execution levels and the design of the DQM. We discuss the issues relating to implementing QoS as a middleware component and to the impact on its overall design. Finally, we present experimental results showing the operation of the DQM with the mpeg applications; the experiments highlight the need for dynamic estimate refinement. Section 1, this section, introduces the paper. Section 2 presents a survey of related work in this area. Section 3 discusses execution levels and the design of the DQM. Section 4 discusses issues related to raising levels and Section 5 discusses dynamic estimate refinement. Section 6 presents the results of our experiments with real level-based applications, and Section 7 contains a summary of this work and the conclusions we have drawn.

2 Background

2.1 Soft real-time application models

Compton and Tennenhouse describe a system in which applications are shed when resource availability reduces below an acceptable point [6]. They argue that applications should cooperatively, dynamically reduce resource requirements. Their approach is to be explicitly guided by the user in selecting which application to eliminate.

Research in imprecise computation at the University of Illinois [8][10] examined the idea of having two parts to each task: a required part and an optional part where the optional part refines the computation performed in the required part, reducing the computational error. A modified task scheduler was used to allocate extra CPU capacity towards the optional parts in such a way as to reduce overall computational error.

Massalin and Pu developed the notion of *software feedback*, wherein job scheduling parameters are modified based on application-specific metrics such as input queue length [18]. This technique has also been applied to application execution [5] such that an application may dynamically modify its processing based upon its performance. The application execution model they describe is strictly best-effort and decentralized, and does not incorporate the notion of any actual QoS guarantees in the operating system environment.

Fan investigates an architecture similar to ours in which applications request a continuous range of QoS commitment [7]. Based upon the current state of the system, the QoS Manager may increase or decrease an application's current resource allocation within this prenegotiated range. Such a system suffers from instability due to the fact that the ranges are continuous and continuously being adjusted, and it lacks a strong mechanism for deciding which applications' allocations to modify and when. It also assumes that any application can be written in such a way as to work reasonably with any resource allocation within a particular range. This assumption is not consistent with the design of the majority of real-time applications.

2.2 Soft real-time scheduling

Jensen's work in Benefit-Based scheduling [12] is relevant to this project. Jensen proposed soft real-time scheduling based on application benefit. Applications would specify a *benefit curve* that indicates the relative benefit to be obtained by scheduling the application at various times with respect to its deadlines. Jensen's goal was to schedule the applications so as to maximize overall system benefit.

Nieh and Lam have developed another system based on the Fair Share scheduling algorithm [16] in which applications are allotted a portion of the CPU based upon their relative importance as measured against the other currently executing applications [21][22]. This allotment changes dynamically depending upon the current requirements of all of the currently executing processes and their relative *importances*. Like Fan's system, Nieh and Lam have based their system on the assumption that soft real-time applications can provide reasonable performance with any resource allocation that the operating system decides to give them.

Our goals and approach are closely related to those of Rialto [13][14]. A major goal of Rialto was to investigate programming abstractions that allow multiple, independent real-time applications to dynamically co-exist and share resources on a hardware platform. They intended to have a system resource planner reason about and participate in overall resource allocations between applications. The major difference between Rialto and this work is in how we deal with system overload. Rialto has a QoS-based scheduler that dynamically allocates system resources (in particular, the CPU) based on prenegotiated QoS guarantees. These guarantees may be renegotiated, and are explicitly enforced by the scheduler. Furthermore, it is up to the applications to decide how to execute in such a way as to effectively utilize the resources that they have been granted. Our work differs from this in two ways. First, the scheduler used for our studies is a general-purpose UNIX scheduler that does not support any notion of deadlines or QoS guarantees. Our DQM relies solely on application-determined missed deadlines and OS reported idle time to inform it whether or not the system is over- or underloaded, demonstrating the feasibility of such a scheme on a general-purpose operating system. Second, our applications provide the DQM with explicit sets of execution levels with corresponding resource requirements and expected benefit, thus allowing the DQM to make resource decisions that more closely reflect the actual operation and associated resource needs of the applications.

Much of the recent research on RT Mach [15] is important for this project. In particular, Processor Capacity Reserves [19] can be used by applications to reserve a particular portion of the CPU. Applications are free to increase their portion of the CPU, given available capacity. Real-time processes and non-real-time processes are treated uniformly, because applications merely request their desired CPU portion. Other efforts at CMU are directed at providing end-to-end reservation services [17]. The Keio-Multimedia Platform at the Japan Advanced Institute of Science and Technology (JAIST) is extending RT Mach to support QoS for continuous media streams [20]. Our overall project approaches operating system support for multimedia applications from a different perspective than these projects. Rather than determining how to map QoS parameters (such as frame rate for video and sample rate for audio) into operating system mechanisms, we attempt to create an architecture in which there can be mediation between applications, enforcement of applications' registered resource usage, and high resource utilization.

2.3 QoS levels

Tokuda developed a system using QoS levels that are similar to ours [26]. His work was done on RT Mach and used Processor Capacity Reserves and real-time kernel threads to manage the execution of the real-time tasks. There are several differences between Tokuda's levels and our own. Tokuda characterizes the levels according to the type of difference between adjacent QoS levels, temporal or spatial, depending on whether the change was to the period of the application or the spatial resolution of the processed data. Our levels are characterized in the DQM by a single number representing average CPU utilization of the algorithm. Level changes involving Tokuda's temporal or spatial changes are automatically allowed for in this representation, as are changes to the algorithms which affect neither temporal nor spatial resolution. Tokuda also uses simply priority to determine the QoS allocation for each application and does not provide any indication of the relative importance of the individual levels within an application. Our per-application and per-level specifications of importance allow for a more accurate allocation of the available resources among the running applications. In addition to using a more general notion of levels, we have developed a middleware implementation that does not rely on the specialized scheduling and resource management provided by a real-time operating system such as RT Mach with Processor Capacity Reserves. This paper specifically addresses the issues that arise when running a middleware implementation without such specialized support.

Abdelzaher et al at the University of Michigan are using a very similar notion of QoS levels to support automated flight control processes distributed over a pool of processors [1]. They have also extended the concept to apply to network resources [2]. Both of their systems are built on top of RT Mach and rely on its real-time support and scheduling. They provide no information about how QoS levels are determined, nor what to do if they are incorrect.

3 Execution levels and the DQM

Our research has focused on supporting soft real-time processes on general-purpose operating systems. Most soft real-time systems soften the real-time behavior of the applications by moderating the percentage of missed deadlines or the amount by which deadlines are missed, with smaller amounts considered better. This is adequate for the class of soft real-time processes for which missed deadlines are acceptable, but not all such processes fall into this category. For example, desktop playback of a fixed-bandwidth network-based continuous media stream does not allow for all deadlines to be missed by a certain amount because eventually the OS will run out of buffer space to hold the queue of frames that is slowly backing up. In this case a preferable solution would be one such as dropping frames or reducing the amount of processing for each frame so that the hard deadlines (enforced by the arrival of new data) can still be met.

In order to give the policy decisions to the applications, we have developed the execution level application execution model. With execution levels, each application specifies a set of algorithmic modes in which it can execute, along with the computational requirements and the corresponding benefit of running in each mode. A middleware QoS manager provides the mechanism for managing soft real-time by managing the level of each running application through a variety of QoS allocation algorithms.

Specifically, each application is characterized by two numbers, the *maximum CPU usage* and the *maximum benefit*. The maximum CPU usage is the fraction of the CPU required to execute the application at its most intensive resource level. The maximum benefit of the application is a user-specified indication of the benefit provided by executing the application when running at its highest performance level - analogous to application priority, importance, or utility in other systems. Each execution level is characterized by three numbers, relative CPU usage, relative benefit, and period. Relative CPU usage specifies the fraction of the maximum CPU usage required by the execution level, relative benefit specifies the fraction of the maximum benefit provided by the execution level, and period specifies the amount of time to allocate for each iteration of the algorithm. Relative values are specified because the maximum CPU usage number depends on the system on which the application is being executed and the maximum benefit will be user-specified, but the relationship between the levels is expected to be constant in most cases and specifiable at application development time. Implicitly we assume that while all of the algorithms correctly implement the desired application, the benefit of the result degrades with a decrease in execution level. An application can be executed at any of the levels, using corresponding resources with corresponding benefit.

The specific execution levels and corresponding CPU usage and benefit are highly application dependent. The levels themselves will be determined by the goals of the application developer. They will incorporate algorithmic trade-offs that represent a range of output qualities. Traditionally, real-time and multimedia application developers make these trade-offs as a matter of routine, selecting the highest quality algorithm that fits within their known computational constraints. With execution levels the developer can incorporate multiple algorithmic options and allow the system to dynamically determine which one is most appropriate at run-time. The CPU usage numbers are directly measured and represent the average CPU usage for each level of an application. The benefit numbers are determined by the application developer. The details of determining appropriate benefit numbers goes beyond the scope of this research. However, a very large body of research has been conducted in other domains to determine acceptable video frame rates, audio jitter and delay, etc. The results of this research apply directly to the problem of determining the relative benefits of different execution levels.

In order to examine QoS-based soft real-time processing with the execution level model, we have developed a prototype system consisting of a middleware QoS manager called a *Dynamic QoS Resource Manager* (*DQM*) and a library of DQM interface and soft real-time support functions called the Soft Real-Time Resource Library (SRL). This prototype system has allowed us to experiment with several different QoS decision algorithms for dynamically adjusting levels among a set of running applications. Like the flexible QoS systems cited above, the current implementation of our DQM works solely with the CPU resource. However, we believe that the concepts described in this paper can be extended in a straightforward manner to encompass other resources such as network bandwidth and memory

The SRL allows an application to specify maximum CPU requirements, maximum benefit, and a set of quadruples

<Level, Resource usage, Benefit, Period>

As with priority specifications in many systems, level 1 represents the highest level and provides the maximum benefit using the maximum amount of resources, and

Max Benefit: 6
Max CPU Usage: 0.75
Num Levels: 6

Level	CPU	Benefit	Period(ms)
1	1.00	1.00	100000
2	0.80	0.90	100000
3	0.65	0.80	100000
4	0.40	0.25	100000
5	0.25	0.10	100000
6	0.00	0.00	100000

Figure 1: Execution levels with CPU usage, Benefit and Period

lower execution levels are represented with larger numbers. For example, an application might provide information such as in Figure 1.

Figure 1 indicates that the maximum amount of CPU that the application will require is 75% of the CPU, when running at it's maximum level, and that at this level it will provide a user-specified benefit of 6. The table further shows that the application can run with relatively high benefit (80%) with 65% of its maximum resource allocation, but that if the level of allocation is reduced to 40%, the quality of the result will be substantially less (25%). The SRL provides the application with the ability to specify the period to be used for each level and, while running, to determine when deadlines have been missed and notify the DQM of such an event. Finally, the SRL dynamically receives information from the DQM about what level the application should be executing and sets a local execution level variable that the application uses to select the algorithm to execute during each period.

The DQM dynamically determines levels for the running applications based on the available resources and the specified benefit of the application. It changes the level of each running application until all applications run without missing deadlines, the system utilization is above some predetermined minimum, and stability has been reached. Resource availability (or the lack thereof) is determined in a few different ways. CPU overload is determined by the occurrence of deadline misses in the running applications. The SRL linked into each application notifies the DQM each time an application misses a deadline. CPU underutilization is determined by examining CPU idle time. System idle time can be determined in several ways including via the operating system, through the UNIX /proc file system, by measuring the CPU usage of a low priority application, and by taking the complement of the CPU usage measurements (or estimates) of the running applications. If the operating system provides idle time information, this information is the most reliable.

Currently the DQM implements several algorithms with various strengths and weaknesses. A previous paper introduced these algorithms and provided a limited comparison of their capabilities [3]. For the purposes of this paper we will use one representative algorithm, *Proportional*, which uses the CPU usage/benefit ratio to determine which application's level to modify in the case of over- or underload. In situations of system overload, it lowers the level of the application with the highest CPU usage/benefit ratio. Similarly, in the event of system underutilization, it raises the level of the application with the lowest CPU usage/benefit ratio. In effect, this algorithms changes the execution level of the application that is furthest from it's fair proportional allocation of the CPU.

4 Measurement issues with raising levels

The DQM uses a static threshold level of measured system idle time to trigger the level-raising algorithm. In order to make good level-raising decisions, reliable resource usage and idle time information is needed. OS-based QoS systems have direct access to this information and make good use of it. Middleware solutions such as ours must make use of the information provided to user-space applications. Both Linux and Solaris (our two OS platforms) provide a /proc filesystem with information about the CPU usage of running applications in user and system space. This information is used by the DQM to trigger the level-raising algorithms. However, there is a problem with this method; the measurements of CPU usage and idle time vary from measurement interval to measurement interval.

Figure 2 shows the execution levels for an experimental execution of the DQM with two synthetic applications run on Linux[1] (with level raising disabled). These applications both have a period of 1/10 of a second, and a maximum usage of 70% of the CPU. The number of levels and relative cpu usage and benefit for each level was randomly generated. The two applications in this example have 8 and 6 levels, respectively. Note that the applications run for 3 seconds (90 periods), then stop.

As can be seen, the execution level of application 1 drops from 1 to 5 between iterations 0 and 13, then remains steady at this level. The estimated CPU usage for application 1 at level 5 is 19%, and the estimated CPU usage for application 2 at level 1 is 70%. This should yield a consistent idle time of 11%. The measurements are made by a separate process that runs at intervals of 1/10 of a second and measures the level and current CPU usage of each application, and system idle time.

Figure 3 shows the measured CPU usage for these same 2 applications, as well as the measured idle time. The measurements can be seen to fluctuate wildly between samples 0 and 13. This is caused by missed deadlines. Even after the levels (and therefore, theoretically, the CPU usage) have stabilized, the measured CPU usage and idle time continues to fluctuate by 10% of the total CPU cycles. However, it should be noted that the sum of the measured CPU usage and the idle time is 100% for every measurement iteration. Measurements on Solaris show similar results.

The observed fluctuation is caused by two factors. The first is phasing of the scheduling of the measurements with the scheduling of each iteration of the applications. This is somewhat avoidable with respect to the CPU usage measurements if we have the SRL measure each application's CPU usage at the end of each period, but is unavoid-

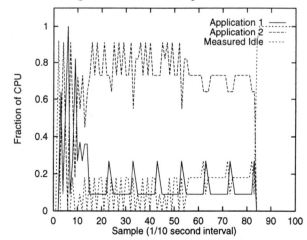

Figure 3: CPU usage for 2 synthetic applications (1)

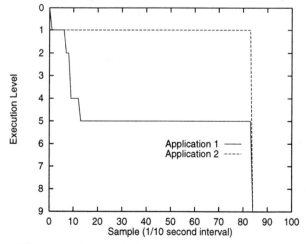

Figure 2: Execution levels for 2 synthetic applications

1. All of the experiments described in this paper were executed on a 200 Mhz Pentium Pro system running Linux 2.0.30. All applications and middleware were executed using the standard Linux scheduler.

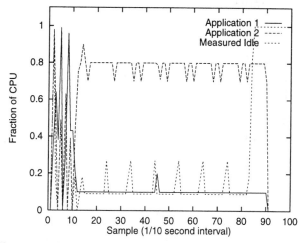

Figure 4: CPU usage for 2 synthetic applications (2)

able with respect to idle time measurement because idle time is a measure of what the applications have not used, and hence there is no perfect time to measure it.

Figure 4 shows the CPU usage and idle time for the same set of applications running with the same algorithm, but this time with the CPU usage measured by the SRL at the end of each iteration of the algorithms (i.e. exactly once per period). The variations seen in this graph are due to the resolution of the CPU usage information provided by the operating system. Both Linux and Solaris provide CPU usage information in hundredths of a second. Reading the usage every tenth of a second gives a granularity of 10%. Note that the idle time is measured slightly less frequently than the CPU usage in this execution, so the graphed peaks in idle time don't match up exactly with the graphed dips in measured CPU usage.

These variations in measured idle time present a problem for middleware determining of when to raise application levels. In particular, the target utilization has to leave at least 10% overhead to account for the measurement inaccuracies.

5 Dynamic Estimate Refinement

Another problem with raising levels occurs when the application resource usage estimates are inaccurate. With underestimates, the system resource utilization will be less than could be achieve with these applications. With over-estimates, the system simply may not stabilize at all. This can occur when the estimates indicate that a level change is feasible, but the actual resource usage is such that it is not. In this case, the level will be raised to take advantage of the available resources, then the application will use more resources than it requested. Then, one more applica-

tions will miss deadlines, causing application levels to be lowered and the cycle will repeat.

There are several reasons why the estimates might be inaccurate. One reason is that the measurements used to calculate the resource usage were simply faulty. A second possible cause of errors is that the measurements were made on a different machine or architecture than the one on which the application is being run. The estimates could also be inaccurate because of an inherent difficulty in measuring the CPU usage of a particular application, either because of measurement error as discussed above or because of variations in the actual amount of work done per iteration. A final cause for inaccuracies in the CPU usage estimates is interference between running applications, e.g. through sharing a system server or resource other than the CPU.

In order to deal with these issues, we have developed a technique called *dynamic estimate refinement*, in which the CPU usage estimates are continuously adjusted using measurements of the actual amount of CPU time used for each level of each application. This allows the system to adjust to the current execution parameters of each application. The current implementation uses a weighted average of the previous estimate and the current measurement, as follows:

current estimate = (previous estimate * weight + measurement) / (weight + 1)

This calculation is executed every 1/10 of a second, each time the CPU usage is measured. The estimate is initialized to the values supplied by the application. Smaller weight factors result in quickly adjusted estimates, but also display some sensitivity to transient changes in measured CPU usage. Larger weight factors slow down the adjustment process, but lead to more stable estimates due to the relative insensitivity to transient changes in the measured CPU usage. As with idle time measurement, the accuracy of the measurement is limited by the resolution of the CPU usage information provided by the operating system.

Figure 5 shows the execution levels for the same two synthetic applications seen above, this time with estimates that are 30% lower than the actual CPU usage of the applications. As can be seen, the level of application 1 changes almost continuously as the DQM tries to adjust the levels to use the available resources efficiently. Note that the applications use level 0 to indicate that they are not running, as seen at the beginning and end of the graphed levels for each application. Figure 6 shows the estimated and measured CPU usage for the same execution. The under-estimated CPU usage results in the worst case situation described above.

Figure 7 shows the results with dynamic estimate refinement. In this case, there is some level changing at the

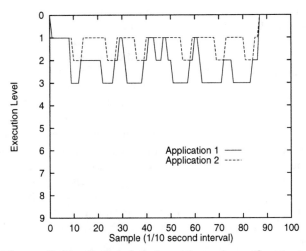

Figure 5: Execution levels with underestimates

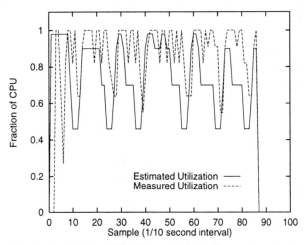

Figure 6: CPU utilization with underestimates

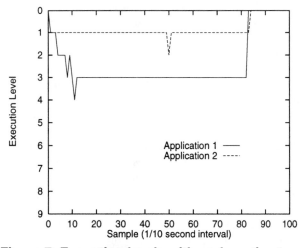

Figure 7: Execution levels with underestimates using dynamic estimate refinement

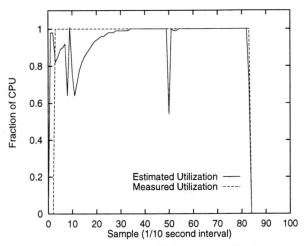

Figure 8: CPU Utilization with underestimates using dynamic estimate refinement

beginning, but the levels quickly stabilize as the estimates are corrected. There is a glitch at sample 50, where the level of application 2 drops to 2 in response to a deadline miss, but it is immediately corrected by the level-raising algorithm. Figure 8 shows the estimated and measured CPU usage for this same run. As can be seen, the incorrect estimates cause some discrepancy between the two numbers, but this is quickly corrected as the applications execute. By sample 33, the estimated and measured CPU usage numbers match exactly.

The graphs in this section were generated with a static raise threshold of 15% and a dynamic estimate refinement weight of 5.

6 Results with real level-based applications

In order to further test the operation of the DQM we developed two level-based soft real-time applications. Both are mpeg players, but they differ in the way that their real-time behavior has been softened. The first, mpeg_size, dynamically adjusts the size of the image displayed on the screen. Since the amount of work is related to how much time is spent drawing the pixels on the screen, this results in a reasonable range of CPU usage numbers over the different levels.

The second application, mpeg_rate, changes the frame rate of the displayed image from 0 frames/second to 10 frames/second. This particular application required no algorithmic changes other than the inclusion of the three SRL functions: dqm_init(), called once at the beginning of the application, dqm_loop(), called each time through the main loop, and dqm_exit(), called at application exit. Figure 9 shows the execution levels for these two applications.

Application 1 - mpeg_size
Max Benefit: 9
Max CPU Usage: 0.89
Num Levels: 8

Level	CPU	Benefit	Period(ms)
1	1.00	1.00	100000
2	0.86	0.90	100000
3	0.73	0.80	100000
4	0.63	0.73	100000
5	0.54	0.65	100000
6	0.46	0.46	100000
7	0.40	0.40	100000
8	0.00	0.00	100000

Application 2 - mpeg_rate
Max Benefit: 9
Max CPU Usage: 0.49
Num Levels: 6

Level	CPU	Benefit	Period(ms)
1	1.00	1.00	100000
2	0.80	0.90	125000
3	0.60	0.75	166666
4	0.40	0.50	250000
5	0.20	0.20	500000
6	0.00	0.00	100000

Figure 9: Execution levels for mpeg_size and mpeg_rate

There are many other ways in which the processing of the mpeg player could have been softened. One obvious method for changing levels is to dynamically change the resolution of the displayed image, displaying a full image each time but using varying size superpixels rather than displaying the full resolution of the image. Depending on the details of the graphics system this technique may or may not result in a large variation in processing time over the various levels. The other obvious technique is to drop frames to achieve a lower CPU usage. Like mpeg_rate, this version would clearly result in the desired variation in CPU usage over the various levels. The choice in which levelization to use is dependent on the goals of the user. If the user wants to see every frame of the image, but doesn't care about the rate at which they are displayed, then mpeg_rate is the one to use. If the user wants the display to run at approximately the rate of the original video, but is willing to sacrifice display resolution or be satisfied with some dropped frames, then these two techniques are good choices.

Figure 10 shows the execution levels that result for these two applications without dynamic estimate refinement and Figure 11 shows the execution levels that result for these two application with dynamic estimate refinement. There are a number of level-changes that occur without dynamic estimate refinement, probably due to

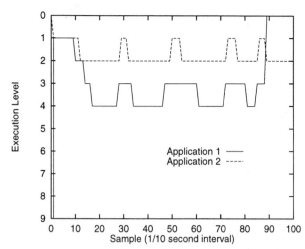

Figure 10: Execution levels for real applications without dynamic estimate refinement

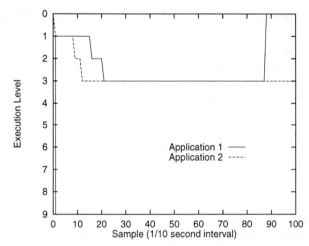

Figure 11: Execution levels for real applications with dynamic estimate refinement

some inaccuracies in the CPU usage estimates. The results with dynamic estimate refinement are significantly better.

Figure 12 shows the execution levels for the same two applications over 10000 samples (just over 15 minutes). There is a small amount of fluctuation in the levels, presumably in response to transient loads in the system, but the levels are generally stable.

7 Conclusion

Soft real-time multimedia applications require certain resource guarantees from the underlying system to be able to provide adequate and stable service. Without such guarantees, application performance varies significantly, and in certain situations applications may fail to run at all. Sev-

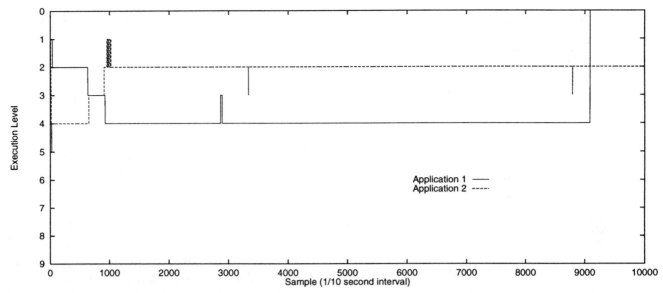

Figure 12: Execution levels for real applications with dynamic estimate refinement over 10000 samples

eral researchers OS based solutions provide (and enforce) QoS resource allocations.

We have developed a QoS based middleware resource management agent called the DQM. The DQM is based on the notion of application specified execution levels that reflect algorithmic modes in which the applications can execute. The DQM uses the execution level information and current system state to dynamically determine appropriate application QoS allocations for the running applications. In this paper we have presented new developments in the design of the DQM, together with significant new results. We have expanded the DQM to work with dynamic application periods and included capabilities for raising application levels. We have also introduced dynamic estimate refinement, a technique for dealing with inaccurate application CPU usage estimates, a significant problem for the level raising algorithms. Finally, we presented two level-based applications, and provided results showing these applications running with the DQM.

In developing the DQM, we have encountered several important issues related to the DQM's role as a middleware component. The biggest issue is that unlike OS-based solutions, a user-space middleware component cannot enforce the QoS allocations. This requires that the applications cooperate, using only the resources that they have been allocated. Rogue applications cannot be managed by the DQM, but we have successfully managed applications whose estimates are incorrect using dynamic estimate refinement. A side effect of the lack of enforcement is that the effect of applications whose usage exceeds their estimates is not confined to themselves. OS based solutions simply cause an application whose usage exceeds its estimate to miss a deadline. Without enforce-

ment, applications whose usage exceeds their estimate may cause a different application to miss its deadline. The centralized nature of the DQM allows global resource level decisions to be made any time any application misses a deadline. Once the estimates have been corrected and levels adjusted appropriately, this is less of a problem. A final issue that we have had to deal with is the lack of detailed CPU usage and idle time information. By averaging the information over longer periods of time, we can get reasonable estimates of resources usage, and by building in a small amount of slack into the idle estimates, we have overcome this problem as much as possible.

8 Acknowledgments

Scott Brandt and Gary Nutt were partially supported by NSF grant number IRI-9307619.

9 References

[1] T.Abdelzaher, E. Atkins, and K. Shin, "QoS Negotiation in Real-Time Systems and its Application to Automated Flight Control," *Proceedings of the 3rd IEEE Real-Time Technology and Applications Symposium*, Jun. 1997.

[2] T. Abdelzaher and K. Shin, "End-host Architecture for QoS-Adaptive Communication", *Proceedings of the 4th IEEE Real-Time Technology and Applications Symposium*, Jun. 1998.

[3] S. Brandt, G. Nutt, T. Berk, and M. Humphrey, "Soft Real-Time Application Execution with Dynamic Quality of Service Assurance", *Proceedings of the 6th IEEE/IFIP International Workshop on Quality of Service*, May 1998.

[4] A. Burns, "Scheduling Hard Real-Time Systems: A Review", *Software Engineering Journal*, May 1991.

[5] S. Cen, C. Pu, R. Staehli, C. Cowan, and J. Walpole, "A Distributed Real-Time MPEG Video Audio Player", *Proceedings of the 5th International Workshop on Network and Operating System Support of Digital Audio and Video*, Apr. 1995.

[6] C. Compton and D. Tennenhouse, "Collaborative Load Shedding", *Proceedings of the Workshop on the Role of Real-Time in Multimedia/Interactive Computing Systems*, Nov. 1993.

[7] C. Fan, "Realizing a Soft Real-Time Framework for Supporting Distributed Multimedia Applications", *Proceedings of the 5th IEEE Workshop on the Future Trends of Distributed Computing Systems*, pp. 128-134, Aug. 1995.

[8] W. Feng and J. Liu, "Algorithms for Scheduling Real-Time Tasks with Input Error and End-to-End Deadlines", *IEEE Transactions on Software Engineering*, Vol. 20, No. 2, Feb. 1997.

[9] H. Fujita, T. Nakajima and H. Tezuka, "A Processor Reservation System Supporting Dynamic QoS Control", *Proceedings of the 2nd International Workshop on Real-Time Computing Systems and Applications*, Oct. 1995.

[10] D. Hull, W. Feng, and J. Liu, "Operating System Support for Imprecise Computation", *Proceedings of the AAAI Fall Symposium on Flexible Computation*, Nov. 1996.

[11] M. Humphrey, T. Berk, S. Brandt, G. Nutt, "The DQM Architecture: Middleware for Application-centered QoS Resource Management", *Proceedings of the IEEE Workshop on Middleware for Distributed Real-Time Systems and Services*, pp. 97-104, Dec. 1997.

[12] E. Jensen and C. Locke and H. Tokuda, "A Time-Driven Scheduling Model for Real-Time Operating Systems", *Proceedings of the 6th IEEE Real-Time Systems Symposium*, pp. 112-122, Dec. 1985.

[13] M. Jones, J. Barbera III, and A. Forin, "An Overview of the Rialto Real-Time Architecture", *Proceedings of the 7th ACM SIGOPS European Workshop*, pp. 249-256, Sep. 1996.

[14] M. Jones, D. Rosu, M. Rosu, "CPU Reservations & Time Constraints: Efficient Predictable Scheduling of Independent Activities", *Proceedings of the 16th ACM Symposium on Operating Systems Principles*, Oct. 1997.

[15] K. Kawachiya, M. Ogata, N. Nishio and H. Tokuda' "Evaluation of QoS-Control Servers on Real-Time Mach", *Proceedings of the 5th International Workshop on Network and Operating System Support for Digital Audio and Video*, pp. 123-126, Apr. 1995.

[16] J. Kay and P. Lauder, "A Fair Share Scheduler", *Communications of the ACM*, 31(1):44-55, Jan. 1988.

[17] C. Lee, R. Rajkumar and C. Mercer, "Experience with Processor reservation and Dynamic QoS in Real-Time Mach", *Proceedings of Multimedia Japan*, Mar. 1996.

[18] H. Massalin, and C. Pu, "Fine-Grain Adaptive Scheduling using Feedback", *Computing Systems*, 3(1):139-173, Winter 1990.

[19] C. Mercer, S. Savage and H. Tokuda, "Processor Capacity Reserves: Operating System Support for Multimedia Applications", *Proceedings of the International Conference on Multimedia Computing and Systems*, pp. 90-99, May 1994.

[20] T. Nakajima and H. Tezuka, "A Continuous Media Application Supporting Dynamic QoS Control on Real-Time Mach", *Proceedings of the 2nd ACM International Conference on Multimedia*, pp. 289-297, 1994.

[21] J. Nieh and M. Lam, "The Design, Implementation and Evaluation of SMART: A Scheduler for Multimedia Applications", *Proceedings of the 16th ACM Symposium on Operating Systems Principles*, Oct. 1997.

[22] J. Nieh and M. Lam, "Integrated Processor Scheduling for Multimedia", *Proceedings of the 5th International Workshop on Network and Operating System Support for Digital Audio and Video*, Apr. 1995.

[23] G. Nutt, "Model-Based Virtual Environments for Collaboration", Technical Report CU-CD-799-95, Department of Computer Science, University of Colorado at Boulder, Dec. 1995.

[24] G. Nutt, T. Berk, S. Brandt, M. Humphrey, and S. Siewert, "Resource Management of a Virtual Planning Room", *Proceedings of the 3rd International Workshop on Multimedia Information Systems*, Sep. 1997.

[25] G. Nutt, S. Brandt, A. Griff, S. Siewert, T. Berk, and M. Humphrey, "Dynamically Negotiated Resource Management for Data Intensive Application Suites", *IEEE Transactions on Knowledge and Data Engineering*, to appear.

[26] H. Tokuda and T. Kitayama, "Dynamic QoS Control based on Real-Time Threads", *Proceedings of the 3rd International Workshop on Network and Operating Systems Support for Digital Audio and Video*, Nov. 1993.

Session 9: Keynote Talk

From POSIX Threads to Ada to Java: A Brief History of Runtime Development for Some Real-Time Programming Languages
Ted Baker, *Florida State University*

Abstract: A hidden but critical part of any real-time application is its runtime environment. If the application is coded in a high level language, the runtime environment includes a runtime system to support the programming language. That is likely to be layered over a real-time kernel, or even a full operating system.

Over the past twenty years, there have been increasing governmental and market pressures for these layers to use off-the-shelf components and standard interfaces. The goal has been to enable the more rapid development of real-time applications, with a higher degree of platform independence. These pressures achieved visible results in the Ada language, the POSIX real-time operating system interfaces, and most recently the proposals for a real-time Java standard.

In the roles of standards writers, implementors and users, the members of the POSIX Ada Real-Time project at the Florida State University have explored the problem of making these standard application program interfaces work for real-time systems. This has included implementation of the POSIX real-time extensions, and implementations of Ada runtime systems over both the POSIX and Java virtual machine interfaces. We have found that the degree to which the promises of these standards are kept depends very much on the ability of the real-time application developer to design within the paradigms supported by the standards, and on the quality of the implementations of the standards.

Profile: **TED BAKER** holds a PhD in Computer Science from Cornell University. His published work spans a wide range of topics, from recursive function theory to real-time operating systems and programming languages. In these latter areas, he and his group at FSU produced one of the first validated Ada cross-compilers for embedded systems. In 1991 he participated on the Ada9X Mapping-Revision Team, as Domain Expert for Real-Time and Systems Programming. Dr. Baker drafted key sections of the Ada 95 reference manual on real-time and systems programming, which have since been adopted as international standards for Ada95. His practical work in this area was realized via his FSU team's multi-tasking runtime system for the Gnu NYU Ada 95 Translator (GNAT). This is believed to have been the first validated implementation of Ada 95 tasking for non-embedded systems, and is perhaps the most widely used Ada implementation today. Based on the POSIX threads API, the runtime system has been successfully ported to number of different execution environments, most recently the Java Virtual Machine.

Dr. Baker is also well known for key foundational results in real-time systems, including the Stack Resource Protocol, Agenda-Based scheduling, the Deadline Sporadic Server, and many others. Currently, Dr. Baker's group is developing validation tests for POSIX real-time Ada bindings, with funds provided by the U.S. Defense Information Systems Agency. He is also participating in a group studying real-time extensions for the Java language, and is porting the GNAT Ada runtime to a "bare machine" implementation, based on an Ada rewrite of Real-Time Linux. Dr. Baker also has been active in software standards related to all types of real-time systems, including the Ada95 language standard, and several POSIX standards. He serves as chair for Language Bindings on the IEEE Portable Applications Standards Committee, and is involved in the POSIX and Ada working groups of both the ISO and IEC.

Session 10: Operating Systems and Runtimes

Techniques for Software Thread Integration in Real-Time Embedded Systems

Alexander G. Dean and John Paul Shen

Department of Electrical and Computer Engineering

Carnegie Mellon University

Pittsburgh, PA 15213

adean@ece.cmu.edu   shen@ece.cmu.edu

Abstract

This paper presents how to perform thread integration to provide low-cost concurrency for general-purpose microcontrollers and microprocessors. A post-pass compiler interleaves multiple threads of control at the machine instruction level for concurrent execution on a uniprocessor and provides very fine-grain multithreading without context switching overhead. Such efficient concurrency allows implementation of real-time functions in software rather than dedicated peripheral hardware.

We investigate a set of code transformations which allow systematic integration of a real-time guest thread into a host thread, producing an integrated thread which meets all real-time requirements. The thread integration concept and the associated code transformations have been applied to example functions chosen from three application domains to evaluate the method's feasibility.

1.0 Introduction

Embedded system designers must work within a design space tightly bounded by system requirements such as cost, size, weight, power and development time. They must trade off design costs with recurring costs, both of which vary over time for each application. Any real-time requirements place additional pressure on these constraints by adding hardware or software components dedicated to timely operation. Hardware solutions increase system size, cost, weight and power. Software solutions complicate timing analysis and verification, and are limited in performance by context switch and interrupt service routine response times. However, CPU chip technology and architecture improvements continue to lower the cost of CPU cycles needed to execute software by about 50% every 18 months.

This paper demonstrates how thread integration (first introduced in [4]) can simplify embedded systems by eliminating hardware dedicated to real-time functions and transferring the work to software. Thread integration is a compiler technology which can automatically interleave multiple threads of computation at the machine instruction level and provide implicit multithreading on a generic uniprocessor. This interleaving involves scheduling at the instruction level and eliminates context switch overhead to allow efficient operation on CPUs ranging from 8 to 64 bits.

Three factors make thread integration difficult. First, the control flow behavior of the two threads may be very different and difficult to reconcile. We use a program representation which simplifies transformations needed to reconcile differing control flow structures. Second, manually integrating assembly code is tedious and error prone. A high-level language is not an appropriate source code representation for real-time thread integration due to the coarse time resolution of the statements. Assembly code must be used as it provides cycle-accurate instruction placement and therefore allows precise scheduling of real-time events. The compiler we use operates on assembly code and performs data flow analysis and register renaming, removing this burden from the programmer. Finally, the behavior of the host thread over time must be known a priori, but may be impossible to predict, as it is equivalent to the halting problem. Embedded system software tends to be deterministic and straightforward to characterize, as it typically has bounded loop iterations and no recursion.

This paper demonstrates how to integrate threads and shows the benefits and costs for three embedded applications. The ultimate goal of our research is the creation of theory and tools for automatically merging a real-time function thread with a host thread, so that the integrated thread requires no extra task-switching once it has begun, allowing nearly all processor cycles to be dedicated to useful work and dramatically increasing the maximum frequency and temporal accuracy of real-time events. The guest thread can emulate a hardware function, allowing elimination of special circuits added to satisfy real-time requirements. This reduces system cost, weight and size, as well as providing device selection flexibility by reducing hardware requirements. This technology is applicable to a broad range of embedded real-time control applications using low- to high-end microprocessors.

Previous work on task fusion by compiler is limited. [8] presents a technique called interleaving for compile-time task scheduling which identifies a task's idle times and schedules other tasks at those times. It is a coarse grain approach and incurs context-switching penalties for each task switch. [19] extends this work to provide non-intrusive real-time task monitoring. However, as the fragment size decreases, the performance penalty exacted by context switching increases. We have found no work other than ours [4] which eliminates this penalty by merging two threads at the assembly instruction level into a single integrated thread. Previous work in code motion with a PDG ([1], [6], [7], [12], [14], [19]) focuses upon reducing program run time.

2.0 Research Methodology

We examine real-time functions from three hypothetical embedded systems to illustrate the benefits of thread integration. In each system, a software function implements a real-time function using busy-waiting code for event scheduling. Thread integration replaces this padding code with instructions from the host function to improve runtime efficiency. The resulting code is then analyzed to determine cycle count and code size. Simulation verifies the correct functioning of the integrated threads.

2.1 Sample Applications

The first application is a small portable computing device such as a hand-held PC (HPC) or portable video game with a high resolution graphic liquid crystal display (LCD). Current HPCs use CPUs with performance of nearly 100 MIPS [16], and future devices will grow faster. Thread integration can use part of this growing CPU capacity to refresh the LCD, eliminating the need for a dedicated LCD controller and its local frame buffer memory if any exists. Thread integration has promise for these markets as it eliminates hardware, cutting system size, cost, weight and time-to-market.

The second application, a digital cellphone integrated into a car, features GSM 06.10 speech compression [5] and uses the CAN 2.0A [2] protocol for communication with other devices within the vehicle. CAN is popular in automotive applications for multiplex communications, reducing the wiring harness size, cost, weight and failure rate while simplifying assembly. Providing a common databus in a vehicle encourages incorporation of features such as hands-free cellphone, navigation aids, entertainment and travel information as well as vehicle customization, opti-

mization, and diagnostics. Thread integration is especially appropriate for the automotive market because of its price sensitivity and size constraints.

The third application, a stand-alone digital cellphone first examined in [4], offers GSM 06.10 speech compression and an I^2C (inter-IC) network [15] for communication with a smart battery. I^2C is popular for embedded systems due to its standardized interface, simplification of hardware, software and printed circuit board design, small device packages, and the wide variety of ICs available. Thread integration can support this application by reducing system hardware cost and increasing software efficiency.

2.2 The Pedigree Compilation Tool

The Pedigree tool suite [12] [13] is being extended to support thread integration. Pedigree is a retargetable, post-pass, program dependence graph-based code transformation and evaluation environment. The Pedigree compiler accepts assembly language programs and uses interprocedural information, profiling information, machine and instruction set architecture descriptions, and scheduling hints to produce optimized code, automatically parallelized optimized code, and provide program visualization information and statistics. Pedigree also contains a functional timing simulator which can be used to evaluate performance.

The Pedigree compiler uses the program dependence graph (PDG) [6], a representation which explicitly identifies control and data dependences. The program's control structure is represented hierarchically, with summary dataflow information added to describe subgraphs. This hierarchical data representation allows efficient code motion and transformations.

The Pedigree tool suite is post-pass; it accepts compiled assembly code as input. It is currently targeted for DEC's Alpha instruction set architecture (ISA), which is a clean 64 bit load-store RISC architecture. The Alpha ISA was chosen for Pedigree for its simplicity and straightforward simulation. Although Alpha processors are not representative of most embedded applications, the Alpha ISA can serve as an expedient research vehicle for illustrating the concept of thread integration for real-time embedded systems. In the future we plan to retarget Pedigree to an ISA more representative of the broad range of embedded controllers (e.g. MIPS, Atmel AVR, Microchip PIC).

3.0 Integration of Real-time Threads

The goal of thread integration (i.e. integrating a guest thread into an existing host thread) is to produce a program with integrated real-time guest thread events which execute at the proper time. In existing systems, this event scheduling can be implemented through busy waiting (the CPU polls inputs to detect event occurrence and executes nops to pass time), or through interrupt-driven context switching (a timer or other signal source triggers execution of the real-time code). Thread integration replaces the filler instructions of the busy-wait version with instructions from the host function, enabling more efficient program execution.

Because the integrated thread has real-time constraints, it is assumed to be uninterruptable. This lack of preemption increases the CPU's maximum interrupt response latency by the worst-case duration of the integrated function. Any other real-time functions requiring a response faster than this must be implemented in hardware. Future work will loosen this constraint. Host and guest function selection are discussed further in [4].

3.1 Program Representation and the PDG

This paper demonstrates compiler-assisted thread integration using the PDG representation of a program, which stores program control and data dependence information concisely and hierarchically, enabling efficient code analysis and motion.

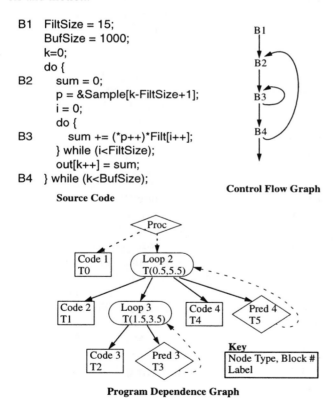

Source Code

Control Flow Graph

Program Dependence Graph

FIGURE 1. Host source code, control flow graph and program dependence graph.

The graph *PDG(N, E)* [6], as extended in [14], contains a control dependence subgraph and a data dependence subgraph. Control nodes include *Code*, *Predicate*, *Group* and *Call* nodes. A predicate node is connected to its children with labeled control edges (e.g. True, False, Any) which describe under which conditions each child is executed. A *Group* node can be further classified as *Multipred* (a group of nodes with multiple immediate control dependences), *Loop*, and *IrrLoop* (an irreducible loop has multiple entry points). A *Proc* node is the root of a PDG and represents a procedure. The nodes are labeled according to the scheme presented in [14]. Figure 1 presents a code fragment with its control flow and program dependence graphs, which are used to illustrate code motion and thread integration. Edges emanating from a single node are ordered from left to right to capture the original lexical order of the code. This enables reconstruction of the CFG by a left-to-right preorder traversal of the PDG. In addition, executing a program visits the PDG in this left-to-right preorder traversal, entering subgraphs rooted by satisfied predicates while repeating loop subgraphs.

The PDG has been used to implement code optimizations which reduce the average execution time of programs on uniprocessors and multiprocessors [6] [7] [1]. This research effort has resulted in a group of code motion, deletion and creation transformations which can be leveraged for thread integration.

3.2 Integration Procedure

Thread integration works by first merging the guest thread into the host thread's PDG by placing it to the right of the host thread, then by moving guest thread nodes towards the left and possibly into the host PDG to meet real-time requirements. The host PDG's hierarchical representation of control and data dependences allows efficient code motion. The application of the various code motions places guest nodes at appropriate locations within the host PDG in order to ensure on-time execution of the guest nodes. This process is guided by timing annotations in the PDG. As the vast majority of program execution is spent in loops, most guest real-time events will need to be executed inside a host loop. Thread integration transforms loops to enable accurate guest node placement for timely execution while allowing trade-offs between execution efficiency and program memory requirements. These transformations also enable efficient integration of guest loops with host loops. In cases requiring extreme timing accuracy, guest code can be scheduled with single cycle accuracy by moving individual host instructions or adding nops for padding.

Thread integration requires several steps before code motion can be performed. First, a PDG is constructed for the host thread, annotated with execution time predictions and processed to normalize timing behavior. The guest thread's PDG is then constructed and processed so each node contains at most one real-time instruction. Next, the guest PDG is appended to the right side of the host PDG as a sub PDG. The initial placement of the entire guest sub PDG to the right of the host PDG effectively implies that the entire guest thread is to be executed after the execution of the host thread. Starting with this initial merging of the two PDG's (or the degenerate integration), code motion is then performed to move each guest node to the left into or between the host nodes according to timing, control dependence and data dependence constraints. This is the actual "integration" process. After the integration process, nodes from the host and guest threads are interleaved in an integrated PDG that meets the real-time execution requirements of the guest thread. Implicit multithreading is achieved by overlapping the execution of the two threads.

For this discussion of code motion, *Node* refers to a generic node, *Host* to a node from the host procedure, *Guest* to a node from the guest procedure, *Code* to a code node, *Proc* to a procedure node, *Pred* to a predicate node, and *Loop* to a loop node.

The Pedigree tool generates a PDG for the host thread annotated with execution time information which is used to guide the placement of real-time guest code. Each host node contains a prediction of its beginning execution time $T_{beg}(Host)$ measured in cycles. This time is derived through path analysis, although profiling can be used. Each loop is annotated with the timing information $[T_{beg}(Host), T_{end}(Host) : T_{iter}(Host)]$. Characteristics of the system's software and hardware can complicate program execution time prediction [10].

- Path analysis determines the timing behavior of the host and guest code. The path analysis requires that the threads have bounded loop iterations and no recursive or dynamic function calls [17]. Much embedded software (including the examples used in this paper) meets these criteria.

- Variations in the use of system resources can affect execution time. Caches, pipelines, superscalar instruction dispatch behavior, virtual memory and variable latency instructions will increase the variability of system performance with different data sets. Embedded real-time systems often lack these features because of cost constraints. In the applications for this paper we assume these features are not used (e.g. no virtual memory), or are configured to operate predictably (locked caches or fast on-chip memory used).

We assume all loop iteration counts are bounded, and differences in execution time for conditionally executed code are eliminated through code motion into or out of predicates as well as padding with nops. The PDG of the guest procedure is constructed and processed to separate each node into a series of nodes with at most one real-time event in each. Nodes in the guest procedure containing operations with real-time constraints are marked with a begin time T_{beg} and the maximum jitter tolerance T_{tol}. The begin time can be derived directly from system requirements, or through some form of a time or task graph [18] [11] [8].

```
B1   outport(ADCtl, ENABLE);
     n = 0;
     do {
B2       Buf[n] = inport(ADData);
         n++;
     } while (n<NumSamples);
```
Guest Source Code

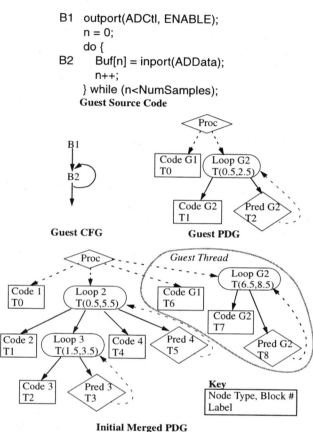

FIGURE 2. Guest code and the initial merged PDG with the host PDG from Figure 1.

An event is called a looping event if it is located within a loop in the guest procedure. Otherwise it is a single event. An event can be described by its timing characteristics. It must be executed at T_{ev} with a tolerance of T_{tol}. A looping event of loop node *Loop*, described by $[T_{beg}(Loop), T_{end}(Loop) : T_{iter}(Loop), T_{comp}(Loop)]$ begins execution at time $T_{beg}(Loop)$, and repeats execution every $T_{iter}(Loop)$ until the last iteration ends at $T_{end}(Loop)$. Each iteration requires $T_{comp}(Loop)$ of computation time, the remainder is idle time.

Figure 2 illustrates how the two graphs are merged into a single PDG by adding the children (and their subgraphs) of the guest PDG after (to the right of) all other children of the host *Proc* node. The merged PDG now represents a procedure in which the host operations are first executed followed by the execution of the guest operations.

During the actual thread integration, each guest node is processed, beginning with the left-most guest child of the *Proc* node. If the node and its subgraph contain no real-time events, they are moved left as far as possible in the PDG by reordering the edges from the *Proc* node. If the node and its subgraph contain a real-time event, the event must be moved to the location or locations which will be executing at the event's desired time. Events which require accurate timing may need to be inserted in a subgraph to improve scheduling options. This subgraph insertion depends upon its control structure; the recursive algorithm of Figure 3 must be used to move the guest nodes.

3.3 Integration of Single Events

Figure 3 shows concepts in the body of the recursive algorithm for integration of single events. The first step for integrating a guest event is finding which host PDG node *Host* will be executing when guest node *Guest*'s event must occur (at $T_{ev}(Guest)$). To begin the integration process, the root node *Proc* is chosen as the parent host node *Par*. Each child of *Par* is inspected to identify the node *Host* which minimizes the error time $T_{err}(Host)$.

$$T_{err}(Host, Guest) \equiv |T_{beg}(Host) - T_{ev}(Guest)|$$

a. If the error time is acceptable, i.e. $|T_{err}(Host, Guest)| <= T_{tol}$, then node *Guest* is moved to execute immediately before *Host*.

If the error time is not acceptable, i.e. $|T_{err}(Host, Guest)| > T_{tol}$, then node *Host* must be entered to find a position in the subgraph with execution time closer to T_{ev}. This traversal depends upon the type of the node *Host*.

b. If *Host* is a code node *Code*, it is split into two nodes $Code_1$ and $Code_2$ at some point between $T_{ev} - T_{tol}$ and $T_{ev} + T_{tol}$. The algorithm is invoked again, with the same parent node *Par*. In that iteration, *Guest* will be moved to between $Code_1$ and $Code_2$.

c. If *Host* is a predicate node *Pred*, the algorithm is invoked repeatedly with *Pred* as the parent *Par* once for each possible value *V* of labels on control edges emanating from *Pred*.

d. If *Host* is a loop node *Loop* iterating from *[1..N]*, it is split into two loops $Loop_B$ and $Loop_E$ iterating from *[1..n]* and *[n+1..N]*.

$$n = round\left(\frac{T_{ev} - T_{beg}(Loop)}{T_{iter}(Loop)}\right)$$

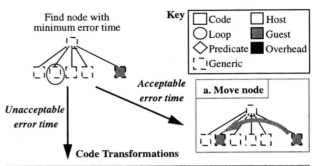

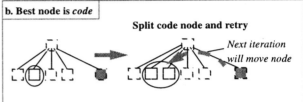

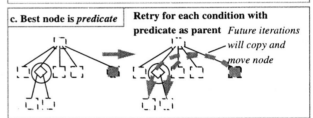

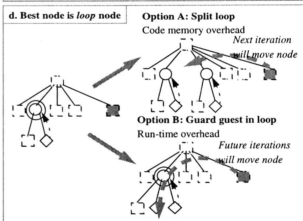

FIGURE 3. Summary of single event integration.

If $T_{err}(Loop_E) > T_{tol}$, one iteration is peeled from the beginning of $Loop_E$ to form a central node $Host_C$ which contains the loop body. The algorithm is invoked again with the same parent node *Par*, and *Guest* will then be inserted into $Host_C$.

An alternative is to insert the guest node guarded by a predicate node. The predicate node activates the guest when a specific loop iteration is reached.

Both of these techniques increase code size. Loop splitting does not directly incur a run-time performance penalty, while guarding the guest does. Since this overhead grows more significant as the loop body size decreases, shorter loops should use splitting while longer loops should use guarded execution.

After performing any code insertion, the resulting program must be rescheduled from the insertion point onward and the beginning execution time predictions updated accordingly.

3.4 Integration of Looping Events

Integrating looping events requires extending the algorithm presented above to allow transformation of the looping event in $Loop_G$ to match the structure of the host procedure. This involves determining how many iterations of the looping event need to be executed within the node $Host$, which executes from $T_{beg}(Host)$ to $T_{end}(Host)$. If $Host$ is not a loop, iterations from $Loop_G$ are peeled off, one at a time, and inserted into $Host$ using single event integration. If $Host$ is a loop $Loop_H$, then it must be combined with $Loop_G$ taking into account the different iteration counts and times for each loop. The number of iterations for both loops ($I(Loop_H)$, $I(Loop_G)$) need not be known at integration time. There may be more than one real-time event $Guest_i$ in the guest loop body $Loop_G$. To integrate two loops, we convert them to top-test form, copy and integrate their bodies and adjust the loop control tests. The integrated loop overlaps execution of as many iterations as possible, while the original guest and host loops perform any remaining work. Figure 4 presents the key concepts, with sections a and b described below. This form of loop integration with unrolling supports variable iteration counts if the unrolled loop tests a counter which can determine whether at least n (the degree of unrolling) more iterations remain. Otherwise each unrolled body must be guarded with a predicate, and timing analysis is further complicated.

Integrating two loops involves fusing the two bodies together and adjusting the execution time per iteration to be an integer multiple of the looping guest event's period. If the guest's idle time is longer than a host iteration, the two loops can simply be fused without any unrolling, using nop padding to fill in remaining idle time. This approach becomes very inefficient as the iteration period mismatch grows. Loop unrolling enables the CPU to perform useful work in place of the busy waiting.

Either the host or guest loop may need to be unrolled, depending upon the iteration time relationship. If the guest must be executed more frequently, it is copied and inserted into the host. Otherwise the guest may have sufficient idle time to allow execution of more than one host iteration, allowing greater efficiency.

a. If $T_{iter}(Loop_G) - T_{comp}(Loop_G) < T_{iter}(Loop_H)$ the guest loop body must be executed more than once per host loop iteration. The guest loop is unrolled to contain n_i guest loop bodies, iterating until the value n stops increasing.

$$ n_i = \left\lceil \frac{T_{iter}(Loop_H) + n_{i-1} \cdot T_{comp}(Loop_G)}{T_{iter}(Loop_G)} \right\rceil $$

This takes into account the additional computation time added by each unrolled body of $Loop_G$. The unrolled guest loop is fused with the host loop body. The result is then padded with nop instructions to bring the execution time per loop iteration to $n*T_{iter}(Loop_G)$.

b. If $T_{iter}(Loop_G) - T_{comp}(Loop_G) > T_{iter}(Loop_H)$ the guest loop body must be executed less than once per host loop iteration, which can be achieved in two ways. The host loop can be unrolled, or execution of the guest can be guarded with a predicate. The first method emphasizes execution efficiency at the expense of more code memory, while the second does the opposite and becomes more attractive for larger host loop bodies.

b1. In the first method, the host loop is unrolled to contain n host loop bodies and is fused with the guest loop body.

$$ n = \left\lfloor \frac{T_{iter}(Loop_G) - T_{comp}(Loop_G)}{T_{iter}(Loop_H)} \right\rfloor $$

b2. The second method uses a predicate node in conjunction with a counter variable to ensure the guest node is executed once every n host loop iterations.

Instructions to initialize the guard counter are inserted before the host loop initialization code. A guard predicate $Pred_{Gi}$ and code $Code_{Gi}$ node pair are added to the host loop body for each guest $Guest_i$ in the guest loop body. A code node $Code_{Ginc}$ to increment the guard counter is also added to the host loop body. The time per iteration for the new host loop is calculated:

$$ T_{iter}(Loop_{Hnew}) = T_{iter}(Loop_H) + \sum_{\forall i} T_{comp}(Code_{Gi}) + T_{comp}(Code_{Ginc}) $$

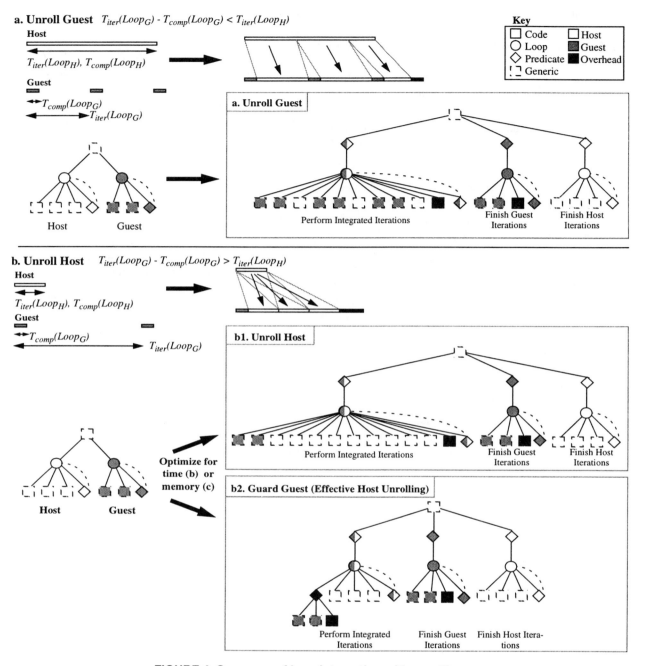

FIGURE 4. Summary of loop integration with unrolling.

The period of the guard counter is n host loop iterations; the counter ranges from 0 to $n-1$.

$$n = \left\lfloor \frac{T_{iter}(Loop_G) - T_{comp}(Loop_G)}{T_{iter}(Loop_{Hnew})} \right\rfloor$$

The delay $I_{del}(Guest_i)$ is measured in host loop iterations from the beginning of the new host loop's first iteration to the guest event $Guest_i$, taking into account the execution of any previous guests $Guest_j$ in this iteration of this guest loop body.

$$I_{del}(Guest_i) = \frac{(T_{ev}(Guest_i) - T_{sta}(Loop_{Hnew}))}{T_{iter}(Loop_{Hnew})} - \frac{\sum_{j=0}^{i-1} T_{comp}(Guest_j)}{T_{iter}(Loop_{Hnew})}$$

These delays determine the placement of the guard predicates (and hence guest nodes) within the new host body, as well as the value for which the predicates check. The predicate for $Guest_i$ is set to match the proper host loop iteration counter value and is placed in the correct location of the loop body by calling *Integrate()*.

Finally, the last guest added to the host loop body is padded with nops lasting T_{pad}. This padding takes into account the computation time of each guest and the time to reset the guard counter variable.

$$T_{pad} = T_{iter}(Guest) - (n \cdot T_{iter}(Loop_{Hnew})) -$$
$$\sum_{\forall i} T_{comp}(Guest_i) - T_{comp}(Code_{Greset})$$

The loop control tests for the integrated loop are formed as the logical product of the tests of both host and guest loops. Unrolling a loop requires changing its counter variable target value to match *n-1* iterations earlier. Any remaining iterations are performed by the original loops, located after the integrated loop. The guest loop is padded and placed immediately after the integrated loop to allow satisfaction of real-time requirements.

4.0 Experimental Results

Three hypothetical applications have been processed to implement real-time guest functions in software to demonstrate benefits of thread integration. This eliminates dedicated hardware in each application to reduce system cost, size and weight. Table 1 summarizes the cost of implementing each application's real-time function in software. The discrete, or non-integrated, software implementation (baseline) in each case uses busy waiting to meet guest function timing requirements, while thread integration increases the software implementation efficiency, reducing the run time at the expense of increased code memory.

The "Run Time Change" columns show how much time is needed to perform the guest's instructions compared with a busy-wait guest implementation. An integrated implementation overlaps host and guest execution and so reduces the time difference below 100%. For example, adding software LCD refresh support to the handheld computer using a discrete busy-wait version requires 2984 cycles per display row. Integrating the LCD refresh function with a graphics line drawing routine reduces the refresh cost to 1673 cycles per display row; now 45% of the refresh work is performed during line drawing. The "Code Memory Change" columns show how much code memory is needed to add the guest function. Thread inte-

gration increases code size (e.g., by splitting or unrolling loops), resulting in significant code expansion. Note that typically only one or two functions will need to be integrated, so the 2x to 6x memory increase is only incurred for the code of those functions, and hence is minor. For example, the handheld cellphone's 1148 byte increase is small in comparison with the 60 kilobytes needed for the voice codec functions.

TABLE 1. Costs of Implementing guest functions in software, without and with thread integration.

System	Discrete		Integrated	
	Run Time Change	Code Memory Change	Run Time Change	Code Memory Change
Handheld Computer	+100% of Guest	+336 bytes	+55.0% of Guest	+1796 bytes
Vehicle Cellphone	+100%	+498	+80.9%	+2460
Handheld Cellphone	+100%	+280	+32.9%	+1148

4.1 Handheld Computer

The first application is a small portable computing device such as a hand-held PC (HPC) or portable video game with a high resolution graphic liquid crystal display (LCD). Current HPCs use CPUs with performance of nearly 100 MIPS [16], and future devices will grow faster. Thread integration uses part of this growing CPU capacity to refresh the LCD, eliminating the need for a dedicated LCD controller and its local frame buffer memory. A line drawing routine is integrated with the LCD row refresh function, improving system efficiency. Thread integration has promise for these markets as it eliminates hardware, cutting system size, cost, weight and time-to-market.

Figure 5 shows the original system hardware architecture. The CPU communicates with an LCD controller (LCDC) [9], which generates control and data signals for the LCD based upon data stored in the frame buffer.

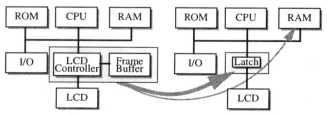

Hardware LCD Refresh   **Software LCD Refresh**

FIGURE 5. Handheld computer hardware components.

A high resolution monochrome LCD (640 by 480 pixels, 1 bit per pixel) displays information and must be refreshed 70 times each second to avoid flickering. Column pixel data is loaded serially into a shift register and then latched every 59.5 μs, driving an entire row simultaneously.

The data and control signals are generated by dedicated LCD controller which requires its own memory or else arbitrated access to the CPU's memory. Using this dedicated hardware solution increases chip count, size and weight, which are typically at a premium in this type of device. Some microcontroller makers address this problem by integrating the LCD controller with the microcontroller. The main disadvantages of such hardware integration are that it limits the designer's options in selecting a microcontroller and may increase device cost.

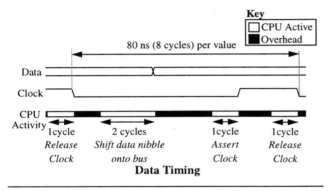

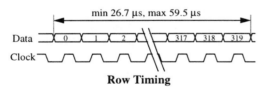

FIGURE 6. LCD refresh timing and CPU activity.

It is possible to generate the LCD control signals in software. A periodic interrupt every 59.5 μs calls a function which shifts a row of data out and clocks the shift registers. The primary bottleneck of this scheme is the low maximum clock speed for common LCD driver shift registers, which ranges from 4 to 12 MHz. As seen in Figure 6, this bottleneck forces a 100 MIPS CPU to spend nearly half of its time during LCD refresh waiting for the shift register, in the form of one and two nop busy waits. Every 59.5 μs, the CPU spends 1280 of its 2984 LCD refresh cycles as busy waits. As a result, the 100 MIPS CPU has 50 MIPS remaining for applications, with 29 MIPS used for the display refresh and 21 MIPS used for busy waits. Thread integration enables the CPU to use those wasted cycles to perform useful work. In this example a fast line drawing routine [3] is integrated with the LCD refresh thread to take advantage of the free time. Figure 7 shows

remaining CPU capacity as a function of line-drawing activity; refreshing the LCD in software requires 50% of the processor's time. The integrated software solution uses

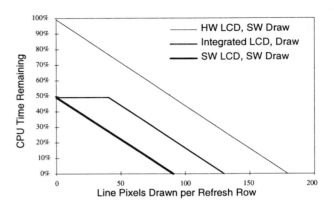

FIGURE 7. CPU capacity vs. line drawing activity.

the idle time in the refresh function to plot up to 40 pixels per display refresh row, freeing up to 21% of the CPU's capacity for other functions. Table 2 presents information on the discrete and integrated threads.

TABLE 2. Handheld computer thread statistics.

Thread	Cycle Count	Idle Cycle Count	Size in Bytes
DrawLine (40 pixels long)	1390	0	616
LCDRow	2984	1280	336
Discrete DrawLine (40 pixels) and LCDRow	4374	1280	952
Integrated DrawLine (40 pixels) and LCDRow	3063	0	2412

Thread integration allows elimination of the LCD controller and its frame buffer. The cost for this integration is 1580 bytes of program memory, 38,400 bytes of data memory for the new frame buffer and 29 MIPS of processor throughput. Thread integration uses nearly all of the idle cycles in LCDRow to perform useful work, and mitigates about half of the performance impact of implementing LCD refresh in software.

4.2 Vehicle Cellphone with External Network

The two digital cellphone examples use GSM 06.10 lossy speech compression [5] integrated with a communication protocol. These applications have tight cost, size, weight and power constraints yet benefit from protocol inclusion. Thread integration is used to eliminate network interface hardware by performing such functions efficiently in software. Both examples integrate a message transmission function into a GSM function which is called once per 20 ms frame; this introduces a message transmission delay of up to 20 ms, which is acceptable for many applications. Message reception is asynchronous and is not integrated; instead a discrete interrupt service routine is used.

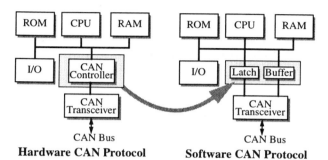

FIGURE 8. Vehicle cellphone hardware components.

This example features a cellphone embedded into a vehicle. With its CAN interface, the phone can signal and react to events in the vehicle, such as muting the stereo during phone calls and automatically calling emergency service dispatchers upon airbag deployment. As the automotive application domain is very price-sensitive, the CPU speed is chosen to be 33 MHz for a 72% load from speech compression. Figure 8 shows a block diagram of the phone's digital architecture for the two network implementations.

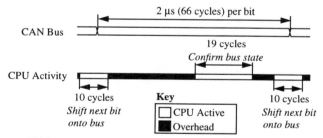

FIGURE 9. CAN message timing and CPU activity.

CAN 2.0A [2] is a robust multimaster bus designed for real-time communication with short messages (up to eight bytes). Transmitters perform bitwise arbitration on unique 11 bit message identifiers to gain access to the bus. During message transmission, the sending node monitors the bus for errors. At the end of the message frame (up to 131 bits), all nodes on the bus assert an acknowledgment flag. Figure 9 shows the timing of operations within each bit cell for this application when using a 33 MHz CPU and 500 kbps

CAN bus. The CAN code requires only 29 cycles of work per 66 cycle bit time, so the CPU utilization of a discrete, busy-wait version is only 44% during message transmission.

Integrating the CAN function with a GSM function (Reflection_Coefficients) allows the CPU to reclaim some of these idle cycles. Figure 10 presents the CPU capacity remaining after message transmission and GSM compression.

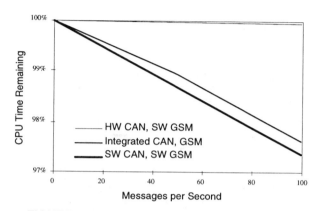

FIGURE 10. CPU capacity vs. message activity.

Thread integration replaces 19% of the idle cycles with useful work. As summarized in table 3, an additional 2062 bytes of program memory are needed for the integrated version as compared with the discrete. Thread integration enables system designers to eliminate a dedicated CAN protocol controller chip, reducing system size, weight and cost.

TABLE 3. Vehicle cellphone thread statistics.

Thread	Cycle Count	Idle Cycle Count	Size in Bytes
Reflection_Coefficients	6344	0	1264
CAN	8674	4847	498
Discrete Reflection_ Coefficients and CAN	14990	4847	1762
Integrated Reflection_ Coefficients and CAN	14436	0	3824

4.3 Cellphone with Internal Network

This handheld cellphone application was presented in detail in [4] and is revisited here for comparison with the other applications. The cellphone communicates with its smart battery using the I^2C protocol, a 100 kbps multimas-

331

ter bus popular for communication within small embedded devices. The message transmission function (I2C) is integrated with an autocorrelation function (Fast_Autocorrelation). I2C implements a subset of the protocol, being limited to sending one byte messages (called Quick Commands in the SMBus extension to I²C) in a system with only one master and regular speed peripherals. The CPU runs at 66 MHz; voice compression requires 30% of the CPU's cycles. The remaining capacity might be used for advanced features such as voice recognition, soft modem/fax, image compression/decompression, and encryption.

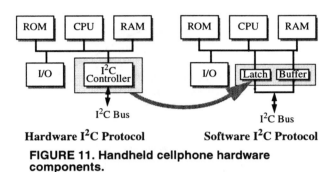

Hardware I²C Protocol　　**Software I²C Protocol**

FIGURE 11. Handheld cellphone hardware components.

Figure 11 shows the two hardware architectures which support the hardware and software implementations of I²C. The hardware I²C version contains a dedicated bus controller, while the software version reduces system hardware.

TABLE 4. Statistics for original and integrated threads

Thread	Cycle Count	Idle Cycle Count	Size in Bytes
Fast_Autocorrelation	25768	0	268
I2C	6612	6404	280
Discrete Fast_Autocorrelation and I2C	32380	6404	548
Integrated Fast_Autocorrelation and I2C	27943	0	1416

Table 4 summarizes characteristics of the two software implementations while Figure 12 plots CPU time required for I²C message transmission based on message rate. The discrete software message transmission function presents a small load for the high-performance CPU (chosen to support the advanced features mentioned previously), but it is reduced further through thread integration. The integrated version supports rates of up to 50 messages per second and is limited by the call frequency of its host function Fast_Autocorrelation. At higher message rates the surplus

messages are transmitted by the less efficient discrete I2C function, which is beyond the knee in the plot.

Integration improves the run time efficiency of the discrete functions but expands the code memory requirement for the two functions from 548 to 1416 bytes. This integration fills the idle time with code from Fast_Autocorrelation efficiently enough to mask 67% of the I²C message transmission time.

In this example, thread integration allows system designers to eliminate a dedicated I²C controller or increase the efficiency of a software implementation at the price of slightly more program memory.

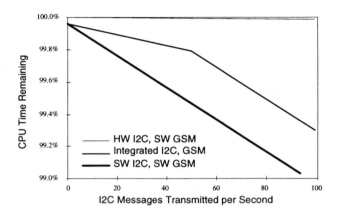

FIGURE 12. CPU time vs. message activity.

5.0 Conclusions and Future Work

In this paper we present techniques for integrating software threads to replace dedicated real-time hardware in embedded systems as well as overlapping the execution of multiple threads to increase overall performance. These techniques can be automated in a compilation tool. We examine the method's feasibility by integrating example real-time threads in several hypothetical embedded systems.

These examples demonstrate the potential savings of hardware components in integrated software implementations. Thread integration allows the system designer to implement new real-time functions in software, speeding time to market and reducing development costs. Moving functions into software enables more of the system cost to match the falling cost of CPU throughput.

We are in the process of adding thread integration techniques to the Pedigree compiler to automate thread integration. We plan to retarget Pedigree to support an ISA more representative of embedded systems. We will extend thread integration to efficiently handle dynamic events which cannot tolerate long latencies.

Acknowledgments

This work was funded by a grant from United Technologies Research Center, East Hartford, CT, 06108, and in part by ONR (N00014-96-1-0347).

References

[1] V.H. Allan, J. Janardhan, R.M. Lee and M. Srinivas, "Enhanced Region Scheduling on a Program Dependence Graph", *Proceedings of the 25th International Symposium and Workshop on Microarchitecture (MICRO-25)*, Portland, OR, December 1-4, 1992.

[2] Robert Bosch GmbH, CAN Specification, Version 2.0.

[3] J.E. Bresenham, "Algorithm for Computer Control of a Digital Plotter", *IBM Systems Journal*, 4(1), 1965, pp. 25-30.

[4] Alexander G. Dean and John Paul Shen, "Hardware to Software Migration with Real-Time Thread Integration", *Proceedings of the 24th EUROMICRO Conference*, Västerås, Sweden, August 25-27, 1998, pp. 243-252.

[5] Jutta Degener, "Digital Speech Compression", *Dr. Dobbs Journal*, December 1994, http://www.ddj.com/ddj/1994/1994_12/degener.htm, http://kbs.cs.tu-berlin.de/~jutta/toast.html.

[6] Jeanne Ferrante, Karl J. Ottenstein and Joe D. Warren, "The Program Dependence Graph and Its Use in Optimization", *ACM Transactions on Programming Languages*, 9(3), July 1987, pp. 319-349.

[7] Rajiv Gupta and Mary Lou Soffa, "Region Scheduling", *Proceedings of the Second International Conference on Supercomputing*, 1987, pp. 141-148.

[8] Rajiv Gupta and Madalene Spezialetti, "Busy-Idle Profiles and Compact Task Graphs: Compile-time Support for Interleaved and Overlapped Scheduling of Real-Time Tasks", *15th IEEE Real Time Systems Symposium*, 1994, pp. 86-96.

[9] Hitachi, HD61830/HD61830B LCDC (LCD Timing Controller) Data Sheet.

[10] Sharad Malik, Margaret Martonosi and Yau-Tsun Steven Li, "Static Timing Analysis of Embedded Software", *ACM Design Automation Conference*, June 1997.

[11] D. Neihaus, "Program Representation and Translation for Predictable Real-Time Systems", *Proceedings of the 12th IEEE Real-Time Systems Symposium*, December 1991, pp. 53-63.

[12] Chris J. Newburn, Derek B. Noonburg and John P. Shen, "A PDG-Based Tool and Its Use in Analyzing Program Control Dependences", *International Conference on Parallel Architectures and Compilation Techniques,* 1994.

[13] Chris J. Newburn, "Pedigree Documentation", Technical Report, CMµART-97-03, Carnegie Mellon Microarchitecture Research Team, Electrical and Computer Engineering Department, Carnegie Mellon University, November 1997.

[14] Chris J. Newburn, "Exploiting Multi-Grained Parallelism for Multiple-Instruction Stream Architectures", Ph.D. Thesis, CMµART-97-04, Electrical and Computer Engineering Department, Carnegie Mellon University, November 1997

[15] Philips Semiconductors, "The I^2C-bus and how to use it (including specifications)", 1995.

[16] Philips Semiconductors, "Optimized MIPS RISC-based Two-ChipPIC Powers Pen-Based, Pocket-Sized Personal Companion Devices", Press release, January 26, 1998

[17] P. Puschner and C. Koza, "Calculating the maximum execution time of real-time programs", *The Journal of Real-Time Systems*, 1(2), September 1989, pp. 160-176.

[18] K. Ramamritham, "Allocating and Scheduling Complex Periodic Tasks", *Proceedings of the 10th International Conference on Distributed Computing Systems*, 1990, pp. 108-115.

[19] Madalene Spezialetti and Rajiv Gupta, "Timed Perturbation Analysis: An Approach for Non-Intrusive Monitoring of Real-Time Computations", *ACM SIGPLAN Workshop on Language, Compiler, and Tool Support for Real-Time Systems*, Orlando, Florida, June 1994

A Worst Case Timing Analysis Technique for Multiple-Issue Machines*

Sung-Soo Lim
Dept. of Computer Engineering
Seoul National University
Seoul, Korea, 151-742

Jung Hee Han
Dept. of Electrical Engineering and Computer Science
University of Michigan, 1301 Beal Ave.
Ann Arbor, MI 48109-2122

Jihong Kim[†]
Dept. of Computer Science
Seoul National University
Seoul, Korea, 151-742

Sang Lyul Min
Dept. of Computer Engineering
Seoul National University
Seoul, Korea, 151-742

Abstract

We propose a worst case timing analysis technique for in-order, multiple-issue machines. In the proposed technique, timing information for each program construct is represented by a directed acyclic graph (DAG) that shows dependences among instructions in the program construct. From this information, we derive for each pair of instructions the distance bounds between their issue times. Using these distance bounds, we identify the sets of instructions that can be issued at the same time. Deciding such instructions is an essential task in reasoning about the timing behavior of multiple-issue machines. In order to reduce the complexity of analysis, the distance bounds are progressively refined through a hierarchical analysis over the program syntax tree in a bottom-up fashion. Our experimental results show that the proposed technique can predict the worst case execution times for in-order, multiple-issue machines as accurately as ones for simpler RISC processors.

1. Introduction

In building a real-time system, the worst case execution times (WCETs) of tasks in the system should be predicted in advance since they are required in schedulability analysis for the system. Results of the WCET prediction should be both *safe* (i.e., the predicted WCET should not be smaller than the real WCET) and *accurate* (i.e., the difference between the predicted WCET and the real WCET should be small). Unsafe prediction causes unexpected deadline misses of tasks that may result in catastrophic consequences. On the other hand, inaccurate prediction leads to a pessimistic schedulability analysis that results in underutilization of system resources.

To obtain accurate prediction for modern high-performance processors, the timing effect of advanced architectural features should be taken into account. For example, several groups including Zhang *et al.*[15], Lim *et al.*[11], Li *et al.*[10], and Healy *et al.*[4] had investigated the prediction techniques for pipelined processors. However, most of existing techniques assume that processors can issue at most one instruction at each cycle, thus cannot produce accurate analysis results for modern multiple-issue machines such as superscalar processors.

In this paper, we propose a worst case timing prediction technique which is applicable to multiple-issue machines. In reasoning about the timing behavior of multiple-issue machines, it is essential to identify the instructions that can be issued at the same time. In the proposed technique, the timing information for each program construct is represented by a directed acyclic graph called an instruction dependence graph (IDG). The IDG shows dependences among instructions in a program. From the IDG, the distance bounds between the issue times of every pair of instructions are derived. Using these distance bounds, we can identify the sets of instructions that can be issued simultaneously. Deriving the distance bounds and identifying simultaneously-issued instructions are two key steps in predicting the WCET of a program on multiple-issue machines.

To reduce the complexity of analysis, our approach is based on an existing hierarchical timing analysis framework called the extended timing schema (ETS) [11]. In this framework, the distance bounds are progressively refined

---

*This work was supported in part by KOSEF under Grant 97-01-02-05-01-3.

[†]Jihong Kim was supported in part by Equipment Award for New Faculty from the College of Natural Sciences, Seoul National University.

over the program syntax tree in a bottom-up fashion. As the distance bounds of surrounding blocks are known during the hierarchical refinements, some adjacent instructions can be merged into a single node of the IDG if they have a constant distance. This merging step reduces the number of nodes maintained by the IDG, thus reducing the complexity of analysis.

The proposed technique is described and validated using a simple in-order, multiple-issue machine model. Since the primary purpose of the work described in this paper is to understand whether the multiple-issue feature can be accurately analyzed to predict the WCETs of programs, we significantly simplify a machine model except for the multiple-issue capability. (This model is described in detail in Section 3.) For the validation purpose, we build a timing tool based on the proposed technique using the multiple-issue machine model, and compare the WCET analysis results from the tool with measurements obtained using simulation. The results show that our technique can predict the WCETs for in-order, multiple-issue machines as accurately as ones for simple RISC processors based on the similar hierarchical technique [11].

The rest of this paper is organized as follows. In Section 2, we explain the ETS that forms the basis of the technique proposed in this paper. In Section 3, we describe our multiple-issue machine model used in this paper. An IDG is formally defined as well in this section. Section 4 presents the key algorithms to derive the distance bounds and to identify the instructions that can be issued simultaneously. In Section 5, we explain how to augment the original ETS framework for the multiple-issue machine model using the distance bounds computed. Experimental results follow in Section 6, and we conclude with future works in Section 7.

2. Extended Timing Schema

Before we discuss the proposed technique, we first describe the extended timing schema (ETS) on which our algorithms are based. The original timing schema is a set of formulas for reasoning about the timing behavior of various language constructs [14]. The ETS extends the timing schema to reflect timing properties of modern architectural features such as pipelining and caching in two aspects: (1) redefinition of the timing information for each program construct and (2) redefinition of the timing formulas using newly introduced operations, concatenation ($\oplus$) and pruning [11].

In the ETS, each program construct is associated with a Worst Case Timing Abstract (WCTA) which is a data structure containing information needed in hierarchical timing analysis. A program construct may have more than one execution path as an **if** statement and the WCETs of these execution paths differ significantly depending on preceding program constructs. Therefore, the worst case execution

	Extended Timing Schema
S: S_1; S_2	$W(S) = W(S_1) \oplus_p W(S_2)$
S: if (exp) then S_1 else S_2	$W(S) = (W(exp) \oplus_p W(S_1)) \cup (W(exp) \oplus_p W(S_2))$
S: while (exp) S_1	$W(S) = (\oplus_{p_{i=1}}^{N}(W(exp) \oplus_p W(S_1))) \oplus_p W(exp)$
S: f(exp_1, . . ., exp_n)	$W(S) = W(exp_1) \oplus_p \ldots \oplus_p W(exp_n) \oplus_p W(f())$

$W(S)$ is the WCTA of a statement **S**. The $\oplus$ operation between two WCTAs, W_1 and W_2, is defined as $W_1 \oplus W_2 = \{w_1 \oplus w_2 | w_1 \in W_1, w_2 \in W_2\}$. The $\oplus_p$ operation is the $\oplus$ operation followed by the pruning operation, and N is the upper bound on the number of the loop iterations.

Table 1. Timing formulas of the extended timing schema.

path of the program construct cannot be determined by analyzing the program construct without considering the preceding program constructs. For this reason, the WCTA of a program construct keeps timing information of every execution path in the program construct that *might* be the worst case execution path. Each execution path of a program construct forms a Path Abstraction (PA) that contains the timing-related information of the execution path. The PA of an execution path encodes the factors that affect the WCET of the execution path. These factors may include the information on the pipelined execution and cache states. The encoding is done in such a way that allows for refinement of the execution path's WCET when the detailed information about the preceding execution paths becomes available. For example, in the case of pipelined execution analysis, the PA is about the use of pipeline stages in the associated execution path. In [11], the PA structure is defined using *reservation tables* which represent the usage of pipeline stages. This information allows for the refinement of the path's execution time once the pipeline usage information of preceding execution paths becomes available.

Two new operations, concatenation ($\oplus$) and pruning, are introduced to form the timing formulas in the ETS. The $\oplus$ operation between two PAs models the execution of one path followed by that of another path and yields the PA of the combined path. During this operation, the execution times of both paths are revised using each other's timing information encoded in their PAs. The pruning operation is performed on a set of PAs for a program construct and prunes the PAs whose associated execution paths cannot be the worst case execution path of the program construct. Table 1 shows the timing formulas of the extended timing schema. The timing formula for **S: S_1; S_2** first enumerates all the possible execution paths within **S**. The pruning operation after the enumeration prunes a subset of the resulting execution paths that cannot be the worst case execution path of the sequential statement. Similarly, the timing formula for an **if** statement first enumerates all the execution paths in the **then** path and those in the **else** path, and the execution paths that cannot be the worst case execution path of the **if** statement are pruned. The timing formula for a loop statement with a loop bound N models a loop unrolled N times. This approach is exact but is computationally intractable for a large N. In [11], Lim *et al.* give an efficient approximate loop timing analysis method using a maximum cycle mean algorithm due to Karp [9].

In summary, in order to perform timing analysis within the ETS framework, the following three components should be decided: (1) determination of the PA structure, (2) definition of the $\oplus$ operation on PAs, and (3) definition of the pruning condition. Once these three components are determined, the worst case timing analysis of a program can be performed mechanically by traversing the program's syntax tree in a bottom-up fashion and applying the timing formulas of the ETS.

3. Multiple-Issue Machine Model and Program Representation

3.1. Multiple-Issue Machine Model

Throughout this paper, we use a simple multiple-issue machine model with the following assumptions:

- Instructions are issued in the order shown in a program (in-order issue). However, each instruction can complete its execution regardless of other instructions' completion (out-of-order completion).

- The delayed branch scheme is used. For a branch instruction, one delay slot is assumed. This assumption is to ignore the effect of the branch prediction results on the execution time. (A worst case timing analysis under branch prediction is one of our main future research topics.)

- All memory accesses are cache hits. This assumption is to ignore the effect of cache misses on the execution time. (Since our approach does not make any assumption on the cache system, previously proposed techniques on the cache analysis [1, 11, 10] can easily be integrated with our approach.)

- Processor can issue up to k instructions simultaneously, where k is provided as a parameter to our analysis. k is equal to or smaller than the number of functional units in the processor (i.e., $k \leq 9$ in our processor model).

We further assume that our machine model has nine functional units as shown in Figure 1 and its instruction set is similar to that used in MIPS R3000/R3010 [8]. In Figure 1,

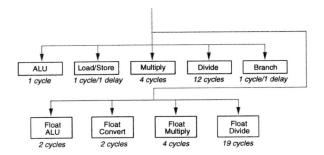

Figure 1. Functional units of target processor model.

each functional unit is shown with the latency of operations performed by the corresponding functional unit. Both the Load/Store and Branch units are assumed to have one delay slot.

3.2. Program Representation

In multiple-issue processors, the amount of exploitable parallelism is restricted by dependences among instructions. Such dependences include *structural dependences* (i.e., resource conflicts) and *data dependences* [7][1]. Structural dependences are caused by multiple instructions competing for the same functional unit. On the other hand, data dependences are caused by multiple instructions that use the same register or memory location. In this paper, we introduce another type of dependences, *order dependences*, that are used to model that instructions are issued in-order in our machine model.

To represent dependences among instructions, we use a directed acyclic graph (DAG), which we call an *instruction dependence graph* (IDG). The IDG representation of a program is similar to popular DAG representation of a program used in compiler research [3, 5]. In an IDG, a node can represent either a single instruction or a sequence of instructions. In the proposed technique, each node of an IDG initially corresponds to a single instruction in a basic block. Through a hierarchical refinement process of our timing analysis technique, several nodes are merged into a single node which represents more than one instruction. Each edge $e = (i, j)$ of an IDG indicates that there is at least one *non-redundant* dependence between the instruction(s) represented by the node i and the instruction(s) represented by the node j. (The exact definition of *redundant* dependences is described below.) Each edge $e = (i, j)$ is associated with a weight ℓ_e (or $\ell_{i,j}$) that represents the minimum cycles

---

[1]There is another type of dependences called *control dependences*. Control dependences are caused by branch instructions. Since we assume the delayed branch scheme in which a compiler resolves control dependences, we do not consider control dependences in our machine model.

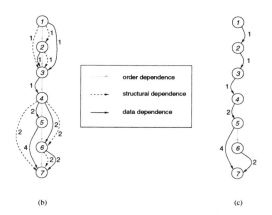

```
1   sll    $25, $12, 0x2      ; $25 <- $12 << 2
2   lui    $1, 0x1000         ; $1  <- 0x1000
3   addu   $1, $1, $25        ; $1  <- $1 + $25
4   lwc1   $f18, 96($1)       ; $f18 <- mem[$1 + 96]
5   mul.s  $f16, $f18, $f18   ; $f16 <- $f18 * $f18
6   add.s  $f18, $f18, $f18   ; $f18 <- $f18 + $f18
7   add.s  $f18, $f18, $f16   ; $f18 <- $f18 + $f16
```

(a)

order dependence

structural dependence

data dependence

(b)   (c)

Figure 2. An example program representation.

required between the issues of the first instructions of the nodes i and j. (For the description convenience, we use the *issue of a node* to mean the issue of the first instruction of a node.)

As an example, consider the basic block shown in Figure 2(a). The basic block contains a sequence of instructions based on the MIPS R3000/R3010 instruction set. Among the instructions, sll, lui, and addu use the ALU functional unit, lwc1 and add.s use the Float ALU functional unit, and mul.s uses the Float Multiply functional unit. The graph shown in Figure 2(b) represents all the dependences among the instructions including redundant dependences. In the dependence graph, since the weights for order dependences are all 0, they are not shown explicitly in the figure. Formally, we define that a dependence $e = (v, w)$ between nodes v and w is redundant if one of the following two conditions is satisfied:

(1) there exists another dependence $e' = (v, w)$ between the same nodes v and w and $\ell_{e'} \geq \ell_e$ (when there are more than one dependence with the same weight between the two nodes, we choose one arbitrarily among them),

(2) there exists a set of dependences, $S = \{e_0, e_1, \ldots, e_p\}$, such that

    (i) $e_0 = (v, i_0), e_p = (i_{p-1}, w)$, and $e_j = (i_{j-1}, i_j)$ for $1 \leq j < p$ and

(ii) $\displaystyle\sum_{i=0}^{p} \ell_{e_i} \geq \ell_e.$

For example, because of rule (2), both of the two dependences between nodes 4 and 6 in Figure 2(b) are redundant. Figure 2(c) shows the corresponding IDG with the redundant dependences eliminated. In an IDG, since all redundant dependences were eliminated, there can be at most one edge between any pair of nodes.

An IDG succinctly represents the timing-related information for a sequence of instructions. However, an IDG alone is generally not sufficient to predict the WCETs. While an IDG contains the complete information on the dependence relationship between the instructions represented by the IDG, more information from the surrounding blocks is necessary to predict the worst case issue patterns that result in the WCETs. For example, if the first instruction of the sequence requires the Float Divide unit, its issue time can vary significantly depending on whether the Float Divide unit is used by the preceding instruction. This type of variation on the issue times makes it difficult to identify the instructions that can be issued simultaneously. To efficiently manage these difficulties, we divide IDG nodes into two types. For the first type of a node (called a *resolved node*), each instruction represented by the node knows which instructions *in the same IDG* use its functional unit and operands. For the second type of a node (called an *unresolved node*), at least one instruction in the node cannot tell when its functional unit or operands may be used, simply by examining the preceding instructions in the same IDG. In our proposed technique, for unresolved nodes, we assume that their executions may be delayed by the maximum possible delay for safe prediction. For accurate prediction, the maximum delay value is reduced as more information from surrounding blocks are known through the hierarchical refinement process. Formally, we define the resolved and unresolved nodes as follows:

Definition 1 A node is said to use a register if the register is one of the source register(s) of an instruction in the node. Let *use(i)* for a node i be the set of registers used by the instruction(s) in the node i.

Definition 2 A node is said to define a register if the register is the destination register of an instruction in the node. Let *def(i)* for a node i be the set of registers defined by the instruction(s) in the node i.

Definition 3 A node is said to occupy a functional unit if an instruction in the node utilizes the functional unit during its execution. Let *occupy(i)* for a node i be the set of functional units occupied by the instruction(s) in the node i.

Definition 4 A node i is said to be resolved if all the registers in *use(i)* and *def(i)* are defined by preceding nodes in

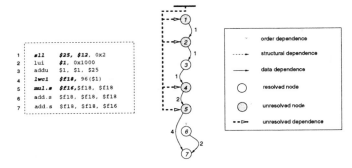

1	*11	$25, $12, 0x2
2	lui	$1, 0x1000
3	addu	$1, $1, $25
4	lwc1	$f18, 96($1)
5	mul.s	$f16,$f18, $f18
6	add.s	$f18, $f18, $f18
7	add.s	$f18, $f18, $f16

order dependence
structural dependence
data dependence
○ resolved node
○ unresolved node
- -▷ unresolved dependence

Figure 3. An IDG with resolved/unresolved nodes.

the same IDG and all the functional units in $occupy(i)$ are occupied by preceding nodes in the same IDG. Otherwise, the node is said to be unresolved. If a node is resolved, we say that all the dependences for the node are resolved. If a node is unresolved, we say that the node has unresolved dependences.

Figure 3 shows the same IDG used in Figure 2 with the resolved/unresolved information augmented. As an example of the unresolved nodes, consider node 4 in the IDG. We can note that $use(4) = \{\ \$1\ \}$, $def(4) = \{\ \$f18\ \}$, and $occupy(4) = \{\ \text{Float ALU}\ \}$ according to Definitions 1, 2, and 3. Among the elements in $use(4)$ and $def(4)$, register $\$f18$ is not defined by nodes 1, 2, and 3. The functional unit Float ALU in $occupy(4)$ is also not occupied by any of the preceding three nodes 1, 2, and 3. Therefore, node 4 is an unresolved node which has unresolved dependences for register $\$f18$ and the Float ALU functional unit. The dotted thick edge from outside of the IDG to node 4 in Figure 3 represents the unresolved dependence. Similarly, nodes 1, 2, and 5 are unresolved nodes as well due to unresolved dependences for registers or functional units.

4. Distance Bounds between Instructions

In this section, we first describe an algorithm for deriving the distance bounds on the issue times of each pair of instructions in a given IDG. (We call this *a bounding step*.) These distance bounds are used to identify the instructions that can be simultaneously issued. (We call this *a multiple issuing step*.) Once the distance bounds are computed for the IDG and the instructions are identified for multiple issues, the IDG can be simplified. (we call this *a merging step*.) For example, if two adjacent instructions have a constant issue distance, without loss of information, we can combine these two instructions into a single IDG node. The merging step reduces the complexity of analysis by reducing the number of nodes that need to be kept in an IDG.

4.1. Definitions and Terminology

We use the following terms and notations in explaining the algorithms:

- We use the term *resources* to refer to both registers and functional units. Let $\mathcal{R} = \{r_1, r_2, \ldots, r_{N_R}\}$ be the set of resources in a processor model where N_R is the total number of resources. N_R is the sum of the number of registers and the number of functional units. (In our processor model, N_R is 73, consisting of 64 registers and 9 functional units.)

- Each resource r_i is associated with the maximum latency z_i, which is defined to be the maximum duration for which an instruction may occupy the resource r_i. If r_i is a functional unit, z_i is the maximum instruction latency among all the instructions that occupy r_i during their executions. Let z_{max} be the maximum z_i for all the functional units. If an r_i is a register, z_i is defined as z_{max}. For a given processor, z_i's can be obtained from the processor manual. In our processor model, z_{max} is 19 cycles which is the latency of instructions for the Float Divide functional unit.

- For an unresolved node i in an IDG, let $unresolved(i)$ be the set of resources that are not resolved in node i. The $unresolved(i)$ set consists of the registers and the functional units that are not resolved in node i. The unresolved registers are the registers in $use(i)$ or $def(i)$ but not in $def(j)$ for $j < i$ while the unresolved functional units are the functional units in $occupy(i)$ but not in $occupy(j)$ for $j < i$.

- For each node i, $max\_latency\_node(i)$ is the time duration from the issue of the first instruction of node i to the completion of the executions of all the instructions in the node i while $min\_latency\_node(i)$ is the time duration from the issue of the first instruction of node i to the issue of the last instruction of node i. $Max\_latency\_node(i)$ is used to assign the maximum possible weight of an edge from node i to a succeeding node and $min\_latency\_node(i)$ is to assign the minimum possible weight of an edge from node i to a succeeding node. For each node i, $max\_latency\_unresolved(i)$ is the maximum of the maximum latencies of the resources in $unresolved(i)$. $Max\_latency\_unresolved(i)$ is used to assign the maximum possible weight of an edge from a preceding node to node i.

4.2. Bounding Step

In order to represent the variation of instruction issue times, we derive the distance bounds between the issue times

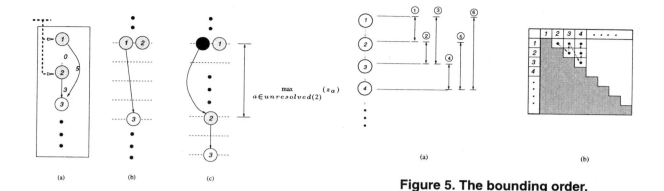

Figure 5. The bounding order.

Figure 4. A bounding step example.

for each pair of nodes. As an example, consider the IDG shown in Figure 4(a) where nodes 1 and 2 have unresolved dependences. In order to compute the distance bounds for each pair of nodes, there are three combinations to consider: the distance bounds for nodes 1 and 2, nodes 2 and 3 and nodes 1 and 3. The lower bound for nodes 1 and 2 occurs when node 2 is issued at the same time as node 1 as shown in Figure 4(b). Such a scenario is possible because node 2 has only an order dependence with node 1. Thus, the lower bound for nodes 1 and 2 is 0. On the other hand, the upper bound occurs when the issue of node 2 is delayed as much as possible from the issue of node 1. Such a scenario is shown in Figure 4(c). In the figure, the black node represents the node that immediately precedes the current program construct. In this scenario, the black node is assumed to have only an order dependence with node 1, so it can be issued at the same time as node 1. Furthermore, we assume that the black node occupies the unresolved resources of node 2 making the unresolved dependences of node 2 be forced to be resolved. To give the upper bound, this unresolved dependence should have the largest possible latency, $\max_{a \in unresolved(2)} (z_a)$, where a is an element of the set of unresolved resources for node 2.

Next, consider the bounds on the distance between nodes 2 and 3. This distance is affected by three weights, $\ell_{2,3}$, $\ell_{1,3}$, and $\ell_{1,2}$. The lower bound can be obviously $\ell_{2,3}$ (= 3), but it can be tightened more. For instance, if the upper bound of the distance between nodes 1 and 2 is less than $(\ell_{1,3} - \ell_{2,3})(= 2)$, the distance between nodes 2 and 3 is guaranteed to be larger than $\ell_{2,3}$ (= 3). Therefore, the lower bound is the larger of (1) $\ell_{2,3}$ and (2) the difference between $\ell_{1,3}$ and the upper bound of the distance between nodes 1 and 2. Similarly, the upper bound is the larger of (1) $\ell_{2,3}$ and (2) the difference between $\ell_{1,3}$ and the lower bound of the distance between nodes 1 and 2. These comparisons require the distance bounds between nodes 1 and 2 to be calculated in advance.

Finally, consider the distance bounds for nodes 1 and 3. The lower bound can be obviously $\ell_{1,3}$ (= 5). However, if the distance between nodes 1 and 2 is guaranteed to be larger than $(\ell_{1,3} - \ell_{2,3})(= 2)$, the distance between nodes 1 and 3 should be computed by summing the distance between nodes 1 and 2 and $\ell_{2,3}(= 3)$. Therefore, the lower bound for nodes 1 and 3 is the larger of (1) $\ell_{1,3}$ and (2) the sum of the lower bound of the distance between nodes 1 and 2 and $\ell_{2,3}$. Similarly, the upper bound on the distance between nodes 1 and 3 is the larger of (1) $\ell_{1,3}$ and (2) the sum of the upper bound of the distance between nodes 1 and 2 and $\ell_{2,3}$.

In calculating the distance bounds, some distance bounds must be computed earlier than others. For example, deriving the distance bounds for nodes 2 and 3 requires the distance bounds for nodes 1 and 2 to be available in advance. Similarly, deriving the distance bounds for nodes 1 and 3 also requires the distance bounds for nodes 1 and 2 to be available in advance. This implies that deriving distance bounds should be performed in the order shown in Figure 5. Figure 5(a) shows the order of calculating distance bounds with a sample IDG. The distance bounds for nodes 1 and 2 are calculated first followed by the calculation of distance bounds for nodes 2 and 3, nodes 1 and 3, and so on. Figure 5(b) shows the order of calculating distance bounds using a table whose cell represents the distance bounds between the row-numbered node and the column-numbered node.

Generalizing the above example, we can compute the distance bounds between two nodes as follows. Let $D_{i,j}^{min}$ and $D_{i,j}^{max}$ be the minimum (required) and maximum (possible) distances between the issue times of nodes i and j ($i < j$), respectively. As shown in Figure 5, the calculation order is: $[D_{1,2}^{min}, D_{1,2}^{max}]$, $[D_{2,3}^{min}, D_{2,3}^{max}]$, $[D_{1,3}^{min}, D_{1,3}^{max}]$, $[D_{3,4}^{min}, D_{3,4}^{max}]$, $[D_{2,4}^{min}, D_{2,4}^{max}]$, $[D_{1,4}^{min}, D_{1,4}^{max}]$, ... In calculating $[D_{i,j}^{min}, D_{i,j}^{max}]$, we consider the nodes that have dependences with node j in the IDG. We classify such nodes into the following three classes according to their positions in the IDG as shown in Figure 6: (1) the nodes preceding node i (i.e., nodes $p_1, p_2, \ldots, p_m$ in Figure 6(b)), (2) node i (Figure 6(c)), and (3) the nodes succeeding node i (i.e.,

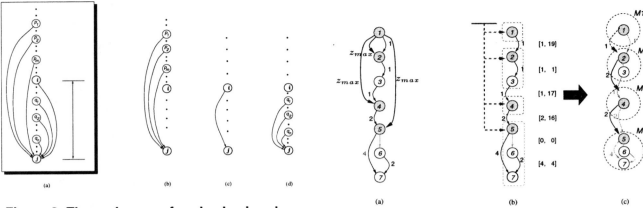

Figure 6. Three classes of nodes having dependences with node j.

Figure 7. IDG modifications for $D_{i,j}^{max}$ calculation and merging operation.

nodes $q_1, q_2, \ldots, q_n$ in Figure 6(d)). In order to calculate $D_{i,j}^{min}$, three candidate lower bound values from the three class are computed separately, and then the largest of three candidate values is chosen to be $D_{i,j}^{min}$. For the first class, we calculate the differences between $\ell_{p_x,j}$ and $D_{p_x,i}^{max}$ where $1 \leq x \leq m$. $\ell_{p_x,j}$ is given in the original IDG and $D_{p_x,i}^{max}$ is calculated at an earlier stage. The largest of these differences is the candidate lower bound value from the first class. For the second class, $\ell_{i,j}$ is the candidate value. For the last class, we calculate the sums of D_{i,q_y}^{min} and $\ell_{q_y,j}$ where $1 \leq y \leq n$. The largest of these sums is the candidate value from the third class.

The maximum distance $D_{i,j}^{max}$ between the issue times of nodes i and j can be obtained when the issue of node j is maximally delayed relative to node i. For safe bounding on the maximum distance, we introduce additional edges (called *max edges*) between node 1 and the unresolved nodes of the IDG. The max edges between node 1 and unresolved node i has a weight of $max\_latency\_unresolved(i)$, thus effectively models the maximum possible delay between a preceding (but yet unknown) node and unresolved node i. Figure 7(a) shows the IDG of Figure 3 with the max edges added. Note that the weights are all z_{max} since the unresolved nodes have registers as their unresolved resources. Using the modified IDG with the max edges, the $D_{i,j}^{max}$ calculation proceeds similarly to the $D_{i,j}^{min}$ calculation. (In order to distinguish the modified IDG and the original IDG, we use $\ell'_{i,j}$ to indicate a weight in the modified IDG. $\ell'_{i,j}$ is defined as follows: $\ell'_{i,j} = \ell_{i,j}$ if $i \neq 1$, $\ell'_{i,j} = max\_latency\_unresolved(j)$ if node j is an unresolved node and $i = 1$, and $\ell_{i,j} = 0$ if there is no edge between nodes i and j in the IDG.) Three candidate upper bound values from the three classes are computed and the largest value is selected as $D_{i,j}^{max}$. For the first class, we calculate the differences between $\ell'_{p_x,j}$ and $D_{p_x,i}^{min}$ where $1 \leq x \leq m$. The largest of these differences is the candidate value from the second class. From the second class, we take $\ell'_{i,j}$ as in the $D_{i,j}^{min}$ calculation. For the third class, we

calculate the sums of D_{i,q_y}^{max} and $\ell'_{q_y,j}$ where $1 \leq y \leq n$. The largest of the sums is the candidate from the last class. The $D_{i,j}^{min}$ and $D_{i,j}^{max}$ calculations can be summarized by the following equations:

$$D_{i,j}^{min} = \max(\max_{1 \leq x \leq m}(\ell_{p_x,j} - D_{p_x,i}^{max}), \ell_{i,j}, \max_{1 \leq y \leq n}(D_{i,q_y}^{min} + \ell_{q_y,j})) \quad (1)$$

$$D_{i,j}^{max} = \max(\max_{1 \leq x \leq m}(\ell'_{p_x,j} - D_{p_x,i}^{min}), \ell'_{i,j}, \max_{1 \leq y \leq n}(D_{i,q_y}^{max} + \ell'_{q_y,j})). \quad (2)$$

Each equation in the above has three elements in the outermost max operation and each element corresponds to each class of nodes.

4.3. Multiple Issuing and Merging Steps

In the multiple issuing step, we identify the instructions that are guaranteed to be issued simultaneously, based on the distance bounds computed in the previous section, and then refine the distance bounds of the IDG to reflect the effect of identified instructions to the IDG representation. In principle, two nodes whose distance bounds are [0, 0] can be issued simultaneously. If a series of nodes have the distance bounds of [0, 0], these nodes can be potentially issued at the same time. However, the number of simultaneously issued instructions cannot be greater than the multiple-issue limit of a target processor. For example, in our machine model where the maximum of k instructions can be issued simultaneously, consider a series of nodes $p, p+1, \ldots, p+q$ such that $[D_{p+i,p+i+1}^{min}, D_{p+i,p+i+1}^{max}] = [0, 0]$ for $0 \leq i < q$. For the nodes, $p, p+1, \ldots, p+q$, we first check if $q+1 \leq k$. If $q + 1 \leq k$, all the nodes in the series are guaranteed to be issued at the same time and no special refinement step is necessary to reflect the effect of the multiple-issue identification. On the other hand, if $q + 1 > k$, not all the nodes in the series can be issued simultaneously. Since our

340

machine model assumes an in-order issue, only the first k nodes, $p, p+1, \ldots, p+k-1$ can be issued at the same time. The remaining nodes, $p+k, \ldots, p+q$, should be issued at least one cycle later than the first k nodes. Therefore, in case that $q+1 > k$, after identifying the first k nodes, the IDG should be modified. To represent that only the first k nodes can be issued simultaneously, we replace an edge between nodes $p+k-1, p+k$ with an edge of a weight 1. Since the new edge will change the distance bounds of the IDG, we recalculate the distance bounds for the affected nodes. A more detailed description on the multiple issuing algorithm can be found in [12].

As it will be described in detail in the next section, an IDG is encoded into the PA structure that represents a program construct, and two successive IDGs are concatenated into a new IDG during the hierarchical refinement process. Repeated concatenations, however, may require a large amount of space to maintain all the nodes of the concatenated IDGs. Therefore, we propose a merging operation on an IDG that reduces the number of nodes in an IDG. (In our proposed technique, a merging operation is performed after the multiple issuing step.) Two adjacent nodes in an IDG are merged into a single node if the lower bound of the distance between two nodes are same as the upper bound of the distance between two nodes. That is, if $D_{j,j+1}^{min}$ is equal to $D_{j,j+1}^{max}$, nodes j and $j+1$ can be merged into a single node. In general, N nodes, $p, p+1, \ldots, p+N-1$, can be merged into a single node (after the multiple issuing step) if $[D_{p,p+1}^{min}, D_{p,p+1}^{max}] = [c_{i_1}, c_{i_1'}]$, $[D_{p+1,p+2}^{min}, D_{p+1,p+2}^{max}] = [c_{i_2}, c_{i_2'}]$, $\ldots$, $[D_{p+N-2,p+N-1}^{min}, D_{p+N-2,p+N-1}^{max}] = [c_{i_{p+N-1}}, c_{i_{p+N-1}'}]$ and $c_{i_k} = c_{i_k'}$ for $1 \le k \le p+N-1$. Figure 7(b)-(c) illustrates the merging operation. The IDG shown in Figure 7(b) includes the distance bounds between nodes as well as the weights between nodes. In Figure 7(b), the nodes that can be merged are shown inside a dotted box. For example, nodes 2 and 3 can be merged because the distance bounds between them are [1, 1]. Nodes 5, 6 and 7 can be merged as well because they have the distance bounds [0, 0] and [4, 4]. Since merged nodes (except for the first node) have a constant distance on their issue times relative to the first node, no information is lost in predicting the WCETs by the merging operation. On the other hand, as the hierarchical analysis proceeds, the number of nodes that can be merged grows rapidly since most of unresolved nodes will be resolved during the hierarchical refinement process. Therefore, the reduction in the number of nodes by the merging operations is substantial.

There are two more factors to consider during the merging operation. First, since the merged node represents several nodes before the merging operations are performed, we have to modify the weights between the merged node and other nodes in the merged IDG. (Note that our definition of a weight between two nodes means the minimum distance

(a)

(b)

Figure 8. A tabular form representation of distance bounds.

between the issues of first instructions of the two nodes.) For example, in Figure 7(c), the weight between merged nodes M_2 and M_3 is computed to be the sum of a constant distance between nodes 2 and 3 and the weight between nodes 3 and 4 in the original IDG. Second, even when a series of nodes have their distance bounds as [0, 0], these nodes are not always merged for accurate prediction of the WCETs. This happens for the following two cases: (1) a series of nodes have distance bounds of [0, 0], but the consecutive nodes start from the first node in the IDG and (2) a series of nodes have distance bounds of [0, 0] but the last node in the IDG is also a part of these nodes. In the first case, if we merged the nodes, we will lose some accuracy when we concatenate with a preceding IDG whose last n nodes have distance bounds [0, 0]. Similarly, in the second case, if we merged the nodes, we will lose some accuracy when we concatenate with a succeeding IDG whose first n nodes have distance bounds [0, 0].

The distance bounds for all combinations of nodes in an IDG can be represented as a tabular form. Figure 8 shows the tabular form representations of the distance bounds for our example. Figure 8(a) shows the distance bounds for original IDG and Figure 8(b) shows the distance bounds after merging is applied to the IDG. This tabular representation is included into the PA structure for a program construct.

5. Extensions to ETS

In this section, we describe the extensions made to the original ETS framework to support the WCET prediction for our multiple-issue machine model. We explain how to encode the IDG for a program construct in the PA structure and define the concatenation ($\oplus$) operation and the pruning operation using the three distance bounds steps described in the previous section.

The PA Structure To take into account the multiple-issue capability in the ETS framework, we define the PA structure of the program construct to include the IDG. To understand why an IDG is used instead of a reservation table which was used for simple pipelined processors, consider Figure 9 that

Figure 9. A reservation table example.

shows a reservation table for a sequence of instructions. In the reservation table, the rows represent the pipeline stages and the columns represent time, and an x in the reservation table specifies the use of the corresponding pipeline stage by an instruction at the indicated cycle. When a reservation table is constructed the issue time of an instruction relative to others in the same basic block is fixed. This static assignment of an issue time to an instruction leads to a severe overestimation of the WCET for multiple-issue processors because when information on the surrounding blocks are known later, the issue times cannot be easily adjusted reflecting the simultaneously issued instructions from the different blocks.

The PA structure for multiple-issue machines is shown in Figure 10. The PA structure for a program construct consists of five tables. The distance bounds derived from the IDG for the program construct are included in a table called bounds_table where each cell corresponds to the distance bounds between the row-numbered node and the column-numbered node. In order to compute the WCET of an IDG and to prune redundant PAs, for each node i in the IDG, the $min\_latency\_node(i)$ and $max\_latency\_node(i)$ are maintained in the PA. Two additional tables, in and out, are used to detect the transition of unresolved nodes to resolved nodes when two PAs are concatenated. The in table contains the information on the unresolved dependences of the IDG which may be refined as the resolved dependences by a preceding IDG at a later stage. For a register, the first node that uses or defines the register is recorded in the in table, while, for a functional unit, the first node that occupies the functional unit in the IDG is recorded in the in table. On the other hand, the out table contains the information on the factors that may cause the unresolved dependences of succeeding IDGs to be refined as the resolved dependences. In the out table, for a register, the last node that defines the register is recorded, and, for a functional unit, the last node that occupies the functional unit is recorded with its latency. When two PAs are concatenated, these five tables from each PA are used to construct new tables for the concatenated PA.

From the PA information, we can derive the WCET of the IDG. Let the WCET of an IDG be the worst case execution time from the issue of the first node to the end of the executions of all the nodes. Then we can calculate the WCET of the IDG as follows. Assume $\mathcal{N}$ to be the set of nodes of the

```
struct PA of a path p {
    struct BOUNDS {
            d_min, d_max ;
    } bounds_table[N_nodes][N_nodes] ;
    min_latency_node[N_nodes] ;
    max_latency_node[N_nodes] ;
    struct IN
            in[N_resources] ;
    struct OUT {
            node ;
            latency ;
    } out[N_resources] ;
};
```

Figure 10. The structure of PA.

IDG and $max\_latency\_node(i)$ to be the maximum of the latencies of the functional units in $occupy(i)$ as defined in Section 4. Then the WCET of an IDG can be computed as follows:

$$T_{worst} = \max_{i \in \mathcal{N}}(D_{1,i}^{max} + max\_latency\_node(i)).$$

This formula produces the time required from the issue of the first instruction of an IDG to the completion of all the instructions in the IDG in the worst case. Once the PA for a whole program is built, we can compute the WCET of the program from the PA in a similar way. However, in the calculation of the WCET for the whole program, we can assume that the instructions in unresolved nodes in the final IDG are issued with the minimal delay because there will be no instructions that can resolve these unresolved dependences. Therefore, the WCET for a program is computed as follows:

$$WCET_{program} = \max_{i \in \mathcal{N}}(D_{1,i}^{min} + max\_latency\_node(i)).$$

The Concatenation and Pruning Operations The second step of augmenting the extended timing schema for multiple-issue machines is to define the semantic of the concatenation ($\oplus$) operation according to the structure of the PA. The concatenation operation on two PAs produces a new PA containing the information on a new IDG constructed by linking two IDGs from the original PAs. In each concatenation, the three bounds steps (the bounding step, the multiple issuing step, and the merging step) are applied to the newly constructed PA. Since the IDG is represented by the five tables, `bounds_table`, `min_latency_node`, `max_latency_node`, `in`, and `out`, the five tables are newly created from the tables in the original PAs.

The concatenation operation on two PAs w_1 and w_2 producing a new PA w_3 consists of the following four steps. Assume that w_2 follows w_1 in a program order. Let N_{w_1} and N_{w_2} denote the number of nodes of the IDGs in w_1 and w_2, respectively. Then, the dimensions of bounds table `bounds_table`$_{w_1}$ for w_1 is $N_{w_1} \times N_{w_1}$, while the dimensions of the bounds table `bounds_table`$_{w_2}$ for w_2 is $N_{w_2} \times N_{w_2}$.

The first step of the concatenation operation is to build a new bounds table `bounds_table`$_{w_3}$ from the original two bounds tables `bounds_table`$_{w_1}$ and `bounds_table`$_{w_2}$. The size of the new `bounds_table` will be initially $(N_{w_1} + N_{w_2}) \times (N_{w_1} + N_{w_2})$. This initial table models the new IDG where two original IDGs from w_1 and w_2 are linked together. Once `bounds_table`$_{w_3}$ is initially filled, we apply the bounding algorithm (to compute the distance bounds), the multiple issuing algorithm (to identify the instructions that can be issued simultaneously) and the merging algorithm (to shrink the table size) to `bounds_table`$_{w_3}$. The new bounds table `bounds_table`$_{w_3}$ is initially filled as follows. Since the distance bounds of instructions within w_1 and the distance bounds of instructions within w_2 are not modified by the concatenation operation, `bounds_table`$_{w_3}$`[i][j]` = `bounds_table`$_{w_1}$`[i][j]` for $1 \leq i, j \leq N_{w_1}$ and `bounds_table`$_{w_3}$`[`N_{w_1}`+i][`N_{w_1}`+j]` = `bounds_table`$_{w_2}$`[i][j]` for $1 \leq i, j \leq N_{w_2}$.

The second step of the concatenation is to check if new dependences exist between a node n_1 of w_1 and a node n_2 of w_2 after two PAs were concatenated. Since the new dependences exist when n_1 and n_2 share the common resources, we compare the `out` table of w_1 and the `in` table of w_2. If a resource r_i is found to be shared by `out` of w_1 and `in` of w_2, a new edge with the weight of `out[i].latency` from w_1 is attached between the corresponding nodes (i.e., node p from w_1 and node q from w_2 if `out[i].node` of w_1 is p and `in[i].node` of w_2 is q). This new edge with the corresponding weight is used in filling `bounds_table`$_{w_3}$`[i][j +` N_{w_1}`]` for $1 \leq i \leq N_{w_1}$ and $1 \leq j \leq N_{w_2}$. Once `bounds_table`$_{w_3}$ is built, we apply the three bounding steps to find the simplified version of `bounds_table`$_{w_3}$.

The next step is to fill the `min_latency_node` and the `max_latency_node` for each node. These latencies are calculated in the merging step. If nodes j and k are found to be merged into node m, the `min_latency_node[`m`]` and the `max_latency_node[`m`]` of the merged node m are obtained by adding the constant distance between the nodes j and k to the `min_latency_node[`k`]` and the `max_latency_node[`k`]` of node k. In this way, the la-

tencies are modified to represent the times from the issue of the first instruction as defined in Section 4.1.

Finally, the contents of `in` and `out` for w_3 are filled using `ins` and `outs` of w_1 and w_2. The `in` of w_3 is filled by copying the contents of `ins` of w_1 and w_2. The contents of `in` of w_1 will override the contents of `in` of w_2. The `out` of w_3 is filled in a similar manner.

The last missing component for applying the ETS is to define the pruning operation. The purpose of a pruning operation is to eliminate the paths that cannot be the worst case execution path. In other words, in the same WCTA, if the WCET of a PA w_1 in the worst case scenario is shorter than the WCET of any other PA w_2 in the best case scenario, a PA w_1 can be safely pruned from the WCTA. The WCET in the best case scenario of a PA w, which we call $T_{best\_worst}(w)$, is defined as follows:

$$T_{best\_worst}(w) = D_{1,m}^{min} + min\_latency\_node(i),$$

where m is the number of nodes in the IDG of a PA w. In this equation, $T_{best\_worst}(w)$ is the minimum delay from the issue of the first instruction to the issue of the last instruction in the IDG. On the other hand, the WCET in the worst case scenario of a PA w, which we call $T_{worst\_worst}(w)$, is defined as follows:

$$T_{worst\_worst}(w) = D_{1,m}^{min} + 2 \times z_{max},$$

where z_{max} is the maximum latency of an instruction in the target processor (as defined in Section 4.1). The worst scenario occurs when the issue of the first instruction in w is maximally delayed by the dependences with the preceding program constructs and the instructions in w maximally delay the issue of the first instruction in the succeeding program constructs. In order to account for two maximal delays (before and after w), we add $2 \times z_{max}$ to $D_{i,m}^{min}$. The pruning condition can be more formally specified as follows:

A PA w in a WCTA W can be pruned without affecting the prediction for the worst case timing behavior of W if $\exists w' \in W$ such that $T_{worst\_worst}(w) < T_{best\_worst}(w')$.

6. Experimental Results

We have performed experiments to validate our approach by building a timing tool based on the proposed technique and comparing the WCET bounds produced by the timing tool to the simulation results measured from a simulator. Figure 11 shows an overview of our timing analysis environment. The timing analyzer takes as input the assembly code, program syntax information, and the call graph along with the user-provided information (e.g., loop bound) to predict the WCET of the program. A modified lcc compiler

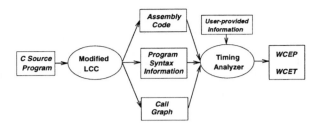

Figure 11. Experiment setup.

benchmarks	description
Arrsum	calculates the sum of 10 array elements.
Fib	computes the 30th element of the Fibonacci sequence.
MM	multiplies two 5 × 5 matrices.
BS	performs binary search over 15 integer array elements.
ISort	sorts 10 integer array elements using the insertion sort algorithm.
InLP	shows more ILP (relative to other benchmarks) by the manual rearrangement of the assembly instructions.

Table 2. The benchmarks used in our experiments.

[11] accepts a C source program and generates the inputs to the timing analyzer.

The predicted WCETs were compared with the measurements obtained from a simulator that models our target multiple-issue machine model. The simulator was built using a software tool, called Visualization-based Microarchitecture Workbench (VMW) [2], that provides a framework for systematically constructing a processor simulator at the microarchitecture level. In VMW, a new processor is specified using several machine specification files and the corresponding processor simulator is automatically generated. (The VMW tool has been successfully used to simulate multiple-issue processors such as superscalar processors (e.g., PowerPC620).) The machine specification for the target multiple-issue machine included a microarchitecture machine organization specification file (71 lines), an instruction syntax specification file (115 lines), an instruction semantic specification file (127 lines), and an instruction timing specification file (543 lines). The simulator assumes the MIPS R3000 instruction-set architecture and displays the machine status during simulations along with the execution times.

Table 2 summarizes the benchmarks used in our experiments. Since the modified lcc compiler was originally developed for simple pipelined machines without employing the special compiler optimizations techniques that can increase instruction-level parallelism (ILP) of the compiled code, the generated assembly code contains relatively small ILP. In order to validate the applicability of our technique on

	single issue		double issue		quadruple issue	
	S	P	S	P	S	P
Arrsum	108	108	92	92	92	92
Fib	227	227	190	190	189	189
MM	4142	4142	3553	3553	3552	3552
BS	101	106	81	84	80	83
ISort	1262	2126	1088	1844	1087	1844
InLP	3331	3331	2498	2498	2290	2290

S: simulation, P: prediction

Table 3. The experimental results.

programs with more ILP, we made a benchmark called *InLP* whose instructions were manually reordered for more ILP after the assembly code was generated from the modified lcc. The analysis results and the simulation results for the benchmarks are compared in Table 3. The results are shown for three different issue numbers: single issue, double issue, and quadruple issue. Because of the small ILP available in the assembly code, as shown in the table, the execution times of the benchmarks (except for *InLP*) are very close each other on a double-issue machine and a quadruple-issue machine.

For the *Arrsum*, *Fib*, *MM*, and *InLP* benchmarks, the analysis results are exactly same as the simulation results because the execution path of each benchmark program is unique. However, for *BS* and *ISort*, the analysis results are larger than the simulation results. The differences between the analysis results and the simulation results are mainly from infeasible paths. As we discussed in [11], we believe that the infeasible path problem exists in any static WCET prediction technique, and the elimination of these paths using dynamic path analysis is an issue orthogonal to the WCET prediction approach. The existing path analysis method (e.g., the work done by Park [13]) can easily be integrated with the proposed method, thus producing tighter WCETs for the *BS* and *ISort* benchmarks.

7. Conclusion and Future Work

In this paper, we described a timing analysis technique that can accurately predict the WCETs of tasks for multiple-issue machines. Our technique is based on the existing extended timing schema (ETS). We enhanced the ETS framework to account for the timing variation resulting from multiple issues of instructions per cycle. The main extension was on the PA structure. Instead of reservation tables used for the original ETS, we maintain an IDG (Instruction Dependence Graph) to represent dependences among instructions and include it in the PA structure. From the IDG, the minimum and maximum distance bounds between the issue times of the instructions are computed. These bounds are used to identify the instructions that can be issued simultaneously. The identification of the constant distance instructions as well as the simultaneously issued instructions allows the IDG to be simplified, reducing the number of necessary nodes to be kept in the IDG. The concatenation operation is redefined to support the combining of two IDGs followed by the IDG simplifications. We also redefined the pruning condition that can eliminate an execution path that cannot be part of the worst case execution path, considering the effect of multiple issues on the execution time.

We also built a timing tool based on the proposed technique and compared the WCET bounds of several benchmark programs predicted by the timing tool to their measurements from a simulator. The results show that the proposed technique can predict the WCETs for in-order, multiple-issue machines in a similar accuracy to the results from simple pipelined processors.

Our work described in this paper strongly suggests that the multiple-issue capability of modern microprocessors can be accurately analyzed to predict the WCETs of programs. However, to estimate the WCETs of tasks for more realistic multiple-issue processors such as commercial superscalar processors, our technique needs to be extended further to handle other advanced architectural features that can cause the timing variation in multiple-issue processors. For example, many superscalar processors execute in an out-of-order, multiple-issue fashion and support the dynamic scheduling, dynamic branch prediction and speculative execution [6]. Since these features all affect the execution time, the proposed technique should be extended to account for these features. Therefore, our current research direction is focused on developing the techniques for modeling these dynamic architectural features and predicting the WCETs taking into account the timing effect of these features.

References

[1] R. Arnold, F. Mueller, D. Whalley, and M. Harmon. Bounding Worst-Case Instruction Cache Performance. In *Proceedings of the 15th Real-Time Systems Symposium*, pages 172–181, 1994.

[2] T. A. Diep and J. P. Shen. VMW: A Visualization-Based Microarchitecture Workbench. *IEEE Computer*, 28(12):57–64, 1995.

[3] J. Ferrante, K. Ottenstein, and J. Warren. The Program Dependence Graph and Its Use in Optimization. *ACM Transactions on Programming Languages and Systems*, 9(3):319–349, July 1987.

[4] C. A. Healy, D. B. Whalley, and M. G. Harmon. Integrating the Timing Analysis of Pipelining and Instruction Caching. In *Proceedings of the 16th Real-Time Systems Symposium*, pages 288–297, December 1995.

[5] J. Hennessy and T. Gross. Postpass Code Optimization of Pipeline Constraints. *ACM Transactions on Programming Languages and Systems*, 5(3):422–448, July 1983.

[6] J. L. Hennessy and D. A. Patterson. *Computer Architecture: A Quantitative Approach 2nd Ed.* Morgan Kaufmann Publishers, San Mateo, CA, 1996.

[7] M. Johnson. *Superscalar Microprocessor Design*. Prentice Hall, 1991.

[8] G. Kane and J. Heinrich. *MIPS RISC Architecture*. Prentice Hall, Englewood Cliffs, NJ, 1991.

[9] R. M. Karp. A Characterization of the Minimum Cycle Mean in a Digraph. *Discrete Mathematics*, 23:309–311, 1978.

[10] Y. S. Li, S. Malik, and A. Wolfe. Cache Modeling for Real-Time Software: Beyond Direct Mapped Instruction Caches. In *Proceedings of the 17th Real-Time Systems Symposium*, pages 254–263, 1996.

[11] S.-S. Lim, Y. H. Bae, G. T. Jang, B.-D. Rhee, S. L. Min, C. Y. Park, H. Shin, K. Park, and C. S. Kim. An Accurate Worst Case Timing Analysis for RISC Processors. *IEEE Transactions on Software Engineering*, 21(7):593–604, July 1995.

[12] S.-S. Lim, J. H. Han, J. Kim, and S. L. Min. A Worst Case Timing Analysis Technique for Multiple-Issue Processors. Technical Report SNU-CE-AN-98-001, Architecture and Network Laboratory, Seoul National University, 1998.

[13] C. Y. Park. Predicting Program Execution Times by Analyzing Static and Dynamic Program Paths. *Real-Time Systems*, 5(1):31–62, March 1993.

[14] A. C. Shaw. Reasoning About Time in Higher-Level Language Software. *IEEE Transactions on Software Engineering*, 15(7):875–889, July 1989.

[15] N. Zhang, A. Burns, and M. Nicholson. Pipelined Processors and Worst-Case Execution Times. *Real-Time Systems*, 5(4):319–343, Oct. 1993.

Efficient Object Sharing in Quantum-Based Real-Time Systems[*]

James H. Anderson, Rohit Jain, and Kevin Jeffay
Department of Computer Science
University of North Carolina
Chapel Hill, NC 27599-3175
{anderson,jain,jeffay}@cs.unc.edu

Abstract

We consider the problem of implementing shared objects in uniprocessor and multiprocessor real-time systems in which tasks are executed using a scheduling quantum. In most quantum-based systems, the size of the quantum is quite large in comparison to the length of an object call. As a result, most object calls can be expected to execute without preemption. A good object-sharing scheme should optimize for this expected case, while achieving low overhead when preemptions do occur. In this paper, we present several new shared-object algorithms for uniprocessors and multiprocessors that were designed based upon this principle. We also present scheduling analysis results that can be used in conjunction with these algorithms.

1. Introduction

In many real-time systems, tasks are scheduled for execution using a scheduling quantum. Under quantum-based scheduling, processor time is allocated to tasks in discrete time units called *quanta*. When a processor is allocated to some task, that task is guaranteed to execute without preemption for Q time units, where Q is the length of the quantum, or until it terminates, whichever comes first. Many real-time applications are designed based on scheduling disciplines such as proportional-share [20] and round-robin scheduling that are expressly quantum-based. Under proportional-share scheduling, each task is assigned a *share* of the processor, which represents the fraction of processing time that that task should receive. Quanta are allocated in a manner that ensures that the amount of processor time each task receives

is commensurate with its share. Round-robin scheduling is a simpler scheme in which each task has an identical share.

Quantum-based execution also arises when conventional priority-based scheduling disciplines, such as rate-monotonic (RM) and earliest-deadline-first (EDF) scheduling, are implemented on top of a timer-driven real-time kernel [14]. In such an implementation, interrupts are scheduled to occur at regular intervals, and scheduling decisions are made when these interrupts occur. The length of time between interrupts defines the scheduling quantum. Timer-driven systems can be seen as a compromise between nonpreemptive and completely preemptive systems. In fact, nonpreemptive and preemptive systems abstractly can be viewed as the extreme endpoints in a continuum of quantum-based systems: a nonpreemptive system results when $Q = \infty$ and a fully preemptive system results when $Q = 0$. Nonpreemptive systems have several advantages over preemptive systems, including lower scheduling overheads (if preemptions are frequent) and simpler object-sharing protocols [8, 13]. Also, timing analysis is simplified because cache behavior is easier to predict. However, these advantages come at the potential expense of longer response times for higher-priority tasks. Quantum-based systems can be seen as a compromise between these two extremes.

In this paper, we consider the problem of efficiently implementing shared objects in quantum-based real-time systems. We consider both uniprocessor and multiprocessor systems. The basis for our results is the observation that, in most quantum-based systems, the size of the quantum is quite large compared to the length of an object call. Indeed, processors are becoming ever faster, decreasing object-access times, while quantum sizes are not changing. Even with the technology of several years ago, one could make the case that object calls are typically short compared to a quantum. As evidence of this, we cite results from experiments conducted by Ramamurthy to compute access times for several common objects [18]. These experiments were performed on a 25 MHz 68030 machine and involved objects ranging from queues to linked lists to medium-sized

[*]Work supported by NSF grant CCR 9510156. The first author was also supported by a Young Investigator Award from the U.S. Army Research Office, grant number DAAH04-95-1-0323, by NSR grant CCR 9732916, and by an Alfred P. Sloan Research Fellowship. The second author was supported by a UNC Board of Governor's Fellowship. The third author was supported by a grant from IBM Corporation.

balanced trees. Both lock-based and lock-free (see below) object implementations were evaluated. Ramamurthy found that, even on a slow 25 MHz machine, all object calls completed within about 100 microseconds, with most taking much less. In contrast, a quantum in the range 1-100 milliseconds is used in most quantum-based systems.[1]

These numbers suggest that, in a quantum-based system, most object calls are likely to execute without preemption. A good object-sharing scheme should optimize for this expected case, while achieving low overhead when preemptions do occur. Clearly, an optimistic object-sharing scheme is called for here, because pessimistically defending against interferences on every object call by acquiring a lock will lead to wasted overhead most of time. In an *optimistic scheme*, objects are accessed in a manner that does not preclude interferences due to concurrent accesses. If an operation on an object *is* interfered with before it is completed, then it has no effect on the object. Any operation that is interfered with must be retried in order to complete. Optimistic schemes perform well when retries are rare, which is precisely the situation in quantum-based systems.

In this paper, we show that it is possible to significantly optimize retry-based shared-object algorithms by directly exploiting the relative infrequency of preemptions in quantum-based systems. The specific assumption we make throughout this paper regarding preemptions is as follows.[2]

Preemption Axiom: *The quantum is large enough to ensure that each task can be preempted at most once across two consecutive object calls.* □

Given the Preemption Axiom, each object call can be retried at most once, i.e., there is a bound on overall object-sharing costs. The Preemption Axiom is quite liberal: not only are object calls of short to medium duration allowed (the case we most expect and optimize for), but also calls that are quite long, approaching the length of an entire quantum.

Our work builds upon recent research by us and others on using lock-free and wait-free shared-object algorithms in real-time systems [3, 4, 5, 6, 15, 19]. Operations on lock-free objects are optimistically performed using a user-level retry loop. Such an operation is atomically validated and committed by invoking a synchronization primitive such as *compare-and-swap* (CAS). The retry loop is executed repeatedly until this validation step succeeds. Wait-free shared objects are required to satisfy an extreme form of lock-freedom that precludes all waiting dependencies among tasks, including potentially unbounded operation retries.

The remainder of this paper is organized as follows. In the first part of the paper (Section 2), we consider the problem of implementing shared objects in quantum-based uniprocessor systems. Our approach is to develop lock-free algorithms that are optimized in accordance with the Preemption Axiom. The Preemption Axiom ensures that each lock-free operation is retried at most once. Thus, if an operation is interfered with due to a preemption, then the retry code can be purely sequential code in which shared data is read and written without using synchronization primitives. In short, the Preemption Axiom automatically converts a lock-free implementation into a wait-free one. In addition to discussing algorithmic techniques, we also show how to account for object-sharing costs in scheduling analysis.

In the second part of the paper (Section 3), we consider the problem of implementing shared objects in quantum-based multiprocessor systems. In a multiprocessor, a retry mechanism by itself clearly is not sufficient, because a task on one processor may be repeatedly interfered with due to object invocations by tasks on other processors. Our approach is to use a retry mechanism in conjunction with a preemptable queue lock [17]. In our approach, a task performs an operation on an object by first acquiring a lock; if a task is preempted before its operation is completed, then its operation is retried. In comparison to previous preemptable queue-lock algorithms [21, 22], ours is quite simple. Its simplicity is mostly due to the fact that it was designed for systems satisfying the Preemption Axiom.

2. Uniprocessor Systems

In this section, we consider the implementation of shared objects in quantum-based uniprocessor systems. We also show how to account for object-sharing costs arising from the proposed implementations in scheduling analysis.

2.1. Implementing Objects

The Preemption Axiom ensures that each lock-free operation is retried at most once. Thus, if an operation is interfered with due to a preemption, then the retry code can be optimized to be purely sequential code in which shared data is accessed without using synchronization primitives.

Implementing read-modify-writes. As an example of an implementation that is optimized in this way, consider Figure 1. This figure shows how to implement read-modify-write (RMW) operations using CAS.[3] A RMW operation on a variable X is characterized by specifying a function f.

---

[1] A quantum of 1-100 milliseconds may not be sufficient for all real-time applications. For systems that employ a very small quantum, the results of this paper may not be applicable.

[2] This axiom can be weakened to allow preemptions by tasks due to external interrupts, provided that each task can be preempted at most once across two consecutive object calls by other tasks that access shared objects, and the time spent servicing external interrupts is accounted for when analyzing schedulability.

[3] CAS($addr, old, new$) is equivalent to the atomic code fragment ⟨ **if** $*addr = old$ **then** $*addr := new$; **return** *true* **else return** *false* **fi** ⟩.

```
procedure RMW(Addr: ptr to valtype; f: function) returns valtype
private variable old, new: valtype
1:    old := *Addr;
2:    new := f(old);
3:    if CAS(Addr, old, new) = false then
4:        old := *Addr;                    /* retry operation */
5:        *Addr := f(old)   /* lines 4-5 execute without preemption */
      fi;
6:    return old
```

Figure 1. Uniprocessor read-modify-write implementation.

Informally, such an operation has the effect of the following atomic code fragment: $\langle x := X;\ X := f(x);\ $ **return** $x \rangle$. Example RMW operations include fetch-and-increment, fetch-and-store, and test-and-set.

The implementation in Figure 1 is quite simple. If the CAS at line 3 succeeds, then the RMW operation atomically takes effect when the CAS is performed. If the CAS fails, then the invoking task must have been preempted between lines 1 and 3. In this case, the Preemption Axiom implies that lines 4 and 5 execute without preemption. Given this implementation, we can conclude that, in any quantum-based uniprocessor system that provides CAS, any object accessed only by means of reads, writes, and read-modify-writes can be implemented in constant time. It should be noted that virtually every modern processor either provides CAS or instructions that can be used to easily implement CAS.

Conditional compare-and-swap. Using similar principles, it is possible to efficiently implement *conditional compare-and-swap* (CCAS), which is a very useful primitive when implementing lock-free and wait-free objects. CCAS has the following semantics.

CCAS(V: **ptr to** *vertype*; *ver*: *vertype*; X: **ptr to** *wdtype*;
                      old, *new*: *wdtype*) **returns** boolean
$\langle$ **if** $*V \neq ver \vee *X \neq old$ **then return** *false* **fi**;
$\quad *X := new$;
$\quad$ **return** *true* $\rangle$

The angle brackets above indicate that CCAS is atomic. As its definition shows, CCAS is a restriction of a two-word CAS primitive in which one word is a compare-only value. Lock-free and wait-free objects can be implemented by using a "version number" that is incremented by each object call [3, 12]. CCAS is useful because the version number can be used to ensure that a "late" CCAS operation performed by a task after having been preempted has no effect.

Figure 2 shows how to implement CCAS using CAS on a quantum-based uniprocessor. The implementation works by packing a task index into the words being accessed. The

```
type wdtype = record val: valtype; task: 0..N end
        /* all fields of wdtype are stored in one word; task indices ... */
        /* ... range over 1..N; the task field should be 0 initially */

procedure CCAS(V: ptr to vertype; ver: vertype;
        W: ptr to wdtype; old, new: wdtype; p: 1..N) returns boolean
private variable w: wdtype
        /* p is assumed to be the identify of the invoking task */

1:    w := *W;
2:    if w.val ≠ old.val then return false fi;
3:    if *V ≠ ver then return false fi;
4:    if CAS(W, w, (old.val, p)) then
5:        if *V ≠ ver then
6:            w := *W;        /* lines 6-8 execute without preemption */
7:            *W := (w.val, 0);
8:            return false
          fi;
9:        if CAS(W, (old.val, p), (new.val, 0)) then return true fi
      fi;
      /* lines 10-13 execute without preemption */
10:   if W->val ≠ old.val then return false fi;
11:   if *V ≠ ver then return false fi;
12:   *W := (new.val, 0);
13:   return true

procedure Read(W: ptr to wdtype) returns wdtype
private variable w: wdtype

14:   w := *W;
15:   if w.task = 0 then return w.val
      else
16:       CAS(W, w, (w.val, 0)); /* lines 16-19 are rarely executed */
17:       w := *W;
18:       CAS(W, w, (w.val, 0));
19:       return w.val
      fi
```

Figure 2. CCAS **implementation. Code for reading a word accessed by** CCAS **is also shown.**

task index field is used to detect preemptions. It is clearly in accordance with the semantics of CCAS for a task T_i to return from line 2 or 3. To see that the rest of the algorithm is correct, observe that a task T_i can find $*V \neq ver$ at line 5 only if it was preempted between lines 3 and 5. Similarly, the CAS operations at lines 4 and 9 can fail only if a preemption occurs. By the Preemption Axiom, this implies that lines 6-8 and 10-13 execute without preemption. It is thus easy to see that these lines are correct. The remaining possibility is that a task T_i returns from line 9. T_i can return here only if the CAS operations performed by T_i at lines 4 and 9 both succeed. The first of these CAS operations only updates the task index field of W; the second updates the value field. We claim that T_i's CAS at line 9 is successful only if no task performs a Read operation on word W or assigns W within its CCAS procedure between the execution of lines 4 and 9 by T_i — note that this property implies that T_i's CCAS can be linearized to its execution of line 5. To see that this property holds, observe that if some other task updates W in its CCAS procedure, then $W->task \neq i$ is established, implying that T_i's CAS at line 9 fails. Also, if some task T_j performs a Read operation on W when $W->task = i$ holds, then it must establish $W->task = 0$, causing T_i's CAS at line 9 to fail. To see this, note that, by the Preemption Axiom, T_j's execution of the Read procedure itself can be preempted at most once. By inspecting the code of this procedure, it can be seen that this implies that T_j must establish $W->task = 0$ during the same quantum as when it reads the value of W.

It is important to stress that our objective here is to design object implementations that perform very well in the absence of preemptions and that are still correct when preemptions do occur. If the code in Figure 2 is never preempted when executed by any task, then lines 6-8, 10-13, and 16-19 are never executed. Thus, in the expected case, this object implementation should perform well.

In the full paper [1], an implementation of a multi-word CAS (MWCAS) object is presented that is based on techniques that are similar to those described above; this implementation is not included here due to lack of space. The semantics of MWCAS generalizes that of CAS to allow multiple words to be accessed simultaneously. MWCAS is a useful primitive for two reasons. First, it simplifies the implementation of many lock-free objects; queues, for instance, are easy to implement with MWCAS, but harder to implement with single-word primitives. Second, it can be used to implement multi-object operations. For example, an operation that dequeues an item off of one queue and enqueues it onto another could be implemented by using MWCAS to update both queues. Our MWCAS implementation is a bit more involved than those described above, and thus may be of interest to readers interested in techniques for implementing more complicated objects.

2.2. Scheduling Analysis

We now turn our attention to the issue of accounting for object-sharing costs in scheduling analysis when object implementations like those proposed in the previous subsection are used. We consider scheduling analysis under the rate-monotonic (RM) and earliest-deadline-first (EDF) scheduling schemes. We also very briefly consider proportional-share (PS) scheduling.

We begin by considering the RM and EDF schemes. In both of these schemes, a periodic task model is assumed. We call each task invocation a *job*. For brevity, we limit our attention to systems in which each task's relative deadline equals its period (extending our results to deal with systems in which a task's relative deadline may be less than its period is fairly straightforward). In our analysis, we assume that each job is composed of distinct nonoverlapping computational fragments or *phases*. Each phase is either a *computation phase* or an *object-access phase*. Shared objects are not accessed during a computation phase. An object-access phase consists of exactly one retry loop. We assume that tasks are indexed such that, if a job of task T_i can preempt a job of task T_j, then $i < j$ (such an indexing is possible under both RM and EDF scheduling). The following is a list of symbols that will be used in our analysis.

- N - The number of tasks in the system. We use i, j, and l as task indices; each is universally quantified over $\{1, \ldots, N\}$.

- Q - The length of the scheduling quantum.

- p_i - The period of task T_i.

- w_i - The number of phases in a job of task T_i. The phases are numbered from 1 to w_i. We use u and v to denote phases.

- x_i - The number of object-access phases in a job of task T_i.

- c_i^v - The worst-case computational cost of the vth phase of task T_i, where $1 \leq v \leq w_i$, assuming no contention for the processor or shared objects. We denote total cost over all phases by $c_i = \sum_{v=1}^{w_i} c_i^v$.

- r_i^v - The cost of a retry if the vth phase of task T_i is interfered with. For computation phases, $r_i^v = 0$. For object-access phases, we usually have $r_i^v < c_i^v$, because retries are performed sequentially. We let $r_i = max_v(r_i^v)$.

- $m_i^v(j, t)$ - The worst-case number of interferences in T_i's v^{th} phase due to T_j in an interval of length t.

- f_i^v - An upper bound on the number of interferences of the retry loop in the vth phase of T_i during a single execution of that phase.

A simple bound on interference costs. The simplest way to account for object interference costs is to simply inflate each task T_i's computation time to account for such costs. This can be done by solving the following recurrence.

$$c_i' = c_i + min[x_i, (\lceil \frac{c_i'}{Q} \rceil - 1)] \cdot r_i \qquad (1)$$

c_i' is obtained here by inflating c_i by r_i for each quantum boundary that is crossed, up to a maximum of x_i such boundaries (since T_i accesses at most x_i objects in total). If task T_i accesses objects with widely varying retry costs, then the above recurrence may be too pessimistic. Let $r_{i,1}$ be the maximum retry cost of any of T_i's object-access phases, let $r_{i,2}$ be the next-highest cost, and so on. Also, let $v_i = min[x_i, (\lceil c_i'/Q \rceil - 1)]$. Then, we can more accurately inflate c_i by solving the following recurrence.

$$c_i' = c_i + \sum_{k=1}^{v_i} r_{i,k} \qquad (2)$$

Once such c_i' values have been calculated, they can be used within scheduling conditions that apply to independent tasks. A condition for the RM scheme is given in the following theorem.

Theorem 1: *In an RM-scheduled quantum-based uniprocessor system, a set of tasks with objects implemented using the proposed retry algorithms is schedulable if the following holds for every task T_i, where $B_i = \min(Q, \max_{j>i}(c_j'))$.*

$$(\exists t : 0 < t \le p_i :: B_i + \sum_{j=1}^{i} \left\lceil \frac{t}{p_j} \right\rceil c_j' \le t) \qquad \square$$

In the above expression, B_i is a blocking term that arises due to the use of quantum-based scheduling [14].[4] The next theorem gives a scheduling condition for the EDF scheme.

Theorem 2: *In an EDF-scheduled quantum-based uniprocessor system, a set of tasks with objects implemented using the proposed retry algorithms is schedulable if the following holds.*

$$\sum_{i=1}^{N} \frac{c_i'}{p_i} \le 1 \wedge$$
$$(\forall i : 1 \le i \le N :: (\forall t : p_1 < t < p_i :: min(Q, c_i') + \sum_{j=1}^{i-1} \lfloor \frac{t-1}{p_j} \rfloor c_j' \le t)) \qquad \square$$

The above condition is obtained by adapting the condition given by Jeffay et al. in [13] for nonpreemptive EDF scheduling. Note that this condition reduces to that of Jeffay et al. when $Q = \infty$ and to that for preemptive EDF scheduling [16] when $Q = 0$.

Bounding interference costs using linear programming. Anderson and Ramamurthy showed that when lock-free objects are used in a uniprocessor system, object interference costs due to preemptions can be more accurately bounded using linear programming [4]. Given the Preemption Axiom, we show that it is possible to obtain bounds that are tighter than those of Anderson and Ramamurthy.

Our linear programming conditions make use of a bit of additional notation. If a job of T_j interferes with the vth

---

phase of a job of T_i, then an additional demand is placed on the processor, because another execution of the retry-loop iteration in T_i's v^{th} phase is required. We denote this additional demand by $s_i^v(j)$. Formally, $s_i^v(j)$ is defined as follows.

Definition 1: Let T_i and T_j be two distinct tasks, where T_i has at least v phases. Let z_j denote the set of objects modified by T_j, and a_i^v denote the set of objects accessed in the vth phase of T_i. Then,

$$s_i^v(j) = \begin{cases} r_i^v & \text{if } j < i \wedge a_i^v \cap z_j \ne \emptyset \\ 0 & \text{otherwise.} \end{cases}$$

Give the above definition of $s_i^v(j)$, we can state an *exact* expression for the worst-case interference cost in tasks T_1 through T_i in any interval of length t.

Definition 2: The total cost of interferences in jobs of tasks T_1 through T_i in any interval of length t, denoted $E_i(t)$, is defined as follows: $E_i(t) \equiv \sum_{j=1}^{i} \sum_{v=1}^{w_j} \sum_{l=1}^{j-1} m_j^v(l,t) s_j^v(l)$. $\square$

The term $m_j^v(l,t)$ in the above expression denotes the worst-case number of interferences caused in T_j's v^{th} phase by jobs of T_l in an interval of length t. The term $s_j^v(l)$ represents the amount of additional demand required if T_l interferes once with T_j's v^{th} phase. The expression within the leftmost summation denotes the total cost of interferences in a task T_j over all phases of all jobs of T_j in an interval of length t.

Expression $E_i(t)$ accurately reflects the worst-case additional demand placed on the processor in an interval $\mathcal{I}$ of length t due to interferences in tasks T_1 through T_i. Precisely evaluating this expression is computationally expensive, so we instead will try to obtain a bound on $E_i(t)$ that is as tight as possible. We do this by viewing $E_i(t)$ as an expression to be maximized. The $m_j^v(l,t)$ terms are the "variables" in this expression. These variables are subject to certain constraints. We obtain a bound for $E_i(t)$ by using linear programming to determine a maximum value of $E_i(t)$ subject to these constraints. We now explain how appropriate constraints on the $m_j^v(l,t)$ variables are obtained. In this explanation, we focus on the RM scheme. Defining similar constraints for the EDF scheme is fairly straightforward. We impose six sets of constraints on the $m_i^v(j,t)$ variables.

Constraint Set 1: $(\forall i,j : j < i :: \sum_{v=1}^{w_i} m_i^v(j,t) \le \lceil \frac{t+1}{p_j} \rceil)$. $\square$

Constraint Set 2: $(\forall i :: \sum_{j=1}^{i} \sum_{v=1}^{w_j} \sum_{l=1}^{j-1} m_j^v(l,t) \le \sum_{j=1}^{i-1} \lceil \frac{t+1}{p_j} \rceil)$. $\square$

Constraint Set 3: $(\forall i,v :: \sum_{j=1}^{i-1} m_i^v(j,t) \le \lceil \frac{t+1}{p_i} \rceil f_i^v)$. $\square$

Constraint Set 4: $(\forall i, v :: f_i^v \le 1)$. □

Constraint Set 5: $(\forall i :: \sum_{j=1}^{i-1} \sum_{v=1}^{w_j} m_i^v(j,t) \le (\lceil \frac{c_i'}{Q} \rceil - 1) \cdot \lceil \frac{t+1}{p_i} \rceil)$. □

Constraint Set 6: $(\forall i :: \sum_{j=1}^{i-1} \sum_{v=1}^{w_j} m_i^v(j,t) \le x_i \cdot \lceil \frac{t+1}{p_i} \rceil)$. □

There first three constraint sets were given previously by Anderson and Ramamurthy [4]. The first set of constraints follows because the number of interferences in jobs of T_i due to T_j in an interval $\mathcal{I}$ of length t is bounded by the maximum number of jobs of T_j that can be released in $\mathcal{I}$. The second set of constraints follows from a result presented in [6], which states that the total number of interferences in all jobs of tasks T_1 through T_i in an interval $\mathcal{I}$ of length t is bounded by the maximum number of jobs of tasks T_1 through T_{i-1} released in $\mathcal{I}$. In the third set of constraints, the term f_i^v is an upper bound on the number of interferences of the retry loop in the vth phase of T_i during a single execution of that phase. The reasoning behind this set of constraints is as follows. If at most f_i^v interferences can occur in the vth phase of a job of T_i, and if there are n jobs of T_i released in an interval $\mathcal{I}$, then at most $n f_i^v$ interferences can occur in the vth phase of T_i in $\mathcal{I}$. In Anderson and Ramamurthy's paper, the f_i^v terms are calculated by solving an additional set of linear programming problems. In our case, they can be bounded as shown in the fourth set of constraints.[5] This is because, by the Preemption Axiom, each object access can be interfered with at most once. The last two constraint sets arise for precisely the same reasons as given when recurrence (1) was explained. The c_i' term in the fifth constraint set can be calculated by solving recurrence (1) or (2).

We are now in a position to state scheduling conditions for the RM and EDF schemes. Recall that $E_i(t)$ is the actual worst-case cost of interferences in jobs of tasks T_1 through T_i in any interval of length t. We let $E_i'(t)$ denote a bound on $E_i(t)$ that is determined using linear programming as described above. For RM scheduling, we have the following.

Theorem 3: *In an RM-scheduled quantum-based uniprocessor system, a set of tasks with objects implemented using the proposed retry algorithms is schedulable if the following holds for every task* T_i*, where* $B_i = \min(Q, \max_{j>i}(c_j'))$.

$$(\exists t : 0 < t \le p_i :: B_i + \sum_{j=1}^{i} \lceil \frac{t}{p_j} \rceil c_j + E_i'(t-1) \le t)$$ □

---

[5]It is actually possible to eliminate Constraint Set 4, because the linear programming solver will always maximize each f_i^v term to be 1. Furthermore, when substituting 1 for f_i^v in Constraint Set 3, the resulting set of constraints implies those given in Constraint Set 6, so these constraints can be removed as well. We did not minimize the constraint sets in this way because we felt that this would make them more difficult to understand, especially when comparing them against those in [4].

This condition is obtained by modifying one proved in [4] by including a blocking factor for the scheduling quantum. For EDF scheduling, we have the following.

Theorem 4: *In an EDF-scheduled quantum-based uniprocessor system, a set of tasks with objects implemented using the proposed retry algorithms is schedulable if the following holds.*

$$(\forall t :: \sum_{j=1}^{N} \lfloor \frac{t}{p_j} \rfloor c_j + E_N'(t-1) \le t)$$ □

This condition was also proved in [4]. Since t is checked beginning at time 0, a blocking factor is not required. As stated, the expression in Theorem 4 cannot be verified because the value of t is unbounded. However, there is an implicit bound on t. In particular, we only need to consider values less than or equal to the least common multiple of the task periods. (If an upper bound on the utilization available for the tasks is known, then we can restrict t to a much smaller range [9].)

Note that, in a quantum-based system, no object access by a task that is guaranteed to complete within the first quantum allocated to a job of that task can be interfered with. Thus, such an access can be performed using a less-costly code fragment that is purely sequential. All of the scheduling conditions presented in this subsection can be improved by accounting for this fact.

In the full paper [1], we show how object-sharing overheads arising from algorithms as proposed here affect lag-bound calculations in proportional-share (PS) scheduled systems. In the PS scheduling literature, the term "client" is used to refer to a schedulable entity. Each client is assigned a *share* of the processor, which represents the fraction of processing time that that client should receive. Quanta are allocated in a manner that ensures that the amount of processor time each client receives is commensurate with its share. The *lag* of a client is the difference between the time a client should have received in an ideal system with a quantum approaching zero, and the time it actually receives in a real system. Stoica et al. showed that optimal lag bounds can be achieved by using *earliest-eligible-virtual-deadline-first* (EEVDF) scheduling [20]. As we show in the full paper, the lag bounds of Stoica et al. can be applied in a system in which our shared-object algorithms are used by simply inflating the cost of a client's request by the cost of one retry loop for every quantum boundary it crosses.

Experimental Comparison. In order to compare the retry-cost estimates produced by the linear programming methods proposed in this paper and in [4], we conducted a series of simulation experiments involving randomly-generated task sets scheduled under the RM scheme. Each task set in these experiments was defined to consist of ten tasks that access up to ten shared objects. 120 task sets

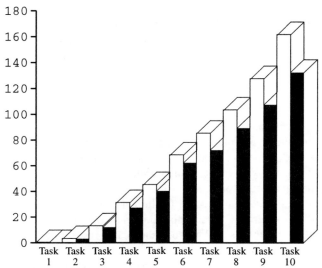

□ Old Condition ■ New Condition

Figure 3. Comparison of linear programming scheduling conditions. Each task's average estimated retry cost is shown.

were generated in total, and for each task set, a retry cost was computed for each task using the two methods being compared. Due to space limitations, the exact methodology we used in generating task sets is not described here; see [1] for details. The results of these experiments are depicted in Figure 3. This figure shows the average retry cost of each task over all generated task sets as computed by each method. As before, tasks are indexed in order of increasing periods. Thus, T_1 has highest priority in all experiments, and as a result, its retry cost is estimated to be zero under both methods. It can be seen in Figure 3 that the method of this paper yields retry-cost estimates for higher-priority tasks that are about 10% to 20% lower than those produced by the method of [4]. In addition to determining retry-cost estimates, we also kept track of how long each schedulability check took to complete. On average, the schedulability check proposed in this paper took 11.7 seconds per task set, while the one proposed in [4] took 235 seconds. This is because of the complicated procedure invoked to compute f_i^v values in the method of [4].

3. Multiprocessor Systems

In this section, we describe a new approach to implementing shared objects in quantum-based multiprocessor systems. Using this retry mechanism, scheduling analysis can be performed on each processor using the uniprocessor scheduling conditions considered in the previous section. In

Section 3.1, we describe this retry mechanism in detail. In Section 3.2, we present results from experiments conducted to evaluate our approach.

3.1. Implementing Objects

In a multiprocessor system, a retry mechanism by itself is not sufficient, because a task on one processor may be repeatedly interfered with due to object invocations performed by tasks on other processors. Our approach is to use a retry mechanism in conjunction with a preemptable queue lock. A *queue lock* is a spin lock in which waiting tasks form a queue [17]. Queue locks are useful in real-time systems because waiting times can be bounded. With a preemptable queue lock, a task waiting for or holding a lock can be preempted without impeding the progress of other tasks waiting for the lock. Given such a locking mechanism, any preempted operation can be safely retried. As before, we can appeal to the Preemption Axiom to bound retries, because retries are caused only by preemptions, not by interferences across processors. The Preemption Axiom is still reasonable to assume if we focus on systems with a small to moderate number of processors (the cost an operation depends on the spin queue length, which in turn depends on the number of processors in the system). We believe that it is unlikely that a real-time application would be implemented on a large multiprocessor, and even if it were, it is unlikely that one object would be shared across a large number of processors.

Queue locks come in two flavors: array-based locks, which use an array of spin locations [7, 11], and list-based locks, in which spinning tasks form a linked list [17]. List-based queue locks have the advantage of requiring only constant space overhead per task per lock. In addition, list-based queue locks exist in which all spins are local if applied on multiprocessors either with coherent caches or distributed shared memory [17]. In contrast, with existing array-based locks, spins are local only if applied in a system with coherent caches.

All work known to us on preemptable queue locks involves list-based locks [21, 22]. This is probably due to the advantages listed in the previous paragraph that (non-preemptable) list-based locks have over array-based ones. However, correctly maintaining a linked list of spinning tasks in the face of preemptions is very trick. Wisniewski et al. handle such problems by exploiting a rather non-standard kernel interface that has the ability to "warn" tasks before they are preempted so that they can take appropriate action in time [22]. In the absence of such a kernel interface, list maintenance becomes quite hard, leading to complicated algorithms. For example, a list-based preemptable queue lock proposed recently by Takada and Sakamura requires a total of 63 executable statements [21]. Our preemptable queue lock is an array-based lock and is quite simple, consisting of only 17 lines of code. In addition, all that we require the kernel to do is to set a shared variable whenever a task is preempted indicating that that task is no longer running. As with other array-based locks, our algorithm has linear space overhead per lock and requires coherent caches in order for spins to be local. However, most modern workstation-class multiprocessors have coherent caches. Also, in many applications, most objects are shared only by a relatively small number tasks, so having linear space per lock shouldn't be a severe problem. In any event, these disadvantages seem to be far outweighed by the fact that our algorithm is so simple.

Our algorithm is shown in Figure 4. For clarity, the lock being implemented has been left implicit. In an actual implementation, the shared variables *Tail*, *State*, and *Pred* would be associated with a particular lock and a pointer to that lock would be passed to *acquire_lock* and *release_lock*.

The *State* array consists of $2N$ "slots", which are used as spin locations. A task T_i alternates between using slots i and $i + N$. T_i appends itself onto the end of the spin queue by performing a *fetch_and_store* operation on the *Tail* variable (line 5). It then spins until either it is preempted, its predecessor in the spin queue is preempted, or its predecessor releases the lock (line 9). In a system with coherent caches, this spin is local. If T_i stops spinning because its predecessor is preempted, then T_i takes its predecessor's predecessor as its new predecessor (lines 12-13). If T_i is preempted before acquiring the lock, then (when it resumes execution) it stops spinning and re-executes the algorithm using its other spin location (line 2). Note that the Preemption Axiom ensures that T_i will not be preempted when it re-executes the algorithm. In addition, by the time T_i acquires the lock and then releases it to another task, no task is waiting on either of its two spin locations, i.e., they can be safely reused when T_i performs future lock accesses. Without the Preemption Axiom, correctly "pruning" a preempted task from the spin queue would be much more complicated. (For multiprocessors, the Preemption Axiom can be relaxed to state that a task can be preempted at most once across two consecutive attempts to complete the *same* object call. If our lock algorithm is used by tasks on P processors, then a task that is preempted may have to wait for $P - 1$ tasks on other processors to complete their object calls when it resumes execution. Thus, the Preemption Axiom is tantamount to requiring that the quantum is long enough to contain $P + 1$ consecutive object calls in total on the P processors across which the object is shared.)

We have depicted the algorithm assuming that each task performs its object access as a critical section with interrupts turned off (see lines 14 and 17). Instead, object accesses could be performed using lock-free code, in which case the entire implementation would be preemptable. It can be seen in Figure 4 that the code fragment at lines 5-6 is required to be executed without preemption. This ensures that the

shared variable
  Tail: 0..2N − 1 **initially** 0;
  State: **array**[0..2N − 1] **of** {WAITING, DONE, PREEMPTED}
                                             initially DONE;
  Pred: **array**[0..N − 1] **of** 0..2N − 1

private variable   /* local to task T_p */
  pred: 0..2N − 1;
  slot: {p, p + N} **initially** p
  /* *slot* is assumed to retain its value across procedure invocations */

procedure *acquire_lock*()
1: **while** *true* **do**   /* can only loop at most twice */
2:      *slot* := (*slot* + N) **mod** 2N;
3:      *State*[*slot*] := WAITING;
4:      *disable interrupts*;
5:      *pred* := *fetch_and_store*(&*Tail*, *slot*); /* join end of spin queue */
6:      *Pred*[*slot* **mod** N] := *pred*;
7:      *enable interrupts*;
8:      **while** *State*[*slot*] ≠ PREEMPTED **do**
9:          **while** *State*[*slot*] = WAITING ∧
                         State[*pred*] = WAITING **do** /* spin */ **od**;
        /*
        * after the spin, *State*[*slot*] = PREEMPTED or
        * *State*[*pred*] = PREEMPTED or *State*[*pred*] = DONE
        */
10:        **if** *State*[*slot*] ≠ PREEMPTED **then**
11:            **if** *State*[*pred*] = PREEMPTED **then**
12:                *pred* := *Pred*[*pred* **mod** N]; /* predecessor is preempted */
13:                *Pred*[*slot* **mod** N] := *pred*;   /* get new predecessor */
            else /* *State*[*pred*] = DONE */
14:                *disable interrupts*;
15:                **if** *State*[*slot*] = WAITING **then return** /* lock acquired */
                                      else *enable interrupts*
            fi
          fi
        fi
      od
  od

procedure *release_lock*()
16: *State*[*slot*] := DONE;
17: *enable interrupts*

Figure 4. Preemptable spin-lock algorithm for quantum-based multiprocessors. In this figure, task indices are assumed to range over $\{0, \ldots, N - 1\}$**.**

predecessor of a preempted task can always be determined. As an alternative to disabling interrupts, if a preemption occurs between lines 5 and 6, then the kernel could roll the preempted task forward one statement when saving its state. This alternative would be necessary in systems in which tasks do not have the ability to disable interrupts.

When a task T_i is preempted while waiting for the lock, the kernel must establish *State*[*slot*] = PREEMPTED. It is not necessary for the kernel to scan state information per lock to do this. The appropriate variable to update can be determined by having a single shared pointer *Stateptr*[*i*] for each task T_i that is used across all locks. Prior to assigning "State[*slot*] := WAITING" in line 3, T_i would first update *Stateptr*[i] to point to *State*[*slot*]. By reading *Stateptr*[i], the kernel would know which state variable to update upon a preemption. (If locks can be nested, then multiple *Stateptr* variables would be required per task.)

3.2. Experimental Comparison

We have conducted performance experiments to compare our preemptable queue lock algorithm to a preemptable queue lock presented last year by Takada and Sakamura [21]. Their lock is designated as the "SPEPP/MCS algorithm" in their paper, so we will use that term here (SPEPP stands for "spinning processor executes for preempted processors"; MCS denotes that this lock is derived from one published previously by Mellor-Crummey and Scott [17]). The SPEPP/MCS algorithm was the fastest in the face of preemptions of several lock algorithms tested by Takada and Sakamura. Our experiments were conducted using the Proteus parallel architecture simulator [10]. Using a simulator made it easy to provide the kernel interface needed by each algorithm. The simulator was configured to simulate a bus-based shared-memory multiprocessor, with an equal number of processors and memory modules. The simulated system follows a bus-based snoopy protocol with write-invalidation for cache coherence. Tasks are assigned to processors and are not allowed to migrate. On each processor, tasks are scheduled for execution using a quantum-based round-robin scheduling policy. The scheduling quantum in our simulation was taken to be 10 milliseconds.

Figure 5 presents the results of our experiments. In this figure, the average time is shown for a task to acquire the lock, execute its critical section, and release the lock. These curves were obtained with a multiprogramming level of five tasks per processor, with each task performing 50 lock accesses. The execution cost of the critical section was fixed at 600 microseconds. Each task was configured to perform a noncritical section between lock accesses, the cost of which was randomly chosen between 0 and 600 microseconds. The simulations we conducted indicate that only the number of processors in the system affects relative performance; simulations for different numbers of lock accesses and multiprogramming levels resulted in similar graphs. The curves in Figure 5 indicate that the time taken to acquire the lock in our algorithm is up to 25% less than that for the SPEPP/MCS algorithm (the time taken to acquire the lock is obtained by subtracting the critical section execution time from the values in Figure 5). We also instrumented the code to measure the time taken to acquire the lock in the best case. For each algorithm, the time taken by a task to acquire the lock is minimized when that task is at the head of the spin queue. The best-case time for acquiring the lock was 100

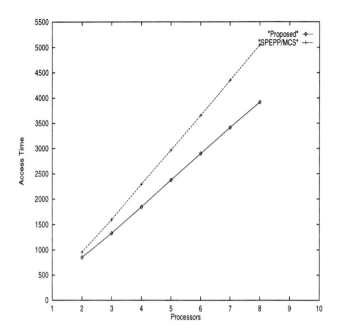

Figure 5. Experimental comparison of preemptable spin-lock algorithms. Curves show average access times (in microseconds).

microseconds for our algorithm, and 200 microseconds for the SPEPP/MCS algorithm.

4. Concluding Remarks

We have presented a new approach to implementing shared objects in quantum-based real-time uniprocessor and multiprocessor systems. In the proposed object implementations, object calls are performed using an optimistic retry mechanism coupled with the assumption that each task can be preempted at most once across two consecutive object calls. We have presented experimental evidence that such implementations should entail low overhead in practice.

In a recent related paper, Anderson, Jain, and Ott presented a number of new results on the theoretical foundations of wait-free synchronization in quantum-based systems [2]. It was shown in that paper that the ability to achieve wait-free synchronization in quantum-based systems is a function of both the "power" of available synchronization primitives and the size of the scheduling quantum. We hope the results of [2] and this paper will spark further research on synchronization problems arising in quantum-based systems.

Acknowledgement: We are grateful to Alex Blate for his help in running simulation experiments. We also acknowledge David Koppelman for his help with the Proteus simulator.

References

[1] J. Anderson, R. Jain, and K. Jeffay Efficient Object Sharing in Quantum-Based Real-Time Systems (expanded version of this paper). Available at http://www.cs.unc.edu/~anderson/papers.html.

[2] J. Anderson, R. Jain, and D. Ott. Wait-free synchronization in quantum-based multiprogrammed systems. In *Proceedings of the 12th International Symp. on Distributed Computing (to appear)*. Springer Verlag, 1998.

[3] J. Anderson, R. Jain, and S. Ramamurthy. Wait-free object-sharing schemes for real-time uniprocessors and multiprocessors. In *Proceedings of the 18th IEEE Real-Time Systems Symp.*, pp. 111–122. 1997.

[4] J. Anderson and S. Ramamurthy. A framework for implementing objects and scheduling tasks in lock-free real-time systems. In *Proceedings of the 17th IEEE Real-Time Systems Symp.*, pp. 92–105. 1996.

[5] J. Anderson, S. Ramamurthy, and R. Jain. Implementing wait-free objects in priority-based systems. In *Proceedings of the 16th ACM Symp. on Principles of Distributed Computing*, pp. 229–238. 1997.

[6] J. Anderson, S. Ramamurthy, and K. Jeffay. Real-time computing with lock-free objects. *ACM Trans. on Computer Systems*, 15(6):388–395, 1997.

[7] T. Anderson. The performance of spin lock alternatives for shared-memory multiprocessors. *IEEE Trans. on Parallel and Distributed Systems*, 1(1):6–16, 1990.

[8] N. C. Audsley, I. J. Bate, and A. Burns. Putting fixed priority scheduling into engineering practice for safety critical applications. In *Proceedings of the 1996 IEEE Real-Time Technology and Applications Symp.*, pp. 2–10, 1996.

[9] S. Baruah, R. Howell, and L. Rosier. Feasibility problems for recurring tasks on one processor. *Theoretical Computer Science*, 118:3–20, 1993.

[10] E. Brewer, C. Dellarocas, A. Colbrook, and W. Weihl. Proteus: A high-performance parallel-architecture simulator. Technical Report MIT/LCS/TR-516, MIT, Cambridge, Massachusetts, 1992.

[11] G. Graunke and S. Thakkar. Synchronization algorithms for shared-memory multiprocessors. *IEEE Computer*, 23:60–69, 1990.

[12] M. Greenwald and D. Cheriton. The synergy between non-blocking synchronization and operating system structure. In *Proceedings of the USENIX Association Second Symp. on Operating Systems Design and Implementation*, pp. 123–136, 1996.

[13] K. Jeffay, D. Stanat, and C. Martel. On non-preemptive scheduling of periodic and sporadic tasks. In *Proceedings of the 12th IEEE Symp. on Real-Time Systems*, pp. 129–139. 1991.

[14] D. Katcher, H. Arakawa, and J.K. Strosnider. Engineering and analysis of fixed priority schedulers. *IEEE Trans. on Software Engineering*, 19(9):920–934, 1993.

[15] H. Kopetz and J. Reisinger. The non-blocking write protocol nbw: A solution to a real-time synchronization problem. In *Proceedings of the 14th IEEE Symp. on Real-Time Systems*, pp. 131–137. 1993.

[16] C. Liu and J. Layland. Scheduling algorithms for multiprogramming in a hard real–time environment. *Journal of the ACM*, 30:46–61, 1973.

[17] J. Mellor-Crummey and M. Scott. Algorithms for scalable synchronization on shared-memory multiprocessors. *ACM Trans. on Computer Systems*, 9(1):21–65, 1991.

[18] S. Ramamurthy. *A Lock-Free Approach to Object Sharing in Real-Time Systems*. PhD thesis, University of North Carolina, Chapel Hill, North Carolina, 1997.

[19] S. Ramamurthy, M. Moir, and J. Anderson. Real-time object sharing with minimal support. In *Proceedings of the 15th ACM Symp. on Principles of Distributed Computing*, pp. 233–242. 1996.

[20] I. Stoica, H. Abdel-Wahab, K. Jeffay, S. Baruah, J. Gehrke, and C. Plaxton. A proportional share resource allocation algorithm for real-time, time-shared systems. In *Proceedings of the 17th IEEE Real-Time Systems Symp.*, pp. 288–299. 1996.

[21] H. Takada and K. Sakamura. A novel approach to multiprogrammed multiprocessor synchronization for real-time kernels. In *Proceedings of the 18th IEEE Real-Time Systems Symp.*, pp. 134–143. 1997.

[22] R. Wisniewski, L. Kontothanassis, and M. Scott. High performance synchronization algorithms for multiprogrammed multiprocessors. In *Proceedings of the Fifth ACM Symp. on Principles and Practices of Parallel Programming*, pp. 199–206. 1995.

Session 11.A: Systems Design and Development Tools II

A Development Framework for Ultra-Dependable Automotive Systems Based on a Time-Triggered Architecture

Bernd Hedenetz

Daimler-Benz Research, HPC T721, D-70546 Stuttgart, Germany

hedenetz@dbag.stg.daimlerbenz.com

Abstract

Today by-wire systems are well-known and utilised in the area of aircraft construction. In the last few years there has been an endeavour in the automotive industry to realise by-wire applications without mechanical or hydraulic backup systems in vehicles. The required electronic systems must be highly reliable and cost-effective due to the constraints of mass production.

A time-triggered architecture is a new approach that satisfies these requirements. The backbone of communication in this architecture is the fault-tolerant Time-Triggered Protocol (TTP), developed by the Vienna University of Technology and the Daimler-Benz Research. The TTP protocol has been designed due to the class C SAE [25] classification for safety critical control applications, like brake-by-wire or steer-by-wire.

For time-triggered architectures a new development process is required to handle the complexity of the systems, accelerate the development and increase the reliability. In this paper we present an approach for the development of distributed fault-tolerant systems based on TTP. The present approach is evaluated by a brake-by-wire case study.

1 Introduction

In the past few years there has been the tendency to increase the safety of vehicles by introducing intelligent assistance systems (e.g., ABS, Brake-Assistant (BA), Electronic Stability Program (ESP), etc.) that help the driver to cope with critical driving situations. These functions are characterised by the active control of the driving dynamics by distributed assistance systems, which therefore need a reliable communication network. The faults in the electronic components, which control these functions, are safety critical. However, the assistance functions deliver only an add-on service in accordance with a fail-safe strategy for the electronic components. If there is any doubt about the correct behavior of the

assistance system, it will be switched off. For by-wire systems without a mechanical backup a new dimension of safety requirements for automotive electronics is reached. After a fault the system has to be fail-operational until a safe state is reached.

For the fail-operational assumption we demand that after any arbitrary fault the system is fully operational. The effective use of the redundancy is important, in order to reduce the production costs for automotive by-wire systems. A major goal is to increase the reliability of the system by adding additional redundancy without increasing the complexity of the system. Therefore, new electronic architectures have to be developed.

Distributed time-triggered architectures (TTA) can be realised through the Time-Triggered Protocol (TTP) which guarantees a global time synchronisation over the whole system and an adequate message transmission.

In this paper we present an approach for the development of distributed fault-tolerant systems based on TTP. This paper is organised as follows: Section 2 gives an overview of the general architecture and elaborates on the time-triggered approach and the communication subsystem. Section 3 gives a short overview about the lifecycle of safety related automotive systems. In Section 4 the development framework for TTA systems is presented. In Section 5 the development approach is demonstrated at the example of a brake-by-wire case study. The paper is concluded in Section 6.

2 Time-Triggered Approach

The TT paradigm of a real-time system is based on a distinctive view of the world: the observer (the computer system) is not driven by the events that happen in its environment. The system decides through the progression of time when to look at the world. Therefore, it is impossible to overload a time-triggered observer.

A TT system takes a snapshot of the world, an observation, at recurring predetermined points in time determined by the current value of a synchronised local clock. This snapshot is disseminated within the computer system by the communication protocol to update the state variables that hold the observed values. The semantic of the periodic messages transported in a TT system is a state-message semantic, i.e., a new version of a message overwrites the previous version and messages are not consumed on reading. This semantic is well suited to handle the transport of the values of the state variables used in control applications. The state message semantic provides a predefined constant load on the communication system and eliminates the problem of dynamic buffer management [23].

2.1 Time-Triggered Protocol (TTP)

For the realisation of a distributed time-triggered architecture a communication network is necessary that provides the features mentioned above. This type of communication belongs mainly to class C of the SAE classification [25].

None of the commonly used in-vehicle communication systems (CAN, A-BUS, VAN, J1850-DLC, J1850-HBCC [26]) meet the requirements for safety related by-wire systems since they were not designed for this case [17]. They are all lacking in being deterministic, in synchronisation and fault tolerance characteristics.

These missing properties are the motivation for developing new approaches for in-vehicle communication systems. As a new start we examine the Time-Triggered Protocol developed by the University of Vienna and Daimler-Benz Research. TTP is especially designed for safety related applications and fulfills these requirements.

TTP is an integrated time-triggered protocol that provides:

- a membership service, i.e., every single node knows about the actual state of any other node of the distributed system
- a fault-tolerant clock synchronisation service (global time-base),
- mode change support,
- error detection with short latency,
- distributed redundancy management.

All these issues are supported implicitly by the protocol itself. A comprehensive description of the TTP protocol is given in [13,14,15]. The TTP protocol has been designed to tolerate any single physical fault in any one of its constituent parts (node, bus) without an impact on the operation of a properly configured cluster [15].

The overall TTP hardware architecture is characterized by both the TTP system architecture and the TTP node architecture as shown in Figure 1. A TTP real-time system consists of a host subsystem, which executes the real-time application and the communication subsystem providing reliable real-time message transmission. The interface between these subsystems is realised by a dual ported RAM (DPRAM) called *Communication Network Interface (CNI)* [16]. The assembly of host and TTP-controller is called *Fail Silent Unit (FSU)*. Two FSUs form a single redundant *Fault-Tolerant Unit (FTU)*. The physical layer consists of two independent transmission channels.

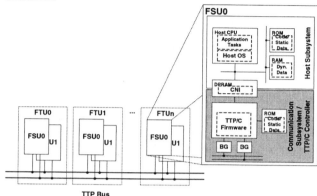

Figure 1: Architecture of a TTP-based fault-tolerant real-time system

2.2 Node Architecture

The overall aim of the node architecture is to fulfill the fail-silence assumption without developing special hardware for fault detection. We use software fault detection methods and low cost hardware mechanisms (such as watchdogs) and mechanisms provided by the CPU (bus error, address error, illegal op-code, privilege violation, division by zero,...). In [12] it is shown that a high degree of fault detection can be achieved by software fault detection mechanisms. We follow this approach for trying to fulfill the fail-silence assumption. Our architecture can be separated into three subsystems (see Figure 2):

- *Communication subsystem*: this part is responsible for the communication between distributed components.
- *Fault-tolerant subsystem*: this part contains safety critical and fault tolerance mechanisms. The safety related application is handled by this subsystem.
- *Application subsystem*: this part includes the safety related tasks, which build the application.

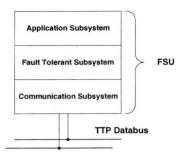

Figure 2: Subsystems of an FSU

2.3 Propagation of TTP

TTP is in discussion in the Brite-EuRam Project „Safety Related Fault Tolerant Systems in Vehicles" (acronym: „X-By-Wire") to be proposed as a European or International Standard [2].

In 1997 the Esprit Project „Time Triggered Architecture" (acronym TTA) has been started with the intention to develop a prototype TTP controller chip [9]. Other aims of the TTA project are the development of tools for the design of TTP systems and the formal verification of parts of the TTP protocol e.g. the clock synchronisation algorithm.

3 Lifecycle

The typical lifecycle for the development of safety related automotive systems consist of the following phases: *system specification*, *system design*, *design verification*, *implementation* and *integration* (see Figure 3). Several, more detailed descriptions of the lifecycle exist, for further study a large number of books [27] and standards are available [10,11]. All steps of the lifecycle have to be supported with tools to manage the complexity of the systems, accelerate the development process and increase the reliability. New tools have to be developed and common used tools have to be adapted to the requirements of TTA systems.

4 Development Process

For TTA systems a new development process is required which supports every phase of the lifecycle. Our aim is to devise a approach for designing complex distributed safety-related automotive systems using *commercial-off-the-shelf* tools to as high a degree as possible. Our approach based on verification of the system design by functional simulation, fault modeling in the models, functional test and fault injection in the real system architecture. Therefore we separate the development process in seven single steps (see Figure 3).

During the first step - *requirement specification* - we specify the functional requirements, the time constrains and the reliability requirements of the system. In the second step - *architectural design* - the structure of the communication network, communication relations between the nodes and the schedule of the application tasks are defined due to the specification. In the next step - *functional design* - we realise the application, e.g., a control loop for an anti blocking system (ABS), as a functional model. For the actual realization of this part we use the tool Statemate™ from i-Logix [7] and MATLAB®/Simulink™ from MathWorks [19]. In the following step - *functional simulation* - the functional models are verified through simulation and the reliability is examined by *fault modeling* into the functional models. In the step - *realisation and integration* - the real architecture is realised and integrated in a vehicle. Therefore we use the capability of automatic code generation of the tools. Additionally, we use monitoring tools to trace the system behavior. In the final step - *test and fault injection* - we execute test and fault injection experiments in the target system to verify the behavior of the real system with respect to the requirement specification.

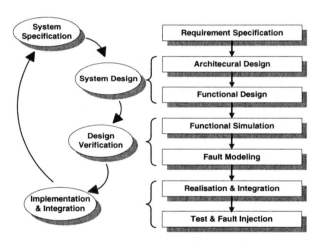

Figure 3: Overview about the development process

4.1 Requirement Specification

System specification is a very sensitive phase. The most faults that lead to critical failures are system-faults, and most design errors are not low-level implementation errors but errors committed at the system specification phase [18]. The description of the requirement specification has to include:
- Identification of the objects in the environment
- which produce or consume data flows.

360

- Definition of the input and output signals for these objects.
- Specification of the functional and time behavior of these objects.
- Specification of the reliability requirements.
- Definition of a fault hypothesis.

To verify the functional models and the system realisation we have to specify the system with a sufficient accuracy. The requirement specification is used to generate test pattern, fault pattern and environment models. Environment models are used as a reference for the functional simulation. Environment models can be described by:
- Statemate^{TM} models,
- Input, output signals (stimulation and reaction),
- Differential equations, and
- C-code.

4.2 Architectural Design

The complexity of a system depends on the number and types of elements and relations and on the amount of their inner states. A method to handle complex systems is the decomposition into smaller subsystems. A common way is to partition the entire system into subsystems with high inner connectivity and few relations crossing the subsystem boundaries [1]. For the design of time triggered architectures we follow this approach; first we design the highest subsystem level, the communication nodes in a TTP communication system. This step is called *global design* and consists of all steps associated with the overall system architecture:
- A time-triggered system is partitioned into a set of components connected by the TTP bus.
- In respect with the reliability requirements, critical components can be replicated.
- The communication relations between the components are defined.
- In the last step, a bus schedule is determined that fulfills the communication requirements of the previous steps.

These steps are typically done by the system manufacturer. The structure is commonly determined by the function which the system has to fulfill. For example, in an automotive steer-by-wire system, redundancy is required for measurement of the steering wheel angle and control of the steering actuator. The redundant nodes have to be distributed that there is no common mode failure - e.g. intruding of water in the ECU - can cause a fatal failure.

4.3 Functional Design

After the global design, the *local design* contains all steps associated with the specification of a single component. The bus message scheduling specified in the global design defines the interface of each component in the value and time domain. The local design consists of the following steps:
- Definition of the software structure of the components.
- Description of the application tasks and their communication relations and time constraints.
- Adding of fault tolerant schemes, e.g. double execution and variable protection through cycle-redundancy checks (CRC).
- Finally, a task schedule which fulfills the functional requirements and time constraints is determined.

The single components in the automotive environment are typically developed by sub-suppliers.

4.4 Functional Simulation

Models of real-time systems have to support different views of a system. A system can be described by four different views:
- Structural view: represents the structure of the subsystems.
- Functional view: describes the functions and processes of the system, the input and output signals, and the information flows between the functions and processes.
- Behavior view: describes the time and dynamic behavior and the internal states of the components.
- Implementation view: represents the realisation of the system by source code.

For the actual realisation of the functional models we use the tools Statemate^{TM} and MATLAB$^®$/Simulink^{TM}. Statemate^{TM} provides a hierarchical modeling approach for the specification and analysis of complex systems. The special feature of Statemate^{TM} is that it puts emphasis on the dynamic verification of the specification. This tool provides facilities for the model execution, in interactive or batch mode, and to instrument the models in order to collect statistics during execution. The model can be either connected to a software environment model (software-in-the-loop) or to a target hardware environment (hardware-in-the-loop). The source code can be generated automatically from the functional specification.

The main benefit of this approach is that the system behavior can be examined from a very early design phase and changes can be made with minor effort.

Statemate[TM] uses three methods for system modeling, *module charts*, *activity charts*, and *statecharts* [5,6]. The module charts describe the structural view of the system while activity charts describe the functional view and are similar to conventional data flow diagrams. Activity charts illustrate the identified sub-functions and the information flows between them. Statecharts describe the behavioral view of the system. Through automatic code generation Statemate[TM] also supports the implementation of the system.

4.4.1 Modeling a TTA System

The Statemate[TM] approach is typically used for reactive systems. Time constraints are only an implicit part of the models. An important property in a TTA is the fulfillment of the time constrains. If the time boundaries are violated the system can not fulfill its duty. We solve this problem by building up a complete model of the TTA system in the Statemate[TM] developing environment. The time constraints of the system architecture are guaranteed by the model of the TTP communication system. The time constraints on the node subsystem are guaranteed by the model of the fault tolerant subsystem.

The *system architecture* is the highest modeling level. This level represents the structure of the system. Every node is also modeled in detail. *Node* represents the node structure and consists of the *fault tolerant subsystem*, the *communication subsystem* and the *application subsystem* (corresponding to Figure 2). The fault tolerant subsystem builds the environment for the safety critical tasks, defined in the application subsystem. The communication subsystem handles the communication services provided by the TTP system (see Figure 4).

For the design of a new system the developer has to define the application dependable parts, the architectural structure of the TTP cluster and the application subsystem, corresponding to the global and local design in Section 4.2 and 4.3. The other parts of the model are available in a model library and can be reused.

4.4.2 Application Functional Specification

Applications on the top of a TTA consist usually of the parts; periodically reading sensor signals, calculation of new system states, and activation of actuators. The function of applications are usually described through statemachines and the control algorithms. The Statemate[TM] environment provide for the specification of statemachines the modeling concept of activity charts and statecharts. The control algorithms are developed with the help of MATLAB[®]/Simulink[TM] or MATRIX$_X$[TM] [28]. The control algorithms can be integrated in Statemate[TM] through C source code or in the case of MATRIX$_X$[TM] directly, due to a common interface.

4.4.3 Application Development Environment

For the developing of applications we use a *software-in-the-loop* simulation environment (see Figure 5). We

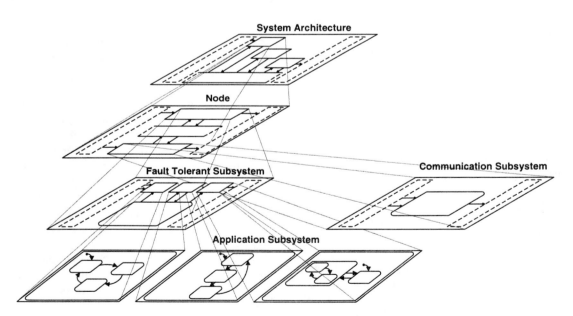

Figure 4: Functional model of a TTA

define a test environment out of the requirement specification, in which the functional model can be tested. We connect the functional model of the TTA system with the behavioral model of the vehicle. This method is called software-in-the-loop. To verify the functional model a set of test patterns have to be defined. The number of test patterns depend on the complexity of the system, the number of signals and the used test strategy. The environment model is realised by using MATLAB®/Simulink™ .

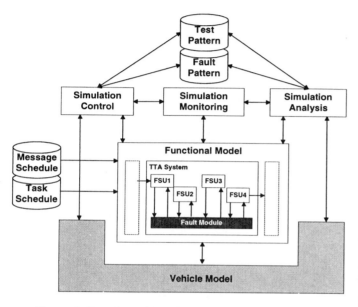

Figure 5: Overview of the simulation environment

The simulation environment consists of five components:

- The *vehicle model* is used as a test environment for the functional modeling. The vehicle model delivers the reactions of the environment to the functional model.
- The *simulation control* stimulates and controls the simulation. Additionally, the test pattern and the vehicle parameters are handled.
- The *simulation monitor* shows the current state of the simulation.
- The *simulation analysis* stores and analyses the reaction of the functional model to the different test and fault pattern.
- The *fault module* allows the fault injection into the functional model. Section 4.5 describes the fault module closer.

If any fault is detected during the simulation, the fault has to be localized and corrected. In addition to the verification of the functional models, faults and open issues in the requirement specification can be detected.

4.5 Fault Modeling

To examine the reliability of the functional specification we introduced a fault module in our simulation environment, which allows us formal analysis of the system behavior in the presence of faults. In our fault hypothesis we claimed to tolerate any single arbitrary fault. To validate this property we use the fault module. The fault module is an optional part of the functional model and is controlled by the simulation control. The behavior of the fault module corresponds to the behavior of the fault injection device (see Section 4.7). So the result between fault modeling and fault injection can be compared and the fault modeling can be verified. Our focuses of fault injection activities on the real system focus on the disturbance of the communication on the TTP transmission channel. Thus the fault injection module is realised for the transmission channels only.

4.6 Realisation and Integration

After finishing the global and local design and verification of the behavior through functional simulation and fault modeling, the complete system is integrated by connecting all components, by downloading and execution of the application software.

For the system integration the opportunity to monitor the global behavior by tracing the bus is important. Therefore we developed, together with an outhouse partner a monitoring tool, which allows us during runtime to monitor and trace the messages on the communication bus, without influencing the system. The inner state of the components like task states, variable values, etc. can be observed via local monitoring. Local monitoring should be applied very carefully, because it changes the behavior, especially the timing behavior of the components.

In industrial projects parts of the system are developed by different project teams or outhouse partners. For the component developer the whole system is typically not available. For the test of a single component a tool which simulates missing nodes is required. Therefore we realised a first prototype tool [3].

4.7 Test and Fault Injection

We have three intentions with the test and the fault injection experiments:
1. Verify the behavior of the TTP bus against the preliminary TTP specification, the TTP protocol is still under current investigation.
2. Verify the behavior of the simulation models for the nodes, the communication subsystem and the fault

module during the developing phase of the simulation environment.

3. Verify the behavior of the real system with respect to the system requirement specification.

4.7.1 Test

The definition of the test pattern is very important for the quality of the test. The aim is to reach as high as possible coverage of the test room with a minimum number of test patterns. The test method has to be understandable and reproducible, therefore, we used a functional test method.

Functional test methods examine the functional behavior and not the code itself. The program is considered as a *black box* [22]. The aim of the functional test is to test the specified requirements as completely as possible. The test specification can be described in a formal and informal way [4]. Formal methods nowadays are only accepted for a few applications in the industry. The most important functional test methods are *equivalent class, boundary test* [20], the *category-partition method* [21], and the *classification tree method* [4]. We generate our test pattern with the help of the classification tree method. It supports the combination of different input signals to generate test patterns. In the first step the relevant classifications are identified with the help of the requirement specification. In the next step the classifications are separated into mathematical disjunctive classes. The classifications and classes can be defined hierarchically and form a classification tree. The test patterns are generated by the combination of the non classifiable basic classes, from each single classification one class is used.

4.7.2 Fault Injection

Fault injection is a method for testing the fault-tolerance of a system with respect to the specified behavior. Fault injection is needed for two different purposes: to test the correct operation of the fault tolerance algorithms/mechanisms and to predict the dependability of the system in a realistic scenario where faults are expected to occur and have to be handled properly [12].

Our present fault injection techniques concentrate on disturbing the transmission channel. Therefore we use a fault injection hardware called *TTP-Stress*, which allows to disturb the communication channel of TTP. In a distributed fault-tolerant system the communication between the nodes is of utmost importance. Faults which are injected:

- Faults of the Physical Communication Layer: short cuts between transmission wires, short cuts to ground

or power supply, loss of connections, faulty bus termination, etc.

- Loss of Frames: the switch off and reconfiguration of nodes can be simulated.
- Change of bits: the message contents can be changed.

The disturbances can be injected for a defined time interval, periodically or permanently. The start trigger is set manually through the user or via an external device, e.g., from a monitoring tool.

TTP supports different physical transmission layers. The currently implemented physical layer is in conformance with the ISO/DIS 11898 CAN [24] standard, i.e., differential transmission on a two-wire broadcast bus with one dominant state and one recessive state. The higher layers defined in the CAN specification (e.g. arbitration) do not apply for TTP.

5 Brake-by-wire Case Study

Automotive applications like brake- or steer-by-wire are typical examples for the use of a time-triggered architecture. We selected a *brake-by-wire* application, which we realised as a case study to evaluate the TTP protocol [8]. This application has several advantages:

- Realistic workload in a hard real-time application.
- Reuse for future realisations.
- Experiences on a real automotive example.

5.1 Requirement Specification

The requirement specification consists of the parts: specification of the system and definition of the test environment.

We realise the system specification in textual form with in-house used methods. So we do not have the opportunity to execute consistence checks in the description of the specification. Therefore we use the system model, which represents a detailed functional specification of the system.

5.2 Architectural System Design

Our fault tolerant architecture consists of a set of two redundant ECU's for the *Brake-by-Wire-Manager (BBW-Manager, BBWM)* and 4 single ECU's, one for each brake (see Figure 6). The ECU's are connected by two replicated busses. In this case study the brake ECU's are not designed redundant, in order to reduce costs, since the failure of a single brake is not considered to be as severe as the failure of the BBW-Manager.

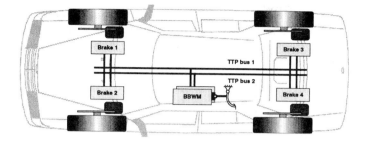

Figure 6: An Example for an TTA Architecture

The functional of the BBW-Manager is to read the sensor values of the brake pedal, the revolution counters of the wheels, the yaw-sensor, the acceleration sensors, and to calculate from these signals the brake force set points for the four brake actuators. The BBW-Manager also manages higher assistance functions like ABS, traction and driving dynamic control. The brake electronics get the brake force set points from the BBW-Manager.

The whole communication between the BBW-Manager, and the brake electronics is based on the fault tolerant TTP system.

In contrast to event triggered systems a TTP system is built upon a static message schedule. Figure 7 depicts the result of this phase, the static synchronous time division multiple access (TDMA) scheme and its constraint that each subsystem has to send exactly once in a TDMA cycle. The messages marked with 'I' are so called I-Frames, used for reintegration of rebooted nodes and do not transmit information for the application layer.

A TDMA slot has a length of about 1.2 msec. New brake force set points are sent every 7.2 msec, which is sufficient for an ABS control loop. The brake control ECU's send their status and the current brake force. These messages are not so time critical as the transmission of the brake force set points. The brake ECU's send their messages only once in a cluster cycle, each 12 TDMA slots. In the remaining slots the brake ECU's send I-Frames for the network management.

5.3 Functional Design

As one example of a component with fail-silent property we describe in this section the realisation of the BBW-Manager. The four brake ECU's are realised in a similar manner. The BBW-Manager has the functionality to calculate the four brake force set points. The brake force set points are safety related and have to be protected from transient and permanent faults. Figure 8 shows the schedule which is periodically executed on the BBW-Manager:

1. *Pedal signal measurement*, of the pedal signals from

the pedal sensors.

2. *Pedal signal plausibility checks*, from the three pedal signals one valid value is calculated. This task is executed three times, to detect faults.
3. *Voter*, a voter task votes from the result of the three plausibility check tasks and starts an exception handling if a fault is detected.
4. *Brake force control*, the brake forces for the four actuators are calculated. This task is also executed three times.
5. *Voter*, a voter task votes from the result of the three brake force control tasks.
6. *TTP-communication*, the brake forces are send to the brakes via the TTP communication network.
7. *Diagnose*, a diagnose task is executed.
8. *Diagnose output*, the diagnose values are transmitted to an extern diagnose device.

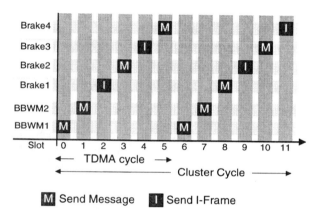

Figure 7: Communication Matrix of the Brake-by-wire Case Study

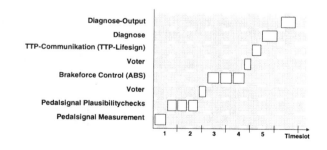

Figure 8: Local Task Schedule of the BBW-Manager

5.4 Functional Simulation

The system model represents the same structure of nodes as the real architecture. As an example we show the functional model of the system architecture (see Figure

9). We only present this part of the model, because the description of the whole model is beyond the scope of this paper.

The activity charts BBWM1_AC and BBWM2_AC represents the BBW-Manager nodes 1 and 2, similar the activity charts BRAKE_ACx the brake nodes. @ is part of the Statemate™ syntax and means that a more detailed description of the activity exists. The external activities SENSORS and ACTUATORS represent the source and sink for the input and output data flows. The external activities MEDL_COMPILER and TADL_COMPILER, the configuration of the communication and task schedule of the nodes.

For the functional simulation first we use the single step mode to verify the model being complete and consistent. After this, we define the test pattern and exercise the simulation in the batch mode. We instrument the simulation for control and collecting of statistics during execution.

5.5 Fault Modeling

The fault module is a optional part of the system model and is represented by the activity chart TTP_STRESS_AC. To compare the results between fault modeling and fault injection the fault model has the same function as the fault injection device (TTP-Stress). In the real system we use a broadcast bus, therefore TTP-Stress can be connected at an arbitrary point with the bus. In the system model every TTP message transmitted on the bus is piped through the fault module. For the verification of the fault module behavior we use the same setup in fault modeling and fault injection.

5.6 Realisation and Integration

For the realisation we use the capability of automatic code generation of Statemate™ and MATLAB®/Simulink™. By using automatic code generation we still have the problem that we use non validated code generators; this problem will be addressed in our future work. As target platforms we use a VxWorks [29] based system for the BBW-Manager and a controller platform without floating point unit for the brake ECU´s. Currently download and execution of automatic generated code is only possible for the BBW-Manager. The complexity of BBW-Manager is much higher than the Brake ECU´s.

For system integration we use bus monitoring and additionally every node sends its internal states via a diagnosis bus to an external monitoring device. So we have the capability of monitoring and logging of all important system states.

5.7 Test and Fault Injection

We use functional test for the verification of our implementation. To define the test pattern out of the

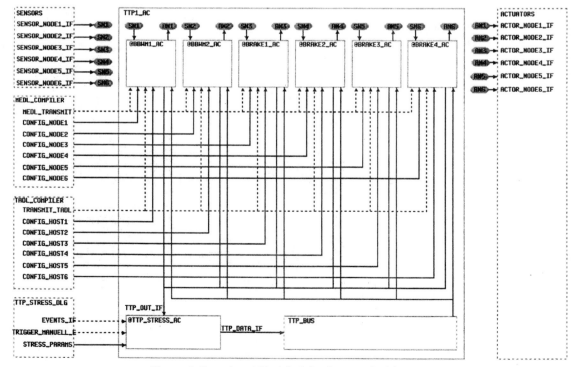

Figure 9: Functional Model of the System Architecture

366

requirement specification we use classifications trees [4].

The test pattern for the fault injection is separated into three groups; verification of the protocol behavior, verification of the fault, and verification of the system behavior under fault conditions.

The verification of the protocol behavior, depends on the protocol specification. We generate the fault pattern manually through examining the TTP specification. For the examination of the system behavior under fault conditions, we use the results of classification tree analysis.

6 Conclusion

In this paper we present a framework for the development of ultra-dependable automotive systems based on a time-triggered architecture. In the first part of the paper we introduce the time-triggered architecture and the time-triggered protocol. We showed that time-triggered architectures are well suited for safety critical automotive by-wire applications. In the second part we describe an approach is for the development of TTP based systems. Our approach based on verification of the system design by functional simulation, fault modeling, functional test and fault injection in the real system. At the end we gave a brief example of how this approach can be used in a brake-by-wire case study.

References

[1] C. Alexander, *Notes On The Synthesis of Form*, Harvard University Press, Cambridge, Massachusetts and London, England, 1964.

[2] E. Dilger, L.A. Johansson, H. Kopetz, M. Krug, P. Lidén, G. McCall, P. Mortara, B. Müller, U. Panizza, S. Poledna, A.V. Schedl, J. Söderberg, M. Strömber, T. Thurner: *Towards an Architecture for Safety Related Fault Tolerant Systems in Vehicles*, Proceedings of the ESREL´97 International Conference, 1997.

[3] Fleisch, Ringler Th. and Belschner, R., *Simulation of Application Software for a TTP Real-Time Subsystem*. Proc. of European Simulation Symposium, Istanbul, Turkey, June 1997.

[4] K. Grimm, M. Grochtmann, *Classification Trees for Partition Testing*, in Software Testing, Verification and Reliablility, Bd. 3, No. 2, pp. 63-82, 1993.

[5] D. Harel, *Statecharts: a visual formalism for complex systems*, Science of Computer Programming, vol. 8, no. 3, pp. 231-274,1987.

[6] D. Harel et al., *On the formal semantics of Statecharts*, in Proc. 2nd IEEE Symposium on Logic in Computer Science, IEEE Press, NY, USA, pp. 54-64, 1987.

[7] D. Harel et al., *Statemate™: a working environment for the development of complex reactive systems*, IEEE Trans. On Software Engineering, vol. SE-16, no. 4, pp. 403-414, 1990.

[8] B. Hedenetz, R. Belschner, *Brake-by-wire without Mechanical Backup by Using a TTP-Communication Network*, SAE International Congress 1998.

[9] G. Heiner, T. Thurner, *Time-Triggered Architecture for Safety-Related Distributed Real-Time Systems in Transportation Systems*, FTCS-28, June 1998.

[10] IEEE Std. 1074.1991, *IEEE Standard for Developing Software Lifecycle Processes*, The Institute of Electrical and Electronics Engineers, Inc., 1991.

[11] ISO/ICE 1508, *Functional safety: safety-related systems*, International Electrotechnical Commission, 1995.

[12] J. Karlsson, P. Folkesson, J. Arlat, Y. Crouzet, G. Leber, *Integration and Comparison of Three Physical Fault Injection Techniques*, Predictably Dependable Computing Systems, Springer Verlag 309-329, 1995.

[13] H. Kopetz, et. al., *A Prototype Implementation of a TTP/C Controller*, Proceedings SAE Congress 1997, Detroit, MI, USA, Febr. 1997. Society of Automotive Engineers, SAE Press. SAE Paper No. 970296.

[14] H. Kopetz, *Real-Time Systems - Design Principles for Distributed Real-Time Systems*, Kluwers Academic Publishers, 1997.

[15] H. Kopetz, G. Grünsteidl, *TTP - A Protocol for Fault-Tolerant Real-Time Systems*, IEEE Computer, pages 14-23, January 1994.

[16] A. Krüger, *Interface design for Time-Triggered Real-Time System Architectures*, doctor thesis, Institut für Technische Informatik, Vienna University of Technology, 1997.

[17] M. Krug, A. V. Schedl, *New Demands for Invehicle Networks*, Proceedings of the 23rd EUROMICRO Conference, pp. 601-606, 1997.

[18] N. Leveson, *Safeware - System safety and computers*, Addison-Wesley, Reading, MA, 1995.

[19] MathWorks, *MATLAB® - The Language of Technical Computing*, MathWorks Inc., MATLAB® 5.1, June 1997.

[20] G.J. Myers, *The Art of Software Testing*, Wiley-Interscience, Chichester, 1979.

[21] T.J. Ostrand, M.J. Balcer, *The Category-Partition Method for Specifying and Generating Functional Test*, in Communications of the ACM, Bd. 31, Nr. 6, Juni 1988.

[22] N. Parrington, M. Roper, *Softwaretest*; Mc Graw-Hill, Hamburg, 1990

[23] S. Poledna, *The Problem of Replica Determinism*, Fault-Tolerant Real-Time Systems, Kluwer Academic Publishers, 1996.

[24] SAE, *Control Area Network: an invehicle serial communication protocol*, SAE Information Report J1583, SAE Handbook, 1990.

[25] SAE, *Class C Application Requirement Considerations*, SAE Recommended Practice J2056/1, SAE, June 1993.

[26] SAE, *Survey of Known Protocols*, SAE Information Report J2056/2, SAE, April 1993.

[27] I. Sommerville, *Software Engineering*, Addison-Wesley Publishing Company, Wokingham, England, 3rd edition, 1989.

[28] URL: http://www.isi.com/products/matrixx/.

[29] URL: http://www.wrs.com/.

Integrated Design Tools for Hard Real-time Systems

Carlos Puchol
Software Production Research Department
Bell Laboratories, Lucent Technologies
Naperville, IL 60566-7050, USA
cpg@research.bell-labs.com

Aloysius K. Mok
Department of Computer Sciences
The University of Texas at Austin
Austin, TX 78712-1188, USA
mok@cs.utexas.edu

Abstract

We propose a toolset for designing real-time systems. The toolset is based on a design methodology for real-time systems. The purpose of a design methodology is to provide a set of procedures and guidelines that, with human intervention and interaction, allow designers to systematically obtain implementations of systems that conform precisely to their design specifications. Our methodology is designed for automation. We present the toolset and case study of the design of a simple VCR system. The methodology is based on a formal model and precise descriptions of the components of the system. The underlying model of our methodology is composed of a control level and a data-flow level that, together with a resource scheduler and the application-specific code, make up the system under design.

1. Introduction

We present a toolset for the design of real-time systems. The toolset is based on a new methodology and integrates the models that the methodology proposes for designing real-time systems. A design methodology for real-time systems is a set of procedures that allows designers to systematically obtain implementations of systems that conform precisely to their design specifications. In this case, the methodology presented is based on a formal model and precise descriptions of the elements at hand.

Computer systems are being used commonly to control devices "in real time." A real-time system is considered to be one that interacts with the environment in a way that the timeliness of its response is important, as well as its logical correctness. Many real-time systems are used for controlling physical processes, where these requirements occur often. In many cases, not only one but several cooperating computing units are used to achieve a common goal such as in a car, an aircraft control system, in a satellite or in a telephone switch. The task of designing and implementing such

systems is a demanding one and is considered to be hard due to the fact that, in most cases, strong reliability specifications are part of the overall system requirement. This is especially the case for complex distributed real-time systems. A system is said to be a *hard* real-time system when timing constraints must be satisfied without exception.

We consider the problem of providing a general, integrated and automated approach to the design of distributed hard real-time systems which not only preserves but makes use of correctness criteria provided by existing analytical techniques. We call this a *design methodology* for the domain of real-time systems. Our methodology considers all the major aspects associated with a real-time system, including (and specially) timeliness. It is based on three fundamental principles:

- Automation: it is subject to be automated via computer-aided design tools;
- Formalization: it is formally defined and subject to analysis, and
- Generality: it applies to a large class of systems.

Current techniques for building real-time systems are largely *ad hoc* legacy processes of trial and error, involving issues such as timeliness, performance and correctness, which are generally dealt with in an informal way. Only in rare cases these systems are built from scratch. There are several design methodologies proposed for real-time system design (e.g. [19, 8]) which adopt some form of software architecture, however, they fail to address thoroughly the central requirements that distinguish real-time systems from non-real-time systems, namely timeliness and reliability requirements.

2. Overview

The methodology we propose follows the underlying architecture of the SARTOR project [16] (Software Automation for Real-Time Systems) and provides an integrated approach to the design and implementation of real-time systems. We propose organizing the system under design as four (interacting) components:

- Asynchronous level
- Synchronous level
- Functional level
- Timing level

We address the issues of integrating the different levels of abstraction to achieve the required properties. We view the first two levels as defining the *control flow* execution patterns of the system, while the last two levels define the *data flow* execution patterns of it. Integrating the control flow and the data flow aspects of the system is the central issue addressed by this work. The purpose of our software architecture is to *define precisely* the subproblems involved in the design of a system and how to *integrate* their solutions to obtain a concrete implementation of it. We therefore do not elaborate on the solutions to most of these subproblems, some of which are quite complex on their own.

Research on techniques for real-time system software has focused largely on the major components for real-time systems, such as scheduling theory, communications, formal specification and formal verification. However, little attention has been devoted to the integration of the results for the implementation of real-time software systems from scratch. Of all the components in a real-time system, the software architecture (the product of this methodology) is the topmost element from a designer's perspective. It defines how the rest of the components in the system behave and interact to satisfy the requirements —from the operating system and databases to the network and the hardware. At present, there is no accepted methodology that can be used to provide a solution to all real-time requirements. To quote the summary of a workshop on the topic ([12]):

> "The workshop revealed sharp differences of opinion with regard to [...] what is the best method to design large, distributed real-time systems, and what should be the relationship between design theory and scheduling theory. The differences confirmed the often mentioned 'disconnect' between design theory and scheduling theory."

Our aim is to fill this gap among the different disciplines in the field and integrate them in a unified, coherent model.

Separation of Concerns

Clearly, scheduling theory is used crucially as part of the design of a hard real-time system, for the system will not meet its timeliness constraints if it is not schedulable. Likewise, the functional requirements of the system (those requirements describing the behavior of the system independent of the timeliness), must be taken into account in the

design of the system for it to behave as required. These aspects of the design are generally considered to be the most important. However, no less important in practice are other issues such as the structural organization and the use of suitable languages for specifying and programming the system. These issues are important in order to manage the complexity of engineering increasingly large systems. Some of these issues, such as specification languages and verification, have already been addressed by the SARTOR project in the past [4]. Our methodology pays attention to all these concerns, including the more pragmatic ones, while satisfying reasonable separation of concerns in the following issues:

- Structural organization: both architecture-based (mapping to a set of resources such as processors and network) and semantics-based (organization of the specification).
- Modular behavior specification: formal description of the system by stepwise definition and composition of the behavior of its parts.
- Resource schedulability requirements: processor, network, devices, etc. Both on an individual basis and in a global basis.
- Code synthesis: automated code generation to accomplish the behavior defined by the specification.
- Timing performance: assurance that timing performance falls within specification.

3. The Methodology

The design methodology is structured in two levels, each organized in two sub-levels each: a control-flow level, which is composed of an asynchronous layer and a synchronous layer, and a data-flow level, which is composed of a functional layer and a timing layer.

The control-flow level allows designers to focus on the design of their systems based on asynchronously-executing processes whose internal behavior can be specified in a synchronous fashion. Most current formalisms allow only for one form of specification (asynchronous or synchronous), with limited support for the other. The internal states of these processes control the execution of real-time tasks.

These tasks form the data-flow level. We decompose this level further by splitting it into a functional layer of tasks (with dependency constraints among them) and a timing layer, which captures individual timing annotations for the tasks. By structuring the system in this way, we clearly identify the structures that designers have to define and the problems that need to be solved individually.

We now outline the underlying architecture of our methodology in two parts, describing the control-flow levels followed by the data-flow levels. We stress that this organization does not imply that some levels subsume or control others —the system is governed by the interaction of the different structures in each level as well as external environment behavior: changes in the control-flow of the system impact on the tasks being executed at the data-flow level; similarly, results from computations in the data-flow levels can influence the control-flow. At any time, an external input can influence one or both or none. The system has a resource scheduler which is driven by the state of the system. The scheduler determines which data-flow components may be present at any time. Figure 1 depicts these relationships among the different structures of the system.

3.1. The Control-Flow Levels

In order to illustrate the design of the top two levels of the architecture, we first overview current approaches to modeling and representing reactive systems.

Current formalisms for reactive, parallel and concurrent finite state systems can be broadly classified in two groups, based on the basic computation model used: the synchronous approach and the asynchronous approach.

In the synchronous approach, systems are represented by concurrent finite state machines (FSMs) that interact typically by means of instantaneous broadcast of events. Composing systems to run concurrently to form a larger system is done by computing the product of the individual state machines, which execute in lockstep. Examples of this approach are formalisms like I/O Automata [15], the S/R model [14], Esterel [1], Lustre [9], SCR [2] and Modechart [13].

In the asynchronous approach, one way to represent systems is by FSMs that interact through point-to-point communication channels (which can themselves provide so-called "synchronous" or "asynchronous" behavior). Other formalisms in this approach use shared-memory to communicate. The FSMs generally execute in an interleaving fashion. Examples of such systems include CSP [10], UNITY [3], SPIN [11] and VFSM [21].

Since most industrial systems have both synchronous and asynchronous components, many current formalisms support fundamentally one model and somehow provide some support for modeling the other, providing to some extent both synchrony and asynchrony. Classifying some formalism as merely synchronous or asynchronous is not therefore entirely accurate. However, no current formalism seems to capture *both* the synchronous and asynchronous aspects of a system in a uniform framework.

In general terms, asynchronous models tend to be more suitable for modeling distributed systems such as network protocols, due to the amount of asynchronous communication involved. Asynchronous models with shared memory are more suitable for parallel systems. On the other hand,

synchronous models are more suitable for uniprocessor environments (where concurrency is used as a modeling tool to enhance the expressive power of the model), or for digital circuits (where concurrency models physics).

Our model provides an integrated approach for modeling both aspects of a system. The top two levels of the architecture provide for this.

Taking a more pragmatic view, one can draw a reasonably accurate simile from modern (non-real-time) operating systems. Large applications are usually structured in terms of processes, which are "loosely coupled" and which run in parallel (potentially distributed). Processes are ideally suited for this purpose because they do not generally share common space and run "in parallel" (physically or virtually). We note that no assumptions are made as to the relative speeds of execution among processes and that they mostly communicate asynchronously. Looking further inside their organization, many of these applications, specially the ones with responsiveness requirements (widely known examples include Wold Wide Web browsers), further decompose its implementation in terms of threads. Threads execute in a lockstep fashion, and while no assumptions are made about their execution speeds, the implementations guarantee fairness constraints for their proper execution. They all share a common space. These would correspond to our synchronous level.

The Asynchronous and Synchronous Levels

We propose a two-fold model for the control-flow of the system under design which incorporates both asynchronous and synchronous behavior. We place asynchronous behavior at the topmost level of the architecture. Communicating *processes* and message *channels* are the essential elements at this level. A process can be obtained by grouping other processes hierarchically or otherwise by assigning a (finite state) behavior to it. Communicating processes may not share resources other than channels and execute independently of each other (except when message dependencies are involved). No assumption is made about their relative speeds. Messages flow from processes through channels, to other processes, where they represent incoming input.

Specifically, the control structure of a system is specified in our architecture (in its most primitive instantiation) by a graph $G = (V, E, f, B)$ where the elements of V are processes and the elements of $E \subseteq V \times V$ are (optionally buffered, typed, multicast and/or timed) channels connecting processes in the system. Each primitive process $p \in V$ (which forms the basis of the asynchronous level) has a unique behavior $f(p) = b \in B$ associated. The behaviors in B (which form the synchronous level), can be defined in their most primitive form as a set of timed finite state machines. Input events to these state machines can come from

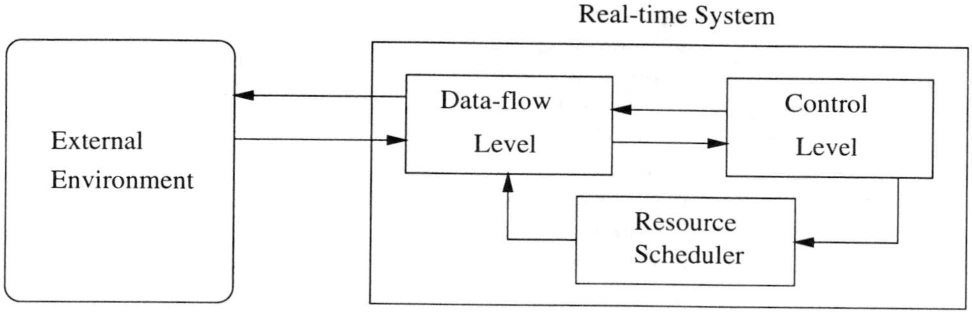

Figure 1. The structure of a real-time system.

the external environment or from messages from other state machines belonging in some other process.

Note that this is the simplest method of describing an instance of our model. In practice, applying the principles of structuring and modularity becomes necessary for bridging the gap between theoretical and practical real-time system specification and implementation. System specification must be understandable and manageable and the formalism needs to provide a path to an implementation with reasonable resources. These are aspects that many formalisms neglect and that limits their use. We consider these aspects in the language support provided for this architecture, thus for the purpose of the argument, we assume one instance of the architecture is defined with the graph model outlined above.

With an instance of these two levels in hand it is easy to realize the following: suppose we have an oracle to solve instances of scheduling problems in zero time and suppose we have the actual information about the hardware configuration of the set of processors and network architecture of the system. The problem of resource *mapping* to the architecture can then be precisely defined and solved for the particular instance. Similarly, one can more precisely define other problems, and integrate their solutions to synthesize code automatically. In the absence of oracles to solve problems in a reasonable time, this method can be used to guide the designers iteratively through the design and implementation process, providing valuable feedback of where any problems of integration/synthesis occur in the instance, based on the outcome of the available tools.

3.2. The Data-Flow Levels

The two levels described above interact with each other through message passing and event broadcast and provide the main structural and behavioral aspects of the system. In the end, systems have to interact with the world and have to execute "cpu-cycle-consuming" operations such as processing signals from a radar, controlling a user interface or recognizing shapes in a digital image. These operations can be decomposed into a set of *tasks* which communicate by

passing data among them and have periodic, end-to-end and data sharing constraints. The behavior at this level can be modeled using a graph-based model such as AND-OR dataflow graphs [20].

It is clear that these tasks may influence the behavior of the system; therefore, we need to integrate them with the top levels of our architecture. It is also clear that the current state of the system may influence the tasks being executed at any time during their execution. In our architecture, tasks communicate with the synchronous level elements (modes and processes) through bi-directional *signals*. These signals are considered "external" inputs for the top levels when sent from the data-flow level to the control level. When the signals flow from the top level to the bottom level tasks considered them just like external inputs.

The Functional and Timing Levels

More specifically, the functional level is obtained by specifying a set of tasks T. The system designer can assign a subset of tasks $t \subseteq T$, each possibly annotated with timeliness constraints (such as periodicity or maximum inter-arrival time), to execute only while specific states $s \subseteq B$ are being executed. In fact, the set of tasks T can be a forest of individual tasks, all of which may execute according to a set of timeliness constraints imposed upon them either individually or on an end-to-end basis for each tree.

In the functional level, these timeliness constraints are fundamental to our ability not only to generate instances of *offline scheduling* problems but also to *synthesize code* that drives the system scheduler to behave correctly as specified.

The last level is the timing level. This level is defined by establishing the worst case execution time for each of the individual tasks in T. This information is part of the input to the offline scheduler.

The offline scheduler must also generate information for the *online scheduler* of the system. In particular, critical information needed for the online scheduler includes which tasks need to be executing along with their parameters (execution time, period, resources, etc.), the order and the time in which tasks need to be added/deleted to/from the current task set. This is known as the *mode change* problem. It is especially important that the offline scheduler solve the mode change problem, since timing constraints need to be met even when the system is in a transient state.

The offline scheduler can gather the information about all the possible tasks sets executing (and using resources) in each processor in the system and the transitions among them from the analysis tools (such as the verification tool or the compiler tool) applied to the top two levels.

4. The Architecture

The top-level view of the design stages is outlined in Figure 2. Our methodology supports an iterative design process where automation and human guidance leads to a final design through these stages. The iterative process consists of attempting a each of the stages sequentially until the final stage is reached. If at any any point in the specification one stage fails, the designer must backtrack to some previous stage and pick another solution to proceed further. Our methodology calls for the tools in each of the stages to provide enough information (when failures occur) to allow the developers to obtain insight to help in the next try at previous stages in the process.

The design process starts by defining the architectural elements of the system, which includes the following information:

- Number of processors in the system
- Cost of communication among them
- Data-flow linear and mutual exclusion dependency constraints
- Attributes per task:

    - direct assignment constraint to a processor
    - exclusion constraint from a processor
    - execution period
    - execution release time
    - code for execution by the task

- Worst case computation time for the code

Section 5 has more specifics on the language used for writing these constraints. Our set of tools allows all this information to be filtered through the different stages in the design process.

The toolset is composed of MC2MSP, XMSP, MC2STRL and MSP2SCHED. Figure 3 depicts the relationships among the tools we use. MC2MSP translates the architectural information into a sequence of *scheduling problem instances*, which are properly fed into XMSP, the graphical version of the MSP.RTL scheduler [17]. MC2MSP is therefore a partitioning algorithm, in a very

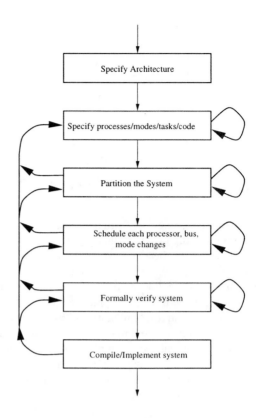

Figure 2. The structure of the design process.

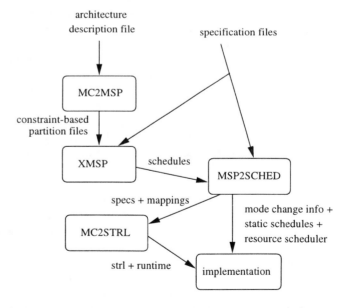

Figure 3. Integration of the tools used.

372

simple form. In general, the number of possible combinations of partitions (mappings from tasks to processors) that the system could be partitioned in may be very large. We argue however, that by allowing input from the designer in the process, the number of possible tasks can be reduced dramatically until one feasible global solution is obtained. Our tools and MSP.RTL assumes a simple, mutually exclusive, non-preemptive bus as the communication medium.

For large systems the process of obtaining one or more feasible partitions can be further automated through iterative use of the scheduler. Once a candidate partition of the system is obtained that the scheduler has been able to schedule, MSP2SCHED, a program that integrated the scheduling information output from XMSP and MC2STRL, the Modechart compiler [18] are used to obtain an implementation by combining the offline scheduler, the compiled specification, the run-time specs, the table of scheduling modes and the mode-change information.

5. VCR example

The following is a specification and outline of the implementation of a simple "digital VCR" application (a VCR-like program to display tuned TV signals and video files) with the following informal specification for its behavior:

A simple VCR can only play and record. It has three ways to record. The user can manually record for any length of time. It has an OTR (One Touch Record) feature which allows the user to start recording immediately for either 30, 60, 120 minutes (time units). It also has an XPR (eXPress Record) feature, which functions like OTR but allows the user to delay the start of the recording for 30, 60 or 90 minutes, and does not interfere with operation of the VCR during this delay. Both OTR and XPR override any user selected mode once they start recording, and XPR will turn the VCR on if it is off when it is time to start recording.

Suppose that we can implement this digital VCR with two processors (say, a digital signal processor for tuning and signal conditioning, and a standard processor for displaying images), interconnected by some bus. In our toolset, the architectural specification of the system is defined in a so-called *project* file such as the one for the VCR example, in the box in this page.

Most of the parts included in this specification are self-explanatory: these sections act like top-level descriptions of each of the parts of the system and their characteristics. The Code section specifies a mapping from code labels (used by the tasks) to actual literal strings that are used during code generation. For each label, a worst-case estimate of the execution time of the code is included in the mapping. The Tasks section maps tasks to code, where each task specification listed includes its period and release time (tasks using identical code under different period or release times are considered to be different).

```
# Project file for the VCR example

Code {
#       alias       comp. time              literal code
        f_tune      2           >           f_tune();
        f_vhs       1           >           f_read();
        f_display   4           >           f_display();
        f_play      4           >           play(NORMAL);
        f_fastplay  1           >           play(FAST);
        f_record    1           >           f_record();
        f_clock     1           >           f_clock();
}

Tasks {
#       Task id     period  release calls
        tune        20      0       f_tune
        vhs         20      0       f_vhs
        display     20      0       f_display
        play        20      0       f_play
        fastplay    10      0       f_fastplay
        record      20      0       f_record
        clock       40      0       f_clock
}

Processors {
#       processor       allowed (- disallowed) tasks
        TUNER           tune vhs
        VIDEO           display play fastplay record
}

Dataflow { comm_delay 4 } {
        depend tune display
        depend vhs play
        depend vhs record
        depend vhs fastplay
}

Specs {
        vcr.mc
}
```

The Processors section specifies the processors in the system, in this case two of them, along with constraints on task assignments. Each processor definition lists the tasks that must run on it and tasks that must *not* run on it (in this case no such tasks have been specified). Unconstrained tasks are left free to be assigned to any processor by the mapping algorithm. The Dataflow section lists a series of dependencies including linear precedence and mutual exclusion among tasks. In addition, it specifies an (optional) parameter for communication delays incurred when any two direct precedence dependencies occur across two different processors. Finally, the Spec section lists the names of the control specifications involved.

Consider the tuner task in the system above. This task has a period of 20 time units, the release time is 0, and when it is invoked by the scheduler, it calls f_tune, which is defined to be a simple call to: "f_tune()." The worst case computation time for the task is estimated to be 2 time units, as specified in the `Code` section. Furthermore, because this task presumably has to access hardware, some hardware available only in the `TUNER` processor, it is constrained to be run there, as defined in the line for the `TUNER` processor. In the `Dataflow` section, a dependency constraint is specified for the `tune` task: every instance of the task must be followed by an instance of the `display` task, which happens to be assigned to processor `DISPLAY`. Any communication among the two tasks takes up to 4 time units, per the definition of `comm_delay`.

5.1. Control domain for the VCR specification

The specification above is obviously a possibly incomplete and inconsistent specification. An overview of the top-level control-flow formal specification in Modechart (modes only), is displayed in Figure 4. It is made up of two parallel components, one that contains the VCR implementation and one that contains the environment model for the implementation (one mode per each button available to the user in the VCR plus two end-of-tape and begin-of-tape signals, EOT/BOT).

The implementation part contains three parallel components. Two of those components are similar and implement the timers used for the OTR and XPR functions. Figure 5 displays the specification for one of the timers. The other component of the VCR mode contains the controller which drives the execution of the VCR.

The timer modes basically rotate around four (main) states on the pressing of the corresponding (OTR/XPR) button. All but the initial state are "active" in that they have accumulated timers. When the last timer expires and the mode returns to the start state, other parts of the specification go into action. The modes depicted smaller in the figure are auxiliary modes to prevent zero cycles from occurring. Note that this specification is actually non-deterministic, very specifically at those times in which the button press coincides with the expiration of one of the 30-unit timers. To solve this, we introduce priorities among conflicting transitions: we add extra labels with negated external events that effectively make one transition take priority over the other. This is an artifact to give a less abstract meaning to the specification, by removing non-determinism.

The controller specification, shown in Figure 6, is made up of an Off mode and an On mode, both of them serial (Off being the default initial mode). Some modes include an "initial" and "final" modes separated by an delay of one time unit. This is also used to prevent zero cycles from occurring. The On mode consists of two modes, the initial Stop mode and the Active mode. The latter is a parallel mode that contains a unit delay that allows for transitions out of active (to Stop if manually done and to Off, if trig-gered automatically or manually).

The transitions not fully displayed in Figure 6 have the following transition expressions as labels (note that the events that start with `->B` correspond to entry events of modes in the environment mode, with the appropriate name, the BOT external even indicates a `beginning of tape` event and the EOT indicates the *end of tape* event):

- T0: `(->XPR_START & !BON) | (->BOTR & !BON)`
- T1: `->BON`
- T2: `->BREC`
- T3: `->BPLAY`
- T4: `->BFWD`
- T5: `->BREW`
- T6: `->BSTOP | ->BOT | ->EOT`
- T7: `->OTR_START | ->XPR_START | ->BOFF`
- T8: `->BOFF`

This specification (viewed as one process) can be extended (most appropriately) for including asynchronous interaction by defining for instance a "remote control" process that runs in parallel asynchronously and which drives the operation of this VCR process by interacting with it through a channel modeling the infra-red communication. This is an (admittedly rather small) example of how two independent processes communicate asynchronously to influence each other. Our model assumes that they both run in parallel, but they only influence each other when they exchange information.

This specification has the BOT and EOT signals as input. We will see below that these signals are the communication medium between the data-flow domain and the control domain.

5.2. Data-flow domain for the VCR specification

Now, assume that we structure the problem in order to implement this digital VCR by defining the following tasks, as seen above in the project file: a *tuner* task that tunes the input channels, a *vhs* task that is capable of decoding signals from a file or cassette, a *display* task that shows the channel input in a window, a *play* task that displays decoded input on the screen, a *fastplay* task that displays decode input on the screen, if only more often and at a lesser quality than regular play, a *record* task that records decoded or channel input into a file, and finally, a *clock* task that displays a clock and counter information in the VCR console.

5.3. Scheduling

Figures 7 to 10 show some of the static schedules for the VCR scheduler. These schedules were obtained by using the MSP.RTL scheduler [17]. Note that these schedules

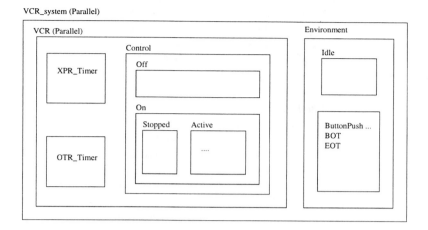

Figure 4. Overview of Modechart VCR system specification.

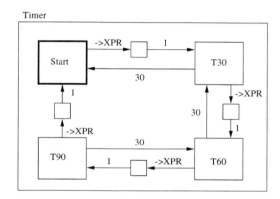

Figure 5. VCR-specific timer specification.

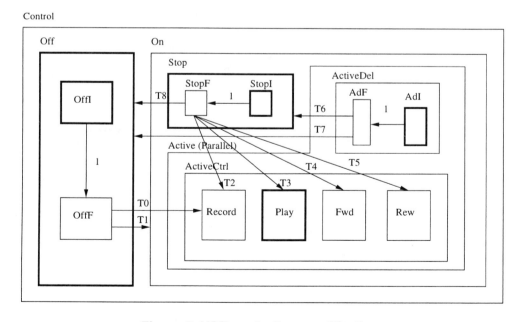

Figure 6. VCR controller specification.

correspond to scheduling modes 0, 1, 5 and 7. These modes have been obtained from the specification and the architecture description. The MC2MSP tool obtains a representation of the possible states that the system may be in and produces a set of major scheduling modes that the system may be in. From the initial mode where no tasks are active, to a mode where all possible tasks are scheduled (regardless of whether some groups of tasks may actually run or not). On one extreme, MC2MSP may generate many scheduling modes with many mode changes. On the other, it may only generate one mode with lots of time allocated to tasks that may not needed. Mode 7, for example, has provisions for all possible tasks included. Details on the interfacing between the specification of the system and the scheduler are presented next.

5.4. Integrating Control and Scheduling

These constraints are indicated in the `Processors` section of the architecture specification file. Similarly, the dependency constraints among tasks are specified in the `Dataflow` section of the specification. In this case, linear dependency among tasks (using the keyword `depend`) and mutual exclusion among tasks (using the keyword `mutex`) may be specified.

These are reasonably high-level constraints imposed on the specification. These constraints are translated into the input language of the offline scheduler MSP.RTL, which is a combination of task mappings to processors, and sets of constraints. Consider the following input file for the VCR example:

```
PROBLEM vcrSP7_1
PROCESSOR bus TUNER VIDEO

PROCESSES /* task info */
clock            (TUNER) 1      0      40
fastplay         (VIDEO) 1      0      10
display          (VIDEO) 4      0      20
play             (VIDEO) 4      0      20
tune             (TUNER) 2      0      20
vhs              (TUNER) 1      0      20
C:tune:display   (bus)   4      0      20
C:vhs:play       (bus)   4      0      20
C:vhs:fastplay   (bus)   4      0      20

CONSTRAINTS
{@(_tune) <= @(^C:tune:display)} AND
{@(_C:tune:display) <= @(^display)} AND
{@(_vhs) <= @(^C:vhs:play)} AND
{@(_C:vhs:play) <= @(^play)} AND
{@(_vhs) <= @(^C:vhs:fastplay)} AND
{@(_C:vhs:fastplay) <= @(^fastplay)}
```

This file, automatically generated from the architectural specification, contains enough information for the scheduler to attempt to solve this particular scheduling problem instance. The file above contains four sections. The first one defines the name of the problem instance (vcrSP7_1). The second one defines the processors in the system, in this case there are three, two as defined (called TUNER and VIDEO) plus one, called bus which has been introduced by MC2MSP because in this instance, there is communication among two tasks that reside in different processors.

The third section, called PROCESSES, contains information partially describing the tasks in this problem instance. These tasks are divided in two groups: regular tasks and communication tasks. The communication tasks are prefixed by C: and are inserted by MC2MSP to represent (for the purposes of scheduling) the communication patterns of the tasks. Each task in this section is mapped to a processor. The three column following the processor assignment are the computation time, the release time and the period for the task. Communication tasks assume the period of the originating task.

The rest of the file contains the CONSTRAINTS section, which is an RTL formula specifying all the properties that a feasible schedule must satisfy. This formula is typically a large conjunction of simpler RTL expressions relating the end of a task with the beginning of the other one. For instance, the formula @(_tune) <= @(^C:tune:display) specifies that for every instance of tasks tune and C:tune:display, the of the end of the first one must occur before or at the beginning of the second one. Linear dependency constraints are similar to these constraints. Mutual exclusion constraints are slightly more complex (they are formed by the disjunction of two simple terms), since they do not enforce order of execution, just exclusion.

It is important to note that tasks at the data flow level may emit signals that are fed back to the control level, thereby influencing the behavior of the while system. In this example, the BOT and EOT signals may be emitted by any of the tasks that display frames in the screen, such as play, record and fastplay. This happens because during the execution of these tasks they may hit the end or beginning of the video stream.

6. Summary and Future Work

We have introduced a methodology and integrated toolset for the design and implementation of real-time systems. The methodology is structured in levels which encourage separation of concerns and smooth integration to obtain a complete, highly reliable system that matches the specifications. The common theme in the architecture is the presence of time as a first-order element in the system. The methodology and toolset call for the adoption of an iterative approach to system design which involves human guidance and automation to obtain insights on the structure and behavior of the system. We illustrate the toolset with a small example of a VCR system.

Figure 7. Initial schedule for the VCR specification (sched. mode 0).

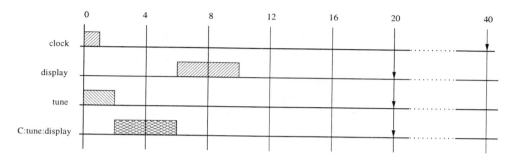

Figure 8. Schedule for the VCR specification (sched. mode 1).

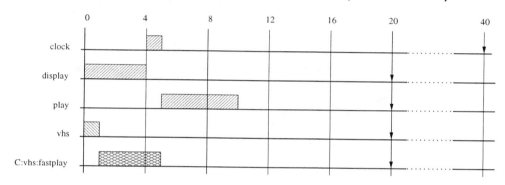

Figure 9. Schedule for the VCR specification (sched. mode 5).

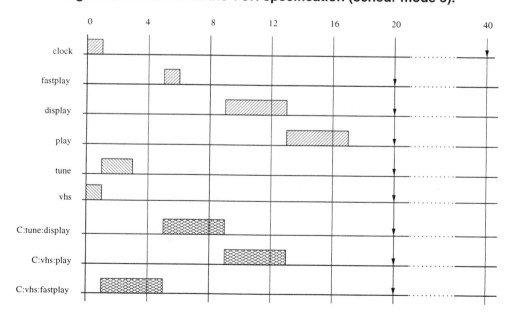

Figure 10. Schedule for the VCR specification (sched. mode 7).

How does this methodology fit in the context of current development methods for real-time systems? We believe that in order for the proposed approach to achieve more generality and completeness, several issues remain to be integrated.

One of the problems that stands out is the problem of linking the specification to the requirements. Currently there is some promising research and development on formal requirements engineering [2]. However, the formal ligature binding the two remains to be an interesting problem to explore.

On the other end of our spectrum, another problem that remains to be explored is how to accurately estimate the (worst-case) timing of code in the context of the increasing complexity of current microprocessor and network architectures and technologies [6]. Compiler technology is reaching unprecedented levels of sophistication and will, in due time, help substantially in tackling this problem. However, even with the help of compiler techniques, issues like cache memories, multi-level caches, distributed caches, non-linear memory architectures, unreliable interrupt latencies, unpredictable bus delays and multi-level bus systems, can raise the complexity bar in the analysis of worst-case execution of tasks. Most modern architectures, specially off-the-shelf products, tend to be optimized for the average case. It is fortunate that processor cycles are becoming more and more of a commodity and may help in providing more comfortable safety bounds for (worst-case) execution of critical tasks.

Modular and compositional verification is one of several emerging topics in research in computer science. The state-explosion problem and the management of infinite-state-space systems can be tackled with exploitation of symmetry, partial orders, abstraction and refinement over the structure of the specifications (e.g. [5, 7, 2]). Our approach would benefit substantially from a compositional verification technique that would integrate both the asynchronous and synchronous approach.

We are currently evaluating alternatives to automating the generation of partitions further in order to automate the collection of schedules and scheduling modes. Because XMSP is a graphical tool, there is currently no provision for automated (or "batch mode") invocation of it. For large systems, it would be specially interesting to invoke the MSP.RTL scheduler in parallel and even to control the limits of execution, in case complex schedules take substantial amounts of time to compute.

References

[1] G. Berry and G. Gonthier. The ESTEREL synchronous programming language: design, semantics, implementation. *Science of Computer Programming*, 19:87–152, 1992.

[2] R. Bharadwaj and C. L. Heitmeyer. Verifying scr requirements specifications using state exploration. In *Proceedings of First ACM SIGPLAN Workshop on Automatic Analysis of Software*, 1997.

[3] K. M. Chandy and J. Misra. *Parallel Program Design*. Addison Wesley, 1988.

[4] P. C. Clements, C. L. Heitmeyer, B. G. Labaw, and A. Rose. MT: A toolset for specifying and analyzing real–time systems. In *Proceedings of the IEEE Real-Time Systems Symposium*, pages 12–22. IEEE Computer Society, December 1993.

[5] E. A. Emerson and K. Namjoshi. Automated verification of parameterized synchronous systems. In *Proceedings of the Computer Aided Verification Conference*, pages 178–187, 1996.

[6] C.-G. L. et. al. Analysys of cache-related preemption delays in fixed-priority preemptive scheduling. In *Proceedings of the IEEE Real-Time Systems Symposium*, pages 264–274, 1996.

[7] P. Godefroid. *Partial-Order Methods for the Verification of Concurrent Systems – An Approach to the State-Explosion Problem*, volume 1032 of *LNCS*. Springer-Verlag, 1996.

[8] H. Gomaa. A software design method for real-time systems. *Communications of the ACM*, 27, Septermber 1984.

[9] N. Halbwachs, P. Caspi, P. Raymond, and D. Pilaud. The synchronous data-flow programming language LUSTRE. *Proceedings of the IEEE*, 79:1305–1320, 1991.

[10] C. Hoare. *Communicating Sequential Processes*. Prentice-Hall, 1985.

[11] G. J. Holzmann. *Design and Validation of Computer Protocols*. Prentice-Hall, 1991.

[12] N. R. Howes. Workshop summary. In D. W. Fife, N. R. Howes, and J. D. Wood, editors, *Proceedings of the Workshop on Large, Distributed, Parallel Architecture, Real-Time Systems*, 1993.

[13] F. Jahanian and A. Mok. Modechart: a specification language for real-time systems. *IEEE Transactions on Software Engineering*, 20(12):933–947, December 1994.

[14] R. P. Kurshan. *Computer-Aided Verification of Coordinating Processes*. Princeton Series in Computer Science, 1994.

[15] N. Lynch and M. Tuttle. An introduction to I/O automata. *CWI-Quarterly*, 2(3):219–246, 1989.

[16] A. Mok. SARTOR – a design environment for real-time systems. In *Proceedings 9th IEEE Computer Security Applications conference (COMPSAC)*, 1985.

[17] A. Mok, D.-C. Tsou, and R. Rooij. The MSP.RTL real-time scheduler synthesis tool. In *Proceedings of the IEEE Real-Time Systems Symposium*. IEEE Computer Society, December 1996.

[18] C. Puchol, A. Mok, and D. Stuart. Compiling Modechart specifications. In *Proceedings of the IEEE Real-Time Systems Symposium*, pages 256–265. IEEE Computer Society, December 1995.

[19] B. Selic, G. Gullekson, and P. T. Ward. *Real-time object-oriented modeling*. John Wiley & Sons, 1994.

[20] S. Sutanthavibul. *"A Data-Flow Model of Real-Time Systems"*. PhD thesis, The University of Texas at Austin, Department of Computer Sciences, May 1990.

[21] F. Wagner. VFSM executable specification. In *CompEuro92*, 1992.

Performance Measurement using Low Perturbation and High Precision Hardware Assists[1]

Alan Mink and Wayne Salamon[2]

Scalable Parallel Systems Group
Information Technology Laboratory
National Inst. of Standards and Tech. (NIST)
Gaithersburg, MD 20899
{amink,wsalamon}@nist.gov

Jeffrey K. Hollingsworth and Ramu Arunachalam[3]

Computer Science Dept.
University of Maryland
College Park, MD 20742

{hollings,ramu}@cs.umd.edu

Abstract

We present the design and implementation of MultiKron PCI, a hardware performance monitor that can be plugged into any computer with a free PCI bus slot. The monitor provides a series of high-resolution timers, and the ability to monitor the utilization of the PCI bus. We also demonstrate how the monitor can be integrated with online performance monitoring tools such as the Paradyn parallel performance measurement tools to improve the overhead of key timer operations by a factor of 25. In addition, we present a series of case studies using the MultiKron hardware performance monitor to measure and tune high-performance parallel computing applications. By using the monitor, we were able to find and correct a performance bug in a popular implementation of the MPI message passing library that caused some communication primitives to run at one half of their potential speed.

1. Introduction

Low cost and low perturbation performance data collection is necessary in high performance computing for both measurement and control purposes. This applies to single processors, parallel processing, heterogeneous distributed environments, and especially real-time environments. Event tracing can be accomplished in software without hardware support, although the perturbation incurred may be substantial and the precision of the available "time" may be too coarse for resolving delays and correlating interprocessor events. Hardware support can significantly reduce the perturbation, improve the time precision, and is a must for tallying high-speed hardware events.

Writing and debugging parallel and real-time programs is a complex and time-consuming task. The correctness of such programs is not only dependent on logical or functional correctness but also on temporal correctness. Temporal correctness can be difficult to guarantee or verify especially in an open system with a dynamic task set due to the timing interactions and unpredictable interleaving of other tasks in the system. Runtime monitoring tools can be a valuable asset in debugging and fine-tuning such systems by providing a means to observe scheduling and timing behavior. Using a monitoring tool one can collect information related to the system behavior such as execution time, CPU usage, blocked time, etc., which can be used to pinpoint temporal errors, restructure computation and ascertain the accuracy of Worst Case Execution Times. Runtime monitoring is also useful during normal operation of the system to verify that the system meets its temporal requirements.

Monitoring tools collect data for both user and system level metrics by inserting software probes into the appropriate functions of the code. Execution of the instrumented code triggers the capture and storage of data by the monitoring system. It is, however, important for the monitoring tool to be as non-intrusive as possible so as not to change the behavior of the underlining task set. Significant intrusion will increase the execution time of the activities being monitored which can lead to tasks missing their deadlines, adversely affecting load balance, or even reducing the ability to schedule hard real-time tasks.

Although many current micro-processors provide hardware counters, there is usually only one clock register. For performance measurement it is necessary to virtualize a clock into a timer (i.e., support start and stop operations). In addition, multiple timers are required to measure the time between different events. In this paper we present the NIST Multikron[4] hardware monitor, which provides 16 high-precision, non-intrusive timers and counters. In addition, Multikron provides minimally intrusive event tracing via an onboard trace memory (or optional external data path).

We describe MultiKron's integration with the Paradyn[18] performance measurement tool. Paradyn provides application performance analysis, visualization, and dynamic insertion and removal of measurement probes. This paper presents the first integration of

---

[1] This NIST contribution is not subject to copyright in the United States. Certain commercial items may be identified but that does not imply recommendation or endorsement by NIST, nor does it imply that those items are necessarily the best available for the purpose.

[2] This work was partially sponsored by DARPA.

[3] Supported in part by NIST CRA #70NANB5H0055, NSF Grants ASC-9703212 and CDA-9401151, and DOE Grant DE-FG02-93ER25176.

---

[4] MultiKron is a registered trademark of NIST.

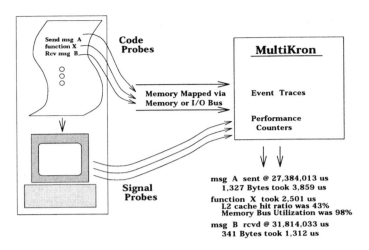

Figure 1: Overview of Measurement Probes.

Paradyn's dynamic instrumentation (insertion and deletion of code during program execution), with a hardware-based counters. The combination of these two systems permits Paradyn to dynamically re-use the finite number of hardware timers on the Multikron system.

The rest of the paper is organized as follows. Section 2 describes the MultiKron measurement hardware. Section 3 describes the integration of MultiKron with the Paradyn Parallel Performance Measurement Tools. Section 4 presents a series of micro-benchmarks and case studies to demonstrate the benefit of hardware-software performance measurement. Section 5 summarizes related work and Section 6 presents our conclusions.

2. Hardware Measurement Environment

The focus of the NIST performance instrumentation work[22] is to provide hardware support in obtaining performance measurement data from parallel computers, as well as uniprocessors, with tolerable perturbation to both the executing processes and the architecture on which they are executing. Current NIST instrumentation consists of the MultiKron_II[19] and the MultiKron_vc[20] custom VSLI chips, and their associated toolkits[21, 23]. The chips are designed to be memory mapped to the local processor(s), via the memory or I/O bus. The MultiKron_II provides both event tracing and 16 performance counters, while the MultiKron_vc provides only performance counters, but 64 thousand of them. Performance counters can be used to count the number of occurrences of a target event or to record the elapsed time between events. Both chips provide a high-precision clock.

The MultiKron toolkits are printed circuit boards (PCBs) that contain a MultiKron chip, interface logic to a standard I/O bus (currently VME, SBus, and PCI), logic for support and management of the MultiKron, and two data storage schemes: a local, dedicated memory on the PCB or an external interface to another machine. The MultiKron chips are not directly useful to experimenters,

since they would likely lack the time or expertise to interface the chips to their machine. Thus, the MultiKron toolkits provide experimenters a quick and easy means to utilize MultiKron instrumentation. These toolkits are designed so that experimenters can plug-in the PCB, install its support software and begin to integrate performance measurement into their experiments.

2.1 MultiKron Instrumentation

During execution of a program under test, performance measurement data are acquired as directed by measurement probes (see Figure 1). There are two types of measurement events, hardware and software. A hardware measurement event is captured via a wire physically connected to an electrical signal in the system being measured. One of the options for the MultiKron performance counters is to count the occurrences of these external signals.

Operationally the MultiKron is a passive, memory-mapped device. Programmers interact with MultiKron via reads and writes to the mapped memory region. To generate traces, a software measurement event is triggered by the execution of a specific statement, a measurement probe, in the application program. A measurement probe can be added to the source code, requiring recompilation, or added directly to the executable code via a binary patch[11]. The probe appears as an assignment statement to a memory mapped MultiKron address. When the measurement probe code is executed, the value from the assignment statement (generally an event ID) is written to the MultiKron, which then appends its current timestamp (precision on the order of 100 ns), the identity of the process, and in multi-processor systems, the identity of the CPU, to form an event trace sample. The trace sample is then buffered and written to the MultiKron data storage interface. Operating system support is necessary during context switches to load the MultiKron with the current process ID. Thus, MultiKron provides a hardware assist to traditional software-based instrumentation systems

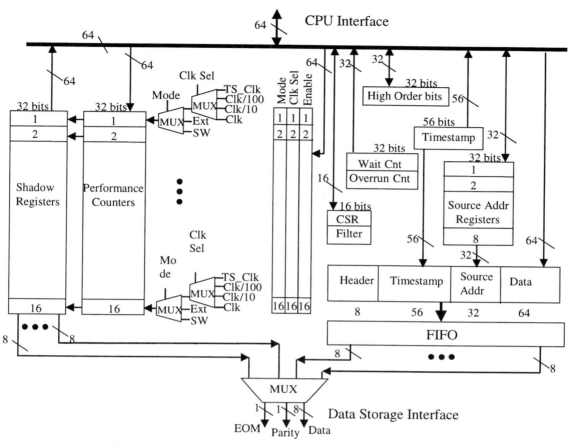

Figure 2: Functional Block Diagram of the MultiKron Chip.

thereby minimizing the perturbation to the executing program by simplifying the probe code to a single write operation and recording the time-stamped samples into its own memory.

The block diagram of the MultiKron_II chip is shown in Figure 2. There are two separate interfaces: a CPU interface to acquire measurement data and control the chip, and a data storage interface to separately store measured data without interfering with normal processor execution. The right hand side of the figure represents the acquisition and buffering of the 20 byte trace event samples. The left-hand side of the figure represents the performance counters and their control. Each counter is controlled by a dedicated sub-field in the Mode, Clk Sel, and Enable registers. The Mode and Clk Sel registers select the signal to be tallied by each counter. The Enable register controls whether each counter is active or inactive. The counters, which can be virtualized for each process with operating system support, can be written directly by the CPU, but only read indirectly via the Shadow Registers. This transparent operation allows the data of all of the performance counters to be simultaneously read out and held constant while the counters continue their programmed activities. This simultaneous read provides a single time view of the measured data without concern for time skew caused by

reading each counter separately at slightly different times. Data records sent to the data storage interface are 20 byte trace event samples, optionally concatenated with the 64 bytes of data from the performance counters.

2.2 The PCI MultiKron Toolkit

The MultiKron toolkit PCBs are designed to be easily re-engineered for different buses. The PCB form factor, connectors, and bus protocol will be different for each bus, but these functions have been isolated from the rest of the board design. The block diagram of the PCI bus toolkit, designed and used for this project, is shown Figure 2. A single programmable logic device (PLD) handles the bus interface logic. A second PLD handles the logic for the rest of the toolkit board, which includes a MultiKron_II chip, a MultiKron_vc chip, a FIFO, and 16M Bytes of DRAM storage. The MultiKron_vc controls its own dedicated SRAM storage, which is normally not directly accessible to the experimenter. The MultiKron_II uses the on-board 16 Mbytes of DRAM to store trace event samples, and this memory is directly accessible to the experimenter.

One of the PCI bus signals, DEVSEL#, is a device active signal. To measure the utilization of the PCI bus we hardwired two versions of the DEVSEL# signal to the

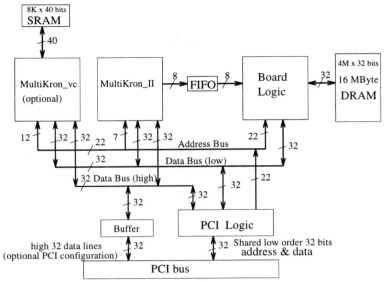

Figure 3: Functional Block Diagram of the PCI Multikron Toolkit.

external input pin of the MultiKron performance counters, numbers 0 and 2. One version is the direct signal, and the other version is the signal enabled only when the toolkit board is active. These signals can be used to determine the overall PCI bus utilization and the time used by the toolkit board. By configuring performance counters number 0 and 2 to use these input signals, they will tally the total number of clock ticks that the PCI bus is busy, and busy only with the toolkit board, respectively. By configuring another performance counter to tally the total number of elapsed clocks, we can compute the percent of time the bus is utilized. The MultiKron clocks are operating at a rate faster than the 33 MHz PCI bus clock, thus yielding a fairly accurate measure of utilization. Each MultiKron performance counter is a 32 bit counter, but "even" numbered counters can be configured as 64 bit counters by concatenating them with their neighboring "odd" numbered counter. Concatenating counters is useful for tallying high frequency events, since a 32 bit counter can overflow quickly, in less than 90 seconds when tied to a 50 MHz clock.

3. Integrating Paradyn and MultiKron

To provide an end-to-end demonstration of the benefits of hardware instrumentation for tuning application programs, we have integrated support for the MultiKron PCI toolkit into the Paradyn Parallel Performance Measurement Tools. To take advantage of the high-resolution, low-overhead timers available with the MultiKron board, we replaced Paradyn's default software-based instrumentation with memory operations on the mapped PCI board. The next sub-section provides a brief overview of the Paradyn tools, its instrumentation, and its data collection

models. Section 3.2 describes the design and implementation of the Paradyn-MultiKron integration.

3.1 Paradyn and Its Data Collection Model

Paradyn is a parallel performance suite designed to scale to long running (multi-hour) executions on large-scale parallel systems. The tools are designed to provide precise information about application performance during program execution, yet keep instrumentation overhead reasonable. To do this, Paradyn uses a mechanism known as *Dynamic Instrumentation*[11] that employs run-time code generation to insert instrumentation into a running program.

The end-to-end requirements of Paradyn are very similar to that of a soft real-time system. In order to provide accurate real-time performance feedback all the different modules (data collection, analysis and visualization) have delay requirements that must be met for the system to be effective. To control the amount of instrumentation overhead, dynamic instrumentation is regulated by a cost model[13] that limits the amount of instrumentation enabled to not exceed a user defined time budget (expressed as the ratio of instrumentation code execution time to application code execution time).

Paradyn's data collection model is based on a hybrid two step process. As the program to be measured executes, data structures record the frequency and duration of instrumented operations. These data structures are then periodically sampled to report performance information to an external process (called the Paradyn deamon) that forwards them to visualization and analysis components. Periodic sampling of these structures provides accurate information about the time varying performance of an application without requiring the large amount of data

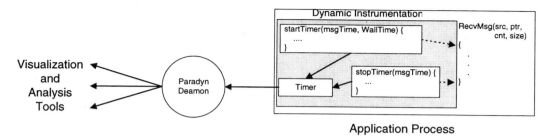

Figure 4: Paradyn's Data Collection Paths.

needed to store event logs of every change in the state of a monitored variable.

To meet the challenges of providing efficient and detailed instrumentation, Dynamic Instrumentation makes some radical changes in the way traditional performance data collection has been done. However, since the approach is designed to be usable by a variety of high level tools, a simple interface is used. The interface is based on two abstractions: **resources** and **metrics**. Resources are hardware or software abstractions that we wish to collect performance information about. For example, procedure, processes, CPU's, and disks are all resources. Metrics are time varying functions that characterize some aspect of a parallel program's performance. Metrics can be computed for any subset of the resources in the system. For example, CPU utilization can be computed for a single procedure executing on one processor or for the entire application.

Metrics definitions are converted into instrumentation *snippets* by a compiler that inserts code into the running application[14]. Figure 4 shows an application program with two snippets inserted: one at the entry to the RecvMsg function and the second at the end of that function. This pair of snippets computes the amount of time that the RecvMsg functions, and any functions it calls, are active. The first snippet starts a wall timer when the application program enters the RecvMsg function. The second snippet stops the timer when the application leaves this function.

3.2 Integrating Paradyn and MultiKron

To integrate Paradyn's instrumentation system with the MultiKron toolkit, we have replaced the software used to implement Paradyn's timers by instructions to trigger

MultiKron's hardware timers. Figure 5 shows the modified data path when using the hardware assist for timers. The application program still has two snippets, but now these snippets consist of assignment statements to the memory mapped control register. In addition to periodically sampling the value of the timer, the Paradyn daemon now directly reads metric values by memory mapping the MultiKron hardware. Timers are implemented by configuring the performance counters in the MultiKron to be incremented by the clock on the MultiKron board. Once configured, starting a timer simply requires a write operation to the memory-mapped location that enables the counter. Likewise stopping a timer also requires a similar operation. Figure 5 shows a slightly simplified version of the implementation (the actual code uses a bit mask to select a specific counter, so the constant is not 1). In addition to a faster access to a clock source, the MultiKron implementation of Paradyn's timers are faster because they provide the abstraction of a timer (e.g., start and stop) rather than the building block of a clock (e.g., return current time). Sampling by the Paradyn daemon is accomplished by having the daemon process also map the MultiKron into its address space.

We have also exported the PCI bus utilization counter in the MultiKron toolkit as a Paradyn metric. This allows online (during execution) visualization of bus utilization along side application (software) specific metrics such as message passing statistics. Isolating bus utilization to specific program components can be difficult due to asynchronous events such as I/O and the unpredictable interleaving of kernel activity with application requests. As a result, the bus utilization metric can only be requested for the entire machine rather than specific procedures, files,

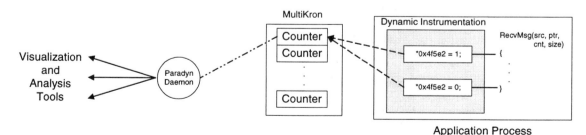

Figure 5: Paradyn Data Collection Using Multikron.

383

or threads. However, for many real-time and parallel applications, only one process per node is executing and so the per-machine measurements are nearly identical to per-process data.

4. Measurement Studies

In order to evaluate the capabilities of the MultiKron and its integration with the Paradyn Parallel Performance Tools, we conducted a series of measurement studies. The first set of experiments was designed to demonstrate the capabilities of the hardware instrumentation of the MultiKron, and to quantify the advantages of using hardware assistance for online performance evaluation tools such as Paradyn.

The second set of experiments was designed to show the benefits of using the combined hardware-software set of tools to understand the performance of parallel and distributed applications. These same benefits and concerns apply to real-time systems, and especially to parallel and distributed real-time systems using the real-time extensions to the Message Passing Interface (MPI)[15]. In these systems, the timing of network and peripheral device activity is of equal concern to those of processor activity. Light-weight data capture mechanisms allow performance measurements to be acquired in real-time systems, even those with tight time budgets. Since this measurement mechanism causes very little perturbation to the executing processes, accurate, undistorted performance information can be obtained down to relatively fine-grained events. In contrast, software based data capture tools are not suited to real-time systems since they can distort performance information, especially for fine-grained events.

4.1 Benefits of using MultiKron Storage

We wished to quantify the benefits of using the on-board memory of the MultiKron to record periodic samples of performance data. By using the MultiKron's storage, a system being measured is able to record periodic samples of the 16 MultiKron performance counters into the on-board memory for offline analysis after the time critical events have been measured. To evaluate this capability, we constructed a test program that can either sample the 16 performance counters and store the values in the system main memory (i.e. request multiple reads over the PCI bus), or request the MultiKron to store a sample containing the current values of the counters in its memory. We than ran the test program varying the frequency of these requests.

The results of comparing the overhead of different sampling frequencies are shown Figure 6. By using the MultiKron to trigger samples, we are able to gather over 100,000 samples per second and only incur a load of less than 5% on the PCI bus. By contrast, a similar level of sampling that directly reads the performance counters results in a PCI bus utilization of over 40%. In addition, the processor utilization to read samples frequently is very high. For example, when polling the maximum possible sampling rate is 122,000 samples per second, which re-

quires all available cycles on the 233 Mhz Pentium II processor used in these experiments.

The implication is that a large set of time trace events with the corresponding set of counters can be assembled with little perturbation to the executing code by using MultiKron type instrumentation. Whereas, reading each counter and the clock individually at each event can cause significant perturbation. Such delays could significantly degrade parallel code performance, but could be catastrophic to real-time codes.

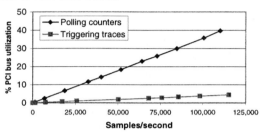

Figure 6: Sampling frequency vs. Bus Utilization.

4.2 Performance of MultiKron Integration

In the original implementation of Paradyn, *gettimeofday* and *getrusage* UNIX system calls are used for wall timer and process timer respectively. In the MultiKron implementation, each start and stop time operation is simply one or two writes to the mapped control registers. A read or write to a MultiKron register is slightly slower than reading or writing a "normal" address. This difference ocurs because the PCI Bus (where the MultiKron is located) is slower than the memory bus. However, this difference is insignificant compared to the time taken by a timer system call.

To quantify the performance gains of using MultiKron compared with software system calls, we wrote a test program to start and stop Paradyn wall timers for each implementation. In the test program, a timer is started and stopped 5 million times. The test program was run on a DEC Alpha with a clock speed of 275 MHz. The aggregate net time to execute each call after factoring out loop overhead is 2.6 micro-seconds (715 processor clock cycles) for the system call-based implementation, and 0.096 micro-seconds (26 processor clock cycles) for the MultiKron version, or 27 times faster. This speedup is due to being able to execute a single memory operation rather than the sequence: read clock, read start time, and then update accumulated time. Also, reading a wall clock on the Alphas requires trapping into the operating system kernel.

4.3 Micro-benchmarks of MultiKron on PCs

We also have installed the PCI MultiKron toolkit on a network of Intel Pentium II's based PCs connected by a Myrinet network. Myrinet[4] is a 1.2 Gbps switched local area network that is designed to provide both low latency and high speed communication. Our experimental configuration consists of a network of eight Pentium IIs with

64 MB of memory each. Inter-node communication is provided by sending messages using the industry standard Message Passing Interface (MPI)[8]. We used the BIP[25] protocol that provides a Myrinet driver which works with the MPICH[7] implementation of MPI developed by Argonne National Laboratory.

Given the high speed of Myrinet, we wanted to use the MultiKron's PCI bus monitor to see if the performance of the PCI bus was a limiting factor in the communication speed between nodes. We constructed a simple ping-pong message-passing program that sends a series of of fixed size messages between two hosts. We also instrumented this program to use the MultiKron PCI bus-monitoring feature to record the average PCI bus utilization for each run. For each message size, the experiment was repeated 10,000 times, and the average of the last 9,000 values is reported. We repeated the measurements for various sized messages from 1024 bytes to 10 megabytes.

Figure 7 shows the results of these measurements. The two curves show the correlation between application level message passing rates and PCI bus utilization as the message size is varied. This graph shows that once the message size exceeds 500 kilobytes, both the transfer rate and bus utilization curves flatten out. The effective transfer rate is about 120 MB/sec and the bus utilization is over 95%. Considering that the maximum speed of the PCI bus is 132 MB/sec (4 byte wide bus at 33MHz) and that the theoretical maximum speed of Myrinet is 150 MB/sec it appears that the PCI bus is the limiting resource.

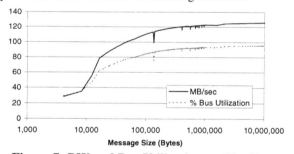

Figure 7: BW and Bus Utilization vs. Pkt Size.

We also used the PCI bus-monitor feature of the Multikron board to find and correct a performance bottleneck in the all-to-all communication primitive in MPICH, a popular implementation of MPI. The PCI bus utilization for two nodes of an eight-node cluster is shown in Figure 8. The graph shows a one-second interval of a test application that executes a series of all-to-all communication requests. As can be seen, there is a large fluctuation in bus utilization, and the average bus utilization for the entire application is only 30%. However, since all-to-all message passing is nothing more than a sequence of point-to-point messages, we would have expected the bus utilization to be similar to that seen in Figure 7. Since each all-to-all message is 1.3 MB (or 163 KB per node), we would have expected an average bus utilization of close to 80%. Also, the average aggregate transfer rate across eight

nodes is 162 MB/sec, which is only 35% higher than the two node case.

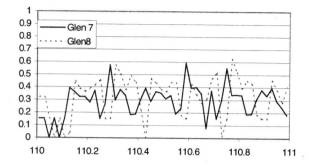

Figure 8: PCI bus utilization vs. time for two nodes.

Qualitatively, the graph shows a large fluctuation in the bus utilization as a function of time. As a result, we suspected that somehow the all-to-all function was not able to send data at the uniformly high rate we had expected. We then looked at the implementation of the function, and discovered that although the function was using non-blocking sends and receives to transmit the data, each node was initiating the sends in the same order. Each process started with virtual node zero and then proceed sequentially to each other node. We suspected that the lower level implementation of non-blocking communication was processing message send requests in a FIFO order. This send pattern would result in contention for each node that was the recipient of several simultaneous sends. To test this theory, we changed the send loop to have each node start by sending data to the node with the next highest node number. The results of this version are shown Figure 9. In this case, the test application achieves an average bus utilization of 58%, and the aggregate communication performance across eight nodes is 316 MB/sec.

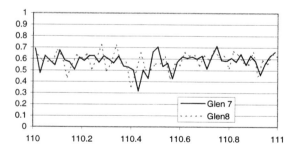

Figure 9: PCI Bus Utilization after tuning.

The micro-benchmarks show the ability of the MultiKron toolkit to reduce the overhead associated with software-based instrumentation and the utility of the PCI bus monitor to isolate performance problems in systems software. In the next section, we consider the utility of the toolkit for measuring application programs.

385

4.4 Application Case Studies

To evaluate the performance of the MultiKron toolkit on real applications, we selected two programs. The first is an out of core LU matrix decomposition that was run on a DEC Alpha cluster. This application shows the integration of MultiKron PCI bus statistics time and counter based metrics triggered by software probes. The second application is an implementation of the Poisson problem (Jacobi integration on a 2-D grid). This application demonstrates how the MultiKron can be used to show that the PCI bus is not a bottleneck.

LU is the dense LU decomposition of an out-of-core matrix[10]. This application is interesting because it is communication, computation and I/O intensive. This implementation of the out-of-core data staging is done using synchronous `read` and `write` operations. In our measurement studies, we used an 8192×8192 double precision matrix (total size 536MB) staged using slabs of 64 columns as a basic unit.

We ran the application on a cluster of four DEC Alpha processors connected via a 155 Mbps ATM network. A time histogram showing the performance of the first several minutes of the application's execution is shown in Figure 11. In this graph, we have requested Paradyn to display three metrics: message bytes transferred, PCI bus utilization, and execution (wall) time spent in the I/O write routine. The bus utilization and execution time curves were generated using data gathered via the MultiKron monitor, and the message bytes metric was computed using Paradyn's software counters. The curves show that the PCI bus utilization is highest during the I/O operations, approximately 30%. We also see that the bus utilization continues past the I/O interval due to the file-system write-behind policy. Once the I/O phase completes, there is a period when none of the metrics show much activity. This middle interval of time is computation that is not captured by the three metrics shown Figure 11. After this middle phase ends, the application enters a communication phase where data transfers to and from the selected process peak at 1.5 MB/sec. During this final phase, the PCI bus utilization is perceptible (slight peaks in the time-histogram), but not a significant bottleneck.

The second application is a solution to the Poisson problem by using Jacobi integration on a 2-D decomposition. Figure 10 shows the performance statistics for this application when it is executed on 2, 4, and 8 nodes of a Myrinet connected cluster of Pentium II machines. For all versions of the application, the program spends a majority of its time performing communication operations. However, despite the majority of time being spent in communication, the fifth column of Figure 10 shows that the PCI bus utilization never exceeds 5%. This data shows the software overhead of the message-passing library dominates the PCI bus utilization. Further investigation into the application confirmed that the reason it spends so much time in communication routines is due to the relatively small message size (average message size is only 15-30 bytes depending on the number of nodes used).

Nodes	Time	Comm	% Comm	PCI
2	14.07	7.79	55.4%	3.9%
4	17.34	10.33	59.6%	4.6%
8	18.99	10.85	57.2%	3.7%

Figure 10: Data for the Decomp Application.

5. Related Work

Several tools to permit runtime verification of real-time requirements exist. Mok[24] developed a language for expressing real-time timing requirements that can be verified at runtime. Chodrow et al [6] have developed a system that permits checking real-time properties during system execution. Their system could benefit from the Multikron monitor since Multikron provides a mechanism to provide high-resolution time-stamped trace records.

Various types of hardware performance measurement have been incorporated into high-performance microprocessors and systems. The IBM RP3[5] included performance-monitoring hardware throughout the system. The Sequent Symmetry's also included hardware to measure bus utilization, bus read and write counts, and cache miss rates. Using this information, tools[12] were able to give the programmer insights that substantially simplified program tuning. Unfortunately, Sequent never widely disclosed the existence of these features due to fears that information obtained using the hardware instrumentation would be used by their competitors. Another early example of hardware performance data comes from the Cray Y-MP[2]. The Y-MP provided a wide variety of hardware-level performance data including information about frequency of specific instructions.

Most current microprocessors also include hardware counters for measuring processor visible events. For example, the Intel Pentium family of processors[17] provides access, via model specific registers (MSR), to data including cache misses, pipeline stalls, instructions executed, misaligned memory accesses, interrupts, and branches. Similar data is also provided for the Ultra Sparc, DEC Alpha[1], IBM Power2[27], and MIPS R10000[28] processors. However, a limitation of this type of instrumentation is that it is only available for processor visible events, and therefore can not track other aspects of the system such as the bus and the I/O system.

Several versions of hardware support for tracing have been developed. The TMP monitor[9] included a general-purpose microprocessor dedicated to instrumentation, and a separate I/O network to gather performance data at a central location. Tsai et al [26] have developed a non-intrusive hardware monitor for real-time systems. Their technique requires a complex processor to track the activity of the primary processor, however they were able to develop a completely non-intrusive monitor as a result.

Malony and Reed[16] developed HYPERMON to measure the performance of an Intel Hypercube. HYPERMON permitted gathering data from each node to a custom designed monitoring node. Like MultiKron, HYPERMON used software-based instrumentation to trigger

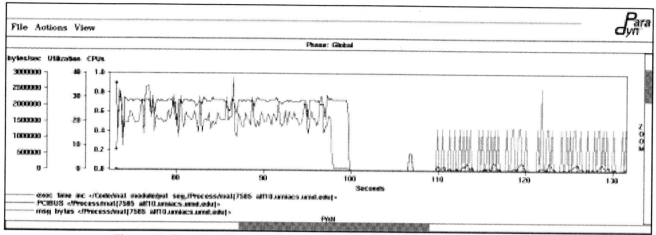

Figure 11: **Paradyn Time Histogram Showing Application and PCI Metrics.**

This graph shows the Paradyn Time-histogram display for three metrics: execution time for the put_seq procedure, PCI Bus utilization, and message bytes transferred. The graph has three distinct phases. In the first phase, the put_seq procedure is active and the PCI bus utilization is about 30%. In the middle phase, none of the three metrics show a significant amount of activity (i.e., the program is performing operations not related to the three metrics). In the final phase, the program is sending messages, but this activity is only inducing a very light load on the bus.

the transfer of events to the hardware tracing facility. One advantage of the MultiKron toolkit and its on-board memory is that a separate data collection network is not required. Instead data can be accumulated on each node, and transferred when the application completes execution. A key enabling trend to make plug-in instrumentation hardware possible has been the migration of high-performance computing platforms to using Commodity Off The Shelf (COTS) nodes with standardized I/O buses.

6. Conclusions

Low perturbation and high precision timers are beneficial in collecting performance data as demonstrated in our experiments. Also, having performance counters throughout the computer system rather than just inside the microprocessor is useful for tuning applications. Application developers are finding I/O bus statistics vital for tuning their applications[3]. As real-time parallel and distributed systems become more complex and pervasive, the utility of these counters will increase.

While many microprocessor vendors are incorporating hardware counters in their design, the interface to these counters is rarely what is necessary for application performance measurement studies. For example, most vendors make their performance counters readable using only privileged instructions. This requires application programs to trap into the operating system to read these counters. The overhead of a trap is tolerable for course grained measurements (i.e., at the beginning and end of a program). However, for fine-grained measurements at the procedure and loop levels, this trap overhead is unacceptable since the time required for even the fastest trap represents a significant fraction of the time of the event to be measured. Operating system vendors should also provide either a virtualized view of the performance counters so

that performance data can be tracked on a per-process or per-thread basis, or provide easy hooks to allow third-party software to have a callback during the context-switch code.

MultiKron type instrumentation includes a larger set of counters, sixteen, compared to microprocessor on-chip counters which generally have two timers. Current on-chip counters do have the advantage of having access to internal chip information that the MultiKron can't get access to, but 32 or more signals must be multiplexed to the limited number of counters. MultiKron also provides for event tracing in addition to counting. Thus, the MultiKron provides an efficient, low perturbation means to collect the information as well as generate it. This is a significant benefit to real-time systems that generally have tight time budgets and are sensitive to the insertion of delays. Event tracing and data collection incur larger implementation costs than do simple counters, and therefore face higher manufacturer resistance.

A performance monitoring tool like the Paradyn and MultiKron combination presented in this paper can be very useful in providing runtime feedback about the scheduling and timing behavior of a set of real-time tasks under different system conditions. Metrics like resource utilization and blocking time can be collected in an efficient way and displayed on a timely basis without affecting the underlining behavior of the task set.

Acknowledgments

We thank Li Zhang for his efforts to port Paradyn's Dynamic Instrumentation system to the DEC Alpha processor. The BIP team provided several explanations and bug-fixes that were critical to using the Myrinet. Mustafa Uysal supplied the implementation of LU used in the case study and helped us to it. The decomposition application was taken from examples supplied in [8].

References

1. DECchip 21064 and DECchip21064A Alpha AXP Microprocessors - Hardware Reference Manual, EC-Q9ZUA-TE, DEC, June 1994.
2. UNICOS File Formats and Special Files Reference Manual SR-2014 5.0, Cray Research Inc.
3. A. C. Arpaci-Dusseau, R. H. Arpaci-Dusseau, D. E. Culler, J. M. Hellerstein, and D. A. Patterson, "Searching for the Sorting Record: Experiences in Tuning NOW-Sort," SIGMETRICS Symposium on Parallel and Distributed Tools. Aug. 1998, Welches, OR, pp. 124-133.
4. N. J. Boden, D. Cohen, R. E. Felderman, A. E. Kulawik, C. L. Seitz, J. N. Seizovi, and W.-K. Su, "MYRINET: A Gigabit Per Second Local Area Network," IEEE-Micro, 15(1), 1995, pp. 29-36.
5. W. C. Brantley, K. P. McAuliffe, and T. A. Ngo, RP3 Performance Monitoring Hardware, in Instrumentation for Future Parallel Computer Systems, M. Simmons, R. Koskela, and I. Bucker, Editors. 1989, Addison-Wesley. pp. 35-47.
6. S. E. Chodrow, F. Jahanian, and M. Donner, "Run-Time Monitoring of Real-Time Systems," Real-Time Systems Symposium. Dec. 1991, pp. 74-83.
7. W. Gropp, E. Lusk, N. Doss, and A. Skjellum, "A high-performance, portable implementation of the MPI message passing interface standard," Parallel Computing, 22(6), 1996, pp. 789-828.
8. W. Gropp, E. Lusk, and A. Skjellum, Using MPI: Portable Parallel Programming with the Message Passing Interace. 1995: MIT Press.
9. D. Haban and D. Wybranietz, "A Hybrid Monitor for Behavior and Performance Analysis of Distributed Systems," IEEE Transactions on Software Engineering, 16(2), 1990, pp. 197-211.
10. B. Hendrickson and D. Womble, "The Torus-wrap Mapping for Dense Matrix Calculations on Massively Parallel Computers," SIAM Journal Scientific Computing, 15(5), 1994, pp. 1201.
11. J. K. Hollingsworth and B. Buck, DyninstAPI Programmer's Guide, CS-TR-3821, University of Maryland, August 1997.
12. J. K. Hollingsworth, R. B. Irvin, and B. P. Miller, "The Integration of Application and System Based Metrics in A Parallel Program Performance Tool," 1991 ACM SIGPLAN Symposium on Principals and Practice of Parallel Programming. April 21-24, 1991, Williamsburg, VA, pp. 189-200.
13. J. K. Hollingsworth and B. P. Miller, "Using Cost to Control Instrumentation Overhead," Theoretical Computer Science, 196(1-2), 1998, pp. 241-258.
14. J. K. Hollingsworth, B. P. Miller, M. J. R. Goncalves, O. Naim, Z. Xu, and L. Zheng, "MDL: A Language and Compiler for Dynamic Program Instrumentation," International Conference on Parallel Architectures and Compilation Techniques (PACT). Nov. 1997, San Francisco, pp. 201-212.
15. A. Kanevsky, A. Skjellumy, and J. Watts, "Standardization of a Communication Middleware for High-Performance Real-Time Systems," RTSS. December 2-5, 1997, San Francisco, CA.
16. A. D. Malony and D. A. Reed, "A Hardware-Based Performance Monitor for the Intel iPSC/2 Hypercube," 1990 International Conference on Supercomputing. June 11-15, 1990, Amsterdam, pp. 213-226.
17. T. Mathisen, "Pentium Secrets," Byte, 19(7), 1994, pp. 191-192.
18. B. P. Miller, M. D. Callaghan, J. M. Cargille, J. K. Hollingsworth, R. B. Irvin, K. L. Karavanic, K. Kunchithapadam, and T. Newhall, "The Paradyn Parallel Performance Measurement Tools," IEEE Computer, 28(11), 1995, pp. 37-46.
19. A. Mink, Operating Principles of Multikron II Performance Instrumentation for MIMD Computers, NISTIR 5571, National Institute of Standards and Technology, Dec. 1994.
20. A. Mink, Operating Principles of MultiKron Virtual Counter Performance Instrumentation for MIMD Computers, NISTIR 5743, National Institute of Standards and Technology, Nov. 1995.
21. A. Mink, Operating Principles of the SBus Mulikron Interface Board, NISTIR 5652, National Institute of Standards and Technology, May 1995.
22. A. Mink, R. Carpenter, G. Nacht, and J. Roberts, "Multiprocessor Performance Measurement Instrumentation," IEEE Computer, 23(9), 1990, pp. 63-75.
23. A. Mink and W. Salamon, Operating Printicples of the PCI Bus Multikron Interface Board, NISTIR 5993, National Institute of Standards and Technology, Mar 1997.
24. A. K. Mok and G. Liu, "Early Detection of Timing Constraint Violations at Runtime," Real-Time Technology and Applications Symposium. 1997, pp. 176-185.
25. L. Prylli and B. Tourancheau, "BIP: a new protocol designed for high performance networking on Myrinet," IPPS Workshop on PC-NOW. 1998, Orlando, FL.
26. J. J. P. Tsai, K. Y. Fang, and H. Y. Chen, "A Noninvasive Architecture to MOnitor Real-time Distributed Systems," IEEE Computer, 23(3), 1990, pp. 11-23.
27. E. H. Welbon, C. C. Chen-Nui, D. J. Shippy, and D. A. Hicks, The POWER2 Performance Monitor, in PowerPC and Power2: Technical Aspects of the New RISC System/6000. 1994, IBM Corporation. p. 45-63.
28. M. Zagha, B. Larson, S. Turner, and M. Itzkowitz, "Performance Analysis Using the MIPS R10000 Performance Counters," Supercomputing. Nov. 1996, Pittsburg, PA.

Session 11.B: Scheduling and Analysis II

Real-Time Scheduling in a Generic Fault-Tolerant Architecture

A. J. Wellings, Lj. Beus-Dukic
Department of Computer Science
University of York
York, YO10 5DD, United Kingdom
{andy, ljerka}@cs.york.ac.uk

D. Powell
LAAS-CNRS
7 Avenue du Colonel Roche
31077 Toulouse Cedex 4, France
dpowell@laas.fr

Abstract

Previous ultra-dependable real-time computing architectures have been specialised to meet the requirements of a particular application domain. Over the last two years, a consortium of European companies and academic institutions has been investigating the design and development of a Generic Upgradable Architecture for Real-time Dependable Systems (GUARDS). The architecture aims to be tolerant of permanent and temporary, internal and external, physical faults and should provide confinement or tolerance of software design faults. GUARDS critical applications are intended to be replicated across the channels which provide the primary hardware fault containment regions. In this paper, we present our approach to real-time scheduling of the GUARDS architecture. We use an extended response-time analysis to predict the timing properties of replicated real-time transactions. Consideration is also given to the scheduling of the inter-channel communications network.

1. Introduction

Most ultra-dependable real-time computing architectures developed in the past have been specialised to meet the particular requirements of the application domain for which they were targeted. This specialisation has led to very costly, inflexible, and often hardware-intensive solutions that, by the time they are developed, validated and certified for use in the field, can already be out-of-date in terms of their underlying hardware and software technology. This problem is exacerbated in some application domains since the systems in which the real-time architecture is embedded may be deployed for several decades, i.e., almost an order of magnitude longer than the typical lifespan of a generation of computing technology.

Over the last two years, a consortium of European companies and academic institutions has been investigating the design and development of a Generic Upgradable Architecture for Real-time Dependable Systems (GUARDS[1]), together with an associated development and validation environment. The end-user companies in the consortium all currently deploy ultra-dependable real-time embedded computers in their systems, but with very different requirements and constraints resulting from the diversity of their application domains: nuclear submarine, railway and space systems. For example, railway applications have the requirement for fail-safe control systems with a safe shutdown rate less than 10^{-9} per hour, whereas space applications have the need for autonomous operations over a 15 year mission with a reliability figure of 0.985 [24].

The overall aim of the GUARDS project is to significantly decrease the lifecycle costs of such embedded systems. The intent is to be able to configure instances of the GUARDS generic architecture that can be shown to meet the very diverse requirements of these (and other) critical real-time application domains.

This paper discusses the real-time aspects of the proposed architecture. In Section 2 we present a brief overview of the architecture. In Section 3 we discuss the structure of applications and how they are scheduled within a channel. Section 4 then considers the replication of applications across channels and how replica determinism is achieved. Section 5 discusses the form of offset analysis that we have used to analyse the resulting real-time transactions. We then consider the implications for scheduling the inter-channel network. Finally, the current status of the project is presented along with our conclusions.

---

[1] GUARDS is partially financed by the European Commission as ESPRIT project no 20716. The consortium consists of three end-user companies: Technicatome (France), Ansaldo Segnalamento Ferroviario (Italy) and Matra Marconi Space France; two technology-provider companies: Intecs Sistemi (Italy), Siemens AG Österreich PSA (Austria); and three academic partners: LAAS-CNRS (France), Pisa Dependable Computing Centre (Italy) and the University of York (United Kingdom).

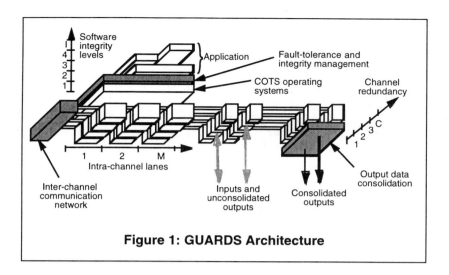

Figure 1: GUARDS Architecture

2. The GUARDS Architecture

To minimise cost and to maximise flexibility, the architecture favours the use of commercial off-the-shelf (COTS) hardware and software components, with application-transparent fault-tolerance implemented primarily by software. The architecture aims to be tolerant of permanent and temporary, internal and external, physical faults and should provide confinement for tolerance of software design faults. A three-pronged approach is being followed to reduce the cost of validation and certification of instances of the architecture:

1. design for validation so as to focus validation obligations on a minimum set of critical components;

2. re-use of already-validated components in different instances; and

3. the support of application components of different criticalities.

Drawing on experience from systems such as SIFT [20], MAFT [16], FTPP [13] and Delta-4 [23], the generic architecture is defined along three axes (see Figure 1) [24]:

- the channel axis (C): channels provide the primary hardware fault containment regions; it is possible to configure instances of the architecture with 1 to 4 channels;

- the intra-channel or multiplicity axis (M): multiple resources can be provided in each channel either for increased performance and/or for use as secondary fault containment regions; and

- the integrity axis (I): spatial and temporal firewalls are implemented, together with a strictly-enforced multi-level integrity policy [28], to protect critical components from residual design faults in less-critical components.

GUARDS critical application tasks are intended to be replicated across the channels. Our approach allows for both diverse or identical implementations of the replicas. However, in the prototypes under construction, it is assumed that only identical copies of tasks are replicated. It should be stressed that it is the application tasks which are replicated, *not* the entire software in a channel. Hence, each channel may run a different mixture of critical and non-critical tasks.

Although the GUARDS architecture favours the use of commercial off-the-shelf components, some parts of the architecture must necessarily be purpose-designed to meet the high dependability requirements. These are identified on Figure 1 as shaded components:

- the inter-channel communication network, needed to ensure inter-channel synchronisation and interactive consistency;

- the output data consolidation system, needed to combine redundant logical outputs into error-free physical outputs to the controlled process; and

- the fault-tolerance and integrity management layer needed to coordinate replicated software components and enforce the integrity policy.

Each channel acts as a shared memory multi-processor system. Figure 2 illustrates the intra-channel architecture. There is an Inter-Channel Network (ICN) manager processor and one or more host processors. Each processor has some dual-ported shared memory which can be accessed over a VME bus or from the local processor. This structure aims to facilitate timing analysis of inter-processor communication. The ICN manager is responsible for handling all communication on the ICN network, performing any required interactive consistency algorithms (we are using the ZA algorithm [12]) and ensuring that the clocks are synchronised between channels (we currently use a converging averaging algorithm [19]).

In the prototype system currently under construction, the ICN network consists of one 10 Mbit/s twisted pair link for each channel in the architecture. Each channel may only write to its private link, but can receive on any of the other links. The links are managed by M68360 Ethernet controllers and the ICN manager itself is an M68040. The host processors can be any processor which can be attached to a VME backplane bus and which supports dual-ported memory.

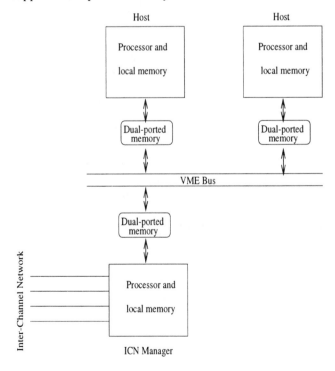

Figure 2: The GUARDS Intra-Channel Architecture

For more details of the rationale for the GUARDS architecture, see [24].

In order to understand the timing properties of the architecture, it is necessary to address the following topics:

- how applications are constructed and scheduled within a channel;

- how applications are replicated across channels and how those replicas are coordinated; and

- how the ICN is scheduled.

These topics are considered in the following sections.

3. Applications and Intra-Channel Scheduling

The approach taken to scheduling real-time applications depends on the computational model required by the application. The computational model defines the form of concurrency supported by GUARDS (for example, tasks, threads, asynchronous communication, etc.) and any restriction that must be placed on application programs to facilitate their timing analysis (for example, bounded recursion). In general, GUARDS applications may conform to a time triggered, event triggered or mixed computational model.

In keeping with the GUARDS requirement of genericity, the architecture and its operating system must be capable of supporting a range of scheduling models. Furthermore, the operating system must ideally be capable of being tailored so that it supports only those primitives required by a particular application. In the prototype architectures being developed we are using VxWorks, QNX and VRTX.

Three scheduling models are defined for GUARDS:

- Cyclic — as typified by the traditional cyclic executive;

- Cooperative — where an application-defined scheduler and the prioritised application tasks themselves explicitly pass control between one another to perform the required dispatching; and

- Pre-emptive — the standard pre-emptive priority scheme.

Table 1 summarises the timing analysis techniques which are used with the three models.

The choice of scheduling model for a particular application will depend on a variety of factors such as:

- the computational model of the application;

- the performance requirements of the application;

- constraints placed on the development process by certification authorities (for example, the particular method of testing or the form of safety case required); and

- the ease with which the proposed application can be maintained with the chosen scheduling model.

Table 1: GUARDS Timing Analysis Techniques

Computational model	Function release	Scheduling model		
		Cyclic	Co-operative	Pre-emptive
Time-triggered	Periodic	Timing analysis by construction	Response time analysis	Rate monotonic analysis
Event-triggered	Sporadic	N/A	Response time analysis	Response time analysis
Mixed	Periodic & sporadic	N/A	Response time analysis	Response time analysis

For the remainder of this paper, we will consider the preemptive model as that is the one which poses the greatest challenges. See [29] for details of how the cyclic and cooperative models are handled.

Our timing analysis for the pre-emptive model is based upon the Response-time Analysis [18], [2]. We assume that any communication between applications is asynchronous through the shared memory. The use of round-robin scheduling on the VME allows all shared memory accesses to be bounded (this is adequate because it is assumed that the number of hosts within a channel is small). Furthermore, we assume the use of a non-blocking algorithm such as that proposed by Simpson [25] to avoid the problems associated with remote blocking.

4. Inter-Channel Replication of Applications

For an application task to be replicated, it must behave deterministically and each replica task must process the same inputs in the same order. At any point where there is potential for replica divergence, the channels must perform an interactive consistency agreement. Unfortunately, the cost of executing interactive consistency agreement protocols can be significant. There is therefore a need to keep their use to a minimum.

There is clearly a trade-off between the frequency of performing comparisons between channels and the overheads (and scheduling constraints) imposed by such comparisons. In MAFT [16], [14], which supports a cooperative computational model, the scheduling table for each site is replicated for fault tolerance. Each local scheduler, as well as selecting the next task for executing on its site, also mirrors the operations performed by the other schedulers. Every time a task is scheduled or completes, the local scheduler broadcasts its details to all sites. The schedulers then perform an interactive consistency agreement to determine which task has started or completed. The local scheduler can then decide whether the action undertaken by a remote scheduler was in error (that is, the task scheduled was different from the one that a local scheduler thought should be scheduled). Data messages between tasks are also broadcast to all sites. The overheads associated with these protocols are large and MAFT requires a separate custom-built processor (called the operations controller) as well as an application processor in each channel. However, the frequency of comparisons allowed by this approach ensures an early detection of errors.

In our approach, agreement is not necessary on every scheduling decision. Rather, we ensure that all replicated tasks read the same internal data. With this mechanism, we can tradeoff fewer agreement communications (and therefore greater efficiency) against early detection of errors. Whichever approach is taken, it is still necessary to perform, interactive consistency or Byzantine agreement, on single-sourced data such as sensor inputs.

In summary, if we assume that each replica does not contain any inherently non-deterministic code (for example, use of the Ada select statement), then it is only necessary to:

- perform interactive consistency (IC) agreement or Byzantine agreement on single-sourced data;

- ensure that all replicas receive the same inputs when those inputs are obtained from other replica tasks (replicated inputs); and

- perform voting on any vital output.

The following subsections indicate how we meet three requirements.

4.1. Agreement on Sensor Inputs

Even when replicated sensors are provided, the values read from them must be considered as single-source values and thus potentially different, even in the absence of faults. So that the replicated tasks in each channel process the same inputs, it is therefore necessary to exchange the values read locally by each channel and to agree on the vector of values that each channel thereby obtains. This is the purpose of interactive consistency agreement (the symmetric equivalent of Byzantine agreement) [21].

The agreed vector of values is then processed by an application-dependent fault-tolerant algorithm, such as mid-value select, that computes a single value from the agreed vector of possibly erroneous input values. To reduce the complexity of the input selection algorithm, it is important to minimize the error between the redundant input values. However, since the tasks are independently scheduled on each channel, they could read their corresponding sensors at significantly different times. This is similar to the input jitter problem where a task (τ) implementing a control law has to read its input on a regular basis. If jitter is a problem, the solution is to split the task into two tasks (τ^{ip}, τ'). τ^{ip} has a release time[2] and a deadline appropriate for the dynamics of the physical quantity being measured by the sensor (to facilitate reaching an agreement on the value of the readings between the replicated sensors). τ' has the original τ's deadline and is executed at an offset from the release time of τ^{ip}. We will discuss what value this offset should have in Section 5.

4.2. Identical Internal Replicated Input

Two cases need to be considered when reader and writer tasks share the same data, according to whether or not there is an explicit precedence constraint between the writer and the reader.

When there is such a constraint, then it can be captured by the scheduling. For example, consider the following types of synchronous interactions:

1.1. Periodic writer – Periodic reader: the writer is given a higher priority than the reader and will produce its data first.[3]

1.2. Periodic writer – Sporadic reader: the writer releases the reader.

1.3. Sporadic writer – Sporadic reader: the writer releases the reader.

In all these cases, if the writer replicas receive the same input and are deterministic then the reader replicas will

always receive the same values. Note that if we have a Sporadic writer and a Periodic reader then there cannot be an explicit precedence constraint between them but only asynchronous communication (see below).

When tasks share data asynchronously (and therefore there is no explicit precedence constraint between the writer and the reader), there are four types of interaction.

2.1. Periodic writer – Periodic reader: the periods of the two tasks do not have a simple relationship.

2.2. Periodic writer – Sporadic reader: the reader is not released by the writer.

2.3. Sporadic writer – Sporadic reader: the reader is not released by the writer.

2.4. Sporadic writer – Periodic reader: there is no relation between the release of the writer and the reader.

In all of these cases, it cannot be guaranteed that each replica reader gets the same data value. It is therefore necessary to either perform an interactive consistency communication between the replicas or to provide some other mechanism to ensure that the replicas read the same value. Barrett at al. [4] and Poledna [22] indicate that where data is being read asynchronously by a replica, it is possible to keep more than one copy of that data (usually two is enough) and use timestamps to ensure that each replica reads the same value. The essence of this approach is to use off-line schedulability analysis [2] to calculate the worst-case response times of each replicated writer. The maximum of these values is added to the release time of the replicas (taking into account any release jitter) to give a time by which all replicas must have written the data (in the worst case). To allow for clock drift between replicas, the maximum drift, ε, is also added. This value is used as a timestamp when the data is written. Hence:

Timestamp =
release time of writer + worst-case release jitter +
worst-case response time of writer replicas + ε (1)

A reader replica simply compares its release time with this data timestamp. If the timestamp is earlier, then the reader can take the data. If the timestamp is later than its release time, then the reader knows that its replicated writer has potentially executed before the other replicated writers. It must therefore take a previous value of the data (the most recent) whose timestamp is earlier than its release time. All reader replicas undertake the same algorithm and consequently get the same value. The scheme has the following properties:

---

[2] We assume that all I/O is periodic in nature.
[3] This is providing the writer does not block and is on the same processor as the reader. If it does block or they are on different processors, the reader must have an offset from the writer equal to at least the response time of the writer.

- all corresponding replicated data items have the same timestamp;

- all replicated writers will have completed writing their data by the local time indicated by the timestamp; and

- all replicated readers will read the most recent data that can be guaranteed to be read by all of them.

We assume that the schedulability analysis algorithms have been correctly implemented. We use budget timers [27] to ensure that tasks do not overrun their worst-case execution time.

Periodic writer

If the writer of the data is periodic (cases 2.1 and 2.2 above), then expression (1) can be used directly. The release time of the writer replicas is common to all replicas and the worst-case response time for the replicas can be calculated by off-line schedulability analysis. Therefore, each writer replica will timestamp its data with the same timestamp and all replicas will have written this data when the local clock at any site is greater that the timestamp.

Sporadic writer

If the writer is sporadic (cases 2.3 and 2.4 above), the release time used depends on how the sporadic was released.

If the writer is released by an interrupt then there is no common release time between replicas that can be used. It is therefore necessary for the replicas to undertake an IC agreement (they agree to use the latest local release time as the common release time). Each replica, τ, is split into two tasks τ^1 and τ^2. τ^1 is given its release time when it is released by the scheduler; it writes this value to the IC network. τ^2 is offset from τ^1 by a value which is equal to the release jitter of τ^1 plus its worst-case response time plus ε. The release jitter is any skew that might occur between the time the interrupts are generated in each channel (it is assumed that this is known by the designer).

If the sporadic writer is released by a periodic task, then its release time is equal to the release time of the periodic task plus the worst-case response time of the periodic task at the point at which the sporadic task is released.

If the writer is in a chain of sporadic tasks that originates from a periodic task, it uses a release time equal to the release time of the periodic task plus the sum of the worst-case response times of all the tasks in the chain. If the writer is a sporadic task which is in a chain of sporadic

tasks triggered by an interrupt, then it uses the same approach only with the agreed release time of the original sporadic task.

4. 3. Output Voting

Where output voting is required, it is again necessary to transform the replicated task writing to the actuators into two tasks (τ' and τ^{op}): τ' sends the output value across the ICN for voting, and τ^{op} reads the majority vote and sends this to the actuator. The deadline of τ' will determine the earliest point when the ICN manager can perform the voting. The offset and deadline of τ^{op} will determine when the voted result must be available and the amount of potential output jitter. Hence, the two tasks have similar timing characteristics to the tasks used for input agreement (Section 4.1). The main difference is that there is a simple majority vote rather than an agreement protocol involving three separate values.

5. Handling Offsets

In Section 4, we considered how to structure the task set of an application so that it can be replicated. The real-time periodic transaction model that has been developed is depicted in Figure 3. A periodic transaction i consists of three tasks τ_i^1, τ_i^2 and τ_i^3. Task τ_i^1 reads a sensor and sends the value to the ICN manager. Task τ_i^2 reads back from the ICN manager the set of values received from all the replicas; it consolidates the values and processes the consolidated reading and eventually produces some data. It sends this data for output consolidation to the ICN manager. Task τ_i^3 reads from the ICN manager the consolidated output value and sends it to the actuator. All communication with the ICN manager is asynchronous via the channel's shared memory.

Of course, Figure 3 is a form of real-time transactions implemented by offsets. Analysis of task sets with offsets is N-P complete [18] and even sub-optimal solutions are complex [1], [3], [26]. The approach we take is based on [5] modified to take into account the fact that the computational times of τ_i^1 and τ_i^3 (respectively C_i^1 and C_i^3) are much less than C_i^2, the computational time of τ_i^2, i.e., $C_i^2 >> max(C_i^1, C_i^3)$. In particular:

1. We assign priorities to competing transactions according to transaction deadlines (D) within the following framework. A task τ_i^1 has a greater priority than task τ_j^1, if $D_i < D_j$. All τ^1 tasks have priorities greater than all τ^3 tasks which have priorities greater than τ^2 tasks.

2. We perform response time analysis [2] on all the τ_j^1 and τ_j^3 tasks and calculate their response times (assuming that they are all released at the same moment in time, i.e., they form a critical instance). All τ_i^2 tasks are ignored at this stage; they have lower priorities.

Task

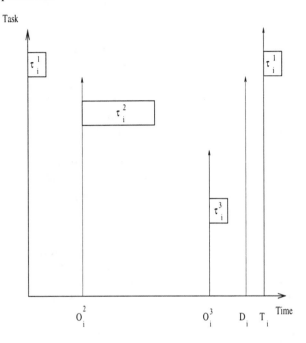

Figure 3: A GUARDS Real-Time Periodic Transaction

3. We assign O_i^2 to be $T_i/3$ and O_i^3 to be $(2*T_i)/3$ where O_i^2 is the offset of τ_i^2, O_i^3 is the offset of τ_i^3, and T_i is the period of the transaction (see Figure 3).

4. We construct a composite task[4] for τ_i as having a period $T/3$ and a computational time which varies: in its first period it is C_i^2, in its second period C_i^1, in its third period C_i^3 and in its fourth period C_i^2 and so on. This assumes $C_i^2 > C_i^1 > C_i^3$. The order of the C values reflects our assumption about their relative sizes. If this is not the case, the C_i values should be ordered in decreasing sizes. This is so that the composite task generates the maximum interference on lower priority tasks, which is essential for the analysis to be non-optimistic.

---

[4] A composite task is used for analysis purposes only. It is a task representing the transaction whose real-time properties are chosen so that the interference it causes on lower priority tasks is not optimistic, and yet the interference is less pessimistic than treating the transaction as three tasks which are released simultaneously [5], [6].

5. We use critical instance response time analysis to analyse each τ_i^2 task. However, for each transaction with a higher priority than τ_i^2, we use its associated composite tasks when calculating its interference on τ_i^2 (i.e. we ignore the input and output tasks associated with the higher priority transactions but include the ones from low priority transactions). This gives us the response times of the τ_i^2 tasks.

Clearly, after having completed the above procedure, a check must be made to ensure that:

1. the response times of the individual tasks are less than the offsets of the next task in the transaction;

2. there is enough time before the offset and after the response to transmit data on the ICN network; and

3. the deadline of the transaction has been met.

If any of these conditions are violated, then it may be possible to modify the offsets of the transaction violating the condition in an attempt to satisfy all the requirements [5].

In the special case where the deadline of the transaction is equal to the period of the transaction then it is possible to optimise the above approach. The first task in the transaction now has the responsibility of writing the result of the voted output (for the previous period) to the actuator and then immediately reading the sensor value. Hence, a transaction now only has two tasks rather than three.

6. Scheduling the ICN Network

In order to perform interactive consistency agreements, in the presence of n arbitrary failures, it is necessary to have the following properties [17]:

1. The system must consist of at least $3n+1$ participants, or $2n+1$ participants with authenticated communication [21].

2. The participants must be inter-connected through $2n+1$ disjoint paths [9].

3. The private values must be exchanged at least $n+1$ times between participants [11].

4. Non-faulty participants must be synchronised to provide a bounded skew and must be able to communicate in bounded time [10].

The GUARDS architecture achieves the final property by

having a TDMA inter-channel network. This is adequate because in the application areas being considered, all input and output is periodic in nature and consequently it is possible to generate a static schedule for the network – even though we are using fixed priority scheduling within each channel.

The basic cycle of the ICN is fixed by either the required channel synchronisation precision or by the maximum I/O frequency in a given mode. The cycle is slotted, with each slot being long enough for 1 fixed-sized message transmission (and up to 3 message receptions). As discussed in Section 4, during system design, each replicated application is represented as a real-time transaction. Following the individual schedulability analysis of each channel, the following characteristics are known for each task participating in replicated transactions:

- Period (T)

- Response-time (R)

- Offset (O)

- Deadline (D)

From this information, it is possible to build the ICN tables – in the same way as cyclic executive schedules can be constructed [7]. Note that all communication with the ICN manager is asynchronous through the channels' shared memory. Consequently, the ICN manager can take the data any time after the producing task's deadline has expired.

Of course, there is a close relationship between the scheduling of the channels and the scheduling of the ICN network. If the off-line tool fails to find an ICN schedule, it will be necessary to re-visit the design of the application.

7. Current Status and Conclusions

At the time of writing, the GUARDS project is in the middle of its implementation phase. A prototype ICN network and its associated managing software has been constructed. Off-line tools are being built around the HRT-HOOD design method [8] and its associated toolset [15].

The experience gained from projects such as SIFT and MAFT, and the requirement to (wherever possible) use COTS components, means that the overheads associated with executing frequent agreement protocols cannot be tolerated. This, coupled with the need to use fixed priority based scheduling, has led us to use a timestamp approach to achieving replica determinism. However, even this

method does not remove the requirement for agreement on sensor input and voting on actuator output. Consequently, we have had to resort to a real-time transaction model incorporating offset analysis.

8. Acknowledgements

The authors would like to acknowledge the contributions made to the ideas presented in this paper by the other GUARDS partners. In particular, we would like to thank Paolo Coppola and Alessandro Paganone of Intecs Sistemi who are implementing the tools needed to support the timing analysis presented in this paper.

Alan Burns has also provided significant input to the ideas expressed in this paper.

9. References

[1]   N. Audsley, *Flexible Scheduling for Hard Real-Time Systems,* D. Phil Thesis, Department of Computer Science, University of York, UK, 1993.

[2]   N. Audsley, A. Burns, M. Richardson, K. Tindell and A. J. Wellings, "Applying New Scheduling Theory to Static Priority Pre-emptive Scheduling", *Software Engineering Journal*, 8 (5), pp.284-292, 1993.

[3]   N. A. Audsley, K. Tindell and A. Burns, "The End of the Line for Static Cyclic Scheduling?", in *Proceedings of the 5th Euromicro Workshop on Real-Time Systems,* (Oulu, Finland), pp.36-41, IEEE Computer Society Press, 1993.

[4]   P. A. Barrett, A. Burns and A. J. Wellings, "Models of Replication for Safety Critical Hard Real-Time Systems", in *Proceedings of 20th IFAC/IFIP Workshop on Real-Time Programming (WRTP'95),* (Fort Lauderdale, Florida, USA), pp.181-188, Pergamon Press, 1995.

[5]   I. Bate and A. Burns, "Schedulability Analysis of Fixed Priority Real-Time Systems with Offsets", in *Proceedings of 9th Euromicro Workshop on Real-Time Systems,* (Toledo, Spain), pp.153-160, IEEE Computer Society Press, 1997.

[6]   I. Bate and A. Burns, "Investigation of the Pessimism in Distributed Systems Timing Analysis", in *Proceedings of 10th Euromicro Workshop on Real-Time Systems,* (Berlin, Germany), pp.107-114, IEEE Computer Society Press, 1998.

[7]   A. Burns, N. Hayes and M. F. Richardson, "Generating Feasible Cyclic Schedules", *Control Engineering Practice*, 3 (2), pp.151 - 162, 1995.

[8]   A. Burns and A. J. Wellings, *Hard Real-Time HOOD: A Structured Design Method for Hard Real-Time Ada Systems,* Elsevier, 1995.

[9]   D. Dolev, "The Byzantine Generals Strike Again", *Journal of Algorithms*, 3 (1), pp.14-30, 1982.

[10] D. Dolev, C. Dwork and L. Stockmeyer, "On the Minimal Synchronism Needed for Distributed Concensus", *Journal of the ACM*, 34 (1), pp.77-97, 1987.

[11] M. Fischer, "A Lower Bound for the Time to Assure Interactive Consistency", *Information Processing Letters*, 14 (4), pp.183-186, 1983.

[12] L. Gong, P. Lincoln and J. Rushby, "Byzantine Agreement with Authentication: Observations and Applications in Tolerating Hybrid and Link Faults", in *Dependable Computing for Critical Applications 6, Dependable Computing and Fault Tolerant Systems,* (R. K. Iyer, M. Morganti, W. K. Fuchs and V. Gligor, Eds.), 10, pp.139-157, IEEE Computer Society Press, 1998.

[13] R. E. Harper and J. H. Lala, "Fault-Tolerant Parallel Processor", *Journal of Guidance Control and Dynamics*, 14 (3), pp.554-563, 1990.

[14] M. C. E. Hugue and P. D. Stotts, "Guaranteed Task Deadlines for Fault-Tolerant Workloads with Conditional Branches", *Real-Time Systems*, 3 (3), pp.275-305, 1991.

[15] Intecs-Sistemi, *HRT-HoodNICE: a Hard Real-Time Software Design Support Tool*, N°ESTEC Contract 11234/NL/FM/(SC) - final report (see also http://www.pisa.intecs.it/products/HRT-HoodNICE/), 1996.

[16] R. M. Keickhafer, C. J. Walter, A. M. Finn and P. M. Thambidurai, "The MAFT Architecture for Distributed Fault Tolerance", *IEEE Transactions on Computers*, 37 (4), pp.398-404, 1988.

[17] J. H. Lala and R. E. Harper, "Architectural Principles for Safety-Critical Real-Time Applications", *Proceedings of the IEEE*, 82 (1), pp.25-40, 1994.

[18] J. Y. T. Leung and J. Whitehead, "On the Complexity of Fixed-Priority Scheduling of Periodic, Real-Time Tasks", *Performance Evaluation (Netherlands)*, 2 (4), pp.237-250, 1982.

[19] J. Lundelius-Welch and N. Lynch, "A New Fault-Tolerant Algorithm for Clock Synchronisation", *Information and Computation*, 77 (1), pp.1-36, 1988.

[20] P. M. Melliar-Smith and R. L. Schwartz, "Formal Specification and Mechanical Verification of SIFT: a Fault-Tolerant Flight Control System", *IEEE Transactions on Computers*, C-31 (7), pp.616-30, 1982.

[21] M. Pease, R. Shostak and L. Lamport, "Reaching Agreement in the Presence of Faults", *Journal of the ACM*, 27 (2), pp.228-234, 1980.

[22] S. Poledna, "Deterministic Operation of Dissimilar Replicated Task Sets in Fault-Tolerant Distributed Real-Time Systems", in *Dependable Computing for Critical Applications 6 (Proc. IFIP 10.4 Work. Conf. held in Grainau, Germany, March 1997),* (M. D. Cin, C. Meadows and W. H. Sanders, Eds.), pp.103-119, IEEE Computer Society Press, 1998.

[23] D. Powell (Ed.), *Delta-4: A Generic Architecture for Dependable Distributed Computing,* Research Reports ESPRIT, Springer-Verlag, 1991.

[24] D. Powell, *Preliminary Definition of the GUARDS Architecture*, LAAS-CNRS, Toulouse, France, N°96277 (GUARDS Report No. D1A1/AO/5000/D) ESPRIT Project 20716, 1997.

[25] H. Simpson, "Four-Slot Fully Asynchronous Communication Mechanism", *IEE Proceedings*, 137 Part E (1), pp.17-30, 1990.

[26] K. Tindell, *Fixed Priority Scheduling of Hard Real-Time Systems,* D.Phil Thesis, Department of Computer Science, University of York, UK, 1993.

[27] H. Tokuda and M. Kotera, "A Real-Time Tool Set for the ARTS Kernel", in *Proceedings IEEE Real-Time Systems Symposium,* pp.289-299, 1988.

[28] E. Totel, J.-P. Blanquart, Y. Deswarte and D. Powell, "Supporting Multiple Levels of Criticality", in *Proceedings of 28th Fault-Tolerant Computing Symposium (FTCS-28),* (Munich, Germany), pp.70-79, IEEE Computer Society Press, 1998.

[29] A. J. Wellings, L. Beus-Dukic and A. Burns, *Computational Models and Time-Related Dependability Mechanisms for GUARDS*, Department of Computer Science, University of York, UK, N°GUARDS D1A4/AO/7012/B, 1996.

Improved Response-Time Analysis Calculations

Mikael Sjödin[1]
[1]Department of Computer Systems
Uppsala University
Sweden

Hans Hansson[2&1]
[2]Dept. of Computer Engineering
Mälardalens Högskola
Sweden

E-mail: {mic,hansh}@docs.uu.se

Abstract

Schedulability analysis of fixed priority preemptive scheduled systems can be performed by calculating the worst-case response-time of the involved processes. The system is deemed schedulable if the calculated response-time for each process is less than its corresponding deadline. It is desirable that the Response-Time Analysis (RTA) can be efficiently performed. This is particularly important in dynamic real-time systems when a fast response is needed to decide whether a new job can be accommodated, or when the RTA is extensively applied, e.g., when used to guide the heuristics in a higher level optimiser.

This paper presents a set of methods to improve the efficiency of RTA calculations. The methods are proved correct, in the sense that they give the same results as traditional (non-improved) RTA. We also present an evaluation of the improvements, by applying them to the particularly time-consuming traffic model used in RTA for ATM communication networks. Our evaluation shows that the proposed methods can give an order of magnitude reduction of the execution time of RTA.

1 Introduction

Schedulability analysis is used to off-line, *á priori*, determine whether all hard real-time jobs in a *real-time system* will meet their deadlines. One method to perform schedulability analysis of fixed priority scheduled systems is to calculate the worst case response-time of each process, i.e., to perform a *Response-Time Analysis* (RTA) [3]. The system is deemed schedulable if the calculated response-time for each process is less than its corresponding deadline.

When designing a real-time system, schedulability analysis is used to assess the timely behaviour of the system. The design process is by nature iterative; possible solutions are evaluated and discarded, or refined, until a satisfactory solution is found. Hence, efficient tool support to make fast evaluations (of e.g., schedulability) is required.

In designing distributed real-time systems a new set of problems arise. Amongst them is allocation of functionality. Automated allocation algorithms typically require schedulability analysis to be carried out many times (tens of thousands of times) as the algorithm evaluates different allocations. Since the bulk of the time consumed by such an allocation algorithm is spent performing schedulability analysis the performance of the schedulability algorithm is crucial for the usability of these allocation tools.

Also related to distributed real-time systems is schedulability analysis of the interconnection network. In some cases (e.g. the Control Area Network (CAN) [16]) the complexity of the schedulability analysis is essentially equivalent to that of CPU scheduling. In other cases the modelling of the communications media requires substantially more complex analysis (e.g. RTA for Asynchronous Transfer Mode (ATM) Networks [5, 12]), yielding long execution times for the schedulability analysis.

Yet another case when the performance of the schedulability analysis is crucial is in dynamic real-time systems where requests for new real-time jobs may arrive at runtime. Schedulability analysis has to be performed before such a job (e.g. a multimedia application) can be admitted to the system. Naturally, in this situation, the schedulability analysis must be performed as fast as possible to allow fast responses to requests for new real-time jobs.

The virtue of Response Time Analysis (RTA) is its high precision (often exact or nearly exact) and great flexibility in choice of process models. A variety of process models has been derived [2], and RTA is also applicable to many other types of resources, e.g. hard disk drives [14] and communications networks [5, 16]. The high precision is very important for the real-time system designer since it allows high utilisation of system hardware. For example, RTA for ATM Networks has for a set of realistic traffic conditions been shown to have higher precision and allow higher resource utilisation than other popular schedulability analysis methods (e.g. Weighted Fail Queueing (WFQ) [9, 10]) for ATM networks [5, 12].

Given the above requirement for high precision and fast schedulability analysis, sometimes combined with computationally demanding models, the need to address performance issues for schedulability analysis is obvious. In this paper we will describe and evaluate four methods to decrease the execution time of response time analysis.

Paper Outline: In section 2 we present response-time analysis in greater detail. Section 3 introduces and proves a theorem needed to show correctness of our proposed methods. In section 4 we present the four methods to improve the RTA execution time. The presented methods are evaluated in the context of RTA for ATM networks in section 5. Finally, in section 6 we make some concluding remarks.

2 Background

Liu and Layland [8] presented an inexact (i.e. sufficient but not necessary) schedulability test for periodic processes scheduled with fixed priorities when priorities are assigned in *rate monotonic* order.

The exact formulation of the worst case response time for fixed priority scheduled processes was introduced by Joseph and Pandya [6]. Audsley et. al. showed how the response time could be calculated with fix-point iteration [3], thus giving an exact (i.e. both sufficient and necessary) schedulability test. Since then Response Time Analysis (RTA) has been extended to handle more complex process models [2], including sporadic processes, kernel overheads, blocking by low priority processes, release jitter, arbitrary large deadlines, etc.

Also, RTA has been successfully applied to resources other than CPUs. Tindell and Burns [14] showed how RTA can be applied to hard disk drives. Tindell et. al. [16] also derive RTA for the *Controller Area Network* (CAN), thus enabling end-to-end schedulability analysis of distributed real-time systems. Lately, Sjödin et. al. [12, 5] presented RTA for ATM Networks, thus allowing guaranteed response times for high bandwidth connections. Other extensions to RTA include analysis of the cache behaviour on modern hardware architectures [4, 7].

2.1 An Example of Response-Time Analysis

In this paper we will present a set of methods to decrease the time of performing RTA. These methods are applicable to a variety of process models, and will be presented using a simple but realistic process model.

The model used include blocking, release jitter and in section 2.2 arbitrary large deadlines are introduced. Each process i is characterised by the following attributes:

C_i the worst case computation time, $C_i > 0$,

T_i the period (or minimum inter-arrival time), $T_i > 0$,

B_i the maximum blocking from lower priority processes, $B_i \geq 0$,

J_i the maximum jitter (i.e. variance from periodicity), $J_i \geq 0$,

D_i the deadline of process i. Initially the deadline is assumed to be less than the period, $D_i \leq T_i$, but in section 2.2 we extend the model to allow arbitrary large deadlines.

It is assumed that the total system utilisation is less than 100% (i.e. $\sum C_i / T_i < 1$). The response-time equation for the above model is [3]:

$$R_i = B_i + C_i + \sum_{j \in hp(i)} \left\lceil \frac{R_i + J_j}{T_j} \right\rceil C_j \qquad (1)$$

where $hp(i)$ denotes the set of processes with higher priority than process i.[1] Since the ceiling function ($\lceil \ \rceil$) does not lend itself for algebraic manipulation equation 1 cannot be expressed in closed form. Instead, to find the value of R_i *fix-point iteration* is performed, as illustrated in equation 2.

$$R_i^{\#n+1} = B_i + C_i + \sum_{j \in hp(i)} \left\lceil \frac{R_i^{\#n} + J_j}{T_j} \right\rceil C_j \qquad (2)$$

The fix-point iteration starts with $R_i^{\#0} = 0$ and terminates when $R_i^{\#n} = R_i^{\#n+1}$ at which point R_i is found.

When performing RTA, equation 1 is evaluated for each process and the calculated response time is compared to the deadline. The system is deemed *schedulable* if all response times are less than or equal to their corresponding deadline (i.e. if $\forall i : R_i \leq D_i$).

2.2 RTA when Deadline is Greater than Period

One extension to the process model used above is to allow the deadline to exceed the period (i.e. remove the requirement that $D_i \leq T_i$) [15]. This extension is particularly useful for real-time communication or distributed real-time systems where end-to-end latencies can be quite high compared to the process periods.

When the deadline is allowed to be greater than the period it is possible to invoke a process a second time before its first invocation has completed its execution. This means that the second invocation is not only delayed by higher priority processes, but also by the first invocation. Thus, to analyse this model we need to investigate the completion-time for a set of invocations of each process. The completion-time for the k-th invocation, I_i^k, (where

---

[1]To simplify presentation we assume that each process has a unique priority.

$k = 0$ for the first invocation) is described by equation 3.[2]

$$I_i^k = B_i + (k+1)C_i + \sum_{j \in hp(i)} \left\lceil \frac{I_i^k + J_j}{T_j} \right\rceil C_j \quad (3)$$

Like equation 1, equation 3 is evaluated with fix-point iteration. I_i^k is evaluated for successive invocations, k-s, until the k-th invocation has completed before the $k+1$-th invocation is released. Let A_i^k denote the release (arrival) of the k-th invocation. The earliest arrival time is defined as

$$A_i^k = \max(kT_i - J_i, 0)$$

The response time for invocation k is the difference between the arrival time and completion time, i.e. $R_i^k = I_i^k - A_i^k$, and the response time for process i, R_i, is the maximum of the calculated invocations. Formally:

$$R_i = \max_{k \in 0 \dots m} R_i^k \quad \text{where}$$
$$R_i^k = I_i^k - A_i^k \quad \text{and}$$
$$m = \min(\{k : I_i^k \le A_i^{k+1}\})$$

3 Convergence of the Fix-Point Iteration

Before addressing performance issues of RTA we will take a close look at equations 1 and 2. It is neither obvious that equation 1 has a solution, nor that the fix-point iteration (equation 2) is guaranteed to find a solution even if solutions exists. In fact, fix-point equations can in general have arbitrary number of solutions (including 0), and fix-point iteration is in general not guaranteed to find any solution even if one exists.

It has been proven [13] that the fix-point iteration in equation 2 will increase monotonically. Thus, we know that the iteration cannot oscillate around possible fix-point solutions. However, monotonicity does not by itself indicate that the fix-point iteration will converge and, more importantly, do not guarantee that the fix-point iteration will find the smallest solution to equation 1 when a solution exists.

In order to show that our methods to decrease analysis time do not change the result of the analysis, we will prove that both the original method (equation 2) and our proposed methods always will find the smallest solution to equation 1, when any solution exists.

Theorem 1: *If any $R_i^{\#n}$ in the fix-point iteration of equation 2 is less than or equal to the smallest solution to equation 1, then the fix-point iteration is guaranteed to converge at the smallest solution (provided that at least one solution exists).*

---

[2]Note the two different superscript notations used for fix-point iteration, $R_i^{\#n}$, and for enumerating process invocations, I_i^k.

Proof: First consider the case that $R_i^{\#n} = R_i^{\#n+1}$. This means that fix-point iteration has converged and that theorem 1 holds.

Next, consider the case that $R_i^{\#n} \neq R_i^{\#n+1}$. We begin by reformulating equation 1 as a function:

$$f(x) = B_i + C_i + \sum_{j \in hp(i)} \left\lceil \frac{x + J_j}{T_j} \right\rceil C_j \quad (4)$$

Fix-point iteration converge when $f(x) = x$. We also note that $f(x)$ is monotonically increasing.

Consider figure 1 which shows an assumed line $y = f(x)$ and the line $y = x$. The graphical interpretation of a fix-point is when the two lines intersect. This example has two fix-points, indicated by the black dots.

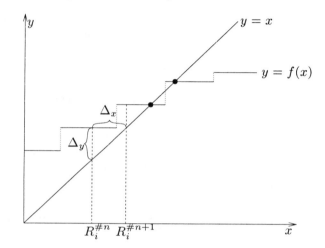

Figure 1. Fix-point iteration n

We prove theorem 1 by showing (1) that no fix-points exists between $R_i^{\#n}$ and $R_i^{\#n+1}$ (i.e. we cannot "miss" a fix-point) and (2) that the difference between $R_i^{\#n}$ and $R_i^{\#n+1}$ cannot be arbitrary small (i.e. we will progress towards the fix-point in a finite number of steps.[3])

(1) Let Δ_y denote the vertical distance between the lines $y = f(x)$ and $y = x$ at $x = R_i^{\#n}$ (see figure 1). The definition of Δ_y is:

$$\Delta_y = f(R_i^{\#n}) - R_i^{\#n} \quad (5)$$

Let Δ_x denote the distance we move horizontal along the x-axis the $n+1$-th fix-point iteration (see figure 1):

$$\Delta_x = R_i^{\#n+1} - R_i^{\#n} \quad (6)$$

---

[3]Convergence in a finite number of steps requires the solutions to equation 1 to be finite. It can be proven, by upper bounding the ceiling expression in equation 1 (in a way similar to that in Method 1 in section 4), that there exists a non-infinite upper bound for solutions to equation 1.

It follows from equations 2 and 4 that

$$R_i^{\#n+1} = f(R_i^{\#n}) \qquad (7)$$

Hence, we can derive the following from equation 6:

$$\Delta_x = R_i^{\#n+1} - R_i^{\#n} \overset{\text{eq. (7)}}{\Longrightarrow}$$
$$\Delta_x = f(R_i^{\#n}) - R_i^{\#n} \overset{\text{eq. (5)}}{\Longrightarrow}$$
$$\Delta_x = \Delta_y$$

Since $\Delta_x = \Delta_y$ and the slope of the line $y = x$ is 1 there can be no intersection of the lines $y = f(x)$ and $y = x$ between $x = R_i^{\#n}$ and $x = R_i^{\#n} + \Delta_x$. Or equivalently, there exists no fix-points between $R_i^{\#n}$ and $R_i^{\#n+1}$.

(2) We observe that if $f(x)$ is increasing it means that at least one of the ceiling expressions in the summation has increased its value (note that each of the ceiling expressions in the sum is monotonically increasing). The value of a ceiling expression increases with at least 1 and the expression is multiplied with a constant (C_j). Thus, the minimum non-zero difference between $R_i^{\#n}$ and $R_i^{\#n+1}$ is $\min(C_j)$ (which is a constant). $\qquad \square$

Theorem 1 holds for any $R_i^{\#n}$, especially $R_i^{\#0}$. Hence, we can safely choose any $R_i^{\#0}$ less than or equal to the least fix-point and be sure to find the least solution to equation 1 with fix-point iteration.

4 Improving the Runtime of the Analysis

The key to improve the runtime of the analysis is to decrease the number of fix-point iterations. In this section we present three methods to directly decrease the number of iterations. In addition we present one method to decrease the number of invocations which has to be investigated when the deadline is greater than the period.

Method 1: A Closed Form Lower Bound for R_i

We can derive a lower bound for R_i by using an approximation of the ceiling ($\lceil \ \rceil$) function in equation 1. We can safely approximate $\lceil X \rceil$ with X (since $\lceil X \rceil \geq X$) to obtain the following inequality from equation 1:

$$R_i \geq B_i + C_i + \sum_{j \in hp(i)} \frac{R_i + J_j}{T_j} C_j$$

Which gives the following lower bound for R_i:

$$R_i \geq \frac{B_i + C_i + \sum\limits_{j \in hp(i)} \dfrac{J_j C_j}{T_j}}{1 - \sum\limits_{j \in hp(i)} \dfrac{C_j}{T_j}} \qquad (8)$$

Let $Rmin_i$ denote the lower bound on R_i described by equation 8. Then, by theorem 1, we can start fix-point iteration at $Rmin_i$, i.e. letting $R_i^{\#0} = Rmin_i$.

Naturally, this method is also applicable to calculating the I_i^k-s (from equation 3) when arbitrary large deadlines are allowed. In that case the term C_i in equation 8 is just replaced by $(k + 1)C_i$.

Method 2: Evaluating in Priority Order

In most cases the order in which the response times, the R_i-s, are calculated does not matter. In those cases we are free to choose the evaluation order which gives the most beneficial run-time performance. By calculating the response times of the processes in descending priority order, starting with the highest priority process, it is possible to reduce the execution time of the analysis.

Intuitively, a lower priority process can not start to execute before all higher priority process has completed. To see how we can utilise this fact, assume that the set of processes has been numbered so that process i has higher priority than process $i+1$. Then, the response time of process i, R_i, is a *level i busy interval*, meaning that during the interval R_i all execution has priority i or higher.

A lower priority processes may execute at priority i or higher if it locks any resource used by a higher priority process. The maximum time lower priority processes can execute during R_i is B_i. Thus, process $i+1$ may start to execute at R_i but may already have executed for B_i time units. Since the response time must include the execution time of process $i+1$, this gives us a lower bound on the maximum response time of $R_i - B_i + C_{i+1}$, i.e. we can assign

$$Rmin_i = R_{i-1} - B_{i-1} + C_i.$$

By theorem 1, we can start fix-point iteration on $Rmin_i$, i.e. $R_i^{\#0} = Rmin_i$.

In the model with arbitrary large deadlines, the completion time of the k-th invocation, I_i^k, represents a level i busy interval. The largest busy interval calculated is the completion time of the last invocation m (where m was defined in section 2.2). Thus, we can use

$$Imin_i^k = I_{i-1}^m - B_{i-1} + (k + 1)C_i.$$

Method 3: Successive Process Invocations

When calculating the response-time for successive invocations of the same process (in the arbitrary large deadline model from section 2.2) it is obvious that invocation $k + 1$ must have a completion time later than invocation k. Letting, $Imin_i^k$ denote the lower bound of invocation k of process i we can assign the lower bound as:

$$Imin_i^k = I_i^{k-1} + C_i \quad \text{if } k \geq 1$$

This method combines excellently with method 2. When combining the two methods we use the level i-1 busy interval as the lower bound for the first invocation only, i.e.

$$Imin_i^0 = I_{i-1}^m - B_{i-1} + B_i + C_i$$

By theorem 1, we can start the fix-point iteration at $Imin_i^k$.

When combining methods 2 and 3 we substantially reduce the complexity of RTA. The original method will restart fix-point iteration at time 0 both for each process and for each process invocation. Thus, the original method is cubic in complexity with respect to the maximum busy interval for the system. Whereas, the combination of method 2 and 3 prevent us from going back in time when starting fix-point iteration. Thus, using method 2 and 3 makes the complexity of RTA linear with respect to the maximum busy interval.

Method 4: Evaluating Fewer Invocations

In the arbitrary large deadline model from section 2.2 there is also the possibility that the jitter, J_i, is larger than the period. This may be true for certain jitter prone application such as multimedia encoding or decoding, especially if the application is part of a long process chain where jitter is accumulated along the chain. Another scenario where the jitter may be larger than the period is when the process model allow *dual period processes*, such as the *sporadic periodic process model* [13] or in the RTA for ATM Networks [5, 12], where the smaller period may be substantially smaller than the jitter.

When the jitter is larger than the period there is a possibility (in the model) that more than one invocation of the same process arrives at time zero (remember: $A_i^k = \max(kT_i - J_i, 0)$). If h is the highest numbered invocation arriving at time zero, then R_i^h must be greater than any R_i^k when $k < h$. This is due to the fact that invocations are served in FIFO order and invocation h is the last one to receive service. Thus, it is not necessary to calculate R_i^k (nor I_i^k) for $k < h$, we can simply start with $k = h$.

5 Evaluation

In order to show the benefits of the methods described in section 4 we evaluated the methods by applying them to the particularly time-consuming model used in the *Response-Time Analysis (RTA) for ATM Networks* [5, 12]. This section begins with an introduction to ATM and a brief presentation of the RTA for ATM Networks, after which the results of our evaluation are presented.

5.1 ATM Networking

Asynchronous Transfer Mode (ATM) [11] is a high performance, connection oriented, network architecture. Over each connection a *stream* of fixed size packets, called *cells*, are transmitted. Each cell is 53 bytes long, consisting of 5 byte header information and 48 byte *payload* (user data). Large messages are segmented and sent in consecutive cells in the stream. The ATM network guarantees that cells within a stream are delivered in the same order as they were transmitted.

Conceptually, an ATM network consists of a set of *source nodes*, *ATM switches*, and *destination nodes*. A source node separates cells within a stream, e.g. with a *leaky bucket* [11], and multiplexes cells from different streams on the outgoing line. Based on stream identifiers in the cell-headers, each switch routes cells from a set of *input ports* to a set of *output ports*. At an output port of an ATM switch a *port controller* multiplexes cells from different streams onto the outgoing line. Eventually the cells reaches their respective destination node.

5.2 RTA for ATM Networks

The RTA for ATM Networks (ATM) uses a traffic model which basically is an extension of the arbitrary large deadline model presented in section 2.2.

However, the ATM model is *non-preemptive*, i.e. once the transmission of an *ATM cell* has started, it cannot be preempted. Also, the ATM model uses two levels of periodicity. One level is the period of (i.e. distance between) the cells constituting one message, the other level is the period of the message. Sjödin [12] presents the details of this model, as well as the equations presented below.

Here we present a slightly simplified version of the RTA for ATM Networks, e.g., we add the restriction that each stream has a unique priority and we only consider a single output port. Each stream is characterised by the following attributes:

N_i the maximum number of cells required for a message, $N_i \geq 1$,

T_i the period, or minimum inter-message time, $T_i > 0$,

t_i denotes the inter-cell delay when a message passes through a cell spacer (i.e. a traffic shaper, such as a leaky bucket) at the source node, $0 \leq t_i \leq T_i/N_i$, and

J_i the maximum jitter,[4] $J_i \geq 0$.

Using the above parameters the number of arrived cells from stream i at time t is expressed by c_i^t and the latest

---

[4]in this simplified version J_i denote both initial message jitter plus any accumulated network jitter

dequeuing time of cell k is denoted by I_i^k, as defined below:

$$c_i^t = ((t + J_i) \text{ div } T_i) N_i +$$
$$\min \left[\left(((t + J_i) \text{ rem } T_i) \text{ div } t_i \right) + 1, N_i \right]$$
$$I_i^k = \left(1 + k + \sum_{j \in hp(i)} c_j^{I_i^k} \right) \tau$$

where τ denotes the time it takes to send one ATM cell and $hp(i)$ denotes the set of streams which have higher priority than stream i. I_i^k is solved with fix-point iteration. In this simplified RTA for ATM networks we calculate the worst case queueing delay, Q_i, for each stream i. Arbitrary large deadlines are allowed and the queueing delay is calculated in a way similar to that in section 2.2:

$$Q_i = \max_{k \in [0 \ldots m]} Q_i^k$$
$$Q_i^k = I_i^k - A_i^k$$
$$A_i^k = \max \left(0, (k \text{ div } N_i) T_i + (k \text{ rem } N_i) t_i - J_i \right)$$
$$m = \min(\{ k : I_i^k \leq A_i^{k+1} \})$$

The methods 2, 3 and 4 (in section 4) are directly applicable to the RTA for ATM. Method 1, using a closed form lower bound, can be slightly adapted. I_i^k can be approximated in a similar way (using approximations of "div" and "min" instead of an approximation of $\lceil \rceil$ as described in section 4). However a better lower bound can be derived for this dual-period model by recognising that the number of cells arrived, c_i^t, is downwards bounded by $\frac{t+J_i}{T_i} N_i$. Thus, we can derive the following lower bound on the dequeuing time:

$$c_i^t \geq \frac{t+J_i}{T_i} N_i \qquad \Rightarrow$$
$$I_i^k \geq \left((1 + k + \sum_{j \in hp(i)} \frac{I_i^k + J_i}{T_i} N_i \right) \tau \quad \Rightarrow$$
$$I_i^k \geq \frac{\left(1 + k + \sum_{j \in hp(i)} \frac{J_j}{T_j} N_j \right) \tau}{1 - \sum_{j \in hp(i)} \frac{N_j \tau}{T_j}}$$

5.3 Evaluation Environment

When performing RTA for ATM networks the analysis time is highly dependent on the load of the system and also on the type of traffic which exists in the system. Thus, to evaluate the proposed methods we use traffic from three different *traffic profiles*. These profiles have been designed to represent different network conditions. The profiles are called "Control", "Ctrl/MM" and "Select".

The profiles and the algorithm to generate traffic scenarios from them have been presented previously [5] and are discussed more thoroughly by Sjödin [12].

We have performed RTA for a single output port of an ATM switch. For simplicity we have assumed that each stream has a unique priority and that priorities are assigned in deadline monotonic order. The reported execution times are from executions on a 233MHz Pentium CPU.

5.4 Results

We have studied the behaviour of the proposed methods in isolation and also how they interact when combined. We present results both for a few selected scenarios (figures 3 and 4) and average values from a larger simulation study (figures 5 and 6). We have selected six scenarios, two from each profile, which we found to be typical for each profile when generating scenarios with approximately 90% load. The scenarios are described in figure 2. (The max and average columns refer to the per stream load and message size.)

Scenario	Nr. of Strms.	% Load			N_i	
		Total	Max	Avrg	Max	Avrg
Control1	213	90.0	7.6	0.42	7	1.4
Control2	225	92.1	7.4	0.41	6	1.5
Ctrl/MM1	34	96.5	27	2.8	199	73
Ctrl/MM2	25	92.2	36	3.7	350	87
Select1	228	90.0	22	0.39	171	30
Select2	193	90.0	22	0.47	171	34

Figure 2. The investigated scenarios

Figure 3(a) shows how each method reduces the number of fix-point iterations needed to analyse each scenario. The percentage values represent the reduction relative the original analysis. Figure 3(b) shows the original execution time and speedup for each method. In the rightmost columns of figure 3 we show the results when combining methods 3 and 4 and methods 2, 3 and 4. We include the results for methods 3+4 since these two methods are specific to the arbitrary large deadline process model (section 2.2). The results indicate that the combination of methods 2+3+4 is the most beneficial combination.

From figure 3 it is evident that methods 2 and 3 (evaluating in priority order and remembering the dequeuing time of the previous invocation respectively) are the two most beneficial methods. We also found that method 1 (using a closed form lower approximation as starting point) together with any of the other methods gives a very small improvement (in the order of a few percent). If fact, when using method 1 together with both the other methods its effect is negligible.

Methods 2 and 3 require no overhead to implement, they simply remember (and utilise) the previous value calculated. Thus, it is no surprise that the reduction of execution times match the reduction in fix-point iterations. Methods 1

Scenario	Original	Method 1	Method 2	Method 3	Method 4	Methods 3+4	Methods 2+3+4
Control1	11671	14%	66%	64%	7%	66%	82%
Control2	16477	13%	62%	69%	8%	70%	84%
CtrlMM1	215297	22%	35%	89%	26%	92%	92%
CtrlMM2	85446	20%	26%	81%	17%	85%	85%
Select1	505688	23%	44%	89%	20%	93%	93%
Select2	573961	23%	42%	89%	20%	93%	93%
Average		19%	46%	80%	16%	83%	88%

(a) Reduction in number of fix-point iterations

Scenario	Original (sec)	Method 1	Method 2	Method 3	Method 4	Methods 3+4	Methods 2+3+4
Control1	1.27	1.1	3.0	3.1	1.1	3.2	6.0
Control2	1.94	1.1	2.7	3.5	1.1	3.7	6.9
CtrlMM1	3.83	1.2	1.6	9.8	1.4	12.8	13.2
CtrlMM2	1.04	1.1	1.4	5.5	1.2	6.5	6.5
Select1	67.55	1.2	1.8	10.3	1.2	14.3	14.7
Select2	64.47	1.2	1.7	10.2	1.2	14.5	14.6
Average		1.2	2.0	7.1	1.2	9.2	10.3

(b) Speedup factor

Figure 3. Relative improvements for different methods (and some combinations)

and 4, however, requires some overhead which causes the decrease in execution time to be less than the decrease in fix-point iterations.

Another interesting aspect of all methods, except method 2, is that their benefit seem to be the largest on the scenarios which are most time consuming to analyse.

Figure 4 shows for method 4 the reduction in number of invocations which had to be investigated. From the figure we observe that the reduction is often substantial. Comparing figure 4 with the "Method 4" column of figure 3(a) we see that the reduction in invocations does not map directly to a reduction in fix-point iterations. On the other hand, combining method 4 with method 3 (in the Average row of 3(b)) we see that method 4 substantially contributes to decreasing the execution time, compared to only using method 3.

Figure 5 shows how the average analysis time changes as the load of the network increases. (To enhance readability of the figure we have chosen to draw only one line for a set of methods whose lines would have coincided in the figure.) In figure 5 we see that method 3 (M.3) is the main contributor to the reduced execution times. However, method 3 is not always the best method and significant improvements can be made by combining method 3 with other methods (see e.g., figure 5(a)). While not formally changing the complexity of RTA from pseudo-polynomial it is clear from figure 5 that the proposed methods significantly

Scenario	Original	Method 4	Reduction
Control1	640	583	9%
Control2	763	685	10%
CtrlMM1	6518	4641	29%
CtrlMM2	6456	4924	24%
Select1	23833	15118	37%
Select2	26879	17157	36%
Average			24%

Figure 4. Reduction in number of investigated invocations

reduce the complexity in a practical sense.

The relative behaviour of methods 2 and 3 is quite different depending on the traffic profile. In the Control profile, which is dominated by short messages with tight deadlines, the impact of method 2 is significantly higher than in the other profiles where longer messages are more common. As message size grows, method 3 becomes more significant (method 3 is only used from the second cell of each stream).

Method 1 and 4 has by themselves very little impact, except for the Select profile, which is by far the most compu-

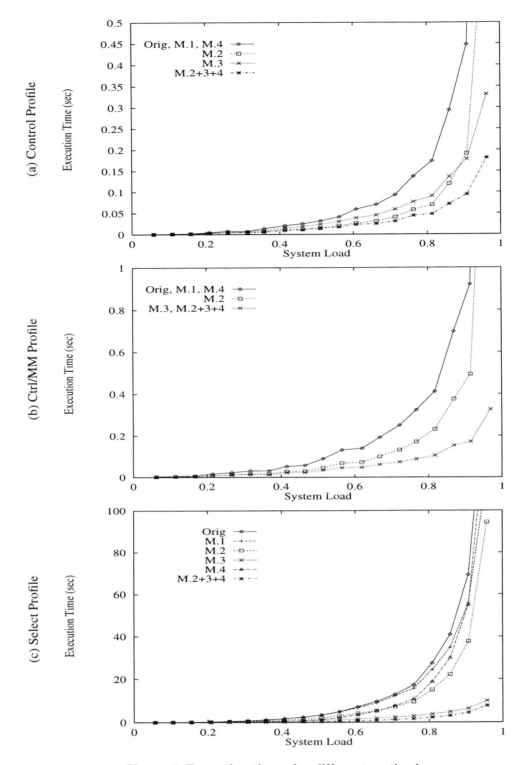

Figure 5. Execution times for different methods

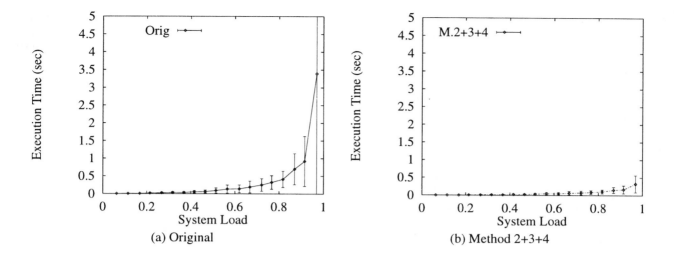

Figure 6. Standard deviations of execution times for Ctrl/MM profile

tationally demanding profile and as such it leaves an opportunity even for these methods to have some impact on the execution time.

Figures 6(a) and 6(b) show the execution times annotated with standard deviations. In these figures we see that not only does the execution time shrink when using the described methods, also the standard deviation of the execution time shrink, thus leading to more predictable execution times of the analysis. This is especially important in dynamic real-time systems where new jobs must be admitted with minimal delay.

Even though method 1 has the smallest effect of the proposed methods its strength is its applicability. Method 1 can be applied in all contexts where it is possible to derive a lower bound on the solution to the fix-point equation. Method 2, however, is applicable when it is possible to evaluate the response times in priority order. To do so can be difficult, for instance, when using Audsley's optimal priority assignment algorithm [1], where the response-time for the lowest priority task is calculated first. Methods 3 and 4 are applicable when deadlines are longer than periods, something which is more frequent in distributed real-time systems.

We also performed a similar evaluation on the classic response time analysis from section 2.1, where only methods 1 and 2 are applicable. The result of this evaluation was in line with the result presented in this section, thus we do not present the actual figures here.

Naturally, the exact impact of each of the described methods are highly dependent on the particular process model used, as well as the profile of the process parameters. However for the traffic model and the profiles consid-

ered here it is clear that the proposed methods dramatically reduce execution time.

6 Conclusions

In this paper we present four methods to decrease the execution time of Response-Time Analysis (RTA) [3]. RTA provides a highly accurate means for determining schedulability of hard real-time systems. RTA is flexible in that it can be used when designing various kinds of real-time systems [2]. This allows the designer of distributed (possibly heterogeneous) real-time systems to use the same method to assess the timely behaviour of the whole system, and to guarantee end-to-end deadlines for distributed applications. The high accuracy (or good precision) implies that the hardware can be highly utilised. High utilisation is of utmost importance in mass-produced real-time systems (e.g. vehicles) where hardware is a dominating factor in the total product cost.

The main motivations to decrease the execution time of the schedulability analysis are threefold. Firstly, the schedulability analysis is used as an evaluation method in the, by nature, iterative design phase of real-time systems development. Secondly, the schedulability analysis can be the core of a higher level optimisation algorithm, such as an algorithm for allocation in distributed real-time systems. Thirdly, in dynamic real-time systems where request for new jobs may arrive during system operation (e.g. in a multimedia communications network) the schedulability analysis is performed at run-time before admitting a new job.

The four presented methods to decrease the execution time of RTA are all easy to implement and require little (or in two cases no) overhead.

- Method 1 utilises a lower bound approximation of the response time to find the exact response time.
- Method 2 utilises the evaluation order when calculating the response time for a complete scenario of processes.
- Method 3 utilises previously calculated information of earlier invocations.
- Method 4 reduce the number of invocations which has to be examined when the jitter is large compared to the period.

The applicability of these methods vary. Method 1 is generally applicable to any kind of RTA. Method 2 requires that the evaluation order can be freely chosen by the implementor of the RTA. This is often, but not always, the case. Methods 3 and 4 are applicable when the deadline of a process is greater than its period. This is normally not the case in single-node real-time systems, but in distributed real-time systems the end-to-end deadline for a transaction can be quite large compared to its period.

We have proved a theorem which shows the correctness of methods 1, 2 and 3. The theorem shows that the original RTA, as well as our proposed improvements, always will find the smallest solution to the response-time equation. Thus, our proposed methods are correct (and exact) in the sense that they do not change the result of the RTA.

We have applied all four methods to the RTA for ATM Networks [5, 12] and evaluated their effects on the execution time. RTA for ATM Networks is a particularly demanding form of RTA where analysis times (without our proposed improvements) can be in the order of minutes (on a 233MHz Pentium CPU). Our evaluation show that each of the methods decrease execution time dramatically (in the range from 15% to 80%), with better relative performance for scenarios which have long execution time. Further, when combining the methods the speedup is typically more than a magnitude. For extremely high loads (above 90%) the benefits are even greater. Also, our evaluation shows that the variance in execution time is dramatically decreased, yielding more predictable execution times of the analysis.

Acknowledgements

Thanks to Prof. T. Baker for helpful discussions leading to the proof of theorem 1. Also, thanks to the anonymous reviewers for their helpful suggestions for improving this paper.

References

[1] N. Audsley. Optimal Priority Assignment and Feasibility of Static Priority Tasks with Arbitrary Start Times. Technical Report YCS-164, Dept. of Computer Science, University of York, England, November 1991. Available at ftp://ftp.cs.york.ac.uk/pub/realtime/papers/YCS164.ps.Z.

[2] N. Audsley, A. Burns, R. Davis, K. Tindell, and A. Wellings. Fixed Priority Pre-emptive Scheduling: An Historical Perspective. *Real-Time Systems*, 8(2/3):129–154, 1995.

[3] N. Audsley, A. Burns, K. Tindell, M. Richardson, and A. Wellings. Applying new scheduling theory to static priority pre-emptive scheduling. *Software Engineering Journal*, 8(5):284–292, 1993.

[4] J. Busquets-Mataix, J. Serrano, R. Ors, P.Gil, and A. Wellings. Adding instruction cache effects to schedulability analysis of preemptive real-time systems. In *Proc. IEEE Real-Time Technology and Applications Symposium*, pages 204–212. IEEE Computer Society Press, June 1996.

[5] A. Ermedahl, H. Hansson, and M. Sjödin. Response-Time Guarantees in ATM Networks. In *Proc. 18th Real-Time Systems Symposium*, pages 274–284. IEEE Computer Society Press, December 1997.

[6] M. Joseph and P. Pandya. Finding Response Times in a Real-Time System. *The Computer Journal*, 29(5):390–395, 1986.

[7] C. Lee, J. Han, Y. Seo, S. Min, R. Ha, S. Hong, C. Park, M. Lee, and C. Kim. Analysis of cache-related preemption delay in fixed-priority preemptive scheduling. In *Proc. 17th Real-Time Systems Symposium*, 1996.

[8] C. Liu and J. Layland. Scheduling algorithms for multiprogramming in a hard-real-time environment. *Journal of the ACM*, 20(1):46–61, 1973.

[9] A. Parekh and R. Gallager. A Generalized Processor Sharing Approach to Flow Control in Integrated Services Networks: The Single Node Case. *IEEE/ACM Transactions on Networking*, 1(3):344–357, June 1993.

[10] A. Parekh and R. Gallager. A Generalized Processor Sharing Approach to Flow Control in Integrated Services Networks: The Multiple Node Case. *IEEE/ACM Transactions on Networking*, 2(2):137–150, April 1994.

[11] C. Partridge. *Gigabit Networking*. Computing Series. Addison-Wesley, 1994. ISBN 0-201-56333-9.

[12] M. Sjödin. Response-Time Analysis for ATM Networks. Department of Computer Systems, Uppsala University, Licentiate Thesis DoCS 97/92, May 1997. URL http://www.docs.uu.se/~mic/lic.ps.gz.

[13] K. Tindell. *Fixed Priority Scheduling of Hard Real-Time Systems*. PhD thesis, University of York, February 1994. Available at ftp://ftp.cs.york.ac.uk/pub/realtime/papers/thesis/ken/.

[14] K. Tindell and A. Burns. Fixed Priority Scheduling of Hard Real-Time Multimedia Disk Traffic. *The Computer Journal*, 37(8):691–697, 1994.

[15] K. Tindell, A. Burns, and A. Wellings. An Extendible Approach for Analysing Fixed-Priority Hard Real-Time Tasks. *Journal of Real-Time Systems*, 6(2):133–151, March 1994.

[16] K. Tindell, H. Hansson, and A. Wellings. Analysing Real-Time Communications: Controller Area Network (CAN). In *Proc. 15th Real-Time Systems Symposium*, pages 259–263. IEEE, IEEE Computer Society Press, December 1994.

Symbolic Schedulability Analysis of Real-time Systems *

Hee-Hwan Kwak, Insup Lee, and Anna Philippou
Department of Computer and Information Science
University of Pennsylvania, USA
{heekwak,annap}@saul.cis.upenn.edu, lee@cis.upenn.edu

Jin-Young Choi
Department of Computer Science and Engineering
Korea University, Korea
choi@formal.korea.ac.kr

Oleg Sokolsky
Computer Command and Control Company, USA
sokolsky@cccc.com

Abstract

We propose a unifying method for analysis of scheduling problems in real-time systems. The method is based on ACSR-VP, a real-time process algebra with value-passing capabilities. We use ACSR-VP to describe an instance of a scheduling problem as a process that has parameters of the problem as free variables. The specification is analyzed by means of a symbolic algorithm. The outcome of the analysis is a set of equations, a solution to which yields the values of the parameters that make the system schedulable. Equations are solved using integer programming or constraint logic programming. The paper presents specifications of two scheduling problems as examples.

1. Introduction

The desire to automate or incorporate intelligent controllers into control systems has lead to rapid growth in the demand for real-time software systems. Moreover, these systems are becoming increasingly complex and require careful design analysis to ensure reliability before implementation. Recently, there has been much work on formal methods for the specification and analysis of real-time systems [8, 10]. Most of the work assumes that various real-time systems attributes, such as execution time, release time, priorities, etc., are fixed *a priori* and the goal is to determine whether a system with all these known attributes would meet required safety properties. One example of safety property is schedulability analysis; that is, to determine whether or not a given set of real-times tasks under a particular scheduling discipline can meet all of its timing constraints.

The pioneering work by Liu and Layland [16] derives schedulability conditions for rate-monotonic scheduling and earliest-deadline-first scheduling. Since then, much work on schedulability analysis has been done which includes various extensions of these results [11, 24, 22, 4, 23, 20, 17, 3]. Each of these extensions expands the applicability of schedulability analysis to real-time task models with different assumptions. In particular, there has been much advance in scheduling theory to address uncertain nature of timing attributes at the design phase of a real-time system. This problem is complicated because it is not sufficient to consider the worst case timing values for schedulability analysis. For example, scheduling anomalies can occur even when there is only one processor and jobs have variable execution times and are nonpreemptable. Also for preemptable jobs with one processor, scheduling anomalies can occur when jobs have arbitrary release times and share resources. These scheduling anomalies make the problem of validating a priority-driven system hard to perform. Clearly, exhaustive simulation or testing is not practical in general except for small systems of practical interest. There have been many different heuristics developed to solve some of these general schedulability analysis prob-

*This research was supported in part by NSF CCR-9415346, NSF CCR-9619910, AFOSR F49620-95-1-0508, AFOSR F49620-96-1-0204 (AASERT), ARO DAAG55-98-1-0393, and ONR N00014-97-1-0505 (MURI).

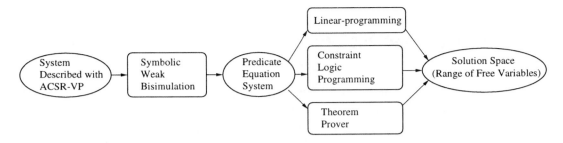

Figure 1. Overview

lems. However, each algorithm is problem specific and thus when a problem is modified, one has to develop new heuristics.

In this paper, we describe a framework that allows one to model scheduling analysis problems with variable release and execution times, relative timing constraints, precedence relations, dynamic priorities, multiprocessors etc. Our approach is based on ACSR-VP and symbolic bisimulation algorithm.

ACSR (Algebra of Communicating Shared Resources) [13], is a discrete real-time process algebra. ACSR has several notions, such as resources, static priorities, exceptions, and interrupts, which are essential in modeling real-time systems. ACSR-VP is an extension of ACSR with value-passing and parameterized processes to be able to model real-time systems with variable timing attributes and dynamic priorities. In addition, symbolic bisimulation for ACSR-VP has been defined. ACSR-VP without symbolic bisimulation has been applied to the simple schedulability analysis problem [5], by assuming that all parameters are ground, i.e., constants. However, it is not possible to use the technique described in [5] to solve the general schedulability analysis problem with unknown timing parameters.

Figure 1 shows the overall structure of our approach. We specify a real-time system with unknown timing or priority parameters in ACSR-VP. For the schedulability analysis of the specified system, we check symbolically whether or not it is bisimilar to a process idling forever. The result is a set of predicate equations, which can be solved using widely available linear-programming or constraint-programming techniques. The solution to the set of equations identifies, if exists, under what values of unknown parameters the system becomes schedulable.

The rest of the paper is organized as follows. Sections 2 and 3 overview the theory of the underlying formal method, ACSR-VP, and introduce symbolic bisimulation for ACSR-VP expressions. Section 4 gives specifications of two scheduling problems, namely the *period assignment problem* and the *start-time assignment problem*. Section 5 illustrates analysis of two instances of these problems. We

conclude with a summary and an outline of future work in Section 6.

2. ACSR-VP

ACSR-VP extends the process algebra ACSR [13] by allowing values to be communicated along communication channels. In this section we present ACSR-VP concentrating on its value-passing capabilities. We refer to the above papers for additional information on ACSR.

We assume a set of variables X ranged over by x, y, a set of values V ranged over by v, and a set of labels L ranged over by c, d. Moreover, we assume a set $Expr$ of expressions (which includes arithmetic expressions) and we let $BExpr \subset Expr$ be the subset containing boolean expressions. We let e and b range over $Expr$ and $BExpr$ respectively, and we write $\vec{z}$ for a tuple $z_1, \ldots z_n$ of syntactic entities.

ACSR-VP has two types of actions: instantaneous communication and timed resource access. Access to resources and communication channels is governed by priorities. A priority expression p is attached to every communication event and resource access. A partial order on the set of events and actions, the preemption relation, allows one to model preemption of lower-priority activities by higher-priority ones.

Instantaneous actions, called *events*, provide the basic synchronization and communication primitives in the process algebra. An event is denoted as a pair (i, e_p) representing execution of action i at priority e_p, where i ranges over τ, the idle action, $c?x$, the input action, and $c!e$, the output action. We use $\mathcal{D}_E$ to denote the domain of events and let λ range over events. We use $l(\lambda)$ and $\pi(\lambda)$ to represent the label and priority, respectively, of the event λ; e.g., $l((c!x, p)) = c!$ and $l((c?x, p)) = c?$. To model resource access, we assume that a system contains a finite set of serially-reusable resources drawn from some set R. An action that consumes one tick of time is drawn from the domain $P(R \times Expr)$ with the restriction that each resource is represented at most once. For example the singleton action $\{(r, e_p)\}$ denotes the use of some resource $r \in R$ at priority

410

level e_p. The action $\emptyset$ represents idling for one unit of time, since no resource is consumed. We let $\mathcal{D}_R$ to denote the domain of timed actions with A, B, to range over $\mathcal{D}_R$. We define $\rho(A)$ to be the set of the resources used by action A, for example $\rho(\{(r_1, p_1), (r_2, p_2)\}) = \{r_1, r_2\}$. We also use $\pi_r(A)$ to denote the priority level of the use of the resource r in the action A; e.g., $\pi_{r_1}(\{(r_1, p_1), (r_2, p_2)\}) = p_1$, and write $\pi_r(A) = 0$ if $r \notin \rho(A)$. The entire domain of actions is denoted by $\mathcal{D} = \mathcal{D}_R \cup \mathcal{D}_E$, and we let α, β range over $\mathcal{D}$. We let P, Q range over ACSR-VP processes and we assume a set of process constants ranged over by C. The following grammar describes the syntax of ACSR-VP processes:

$$P \quad ::= \quad \text{NIL} \mid A : P \mid \lambda.P \mid P + P \mid P\|P \mid$$
$$b \to P \mid P\backslash F \mid [P]_I \mid C(\vec{x}).$$

In the input-prefixed process $(c?x, e).P$ the occurrences of variable x is bound. We write $\mathbf{fv}(P)$ for the set of free variables of P. Each agent constant C has an associated definition $C(\vec{x}) \stackrel{\text{def}}{=} P$ where $\mathbf{fv}(P) \subseteq \vec{x}$ and $\vec{x}$ are pairwise distinct. We note that in an input prefix $(c?x, e).P$, e should not contain the bound variable x, although x may occur in P.

An informal explanation of ACSR-VP constructs follows: The process NIL represents the inactive process. There are two prefix operators, corresponding to the two types of actions. The first, $A : P$, executes a resource-consuming action during the first time unit and proceeds to process P. On the other hand $\lambda.P$, executes the instantaneous event λ and proceeds to P. The process $P + Q$ represents a nondeterministic choice between the two summands. The process $P\|Q$ describes the concurrent composition of P and Q: the component processes may proceed independently or interact with one another while executing instantaneous events, and they synchronize on timed actions. Process $b \to P$ represents the conditional process: it performs as P if boolean expression b evaluates to *true* and as NIL otherwise. In $P\backslash F$, where $F \subseteq L$, the scope of labels in F is restricted to process P: components of P may use these labels to interact with one another but not with P's environment. The construct $[P]_I$, $I \subseteq R$, produces a process that reserves the use of resources in I for itself, extending every action A in P with resources in $I - \rho(A)$ at priority 0.

The semantics of ACSR-VP processes may be provided as a labeled transition system, similarly to that of ACSR. It additionally makes use of the following ideas: Process $(c!e_1, e_2).P$ transmits the value obtained by evaluating expression e_1 along channel c, with priority the value of expression e_2, and then behaves like P. Process $(c?x, p).P$ receives a value v from communication channel c and then behaves like $P[v/x]$, that is P with v substituted for variable x. In the concurrent composition $(c?x, p_1).P_1\|(c!v, p_2).P_2$, the two components of the parallel composition may syn-

chronize with each other on channel c resulting in the transmission of value v and producing an event $(\tau, p_1 + p_2)$.

3. Semantics and Analysis

3.1. Unprioritized Symbolic Graphs with Assignment

Consider the simple ACSR-VP process $P \stackrel{\text{def}}{=} (in?x, 1).(out!x, 1).\text{NIL}$ that receives a value along channel in and then outputs it on channel out, and where x ranges over integers. According to traditional methods for providing semantic models for concurrent processes, using transition graphs, process P in infinite branching, as it can engage in the transition $(in?n, 1)$ for every integer n. As a result standard techniques for analysis and verification cannot be applied to such processes.

Several approaches have been proposed to deal with this problem for various subclasses of value-passing processes [9, 15, 19, 12]. One of these advocates the use of *symbolic* semantics for providing finite representations of value-passing processes. This is achieved by taking a more conceptual view of value-passing than the one employed above. More specifically consider again process P. A description of its behavior can be sufficiently captured by exactly two actions: an input of an integer followed by the ouput of this integer. Based on this idea the notion of symbolic transition graphs [9] and transition graphs with assignment [15] were proposed and shown to capture a considerable class of processes.

In this section we present symbolic graphs with assignment for ACSR-VP processes. As it is not the intention of the paper to present in detail the process-calculus theory of this work, we only give an overview of the model and we refer to [12] for a complete discussion.

3.2. Symbolic Transition Graphs with Assignment

A *substitution*, or *assignment* is a function $\theta : X \to Expr$, such that $\theta(x) \neq x$ for a finite number of $x \in X$. Given a substitution θ, *domain* of θ is the set of variables $D(\theta) = \{x \mid \theta(x) \neq x\}$. A substitution whose domain is empty is called the *identity substitution*, and is denoted by Id. When $|D(\theta)| = 1$, we use $[\theta(x)/x]$ for the substitution θ. Given two substitutions θ and σ, the *composition* of θ and σ is the substitution denoted by $\theta; \sigma$ such that for every variable x, $\theta; \sigma(x) = \sigma(\theta(x))$. We often write $\theta\sigma$ for $\theta; \sigma$.

An SGA is a rooted directed graph where each node n has an associated finite set of free variables $\mathbf{fv}(n)$ and each edge is labeled by a guarded action with assignment. Note that a node in SGA is a ACSR-VP term. Furthermore, we use ϵ to denote the empty action the purpose of which is explained later.

Definition 3.1 (SGA) A Symbolic Graph with Assignment (SGA) for ACSR-VP is a rooted directed graph where each node n has an associated ACSR-VP term and each edge is labeled by boolean, action, assignment, (b, α, θ) or by boolean, the empty action and assignment, (b, ϵ, θ). □

Given an ACSR-VP process, the corresponding SGA can be generated using the rules in Figure 2. Note that the purpose of action ϵ is to decorate transitions that involve no action, but are nonetheless necessary for registering substitutions, see Rule (3). Transition $P \overset{b,\alpha,\theta}{\longmapsto} P'$ denotes that given the truth of boolean expression b, P can evolve to P' by performing action α and putting into effect the assignment θ. The interpretation of these rules is straightforward and we explain them by an example: Consider the following process.

$$P(x) \overset{\text{def}}{=} (x < 2) \rightarrow (a!1, 1).P'(x+1)$$
$$P'(x) \overset{\text{def}}{=} (x < 3) \rightarrow P(1)$$

Process $P(1)$ can output $a!1$ infinitely many times. Applying the rules above gives rise to the SGA in Figure 3(a).

One possible interpretation of our SGA can be given along the lines of programming languages: Process P can be thought of as a procedure, so that $P(1)$ represents a call of P with actual parameter 1 which is accepted by P with formal parameter x declared in P's body. According to its definition, P checks if $x < 2$ and if this boolean expression holds, P outputs $a!1$ and calls process P' with actual parameter $x + 1$. Process P' then checks the validity of condition $x < 3$. If this is satisfied, process P' calls P with actual parameter 1.

Although introduction of the empty action ϵ appears useful in constructing SGA's from process terms it is possible to remove them by means of a fixpoint of a normalization function. For example, given the SGA in Figure 3(a), by applying the normalization process the NSGA in Figure 3(b) is obtained.

We say that an a normalized SGA (NSGA) $(N, E, \mapsto)$ is *finite* if $|N|$ is finite. For the remainder of the paper we only consider finite NSGA's.

3.3. The prioritized Symbolic Transition System

We have illustrated how ACSR-VP processes can be given finite representations as SGA's via the symbolic transition relation $\mapsto$. However, this relation makes no arbitration between actions with respect to their priorities. To achieve this, we refine the relation $\mapsto$ to obtain the prioritized symbolic transition system $\mapsto_\pi$. This is based on the notion of *preemption* which incorporates our treatment of priority, and in particular on relation $\succ$, the *preemptive relation*, a transitive, irreflexive relation on actions [2]. Then

for two actions α and β, $\alpha \succ \beta$ denotes that α preempts β, which implies that in any real-time system, if there is a choice between the two actions, α will always be executed. For example $(c?x, 2) \succ (c?x, 1)$ and $\{(r, 2)\} \succ \{(r, 0)\}$.

Extending the notion of preemption in the value-passing setting involves dealing with the presence of free variables in process descriptions. For example, given actions $\alpha = (c?x, y_1)$ and $\beta = (c?x, y_2)$, whether $\alpha \succ \beta$ or $\beta \succ \alpha$ depends on the values to which variables y_1 and y_2 are instantiated. This idea can easily be incorporated to yield the prioritized transition relation $\mapsto_\pi$. For the precise definition we refer the reader to [12]. We illustrate this with an example. Consider process P:

$$P(x) \overset{\text{def}}{=} (a?y, 1).P'(x,y)$$
$$P'(x,y) \overset{\text{def}}{=} (y \le 1) \rightarrow (a!(x+y), y).NIL$$
$$+ (y \le 2) \rightarrow (a!(x+y), 2).NIL$$

The unprioritized NSGA for P and its prioritized version, Q are shown in Figure 4. Note that transition $P' \overset{y \le 1, (a!(x+y), y), \text{Id}}{\longmapsto} NIL$ is preempted by $P' \overset{y \le 2, (a!(x+y), 2), \text{Id}}{\longmapsto} NIL$ since whenever the former is enabled, the latter is also enabled with a higher priority (that is, whenever $y \le 1$, $y \le 2$ and $y < 2$).

3.4. Weak Bisimulation

Various methods have been proposed for the verification of concurrent processes. Central among them is observational equivalence that allows to compare an implementation with a specification of a given system. Observational equivalence is based on the idea that two equivalent systems exhibit the same behavior at their interfaces with the environment. This requirement was captured formally through the notion of *bisimulation* [18], a binary relation on the states of systems. Two states are bisimilar if for each single computational step of the one there exists an appropriate matching (multiple) step of the other, leading to bisimilar states.

In this setting, bisimulation for symbolic transition graphs is defined in terms of relations parametrized on boolean expressions, of the form $\simeq^b$, where $p \simeq^b q$ if and only if, for each interpretation satisfying boolean b, p and q are bisimilar in the traditional notion. In [12] the authors have proposed weak version of bisimulations for SGA's, that is observational equivalences that abstract away from internal system behavior (both for late and early semantics). Furthermore, algorithms were presented for computing these equivalences. Given two closed processes whose symbolic transition graphs are finite, the algorithm constructs a predicate equation system that corresponds to the most general condition for the two processes to be weakly bisimilar.

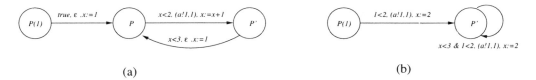

$$\text{(1)} \quad \frac{\quad - \quad}{\alpha.P \overset{true,\alpha,\mathsf{Id}}{\longmapsto} P} \qquad \text{(2)} \quad \frac{C(\vec{v}) \overset{b,\epsilon,\theta}{\longmapsto} C}{\alpha.C(\vec{v}) \overset{b,\alpha,\theta}{\longmapsto} C}$$

$$\text{(3)} \quad \frac{\quad - \quad}{C(\vec{v}) \overset{true,\epsilon,\vec{x}:=\vec{v}}{\longmapsto} C} \quad C(\vec{x}) \overset{\text{def}}{=} P \qquad \text{(4)} \quad \frac{P \overset{b,\alpha,\theta}{\longmapsto} P'}{\mathsf{C} \overset{b,\alpha,\theta}{\longmapsto} P'} \quad C(\vec{x}) \overset{\text{def}}{=} P$$

$$\text{(5)} \quad \frac{P \overset{b,\alpha,\theta}{\longmapsto} P'}{b' \to P \overset{b \wedge b',\alpha,\theta}{\longmapsto} P'}$$

$$\text{(6)} \quad \frac{P \overset{b,\alpha,\theta}{\longmapsto} P'}{P + Q \overset{b,\alpha,\theta}{\longmapsto} P'} \qquad \text{(7)} \quad \frac{P \overset{b,\alpha,\theta}{\longmapsto} P'}{Q + P \overset{b,\alpha,\theta}{\longmapsto} P'}$$

$$\text{(8)} \quad \frac{P \overset{b,\lambda,\theta}{\longmapsto} P'}{P \backslash F \overset{b,\lambda,\theta}{\longmapsto} P' \backslash F} \quad \begin{array}{l} \tau \notin F \\ l(\lambda) \notin F \end{array} \qquad \text{(9)} \quad \frac{P \overset{b,A,\theta}{\longmapsto} P'}{P \backslash F \overset{b,A,\theta}{\longmapsto} P' \backslash F}$$

$$\text{(10)} \quad \frac{P \overset{b,\lambda,\theta}{\longmapsto} P'}{[P]_I \overset{b,\lambda,\theta}{\longmapsto} [P']_I} \qquad \text{(11)} \quad \frac{P \overset{b,A_1,\theta}{\longmapsto} P'}{[P]_I \overset{b,A_1 \cup A_2,\theta}{\longmapsto} [P']_I} \quad A_2 = \{(r,0) \mid r \in I - \rho(A_1)\}$$

$$\text{(12)} \quad \frac{P \overset{b_1,A_1,\theta_1}{\longmapsto} P' \quad Q \overset{b_2,A_2,\theta_2}{\longmapsto} Q'}{P \| Q \overset{b_1 \wedge b_2, A_1 \cup A_2, \theta_1 \cup \theta_2}{\longmapsto} P' \| Q'} \quad \rho(A_1) \cap \rho(A_2) = \emptyset$$

$$\text{(13)} \quad \frac{P \overset{b,\alpha,\vec{x}:=\vec{e}}{\longmapsto} P'}{P \| Q \overset{b,\alpha,\vec{x},\vec{y}:=\vec{e},\vec{y}}{\longmapsto} P' \| Q} \quad \mathbf{fv}(Q) = \{\vec{y}\} \qquad \text{(14)} \quad \frac{P \overset{b,\alpha,\vec{x}:=\vec{e}}{\longmapsto} P'}{Q \| P \overset{b,\alpha,\vec{x},\vec{y}:=\vec{e},\vec{y}}{\longmapsto} Q \| P'} \quad \mathbf{fv}(Q) = \{\vec{y}\}$$

$$\text{(15)} \quad \frac{P \overset{b_1,(c?z,e_1),\theta_1}{\longmapsto} P' \quad Q \overset{b_2,(c!e_2,e_3),\theta_2}{\longmapsto} Q'}{P \| Q \overset{b_1 \wedge b_2,(\tau,e_1+e_3),(\theta_1 \cup \theta_2);\{z:=e_2\}}{\longmapsto} P' \| Q'} \quad z \notin \mathbf{fv}(P) \cup \mathbf{fv}(Q)$$

Figure 2. Rules for constructing Symbolic Graphs with Assignment

Figure 3. SGA (a) and Normalized SGA (b)

Recall process $P(x)$ from section 3.3. Furthermore, consider the following process with bound variable x':

$$R(x') \overset{\text{def}}{=} (a?y', 1).R'(x', y')$$
$$R'(x', y') \overset{\text{def}}{=} (y' \le 2) \to (a!(x' + y' + 1), 2).NIL$$

The prioritized NSGA for R is similar to Q with the exception that after receiving a value via channel a, R outputs value $x' + y' + 1$. Applying the symbolic bisimulation algorithm for processes P and R, we obtain the following predicate equation system.

$$X_{00}(x, x') = \forall z X_{11}(z, x, x')$$
$$X_{11}(z, x, x') = z \le 2 \to z \le 2 \wedge x + z = x' + z + 1$$
$$\wedge\, z \le 2 \to z \le 2 \wedge x' + z + 1 = x + z$$

This equation system can easily be reduced to the equation $X_{00}(x, x') \equiv x = x' + 1$, which allows us to conclude that $P(x)$ and $R(x')$ are bisimilar if and only if $x = x' + 1$ holds. In general, since we are dealing with a domain of linear expressions, predicate equations obtained from the bisimulation algorithm can be solved using integer programming techniques [21].

4. Real-time System Scheduling

In this section, we show how several problems of real-time system scheduling can be specified and analyzed using ACSR-VP. According to [25], real-time scheduling problems can be categorized into the following three groups: priority assignment, execution synchronization, and schedu-

Figure 4. SGA of P and Q

lability analysis problems. The priority assignment problem requires assigning priorities to jobs so that the system schedulability is maximized. The execution synchronization problem is the problem of deciding when and how to release jobs so that the precedence constraints are satisfied and the system schedulability, as well as other performance concerns, are optimized. Schedulability analysis problem is the problem of verifying that a system is schedulable, given a certain priority assignment method and execution synchronization method.

Classic examples of solutions to these problems include the rate-monotonic priority assignment problem on a single processor [16]. It uses static priority assignment, where the priority of each job is assigned in the inverse order of period; the job with shortest period has the highest priority. Deadline-monotonic priority assignment was proposed by [14], where the system has jobs with arbitrary relative deadlines. Dynamic priority assignment problem has been addressed by earliest-deadline first algorithms.

The same groups of problems can be considered in the presence of end-to-end scheduling constraints. Gerber *et al.* [6] proposed the method to guarantee a system's end-to-end requirements of real-time systems. In [27], Tindell *et al.* attempted to compute upper bounds on the end-to-end response time. They also proposed priority assignment in distributed system where jobs have end-to-end deadlines. In [1], Bettati studied the problem of scheduling a set of jobs with arbitrary release times and end-to-end deadlines.

We propose to address real-time scheduling problems by means of analysis based on ACSR-VP. In this approach, a specific instance of a problem is specified as an ACSR-VP expression and symbolically analyzed. In this paper, we illustrate our approach by giving general solutions to two scheduling problems. The first problem is the *period assignment problem* (Section 4.1). It can be viewed as an variant of schedulability analysis problem. The second problem is the *start-time assignment problem* (Section 4.2). It is a version of the execution synchronization problem with end-to-end scheduling. Our methods of solving these problems are optimal in the sense that if the method can not find the period or start-time assignment, then the system can not be scheduled for any assignment of periods (respectively, start times).

4.1. Shortest Job First Scheduling

We define the *period assignment problem* as follows. Consider a set of n preemptable periodic jobs sharing a processor. We apply the shortest job first scheduling algorithm to schedule these n jobs. Each job is characterized by two parameters: execution time and period. We assume that the deadline for each task is the same as its period. Execution times $E_1, \ldots, E_n$, and periods $P_1, \ldots, P_{k-1}, P_{k+1}, \ldots, P_n$ are known. We have to determine the period of the kth job.

We model each job in the set as the following ACSR-VP process:

$$
\begin{aligned}
Job_i(e_i, p_i, s_i, t_i) &\stackrel{\text{def}}{=} \\
&(s_i < e_i) \wedge (t_i < p_i) \rightarrow \\
&\quad \{(cpu, MAX - e_i)\} : Job_i(e_i, p_i, s_i + 1, t_i + 1) \\
&\quad + \emptyset : Job_i(e_i, p_i, s_i, t_i + 1) \\
&+ (s_i = e_i) \wedge (t_i \leq p_i) \rightarrow Wait_i(e_i, p_i, t_i) \\
Wait_i(e_i, p_i, t_i) &\stackrel{\text{def}}{=} \\
&(t_i < p_i) \rightarrow \emptyset : Wait_i(e_i, p_i, t_i + 1) \\
&+ (t_i = p_i) \rightarrow Job_i(e_i, p_i, 0, 0)
\end{aligned}
$$

Process $Job_i(e_i, p_i, s_i, t_i)$ represents a job with execution time e_i and period p_i, which has accumulated s_i units of processing time in the current period. The current period has started t_i time units ago. As long as the job is not finished ($s_i < e_i$) and the current period is not over ($t_i < p_i$), the job competed with other job for access to the CPU, which is represented by resource cpu. The priority of the job is $MAX - e_i$, where $MAX = \max(E_i)$. That is, the shortest job has the highest priority. If the job is preempted by a higher-priority process, it idles in that time unit. alternatively, if the job has completed ($s_i = e_i$), it turns into process $Wait_i(e_i, p_i, t_i)$, which idles until the end of the current period and restarts itself.

Assuming that, initially, all jobs are started at time 0, we can capture behavior of the whole system as

$$
\begin{aligned}
SJF(prd) &\stackrel{\text{def}}{=} [Job_1(E_1, P_1, 0, 0) \parallel \cdots \parallel Job_k(E_k, prd, 0, 0) \\
&\quad \parallel \cdots \parallel Job_n(E_n, P_n, 0, 0)]_{\{cpu\}}.
\end{aligned}
$$

The free variable prd represents the period of Job_k, which has to be determined. Notice that *Closure* operator is used in *SJF(prd)* process to prevent resource cpu from being idle when there is a job waiting to be executed.

Note that process $Job_i(e_i, p_i, s_i, t_i)$ will deadlock if it has not finished executing by the end of its period. The

414

composite process $SJF(prd)$ will also deadlock when one of its constituent processes deadlocks. We can use this property of the specification to determine admissible range for values of prd. We can apply the symbolic weak bisimulation algorithm to analyze the equivalence of $SJF(prd)$ and process $\emptyset^\infty$, which never deadlocks. This gives us a set of conditions on prd. These conditions, when satisfied, will guarantee that $SJF(prd)$ never deadlocks, that is, that no job misses its deadline.

4.2. Scheduling with Constraints

In this section, we use ACSR-VP to specify an end-to-end scheduling problem introduced in [7]. We are given a set of jobs running on a single processor, and the order of execution of jobs is fixed. The system is non-preemptable; that is, a job always finishes before the next one is started. The order of job execution is assumed to be fixed and known. Jobs have variable execution times denoted, for i^{th} job, $[e_i^-, e_i^+]$. Additionally, there is a set of constraints on absolute and relative times of initiation and completion of jobs. The goal is to statically determine the range of start times for each job so that there are no conflicts between the jobs and all constraints are satisfied. We call this problem the *start-time assignment problem*.

Constraints that we consider in this problem are linear inequalities over start times and execution times of the jobs. Examples of constraints are "Job a should start no earlier than time t ($s_a \geq t$);" "Job a should be finished before time t ($s_a + e_a \leq t$);" "Job a should be finished within t time units after job b finishes ($s_b + e_b \leq s_a + e_a + t$)." A concrete example of this problem is shown in Section 5.2.

Deriving the start-time assignments for arbitrary constraints is an NP-hard problem [7]. The complexity of a brute-force search is exponential with respect to the bounds of execution times and the number of jobs [26], making this approach impractical for most real-life systems. As in [7], we limit ourselves to constraints with at most two variables. A natural approach for solving this problem is to employ linear programming. However, applying linear-programming techniques to start-time assignment problem directly requires us to encode the scheduling algorithm into the linear constraints.

Our method lets us circumvent this problem. We construct an ACSR-VP specification of the set of jobs together with their constraints. The symbolic semantics of ACSR-VP allows us to produce a predicate equation system that can be solved by well-known techniques such as linear programming or constraint logic programming.

Each $Job_i, i \in \{1, \ldots, n\}$, is specified as follows:

$Job_i(t_i, s_i) \stackrel{\text{def}}{=}$
$\quad (t_i < s_i) \rightarrow \emptyset : Job_i(t_i + 1, s_i)$
$\quad + (Start!, n + 1 - i).(t_i = s_i \rightarrow Job_i'(0, t_i, s_i))$

$Job_i'(r_i, t_i, s_i) \stackrel{\text{def}}{=}$
$\quad (r_i < e_i^-) \rightarrow \{(cpu, 1)\} : Job_i'(r_i + 1, t_i + 1, s_i)$
$\quad + (r_i = e_i^-) \rightarrow Job_i''(0, t_i, s_i)$
$Job_i''(e_i, t_i, s_i) \stackrel{\text{def}}{=}$
$\quad (e_i < e_i^+ - e_i^-) \rightarrow \{(cpu, 1)\} : Job_i''(e_i + 1, t_i + 1, s_i)$
$\quad + (e_i \leq e_i^+ - e_i^-) \rightarrow (Finished!, 1).IDLE$

The job process uses signals $Start$ and $Finish$ to communicate with the constraint process discussed below. Job_i represents behavior of the job before its start time s_i comes. At that moment, Job_i sends an event $Start$ to synchronize with $Constraint_i$, and becomes Job_i'. Job_i' represents the mandatory execution time of the job, that is, until the lower bound on its execution time e_i^- arrives. Then Job_i' becomes Job_i'', which continually offers the choice between completing the job by sending event $Finished$ to the corresponding constraint, or continuing the execution until the upper bound of execution time (e_i^+) is reached. After the execution is completed, the job becomes idle, represented by ACSR-VP process $IDLE \stackrel{\text{def}}{=} \emptyset : IDLE$.

Constraints are represented by a collection of processes $Constraint_i, i \in \{1, \ldots, n\}$. $Constraint_i$ models the state of the system that Job_{i-1} is finished but Job_i is not started yet. Upon event $Start$, it becomes $Constraint_i'$, which models the state of the system that Job_i is in execution. Event $Finished$ turns $Constraint_i'$ into $Constraint_i''$, which represents the state of the system after Job_i is finished. $Constraint_i''$ checks if the timing conditions related to Job_i are satisfied and deadlocks if the condition fails.

$Constraint(t) \quad \stackrel{\text{def}}{=} Constraint_1(t)$
$Constraint_1(t) \quad \stackrel{\text{def}}{=} (Start?, 1).Constraint_1'(t)$
$\qquad\qquad\qquad + \emptyset : Constraint_1(t + 1)$
$Constraint_1'(t) \quad \stackrel{\text{def}}{=} (Finished?, 1).Constraint_1''(t)$
$\qquad\qquad\qquad + \emptyset : Constraint_1'(t + 1)$
$Constraint_1''(t) \quad \stackrel{\text{def}}{=} b_1 \rightarrow \emptyset : Constraint_2(t, 1)$
$\qquad\qquad\qquad \vdots$
$Constraint_n(t, \vec{v}) \stackrel{\text{def}}{=} (Start?, 1).Constraint_n'(t, \vec{v})$
$\qquad\qquad\qquad + \emptyset : Constraint_n(t + 1, \vec{v})$
$Constraint_n'(t, \vec{v}) \stackrel{\text{def}}{=} (Finished?, 1).Constraint_n''(t, \vec{v})$
$\qquad\qquad\qquad + \emptyset : Constraint_n'(t + 1, \vec{v})$
$Constraint_n''(t, \vec{v}) \stackrel{\text{def}}{=} b_n \rightarrow \emptyset : IDLE$

To perform the analysis of the problem, we compose the job processes together with the constraint process:

$System(Start_1, \cdots, Start_2) \stackrel{\text{def}}{=}$
$\quad (Constraint(0) \parallel Job_1(0, Start_1) \parallel \cdots$
$\quad \parallel Job_n(0, Start_n)) \backslash \{Start, Finished\}$

The resulting system will deadlock if the constraints are not satisfied. Again, we can apply the symbolic algorithm to

415

this ACSR-VP process to obtain the set of predicate equations. The solution to these equations will give us the range of admissible start times for each of the jobs.

The proposed technique gives, to our knowledge, the first static algorithm for the problem. The method proposed in [7] contains a static component that analyzes constraints, and a dynamic component. The static component produces a calendar, a set of functions that is used by the dynamic component to compute start times.

Moreover, ACSR-VP specification allows us to remove the requirement of a fixed total order on job execution. A slightly more complex specification of the constraints can be constructed that will use the partial order induced by the constraints instead. The resulting specification still yields to analysis in many practical cases.

5. Examples

In this section, we present results of analysis of the two scheduling problems outlined in Section 4. To make examples manageable, we consider small instances of the problems.

5.1. Shortest Job First Scheduling

Consider the system containing two jobs. The first job has execution time 1 and period 2. The execution time of the second job is 2 and the admissible range of its period has to be determined by the algorithm. Job 1, therefore, has the higher priority of the two. The ACSR-VP specifications of the jobs are as follows:

$$Job_1 \stackrel{\text{def}}{=} \{(cpu, 2)\} : \emptyset : Job_1$$
$$Job_2(t, p) \stackrel{\text{def}}{=} (t < p) \rightarrow (\{(cpu, 1)\} : Job_2'(t + 1, p)$$
$$+ \emptyset : Job_2(t + 1, p))$$
$$Job_2'(t, p) \stackrel{\text{def}}{=} (t < p) \rightarrow (\{(cpu, 1)\} : Job_2''(t + 1, p)$$
$$+ \emptyset : Job_2'(t + 1, p))$$
$$Job_2''(t, p) \stackrel{\text{def}}{=} (t = p) \rightarrow Job_2(0, p)$$
$$+ (t < p) \rightarrow \emptyset : Job_2''(t + 1, p)$$

We simplified the specification for Job_1, since it has the highest priority in the system and will never need idling. $Job_2(t, p)$ represent the job that has not have access to the processor in the current period, $Job_2'(t, p)$ is the same job after it has used the processor for one time units, and $Job_2''(t, p)$ represent its idling state.

The whole system is specified as $SJF(prd) \stackrel{\text{def}}{=} [Job_1 \| Job_2(0, prd)]_{\{cpu\}}$. When we analyze this specification, the symbolic algorithm produces the following set of equations:

$$X_{00}(prd) = 0 < prd \wedge X_{12}(1, prd)$$
$$X_{12}(t, p) = t < p \wedge X_{01}(t + 1, p)$$

$$X_{01}(t, p) = t < p \wedge X_{11}(t + 1, p)$$
$$X_{11}(t, p) = t < p \wedge X_{03}(t + 1, p)$$
$$X_{03}(t, p) = ((t < p \wedge X_{13}(t + 1, p))$$
$$\vee (t = p \wedge 0 < p \wedge X_{12}(1, p)))$$
$$\wedge (t < p \rightarrow X_{13}(t + 1, p))$$
$$\wedge ((t = p \wedge 0 < p) \rightarrow X_{12}(1, p))$$
$$X_{13}(t, p) = ((t = p \wedge 0 < p \wedge X_{01}(1, p))$$
$$\vee (t < p \wedge X_{03}(t + 1, p)))$$
$$\wedge ((t = p \wedge 0 < p) \rightarrow X_{01}(1, p))$$
$$\wedge (t < p \rightarrow X_{03}(t + 1, p))$$

When the predicate variable X_{00} is true, we can conclude that *SJF(prd)* is schedulable. Since all the boolean expression in the predicate equations are linear, we can use a constraint solver or a constraint logic programming tool to solve the predicate equations. We used SICStus tool to conclude that the system is schedulable when $prd \geq 4$.

5.2. Scheduling with Constraints

Consider a system with two jobs, Job_1 and Job_2, shown in Figure 5. Let e_1 and e_2 be respective execution times of Job_1 and Job_2, and s_1 and s_2, their start times. The bounds on execution times of Job_1 and Job_2 are $5 \leq e_1 \leq 7$ and $3 \leq e_2 \leq 4$. There are four timing constraints:

1. Job_1 should be finished before or at 12 ($s_1 + e_1 \leq 12$).

2. Job_2 should be finished within 10 time units after Job_1 finishes ($s_2 + e_2 \leq s_1 + e_1 + 10$).

3. Job_2 should be finished before or at 25 ($s_2 + e_2 \leq 25$).

4. Job_2 should start after or at 14 ($s_2 \geq 14$).

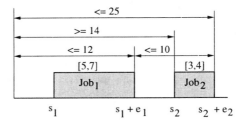

Figure 5. An Instance of the Start-time Assignment Problem

Since the order of the tasks is clear from the constraints and the constraints themselves are simple enough, we chose to incorporate them directly into the ACSR-VP specifications of the jobs instead. The resulting specification is as follows:

$$System(t, s_1, s_2) \stackrel{\text{def}}{=}$$
$$(t \leq 12 - 7) \rightarrow$$

$$((t < s1) \rightarrow \emptyset : System(t+1, s_1, s_2)$$
$$+(t = s_1) \rightarrow \{(cpu, 1)\} : Job_1(0, t+5, s_2))$$
$$Job_1(e, t, s_2) \stackrel{\text{def}}{=}$$
$$(e < 7 - 5) \rightarrow \{(cpu, 1)\} : Job_1(e+1, t+1, s_2)$$
$$+ (e \leq 7 - 5) \rightarrow System'(t, 14, s_2)$$
$$System'(f_1, t, s_2) \stackrel{\text{def}}{=}$$
$$(f_1 \leq 12 \wedge t \leq 25 - 4) \rightarrow$$
$$((t < s_2) \rightarrow \emptyset : System'(f_1, t+1, s_2)$$
$$+(t = s_2) \rightarrow \{(cpu, 1)\} : Job_2(f_1, 0, t+3, s_2))$$
$$Job_2(f_1, e, t, s_2) \stackrel{\text{def}}{=}$$
$$(e < 4 - 3) \rightarrow \{(cpu, 1)\} : Job_2(f_1, e+1, t+1, s_2)$$
$$+ (e \leq 4 - 3) \rightarrow End(f_1, t, s_2)$$
$$End(f_1, t, s_2) \stackrel{\text{def}}{=}$$
$$(f_1 \leq 12 \wedge t - f_1 \leq 10 \wedge s_2 \geq 14) \rightarrow IDLE$$

Process $System$ represents the system, in which the jobs are scheduled to start at times s_1 and s_2 but has not been started yet. The process evolves into Job_1 at time s_1. After Job_1 completes at time f_1, process $System'$ is idle until it's time to start Job_2. Finally, the process End checks that all end-to-end constraints are satisfied. The system is started at time 0 and will be deadlock-free for the admissible values of s_1 and s_2. The symbolic weak bisimulation algorithm generates the predicate equations system shown below. The equations were solved with the help of SICStus tool. The generated solutions are listed in Table 1.

$$X_0(t, s_1, s_2) =$$
$$(t \leq 5 \wedge t < s_1) \rightarrow X_1(t+1, s_1, s_2)$$
$$\wedge \ (t < 5 \wedge t = s_1) \rightarrow X_2(0, t+5, s_2)$$
$$\wedge \ ((t \leq 5 \wedge t < s_1 \wedge X_1(t+1, s_1, s_2))$$
$$\vee (t < 5 \wedge t = s_1 \wedge X_2(0, t+5, s_2)))$$
$$X_1(t, s_1, s_2) =$$
$$(t \leq 5 \wedge t < s_1) \rightarrow X_1(t+1, s_1, s_2)$$
$$\wedge \ (t \leq 5 \wedge t = s_1) \rightarrow X_2(0, t+5, s_2)$$
$$\wedge \ ((t \leq 5 \wedge t < s_1 \wedge X_1(t+1, s_1, s_2))$$
$$\vee (t \leq 5 \wedge t = s_1 \wedge X_2(0, t+5, s_2)))$$
$$X_2(e, s_1, s_2) =$$
$$(e < 2) \rightarrow X_2(e+1, t+1, s_2)$$
$$\wedge \ (e \leq 2 \wedge t \leq 12 \wedge 14 < s_2) \rightarrow X_3(t, 15, s_2)$$
$$\wedge \ (e \leq 2 \wedge t \leq 12 \wedge 14 = s_2) \rightarrow X_4(t, 0, 17, s_2)$$
$$\wedge \ ((e < 2 \wedge X_2(e+1, t+1, s_2))$$
$$\vee (e \leq 2 \wedge t \leq 12 \wedge 14 < s_2 \wedge X_3(t, 15, s_2))$$
$$\vee (e \leq 2 \wedge t \leq 12 \wedge 14 = s_2 \wedge X_4(t, 0, 17, s_2)))$$
$$X_3(f_1, t, s_2) =$$
$$(f_1 \leq 12 \wedge t \leq 21 \wedge t < s_2) \rightarrow X_3(f_1, t+1, s_2)$$
$$\wedge \ (f_1 \leq 12 \wedge t \leq 21 \wedge t = s_2) \rightarrow X_4(f_1, 0, t+3, s_2)$$
$$\wedge \ ((f_1 \leq 12 \wedge t \leq 21 \wedge t < s_2 \wedge X_3(f_1, t+1, s_2))$$
$$\vee (f_1 \leq 12 \wedge t \leq 21 \wedge t = s_2 \wedge X_4(f_1, 0, t+3, s_2)))$$
$$X_4(f_1, e, t, s_2) =$$
$$(e < 1 \rightarrow X_4(f_1, e+1, t+1, s_2)$$
$$\wedge \ (e \leq 1 \wedge f_1 \leq 12 \wedge t - f_1 \leq 10 \wedge s_2 \geq 14) \rightarrow X_5$$
$$\wedge \ ((e < 1 \wedge X_4(f_1, e+1, t+1, s_2))$$
$$\vee (e \leq 1 \wedge f_1 \leq 12 \wedge t - f_1 \leq 10 \wedge s_2 \geq 14 \wedge X_5))$$
$$X_5 = true$$

s_1	3	4	4	5	5	5
s_2	14	14	15	14	15	16

Table 1. Solutions of Start-time Assignment Problem

6. Conclusions

We have described a formal framework for the specification and analysis of real-time scheduling problems. Our framework is based on ACSR-VP and symbolic bisimulation. The major advantage of our approach is that the same framework can be used for scheduling problems with different assumptions and parameters. In other scheduling-theory based approaches, new analysis algorithms need to be devised for problems with different assumptions since applicability of a particular algorithm is limited to specific system characteristics.

We believe that ACSR-VP is expressive enough to model any real-time system. In particular, our method is appropriate to model many complex real-time systems and can be used to solve the *priority assignment problem*, *execution synchronization problem*, and *schedulability analysis problem*. It is, in most cases, efficient in the sense that resulting predicate equation systems can be solved with existing techniques such as linear programming or constraint programming, which can solving linear equation constraints efficiently in practice [21].

The novel aspect of our approach is that schedulability of real-time systems can be described formally and analyzed automatically, all within a process-algebraic framework. It has often been noted that scheduling work is not adequately integrated with other aspects of real-time system development [3]. Our work is a step toward such an integration, which helps to meet our goal of making the timed process algebra ACSR a useful formalism for supporting the development of reliable real-time systems. Our approach allows the same specification to be subjected to the analysis of both schedulability and functional correctness.

There are several issues that we need to address to make our approach practical. We showed that resulted predicate equation systems can be solved with constraint logic programming or linear programming. We plan to investigate when resulting equation systems are simple or difficult to solve. In general, we may have to use a more powerful technique such as theorem prover; however, it is not clear whether any reasonable real-time system scheduling problem can result in such a complex equation system. We are currently augmenting PARAGON, the toolset for ACSR, to support the full syntax of ACSR-VP directly and implementing a symbolic bisimulation algorithm. This toolset will allow us to experimentally evaluate the effectiveness of our approach with a number of large scale real-time systems.

References

[1] R. Bettati. *End-to-end Scheduling to Meet Deadlines in Distributed Systems*. PhD thesis, University of Illinois at Urbana-Champaign, 1994.

[2] P. Brémond-Grégoire, I. Lee, and R. Gerber. ACSR: An Algebra of Communicating Shared Resources with Dense Time and Priorities. In *Proc. of CONCUR '93*, 1993.

[3] A. Burns. Preemptive priority-based scheduling: An appropriate engineering approach. In S. H. Song, editor, *Advances in Real-Time Systems*, chapter 10, pages 225–248. Prentice Hall, 1995.

[4] M. Chen and K. Lin. Dynamic Priority Ceilings: A Concurrency Control Protocol for Real-Time Systems. *Real-Time Systems*, 2(4):325–346, 1990.

[5] J.-Y. Choi, I. Lee, and H.-L. Xie. The Specification and Schedulability Analysis of Real-Time Systems using ACSR. In *Proc. of IEEE Real-Time Systems Symposium*, December 1995.

[6] R. Gerber, D. Kang, S. Hong, and M. Saksena. End-to-End Design of Real-Time Systems. In D. Mandrioli and C. Heitmeyer, editors, *Formal Methods in Real-Time Computing*. John Wiley & Sons, 1996.

[7] R. Gerber, W. Pugh, and M. Saksena. Parametric Dispatching of Hard Real-Time Tasks. *IEEE Transactions on Computers*, 44(3), March 1995.

[8] C. Heitmeyer and D. Mandrioli. *Formal Methods for Real-Time Computing*. Jonh Wiley and Sons, 1996.

[9] M. Hennessy and H. Lin. Symbolic bisimulations. *Theoretical Computer Science*, 138:353–389, 1995.

[10] M. Joseph. *Real-Time Systems: Specification, Verification and Analysis*. Prentice Hall Intl., 1996.

[11] M. Joseph and P. Pandya. Finding Response Times in a Real-Time System. *Computer Journal*, 29(5):390–395, 1986.

[12] H. Kwak, J. Choi, I. Lee, and A. Philippou. Symbolic weak bisimulation for value-passing calculi. *Technical Report, MS-CIS-98-22, Department of Computer and Information Science, University of Pennsylvania*, 1998.

[13] I. Lee, P. Brémond-Grégoire, and R. Gerber. A Process Algebraic Approach to the Specification and Analysis of Resource-Bound Real-Time Systems. *Proceedings of the IEEE*, pages 158–171, Jan 1994.

[14] J. Leung and J. Whitehead. On the complexity of fixed-priority scheduling of periodic, real-time tasks. *Performance Evaluation*, pages 2:237–250, 1982.

[15] H. Lin. Symbolic graphs with assignment. In U.Montanari and V.Sassone, editors, *Proceedings CONCUR 96*, volume 1119 of *Lecture Notes in Computer Science*, pages 50–65. Springer-Verlag, 1996.

[16] C. L. Liu and J. W. Layland. Scheduling Algorithms for Multi-programming in A Hard-Real-Time Environment. *Journal of the Association for Computing Machinery*, 20(1):46 – 61, January 1973.

[17] J. W. S. Liu and R. Ha. Efficient methods of validating timing constraints. In S. H. Song, editor, *Advances in Real-Time Systems*, chapter 9, pages 199–233. Prentice Hall, 1995.

[18] R. Milner. *Communication and Concurrency*. Prentice-Hall, 1989.

[19] P. Paczkowski. Characterizing bisimilarity of value-passing parameterised processes. In *Proceedings of the Infinity Workshop on Verification of Infinite State Systems*, pages 47–55, 1996.

[20] R. Rajikumar, L. Sha, and J. Lehoczky. Real-Time Synchronization Protocols for Multiprocessors. In *Proc. of IEEE Real-Time Systems Symposium*, pages 259–272, 1989.

[21] R. Saigal. *Linear Programming : A Modern Integrated Analysis*. Kluwer Academic Publishers, 1995.

[22] L. Sha, R. Rajkumar, and J. Lehoczky. Priority Inheritance Protocols: An Approach to Real-time Synchronization. *IEEE Transactions on Computers*, 39(9):1175–1185, September 1990.

[23] L. Sha, R. Rajkumar, J. Lehoczky, and K. Ramamritham. Mode change Protocols for Priority Driven Preemptive Scheduling. *Real-Time Systems: The International Journal of Time Critical Computing Systems*, 1(3), December 1989.

[24] B. Sprunt, L. Sha, and J. Lehoczky. Aperiodic Task Scheduling for Hard-Real-Time Systems. *Real-Time Systems: The International Journal of Time Critical Computing Systems*, 1(1):27–60, 1989.

[25] J. Sun. *Fixed-priority End-to-end Scheduling in Distributed Real-time Systems*. PhD thesis, University of Illinois at Urbana-Champaign, 1997.

[26] J. Sun and J. W. Liu. Bounding Completion Times of Jobs with Arbitrary Release Times and Variable Execution Times. In *Proceedings of 17 th IEEE Real-Time Systems Symposium*, December 1996.

[27] K. Tindell and J. Clark. Holistic Schedulability Analysis for Distributed Hard Real-time Systems. *Microprogramming*, 50(2):117–134, April 1994.

Session 12.A: Dependability and Fault Tolerance

Fault-Tolerant Clock Synchronization in CAN

Luís Rodrigues
FCUL*
ler@di.fc.ul.pt

Mário Guimarães[†]
IST-UTL
Mario.Guimaraes@inesc.pt

José Rufino
IST-UTL[‡]
ruf@digitais.ist.utl.pt

Abstract

This paper presents a new fault-tolerant clock synchronization algorithm designed for the Controller Area Network (CAN). The algorithm provides all correct processes of the system with a global timebase, despite the occurrence of faults in the network or in a minority of processes. Such global time-frame is a requirement of many distributed real-time control systems.

Designing protocols for CAN is justified by the increasing use of this network in industrial automation applications. CAN owns a number of unique properties that can be used to improve the precision and performance of a clock synchronization algorithm. Unfortunately, some of its features also make the implementation of a fault-tolerant clock synchronization service a non-trivial task. Our algorithm addresses both the positive and the negative aspects of CAN.

1. Introduction

The availability of a global timebase in all correct processes, despite the occurrence of faults in a minority of processes or in the network itself, is a requirement of many distributed real-time control systems. For instance, synchronized clocks can be used for the synchronization of external actions, distributed trace of events, measurement of actions that spawn multiple processes and the development of (higher level) fault-tolerant distributed algorithms.

A common solution for the global time-base problem consists in using the node hardware clock to create a virtual clock at each process, which is locally read. All virtual clocks are internally synchronized by a *clock synchronization algorithm*. Surveys of existing clock synchronization algorithms can be found in [17, 13]. Clock synchronization algorithms differ on issues such as the precision they

achieve (i.e., how far clocks can be from each other), number and type of tolerated faults, number and size of messages exchanged, etc. Naturally, the solution for clock synchronization deeply depends on the properties of the underlying network.

The Controller Area Network (CAN) [14, 8] is a communication bus for message transaction in small-scale distributed environments. Originally designed to reduce cabling complexity and saving wiring costs in automotive applications, CAN gathers nowadays an increasing acceptance in other areas, like control and automation. In the design and implementation of real-time distributed control systems, CAN represents a very cost-effective *field-bus* solution for real-time sensing and actuating in harsh environments with strict timeliness and reliability requirements.

This paper presents a new clock synchronization algorithm designed for CAN. The paper discusses the CAN properties that can be used to improve the precision of clock synchronization and the properties that make the implementation of a fault-tolerant version of such service a non-trivial task. The algorithm can be implemented exclusively in software, tolerates process and network faults, and provides precision and accuracy preservation in the order of a few microseconds. The algorithm is inspired of the generic *a posteriori agreement* algorithm for broadcast networks [22, 23] and of a non fault-tolerant algorithm specially designed for CAN [4], but differs significantly from these algorithms. We have named our new algorithm "phase-decoupled" *a posteriori* agreement.

The paper is organized in three major parts. The first part provides the background: Section 2 provides a brief description of CAN operation, discussing its relevant properties; Section 3 introduces the clock synchronization problem; related work is surveyed in Section 4. The second part describes our work: the design approach is sketched in Section 5; a straightforward implementation of the *a posteriori* agreement on CAN is described Section 6; the new "phase-decoupled" *a posteriori* agreement algorithm is presented in Section 7. The last part is concerned with improvements and performance issues: use of CAN message priorities is discussed in Section 8 and the performance is analyzed in

---

*Faculdade de Ciências da Universidade de Lisboa

[†]Currently at Inesc, Portugal.

[‡]Instituto Superior Técnico da Universidade Técnica de Lisboa

CAN1 - Validity: if a correct node broadcasts a message, then the message is eventually delivered to a correct node.

CAN2 - Best-effort Agreement: if a message is delivered to a correct node, then the message is eventually delivered to all correct nodes, if the sender remains correct.

CAN3 - At-least-once Delivery: any message delivered to a correct node is delivered at least once (a message is automatically retransmitted if an error occurs).

CAN4 - Non-triviality: any message delivered to a correct node was broadcast by a node.

CAN5 - Bounded Transmission Delay : the time elapsed between the request of a broadcast and the corresponding message delivery at any correct node is bounded by two known values $\Gamma^{min} < \Gamma^{max}$.

CAN6 - Tightness: if the sender remains correct, the last retransmission of the same message is delivered to any two correct nodes at real time values that differ, at most, by a known interval $\Delta\Gamma_{tight}$.

Figure 1. CAN Properties

Section 9. Section 10 concludes the paper.

2. Controller Area Network

CAN is a bus with a multi-master architecture [14, 8]. The transmission medium is usually a twisted pair cable. The network maximum length depends on data rate; typical values are: 40m @ 1 Mbps; 1000m @ 50 kbps. Bus state takes one out of two values: *recessive*, which only appears on the bus when all the nodes send recessive bits; *dominant*, which only needs to be sent by one node to stand on the bus.

Any message sent by a CAN node must be tagged with a network-wide unique identifier. Access control to the shared bus uses a *carrier sense multi-access with deterministic collision resolution* (CSMA/DCR) scheme. Bus access conflicts are resolved through the bitwise comparison of message unique identifiers: if the transmitted identifier bit is recessive and a dominant bit is monitored, the node gives up from transmitting and starts to receive incoming data; the node transmitting the message with the lowest identifier goes through and gets the bus. If the arbitration process is lost, a new attempt to send the message is made when the bus is released.

The CAN network can be modeled by the set of properties summarized in Figure 1. We note that only the properties relevant for clock synchronization are listed: a more precise model can be found in [16]. Properties CAN1 to CAN4 are a consequence of the comprehensive set of error detection, error signaling and error recovery features of the CAN network. Messages corrupted by errors are discarded at correct receivers and automatically submitted for retransmission by a correct sender. This procedure secures property CAN1. Unfortunately, it also allows the same message to be received by a correct node more than once [16] (property CAN3). When no CAN protocol violation is detected until the last but one bit of a message, any correct receiver will always locally accept that message, even if the following bit gets corrupted. Conversely, a correct sender will consider such corruption an error and it will retransmit the message.

Properties CAN5 and CAN6 describe system behavior in the time domain. Ensuring property CAN5 depends on multiple factors: traffic patterns, latency classes and offered load bounds, as well as their relation with CAN message identifiers[20, 24]; error patterns and maximum error recovery latency [15]. Property CAN6 is crucial for achieving a high precision on synchronized clocks. The upper bound of message reception real time variance ($\Delta\Gamma_{tight}$) has two different contributions [10]: the maximum variance on the network physical propagation delay $\Delta\Gamma_{prp}$; the maximum variation of message processing time at any correct receiver, $\Delta\Gamma_{rec}$. By correct design, $\Delta\Gamma_{rec}$ can be bounded by values in the order of a few microseconds (some controllers offer dedicated support to minimize this bound [21]). On the other hand, CAN is particularly advantageous with regard to variation of $\Delta\Gamma_{prp}$: the bus transmission line is operated in a *quasi-stationary* mode, giving enough time for bit signal stabilization along the bus before performing sampling. The exact value of $\Delta\Gamma_{prp}$ depends on the bus lenght and on network configuration parameters, but it is always a small fraction of the network bit time (10%-30%).

3. Clock synchronization

The goal of clock synchronization is to establish a global timebase in a distributed system composed of a set of processes $\mathcal{P}$ which can interact exclusively by message passing. Processes can only observe time through a *clock*. One commonly used solution to achieve this goal is to provide each process p ($p \in \mathcal{P}$) in the distributed system with an imperfect physical clock pc_p (notation closely follows that of [17]). The clock at a correct process p can then be viewed as implementing, in hardware, an increasing continuous[1] function pc_p that maps (non-observable) real time[2] t to a clock time $pc_p(t)$. Through a clock synchronization algorithm it is possible to derive, from the physical clock at each process p, a virtual clock vc_p satisfying the *precision* (VC1), *rate* (VC2), and *accuracy* (VC3) properties, presented in

[1]It is known that digital clocks have a finite granularity and increase by ticks [10]. However, for sake of clarity, we chose to simplify our expressions in this matter.

[2]In an assumed Newtonian time frame.

PC - Physical clocks; VC - Virtual clocks
(for some positive constants μ and ρ, $\forall_{k,l} \in \mathcal{P}$)

PC1- Initial value,
$$pc_k(0): 0 \leq pc_k(0) \leq \mu$$

PC2- Rate,
$$\exists \rho: 0 \leq 1 - \rho \leq \frac{pc_k(t_2) - pc_k(t_1)}{t_2 - t_1} \leq 1 + \rho \quad \text{for } 0 \leq t_1 < t_2$$

VC1 - Precision,
$$\exists \delta_v: |vc_k(t) - vc_l(t)| \leq \delta_v \quad \text{for } 0 \leq t$$

VC2 -Rate,
$$\exists \rho_v: 1 - \rho_v \leq \frac{vc_k(t_2) - vc_k(t_1)}{t_2 - t_1} \leq 1 + \rho_v \quad \text{for } 0 \leq t_1 < t_2$$

VC3 - Accuracy,
$$\exists \alpha_v: |vc_k(t) - t| \leq \alpha_v \quad \text{for } 0 \leq t$$

Figure 2. Summary of Clock Properties.

Figure 2.

Precision δ_v characterizes how closely virtual clocks are synchronized to each other, ρ_v is the drift rate of virtual clocks. Accuracy α_v characterizes how closely virtual clocks are synchronized to real time. Due to the nonzero drift rate of physical clocks, accuracy cannot be ensured without some external source of real time. However, a good algorithm should maintain clocks as close as possible to the best real time source available, which may be one of the correct clocks in the system. In that sense, minimizing[3] ρ_v, should *preserve* accuracy, and that term will be used in this paper when informally discussing these attributes.

Since physical hardware clocks can be permanently drifting from each other, virtual clocks must be resynchronized from time to time. A clock synchronization algorithm should then be able to: (i) generate a periodic resynchronization event. The time interval between successive synchronizations is called the resynchronization interval, denoted T; (ii) provide each correct process with a value to adjust the virtual clocks in such a way that *precision* and *rate* hold. The clock adjustment can be applied instantaneously or spread over a time interval. In both techniques, for the sake of convenience, the adjustment is usually modeled by the start of a new virtual clock upon each resynchronization event [5, 17].

The worst-case clock precision δ_v is obtained by adding to the precision δ_{vi} achieved with the synchronization the drift between clocks during the resynchronization interval T, that is $\delta_v = \delta_{vi} + 2\rho T$. The physical clock drift ρ is typically of the order of 10^{-4} to 10^{-6} and the resynchronization

---

[3]In any case, limited to ρ [18].

interval T can be selected such that the desired precision is guaranteed. If the algorithm exhibits a good precision enhancement property a longer resynchronization interval can be chosen.

4. Related work

Software based clock synchronization protocols can be fully generic or tailored for certain classes of networks. In this paper we are looking for solutions that can exploit the CAN properties mentioned in Section 2, namely the ability to generate a "simultaneous" event through the broadcast of a message. Thus we will concentrate our attention on two algorithms that are targeted for networks with these properties.

4.1. A posteriori agreement

The *a posteriori agreement* for clock synchronization [22, 23] is a technique that uses tightness property of some networks (see CAN6) to avoid the influence of the network access delay variability on the precision of virtual clocks. An aim of the *a posteriori agreement* technique is to improve precision by making the clock synchronization algorithm depend on $\Delta\Gamma_{tight}$, instead of depending on the variance of message delivery ($\Delta\Gamma = \Gamma^{max} - \Gamma^{min}$, according to property CAN5) or on the worst-case message delivery (Γ^{max}). The improvement on clock precision is high because $\Delta\Gamma_{tight} << \Delta\Gamma$ (note that $\Delta\Gamma$ also includes the network access delay variance).

Synchronization starts with each process disseminating a *start* message at a pre-agreed instant on its clock. Reception of *start* messages trigger the start of a new virtual clock. Note that, due to process or network faults, not all broadcasts will be received by all correct processes. Thus, clocks triggered by a *start* message must be kept merely as candidates for synchronization until an agreement is obtained on a broadcast yielding high precision. This agreement can be used to select an adjustment to the absolute value of the elected clock, in order to yield the best accuracy preservation possible. Since the agreement is executed after the candidate virtual clocks have been started, the algorithm was called *a posteriori agreement*. As a consequence of this approach, the resulting precision is mainly limited by $\Delta\Gamma_{tight}$ and marginally by the time required to reach agreement (Γ^{max}_{agreem}). The precision achieved by the *a posteriori agreement* algorithm was proven [22, 23] to be limited by:

$$\delta_{vi} \geq (1 + \rho)\Delta\Gamma_{tight} + 2\rho\Gamma^{max}_{agreem}$$

The general algorithm is communication and agreement protocol independent, i.e., the choice of different communication infrastructures and agreement protocols would lead to different implementations of the algorithm. An implementation of the *a posteriori* technique for local area networks such as Ethernet and Token-Bus has been proposed [23]. However, the bandwidth and message size required by such implementation is not supported by the maximum data field size (8 bytes) allowed in CAN messages. Our work departs from designing a specialization of the original *a posteriori* protocol that defines an agreement protocol tailored to the CAN network.

4.2. CAN oriented algorithms

Gergeleit and Streich have proposed a clock synchronization algorithm for CAN based on a master-slave configuration [4]. The algorithm can be seen as a non fault-tolerant implementation of the *a posteriori* agreement approach. The master periodically emits a *start* message that triggers the start of a new virtual clock in all the slaves. CAN properties guarantee that, if the master survives, these virtual clocks are precise. Accuracy is achieved by calculating the adjustment *a posteriori*. Since the algorithm is not fault-tolerant, no agreement protocol needs to be executed. The master sends an absolute clock value based on its own measurement of the delay incurred for the dissemination of the *start* message (typically, the master will be connected to an external source of time) and all slaves adjust their clocks accordingly. To reduce traffic, the master reference value required for the adjustment is piggybacked in the next *start* message.

A positive aspect of this algorithm is its low bandwidth consumption. A single message at every synchronization round is enough to keep the clocks synchronized. The major drawback is its complete lack of tolerance with regard to the failure of the master process. To overcome this drawback it was suggested to use multiple cooperating masters using a token-based approach; in each synchronization round a different master would be responsible for ensuring synchronization [1]. Unfortunately, since CAN does not guarantee reliable delivery when the sender fails [16], it is possible for a failed master to leave the system in an inconsistent state.

4.3. Other approaches

A major limitation of all known software clock synchronization algorithms designed for arbitrary networks, is that precision is limited either by the variance of the message delivery delay [12], or worse, by its upper bound [18]. This problem may be minimized with hardware support, either by implementing clock synchronization exclusively by hardware [7, 11] or by using hybrid schemes [13] which attempt at reducing that variance, for instance, using clock synchronization units that are able to timestamp messages [9] and receive GPS signaling. Although designing

specifically for CAN, our goal is to allow the use of "off-the-shelf" components. Statistical techniques can also be used to minimize the effect of the network variance [2]. The work of [3] provides an interesting integration of internal and external clock synchronization but, being based on remote clock reading, it is not clear how it can be adapted to exploit CAN tightness.

5   Design overview

The CAN owns a number of characteristics that offer the potential for achieving highly precise clock synchronization, in particular it exhibits a network tightness in the order of a few microseconds and built-in error handling facilities. On the other hand, it has a low bandwidth (compared with today's LANs) and supports only small messages which favors simple protocols. Also, only best-effort agreement is provided (i.e., in case of sender failure the message may be received by just a subset of the nodes) which difficults agreement on clock values.

As seen in the previous sections, some clock synchronization algorithms have been designed specifically for CAN. However, these protocols exhibit limited or no fault-tolerance features, having thus limited applicability for dependable applications. On the other hand, most of the generic algorithms described in the literature cannot make explicit use of the unique (positive) features of CAN.

The *a posteriori* agreement approach seems suitable for CAN since the precision achieved is in the order of the network tightness. Our work is based on the idea of applying the *a posteriori* technique to CAN. However, limitations of a straightforward implementation of this technique, lead us to develop a new algorithm, particularly suited for the CAN network.

6. What's missing for *a posteriori* agreement on CAN

To motivate the need for a new algorithm, we describe first a straightforward implementation of the *a posteriori agreement technique* for CAN. The algorithm is obtained by enhaning the generic *a posteriori* algorithm described in [22, 23] with a CAN-specific agreement protocol. The proposal of an agreement protocol suited to CAN is also a contribution of this work.

The resulting algorithm offers excellent precision and requires only two phases of message exchanges. On the other hand, it requires a large number of messages in the first phase and does not provide good accuracy. A run of this basic algorithm requires at least $n(n + 1)$ messages; in the next section, we will describe an algorithm that lowers the number of messages required down to $3n$.

The algorithm is fully decentralized. In order to tolerate f faults, at least $2f + 1$ processes must try to generate a simultaneous event (for clarity, we will simply assume that all processes try to do so). No matter how many processes trigger the synchronization algorithm, all correct processes need participate in the agreement to select one of the simultaneous events as the source of the clock for the next synchronization interval. We assume that there is a total order of the processes identifiers; this order is used to rank votes on the agreement phase of the algorithm.

A pseudo-code description of the algorithm is given in Figure 3. Let T denote the resynchronization interval. Each period is initiated by a process p when its virtual clock reaches iT, the time for synchronization round i, by broadcasting a $\langle start, i\rangle$ message on the network (l. 107). If the sender does not fail, CAN guarantees that this message will be eventually received by all correct processes at approximately the same time (properties CAN2 and CAN6). Note however, that the occurrence of faults may lead to message retransmission by the CAN protocol "cast in silicon". Thus, duplicates of the same $\langle start\rangle$ message can be received (property CAN3). Each time a $start$ message is received a new candidate clock is started (duplicates restart this clock). Typically, several processes will send a $start$ message at approximately the same time. Only tight events may be eligible as candidates. In CAN, only the sender can detect reliably when a message is delivered to all correct processes. Thus, only the sender can safely propose its own message (and associated clock) as a valid candidate.

When a new candidate clock is started, it is started with some dummy pre-defined value (l. 113). In fact, candidate clocks may be precise but are inaccurate because there is a variable and unpredictable delay in the dissemination of the $start$ message. At the end of the agreement, the selected clock is adjusted to a value that best preserves the accuracy. In this basic algorithm, this adjustment is computed by the sender of the associated $start$ message, based on the local measurements, at each process, of the virtual time at which the corresponding message was locally received. Let $rt^{i,p}$ denote the reception time of the $\langle start, i\rangle$ message from p, according to vc_q^{i-1}. In order to make this information available at the sender, every $\langle start, i\rangle$ message is acknowledged directly to the sender p by every process q, with an $\langle ack, i, p, rt^{i,p}\rangle$ message (l. 119).

The protocol proceeds with a second phase of message exchange where the processes agree on which candidate clock should be used for the next round. This phase is initiated by a sender p when: it detects the succesfull transmission of its own $start$ message; at least $f + 1$ $start$ messages have been received; it has received all the associated ack messages or the corresponding AckTimer has expired (l. 124). When these conditions are satisfied, the sender computes the adjustement for its own clock, by selecting the

```
100   // variable description
101   //    voted^i: voted candidate.
102   //    RT^i[]: reception times.
103   //    Δ^i: adjustment for this candidate.
104   //    starts^i, acks^i, and votes^i: counters
105   starts^i := 0; acks^i := 0;
106   voted^i := NONE;

107   when vc^{i-1}(NOW) = iT
108      and voted^i = NONE do
109         broadcast (⟨start, i⟩);

110   when received S=⟨start, i⟩ from q do
111      rt^{i,q} := vc^{i-1} (NOW);
112      // start new candidate clock
113      cc^{i,q} (NOW) := 0;
114      if not-duplicate(S) then starts^i := starts^i + 1;
115      if p = q then // my own start message
116         acks^i := acks^i+1;
117         RT^i[p] :=rt^{i,q}
118      else
119         unicast (⟨ack, i, rt^{i,q}⟩);
120         if notstarted(AckTimer) then start(AckTimer);

121   when received A=⟨ack, i, rt^{i,p}⟩ from q ≠ p do
122      RT^i[q] :=rt^{i,p}
123      if not-duplicate(A) then acks^i := acks^i + 1;

124   when transmission-confirmed (⟨start, i⟩)
125      and starts^i ≥ f + 1
126      and (acks^i = N or expired(AckTimer))
127      and voted^i = NONE do
128         N := acks^i;
129         voted^i := p;
130         votes^i := 0;
131         Δ^i := median(∀_x RT^i[x] > 0);
132         broadcast(⟨vote, i, p, Δ^i⟩);

133   when received V=⟨vote, i, v, Δ^v ⟩ from q ≠ p
134      and not-duplicate(V) do
135         if not-started(VoteTimer) then start(VoteTimer);
136         if rank(v) > rank(voted^i) then do
137            voted^i := v;
138            votes^i := 1;
139            Δ^i := Δ^v;
140            broadcast(⟨vote, i, v, Δ^v⟩ );
141         if voted^i = v then votes^i := votes^i +1;

142   when expired(VoteTimer) or votes^i = N
143      and voted^i ≠ NONE do
144         vc^i := cc^{i,voted^i} + Δ^i;
145         N:= votes^i;
```

Figure 3. *A posteriori* **algorithm for CAN**

median value of the receive times returned in the *ack* messages and broadcasts a $\langle vote$, i, p, $\Delta^{adjust,p} \rangle$ message (l. 132). When another process q receives the *vote* message, it confirms this choice by sending a similar *vote* message (l. 140). In the best case, all processes vote on the same candidate clock and this phase ends as soon as the same vote is received from every correct process (l. 142). If two or more senders receive (approximately at the same time) the confirmation of the transmission of their own *start* messages, concurrent votes for different candidates will be issued. In this case, the vote with higher rank is preferred (this means that a process may change its vote during this phase). This voting protocol is similar to the election algorithm described in [19]. It should be noted that the adjustment computed by this algorithm may be inaccurate because there is no way to match the acknowledgement (that carry the values needed to compute the adjustment) with the appropriate retransmission of the start message (that triggered the clock being adjusted). Our new protocol adresses this aspect.

The protocol is further complicated due to the possibility of process failures. In such case, some *ack* or *vote* messages will be missing. To prevent deadlock, a simple timeout mechanism is used in both phases: if an *ack* (or *vote*) message is missing after a pre-defined time limit the faulty processes are marked as failed. Note that the CAN properties guarantee the reliable and timely delivery of messages when the sender is correct. Thus, the protocol embodies a minimal fault-detection functionality that can be provided as input for a complementary membership service.

Assume that all processes issue a *start* message. According to the *a posteriori* agreement algorithm, all processes must acknowledge these start messages. Finally, in the best case, all processes vote on the same candidate clock. Thus, the protocol requires at least n start messages, each requiring $n - 1$ acknowledgements and n additional vote messages, for a total of $n + n(n-1) + n = n(n+1)$ messages. The worst-case is much higher than this: *start* messages may need to be retransmitted and all retransmissions need an acknowledgement from every process; several processes may concurrently vote for their own candidate clock, resulting in a cascade of voting messages. In the next section, we will present a "phase-decoupled" algorithm that alleviates these problems.

7. The new "phase-decoupled" *a posteriori* algorithm

The "phase-decoupled" *a posteriori* algorithm addresses the drawbacks of the basic *a posteriori* algorithm in face of the properties of the CAN network, namely the large number of acknowledgement messages, the potentially large number of concurrent votes, and the inaccuracy of clock adjustments (due to automatic retransmissions). These prob-

lems are solved using different mechanisms.

In the original *a posteriori* agreement protocol, acknowledgement messages are used for two different purposes: to disseminate reception times (used to compute the adjustment) and to ensure (and detect) reliable delivery of the *start* message. In CAN, reliable delivery is guaranteed as long as the sender remains correct. Thus, acknowledgements are only needed to disseminate reception times. The proposed modification is based on the observation that only the selected clock needs to be adjusted and that the number of messages is strongly reduced if the reception times for the other clocks are not disseminated. This can be achieved by voting on the candidate clock before the acknowledgment phase. Since reception times are no longer available at voting time, the reduction on the number of messages is achieved at the cost of "decoupling" the start phase from the adjustment computation phase (which are overlapped in the simple protocol), thus the name of the new protocol.

Decoupling these two phases has another advantage in terms of accuracy of clock synchronization. Since acknowledgements are only produced when the *start* is stable (i.e., when it has already been successfully transmitted), all disseminated reception times refer to the last correct transmission. This allows the final adjustment to be computed based on accurate reception times.

The problem of concurrent votes is a consequence of the precision of clock synchronization. Since all clocks exhibit approximately the same time, all processes will reach iT at approximately the same real time, all processes will send a start message concurrently, and so on. Although the network will enforce a serialization of all these messages, the delays incurred by such serialization are not enough to prevent concurrent executions. It should be noted that, with most existing CAN controllers, it is difficult to cancel in due time a message submitted for transmission. In the "phase-decoupled" algorithm this problem is solved using a simple Time-Division Multiplexing (TDM) approach: each processes delays its own vote by a period that is inversely proportional to its rank. This artificially extends the agreement phase but, as seen in Section 4.1, this is not the major factor on the final precision.

A pseudo-code description of the "phase-decoupled" algorithm is given in Figure 4. As in the basic algorithm, processes transmit a *start* message when their virtual clock reaches the time to resynchronize (l. 210). Unlike the basic algorithm, *start* messages do not generate acknowledgements. Instead, when enough start messages have been observed, the voting phase is immediately started (l. 220).

The voting phase is similar to that of the basic algorithm with some minor changes. One of the differences its that, instead of the final adjustment, voting messages disseminate the reception time of the associated start message (l. 226). The other difference is that each process delays the vote on

```
200    // variable description
201    //   voted^i: voted candidate.
202    //   RT^i[]: reception times.
203    //   Δ^i: adjustment for this candidate.
204    //   adjuster^i: proposer of the adjustment.
205    //   starts^i
206    //   votes^i, and adjusts^i: counters
207    starts^i := 0;
208    voted^i := NONE;
209    adjuster^i := NONE;

210    when vc^{i-1}(NOW) = iT
211      and voted^i = NONE do
212        broadcast(⟨start, i⟩);

213    when received S=⟨start, i⟩ from q do
214      rt^{i,q} := vc^{i-1}(NOW);
215      // start new candidate clock
216      cc^{i,q}(NOW) := 0;
217      if not-duplicate(S) then starts^i := starts^i + 1;

218    when transmission-confirmed(⟨start, i⟩)do
219      start(VoteTDMTimer, rank(p));

220    when expired(VoteTDMTimer)
221      and starts^i ≥ f + 1
222      and voted^i = NONE do
223        voted^i := p;
224        votes^i := 1;
225        RT^i[p] := rt^{i,p};
226        broadcast(⟨vote, i, p, rt^{i,p}⟩);

227    when received V = ⟨vote, i, v, rt^{i,v}⟩) from q ≠ p
228      and not-duplicate(V) do
229        if not-started(VoteTimer) then start(VoteTimer);
230        RT^i[q] := rt^{i,v};
231        if rank(v) > rank(voted^i)
232          or voted^i = NONE then
233            voted^i := v;

234            votes^i := 1;
235            broadcast(⟨vote, i, v, rt^{i,v}⟩);
236        else-if voted^i = v
237          and (i = 0
238          or (i > 0 and rt^{i,v} > 0)) then
239            votes^i := votes^i+1;

240    when expired(VoteTimer)
241      or votes^i = N do
242        start(AdjustTDMTimer, rank(p));

243    when expired(AdjustTDMTimer)
244      and adjuster^i = NONE do
245        adjuster^i := p;
246        adjusts^i := 0;
247        N := votes^i;
248        Δ^i := median(∀_x RT^i[x] > 0);
249        broadcast(⟨adjust, i, p, Δ^i⟩);

250    when received D=⟨adjust, i, a, Δ^a⟩ from q ≠ p
251      and not-duplicate(D) do
252        if not-started(AdjustTimer) then start(AdjustTimer);
253        if rank(a) > rank(adjuster^i)
254          or adjuster^i = NONE then
255            adjuster^i := a;
256            adjusts^i := 1;
257            Δ^i := Δ^a;
258            broadcast(⟨adjust, i, a, Δ^a⟩);
259        else-if adjuster^i = a
260          and (i = 0
261          or (i > 0 and rt^{i,v} > 0))then
262            adjusts^i := adjusts^i+1;

263    when expired(AdjustTimer)
264      or adjusts^i = N do
265        vc^i := cc^{i,voted^i} + Δ^i;
266        N:= adjusts^i;
```

Figure 4. The "phase-decoupled" algorithm

its own clock by an amount of time that is dependent of its rank (l. 218). If correct, the process with higher rank will propose its own clock first and the other processes will confirm this vote. Only in the case of failure, the process with succeeding rank will issue a different vote message. As before, timeouts are used to terminate the voting phase in case of missing votes.

At the end of the voting phase, all correct clocks have agreed on the same candidate clock (l. 240). However, different processes can have different sets of votes. Note that if a process fails during the transmission of its own vote the CAN does not ensures the reliable delivery of this message. Thus, processes cannot apply a local function to compute the adjustment for the selected clock: an additional agreement phase needs to be performed. This second phase is quite similar to the voting phase. The process with higher rank will locally compute the adjustment and disseminate it

using an *adjust* message (l. 249). This message needs to be confirmed by all correct processes (l. 258). Again, in case of failure of the process with higher rank, all other processes would, in turn, compute and propose an adjustment for the selected clock.

8. CAN message priorities

The CAN priority based arbitration scheme allows the assignment of a different priority to each protocol message. This section discusses how this feature can be exploited to promote faster protocol termination. Our proposal assumes that the message identifiers are constructed using three fields, namely *protocol priority*, *message priority* and *rank priority*.

The *protocol priority* field is mapped onto the high priority bits of the message identifier and reflects the relative priority of clock synchronization with regard to other activities in the system. A positive feature of our algorithm is that, as long as enough bandwidth is reserved to execute the protocol in due time, the use of the higher CAN priorities is not required in order to achieve good precision.

The *message priority* field reflects the relative priorities of protocol messages with regard to each other. Here, message urgency increases as the algorithm execution approaches its final phase (that is, the *adjust* messages have higher priority than the *vote* messages, which in turn have higher priority than *starts*). The rationale is that, as soon an a new protocol phase is started, messages regarding previous phases become obsolete and should be given a lower priority (the time-division multiplexing scheme minimizes the number of these messages).

Finally, the *rank priority* field ensures that messages of the same type are given a priority which reflects the rank of their senders. This means that the vote (or adjust) from the process of higher rank (which is bound to win the election) is given a higher priority than other votes.

The use of the CAN arbitration scheme complements the time-division multiplexing technique when, due to processing or network transient overloads, requests from different processes compete for network access. In the performance section, this CAN-based message ordering scheme was used in all simulations.

9. Performance

This section discusses the performance of the "phase-decoupled" *a posteriori* algorithm in terms of number of messages exchanged, precision and accuracy preservation.

9.1. Number of messages

The minimum number of messages generated by an execution of the algorithm is n starts, n votes and n adjusts, for a total of $N_{min} = 3n$ messages[4]. Worst-case values depend on the number of faults and on system configuration. If all nodes configured to generate a start message reach the synchronization point approximately at the same time, the first phase of the algorithm generates n messages. Nodes should then vote for electing a candidate clock. In the worst-case, each node begins voting on its own clock, changing afterwards the vote, successively, to higher rank clocks. This means each node generates a number of messages equal to its rank numbering; the sum of the messages generated by all the nodes represents the sum of the first n terms of an

---

[4]Actually, through a network management interface, it is possible to load a configuration where only $2f + 1$ processes are required to send a start message. However, to simplify the explanation, we have selected a configuration where all nodes run the same code.

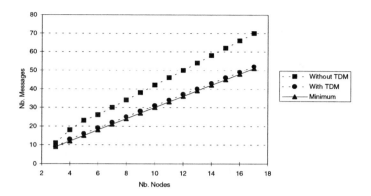

Figure 5. Variation of generated messages with number of nodes

arithmetic sequence with ratio one. This model applies also to the adjustment phase. Thus:

$$N_{max} = n + \frac{n}{2}(1+n) + \frac{n}{2}(1+n) = n^2 + 2n$$

Naturally, the average number of messages exchanged on a typical execution environment is much less than N_{max}. The purpose of the time-division multiplexing scheme on the voting and adjust phases is to approximate the average number of messages exchanged to N_{min}. To evaluate the effectiveness of our approach, we have used the MIT LCS Advanced Network Architecture group's network simulator (NETSIM [6]). In this experiment, we have considered the CAN 2.0B @ 1 Mbps and we have set the time-division multiplexing timers for a value of $400\mu s$. This value is 2.5 times bigger than the time required to propagate a message ($160\mu s$) but is still small enough to have a minor impact on clock precision in case of process crashes (each timeout adds $400\mu s$ to the agreement phase, thus even two consecutive failures would affect the precision in less than $10^{-3}\mu s$). The results for a fault-free scenario are shown in Figure 5, where the use of the time-division multiplexing method is compared with a scenario that does not use such technique. It is clear that the number of messages generated in the former case closely approximates the minimum number of messages required by the algorithm.

9.2. Precision and accuracy preservation

The precision achieved by an algorithm based on the *a posteriori* agreement technique was proven [23] to be limited by:

$$\delta_{vi} \geq (1 + \rho)\Delta\Gamma_{tight} + 2\rho\Gamma_{agreem}^{max}$$

Additionally, at each resynchronization there is a potential accuracy loss of, approximately, $(1 + \rho)\Delta\Gamma_{tight}$ (see [23] for exact formulas).

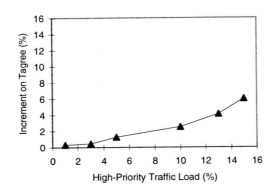

Figure 6. Average agreement time versus network load

Intended precision (μs)	T (s)	Worst-case accuracy loss ($\mu s/hour$)
50	20	3600 + 1800
100	45	3600 + 800
200	95	3600 + 370
300	145	3600 + 240

Table 1. Resynchronization interval

The parameters needed to compute results are: $\Delta\Gamma_{tight}$, which depends on maximum network propagation delay variance and on the maximum variance of timestamping processing overheads that can be observed at any correct receiver; ρ, that depends on the specifications and operational condition of the clock; and Γ_{agreem}^{max} which depends on the number of tolerated faults, resulting number of messages exchanged, configuration of the time-division multiplexing timers using for voting phases, and on background traffic of higher priority.

To evaluate the impact of the high-priority traffic load on the time required to reach agreement we have run a series of simulations of our protocol under different traffic loads. The results are depicted in Figure 6. It can be seen that even a traffic load of high-priority background traffic in the order of 15% has a small impact on the agreement time (which in turn has only a minor impact on clock precision).

Table 1 presents the resynchronization interval required for different values of worst-case precision. It also shows the maximum accuracy loss per hour of operation using such a resynchronization interval. We have considered a value of $10\mu s$ for $\Delta\Gamma_{tight}$ (a conservative value) and a value of $\rho = 10^{-6}$, common for crystal based clocks. The worst-case accuracy loss has two components, one that depends exclusively of the drift of physical clocks (without external synchronization, this is also the best accuracy preserva-

tion achievable [18]), and other that represents the protocol-induced accuracy loss. If required, the *a posteriori agreement* technique can be extended to perform external synchronization [23]. Nevertheless, it is important to exhibit a small accuracy loss even when external synchronization is used (this makes the system robust to transient faults of the external source).

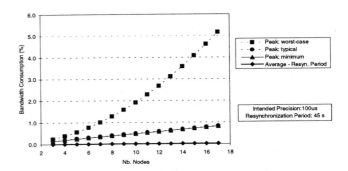

Figure 7. Bandwidth consumption (T=45s)

As it can be seen, to offer a precision in the order of $100\mu s$ (which is less than the average time required to disseminate a message in the CAN) clocks need to be synchronized only once every $45s$ and the protocol induced accuracy loss is much smaller than the accuracy loss due to the drift of the physical clocks. Figure 7 shows the CAN bandwidth consumption due to the protocol traffic in this scenario for different number of nodes. Since clock synchronization traffic exhibits a bursty behavior, the figure shows worst-case, minimum and typical values of bandwidth consumption during the execution of the protocol. Again, it should be noted that typical values are much lower than the theoretical worst-case value. The figure also shows the average bandwidth consumption over the entire synchronization period (lower line); naturally these values are very small.

10. Conclusions and future work

Designing clock synchronization protocols for CAN is justified by the increasing use of this network in industrial automation applications. Our work departures from a straightforward implementation of the *a posteriori* algorithm on CAN, which is obtained by enriching the generic algorithm described in [23] with a CAN-specific agreement protocol. This approach has several limitations, namely the large number of messages exchanged and the low accuracy of clock synchronization. It is interesting to observe that an optimization for local area networks (the use of acknowledgements for the dual purpose of reliability and clock value collection) actually degrades the performance on CAN. A new "phase-decoupled" *a posteriori* agreement algorithm that carefully addresses the limitations of CAN was presented. The algorithm offers a tight precision and good accuracy with a reasonable cost. For instance, to ensure a precision of $100\mu s$, clocks have to be synchronized only once every $45s$ and the accuracy loss is only in the order of $4.2ms$ per hour.

It was shown that the a posteriori agreement technique can be combined in an hierarchical manner with other synchronization algorithms to provide clock synchronization beyond the borders of a single broadcast segment [23]. A similar approach could be used here to synchronize several CAN buses. The integration of this technique with the approach suggested in [3], would also allow to support both internal and external synchronization.

References

[1] E. Christer, H. Thane, and M. Gustafsson. A communication protocol for hard and soft real-time computer systems. In *Proc. of the European Workshop on Real-Time Systems (EURWRTS)*, L'Aquila, Italy, Jun. 1996.

[2] F. Cristian. Probabilistic clock synchronization. *Distributed Computing*, 3(3):146–148, 1989.

[3] C. Fetzer and F. Cristian. Integrating external and internal clock synchronization. *Journal of Real-Time Systems*, 12(2), 1997.

[4] M. Gergeleit and H. Streich. Implementing a distributed high-resolution real-time clock using the CAN-Bus. In *Proc. of the 1st International CAN-Conference*, Mainz, Germany, Sep. 1994.

[5] J. Halpern, B. Simons, R. Strong, and D. Dolev. Fault-tolerant clock synchronization. In *Proceedings of the 3Rd ACM Symp. on Principles of Distributed Computing*, pages 89–102, Vancouver Canada, Aug. 1984.

[6] A. Heybey. The network simulator version 2.1. Technical report, M.I.T., Sep. 1990.

[7] A. Hopkins, T. Smith, and J. Lala. FTMP - A highly reliable fault-tolerant multiprocessor for aircraft. *Proceedings of the IEEE*, 66(10):1221–1240, Oct. 1978.

[8] ISO. *ISO International Standard 11898 - Road vehicles - Interchange of digital information - Controller Area Network (CAN) for high-speed communication*, Nov. 1993.

[9] H. Kopetz and W. Ochsenreiter. Clock syncronization in distributed real-time systems. *IEEE Transactions on Computers*, C-36(8):933–940, Aug. 1987.

[10] H. Kopetz and W. Schwabl. Global time in distributed real-time systems. Technical Report 15/89, Technische Universitat Wien, Wien Austria, Oct. 1989.

[11] C. Krishna, K. Shin, and R. Butler. Ensuring fault tolerance of phase-locked clocks. *IEEE Transac. Computers*, C-43(8):752–756, Aug. 1985.

[12] J. Lundelius and N. Lynch. An upper and lower bound for clock synchronization. *Information and Control*, (62):190–204, 1984.

[13] P. Ramanathan, K. Shin, and R. Butler. Fault-tolerant clock synchronization in distributed systems. *IEEE, Computer*, 23(10):33–42, Oct. 1990.

[14] Robert Bosch GmbH. *CAN Specification Version 2.0*, Sep. 1991.

[15] J. Rufino and P. Veríssimo. A study on the inaccessibility characteristics of the Controller Area Network. In *Proc. of the 2nd International CAN Conference*, London, England, Oct. 1995.

[16] J. Rufino, P. Verissimo, G. Arroz, C. Almeida, and L. Rodrigues. Fault-tolerant broadcasts in CAN. In *Digest of Papers, The 28th IEEE International Symposium on Fault-Tolerant Computing*, Munich, Germany, Jun. 1998.

[17] F. Schneider. Understanding protocols for byzantine clock synchronization. Technical report, Cornell University, Ithaca, New York, Aug. 1987.

[18] T. Srikanth and S. Toueg. Optimal clock synchronization. *Journal of the Association for Computing Machinery*, 34(3):627–645, Jul. 1987.

[19] A. Tanenbaum. *Modern Operating Systems*. Prentice Hall, 1992.

[20] K. Tindell and A. Burns. Guaranteeing message latencies on Controler Area Network. In *Proc. of the 1st International CAN Conference*, Mainz, Germany, Sep. 1994.

[21] K. Turski. A global time system for CAN networks. In *Proc. of the 1st International CAN Conference*, pages 3.2–3.7, Mainz, Germany, Sep. 1994.

[22] P. Veríssimo and L. Rodrigues. A posteriori agreement for fault-tolerant clock synchronization on broadcast networks. In *Digest of Papers, The 22nd International Symposium on Fault-Tolerant Computing*, Boston, USA, Jul. 1992. IEEE.

[23] P. Veríssimo, L. Rodrigues, and A. Casimiro. Cesiumspray: a precise and accurate global time service for large-scale systems. *Journal of Real-Time Systems*, 12(3):243–294, 1997.

[24] K. Zuberi and K. Shin. Non-preemptive scheduling of messages on Controller Area Networks for real-time control applications. In *Proc. of the IEEE Real-Time Technology and Application Symposium*, pages 240–249, Chicago, Illinois, USA, May 1995. IEEE.

Using Light-Weight Groups to Handle Timing Failures in *Quasi-Synchronous* Systems

Carlos Almeida

Instituto Superior Técnico - Universidade Técnica de Lisboa

DEEC, Av. Rovisco Pais - 1096 Lisboa Codex - Portugal

cra@digitais.ist.utl.pt

Paulo Veríssimo

Faculdade de Ciências da Universidade de Lisboa

Bloco C5, Campo Grande, 1700 Lisboa - Portugal

pjv@di.fc.ul.pt

Abstract

In a quasi-synchronous *environment worst-case times associated with a given activity are usually much higher than the average time needed for that activity. Using always those worst-case times can make a system useless. However, not using them may lead to timing failures. On the other hand, fully synchronous behavior is usually restricted to small parts of the global system. In a previously defined architecture we use this small synchronous part to control and validate the other parts of the system. In this paper we present a light-weight group protocol that together with the previously defined architecture makes it possible to efficiently handle timing failures in a* quasi-synchronous *system. This is specially interesting when active replication is used. It provides application support for a fail-safe behavior, or controlled (timely and safe) switching between different qualities of service.*

1. Introduction

In the last few years there has been a proliferation of computers and communication networks. This creates the potential for the development of new classes of applications. Applications that until now were only centralized are now intended to run in a distributed environment. This new infrastructure also creates the potential for the existence of a set of new services with new requirements. Issues such as fault-tolerance and real-time characteristics are examples of aspects that must be addressed in this new context.

Although these problems are reasonable well understood in the context of synchronous systems, they are very d-

ifficult to solve (if even possible) in systems that are not fully synchronous, which is the case of these new infrastructures. Some new communication network technologies (e.g. ATM [11]) have improved the synchronism properties of these distributed environments, however they are not always fully synchronous. They are at most what we call *quasi-synchronous* [26]. Only a small part of the system can be considered as synchronous. The rest has a more dynamic behavior exhibiting, for a given activity, worst-case delays that are much higher than the normal delays[1] (see Figure 1).

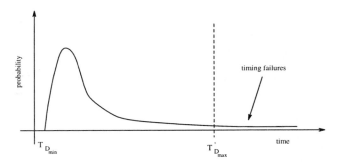

Figure 1. Distribution function for message delivery time (T_D) in a *quasi-synchronous* system. The worst-case is much higher than the normal case. Assuming as maximum a value closer to the normal case (due to practical reasons) increases the probability of having timing failures.

In this type of environment, the development of distribut-

---

[1] These delays can be related to execution if it is a CPU related activity, or transmission in the case of a network related activity.

ed fault-tolerant real-time applications is a difficult task. However, there is a demand for such applications, and therefore providing support for their development is of utmost importance.

We have been addressing these problems and in previous documents we have presented: the *quasi-synchronous* model [26]; group communication protocols that take into account the characteristics of these systems and provide message early-delivery [2]; and a timing failure detection service that has a key role in the proposed architecture [3]. In this paper we describe the protocols associated with the management of a hierarchy of groups, and explain how by using light-weight groups we can handle timing failures in a *quasi-synchronous* system.

The paper is organized as follows: in the next section we briefly describe our *quasi-synchronous* approach. In Section 3 we give a short reference to some related work. In Section 4 we present the group management protocols. In Section 5 we present and discuss some results obtained using simulation. The paper ends with the conclusions and some considerations about future work.

2. The quasi-synchronous approach

A synchronous system is one that exhibits known bounds on process execution times, message transmission delay and local clock rate drift. An asynchronous system is one where there are no such bounds. However, practical scenarios are not usually so well defined. Most systems, although not being fully synchronous, are not completely asynchronous either. They exhibit some form of synchronism. In this category are what we call *quasi-synchronous* systems [26].

A *quasi-synchronous* system can be modeled as if it was a synchronous system, in the sense that there are bounds on process execution times, message transmission delay and local clock rate drift, but some or all of those bounds are not precisely known, or have values that are too far from the normal case, that in practice one must use other values (closer to the normal case). In both cases it means that there is a non-null probability that the values we pick are not correct. This is a realistic scenario when there are situations of overload. Better synchronism properties are restricted to a small part of the system: a few high priority activities, and a small bandwidth channel for high priority messages.

Our approach is to use this small synchronous part of the system to build components able to control and validate the other parts of the system, thus making it possible to achieve safety in a timely fashion. This approach does not solve all timeliness problems *per se*, but can be used by applications to reach a safe state before stopping, or switch in a controlled manner between several different qualities of service. Together with group communication protocols and a hierarchy of group management it can also provide an efficient support

for the use of active replication. As we show in this paper this approach can be very useful in the handling of timing failures. Using active replication to tolerate timing failures is possible if we can assume an independent failure mode. Although the assumption of an independent failure mode is not always realistic, there are many scenarios where it can be considered. This is what happens in some of our applications of concern. The distributed telecommunications information network database components suffer sporadic timing failures due to overload, caused by request arrival and local processing unpredictability. Making replicated requests may be a solution to mask these sporadic timing failures.

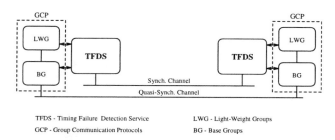

TFDS - Timing Failure Detection Service   LWG - Light-Weight Groups
GCP - Group Communication Protocols   BG - Base Groups

Figure 2. Use of the Timing Failure Detection Service

The proposed architecture is represented in Figure 2. It uses a timing failure detection service (TFDS) to disseminate with timeliness guarantees control information that is used by the communication protocols to validate their properties [3]. The implementation of TFDS may require the use of a specific network or a dedicated channel in a more generic network. We are exploiting several approaches. Depending on what is available and on the existing resources for a given application one may choose the approach that best fits in a given scenario. If an ATM network is available, for example, TFDS can be implemented using a channel with better guarantees than the channels used for normal communication.

Group communication protocols and group management are a powerful tool to support the development of applications that require the use of replication. Replication is often used as a way to increase availability and dependability. However, its existence implies replica management and communication support. This is specially important when there is a need for consistent dynamic updates in the presence of failures, including timing failures. This is a situation where our approach can be very helpful. By using TFDS as an oracle it is possible to detect timing failures (e.g. delays in updates) in a timely fashion. This in conjunction with a hierarchical structure for group management allows an efficient handling of timing failures.

In our architecture (see Figure 2) we use two layers for

group management. At low level there is a basic group layer (BG) corresponding to traditional group management (a participant leaves the group when it wants, or when it crashes). On top of the BG layer there is a layer with lightweight groups (LWG). A participant may leave the LWG group even when the BG group is still operational. This makes it possible to efficiently enforce safety properties when timing failures are detected. With the help of TFDS we can *force* a *fail stop mode* related to timing failures. A given participant is only considered active (able to generate messages) if it is in a consistent state (up-to-date). Keeping the BG layer operational reduces recovery time because late messages can still be collected.

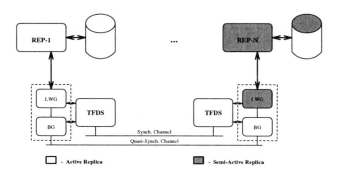

Figure 3. Use of TFDS and LWG in a distributed and replicated real-time database

The use of TFDS and LWG in a distributed and replicated real-time database is represented in Figure 3. The database application runs on top of TFDS and group communication protocols. When a given replica fails to receive the update in the specified time (detected by TFDS), it is temporarily disconnected from the group of active replicas (this is represented in gray in the figure). As there are two different group layers, only the upper layer is disconnected from the group when a timing failure is detected. The disconnection avoids consistency and contamination problems [21]. As the replica is not in a consistent state, it is prevented to respond to queries. However, keeping the low layer active, the replica may continue to receive updates thus minimizing the recovery time. This replica can be seen as a *semi-active replica*. As soon as the replica reaches a consistent state again, it may rejoin the group and become an active replica. Recovery can be done by means of state transfer, but, provided that there are some execution idle times between requests, it is faster to collect and execute late messages to catch-up. Message order can be enforced using the control information available from TFDS.

2.1. Feasibility of the assumptions on synchrony

The assumption of a channel with *better* characteristics is a reasonable assumption in scenarios usually available in real-time environments. Even in a real-time networks such as Token-bus, only high priority messages have hard real-time guarantees. In order to have guarantees for all messages, the configuration and network load must be completely controlled. In more general network architectures, it is normally possible to give guarantees to the highest priority messages. An example of such a network technology where different guarantees are given to different channels, is ATM (Asynchronous Transfer Mode) [11]. In this case it is possible to reserve channels with a given bandwidth and with a given level of guarantee associated with them. More recently a new type of network was standardized, called Iso-Ethernet [7], where traditional Ethernet and ISDN channels (Integrated Services Digital Network) coexist, with the latter having temporal guarantees. In some scenarios, it is also possible to have a dedicated network, as it is sometimes used for clock synchronization, for example. In the context of new telecommunications infrastructures, there are also examples of services that make our approach more viable, such as the short message service of GSM (SMS-GSM) and the foreseen message services of low earth orbit satellite constellations (LEO-Iridium)[9].

In a generic way, the fact that we only need a small bandwidth for the synchronous channel (the amount of information to transmit on the synchronous channel is much smaller than the amount of information to transmit on a normal channel), makes it easier to obtain. Note that there is usually an almost constant relation between latency and throughput in all networks. A low latency is usually obtained at the cost of having a decrease in throughput. When a high throughput is not needed, it makes it easier to obtain a channel with better temporal guarantees. In the limit, "a zero bandwidth" channel would provide very good temporal guarantees with probability 1!

Another aspect that we assume in this paper and we do not address here is clock synchronization. There is however, published work about this subject that show how that can be done in similar environments [27, 16]. Anyway, the precision and granularity of the clocks will only impose limitations on application time granularity not in the feasibility of the model, and the availability of a synchronous channel can make it easier to obtain.

3. Related work

The way we address some problems in our work has similarities with other works, even if in different contexts. For example, the idea of using early-delivery protocols, that we address in [2], appears in some other papers, and we used the work of Gopal *et al.* [20] as a starting point. In our paper we introduced extensions in order to be able to provide early-delivery to all participants of the communication group.

The use of a failure detection service together with the communication protocols, that we address in [3], can also be related to work done by the Isis Group [24, 8] to *solve* the problem of consensus in an asynchronous system [17]. The major difference between the two scenarios is that we want to reach agreement in a known bounded time and also detect timing failures. This puts some special requirements on the failure detection service – it must be implemented using a synchronous channel. Our timing failure detection service is also extended to provide the dissemination of control information.

Another work that deals with systems that are not completely synchronous is the one described by Dwork *et al.* in [12] about *partial synchrony*. However, they are mainly concerned with safety properties not related with time, assuming a liveness perspective, whereas we are deeply concerned with time under the perspective of timeliness. This essentially means having safety in a bounded time in a *quasi-synchronous* system. That is why we have to pick *a priori* a given value as the bound for message delay. In [12] the bound is not known or the point in time when it starts to hold is not known.

More recently there has been another work that has some similarities to our work from the point of view of goals [15]. That work is based on a model called *Timed Asynchronous* [10]. That system model assumes that processes have access to local clocks that although not synchronized have a bounded drift rate. The fault model assumes that processes may crash or experience performance failures and messages can have omissions or performance failures. On top of this model a datagram service is built that has knowledge about failures (*fail-aware*) [13]. It calculates an upper bound for message transmission delay using round trip delays and local clocks (not synchronized). Based on that calculus a message is classified either as *fast* or *slow*. This information can be used by upper layers to build, for example, a membership service able to define logical partitions [14]. This way it is possible to have applications with a fail-safe behavior [15].

Although with some similar goals (support for the development of real-time applications on environments that are not fully synchronous), the work just described is based on a system model (*Timed Asynchronous*) that is "more asynchronous" than our *Quasi-Synchronous* model. This way the qualities of service that can be offered in each environment are not exactly the same. Both models make it possible to build applications with a fail-safe shutdown. However, the Quasi-Synchronous model provides more flexibility for system reconfiguration. Because of the timely control information provided by TFDS, it is possible to reach an agreement before making a decision about the way that reconfiguration

should be done.

The use of light-weight groups (that is the focus of this paper) is also something that has been used by other researchers [23, 19, 25]. However, they were used in a different perspective not related to real-time and the handling of timing failures.

Having group members that exclude themselves from the group upon failure detection is also used in [1]. However, they do not use a hierarchical structure for groups and the excluding members do so by crashing. Another difference is that in our case it is possible to reach an agreement before making the decision to leave or not the group.

4. Group management and timing failures

As we explained above, in order to handle the uncertainty inherent to a quasi-synchronous system we propose the use of a hierarchy of groups. At a low level, communication is addressed to base groups (BG) whose elements remain in the group as long as they do not crash. At a higher level there are light-weight groups (LWG). A LWG group is mapped to a BG group, however its elements are only considered as active elements as long as they do not experience timing failures. When a timing failure is detected (a message that is received late) the faulty element leaves the LWG group. At the BG group level that element is still operational and can collect late messages in order to have a fast recovery.

4.1. Basic model

Our protocols for the management of groups are supported on the Timing Failure Detection Service (TFDS). TFDS works as an oracle that periodically disseminates control information among all nodes containing group participants. Each node has a TFDS instance. The period of TFDS is Π_F and the latency is Δ_F. TFDS is implemented on top of a small bandwidth synchronous channel. We also assume synchronized clocks. Generic communication is done using channels with more relaxed synchronism properties where it is possible to have timing failures. Messages are supposed to be disseminated within a time interval $T_{Dis_{max}}$. If a message with timestamp T_m is received after $T_m + T_{Dis_{max}}$ there is a timing failure.

When agreement is required, a message is not immediately delivered upon reception. Instead, there is an additional latency increment in order to be able to make the decision about delivering or not. This increment is λ and is related to TFDS parameters: $\lambda \geq \Pi_F + \Delta_F$.

Messages are ordered accordingly to their timestamps T_m that are generated by the sender at send time using the current value of its clock (which is synchronized). Messages are kept in a delivery queue but are only delivered when there are guarantees about the order and agreement (depending on the quality of service desired). Those guarantees are obtained through the control information disseminated by TFDS. Early-delivery is provided if those guarantees are obtained before the deadline for delivery ($T_m + T_{Dis_{max}} + \lambda$). For a more detailed description of the early-delivery group communication protocols and TFDS, the interested reader is referred to [2] and [3].

The protocols for group management, both BG and LWG, also use the delivery queue and TFDS in order to achieve a consistent behavior. Membership changes are done in a consistent way by all participants and are ordered with respect to message delivery. Messages are delivered in the same view by all correct participants. This is related to virtual synchrony that was first introduced in the Isis system [6] and has been used since then by other researchers, sometimes with some modifications [18].

4.2. Light-weight groups

As we said above, timing failures are handled at LWG level and crash failures are handled at BG level. A timing failure will force a LWG participant to leave the group. After recovering by collecting late messages it will request to join again the group. Recovering can also be done by state transfer. However, collecting late messages is usually faster. So, in this paper we consider the state transfer only in the context of base groups. The procedure would be similar for LWG.

Leave

A timing failure occurs when a given message m with timestamp T_m takes more than the assumed maximum time $T_{Dis_{max}}$ to be disseminated to all participants of the group, i.e., there is at least one participant for which we have

$$T(reception) > T_m + T_{Dis_{max}}.$$

When this happens, in order to provide a fail-stop behavior related to timing failures, the participant that did not receive the message in time must leave the LWG group (switch from active to not active). Furthermore, the other participants must also remove the failed member from their list of active members (view). This operations must be done in a consistent way by all participants, and the "leave" operation must be ordered with respect to message deliveries: all participants see the same order.

This is achieved by doing that operation at message delivery time ($T_m + T_{Dis_{max}} + \lambda$). Note that messages are ordered by their timestamps and there is a total order. As $\lambda \geq \Pi_F + \Delta_F$, between $T_m + T_{Dis_{max}}$ and $T_m + T_{Dis_{max}} + \lambda$, TFDS will disseminate to all participants the information about who has received or not the message by $T_m + T_{Dis_{max}}$. This way, a consistent decision

can be made by all participants, and faulty participants are removed from the view (membership).

Although the failure is due to the fact that a message m was not received until $T_m + T_{Dis_{max}}$, that failure is not effective until $T_m + T_{Dis_{max}} + \lambda$, the delivery deadline. Only at the delivery deadline an inconsistent state is reached when/if the other participants deliver the message. Between $T_m + T_{Dis_{max}}$ and $T_m + T_{Dis_{max}} + \lambda$ the participant can still be considered as correct because the missing/late message does not affect yet the "visible" state of that participant. Moreover, only at delivery time it is possible to have a consistent view of the situation.

At delivery time a consistent decision is made by all participants. A fail-stop behavior is enforced by the "failed" element itself by switching from active to not active. Note that the TFDS instance associated with the failed participant is still operational. As we are only assuming timing failures in the generic communication channel, TFDS is supposed to be full operational and so protocol correction can be ensured (crash failures are handled at BG level).

Messages in transit

It is possible to have messages that were already sent when a given participant fails, but were not accepted yet by all the other participants of the group. Those messages are supposed to be delivered and they must be taken into account to define order of delivery. TFDS provides the required information to achieve this. In the case of a crash, that situation is detected by not receiving the information periodically disseminated by TFDS. Such case implies not having early-delivery. It is necessary to wait the maximum time in order to make sure that a "flush" is done. As we do not have the information usually provided by TFDS, we do not know if there are messages in transit, and so we must wait to possibly receive those messages.

Join

When a given participant that was out of the group reaches a correct state again (from the point of view of order and agreement) it can request to rejoin the group. For that it can "send" a "join message" using TFDS. This "message" is timestamped as a regular message and inserted in the message queue accordingly to the timestamp. This way there is a "flush" of previous messages corresponding to the view where this participant did not belong.

When a given participant is in recovering mode, it can reach an up-to-date state by collecting late messages or by asking for a state transfer. For LWG we consider here only the first case. A state transfer would be handled in a manner similar to the one described for the base groups.

Messages with a timestamp greater than the timestamp of the request to join ($T_m > T_j$) are delivered after the join and need to have the confirmation from the new participant. Order is ensured by TFDS. Messages with a timestamp $T_m < T_j$ are delivered before the join and so do not have the confirmation from the new participant that is not an active member at that point.

All correct participants deliver a given message in the same view. They all know who accepts/delivers. However, a given message can be sent in a view different from the view in which it is delivered. A participant can leave a view before delivering a message sent in that view.

A given participant can deliver a message sent in a view to which it did not belong, provided that it had already request the join at that point. When the message was sent it was not an active member but it had already requested to join. The "join" will be "delivered" before the message.

In this mode of operation a sender does not know with accuracy at sending time which is the view in which the message will be delivered. All possible participants are potential elements of the view. Consistency is ensured by TFDS that remains operational even when a given participant (from a LWG) experiences a timing failure.

Locally, a participant only becomes an active member when/if it is in a consistent state. This behavior makes it possible to optimize the join by requesting it sooner.

4.3. Base groups

The protocol used for the management of base groups (BG) is also supported on TFDS. The control information is disseminated by TFDS with a period Π_F and a latency Δ_F. The protocol is intended to handle crash failures. The absence of a periodic message from the TFDS instance of a given participant p means that participant p has crashed. As TFDS uses a synchronous channel, the absence of information is assumed as a crash. Timing failures only occur in generic communication channels.

Leave

As explained above, the detection of a crash failure is done by not receiving the periodic information disseminated by TFDS. If by time $\Pi_F^i + \Delta_F$ the information related to period i is not received from a given participant p, it means that p has crashed. All correct participants detect this situation. However, they do not update their membership list immediately. This is necessary in order to ensure the correctness of the early-delivery protocols.

The exact moment of crash is not known with accuracy. It can be in the interval $[\Pi_F^{i-1}, \Pi_F^i]$. This means that it is possible that there are messages sent by the failed participant that are still in transit. The last one can have a timestamp $T_m = \Pi_F^i$. So, it is necessary to wait until $\Pi_F^i + T_{Dis_{max}} + \lambda$. This can be handled by inserting

a fictitious message with timestamp Π_F^i when the failure is detected. This "message" will be "delivered" at normal delivery time $(T_m + T_{Dis_{max}} + \lambda$, being $T_m = \Pi_F^i)$. This "delivery" corresponds to the indication of participant failure and respective membership update. During this period of time it may not be possible to provide early-delivery.

Join

TFDS has a reserved slot for each possible participant. This is used to request the join. When a participant restarts at time Π^0, it sends the request to join. At time $\Pi^0 + \Delta_F$ all correct participants know about the request. At this point the new participant is considered an "observer", not a full member. It starts to accept (without delivering) messages with timestamps $T_m > \Pi^0 + \Delta_F$. Other messages are discarded (they will be taken into account in the state transfer).

At time $T_i = \Pi^0 + \Delta_F + T_{Dis_{max}} + \lambda$ the group coordinator (for example the one with the lowest identifier) sends a state transfer to the joining participant. This time interval is necessary in order for the state transfer to take into account possible messages that were in transit $(T_m < \Pi^0 + \Delta_F)$.

At time $T_i + T_{Dis_{max}} + \lambda$ the new participant updates its state based on the state transfer and on the messages it collected in the mean time $(T_m > \Pi^0 + \Delta_F)$ and becomes an active member of the group. All other participants also update their membership list.

5. Discussion of results

In order to have a better idea about the behavior of the proposed architecture and protocols, we made some simulations corresponding to possible situations of target applications. In this section we present the results associated with the scenario where we use TFDS and light-weight groups to handle timing failures. A more complete study of several scenarios can be found in [4].

5.1. Simulation characteristics

The simulations that we present here were obtained using NETSIM [22], a simulator developed by the "MIT LCS Advanced Network Architecture" group. This simulator allows the specification of a network of components that exchange messages. It offers a graphical interface for visualization and parameterization of network topology and components. Essentially it works as an event manager. Events are generated by components accordingly to protocol implementations.

For generic communication data channels we used an Ethernet network at 10Mbits/s with support for multicast. We do not consider collisions but we consider transmission delay and medium occupation. Messages wait in queues until transmission is possible. Transmission duration takes into account message size. As we are mainly concerned with timing failures, we do not consider here omissions. That would imply the use of retransmissions in order to have reliability. We assume it included at this level. A specific treatment of this issue is not our main goal, that is why we did not address it here. From a practical point of view it would mean essentially an increase of message dissemination time. This means that the time values represented in the Figures [4-7] would be higher in a real setting. However, for our study relative values are more important than the absolute values. Absolute values will depend always on system and application time granularity.

Messages are generated in a random fashion following a Poisson distribution. For message size we used 1000 bytes. There is time associated with message processing. This time takes into account not only the time required to process the message but also possible CPU load related to other activities due for example to the existence of other applications. This situation corresponds to extra load that is independent of the message being processed and may differ between different processors. It is also modeled as a Poisson distribution. This aspect of load independence between different processors is important when considering active replication.

For TFDS we assume the existence of a synchronous channel with timeliness guarantees. The simulation of that channel if done in an independent fashion generating reception events directly on the destination accordingly to the period and latency considered for that service. For the simulations presented in this paper, we used $\Pi_F = 500\mu s$ and $\Delta_F = 100\mu s$.

5.2. Simulation scenarios

When application requirements implies agreement between all correct replicas about who has received or not a given message, system response time is conditioned by the time required for message dissemination and its worst case $(T_{Dis_{max}})$.

It is possible to still offer an early-delivery service, but if unanimity is wanted, it is always necessary to wait for reception confirmation from the latest replica. The value assumed for $T_{Dis_{max}}$ is the waiting threshold. If by that time (more precisely, $T_m + T_{Dis_{max}}$) there is a replica that has not received the message, then there are two options: the message is discarded; or the late replica is excluded from the group. In any case the decision must be made in a consistent way by all correct replicas (in the second option, late replicas are considered not correct and leave the group).

The maximum message delivery time $(T_{D_{max}})$ is, however, $T_{D_{max}} = T_{Dis_{max}} + \lambda$. The latency increase $(\lambda = \Pi_F + \Delta_F)$ is necessary to have the information needed to make a consistent decision. This way, if from

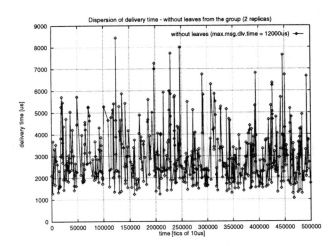

Figure 4. Scenario (a) - Active replication with updates (dispersion of delivery time). Use of TFDS and LWG. No leaves (maximum message delivery time = $12000\mu s$, 2 replicas).

the application point of view we want to select a given maximum message delivery time $(T_{D_{max}})$, then we have to parameterize the communication protocols so as to choose the right waiting threshold $T_{Dis_{max}}$. This value is obtained by subtracting $\Pi_F + \Delta_F$ from the application chosen value. For example, if the application wants a maximum message delivery time of, say, $T_{D_{max}} = 6000\mu s$, then (assuming $\Pi_F = 500\mu s$ and $\Delta_F = 100\mu s$) we will have:

$$T_{Dis_{max}} = 6000 - \Pi_F - \Delta_F = 6000 - 500 - 100 = 5400\mu s.$$

Thus, the waiting threshold to decide about the timing failure will be $5400\mu s$, in order to make sure that the maximum message delivery time is $6000\mu s$.

When timeliness is a key factor, the possibility of "ignoring" (temporarily disconnecting from the group) late participants makes it possible to reduce system response time. It is however important to have an efficient group management so as to avoid excessive overhead. This is achieved by the use of Light-Weight Groups (LWG) as explained before. When there is a timing failure (late reception of a message by a given replica), that replica leaves the group so as to avoid system inconsistency. However, it continues to be a member of the Base Group (BG) and keeps collecting late messages in order to have a faster recovery. This group management is done in a controlled way with the help of TFDS, as previous explained.

The simulation scenario that we present here is intended to show the effect of using LWG and TFDS as a way to improve system response time in a situation where there are dynamic updates in a set of replicas. This scenario is subdivided into four scenarios (a, b, c, d) in order to better

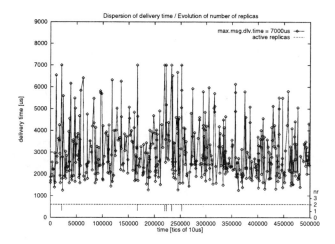

Figure 5. Scenario (b) - Active replication with updates (dispersion of delivery time). Use of TFDS and LWG. Leaves and joins (maximum message delivery time = $7000\mu s$, 2 replicas).

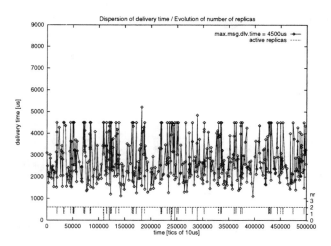

Figure 6. Scenario (c) - Active replication with updates (dispersion of delivery time). Use of TFDS and LWG. Leaves and joins (maximum message delivery time = $4500\mu s$, 2 replicas).

clarify the results obtained. This way we start by considering the situation in which group elements are stable, i.e. there are no leaves from the group. This happens because the value chosen for maximum message delivery time ($T_{D_{max}}$) is high enough to avoid being reached. Figure 4 corresponds to that situation. The value used for $T_{D_{max}}$ was $12000\mu s$ (implying $T_{Dis_{max}} = 11400\mu s$, used as threshold to define if a given replica experiences or not a timing failure). The figure represents the dispersion of message delivery time for a given time interval. It is a situation where there is active replication using 2 replicas, and it is necessary to keep consistency between them. It implies that the decision about delivering or not a given message can only be made after message reception by both replicas. As can be seen in the figure, although for most cases delivery time is between $1000\mu s$ and $5000\mu s$, there are other cases where it can reach, or even exceed, $8000\mu s$.

In order to reduce these delays we can assume a lower maximum message delivery delay, thus lowering also the threshold $T_{Dis_{max}}$, which forces the decision to be made early. The reduction of delivery time is obtained at the expense of excluding late replicas. This operation must be done in a consistent way (which is achieved with the help of TFDS) and furthermore there is a tradeoff between timeliness and number of active replicas. If the threshold is too low there is the possibility of excluding most replicas (in the limit, all replicas). Anyway, a careful use of this mechanism allows to obtain significant improvements in the system response time.

Figures 5 and 6 show the results obtained when maximum message delivery time $T_{D_{max}}$ is $7000\mu s$ and $4500\mu s$,

respectively. The figures also show (bottom) the evolution of the number of active replicas (leaves and joins). As can be seen in Figure 5, by reducing $T_{D_{max}}$ to $7000\mu s$ makes it possible to have a delivery time always less or equal to that value. This is possible because when a replica is late it is excluded from the group, as can be seen in bottom part of the figure. This exclusion is usually very short because, as explained before, late messages are still received, allowing a fast recovery. The re-integration in the group (join) is done in a controlled way using TFDS.

As can be seen in Figure 5, for $T_{D_{max}} = 7000\mu s$, there are few situations where it is necessary to exclude a replica. This means that it might be possible to have an acceptable system behavior even with a lower threshold. In Figure 6 it is shown the results obtained when $T_{D_{max}}$ is $4500\mu s$. In this situation, system response time is reduced to values less or equal to $4500\mu s$ in almost all cases. However, there are a few cases where there are temporarily no active replicas. In those situations, it is not possible to guarantee the maximum message delivery time assumed. In Figure 6 there are two situations in which the message is delivered after the deadline. Delivering or not messages that are in these situations is optional. One can choose to discard the message and not deliver it to any replica. The final decision is application dependent. It might be acceptable to have a small percentage of messages being delivered with some delay (this is a typical scenario in soft real-time applications).

In cases where it is important to minimize the possibility of excluding all active replicas, one possible solution is to increase the number of active replicas. This way the probability of having all replicas late at the same time is

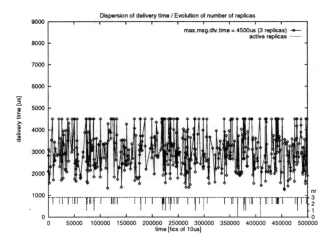

Figure 7. Scenario (d) - Active replication with updates (dispersion of delivery time). Use of TFDS and LWG. Leaves and joins (maximum message delivery time = $4500\mu s$, 3 replicas).

reduced. Figure 7 shows the results obtained when we use 3 replicas instead of 2. In this situation, for the same threshold ($T_{D_{max}} = 4500\mu s$), during the observation period, there were only two cases where all replicas received the same message late. (Even in that situation, the delivery was done before the assumed deadline.) These results show the potential of our approach.

5.3. Improvements and limitations

The results presented in this section show that by using the proposed architecture it is possible to improve in a significant way the behavior of a real-time system that runs in an environment that is not fully synchronous (quasi-synchronous). There are improvements both at system timeliness level and logical safety level.

By restricting synchronism properties to a few system modules, which makes its implementation viable in a larger setting, it is possible to build an infrastructure that supports the development of fault tolerant real-time applications in scenarios where is was not possible before.

It is not our goal to support the development of critical hard real-time applications on environments that are not fully controlled. It is our goal to use an approach that allows the improvement of real-time characteristics, and at same time improve the validation of situations where timeliness goals are not fully achieved.

In a generic way, we can consider two fundamental aspects in our approach:

1. Use of a best-effort policy at "normal" system components level trying however to introduce optimizations.

2. Add validation mechanisms that by having better synchronism properties make it possible to control the other system components, thus providing safety.

The first aspect *per se* improves the support for soft real-time applications. However, it is the second aspect that introduces a more significant improvement in the system. It makes it possible to support hard real-time applications provided that they have a fail-safe state. So, we use a best-effort policy to try to fulfill application timeliness requirements, but we also validate safety properties. If, by the assumed deadline, it is not possible to obtain the desired results, one can opt to stop in a fail-safe state (hard real-time), or one can relax timeliness requirements and wait for late results (soft real-time).

The characteristics of the validation mechanism that we refer above (TFDS) puts some restrictions on the type of environment where it is possible to obtain its implementation. The need of a synchronous channel in order to have timeliness guarantees limits its utilization. However, as we have already said, we only need a small bandwidth channel for control information, not generic data. New network technologies such as ATM (*Asynchronous Transfer Mode*) are also improving this scenario, thus making the use of our approach more viable.

6. Conclusions and future work

The work presented in this paper is part of a more generic architecture that aims at providing an infrastructure to support the development of fault-tolerant distributed real-time applications. Our target applications are mainly those with dynamic characteristics or those that run on environments that are not completely synchronous (*quasi-synchronous*).

In previous documents we have presented our *quasi-synchronous* model, group communication protocols that provide early-delivery, and a timing failure detection service that is a key component in the proposed architecture. In this paper we presented group management protocols supported on that previous defined architecture. They are structured in a hierarchical way providing a layer of light-weight groups. As shown in the paper, this is used to efficiently handle timing failures in a *quasi-synchronous* system. These results are very important to a new class of applications that is appearing due to the widespread use of computers and communication networks.

The results presented so far are mainly related to communications. In order to obtain a "full" system we need to also address similar problems related to processing. We are now addressing those problems in the DDRAFT system [5].

Acknowledgments

We would like to thank José Rufino for many helpful discussions and comments.

References

[1] T. Abdelzaher, A. Shaikh, F. Jahanian, and K. Shin. RT-CAST: Lightweight multicast for real-time process groups. In *Proceedings of Real-Time Technology and Applications Symposium*, Boston, MA, June 1996. IEEE.

[2] C. Almeida and P. Veríssimo. An adaptive real-time group communication protocol. In *Proceedings of the First IEEE Workshop on Factory Communication Systems*, Leysin, Switzerland, Oct. 1995.

[3] C. Almeida and P. Veríssimo. Timing failure detection and real-time group communication in *quasi-synchronous* systems. In *Proceedings of the 8th Euromicro Workshop on Real-Time Systems*, L' Aquila, Italy, June 1996. Also available as INESC technical report RT/20-95.

[4] C. Almeida and P. Veríssimo. Timing failure detection service: Architecture and simulation results. Technical Report CTI RT-97-05, Instituto Superior Técnico, Lisboa, Portugal, Dec. 1997.

[5] C. Almeida and P. Veríssimo. DDRAFT: Supporting dynamic distributed real-time applications with fault-tolerance. Technical Report CTI RT-98-02, Instituto Superior Técnico, Lisboa, Portugal, Feb. 1998.

[6] K. P. Birman. Virtual synchrony model. Technical report, Cornell University, July 1993.

[7] R. Brand. Iso-Ethernet: Bridging the gap from WAN to LAN. *Data Communications*, July 1995.

[8] T. Chandra and S. Toueg. Unreliable failure detectors for asynchronous systems (preliminary version). Technical report, Department of Computer Science, Cornell University, Ithaca, USA, July 1991.

[9] G. Comparetto and R. Ramirez. Trends in mobile satellite technology. *Computer*, 30(2):44–52, Feb. 1997.

[10] F. Cristian and C. Fetzer. The timed asynchronous system model. Technical Report CSE97-519, Dept. of Computer Science, UCSD, La Jolla, CA 92093-0114, January 1997.

[11] M. de Prycker. *Asynchronous Transfer Mode: Solution For Broadband ISDN (Third Edition)*. Number ISBN 0-13-342171-6. Prentice Hall, 1995.

[12] C. Dwork, N. Lynch, and L. Stockmeyer. Consensus in the presence of partial synchrony. *Journal of the ACM*, 35(2):288–323, Apr. 1988.

[13] C. Fetzer and F. Cristian. A fail-aware datagram service. Technical Report CS96-498, Department of Computer Science and Engineering, University of California, San Diego, La Jolla, CA 92093-0114, November 1996.

[14] C. Fetzer and F. Cristian. A fail-aware membership service. Technical Report CS96-503, Department of Computer Science and Engineering, University of California, San Diego, La Jolla, CA 92093-0114, November 1996.

[15] C. Fetzer and F. Cristian. Fail-awareness: An approach to construct fail-safe applications. In *Proceedings of 27th Annual International Symposium on Fault-Tolerant Computing*, Seattle, Washington, USA, June 1997.

[16] C. Fetzer and F. Cristian. Integrating external and internal clock synchronization. *Journal of Real-Time Systems*, 12(2), 1997.

[17] M. J. Fischer, N. A. Lynch, and M. S. Paterson. Impossibility of distributed consensus with one faulty process. *Journal of the Association for Computing Machinery*, 32(2):374–382, Apr. 1985.

[18] R. Friedman and R. van Renesse. Strong and weak virtual synchrony in horus. Technical Report TR-95-1537, Cornell University, Ithaca, USA, August 1995.

[19] B. Glade, K. Birman, R. Cooper, and R. Renesse. Lightweight process groups in the isis system. *Distributed System Engineering*, (1):29–36, 1993.

[20] A. Gopal, R. Strong, S. Toueg, and F. Cristian. Early-delivery atomic broadcast. In *Proc. of Ninth ACM Symposium on Principles of Distributed Computing*, Quebec City, Canada, August 1990.

[21] A. Gopal and S. Toueg. Inconsistency and contaminations. In *Proceedings of the Tenth ACM Annual Symposium on Principles of Distributed Computing*, pages 257–272, Montreal, Quebec, 1991.

[22] A. Heybey. The network simulator version 2.1. Technical report, M.I.T., USA, September 1990.

[23] D. Powell, editor. *Delta-4 - A Generic Architecture for Dependable Distributed Computing*. ESPRIT Research Reports. Springer Verlag, Nov. 1991.

[24] A. M. Ricciardi and K. P. Birman. Using process groups to implement failure detection in asynchronous environemnts. Technical Report TR 91-1188, Cornell University, Department of Computer Science, 1991.

[25] L. Rodrigues, K. Guo, A. Sargento, R. van Renesse, B. Glade, P. Veríssimo, and K. Birman. A dynamic light-weight group service. In *Proceedings of the 15th IEEE Symposium on Reliable Distributed Systems*, Niagara on the Lake, Canada, Oct. 1996. (also available as Cornell University Technical Report, TR96-1611).

[26] P. Veríssimo and C. Almeida. Quasi-synchronism: a step away from the traditional fault-tolerant real-time system models. *Bulletin of the Technical Committee on Operating Systems and Application Environments (TCOS), IEEE Computer Society*, 7(4):35–39, Winter 1995.

[27] P. Veríssimo, L. Rodrigues, and A. Casimiro. Cesiumspray: a precise and accurate global time service for large-scale systems. *Journal of Real-Time Systems*, 12(3):243–294, 1997.

Dependable System Upgrade

Lui Sha[1]
Department of Computer Science
University of Illinois at Urbana Champaign
DCL, 1304 W. Springfield
Urbana, IL, 61801
September, 1998

lrs@cs.uiuc.edu, 217 244-1887

Abstract — *The rate of innovations in technologies has far exceeded the rate of adopting them in at least the past 20 years. To fully realize the potential of innovations, a paradigm shift is needed, from a focus on enabling technologies for completely new installations to one which is designed to mitigate the risk and cost of bringing new technologies into functioning systems.*

In this paper, we show that real time control software can be dependably upgrade online via the use of analytically redundant controllers.

1.0 Introduction

Computers and computer networks have revolutionized the production of goods and the delivery of services. However, the existing computing infrastructure also introduces formidable barriers to continuous process improvement, equipment upgrades, and agility in responding to changing markets and increased global competition. Consider the following anecdotal scenarios from industry.

Process improvement: A research department developed a process modification that improved significantly the product yield and quality. With a relatively minor modification of the processing sequence, and new set-points for key process variables, the improvements were demonstrated in the laboratory. Nevertheless, these improvements were never implemented in the plant, because the line manager persuaded management that it couldn't be done cost effectively. Although the required software modifications are simple logic modifications, the process sequence is controlled by a set of networked PLCs coordinating many valves, sensors and PID loops. The last time a modification was at-

tempted on the code, it took the process down completely, costing thousands of dollars in downtime. The line manager wanted no part of installing the so-called process improvements developed by the research department.

Such problems are pervasive in real time systems, in spite of the fact that "hot swapping" of hardware components has been practiced successfully in high availability systems for a long period of time. Industry needs a computing infrastructure in which upgrades will be safe and predictable, with negligible down-time

A important technical challenges is how to perform fault tolerant online upgrade of real time software applications. In this paper, we will examine this subject in the context of process controls.

Two important objectives of the Simplex architecture are to 1) maintain a given level of system performance and functionality in spite of faults that can be introduced by changes and 2) permit the changes of a real time application software without the need to shutting down its normal operations. These objectives are realized by the use of analytic redundancy and real time dynamic component binding. In Section 2, we will present the notion of analytic redundancy and its applications. In Section 3, we examine the timing considerations. In Section 4, we will review the software architecture. Finally, we summarize the findings in Section 5.

2.0 Software Fault Tolerance Using Analytic Redundancy

---

[1] This paper was written when the author was at CMU.

In this section, we will first present the software fault model, followed by a brief description on the use of analytically redundant controllers.

2.1 Software Fault Model

What can go wrong when application software is modified? From the viewpoint of detection and recovery, the faults can be classified into three types: 1) resource sharing fault: corrupting other modules' code and data; 2) timing fault: failure to meet timing requirements; 3) semantic faults: producing wrong values.

Resource sharing faults can be addressed by address space protections and the protection of shared critical resources such as I/O channels. Timing faults can be addressed by real time scheduling methods such as generalized rate monotonic scheduling (GRMS) [3, 4]. Since both address space protection and GRMS are well established technologies, we will focus on semantic faults in this paper.

2.2 Analytically Redundant Controllers and The Recovery Region

A real time control system is typically characterized by a set of system quality attributes such as reliability, performance, and stability. When an attribute $Q_i()$ is a measure, component C_1 is said to be analytically redundant to C_2 with respect to the minimal requirement of the quality attribute $Q_i()$, if $Q_i(C_1) \le Q_i(C_2)$ and $Q_i(C_1) \ge R_i$, where R_i is the minimal requirement of $Q_i()$.[2] The application of analytic redundancy in Simplex architecture for real time control applications is realized by the use of analytically redundant controllers. The integrity of the system is guaranteed by a reliable controller. The reliable controller should utilize well understood control technologies and is simple with respect to existing high assurance software development technology.

_____

[2] Alternatively, if $Q_i()$ represents an undesirable attribute, then we would, instead, require $Q_i(C_1)$ less than some bound.

On the other hand, high performance controllers are designed to optimize the control performance such as faster response to commands, small tracking errors, and the reduction of energy usage, etc. The high performance controller may utilize new technologies such as neuronet, which can provide a high degree of control performance but its property could be diffi-

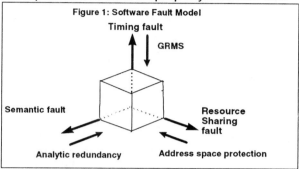

Figure 1: Software Fault Model

cult to analyze. The high performance controller and the reliable controller form an analytically redundant pair of controllers. One has a high degree of control stability and software reliability but with limited control performance, whereas the other has a high degree of control performance but with a lower degree of software reliability and control stability. The reliable controller is analytically redundant to the high performance controller in performance, assuming that the reliable controller can provide the minimal performance that is acceptable by the applications. The high performance controller is analytically redundant to the reliable controller with respect to the quality attributes software reliability and control stability, assuming that the

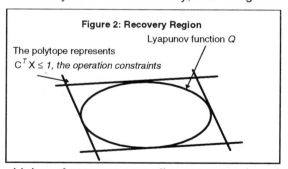

Figure 2: Recovery Region

Lyapunov function Q

The polytope represents $c^T x \le 1$, the operation constraints

high performance controller can meet the minimal software reliability and control stability requirements.

When we combine the usage of reliable controller and high performance controller, we need to know 1) when to let the reliable controller to take over the control of the system from a faulty high performance controller; and 2) the reliable controller would not unduly restrict the state space used by the high performance controller. Both of these two problems can formulated as the recovery region design problem.

In the operation of a plant (or a vehicle), there is a set of state constraints, called operation constraints, representing the safety, device physical limitations, environmental and other operation requirements. The operation constraints can be represented as a normalized polytope, $C^T X \leq 1$, in the N-dimensional state space of the system under control (See Figure 2). Each line on the boundary represents a constraint, for example, the rotation of the engine must be no greater than K RPM. In order not to violate the operation constraints, we must switch the control from the faulty high performance controller to the reliable controller at appropriate moments before the operation constraints are violated, so that after the switch, all the future trajectories under the reliable controller will not violate the operation constraints.

Legal states are the set of plant states that do not violate the operation constraints. The recovery region associated with a reliable controller is defined as the subset of legal states that the system under the controller is guaranteed not to leave. Furthermore, from any state in the recovery region, the system can reach a neighborhood of some set point (desirable states) under the reliable controller. To ensure that operation constraints are observed in spite of faults in experimental high performance controllers, we have to insist that the trajectories of high performance controllers must lie within the recovery region.

Geometrically, a Lyapunov function for a dynamic system with a given controller defines a N-dimensional ellipsoid in the N dimensional system state space as illustrated in Figure 2. A Lyapunov function has the important property that as long as the system is in the ellipsoid defined by Lyapunov function, the system states under the given controller will stay within the ellipsoid and converge to the equilibrium position[5]. This implies that the recovery region associated with the reliable controller can be modeled by a Lyapunov function and the boundary of the ellipsoid defined by the Lyapunov function represents the switching rule. To ensure that the system under the control of a problematic controller never violate the opera-

tion constraints, we must switch the control from this problematic controller to the reliable controller before the system state is outside of the ellipsoid. It should be noted that in practice, the system state cannot be known instantaneously and exactly. Nevertheless, we shall assume this ideal condition in this section and deal with the state observation problem later.

Lyapunov function is not unique for a given system and controller. In order not to unduly restrict the state space that can be used by the

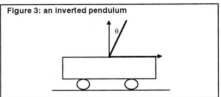
Figure 3: an inverted pendulum

high performance controllers, we need to find the largest ellipsoid within the polytope that represents the operation constraints. Mathematically, finding the largest ellipsoid inside a polytope is a type of linear programming problem known as Linear Matrix Inequality (LMI) problems[10]. Thus, we can use Lyapunov theory and the LMI tools[3] to solve our recovery region problem. For example, giving a dynamic system $X' = A^* X + B K X$, Where X is the system state, A^* is the system equation and K represents a controller. We can first choose K by using well understood controller design with a robust stability, i.e., the system stability region is insensitive to model uncertainty[5]. Such designs are well understood and can be designed analyzed using software packages such as the control toolbox in MATLAB.

The system under the control of this reliable controller is $X' = A X$, where $A = (A^* + B K)$, where the stability condition is represented by $A^T Q + Q A < 0$, and Q is the Lyapunov function. The operational constraints are represented by a normalized polytope, $C^T X \leq 1$. The largest ellipsoid inside the polytope can be found by minimizing $(log\ det\ Q^{-1})$ [10], subject to stability condition. The resulting Q defines the largest normalized ellipsoid $X^T Q X = 1$ inside the polytope (See Figure 2).

2.3 Experimental Data

[3] The software package that we used to find the largest ellipsoid was developed by Steven Boyd's group at Stanford.

The use of recovery region can be illustrated by the fault tolerant upgrade of the software controlling an inverted pendulum, which can be moved from one end to the other on a 6 feet long track, as illustrated in Figure 3. The controller must keep the rod from falling down in addition to move the cart to commanded positions. We are interested in the dependable upgrade of the high performance controller. There are three controllers: the reliably controller as discussed before, a baseline high performance controller and a new experimental controller. The baseline controller can move the inverted pendulum reasonably fast while keeping the rod in upright position. However, we would like to try a new type of control designs that is supposed to be able to move the inverted pendulum much faster. So we will begin the following experiment. We start the system under the control of the baseline controller and then pass the control to the new experimental controller. Both the baseline controller and the reliable controller are running in parallel but their outputs are not used until we need them. Figure 4 is a sample of the experimental data logged in the laboratory. In Figure 4, the horizontal axis represents time. The vertical axis represents how far away the system state is from the center of recovery region. Suppose that the system is under the control of the new experimental controller. Each period it generates an output U_new(k+1) to be used at the beginning of next period. If this output U_new(k+1) will cause the system state to go outside of the bound of the ellipsoid, we will switch to the reliable controller. This check is done by checking if $X^T Q X < 1$, where X would be the system state if we were to use U_new(K+1).

We now review sample data for one of the experiments. At time t ~ 4.3 sec, the control experiment is initialized. Next, the output of the experimental controller is used. The system under the control of the experimental controller stays well within the recovery region until t ~ 11.2 second. At that moment, a bug was triggered and generates an output which, if used, will put the system state outside of the recovery region, indicated by a spike that exceeds 1. The decision rule therefore uses the output from the reliable controller in stead. At time t ~ 13.4 second, the system passes the control to the baseline controller, which moves the inverted pendulum to the command position.

Finally, we provide a physical interpretation of the data that gives a more intuitive understanding of the experiment. The inverted pendulum has a four dimensional state vector, (angle, angle velocity, track and track velocity). The ellipsoid that represents the recovery region uses the coordination system that is mounted on the center of the cart as illustrated in Figure 3. This means that the responsibility of the reliable controller is to put the inverted pendulum to the state of (0, 0, 0, 0). That is, to keep the rod stop moving at upright position and the cart stop moving at the track position at which the reliable controller was invoked. From time t ~ 4.3 to 11.2 second, we can see that $X^T Q X$ values form a relatively large wave patter. This is due to the rod shaking back and forth modestly while it is being moved to the commanded position. But it is well within the recovery region. At time ~ 11.2, the large spike of $X^T Q X$ value means that if the U_new(k+1) will put the rod in a state of large angle and large angular velocity, which cannot be recovered by the reliable controller. The small $X^T Q X$ value after the reliable controller in control means that the rod is steadily balanced at the position at which the reliable controller has taken over. The small $X^T Q X$ "waves" after the baseline controller taking over means that the rod is shaking very little when the cart

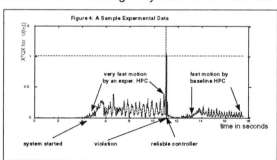

is moved from current position to the commanded position.

Readers may ask the question that how difficult is the computation of the Lyapunov function and can it be scaled up for complex real world applications? The computation of the recovery requires itself is straightforward application of a software package. However, the package requires the system model and the reliable control. In vehicular control applications such as flight control applications, the aircraft model often already exists due to the need of simulation and design modification. However, the reliable controller needs to be designed.

To apply this approach to large systems with many control loops, we can create a hierarchy of recovery regions at different levels of abstraction. For example, in an aircraft auto-landing application, the auto-landing recovery region concerns only about the states of aircraft dynamics as it approaches the run-way: will the experimental auto-landing controller put the aircraft in states, in which the aircraft cannot be safely landed by the pilot or by the existing auto-landing controller?[4] Recovery regions for higher and lower level subsystems can be developed accordingly.

3.0 Timing Considerations

In the previous sections, we assume that decision rule can know the system state instantaneously and accurately. In reality, there are noises in sensor readings and the use of low pass filters to reduce noise introduces delays in plant state information. Fortunately, the worst case phase delay introduced by a low pass filter can be easily computed from the filter design and the given bandwidth of the plant dynamics.

In addition to filtering delays, there are real time scheduling delays as illustrated in Figure 5. Since the sensor noises usually have much high frequency than the bandwidth of motions, it is often the case that the scheduling delay is larger than the low pass filter delays.[5] Suppose that the plant is under the control of a new (experimental) high performance controller. During a time interval (k, (k+1)), the decision rule needs to determine if the system under the control of the new controller will stay within the recovery region illustrated in Figure 2. During this interval, the output by the new controller at time k, U_new(k), has already been sent to the plant. The output selected by the decision rule will be sent to the plant at time (k+1). As a result, the effect of the decision at interval (k, (k+1)) can only be seen at the system state sampled at time k + 2, X(k+2).

---

[4] CMU and Lockheed Martin have been sponsored by DARPA and the Air Force Research Laboratory to investigate the application and generalization of Simplex architecture for reliable flight control software upgrades.

[5] If the bandwidths of noise and motion overlap each other, Kalman filter may be called for. Kalman filter does not generate delays but it is computationally intensive.

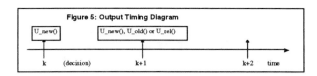

Figure 5: Output Timing Diagram

To select the correct control, the plant state read at time k, X(k), is projected forward in time to estimate the plant state X(k+1). The projection computation uses the plant model, control U_new(k) for the duration which is the sum of the filtering delay and one sampling period. Next, the plant state projected forward in time one period again to estimate X(k+2), using the plant model, U_new(k+1) and X(k+1). If U_new(k+1) will cause plant state X(k+2) to go outside of the recovery region, the decision rule will use reliable controller's output, U_rel(k+1), instead, until the plant reaches a state that can be controlled by the baseline controller.

Readers might asked the question: what if at time k, U_new(k) has already cause the plant's state at time (k+1) to be outside of the recovery region and hence the system may no longer be recoverable. In this case there is nothing can be done by the decision rule during the interval (k, (k+1)). Fortunately, this cannot happen if the plant is initialized correctly. Suppose that X(0) is inside the recovery region and the control U(0) is correct. It follows that X(1) will be within the recovery region. During the time interval (0, 1), we may use the new controller's output U_new(1) if the estimated plant state X(2) is within the recovery region. The next decision point is in the interval (1, 2). U_new(2) will be considered only if U_new(1) causes the system state X(2) to stay within the recovery region. In other words, U_new(k+1) will be considered at all only if U_new(k) causes X(k+1) to stay within the recovery region. Otherwise, U_new(k) would already be rejected during interval ((k-1), k). Thus, as long as the system is initialized correctly, our decision rule will keep the system to stay within the recovery region.

So far, we implicitly assume that the estimated system state is always correctly. In real life, there is always errors in the estimated plant state. To compensate for estimation error, we need to use a smaller practical recovery region within the theoretical recovery region computed under the perfect state information assumption. The shortest distance between the two regions' boundaries is the margin for estimation errors.

As a rule, the estimation errors grow larger as the duration for projection grows longer. This can be modeled as, e.g., $t\sigma^2$, a commonly used time series model to account for the effect of the time in predicting future states of the system; where σ^2 represents the intrinsic error in the state estimation and t represents the duration of projection. Recall that t equals to two sample periods plus the filtering delay. Thus, even if a slower sampling rate is allowed by the design of the controller, it will still increase the state estimation error, $t\sigma^2$. The same can be said about the effect of filtering delay. The increase in the state estimation errors will, in turn, force us to increase the estimation error margins and thus result in a reduction of the size of the practical recovery region. On the other hand, a slower sampling rate improves system schedulability. Thus, if the normal system operation is far away from the boundary of operation constraints and if the reduction of control performance is modest, slowing down the sampling rate to improve the system schedulability is a wise choice. In a more complex situation, we need to define the penalty functions for the reduction of recovery region sizes and the reduction of control performance as functions of sampling rates. This would allow us to optimize the overall system schedulability and performance. The detail analysis of this system optimization is, however, beyond the scope of this paper and will be reported in a different paper. What we want to emphasize in this paper is that schedulability analysis, filter design, controller design and the recoverable region design are intimately related. It is a good idea to integrate the controller and scheduler design into unified system design methodology.

4.0 Software Architecture

We now review the software architecture known as the Simplex architecture. An adage of architecture is that *form follows function*. The fundamental construction in the Simplex architecture is an *analytically redundant unit* (ARU) that is designed to support the use of analytically redundant controllers (Figure 6). Within an ARU, the replacement unit construction and the replacement transaction facility supports online upgrade of controllers.

4.1 An Analytically Redundant Unit

Each ARU implements a major subsystem, for example, an auto-pilot or an engine controller. The software implementing the reliable controller and switching rule will be referred to as the high assurance component. Its development should follow an appropriate high assurance software development procedure, because it directly impacts the system reliability on critical control functions[6]. The high performance component may contain one or more high performance controllers, typically one is the existing baseline high performance controller and the other is an experimental new high performance controller to be tested in the plant. In addition, there is an optional performance monitoring and data logging component.

The software architecture must ensure that the less reliable high performance control software cannot interfere with the execution of the high assurance application kernel. Currently, in safety critical applications, the only practical solution is to run the reliable controller on a separate fault tolerant hardware with certified runtime. In non-safety critical real time control applications, these two types of software can reside on the same computer and be separated by address spaces and timing firewalls using, for example, sporadic servers[3, 4].

Figure 6 also indicates that the reliable controller and the high performance controllers can use different sets of input sensors. Indeed, analytically controllers need not be alternative computations to the same set of inputs as required by both recovery blocks[9] and N-version programming[11]. The reliable controller and the high performance controllers are executing in parallel, generating three candidate control outputs, U_rel(), U_new() and U_bas() for the decision to choose.

---

[6] In safety critical applications, DO 178B for flight software is a practical development and certification procedure. This standard also covers the certification of the runtime together with the application.

Figure 7 illustrates the selection of controllers within an analytically redundant unit. The vertical axis represents control performance levels while the horizontal axis represents time. At time t_0, the system starts with the baseline controller. At time t_1, under operator command, the system is switched to an upgraded new high performance control online. Unfortunately, this new controller has bugs and the system is switched to reliable controller at time t_2. As the system is stabilized by the reliable controller, the system control is automatically switched back to the baseline controller at time t_3. In the mean time, engineers can debug the new controller, recompile it and then ask the operator to try the fixed new controller again at time t_4. Once the new experimental controller is sufficiently tested, it can be considered as the baseline controller and the old baseline controller is deleted to reduce the workload on the system. It is important to note that testing cannot and need not be exhaustive. Under Simplex architecture, a high performance controller with a reasonable mean time to failure is acceptable, since it can be restarted while the system is under the control of the reliable controller.

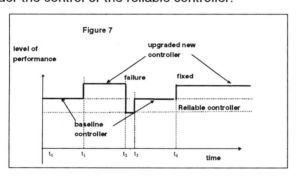

4.2 Dynamic Component Binding

The upgrade of the high performance controller described in the previous section can be done without shutting the system operations. The following provides an overview of the dynamic component binding service provided by Simplex architecture as illustrated in Figure 8.

Real time scheduling service: In simplex architecture, all the real time computation and real time communication is explicitly scheduled by GRMS[3,4], which provides a simple analytic solutions to many practical real time scheduling problems including: scheduling periodic and aperiodic tasks, task synchronization, transient overloads, bus and network scheduling.

Real time group communication service: the Simplex architecture middleware provides a real time publication and subscription service to application software modules[6]. This service is a real time service similar to the group communication facility found in [7]. It decouples data producers and data consumers. Data producers will "publish" data at the service while applications that need the data will "subscribe" the data at the service. This way, we can change the data publisher transparently with respect to data subscribers. For example, we can change the controller software transparently from the viewpoint of the D/A converter at the actuator.

Replacement units: replacement units are virtual or physical computers that are used to encapsulate a set of computation activities. Within a computer, it is typically implemented as a real time process together with a standardized communication interface. The communications

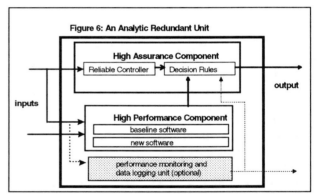

Figure 6: An Analytic Redundant Unit

are carried out via the real time publication and subscription service. Replacement units can be added, deleted or replaced during runtime. A detailed review on the implementation of replacement units can be found in [8].

Replacement transaction facility: The fundamental operation provided by the Simplex Architecture for replacement unit management is the replacement transaction. During this replacement transaction, state information (e.g. those relating to controllers or filters) may need to be transferred from the *old unit* to the *new unit*. Alternatively, the *new unit* may capture the dynamic state information of physical systems through plant input data. Without state information, there may be undesirable transients in the behavior of the new replacement unit when it comes online. Hence, the replacement transaction of a single replacement unit is carried out in stages:

1. A *new unit* is created and its communication channels are connected using the lowest background priority. Once the creation is completed, its priority will be raised to what is assigned by GRMS.
2. Plant input data and other state information, if any, are provided to the *new unit*. The *new unit* begins computations. The output of the unit is monitored but not used.
3. The replacement transaction waits for the output of the *new unit* converges to a user provide criteria. Once the convergence is reached. The output of the old unit is turned off and the new unit is turned on. Alternatively, one can use application provided procedures to smooth out the transition from an old controller to a new controller.

A two-phase protocol is used when multiple replacement units are to be replaced simultaneously. The first phase is to wait for all *the new units* to reach a steady state (step 3 above). The second phase is a distributed action that simultaneously switches on all the *new units* and switches off all the (old) *baseline units*. The granularity of "simultaneity" is models as to finish the work within a single sample period. The replacement transaction must finish with a prescribed duration or it will be aborted.

When a replacement unit needs to be deleted, we first set its priority to the lowest background level. We then disconnect its communication channels and destroy the process used by the replacement unit at background priority. We use low background priority to create or destroy replacement unit, because they are time consuming operations and we don't want to interfere with the real time loops.

5.0 Summary

The downtime of a large industrial operation is often prohibitively expensive and a failure could have disastrous consequences. Lacking an effective approach to mitigate the risks associated with inserting new control and computing technologies into deployed systems, many real time control systems are forced to keep outdated technologies.

A paradigm shift is needed, from a focus on enabling technologies for completely new installations to one which is designed to mitigate the risk and cost of bringing new technology into functioning systems. Industry needs a new computing infrastructure in which upgrades will

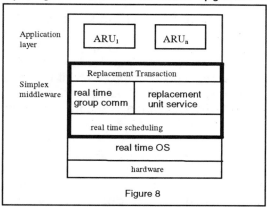

Figure 8

be easy and reliable, with negligible down-time.

The notion of upgrading real time control software without shutting down the normal operations and in spite of the errors that can be introduced by the upgrades is an attractive one. Giving that the real time control software architecture is dominated by static architectures, the feasibility of a fault tolerant and dynamically upgradable software architecture needs to be convincingly demonstrated.

As a result, we have made a serious effort in the development of interactive demonstrations in the past few years. The first implementation of Simplex architecture was on an inverted pendulum[7]. The next demonstration was on CMU's Semi-conductor wafer making facility[8]. The third demonstration was a submarine diving control prototype[9]. The fourth demonstration prototype is a system survivability demonstration which uses two inverted pendulum that carries a rod on their tips. Thus their motions must be coordinated via communications across a network that is open to attacks.[10] Recently, together with

[7] This work was sponsored by the ONR and it has laid the foundation of the Simplex architecture.
[8] This work was done as a CMU graduate student project.
[9] This work was sponsored by the ONR and the New Attack Submarine Program Office, NAVSEA PMS-450.
[10] This work was sponsored by the ONR and it has laid the foundation of using analytic redundancy for system survivability applications.

Lockheed Martin, we have successful demonstrated of the dependable upgrade of the F16 auto-pilot on Lockheed Martin's flight simulator[11], exhibited by the Air Force at the April 1998 Software Technology Conference at Salt Lake City.

Based on the results we have so far, we believe that, dynamic real time fault tolerant architecture is not only desirable but also feasible. In this paper, we have reviewed some of the fundamental concepts of Simplex architectures and will soon report specific findings and lesson learned in the experimental and theoretical investigations we have done so far.

ACKNOWLEDGMENTS

This work described here has been sponsored in part by ONR, by NAVSEA PMS-450, by JSF program office, by DARPA EDCS program and by AFRL.

Since the author conceived the Simplex architecture in 1992, many have contributed to its development. I want to thank Michael Gagliardi, Ted Marz, Ragunathan Rajkumar, Peter Feiler, Neal Altman, John Walker and Jonathan Preston for their contributions to the system design, development and demonstrations and to thank Danbing Seto, Mark Klein, John Lehoczky and Bruce Krogh for their contributions to the theoretical aspects of our studies. Our thinking in system recoverability is also shaped by the excellent work of Karl Astrom's group, especially Anders Rantzer and Mikael Johanssonon on the use of LMI for the maximal recovery region problem. Finally, I want to thank Ben Calloni for his helpful comments and suggestions.

REFERENCES

[1] Sha, L., Rajkumar, R., and Gagliardi, M., *Evolving Dependable Real Time Systems*, the proceedings of IEEE Aerospace Conference, 1996..

[2] Gray, J, *A Census of Tandem System Availability Between 1985 and 1990*, IEEE Transaction on Reliability, Oct. 1990.

[3] Sha, L., Rajkumar, R., and Sathaye, S., *Generalized Rate Monotonic Scheduling Theory: A Framework of Developing Real-time Systems,* IEEE Proceedings, Jan., 1994.

[4] Klein, M., Ralya, T. Pollak, B., Obenza, R. and Harbour, M. G. *A Practitioner's Handbook for Real-time Analysis,* Kluwer Academic Publishers, 1993

[5] Franklin, G. F., Powell, J. D., Emani-Naeini, A. E., Feedback Control of Dynamic Systems, Addison Welsley, 1991.

[6] Rajkumar, R., Gagliardi, M. and Sha, L., *The Real-time Publisher/Subscriber IPC Model for Distributed Real-time Systems: Design and Implementation,* The proceedings of the 1st IEEE Real-time Technology and Applications Symposium, May 1995.

[7] Birman, K. P., *The Process Group Approach to Reliable Distributed Computing*, TR-91-1216, CS Department, Cornell University.

[8] Gagliardi, M., Rajkumar, R., Sha, L.*, Designing for Evolvability: Building Blocks for Evolvable Real-Time Systems*, Real-Time Applications Symposium, 1996.

[9] B. Randell. System structure for software fault tolerance. IEEE Transactions on Software Engineering, 1(2):220--232, June 1975.

[10] Boyd, S., Ghaoul, L. E., Feron, E., and Balakrishnan, V., Linear Matrix Inequality in Systems and Control Theory, SIAM Studies in Applied Mathematics, p.p. 70.

[11] Algirdas Avizienis: The N-Version Approach to Fault-Tolerant Software. TSE 11(12): 1491-1501 (1985)

[12] Seto, D., Krogh, B. H., Sha, L., and Chutinan, Dynamic Control System Upgrade Using Simplex Architecture, IEEE Control, August, 1998.

---

[11] This work is carried out jointly by CMU and Lockheed Martin under the INSERT program sponsored by DARPA and AFRL.

Session 12.B: Communications and Networks

Statistical Delay Guarantee of Virtual Clock

Pawan Goyal
goyal@research.att.com
Networking and Distributed Systems Center
AT&T Labs - Research
180 Park Avenue, Florham Park, NJ 07932

Harrick M. Vin
vin@cs.utexas.edu
Department of Computer Sciences
University of Texas at Austin
Taylor Hall 2.124, Austin, TX 78712

Abstract

In this paper, we derive a statistical delay guarantee of the generalized Virtual Clock scheduling algorithm. We define the concept of an equivalent fluid and packet source and prove a theorem that relates the departure time of a packet in a fluid FCFS multiplexor to its departure time in a packet multiplexor that uses generalized Virtual Clock algorithm for scheduling packets. This theorem enables us to use extant analyses of fluid FCFS multiplexors for providing statistical QoS guarantees in a network that employs the generalized Virtual Clock algorithm. We utilize the extant analysis of FCFS fluid multiplexors serving two-state on-off sources with exponentially distributed on and off durations to evaluate the increase in utilization yielded by our analysis technique. Our experiments demonstrate that for one of the source models employed in the literature, our technique can increase utilization by upto 400% compared to previously know statistical analysis methods.

1 Introduction

Integrated services networks are required to support a variety of applications (e.g., audio and video conferencing, multimedia information retrieval, ftp, telnet, WWW, etc.) with a wide range of Quality of Service (QoS) requirements. Whereas continuous media applications such as audio and video conferencing require a network to provide QoS guarantees with respect to bandwidth, packet delay, and loss; applications such as telnet and WWW require low packet delay and loss. Throughput intensive applications like ftp, on the other hand, require network resources to be allocated such that the throughput is maximized. A network meets these requirements primarily by appropriately *scheduling* its resources.

To appropriately schedule network bandwidth, several packet scheduling algorithms have been proposed in the literature [3, 4, 5, 7, 9, 11, 13, 14, 15, 21]. Furthermore,

to enable the network to provide bounds on end-to-end delay as well as throughput guarantees to various flows, several analyses of these algorithms have been carried out [6, 8, 10, 13]. These techniques enable a network to provide deterministic bounds on QoS. Though these techniques are appropriate when the packet sources can be well characterized deterministically, they lead to underutilization of resources when the sources have significant statistical variations [12]. Analysis techniques for packet scheduling algorithms that enable a network to provide statistical guarantees and, thus, achieve higher utilization of resources have largely remained unexplored [1].

In this paper, we take a step towards addressing this problem by deriving a statistical delay guarantee of the generalized Virtual Clock scheduling algorithm [10]. We first model the sources as fluid processes and analyze the queuing behaviour of a FCFS fluid multiplexor. We then define the concept of an *equivalent* fluid and packet source and prove a theorem that relates the departure time of a packet in a fluid FCFS multiplexor to its departure time in a packet multiplexor that uses generalized Virtual Clock algorithm for scheduling packets. This theorem enables us to use extant analyses of fluid FCFS multiplexors for providing statistical QoS guarantees in a network that employs the generalized Virtual Clock algorithm. We utilize the analysis of FCFS fluid multiplexors serving two-state on-off sources with exponentially distributed on and off durations presented in [2] to evaluate the increase in utilization yielded by our analysis technique. Our experiments demonstrate that for one of the source models employed in the literature, our technique can increase utilization by upto 400% compared to previously know statistical analysis methods.

The rest of the paper is organized as follows. In Section 2, we derive the statistical delay guarantee of generalized Virtual Clock algorithm. We present the results of our experiments and related work in Sections 3 and 4, respectively. Finally, Section 5 summarizes the results of this paper.

2 Analysis of Generalized Virtual Clock

Several data and continuous media sources such as audio and video have an intrinsic rate of traffic generation that varies over time. Hence, they can be modeled as fluid processes generating fluid at time varying rates. Let the rate of fluid generation for source f at time t be $\widehat{R}_f(t)$. To determine delay and loss incurred by the fluid sources, consider a multiplexor serving Q sources. Let the scheduling algorithm at the multiplexor be FCFS and the stochastic behaviour of the Q sources be such that the queue length at the multiplexor at any time t, denoted by $\widehat{W}(t)$, is given as:

$$P\left(\widehat{W}(t) > \gamma\right) \leq G(\gamma)$$

Let us assume that function $G(\gamma)$ can be determined from the statistical characterization of the fluid sources. Hence, the delay and loss behaviour of the fluid sources is known. Since in computer networks sources transmit data as packets, our objective is to use function $G(\gamma)$ to determine QoS guarantees in an *equivalent* packet system. Clearly, this can be achieved only if appropriate packet scheduling algorithm is employed by the packet multiplexor. We choose generalized Virtual Clock (VC) as the packet scheduling algorithm. To achieve our objective, we:

- Define the concept of equivalent fluid and packet arrival processes (Section 2.1),

- Relate the departure time of a packet in the multiplexor employing the VC scheduling algorithm to the departure time of the last bit of the packet in the FCFS fluid multiplexor when the arrival processes at the packet and fluid multiplexors are equivalent (Section 2.2), and

- Derive the QoS guarantees for sources in a generalized VC multiplexor using the relationship between the fluid and packet system (Section 2.3).

In the following sections, we will use the following terminology. We will refer to the sequence of packets transmitted by a source to a destination as a flow. A flow is served by a sequence of packet switches (routers). We will refer to the output port of a switch as a server. The jth packet of a flow and its arrival time will be denoted by p_f^j and $A(p_f^j)$, respectively.

2.1 Equivalent Fluid and Packet Processes

Consider a fluid source f generating fluid at rate $\widehat{R}_f(t)$. Then, a packet source can be considered equivalent to a fluid source if it generates a packet *exactly* at the time at which the first bit of the packet would be generated in the fluid

source. This notion of equivalence is strong. Instead, we consider a packet source to be equivalent to the fluid source if it generates a packet *no later than* the time at which the first bit of the packet would be generated in the fluid source.

To formalize this notion of equivalence, we define a rate function for flow f, denoted by $R_f(t)$, based on *expected arrival time* of packets. The expected arrival time of a packet is the time at which the first bit of the packet would be generated in the fluid system. To formally define it, let r_f^j be the rate at which p_f^j is generated. Then, the expected arrival time of p_f^j, denoted by $EAT(p_f^j, r_f^j)$, is defined as:

$$EAT(p_f^j, r_f^j) = \max\left\{A(p_f^j), EAT(p_f^{j-1}, r_f^{j-1}) + \frac{l_f^{j-1}}{r_f^{j-1}}\right\}$$

where $EAT(p_f^0, r_f^0) + \frac{l_f^0}{r_f^0} = 0$. We define $R_f(t)$ to be the rate at which p_f^j is generated in the time interval between its expected arrival time and the time at which its last bit would be generated in a fluid flow system. In a fluid flow system, if the first bit of p_f^j is generated at time $EAT(p_f^j, r_f^j)$, its last bit would be generated at time $EAT(p_f^j, r_f^j) + \frac{l_f^j}{r_f^j}$. Hence, $R_f(t)$ is formally defined as:

$$R_f(t) = \begin{cases} r_f^j & \text{if } \exists j \ni \left(EAT(p_f^j, r_f^j) < t \right. \\ & \left. \leq EAT(p_f^j, r_f^j) + \frac{l_f^j}{r_f^j}\right) \\ 0 & \text{otherwise} \end{cases}$$

We define a packet source and fluid source to be equivalent if $\widehat{R}_f(t) = R_f(t)$. Observe that $R_f(t)$ changes only at discrete time instants and does not vary during interval $[EAT(p_f^j, r_f^j), EAT(p_f^j, r_f^j) + \frac{l_f^j}{r_f^j}]$. Hence, $\widehat{R}_f(t) = R_f(t)$ only if fluid source changes rates at discrete time instants. We assume that this assumption is satisfied by the fluid source.

An important aspect of this notion of equivalence is that it only requires a packet of a flow to arrive no later than the time its first bit is generated in the fluid source; a packet may actually arrive much earlier than that. Thus, there are infinitely many packet arrival processes that would be considered equivalent to a fluid process. To illustrate this, consider an example fluid source that has rate $0.5pkt/s$ in $(1, 5]$, $1pkt/s$ in $(5, 7]$, and 0 elsewhere. Then, a packet source would be equivalent to the fluid source as long as packets 1,2,3, and 4 arrive by time 1,3,5, and 6, respectively. Figure 1 illustrates two packet arrival sequences that satisfy this assumption and thus are equivalent to the fluid source.

We now use this concept of equivalence to derive a new delay guarantee of generalized Virtual Clock algorithm.

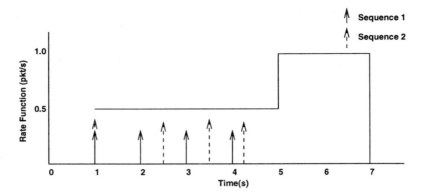

Figure 1. Equivalence of Fluid and Packet Sources

2.2 Delay Guarantee of Generalized Virtual Clock

The generalized Virtual Clock (VC) scheduling algorithm, defined in [10], is a generalization of Virtual Clock presented in [22]. This generalization is based on the observation that since several continuous media and data sources generate data at time varying rates, a scheduling algorithm should be able to allocate variable rate to the packets of a flow. Specifically, it is defined as follows:

1. On arrival, packet p_f^j is stamped with virtual clock value, denoted by $VC(p_f^j, r_f^j)$, computed as:

$$VC(p_f^j, r_f^j) = EAT(p_f^j, r_f^j) + \frac{l_f^j}{r_f^j}$$

where r_f^j is the rate assigned to p_f^j.

2. Packets are serviced in the increasing order of the virtual clock values.

Consider a VC server serving Q flows. It was shown in [10] that if C is the capacity of the server and $\sum_{n \in Q} R_n(t) \leq C$ for all t, then the VC server guarantees that the departure time of a packet, denoted by $L_{VC}(p_f^j)$, is given as:

$$L_{VC}(p_f^j) \leq VC(p_f^j, r_f^j) + \frac{l_{max}}{C} \qquad (1)$$

where l_{max} is the maximum packet length served by a server. Our concept of *equivalence* between fluid and packet sources allows another interpretation of this guarantee. Let the rate assigned to a packet be the rate at which it is generated in the fluid system. Observe that when $\sum_{n \in Q} R_n(t) \leq C$ then buffer does not build up in a FCFS fluid server serving the *equivalent* Q fluid flows. Hence, the last bit of a packet departs at the time at which it arrives. Let $\widehat{L}(p_n^j)$ denote the time at which the last bit of

packet p_f^j departs in the fluid FCFS server. Then, since the last bit of packet is generated at time $VC(p_f^j, r_f^j) = EAT(p_f^j, r_f^j) + \frac{l_f^j}{r_f^j}$, we conclude that:

$$L_{VC}(p_f^j) \leq \widehat{L}(p_f^j) + \frac{l_{max}}{C}$$

Hence, the departure time of a packet in a VC server is at most $\frac{l_{max}}{C}$ more than its departure time (i.e., the departure time of the last bit) in the FCFS fluid server serving equivalent fluid flows.

The above delay guarantee of a VC server and the relationship between the departure time of a packet in a VC server and equivalent FCFS fluid server holds only when $\sum_{n \in Q} R_n(t) \leq C$ for all t. When flows have significant statistical variations in their rate, i.e., $R_n(t)$ varies significantly over time, then ensuring that $\sum_{n \in Q} R_n(t) \leq C$ may lead to significant underutilization of resources. To achieve higher utilization of resources, it is desirable to derive the delay guarantee of a VC server when $\sum_{n \in Q} R_n(t) > C$. We achieve this objective in Theorem 1 by relating the departure time of packet in a VC server to its departure time in a FCFS fluid flow server serving equivalent fluid flows *without* putting any constraints on the rate functions.

In what follows, we will use the following terminology. We will consider the arrival and departure time of a packet in the fluid server to be the arrival and departure time of its first and last bit, respectively.

Theorem 1 *If the flows served by a VC server and a FCFS fluid server are equivalent, then the departure time of packet p_f^j in a VC server is given as:*

$$L_{VC}(p_f^j) \leq \widehat{L}(p_f^j) + \frac{l_{max}}{C}$$

Proof: Let $W(t_1, t_2)$ and $\widehat{W}(t_1, t_2)$ denote the work done by the VC server and FCFS fluid server, respectively, in

$[t_1, t_2]$. Also, let $T(w)$ be the time taken to complete work w. Now, consider packet p_f^j. Define t_0, t_1, and t_2 as follows (see Figure 2):

- $t_2 = L_{VC}(p_f^j)$.

- t_0 and t_1: Let t_0 be the largest time instant less than t_2 in the busy period of the VC server in which p_f^j is served at which a packet with Virtual Clock value greater than that of p_f^j is scheduled. Let t_1 be the time at which such a packet finishes service. If such a packet does not exist, set t_0 and t_1 to the beginning of the busy period of the VC server.

Observe that packet p_f^j arrives only after t_0 in the VC server. This can be observed by considering two cases:

- t_0 is the beginning of the busy period: In this case it is trivially true.

- t_0 is not the beginning of the busy period: From the definition of t_0 we know that a packet with virtual clock value greater than that of p_f^j was scheduled at t_0. Since a VC server schedules packets in increasing order of virtual clock values, we conclude that p_f^j could not have arrived by t_0.

Hence, p_f^j arrives only after t_0 in the VC server. Since the fluid and packet arrival processes are equivalent and a packet can arrive only earlier in the packet system, we conclude that p_f^j can arrive only after t_0 in the fluid system. Hence, $t_0 < \widehat{L}(p_f^j)$. Therefore, we get:

$$t_0 + T(\widehat{W}(t_0^+, \widehat{L}(p_f^j))) \le \widehat{L}(p_f^j)$$

Since $T(w) \ge \frac{w}{C}$, we get:

$$t_0 + \frac{\widehat{W}(t_0^+, \widehat{L}(p_f^j)))}{C} \le \widehat{L}(p_f^j) \qquad (2)$$

To determine the relationship between $\widehat{L}(p_f^j)$ and $L_{VC}(p_f^j)$, our objective now is to relate $\widehat{W}(t_0^+, \widehat{L}(p_f^j))$ to variables in the VC server. To do so, we relate $\widehat{W}(t_0^+, \widehat{L}(p_f^j)))$ to $W(t_1, t_2)$. Observe that:

- *Packets served by the VC server in $[t_1, t_2]$ are served by the fluid server after t_0*: First, observe that packets served in $[t_1, t_2]$ arrive only after t_0 in the VC server. Consider two cases:

  - t_0 is the beginning of the busy period: The claim holds trivially in this case.

  - t_0 is not the beginning of the busy period: In this case, from the definition of t_0 we know that a packet with virtual clock value greater than

the virtual clock values of the packets served in $[t_1, t_2]$ was scheduled at t_0. Since a VC server serves packets in increasing order of virtual clock values, the packets served in $[t_1, t_2]$ could not have arrived by t_0.

Hence, packets served in $[t_1, t_2]$ in the VC server arrive only after t_0 in the VC server. Since fluid and packet processes are equivalent, a packet can arrive only earlier in a VC server than in the fluid system. Hence, we conclude that the packets served by the VC server in $[t_1, t_2]$ arrive only after t_0 in the fluid server also and are consequently served after t_0.

- *Packets served by the VC server in $[t_1, t_2]$ are served by the fluid server by $\widehat{L}(p_f^j)$*: In the fluid arrival process, the last bit of a packet is generated at time equal to the Virtual Clock value of the packet. Since the fluid multiplexor is FCFS, we conclude that the packets depart the fluid server in the order of their Virtual Clock values (packets with equal virtual clock values depart simultaneously). Hence, all packets with Virtual Clock value less than or equal to that of p_f^j will be served in the fluid server by $\widehat{L}(p_f^j)$. Since all the packets served in time interval $[t_1, t_2]$ by VC server have virtual clock value less than or equal to that of p_f^j, we conclude that they will be served by the fluid server by $\widehat{L}(p_f^j)$.

Thus, we conclude that the packets served by the VC server in $[t_1, t_2]$ will be served by the fluid server in $[t_0^+, \widehat{L}(p_f^j)]$. Therefore, we get:

$$W(t_1, t_2) \le \widehat{W}(t_0^+, \widehat{L}(p_f^j)) \qquad (3)$$

Using (3) to substitute in (2), we get:

$$t_0 + \frac{W(t_1, t_2)}{C} \le \widehat{L}(p_f^j)$$

Since the VC server is busy in $[t_1, t_2]$, $W(t_1, t_2) = (t_2 - t_1)C$. Hence,

$$t_0 + \frac{(t_2 - t_1)C}{C} \le \widehat{L}(p_f^j)$$

$$t_2 \le \widehat{L}(p_f^j) + (t_1 - t_0)$$

Since $t_2 = L_{VC}(p_f^j)$ and $t_1 - t_0 \le \frac{l_{max}}{C}$, we get:

$$L_{VC}(p_f^j) \le \widehat{L}(p_f^j) + \frac{l_{max}}{C}$$

∎

Note that we have made no assumptions about the rate functions in Theorem 1. The Theorem yields (1) when

453

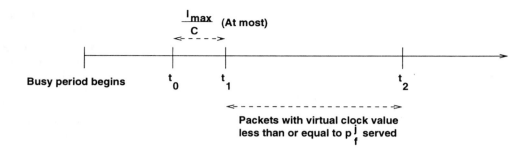

Figure 2. Timeline in the Virtual Clock server

$\sum_{n \in Q} R_n(t) \leq C$ but continues to hold even when $\sum_{n \in Q} R_n(t) > C$. Thus, it subsumes the previous theorems on Virtual Clock. Furthermore, to the best of our knowledge, this is the only result that relates the departure time of a packet in a fluid FCFS server to that in a packet server.

The relationship between the fluid analysis and the packet analysis only requires $R_n(t) = \widehat{R}_n(t)$. As we had observed earlier, there are infinitely many packet arrival process that satisfy this assumption. Thus, the relationship between fluid and packet analysis for a Virtual Clock server holds for infinitely many realizations of a fluid process. This weaker notion of equivalence is desirable in packet networks because due to variation in packet processing times as well as granularity of timers at the host operating system, packets may not be generated *exactly* at the time they are required to be. Furthermore, this weaker notion of equivalence provides protection from flows that misbehave either intentionally or due to faulty hardware.

The above theorem can be misinterpreted as being the same as Theorem 1 of [13] that relates the departure time of a packet in a Packet-by-packet Generalized Processor Sharing (PGPS) server to its departure time in a fluid Generalized Processor Sharing (GPS) server. However, there are several important differences. To elucidate the differences, let us briefly review Theorem 1 of [13]. The theorem states that if $L_{PGPS}(p_f^j)$ is the departure time of packet p_f^j in a PGPS server and $L_{GPS}(p_f^j)$ is its departure time in a GPS server under the *same arrival sequence* of packets, then:

$$L_{PGPS}(p_f^j) \leq L_{GPS}(p_f^j) + \frac{l_{max}}{C} \qquad (4)$$

There are two important aspects of (4).

- (4) is derived under the assumption that, in a GPS server, fluid amount equivalent to the length of a packet arrives exactly at the time instant at which the packet arrives in the PGPS server. This is in contrast to our notion of equivalence between fluid and packet sources in which the packet can arrive in the packet system significantly before it starts arriving in the fluid system.

- The fluid server uses the GPS scheduling algorithm. This is in contrast to Theorem 1 where the fluid server is a FCFS server.

We demonstrate the importance of these differences by illustrating through an example that a result which is analogous to (4) does not hold for Virtual Clock. Let $L_{F-VC}(p_f^j)$ be the departure time of a packet in a fluid VC server when fluid equivalent to the length of a packet arrives exactly at the time at which the packet arrives. Then, a claim analogous to (4) would be:

$$L_{VC}(p_f^j) \leq L_{F-VC}(p_f^j) + \frac{l_{max}}{C} \qquad (5)$$

The following example demonstrates that this claim is incorrect.

Example 1 *Consider a server with capacity $3bits/s$. Let it serve three flows each with rate of $1bit/s$. Let the length of packets transmitted by flows 1 and 3 be 1 bit and that by flow 2 be 2 bits. Let flows 1 and 2 send 9 and 7 packets, respectively, at time 0. Let flow 1 send an additional packet at time 7^+, and flow 3 infinite number of packets at time $7\frac{2}{3}$. Now, consider the departure time of p_1^{10} in fluid Virtual Clock and Virtual Clock servers.*

- *Fluid Virtual Clock: The virtual clock values of p_2^7 and p_1^{10} are 14 and 10, respectively. Hence, the fluid Virtual Clock server will service p_1^{10} before p_2^7. Consequently,*

$$L_{F-VC}(p_1^{10}) = 7^+ + \frac{1}{3} \qquad (6)$$

- *Virtual Clock: p_1^{10} can not be scheduled until p_2^7 finishes at time $7\frac{2}{3}$. But at time $7\frac{2}{3}$, packets from flow 3 arrive. The virtual clock values for flow 3 packets are given as:*

$$VC(p_3^k, 1) = 7\frac{2}{3} + k \qquad (7)$$

Hence, we conclude that virtual clock value of packet p_3^2 is less than virtual clock value of p_1^{10}. Consequently, packets p_3^1 and p_3^2 will be served before p_1^{10}

454

is served. Hence, we get:

$$L_{VC}(p_1^{10}) = 7\frac{2}{3} + \frac{2}{3} \tag{8}$$

From (6) and (8) we conclude that (5) does not hold.

The example can be extended to demonstrate that the departure time in the packet system can be arbitrarily away from the departure time in the fluid system. This example also demonstrates that our concept of equivalence between fluid and packet sources is central to the derivation of Theorem 1.

2.3 Determining QoS Guarantees for Flows

Our objective is to determine the QoS guarantees for flows being served by a generalized VC server. As outlined before, we achieve this objective by:

- Using fluid flow analysis of FCFS fluid flow server serving equivalent flows to determine the QoS guarantees for the flows, and

- Utilizing Theorem 1 to determine the QoS guarantees for the generalized VC server.

Consider a FCFS fluid flow server serving flows that are equivalent to the flows in a generalized VC server. Let infinite buffer be available at the fluid server. Furthermore, let the behaviour of flows be such that $P\left(\widehat{W}(t) > \gamma\right) \leq G(\gamma)$. Let us assume that the function $G(\gamma)$ is known. Now, consider an equivalent VC server. Since the VC server will have finite buffer in practice, let it serve only packets for which

$$L_{VC}(p_f^j) \leq VC(p_f^j, r_f^j) + d + \frac{l_{max}}{C} \tag{9}$$

where d depends on the available buffer space, denoted by B, at the server (one possible relationship between d and B is $B = C \cdot d$). Thus, in the VC server packets for which (9) is not satisfied are dropped. Hence, the loss rate for a flow is given by the probability of (9) not being satisfied. Our objective now is to employ the fluid analysis and Theorem 1 to determine the loss rate.

Observe that in the fluid server the last bit of a packet is generated at its virtual clock value. Hence, in the fluid server:

$$\widehat{L}(p_f^j) \leq VC(p_f^j, r_f^j) + \frac{\widehat{W}(t_0)}{C} \tag{10}$$

where $t_0 = VC(p_f^j, r_f^j)$. From Theorem 1 we know that

$$L_{VC}(p_f^j) \leq \widehat{L}(p_f^j) + \frac{l_{max}}{C} \tag{11}$$

Using (10) and (11), we get:

$$L_{VC}(p_f^j) \leq VC(p_f^j, r_f^j) + \frac{\widehat{W}(t_0)}{C} + \frac{l_{max}}{C} \tag{12}$$

From (12) and (9), we conclude that if we drop packet p_f^j when it does not satisfy (9), then $\frac{\widehat{W}(t_0)}{C} > d$. Thus, if we assume that all the flows are independent and the state of the queue observed by a flow is the same as the time average of the queue, then the probability of loss of a packet, denoted by q, can be approximated as :

$$q = P\left(\frac{\widehat{W}(t)}{C} > d\right)$$

Since $P\left(\widehat{W}(t) > \gamma\right) \leq G(\gamma)$, we get:

$$q = G(C \cdot d) \tag{13}$$

Thus, given d and $G(\gamma)$, the loss rate for a flow can be determined using (13). Furthermore, a bound on the departure time of packets is determined using (9).

Our objective now is to determine the maximum delay incurred by packets at the VC server using (9). Recall that Theorem 1 and consequently (9) holds for infinitely many arrival processes. To determine the maximum packet delay incurred by packets in the VC server, we need to constrain the packet arrival process. Hence, we assume that the packets arrive at their expected arrival time. Thus,

$$VC(p_f^j, r_f^j) - A(p_f^j) = VC(p_f^j, r_f^j) - EAT(p_f^j, r_f^j) = \frac{l_f^j}{r_f^j} \tag{14}$$

Hence, using (9) and (14), we conclude that delay for packet p_f^j, denoted by d_f^j, is given as:

$$d_f^j \leq \frac{l_f^j}{r_f^j} + d + \frac{l_{max}}{C}$$

Hence, the maximum delay incurred by packets of flow f is $d_f^{max} = \max\{d_f^j\}$ where the maximum is over all packets of the flow. Thus, using the analysis of a fluid FCFS server, we can determine the delay and loss guarantees for a flow in a generalized VC server. Our objective now is to extend this analysis to a network of servers.

We extend the above single server analysis to multiple servers by employing the methodology in [20]. We assume that all the servers in the network employ generalized Virtual Clock as the packet scheduling algorithm. Furthermore, we assume that the mechanisms required for allocating variable rate in a VC server to the packets of a flow (such as the fast reservation protocol in [16]) are available. Finally, we assume that jitter controller as in [20] is employed at each server to reconstruct the traffic pattern of each flow at each server on the path. Let there be K servers on the path of flow f and i^{th} server on the path be server i. Also, let q^i and $d_f^{max,i}$ be the packet loss probability and the maximum packet delay at server i determined using the single server analysis. Then, as shown in [20], the maximum end-to-end delay is $\sum_{i=1}^{i=K} d_f^{max,i}$ and the packet loss probability is $\sum_{i=1}^{i=K} q^i$.

In the next section, we evaluate the increase in utilization yielded by our analysis.

3 Experimental Evaluation

We determine the increase in utilization when a network provides statistical guarantee to on/off sources with exponentially distributed on and off periods. An on/off source is a two state process that is either in an "on" state or in an "off" state. It generates data at a constant rate R in the on state and no data in the off state. The time spent by it in on and off state are exponentially distributed. Thus, if I_{on} and I_{off} denote the average time spent by the source in on and off state, respectively, then the source is completely characterized by the tuple (I_{on}, I_{off}, R). We choose two specific values for the tuple and term the resultant sources EXP1 and EXP2:

- EXP1: For this source, $I_{on} = 312ms$, $I_{off} = 325ms$, and $R = 64Kb/s$. This model has been considered appropriate for audio source [12].

- EXP2: For this source, $I_{on} = 9.76ms$, $I_{off} = 90ms$, and $R = 1Mb/s$. This is one of the source models used in [12] and may be appropriate for some data sources.

In both the models, we assume that only complete packets are generated, i.e., if the source would make a transition to off state before a complete packet can be generated, no packet is generated.

For ease of analysis, we consider networks that only serve either EXP1 or EXP2 sources but not both. Furthermore, we assume that the load on each server on the path of a flow is same, i.e, each server serves same number of flows. In such a case, if d_f^{max} and q are the maximum delay and packet loss probability at a single server, then the maximum end-to-end delay is $K d_f^{max}$ and the packet loss probability is Kq. Thus, we can determine the end-to-end delay and loss probability from the single server analysis.

To determine the loss probability and maximum delay for a flow in a VC server, we require the function $G(\gamma)$ for a FCFS fluid server serving equivalent fluid flows. The steady state distribution of queue length of a FCFS fluid server when all the sources are identical on/off fluid sources with exponentially distributed periods has been derived in

[2]. Thus, function $G(\gamma)$ such that $P(\widehat{W}(t) > \gamma) \leq G(\gamma)$ when $t \to \infty$ is known. As argued in [18], $P(\widehat{W}(t) > \gamma) \leq G(\gamma)$ even when t is finite. Hence, we can determine the delay and loss probability in the fluid FCFS server. Thus, using the analysis presented in Section 2.3 we can use it to determine the delay and loss probability in the VC server.

We now present our evaluation for EXP1 and EXP2 sources when the capacity of each of the servers in the network is $10Mb/s$ and the packet size is 512 bits.

- EXP1: Figures 3(a), 3(b), and 3(c) plot the end-to-end delay versus number of flows for 1, 5, and 10 server paths, respectively, for EXP1 flows. As Figure 3(a) demonstrates, the maximum delay for 269 flows is 13.8 ms when the desired loss probability is 10^{-6} and there is one server on the path. This illustrates that our analysis matches the performance of the measurement based admission control algorithm in [12] which accepts 250 flows on an average. The figures also show that the end-to-end delay increases with increase in the number of servers. For example, the delay increases to 81.9 ms for 269 flows when the number of servers increases to 5.

To validate the analytical predictions, we simulated a VC server serving 269 EXP1 flows for 1000 seconds. In conformance with the predictions, no packet was lost in the simulation.

- EXP2: Figures 4(a), 4(b), and 4(c) plot the end-to-end delay versus number of flows for 1, 5, and 10 server paths, respectively, for EXP2 flows. As Figure 4(a) demonstrates, the maximum delay for 79 flows is 41 ms when the desired loss probability is 10^{-6} and there is one server on the path. This illustrates that our analysis matches the performance of the measurement based admission control algorithm in [12] which accepts 75 flows on an average. Also, the maximum delay incurred by a packet was found to be 42ms through simulations in [12]. Thus, the analytical predictions conform with simulation observations reported in the literature. The figures also show that as in the case of EXP1, the end-to-end delay increases with increase in the number of servers. For example, the delay increases to 221.7 ms for 79 flows when the number of servers increases to 5.

To validate the analytical predictions, we conducted several simulations. In each simulation, a VC server served fixed number of EXP2 flows. Each simulation was conducted for 1000 seconds and packets that violated (9) were dropped. For a given number of flows, the delay term d in (9) was determined from Figure 4(a) for loss probability of 10^{-3}. Figure 5 plots the experimentally observed loss rates averaged

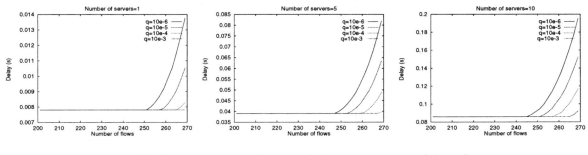

Figure 3. EXP1 source: (a) 1 Server, (b) 5 Servers, and (c) 10 Servers

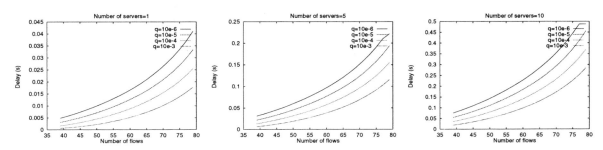

Figure 4. EXP2 source: (a) 1 Server, (b) 5 Servers, and (c) 10 Servers

over all the flows for varying number of flows. Observe that the average loss rate is significantly below 10^{-3}. Furthermore, we found that the loss rate for all the flows was below 10^{-3} (in fact the loss rates for all the flows was significantly below 10^{-3}). Hence, we conclude that the simulations confirm the analytical predictions.

If the network were to provide deterministic guarantees, then at most 160 EXP1 flows ($\frac{10Mbs}{64Kb/s} = 160$) and 10 EXP2 flows ($\frac{10Mbs}{1Mb/s} = 10$) could have been accepted regardless of the maximum acceptable end-to-end delay and the number of servers on the path. In contrast, from Figures 3(b) and 4(b) we conclude that our analysis allows the network to accept 269 EXP1 flows and 79 flows when the number of servers on the path is 5, the desired loss probability is 10^{-6}, and maximum end-to-end delay of 81.9 ms and 221.7 ms is acceptable for EXP1 and EXP2 flows, respectively. This demonstrates that our analysis enables a network to achieve significantly higher utilization when statistical guarantees are acceptable.

4 Related Work

Statistical guarantees of Generalized Processor Sharing (GPS) when the sources have *exponentially bounded burstiness* have been derived in [18, 19, 23]. Our approach is different from the approach taken in [19, 23]. Whereas [19, 23] focus on analyzing the behaviour of a fluid GPS server, we

leverage off existing analysis for FCFS fluid servers and focus on determining the performance guarantees of an equivalent packet system. In contrast to a VC server, extant analysis of fluid FCFS servers can not be employed for PGPS server. Other differences between the guarantees of a PGPS and a VC server have been discussed at length in Section 2.2.

An approach for providing statistical QoS guarantees to flows in a VC server has also been presented in [17]. The approach in [17] employs the *deterministic* delay guarantee of a VC server to provide statistical guarantees as follows. It assumes that packets that cause $\sum_{n \in Q} R_n(t)$ to exceed C are dropped. Hence, the packet loss probability, denoted by q, is approximated as:

$$q = P\left(\sum_{n \in Q} R_n(t) > C\right) \qquad (15)$$

Since in a fluid server with zero buffer loss occurs whenever $\sum_{n \in Q} R_n(t)$ exceeds C, we term this the *Zero Buffer* approach. The loss probability q is determined using the probability distribution of the rate function of each flow. The single server analysis is extended to multiple servers in a manner analogous to ours. The key difference between this and our approach is that whereas in this approach packets that cause $\sum_{n \in Q} R_n(t)$ to exceed C are dropped, we buffer packets that may lead to violation of this condition and drop only packets that violate (9). Thus, our approach utilizes additional buffer in servers and, hence, is termed *Finite Buffer* approach. The advantage of Finite Buffer ap-

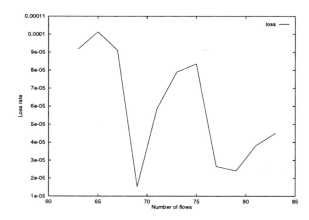

Figure 5. The loss rate for EXP2 sources determined through simulations

proach over Zero Buffer is that it provides additional flexibility to a network and enables it to achieve higher utilization when the maximum acceptable delay for flows is higher than the minimum that can be guaranteed. To demonstrate this, we determine the number of EXP1 and EXP2 flows that can be admitted using the Zero Buffer approach.

The probability distribution of the rate function for EXP1 and EXP2 sources is determined as follows. The probability of being in on state, denoted by p_{on} is $p_{on} = \frac{I_{on}}{I_{on}+I_{off}}$, and being in off state, denoted by p_{off}, is $1 - p_{on}$. Thus, $P(R_f(t) = R) = p_{on}$ and $P(R_f(t) = 0) = p_{off}$. Hence, the distribution of the rate function of the EXP1 and EXP2 sources is known. Thus, the maximum number of EXP1 and EXP2 flows that can be admitted for a given packet loss probability in Zero Buffer approach can be determined using (15) and its extension to the multiple server case. Figures 6(a) and 6(b) plot the number of flows admitted for different number of servers on the path and different end-to-end loss probability for EXP1 and EXP2 sources, respectively. The figures demonstrate that 251 EXP1 and 20 EXP2 flows are admitted when the desired loss probability is 10^{-6} and there is one server on the path. The number of admissible EXP1 and EXP2 flows decreases to 246 and 18, respectively, when the number of servers increases to 5.

Figures 3, 4, and 6 show that the achievable utilization is always higher using the Finite Buffer approach for both EXP1 and EXP2 sources. To observe the increase in utilization, let the number of servers on the path and the desired packet loss probability be 5 and 10^{-6}, respectively. Then the number of admissible EXP1 flows when the delay requirement is 82 ms is 269 and 246 in Finite Buffer and Zero Buffer, respectively. Similarly, the number of admissible EXP2 flows when the delay requirement is 222 ms is 79 and 18 in Finite Buffer and Zero Buffer, respectively. The increase in utilization is higher in EXP2 than in EXP1 as EXP2 source has higher peak to average ratio and, hence, is more bursty. Thus, the additional flexibility provided by our

approach (Finite Buffer) enables a network to achieve significantly higher utilization than the approach (Zero Buffer) in [17].

5 Conclusions

In this paper, we derived a statistical delay guarantee of the generalized Virtual Clock scheduling algorithm. We defined the concept of an *equivalent* fluid and packet source and proved a theorem that relates the departure time of a packet in a fluid FCFS multiplexor to its departure time in a packet multiplexor that uses generalized Virtual Clock algorithm for scheduling packets. This theorem enables us to use extant analyses of fluid FCFS multiplexors for providing statistical QoS guarantees in a network that employs the generalized Virtual Clock algorithm. We utilized the analysis of FCFS fluid multiplexors serving two state on-off sources with exponentially distributed on and off durations presented in [2] to evaluate the increase in utilization yielded by our analysis technique. Our experiments demonstrate that for one of the source models employed in the literature, our technique can increase utilization by upto 400% compared to previously know statistical analysis methods.

References

[1] Workshop on packet scheduling held in conjunction with SIGCOMM'96. August 1996.

[2] D. Anick, D. Mitra, and M. Sondhi. Stochastic theory of a data handling system with multiple sources. *Bell Systems Technical Journal*, 61:1871–1894, 1982.

[3] J. Bennett and H. Zhang. WF^2Q: Worst-case fair weighted fair queuing. In *Proceedings of INFOCOM'96*, pages 120–127, March 1996.

[4] J. Bennett and H. Zhang. Hierarchical packet fair queuing algorithms. *IEEE/ACM Transactions on Networking*, 5(5), October 1997.

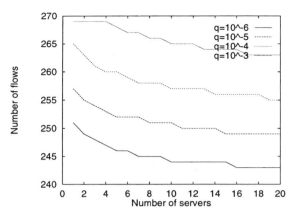 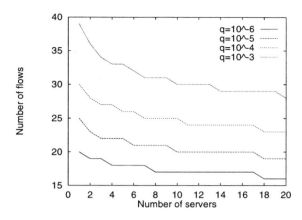

Figure 6. (a) EXP1 Source (b) EXP2 source

[5] N. Figuera and J. Pasquale. Leave-in-time: A new service discipline for real-time communication in a packet-switching data network. In *Proceedings of ACM SIGCOMM'95*, pages 207–218, 1995.

[6] L. Georgiadis, R. Guerin, V. Peris, and K. Sivarajan. Efficient network qos provisioning based on per node traffic shaping. In *Proceedings of INFOCOM'96*, pages 102–110, March 1996.

[7] P. Goyal. *Packet Scheduling Algorithms for Integrated Services Networks*. PhD thesis, Department of Computer Sciences, The University of Texas at Austin, 1997.

[8] P. Goyal, S. S. Lam, and H. M. Vin. Determining end-to-end delay bounds in heterogeneous networks. *ACM/Springer-Verlag Multimedia Systems Journal*, 5(3):157–163, May 1997. Also appeared in the Proceedings of the Workshop on Network and Operating System Support for Digital Audio and Video, Pages 287-298, April 1995.

[9] P. Goyal and H. M. Vin. Fair airport scheduling algorithms. In *Proceedings of the Workshop on Network and Operating System Support for Digital Audio and Video*, pages 273–282, May 1997.

[10] P. Goyal and H. M. Vin. Generalized guaranteed rate scheduling algorithms: A framework. *IEEE/ACM Transactions on Networking*, 5(4):161–171, August 1997.

[11] P. Goyal, H. M. Vin, and H. Cheng. Start-time fair queuing: A scheduling algorithm for integrated services packet switching networks. *IEEE/ACM Transactions on Networking*, 5(5), October 1997.

[12] S. Jamin, P. Danzig, S. Shenker, and L. Zhang. A measurement based admission control algorithm for integrated services packet networks. In *Proceedings of ACM SIGCOMM'95*, pages 2–13, 1995.

[13] A. Parekh. *A Generalized Processor Sharing Approach to Flow Control in Integrated Services Networks*. PhD thesis, Department of Electrical Engineering and Computer Science, MIT, 1992.

[14] D. Stiliadis. *Traffic Scheduling in Packet-Switched Networks: Analysis, Design and Implementation*. PhD thesis, Department of Computer Science and Engineering, University of California at Santa Cruz, 1996.

[15] S. Suri, G. Varghese, and G. Chandramenon. Leap forward virtual clock: A new fair queuing scheme with guaranteed delays and throughput fairness. In *Proceedings of INFOCOM'97*, April 1997.

[16] J. S. Turner. Managing bandwidth in atm networks with bursty traffic. *IEEE Network*, 6(5):5–58, September 1992.

[17] G. Xie and S. S. Lam. Real-time block transfer under a link sharing hierarchy. In *Proceedings of INFOCOM'97*, April 1997.

[18] O. Yaron and M. Sidi. Performance and stability of communication networks via robust exponential bounds. In *IEEE/ACM Transactions on Networking*, volume 1, pages 372–385, 1993.

[19] O. Yaron and M. Sidi. Generalized processor sharing networks with exponentially bounded burstiness arrivals. In *Proceedings of INFOCOM'94*, 1994.

[20] H. Zhang. *Service Disciplines for Integrated Services Networks*. PhD thesis, Department of Electrical Engineering and Computer Science, University of California at Berkeley, 1993.

[21] H. Zhang. Service disciplines for guaranteed performance service in packet-switching networks. *Proceedings of the IEEE*, 83(10), October 1995.

[22] L. Zhang. VirtualClock: A new traffic control algorithm for packet switching networks. In *Proceedings of ACM SIGCOMM'90*, pages 19–29, Aug. 1990.

[23] Z. L. Zhang, D. Towsley, and J. Kurose. Statistical analysis of generalized processor sharing discipline. In *Proceedings of ACM SIGCOMM'94*, pages 68–77, 1994.

459

Realizing Services for Guaranteed-QoS Communication on a Microkernel Operating System

Ashish Mehra[†], Anees Shaikh, Tarek Abdelzaher, Zhiqun Wang, and Kang G. Shin

Real-Time Computing Laboratory
University of Michigan
Ann Arbor, MI 48109–2122
{*ashaikh,zaher,zqwang,kgshin* } *@eecs.umich.edu*

[†]Server and Enterprise Networking
IBM T.J. Watson Research Center
Yorktown Heights, NY 10598-0704
mehraa@watson.ibm.com

Abstract

Provision of end-to-end QoS guarantees on communication necessitates appropriate support in the end systems (i.e., hosts) and network routers that form the communication fabric. This paper focuses on the architectural and implementation challenges involved in realizing QoS-sensitive host communication subsystems on contemporary microkernel operating systems with limited real-time support. We motivate and describe the components constituting our integrated service architecture that together ensure QoS-sensitive handling of network traffic at both sending and receiving hosts and demonstrate a communication framework that can implement alternative QoS models by applying appropriate policies. An experimental evaluation in a controlled configuration demonstrates the efficacy with which QoS guarantees are maintained, despite limitations imposed by the underlying operating system.

1 Introduction

With the continued upsurge in the demand for networked multimedia and real-time applications, a key issue is to identify and resolve the challenges of realizing QoS-sensitive communication subsystems at end systems (i.e., network clients and servers). Traditional design of communication subsystems has centered around optimizing average performance without regard to the performance variability experienced by applications or end users. As such, simple and efficient schemes have been employed for traffic and resource management, as exemplified by the first-come-first-serve service policy. Provision of QoS guarantees, however, requires sophisticated traffic and resource management functions within the communication subsystem, and hence significantly impacts its structure and performance.

In this paper we explore QoS-sensitive communication subsystem design for contemporary operating systems. We describe the general architecture, implementation, and evaluation of a guaranteed QoS communication service for a microkernel operating system. Microkernel operating systems continue to play an important role in operating system design [20], and are being extended to

support real-time and multimedia applications [31]. We describe how to map the architectural components of a QoS-sensitive communication subsystem onto the support furnished by the operating system in order to provide appropriate QoS guarantees. We discuss the difficulties in realizing real-time behavior on such platforms and our approach to providing predictability within platform limitations. While we have focused on a microkernel operating system, we believe that our design approach and issues highlighted are equally applicable, although with necessary modifications, to the in-kernel protocol stacks of monolithic Unix-like operating systems [5, 14].

When implementing the service architecture, lack of appropriate operating system mechanisms for scheduling and communication may negatively impact real-time communication performance. Accordingly, we have developed compensatory mechanisms in the communication subsystem to reduce the effects of platform unpredictability. For purposes of admission control, we parameterize the communication subsystem via detailed profiling of the send and receive data paths. Based on this parameterization, we identify the relevant overheads and constraints and propose run-time resource management mechanisms that, along with an admission control procedure, bound and account for these overheads. Execution profiling is, therefore, a key component of our architecture. An experimental evaluation in a controlled configuration demonstrates the efficacy with which QoS guarantees are maintained, within limitations of the inherent unpredictability imposed by the underlying operating system.

For application-level QoS guarantees, an end system must provide adequate computation as well as communication resources to simultaneously executing applications. We focus on QoS-sensitive communication subsystem design while recognizing that real-time performance cannot be fully guaranteed without additional support from the operating system kernel. Such support could be in the form of processor capacity reserves for the service [28] or appropriate system partitioning [7], and are beyond the scope of this paper.. We envision a system structure with the *communication subsystem* distinct from the *computation subsystem*. The communication subsystem handles all activities and resources involved in transmission and reception of data to and from the network. The computation subsystem, on the other hand, comprises all application processes and threads that perform tasks other than communication processing.

We believe that the communication subsystem is a resource

[†]The work of this author was performed at the University of Michigan. The work reported in this paper was supported in part by the National Science Foundation under grant MIP–9203895 and the Defense Advanced Research Project Agency under grant DOD-C-F30602-95-1-0044. Any opinions, findings, and conclusions or recommendations expressed in this paper are those of the authors and do not necessarily reflect the views of NSF or DARPA.

management domain distinct from the computation subsystem, since the QoS requirements and traffic characteristics of applications might not necessarily be tied to application importance. While we do not consider integration of QoS-sensitive communication and computation subsystems in this paper, we argue that the architectural support described in this paper is complementary to the underlying operating system support required for application-level QoS guarantees. We are currently investigating architectural approaches to integrate the two subsystems in a flexible manner.

Our primary contribution lies in realizing and demonstrating a QoS-sensitive communication subsystem that partially compensates for the unpredictability in a contemporary operating system, while exploiting the available support for provision of QoS guarantees on communication. This includes integration of the architectural components providing QoS guarantees with local communicaiton resources and management policies, support for dynamic scheduling of all communication processing, and detailed prameterization of the communication subsystem to incorporate underlying platform overheads for acccurate admission control. The insights gained from our work can benefit system designers and practitioners contemplating addition of elaborate QoS support in existing operating systems.

In the next section we note related work in the design of QoS-sensitive communication services. Section 3 presents the goals and architecture of the real-time (guaranteed-QoS) communication service. The components of the architecture are described in Section 4. Section 5 describes our prototype implementation and the issues faced in its realization on a platform with limited real-time support. Section 6 follows with results of an experimental evaluation of our implementation and Section 7 concludes the paper with a summary and directions for future work.

2 Related Work

A number of approaches are being explored to realize QoS-sensitive communication and computation in the context of distributed multimedia systems. An extensive survey of QoS architectures is provided in [9], which provides a comprehensive view of the state of the art in the provisioning of end-to-end QoS.

Network and protocol support for QoS: The Tenet real-time protocol suite [4] is an implementation of real-time communication on wide-area networks (WANs), but it did not address the problem of QoS-sensitive protocol processing inside hosts. Further, it does not incorporate implementation constraints and their associated overheads, or QoS-sensitive processing of traffic at the receiving host. While we focus on end-host design, support for QoS or preferential service in the network is being examined for provision of integrated and differentiated services on the Internet [6, 8, 12]. The signalling required to set up reservations for application flows can be provided by RSVP [34], which initiates reservation setup at the receiver, or ST-II [13], which initiates reservation setup at the sender.

QoS architectures: The OMEGA [30] end point architecture provides support for end-to-end QoS guarantees with a focus on an integrated framework for the specification and translation of application QoS requirements, and allocation of the necessary resources. OMEGA assumes appropriate support from the operating system for QoS-sensitive application execution, and the network

subsystem for provision of transport-to-transport layer guarantees (the subject of this paper). QoS-A [10] is a communication subsystem architecture which provides features similar to our service, but its realization would necessitate architectural mechanisms and extensions like those presented in this paper. A novel RSVP-based QoS architecture supporting integrated services in TCP/IP protocol stacks is described in [5]. A native-mode ATM transport layer has been designed and implemented in [3]. These architectures provide support for traffic policing and shaping but not for scheduling protocol processing and incorporating implementation overheads and constraints.

Operating system support for QoS-sensitive communication: Real-time upcalls (RTUs) [17] are used to schedule protocol processing for networked multimedia applications via event-based upcalls [11]. In contrast to RTUs, our approach adopts a thread-based execution model for protocol processing, schedules threads via a modified earliest-deadline-first (EDF) policy [22], and accounts for a number of implementation overheads. Similar to our approach, rate-based flow control of multimedia streams via kernel-based communication threads is also proposed in [33]. However, in contrast to our notion of per-connection threads, a coarser notion of per-process kernel threads is adopted. Also, the architecture outlined in [33] does not provide signalling and resource management services within the communication subsystem.

Explicit operating system support for communication is a focus of the Scout operating system, which uses paths as a fundamental operating system structuring technique [29]. A path can be viewed as a logical channel through a multilayered system over which I/O data flows. As we demonstrate, the CORDS path abstraction [16], similar to Scout paths, provides a rich framework for development of real-time communication services. Our architecture generalizes and extends the path abstraction to provide dynamic allocation and management of communication resources according to application QoS requirements. Recently, processor capacity reserves in Real-Time Mach [28] have been combined with user-level protocol processing [23] for predictable protocol processing inside hosts [21]. However, no support is provided for traffic enforcement or the ability to control protocol processing priority separate from application priority.

3 Real-Time Communication Service Architecture

Our primary goal is to provide applications with a service to request and utilize guaranteed-QoS unicast connections between two hosts. The overall service is currently being utilized in the AR-MADA project [1], which implements a set of communication and middleware services that support end-to-end guarantees and fault-tolerance in embedded real-time distributed applications.

Common to QoS-sensitive communication service models are the following three architectural requirements: (i) maintenance of per-connection QoS guarantees, (ii) overload protection via per-connection traffic enforcement, and (iii) fairness to best-effort traffic [25]. Earlier work in [25] presented and justified a high-level architectural design in the context of a specific communication service model. We generalize the architecture to apply to a number of service models, and focus on techniques and issues that arise in implementing the generic architectural components.

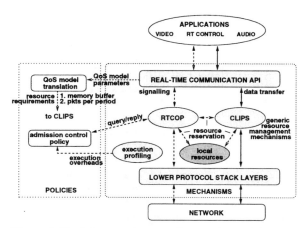

Figure 1. Real-time communication service architecture

Figure 1 illustrates the high-level software architecture of our guaranteed-QoS service at end-hosts. The core functionality of the communication service is realized via three components that interact to provide guaranteed-QoS communication. Applications use the service via the real-time communication application programming interface (RTC API); RTCOP coordinates end-to-end signalling for resource reservation and reclamation during connection set-up or tear-down; and CLIPS performs run-time management of resources for QoS-sensitive data transfer. Since platform-specific overheads must be characterized before QoS guarantees can be ensured, an execution profiling component is added to measure and parameterize the overheads incurred by the communication service on a particular platform, and make these parameters available for admission control decisions. The control path taken through the architecture during connection setup is shown in Figure 1 as dashed lines. Data is then transferred via RTC API and CLIPS as indicated by the solid lines.

Together, these components provide per-connection communication resource management, including signalling, admission control and resource reservation, traffic enforcement, buffer management, and CPU and link scheduling. We organize these functions into reusable core mechanisms that can implement alternative QoS communication paradigms given the appropriate policies.

We have approached the architectural component design with the goal of separating mechanisms that provide QoS-sensitive communication from the policies that dictate the nature of QoS guarantees. A relaxed admission control policy, for example, coupled with these component mechanisms could be used to implement a statistical guarantee model. Similarly, changing the policy for expression of application QoS requirements, along with a suitable admission control policy, facilitates QoS negotiation and adaptation, as is demonstrated in [2].

4 Architecture Component Design

Below, we discuss the salient features of each architectural component of the service along with its interaction with other components to provide QoS guarantees. We also describe how the components are used to realize a particular service model.

4.1 RTC Application Interface

The programming interface exported to applications comprises routines for connection establishment and teardown, message transmission and reception on established connections, and initialization and support routines. Table 1 lists some of the main routines currently available in RTC API. The API has two parts: a top half that interfaces to applications and is responsible for validating application requests and creating internal state, and a bottom half which interfaces to RTCOP for signalling (i.e., connection setup and teardown), and to CLIPS for QoS-sensitive data transfer.

The design of RTC API is based in large part on the well-known socket API in BSD Unix. Each connection endpoint is a pair (IPaddr, port) formed by the IP address of the host (IPaddr) and an unsigned 16-bit port (port) unique on the host, similar to an INET domain socket endpoint. In addition to unique endpoints for data transfer, an application may use several endpoints to receive signalling requests from other applications. Applications willing to be receivers of real-time traffic register their signalling ports with a name service or use well-known ports. Applications wishing to create connections must first locate the corresponding receiver endpoints before signalling can be initiated.

The key aspect which distinguishes RTC API from the socket API is that the receiving application *explicitly approves* connection establishment and teardown. When registering its intent to receive signalling requests, the application specifies an agent function that is invoked in response to connection requests. This function, implemented by the receiving application, determines whether sufficient application-level resources are available for the connection and, if so, reserves necessary resources (e.g., CPU capacity, buffers, etc.) for the new connection.

The QoS-parameters passed to rtcCreateConnection are translated, for generality, into abstract resource requirements. These are, (i) a specified message buffer size to be reserved for the connection, and (ii) a specified number of packets to be transmitted per specified period. These parameters are passed to CLIPS so that it can perform resource management. In addition, optional (QoS model-specific) parameters can be specified and interpreted by the admission policy. Typically, such parameters would constitute additional constraints, such as message deadline for example that affect admission control decisions.

4.2 Resource Reservation with RTCOP

Requests to create and destroy connections initiate the Real-Time Connection Ordination Protocol (RTCOP), a distributed end-to-end signalling protocol. RTCOP is composed of *request and reply handlers* that manage signalling state and interface to the admission control policy, and a *communication module* that handles the task of reliably forwarding signalling messages. This separation allows simpler replacement of admission control policies or connection state management algorithms without affecting communication functions. Note that signalling and connection establishment are non-real-time (but reliable) functions. QoS guarantees apply to the data sent on an established connection but signalling requests are sent as best-effort traffic.

When processing a new signalling request, the request handler at each hop invokes an admission control procedure to decide

Function	Parameters	Operation Performed
`rtcInit`	none	service initialization
`rtcGetParameter`	chan id, param type	query parameter on specified real-time connection
`rtcRegisterPort`	local port, agent function	register local port and agent for signalling
`rtcUnRegisterPort`	local port	unregister local signalling port
`rtcCreateConnection`	remote host/port, max rate, max burst size, max msg size, max delay	create connection with given parameters to remote endpoint ; return connection id
`rtcAcceptConnection`	local port, chan id, remote host/port	obtain the next connection already established at specified local port
`rtcDestroyConnection`	chan id	destroy specified real-time connection
`rtcSendMessage`	chan id, buf ptr	send message on specified real-time connection
`rtcRecvMessage`	chand id, buf ptr	receive message on specified real-time connection

Table 1. Routines comprising `RTC API`

whether or not sufficient resources are available for the new request. When a connection is admitted at all nodes on the route, the reply handler at the destination node generates a positive acknowledgment on the reverse path to the source to commit connection resources. These resources include packet and message buffers and a `CLIPS` connection handler thread.

The communication module handles the basic tasks of sending and receiving signalling messages, as well as forwarding data packets to and from the applications. Most of the protocol processing performed by the communication module is in the control path during processing of signalling messages. In the data path it functions as a simple transport protocol, forwarding data packets on behalf of applications, much like UDP.

`RTCOP` exports an interface to `RTC API` for specification of connection establishment and teardown requests and replies, and selection of logical ports for connection endpoints. The `RTC API` uses the latter to reserve a signalling port in response to a request from the application, for example. `RTCOP` also interfaces to an underlying routing engine to query an appropriate route before initiating signalling for a new connection. In general, the routing engine should find a route that can support the desired QoS requirements. However, for simplicity we use static (fixed) routes for connections since it suffices to demonstrate the capabilities of our architecture and implementation.

4.3 CLIPS-based Resource Scheduling

The Communication Library for Implementing Priority Semantics (CLIPS), implements the necessary resource-management mechanisms to realize QoS-sensitive real-time data transfer. It provides a simple interface that exports the abstraction of a guaranteed-rate communication endpoint, where the guarantee is in terms of the number of packets sent during a specified period. The endpoint also has an associated configurable buffer to accomodate bursty sources. We call this combination a *clip*. To control jitter, `CLIPS` also accepts a deadline parameter. Within each period packets will be transmitted (via the clip) by the specified deadline measured from the start of the period.

Internal to `CLIPS`, each clip is provided with a *message queue* to buffer messages generated or received on the corresponding endpoint, a *communication handler thread* to process these messages, and a *packet queue* to stage packets waiting to be transmitted or received. Once a pair of clips are created for a connection, messages can be transferred in a prioritized fashion using the `CLIPS API`. The `CLIPS` library implements the key functional

components illustrated in Figure 2.

QoS-sensitive scheduling: The communication handler thread of a clip executes in a continuous loop either dequeuing outgoing messages from the clip's message queue and fragmenting them (at the source host), or dequeuing incoming packets from the clip's packet queue and reassembling messages (at the destination host). Each message must be sent within a given local delay bound (deadline) that is specified to the clip as a QoS parameter. To achieve the best schedulable utilization, communication handlers are scheduled based on an earliest-deadline-first (EDF) policy. Since most operating systems do not provide EDF scheduling, `CLIPS` implements it with a user-level scheduler layered on top of the operating system scheduler. The user-level scheduler runs at a static kernel priority and maintains a list of all kernel threads registered with it, sorted by increasing deadline. At any given time, the `CLIPS` scheduler blocks all of the registered threads using kernel semaphores except the one with the earliest deadline, which it considers in the running state. The running thread will be allowed to execute until it explicitly terminates or yields using a primitive exported by `CLIPS`. In the context of executing this primitive, the scheduler blocks the thread on a kernel semaphore and signals the thread with the next earliest deadline. This arrangement implements non-preemptive EDF scheduling within a single protection domain.

Policing and communication thread scheduling: Each communication handler is assigned a *budget* to prevent a communication client from monopolizing resources. The budget is expressed in terms of a maximum number of packets to be processed per period and is replenished at the start of a new period. Communication handlers call the CLIPS scheduler after processing each packet to decrement the budget. To police non-conformant sources, the handler is blocked when its budget expires. A handler is rescheduled for execution when the budget is replenished. We implement a "cooperative preemption" mechanism that prevents handlers with large periods and budgets from inflicting unacceptable jitter on the execution of handlers with smaller periods. Each handler participates in cooperative preemption by voluntarily yielding the CPU after processing a small number of packets. If no handler of higher priority is ready for execution at that time, `CLIPS` returns control to the yielding handler immediately. Otherwise, the higher priority handler is executed. Thus, a handler may be rescheduled by the communication thread scheduler when the it blocks due to expiration of its budget, or when it yields the CPU.

QoS-sensitive link bandwidth allocation: Modern operating sys-

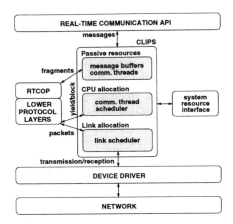

Figure 2. Functional structure of `CLIPS`.

tems typically implement FIFO packet transmission over the communication link. While we cannot avoid FIFO queuing in the kernel's network device, `CLIPS` implements a dynamic priority-based *link scheduler* at the bottom of the user-level protocol stack to schedule outgoing packets. The link scheduler implements the EDF scheduling policy using a priority heap for outgoing packets. To prevent a FIFO accumulation of outgoing packets in the kernel (e.g., while the link is busy), the `CLIPS` link scheduler does not release a new packet until it is notified of the completion of previous packet transmission. Best-effort packets are maintained in a separate packet heap within the user-level link scheduler and serviced at a lower priority than those on real-time clips.

4.4 Execution profiling

The execution profiling component is invoked when the system is deployed on a new platform, or upon system upgrades. It abstracts the communication overheads and costs of the host hardware and software platform and makes them available to admission control to account for protocol processing delay, packet transmission latency, message send delay, etc. Details of our profiling methodology, including measured parameters of our service implementation, are available in [26].

4.5 Service Model Instantiation

Our real-time communication architecture may be used to realize a family of service models that differ in the choice of QoS-parameters and admission control policy, as long as QoS parameters can be converted into a rate constraint (maximum number of packets sent per period), a storage constraint (maximum packet buffer size), and a deadline on each node. We have implemented a communication paradigm amenable to such an abstraction, namely the real-time channels model [15, 19]. A real-time channel is a unicast virtual connection between a source and destination host with associated performance guarantees on message delay and available bandwidth. In requesting a new channel, the application specifies its message generation process to allow the communication subsystem to compute resource requirements and decide whether it can guarantee the desired quality-of-service. The generation process is expressed in terms of the maximum message size (M_{max}), maximum message rate (R_{max}), and maximum message burst size (B_{max}). The burst parameter serves to bound the short-term variability in the message rate and partially determines the necessary

buffer size (i.e. in time t, the number of messages generated must be no more than $B_{max} + t \cdot R_{max}$). The QoS requirement is expressed as an upper bound on end-to-end communication delay from the sending application to the receiving application. This deadline parameter influences admission control decisions at all nodes in the route during signalling.

The admission control policy for real-time channels implements the `D_order` algorithm to perform schedulability analysis for CPU and link bandwidth allocation. Details on `D_order` and subsequent extensions to account for CPU preemption costs and the relationship between CPU and link bandwidth are available in [19] and [24], respectively.

5 Service Implementation

Our experimental testbed and implementation environment is based on the MK 7.2 microkernel operating system from the Open Group Research Institute. The hardware platform consists of several 133 MHz Pentium-based PCs connected by a Cisco 2900 Ethernet switch operating at 10MB/s.

While not a full-fledged real-time OS, MK 7.2 includes several features that facilitate provision of QoS guarantees. Specifically, though it provides only preemptive fixed-priority scheduling, the 7.2 release includes the `CORDS` (Communication Object for Real-time Dependable Systems) protocol environment [16] in which our implementation resides. `CORDS` is based on the *x*-kernel object-oriented networking framework originally developed at the University of Arizona [18], with some significant extensions for controlled allocation of system resources. `CORDS` is also available for Windows NT and, as such, serves as a justifiable vehicle for exploring the realization of communication services on modern microkernels with limited real-time support.

5.1 Service Configuration

Figure 3(a) shows the software configuration for the guaranteed-QoS communication service. While the `CORDS` framework can be used at user-level as well as in the kernel, we have developed the prototype implementation as a user-level `CORDS` server. There are several reasons for this choice as discussed in Section 5.2 below, the most obvious being the ease of development and debugging, resulting in a shorter development cycle. Applications link with the `librtc` library and communicate real-time connection requests and data via IPC with the user-level `CORDS` server.

The service protocol stack is configured within the server as shown in Figure 3(b). `RTC API` interfaces with applications via Mach Interface Generator (MIG) stubs, translating application requests to specific invocations of operations on `RTCOP` (for signalling) or `CLIPS` (for data transfer). `RTCOP` serves as a transport protocol residing above a two-part network layer composed of `RTROUTER` and `IP`. Though we currently use default IP routing, we provide `RTROUTER` as a go-between protocol to keep the routing interface independent of IP so that `RTCOP` may eventually work with more sophisticated routing protocols that support QoS- or policy-based routing. The `IP`, `ETH`, and `ETHDRV` protocols are standard implementations distributed with the `CORDS` framework. `ETH` is a generic hardware-independent protocol that provides an interface between higher level protocols and the actual Ethernet driver. `ETHDRV` is specific to the user-level implementation of the

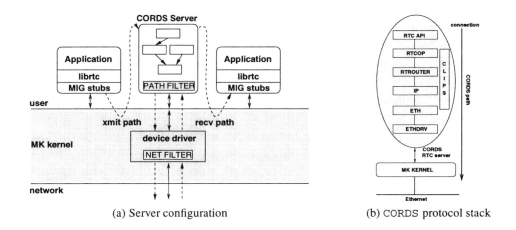

(a) Server configuration

(b) CORDS protocol stack

Figure 3. Service implementation as CORDS server: In (a) the communication path used by applications is shown; (b) illustrates the configurable protocol stack.

CORDS server. It is an out-of-kernel device driver that interacts with the network device driver in the Mach kernel through system calls to a Mach device control port. Note that CLIPS spans the protocol stack, providing scheduling and resource management services at both the message and packet levels.

When an application sends a message to the CORDS server for transmission on an established real-time connection, an API thread waiting on the corresponding Mach port first deposits it into a connection-specific message queue. CLIPS then schedules the connection's handler thread to perform protocol processing and fragment the message into packets. These packets are labeled with their local deadline and staged in the CLIPS packet heap. From this point the CLIPS link scheduler thread retrieves packets and transmits them according to their dealines. A packet arriving at the receiving host is demultiplexed into its connection-specific packet buffer when it enters the CORDS server from the kernel. The connection handler thread, scheduled by CLIPS, retrieves the packet and shepherds it up the protocol stack performing protocol processing and message reassembly. Once reassembled, the message is deposited in the connection message queue and the corresponding API thread is notified of the message arrival (if it is waiting). Finally, the API thread constructs a MIG message containing the data and delivers it to the application task.

5.2 Implementation Issues and Platform Support

Below we highlight several issues and challenges in implementing the communication service. We discuss limitations in the underlying platform that lead to unpredictable behavior and the compensatory mechanisms that we used to circumvent them. We also describe platform features that are useful in realizing a real-time communication service and their use in our implementation.

Server-based implementation: While a server-based implementation is natural for a microkernel operating system, it may perform poorly compared to user-level protocol libraries due to excessive data copying and context switching [23, 32]. Implementing the service as a protocol library, however, distributes the functions of admission control and run-time resource management among several address spaces. Since applications may each compete for communication resources, controlling system-wide resources is

more effectively done when these functions are localized in a single domain. Moreover, in the worst case, compared to user-level protocol libraries a server configuration only suffers from additional context switches. While this has significant implications for small messages, the relative degradation in performance is not as significant for large data transfers performed by the guaranteed-QoS communication service, although it may affect connection admissibility. Once developed and debugged, the server can be moved into the kernel to improve performance and predictability. Our design approach and lessons learned are applicable to communication subsystems realized as user-level libraries, co-located kernel servers, or integrated kernel implementations.

Network device interface: A server-based implementation presents a number of problems for data input and output in our architecture. The bottom layer of the protocol stack interfaces with the kernel device driver via the kernel's IPC mechanism. Device output is initiated by the CLIPS link scheduler, as close as possible to the device driver without being in the kernel. The kernel device driver cannot directly invoke the user-level link scheduler in response to transmission completion interrupts unless the OS supports mapped device drivers or user-level upcalls. In the absence of such support, user-level link scheduling cannot be done in interrupt context. Instead, we utilize user-level threads to perform synchronous device transfers and link scheduling is realized in the context of a high priority thread.

Resource reservation with Paths: Resource reservation must be coordinated in an end-to-end fashion along the route of each connection during connection establishment. CORDS provides two abstractions, *paths* and *allocators*, for reservation and allocation of system resources within the CORDS framework. Resources associated with paths include dynamically allocated memory, input packet buffers, and input threads that shepherd messages up the protocol stack [16]. Paths, coupled with allocators, provide a capability for reserving and allocating resources at any protocol stack layer on behalf of a particular connection, or class of messages. With packet demultiplexing at the lowest level at the receiver (i.e., performed in the device driver), it is possible to isolate packets on different paths from each other early in the protocol stack. Incoming packets are stored in buffers explicitly tied to the appropriate path and serviced by threads previously allocated to that path. Moreover, threads reserved for a path may be assigned one of several scheduling policies and priority levels. We use paths to facilitate per-connection resource reservation during connection setup.

Packet classification: Proper handling of prioritized real-time data at the receiving host requires that packet priority be identified as early as possible in the protocol stack, and that packets be served accordingly. CORDS associates outgoing packets with paths and demultiplexes incoming traffic into per-path buffers, essentially acting as a specialized packet filter. The data link device driver examines outgoing packets and adds an appropriate path identifier to allow early path-based demultiplexing at the receiver. This allows packet handling to be done in path-dependent order and facilitates imposing relative priorities among paths (e.g., packets of one path can be served before those of another). While this technique is natural for networks supporting a notion of virtual circuit identifiers (VCI) such at ATM, it is not so for traditional data link technologies such as Ethernet. In the case of Ethernet, the CORDS driver adds a new *path identifier* to the data link header. This creates a non-standard Ethernet header that would not be understood by hosts not running the CORDS framework.

Packet queuing: While packet classification, as discussed above, occurs in the QoS-sensitive communication server, we cannot assume that the kernel supports prioritized packet processing. The in-kernel network device driver simply relays received packets to the communication server in FIFO order via the available IPC mechanism, in our case Mach ports. This FIFO ordering does not respect connection QoS requirements, however, since urgent packets can suffer unbounded priority inversion when preceded by an arbitrary number of less urgent packets in the queue. Also, since the same queue is used for real-time and non-real-time traffic, depending on packet arrival-time patterns, real-time data maybe dropped when the queue is filled by non-real-time packets. These two problems cannot be solved without modifying the kernel device driver. To ameliorate this unpredictability, a high priority thread waits on the communication server's input port and dequeues incoming packets as soon as they arrive, depositing them in their appropriate path-specific queues. This prevents FIFO packet accumulation in the kernel and allows the server to service packets in priority order according to the connection path.

Application-server IPC: A problem similar to the above arises when applications use kernel-level IPC mechanisms to send messages via the QoS-sensitive communication server. Unless synchronous communication (e.g., RPC) is used to send messages to the server, successive application messages will accumulate in the kernel buffers for delivery to the server. In a QoS-sensitive system the length of such a queue should be derived from the application traffic specification, for example based on message rate, size, and burst. If the queue is too small, application messages may be dropped or require retransmission from the application. If the queue is overly long, application messages may reside in it longer than anticipated and result in deadline violations. We do not assume that we can control allocation of the kernel-level IPC queues. Our strategy is to drain them as fast as possible, transferring messages to connection-specific queues in the communication server, which are sized in accordance with the connection's traffic specification. We dedicate an API thread per connection within the server whose function is to consume messages from the corre-

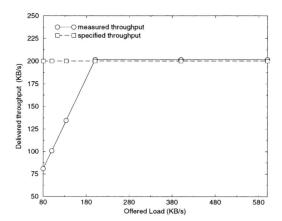

Figure 4. Traffic enforcement on a single real-time channel: $R_{max} = 5$ **msg/sec,** $M_{max} = 40$**KB,** $B_{max} = 10$, **and** $D = 200$**ms.**

sponding Mach port queue. Once an application sends a message to the server, the corresponding API thread reads it from the Mach port and queues it for the corresponding communication handler. The thread, whose execution time is charged to the handler's budget, runs at handler priority, and is allowed to continue running at background priority when the handler's budget expires. Like the handler, the API thread adheres to the cooperative preemption model by yielding to waiting, higher priority messages after processing a fixed amount of message data.

Dynamic path creation and deletion: Real-time connections may be created and deleted repeatedly over an application's lifetime requiring that paths be dynamic entities with appropriate teardown and resource reclamation mechanisms. The CORDS framework envisions a relatively static use of paths, with a single path for best-effort traffic and a few paths for different classes of traffic. That is, there are never more than perhaps ten active paths, all of these long-lived and preconfigured. Accordingly, the CORDS path library does not support path teardown or resource reclamation operations. To facilitate a one-to-one association between real-time connections and paths, we have extended CORDS to support path destruction and reclamation of resources associated with a path. These mechanisms are invoked by RTCOP during signalling of teardown messages from connection source to destination.

6 Experimental Evaluation

We conducted several experiments to evaluate the efficacy of our prototype implementation. The experiments demonstrate two key aspects of the QoS support provided: traffic enforcement (i.e., policing and shaping) on a single connection, and traffic isolation between multiple real-time and best-effort connections. We show that reasonably good QoS-guarantees can be achieved despite the lack of real-time scheduling and communication support in the kernel.

The experimental setup consists of two hosts communicating on a private segment through the Ethernet switch. To avoid interference from the Unix server, we suppress extraneous network traffic (e.g., ARP requests and replies) and configure the CORDS server to receive all incoming network traffic. This allows us to

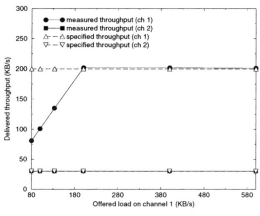

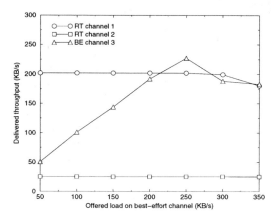

(a) Isolation between real-time channels   (b) Isolation between best-effort and real-time traffic

Figure 5. In (a) channel 1 has the same specification as in Figure 4 and channel 2 has $R_{max} = 2$ msg/sec, $M_{max} = 15$ KB, $B_{max} = 10$, and $D = 100$ ms. In (b) channel 1 has a specification of $R_{max} = 10$ msg/sec, $M_{max} = 20$ KB, $B_{max} = 10$, and $D = 200$ ms and channel 2 has $R_{max} = 5$ msg/sec, $M_{max} = 5$ KB, $B_{max} = 10$, and $D = 100$ ms.

limit the background CPU load on each host and accurately control network traffic between them. For each experiment reported below, connections are created between MK client tasks running at the two hosts. Connection parameters are specified according to the real-time channel model, namely as maximum message size (M_{max}), maximum message burst (B_{max}), message rate (R_{max}), and message deadline (D). Message traffic is generated by threads running within the MK client task at the source and consumed by threads running within the destination client. Our evaluation metric is the per-connection application-level throughput delivered to the receiving task at the destination host.

6.1 Traffic Enforcement

For this experiment, we establish a real-time channel with a specified rate of 200 KB/s and a 200 ms deadline. The actual offered load on the channel is varied, however, by changing the interval between generation of successive messages, ranging from 500 ms to 0 ms (i.e., continuous traffic generation).

As shown in Figure 4, the delivered throughput increases linearly with the offered load until the offered load equals the specified channel rate. For example, at an offered load of 100 KB/s (corresponding to a message generation interval of 400 ms), the delivered throughput is 100 KB/s. Similarly, at an offered load of 200 KB/s, the delivered throughput is 200 KB/s. For offered loads beyond the specified channel rate, however, the delivered throughput equals the specified channel rate. This continues to be the case even under continuous message generation (message generation interval of 0 ms). These measurements show that the traffic enforcement mechanisms effectively prevent a real-time connection from violating its specified rate.

6.2 Traffic Isolation

In addition to proper traffic enforcement, recall that one of the architectural goals of the guaranteed-QoS communication service is to ensure isolation between different QoS and best-effort connections. We first consider traffic isolation between multiple real-time channels subject to traffic violation by a real-time channel. Two

real-time channels are established between the hosts, one representing a high-rate channel (channel 1) and the other representing a low-rate channel (channel 2). The high-rate channel has the same traffic and deadline specification as before, i.e. a specified rate of 200 KB/s. The low-rate channel has a specified channel rate of 30 KB/s. Message generation on channel 2 is continuous, so that it sends at a persistent 30 KB/s. Channel 1 is controlled in order to vary the offered load.

Figure 5(a) shows the delivered throughput on channels 1 and 2 as a function of the offered load on channel 1. Once again, the delivered throughput on channel 1 increases linearly with the offered load until the offered load equals the specified channel rate (200 KB/s). Subsequent increase in offered load has no effect on the delivered throughput which stays constant at the specified channel rate. The delivered throughput on channel 2, on the other hand, remains constant at approximately 30 KB/s (its specified channel rate) regardless of the offered load on channel 2. That is, traffic violations on one connection (even continuous message generation) do not affect the delivered QoS for another connection.

We also consider traffic isolation between real-time and best-effort traffic under increasing best-effort load. For this experiment we create an additional best-effort channel in addition to two real-time channels. As before, one real-time channel (channel 1) represents a high-rate channel with a specified rate of 200 KB/s. The other real-time channel (channel 2) is a low-rate channel with rate 25 KB/s. Message generation on channels 1 and 2 is continuous, i.e., with a message generation interval of 0 ms. The offered load on the best-effort channel (channel 3) is varied from 50 KB/s to 350 KB/s by controlling the message generation interval.

Figure 5(b) plots the delivered throughput on each channel as a function of the offered best-effort load. A number of observations can be made from these measurements. First, the delivered throughput on channels 1 and 2 are roughly independent of the offered best-effort load. That is, real-time traffic is effectively isolated from best-effort traffic, except under very high best-effort loads as explained below. Second, best-effort traffic utilizes any excess capacity not consumed by real-time traffic, as evidenced by the roughly linear increase in delivered throughput on channel 3 as a function of the offered load. Once the system reaches saturation (beyond a best-effort offered load of approximately 250 KB/s), however, best-effort throughput declines sharply due to buffer overflows and the resulting packet loss at the receiver.

Under very high best-effort loads, the delivered throughput on channel 1 declines slightly. We believe that this is due to the overheads of receiving and discarding best-effort packets, which have not been accounted for in the admission control procedure. These overheads impact the delivered throughput on high-rate connections more than low-rate connections, as evidenced by the constant throughput delivered to channel 2 even under very high best-effort load.

6.3 Fairness to Best-Effort Traffic

While the load offered by real-time connections in the previous experiments was persistent (always greater than the reserved capacity), this experiment focuses on utilization of any reserved capacity not utilized by a real-time connection. It is desirable that this unused capacity be utilized by best-effort traffic, as per our goal of fairness. Other real-time connections should not be allowed to consume this excess capacity at the expense of best-effort traffic. We create two real-time channels and a best-effort channel as before. While the offered load on channel 2 is continuous, channel 1 only offers a load of 100 KB/s even though it is allocated a capacity of 200 KB/s. We consider two cases of message generation on channel 1, as explained below. In case 1, channel 1 carries 20 KB messages at 5 messages/second (half the specified rate). In case 2, it generates 10 KB messages at 10 messages/second.

Figure 6 plots the delivered throughput on all the channels as a function of the offered load on the best-effort channel (channel 3). Channel 1 receives a constant 100 KB/s throughput independent of the offered best-effort load. Similarly, channel 2 receives its allocated capacity of 25 KB/s. In case 1, Channel 3's delivered throughput increases linearly with the offered load until an offered load of 250 KB/s. Beyond this load, the delivered best-effort throughput falls as before, but continues to be higher than that obtained in Figure 5(b) when real-time channels were using their full reserved capacity.

We found, though, that best-effort traffic is unable to fully utilize the unused capacity left by channel 1. We suspect that this effect is primarily due to packet losses caused by buffer overflow at the receiver, either in the adapter or in the kernel device port queue used by the CORDS server to receive incoming packets. To validate this, we ran additional experiments with case 2, in which channel 1 generates smaller messages (10 KB) at a higher rate to offer the same average load of 100 KB/s. As can be seen in Figure 6, the delivered best-effort throughput in this case continues to increase linearly beyond 250 KB/s and shows no decline even for a best-effort load of 350 KB/s. These results suggest that best-effort traffic is able to fully utilize unused capacity when real-time traffic is less bursty (i.e., has fewer packets in each message).

6.4 Further Observations

With the user-level CORDS server configuration, the receiving task is able to receive packets at an aggregate rate of 450-500 KB/s (depending on the number of packets in a message), even though the sender can send at a maximum rate of approximately 750 KB/s.

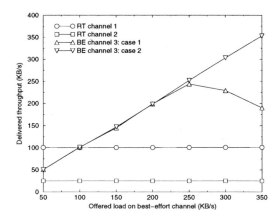

Figure 6. Channels 1 and 2 have the same parameters as in Figure 5(b) but channel 1 underutilizes its reservation. In case 1, channel 1 generates 20 KB messages at 5 msg/s; in case 2, it generates 10 KB messages at 10 msg/s.

This discrepancy is most likely due to CPU contention between the receiving application task and the CORDS server and the resulting context switching overheads, and the high cost of IPC across the client and server. Another reason could be the unnecessary copy performed by the lowest layer (ETHDRV) of the CORDS protocol stack whenever packets from multiple paths arrive in an interleaved fashion. Since this occurs frequently with multiple channels and under high traffic load, it is likely that this extra copy is slowing down the receiver significantly; this extra copy can only be eliminated by redesigning path buffer management in the CORDS framework. More importantly, none of these effects are accounted for in the admission control procedure, and must be addressed when the communication subsystem is integrated more closely within the host operating system. We expect to see significant improvements in the base performance for an in-kernel realization of our prototype implementation.

7 Summary and Future Work

In this paper we have described our experiences with the design, implementation, and evaluation of a guaranteed-QoS communication service implemented on a contemporary microkernel operating system with limited real-time supprt. We designed three primary components that provide general mechanisms for real-time communication, including support for signalling and resource reservation, traffic enforcement, buffer management, and CPU and link scheduling. A fourth execution profiling component is responsible for the essential task of characterizing platform-specific communication overheads. When combined with with specific policies for admission control and interpretation of QoS parameters, these components can be used to implement several QoS-sensitive communication models.

We have tested our prototype with transmission of stored compressed video and playout using mpeg_play. We plan to conduct further experiments with a number of stored video traces. To allow for QoS-adaptation, we have implemented an end-host architecture for adaptive-QoS communication services [2]. In [26] we describe the complex process of parameterizing the overheads of the communication subsystem and target platform. These efforts illustrate the need for an automated approach to profiling and system parameterization. We have, therefore, also begun to explore self-parameterizing protocol stacks for QoS-sensitive communication subsystems [27].

References

[1] T. Abdelzaher, S. Dawson, W. Feng, S. Ghosh, F. Jahanian, S. Johnson, A. Mehra, T. Mitton, J. Norton, A. Shaikh, K. Shin, V. Vaidyan, Z. Wang, and H. Zou. ARMADA middleware suite. In *Proc. of IEEE Workshop on Middleware for Distributed Real-Time Systems and Services*, pages 11–18, San Francisco, CA, December 1997.

[2] T. Abdelzaher and K. Shin. End-host architecture for QoS-adaptive communication. In *to appear in Proc. Real-Time Technology and Applications Symposium*, Denver, Colorado, June 1998.

[3] R. Ahuja, S. Keshav, and H. Saran. Design, implementation, and performance of a native mode ATM transport layer. In *Proc. IEEE INFOCOM*, pages 206–214, March 1996.

[4] A. Banerjea, D. Ferrari, B. Mah, M. Moran, D. C. Verma, and H. Zhang. The Tenet real-time protocol suite: Design, implementation, and experiences. *IEEE/ACM Trans. Networking*, 4(1):1–11, February 1996.

[5] T. Barzilai, D. Kandlur, A. Mehra, D. Saha, and S. Wise. Design and implementation of an RSVP-based quality of service architecture for integrated services Internet. In *Proc. Int'l Conf. on Distributed Computing Systems*, May 1997.

[6] S. Blake, D. Black, M. Carlson, E. Davies, Z. Wang, and W. Weiss. An architecture for differentiated services. Internet Draft (draft-ietf-diffserv-arch-01.txt), August 1998.

[7] G. Bollella and K. Jeffay. Supporting co-resident operating systems. In *Proc. Real-Time Technology and Applications Symposium*, pages 4–14, June 1995.

[8] R. Braden, D. Clark, and S. Shenker. Integrated services in the Internet architecture: An overview. *Request for Comments RFC 1633*, July 1994. Xerox PARC.

[9] A. T. Campbell, C. Aurrecoechea, and L. Hauw. A review of QoS architectures. *Multimedia Systems Journal*, 1996.

[10] A. T. Campbell, G. Coulson, and D. Hutchison. A quality of service architecture. *Computer Communication Review*, April 1994.

[11] D. D. Clark. The structuring of systems using upcalls. In *Proc. ACM Symp. on Operating Systems Principles*, pages 171–180, 1985.

[12] D. D. Clark, S. Shenker, and L. Zhang. Supporting real-time applications in an integrated services packet network: Architecture and mechanism. In *Proc. of ACM SIGCOMM*, pages 14–26, August 1992.

[13] L. Delgrossi and L. Berger. Internet stream protocol version 2 (ST-2) protocol specification - version ST2+. *Request for Comments RFC 1819*, August 1995. ST2 Working Group.

[14] R. Engel, D. Kandlur, A. Mehra, and D. Saha. Exploring the performance impact of QoS support in TCP/IP protocol stacks. In *Proc. IEEE INFOCOM*, San Francisco, CA, March 1998.

[15] D. Ferrari and D. C. Verma. A scheme for real-time channel establishment in wide-area networks. *IEEE Journal on Selected Areas in Communications*, 8(3):368–379, April 1990.

[16] F.Travostino, E.Menze, and F.Reynolds. Paths: Programming with system resources in support of real-time distributed applications. In *Proc. IEEE Workshop on Object-Oriented Real-Time Dependable Systems*, February 1996.

[17] R. Gopalakrishnan and G. M. Parulkar. A real-time upcall facility for protocol processing with QoS guarantees. In *Proc. ACM Symp. on Operating Systems Principles*, page 231, December 1995.

[18] N. C. Hutchinson and L. L. Peterson. The *x*-Kernel: An architecture for implementing network protocols. *IEEE Trans. Software Engineering*, 17(1):1–13, January 1991.

[19] D. D. Kandlur, K. G. Shin, and D. Ferrari. Real-time communication in multi-hop networks. *IEEE Trans. on Parallel and Distributed Systems*, 5(10):1044–1056, October 1994.

[20] D. G. Korn. Porting UNIX to windows NT. In *Proc. USENIX Winter Conference*, January 1997.

[21] C. Lee, K. Yoshida, C. Mercer, and R. Rajkumar. Predictable communication protocol processing in Real-Time Mach. In *Proc. of 2nd Real-Time Technology and Applications Symposium*, June 1996.

[22] C. Liu and J. Layland. Scheduling algorithms for multi-programming in hard real-time environment. *Journal of the ACM*, 1(20):46–61, January 1973.

[23] C. Maeda and B. N. Bershad. Protocol service decomposition for high-performance networking. In *Proc. ACM Symp. on Operating Systems Principles*, pages 244–255, December 1993.

[24] A. Mehra, A. Indiresan, and K. Shin. Resource management for real-time communication: Making theory meet practice. In *Proc. 2nd Real-Time Technology and Applications Symposium*, pages 130–138, June 1996.

[25] A. Mehra, A. Indiresan, and K. Shin. Structuring communication software for quality of service guarantees. In *Proc. 17th Real-Time Systems Symposium*, pages 144–154, December 1996.

[26] A. Mehra, A. Shaikh, T. Abdelzaher, Z. Wang, and K. Shin. Realizing services for guaranteed-QoS communication on a microkernel operating system. Technical Report CSE-TR-375-98, University of Michigan, Dept. of Electrical Engineering and Computer Science, Ann Arbor, MI, September 1998.

[27] A. Mehra, Z. Wang, and K. Shin. Self-parameterizing protocol stacks for guaranteed quality of service. available at ftp://rtcl.eecs.umich.edu/outgoing/ashish/selfparam.ps, June 1998.

[28] C. W. Mercer, S. Savage, and H. Tokuda. Processor capacity reserves for multimedia operating systems. In *Proceedings of the IEEE International Conference on Multimedia Computing and Systems*, May 1994.

[29] D. Mosberger and L. L. Peterson. Making paths explicit in the Scout operating system. In *Proc. USENIX Symp. on Operating Systems Design and Implementation*, pages 153–168, October 1996.

[30] K. Nahrstedt and J. M. Smith. Design, implementation and experiences of the OMEGA end-point architecture. *IEEE Journal on Selected Areas in Communications*, 14(7):1263–1279, September 1996.

[31] S. Sommer and J. Potter. Operating system extensions for dynamic real-time applications. In *Proc. 17th Real-Time Systems Symposium*, pages 45–50, December 1996.

[32] C. A. Thekkath, T. D. Nguyen, E. Moy, and E. Lazowska. Implementing network protocols at user level. *IEEE/ACM Trans. Networking*, 1(5):554–565, October 1993.

[33] D. K. Y. Yau and S. S. Lam. An architecture towards efficient OS support for distributed multimedia. In *Proc. Multimedia Computing and Networking (MMCN '96)*, January 1996.

[34] L. Zhang, S. Deering, D. Estrin, S. Shenker, and D. Zappala. RSVP: A new resource ReSerVation Protocol. *IEEE Network*, pages 8–18, September 1993.

Scheduling Communication Networks Carrying Real-Time Traffic

John P. Lehoczky
Department of Statistics
Carnegie Mellon University
Pittsburgh, PA 15213

Abstract

This paper presents new methods to analyze the performance of certain scheduling algorithms for communication networks carrying real-time traffic and operating in a packet switched mode. The real-time traffic consists of distinct sessions each of which transmits packets with hard deadlines. Edf and fifo scheduling policies are analyzed in detail. For the single node case, methods based on real-time queueing theory and heavy traffic queueing theory are applied to develop closed-form expressions for the fraction of packets which miss their deadline as a function of the characteristics of the sessions using the node. The results are extended to a two-node non-Jackson network. Simulations illustrate the excellent accuracy of the closed-form expressions. The formulas developed are used to design system parameters that can attain desired levels of packet lateness. [1] [2]

1   Introduction

Over the last decade, information technology has dramatically increased. There are now many different types of communication services available and an ever increasing demand for those services. Real-time communication services, while currently a small portion of the total demand, are of increasing importance. Given the dramatic increase in demand, the implementation and evolution of high speed networks is occurring far faster than our ability to develop models and analysis techniques to understand, then to control these networks. Communication engineering expertise can develop effective protocols and rules of thumb for network administration; however, analytic methodologies

and closed-form expressions for system performance measures would be of substantial value in this rapidly evolving domain. This paper introduces methods to analyze communication networks carrying real-time traffic that exhibit substantial randomness.

There has been important recent work that does develop analytic methods to determine stability and calculate delay. Cruz [2], [3] developed a calculus for network delay in the single and multiple node cases. The theory he developed is different from standard queueing theoretic models, because he uses non-probabilistic data stream arrival models which satisfy burstiness constraints. Using this assumption he is able to derive bounds on delay and buffering requirements for network elements. Parekh and Gallager [9], [10] studied a new network resource allocation policy called the weighted (or generalized) processor sharing (wps) algorithm and combined this with a leaky bucket admission control policy. For these scheduling and control mechanisms, the authors developed worst-case packet delay and worst-case session backlogs for both the single node and multiple node cases. Related research was published by Chang [1]. He also addressed the stability problem by determining conditions on queueing networks that result in bounded queue lengths and bounded delays for customers and gave conditions for the queue length distribution to have an exponential tail. This and related research is too substantial to summarize here; the reader is referred to the survey by Zhang [12] that presents a wide range of service disciplines, bounds on performance and a discussion of design tradeoffs.

One drawback of the work to date is that it focuses on performance bounds, and the bounds that are derived may be quite pessimistic. It is, therefore, important to find methods that would offer realistic answers but would be reasonably robust to the assumptions made. A second drawback is that the methods do not apply directly to real-time traffic for which performance is measured at the packet level, rather than at an aggregated level. Real-time traffic can be more

[1] Key Words: Real-time communication systems, real-time queueing theory, heavy traffic queueing network theory.

[2] This research was supported in part by the Office of Naval Research contract N00014-92-J-1524 and by DARPA under F30602-96-1-0160 and N66001-97-C-8527. My thanks go to Hui Zhang and Raj Rajkumar of CMU for many useful discussions about communication systems carrying real-time traffic and to Shu-Ngai Yeung who performed the simulation experiments.

than just traffic requiring a small latency. In two-way voice and video, there are requirements on each packet to reach its destination within a time constraint, not just a requirement on the average delay per packet. Current analytic methods which assess whether each packet meets its timing requirement requires a very deterministic traffic flow with nearly deterministic processing times. For more stochastic situations, new analytic methods are needed.

Recently, a new queueing theory methodology called *real-time queueing theory* has been developed that allows one to keep track of the timing behavior of each of the tasks in the system. The theory assumes that heavy traffic conditions prevail, i.e. the traffic intensity at the node approaches 1. The theory focuses on the *lead-time* of each task, where lead-time is defined to be the time until the task's deadline expires, a quantity that decreases at unit rate until the task finishes processing. Under certain assumptions, the theory shows the system can be decomposed hierarchically. First, one can study the occupancy of the queue using ordinary queueing theoretic methods (including heavy traffic theory). Second, conditional on the occupancy of the queueing system, one can construct the instantaneous lead-time profile (vector of task lead-times) of the tasks which are currently in the system. In heavy traffic, the conditional lead-time profile is nearly deterministic, its shape being characterized by the traffic intensity, the deadline distribution associated with all tasks and the scheduling policy used to service those tasks. One can use this hierarchical characterization to determine system performance measures. For example, to determine the fraction of packets or tasks which will finish late, one can examine the lead-time profile for each queue length to see if any customers are late. Then one can average these conditional results using the heavy traffic approximation to the queue length distribution. The theoretical foundations for the single node case with a single traffic flow, general task deadlines and edf scheduling have been given by Doytchinov, Lehoczky and Shreve (DLS) [4]. This model permits task arrivals to be general renewal process and task service requirements to be independent but have a general common distribution. Further results for the Markov case were developed by Lehoczky [6] and [7].

The initial work on real-time queueing theory has its own shortcomings for addressing modern communication systems. For example, to date it has been assumed that there is a single arrival process rather than allowing for many distinct flows or sessions to arrive at a node. In addition, one needs to introduce

traffic flow regulators and shapers to capture the true nature of these networks. Finally, it has been found that network arrival processes are often self-similar, a structure that is different from renewal processes. However, it seems that treating the general problem is too ambitious an initial goal. Consequently, in this paper, we will focus on the development of methodology that allows us: (1) to study the superposition of many streams of real-time traffic, (2) to calculate, often in closed-form, real-time traffic performance measures and (3) to calculate analytically the resource requirements needed by a set of applications to ensure that their timing requirements are met. In this paper, we use the fraction of session packets that arrive late as our performance measure, and we seek to determine the resources required so that a particular level of performance is achieved. Other performance measures can also be considered using similar analytic techniques. We will focus on the single node case and on a two-node network which is *not* a Jackson network. While there are significant limitations to the model presented, the results of the analysis allow a number of important questions to be addressed. For example, the formulas developed can be used directly to gain insight into the benefits of resource sharing policies compared with resource reservation policies in real-time systems. The formulas can be used to develop admission control policies and resource allocation policies, e.g. how much of the system's resources must be allocated to the real-time sessions to ensure that their timing requirements are met? Given a current set of applications on the system, can we admit a new application and still ensure that all timing requirements are met? The formulas can also give analytic insight into the differences in performance of various scheduling algorithms. While the models studied in this paper ignore important aspects of real systems, the work is a first step in the development of analytic methods for real-time communication systems.

This paper is organized as follows. Section 2 introduces the specific model and assumptions. Section 3 presents a simple example to fix the ideas. Section 4 presents the methodology to assess lateness for real-time communication systems along with simulation results to illustrate the accuracy of the real-time queueing theory approximations. Section 5 presents a two-node non-Jackson network, its analysis and simulation results. Space limitations prevent a full presentation the expressions for the lateness probabilities for edf and fifo in the network case. Only the broad ideas and simulation results are presented. Section 6 presents a summary and some conclusions.

2 The Basic Model: One Node

In this section, we introduce the basic model and assumptions for the single node case.

A1: The node consists of a single server which processes packets at rate 1.

A2: Input traffic consists of S independent sessions transmitting packets. These session packets are enqueued in separate buffers. The ith session, $1 \leq i \leq S$ has an associated renewal arrival process of packets. The interarrival times between packets are random with distribution function F_i, mean value $1/\lambda_i$ and coefficient of variation (variance divided by the squared mean) α_i^2. For periodic arrival processes, $\alpha_i = 0$.

A3: Packets from session i have random service requirements given by the probability distribution G_i with mean $1/\mu_i$ and coefficient of variation β_i^2. For constant service times, $\beta_i = 0$.

A4: Each packet from session i has a constant hard deadline given by d_i, $1 \leq i \leq S$. All packets are served, even if they depart late from the node.

A5: The server processes packets using a *head-of-the-line* policy, that is only packets at the head of a session queue are eligible to be processed. Earliest Deadline First (edf), fifo and weighted processor sharing (ps and wps) are considered. Preemption is permitted, preemption is preempt-resume, and preemption is assumed to result in no overhead.

Several comments about the assumptions are in order. First, the assumption of preemption is inappropriate for real communication systems where whole packets must be transmitted. In this paper we study systems in heavy traffic which often have long queues. In such systems where the service time represents a small part of each packet's total delay, there is essentially no performance difference between full preemption and head-of-the-line preemption. Second, we assume renewal process arrival models rather than arrival processes that exhibit long-range memory or self-similar behavior, a class of arrival processes thought to model traffic in large networks. Nevertheless, we are focusing on session-based real-time traffic such as that arising from video-conferencing. We expect such applications to produce periodic packets of possibly random length. The renewal process arrivals and general service time distributions offers a good starting point for an important class of real-time traffic. Finally, since session packets are queued in buffers and session packets ordinarily arrive in deadline order, it is optimal to serve only packets at the head of each queue, and we consider only such policies. There are several ways to allocate service capacity to the packets at the head of each queue.

First, packets could be served in fifo order. The server would service the packet at the head of the session queues with the earliest arrival time (assuming this information is available in the packet headers). This service discipline does not take packet deadlines into consideration, consequently it is generally not a suitable scheduling policy for real-time traffic. Still, fifo is easily implemented with a single buffer and can offer reasonable performance for these systems since each session's packets are kept in deadline order. For fifo, the fraction of a session's packets which are late should depend upon the system traffic intensity and the timing requirements (deadline) of that session.

Second, packets could be served using edf. With edf, the server would select the packet at the head of each of the session queues having the shortest lead-time (assuming that the packet deadline information was available in the packet header). Since we assume that session packets arrive in deadline order, this discipline would be equivalent to having a single buffer in which all packets are kept in edf order. The edf queue discipline is known to possess certain optimality properties (see Panwar and Towsley [8] and Hong, Tan and Towsley [5]) in the sense of minimizing lateness probabilities. In fact, the edf scheduling policy will result in roughly equal packet lateness probabilities for each of the sessions, independent of their arrival, service or deadline parameters. Thus, this discipline will offer a certain fairness property to the sessions, namely each session will have (in the long run) a constant fraction of its packets which finish late, and that fraction will be determined by considering all of the session characteristics together, not individually. Of course, it is possible that we might consider lateness for one session to be more tolerable than for other sessions. If this were the case, then either the number of sessions which is admitted must be reduced or standard edf must not be used.

Third, packets could be served using wps, see Parekh and Gallager [9, 10], Chang [1] and Zhang [12] for a thorough discussion of the various forms of this scheduling policy and for delay bounds. This class of policies assigns a set of weights to each of the sessions, $w_i, 1 \leq i \leq S$. At any instant, there will be a subset of sessions, $\mathcal{S}_{ne} \subset \{1, 2, \ldots, S\}$ with non-empty buffers. The processor then allocates the fraction $w_i / \sum_{j \in \mathcal{S}_{ne}} w_j$ to each session $j \in \mathcal{S}_{ne}$. In this way, any session i is guaranteed to receive at least a fraction $w_i / \sum_{j=1}^{S} w_j$ independent of how many packets any other session may transmit. If a session floods its own buffer, all other sessions are protected. While processor sharing does not consider packet timing requirements as is, therefore, not designed to support real-time systems, one could ask if there is a way to assign the weights in wps to meet the packet timing requirements. It is not clear how one should assign the weights to best support real-time traffic requirements. Although the ps and wps scheduling policies are not analyzed in detail in this paper, the methodology presented herein can be used for such an analysis, and the results will be presented elsewhere.

3 A Simple Example

A simple example may help to clarify the ideas presented in the previous section concerning the performance measure we have chosen to study: the fraction of each session's packets which finish after their deadline, i.e. are late. In this example, we consider a single node which is processing 4 mutually independent sessions. Each session has an arrival process of packets governed by a renewal process with rate λ_i, $1 \leq i \leq 4$. All packets from all sessions have a mean service time of 1. We consider three basic cases: (1) arrivals from each session are governed by a Poisson process and packets have exponential service requirement, (2) arrivals are Poisson and packets have constant service requirements, and (3) arrivals are periodic and packets have exponential service requirements. These three offer a range of cases, one with both arrivals and services being random, while the other two keep the service times (2) or arrival times (3) deterministic. It turns out that (2) and (3) have very similar performance behavior in heavy traffic, and the methods developed in this paper indicate that those two should be indistinguishable. Thus, to conserve space, we only present results for cases (1) and (2) in this paper and omit (3). Each stream has a common constant packet deadline given by d_i, $1 \leq i \leq 4$. For wps, the weights were chosen to equalize the traffic intensities for each session, namely $w_i = \lambda_i / (\lambda_1 + \cdots + \lambda_4)$, $1 \leq i \leq 4$. The results for the four different scheduling policies used with a particular choice of parameter values are presented in Table 1, the left-side for exponential service times and the right-side for constant service times. The simulation experiment consisted of 50 independent runs of 2 million packet arrivals each[3]. The session arrival rates and deadlines are chosen only for pedagogical purposes to help understand the be-

havior of the various scheduling policies for real-time traffic, not to be representative of any real situation. In Table 1, the arrival rates and deadlines are in direct relation and span a wide enough range of values that significant packet lateness will occur for all the scheduling policies. Notice that we are simulating a heavy traffic case, the traffic intensity on the server is .95. This is the most important case to consider, since one would generally want share the available real-time traffic capacity to maximize efficiency, as opposed to reserving capacity for each session even though much of it may be wasted.

The simulations give clear insights into the behavior of the various scheduling policies. First, the results for the two cases presented are very consistent, the only difference being that the fraction of late packets is substantially smaller when service times are constant compared with the case in which service times have an exponential distribution. While the quantitative relationship between the loss probabilities in these two cases is not clear, it is obvious that the reduction in variability that arises when service times are constant should substantially reduce queue lengths and packet lateness probabilities.

Second, the simulations indicate that edf is the superior scheduling policy for minimizing overall packet lateness. This is not surprising given the optimality properties that edf possesses in uniprocessor real-time scheduling theory. It is also clear that lateness probabilities are constant under edf, with approximately 7% of each session's packets being late for exponential service times and .5% being late for constant service time. Thus, edf does appear to offer equal lateness probability to all sessions independent of their traffic intensities and their deadlines. It will be seen that this common lateness probability can be predicted from the overall traffic intensity and the expected deadline of a randomly selected packet. A closed-form expression for this probability is given in the next section.

Third, fifo results in a slightly higher overall lateness probability than edf, and the fraction of late packets differs for the different sessions, with shorter deadline sessions having higher lateness probabilities. The relatively small overall difference between fifo and edf is partly from the fact that the session buffers are kept in edf order (the same as fifo order within session). This helps to bring fifo into line with edf and allows it to come close to edf performance.

Fourth, standard processor sharing behaves significantly worse than fifo in terms of overall packet lateness. The behavior is more complex that with edf and fifo. For traffic flows in which the worst case traffic in-

---

[3]The standard errors and variability of the results are discussed in the next section.

	Exponential Service					Constant Service				
Session	1	2	3	4	Total	1	2	3	4	Total
Arrival Rate	.05	.15	.25	.50	.95	.05	.15	.25	.50	.95
Deadline	30	40	50	60		30	40	50	60	
Service Rate	1	1	1	1		1	1	1	1	
% Late EDF	.0711	.0711	.0711	.0710	.0711	.0048	.0049	.0049	.0049	.0049
% Late FIFO	.2219	.1345	.0813	.0492	.0802	.0496	.0178	.0064	.0023	.0114
% Late PS	.0005	.0004	.0011	.1732	.0915	.0000	.0000	.0000	.0358	.0188
% Late WPS	.4510	.2163	.1082	.0332	.1038	.3506	.0858	.0233	.0023	.0393

Table 1: Lateness Probabilities for Poisson Arrivals and Exponential or Constant Service Times

tensity is not in heavy traffic, we would expect little, if any, packet lateness. By worst case traffic intensity, we mean the situation in which all packet buffers are busy. In the examples, consider sessions 1 and 2. If all 4 session buffers are non-empty, then all sessions receive a .25 service rate. Under these conditions, the instantaneous traffic intensity for flows 1 and 2 are $.05/.25 = .2$ and $.15/.25 = .6$ respectively, both far less than 1. Consequently, it should be very rare for any packets in those sessions to miss their deadlines. For session 3, the worst case traffic intensity is $.25/.25 = 1.0$, a situation which, by itself, should result in substantial lateness. However, sessions 1 and 2 will often not be present, so session 3 will only infrequently face the worst case, then only for a short period. Consequently, packet lateness for session 3 should be rare. Session 4, however, will face a traffic intensity of 1.0 if any of the other 3 sessions buffers is non-empty, and the traffic intensity could reach 1.5 or 2.0 if two or three of the buffers are non-empty. In spite of the long deadlines for session 4 packets, given that it will face such high traffic intensities, we should expect substantial lateness. This is borne out in both tables. Consequently, for ps, the session traffic intensity appears to play a primary role.

Fifth, for the set of weights chosen (which equalized the traffic intensity of all sessions), the performance for wps is quite different from ps. While equalization of the traffic intensities might seem to be a reasonable strategy, for real-time systems, one must take the deadlines into account. Furthermore, as one decreases the weight assigned to a particular session (from ps which assigns $w_i = .25$, $1 \leq i \leq 4$), the variance of the service time for that session increases, and as this variance parameter increases, that session's performance (say in terms of packets lateness) will decrease. Thus, one would like to decrease the weight on the first flow, but only to a limited extent, given it has a very short deadline. Clearly, it would be of substantial value to have formulas for the sessions' performance measure as

a function of the weights assigned and the other session characteristics. The methods developed in this paper can be used to develop such formulas, although this is not done in this paper.

4 Heavy Traffic Analysis: One Node Case

4.1 Background

Our approach to developing analytic methods for the network scheduling problem is based on heavy traffic theory and real-time queueing theory. These two theories can be applied when the traffic intensity on the server approaches 1. In that case, under very general circumstances (including fairly general arrival and service process assumptions, multiple application types and general routing schemes) the occupancy of a queueing network can be treated as a reflected Brownian motion process with drift for the single node case and as a reflected Brownian network process with drift for the network case. The initial research on heavy traffic queueing focused on a description of the standard queueing performance measures under heavy traffic conditions. Much of the heavy traffic network research focuses entirely on the queue length or workload process at each node and not on the lead-times of tasks in the network. Nevertheless, some recent research is relevant to the problems being addressed in this paper. For example, Williams [11] gives an analysis of the queueing aspects of networks in which general head-of-the-line service policies are considered. The heavy traffic queueing literature is too large to summarize in this paper; the interested reader should consult DLS [4] for a discussion of the relevant literature and numerous references.

The new methodology of real-time queueing theory builds on the heavy traffic queueing network literature, but addresses the problems from the viewpoint of real-time systems and the ability of a system to meet task timing requirements. This theory models the dynamics of the lead-times of packets (time until the deadline elapses). In the single node case, one must focus not only on $Q(t)$, the occupancy of a buffer, but on the higher dimensional quantity, $(Q(t), L_1(t), \ldots, L_{Q(t)}(t))$, where $L_i(t)$ represents the lead-time (at time t) of the ith packet in the buffer. Lehoczky [6] showed that one should consider the marginal behavior of $Q(t)$ (which in heavy traffic is given by a reflected Brownian motion) and the conditional behavior of $(L_1(t), \ldots, L_{Q(t)}(t))$ given $Q(t)$. In heavy traffic, this vector has nearly deterministic behavior. This behavior (called the lead-time profile) can be computed analytically and depends upon $Q(t)$, the scheduling policy and the initial deadlines of the packets. The mathematical foundations for the single node case with edf service are given in DLS [4].

Heavy traffic queueing theory studies a sequence of queueing systems whose traffic intensities approaches unity. The traffic intensity parameter for the nth system, $\rho^{(n)}$, is characterized by $\rho^{(n)} = 1 - (\gamma/\sqrt{n})$. This is often achieved by letting the associated arrival and service rates be given by $\lambda^{(n)} = \lambda(1 - (\gamma/\sqrt{n}))$ and $\mu^{(n)} = \lambda$ for $n \to \infty$. The occupancy of the queue is then of the order of $\sqrt{n}$, and packet delays are also of the order of $\sqrt{n}$. The heavy traffic scaling requires that time be scaled by a factor n and space (or queue occupancy) by $\sqrt{n}$. This means that in the heavy traffic scaling, during the time any single packet or task is in the system, the queue length will be essentially constant. Thus, for any given queue length, many packets will be flowing through the system before that length changes appreciably. Consequently, there is an averaging effect which leads to near deterministic profiles. If we use the deterministic profiles, then there will be a deterministic relationship between packet lateness and queue length. Once that relationship is determined, we can calculate performance characteristics involving packet lateness in terms of queue lengths. This requires only the equilibrium distribution for the queue length process in heavy traffic. For the single node case, this will be exponential with parameters given by the mean and variance of the arrival and service processes. We specify this distribution next.

4.2   EDF Scheduling

DLS [4] proved that for a single flow of arriving tasks with initial deadlines given by the c.d.f. G and common service distribution, conditional on $Q(t) = Q$, the empirical lead-time profile (i.e. the empirical c.d.f. derived from $(L_1, \ldots, L_Q)$) converges, as the traffic

intensity converges to 1 to the c.d.f. H defined by

$$H(x) = \lambda \int_{L(Q)}^{x} (1 - G(u))du, \quad L(Q) \le x < \infty,$$

where $L(Q)$ is defined by the relation

$$Q = \lambda \int_{L(Q)}^{\infty} (1 - G(u))du.$$

Recall that $\lambda^{(n)} = \lambda(1 - (\gamma/\sqrt{n}))$ and $\mu^{(n)} = \lambda$, so in the example given in sections 3 and 4, $\lambda = 1$.

The case of multiple independent sessions in which all session packets have a common deadline and all packets have an identical service distribution (e.g. exponential or constant), is a special case of this result. We simply define G to be given by the discrete distribution $\{(d_i, p_i), 1 \le i \le S\}$ where $p_i = \lambda_i / \sum_{j=1}^{S} \lambda_j$.

It is convenient to define $E(D) = \sum_{j=1}^{S} d_j p_j$, the expected deadline. Then it is easy to determine that for $L(Q) \le \min_{\{1 \le i \le S\}} d_i$,

$$L(Q) = Q/\lambda - E(D).$$

Note that $L(Q)$ represents the first order approximation to the lead-time of the packet with the shortest lead-time. Now, a packet becomes late when its lead-time becomes negative, and the shortest lead-time becomes negative when $L(Q) \le 0$, or equivalently, when $Q \ge \lambda E(D)$. Consequently, packets departing the system from any session will be late when $Q \ge \lambda E(D)$. For edf, all sessions will have a common fraction of late packets.

Thus we can approximate the packet lateness probability by equating packet lateness with the event $\{Q \ge \lambda E(D)\}$ and computing this probability approximately using standard heavy traffic theory. For the single node with independent renewal process input and independent packet service times, the queue length process can be modeled as a reflected Brownian motion with drift $a = \rho - 1$ and variance $\sigma^2 = \sum_{i=1}^{S} \lambda_i(\alpha_i^2 + \beta_i^2)/\mu_i^2$. For such a drifted, reflected Brownian motion, the equilibrium queue length distribution will be exponential with parameter $2a/\sigma^2$. Consequently, the probability that the queue length exceeds the critical value $\lambda E(D)$ is given by $\exp(-2a\lambda E(D)/\sigma^2)$. This applies to the general case, but the examples presented have been simplified in that $\alpha_i = 0$ or 1 depending upon whether the arrival processes are Poisson or periodic and $\beta_i = 0$ or 1 depending upon whether the packet service distributions are exponential or constant. Furthermore, each session has the same mean service time. This gives a simple closed-form expression for the fraction of late

	Exponential Service				Constant Service			
Session	1	2	3	4	1	2	3	4
Arrival Rate	.05	.15	.25	.50	.05	.15	.25	.50
Deadline	30	40	50	60	30	40	50	60
Service Rate	1	1	1	1	1	1	1	1
Simulated % Late EDF	.0711	.0711	.0711	.0710	.0048	.0049	.0049	.0049
RTQT Approx. % Late EDF	.0660	.0660	.0660	.0660	.0044	.0044	.0044	.0044
Service Rate	1.082	1.082	1.082	1.082	1.014	1.014	1.014	1.014
Simulated % Late EDF	.0009	.0009	.0009	.0009	.0012	.0012	.0012	.0012
RTQT Approx. % Late EDF	.0010	.0010	.0010	.0010	.0010	.0010	.0010	.0010
Service Rate	1.130	1.130	1.130	1.130	1.036	1.036	1.036	1.036
Simulated % Late EDF	.00006	.00007	.00007	.00007	.00011	.00012	.00012	.00011
RTQT Approx. % Late EDF	.00010	.00010	.00010	.00010	.00010	.00010	.00010	.00010

Table 2: Simulated and RTQT Approximation (Poisson Arrivals): EDF Lateness Probabilities

packets given by $\rho^{\lambda E(D)}$ for exponentially distributed service times and $\rho^{2\lambda E(D)}$ for constant service times. Note that the lateness probability approximation depends only on the first two moments of the renewal arrival process and the packet service time distribution and on the first moment of the deadline distributions of the packets in different sessions. Thus very complicated systems can be analyzed with reasonable accuracy using the real-time queueing theory methods, even though an exact analysis is impossible.

To illustrate this lateness approximation, we return to the example presented in Table 1, where $E(D) = 53$, $\rho = .95$ and $\lambda = 1$. Consequently, we approximate packet lateness for the edf scheduling policy by $.95^{53} = .0660$ when the service times are exponential. This is very close to the .0711 value found in the simulation. For the constant service time case, real-time queueing theory predicts a loss fraction of $.95^{2\cdot53} = .0044$. This also compares favorably with the simulation result of .0049. This lateness probability is predicted to be identical for each of the sessions, in spite of their different arrival rates and deadlines, and this prediction is clearly borne out.

Thus, it appears that the two-step methodology of (1) determining (using real-time queueing theory) the queue length conditions for which packets should be finishing late, then (2) approximating the probability of this queue length condition using heavy traffic queueing theory is remarkably effective for edf. One can use the closed-form expressions given in this section to find a change in the systems parameters that will result in some target value for the fraction of packets that are lost. For example, suppose that we allocate more processing capacity or more bandwidth to the real-time tasks, so that the service rate is increased. By how much does the service rate need to be increased in order for the fraction of packets that are late to be reduced to some goal, say α. For exponential service times, one simply needs to solve find a service rate that gives a traffic intensity ρ satisfying $\rho^{\lambda E(D)} = \alpha$, or $\rho = \exp(\log(\alpha)/(\lambda E(D)))$. For constant service rates, we need to choose $\sqrt{\rho} = \exp(\log(\alpha)/(\lambda E(D)))$. Table 2 gives results when we choose $\alpha = .001$ and $\alpha = .0001$. The results in this table show that the real-time queueing approximations are quite accurate; however, they also appear to systematically underestimate or overestimate the true packet loss probabilities. It will be interesting to develop continuity corrections in the above formulates which more accurately estimates these lateness probabilities; however, these relatively crude, first-order formulas provide remarkable accuracy. It should also be noted that in this high traffic intensity situation ($\rho = .95$), the fraction of packets which are late exhibits great variability. The simulation study consisted of 50 independent runs of 2 million packet arrivals each, starting from emptiness. The runs were used to calculate standard errors for the packet loss probabilities. The simulated loss probability is $.0711 \pm .0001$ for exponential service and $.0049 \pm .0001$ for constant service. While the loss probabilities were accurately estimated, there is great variability. For example, in the exponential service case, session packet loss ranged (over different runs) from .0582 to .0860. For constant service, this range was .0018 to .0092. Judged in light of this large variability, the relatively crude real-time queueing approximations of .0660 and .0044 appear remarkably accurate. It also appears that one can accurately estimate the processing or bandwidth capacity required to attain a desired level of packet lateness. In the third section of Table 1, we note that only a 13% increase in service rate is needed to reduce the packet loss rate to .0001 for all session in the exponential case, and only a 3.6% increase is required in the constant service case.

4.3 FIFO Scheduling

We next turn to fifo scheduling. As was mentioned before, fifo is a scheduling policy which does not consider packet deadlines. Consequently, to analyze the real-time behavior of fifo, for example to determine the packet lateness probabilities, we proceed in two steps. First, we ignore packet deadlines completely and assume that each packet has a zero deadline. The lead-time is then the negative of the time spent in queue. When a packet leaves the system, we can add its lead-time to its deadline (i.e. subtract its time in queue from the deadline) to determine its true lead-time at departure. That value is negative if and only if the packet is late. Using this idea, we can determine a condition for lateness for each individual session.

The lead-time profile assuming all packets have 0 deadlines conditional on Q is given by a uniform distribution on the interval $[-\frac{Q}{\lambda}, 0]$. If a packet from session i departs when the queue length is Q, then we add back its true deadline, d_i, to obtain its true lead-time. Consequently, a packet from session i is late if and only if $Q > \lambda d_i$. This gives conditions on the total system occupancy, Q, for which each session will have late packets. We can now use the standard heavy traffic queueing approximations described in the edf analysis to determine approximations for the fraction of packets in each session that are late. Packets in session i will have approximate lateness probability given by $\rho^{\lambda d_i}$, $1 \leq i \leq S$ for exponential service times and $\rho^{2\lambda d_i}$, $1 \leq i \leq S$ for constant service times. These values are presented in Table 3 as are the simulation results.

The theoretical approximation for the lateness probability compares very favorably to the simulated value, session by session. Also, one can use the formulas to determine processing and bandwidth capacity needed to achieve target levels of packet lateness. In the fifo case, the session with the shortest packet deadlines will be the one that determines the choice of the capacity. For exponential service times, an 19.5% (29.3%) increase results in all packet loss levels falling below .001 (.0001). These should be compared with the 8.2% (13%) values for edf. For constant service times, the capacity increases needed for fifo are 6.5% (10.7%) to reach a .001 (.0001) packet loss rate. These capacity increases should be compared with the 1.4% (3.6%) values for edf. One can easily see the superiority of edf over fifo. The loss probabilities derived from

the formulas are reasonably close but systematically differ from the simulated values. Presumably, these first order approximations can be improved through the use of continuity corrections, but this and a more complete study of the performance of this method are topics for further research. Even so, these preliminary results show great promise.

5 A Two-Node Non-Jackson Network

In this section, we illustrate that the methods developed in Section 4 can be extended to networks using the ideas developed by Lehoczky [7].

We consider a particular two node network. Suppose that there are S_1 sessions sending packets first to node 1. Sessions $1, \ldots, S_1 - 1$ receive service from node 1, then leave the network. Session S_1 packets, upon departing from node 1, are transmitted to node 2 for processing, after which they exit from the network. Similarly, suppose that there are S_2 sessions sending packets first to node 2. Sessions $1, \ldots, S_2 - 1$ receive service from node 2, then leave the network. Session S_2 packets, upon departing from node 2, are transmitted to node 1 for processing, after which they exit from the network. There are $S_i + 1$ session buffers at node i, $i = 1, 2$. We assume that each session j arriving from outside the network to node i has its own arrival rate, λ_{ij}, service rate, μ_{ij}, and deadline, d_{ij}. For simplicity in this example, we assume all session packets at all nodes have mean service time 1.

The treatment of packet deadlines must be handled carefully. Packets arriving from outside the network have end-to-end deadlines. Packets visiting both nodes should have longer end-to-end deadlines than packets visiting only one node before leaving the network. However, if its deadline is long and a scheduling policy such as edf is used, then packets from that session will have relatively low priority and likely miss their deadlines more frequently than desired. To deal with this problem, we divide the end-to-end deadline by 2 to create a local or "per-hop" deadline. When a packet leaves its first node en route to its second, the per-hop deadline is added back into its lead-time.

5.1 EDF Scheduling at Both Nodes

We begin with some notation. Let $\lambda_{ij}, 1 \leq i \leq 2; 1 \leq j \leq S_i$ denote the arrival rates and deadlines of sessions arriving to node i from outside the network. Define $(\lambda_{10}, d_{10}) = (\lambda_{2S_2}, d_{2S_2})$, $(\lambda_{20}, d_{20}) = (\lambda_{1S_1}, d_{1S_1})$ for the transitional sessions. Next define $p_{ij} = \lambda_{ij} / \sum_{k=0}^{S_i} \lambda_{ik}$ for $i = 1, 2$ and $0 \leq j \leq S_i$. The lead-times for the transitional packets will depend upon the lead-times of the departing packets at

	Exponential Service				Constant Service			
Session	1	2	3	4	1	2	3	4
Arrival Rate	.05	.15	.25	.50	.05	.15	.25	.50
Deadline	30	40	50	60	30	40	50	60
Service Rate	1	1	1	1	1	1	1	1
Simulated % Late FIFO	.2219	.1345	.0813	.0492	.0496	.0178	.0064	.0023
RTQT Approx. % Late FIFO	.2146	.1285	.0769	.0461	.0461	.0165	.0059	.0021
Service Rate	1.195	1.195	1.195	1.195	1.065	1.065	1.065	1.065
Simulated % Late FIFO	.00060	.00005	.00000	.00000	.00083	.00008	.00001	.00000
RTQT Approx. % Late FIFO	.00102	.00010	.00001	.00000	.00105	.00011	.00001	.00000
Service Rate	1.293	1.293	1.293	1.293	1.107	1.107	1.107	1.107
Simulated % Late FIFO	.00003	.00000	.00000	.00000	.00006	.00000	.00000	.00000
RTQT Approx. % Late FIFO	.00010	.00000	.00000	.00000	.00010	.00000	.00000	.00000

Table 3: Simulated and RTQT Approximation (Poisson Arrivals): FIFO Lateness Probabilities

	Exponential Service					Constant Service				
Session Nodes 1,2	1	2	3	4	Hop #2	1	2	3	4	Hop #2
Arrival Rate Node 1	.10	.15	.10	.30	.30	.10	.15	.10	.30	.30
Arrival Rate Node 2	.15	.10	.10	.30	.30	.15	.10	.10	.30	.30
Deadlines Node 1	30	35	40	45	30	30	35	40	45	30
Deadlines Node 2	20	30	40	30	45	20	30	40	30	45
Service Rate Nodes 1,2	1	1	1	1	1	1	1	1	1	1
Sim. EDF % Late at 1	.1184	.1183	.1181	.1182	.1381	.0106	.0106	.0106	.0106	.0109
RTQT Pred. Late at 1	.1246	.1246	.1246	.1246	.1546	.0114	.0114	.0114	.0114	.0127
Sim. EDF % Late at 2	.1250	.1247	.1249	.1248	.1323	.0097	.0097	.0097	.0098	.0097
RTQT Pred. Late at 2	.1357	.1357	.1357	.1357	.1455	.0128	.0128	.0128	.0128	.0130

Table 4: Simulated and RTQT Approximation (Poisson Arrivals): EDF Lateness Probabilities

	Exponential Service					Constant Service				
Session Nodes 1,2	1	2	3	4	Hop #2	1	2	3	4	Hop #2
Arrival Rate Node 1	.10	.15	.10	.30	.30	.10	.15	.10	.30	.30
Arrival Rate Node 2	.15	.10	.10	.30	.30	.15	.10	.10	.30	.30
Deadlines Node 1	30	35	40	45	30	30	35	40	45	30
Deadlines Node 2	20	30	40	30	45	20	30	40	30	45
Service Rate Nodes 1,2	1	1	1	1	1	1	1	1	1	1
Sim. EDF % Late at 1	.2221	.1731	.1349	.1047	.1970	.0391	.0229	.0134	.0078	.0178
RTQT Pred. Late at 1	.2146	.1661	.1285	.0994	.1879	.0461	.0276	.0165	.0099	.0152
Sim. EDF % Late at 2	.3657	.2209	.1334	.2210	.0605	.1157	.0388	.0133	.0389	.0018
RTQT Pred. Late at 2	.3585	.2146	.1285	.2146	.0555	.1285	.0461	.0165	.0461	.0010

Table 5: Simulated and RTQT Approximation (Poisson Arrivals): FIFO Lateness Probabilities

the other node. Let $\mathbf{L} = (L_1, L_2)$ where L_i denotes the lead-time of departing packets at node i, $i = 1, 2$. These are random processes, varying with time, but using real-time queueing theory they are deterministically related to $\mathbf{Q} = (Q_1, Q_2)$, in a way developed in Section 4.2 for edf and Section 4.3 for fifo. Hence the instantaneous lead-times of the transitional packets are $d_{10}^*(\mathbf{L}) = d_{10} + L_2$, and $d_{20}^*(\mathbf{L}) = d_{20} + L_1$. Now, the lead-time distributions depend on $\mathbf{L}$; however, those distributions, when combined with $\mathbf{Q}$, uniquely determine $\mathbf{L}$. Thus, we must solve a fixed-point problem to define a one-to-one correspondence between $\mathbf{L}$ and $\mathbf{Q}$. The solution to the fixed-point problem will depend on the scheduling policy. Since our performance measure is the fraction of late packets, for node i packets, were interested in $\{\mathbf{Q} | L_i \leq 0\}$ for $i = 1, 2$. For transitional packets exiting the system from node 2, packet lateness corresponds to $\{\mathbf{Q} | L_1 \leq -d_{20}\} \cup \{\mathbf{Q} | L_1 > -d_{20} \cap L_2 \leq 0\}$ where the first event corresponds to packets that arrive at node 2 after their end-to-end deadline has elapsed. Lateness of transitional packets exiting the system from node 1, corresponds to $\{\mathbf{Q} | L_2 \leq -d_{10}\} \cup \{\mathbf{Q} | L_2 > -d_{10} \cap L_1 \leq 0\}$. Once these sets of queue lengths have been determined, we use heavy traffic theory to determine their probability. Even though the network is not a Jackson network, the heavy traffic approximation will be of product form, hence a product of exponentials.

While the probabilities are straightforward to compute, they are difficult to represent in closed form. One simple case occurs with fifo service and equal traffic intensities of ρ at both nodes. The fraction of transitional packets that will finish late is given by $\rho^{2d_{i0}}(1 - d_{i0} \log(\rho))$, for $i = 1, 2$, where $2d_{i0}$ is the end-to-end deadline for transitional packets exiting node i.

We present simulation results for edf in Table 4 and fifo in Table 5. Once again, one can also determine service rates such that a given level of lateness is attained for any particular session.

6 Summary and Conclusions

In this paper, we have presented a new analysis of edf and fifo scheduling algorithms for communication networks carrying real-time traffic. Closed form expressions predicting the fraction of late packets for each session were developed. Those expressions were remarkably accurate for the limited simulation results that were presented. Furthermore, they were used to solve certain system design questions. A more systematic study is needed to determine the accuracy of this approximation and improvements of them, but the preliminary results are very promising.

The concepts were applied to a two-node non-Jackson network. Analytic formulas were again developed to predict the fraction of late packets for every session, and those formulas compared well with simulation results. These formulas can be used to solve design questions.

There are many extensions possible for this model, beyond simply increasing the number of nodes in the network. It will be important to develop analyses for traffic controllers, such as the leaky-bucket admission control algorithm. The heavy traffic methods presented in this paper should offer a viable approach to such analyses, and it is hoped that this paper will stimulate interest in these topics.

References

[1] Chang, C.-S., "Stability, queue length, and delay of deterministic and stochastic queueing networks," *IEEE Transactions on Automatic Control*, 39, May 1994, 913-931.

[2] Cruz, R. L., "A calculus for network delay, Part 1: Network elements in isolation," *IEEE Transactions on Information Theory*, 37, January, 1991, 114-131.

[3] Cruz, R. L., "A calculus for network delay, Part II: Network Analysis," *IEEE Transactions on Information Theory*, 37, January, 1991, 132-141.

[4] Doytchinov, B., Lehoczky, J.P. and Shreve, S., "Real-time queues in heavy traffic with earliest deadline first queue discipline," Technical Report, Dept. Mathematical Sciences, Carnegie Mellon Univ., July, 1998.

[5] Hong, J., Tan, X., and Towsley, D., "A performance analysis of minimum laxity and earliest deadline scheduling in a real-time system," *IEEE Trans. Computers*, 38(12), Dec., 1989, 1736-1744.

[6] Lehoczky, J.P., "Real-time queueing theory," *Proc IEEE Real-Time Systems Symp.*, Dec. 1996, 186-195.

[7] Lehoczky, J.P., "Real-time queueing network theory," *Proc. Real-Time Systems Symp.*, December 1997, 58-67.

[8] Panwar, S., and Towsley, D., "On the optimality of the STE rule for multiple server queues that serve customers with deadlines," COINS TR 88-81, Univ. Mass., 1988.

[9] Parekh, A.,K. and Gallager, R.G., "A generalized processor sharing approach to flow control in integrated services networks: The single node case," *IEEE/ACM Trans. Networking,* 1, June 1993, 344-357.

[10] Parekh, A.,K. and Gallager, R.G., "A generalized processor sharing approach to flow control in integrated services networks: The multiple node case," *IEEE/ACM Trans. Networking,* 2, April, 1994, 137-150.

[11] Williams, R. J., "Diffusion approximations for open multiclass queueing networks: sufficient conditions involving state space collapse," Dept. Math., U.C. San Diego, 1997.

[12] H. Zhang, "Service Disciplines For Guaranteed Performance Service in Packet-Switching Networks," *Proc. IEEE*, 83(10), Oct. 1995, 1374-1399.

Proportional Share Scheduling of Operating System Services for Real-Time Applications[*]

Kevin Jeffay, F. Donelson Smith, Arun Moorthy, James Anderson
University of North Carolina at Chapel Hill
Department of Computer Science
Chapel Hill, NC 27599-3175
{jeffay,smithfd,moorthy,anderson}@cs.unc.edu

Abstract

While there is currently great interest in the problem of providing real-time services in general purpose operating systems, the issue of real-time scheduling of internal operating system activities has received relatively little attention. Without such real-time scheduling, the system is susceptible to conditions such as *receive livelock* — a situation in which an operating system spends all its time processing arriving network packets, and application processes, even if scheduled with a real-time scheduler, are starved. We investigate the problem of scheduling operating system activities such as network protocol processing in a proportional share manner. We describe a proportional share implementation of the FreeBSD operating system and demonstrate that it solves the receive livelock problem. Packets are processed within the operating system only at the cumulative rate at which the destination applications are prepared to receive them. If packets arrive at a faster rate then they are discarded after consuming minimal system resources. In this manner the performance of "well behaved" applications is unaffected by "misbehaving" applications. We demonstrate this effect by running a set of multimedia applications under a variety of network conditions on a set of increasingly sophisticated proportional share implementations of FreeBSD and comparing their performance. This work contributes to our knowledge of the engineering of proportional share real-time systems.

1. Introduction

Applications such as interactive multimedia and immersive virtual environments, require real-time computation and communication services from the operating system in order to be effective. As applications such as these are increasingly being hosted on general purpose (rather than specialized real-time) operating systems, there is great interest in migrating real-time systems technology to desktop operating systems. A recent development in the area of real-time support in general purpose operating systems is the use of proportional share resource allocation for providing real-time services [3, 7, 9, 13]. In a proportional share

system, processes make progress at a precise, uniform rate according to the share of system resources they are to receive. Processes appear to execute on a dedicated virtual processor whose capacity is a fraction of that of the actual processor. Proportional share resource allocation is particularly well-suited to the problem of providing real-time services within a general purpose operating system because its underlying scheduling mechanism is a quantum-based round-robin-like scheduler and because one can implement a proportional share system without introducing any new application-level concepts or mechanisms. This means that existing applications can be made to execute in a predictable, real-time manner without modifying the application.

Previous operating system work in proportional share resource allocation has considered only the problem of scheduling user processes. In particular, the problem of scheduling operating system activity such as network protocol processing has not been addressed. This is significant because much of the processing in the operating system occurs asynchronously with respect to system calls made by applications. If the execution of operating system activities is not managed carefully, the operating system may consume an inordinate amount of resources and nullify the benefits of real-time scheduling for application processes.

For example, consider the *receive livelock* problem described by Druschel and Banga, and by Mogul and Ramakrishnan [6, 23]. In most general purpose operating systems, the processing of inbound network packets is the highest priority activity after the processing of clock interrupts. This is the case because the network interface is arguably the most real-time device on a general purpose computer. Since one cannot typically control the rate at which packets arrive at a computer, when packets are not processed "fast enough," it is possible that packets may be lost at the network interface. Said another way, unlike most other devices attached to a computer, the operating system cannot force the network interface to stop generating service requests without running the risk of losing data. On modern high-speed networks, packets can arrive at

---

[*] Work supported by grants from the National Science Foundation (grants CCR-9510156, & CCR-9732916) and the IBM Corporation.

high enough rates that the process of responding to network interrupts and performing the necessary protocol processing can saturate the system. The system will spend all of its time preparing packets to be received by applications and there will be no time for applications to actually receive and process any packets. Thus in the worst case, all inbound data is lost. Every packet is partially processed (by the operating system) while none are fully processed (by the destination application). The receive livelock problem has been observed on server machines such as web servers, file servers, and DNS name servers, that are attached to high-speed networks such as 100 Mbps FDDI rings [6].

The essence of the receive livelock problem is the static priority scheduling mechanisms employed in most operating systems (including most real-time operating systems). If the highest priority processing consumes all of the system's resources then all other processes starve. The solution therefore, is (1) to bound the resources consumed by the network interface, and (2) to ensure that if a packet is received at the network interface it will be processed by the destination application. An approach to the first problem investigated by Mogul and Ramakrishnan, is to poll for newly arrived network packets under times of high load. This technique worked well, however, by itself, polling could not ensure that packets received are eventually processed by the application. This is because ultimately, their system was not a real-time system and did not support integrated application and operating system processing. To address the second problem, Druschel and Banga developed a network subsystem architecture for processing packets according to application-level priorities. We adopt their architecture but implement it using proportional share technology. Moreover, we provide a real-time solution by integrating application and kernel-level scheduling. When combined with proportional share scheduling of user processes, we demonstrate that proportional share scheduling of packet and protocol processing provides a means for precisely controlling the resources consumed by the network subsystem. Network processing will occur at the rates at which applications are prepared to receive packets and hence all data received is eventually processed by the application. Moreover, our solution protects applications from "misbehaving" senders. If a remote sender transmits messages to an application on our machine at a higher rate than the receiving application can process, the "excess" messages are dropped at the network interface after only minimal processing. Thus applications whose senders are "well behaved" are unaffected by these errant processes.

While we are advocates of proportional share technology, we recognize that other solutions to the problems we outline herein are possible (*e.g.*, [23]). Whether or not one views a particular resource allocation approach as being intrinsically better or worse than any other will depend on factors such as the nature of real-time guarantees required by applications, the extent to which it is considered acceptable to modify the internal structures of the operating system or its API, and the extent to which it is considered acceptable to modify applications to take advantage of the new real-time services. Our goal is to understand the cost of providing real-time services transparently to applications that are unaware of their existence. We seek to understand the complexity of providing such services in conventional operating systems and how such services are likely to perform.

Our work makes the following contributions. First we demonstrate a model for proportional share scheduling of operating system services through minimal modifications to the existing operating system. We show how a monolithic, single-threaded operating system kernel such as the FreeBSD kernel can be extended to allow proportional share execution of network packet and protocol processing. Second, we demonstrate that proportional share execution of the network packet and protocol processing solves the receive livelock problem. We show that packets are received only at the rates at which applications are able to process them and how unmodified applications process the packets that are received in real time.

The following section discusses related work in the design of real-time operating systems. Section 3 briefly reviews the main concepts of proportional share resource allocation. Section 4 describes the network protocol processing components of FreeBSD and describes their proportional share implementation. Section 5 evaluates the implementation by demonstrating both the effects of the receive livelock problem and its elimination through proportional share scheduling of the network interface. We conclude in Section 6 with some comments for future investigations.

2. Related Work

Research into the design and construction of real-time operating systems can be crudely partitioned into three categories: the development of brand new real-time operating systems, the extension of existing operating systems to support real-time processing, and the provision of real-time execution facilities by virtualizing the underlying hardware and executing a largely unmodified general purpose operating system on the resulting virtual machine. The most recent example of a new real-time operating system is the Rialto operating system developed at Microsoft [15]. Recent examples of the real-time extensions to existing operating systems are more numerous and include Real-Time Mach [21], the Processor Capacity Reserves variant of Real-Time Mach [18], the SMART Solaris system [7], and variants of Linux [16]. Of particular note here are extensions to UNIX kernels to support proportional share scheduling. These include the SFQ SVR4 UNIX system [3], the Mach- and FreeBSD-based Lottery Scheduling implementations [13], and the EEVDF version of FreeBSD [9]. Each of these systems supports only proportional share execution of user processes. Examples of the providing real-time services through virtual machine emulation include Real-Time Linux [17], the Real-Time IBM Microkernel [22], and a real-time HAL extension for Windows NT [12].

Our approach falls under the category of extending an existing operating system to support proportional share processing. From our perspective the most relevant related work is the work done within the context of the Processor Capacity Reserves (PCR) extensions to Real-Time Mach (RT Mach) [18, 20]. In this work, the RT Mach developers were also concerned with the impact of network protocol processing and explicitly scheduled this process as a real-time process using the PCR abstraction. Protocol processing was performed in a user-level process and hence scheduling its execution was straightforward as real-time scheduling of user processes is the cornerstone of RT Mach. The PCR abstraction ensures that real-time activities do not execute for longer than they are expected to. Thus, although the RT Mach developers were primarily interested in showing the utility of integrated protocol and application scheduling, it is likely that a PCR system could be made immune to the receive livelock problem.

Our work differs in two respects. First, we are dealing a differently structured host operating system. Unlike the original microkernel origins of RT Mach which enable user-level execution of system processes, we are dealing with a monolithic, single-threaded operating system. Our challenge here is to schedule kernel "processes" without rewriting the kernel so as to create physical, schedulable processes. Second, whereas RT Mach employs rate-monotonic scheduling technology, we are experimenting with proportional share resource allocation. Ultimately we hope to show that real-time execution of operating systems services is possible in a proportional share system without having to resort to explicitly restructure the kernel to make it multi-threaded.

3. Proportional Share Resource Allocation

In a proportional share (PS) system each shared resource r is allocated in discrete quanta of size at most q_r. At the beginning of each time quantum a process is selected to use the resource. Once the process acquires the resource, it may use the resource for the entire time quantum, or it may release the resource before the time quantum expires. For a given resource, we associate a *weight* with each process that determines the relative *share* of the resource that the process should receive. Let w_i denote the weight of process i, and let $A(t)$ be the set of all processes active at

time t. Define the (instantaneous) share $f_i(t)$ of process i at time t as

$$f_i(t) = \frac{w_i}{\sum_{j \in A(t)} w_j} \qquad (1)$$

A share represents a fraction of the resource's capacity that is "reserved" for a process. If the resource can be allocated in arbitrarily small sized quanta, and if the process's share remains constant during any time interval $[t_1, t_2]$, then the process is entitled to use the resource for $(t_2 - t_1)f_i(t)$ time units in the interval. As processes are created/destroyed or blocked/released, the membership of $A(t)$ changes and hence the denominator in (1) changes. Thus in practice, a process's share of a given resource will change over time. As the total weight of processes in the system increases, each process's share of the resource decreases. As the total weight of processes in the system decreases, each process's share of the resource increases. When a process's share varies over time, the service time that process i should receive in any interval $[t_1, t_2]$, is

$$S_i(t_0, t_1) = \int_{t_1}^{t_2} f_i(t) \, dt \qquad (2)$$

time units.

Equations (1) and (2) correspond to an ideal "fluid-flow" system in which the resource can be allocated in arbitrarily small units of time. In practice one can implement only a discrete approximation to the fluid system. When the resource is allocated in discrete time quanta it is not possible for a process to always receive exactly the service time it is entitled to in all time intervals. The difference between the service time that a process should receive at a time t, and the time it actually receives is called the service time lag (or simply lag). Let t_0^i be the time at which process i becomes active, and let $s(t_0^i, t)$ be the service time process i receives in the interval $[t_0^i, t]$. Then if process i is active in the interval $[t_0^i, t]$, its lag at time t is defined as

$$lag_i(t) = S_i(t_0^i, t) - s_i(t_0^i, t). \qquad (3)$$

Since the lag quantifies the allocation accuracy, we use it as our primary metric for evaluating the performance of PS scheduling algorithms. Previously we have shown that one can schedule a set of processes in a PS system such that the lag is bounded by a constant over all time intervals [9]. This means that a PS system's deviation from a system with perfectly uniform allocation is bounded and thus, as explained below, real-time execution is possible.

3.1 Scheduling to Minimize Lag

The goal in proportional share scheduling is to minimize the maximum possible lag. This is done by conceptually tracking the lag of processes and at the end of each quantum, considering only processes whose lag is positive [9]. If a process's lag is positive then it is "behind schedule" compared to the perfect fluid system — it should have accumulated more time on the CPU than it has up to the current time. If a process's lag is positive it is considered eligible to execute. If its lag is negative, then the process has received more processor time than it should have up to the current time and it is considered ineligible to execute

When multiple processes are eligible, they are scheduled using an *earliest deadline first* rule, where a process's deadline is equal to its estimated execution time cost divided by its share of the CPU $f_i(t)$. This deadline represents a point in the future when the process should complete execution if it receives exactly its share of the CPU. For example, if a process's weight is such that its share of the CPU at the current time is 10% and it requires 2 *ms* of CPU time to complete execution, then its deadline will be 20 *ms* in the future. If the process actually receives 10% of the CPU, over the next 20 *ms* it will execute for 2 *ms*.

In [9] it was shown that this proportional share version of deadline scheduling provides optimal (*i.e.*, minimum possible) lag bounds. This algorithm forms the basis for the *PS* implementation described in Section 4.

3.2 Realizing Real-Time Execution

In principle, there is nothing "real-time" about proportional share resource allocation. Proportional share resource allocation is concerned solely with *uniform* allocation (often referred to in the literature as *fair* allocation). A *PS* scheduler achieves uniform allocation if it can guarantee that processes' lags are always bounded.

Real-time computing is achieved in a *PS* system by (*i*) ensuring that a process's share of the CPU (and other required resources) remains constant over time, and by (*ii*) scheduling processes such that each process's lag is always bounded by a constant. If these two conditions hold over an interval of length t for a process i, then process i is guaranteed to receive $(f_i \times t) \pm \varepsilon$ units of the resource's capacity, where f_i is the fraction of the resource reserved for process i, and ε is the allocation error, $0 \leq \varepsilon \leq \delta$, for some constant δ [9]. Thus, although real-time allocation is possible, it is not possible to provide hard and fast guarantees of adherence to application-defined timing constraints. Said another way, all guarantees have an implicit, and fundamental, "$\pm \varepsilon$" term. In the implementation described below ε is a set-able parameter, but is fixed at 1 *ms*.

Our deadline-based scheduling algorithm ensures that each process's lag is bounded by a constant [9] (condition (*i*)). To ensure a process's share remains constant over time (condition (*ii*)), whenever the total weight in the system changes, a "real-time" process's weight must be adjusted so that its initial share (as given by equation (1)) does not change. For example, if the total weight in the system increases (*e.g.*, because new processes are created), then a real-time process's weight must increase by a proportional amount. Adjusting the weight to maintain a constant share is simply a matter of solving equation (1) for w_i when $f_i(t)$ is a constant function. (Note that w_i appears in both the numerator and denominator of the right-hand side of (1).)

4. Realizing Proportional Share Execution of Operating System Activities: A Case Study

The challenges in realizing proportional share execution of operating system activities are numerous. They include:

- Identifying "threads" of control within the operating system kernel that need to be scheduled and subjecting them to the purview of a *PS* scheduler.

- Assigning weights and shares to kernel activities.

- Ensuring mutually exclusive access to shared data structures in the kernel.

- Assigning buffer capacity in a proportional manner at asynchronous kernel boundaries.

We illustrate these problems using the network packet and protocol processing portions of the FreeBSD operating system as an example. For brevity, we consider only processing associated with the receipt of inbound packets. (Processing of outbound packets turns out to be an easier problem.)

4.1 Scheduling of Operating System Activities in FreeBSD

FreeBSD is a derivative of the 4.4 BSD Operating System [5]. Network processing occurs in three distinct layers in FreeBSD: the *socket layer*, the *protocol layer*, and the *device interface* layer. Figure 1 illustrates these layers for UDP packets. The layers for other transport protocols are similar. Processing within each layer is controlled by events external to the kernel such as hardware interrupts from the network interface or software interrupts from user processes making system calls to receive network messages. Interrupts from the network interface device are serviced by a device-specific interrupt handler that is executed at a high priority level (called *splimp*) that preempts all other network-related processing and is preemptable only by interrupts from the hardware clock. The device driver copies data from buffers on the adapter card into a chain of fixed-size kernel memory buffers (called *mbufs*) sufficient to hold the entire packet plus auxiliary data such as queue pointers. This chain of *mbufs* is passed on a procedure call to a general interface input routine for a class of input devices (*e.g.*, Ethernet). This procedure uses the type field from the Ethernet header to determine which protocol (*e.g.*, IP) should receive the packet and enqueues the packet on that protocol's input queue. It then posts a software interrupt (with an intermediate priority, *splnet*) that will cause the protocol layer to be executed when no higher priority hardware or software activities are pending. It then returns from interrupt processing at the *splimp* level.

Processing by the protocol layer occurs asynchronously with respect to the device driver processing. When the software interrupt posted by the device driver at priority *splnet* is the highest priority, the protocol-layer input routine is entered. It executes a main loop in which each iteration removes the *mbuf* chain at the head of the input queue and passes it to the appropriate processing routines for IP and UDP. To protect the input queue data structure shared by the protocol layer and the interface layer, the protocol layer dequeue function temporarily raises its priority to the *splimp* level to prevent preemption by the device driver. The *mbuf* chain is then processed completely in the protocol layer and finally enqueued on the receive queue for the destination socket. If any process is blocked in a kernel system call awaiting input on the socket, it is unblocked. Software interrupt porcessing returns when no more *mbufs* remain on the protocol input queue.

The kernel socket layer code executes when a process invokes some form of receive system call on a socket descriptor and runs at the lowest-priority software interrupt level (*spl0*). This priority is used for all normal kernel processing so the socket code can execute when no higher priority interrupts are pending. When there is a receive system call active for the socket, data to be received is copied into the receiving process's local buffers from the *mbuf* chain(s) at the head of that socket's receive queue. This queue is protected by a locking mechanism and by temporarily raising the socket layer priority to *splnet* to prevent preemption by the protocol layer. When there is sufficient data on the socket receive queue to satisfy the current request, the kernel completes the system call and returns to the user process.

For a more complete description of these functions see [5] and [19].

4.2 *PS* Scheduling of Operating System Activities in FreeBSD

Conceptually each layer of protocol processing represents a separate logical process that must be scheduled. These layers are not processes in the traditional sense but instead are more akin to procedure calls that are called by a software interrupt dispatching mechanism that is invoked upon the completion of every system call or quantum expiration. The existing dispatching mechanism is, in essence, a sim-

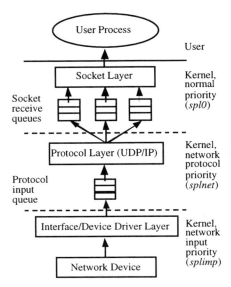

Figure 1: FreeBSD, UDP, network input processing.

ple static priority scheduler. We have modified the FreeBSD software interrupt dispatching mechanism to dispatch kernel activities only at quantum expirations. This has the positive effect of ensuring that user processes execute for a full quantum once scheduled, but also the negative effect of delaying kernel activities. This effect can be mitigated, however, by an appropriate choice of a quantum duration. In the experiments described below we used a 1 *ms* quantum (compared to the default FreeBSD quantum of 100 *ms*) without ill-effect.

In addition to dispatching software interrupts at quantum boundaries, we also assign a weight to each interrupt and perform an eligibility and deadline test for each interrupt [9]. Software interrupts are considered equally with user processes and either the eligible user process or eligible software interrupt with the earliest deadline is scheduled next. One complexity here is that kernel activities communicate and synchronize through shared memory in the kernel. Previously, the software interrupt priority structure was used to ensure shared data in the kernel is accessed in a mutually exclusive manner. We can no longer use these mechanisms because in order for the lag bounds guaranteed by the theory to hold, a process must be able to execute for its entire quantum once scheduled. Thus when a software interrupt handler executes, we must ensure that no shared data structures within the kernel are locked when a quantum expires.

In general, there are several approaches to solving this problem. For the FreeBSD network protocol processing code, each software interrupt routine consists of a loop that removes a packet from one queue, performs some processing and then inserts the packet on a second queue. These loops typically execute until the source queue is empty. We modified these loops to execute until either the source queue is empty or until a maximum number of packets has been processed. In the latter case the interrupt routine will reschedule itself (post another software interrupt for itself) and then terminate. The maximum number of packets to be processed is chosen to be the maximum number of packets that are guaranteed to be processed to completion within one quantum. Bounding the number of packets processed in this way ensures that software interrupt processing is never preempted by a quantum expiry and hence that shared data structures are always in a consistent state at the end of each quantum. Note that although this technique appears at first to reduce performance (because kernel activities may not execute for an entire quantum), the actual rate at which activities are performed depends on the share of the processor they are assigned and not on how long they actually execute once scheduled. Moreover, by adopting this approach we need not include any synchronization code in the packet processing code and hence overall this code is more efficient.

The maximum number of packets that could be processed was determined by hand timing the loops to determine the maximum number of packets that could be processed within a quantum. The time to process a packet is, for the most part, independent of the size of a packet (much of the processing consists of pointer manipulations) and in all cases is bounded. These measurements were also used to determine the cost of a particular kernel activity and used by the dispatcher to compute deadlines for kernel activities as described in Section 3.1.

4.3 *PS* Scheduling of User Processes

User processes are scheduled using the FreeBSD scheduler modified to perform the eligibility and deadline calculations. Process descriptors were changed to record a weight and share for each process as well as a measure of its current execution time cost. Processes can either assign their own weights or have them assigned by a separate manager process. If programs are written with knowledge of our kernel modifications they can alter their weights through a system call. Pre-existing programs receive a default weight that ensures they make progress as in a time-sharing system. This weight (and the weight of any user process) can be changed by the manager process. By manipulating a process's weight, its rate of progress relative to the other processes in the system can be controled. By manipulating a process's share, one can control its absolute rate of progress independent of the other processes in the system. If the manager sets a process's share, the kernel determines what weight the process should have in order to guarantee that it receives the appropriate share [10].

The kernel records a bit indicating whether a process has a fixed weight or a fixed share. Processes with a fixed share are "real-time" processes and their weights will be adjusted to maintain a constant share whenever the total weight of processes in the system changes (*i.e.*, whenever a process is created or destroyed). Beyond the fixed weight/share dichotomy, there is no distinction between real-time and non-real-time processes in the kernel. Any process can become a real-time process at any time so long as the total shares of all real-time processes remains less than 1.0.

To schedule a process the kernel needs an estimate of the process's execution time. The estimated execution time is used to determine the process's deadline as outlined in Section 3.1. We use a simple heuristic of monitoring the exe-

cution time consumed by processes between system calls and assume that the execution time used in the recent past is a good indicator of the time a process will require in the near future. We use the standard FreeBSD execution time monitoring infrastructure to record the elapsed execution time of processes.[1] When a process performs network I/O a new deadline is computed for the process based on the amount of execution time consumed since the last I/O operation. For processes with a regular structure (such as most cyclic real-time processes) this heuristic should work quite well. For the multimedia processing load considered in our experiments (see Section 5), this simple heuristic was sufficient. Moreover, if execution time estimates are inaccurate the kernel will be able to detect this fact. If the execution time estimate for a process is too low then the process will not have made another system call by its deadline. If the estimate is too high, the process will complete its current execution before its deadline. Thus one can employ software phased-locked loops to further refine the estimates of execution time[4].

Note, however, that if the estimate of a process's execution time is inaccurate, it effects only the performance of that process. Independent of the execution time estimate, a process can never consume more than its share of the processor (and shares are determined by weights not costs). Thus if an estimate of a process's execution time is overly optimistic or if a programmer willfully specifies an execution time that is too low, the performance of other processes is unaffected.

4.4 Assigning Weights to Kernel Activities

Kernel processing is scheduled together with user processing; each according to its weight. Weights for user processes are either set by the processes directly or by the manager process. Weights for kernel activities are derived from user weights. For the purpose of defining weights, we distinguish between two types of kernel processing: per user process activity and demultiplexing activity. Per user process activities consist of the kernel processing associated with system calls made by user processes. When a system call is made it is considered a logical extension of the invoking process and execution of the appropriate kernel activity is performed (scheduled) with the same weight as the invoking process. For example, when a process attempts to receive a message from a socket, the socket layer processing is performed with the same weight as the receiving process. In this manner kernel processing directly related to an individual process occurs at the same rate at which the process executes.

---

[1] Note that because software interrupts are now scheduled, timings of user activities are more accurate than in unmodified FreeBSD (as was the case in [23]). Previously, software interrupt processing was charged to the user process executing at the time of the interrupt.

Other kernel activities such as IP processing are performed on behalf of a collection of processes. For example, when the IP processing software interrupt is posted after a packet arrives, the ultimate destination of the packet is not known and hence the rate at which it should be processed cannot be determined (without actually processing the packet!). In this case, IP processing needs to make progress at the sum of the rates of all processes there are currently receiving packets from the network. To ensure this is the case, whenever a user process binds to a socket, the kernel records its weight and adds a corresponding amount of weight to the weight of the IP processing kernel activity.

One subtlety here is that whereas user processes may measure rates in arbitrary units (*e.g.*, execution time received per second), IP processing makes progress in units of packets processed per time unit. Thus a user process's weight must be mapped into a IP weight by estimating how many packets a user process is likely to receive per unit time. To do this, we use the deadline of a process as an estimate of its period and assume that the process will receive one packet per period. For example, if a process's weight is such that its share is 10% of the CPU, and the process's measured execution time is 2 *ms*, its period (the product of dividing its execution time by its share) will be 20 *ms*. Thus the weight of the IP activity needs to be set so as to ensure that IP processing is performed at least once every 20 *ms*. Therefore, whenever a process with deadline d binds to a socket, the weight of the IP activity is increased so that the share of the activity increases by c/d, where c is the cost of IP processing for a single packet (a constant). In addition, the weight of the IP processing activity is further inflated to increase its share by a configurable amount that is sufficient to ensure that non-requested IP packets (*e.g.*, ARPs and other broadcast packets) can be processed without effecting the performance of user packet processing.

4.5 Proportional Share Allocation of Kernel Buffers

A final issue to consider is the allocation of buffer space within the kernel. Just as processes require a share of the CPU in order to make progress, they also require a share of the buffers available in each of the interface and protocol processing layers within the kernel. In FreeBSD, at most 50 packets can be queued pending processing by the IP layer. If these queue entries are allocated to arriving packets in a FCFS manner, it is possible that applications expecting to receive packets at a slow rate may be adversely effected by applications that either are not processing packets fast enough or whose senders "misbehave" by sending packets at a higher rate than the application is prepared to receive. For example, consider a scenario wherein an audio phone application expects to receive one packet every 20 *ms*, and a file transfer program expects to receive 200

packets/second (one packet every 5 *ms* on average). In this case the IP processing activity will be assigned a weight so as to ensure it is able to process at least 50 + 200 = 250 packets/second. If the file transfer sender does not pace its transmission or if it sends at a higher than expected average rate, the device interface queue may become full with unprocessed file transfer packets and when an audio phone packet arrives, it is dropped for lack of space. In this case a "misbehaving" non-real-time application is negatively impacting a "well behaved" real-time application.

The solution, a variant of that proposed by Druschel and Banga [23], is to allocate queue capacity (a number of queue entries) for packets destined for user processes in proportion to the rate at which the process is expected to receive packets. For example, if a user process currently is expecting to receive 1 packet every 20 *ms*, and the period of the IP processing activity is currently 10 *ms*, then at least one queue entry should be reserved for this process. (In practice, one would reserve more entries to deal with a less than periodic arrival process.) If a user process is executing fast enough to receive 1 packet every 5 *ms*, then at least 2 queue entries should be reserved for this process.

In addition to reserving queue entries for user processes, the IP processing activity also has to internally schedule the processing of individual packets. That is, it cannot simply service packets in FCFS order as this would hurt well-behaved applications when other applications are having packets delivered at inappropriate rates. Although queue entries are reserved for user processes, it is likely that at any given time there will exist more packets than the IP activity can process in one quantum, and hence the IP activity must explicitly determine which packets to service first in order to ensure that well-behaved applications do not lose packets. To do this, we simply recursively implement another instance of a proportional share scheduler inside the IP activity to select the packet to process next. Whenever the IP activity is scheduled, it internally sub-allocates its quantum to packet processing by assigning eligible times and deadline to packets based on the weights of the user process that will receive the packet. Combined, the hierarchical scheduling mechanism and queue entry reservation system ensure that when a packet for a well-behaved application arrives at the network interface, it is guaranteed to be processed at the IP layer and delivered to the user process, independent of how other applications are receiving packets. Said another way, packets for misbehaving applications are dropped as early as possible after only minimal processing.

Note that all we are doing here is managing buffers in precisely the same way routers manage buffers under fair queueing-based service disciplines [1, 2, 8, 14].

5. Experimental Results

We modified the FreeBSD 2.2.2-RELEASE system to support proportional share scheduling and ran a suite of experiments to assess the impact of proportional share execution of packet and network protocol processing. Our experiments were conducted on a 200Mhz Pentium Pro with 64 MB of memory. The network interface was a 3Com 3C595 (*vx0*) 10/100 Ethernet adapter running at 10Mbps. We used three simple applications that we believe are indicative of the types of real-time and non-realtime processing that is likely to be performed on a general purpose workstation. The applications were:

- an audio player application that handles incoming 100 byte messages at a rate of 50/second and computes for 1 millisecond on each message (requiring 5% of the CPU on average),

- a motion-JPEG receiver that handles incoming 1470 byte messages at a rate of 90/second and computes for 5 milliseconds on each message (requiring 45% of the CPU on average), and

- file transfer program that handles incoming 1470 byte messages at a rate of 200/second and computes for 1 millisecond on each message (requiring 20% of the CPU on average).

Each of these programs consists of a simple main loop consisting of a *read()* operation on a UDP socket bound to a specific port followed by a computation phase with a known execution time. In addition to these three receiving processes we also ran another process that executed the Dhrystone benchmark program to simulate a compute intensive program.

Each of these programs was run as a separate process on the modified FreeBSD system and assigned a processor share according to its CPU utilization and execution rate. (The Dhrystone was not explicitly assigned a weight. Instead FreeBSD assigned it a weight that resulted in it receiving whatever share of the CPU remained allocated.) We wrote three programs to act as sending processes and send messages with the desired size and rate to the corresponding receiver. We ran one of these programs on each of three additional machines (all 200 Mhz or greater Pentiums) running FreeBSD v2.2.2, all connected to an unloaded 10Mbps Ethernet along with the machine running the modified FreeBSD kernel.

The experimental setup is illustrated in Figure 2.

With this experimental setup we conducted a number of experiments where we investigated the effects of different possibilities for the scheduling within the modified FreeBSD kernel. For each experiment, three variations of the traffic generated by the sending processes were used: (1) all three senders' message transmission rates were constant and uniform, (2) all three senders' message rates were made bursty by selecting a random inter-message delay exponentially distributed with a mean equal to the previous uniform constant rate, and (3) the audio and video senders message rates were constant as in (1), but the file sender "misbehaved" and sent messages at a rate of 1,000/second instead of 200/second. Instrumentation was added to the modified kernel and the user processes to collect performance data. The primary data of interest are (*a*) the number of messages received by each process during a fixed length interval (1 minute in our case), (*b*) the number of packets dropped at the queue between the interface/device driver layer and the IP/UDP protocol layer, and (*c*) the number of packets dropped at the socket receive queue (see Figure 1).) For the Dhrystone benchmark we recorded only the number of iterations completed in our measurement interval. Over our measurements intervals we would nominally expect that the audio player would receive 3,000 packets (50×60), the video player would receive 5,400 packets, and the file transfer would receive 12,000 packets. In addition, we would never like to observe any loss at the socket layer. As we explain below, loss here would be an indication that too much processing time is being spent processing packets in the kernel and that because of this user processes are not able to run.

To establish an unmodified FreeBSD baseline, we first ran our applications on a FreeBSD with a 1 *ms* clock tick and a 1 *ms* scheduling quantum. These results are given in Table 1. The audio and file transfer applications executed at their sender's rate because they require little compute time and are mostly I/O bound, blocked on a socket receive. The video application has a high CPU usage (45%) and is subjected to the FreeBSD aging mechanism which reduces its priority. Because of this, it is unable to receive all of its packets and some are dropped at the socket receive queue. The effect under bursty senders is similar.

When the file transfer sender misbehaves, we see the effects of fixed priority scheduling on in-

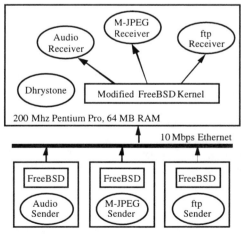

Figure 2: Experimental configuration

Table 1: Unmodified FreeBSD, 1 *ms* clock, 1 *ms* quantum. [2]

	Constant Rate Senders			Bursty Senders			Misbehaved File Sender		
	Packets (Iterations)	Drops at socket	Drops at IP	Packets (Iterations)	Drops at socket	Drops at IP	Packets (Iterations)	Drops at socket	Drops at IP
Audio Application	3,000 (0.5)	0	0	2,938 (15.6)	0	0	2,999 (0.5)	0	0
M-JPEG Application	3,313 (19.1)	2,110 (19.4)	0	3,466 (25.2)	1,703 (10.4)	0	2,456 (15.6)	2,967 (16.4)	0
File Transfer	11,996 (0.5)	0	0	10,897 (58.1)	0	0	11,862 (40.8)	48,043 (39.2)	0
Dhrystone	7,333,439 (49,227)	N/A	N/A	7,660,042 (37,347)	N/A	N/A	5,479,480 (48,454)	N/A	N/A

Table 2: Modified FreeBSD, proportional share for user processes only.

	Constant Rate Senders			Bursty Senders			Misbehaved File Sender		
	Packets (Iterations)	Drops at socket	Drops at IP	Packets (Iterations)	Drops at socket	Drops at IP	Packets (Iterations)	Drops at socket	Drops at IP
Audio Application	2,999 (0.9)	0	0	2,927 (18.1)	0	0	2,999 (0.9)	0	0
M-JPEG Application	5,454 (0.0)	0	0	5,126 (92.6)	0	0	5,454 (0.0)	0	0
File Transfer	11,996 (0.5)	0	0	10,483 (12.0)	0	0	12,000 (0.0)	47,952 (3.8)	0
Dhrystone	4,593,536 (46,257)	N/A	N/A	6,115,263 (235,175)	N/A	N/A	915,343 (26,109)	N/A	N/A

terrupt handling and protocol processing. CPU cycles are used for packets that are eventually dropped at the socket layer taking cycles away from the video and Dhrystone processes (since these processes consume the most CPU time they are aged quickly and soon execute at the lowest priority). Even though more file transfer packets are handled, many more are dropped as are video packets. However, because all packets received are processed up to the socket layer (where there are separate queues for each port), the audio application is still able to receive all its packets.

With this baseline established, we modified the FreeBSD kernel for proportional share scheduling of the user processes. In this case, the interface/device driver layer processing and the network protocol layer processing was executed according to the normal kernel software interrupt level mechanism and priorities. (For all proportional share experiments, we used a clock tick of 1 *ms* and a quantum of 1 *ms*.) The results of this experiment are given in Table 2.

With constant rate senders these results show the benefits of proportional share allocation. Compared with the results in Table 1, the video player now receives all its packets at the expense of the Dhrystone process. Moreover, no packets are dropped at any queue. With bursty senders no packets are dropped but some reduction in the rate of packet reception occurs due to the bursty nature of the senders and our relatively short observation interval. For the case with the misbehaving file transfer sender we are able to maintain the desired rate of progress for all real-time processes. In addition we see the effects of interrupt and protocol processing at a fixed priority in the kernel in the form of a further slowdown of Dhrystone (compared to the constant rate case) and in the loss of file transfer packets at the socket layer. This shows how CPU cycles are still being allocated with fixed priority to processing packets that will never be handled by the application process.

The next design choice we considered was to also explicitly schedule the packet and network protocol processing along with the user processes in a proportional share manner. Given the cost of processing a single packet and the

---

[2] Each entry in each table reports an average and standard deviation (in parenthesis) over a set of runs.

rates at which user processes were estimated to receive, FreeBSD computes a scheduling period for the protocol layer of 10 *ms.* using the procedure outlined in Section 4.4. With this period and its computed share, the protocol processing layer will process 4 packets every 10 *ms.* (note that on average 3.4 packets are expected to arrive in a 10 *ms* interval). The protocol-layer input queue had the same limit on the maximum number of packets that could be enqueued as in normal FreeBSD (50 packets). The results for this experiment are given in Table 3.

For constant rate and bursty senders there is essentially no difference between the proportional share scheduling of user processes only and the combined proportional share scheduling of kernel and user activities. There is, however, a dramatic effect on the results when the file sender misbehaves. As expected, the protocol layer processes at most 24,000 packets (4 packets/10 *ms* for 60 seconds) but because the aggregate number of packets received is over 68,000, the IP protocol layer input queue (with its maximum of 50 entries) is constantly overflowed. More importantly, since the audio sender is sending at the lowest rate (50 packets/second), it is more likely have its packets dropped at the protocol layer input queue. This illustrates why it is important to allocate buffer resources as well as CPU resources to achieve the desired scheduling goals. Note that in this case the performance of the Dhrystone is much improved. Since the real-time processes execute at reduced rates (for lack of data), there are more cycles to be consumed by the Dhrystone.

Following on the architecture of Druschel and Barga [23], we next established an input queue for each socket (destination process) at the asynchronous boundary between the interface/device driver layer and the protocol layer. The queue for each destination process had a limit on the maximum number of packets that could be enqueued based on the scheduling period for the protocol processing and the expected receiving rate for a destination (plus 1 or 2 additional packets to buffer short bursts). The input queue limits were: audio player = 2, video player = 2, and file transfer = 3 packets. The protocol layer processed each of the three queues to exhaustion each time it was run (*i.e.*, every 10 *ms*). These results are given in Table 4.

Again for constant rate and bursty senders there are few differences between this case and the previous one except when the file sender rate increases. With per-destination input queues allocated according to the expected rate of receiving packets, we in effect reserve buffers for the audio and video receivers and thus enable them to achieve the desired rate of packet processing. The particular allocations we used were sufficient for some of the file packets to be processed by the protocol layer only to be discarded at the socket receive queue (because in order to absorb short-lived

bursts, strictly speaking the number of buffers reserved was larger than necessary), however, the majority of packets were discarded at the network interface.

The final design variation we considered was to add a form of proportional share scheduling to the IP/UDP layer processing. In this case, the input queue for each destination was serviced only if the eligible time for receiving the packet at the head of the queue had passed. These results are given in Table 5.

These results show the effect of allocating both CPU and buffer space with the desired results achieved for the all cases of senders. In each case, the processing rates for all applications were as required and all packet drops were pushed down to the point were the minimum resources were expended before the drop occurred.

6. Summary & Contributions

As commodity computers become powerful enough to execute next generation networked multimedia applications, there will be a strong demand for real-time computing and communication support in desktop operating systems. We are advocating the use of proportional share resource allocation technology as the foundation for these services. In this paper investigated the problem of proportional share execution of operating system services. We argued, and demonstrated empirically, that without real-time management of the network interface and protocol processing, the positive effects of real-time scheduling of user processes can easily be nullified. We also demonstrated that it is possible to modify a single threaded monolithic FreeBSD UNIX kernel such that packet and network protocol processing is performed in a proportional share manner. In particular, the parameters needed to schedule kernel activities, namely the weights and costs of each activity, can be either derived from user processes' scheduling parameters or estimated by simple measurement of the code. Moreover, the proportional share framework makes it easy to develop hierarchical resource allocators such as a fair queuing-based buffer manager we employed at the network device interface to further improve throughput for real-time applications.

The result of our research is a proportional share version of FreeBSD that supports integrated application and kernel scheduling and solves the receive livelock problem. Packets are processed only if the destination process is capable of receiving them and all packets received are processed by the application.

Our work contributes to the state of the art in the engineering of proportional share real-time operating systems. While the present work is largely a proof of concept and a preliminary examination of the design space for realizing proportional share services, in the future we hope to per-

Table 3: Modified FreeBSD, *PS* for user processes and protocol processing (one protocol-layer input queue).

	Constant Rate Senders			Bursty Senders			Misbehaved File Sender		
	Packets (Iterations)	Drops at socket	Drops at IP	Packets (Iterations)	Drops at socket	Drops at IP	Packets (Iterations)	Drops at socket	Drops at IP
Audio Application	3,001 (1.4)	0	0	2,992 (5.0)	0	0	757 (341.8)	0	2,244 (341.6)
M-JPEG Application	5,457 (4.2)	0	0	5,225 (8.2)	0	0	2,004 193.0)	0	3,448 (194.9)
File Transfer	12,005 (8.0)	0	0	10,532 (171.3)	0	0	11,999 (0.5)	15,211.0 (297.9)	32,745 (299.5)
Dhrystone	4,970,544 (32,032)	N/A	N/A	6,034,405 (71,884)	N/A	N/A	8,794,017 (340,194)	N/A	N/A

Table 4: *PS* scheduling of user processes and protocol processing with destination queues (no packet scheduling).

	Constant Rate Senders			Bursty Senders			Misbehaved File Sender		
	Packets (Iterations)	Drops at socket	Drops at IP	Packets (Iterations)	Drops at socket	Drops at IP	Packets (Iterations)	Drops at socket	Drops at IP
Audio Application	2,999 (0.9)	0	0	2,958 (17.2)	0	0	2,999 (0.5)	0	0
M-JPEG Application	5,454 (0.5)	0	0	5,215 (11.9)	0	1.3 (0.5)	5,454 (0.5)	0	0
File Transfer	12,005 (3.3)	0	0	10,887 (17.8)	0	7.7 (0.9)	12,003 (5.2)	31,044 (10.1)	16,906 (0.5)
Dhrystone	4,805,747 (63,697)	N/A	N/A	5,817,508 (7,932)	N/A	N/A	1,079,076 (39,830)	N/A	N/A

Table 5: *PS* scheduling of user processes and protocol processing with destination queues and packet scheduling.

	Constant Rate Senders			Bursty Senders			Misbehaved File Sender		
	Packets (Iterations)	Drops at socket	Drops at IP	Packets (Iterations)	Drops at socket	Drops at IP	Packets (Iterations)	Drops at socket	Drops at IP
Audio Application	3,000 (0.0)	0	0	2,966 (8.2)	0	4.0 (5.7)	3,000 (0.0)	0	0
M-JPEG Application	5,454 (0.0)	0	0	5,221 (22.8)	0	6.3 (4.1)	5,454 (0.5)	0	0
File Transfer	11,999 (0.8)	0	0	10,893 (45.7)	0	0.7 (0.5)	12,000 (0.5)	0	47,983 (1.2)
Dhrystone	4,652,845 (15,045)	N/A	N/A	5,788,270 (66,791)	N/A	N/A	1,261,473 (37,910)	N/A	N/A

form a more exhaustive examination of these design issues. In particular, we are working on proportional share allocation of non-preemptible resources in the kernel such as disk bandwidth.

7. References

[1] A. Demers, S. Keshav, S. Shenkar, *Analysis and Simulation of a Fair Queueing Algorithm*, Jour. of Internetworking Research & Experience, Oct. 1990, pp. 3-12.

[2] S. J. Golestani, *A Self-Clocked Fair Queueing Scheme for Broadband Applications*, Proc., IEEE IN-FOCOM '94, April 1994, pp. 636-646.

[3] P. Goyal, X. Guo H. M. Vin, *A Hierarchical CPU Scheduler for Multimedia Operating Systems*, Proc., USENIX Symp. on Operating Systems Design and Implementation, Seattle, WA, Oct. 1996, pp. 107-121.

[4] H. Massalin, C. Pu, *Fine-Grain Adaptive Scheduling Using Feedback, Computing Systems*, Vol. 3, No. 1, 1990, pp. 139-173.

[5] M. K. McKusick, K. Bostic, M.J. Karels J. S. Quarterman. *The Design and Implementation of the 4.4BSD UNIX Operating System*, Addison-Wesley, 1996.

[6] J. Mogul, K. Ramakrishnan, *Eliminating Receive Livelock in an Interrupt-Driven Kernel*, ACM Transactions on Computer Systems, Vol. 15, No. 3, August 1997, pp. 217-252 .

[7] J. Nieh, M. S. Lam. *The Design, Implementation and Evaluation of SMART: A Scheduler for Multimedia Applications*, Proc., Sixteenth ACM Symp. on Operating Systems Principles, Saint-Malo, France, Oct. 1997, pp. 184-197.

[8] A. K. Parekh, R. G. Gallager, *A Generalized Processor Sharing Approach To Flow Control in Integrated Services Networks-The Single Node Case*, ACM/IEEE Transactions on Networking, Vol. 1, No. 3, 1992, pp. 344-357.

[9] I. Stoica, H. Abdel-Wahab, K. Jeffay, S. Baruah, J. Gehrke, C. Plaxton, *A Proportional Share Resource Allocation Algorithm for Real-Time, Time-Shared Systems*, Proc. 17th IEEE Real-Time Systems Symposium, Dec. 1996, pp. 288-299.

[10] I. Stoica, H. Abdel-Wahab, K. Jeffay, *On the Duality Between Resource Reservation and Proportional Share Resource Allocation*, Proc. Multimedia Computing and Networking 1997, SPIE Proceedings Series, Vol. 3020, Feb. 1997, pp. 207-214.

[11] H. Tokuda, T. Kitayama, *Dynamic QOS Control Based on Real-Time Threads*, Proc., Workshop on Network and Operating System Support for Digital Audio and Video, Lancaster, UK, Nov. 1993, Lecture Notes in Computer Science, Vol. 846, pp. 124-137.

[12] VenturCom Inc., Real-time Extension 4.1 for Windows NT, http://www.venturcom.com/prod_serv/nt/rtx/index.html., 1997.

[13] C. Waldspurger, W. Weihl. *Lottery Scheduling: Flexible Proportional Share Resource Management*, Proc. USENIX Symp. on Operating System Design and Implementation, Nov. 1994, pp. 1-12.

[14] L. Zhang, *VirtualClock: A New Traffic Control Algorithm for Packet-Switched Networks*, ACM Transactions on Computer Systems, vol. 9, no. 2, May 1991, pp. 101-124.

[15] M.B. Jones, D. Rosu, M.-C. Rosu, *CPU Reservations & Time Constraints: Efficient, Predictable Scheduling of Independent Activities*, Proc., Sixteenth ACM Symposium on Operating Systems Principles, Saint-Malo, France, October 1997, pp. 198-211.

[16] B. Srinivasan, S. Pather, F. Ansari, D. Niehaus. *A Firm Real-Time System Implementation Using Commercial Off-The-Shelf Hardware and Free Software*, Proc., IEEE Real-Time Technology and Applications Symp., Denver, CO, June 1998, pp. 112-120.

[17] M. Barbarnov, V. Yodaiken, *Real-Time Linux*, Technical Report, Department of Computer Science, New Mexico Institute of Mining and Technology, undated.

[18] C.W. Mercer, S. Savage, H. Tokuda, *Processor Capacity Reserves: Operating System Support for Multimedia Applications*, IEEE Intl. Conf. on Multimedia Computing and Systems, Boston, MA, May 1994, pp. 90-99.

[19] G.R. Wright, W.R. Stevens, *TCP/IP Illustrated, Volume 2, The Implementation*, Addison-Wesley, Reading MA, 1995.

[20] C. Lee, K. Yoshida, C. Mercer, R. Rajkumar, *Predictable Communication Protocol Processing in Real-Time Mach*, Proc., IEEE Real-time Technology and Applications Symposium, Boston, MA, June 1996, pp. 220-229.

[21] H. Tokuda, T. Nakajima, P., Rao, *Real-Time Mach: Towards a Predictable Real-Time System*, Proc.USENIX Mach Workshop, Burlington, VT, October 1990, pp. 73-82.

[22] G. Bollella, K. Jeffay, *Support For Real-Time Computing Within General Purpose Operating Systems: Supporting co-resident operating systems*, Proc., IEEE Real-Time Technology and Applications Symposium, Chicago, IL, May 1995, pp. 4-14.

[23] P. Druschel, G. Banga, *Lazy Receiver Processing: A Network Subsystem Architecture for Server Systems*, Proc., USENIX Symp. On Operating System Design and Implementation, Seattle, WA, Oct. 1996, pp. 261-275.

Author Index

Notes

Notes

IEEE
COMPUTER
SOCIETY

Press Activities Board

IEEE Computer Society Publications

The world-renowned Computer Society publishes, promotes, and distributes a wide variety of authoritative computer science and engineering texts. These books are available in two formats: 100 percent original material by authors preeminent in their field who focus on relevant topics and cutting-edge research, and reprint collections consisting of carefully selected groups of previously published papers with accompanying original introductory and explanatory text.

Submission of proposals: For guidelines and information on Computer Society books, send e-mail to cs.books@computer.org or write to the Project Editor, IEEE Computer Society, P.O. Box 3014, 10662 Los Vaqueros Circle, Los Alamitos, CA 90720-1314. Telephone +1 714-821-8380. FAX +1 714-761-1784.

IEEE Computer Society Proceedings

The Computer Society also produces and actively promotes the proceedings of more than 130 acclaimed international conferences each year in multimedia formats that include hard and softcover books, CD-ROMs, videos, and on-line publications.

For information on Computer Society proceedings, send e-mail to cs.books@computer.org or write to Proceedings, IEEE Computer Society, P.O. Box 3014, 10662 Los Vaqueros Circle, Los Alamitos, CA 90720-1314. Telephone +1 714-821-8380. FAX +1 714-761-1784.

Additional information regarding the Computer Society, conferences and proceedings, CD-ROMs, videos, and books can also be accessed from our web site at http://computer.org/cspress

4/16/98